PHILIP'S

WORLD ATLAS

PHILIP'S

WORLD ATLAS

Published in Great Britain in 1999
by George Philip Limited,
a division of Octopus Publishing Group Limited,
2–4 Heron Quays, London E14 4JP

This edition produced for Borders, 1999

Cartography by Philip's

ISBN 0–540–07833–6

A CIP catalogue record for this book is available from the British Library.

Printed in China

Details of other Philip's titles and services can be found on our website at:
www.philips-maps.co.uk

Philip's World Maps

The reference maps which form the main body of this atlas have been prepared in accordance with the highest standards of international cartography to provide an accurate and detailed representation of the Earth. The scales and projections used have been carefully chosen to give balanced coverage of the world, while emphasizing the most densely populated and economically significant regions. A hallmark of Philip's mapping is the use of hill shading and relief colouring to create a graphic impression of landforms: this makes the maps exceptionally easy to read. However, knowledge of the key features employed in the construction and presentation of the maps will enable the reader to derive the fullest benefit from the atlas.

MAP SEQUENCE

The atlas covers the Earth continent by continent: first Europe; then its land neighbour Asia (mapped north before south, in a clockwise sequence), then Africa, Australia and Oceania, North America and South America. This is the classic arrangement adopted by most cartographers since the 16th century. For each continent, there are maps at a variety of scales. First, physical relief and political maps of the whole continent; then a series of larger-scale maps

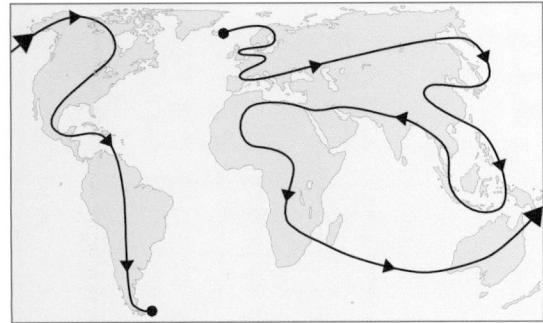

of the regions within the continent, each followed, where required, by still larger-scale maps of the most important or densely populated areas. The governing principle is that by turning the pages of the atlas, the reader moves steadily from north to south through each continent, with each map overlapping its neighbours. A key map showing this sequence, and the area covered by each map, can be found on the endpapers of the atlas.

MAP PRESENTATION

With very few exceptions (e.g. for the Arctic and Antarctic), the maps are drawn with north at the top, regardless of whether they are presented upright or sideways on the page. In the borders will be found the map title; a locator diagram showing the area covered and the page numbers for maps of adjacent areas; the scale; the projection used; the degrees of latitude and longitude; and the letters and figures used in the index for locating place names and geographical features. Physical relief maps also have a height reference panel identifying the colours used for each layer of contouring.

MAP SYMBOLS

Each map contains a vast amount of detail which can only be conveyed clearly and accurately by the use of symbols. Points and circles of varying sizes locate and identify the relative importance of towns and cities; different styles of type are employed for administrative, geographical and regional place names to aid identification. A variety of pictorial symbols denote landscape features such as glaciers, marshes and coral reefs, and man-made structures including roads, railways, airports, canals and dams. International borders are shown by red lines. Where neighbouring countries are in dispute, for example in parts of the Middle East, the maps show the *de facto* boundary between nations, regardless of the legal or historical situation. The symbols are explained on the first page of the World Maps section of the atlas.

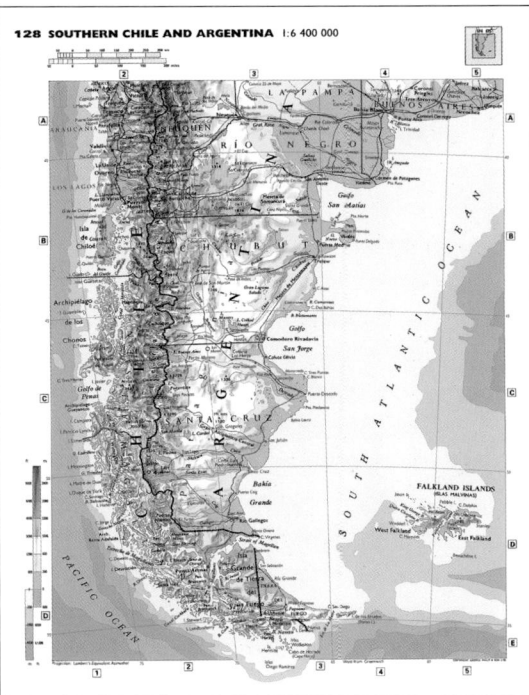

MAP SCALES

1:16 000 000
1 inch = 252 statute miles

The scale of each map is given in the numerical form known as the 'representative fraction'. The first figure is always one, signifying one unit of distance on the map; the second figure, usually in millions, is the number by which the map unit must be multiplied to give the equivalent distance on the Earth's surface. Calculations can easily be made in centimetres and kilometres, by dividing the Earth units figure by 100 000 (i.e. deleting the last five 0s). Thus 1:1 000 000 means 1 cm = 10 km. The calculation for inches and miles is more laborious, but 1 000 000 divided by 63 360 (the number of inches in a mile) shows that 1:1 000 000 means approximately 1 inch = 16 miles. The table below provides distance equivalents for scales down to 1:50 000 000.

LARGE SCALE		
1:1 000 000	1 cm = 10 km	1 inch = 16 miles
1:2 500 000	1 cm = 25 km	1 inch = 39.5 miles
1:5 000 000	1 cm = 50 km	1 inch = 79 miles
1:6 000 000	1 cm = 60 km	1 inch = 95 miles
1:8 000 000	1 cm = 80 km	1 inch = 126 miles
1:10 000 000	1 cm = 100 km	1 inch = 158 miles
1:15 000 000	1 cm = 150 km	1 inch = 237 miles
1:20 000 000	1 cm = 200 km	1 inch = 316 miles
1:50 000 000	1 cm = 500 km	1 inch = 790 miles
SMALL SCALE		

MEASURING DISTANCES

Although each map is accompanied by a scale bar, distances cannot always be measured with confidence because of the distortions involved in portraying the curved surface of the Earth on a flat page. As a general rule, the larger the map scale (i.e. the lower the number of Earth units in the representative fraction), the more accurate and reliable will be the distance measured. On small-scale maps such as those of the world and of entire continents, measurement may only

be accurate along the 'standard parallels', or central axes, and should not be attempted without considering the map projection.

MAP PROJECTIONS

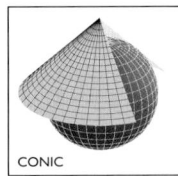

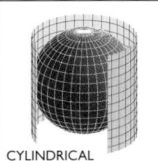

Unlike a globe, no flat map can give a true scale representation of the world in terms of area, shape and position of every region. Each of the numerous systems that have been devised for projecting the curved surface of the Earth on to a flat page involves the sacrifice of accuracy in one or more of these elements. The variations in shape and position of landmasses such as Alaska, Greenland and Australia, for example, can be quite dramatic when different projections are compared.

For this atlas, the guiding principle has been to select projections that involve the least distortion of size and distance. The projection used for each map is noted in the border. Most fall into one of three categories – conic, cylindrical or azimuthal – whose basic concepts are shown above. Each involves plotting the forms of the Earth's surface on a grid of latitude and longitude lines, which may be shown as parallels, curves or radiating spokes.

LATITUDE AND LONGITUDE

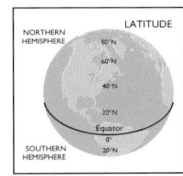
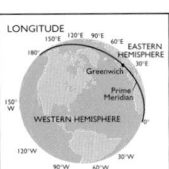
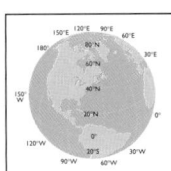

Accurate positioning of individual points on the Earth's surface is made possible by reference to the geometrical system of latitude and longitude. Latitude *parallels* are drawn west–east around the Earth and numbered by degrees north and south of the Equator, which is designated 0° of latitude. Longitude *meridians* are drawn north–south and numbered by degrees east and west of the *prime meridian*, 0° of longitude, which passes through Greenwich in England. By referring to these co-ordinates and their subdivisions of minutes (1/60th of a degree) and seconds (1/60th of a minute), any place on Earth can be located to within a few hundred yards. Latitude and longitude are indicated by blue lines on the maps; they are straight or curved according to the projection employed. Reference to these lines is the easiest way of determining the relative positions of places on different maps, and for plotting compass directions.

NAME FORMS

For ease of reference, both English and local name forms appear in the atlas. Oceans, seas and countries are shown in English throughout the atlas; country names may be abbreviated to their commonly accepted form (e.g. Germany, not The Federal Republic of Germany). Conventional English forms are also used for place names on the smaller-scale maps of the continents. However, local name forms are used on all large-scale and regional maps, with the English form given in brackets only for important cities – the large-scale map of Russia and Central Asia thus shows Moskva (Moscow). For countries which do not use a Roman script, place names have been transcribed according to the systems adopted by the British and US Geographic Names Authorities. For China, the Pin Yin system has been used, with some more widely known forms appearing in brackets, as with Beijing (Peking). Both English and local names appear in the index, the English form being cross-referenced to the local form.

Contents

Europe

Europe: Physical
1:17 800 000
6

Europe: Political
1:17 800 000
7

Scandinavia
1:4 400 000

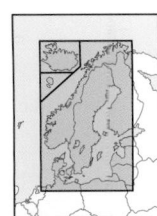

8–9

Denmark and Southern Sweden
1:2 200 000

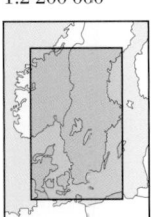

10–11

England and Wales
1:1 800 000

12–13

Scotland
1:1 800 000

14

Ireland
1:1 800 000

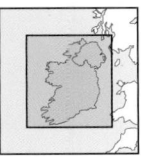

15

British Isles
1:4 400 000

16

Netherlands, Belgium and Luxembourg
1:2 200 000

17

Northern France
1:2 200 000

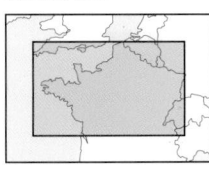

18–19

Southern France
1:2 200 000

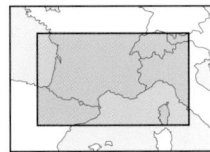

20–21

Middle Europe
1:4 400 000

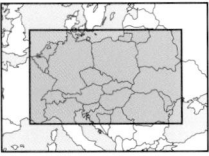

22–23

Germany and Switzerland
1:2 200 000

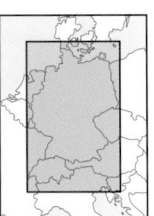

24–25

Austria, Czech Republic and Slovak Republic
1:2 200 000

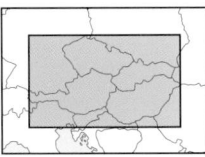

26–27

Northern Italy, Slovenia and Croatia
1:2 200 000

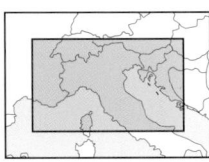

28–29

Southern Italy
1:2 200 000

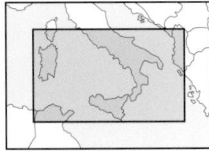

30–31

Eastern Spain
1:2 200 000

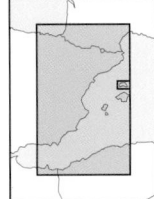

32–33

Western Spain and Portugal
1:2 200 000

34–35

Malta, Crete, Corfu, Rhodes and Cyprus
1:900 000 / 1:1 200 000

36

Balearics, Canaries and Madeira
1:900 000 / 1:1 800 000

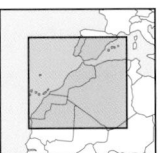

37

Southern Greece
1:2 200 000

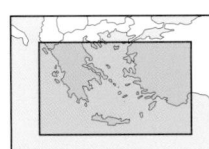

38–39

Northern Greece, Bulgaria and Albania
1:2 200 000

40–41

Hungary, Romania and the Lower Danube
1:2 200 000

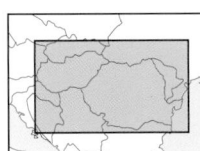

42–43

Poland and the Southern Baltic
1:2 200 000

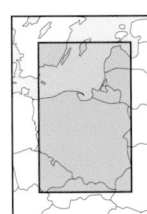

44–45

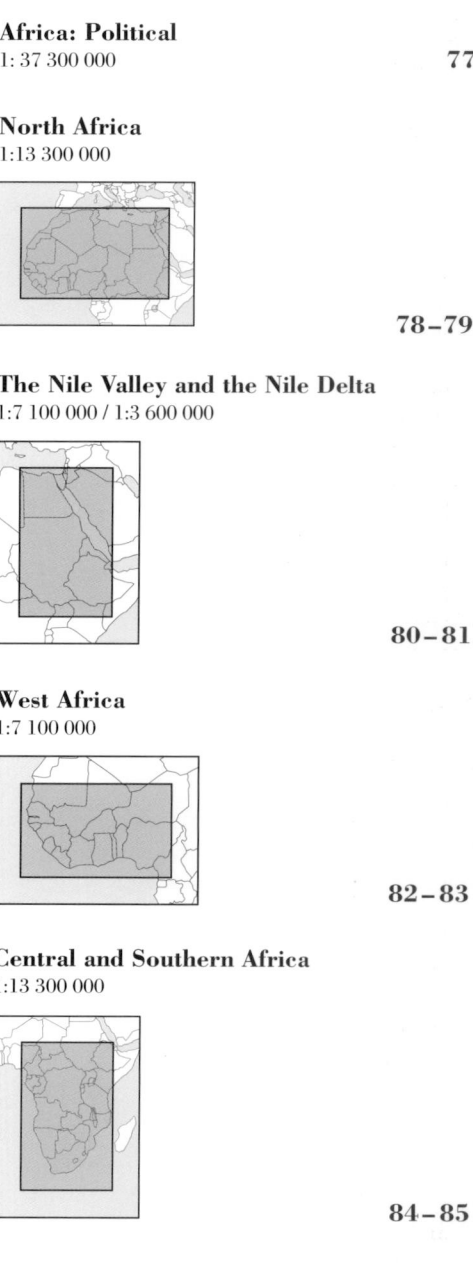

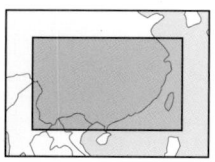
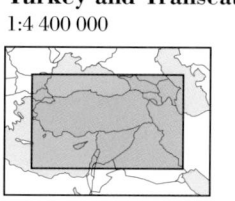

East Africa
1:7 100 000

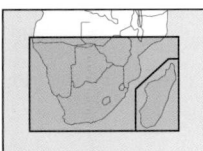

86–87

Southern Africa
1:7 100 000

88–89

Australia and Oceania

Australia and Oceania:
Physical and Political
1:44 400 000   **90**

New Zealand
1:5 300 000

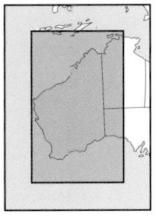

91

Western Australia
1:7 100 000

92–93

Eastern Australia
1:7 100 000

94–95

Pacific Ocean
1:48 000 000   **96–97**

North America

North America: Physical
1:31 100 000   **98**

North America: Political
1:31 100 000   **99**

Canada and Alaska
1:13 300 000 / 1:26 700 000

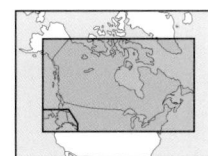

100–101

Eastern Canada
1:6 200 000

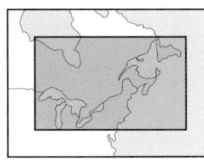

102–103

Western Canada
1:6 200 000

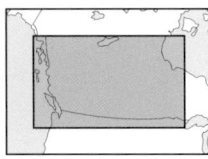

104–105

United States and Hawaii
1:10 700 000 / 1:8 900 000

106–107

Eastern United States
1:5 300 000

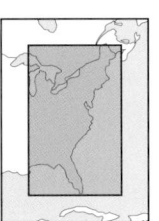

108–109

North-eastern United States
1:2 200 000

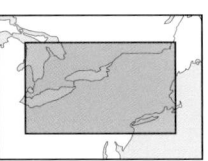

110–111

Middle United States
1:5 300 000

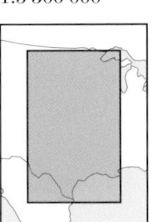

112–113

Western United States
1:5 300 000

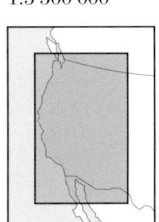

114–115

Central and Southern California
and Washington
1:2 200 000

116–117

Mexico
1:7 100 000

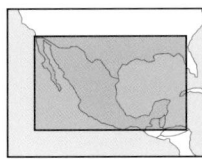

118–119

Central America and the West Indies
1:7 100 000

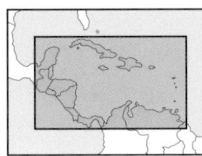

120–121

South America

South America: Physical
1:31 100 000   **122**

South America: Political
1:31 100 000   **123**

South America – North
1:14 200 000

124–125

Central South America
1:7 100 000

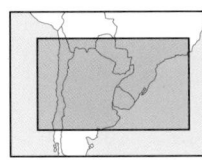

126–127

South America – South
1:14 200 000

128

Index to World Maps

129–224

World Statistics: Countries

This alphabetical list includes all the countries and territories of the world. If a territory is not completely independent, then the country it is associated with is named. The area figures give the total area of land, inland water and ice.

Units for areas and populations are thousands. The population figures are 1998 estimates. The annual income is the Gross National Product per capita in US dollars. The figures are the latest available, usually 1997.

Country/Territory	Area km² Thousands	Area miles² Thousands	Population Thousands	Capital	Annual Income US $
Afghanistan	652	252	24,792	Kabul	600
Albania	28.8	11.1	3,331	Tirana	750
Algeria	2,382	920	30,481	Algiers	1,490
American Samoa (US)	0.20	0.08	62	Pago Pago	2,600
Andorra	0.45	0.17	75	Andorra La Vella	16,200
Angola	1,247	481	11,200	Luanda	340
Anguilla (UK)	0.1	0.04	11	The Valley	6,800
Antigua & Barbuda	0.44	0.17	64	St John's	7,330
Argentina	2,767	1,068	36,265	Buenos Aires	8,750
Armenia	29.8	11.5	3,422	Yerevan	530
Aruba (Netherlands)	0.19	0.07	69	Oranjestad	15,890
Australia	7,687	2,968	18,613	Canberra	20,540
Austria	83.9	32.4	8,134	Vienna	27,980
Azerbaijan	86.6	33.4	7,856	Baku	510
Azores (Portugal)	2.2	0.87	238	Ponta Delgada	–
Bahamas	13.9	5.4	280	Nassau	11,940
Bahrain	0.68	0.26	616	Manama	7,840
Bangladesh	144	56	125,000	Dhaka	270
Barbados	0.43	0.17	259	Bridgetown	6,560
Belarus	207.6	80.1	10,409	Minsk	2,150
Belgium	30.5	11.8	10,175	Brussels	26,420
Belize	23	8.9	230	Belmopan	2,700
Benin	113	43	6,101	Porto-Novo	380
Bermuda (UK)	0.05	0.02	62	Hamilton	31,870
Bhutan	47	18.1	1,908	Thimphu	390
Bolivia	1,099	424	7,826	La Paz/Sucre	950
Bosnia-Herzegovina	51	20	3,366	Sarajevo	300
Botswana	582	225	1,448	Gaborone	4,381
Brazil	8,512	3,286	170,000	Brasília	4,720
Brunei	5.8	2.2	315	Bandar Seri Begawan	15,800
Bulgaria	111	43	8,240	Sofia	1,140
Burkina Faso	274	106	11,266	Ouagadougou	240
Burma (= Myanmar)	677	261	47,305	Rangoon	1,790
Burundi	27.8	10.7	5,531	Bujumbura	180
Cambodia	181	70	11,340	Phnom Penh	300
Cameroon	475	184	15,029	Yaoundé	650
Canada	9,976	3,852	30,675	Ottawa	19,290
Canary Is. (Spain)	7.3	2.8	1,494	Las Palmas/Santa Cruz	–
Cape Verde Is.	4	1.6	399	Praia	1,010
Cayman Is. (UK)	0.26	0.10	35	George Town	20,000
Central African Republic	623	241	3,376	Bangui	320
Chad	1,284	496	7,360	Ndjaména	240
Chile	757	292	14,788	Santiago	5,020
China	9,597	3,705	1,236,915	Beijing	860
Colombia	1,139	440	38,581	Bogotá	2,280
Comoros	2.2	0.86	545	Moroni	450
Congo	342	132	2,658	Brazzaville	660
Congo (= Zaïre)	2,345	905	49,001	Kinshasa	110
Cook Is. (NZ)	0.24	0.09	20	Avarua	900
Costa Rica	51.1	19.7	3,605	San José	2,640
Croatia	56.5	21.8	4,672	Zagreb	4,610
Cuba	111	43	11,051	Havana	1,300
Cyprus	9.3	3.6	749	Nicosia	13,420
Czech Republic	78.9	30.4	10,286	Prague	5,200
Denmark	43.1	16.6	5,334	Copenhagen	32,500
Djibouti	23.2	9	650	Djibouti	850
Dominica	0.75	0.29	78	Roseau	3,090
Dominican Republic	48.7	18.8	7,999	Santo Domingo	1,670
Ecuador	284	109	12,337	Quito	1,590
Egypt	1,001	387	66,050	Cairo	1,180
El Salvador	21	8.1	5,752	San Salvador	1,810
Equatorial Guinea	28.1	10.8	454	Malabo	530
Eritrea	94	36	3,842	Asmara	570
Estonia	44.7	17.3	1,421	Tallinn	3,330
Ethiopia	1,128	436	58,390	Addis Ababa	110
Faroe Is. (Denmark)	1.4	0.54	41	Tórshavn	23,660
Fiji	18.3	7.1	802	Suva	2,470
Finland	338	131	5,149	Helsinki	24,080
France	552	213	58,805	Paris	26,050
French Guiana (France)	90	34.7	162	Cayenne	10,580
French Polynesia (France)	4	1.5	237	Papeete	7,500
Gabon	268	103	1,208	Libreville	4,230
Gambia, The	11.3	4.4	1,292	Banjul	320
Georgia	69.7	26.9	5,109	Tbilisi	840
Germany	357	138	82,079	Berlin/Bonn	28,260
Ghana	239	92	18,497	Accra	370
Gibraltar (UK)	0.007	0.003	29	Gibraltar Town	5,000
Greece	132	51	10,662	Athens	12,010
Greenland (Denmark)	2,176	840	59	Nuuk (Godthåb)	15,500
Grenada	0.34	0.13	96	St George's	2,880
Guadeloupe (France)	1.7	0.66	416	Basse-Terre	9,200
Guam (US)	0.55	0.21	149	Agana	6,000
Guatemala	109	42	12,008	Guatemala City	1,500
Guinea	246	95	7,477	Conakry	570
Guinea-Bissau	36.1	13.9	1,206	Bissau	240
Guyana	215	83	820	Georgetown	690
Haiti	27.8	10.7	6,781	Port-au-Prince	330
Honduras	112	43	5,862	Tegucigalpa	700
Hong Kong (China)	1.1	0.40	6,707	–	22,990
Hungary	93	35.9	10,208	Budapest	4,430
Iceland	103	40	271	Reykjavik	26,580
India	3,288	1,269	984,000	New Delhi	390
Indonesia	1,905	735	212,942	Jakarta	1,110
Iran	1,648	636	64,411	Tehran	4,700
Iraq	438	169	21,722	Baghdad	2,000
Ireland	70.3	27.1	3,619	Dublin	18,280
Israel	27	10.3	5,644	Jerusalem	15,810
Italy	301	116	56,783	Rome	20,120
Ivory Coast (Côte d'Ivoire)	322	125	15,446	Yamoussoukro	690
Jamaica	11	4.2	2,635	Kingston	1,560
Japan	378	146	125,932	Tokyo	37,850
Jordan	89.2	34.4	4,435	Amman	1,570
Kazakstan	2,717	1,049	16,847	Astana	1,340
Kenya	580	224	28,337	Nairobi	330
Kiribati	0.72	0.28	85	Tarawa	920
Korea, North	121	47	21,234	Pyŏngyang	1,000
Korea, South	99	38.2	46,417	Seoul	10,550
Kuwait	17.8	6.9	1,913	Kuwait City	17,390
Kyrgyzstan	198.5	76.6	4,522	Bishkek	440
Laos	237	91	5,261	Vientiane	400
Latvia	65	25	2,385	Riga	2,430

Country/Territory	Area km² Thousands	Area miles² Thousands	Population Thousands	Capital	Annual Income US $
Lebanon	10.4	4	3,506	Beirut	3,350
Lesotho	30.4	11.7	2,090	Maseru	670
Liberia	111	43	2,772	Monrovia	770
Libya	1,760	679	4,875	Tripoli	6,510
Liechtenstein	0.16	0.06	32	Vaduz	33,000
Lithuania	65.2	25.2	3,600	Vilnius	2,230
Luxembourg	2.6	1	425	Luxembourg	45,360
Macau (China)	0.02	0.006	429	Macau	7,500
Macedonia	25.7	9.9	2,009	Skopje	1,090
Madagascar	587	227	14,463	Antananarivo	250
Madeira (Portugal)	0.81	0.31	253	Funchal	–
Malawi	118	46	9,840	Lilongwe	220
Malaysia	330	127	20,993	Kuala Lumpur	4,680
Maldives	0.30	0.12	290	Malé	1,080
Mali	1,240	479	10,109	Bamako	260
Malta	0.32	0.12	379	Valletta	12,000
Marshall Is.	0.18	0.07	63	Dalap-Uliga-Darrit	1,890
Martinique (France)	1.1	0.42	407	Fort-de-France	10,000
Mauritania	1,030	412	2,511	Nouakchott	450
Mauritius	2.0	0.72	1,168	Port Louis	3,800
Mayotte (France)	0.37	0.14	141	Mamoundzou	1,430
Mexico	1,958	756	98,553	Mexico City	3,680
Micronesia, Fed. States of	0.70	0.27	127	Palikir	2,070
Moldova	33.7	13	4,458	Chişinău	540
Monaco	0.002	0.0001	32	Monaco	25,000
Mongolia	1,567	605	2,579	Ulan Bator	390
Montserrat (UK)	0.10	0.04	12	Plymouth	4,500
Morocco	447	172	29,114	Rabat	1,250
Mozambique	802	309	18,641	Maputo	90
Namibia	825	318	1,622	Windhoek	2,220
Nauru	0.02	0.008	12	Yaren District	10,000
Nepal	141	54	23,698	Katmandu	210
Netherlands	41.5	16	15,731	Amsterdam/The Hague	25,820
Netherlands Antilles (Neths)	0.99	0.38	210	Willemstad	10,400
New Caledonia (France)	18.6	7.2	192	Nouméa	8,000
New Zealand	269	104	3,625	Wellington	16,480
Nicaragua	130	50	4,583	Managua	410
Niger	1,267	489	9,672	Niamey	200
Nigeria	924	357	110,532	Abuja	260
Northern Mariana Is. (US)	0.48	0.18	50	Saipan	11,500
Norway	324	125	4,420	Oslo	36,090
Oman	212	82	2,364	Muscat	4,950
Pakistan	796	307	135,135	Islamabad	490
Palau	0.46	0.18	18	Koror	5,000
Panama	77.1	29.8	2,736	Panama City	3,080
Papua New Guinea	463	179	4,600	Port Moresby	940
Paraguay	407	157	5,291	Asunción	2,010
Peru	1,285	496	26,111	Lima	2,460
Philippines	300	116	77,736	Manila	1,220
Poland	313	121	38,607	Warsaw	3,590
Portugal	92.4	35.7	9,928	Lisbon	10,450
Puerto Rico (US)	9	3.5	3,860	San Juan	7,800
Qatar	11	4.2	697	Doha	11,600
Réunion (France)	2.5	0.97	705	Saint-Denis	4,500
Romania	238	92	22,396	Bucharest	1,420
Russia	17,075	6,592	146,861	Moscow	2,740
Rwanda	26.3	10.2	7,956	Kigali	210
St Kitts & Nevis	0.36	0.14	42	Basseterre	5,870
St Lucia	0.62	0.24	150	Castries	3,500
St Vincent & Grenadines	0.39	0.15	120	Kingstown	2,370
San Marino	0.06	0.02	25	San Marino	20,000
São Tomé & Príncipe	0.96	0.37	150	São Tomé	330
Saudi Arabia	2,150	830	20,786	Riyadh	6,790
Senegal	197	76	9,723	Dakar	550
Seychelles	0.46	0.18	79	Victoria	6,850
Sierra Leone	71.7	27.7	5,080	Freetown	200
Singapore	0.62	0.24	3,490	Singapore	32,940
Slovak Republic	49	18.9	5,393	Bratislava	3,700
Slovenia	20.3	7.8	1,972	Ljubljana	9,680
Solomon Is.	28.9	11.2	441	Honiara	900
Somalia	638	246	6,842	Mogadishu	500
South Africa	1,220	471	42,835	C. Town/Pretoria/Bloem.	3,400
Spain	505	195	39,134	Madrid	14,510
Sri Lanka	65.6	25.3	18,934	Colombo	800
Sudan	2,506	967	33,551	Khartoum	800
Surinam	163	63	427	Paramaribo	1,000
Swaziland	17.4	6.7	966	Mbabane	1,210
Sweden	450	174	8,887	Stockholm	26,220
Switzerland	41.3	15.9	7,260	Bern	44,220
Syria	185	71	16,673	Damascus	1,150
Taiwan	36	13.9	21,908	Taipei	12,400
Tajikistan	143.1	55.2	6,020	Dushanbe	330
Tanzania	945	365	30,609	Dodoma	210
Thailand	513	198	60,037	Bangkok	2,800
Togo	56.8	21.9	4,906	Lomé	330
Tonga	0.75	0.29	107	Nuku'alofa	1,790
Trinidad & Tobago	5.1	2	1,117	Port of Spain	4,230
Tunisia	164	63	9,380	Tunis	2,090
Turkey	779	301	64,568	Ankara	3,130
Turkmenistan	488.1	188.5	4,298	Ashkhabad	630
Turks & Caicos Is. (UK)	0.43	0.17	16	Cockburn Town	5,000
Tuvalu	0.03	0.01	10	Fongafale	600
Uganda	236	91	22,167	Kampala	320
Ukraine	603.7	233.1	50,125	Kiev	1,040
United Arab Emirates	83.6	32.3	2,303	Abu Dhabi	17,360
United Kingdom	243.3	94	58,970	London	20,710
United States of America	9,373	3,619	270,290	Washington, DC	28,740
Uruguay	177	68	3,285	Montevideo	6,020
Uzbekistan	447.4	172.7	23,784	Tashkent	1,010
Vanuatu	12.2	4.7	185	Port-Vila	1,290
Venezuela	912	352	22,803	Caracas	3,450
Vietnam	332	127	76,236	Hanoi	320
Virgin Is. (UK)	0.15	0.06	13	Road Town	–
Virgin Is. (US)	0.34	0.13	118	Charlotte Amalie	12,000
Wallis & Futuna Is. (France)	0.20	0.08	15	Mata-Utu	–
Western Sahara	266	103	280	El Aaiún	300
Western Samoa	2.8	1.1	224	Apia	1,170
Yemen	528	204	16,388	Sana	270
Yugoslavia	102.3	39.5	10,500	Belgrade	2,000
Zambia	753	291	9,461	Lusaka	380
Zimbabwe	391	151	11,044	Harare	750

World Statistics: Cities

This list shows the principal cities with more than 500,000 inhabitants (for Brazil, China and India only cities with more than 1 million inhabitants are included). The figures are taken from the most recent census or population estimate available, and as far as possible are the population of the metropolitan area, e.g. greater New York, Mexico or Paris. All the figures are in thousands. Local name forms have been used for the smaller cities (e.g. Kraków).

AFGHANISTAN
Kabul 1,565
ALGERIA
Algiers 2,168
Oran 916
ANGOLA
Luanda 2,418
ARGENTINA
Buenos Aires 11,256
Córdoba 1,208
Rosario 1,118
Mendoza 773
La Plata 642
San Miguel de Tucumán 622
Mar del Plata 512
ARMENIA
Yerevan 1,248
AUSTRALIA
Sydney 3,770
Melbourne 3,217
Brisbane 1,489
Perth 1,262
Adelaide 1,080
AUSTRIA
Vienna 1,595
AZERBAIJAN
Baku 1,720
BANGLADESH
Dhaka 6,105
Chittagong 2,041
Khulna 877
Rajshahi 517
BELARUS
Minsk 1,700
Homyel 512
BELGIUM
Brussels 948
BENIN
Cotonou 537
BOLIVIA
La Paz 1,126
Santa Cruz 767
BOSNIA-HERZEGOVINA
Sarajevo 526
BRAZIL
São Paulo 16,417
Rio de Janeiro 9,888
Salvador 2,211
Belo Horizonte 2,091
Fortaleza 1,965
Brasília 1,821
Curitiba 1,476
Recife 1,346
Pôrto Alegre 1,288
Manaus 1,157
Belém 1,144
Goiânia 1,004
BULGARIA
Sofia 1,116
BURKINA FASO
Ouagadougou 690
BURMA (MYANMAR)
Rangoon 2,513
Mandalay 533
CAMBODIA
Phnom Penh 920
CAMEROON
Douala 1,200
Yaoundé 800
CANADA
Toronto 4,344
Montréal 3,337
Vancouver 1,831
Ottawa-Hull 1,022
Edmonton 885
Calgary 831
Québec 693
Winnipeg 677
Hamilton 643
CENTRAL AFRICAN REP.
Bangui 553
CHAD
Ndjaména 530
CHILE
Santiago 5,067
CHINA
Shanghai 15,082
Beijing 12,362
Tianjin 10,687
Hong Kong (SAR)* 6,502
Chongqing 3,870
Shenyang 3,860
Wuhan 3,520
Guangzhou 3,114
Harbin 2,505
Nanjing 2,211
Xi'an 2,115
Chengdu 1,933
Dalian 1,855
Changchun 1,810
Jinan 1,660
Taiyuan 1,642
Qingdao 1,584
Fuzhou, Fujian 1,380
Zibo 1,346
Zhengzhou 1,324
Lanzhou 1,296
Anshan 1,252
Fushun 1,246
Kunming 1,242
Changsha 1,198
Hangzhou 1,185
Nanchang 1,169
Shijiazhuang 1,159
Guiyang 1,131
Ürümqi 1,130
Jilin 1,118
Tangshan 1,110
Qiqihar 1,104
Baotou 1,033
Hefei 1,000
COLOMBIA
Bogotá 6,004
Cali 1,985
Medellin 1,970
Barranquilla 1,157
Cartagena 812
CONGO
Brazzaville 937
Pointe-Noire 576
CONGO (ZAÏRE)
Kinshasa 1,655
Lubumbashi 851
Mbuji-Mayi 806
COSTA RICA
San José 1,220
CROATIA
Zagreb 931
CUBA
Havana 2,241
CZECH REPUBLIC
Prague 1,209
DENMARK
Copenhagen 1,362
DOMINICAN REPUBLIC
Santo Domingo 2,135
Santiago 691
ECUADOR
Guayaquil 1,973
Quito 1,487
EGYPT
Cairo 9,900
Alexandria 3,431
El Gîza 2,144
Shubra el Kheima 834
EL SALVADOR
San Salvador 1,522
ETHIOPIA
Addis Ababa 2,112
FINLAND
Helsinki 532
FRANCE
Paris 9,319
Lyon 1,262
Marseille 1,087
Lille 959
Bordeaux 696
Toulouse 650
Nice 516
GEORGIA
Tbilisi 1,300
GERMANY
Berlin 3,470
Hamburg 1,706
Munich 1,240
Cologne 964
Frankfurt 651
Essen 616
Dortmund 600
Stuttgart 587
Düsseldorf 571
Bremen 549
Duisburg 535
Hanover 524
GHANA
Accra 949
GREECE
Athens 3,097
GUATEMALA
Guatemala 1,167
GUINEA
Conakry 1,508
HAITI
Port-au-Prince 1,255
HONDURAS
Tegucigalpa 813
HUNGARY
Budapest 1,885
INDIA
Bombay (Mumbai) 12,572
Calcutta 10,916
Delhi 7,207
Madras (Chennai) 5,361
Hyderabad 4,280
Bangalore 4,087
Ahmadabad 3,298
Pune 2,485
Kanpur 2,111
Nagpur 1,661
Lucknow 1,642
Surat 1,517
Jaipur 1,514
Coimbatore 1,136
Vadodara 1,115
Indore 1,104
Patna 1,099
Madurai 1,094
Bhopal 1,064
Vishakhapatnam 1,052
Varanasi 1,026
Ludhiana 1,012
INDONESIA
Jakarta 11,500
Surabaya 2,701
Bandung 2,368
Medan 1,910
Semarang 1,366
Palembang 1,352
Tangerang 1,198
Ujung Pandang 1,092
Bandar Lampung 832
Malang 763
Padang 721
Pakanbaru 558
Samarinda 536
Banjarmasin 535
Surakarta 516
IRAN
Tehran 6,750
Mashhad 1,964
Esfahan 1,221
Tabriz 1,166
Shiraz 1,043
Ahvaz 828
Qom 780
Bakhtaran 666
Karaj 588
IRAQ
Baghdad 3,841
Diyala 961
As Sulaymaniyah 952
Arbil 770
Al Mawsil 664
Kadhimain 521
IRELAND
Dublin 952
ISRAEL
Tel Aviv-Yafo 1,502
Jerusalem 591
ITALY
Rome 2,775
Milan 1,369
Naples 1,067
Turin 962
Palermo 698
Genoa 678
IVORY COAST
Abidjan 2,500
JAMAICA
Kingston 644
JAPAN
Tokyo-Yokohama 26,836
Osaka 10,601
Nagoya 2,152
Sapporo 1,757
Kyoto 1,464
Kobe 1,424
Fukuoka 1,285
Kawasaki 1,203
Hiroshima 1,109
Kitakyushu 1,020
Sendai 971
Chiba 857
Sakai 803
Kumamoto 650
Okayama 616
Sagamihara 571
Hamamatsu 562
Kagoshima 546
Funabashi 541
Higashiosaka 517
Hachioji 503
JORDAN
Amman 1,300
Az-Zarqā 609
KAZAKHSTAN
Almaty 1,150
Qaraghandy 573
KENYA
Nairobi 2,000
Mombasa 600
KOREA, NORTH
Pyŏngyang 2,639
Hamhung 775
Chŏngjin 754
Chinnampo 691
Sinŭiju 500
KOREA, SOUTH
Seoul 11,641
Pusan 3,814
Taegu 2,449
Inchon 2,308
Taejón 1,272
Kwangju 1,258
Ulsan 967
Sŏngnam 869
Puch'on 779
Suwŏn 756
Anyang 590
Chŏnju 563
Chŏngju 531
Ansan 510
P'ohang 509
KYRGYZSTAN
Bishkek 584
LATVIA
Riga 846
LEBANON
Beirut 1,900
Tripoli 500
LIBYA
Tripoli 1,083
LITHUANIA
Vilnius 580
MACEDONIA
Skopje 541
MADAGASCAR
Antananarivo 1,053
MALAYSIA
Kuala Lumpur 1,145
MALI
Bamako 800
MAURITANIA
Nouakchott 735
MEXICO
Mexico City 15,048
Guadalajara 2,847
Monterrey 2,522
Puebla 1,055
León 872
Ciudad Juárez 798
Tijuana 743
Culiacán Rosales 602
Mexicali 602
Acapulco de Juárez 592
Mérida 557
Chihuahua 530
San Luis Potosí 526
Aguascalientes 506
MOLDOVA
Chişinău 700
MONGOLIA
Ulan Bator 627
MOROCCO
Casablanca 3,079 ►
Rabat-Salé 1,344
Fès 735
Marrakesh 621
MOZAMBIQUE
Maputo 2,000
NEPAL
Katmandu 535
NETHERLANDS
Amsterdam 1,101
Rotterdam 1,076
The Hague 694
Utrecht 548
NEW ZEALAND
Auckland 997
NICARAGUA
Managua 864
NIGERIA
Lagos 10,287
Ibadan 1,365
Ogbomosho 712
Kano 657
NORWAY
Oslo 714
PAKISTAN
Karachi 9,863
Lahore 5,085
Faisalabad 1,875
Peshawar 1,676
Gujranwala 1,663
Rawalpindi 1,290
Multan 1,257
Hyderabad 1,107
PARAGUAY
Asunción 945
PERU
Lima-Callao 6,601
Callao 638
Arequipa 620
Trujillo 509
PHILIPPINES
Manila 9,280
Quezon City 1,989
Davao 1,191
Caloocan 1,023
Cebu 662
Zamboanga 511
POLAND
Warsaw 1,638
Lódz 825
Kraków 745
Wroclaw 642
Poznań 581
PORTUGAL
Lisbon 2,561
Oporto 1,174
ROMANIA
Bucharest 2,060
RUSSIA
Moscow 9,233
Petersburg 4,883
Nizhniy Novgorod 1,425
Novosibirsk 1,400
Yekaterinburg 1,300
Samara 1,200
Omsk 1,200
Chelyabinsk 1,100
Kazan 1,100
Ufa 1,100
Volgograd 1,003
Perm 1,000
Rostov 1,000
Voronezh 908
Saratov 895
Krasnoyarsk 869
Togliatti 689
Simbirsk 678
Izhevsk 654
Krasnodar 645
Vladivostok 632
Yaroslavl 629
Khabarovsk 618
Barnaul 596
Irkutsk 585
Novokuznetsk 572
Ryazan 536
Penza 534
Orenburg 532
Tula 532
Naberezhnyye-Chelny 526
Kemerovo 503
SAUDI ARABIA
Riyadh 1,800
Jedda 1,500
Mecca 630
SENEGAL
Dakar 1,571
SIERRA LEONE
Freetown 505
SINGAPORE
Singapore 3,104
SOMALIA
Mogadishu 1,000
SOUTH AFRICA
Cape Town 2,350
East Rand 1,379
Johannesburg 1,196
Durban 1,137
Pretoria 1,080
West Rand 870
Port Elizabeth 853
Vanderbijlpark-Vereeniging 774
Soweto 597
Sasolburg 540
SPAIN
Madrid 3,029
Barcelona 1,614
Valencia 763
Sevilla 719
Zaragoza 607
Málaga 532
SRI LANKA
Colombo 1,863
SUDAN
Nyala 1,267
Khartoum 925
Sharg el Nil 879
SWEDEN
Stockholm 1,744
Göteburg 775
SWITZERLAND
Zürich 1,175
Bern 942
SYRIA
Aleppo 1,591
Damascus 1,549
Homs 644
TAIWAN
Taipei 2,653
Kaohsiung 1,405
Taichung 817
Tainan 700
Panchiao 544
TAJIKISTAN
Dushanbe 524
TANZANIA
Dar-es-Salaam 1,361
THAILAND
Bangkok 5,572
TOGO
Lomé 590
TUNISIA
Tunis 1,827
TURKEY
Istanbul 7,490
Ankara 3,028
Izmir 2,333
Adana 1,472
Bursa 1,317
Konya 1,040
Gaziantep 930
Icel 908
Antalya 734
Diyarbakir 677
Kocaeli 661
Urfa 649
Kayseri 648
Manisa 641
Hatay 561
Samsun 557
Eskisehir 508
Balikesir 501
TURKMENISTAN
Ashkhabad 536
UGANDA
Kampala 773
UKRAINE
Kiev 2,630
Kharkiv 1,555
Dnipropetrovsk 1,147
Donetsk 1,088
Odesa 1,046
Zaporizhzhya 887
Lviv 802
Kryvyy Rih 720
Mariupol 510
Mykolayiv 508
UNITED KINGDOM
London 8,089
Birmingham 2,373
Manchester 2,353
Liverpool 852
Glasgow 832
Sheffield 661
Nottingham 649
Newcastle 617
Bristol 552
Leeds 529
UNITED STATES
New York 16,329
Los Angeles 12,410
Chicago 7,668
Philadelphia 4,949
Washington, DC 4,466
Detroit 4,307
Houston 3,653
Atlanta 3,331
Boston 3,240
Dallas 2,898
Minneapolis-St Paul 2,688
San Diego 2,632
St Louis 2,536
Phoenix 2,473
Baltimore 2,458
Pittsburgh 2,402
Cleveland 2,222
San Francisco 2,182
Seattle 2,180
Tampa 2,157
Miami 2,025
Newark 1,934
Denver 1,796
Portland (Or.) 1,676
Kansas City (Mo.) 1,647
Cincinnati 1,581
San Jose 1,557
Norfolk 1,529
Indianapolis 1,462
Milwaukee 1,456
Sacramento 1,441
San Antonio 1,437
Columbus (Oh.) 1,423
New Orleans 1,309
Charlotte 1,260
Buffalo 1,189
Salt Lake City 1,178
Hartford 1,151
Oklahoma 1,007
Jacksonville (Fl.) 665
Omaha 663
Memphis 614
El Paso 579
Austin 514
Nashville 505
URUGUAY
Montevideo 1,378
UZBEKISTAN
Tashkent 2,107
VENEZUELA
Caracas 2,784
Maracaibo 1,364
Valencia 1,032
Maracay 800
Barquisimeto 745
Ciudad Guayana 524
VIETNAM
Ho Chi Minh City 4,322
Hanoi 3,056
Haiphong 783
YEMEN
Sana 972
Aden 562
YUGOSLAVIA
Belgrade 1,137
ZAMBIA
Lusaka 982
ZIMBABWE
Harare 1,189
Bulawayo 622

* SAR = Special Administrative Region of China

World Statistics: Climate

Rainfall and temperature figures are provided for more than 70 cities around the world. As climate is affected by altitude, the height of each city is shown in metres beneath its name. For each location, the top row of figures shows the total rainfall or snow in millimetres, and the bottom row the average temperature in degrees Celsius; the average annual temperature and total annual rainfall are at the end of the rows. The map opposite shows the city locations.

CITY	JAN.	FEB.	MAR.	APR.	MAY	JUNE	JULY	AUG.	SEPT.	OCT.	NOV.	DEC.	YEAR
EUROPE													
Athens, Greece	62	37	37	23	23	14	6	7	15	51	56	71	402
107 m	10	10	12	16	20	25	28	28	24	20	15	11	18
Berlin, Germany	46	40	33	42	49	65	73	69	48	49	46	43	603
55 m	−1	0	4	9	14	17	19	18	15	9	5	1	9
Istanbul, Turkey	109	92	72	46	38	34	34	30	58	81	103	119	816
14 m	5	6	7	11	16	20	23	23	20	16	12	8	14
Lisbon, Portugal	111	76	109	54	44	16	3	4	33	62	93	103	708
77 m	11	12	14	16	17	20	22	23	21	18	14	12	17
London, UK	54	40	37	37	46	45	57	59	49	57	64	48	593
5 m	4	5	7	9	12	16	18	17	15	11	8	5	11
Málaga, Spain	61	51	62	46	26	5	1	3	29	64	64	62	474
33 m	12	13	16	17	19	29	25	26	23	20	16	13	18
Moscow, Russia	39	38	36	37	53	58	88	71	58	45	47	54	624
156 m	13	−10	−4	6	13	16	18	17	12	6	−1	−7	4
Odesa, Ukraine	57	62	30	21	34	34	42	37	37	13	35	71	473
64 m	−3	−1	2	9	15	20	22	22	18	12	9	1	10
Paris, France	56	46	35	42	57	54	59	64	55	50	51	50	619
75 m	3	4	8	11	15	18	20	19	17	12	7	4	12
Rome, Italy	71	62	57	51	46	37	15	21	63	99	129	93	744
17 m	8	9	11	14	18	22	25	25	22	17	13	10	16
Shannon, Ireland	94	67	56	53	61	57	77	79	86	86	96	117	929
2 m	5	5	7	9	12	14	16	16	14	11	8	6	10
Stockholm, Sweden	43	30	25	31	34	45	61	76	60	48	53	48	554
44 m	−3	−3	−1	5	10	15	18	17	12	7	3	0	7
ASIA													
Bahrain	8	18	13	8	<3	0	0	0	0	0	18	18	81
5 m	17	18	21	25	29	32	33	34	31	28	24	19	26
Bangkok, Thailand	8	20	36	58	198	160	160	175	305	206	66	5	1,397
2 m	26	28	29	30	29	29	28	28	28	28	26	25	28
Beirut, Lebanon	191	158	94	53	18	3	<3	<3	5	51	132	185	892
34 m	14	14	16	18	22	24	27	28	26	24	19	16	21
Bombay (Mumbai), India	3	3	3	<3	18	485	617	340	264	64	13	3	1,809
11 m	24	24	26	28	30	29	27	27	27	28	27	26	27
Calcutta, India	10	31	36	43	140	297	325	328	252	114	20	5	1,600
6 m	20	22	27	30	30	30	29	29	29	28	23	19	26
Colombo, Sri Lanka	89	69	147	231	371	224	135	109	160	348	315	147	2,365
7 m	26	26	27	28	28	27	27	27	27	27	26	26	27
Harbin, China	6	5	10	23	43	94	112	104	46	33	8	5	488
160 m	−18	−15	−5	6	13	19	22	21	14	4	−6	−16	3

CITY	JAN.	FEB.	MAR.	APR.	MAY	JUNE	JULY	AUG.	SEPT.	OCT.	NOV.	DEC.	YEAR
ASIA (continued)													
Ho Chi Minh, Vietnam	15	3	13	43	221	330	315	269	335	269	114	56	1,984
9 m	26	27	29	30	29	28	28	28	27	27	27	26	28
Hong Kong, China	33	46	74	137	292	394	381	361	257	114	43	31	2,162
33 m	16	15	18	22	26	28	28	28	27	25	21	18	23
Jakarta, Indonesia	300	300	211	147	114	97	64	43	66	112	142	203	1,798
8 m	26	26	27	27	27	27	27	27	27	27	27	26	27
Kabul, Afghanistan	31	36	94	102	20	5	3	3	<3	15	20	10	338
1,815 m	−3	−1	6	13	18	22	25	24	20	14	7	3	12
Karachi, Pakistan	13	10	8	3	3	18	81	41	13	<3	3	5	196
4 m	19	20	24	28	30	31	30	29	28	28	24	20	26
Kazalinsk, Kazakstan	10	10	13	13	15	5	5	8	8	10	13	15	125
63 m	−12	−11	−3	6	18	23	25	23	16	8	−1	−7	7
New Delhi, India	23	18	13	8	13	74	180	172	117	10	3	10	640
218 m	14	17	23	28	33	34	31	30	29	26	20	15	25
Omsk, Russia	15	8	8	13	31	51	51	51	28	25	18	20	318
85 m	−22	−19	−12	−1	10	16	18	16	10	1	−11	−18	−1
Shanghai, China	48	58	84	94	94	180	147	142	130	71	51	36	1,135
7 m	4	5	9	14	20	24	28	28	23	19	12	7	16
Singapore	252	173	193	188	173	173	170	196	178	208	254	257	2,413
10 m	26	27	28	28	28	28	28	27	27	27	27	27	27
Tehran, Iran	46	38	46	36	13	3	3	3	3	8	20	31	246
1,220 m	2	5	9	16	21	26	30	29	25	18	12	6	17
Tokyo, Japan	48	74	107	135	147	165	142	152	234	208	97	56	1,565
6 m	3	4	7	13	17	21	25	26	23	17	11	6	14
Ulan Bator, Mongolia	<3	<3	3	5	10	28	76	51	23	5	5	3	208
1,325 m	−26	−21	−13	−1	6	14	16	14	8	−1	−13	−22	−3
Verkhoyansk, Russia	5	5	3	5	8	23	28	25	13	8	8	5	134
100 m	−50	−45	−32	−15	0	12	14	9	2	−15	−38	−48	−17
AFRICA													
Addis Ababa, Ethiopia	<3	3	25	135	213	201	206	239	102	28	<3	0	1,151
2,450 m	19	20	20	20	19	18	18	19	21	22	21	20	20
Antananarivo, Madag.	300	279	178	53	18	8	8	10	18	61	135	287	1,356
1,372 m	21	21	21	19	18	15	14	15	17	19	21	21	19
Cairo, Egypt	5	5	5	3	3	<3	0	0	<3	<3	3	5	28
116 m	13	15	18	21	25	28	28	28	26	24	20	15	22
Cape Town, S. Africa	15	8	18	48	79	84	89	66	43	31	18	10	508
17 m	21	21	20	17	14	13	12	13	14	16	18	19	17
Jo'burg, S. Africa	114	109	89	38	25	8	8	8	23	56	107	125	709
1,665 m	20	20	18	16	13	10	11	13	16	18	19	20	16

CITY	JAN.	FEB.	MAR.	APR.	MAY	JUNE	JULY	AUG.	SEPT.	OCT.	NOV.	DEC.	YEAR
AFRICA (continued)													
Khartoum, Sudan	<3	<3	<3	<3	3	8	53	71	18	5	<3	0	158
390 m	24	25	28	31	33	34	32	31	32	32	28	25	29
Kinshasa, Congo (Z.)	135	145	196	196	158	8	3	3	31	119	221	142	1,354
325 m	26	26	27	27	26	24	23	24	25	26	26	26	25
Lagos, Nigeria	28	46	102	150	269	460	279	64	140	206	69	25	1,836
3 m	27	28	29	28	28	26	26	25	26	26	28	28	27
Lusaka, Zambia	231	191	142	18	3	<3	<3	0	<3	10	91	150	836
1,277 m	21	22	21	21	19	16	16	18	22	24	23	22	21
Monrovia, Liberia	31	56	97	216	516	973	996	373	744	772	236	130	5,138
23 m	26	26	27	27	26	25	24	25	25	26	26	26	26
Nairobi, Kenya	38	64	125	211	158	46	15	23	31	53	109	86	958
820 m	19	19	19	19	18	16	16	16	18	19	18	18	18
Timbuktu, Mali	<3	<3	3	<3	5	23	79	81	38	3	<3	<3	231
301 m	22	24	28	32	34	35	32	30	32	31	28	23	29
Tunis, Tunisia	64	51	41	36	18	8	3	8	33	51	48	61	419
66 m	10	11	13	16	19	23	26	27	25	20	16	11	18
Walvis Bay, Namibia	<3	5	8	3	3	<3	<3	3	<3	<3	<3	<3	23
7 m	19	19	19	18	17	16	15	14	14	15	17	18	18
AUSTRALIA, NEW ZEALAND AND ANTARCTICA													
Alice Springs, Aust.	43	33	28	10	15	13	8	8	8	18	31	38	252
579 m	29	28	25	20	15	12	12	14	18	23	26	28	21
Christchurch, N.Z.	56	43	48	48	66	66	69	48	46	43	48	56	638
10 m	16	16	14	12	9	6	6	7	9	12	14	16	11
Darwin, Australia	386	312	254	97	15	3	<3	3	13	51	119	239	1,491
30 m	29	29	29	29	28	26	25	26	28	29	30	29	28
Mawson, Antarctica	11	30	20	10	44	180	4	40	3	20	0	0	362
14 m	0	−5	−10	−14	−15	−16	−18	−18	−19	−13	−5	−1	−11
Perth, Australia	8	10	20	43	130	180	170	149	86	56	20	13	881
60 m	23	23	22	19	16	14	13	13	15	16	19	22	18
Sydney, Australia	89	102	127	135	127	117	117	76	73	71	73	73	1,181
42 m	22	22	21	18	15	13	12	13	15	18	19	21	17
NORTH AMERICA													
Anchorage, USA	20	18	15	10	13	18	41	66	66	56	25	23	371
40 m	−11	−8	−5	2	7	12	14	13	9	2	−5	−11	2
Chicago, USA	51	51	66	71	86	89	84	81	79	66	61	51	836
251 m	−4	−3	2	9	14	20	23	22	19	12	5	−1	10
Churchill, Canada	15	13	18	23	32	44	46	58	51	43	39	21	402
13 m	−28	−26	−20	−10	−2	6	12	11	5	−2	−12	−22	−7
Edmonton, Canada	25	19	19	22	43	77	89	78	39	17	16	25	466
676 m	−15	−10	−5	4	11	15	17	16	11	6	−4	−10	3
Honolulu, USA	104	66	79	48	25	18	23	28	36	48	64	104	643
12 m	23	18	20	20	22	24	25	26	26	24	22	19	22
Houston, USA	89	76	84	91	119	117	99	99	104	94	89	109	1,171
12 m	12	13	17	21	24	27	28	29	26	22	16	12	21

CITY	JAN.	FEB.	MAR.	APR.	MAY	JUNE	JULY	AUG.	SEPT.	OCT.	NOV.	DEC.	YEAR
NORTH AMERICA (continued)													
Kingston, Jamaica	23	15	23	31	102	89	38	91	99	180	74	36	800
34 m	25	25	25	26	26	28	28	28	27	27	26	26	26
Los Angeles, USA	79	76	71	25	10	3	<3	<3	5	15	31	66	381
95 m	13	14	14	16	17	19	21	22	21	18	16	14	17
Mexico City, Mexico	13	5	10	20	53	119	170	152	130	51	18	8	747
2,309 m	12	13	16	18	19	19	17	18	18	16	14	13	16
Miami, USA	71	53	64	81	173	178	155	160	203	234	71	51	1,516
8 m	20	20	22	23	25	27	28	28	27	25	22	21	24
Montréal, Canada	72	65	74	74	66	82	90	92	88	76	81	87	946
57 m	−10	−9	−3	−6	13	18	21	20	15	9	2	−7	6
New York City, USA	94	97	91	81	81	84	107	109	86	89	76	91	1,092
96 m	−1	−1	3	10	16	20	23	23	21	15	7	2	11
St Louis, USA	58	64	89	97	114	114	89	86	81	74	71	64	1,001
173 m	0	1	7	13	19	24	26	26	22	15	8	2	14
San José, Costa Rica	15	5	20	46	229	241	211	241	305	300	145	41	1,798
1,146 m	19	19	21	21	22	21	21	21	21	20	20	19	20
Vancouver, Canada	154	115	101	60	52	45	32	41	67	114	150	182	1,113
14 m	3	5	6	9	12	15	17	17	14	10	6	4	10
Washington, DC, USA	86	76	91	84	94	99	112	109	94	74	66	79	1,064
22 m	1	2	7	12	18	23	25	24	20	14	8	3	13
SOUTH AMERICA													
Antofagasta, Chile	0	0	0	<3	<3	3	5	3	<3	3	<3	0	13
94 m	21	21	20	18	16	15	14	14	15	16	18	19	17
Buenos Aires, Arg.	79	71	109	89	76	61	56	61	79	86	84	99	950
27 m	23	23	21	17	13	9	10	11	13	15	19	22	16
Lima, Peru	3	<3	<3	<3	5	5	8	8	8	3	3	<3	41
120 m	23	24	24	22	19	17	17	16	17	18	19	21	20
Manaus, Brazil	249	231	262	221	170	84	58	38	46	107	142	203	1,811
44 m	28	28	28	27	28	28	28	28	29	29	29	29	28
Paraná, Brazil	287	236	239	102	13	<3	3	5	28	127	231	310	1,582
260 m	23	23	23	23	23	21	21	22	24	24	24	23	23
Rio de Janeiro, Brazil	125	122	130	107	79	53	41	43	66	79	104	137	1,082
61 m	26	26	25	24	22	21	21	21	21	22	23	25	23

World Statistics: Physical Dimensions

Each topic list is divided into continents and within a continent the items are listed in order of size. The order of the continents is as in the atlas, Europe through to South America. The lists down to this mark > are complete; below they are selective. The world top ten are shown in square brackets; in the case of mountains this has not been done because the world top 30 are all in Asia. The figures are rounded as appropriate.

WORLD, CONTINENTS, OCEANS

THE WORLD	km²	miles²	%
The World	509,450,000	196,672,000	–
Land	149,450,000	57,688,000	29.3
Water	360,000,000	138,984,000	70.7
Asia	44,500,000	17,177,000	29.8
Africa	30,302,000	11,697,000	20.3
North America	24,241,000	9,357,000	16.2
South America	17,793,000	6,868,000	11.9
Antarctica	14,100,000	5,443,000	9.4
Europe	9,957,000	3,843,000	6.7
Australia & Oceania	8,557,000	3,303,000	5.7
Pacific Ocean	179,679,000	69,356,000	49.9
Atlantic Ocean	92,373,000	35,657,000	25.7
Indian Ocean	73,917,000	28,532,000	20.5
Arctic Ocean	14,090,000	5,439,000	3.9

SEAS

South China Sea	2,974,600	1,148,500
Bering Sea	2,268,000	875,000
Sea of Okhotsk	1,528,000	590,000
East China & Yellow	1,249,000	482,000
Sea of Japan	1,008,000	389,000
Gulf of California	162,000	62,500
Bass Strait	75,000	29,000

ATLANTIC	km²	miles²
Caribbean Sea	2,766,000	1,068,000
Mediterranean Sea	2,516,000	971,000
Gulf of Mexico	1,543,000	596,000
Hudson Bay	1,232,000	476,000
North Sea	575,000	223,000
Black Sea	462,000	178,000
Baltic Sea	422,170	163,000
Gulf of St Lawrence	238,000	92,000

INDIAN	km²	miles²
Red Sea	438,000	169,000
The Gulf	239,000	92,000

MOUNTAINS

EUROPE		m	ft
Elbrus	Russia	5,642	18,510
Mont Blanc	France/Italy	4,807	15,771
Monte Rosa	Italy/Switzerland	4,634	15,203
Dom	Switzerland	4,545	14,911
Liskamm	Switzerland	4,527	14,852
Weisshorn	Switzerland	4,505	14,780
Taschorn	Switzerland	4,490	14,730
Matterhorn/Cervino	Italy/Switz.	4,478	14,691
Mont Maudit	France/Italy	4,465	14,649
Dent Blanche	Switzerland	4,356	14,291
Nadelhorn	Switzerland	4,327	14,196
> Grandes Jorasses	France/Italy	4,208	13,806
Jungfrau	Switzerland	4,158	13,642
Barre des Ecrins	France	4,103	13,461
Gran Paradiso	Italy	4,061	13,323
Piz Bernina	Italy/Switzerland	4,049	13,284
Eiger	Switzerland	3,970	13,025
Monte Viso	Italy	3,841	12,602
Grossglockner	Austria	3,797	12,457
Wildspitze	Austria	3,772	12,382
Monte Disgrazia	Italy	3,678	12,066
Mulhacén	Spain	3,478	11,411
Pico de Aneto	Spain	3,404	11,168
Marmolada	Italy	3,342	10,964
Etna	Italy	3,340	10,958
Zugspitze	Germany	2,962	9,718
Musala	Bulgaria	2,925	9,596
Olympus	Greece	2,917	9,570
Triglav	Slovenia	2,863	9,393
Monte Cinto	France (Corsica)	2,710	8,891
Gerlachovka	Slovak Republic	2,655	8,711
Galdhöpiggen	Norway	2,468	8,100
Hvannadalshnúkur	Iceland	2,119	6,952
Ben Nevis	UK	1,343	4,406

ASIA		m	ft
Everest	China/Nepal	8,848	29,029
K2 (Godwin Austen)	China/Kashmir	8,611	28,251
Kanchenjunga	India/Nepal	8,598	28,208
Lhotse	China/Nepal	8,516	27,939
Makalu	China/Nepal	8,481	27,824
Cho Oyu	China/Nepal	8,201	26,906
Dhaulagiri	Nepal	8,172	26,811
Manaslu	Nepal	8,156	26,758
Nanga Parbat	Kashmir	8,126	26,660
Annapurna	Nepal	8,078	26,502
Gasherbrum	China/Kashmir	8,068	26,469
Broad Peak	China/Kashmir	8,051	26,414
Xixabangma	China	8,012	26,286
Kangbachen	India/Nepal	7,902	25,925
Jannu	India/Nepal	7,902	25,925
Gayachung Kang	Nepal	7,897	25,909
Himalchuli	Nepal	7,893	25,896
Disteghil Sar	Kashmir	7,885	25,869
Nuptse	Nepal	7,879	25,849
Khunyang Chhish	Kashmir	7,852	25,761
Masherbrum	Kashmir	7,821	25,659
Nanda Devi	India	7,817	25,646
Rakaposhi	Kashmir	7,788	25,551
Batura	Kashmir	7,785	25,541
Namche Barwa	China	7,756	25,446
Kamet	India	7,756	25,446
Soltoro Kangri	Kashmir	7,742	25,400
Gurla Mandhata	China	7,728	25,354
Trivor	Pakistan	7,720	25,328
> Kongur Shan	China	7,719	25,324
Tirich Mir	Pakistan	7,690	25,229
K'ula Shan	Bhutan/China	7,543	24,747
Pik Kommunizma	Tajikistan	7,495	24,590
Demavend	Iran	5,604	18,386
Ararat	Turkey	5,165	16,945
Gunong Kinabalu	Malaysia (Borneo)	4,101	13,455
Yu Shan	Taiwan	3,997	13,113
Fuji-San	Japan	3,776	12,388

AFRICA		m	ft
Kilimanjaro	Tanzania	5,895	19,340
Mt Kenya	Kenya	5,199	17,057
Ruwenzori			
(Margherita)	Uganda/Congo (Z.)	5,109	16,762
Ras Dashan	Ethiopia	4,620	15,157
Meru	Tanzania	4,565	14,977
Karisimbi	Rwanda/Congo (Z.)	4,507	14,787
Mt Elgon	Kenya/Uganda	4,321	14,176
Batu	Ethiopia	4,307	14,130
Guna	Ethiopia	4,231	13,882
Toubkal	Morocco	4,165	13,665
Irhil Mgoun	Morocco	4,071	13,356
Mt Cameroon	Cameroon	4,070	13,353
Amba Ferit	Ethiopia	3,875	13,042
Pico del Teide	Spain (Tenerife)	3,718	12,198
Thabana Ntlenyana	Lesotho	3,482	11,424
Emi Koussi	Chad	3,415	11,204
> Mt aux Sources	Lesotho/S. Africa	3,282	10,768
Mt Piton	Réunion	3,069	10,069

OCEANIA		m	ft
Puncak Jaya	Indonesia	5,029	16,499
Puncak Trikora	Indonesia	4,750	15,584
Puncak Mandala	Indonesia	4,702	15,427
Mt Wilhelm	Papua NG	4,508	14,790
> Mauna Kea	USA (Hawaii)	4,205	13,796
Mauna Loa	USA (Hawaii)	4,170	13,681
Mt Cook (Aoraki)	New Zealand	3,753	12,313
Mt Balbi	Solomon Is.	2,439	8,002
Orohena	Tahiti	2,241	7,352
Mt Kosciuszko	Australia	2,237	7,339

NORTH AMERICA		m	ft
Mt McKinley			
(Denali)	USA (Alaska)	6,194	20,321
Mt Logan	Canada	5,959	19,551
Citlaltepetl	Mexico	5,700	18,701
Mt St Elias	USA/Canada	5,489	18,008
Popocatepetl	Mexico	5,452	17,887

NORTH AMERICA (continued)		m	ft
Mt Foraker	USA (Alaska)	5,304	17,401
Ixtaccihuatl	Mexico	5,286	17,342
Lucania	Canada	5,227	17,149
Mt Steele	Canada	5,073	16,644
Mt Bona	USA (Alaska)	5,005	16,420
Mt Blackburn	USA (Alaska)	4,996	16,391
Mt Sanford	USA (Alaska)	4,940	16,207
Mt Wood	Canada	4,848	15,905
Nevado de Toluca	Mexico	4,670	15,321
Mt Fairweather	USA (Alaska)	4,663	15,298
Mt Hunter	USA (Alaska)	4,442	14,573
Mt Whitney	USA	4,418	14,495
Mt Elbert	USA	4,399	14,432
Mt Harvard	USA	4,395	14,419
Mt Rainier	USA	4,392	14,409
> Blanca Peak	USA	4,372	14,344
Longs Peak	USA	4,345	14,255
Tajumulco	Guatemala	4,220	13,845
Grand Teton	USA	4,197	13,770
Mt Waddington	Canada	3,994	13,104
Mt Robson	Canada	3,954	12,972
Chirripó Grande	Costa Rica	3,837	12,589
Pico Duarte	Dominican Rep.	3,175	10,417

SOUTH AMERICA		m	ft
Aconcagua	Argentina	6,960	22,834
Bonete	Argentina	6,872	22,546
Ojos del Salado	Argentina/Chile	6,863	22,516
Pissis	Argentina	6,779	22,241
Mercedario	Argentina/Chile	6,770	22,211
Huascaran	Peru	6,768	22,204
Llullaillaco	Argentina/Chile	6,723	22,057
Nudo de Cachi	Argentina	6,720	22,047
Yerupaja	Peru	6,632	21,758
N. de Tres Cruces	Argentina/Chile	6,620	21,719
Incahuasi	Argentina/Chile	6,601	21,654
Cerro Galan	Argentina	6,600	21,654
Tupungato	Argentina/Chile	6,570	21,555
> Sajama	Bolivia	6,542	21,463
Illimani	Bolivia	6,485	21,276
Coropuna	Peru	6,425	21,079
Ausangate	Peru	6,384	20,945
Cerro del Toro	Argentina	6,380	20,932
Siula Grande	Peru	6,356	20,853
Chimborazo	Ecuador	6,267	20,561
Alpamayo	Peru	5,947	19,511
Cotapaxi	Ecuador	5,896	19,344
Pico Colon	Colombia	5,800	19,029
Pico Bolivar	Venezuela	5,007	16,427

ANTARCTICA		m	ft
Vinson Massif		4,897	16,066
Mt Kirkpatrick		4,528	14,855
Mt Markham		4,349	14,268

OCEAN DEPTHS

ATLANTIC OCEAN	m	ft	
Puerto Rico (Milwaukee) Deep	9,220	30,249	[7]
Cayman Trench	7,680	25,197	[10]
Gulf of Mexico	5,203	17,070	
Mediterranean Sea	5,121	16,801	
Black Sea	2,211	7,254	
North Sea	660	2,165	
Baltic Sea	463	1,519	
Hudson Bay	258	846	

INDIAN OCEAN	m	ft	
Java Trench	7,450	24,442	
Red Sea	2,635	8,454	
Persian Gulf	73	239	

PACIFIC OCEAN	m	ft	
Mariana Trench	11,022	36,161	[1]
Tonga Trench	10,882	35,702	[2]
Japan Trench	10,554	34,626	[3]
Kuril Trench	10,542	34,587	[4]
Mindanao Trench	10,497	34,439	[5]
Kermadec Trench	10,047	32,962	[6]

PACIFIC OCEAN (continued)

	m	ft	
Peru–Chile Trench	8,050	26,410	[8]
Aleutian Trench	7,822	25,662	[9]

ARCTIC OCEAN

	m	ft
Molloy Deep	5,608	18,399

LAND LOWS

		m	ft
Dead Sea	Asia	−403	−1,322
Lake Assal	Africa	−156	−512
Death Valley	N. America	−86	−282
Valdés Peninsula	S. America	−40	−131
Caspian Sea	Europe	−28	−92
Lake Eyre North	Oceania	−16	−52

RIVERS

EUROPE

		km	miles
Volga	Caspian Sea	3,700	2,300
Danube	Black Sea	2,850	1,770
Ural	Caspian Sea	2,535	1,575
Dnepr (Dnipro)	Black Sea	2,285	1,420
Kama	Volga	2,030	1,260
Don	Black Sea	1,990	1,240
Petchora	Arctic Ocean	1,790	1,110
Oka	Volga	1,480	920
Belaya	Kama	1,420	880
Dnister (Dniester)	Black Sea	1,400	870
Vyatka	Kama	1,370	850
Rhine	North Sea	1,320	820
N. Dvina	Arctic Ocean	1,290	800
Desna	Dnepr (Dnipro)	1,190	740
Elbe	North Sea	1,145	710
Wisla	Baltic Sea	1,090	675
Loire	Atlantic Ocean	1,020	635

ASIA

		km	miles
Yangtze	Pacific Ocean	6,380	3,960 [3]
Yenisey–Angara	Arctic Ocean	5,550	3,445 [5]
Huang He	Pacific Ocean	5,464	3,395 [6]
Ob–Irtysh	Arctic Ocean	5,410	3,360 [7]
Mekong	Pacific Ocean	4,500	2,795 [9]
Amur	Pacific Ocean	4,400	2,730 [10]
Lena	Arctic Ocean	4,400	2,730
Irtysh	Ob	4,250	2,640
Yenisey	Arctic Ocean	4,090	2,540
Ob	Arctic Ocean	3,680	2,285
Indus	Indian Ocean	3,100	1,925
Brahmaputra	Indian Ocean	2,900	1,800
Syrdarya	Aral Sea	2,860	1,775
Salween	Indian Ocean	2,800	1,740
Euphrates	Indian Ocean	2,700	1,675
Vilyuy	Lena	2,650	1,645
Kolyma	Arctic Ocean	2,600	1,615
Amudarya	Aral Sea	2,540	1,575
Ural	Caspian Sea	2,535	1,575
Ganges	Indian Ocean	2,510	1,560
Si Kiang	Pacific Ocean	2,100	1,305
Irrawaddy	Indian Ocean	2,010	1,250
Tarim–Yarkand	Lop Nor	2,000	1,240
Tigris	Indian Ocean	1,900	1,180

AFRICA

		km	miles
Nile	Mediterranean	6,670	4,140 [1]
Congo	Atlantic Ocean	4,670	2,900 [8]
Niger	Atlantic Ocean	4,180	2,595
Zambezi	Indian Ocean	3,540	2,200
Oubangi/Uele	Congo (Zaïre)	2,250	1,400
Kasai	Congo (Zaïre)	1,950	1,210
Shaballe	Indian Ocean	1,930	1,200
Orange	Atlantic Ocean	1,860	1,155
Cubango	Okavango Swamps	1,800	1,120
Limpopo	Indian Ocean	1,600	995
Senegal	Atlantic Ocean	1,600	995
Volta	Atlantic Ocean	1,500	930

AUSTRALIA

		km	miles
Murray–Darling	Indian Ocean	3,750	2,330
Darling	Murray	3,070	1,905
Murray	Indian Ocean	2,575	1,600
Murrumbidgee	Murray	1,690	1,050

NORTH AMERICA

		km	miles
Mississippi–Missouri	Gulf of Mexico	6,020	3,740 [4]
Mackenzie	Arctic Ocean	4,240	2,630
Mississippi	Gulf of Mexico	3,780	2,350
Missouri	Mississippi	3,780	2,350
Yukon	Pacific Ocean	3,185	1,980
Rio Grande	Gulf of Mexico	3,030	1,880

NORTH AMERICA (continued)

		km	miles
Arkansas	Mississippi	2,340	1,450
Colorado	Pacific Ocean	2,330	1,445
Red	Mississippi	2,040	1,270
Columbia	Pacific Ocean	1,950	1,210
Saskatchewan	Lake Winnipeg	1,940	1,205
Snake	Columbia	1,670	1,040
Churchill	Hudson Bay	1,600	990
Ohio	Mississippi	1,580	980
Brazos	Gulf of Mexico	1,400	870
St Lawrence	Atlantic Ocean	1,170	730

SOUTH AMERICA

		km	miles
Amazon	Atlantic Ocean	6,450	4,010 [2]
Paraná–Plate	Atlantic Ocean	4,500	2,800
Purus	Amazon	3,350	2,080
Madeira	Amazon	3,200	1,990
São Francisco	Atlantic Ocean	2,900	1,800
Paraná	Plate	2,800	1,740
Tocantins	Atlantic Ocean	2,750	1,710
Paraguay	Paraná	2,550	1,580
Orinoco	Atlantic Ocean	2,500	1,550
Pilcomayo	Paraná	2,500	1,550
Araguaia	Tocantins	2,250	1,400
Juruá	Amazon	2,000	1,240
Xingu	Amazon	1,980	1,230
Ucayali	Amazon	1,900	1,180
Marañón	Amazon	1,600	990
Uruguay	Plate	1,600	990

LAKES

EUROPE

		km²	miles²
Lake Ladoga	Russia	17,700	6,800
Lake Onega	Russia	9,700	3,700
Saimaa system	Finland	8,000	3,100
Vänern	Sweden	5,500	2,100
Rybinskoye Res.	Russia	4,700	1,800

ASIA

		km²	miles²
Caspian Sea	Asia	371,800	143,550 [1]
Lake Baykal	Russia	30,500	11,780 [8]
Aral Sea	Kazakstan/Uzbekistan	28,687	11,086 [10]
Tonlé Sap	Cambodia	20,000	7,700
Lake Balqash	Kazakstan	18,500	7,100
Lake Dongting	China	12,000	4,600
Lake Ysyk	Kyrgyzstan	6,200	2,400
Lake Orumiyeh	Iran	5,900	2,300
Lake Koko	China	5,700	2,200
Lake Poyang	China	5,000	1,900
Lake Khanka	China/Russia	4,400	1,700
Lake Van	Turkey	3,500	1,400

AFRICA

		km²	miles²
Lake Victoria	E. Africa	68,000	26,000 [3]
Lake Tanganyika	C. Africa	33,000	13,000 [6]
Lake Malawi/Nyasa	E. Africa	29,600	11,430 [9]
Lake Chad	C. Africa	25,000	9,700
Lake Turkana	Ethiopia/Kenya	8,500	3,300
Lake Volta	Ghana	8,500	3,300
Lake Bangweulu	Zambia	8,000	3,100
Lake Rukwa	Tanzania	7,000	2,700
Lake Mai-Ndombe	Congo (Zaïre)	6,500	2,500
Lake Kariba	Zambia/Zimbabwe	5,300	2,000
Lake Albert	Uganda/Congo (Z.)	5,300	2,000
Lake Nasser	Egypt/Sudan	5,200	2,000
Lake Mweru	Zambia/Congo (Z.)	4,900	1,900
Lake Cabora Bassa	Mozambique	4,500	1,700
Lake Kyoga	Uganda	4,400	1,700
Lake Tana	Ethiopia	3,630	1,400

AUSTRALIA

		km²	miles²
Lake Eyre	Australia	8,900	3,400
Lake Torrens	Australia	5,800	2,200
Lake Gairdner	Australia	4,800	1,900

NORTH AMERICA

		km²	miles²
Lake Superior	Canada/USA	82,350	31,800 [2]
Lake Huron	Canada/USA	59,600	23,010 [4]
Lake Michigan	USA	58,000	22,400 [5]
Great Bear Lake	Canada	31,800	12,280 [7]
Great Slave Lake	Canada	28,500	11,000
Lake Erie	Canada/USA	25,700	9,900
Lake Winnipeg	Canada	24,400	9,400
Lake Ontario	Canada/USA	19,500	7,500
Lake Nicaragua	Nicaragua	8,200	3,200
Lake Athabasca	Canada	8,100	3,100
Smallwood Reservoir	Canada	6,530	2,520
Reindeer Lake	Canada	6,400	2,500
Nettilling Lake	Canada	5,500	2,100
Lake Winnipegosis	Canada	5,400	2,100

SOUTH AMERICA

		km²	miles²
Lake Titicaca	Bolivia/Peru	8,300	3,200
Lake Poopo	Peru	2,800	1,100

ISLANDS

EUROPE

		km²	miles²	
Great Britain	UK	229,880	88,700	[8]
Iceland	Atlantic Ocean	103,000	39,800	
Ireland	Ireland/UK	84,400	32,600	
Novaya Zemlya (N.)	Russia	48,200	18,600	
W. Spitzbergen	Norway	39,000	15,100	
Novaya Zemlya (S.)	Russia	33,200	12,800	
Sicily	Italy	25,500	9,800	
Sardinia	Italy	24,000	9,300	
N.E. Spitzbergen	Norway	15,000	5,600	
Corsica	France	8,700	3,400	
Crete	Greece	8,350	3,200	
Zealand	Denmark	6,850	2,600	

ASIA

		km²	miles²	
Borneo	S. E. Asia	744,360	287,400	[3]
Sumatra	Indonesia	473,600	182,860	[6]
Honshu	Japan	230,500	88,980	[7]
Sulawesi (Celebes)	Indonesia	189,000	73,000	
Java	Indonesia	126,700	48,900	
Luzon	Philippines	104,700	40,400	
Mindanao	Philippines	101,500	39,200	
Hokkaido	Japan	78,400	30,300	
Sakhalin	Russia	74,060	28,600	
Sri Lanka	Indian Ocean	65,600	25,300	
Taiwan	Pacific Ocean	36,000	13,900	
Kyushu	Japan	35,700	13,800	
Hainan	China	34,000	13,100	
Timor	Indonesia	33,600	13,000	
Shikoku	Japan	18,800	7,300	
Halmahera	Indonesia	18,000	6,900	
Ceram	Indonesia	17,150	6,600	
Sumbawa	Indonesia	15,450	6,000	
Flores	Indonesia	15,200	5,900	
Samar	Philippines	13,100	5,100	
Negros	Philippines	12,700	4,900	
Bangka	Indonesia	12,000	4,600	
Palawan	Philippines	12,000	4,600	
Panay	Philippines	11,500	4,400	
Sumba	Indonesia	11,100	4,300	
Mindoro	Philippines	9,750	3,800	

AFRICA

		km²	miles²	
Madagascar	Indian Ocean	587,040	226,660	[4]
Socotra	Indian Ocean	3,600	1,400	
Réunion	Indian Ocean	2,500	965	
Tenerife	Atlantic Ocean	2,350	900	
Mauritius	Indian Ocean	1,865	720	

OCEANIA

		km²	miles²	
New Guinea	Indon./Papua NG	821,030	317,000	[2]
New Zealand (S.)	Pacific Ocean	150,500	58,100	
New Zealand (N.)	Pacific Ocean	114,700	44,300	
Tasmania	Australia	67,800	26,200	
New Britain	Papua NG	37,800	14,600	
New Caledonia	Pacific Ocean	19,100	7,400	
Viti Levu	Fiji	10,500	4,100	
Hawaii	Pacific Ocean	10,450	4,000	
Bougainville	Papua NG	9,600	3,700	
Guadalcanal	Solomon Is.	6,500	2,500	
Vanua Levu	Fiji	5,550	2,100	
New Ireland	Papua NG	3,200	1,200	

NORTH AMERICA

		km²	miles²	
Greenland	Atlantic Ocean	2,175,600	839,800	[1]
Baffin Is.	Canada	508,000	196,100	[5]
Victoria Is.	Canada	212,200	81,900	[9]
Ellesmere Is.	Canada	212,000	81,800	[10]
Cuba	Caribbean Sea	110,860	42,800	
Newfoundland	Canada	110,680	42,700	
Hispaniola	Dom. Rep./Haiti	76,200	29,400	
Banks Is.	Canada	67,000	25,900	
Devon Is.	Canada	54,500	21,000	
Melville Is.	Canada	42,400	16,400	
Vancouver Is.	Canada	32,150	12,400	
Somerset Is.	Canada	24,300	9,400	
Jamaica	Caribbean Sea	11,400	4,400	
Puerto Rico	Atlantic Ocean	8,900	3,400	
Cape Breton Is.	Canada	4,000	1,500	

SOUTH AMERICA

		km²	miles²	
Tierra del Fuego	Argentina/Chile	47,000	18,100	
Falkland Is. (East)	Atlantic Ocean	6,800	2,600	
South Georgia	Atlantic Ocean	4,200	1,600	
Galapagos (Isabela)	Pacific Ocean	2,250	870	

World: Regions in the News

YUGOSLAVIA
Population 10,500,000
(Serb 62.6%, Albanian 16.5%,
Montenegrin 5%, Hungarian 3.3%,
Muslim 3.2%)
Serbia Population: 5,799,800
(Serb 87.7%, excluding the
provinces of Kosovo and
Vojvodina)
Kosovo Population: 2,084,4000
(Albanian 81.6%, Serb 9.9%)
Vojvodena Population: 1,980,830
(Serb 56.8%, Hungarian 16.9%)
Montenegro Population: 635,000
(Montenegrin 61.9%, Muslim
14.6%, Albanian 7%)

CROATIA
Population: 4,672,000
(Croat 78.1%, Serb 12.2%)

SLOVENIA
Population: 1,972,000
(Slovene 88%, Croat 3%, Serb 2%)

MACEDONIA (F. Y. R. O. M.)
Population: 2,009,000
(Macedonian 64%, Albanian 21.7%,
Turkish 5%, Romanian 3%,
Serb 2%)

BOSNIA-HERZEGOVINA
Population: 3,366,000
(Muslim 49%, Serb 31.2%,
Croat 17.2%)

Map legend:
- –·–·– International boundaries
- –··–··– Republic boundaries
- – – – Province boundaries
- ■ Capital cities
- ———— Dayton Peace Agreement Boundary
- Muslim–Croat Federation
- Bosnian Serb Republic

0   100   200 km

FORMER YUGOSLAVIA AND KOSOVO

The former Yugoslavia, a federation of six republics, split apart in 1991–2. Fearing Serb domination, Croatia, Slovenia, Macedonia and Bosnia-Herzegovina declared themselves independent. This left two states, Serbia and Montenegro, to continue as Yugoslavia. The presence in Croatia and Bosnia-Herzegovina of Orthodox Christian Serbs, Roman Catholic Croats, and Muslims led to civil war and 'ethnic cleansing'. In 1995, the war ended when the Dayton Peace Accord affirmed Bosnia-Herzegovina as a single state partitioned into a Muslim-Croat Federation and a Serbian Republic.

But the status of Kosovo, a former autonomous Yugoslav region, remained unresolved. Kosovo's autonomy had been abolished in 1989 and the Albanian-speaking, Muslim Kosovars were forced to accept direct Serbian rule. After 1995, support grew for the rebel Kosovo Liberation Army. The Serbs hit back and thousands of Kosovars were forced to flee their homes. In March 1999, NATO launched an aerial offensive in an attempt to halt the 'ethnic cleansing'. A Serb military withdrawal from Kosovo was finally agreed in June 1999.

KOSOVO
0   20   40 km
- ■ Capital city
- ● Other towns
- –·–·– International boundaries

NO-FLY ZONE
0   100   200 km
- ■ Capital cities
- ● Cities
- ⧄ Kurdish region
- No-fly zone

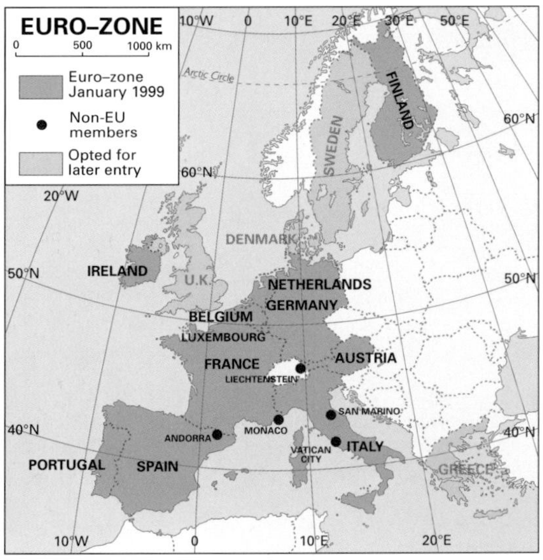

EURO–ZONE
0   500   1000 km
- Euro–zone January 1999
- ● Non-EU members
- Opted for later entry

THE EURO
The euro (€) is the single currency which will eventually replace the national currencies of the countries of the European Economic and Monetary Union (EMU). Euro notes and coins will come into circulation in January 2000. The euro will be used alongside national currencies until July 2002 when it will become the sole legal tender in the EMU countries.

1 euro (€) = US$ 1.66* = £ 0.66*
*market rate 24.05.99

THE NEAR EAST
0   25   50 km
- –··–··– 1949 Armistice Line
- – – – 1974 Cease–fire Line
- *Efrata* ● Main Jewish settlements in the West Bank and Gaza Strip
- *Halhul* ■ Main Palestinian Arab towns in the West Bank and Gaza Strip
- *'Ammān* ■ Capital cities

THE CONGO
0   500   1000 km
- ■ Capital cities
- ● Cities
- –·–·– International boundaries
- Neighbouring countries involved in the conflict in the Congo

CONGO
The Congo gained independence from Belgium in 1960 and was re-named Zaïre in 1971. Ethnic rivalries caused instability until 1965, when the country became a one-party state, ruled by President Mobuto. The government allowed the formation of political parties in 1990, but elections were repeatedly postponed. In 1996, fighting broke out in eastern Zaire, as the Tutsi-Hutu conflict in Burundi and Rwanda spilled over. The rebel leader Laurent Kabila took power in 1997, ousting Mobutu and re-naming the country. A rebellion against Kabila broke out in 1998. Rwanda and Uganda supported the rebels, while Angola, Chad, Namibia and Zimbabwe sent troops to assist Kabila.

ISRAEL
Population: 5,644,000 (inc. East Jerusalem and Jewish settlers in the areas under Israeli administration. Jewish 82%, Arab Muslim 13.8%, Arab Christian 2.5%, Druze 1.7%)

West Bank
Population: 1,122,900 (Palestinian Arabs 97% [of whom Arab Muslim 85%, Jewish 7%, Christian 8%])

Gaza Strip
Population: 748,400 (Arab 98%)

JORDAN
Population: 4,435,000 (Arab 99% [of whom about 50% are Palestinian Arab])

LEBANON
Population: 3,506,000 (Arab 93% [of whom 83% are Lebanese Arab and 10% Palestinian Arab])

WORLD MAPS

SETTLEMENTS

■ PARIS   ■ Berne   ◉ Livorno   ◉ Brugge   ◎ Algeciras   ○ Frejus   ○ Oberammergau   ○ Thira

Settlement symbols and type styles vary according to the scale of each map and indicate the importance
of towns on the map rather than specific population figures

∴ Ruins or Archæological Sites   Wells in Desert

ADMINISTRATION

——— International Boundaries

– – – – International Boundaries
(Undefined or Disputed)

·········· Internal Boundaries

⬭ National Parks

Country Names
NICARAGUA

Administrative
Area Names

KENT

CALABRIA

International boundaries show the *de facto* situation where there are rival claims to territory

COMMUNICATIONS

——— Principal Roads

——— Other Roads

✈ Airfields

——— Principal Railways

⊕ Other Railways

⊣- - -⊢ Railway Tunnels

⊣- - -⊢ Road Tunnels

– – – Railways
Under Construction

·········· Principal Canals

⋈ Passes

PHYSICAL FEATURES

～～ Perennial Streams

– – – Intermittent Streams

⬭ Perennial Lakes

⬭ Intermittent Lakes

Swamps and Marshes

Permanent Ice
and Glaciers

▲ 8848 Elevations in metres

▼ 8500 Sea Depths in metres

1134 Height of Lake Surface
Above Sea Level in metres

ELEVATION AND DEPTH TINTS

Height of Land above Sea Level   Land Below Sea Level   Depth of Sea

in metres	6000	4000	3000	2000	1500	1000	400	200	0						
										6000	12 000	15 000	18 000	24 000	in feet
in feet	18 000	12 000	9000	6000	4500	3000	1200	600							
									0	200	2000	4000	5000	6000	8000	in metres

Some of the maps have different contours to highlight and clarify the principal relief features

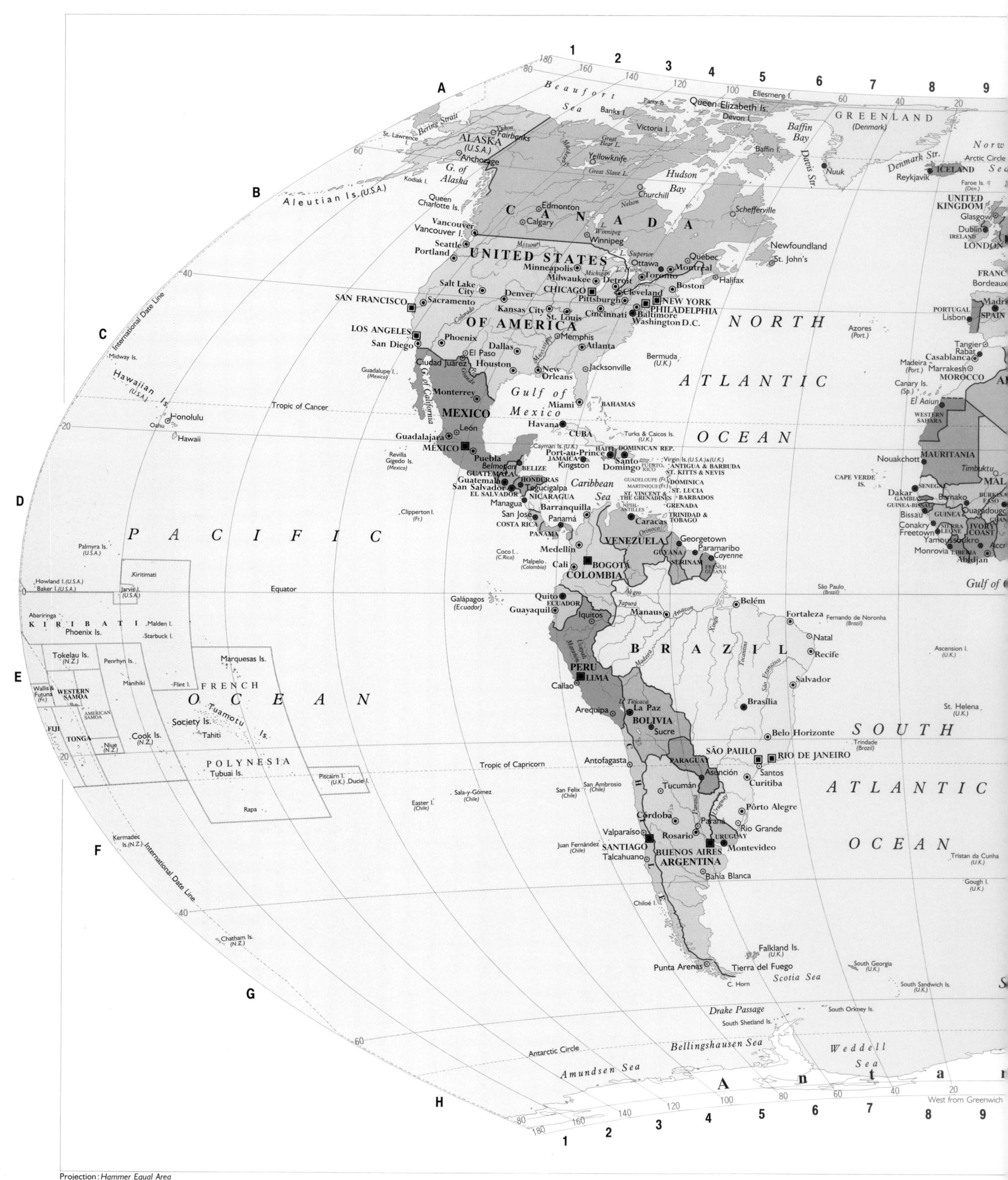

Projection: *Hammer Equal Area*

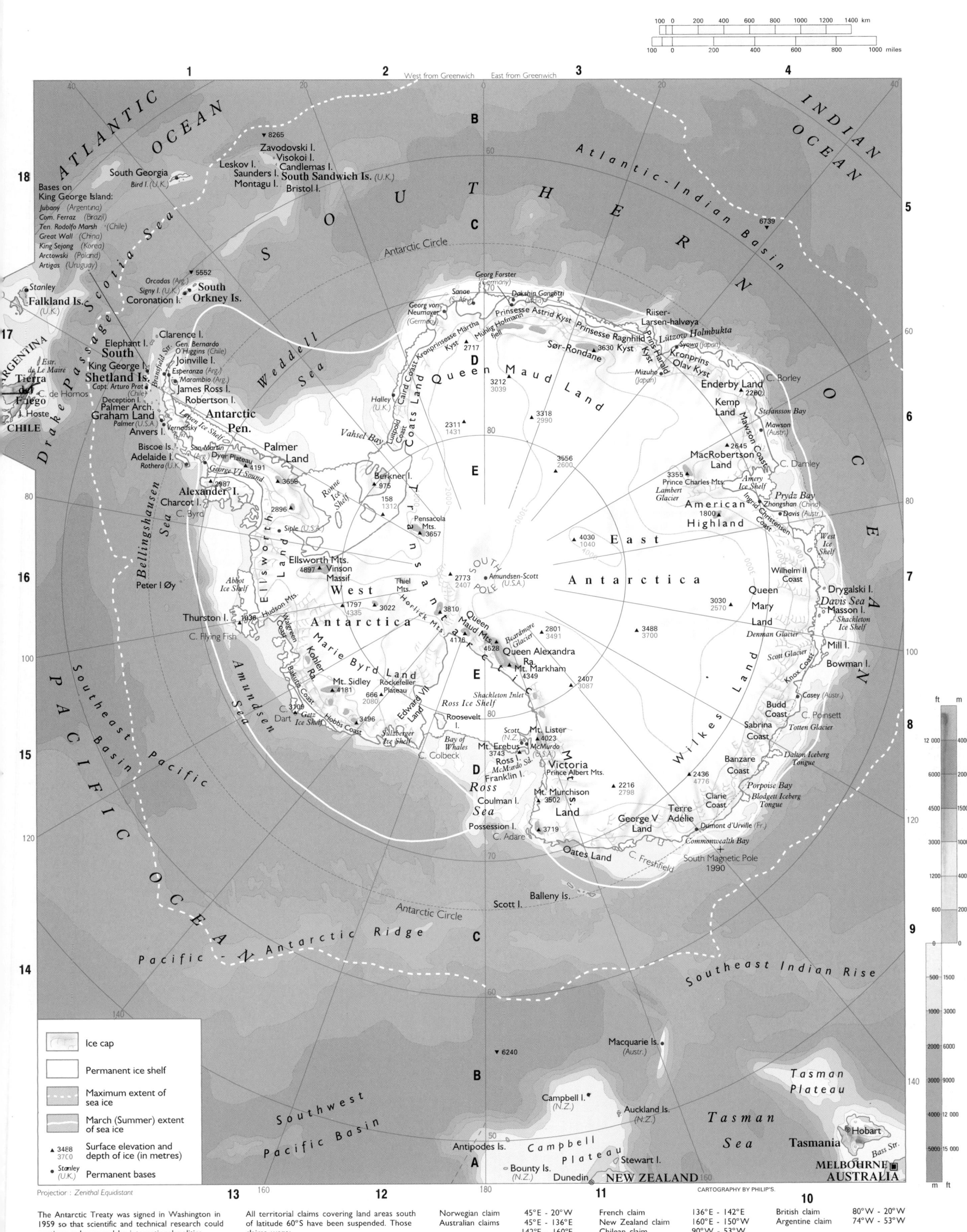

Bases on
King George Island:
Jubany (Argentina)
Com. Ferraz (Brazil)
Ten. Rodolfo Marsh (Chile)
Great Wall (China)
King Sejong (Korea)
Arctowski (Poland)
Artigas (Uruguay)

Legend

	Ice cap
	Permanent ice shelf
	Maximum extent of sea ice
	March (Summer) extent of sea ice
▲ 3488 37C0	Surface elevation and depth of ice (in metres)
• Stanley (U.K.)	Permanent bases

Projection : Zenithal Equidistant

CARTOGRAPHY BY PHILIP'S

The Antarctic Treaty was signed in Washington in 1959 so that scientific and technical research could continue unhampered by international politics.

All territorial claims covering land areas south of latitude 60°S have been suspended. Those claims were:

Norwegian claim	45°E - 20°W	
Australian claims	45°E - 136°E	
	142°E - 160°E	
French claim	136°E - 142°E	
New Zealand claim	160°E - 150°W	
Chilean claim	90°W - 53°W	
British claim	80°W - 20°W	
Argentine claim	74°W - 53°W	

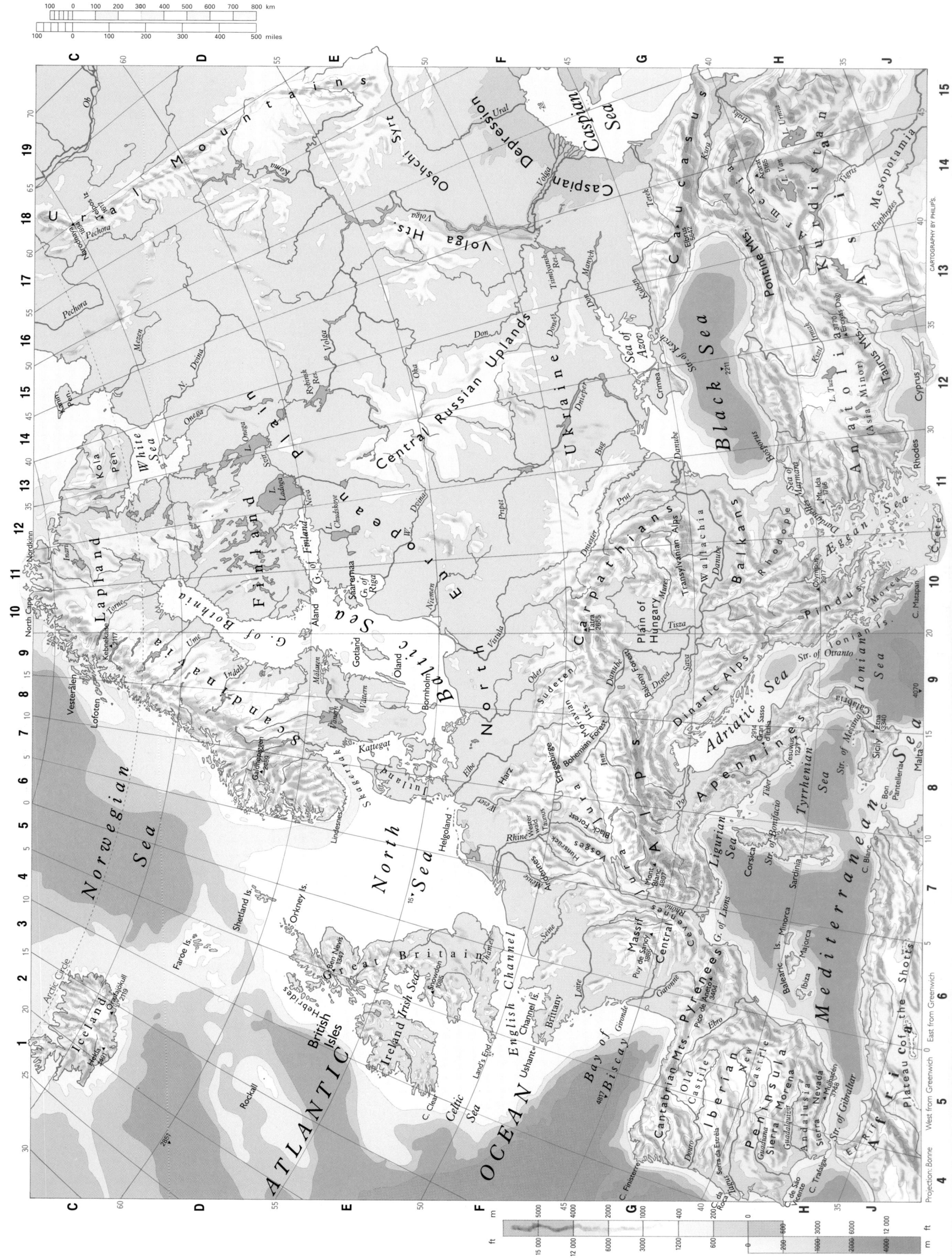

Projection: Bonne

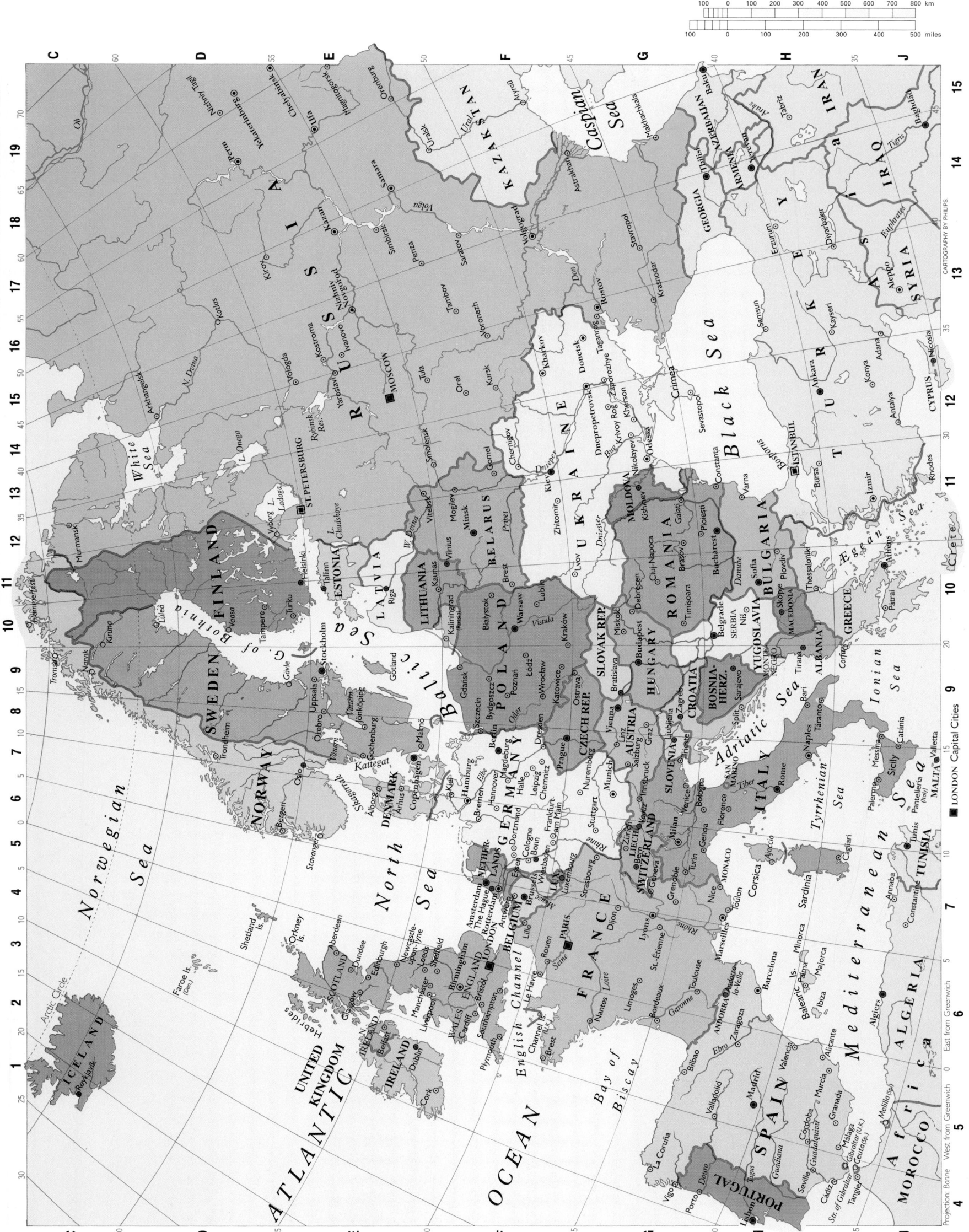

50   0   25   50   75   100   125   150   175 km
50   0   25   50   75   100   125 miles

RUSSIA

Maanselkä

F i n l a n d

L a p p l a n d

Varanger-halvøya
Nordkinn-halvøya
Laksefjorden
Tanafjorden
Varangerfjorden
Vardø
Vadsø
Kirkenes
Nikel
Nordkapp
Magerøya
Honningsvåg
Porsangen
Seiland
Sørøya
Kvaløya
Hammerfest
Alta
Altafjorden
Kautokeino
Karasjok
Lakselv
Utsjoki
Inari
Inarijärvi
Ivalo
Sodankylä
Salla
Rovaniemi
Kemijärvi
Kemijoki
Ounasjoki
Kittilä
Enontekiö
Muonio
Kolari
Pello
Ylitornio
Haparanda
Tornio
Kemi
Keminmaa
Oulu
Oulujoki
Oulujärvi
Muhos
Haukipudas
Kalajoki
Raahe

P e r ä p o h j o l a

N o r r b o t t e n
Kiruna
Gällivare
Jokkmokk
Boden
Luleå
Piteå
Kalix
Överkalix
Övertorneå
Skellefteå
Umeå
Arvidsjaur
Arjeplog
Storuman
Lycksele
Vilhelmina
Sorsele

Lule älv
Råne älv
Skellefte älv
Torne älv
Pite älv
Kalix älv

N O R W A Y

Tromsø
Narvik
Harstad
Sortland
Andenes
Andøya
Langøya
Hinnøya
Vesterålen
Senja
Lofoten
Svolvær
Vestfjorden
Bodø
Fauske
Mo i Rana
Mosjøen
Vefsna
Brønnøysund
Sandnessjøen
Alsten
Vega
Leka
Rørvik
Namsos
Grong
Steinkjer
Levanger
Verdalsøra
Trondheim
Orkanger
Melhus

Trøndelag
Helgeland
Nordland

Kjølen

Jämtland
Ångermanland
Ångermanälven
Strömsund
Östersund
Sollefteå
Örnsköldsvik
Härnösand

Arctic Circle

O C E A N

S E A

Vänern

ICELAND
Reykjavík
Keflavík
Akranes
Akureyri
Húsavík
Egilsstaðir
Seyðisfjörður
Höfn
Vík
Heimaey
Vestmannaeyjar
Surtsey
Vatnajökull
Hofsjökull
Langjökull
Mýrdalsjökull
Snæfellsjökull
Drangajökull
Hvannadalshnúkur 2000
Hekla 1491
Hvítá
Þjórsá
Jökulsá á Fjöllum
Hunaflói
Skagafjörður
Eyjafjörður
Ísafjörður
Grímsey
Bolungarvík
Geysir

FÆROE ISLANDS (Føroyar)
Tórshavn
Streymoy
Eysturoy
Vágar
Suðuroy
Sandoy
Bordoy
Nólsoy
Viðoy
Klaksvík

Arctic Circle
20 West from Greenwich

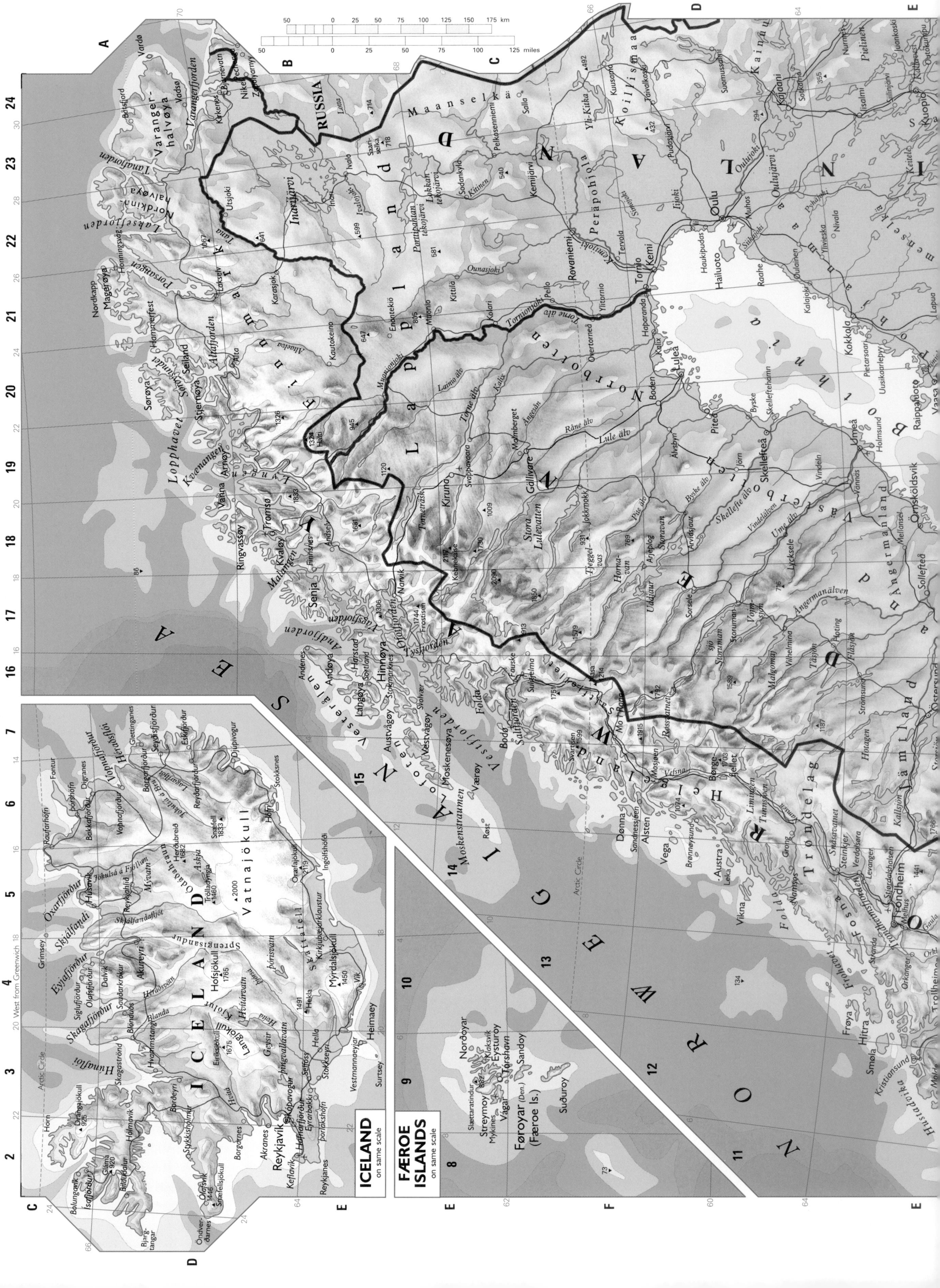

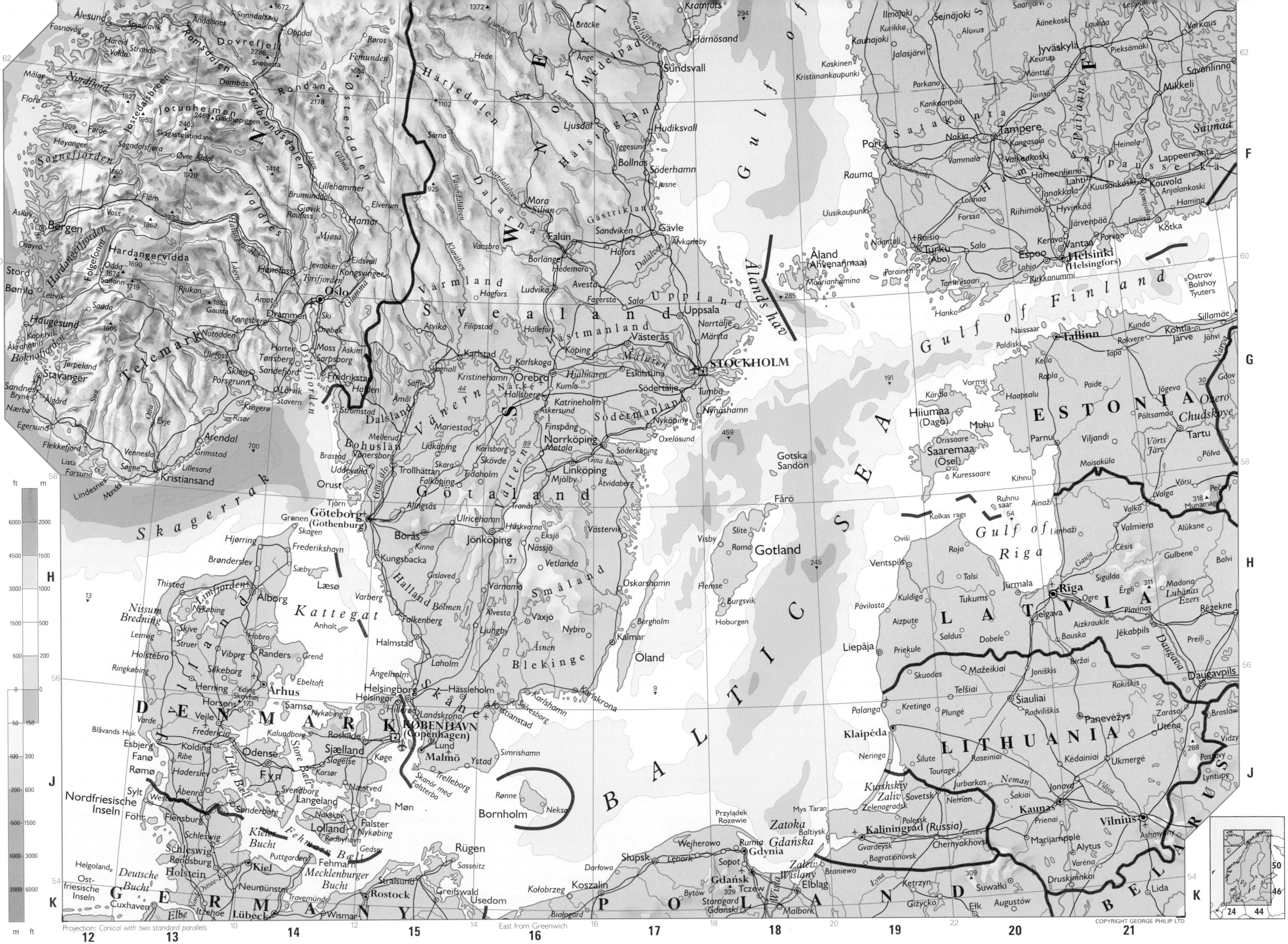

BALTIC SEA

FINLAND

Gulf of Finland

ESTONIA

LATVIA

Gulf of Riga

LITHUANIA

RUSSIA

POLAND

GERMANY

DENMARK

NORWAY

SWEDEN

Sweeland

Götaland

Svealand

Norrland

Dalarna

Värmland

Halland

Skåne

Bohuslän

Gotland

Öland

Bornholm

Rügen

Kattegat

Skagerrak

Ålands hav

Gulf of Bothnia

Helsinki (Helsingfors)
Tampere
Turku (Åbo)
Espoo
Vantaa
Lahti
Jyväskylä
Mikkeli
Kotka
Rauma
Pori
Hanko

Tallinn
Tartu
Pärnu
Narva
Hiiumaa (Dagö)
Saaremaa (Ösel)
Muhu

Riga
Jūrmala
Daugavpils
Liepāja
Ventspils
Klaipėda
Šiauliai
Jelgava

Vilnius
Kaunas
Panevėžys
Kaliningrad (Russia)
Gdańsk
Gdynia
Sopot
Elbląg

STOCKHOLM
Uppsala
Västerås
Örebro
Eskilstuna
Norrköping
Linköping
Jönköping
Göteborg (Gothenburg)
Malmö
Helsingborg
Borås
Gävle
Sundsvall
Falun
Karlstad
Kalmar
Visby
Karlskrona

Oslo
Bergen
Kristiansand
Stavanger
Drammen
Oslofjorden

KØBENHAVN (Copenhagen)
Århus
Ålborg
Odense
Esbjerg

Kiel
Lübeck
Rostock
Flensburg

Projection: Conical with two standard parallels

COPYRIGHT GEORGE PHILIP LTD

East from Greenwich

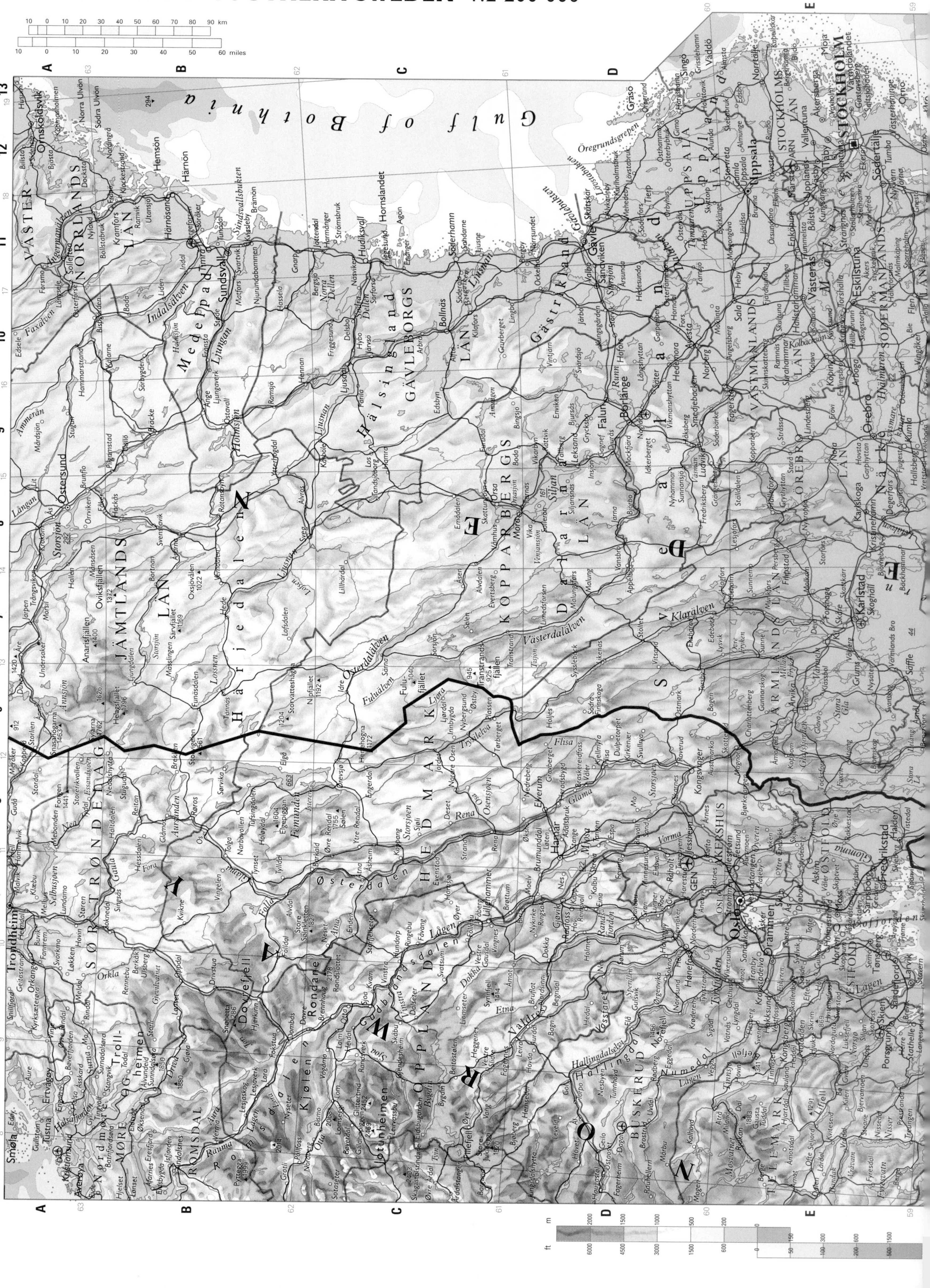

Gulf of Bothnia

VÄSTER- NORRLANDS LÄN

JÄMTLANDS LÄN

Härjedalen

Medelpad

Hälsingland

GÄVLEBORGS LÄN

Gästrikland

KOPPARBERGS LÄN

DALARNA LÄN

VÄRMLAND

VÄSTMANLANDS LÄN

ÖREBRO LÄN

UPPSALA LÄN

STOCKHOLMS LÄN

STOCKHOLM

Uppsala

Gävle

Sundsvall

Östersund

Storsjön

Siljan

Falun

Borlänge

Hudiksvall

Söderhamn

Bollnäs

Härnösand

Örnsköldsvik

SØR-TRØNDELAG

Trondheim

MØRE OG ROMSDAL

Dovrefjell

Rondane

Jotunheimen

OPPLAND

HEDMARK

Østerdalen

Lillehammer

Hamar

Gudbrandsdalen

BUSKERUD

TELEMARK

AKERSHUS

OSLO

VESTFOLD

ØSTFOLD

Fredrikstad

Drammen

Glomma

Klarälven

Västerdalälven

Österdalälven

Ljusnan

Indalsälven

Ljungan

Storsjön

Skien

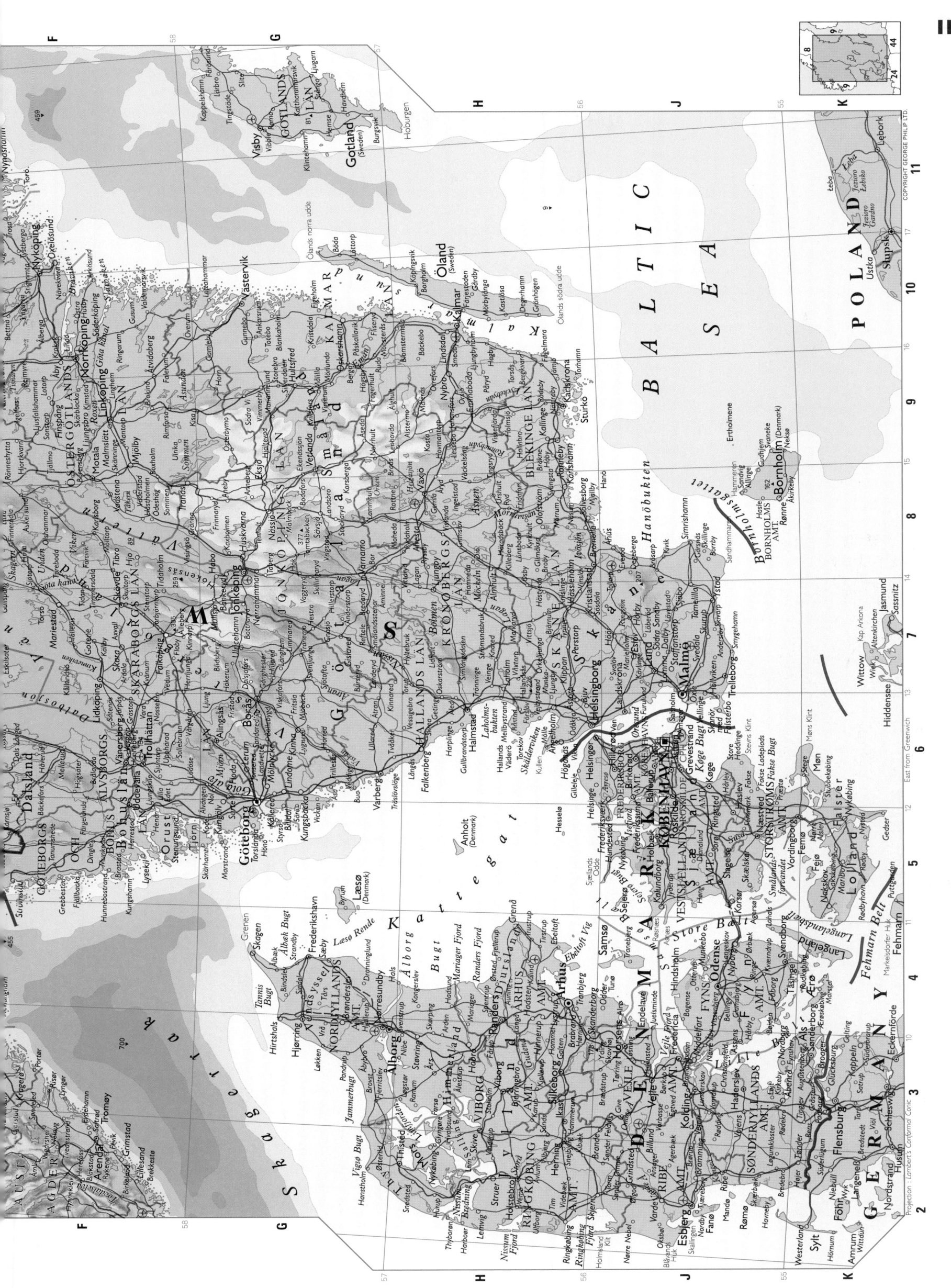

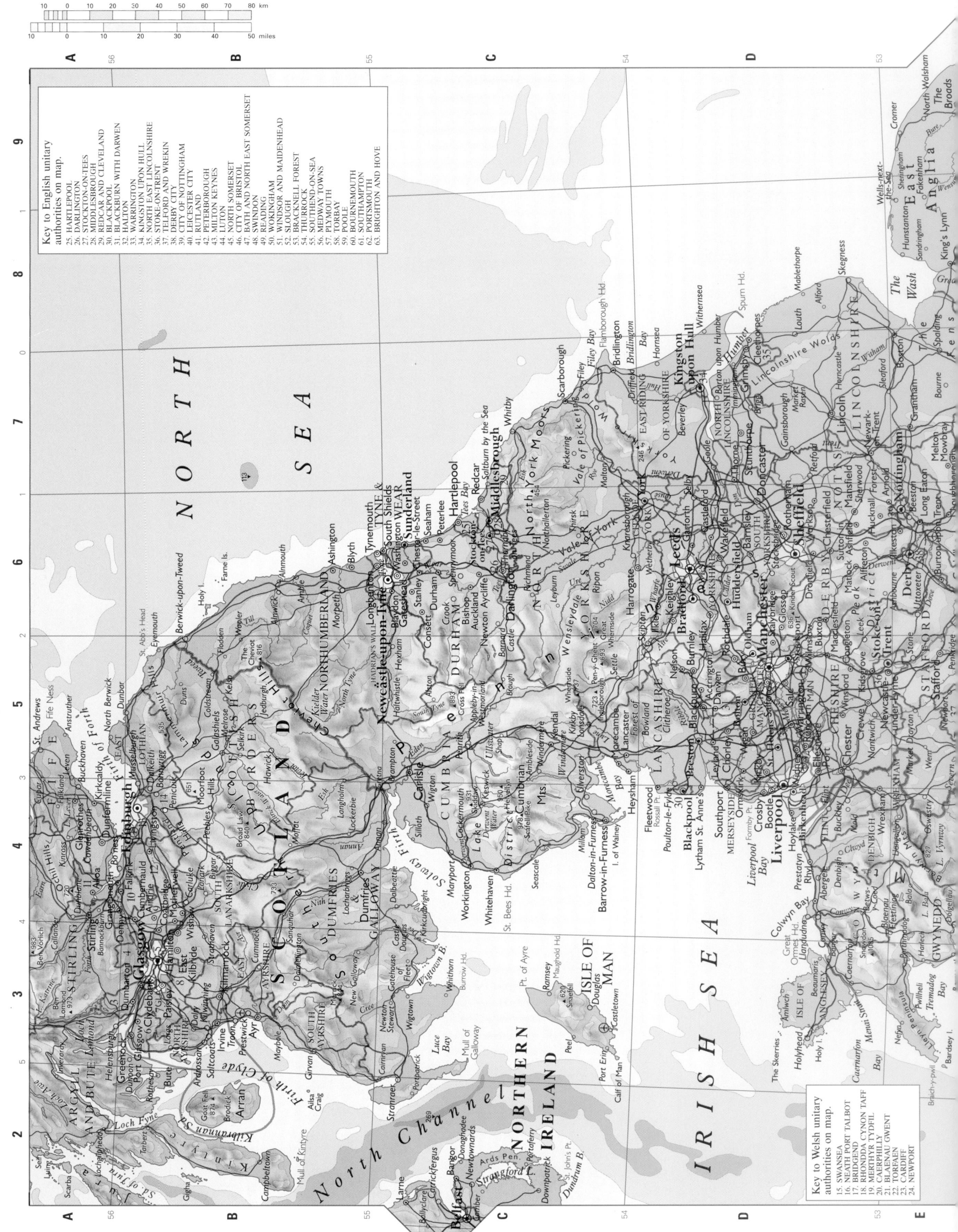

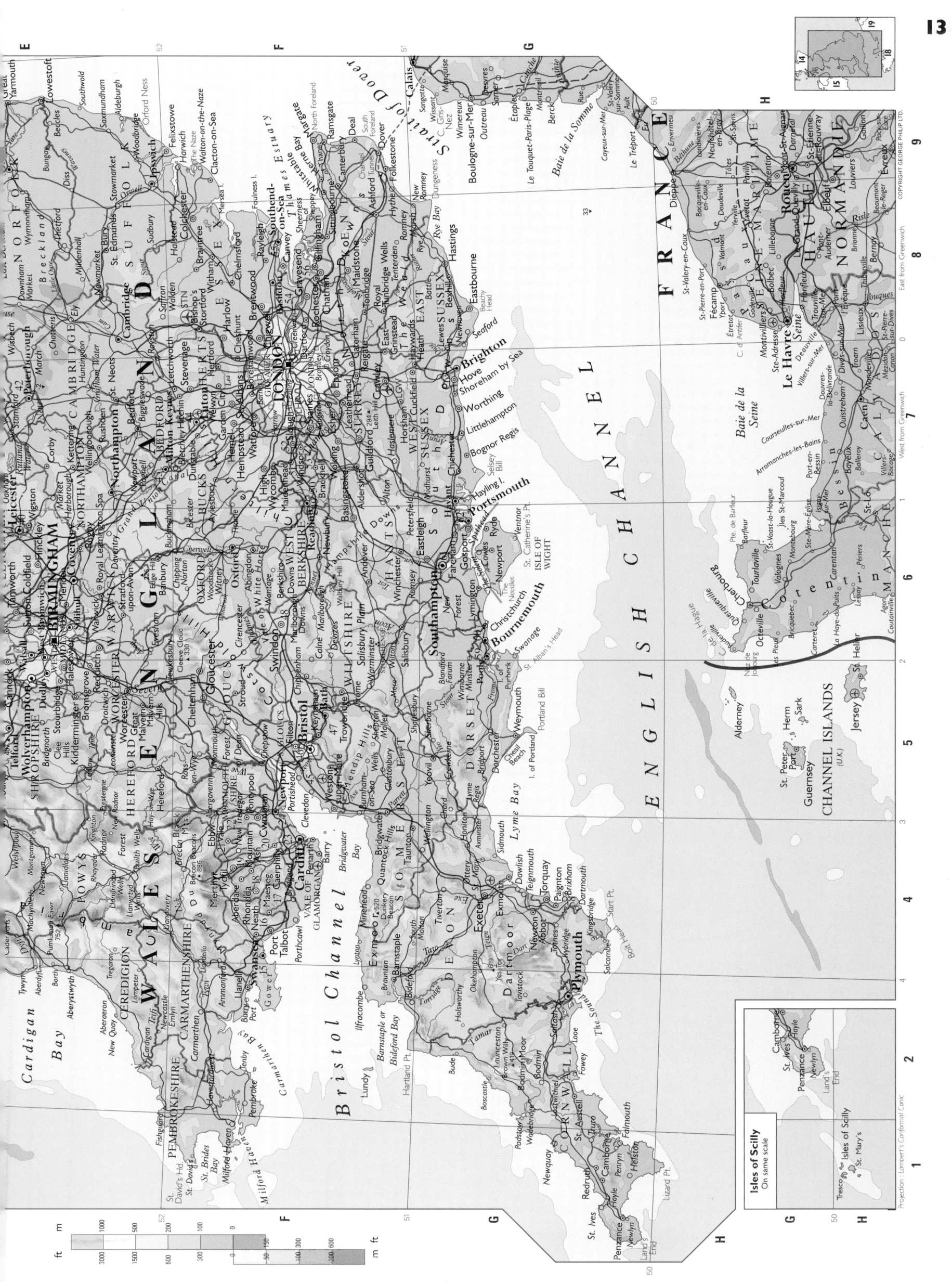

10 0 10 20 30 40 50 60 70 80 km
10 0 10 20 30 40 50 miles

Key to Scottish unitary authorities on map

1. CITY OF ABERDEEN
2. DUNDEE CITY
3. WEST DUNBARTONSHIRE
4. EAST DUNBARTONSHIRE
5. CITY OF GLASGOW
6. INVERCLYDE
7. RENFREWSHIRE
8. EAST RENFREWSHIRE
9. NORTH LANARKSHIRE
10. FALKIRK
11. CLACKMANNANSHIRE
12. WEST LOTHIAN
13. CITY OF EDINBURGH
14. MIDLOTHIAN

ORKNEY IS.
On same scale

SHETLAND IS.
On same scale

SCOTLAND

ATLANTIC OCEAN

NORTH SEA

ENGLAND

NORTHERN IRELAND

North Channel

Projection : Lambert's Conformal Conic

West from Greenwich

COPYRIGHT GEORGE PHILIP LTD.

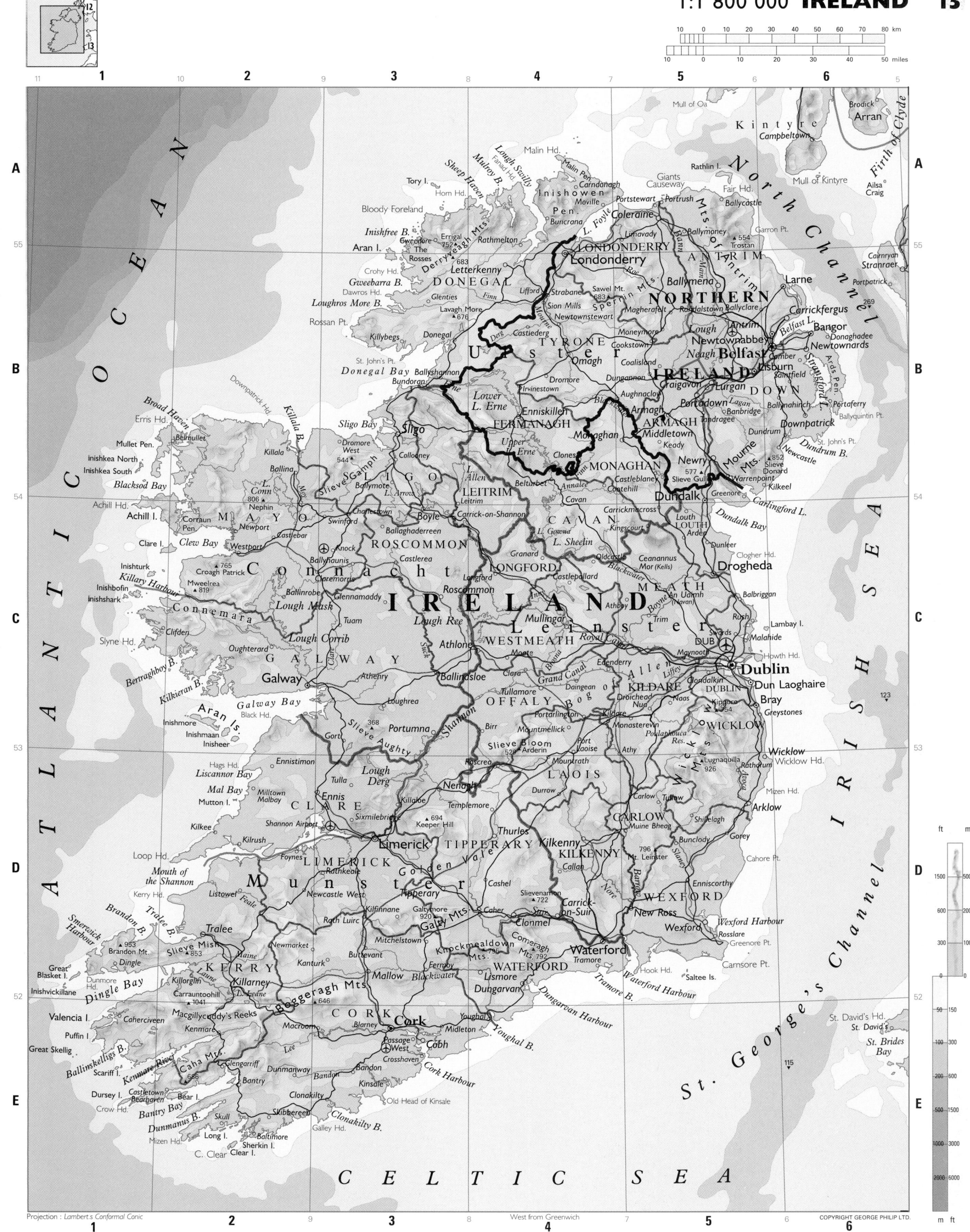

50 0 25 50 75 100 125 150 175 km
50 0 25 50 75 100 125 miles

17
18 19

ATLANTIC OCEAN

Shetland Is.
Unst
Fetlar
Yell
Foula
Mainland
Lerwick
Fair Isle

1224

316

Westray Sanday
Orkney Is.
Mainland Stronsay
Hoy Kirkwall
South
Ronaldsay
C. Wrath
Thurso
Pentland Firth
Wick
Helmsdale

NORWAY
Bergen
Askøy
Haugesund
Stord
Bømlo
Stavanger
Kopervik
Åkrahamn
Sandnes
Bryne
Nærbø

Lewis
Stornoway
Harris
St. Kilda
North Uist
Benbecula
South Uist
Barra

Outer Hebrides
789
North Minch
Ullapool
Lairg
Golspie
Tain
Invergordon
Dingwall
Moray Firth
Nairn
Elgin Buckie Banff Fraserburgh
Inverness Huntly Peterhead
North West Highlands
L. Ness
1182
Aviemore
Don Inverurie
Aberdeen
Ballater Stonehaven

Skye
Raasay
Portree
Maliag
Rhum
Eigg
Coll
Tiree
Mull
Tobermory
Oban
Colonsay

Inner Hebrides

SCOTLAND
Ben Nevis
1342
Fort William
Grampian Mts.
1311
Dee
1214
Forfar
Arbroath
Montrose
Perth
Dundee
St. Andrews

238

NORTH SEA

Jura
Islay
Campbeltown
Arran
North Channel
Firth of Clyde
Greenock
Paisley
Glasgow
East Kilbride
Hamilton
973
L. Lomond
Stirling
Dunfermline
Kirkcaldy
Glenrothes
Dunbar
Edinburgh
Galashiels
Southern Uplands
816
Berwick-upon-Tweed
Kilmarnock
Irvine
Ayr
Jedburgh
Hawick
840
Cheviot Hills
Alnwick

Malin Hd.
Buncrana
Coleraine
Letterkenny
Ballymena
Larne
Aran I.
Lifford
NORTHERN IRELAND
Londonderry
Ulster
Antrim
Bangor
Belfast
Omagh
Portadown
Lisburn
Lurgan
Lough
Neagh
Dumfries
Annan
Kirkcudbright
Stranraer
Mull of Galloway
Whitehaven
Workington
Carlisle
Hexham
Gateshead Durham
Newcastle-upon-Tyne
South Shields
Sunderland
Hartlepool
Redcar
893
Pennines
Darlington
Middlesbrough
Stockton-on-Tees
16

Donegal
Bundoran
Lower L. Erne
Enniskillen
Omagh
Clones
Castleblaney
Newry
Armagh
Cumbrian Mts.
978
Barrow-in-Furness
Lancaster
Scarborough
Bridlington

Ballina
Sligo
Leitrim
Cavan
Dundalk
Drogheda
UNITED
Douglas
I. of Man
Harrogate
York
Beverley
Kingston upon Hull

Achill I.
L. Conn
Castlebar
Westport
L. Mask
Connemara
Galway
IRELAND
Roscommon
Longford
Lough Ree
Athlone
Mullingar
Boyne
KINGDOM
IRISH SEA
Blackpool
Preston
Blackburn
Burnley
Keighley
Bradford
Huddersfield
Halifax
Barnsley
Leeds
636
Scunthorpe
Doncaster
Grimsby
Rotherham
Louth
Humber

Lough Corrib
Ballinasloe
Tullamore
Birr
Port Laoise
Athy
Dublin
Dun Laoghaire
Bray
Anglesey
Holyhead
Bangor
Colwyn Bay
Chester
Liverpool
Manchester
Warrington
Stockport
Oldham
Chesterfield
Crewe
Sheffield
Mansfield
Lincoln
Skegness
The Wash

Galway B.
Aran Is.
Ennis
Lough Derg
Nenagh
Thurles
Carlow
Kilkenny
Wexford
Arklow
Wicklow Mts.
926
Snowdon
1085
Wrexham
Pwllheli
Stoke on Trent
Stafford
Derby
Nottingham
Trent
Granthan
King's Lynn
Cromer

953
Kilrush
Limerick
Tipperary
Clonmel
Carrick-on-Suir
Galtee Mts.
Cambrian Mts.
Shrewsbury
Welshpool
Telford
ENGLAND
Leicester
Nuneaton
Corby
Peterborough
Thetford
Ely
Norwich
Great Yarmouth
Lowestoft

Shannon
Listowel
Tralee
Mallow
Blackwater
Dungarvan
Cardigan Bay
Aberystwyth
Welshpool
BIRMINGHAM
Redditch
Rugby
Royal Leamington Spa
Northampton
Bedford
Cambridge
Bury St. Edmunds
Ipswich

NETHERLANDS
's-Gravenhage
(Den Haag)
ROTTERDAM
Dordrecht
Hoek van Holland
Texel
Den Helder
Haarlem
Alkmaar

Dingle
Killarney
Carrauntoohil
Valencia
Macgillycuddy's Reeks
Bandon
Kinsale
Cork
Cóbh
Youghal
WALES
Carmarthen
Merthyr Tydfil
Neath
886
Cwmran
Brecon
Hereford
Worcester
Cheltenham
Gloucester
Cotswold Hills
Oxford
High Wycombe
Hemel Hempstead
Luton
Stevenage
Harlow
Milton Keynes
Colchester
Chelmsford
Felixstowe

C. Clear
Bantry
Llanelli
Swansea
Port Talbot
Rhondda
Pembroke
Milford Haven
Haverfordwest
Fishguard
Cardiff
Newport
Bristol
Bath
Barry
Swindon
Newbury
Reading
Slough
Basildon
LONDON
Thames
Southend-on-Sea
Margate
36

Newquay
Bude
Barnstaple
Exmoor
Weston-super-Mare
Taunton
Yeovil
Salisbury
Winchester
Guildford
Crawley
Maidstone
Ashford
Folkestone
Dover
Canterbury
Chatham
Reigate
Dunkerque
Zeebrugge
Oostende
Brugge
Gent
Mechelen
BELGIUM
BRUSSELS
(Bruxelles)

CELTIC SEA
618
Dartmoor
Exeter
Exmouth
Torbay
Poole
Weymouth
Bournemouth
Southampton
Portsmouth
Fareham
Havant
Worthing
Brighton
Eastbourne
Hastings
Isle of Wight
Newport
Calais
Boulogne
Gris-Nez
Le Touquet-Paris-Plage
33
Lille
Tourcoing
Tournai
Béthune
Bruay-la-Buissière
Lens
Valenciennes
Cambrai

Land's End
Penzance
Falmouth
St. Austell
Truro
Plymouth
Isles of Scilly

English Channel
Str. of Dover
Dieppe
Fécamp
Le Tréport
Abbeville
Amiens
St. Quentin
Picardie
FRANCE

C. de la Hague
Pte. de Barfleur
Alderney
Guernsey
St. Peter Port
Sark
Channel Is.
(U.K.)
St. Helier
Jersey
Cherbourg
Valognes
Bayeux
Caen
Lisieux
Elbeuf
Rouen
Bolbec
Seine
Trouville-sur-Mer
Pays de Caux
Cotentin

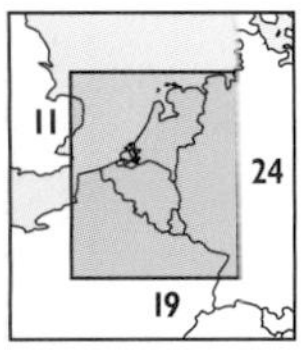

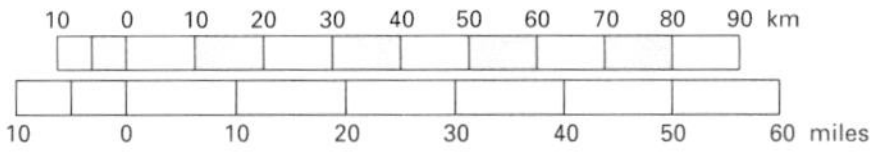

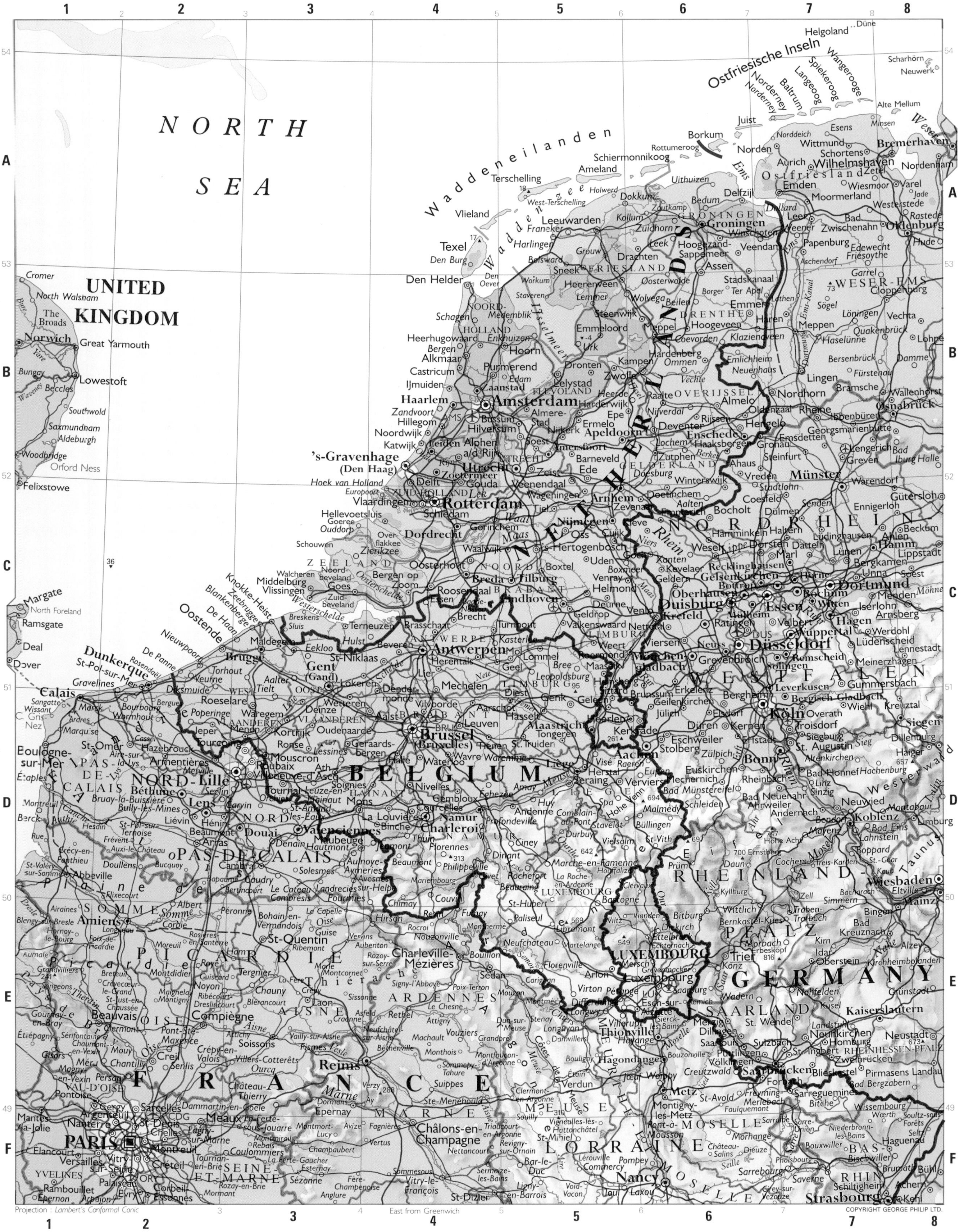

NORTH SEA

UNITED KINGDOM

NETHERLANDS

BELGIUM

FRANCE

GERMANY

LUXEMBOURG

Amsterdam · 's-Gravenhage (Den Haag) · Rotterdam · Utrecht · Groningen · Brussel (Bruxelles) · Antwerpen · Gent (Gand) · Luxembourg · Köln · Düsseldorf · Dortmund · Paris · Strasbourg

Projection : Lambert's Conformal Conic

East from Greenwich

COPYRIGHT GEORGE PHILIP LTD.

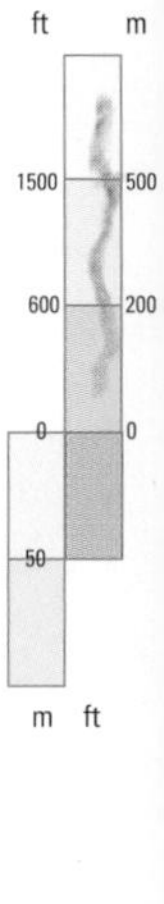

Underlined towns give their name to the
administrative area in which they stand.

DÉPARTEMENTS IN THE PARIS AREA
1. Ville de Paris   3. Val-de-Marne
2. Seine-St-Denis   4. Hauts-de-Seine

Projection : Lambert's Conformal Conic

West from Greenwich

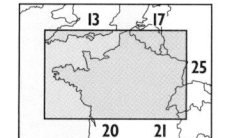

Underlined towns give their name to the
administrative area in which they stand.

COPYRIGHT GEORGE PHILIP LTD.

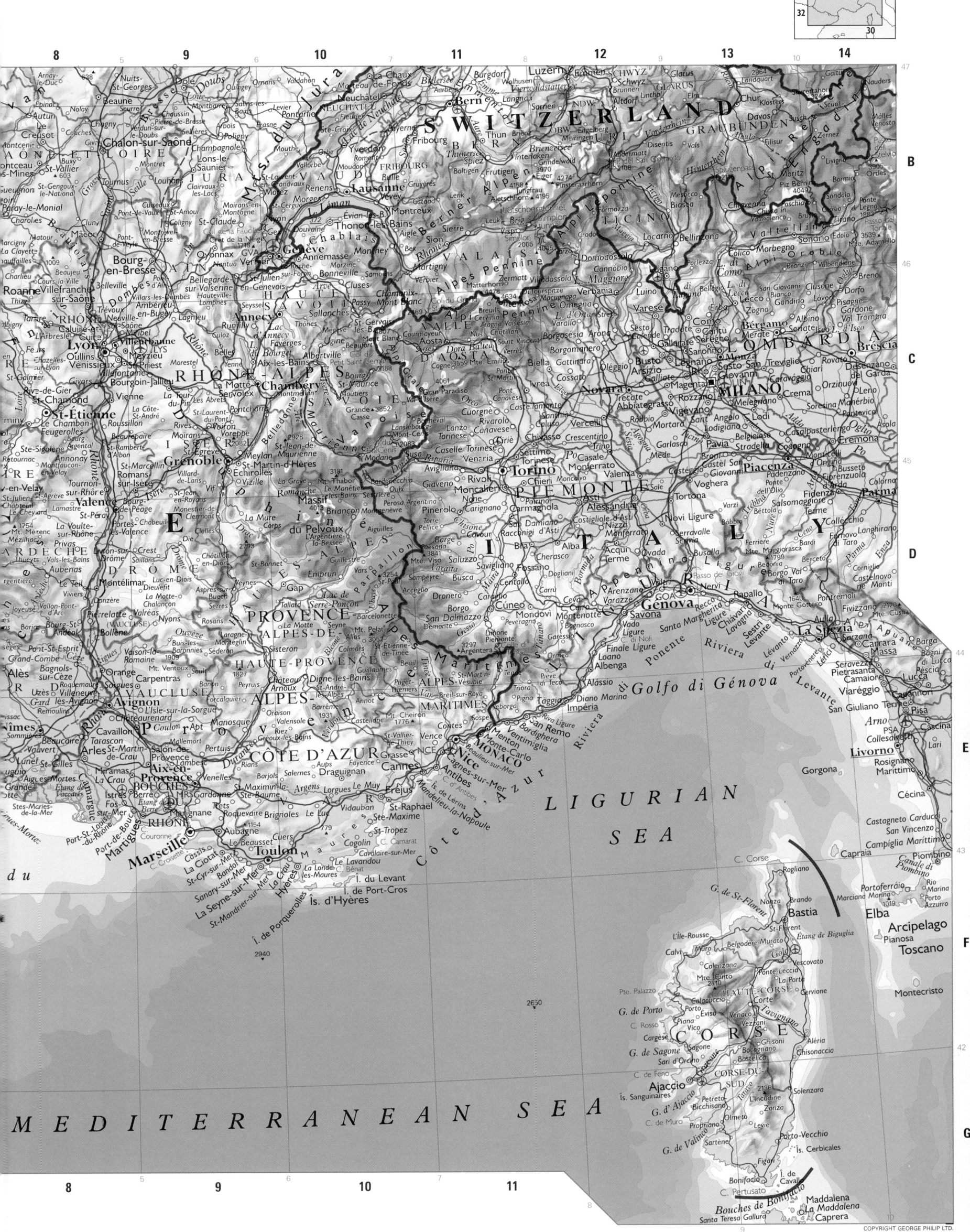

9
46
16
18
20
48
40
41

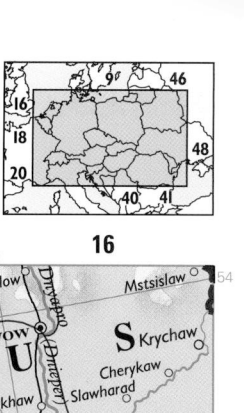

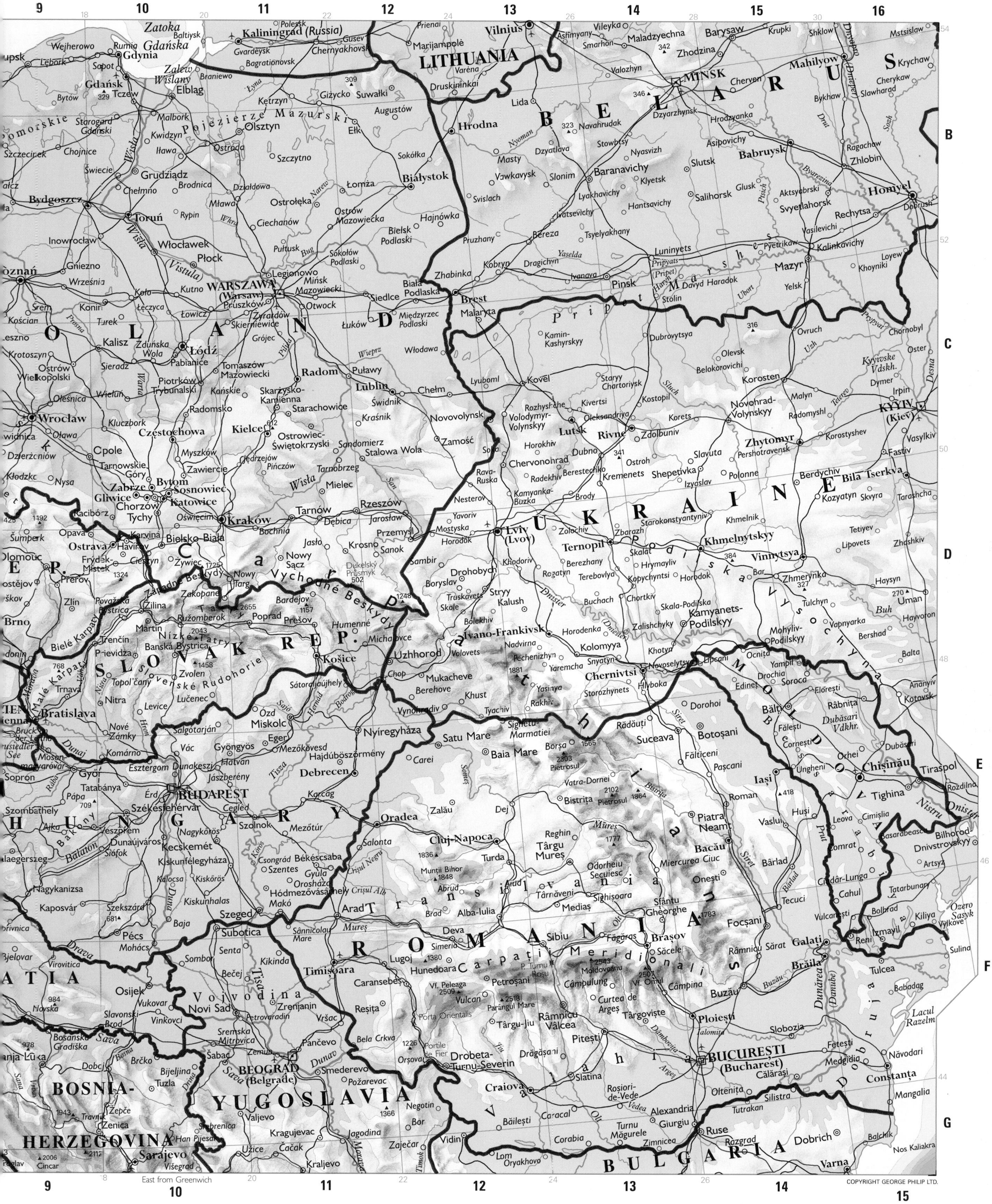
LITHUANIA
BELARUS
POLAND
UKRAINE
SLOVAK REP.
HUNGARY
ROMANIA
MOLDOVA
YUGOSLAVIA
BOSNIA-HERZEGOVINA
BULGARIA
Vilnius
MINSK
WARSZAWA (Warsaw)
Kaliningrad (Russia)
Zatoka Gdańska
Gdańsk
Gdynia
Elbląg
Olsztyn
Toruń
Bydgoszcz
Poznań
Łódź
Wrocław
Katowice
Kraków
Lublin
Białystok
Brest
Hrodna
Baranavichy
Pinsk
Babruysk
Homyel
Mahilyow
KYYIV (Kiev)
Zhytomyr
Rivne
Lutsk
Lviv (Lvov)
Ternopil
Khmelnytskyy
Vinnytsya
Chernivtsi
Ivano-Frankivsk
Uzhhorod
Košice
Prešov
Bratislava
BUDAPEST
Miskolc
Debrecen
Nyíregyháza
Szeged
Pécs
Győr
Oradea
Cluj-Napoca
Timişoara
Arad
Braşov
Sibiu
Iaşi
Chişinău
Tiraspol
Galaţi
Brăila
Constanţa
BUCUREŞTI (Bucharest)
Ploieşti
Craiova
BEOGRAD (Belgrade)
Novi Sad
Sarajevo
Varna
Ruse
Dobrich
Pripet Marshes
Carpaţii Meridionali
Transilvania
Podil's'ka Vysochyna
Vojvodina
Dobrogea
Wisła (Vistula)
Dunărea (Danube)
Dnister
Prut
Siret
Tisza
Sava
Drava
East from Greenwich
9
10
11
12
13
14
15
16
B
C
D
E
F
G

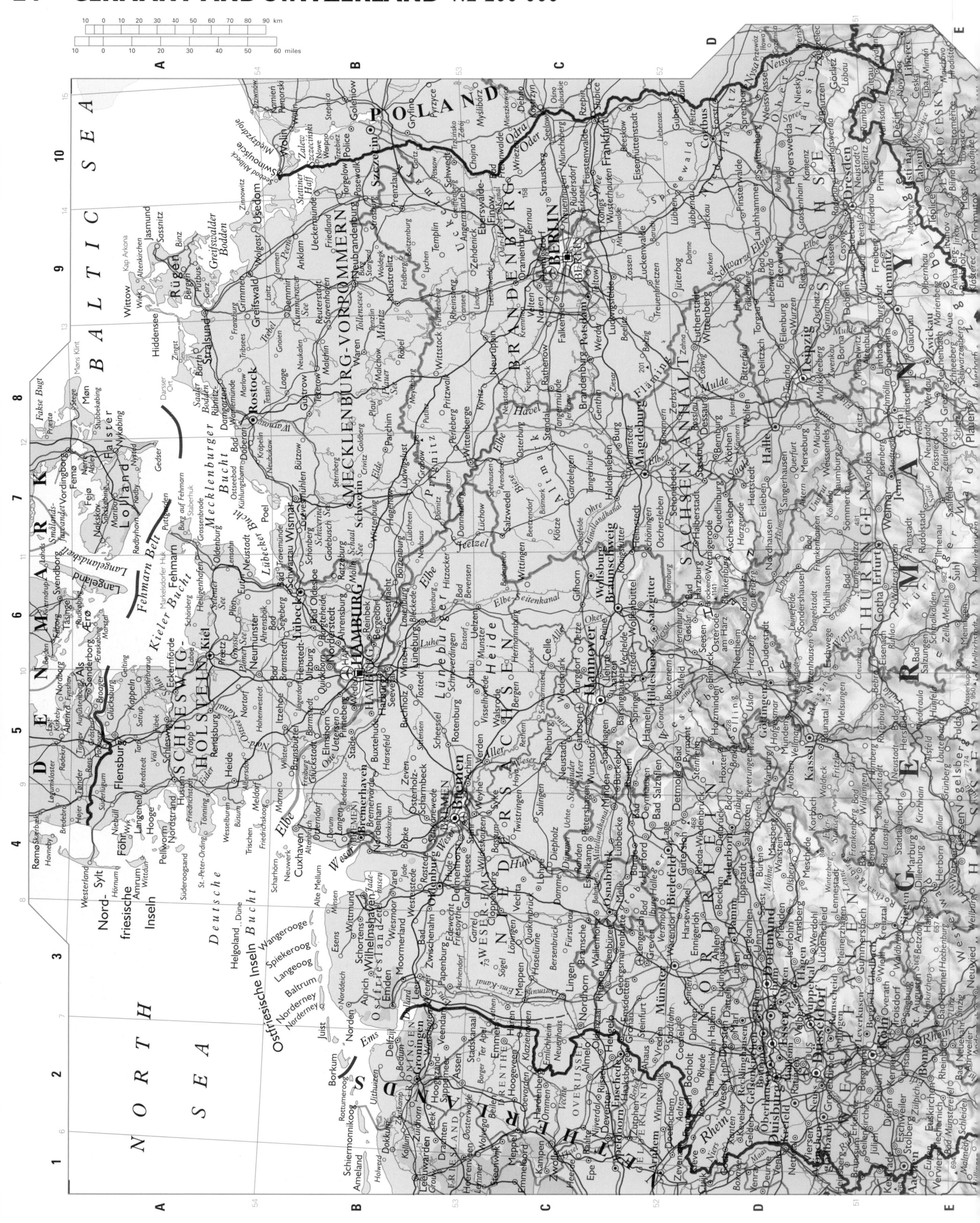

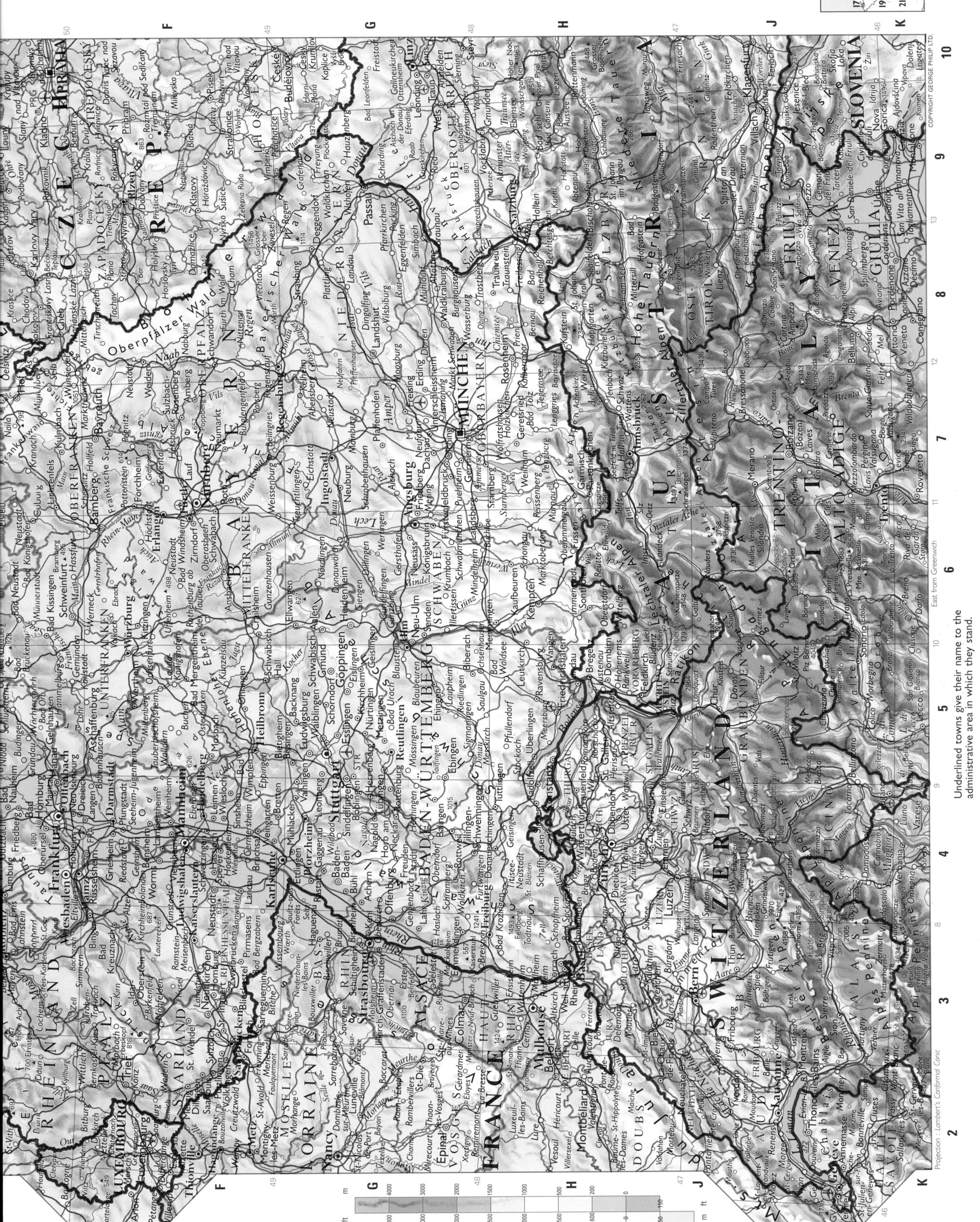

Underlined towns give their name to the
administrative area in which they stand.

Projection : Lambert's Conformal Conic

East from Greenwich

COPYRIGHT GEORGE PHILIP LTD.

Underlined towns give their name to the
administrative area in which they stand.

Projection : Lambert's Conformal Conic

East from Greenwich

Underlined towns give their name to the
administrative area in which they stand.

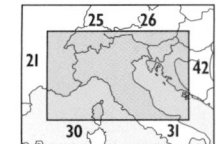

Administrative divisions in Croatia:
1. Brodsko-Posavska
2. Koprivničko-Križevačka
3. Krapinsko-Zagorska
4. Medimurska
6. Požeško-Slavonska
7. Varaždinska
8. Virovitičko-Podravska
10. Zagrebačka

Inter-entity boundaries as agreed
at the 1995 Dayton Peace Agreement.

COPYRIGHT GEORGE PHILIP LTD.

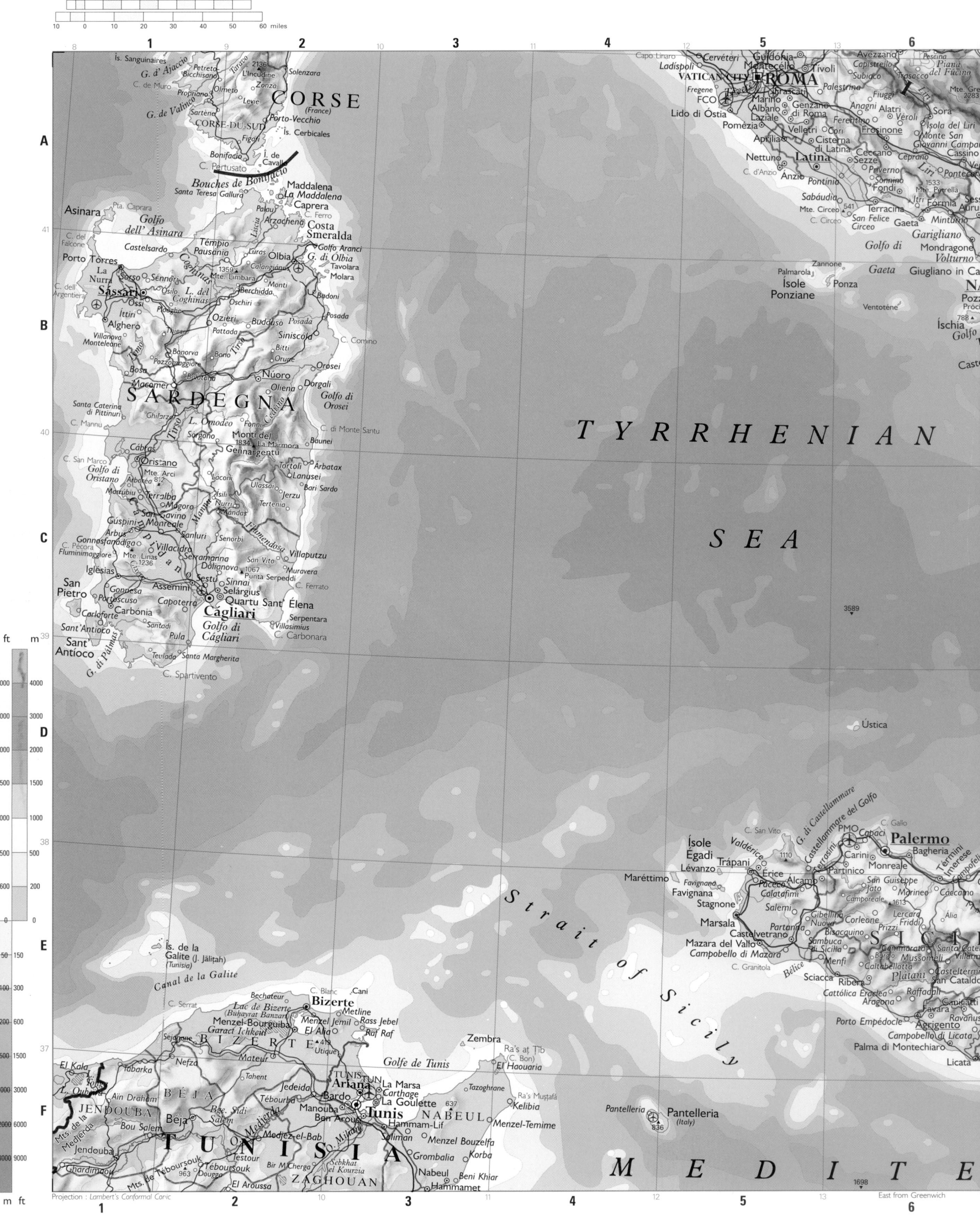

Underlined towns give their name to the
administrative area in which they stand.

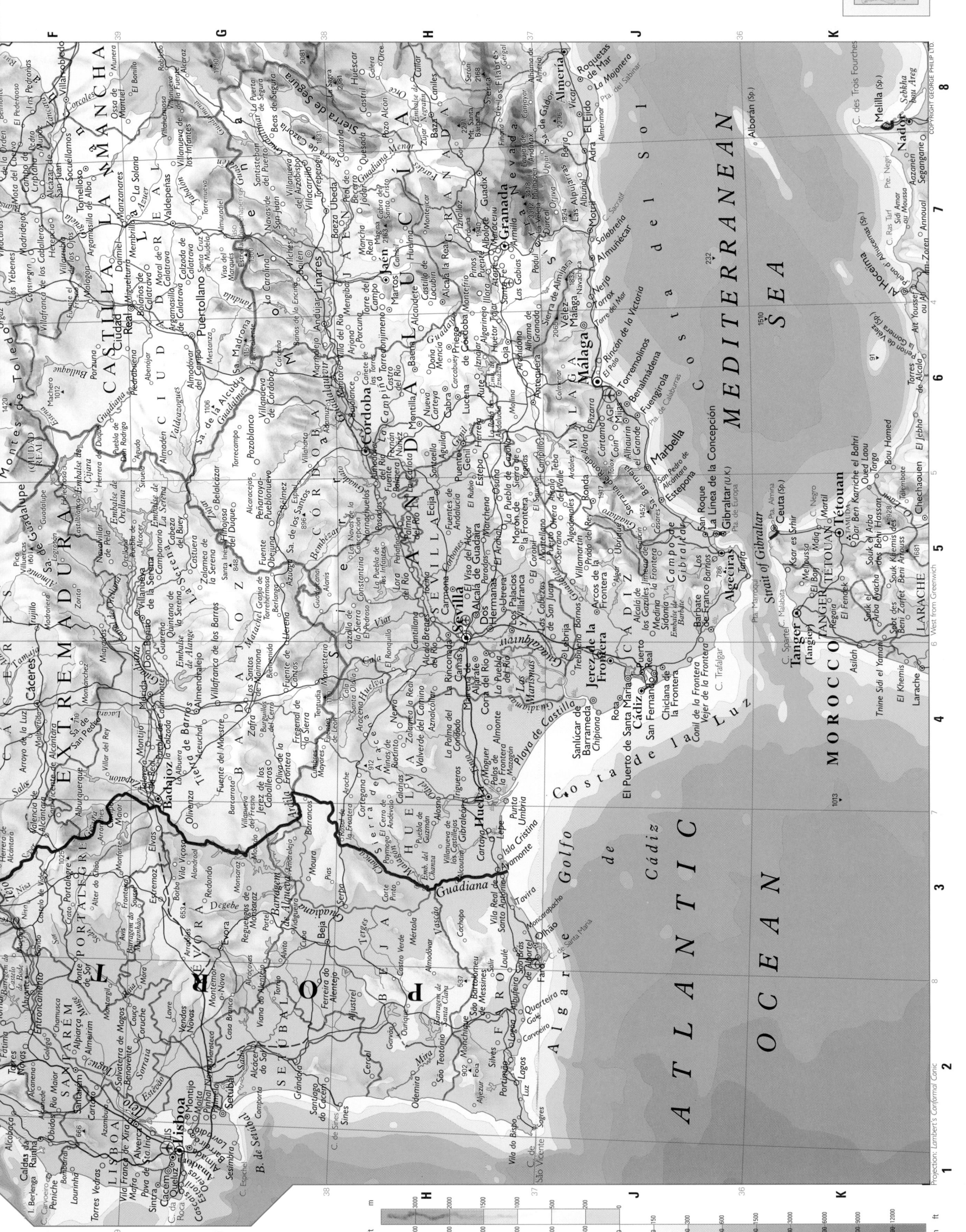

Projection: Lambert's Conformal Conic

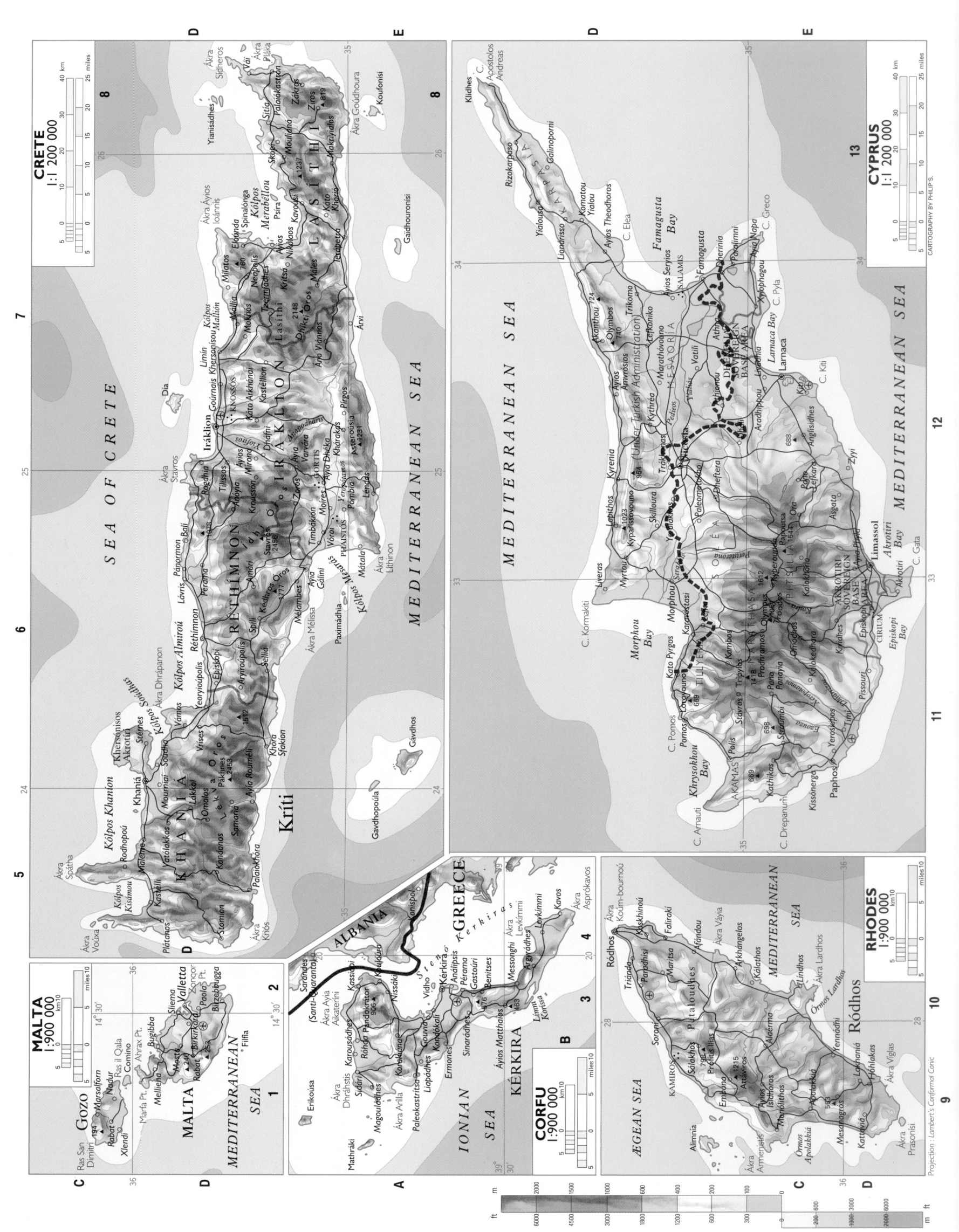

CRETE
1:1 200 000

MALTA
1:900 000

CORFU
1:900 000

RHODES
1:900 000

CYPRUS
1:1 200 000

SEA OF CRETE

MEDITERRANEAN SEA

Kríti

IONIAN SEA

ALBANIA

GREECE

KÉRKIRA

AEGEAN SEA

Ródhos

MEDITERRANEAN SEA

Famagusta Bay

Morphou Bay

MEDITERRANEAN SEA

CARTOGRAPHY BY PHILIP'S

Projection: Lambert's Conformal Conic

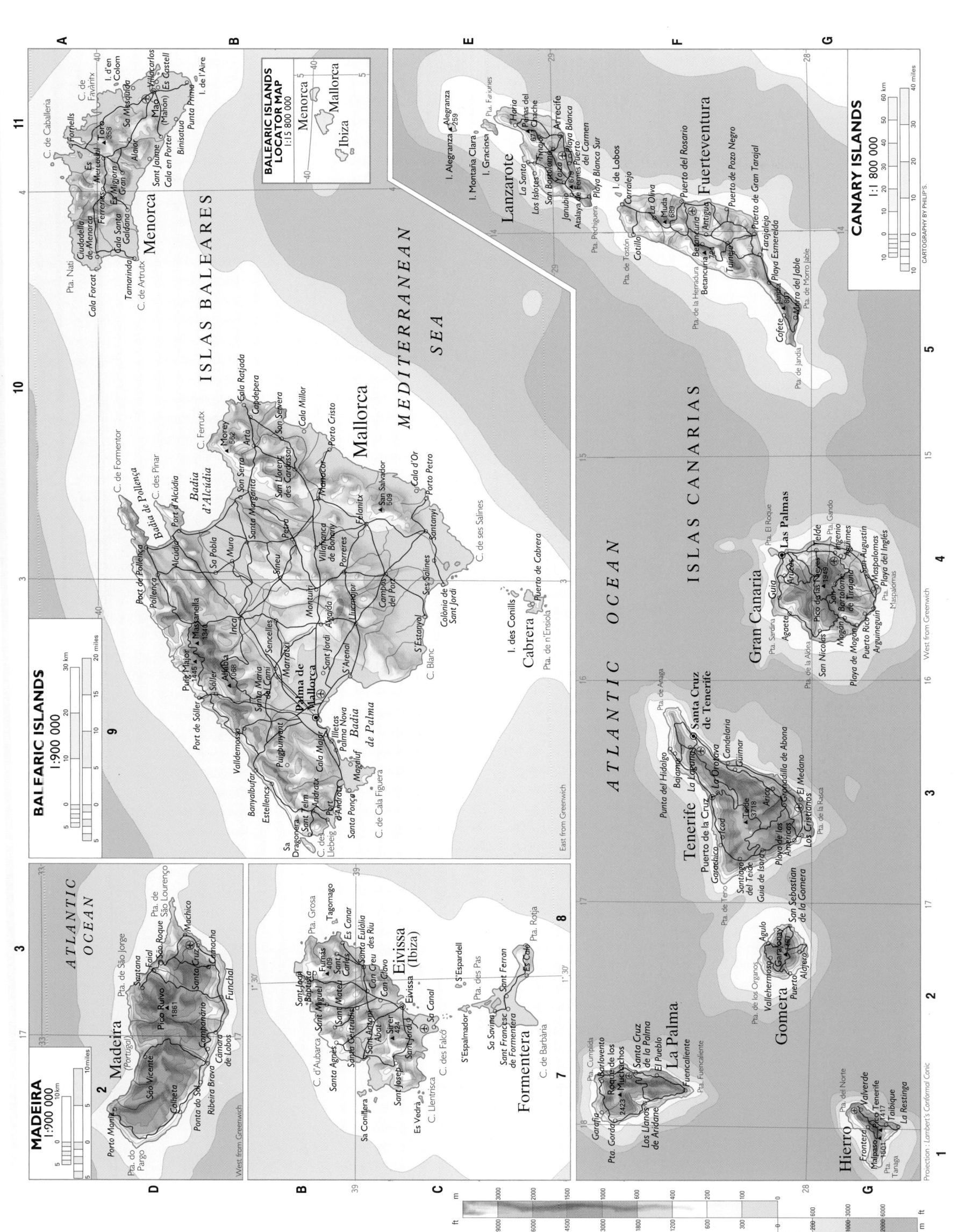

BALEARIC ISLANDS LOCATOR MAP
1:15 800 000

Menorca
Mallorca
Ibiza

BALEARIC ISLANDS
1:900 000

MADEIRA
1:900 000

CANARY ISLANDS
1:1 800 000

CARTOGRAPHY BY PHILIP'S.

Menorca

ISLAS BALEARES

MEDITERRANEAN SEA

Mallorca

Cabrera

ATLANTIC OCEAN

Madeira
(Portugal)

Eivissa
(Ibiza)

Formentera

ISLAS CANARIAS

Lanzarote

Fuerteventura

Gran Canaria

Tenerife

Gomera

La Palma

Hierro

Projection : Lambert's Conformal Conic

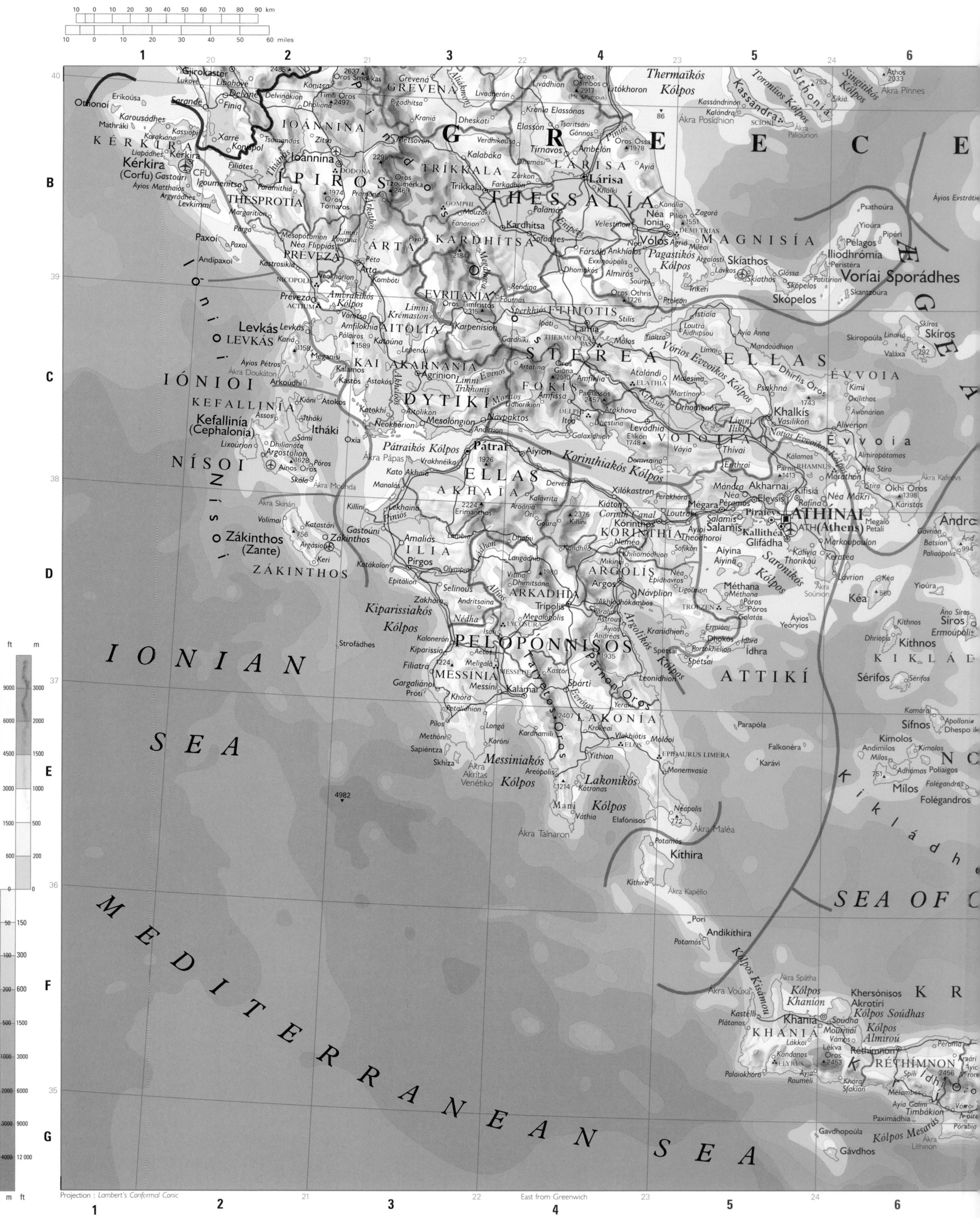

Projection : Lambert's Conformal Conic

East from Greenwich

- - - - Inter-entity boundaries as agreed at the 1995 Dayton Peace Agreement.

Underlined towns give their name to the
administrative area in which they stand.

COPYRIGHT GEORGE PHILIP LTD.

Administrative divisions in Croatia:
1. Brodsko-Posavska
2. Koprivničko-Križevačka
4. Medimurska
5. Osječko-Baranjska
6. Požeško-Slavonska
8. Virovitičko-Podravska
9. Vukovarsko-Srijemska

- - - - Inter-entity boundaries as agreed
at the 1995 Dayton Peace Agreement.

Underlined towns give their name to the administrative area in which they stand.

COPYRIGHT GEORGE PHILIP LTD.

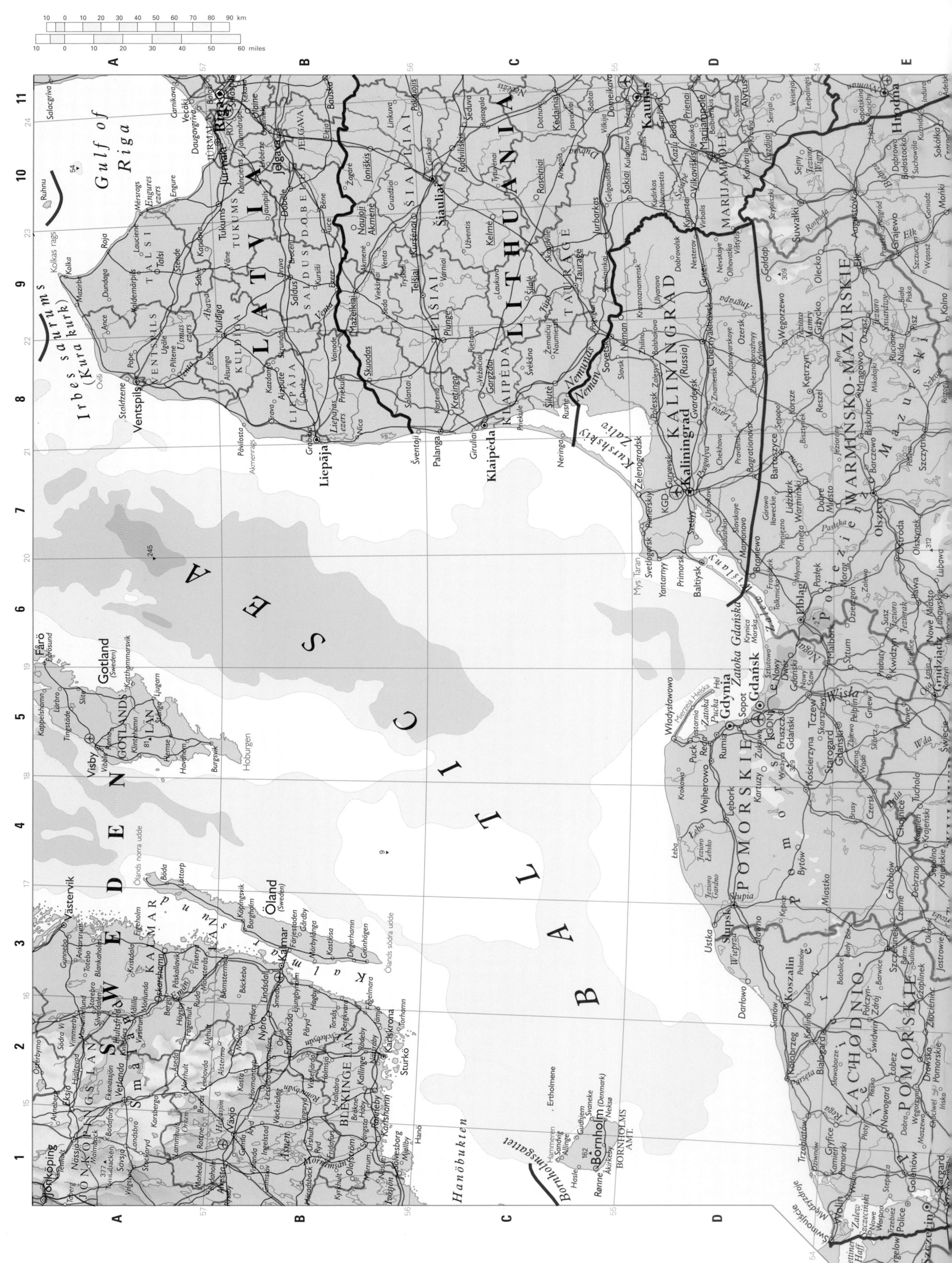

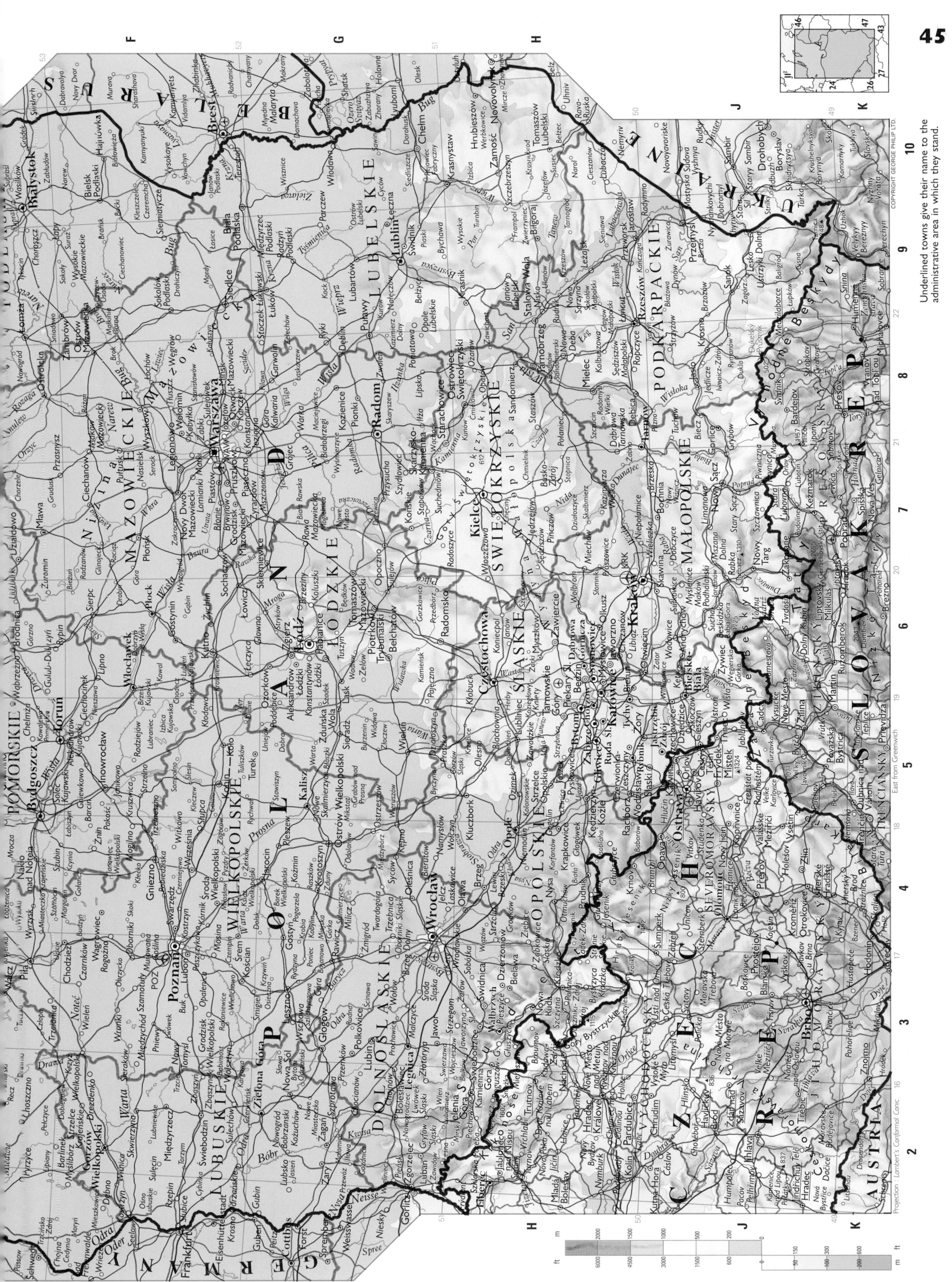

Underlined towns give their name to the
administrative area in which they stand.

COPYRIGHT GEORGE PHILIP LTD.

Projection: Lambert's Conformal Conic

East from Greenwich

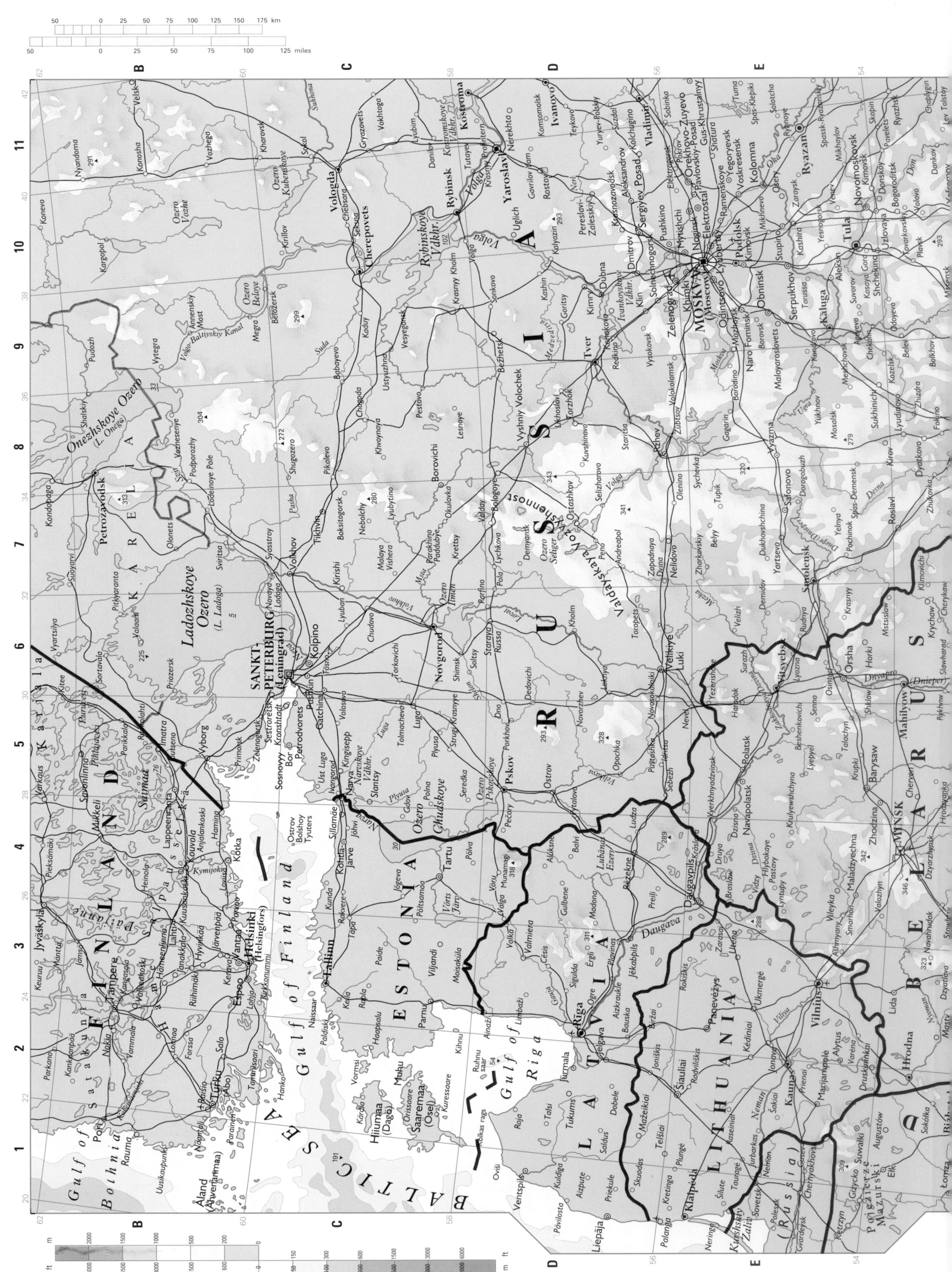

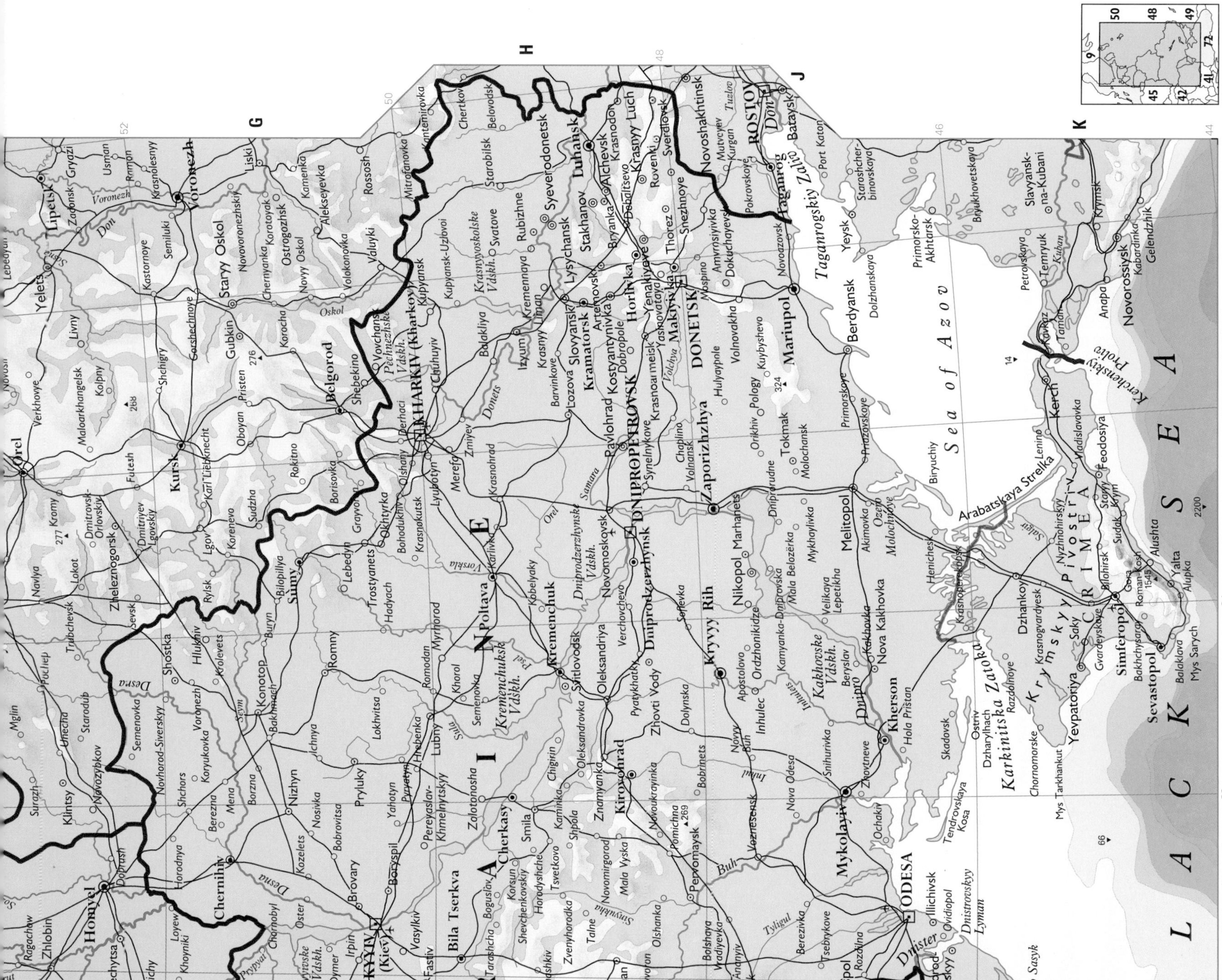

East from Greenwich

CARTOGRAPHY BY PHILIP'S

Projection: Conical with two standard parallels

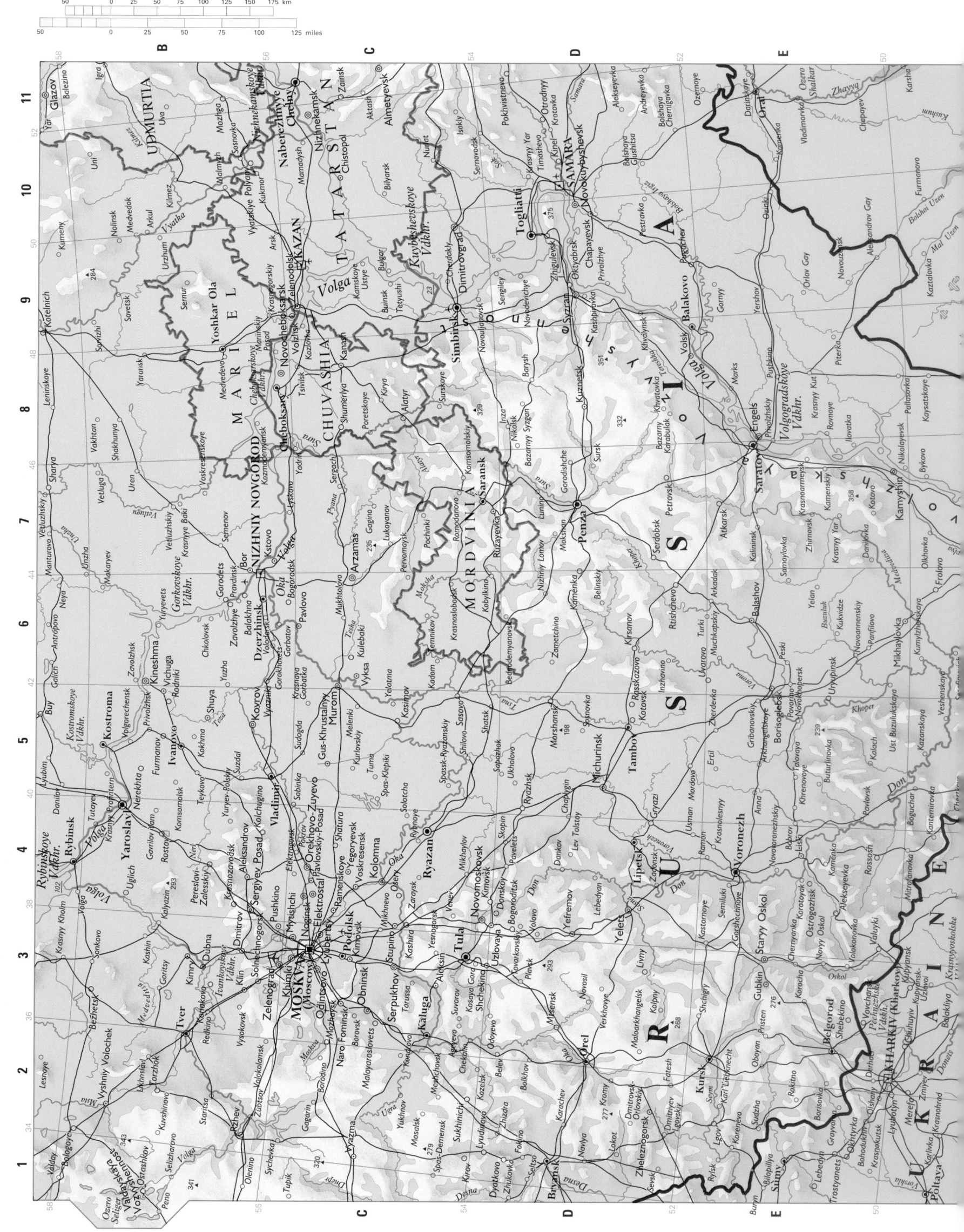

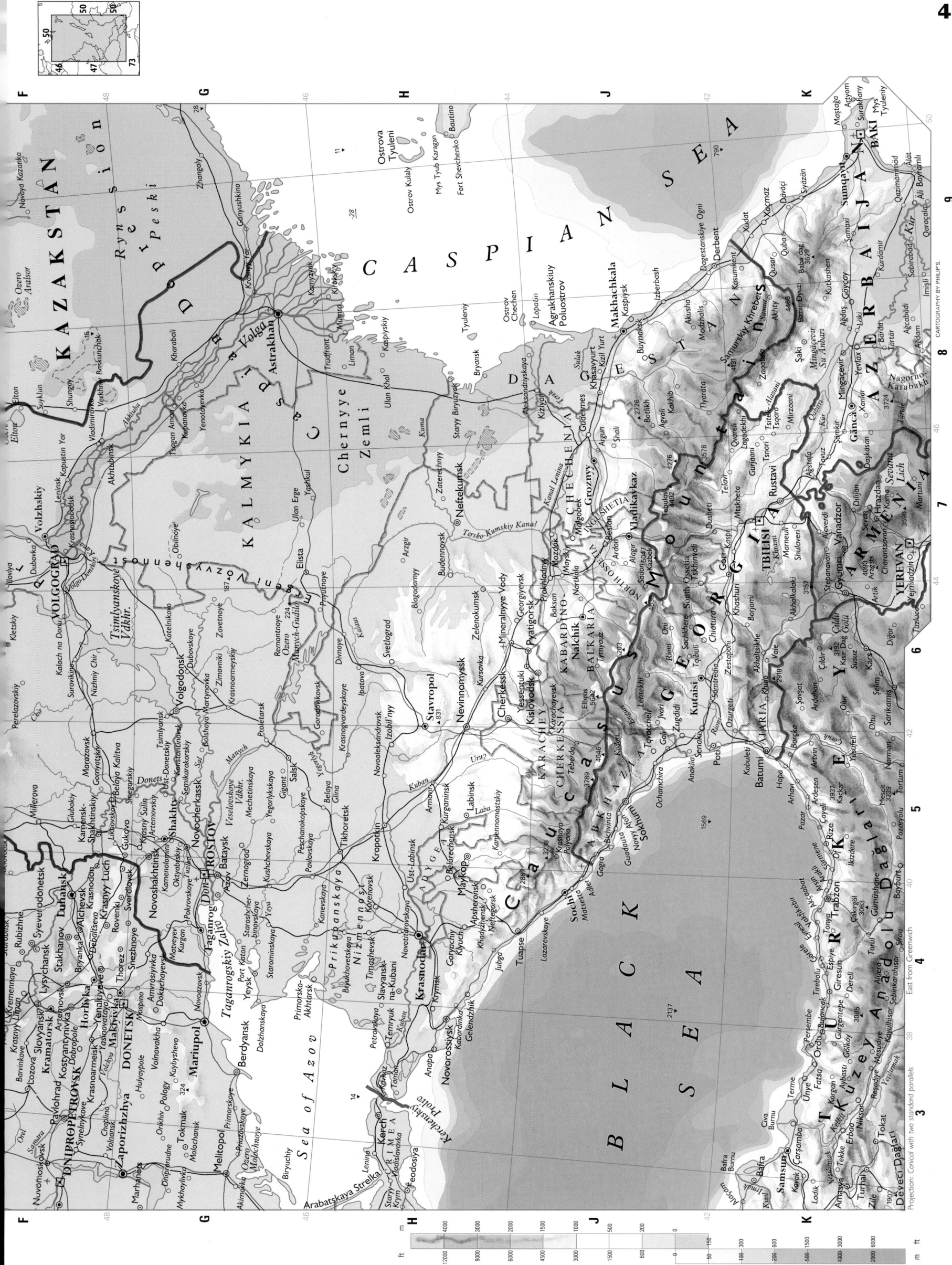

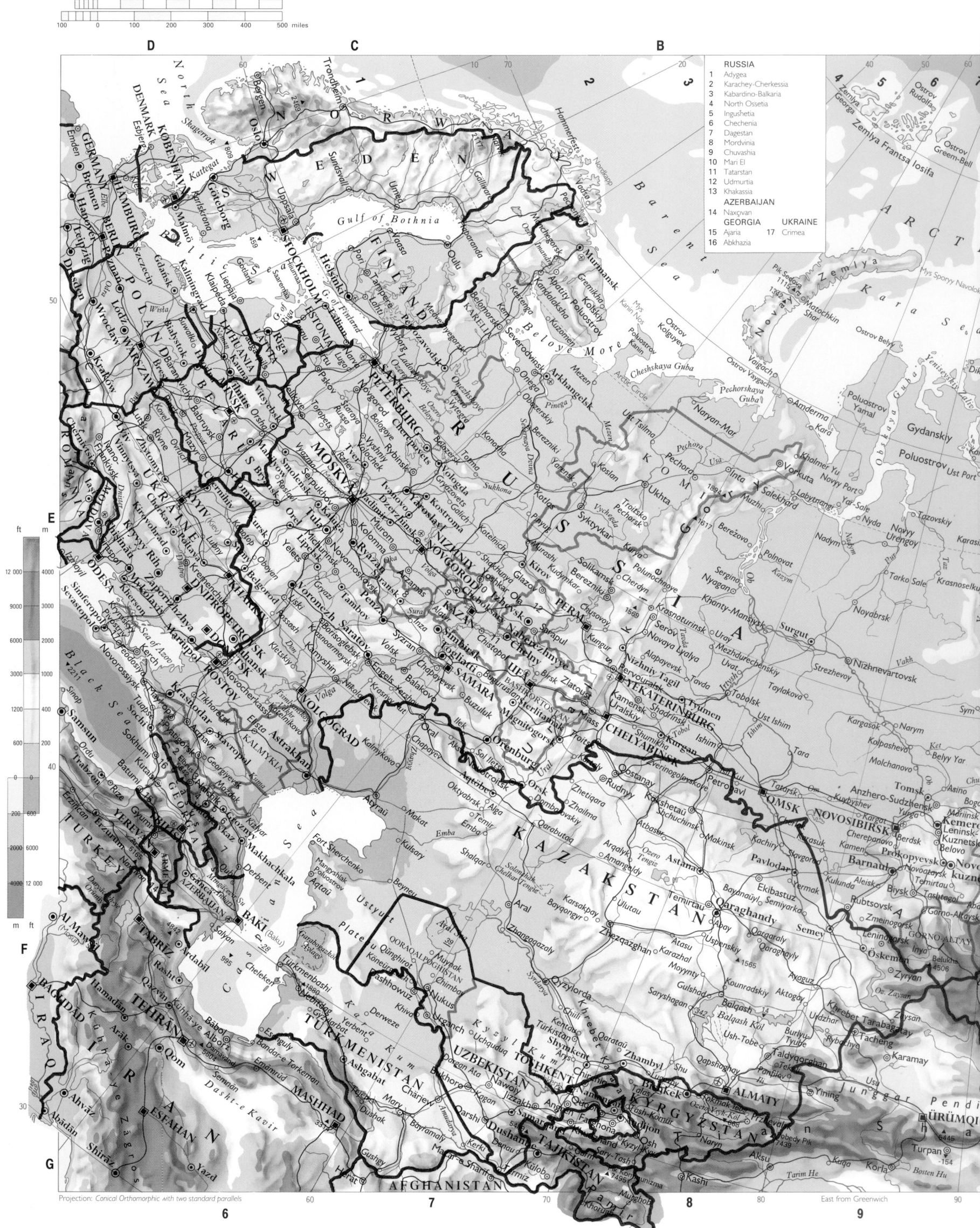

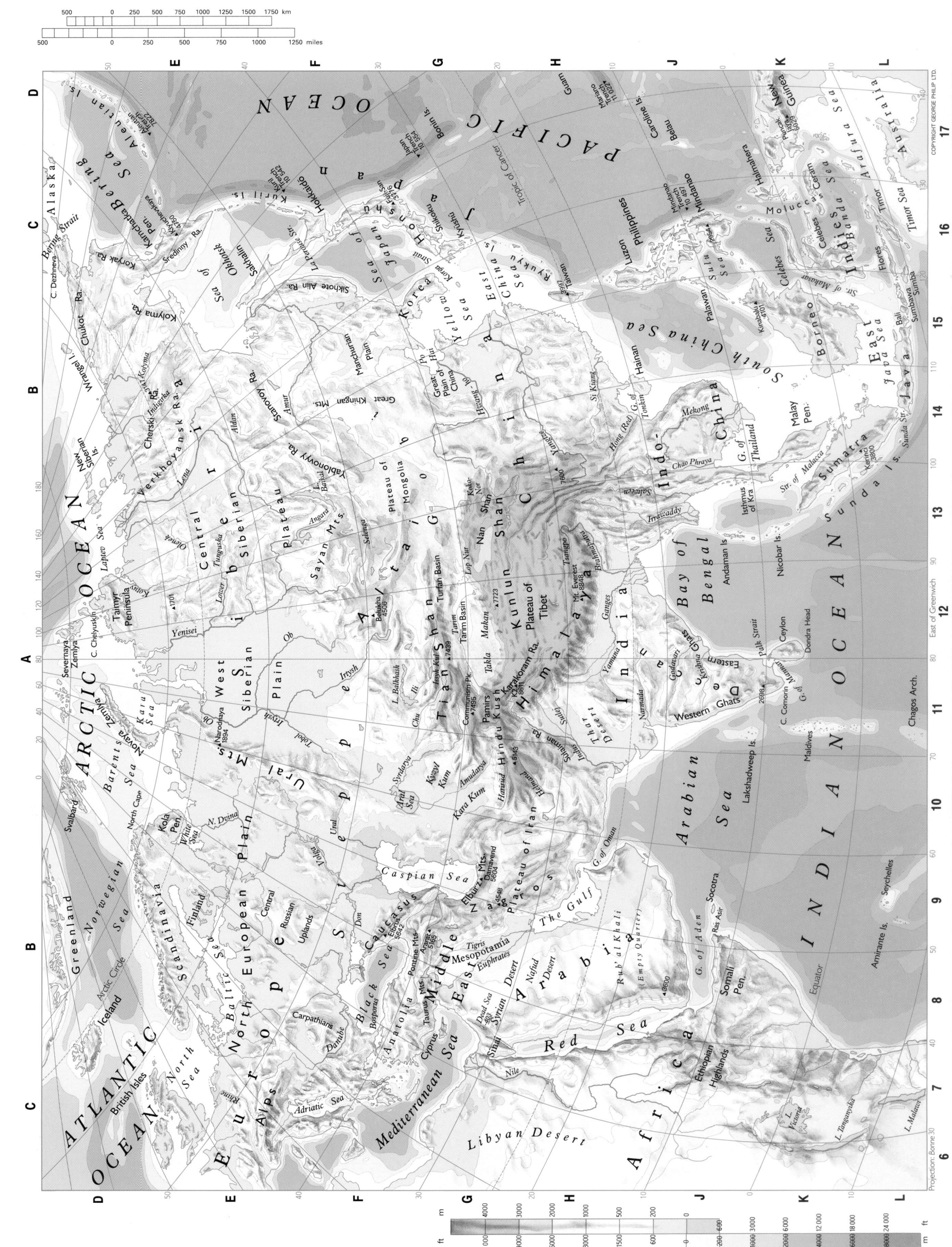

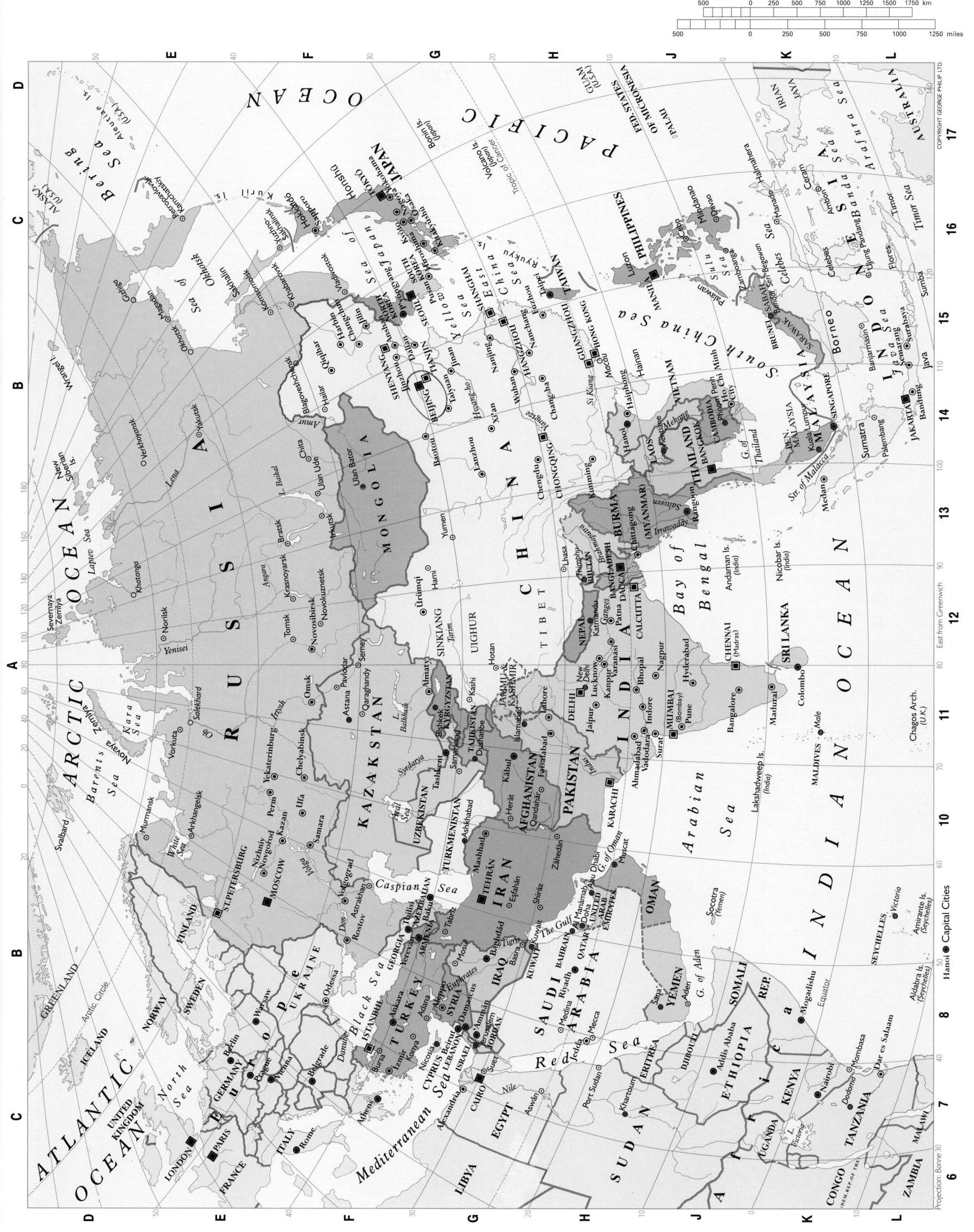

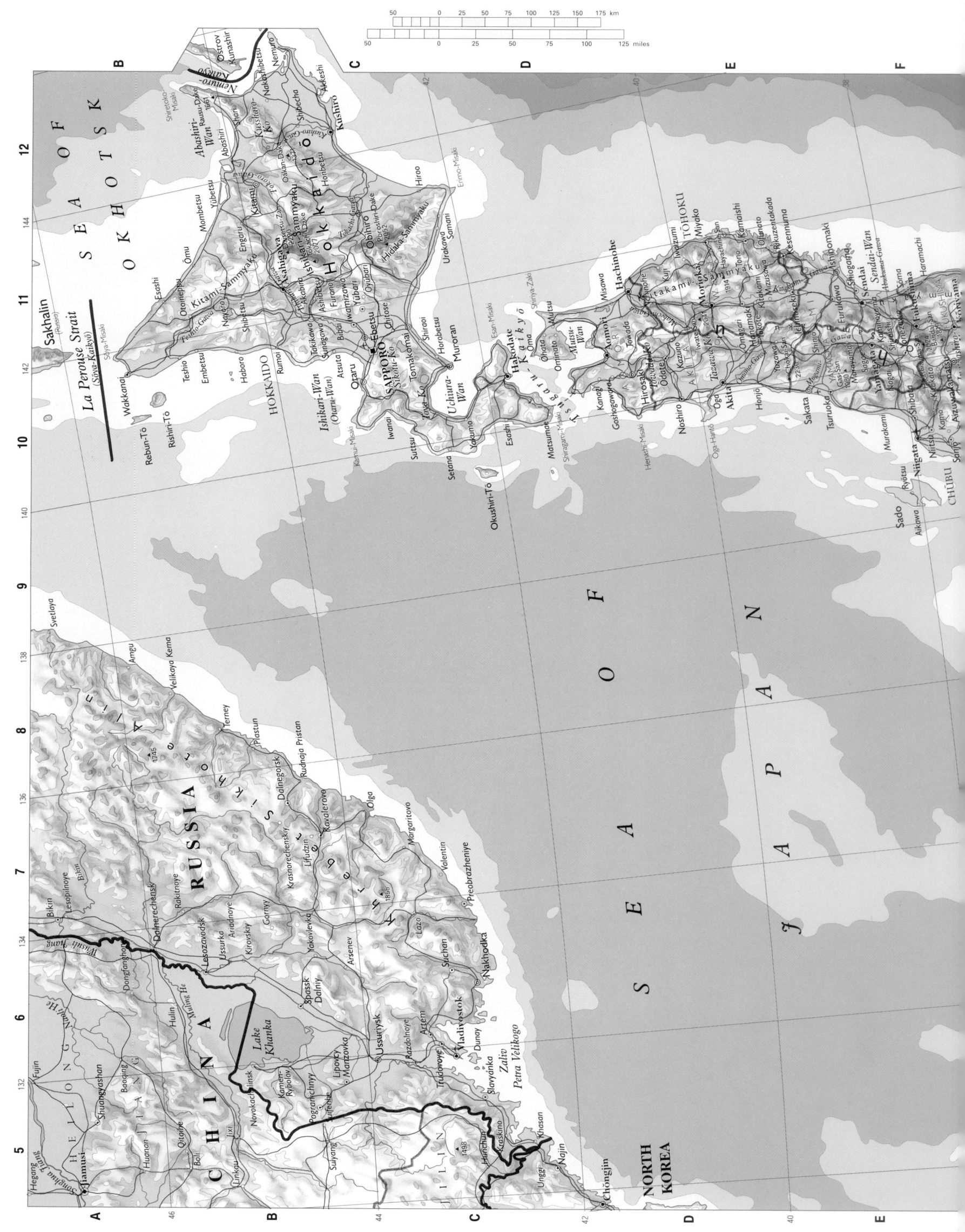

50 0 25 50 75 100 125 150 175 km

50 0 25 50 75 100 125 miles

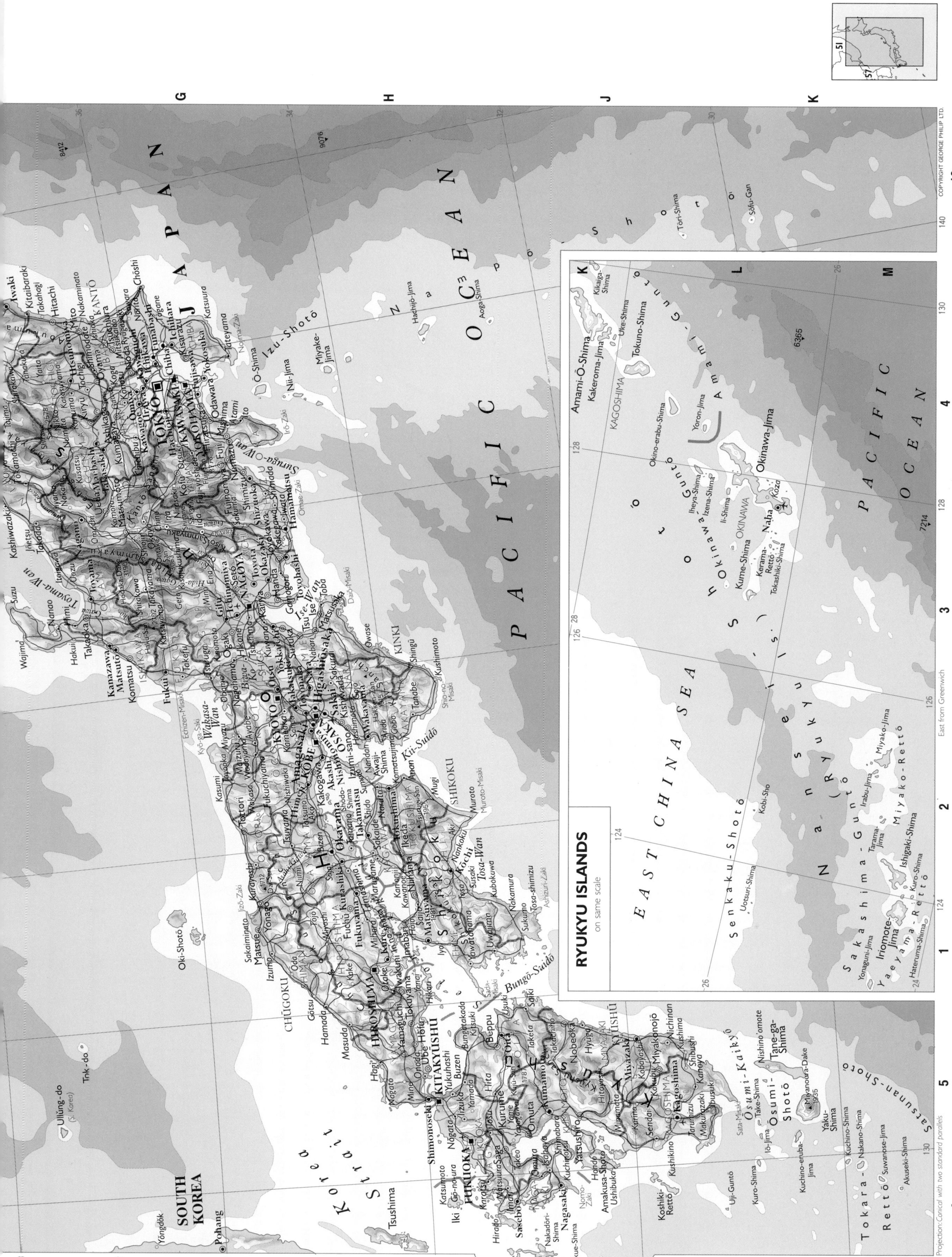

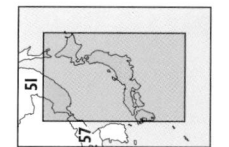

RYUKYU ISLANDS
on same scale

Projection: Conical with two standard parallels

COPYRIGHT GEORGE PHILIP LTD.

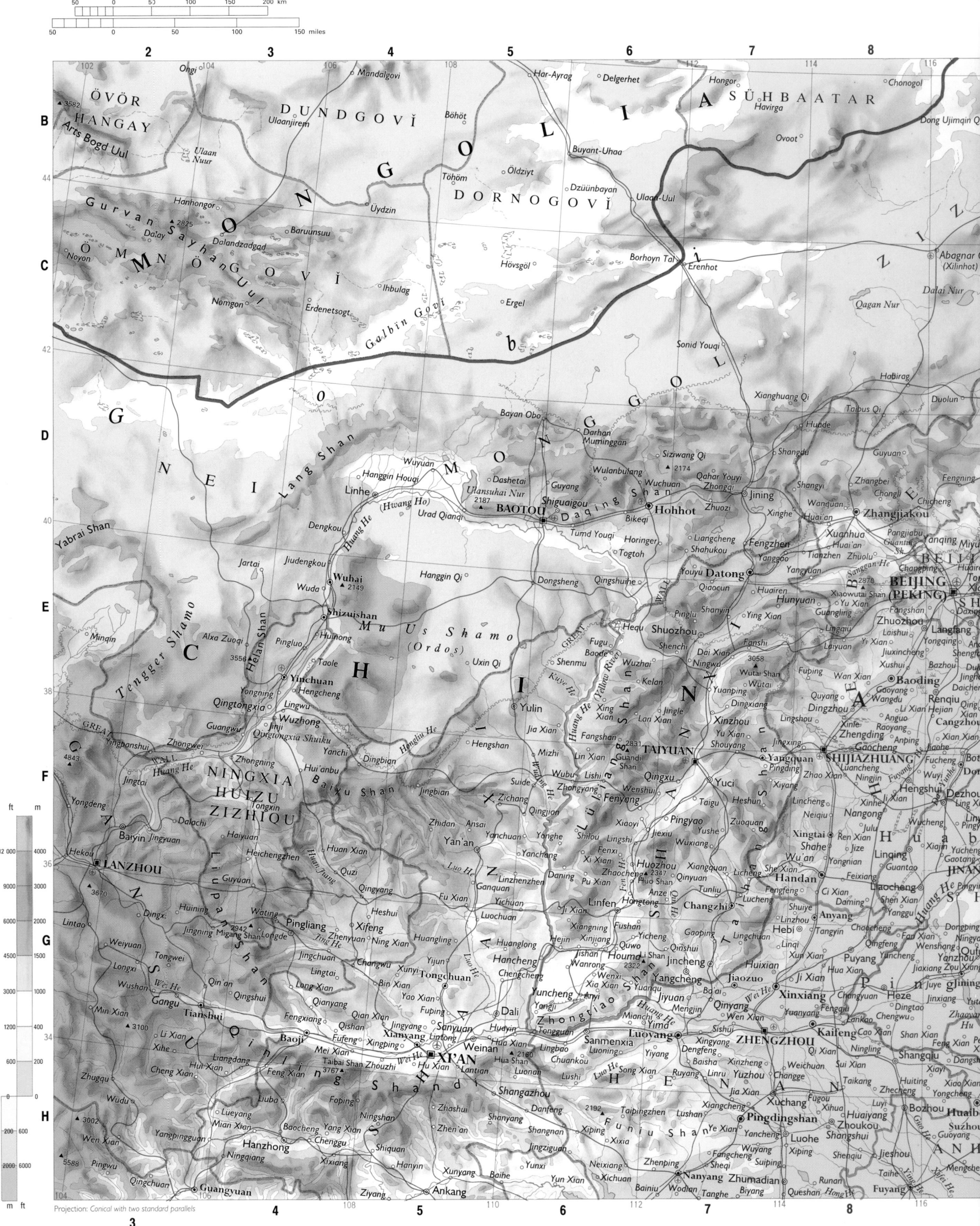

Projection: Conical with two standard parallels

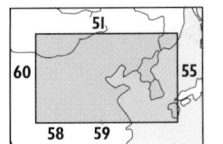

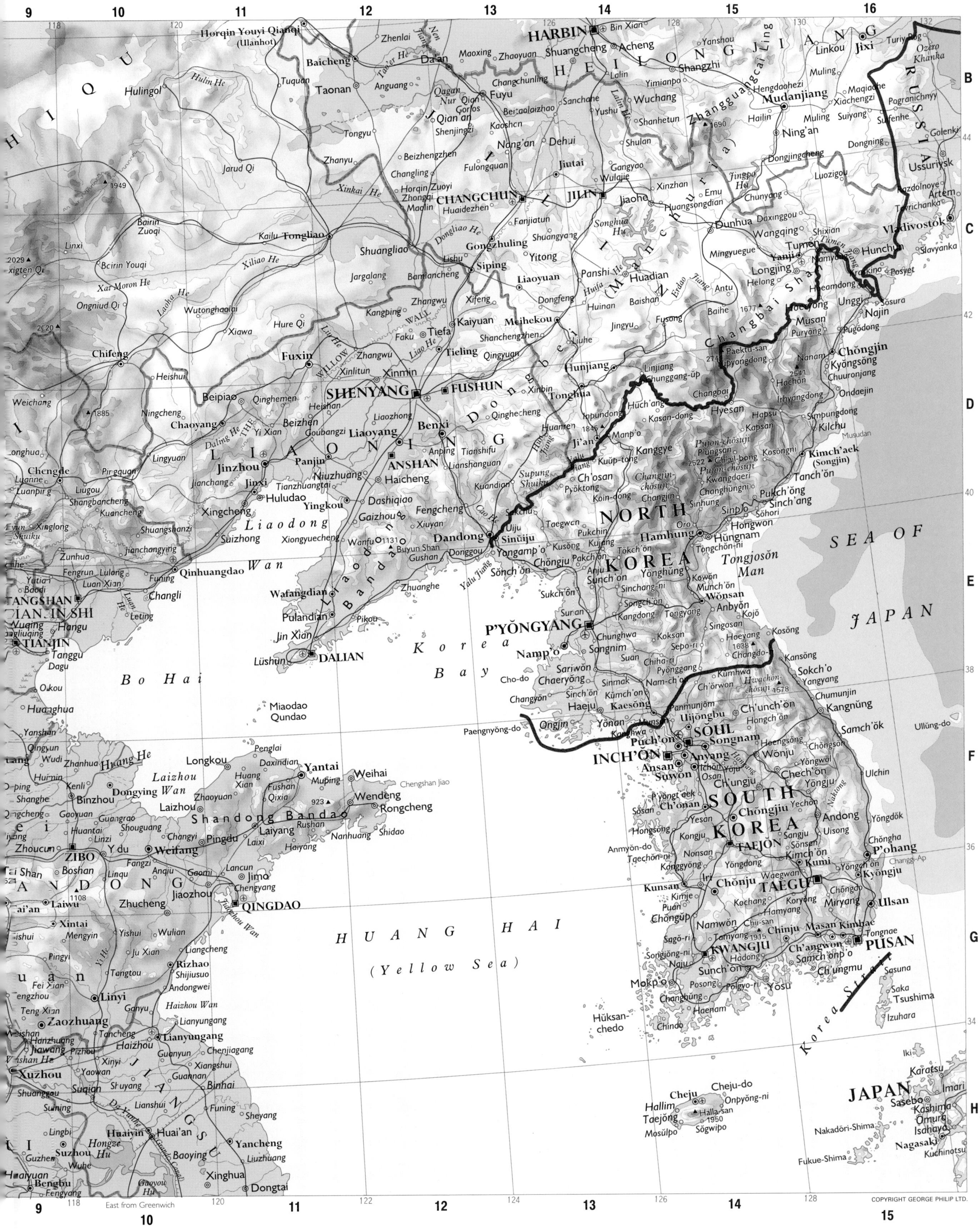

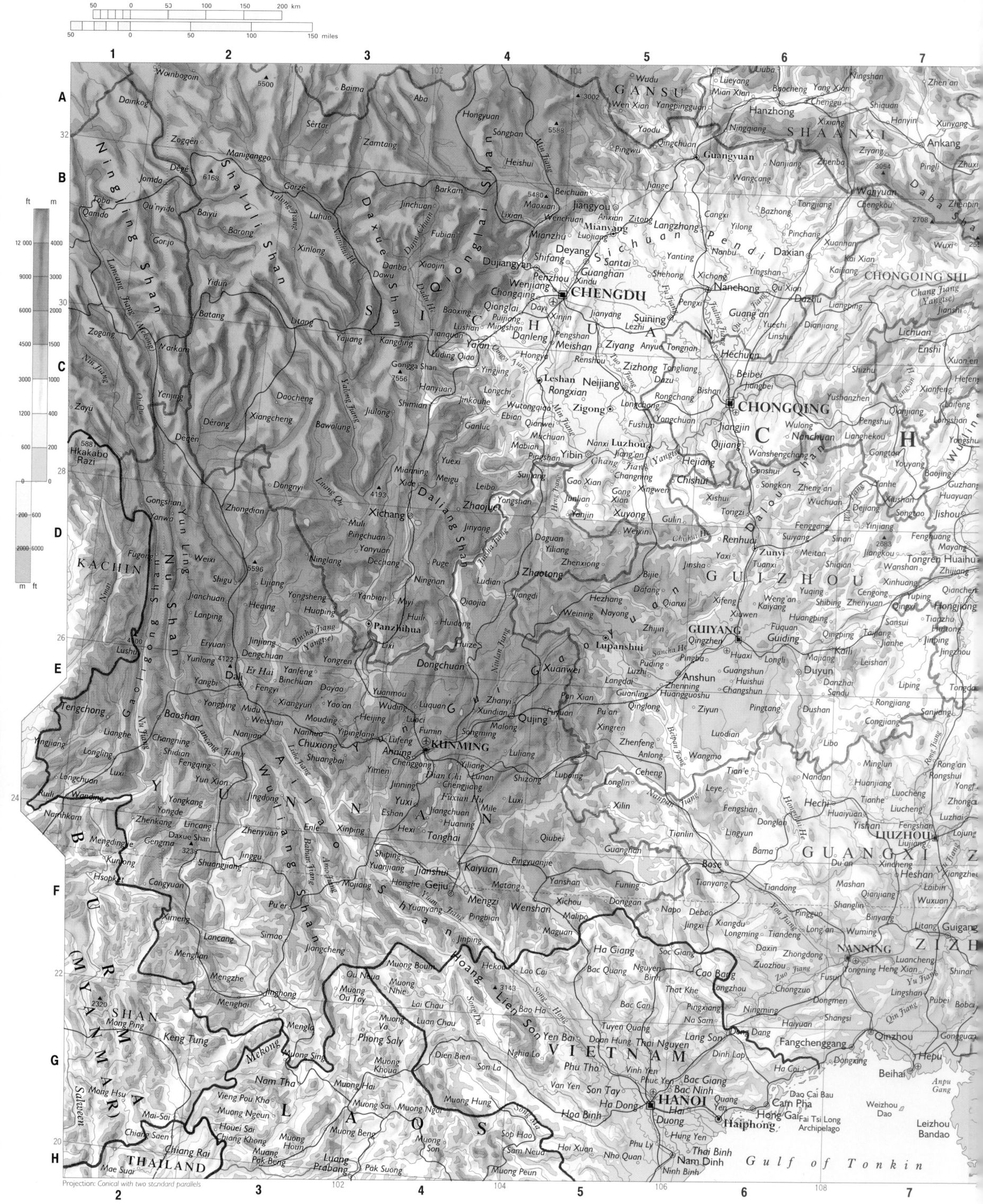

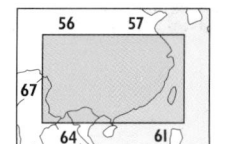

Provinces: HENAN, ANHUI, JIANGSU, HUBEI, ZHEJIANG, HUNAN, JIANGXI, FUJIAN, GUANGDONG, GUANGZU, TAIWAN

Major cities: NANJING, SHANGHAI, SHANGHAI SHI, WUHAN, HANGZHOU, CHANGSHA, NANCHANG, GUANGZHOU, HONG KONG (XIANGGANG), T'AIPEI, KAOHSIUNG, Huainan, Hefei, Ningbo, Wenzhou, Fuzhou, Xiamen, Shantou, Shenzhen, Macau, Kowloon

Water bodies: Chang Jiang (Yangtse), Tai Hu, Chao Hu, Poyang Hu, Dongting Hu, Hongze Hu, SOUTH CHINA SEA, Luzon Strait, Taiwan Strait

Tropic of Cancer

59
61 63

50 0 100 150 200 250 300 km
50 0 50 100 150 200 miles

A

Itbayat I.
Batanes Is.
Batar I.

Balintang Channel

B

Calayan I. Babuyan I.
Dalupiri I.
Babuyan Islands Camiguin I.
Fuga I.
Mayraira Pt. *Babuyan Channel*

PACIFIC

C

Bacarra Bangui Claveria
San Nicolas Aparri Santa Ana
Batac Laoag Kabugao Gonzaga Gattaran
2360 Tuao
Cabugao Tuguegarao
Vigan Santa Maria Bangued
Candon Bontoc Lubuagan Mt. Cresta 1685
Tagudin Balaoan San Mateo Ilagan Palanan Pt.
San Fernando Mt. Pulog 2928 Santiago Palanan
Lingayen Gulf Baguio Cordon C. San Ildefonso
Bolinao Rosario Solano Bayombong
Alaminos Dagupan Mt. Anacuao 1852

OCEAN

O C E A N

D

San Carlos San Manuel Baler Bay
Santa Cruz Bayambang San Jose Baler
Camiling Moncada Cuyapo Victoria
Masinloc Iba Tarlac 2037 La Paz Cabanatuan Dingalan
Concepcion 1780 Gapan
San Antonio Mt Pinatubo Angeles San Fernando Polillo Is.
Olongapo Orani Malabon Patnanongan I.
Bataan Caloocan City Jomalig I.
Manila Bay Quezon City
Cavite MANILA Lamon Bay
Dasmariñas Pasay Santa Cruz Paracale
Nasugbu Tagaytay L. de Bay Lucban Labo
Balayan Lipa San Pablo Atimonan Daet
Lemery Lucena Lobez Catanauan
Batangas Tayabas Bay Calabanga San Andres
Lubang Is. Boac Naga Catanduanes Virac

PHILIPPINES

E

C. Calavite Verde I. Pass Marinduque Iriga Ligao Rapu Rapu I.
Mamburao Calapan Victoria Tablas Strait Tabaco Mayon Vol
Mindoro Mt. Baco 2487 Pinamalayan Legazpi Sorsogon
Sablayan Burias I. *SIBUYAN* Donsol Gubat San Bernardino Str.
Bongabong Bulan
Romblon Ticao I. Irosin Allen Laoang Mondragon
San Jose Roxas Tablas I. Sibuyan I. *SEA* Catarman Gamay
Odiongan Masbate Calbayog Arteche
Busuanga I. Mandaon Oras
Semirara Is. Masbate Taft *Samar*
Catbalogan Borongan

F

Culion I. Pandan Placer Bilinan Catarman
Calamian Kalibo Roxas *VISAYAN* Caibiran Santa Rita
Group Dao *SEA* Calubian Basey
Linapacan Str. Tibiao 2117 Bantayan Carigara Tacloban General MacArthur
Taytay Bugasong Ajuy Palompon Leyte Guiuan
Cuyo Is. *Panay* Pototan Passi Cadiz Bogo *Leyte* Ormoc Dulag Homonhon I.
Cuyo Iloilo Silay Sagay Tuburan Danao Abuyog
Cuyo West Pass San Jose Bacolod San Carlos Camotes Is.
Dumaran I. Guimaras Jordan Victorias Mandaue *Sea* Sogod San Juan Dinagat I.

G

Palawan 1593 Himamaylan Kabankalan La Carlota Cebu Maasin Dinagat I.
Irahuan Honda Bay Hinigaran Binalbagan Carcar Panaon I. Surigao Siargao I.
Puerto Princesa Cagayan Is. Sipalay Argao Bohol I. Placer 10 497
Negros Bais Oslob Tagbilaran Bucas Grande I.
Mt. Mantalingajan Hinoba-an Dumaguete *BOHOL* Carrascal
2085 Tanjay Siquijor I. Mainit 2012 Tandag
Siaton Zamboanguita Camiguin I. Cabadbaran Tago

H

C. Buliluyan Bugsuk I. *SULU* Dapitan Talisayan Nasipit Marihatag
Balabac I. *SEA* Dipolog Alubijid Butuan Bayugan Lianga
Balambangan Bangi Manukan Oroquieta Esperanza Talacogan Hinatuan
Kuddat Senaja Labason Sindangan Ozamiz Iligan Bay Opol Cagayan de Oro Bislig
Langkon Cagayan Sulu I. Kapatagan Iloilo Tubod Iligan 2938 Malaybalay
Jembongan Siocon Pagadian *Mindanao* Bunawan Cateel
Suba Talan Turtle Is. Margosatubi 2815 L. Lanao Baganga
Tenghilan Kota Belud Pangutaran Sibuco Malabang Parang Midsayap Panabo Tagum
Kota Kinabalu G. Kinabalu 4101 Group Olutanga Illana Cotabato Pikit Pantukan Manay
Papar Telok Labuk Sandakan Basilan I. Bay Datu Piang Mt. Apo 2954 Davao Mati
Jolo Group *Moro Gulf* Talayan Digos San Isidro
SABAH Lamitan Kalamansig Davao
Isabela Lebak Koronadal Gulf Malita
MALAYSIA Zamboanga Palimbang 2083 General C. San Agustin
Borneo Pilas Samales Santos
Group Group Kiamba Sarangani Bay
Jolo Tinaca Pt.
Silam Tawi-tawi Group *CELEBES* Sarangani Is.
Tapul Group
Siasi I. *SEA*
Sibutu Group
INDONESIA Kep. Talaud

SOUTH CHINA SEA

SULU SEA

Mindanao Trench

ft m
9000 3000
6000 2000
4500 1500
3000 1000
1200 400
600 200
0 0
200 600
4000 12 000
8000 24 000
m ft

Projection: Lambert's Conformal Conic
East from Greenwich
COPYRIGHT, GEORGE PHILIP LTD.

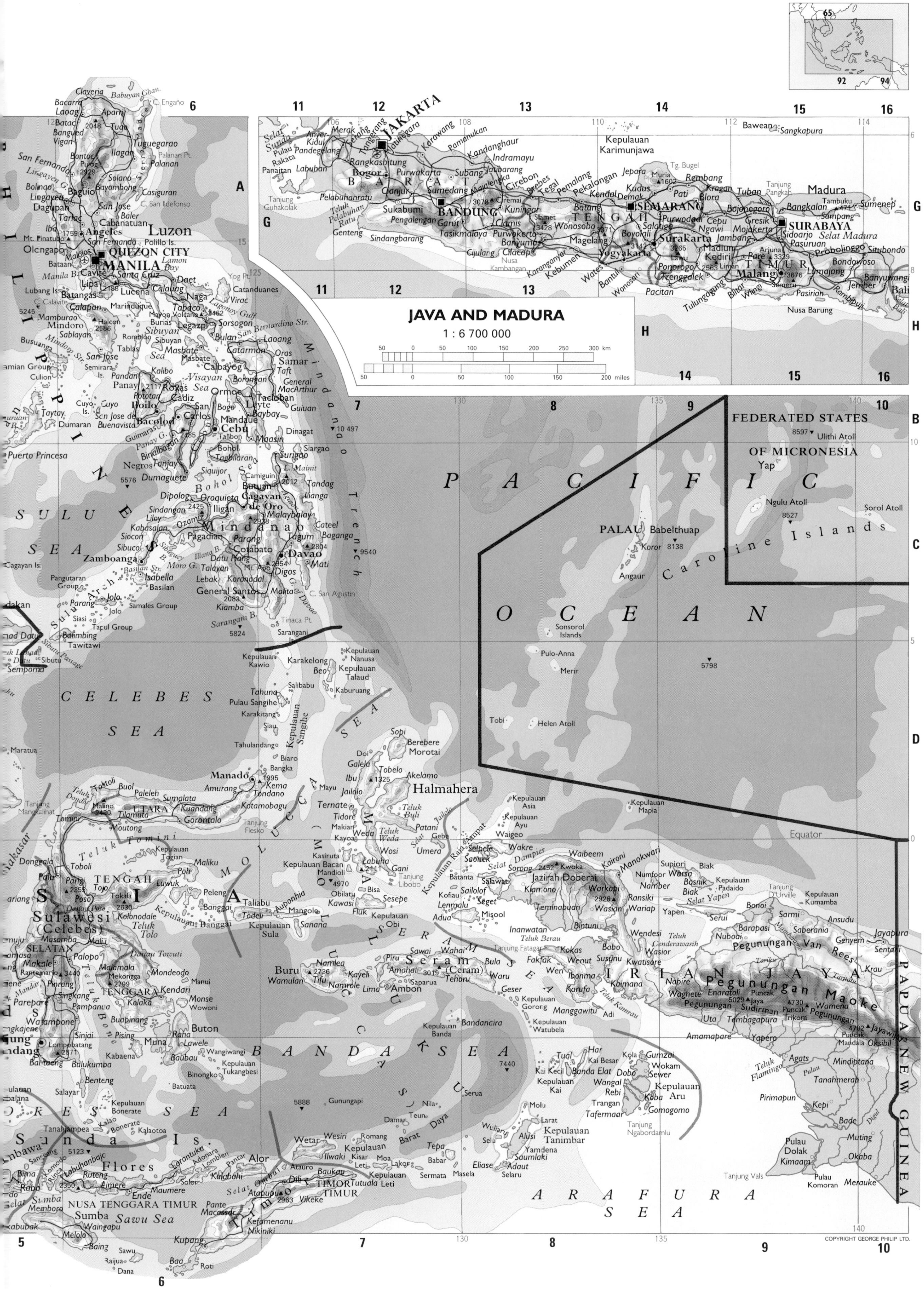

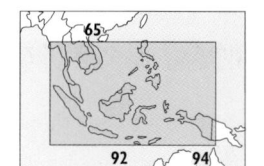

JAVA AND MADURA

1 : 6 700 000

COPYRIGHT GEORGE PHILIP LTD.

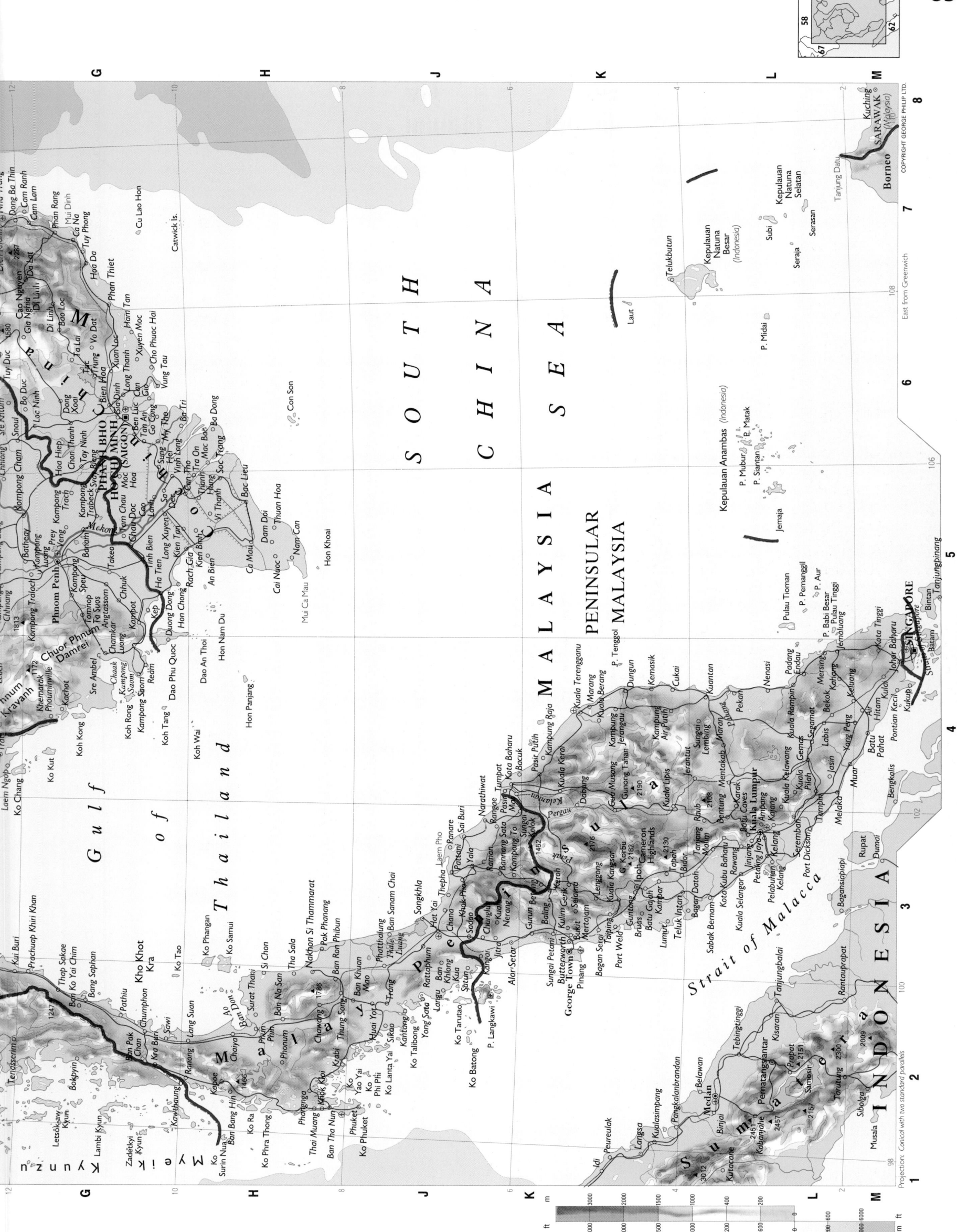

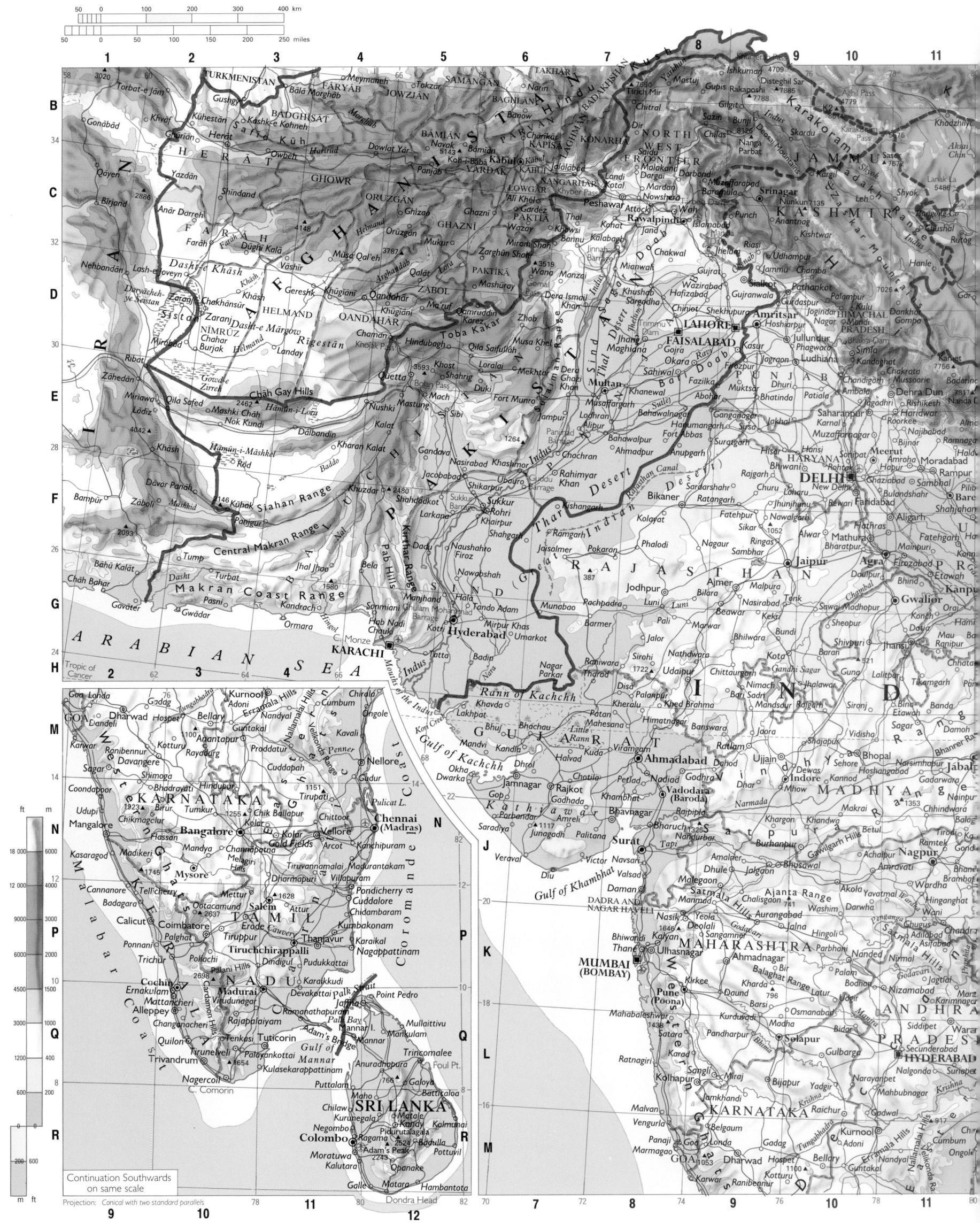

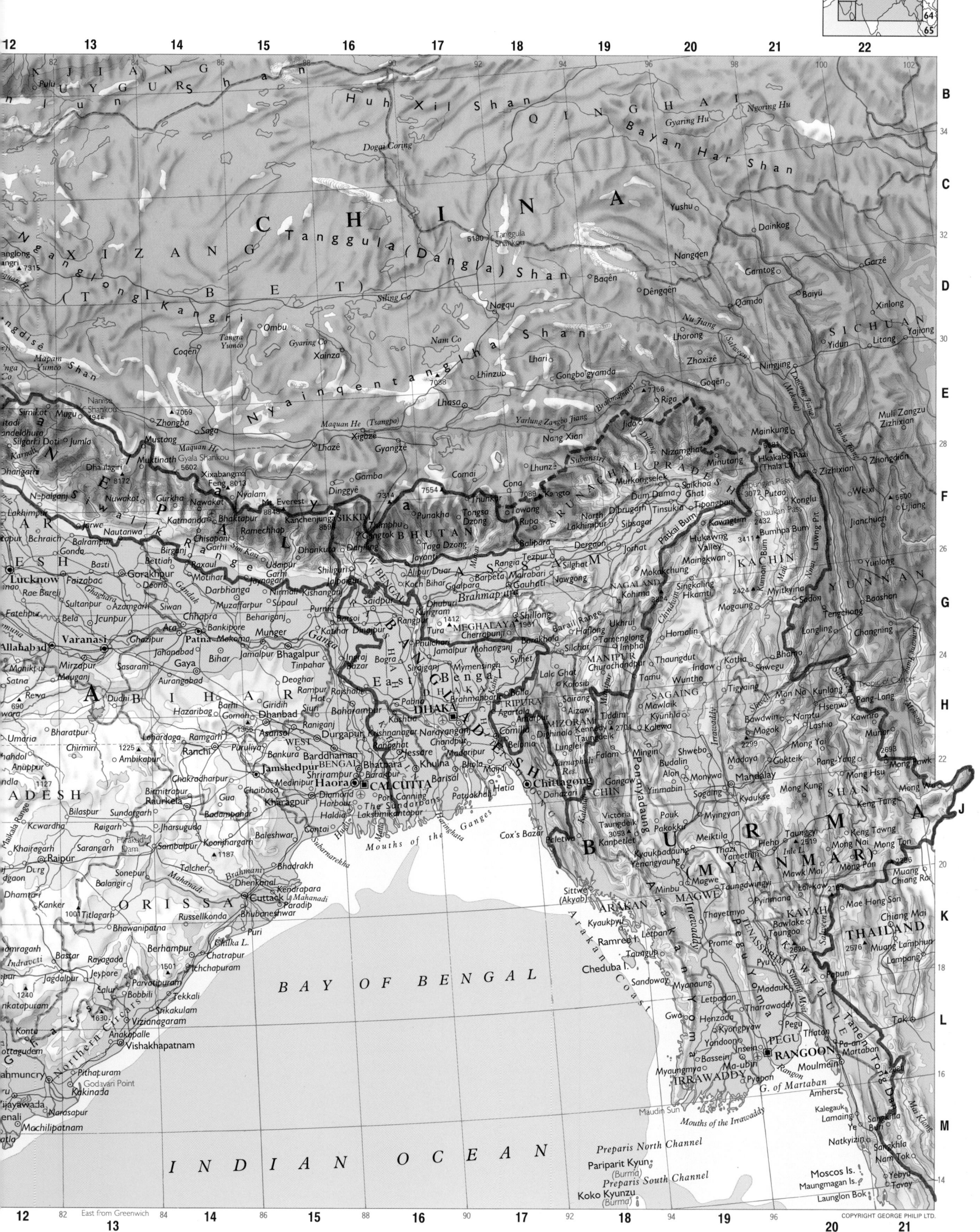

B

34

C

32

CHINA

D

XIZANG (TIBET)

30

Tanggula (Dangla) Shan

QINGHAI

Bayan Har Shan

E

SICHUAN

28

NEPAL

F

Mt. Everest 8848

SIKKIM

BHUTAN

ARUNACHAL PRADESH

KACHIN

YUNNAN

26

Lucknow

W BENGAL

ASSAM

NAGALAND

G

Varanasi

BENGAL

MEGHALAYA

Allahabad

BANGLADESH

MANIPUR

SAGAING

24

A   BIHAR

East Bengal

DHAKA

TRIPURA

MIZORAM

H

WEST

CALCUTTA

Chittagong

CHIN

22

Jamshedpur

Haora

SHAN

J

ADESH

BURMA (MYANMAR)

20

ORISSA

ARAKAN

MAGWE

KAYAH

THAILAND

K

BAY OF BENGAL

KAWTHULE

18

L

RANGOON

16

IRRAWADDY

G. of Martaban

G

M

INDIAN OCEAN

14

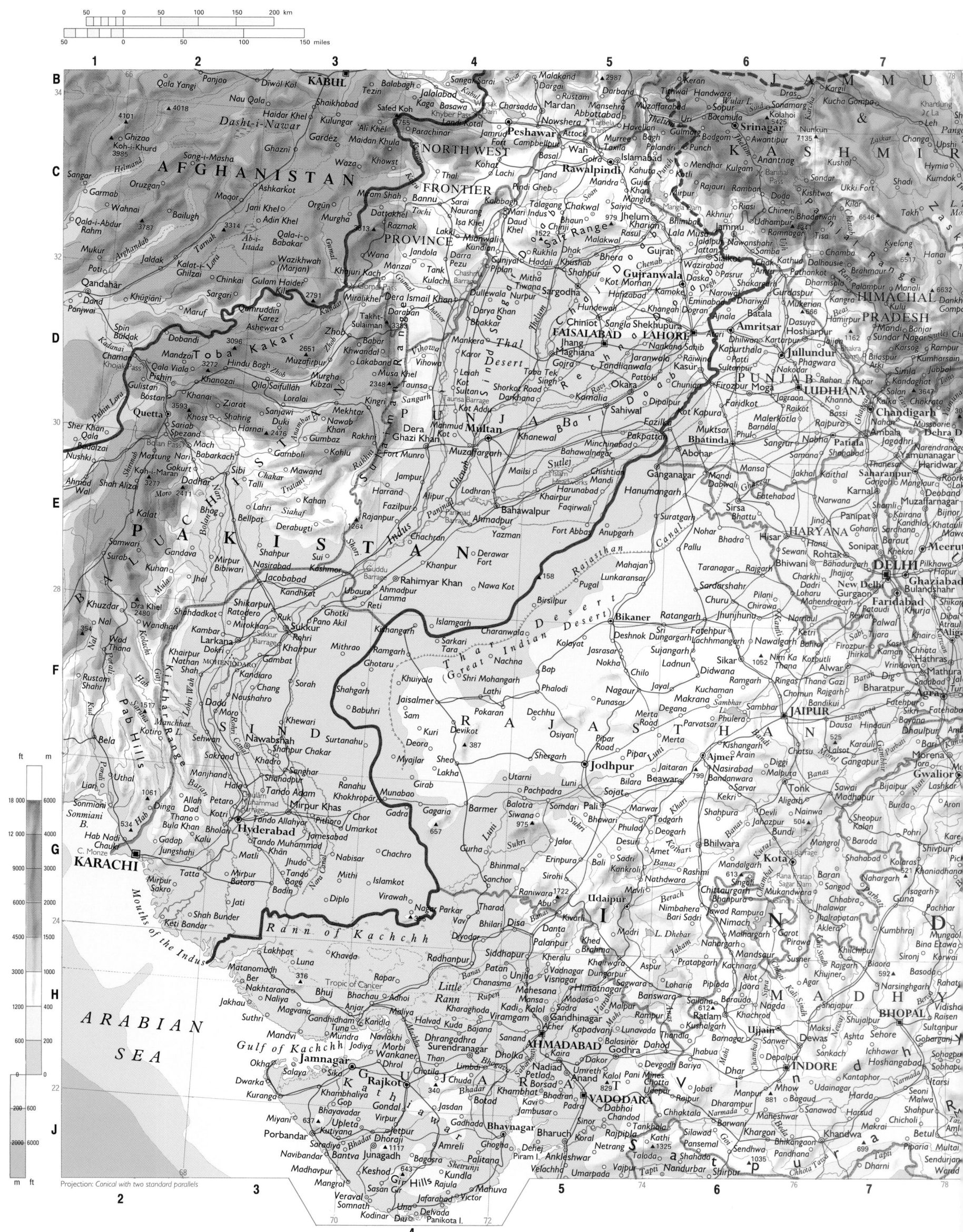

60
66
67
66

JAMMU AND KASHMIR
On same scale as Main Map
CHINA
NORTH WEST FRONTIER
PUNJAB
JAMMU & KASHMIR
HIMACHAL PRADESH
Karakoram Range
Zaskar Mountains
Deosai Mts.
Kunlun Shan
Srinagar
Rawalpindi
Islamabad
Jammu
Leh
Gilgit
K2 8611
CHINA
Nganglong Kangri
Gangdisê Shan
XIZANG (TIBET)
Yarlung Zangbo Jiang (Brahmaputra)
NEPAL
Katmandu
Mt. Everest 8848
SIKKIM
BHUTAN
BANGLADESH
DHAKA
UTTAR PRADESH
LUCKNOW
KANPUR
Allahabad
VARANASI
PATNA
BIHAR
WEST BENGAL
CALCUTTA
MADHYA PRADESH
Jabalpur
Ranchi
Jamshedpur
Mouths of the Ganges
The Sandheads
East from Greenwich
A
B
C
D
E
F
G
H
J
8
9
10
11
12
13
5
6
7

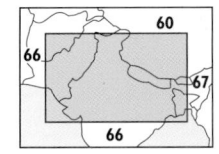

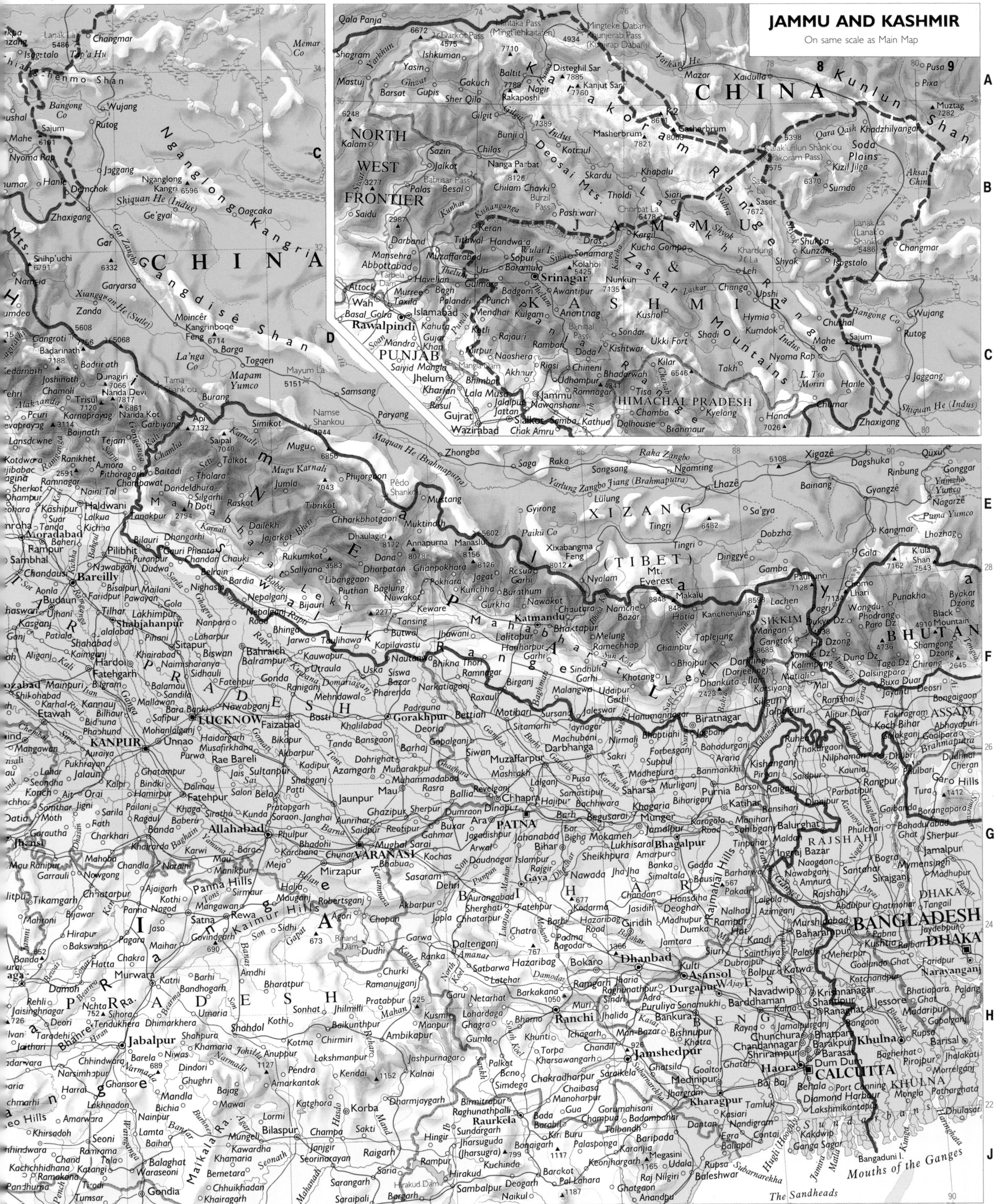

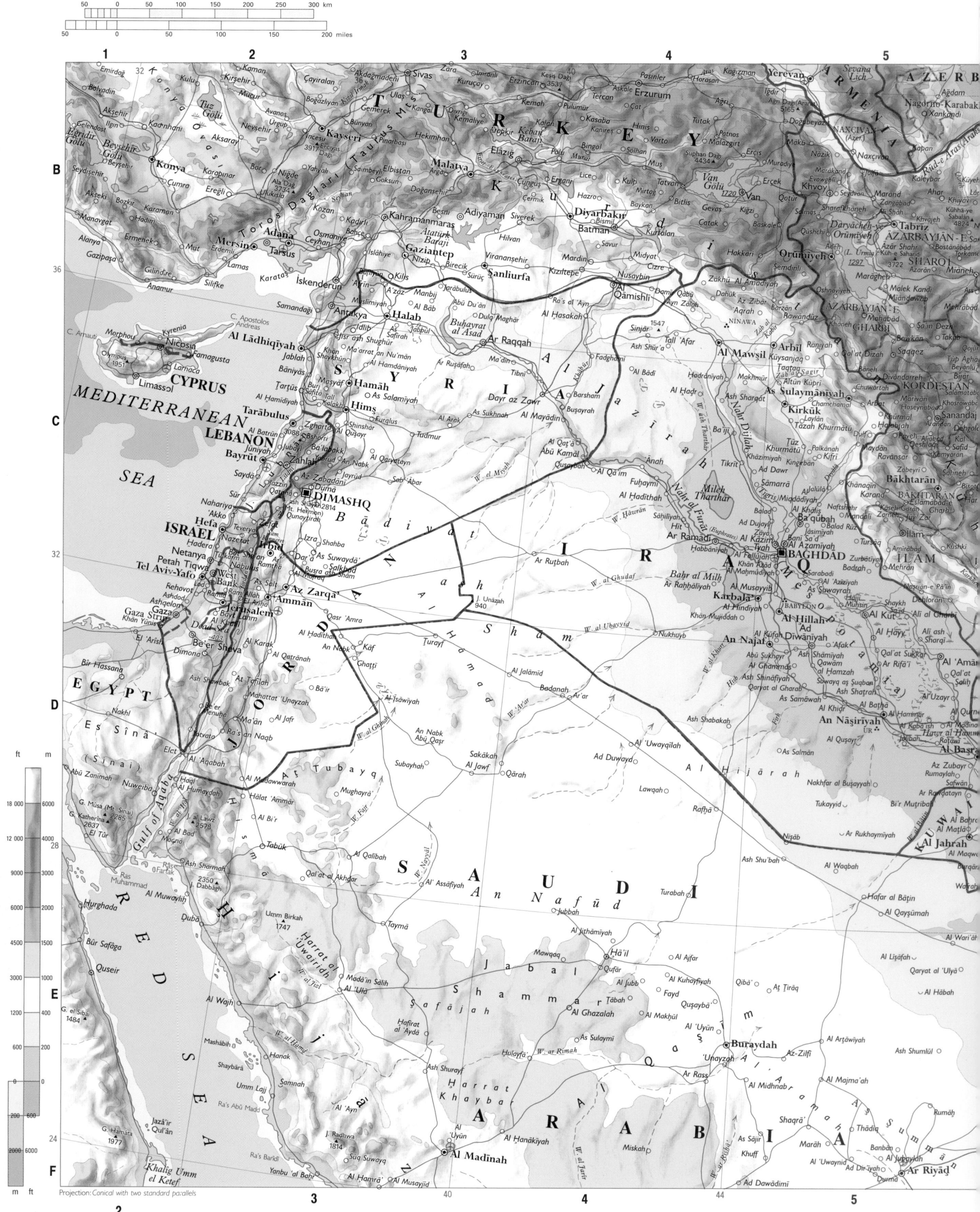

Projection: Conical with two standard parallels

49
50
72
66
80
74

6
7
8
9
10
B
C
D
E
F
CASPIAN
SEA
TURKMENISTAN
Kara Kum
Kopet Dagh
Ashgabat
Türkmenbashi
Cheleken Yarymadasy
Ostrov Ogurchinskiy
Khrebet Bolshoy Balkhan 1880
Nebitdag
Gazanjyk
Gyzylarbat
26 Bakinskikh Komissarov
Gyzyletrek
Mary
Bayramaly
Yoloten
Tejen
Dushak
Sarakhs
Chärjew
Amudarya
Dashköpri
BAKI
Qazimämmäd
Älät
Neftçala
Länkäran
Ästärä
Ardabil
Tälesh
Bandar-e Anzalī
Rasht
Āstāneh
Lāhījān
Fowman
Rūd Sar
GĪLĀN
Rāmsar
Tonekābon
Now Shahr
Bābol Sar
Bābol
Sārī
Neka
Behshahr
MĀZANDARĀN
Āmol
Qā'emshahr
Reshteh-ye Kūhha-ye Alborz
Gorgān
Bandar-e Torkeman
Gonbad-e Kāvūs
Gomīshān
Ramīān
Kord Kūy
Bastām
Shāhrūd
Emāmrūd
Dāmghān
Semnān
SEMNĀN
Qazvin
Karaj
TEHRĀN
Tajrish
Eslāmshahr
Rey
Damāvand
Damavand 5604
Varāmīn
Garmsār
MARKAZĪ
Sāveh
Qom
Daryācheh-ye Namak
Kāshān
Arāk
Malāyer
Borūjerd
Khorramābād
Dasht-e Kavīr
Quchān
Shīrvān
Bojnūrd
Mashhad
Sabzevār
Neyshābūr
Kūh-e Bīnālūd
Kūh-e Sorkh
Torbat-e Heydarīyeh
Torbat-e Jām
Kāshmar
KHORĀSĀN
Gonābād
Ferdows
Qāyen
Bīrjand
Tabas
Khvor
Mehr Jān
Anārak
IRAN
Esfahān
EŞFAHĀN
Najafābād
Khomeynī Shahr
Nā'īn
Ardakān
Yazd
YAZD
Bāţlāq-e Gavkhūnī
Bāfq
Mehrīz
Shahr-e Kord
CHAHĀR MAḨĀLL VA BAKHTĪĀRĪ
Dezfūl
Shūshtar
Masjed Soleymān
Ahvāz
KHŪZESTĀN
Khorramshahr
Ābādān
Bandar-e Khomeynī
Bandar-e Ma'shur
KOHKĪLŪYEH VA BŪYER AHMADĪ
Yāsūj
Kūh-e Dinār 4431
Zāgros
Dasht-e Lūt
Kermān
KERMĀN
Rafsanjān
Sīrjān
Bam
Zarand
Kūh-e Hazārān 4419
Namakzār-e Shahdād
Shahdād
Neyrīz
Darāb
Fasā
Shīrāz
PERSEPOLIS
FARS
Marv Dasht
Kāzerūn
Būshehr
BŪSHEHR
Daryācheh-ye Tashk
Zāhedān
Zābol
Sīstān
Daryācheh-ye Sīstān
Kūh-e Taftān 4042
Īrānshahr
SĪSTĀN VA BALŪCHESTĀN
Hāmūn-e Jaz Mūrīān
Bandar 'Abbās
HORMOZGĀN
Qeshm
Hormoz
Mīnāb
Kūhha-ye Bashākerd
Jāsk
Chāh Bahār
Makran
Hamun-i Mashkel
PAKISTAN
Mīrjāveh
AFGHANISTAN
HERĀT
Herāt
FARĀH
Farāh
NĪMRŪZ
Zaranj
Dasht-e Mārgow
Gowd-e Zirreh
Shindand
Safīd Kūh
Kuwait
Al Aḩmadī
Al Khafjī
Ra's al Mish'āb
As Saffānīyah
Al Jubayl
Ad Dammām
Al Qaţīf
Az Zahrān
Al Khubar
Al Manāmah
BAHRAIN
Al Hufūf
Ad Dawhah
QATAR
Al Jāfūrah
THE GULF
Str. of Hormuz
Ra's Masandam (Oman)
Ra's al Khaymah
Umm al Qaywayn
'Ajmān
Ash Shāriqah
Dubayy
Al Fujayrah
Abū Z̧aby
Al 'Ayn
UNITED ARAB EMIRATES
Al Ḩajar al Gharbī
OMAN
Şuḩār
Gulf of Oman
Qeys
Lāvan
Hendorābī
Sīrrī
Abū Mūsá
Dās
Dalmā
Şīr Banī Yās
Ruwais
East from Greenwich
52
56
60

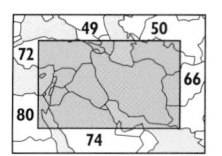

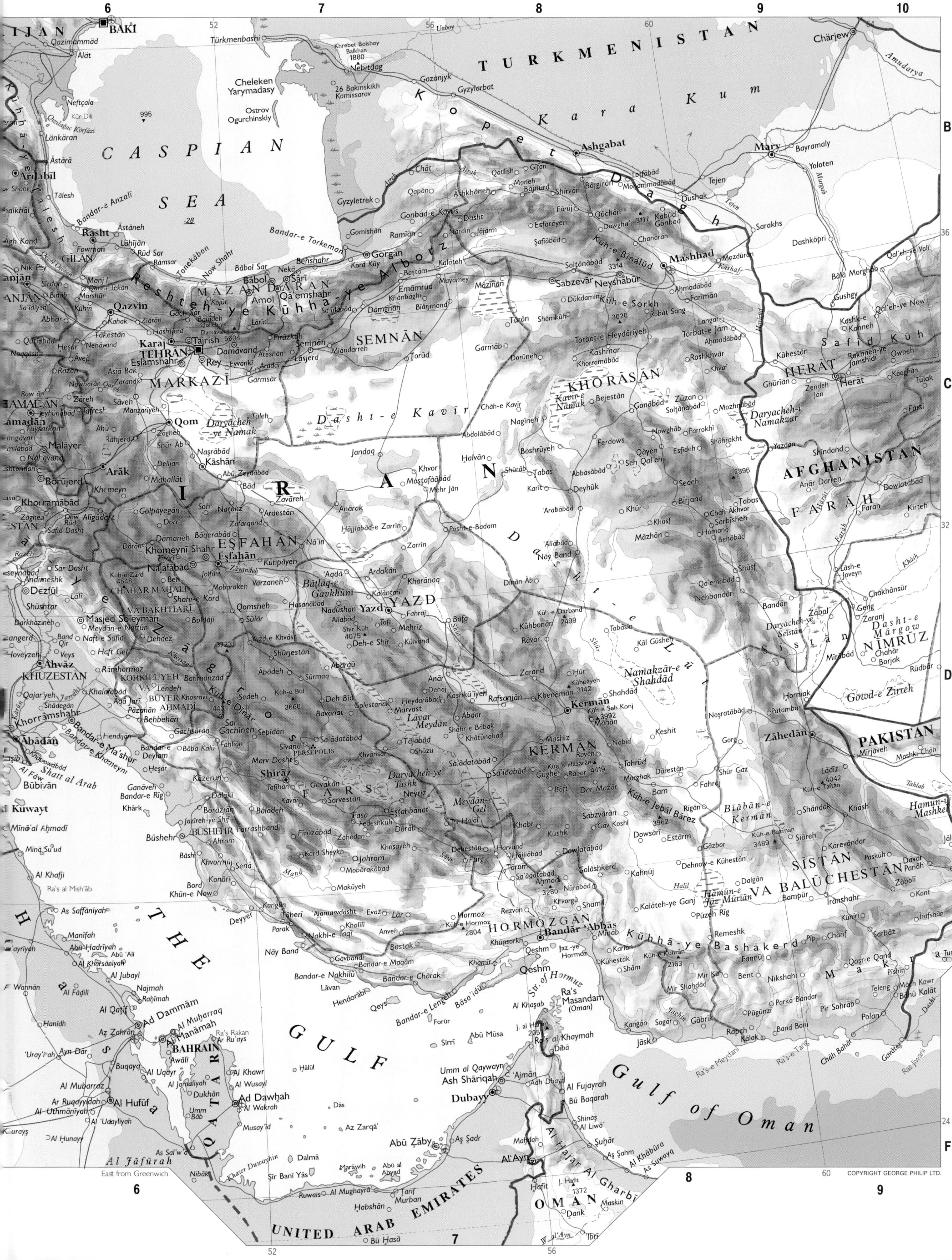

Division between Greeks and Turks
in Cyprus; Turks to the North.

47 49
41 39
80 70 71

CASPIAN SEA

RUSSIA

Sochi · Mtsesto · Adler · Teberda · Elbrus 5642 · KABARDINO-BALKARIA · 5203 · Groznyy · Argun · Khasavyurt · Makhachkala · Kaspiysk · Izberbash

Gagra · Bichvinta · Kodori · 4046 · CHECHENIA · 2726 · Buynaksk · DAGESTAN

Guadauta · Novyy Afon · Sokhumi · NORTH OSSETIA · Vladikavkaz · Kazbek 5047 · Botlikh · 4492 · Agvali · Kakhib · Akusha · Madzhalis · Ogni · Derbent · 790

ABKHAZIA · Ochamchira · Gali · Zugdidi · Jvari · Alagir · Ardon · Sadon · 4276 · 3578 · Tlyarata · Akusha · Kasumkent · Xüdat · 42

GEORGIA · Anaklia · Senaki · Kutaisi · Tqvarcheli · Sachkhere · Oni · South Ossetia · Tskhinvali · Dusheti · 4131 · Samurskiy Khrebet · Samur · Akhty · 4466 · Qusar · Xaçmaz

Poti · Rioni · Samtredia · Zestaponi · Khashuri · Gori · Kaspi · Mtskheta · Telavi · Lagodekhi · Zaqatala · Baba dag 3629 · Quba · Däväçi

1569 · Kobuleti · Ozurgeti · Borjomi · **TBILISI** · Khrami · Marneuli · Gurjaani · Tsnori · Tsiteli · Alazani · Şaki · Kutkashen · Siyäzän

Batumi · **ATARIA** · Khulo · Akhaltsikhe · Vale · 2918 · Akhalkalaki · Shulaveri · Rustavi · Agstafa · Kür · Mingäçevir Su Anbarı · Ağdaş · Göyçay · Şamaxı · Maştağa · Artyom

Hopa · Arhavi · Borçka · Şavşat · 3157 · Stepanavan · Alaverdi · Tovuz · Şämkir · Mingäçevir · Xanlar · **Gäncä** · Barda · Lǎki · **BAKI** · Surakhany

Pazar · Ardeşen · Artvin · Ardahan · Çıldır · Kısır Dağ 3192 · Gyumri · Vanadzor · Dilijan · Sevan · Daşkäsän · Kürdämir · Qazımämmäd · Älät

AZERBAIJAN · Nagorno-Karabakh · Xankändi · Ağcabädi · Ağdam · Sabirabad · Äli Bayramlı · Salyan · Biläsuvar

Of · Rize · İkizdere · Kaçkar 3937 · Yusufeli · Olur · Şenim · **ARMENIA** · Aragats 4090 · Charantsavan · Hrazdan · Kama · Sevana Lich · 3724 · Tärtär · 3616 · İmişli · Qaracala · Kür Dili · Neftçala

Trabzon · Çakırgöl 3063 · Gümüşhane · Mescit 3239 · Kars · Sarikamiş · Susuz · Digor · Artik · **YEREVAN** · Ejmiadzin · 3598 · Martuni · Yeghegnadzor · Goris · Kapan · 3904 · Masallı · Özbalağac Körfäzi

Giresun · Tirebolu · Eynesil · Görele · Vakfıkebir · Araklı · Arsin · Sürmene · Tonya · Bayburt · Narman · Tortum · Horasan · Karakurt · Kağızman · Iğdır · Ararat · Yeghegnadzor · 2477 · Port İliç · Länkäran · Astara

Dereli · Şebinkarahisar · Kelkit · Şiran · Bayburt · Pasinler · Erzurum · Aşkale · Tekman · Karayazı · Tuzluca · **NAXÇIVAN (Azerbayjan)** · Naxçıvan · Culfa · Ordubad · Jolfa · Germi · Ahar · Namin · Ardabil · 4824 · Talesh · Rasht

Şiran · Erzincan · İliç · Kemah 3239 · Pülümür · Çat · Tercan · Hınıs · Malazgirt · Ağrı 5165 · Doğubayazıt · Maku · Khvoy · Evoğhli · Marand · Seydvän · Tabriz · Bostänäbäd · Sarab · Nir · Khalkhäl · Bandar-e Anzali

Anadolu Dağları · Kemaliye · Kemah · Munzur Dağları · Tunceli · Varto · Bingöl · Muş · Suphan Dağı 4434 · Adilcevaz · Erciş · Muradiye · Özalp · Nazik · 3347 · Sharafkhäneh · Daryächeh-ye Orümiyeh · Köh-e Sahand 3722 · Azar Shahr · Märagheh · Azarän · Miäneh · 3327 · Zanjän

Keban Barajı · Keban · Elâzığ · Maden · Palu · Genç · Bingöl Dağları · Van Gölü 1720 · Van · Saray · Qoṭür · 3282 · Salmäs · Qüshchi · 1297 · Orümiyeh (Urmia) · Lake Urmia · Miändowäb · Nik Pey · Abhar · Sırdän · Binäb

Malatya 2545 · Ergani · Çermik · Güneydoğu Toroslar · Lice · Kulp · Bitlis · Gevaş · Çatak · Başkale · 3752 · 3878 · Benäb · Malek Kandi · Mehräbäd · Tup Äghäj

Eskimalatya · Silvan · Diyarbakır · Kurtalan · Batman · Siirt · **Hakkâri Dağları** · Hakkâri · Cilo Dağı 4135 · Yüksekova · Semdinli · Nägadeh · Mahäbäd · Şa'in Dezh · Takäb · Qütiäbäd · Hamadän

Siverek · Bismil · Dicle Nehri · Gerçüş · Şirnak · Eruh · Beytüşşebap · Uludere · **KURDISTAN** · Bowkän · Saqqez · Divändarreh · Bijär · Razan

Hilvan · Derik · Mardin · Midyat · Cizre · Silopi · Zakhu · Al Amädiyah · Az Zibär · 3667 · Rawändüz · Bäneh · Sanandaj · Dehgolän · Qorveh · Bahär · Asadäbäd

Şanlıurfa (Urfa) · Viranşehir · Kızıltepe · Nusaybin · Al Qämishlı · Ayn Zäläh · Dihök · 'Aqrah · Qal'at Dizäh · 3163 · Saqqez · Mariván · Khosrowäbäd · Kämyärän · Tüysarkän · Malâyer · Nahävand

Ra's al 'Ayn · Al Ḥasakah · Tall 'Afar 1460 · Sinjär · NINAWA · Zäb al Kabir · Arbil · Küysanjaq · Altün Küpri · Bäneh · Chamchamal · Arbat · Qeshläq · Kal Safid · Soriqor · Oshtorinän · Borüjerd

Ar Raqqah · Bahret Assad · Fadghämi · Al Ḥadr · **Al Mawşil (Mosul)** · Taqtaq · Taqtaq · As Sulaymäniyah · Hoseynäbäd · Páveh · 3280 · Bisotün · Harsin

Nahr al Furät (Euphrates) · Ma'dan · Ar Ruşäfah · Tibni · Barsham · Khäbür · Ash Sharqät · Kirkük · Tazah Khurmätü · **Bäkhtarän** · Karand · Eslämäbäd-e Gharb · Nahävand

Dayr az Zawr · Buşayrah · **Al Jazirah (Mesopotamia)** · Makhmur · Zäb aş Şaghir · Tüz Khurmätü · Maydän · Kifri · 3350 · Şehneh · Kängävär · Mäläyer · Bäkhtarän

Al Mayädin · Al Hadr · Tikrit · Ad Dawr · Sämarrä · Ba'ij · Nahr Dijlah · Diyälä · Jalülä · Ravänsar · Şorqor · Borüjerd

1390 · As Sukhnah · Al Qaṭ'a · Abü Kamäl · Qusayrah · 'Änah · Al Qä'im · Fuhaymi · Al Ḥadithah · Ad Dujayl · Balad Rüz · Mandali · 2656 · Iläm · Khorramäbäd

Tudmur PALMYRA · Al Arak · **Nahr al Furät (Euphrates)** · Mileh Tharthär · Ad Dujayl · Al Miqdädiyah · Ba'qübah · Jäsimiyah · Banï Sa'd · Turṣäq · Badrah · Jüy Zar · Andimeshk · Dezful · Shüsh

Al Rutbah · W. Rutqa · W. Hawrän · Hit · Habbäniyah · **BAGHDAD** BABYLON · Al Käzim Tyah · Zurbätiyah · Mehrän · Dehloran

IRAQ · Ar Ramädi · Al Fallüjah · Al Maḥmüdiyah · As Suwayrah · Nahr Dijlah (Tigris) · Al 'Azizïyah · Al Küt · Shaykh Sa'd · Alï al Gharbï · 'Alï ash Sharqï · Karkheh

Nukhayb · W. al Ubayyiḍ · Al Musayyib · Karbalä · Bahr al Milḥ · Al Ḥillah · An Nu'mäniyah · Al Hay · Ḥawr as Sa'diyah · Al Amärah · Süsangerd

940 · 'Unäzah · Ar Raḥḥäliyah · **ash Shäm** · Bahr al Milḥ · Al H ndïyah · Ash Shämïyah · 'Afak · Al Küfah · Ad Diwänïyah · Ash Shämïyah · Qal'at Sukkar

An Najaf

ft m
9000 3000
6000 2000
4500 1500
3000 1000
1500 500
600 200
150 50
0 0
150 50
600 200
1500 500
3000 1000
6000 2000
9000 3000
m ft

East from Greenwich

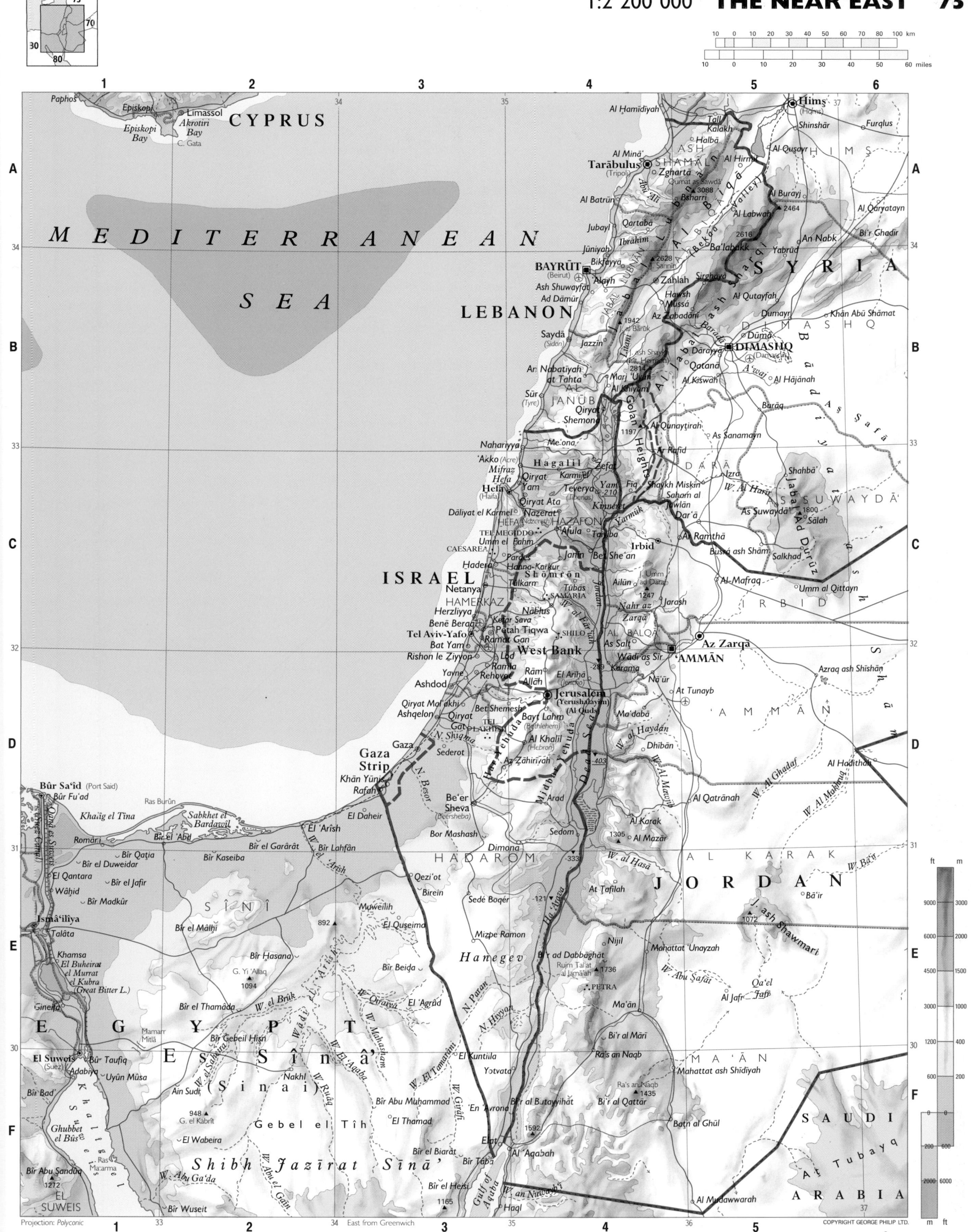

10 0 10 20 30 40 50 60 70 80 100 km
10 0 10 20 30 40 50 60 miles

CYPRUS

Paphos
Episkopi
Episkopi Bay
Limassol
Akrotiri Bay
C. Gata

M E D I T E R R A N E A N

S E A

LEBANON

Al Hamidiyah
Hims (Homs)
Tall Kalakh
Shinshar
Furqlus
Al Mina
Tarabulus (Tripoli)
ASH SHAMAL
Zgharta
Qurnat as Sawda 3088
Al Hirmil
Al Qusayr
HIMS
Al Batrun
Bsharri
2464
Al Qaryatayn
Jubayl
Qartaba
Ibrahim
Al Labweh
Bi'r Ghadir
2616
Juniyah
Bikfayya
Ba'labakk
Yabrud
An Nabk
BAYRUT (Beirut)
2628 Sannin
Sirghaya
Ash Shuwayfat
Zahlah
Hawsh Mussa
Al Qutayfah
Khan Abu Shamat
Alayh
Ad Damur
Az Zabadani
Dumayr
1942 Al Baruk
Sayda (Sidon)
Lash Shayk Jt. Hermon 2814
Darayya
DIMASHQ
Duma
DIMASHQ (Damascus)
Jazzin
Marj 'Uyun
Al Kiswah
Qatana
A'waj
Al Hajanah
An Nabatiyah at Tahta
Al Qunaytirah
Al Jaharra
Buraq
AL JANUB
Qiryat Shemona
Golan Heights
1197
Ar Rafid
As Sanamayn
SYRIA
Nahariyya
Me'ona
Zefat
DARA
Izra
Shahba'
'Akko (Acre)
Hagalil
Karmi'el
Fiq
Shaykh Miskin
W. Al Harir
Mifraz Hefa
Qiryat Yam
Teverya
Yam -210
Dar'a
1800 Salah
AS SUWAYDA
Hefa (Haifa)
Qiryat Ata
Nazerat
Kinneret
Yarmuk
Saham al Jowlan
As Suwayda
Daliyat el Karmel
Nazereth
HAZAFON
Afula
Tayba
Irbid
Busra ash Sham
Salkhad
Jabal ad Duruz
TEL MEGIDDO
Umm el Fahm
Jinin
Bet She'an
Al Ramtha
CAESAREA
Pardes Hanna-Karkur
Shomron
Tubas
Ailun
Umm ad Daraj
Al Mafraq
Umm al Qittayn
Hadera
Tulkarm
SAMARIA 1247
Jarash
IRBID
ISRAEL
Netanya
Nablus
Nahr az Zarqa
HAMERKAZ
Herzliyya
Kefar Sava
SHILO
Benё Beraq
Ramat Gan
Az Zarqa
Tel Aviv-Yafo
Petah Tiqwa
AL BALQA
Bat Yam
As Salt
AMMAN
Rishon le Ziyyon
Lod
West Bank
Wadi as Sir
Karama
Azraq ash Shishan
Yavne
Ramla
Ram Allah
-289
Na'ur
Rehovot
El Arih (Jericho)
403
Ashdod
Jerusalem (Yerushalayim) (Al Quds)
Ma'daba
'AMMAN
Qiryat Mal'akhi
Bet Shemesh
Bayt Lahm (Bethlehem)
W. al Haydan
Ashqelon
Qiryat Gat
TEL LAKHISH
Dhiban
Gaza
N. Shiqma
Al Khalil (Hebron)
Dead Sea
Gaza Strip
Sederot
Az Zahiriya
Bur Sa'id (Port Said)
Bur Fu'ad
Khan Yunis
Rafah
Bur Sa'id
Ras Burun
N. Besor
Be'er Sheva (Beersheba)
Arad
Al Karak
1305 Al Mazar
Khalig el Tina
Sabkhet el Bardawil
El Daheir
Bor Mashash
AL KARAK
Romani
Bir el Abd
Bir el Gararat
Bir Lahfan
Dimona
-333
W. al Hasa
JORDAN
W. Bair
El Qantara
Bir Qatia
Bir el Duweidar
Bir Kaseiba
Arish
HADAROM
Sedom
El Jafir
Bir el Jafir
Wahid
Bir Madkur
N. Arish
Qezi'ot
Birein
At Tafilah
Ba'ir
Isma'iliya
Talata
SINI
Sede Boqer
-121
Ha 'Arava
Ras an Naqb
1072
Khamsa
El Buheirat el Murrat el Kubra (Great Bitter L.)
892
Bir Hasana
Muweilih
El Quseima
Mizpe Ramon
Nijil
Mahattat 'Unayzah
Mahattat ash Shidiyah
Gineifa
G. Yi 'Allaq
1094
Bir Beida
El 'Agrud
Hanegev
Bi'r ad Dabbaghat
Rujm Tal'at al Jama'ah
W. Abu Safat
Qa'el Jafr
EGYPT
Mamarr Mitla
Bir Gebeil Hisn
W. el Brik
Sede Boqer
N. Paran
1736
PETRA
Ma'an
El Suweis (Suez)
Bur Taufiq
Adabiya
Uyun Musa
Ain Sudr
Nakhl
W. Riuq
Bir Abu Muhammad
En 'Avrona
Bi'r al Mari
MA'AN
Bir Bad
Ghubbet el Bus
948 G. el Kabrit
Gebel el Tih
El Thamad
1435 Ra's an Naqb
Bir Abu Sanduq
1272
EL SUWEIS
El Wabeira
Bir el Thamada
W. el Salwia
Wadi el Arish
El Kuntila
Yotvata
Bi'r al Butayyihat
Batn al Ghul
SAUDI ARABIA
Ras Maqarma
Shibh Jazirat Sina
W. Abu Ga'da
Bir el Heisi
1165
Elat
1592
Bi'r al Qattar
At Tubayq
Bir Wuseit
Bir Taba
Al Aqaba
Gulf of Aqaba
W. an Nira
Haql
Al Mudawwarah

Projection: Polyconic
East from Greenwich
COPYRIGHT GEORGE PHILIP LTD.

ft m
9000 3000
6000 2000
4500 1500
3000 1000
1200 400
600 200
0 0
200 600
2000 6000
m ft

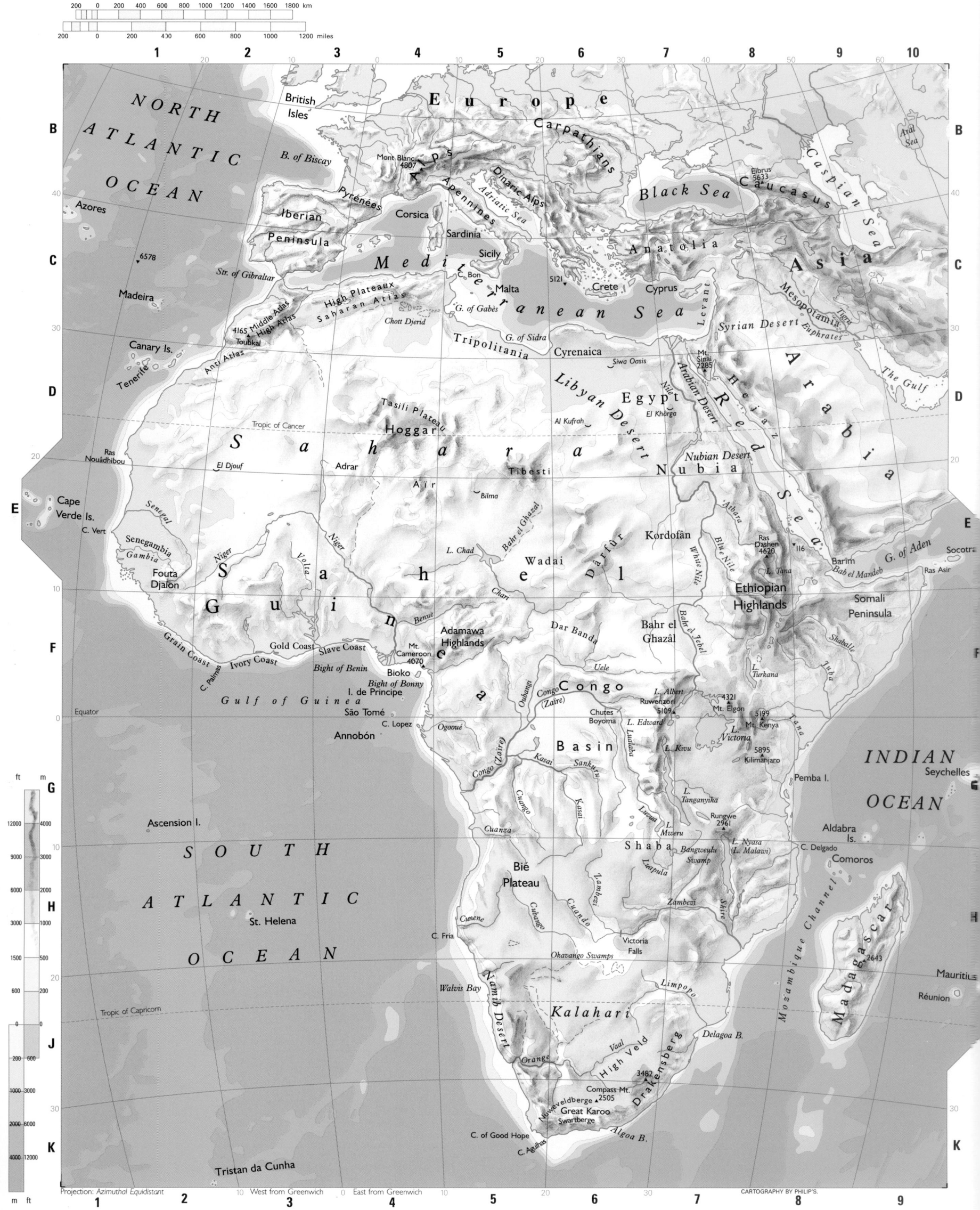

200 0 200 400 600 800 1000 1200 1400 1600 1800 km
200 0 200 430 600 800 1000 1200 miles

NORTH
ATLANTIC
OCEAN

Europe

British
Isles

B. of Biscay

Carpathians

Mont Blanc
4807

Alps

Dinaric Alps

Elbrus
5633

Black Sea

Caucasus

Caspian Sea

Aral Sea

Azores

Iberian
Peninsula

Pyrénées

Apennines

Adriatic Sea

Anatolia

Asia

Madeira

6578

Corsica

Sardinia

Sicily

Malta

C. Bon

5121

Crete

Cyprus

Mediterranean Sea

Levant

Mesopotamia

Tigris

Canary Is.

Tenerife

High Plateaux

Middle Atlas

4165 High Atlas

Toubkal

Anti Atlas

Saharan Atlas

Chott Djerid

G. of Gabès

G. of Sidra

Tripolitania

Cyrenaica

Libyan Desert

Siwa Oasis

Egypt

Nile

El Khârga

Mt. Sinai
2285

Arabian Desert

Hejaz

Red Sea

Syrian Desert

Euphrates

Arabia

The Gulf

Ras
Nouâdhibou

El Djouf

Sahara

Adrar

Hoggar

Tasili Plateau

Aïr

Bilma

Tibesti

Al Kufrah

Nubian Desert

Nubia

Tropic of Cancer

Cape
Verde Is.

C. Vert

Senegal

Senegambia

Gambia

Fouta
Djalon

Niger

Volta

Niger

Sahel

Guinea

L. Chad

Bahr el Ghazal

Wadai

Chari

Darfûr

Kordofân

Sahel

White Nile

Albara

Blue Nile

Ras
Dashen
4620

116

Barim

Bab el Mandeb

G. of Aden

Socotra

Ras Asir

L. Tana

Ethiopian
Highlands

Somali
Peninsula

Grain Coast

C. Palmas

Ivory Coast

Gold Coast

Slave Coast

Bight of Benin

Mt.
Cameroon
4070

Bioko

I. de Principe

Adamawa
Highlands

Benue

Ubangi

Dar Banda

Uele

Bahr el
Ghazâl

Bahr el Jebel

Shaballe

Juba

L.
Turkana

Equator

São Tomé

Annobón

Bight of Bonny

Gulf of Guinea

C. Lopez

Ogooué

Congo
(Zaire)

Congo

L. Albert

Ruwenzori
5109

Chutes
Boyoma

L. Edward

L. Luindi

Congo

Basin

Kasai

Sankuru

Mt. Elgon
4321

5199

Mt. Kenya

L.
Victoria

5895

Kilimanjaro

L. Kivu

Tana

Pemba I.

INDIAN

OCEAN

Seychelles

Ascension I.

SOUTH

ATLANTIC

St. Helena

OCEAN

Congo (Zaire)

Cuango

Kasai

Cuanza

Shaba

Lualaba

L.
Tanganyika

L. Mweru

Rungwe
2961

Bangweulu
Swamp

Luapula

L. Nyasa
(L. Malawi)

C. Delgado

Aldabra
Is.

Comoros

Bié
Plateau

Cunene

C. Fria

Cubango

Cuando

Zambezi

Zambezi

Shire

Victoria
Falls

Okavango Swamps

Mozambique Channel

Madagascar

2643

Mauritius

Réunion

Tropic of Capricorn

Walvis Bay

Namib Desert

Kalahari

Limpopo

Delagoa B.

Vaal

High Veld

Drakensberg

Orange

Nieuveldberge

Great Karoo

Compass Mt.
2505

3482

Swartberge

Algoa B.

C. of Good Hope

C. Agulhas

ft m

12000 4000

9000 3000

6000 2000

3000 1000

1500 500

600 200

0 0

200 600

1000 3000

2000 6000

4000 12000

m ft

Tristan da Cunha

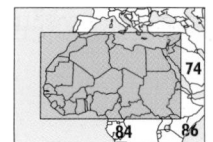

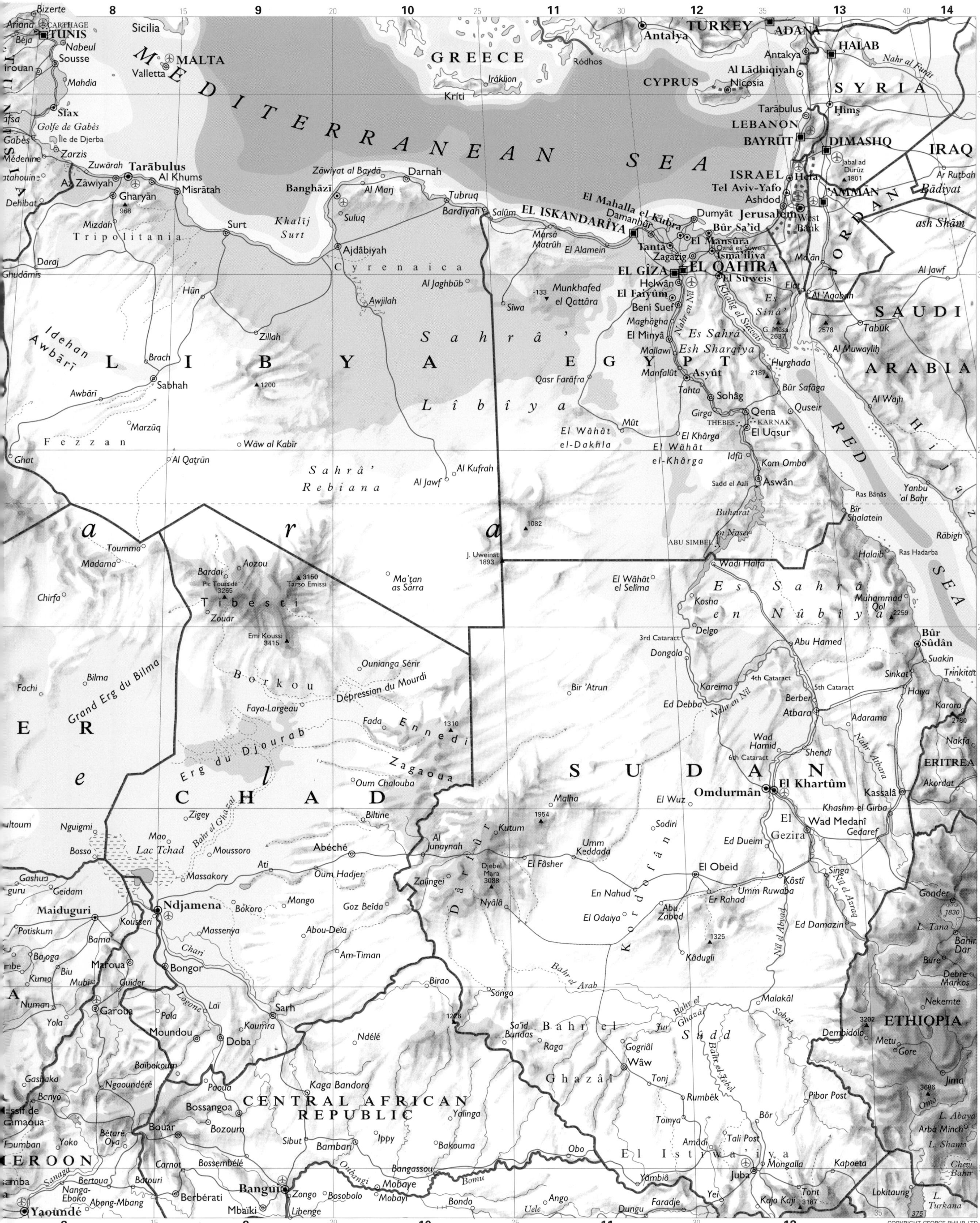

MEDITERRANEAN SEA

GREECE

TURKEY

Antalya ADANA

Ródhos HALAB

Kríti Al Ládhiqiyah Antakya **SYRIA**

CYPRUS Nicosia Himş IRAQ

Tarābulus Ar Ruţbah

LEBANON DIMASHQ Bādiyat

BAYRŪT Jabal ad ash Shām

ISRAEL Durūz 1801

Tel Aviv-Yafo Hefa AMMĀN

El Mahalla el Kubra Dumyât Jerusalem West Ma'ān

Damanhûr Bûr Sa'id Bank

Banghāzī El Marj Tubruq EL ISKANDARÎYA El Mansûra

Al Marj Bardîyah Salûm Tanta Qanâ es Suweis Ma'ān

Sicilia MALTA

Bizerte Ariana CARTHAGE

TUNIS Valletta

Nabeul Mahdia Darnah

Sousse Zāwiyat al Baydā

Sfax Al Khums Zuwārah **Tarābulus** Suluq Surt Marsá El Alamein Zagazig Isma'îliya

Golfe de Gabès Az Zāwiyah Misrātah Matrûh EL GÎZA **EL QAHIRA**

Gabès Gharyān 968 Khalīj Helwân El Suweis

Île de Djerba Mizdah Surt El Faiyûm Es El 'Aqabah

Zarzis Ajdâbiyah Beni Suef Sînâ'

Médenine Tripolitania Cyrenaica Maghâgha G. Mûsa 2578 Tabûk

Dehibat Al Jaghbūb Munkhafed El Minyâ 2637 Al Muwaylih **SAUDI**

Daraj Hūn el Qattâra Mallawi Es Sahrâ Hurghada

Ghudāmis -133 Manfalût Esh Sharqîya

Siwa Asyût 2187 **ARABIA**

LIBYA Sahrâ' Qasr Farâfra Tahta Bûr Safâga Al Wajh

Brach Zillah Sohâg Quseir Hijâz

Awbārī Sabhah Lîbîya Girga Qena RED

Marzūq El Wâhât Mût THEBES KARNAK

Fezzan Wāw al Kabīr el-Dakhla El Khârga El Uqsur Al Wajh

Ghat Al Qaţrūn Sahrâ' Idfû

Rebiana El Wâhât Kom Ombo

el-Khârga Aswân Ras Bânâs SEA

a 1082 Sadd el Aali Bûr

r Buhairat Shalatein Râbigh

Ma'tan a en Naser Yanbu

Toumma as Sarra ABU SIMBEL al Bahr

Madama J. Uweinat Wadi Halfa Halaib Ras Hadarba

Chirfa Aozou 1893 El Wâhât Kosha Muhammad

Bardai 3150 el Selîma Qol 2259

Pic Toussidé 3285 Tarso Emissi Es Sahrâ Delgo Bûr

Tibesti en Nûbiya 3rd Cataract Abu Hamed **Sûdân**

Zouar Emi Koussi Dongola Suakin

3415 Kareima 4th Cataract Sinkat Trinkitat

Bilma Berber 5th Cataract

Fachi Grand Erg du Bilma Borkou Ouninga Sérir Bir 'Atrun Ed Debba Atbara Haiya

Erg du Djourab Dépression du Mourdi Adarama Karora 2180

Faya-Largeau Fada 1310 Wad Nakfa

Zagaoua Ennedi Hamid Shendî **ERITREA**

Oum Chalouba 6th Cataract Akordat

CHAD Malha Omdurmân El Khartûm Kassalâ

Zigey Biltine 1954 El Wuz Khashm el Girba

Nguigmi Mao Bahr el Ghazal Kutum Sodiri El Wad Medanî

Bosso Lac Tchad Moussoro Ati Al Umm Gezira Gedaref

Gashua Geidam Massakory Abéché Junaynah Keddada Ed Dueim 1830

Maiduguri Kousséri Ôum Hadjer El Fâsher El Obeid Kôstî L. Tana

Potiskum Bama Ndjamena Bôkoro Zalingei Djebel En Nahud Abu Er Rahad Singa Gonder Bahir

Bajoga Mongo Marra Nyâlâ Zabad Umm Ruwaba Dar

Biu Mubi Guider Massenya 3088 Goz Beïda Ed Damazin Bure

Numan Maroua Chari Am-Timan En Nahud El Odaiya 1325 Debre

Yola Bongor Kâdugli Markos

Garoua Pala Birao Bahr el Arab Malakâl Nekemte

Baïbokoum Laï Sarh Songo 3202 Metu **ETHIOPIA**

Moundou Koumra Doba 1276 Sa'id Gogrial Dembidola Gore

Bétaré Ndélé Bundas Bahr el Wâw

Oya Baïbokoum Raga Tonj Rumbêk 3886 Jima

Bouar Bozoum Ghazâl Bôr L. Abaya

Ngaoundéré Paoua Kaga Bandoro Yalinga Toinya Tali Post Arba Minch

Bossangoa **CENTRAL AFRICAN** Bakouma Amadi L. Shala

Benyó **REPUBLIC** Ippy Obo El Istwa'iya Kapoeta

Gashaka Bétaré Sibut Bambari Mongalla Chew

Yoko Bossembélé Bakouma Yei Kajo Kaji Bahr

Nanga- Carnot Bangassou Juba Torit 3187 L. Turkana

Eboko **Bangui** Moboye Yambiô Lokitaung

Yaoundé Berbérati Zongo Mobayi Bondo Faradje Dungu

Mbaïki Libenge Uele

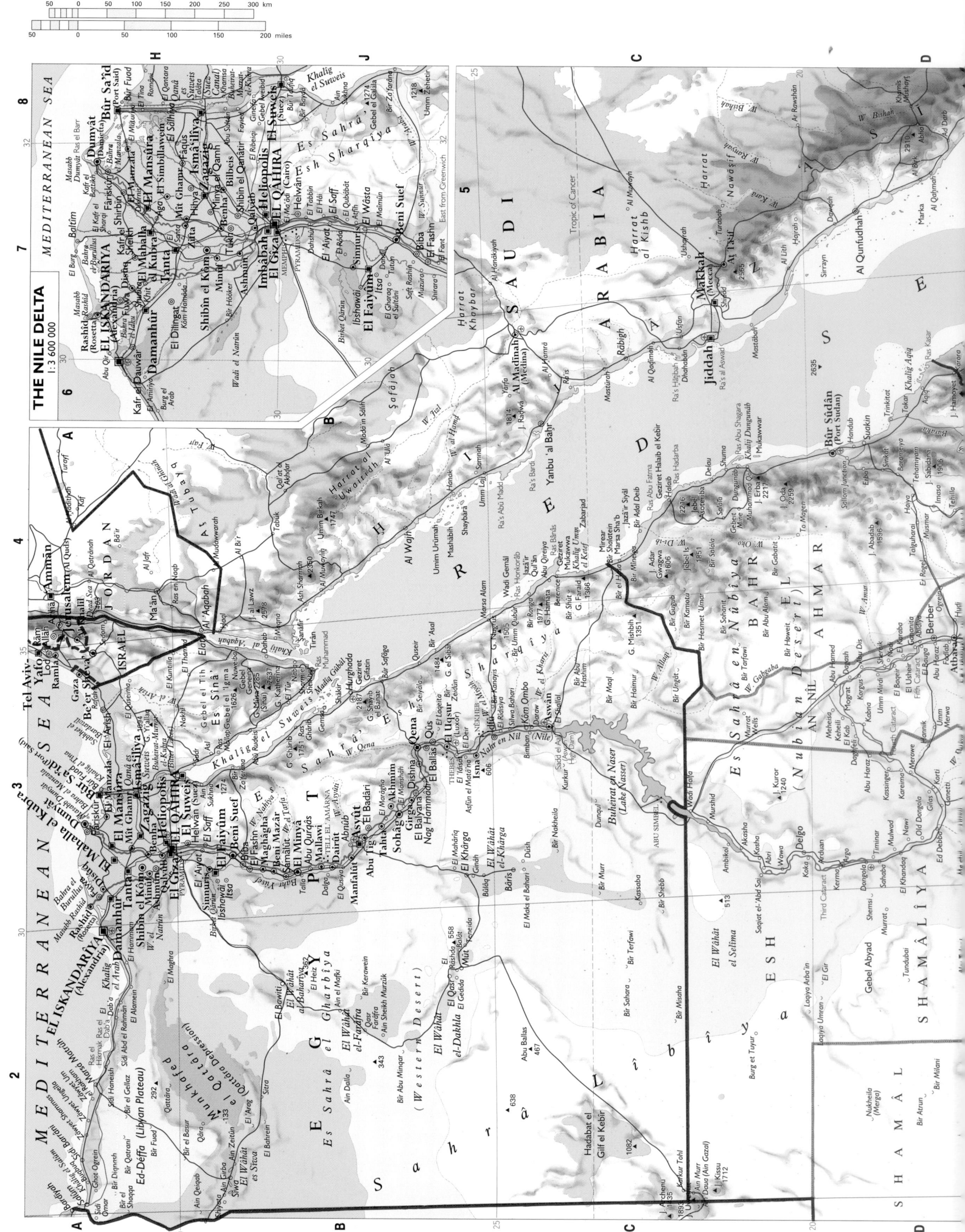

THE NILE DELTA 1:3 600 000

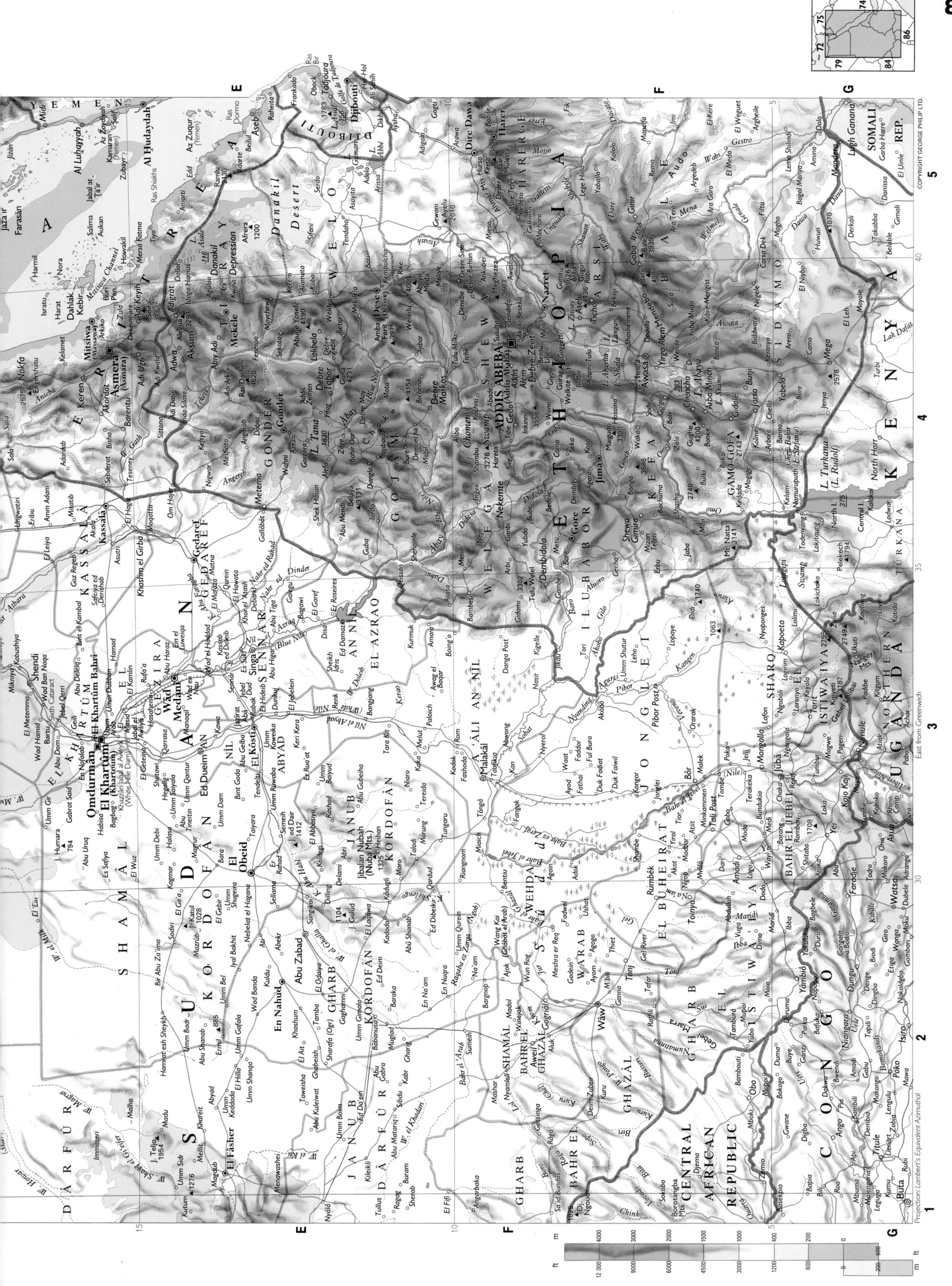

Projection: Lambert's Equivalent Azimuthal

East from Greenwich

Projection : Lambert's Equivalent Azimuthal

West from Green

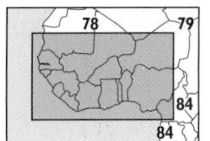

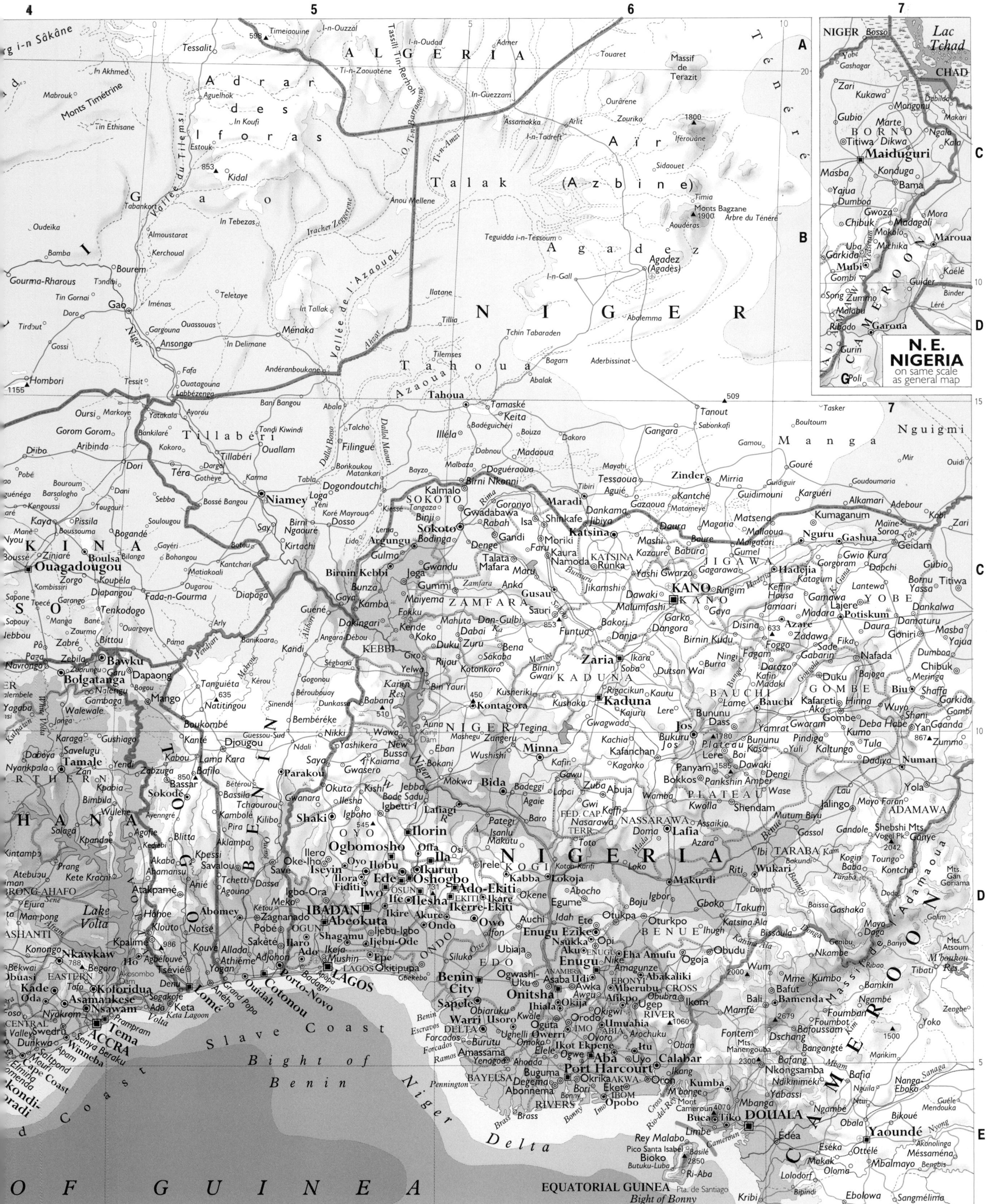

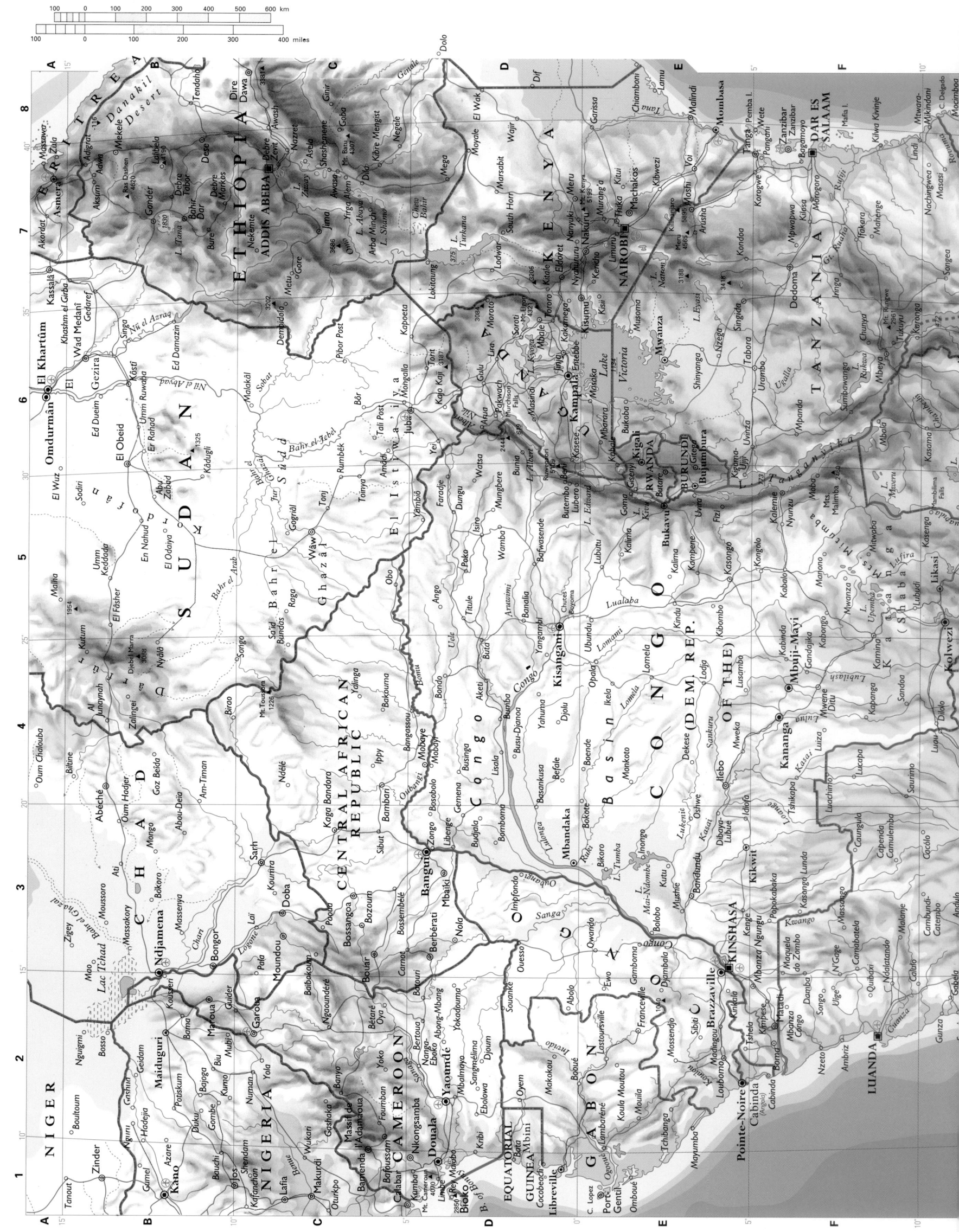

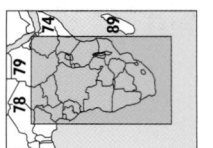

MADAGASCAR
On same scale as
General Map

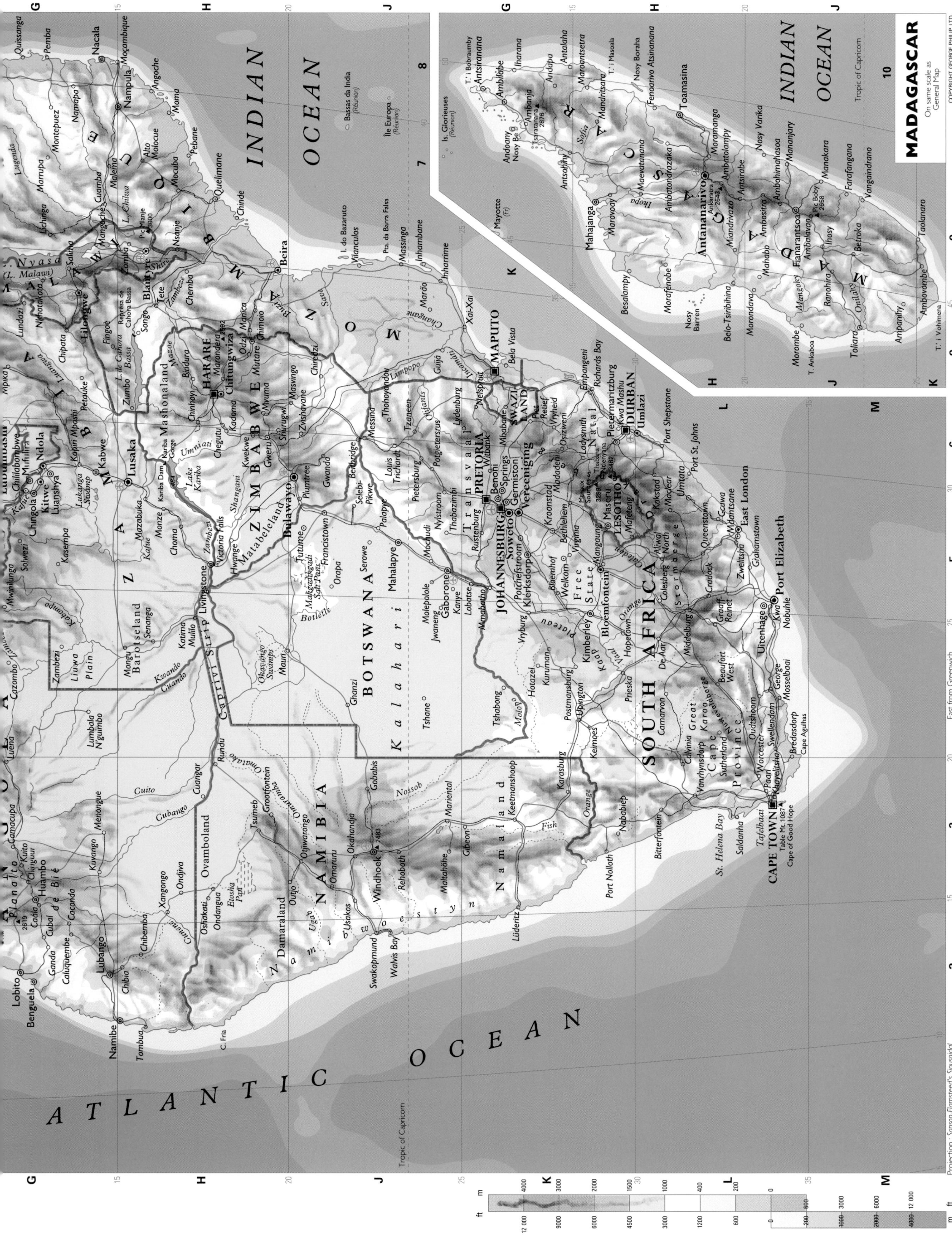

COPYRIGHT GEORGE PHILIP LTD.

INDIAN OCEAN

ATLANTIC OCEAN

SOUTH AFRICA

NAMIBIA

BOTSWANA

ZIMBABWE

ANGOLA

ZAMBIA

MALAWI

MOZAMBIQUE

Projection : Sanson-Flamsteed's Sinusoidal

East from Greenwich

Tropic of Capricorn

Projection: Lambert's Equivalent Azimuthal

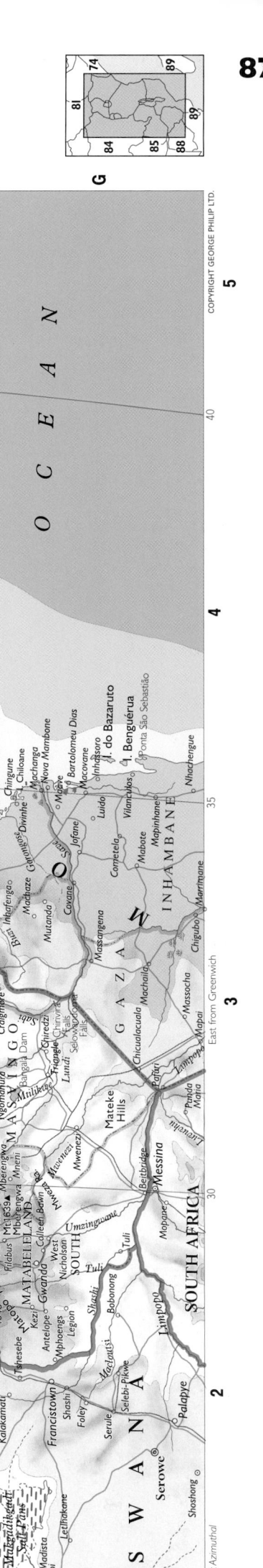

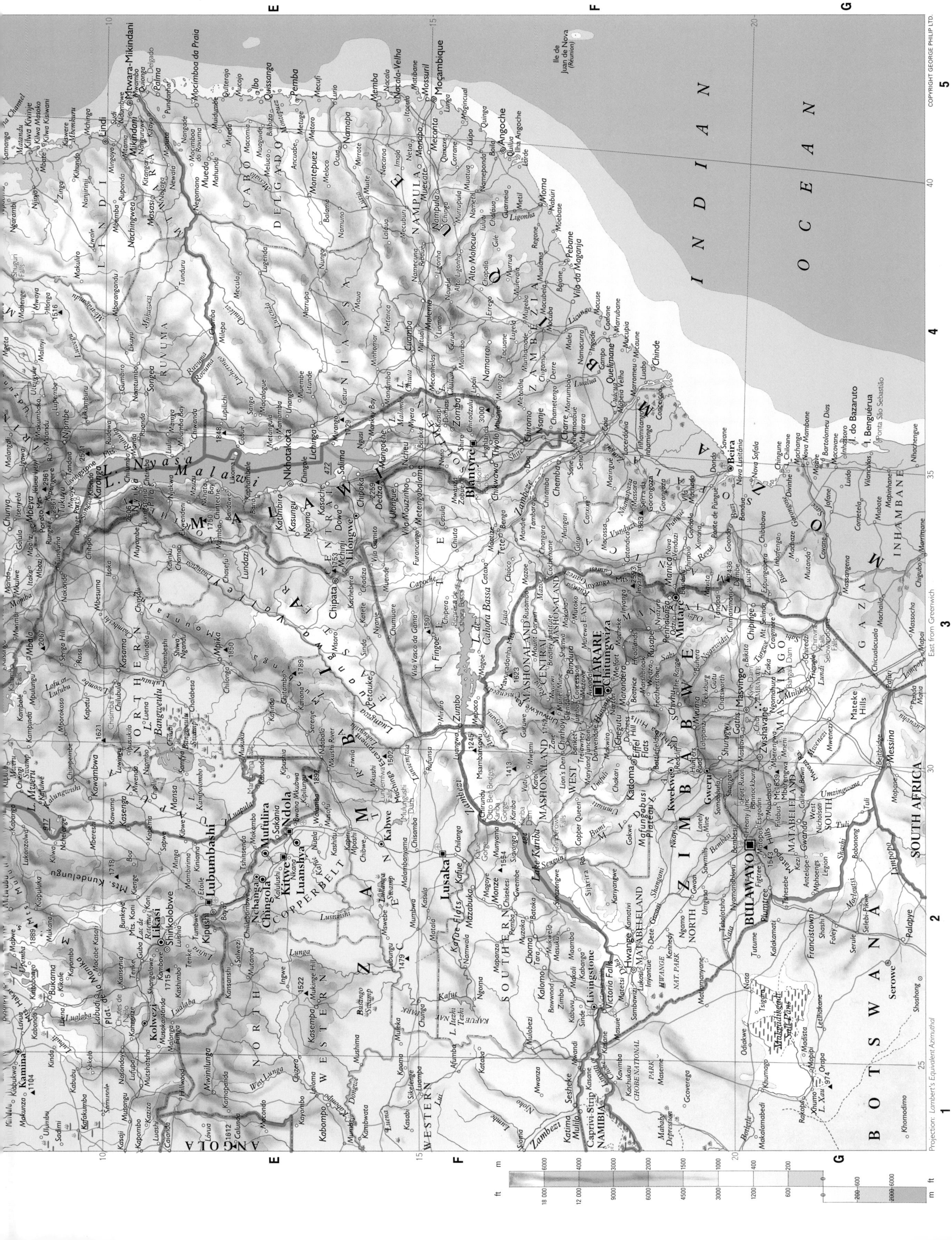

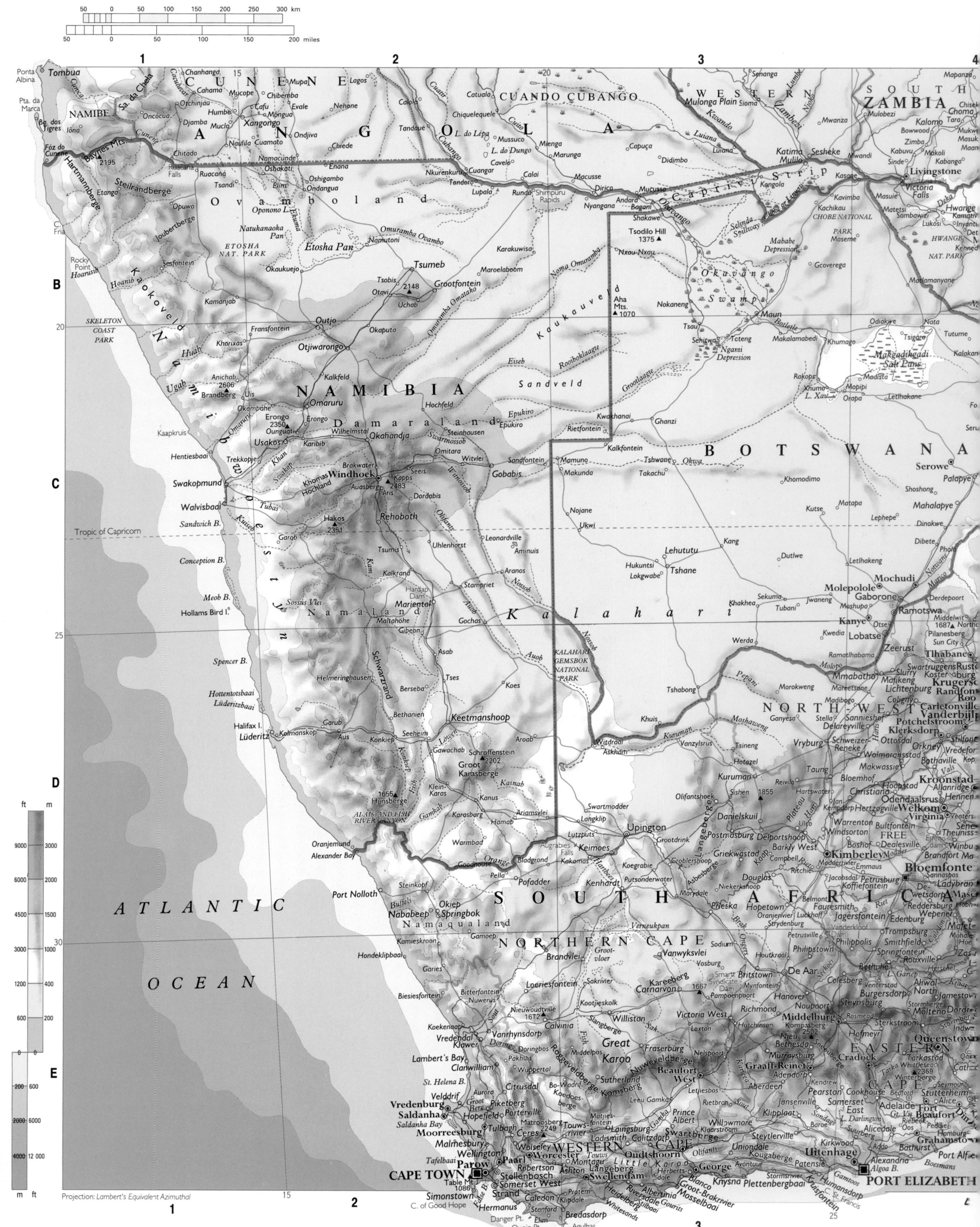

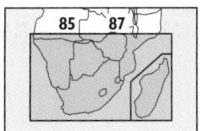

85
87

ZIMBABWE
MASHONALAND CENTRAL
MASHONALAND WEST
MASHONALAND EAST
MATABELELAND
MASVINGO
MANICALAND
HARARE
Chitungwiza
Kadoma
Gweru
Bulawayo
Masvingo
Mutare
Zvishavane
Kwekwe
Lake Kariba
MALAWI
TETE
ZAMBEZIA
MOZAMBIQUE
SOFALA
MANICA
INHAMBANE
GAZA
MAPUTO
Tete
Quelimane
Beira
Chimoio
Inhambane
Maputo
Xai-Xai
Angoche
Chinde
Nsanje
Chiromo
Vila da Maganja
Pebane
Moma
Dondo
Nova Sofala
I. do Bazaruto
I. Benguérua
Vilanculos
Massinga
Chibuto
Manjacaze
Guijá
Messina
Louis Trichardt
Pietersburg
Potgietersrus
NORTHERN
MPUMALANGA
GAUTENG
PRETORIA
JOHANNESBURG
Benoni
Springs
Vereeniging
Witbank
Middelburg
Nelspruit
SWAZILAND
Mbabane
Manzini
KWAZULU NATAL
Newcastle
Ladysmith
Pietermaritzburg
DURBAN
KwaMashu
Umlazi
Empangeni
Richards Bay
LESOTHO
EASTERN CAPE
Umtata
East London
Port Shepstone
Margate
INDIAN OCEAN
MOZAMBIQUE CHANNEL
MADAGASCAR
ANTSIRANANA
MAHAJANGA
TOAMASINA
ANTANANARIVO
FIANARANTSOA
TOLIARA
Antsiranana
Mahajanga
Toamasina
Antananarivo
Antsirabe
Fianarantsoa
Toliara
Morondava
Maintirano
Taolanaro
Manakara
Mananjary
Farafangana
Antalaha
Sambava
Iharana
Nosy Bé
Nosy Boraha
Is. Glorieuses (Fr.)
Ile de Júan de Nova (Fr.)
Tropic of Capricorn
Tanjon' i Bobaomby
Tanjon' i Vohimena
MADAGASCAR
On same scale as General Map
East from Greenwich
5
6
7
8
9
A
B
C
D
E
COPYRIGHT GEORGE PHILIP LTD.

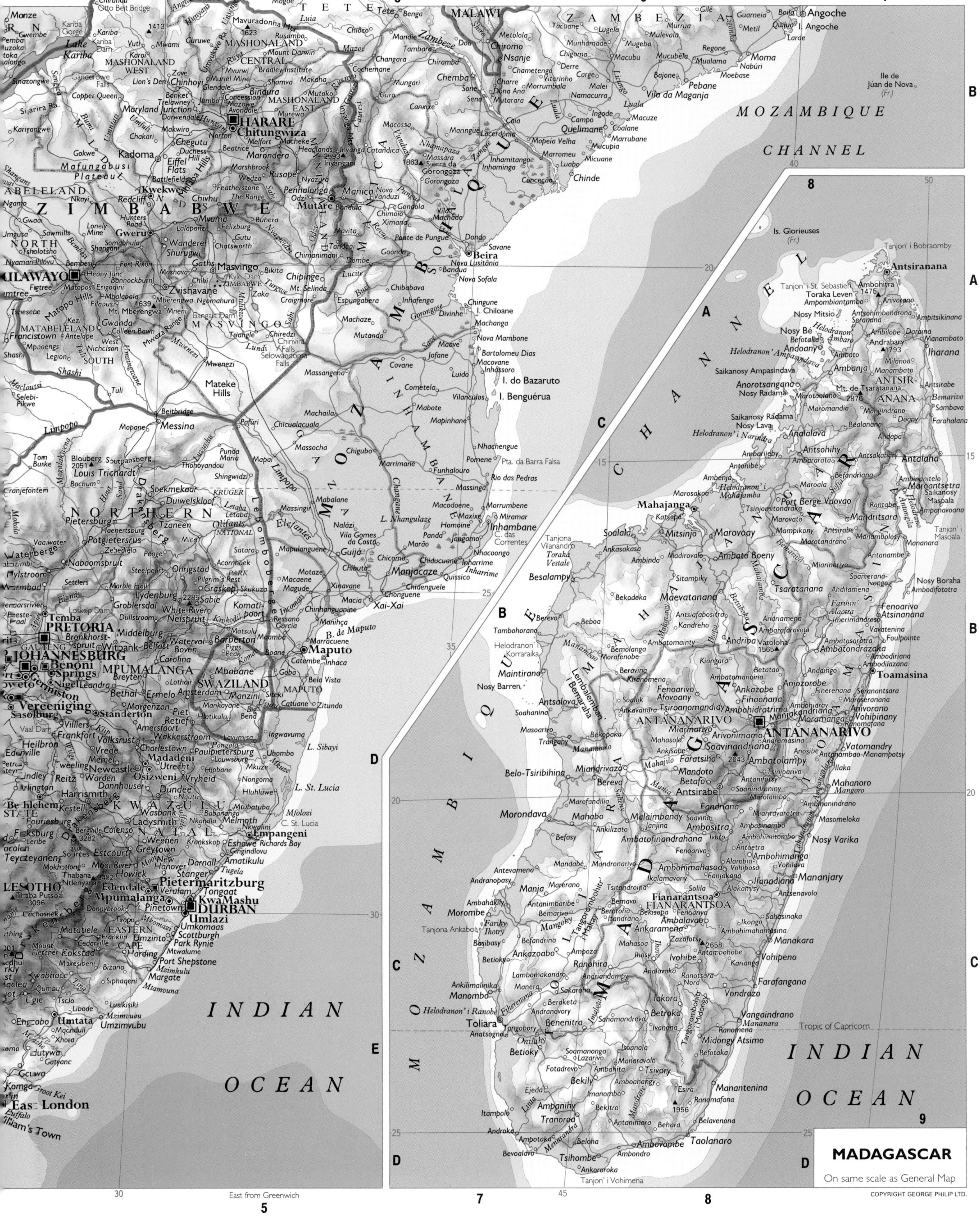

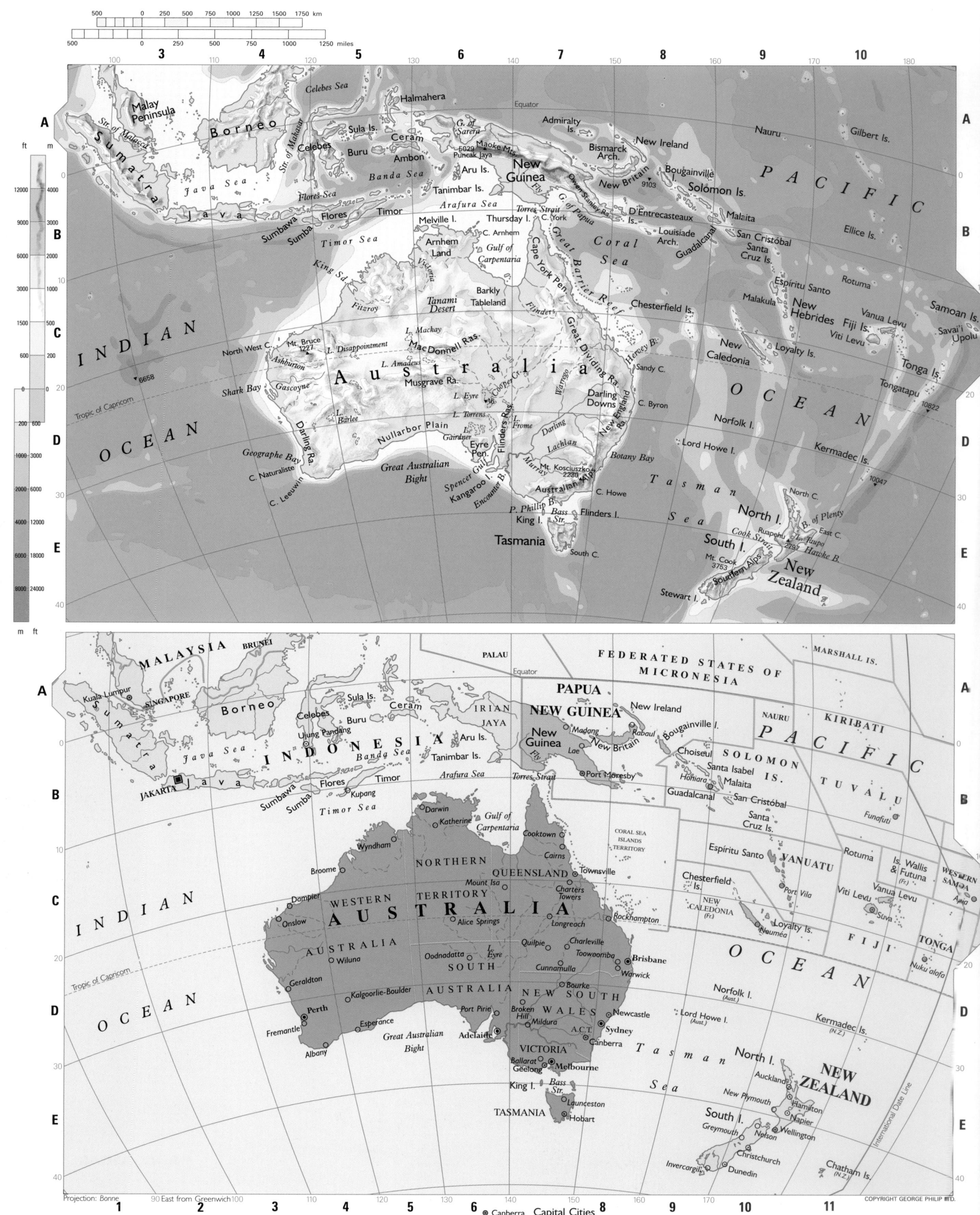

Projection: Bonne   90 East from Greenwich 100

⊛ Canberra   Capital Cities

COPYRIGHT GEORGE PHILIP LTD.

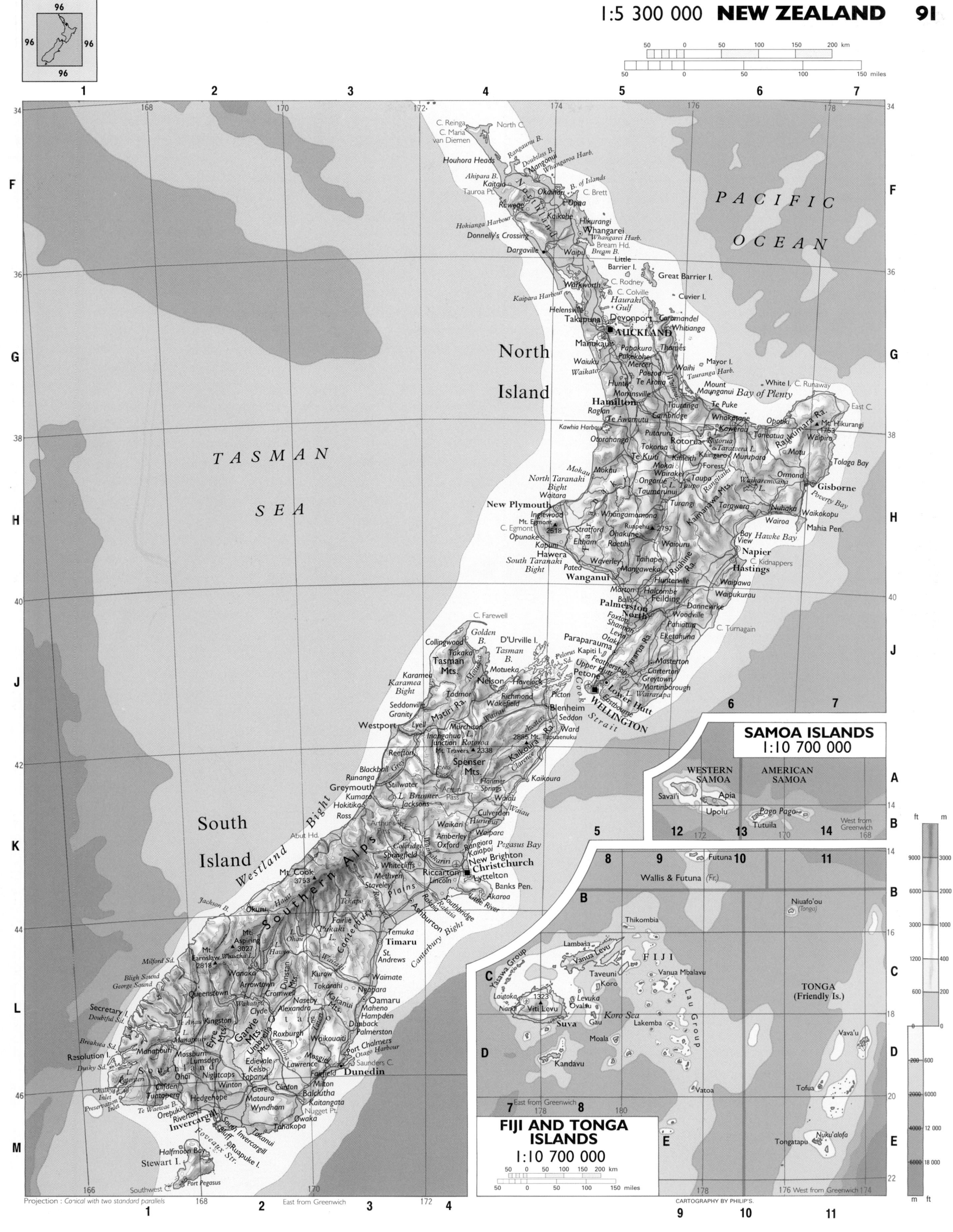

50   0   50   100   150   200 km
50   0   50   100   150 miles

96
96   **96**
96
1

1   2   3   4   5   6   7

34   168   170   172   174   176   178   34

F   *C. Reinga*   *North C.*   *PACIFIC*   F
C. Maria
van Diemen
Houhora Heads
Rangaunu B.
Ahipara B.   *Mangonui*   *OCEAN*
Kaitaia   *Whangaroa Harb.*
Tauroa Pt.   *Okaihau*   *B. of Islands*   *C. Brett*
Rawene   *Opaa*
Hokianga Harbour   *Kaikohe*   *Hikurangi*
Whangarei
Donnelly's Crossing   *Waipu*   *Whangarei Harb.*
Dargaville   *Bream Hd.*
Bream B.   *Little*
36   *Barrier I.*   36
Kaipara Harbour   *Warkworth*   *Great Barrier I.*
C. Rodney   *Cuvier I.*
Helensville   *C. Colville*
Hauraki   *Coromandel*
Takapuna   *Devonport*   *Gulf*   *Whitianga*
G   *AUCKLAND*   *North*   G
Manukau   *Papakura*   *Thames*
Waiuku   *Pukekohe*   *Mercer*   *Waihi*   *Mayor I.*
Waikato   *Paeroa*   *Tauranga Harb.*
Huntly   *Te Aroha*   *Mount*   *White I.*   *C. Runaway*
Morrinsville   *Maunganui Bay of Plenty*   *Island*
Hamilton   *Tauranga*   *Te Puke*   *East C.*
Raglan   *Cambridge*   *Whakatane*   *Opotiki*
Te Awamutu   *Kawerau*   *Mt. Hikurangi*
38   *Kawhia Harb.*   *Putaruru*   *Rotorua*   *Tarawera*   *1753*   38
Otorohanga   *Taratiueri*   *Te Karaka*   *Tolaga Bay*
Te Kuiti   *Kinleith*   *Rotorua*   *Murupara*   *Motu*
Mokau   *Mokai*   *Kaingaroa*   *Whakaremoana*
North Taranaki   *Mokau*   *Wairaket*   *Forest*   *Ormond*
Bight   *Ongarue*   *Taupo*   *Gisborne*
Waitara   *Taumarunui*   *L. Taupo*   *Rangitaiki*   *Poverty Bay*
New Plymouth   *Turangi*   *Kaimanawa Mts.*   *Nuhaka*   *Waikokopu*
H   *Inglewood*   *Whangamomona*   *Tongariro*   *Wairoa*   H
C. Egmont   *Mt. Egmont*   *Ruapehu*   *2797*   *Mahia Pen.*
2518   *Stratford*   *Ohakune*   *Bay*   *Hawke Bay*
Opunake   *Eltham*   *Raetihi*   *View*
Kapuni   *Waiouru*   *Napier*
Hawera   *Taihape*   *Ruahine*   *C. Kidnappers*
South Taranaki   *Waverley*   *Mangaweka*   *Ra.*   *Hastings*
Bight   *Patea*   *Morton*   *Hunterville*   *Waipawa*
40   *Wanganui*   *Halcombe*   *Feilding*   *Waipukurau*   40
Balls   *Dannevirke*
Palmerston   *Woodville*
North   *Pahiatua*
Foxton   *Shannon*   *Eketahuna*
C. Farewell   *Levin*   *Tararua Ra.*   *C. Turnagain*
Golden   *Otaki*
B.   *D'Urville I.*   *Paraparaumu*   *Masterton*
Collingwood   *Tasman*   *Kapiti I.*   *Featherston*   *Carterton*
Takaka   *B.*   *Pelorus*   *Upper Hutt*   *Greytown*
J   *Karamea*   *Motueka*   *Sd.*   *Petone*   *Martinborough*   J
Tasman   *Cook*   *Wairarapa*
Mts.   *Nelson*   *Havelock*   *Picton*   *Lower Hutt*
Karamea   *Richmond*   *WELLINGTON*
Bight   *Tadmor*   *Wakefield*   *Blenheim*
Seddonville   *Maitai Ra.*   *Seddon*   *Cook*
Granity   *Murchison*   *Ward*   *Strait*   6   7
Westport   *Lyell*   *Inangahua*   *2885 Mt. Tapuaenuku*
Junction   *Rotoroa*   **SAMOA ISLANDS**
Reefton   *Mt. Travers ▲2338*   *Kaikoura*   **1:10 700 000**
42   *Blackball*   *Grey*   *Spenser*   *Clarence*   42
Runanga   *Mts.*   *Hanmer*   A   *WESTERN*   *AMERICAN*   A
Greymouth   *Springs*   *SAMOA*   *SAMOA*
Kumara   *Lewis*   *Waiau*   *14*
Hokitika   *L. Brunner*   *Pass*   *Saval'i*   *Apia*
Ross   *Jacksons*   *Culverden*   *Upolu*   *Pago Pago*   *West from*
Hurunui   *Waikari*   B   *Tutuila*   *Greenwich*   B
Waikari   *Amberley*   *172*   *170*   *168*
5   **12**   **13**   **14**
Waipara
K   *Abut Hd.*   *Oxford*   *Pegasus Bay*   5   **8**   **9**   *Futuna*   **10**   **11**   K
South   *Rangiora*   *14*
Island   *Sheffield*   *New Brighton*
Whitecliffs   *Christchurch*   B   *Wallis & Futuna (Fr.)*   B
Mt. Cook   *Springfield*   *Riccarton*   *Lyttelton*   *Niuafo'ou*
3753   *Methven*   *Lincoln*   *Banks Pen.*   *(Tonga)*
Staveley   *Akaroa*   *16*   *Thikombia*
Tekapo   *Little River*   C   *Lambasa*   *FIJI*   C
Jackson B.   *Canterbury*   *Southbridge*   *Yasawa Group*   *Vanua Levu*   *Vanua Mbalavu*
Okuru   *Haast*   *Fairlie*   *Plains*   *Rakaia*   *Taveuni*   *TONGA*
44   *Mt. Aspiring*   *Geraldine*   *Koro*   *(Friendly Is.)*   44
3027   *Pukaki*   *Ashburton Bight*   *Lautoka 1323*   *Levuka*   *Lau*
Wanaka   *Temuka*   *Nandi*   *Viti Levu*   *Ovalau*   *Group*
Mt. Earnslaw   *L. Ohau*   *St. Andrews*   *Suva*   *Gau*   *Koro Sea*   *Lakemba*   *Vava'u*
2818   *Timaru*   *18*
Milford Sd.   *Arrowtown*   *Waitaki*   D   *Moala*   D
Bligh Sound   *Cromwell*   *Waimate*   *Kandavu*   *Vatoa*   *Tofua*   *20*
George Sound   *Queenstown*   *Kurow*   *Ngapara*
Clyde   *Tokarahi*   *Oamaru*   7   *178*   *8*   *180*
Secretary I.   *Wakatipu*   *Alexandra*   *Maheno*   *East from Greenwich*   E   *Tongatapu*   E
L   *Doubtful Sd.*   *Naseby*   *Hampden*   **FIJI AND TONGA**   *Tongatapu*   *Nuku'alofa*   L
L. Anau   *Roxburgh*   *Dunback*   **ISLANDS**   *22*
Garvie   *Palmerston*
Mts.   *Port Chalmers*   **1:10 700 000**
Resolution I.   *Dunstan*   *Waikouaiti*   9   10   11
Dusky Sd.   *Manapouri*   *Mts.*   *Otago Harbour*
Breaksea Sd.   *Massburn*   *Edievale*   *Mosgiel*   *Saunders C.*
Lumsden   *Milton*   *Fairfield*   50   0   50   100   150   200 km
Southland   *Ohai*   *Clinton*   **Dunedin**
Nightcaps   *Tapanui*   *Balclutha*   50   0   50   100   150 miles
Winton   *Gore*   *Kaitangata*
Chalkey Inlet   *Tuatapere*   *Mataura*   *Nugget Pt.*
Orepuki   *Riverton*   *Wyndham*   *Owaka*
M   *Preservation Inlet*   *Hedgehope*   *Tahakopa*   M
Te Waewae B.   *Riverton*
Invercargill   *Bluff*   *Invercargill*   *Ruapuke I.*
Foveaux Str.
Halfmoon Bay
Stewart I.
Southwest C.   *Port Pegasus*

166   168   170   172   174   176   178   174

1   2   3   4   9   10   11
Projection : Conical with two standard parallels   East from Greenwich   CARTOGRAPHY BY PHILIP'S.

TASMAN

SEA

South
Island

Westland Bight

Southern Alps

ft   m
9000   3000
6000   2000
3000   1000
1200   400
600   200
0
200   600
2000   12 000
4000   12 000
6000   18 000
m   ft

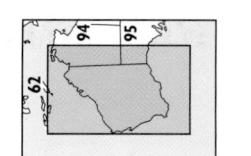

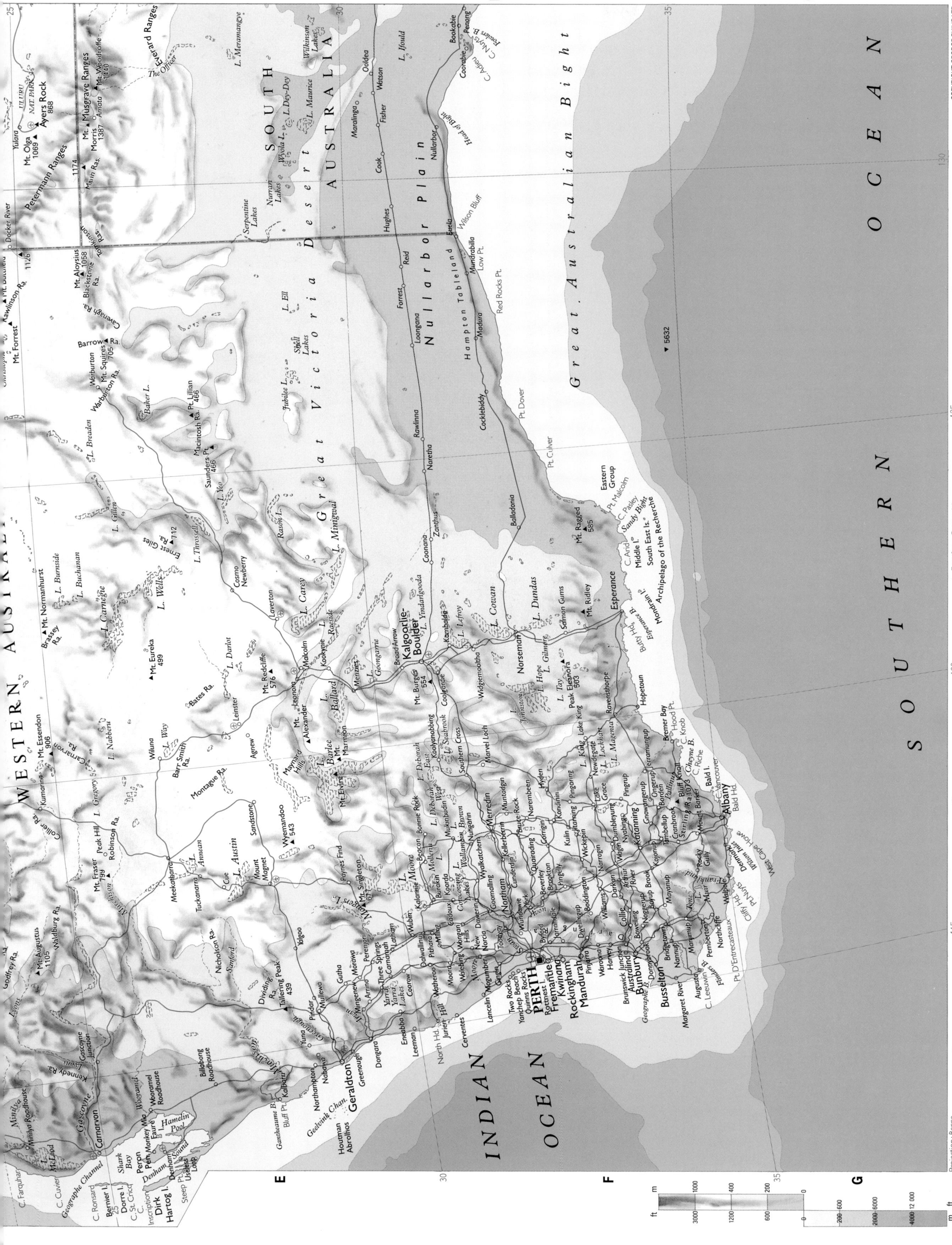

W E S T E R N   A U S T R A L I A

S O U T H   A U S T R A L I A

I N D I A N   O C E A N

S O U T H E R N   O C E A N

Great Victoria Desert

Nullarbor Plain

Hampton Tableland

Great Australian Bight

Nullarbor

PERTH
Fremantle
Rockingham
Kwinana
Mandurah
Bunbury
Busselton
Albany
Geraldton
Carnarvon
Kalgoorlie-Boulder
Norseman
Esperance

Projection: Bonne

East from Greenwich

m ft
1000
400
200
3000
1200
600
200–600
2000
4000   12 000
6000

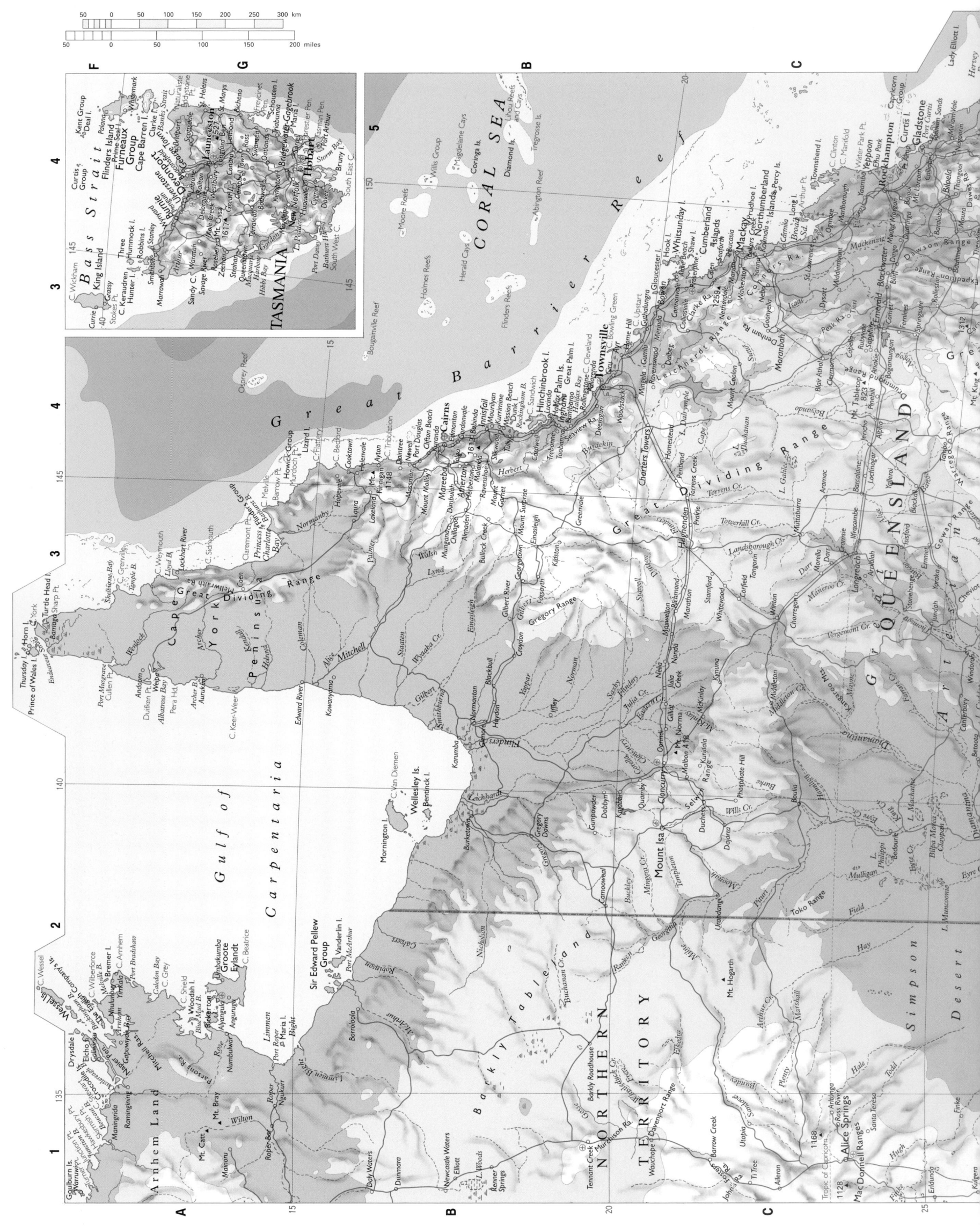

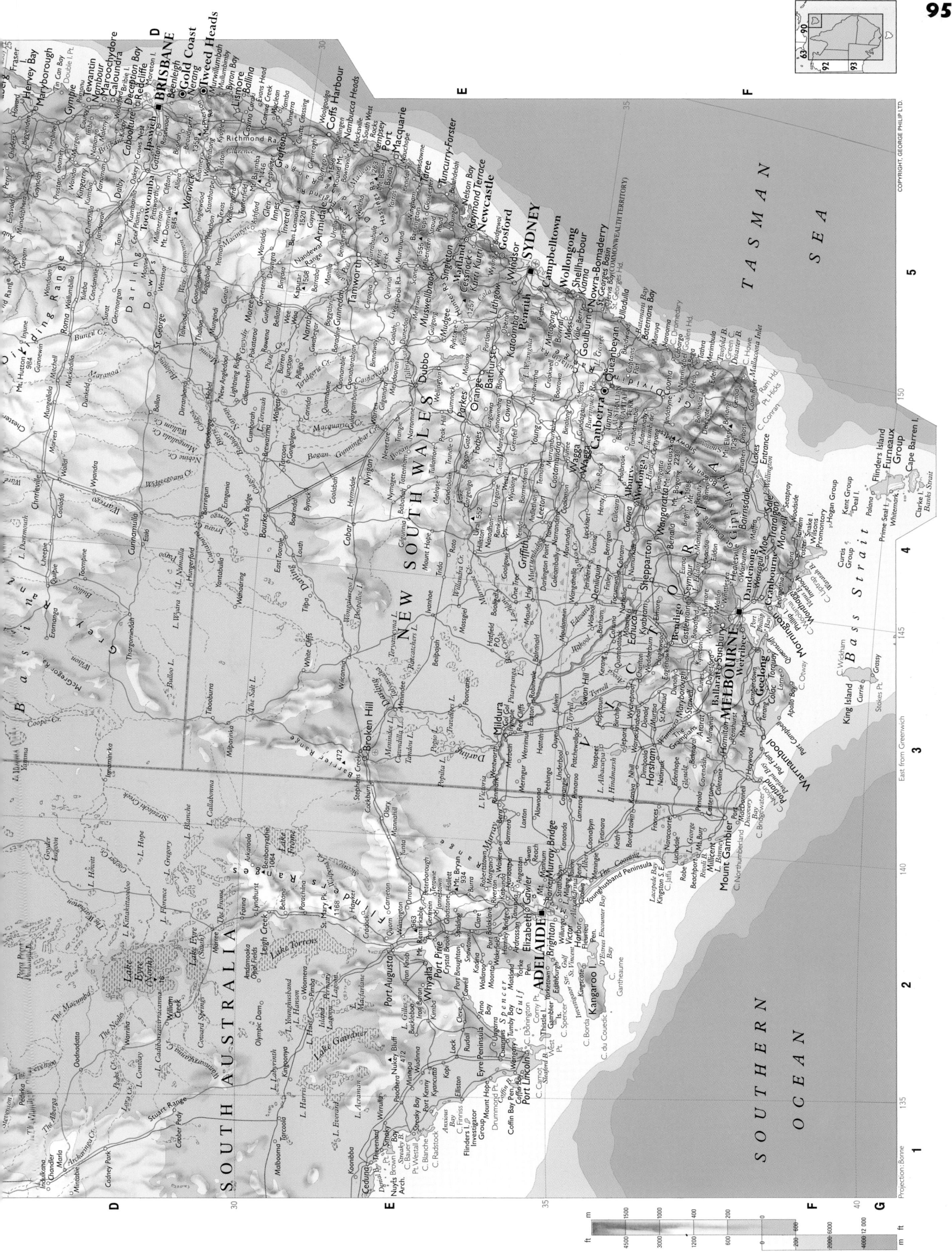

R U S S I A

MOSKVA
Volga
Yekaterinburg
Tomsk
Novosibirsk
Astana (Aqmola)
Semey
Irkutsk
Oz. Baykal
Chita
Ob'
Lena
Okhotsk
Sea of Okhotsk
Poluostrov Kamchatka
Komandorskiye Ostrova (Russia)
Near Is. (U.S.A.)
Andreanof
Bering Sea

KAZAKSTAN
Aral Sea
Balqash Köl
Almaty
Ürümqi
Ulaanbaatar
MONGOLIA
Blagoveshchensk
Amur
Khabarovsk
Sakhalin
Kuril'skiye Ostrova (Russia)
La Perouse Str.
Kuril Trench
Petropavlovsk-Kamchatskiy
▼10,542
▼7822
Aleutian
Aleutian Trench

Toshkent
KYRGYZSTAN
TAJIKISTAN
Altai
C H I N A
Changchun
SHENYANG
Harbin
Vladivostok
Hakodate
Sapporo
Sea of Japan

AFGHANISTAN
Kabul
Srinaga
PAKISTAN
Kunlun Shan
XIZANG
Lanzhou
Xi'an
BEIJING
TIANJIN
Taiyuan
NORTH KOREA
SOUTH KOREA
SOUL
Dalian
Qingdao
Nagoya
Kyoto
Osaka
TOKYO
Yokohama
JAPAN
Shikoku
Kyushu
Sendai
Fuji-San ▲3776
Emperor Seamount Chain

DELHI
Lahore
Kanpur
Himalaya
Mt Everest ▲8848
Lhasa
CHONGQING
Wuhan
Nanjing
Huang He
Yellow Sea
Kitakyushu
SHANGHAI
HANGZHOU
East China Sea
10,554
Japan Trench
Midway Is. (U.S.A.)
Lisianski I. (U.S.A.)

Hyderabad
INDIA
CALCUTTA
DHAKA
BANGLADESH
Ganga
Brahmaputra
Irrawaddy
Mandalay
BURMA
LAOS
Kunming
Changsha
Fuzhou
Taipei
GUANGZHOU
HONG KONG
Macau
TAIWAN
Ryukyu-retto (Japan)
Kazan-Retto (Japan)
Minami-Tori-Shima (Japan)
Ogasawara Gunto (Japan)
South Honshu Ridge
Wake I. (U.S.A.)
Necker Ridge
P A C I F I C

CHENNAI (Madras)
SRI LANKA
Colombo
Salween
Mekong
Hanoi
Hainan
C. Engano
Luzon
Paracel Is.
MANILA
PHILIPPINES
NORTHERN MARIANAS (U.S.A.)
Saipan
MARSHALL IS.
Enewetak Atoll
Bikini Atoll

Bay of Bengal
Rangoon
THAILAND
BANGKOK
CAMBODIA
Phnom Penh
VIETNAM
Phanh Bho Ho Chi Minh
South China Sea
Mindoro
Palawan
Samar
10,497
GUAM (U.S.A.)
11,022
Mariana Trench
Yap
Koror
Caroline Is.
Truk
Micronesia
Marcus
International Dateline

Andaman Is. (India)
Nicobar Is. (India)
G. of Thailand
MALAYSIA
Sulu Sea
Mindanao
Mindanao Trench
PALAU
FEDERATED STATES OF MICRONESIA
Palikir
Pohnpei
Jaluit I.
Dalap-Uliga-Darrit

Kuala Lumpur
SINGAPORE
Sumatera
PEN. MALAYSIA
SARAWAK
BRUNEI
Borneo
SABAH
4101
Celebes Sea
Sulawesi
Halmahera
Seram
Maluku
Buru
Melanesia
NAURU
Tarawa
Butaritari
Gilbert Is.
Banaba
Howland I. Baker I.
O

Palembang
Java Sea
JAKARTA
Jawa
Surabaya
Bali
Flores Sea
Sumbawa
Sumba
Flores
Banda Sea
Timor
7440
I N D O N E S I A
Ujung Pandang
IRIAN JAYA
Puncak Jaya ▲5029
New Guinea
PAPUA NEW GUINEA
Admiralty Is.
New Ireland
Bismarck Arch.
Rabaul
New Britain
Lae
Bougainville
SOLOMON IS.
Phoenix Is.
Enderbury
Abariringa
KI

INDIAN
Cocos Is. (Austral.)
Christmas I. (Austral.)
Java Trench
Selat Sunda
Sunda Islands
Arafura Sea
Torres Strait
C. York
Port Moresby
Honiara
Guadalcanal
Santa Cruz I.
9185
Fongafale
TUVALU
Tokelau (N.Z.)

OCEAN
North West C.
C. Arnhem
Gulf of Carpentaria
Darwin
Broome
Mount Isa
Cairns
Townsville
Coral Sea
Louisiade Arch.
Is. Chesterfield
VANUATU
Espíritu Santo
Port Vila
NEW CALEDONIA (Fr.)
7570
Noumea
Rotuma
Is. Wallis & Futuna (Fr.)
Vanua Levu
Viti Levu
Suva
FIJI
WESTERN SAMOA
Apia
Nuku'alofa
10,822
Tonga Trench

AUSTRALIA
Geraldton
Alice Springs
L. Eyre
Murray
Darling
Brisbane
Norfolk I. (Austral.)
Lord Howe I. (Austral.)
Kermadec Is. (N.Z.)
Kermadec Trench
10,0

Perth
Great Australian Bight
Albany
Adelaide
Canberra
Sydney
Mt. Kosciuszko ▲2237
Melbourne
Bass Str.
Tasmania
Hobart
Tasman Sea
Mt. Cook ▲3752
Auckland
Cook Strait
Chatham (N.Z.)
NEW ZEALAND
Wellington
Christchurch
Dunedin
Invercargill
Bounty Is. (N.Z.)
Antipodes Is. (N.Z.)
Auckland Is. (N.Z.)
Campbell I. (N.Z.)
Macquarie Is. (Austral.)

Nouvelle Amsterdam (Fr.)
I. St. Paul (Fr.)
Mid-Indian Ridge
Is. Crozet (Fr.)
Kerguelen (Fr.)
Heard I. (Austral.)

ft | m
12 000 | 4000
9000 | 3000
6000 | 2000
1500 | 500
600 | 200
0 | 0
200 | 600
1000 | 3000
2000 | 6000
4000 | 12 000
6000 | 18 000
8000 | 24 000
m ft

Projection: Mollweide's Homolographic   East from Greenwich

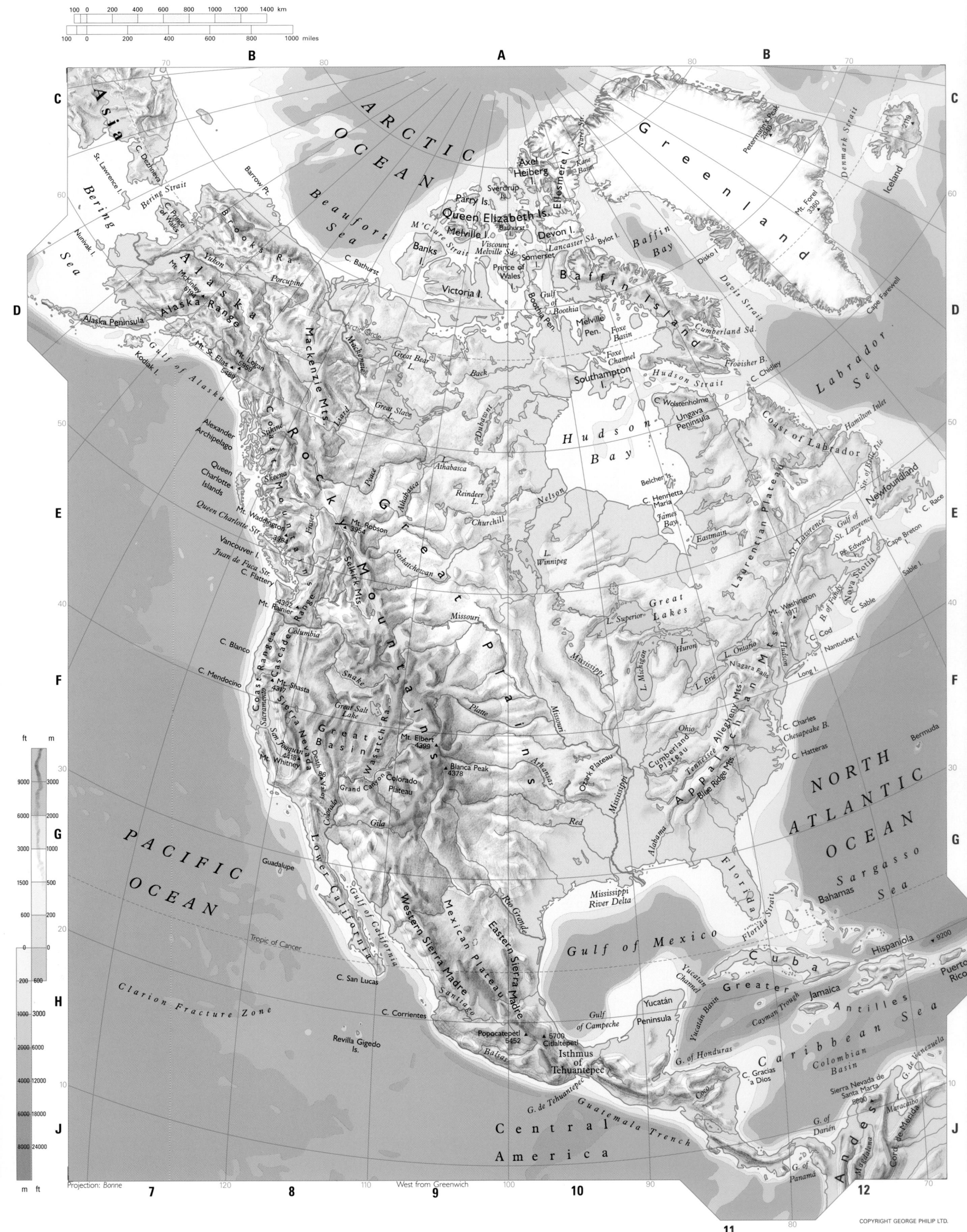

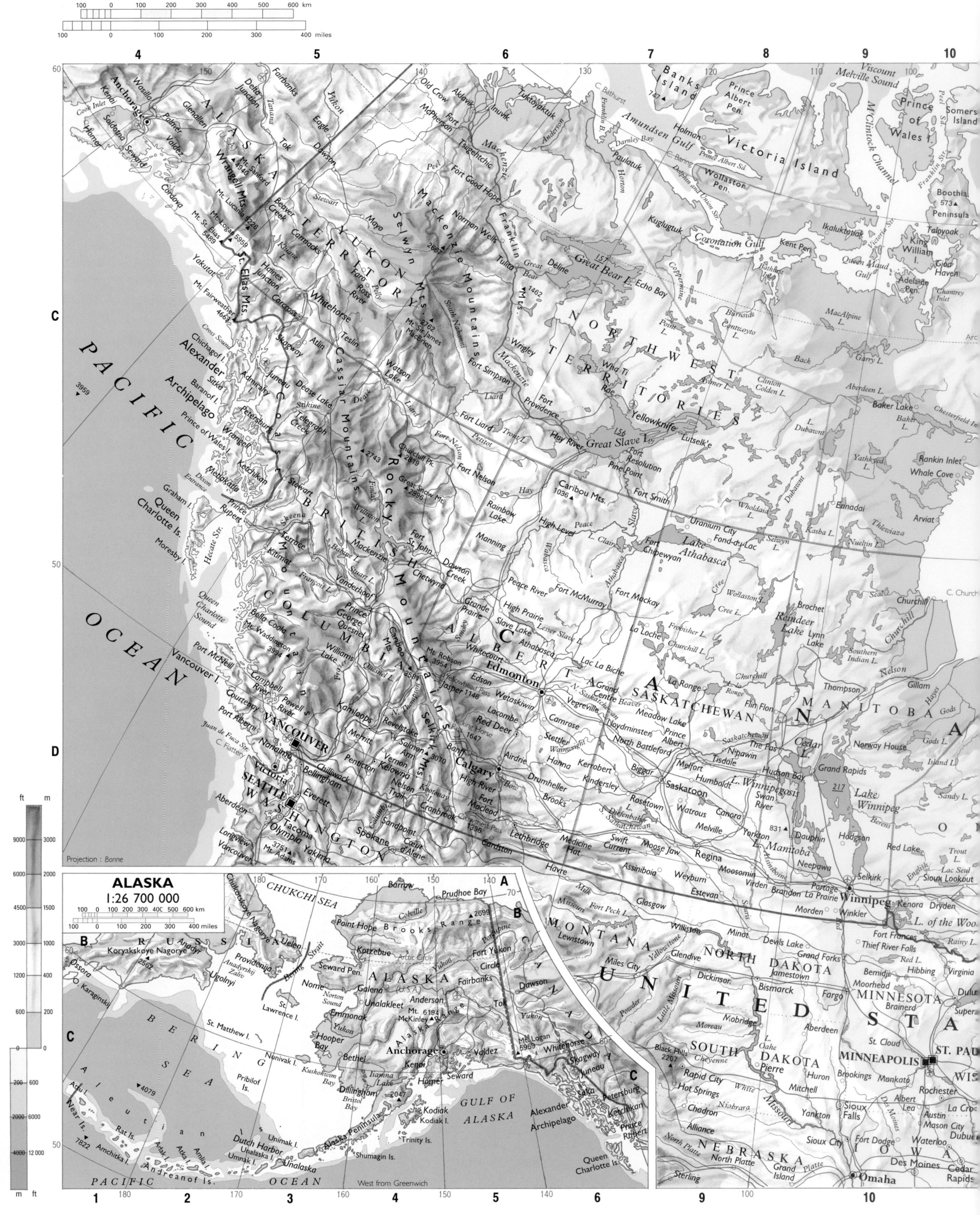

ALASKA
1:26 700 000

Projection : Bonne

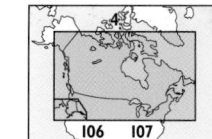

11 12 13 14 15 16

B

Devon I.
Lancaster Sound
Arctic Bay
Borden
Pen.
Bylot I.
Eclipse Sd.
Pond Inlet
Brodeur
Peninsula
C. Adair
Baffin Bay
Nunavik
Uummannaq
Ammassalik
C. Raper
Clyde River
Qeqertarsuaq
Qeqertarsuaq
Ilulissat
Qasigiannguit
Kangerlussuaq

GREENLAND
(KALAALLIT NUNAAT)
(Denmark)

Kong Frederik VI's Kyst

Fury and Hecla Str.
Igloolik
Simpson
Pen.
Pelly Bay
Melville
Peninsula
Foxe
Basin
Prince
Charles
I.
Air
Force
Sanirajak
Home B.
Qikiqtarjuaq
C. Dyer
Cumberland
Peninsula
Pangnirtung
Hoare B.
Sisimiut
Maniitsoq
Nuuk

C

Rae Isthmus
Repulse
Bay
Circle
NUNAVUT
Netilling L.
Foxe
Pen.
Southampton
I.
Salliq
Bell
Pen.
Nottingham
Cape Dorset
Salisbury
Meta
Incognita
Iqaluit
Hall
Peninsula
Kimmirut
Frobisher Bay
Resolution I.
Arsuk
Qeqertarsuatsiaat
Paamiut
Nanortalik
Qaqortoq
Uummannarsuaq

ATLANTIC

Juligaarjuk
Coats
I.
Mansel
I.
Ivujivik
Salluit
Quaqtaq
Akpatok I.
C. Chidley

Labrador
Sea

3809

Hudson
Bay
257
Ottawa Is.
Sleeper Is.
King George Is.
Baker's
Dozen
Is.
Belcher Is.
Kuujjuarapik
Inukjuak
Puvirnituq
Kangiqsujuaq
Péninsule
d'Ungava
Arnaud
Kangirsuk
Ungava Bay
Kangiqsualujjuaq
Hebron
Nain
Hopedale
Harrison
Rigolet
Cartwright
Port Hope Simpson
Belle Isle

50

Tatnam
Peawanuck
Winisk
Severn
Big
Trout L.
C. Henrietta
Maria
Pte. Louis
XIV
James Bay
Akimiski I.
Attawapiskat
Fort Albany
A
Chisasibi
La Grande
Kanaaupscow
Rés. de
Caniapiscau
1135
Schefferville
Petitsikapau
Esker
Labrador
City
Fermont
Ashuanipi
Smallwood
Res.
Labrador
North West River
Happy Valley
Goose Bay
Churchill
Falls
Churchill
St-Augustin
C. Bauld
St. Anthony
Str. of Belle Isle
Deer
Lake
Grand
Falls
Bonavista

D

TARIO
Albany
Moosonee
Wemindji
Eastmain
Eastmain
Waskaganish
Rupert
L.
Albanel
Mistassini
L. Bienville
Nottaway
Rés.
Manicouagan
Gagnon
Moisie
Havre-
St-Pierre
Natashquan
I. d'Anticosti
814
Corner Brook
Stephenville
Newfoundland
Grand
Falls
Gander
Carbonear
St. John's
Placentia
C. Race

L. St. Joseph
L.
Nipigon
Nipigon
Nakina
Kenogami
Geraldton
Marathon
Oba
Hearst
Kapuskasing
Cochrane
Abitibi L.
Timmins
Amos
Matagami
Chibougamau
Rés. Gouin
Dolbeau
St-Jean
Roberval
Chicoutimi
Jonquière
Rimouski
Matane
Gaspé
Pen. de Gaspé
Campbellton
Bathurst
Miramichi
PR. EDWARD I.
Summerside
Charlottetown
Sydney
Glace Bay
North C.
ST-PIERRE et MIQUELON
(Fr.)
Marystown
Placentia
6309

Thunder Bay
Lake Superior
Houghton
183
Sault Ste.
Marie
Elliot
Lake
Sudbury
L. Nipissing
North
Bay
Pembroke
Huntsville
Chapleau
Wawa
New
Liskeard
Kirkland
Lake
Rouyn-
Noranda
Val-d'Or
La Tuque
Mont-
Cabonga
Mont-
Laurier
1190
Québec
Lévis
Thetford
Mines
Woodstock
Fredericton
NEW
BRUNSWICK
Moncton
Amherst
Kentville
Truro
New Glasgow
Antigonish
Port Hawkesbury
Sable I.
(Nova Scotia)

40

Ironwood
Marquette
MI
Manistique
Escanaba
Menominee
Wausau
WISCONSIN
Green
Bay
Appleton
Sheboygan
MILWAUKEE
Madison
Racine
Kenosha
Rockford
Chicago
Gary
South Bend
INDIANA
ILLINOIS
OHIO
Detroit
Windsor
Toledo
CLEVELAND
Erie
PENNSYLVANIA
Houghton
Petoskey
Traverse City
Cadillac
MICHIGAN
Lake
Huron
Georgian
Bay
Manitoulin
Parry
Sound
Barrie
Owen Sound
Peterborough
TORONTO
Hamilton
Kitchener
London
Sarnia
Niagara
Falls
BUFFALO
Rochester
Syracuse
Belleville
Kingston
Oshawa
L. Ontario
Flint
Grand Rapids
Lansing
Saginaw
Sault Ste.
Marie
Montmagny
St-Hyacinthe
Sherbrooke
Shawinigan
Trois-Rivières
Joliette
MONTRÉAL
Hull
Ottawa
Cornwall
L. Champlain
VERMONT
Montpelier
NEW
HAMPSHIRE
Concord
Manchester
MAINE
Augusta
Lewiston
Portland
Bangor
Yarmouth
B. of Fundy
Digby
Bridgewater
Liverpool
NOVA SCOTIA
Halifax
Dartmouth
Saint
John
C. Sable

E

Elmira
Binghamton
Jamestown
Scranton
Allentown
Trenton
Newark
N.J.
NEW YORK
NEW HAVEN
Bridgeport
HARTFORD
CONN.
Springfield
Albany
Providence
R.I.
BOSTON
MASS.
C. Cod

90 11 80 12 70 West from Greenwich 60 COPYRIGHT GEORGE PHILIP LTD.

13 14

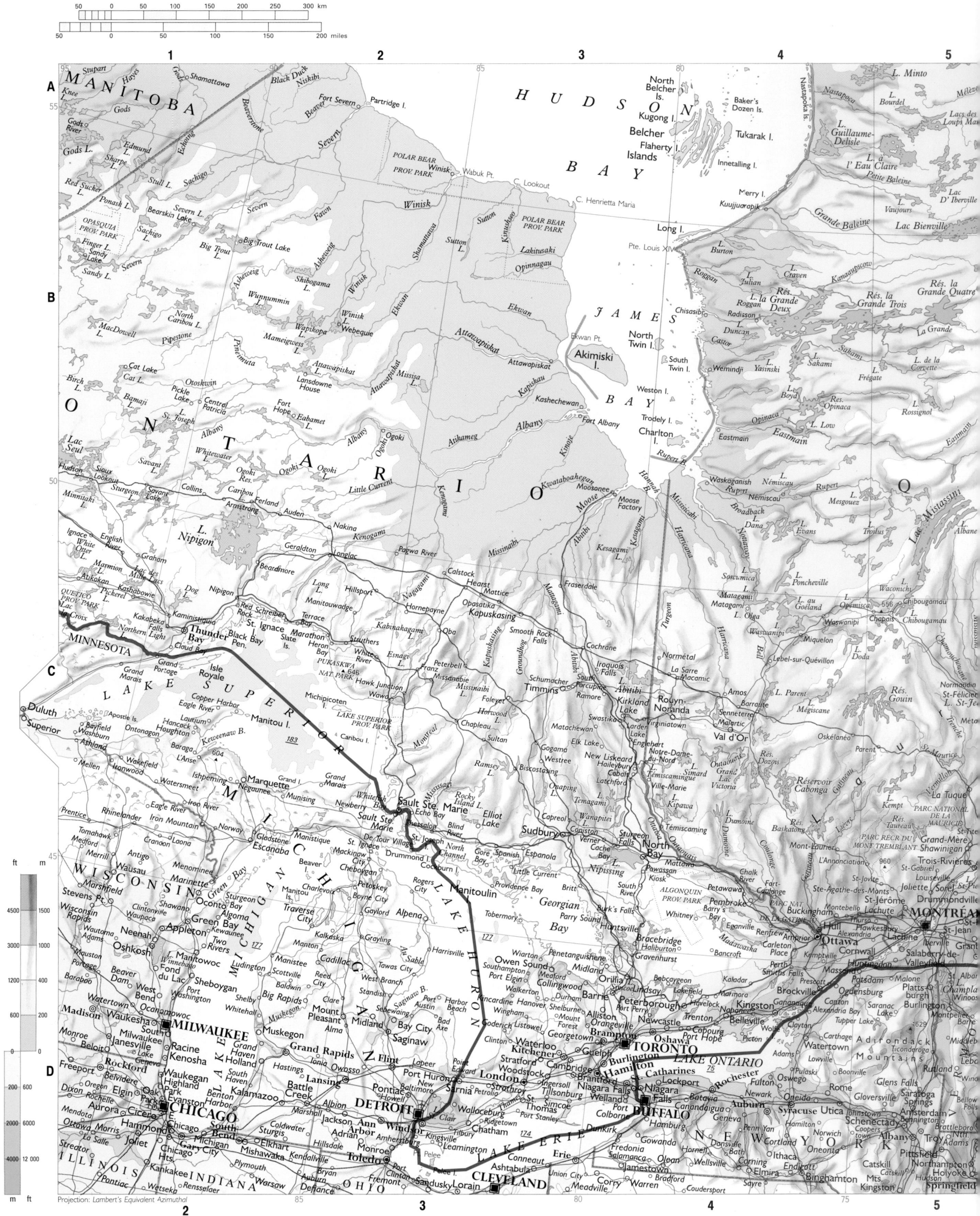

Projection: Lambert's Equivalent Azimuthal

101
105
112
108

6
7
8
9
A
B
C
D
LABRADOR SEA
NEWFOUNDLAND
Labrador
Newfoundland
QUÉBEC
Smallwood Reservoir
Rés. de Caniapiscau
Rés. Manicouagan
Mealy Mts.
Long Range Mts.
Str. of Belle Isle
Î. d'Anticosti
Dét. de Jacques-Cartier
Dét. d'Honguedo
GULF OF ST. LAWRENCE
St. Lawrence
Pén. de Gaspé
Mts. Chic-Chocs
Chaleur Bay
Îs. de la Madeleine (Québec)
Cabot Strait
PRINCE EDWARD ISLAND
Cape Breton Island
NEW BRUNSWICK
NOVA SCOTIA
MAINE
NEW HAMPSHIRE
Bay of Fundy
ST-PIERRE ET MIQUELON (France)
Sable I. (Nova Scotia)
ATLANTIC OCEAN
UNITED STATES
Nain
Hopedale
Makkovik
Postville
Rigolet
Cartwright
Happy Valley-Goose Bay
North West River
Churchill Falls
Labrador City
Wabush
Fermont
Schefferville
Sept-Îles
Port-Cartier
Baie Comeau
Havre-St-Pierre
Natashquan
Blanc-Sablon
St. Anthony
Corner Brook
Stephenville
Grand Falls Windsor
Gander
St. John's
Channel-Port aux Basques
Gaspé
Rimouski
Chicoutimi
Jonquière
Québec
Lévis
Sherbrooke
Campbellton
Bathurst
Edmundston
Fredericton
Moncton
Saint John
Charlottetown
Summerside
Sydney
Glace Bay
Truro
Halifax
Dartmouth
Yarmouth
Bangor
Augusta
Portland
Lewiston
Manchester
Lowell
BOSTON
Quincy
Brockton
West from Greenwich
70
65
60
55
50
45
COPYRIGHT GEORGE PHILIP LTD.

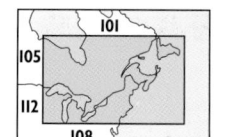

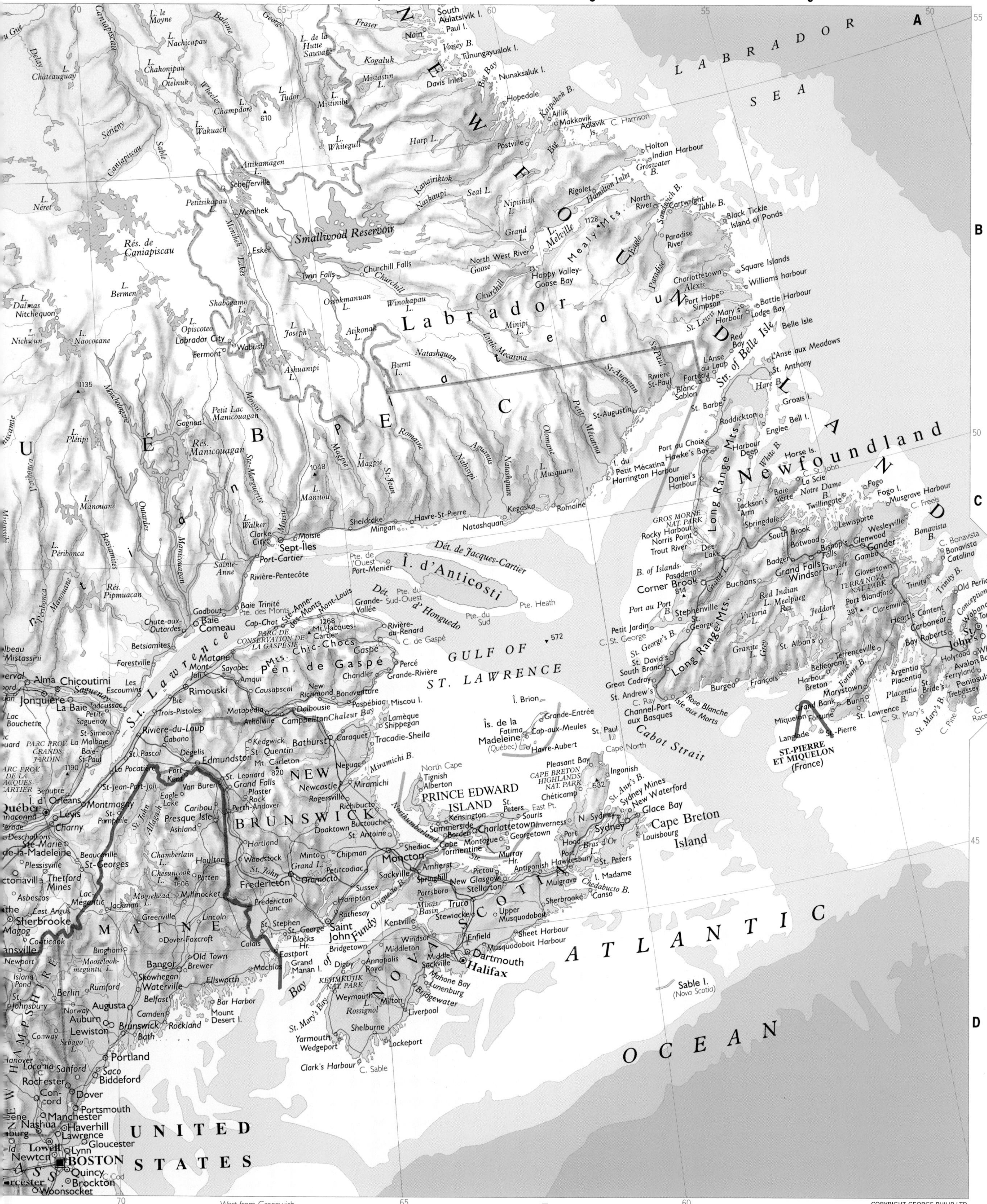

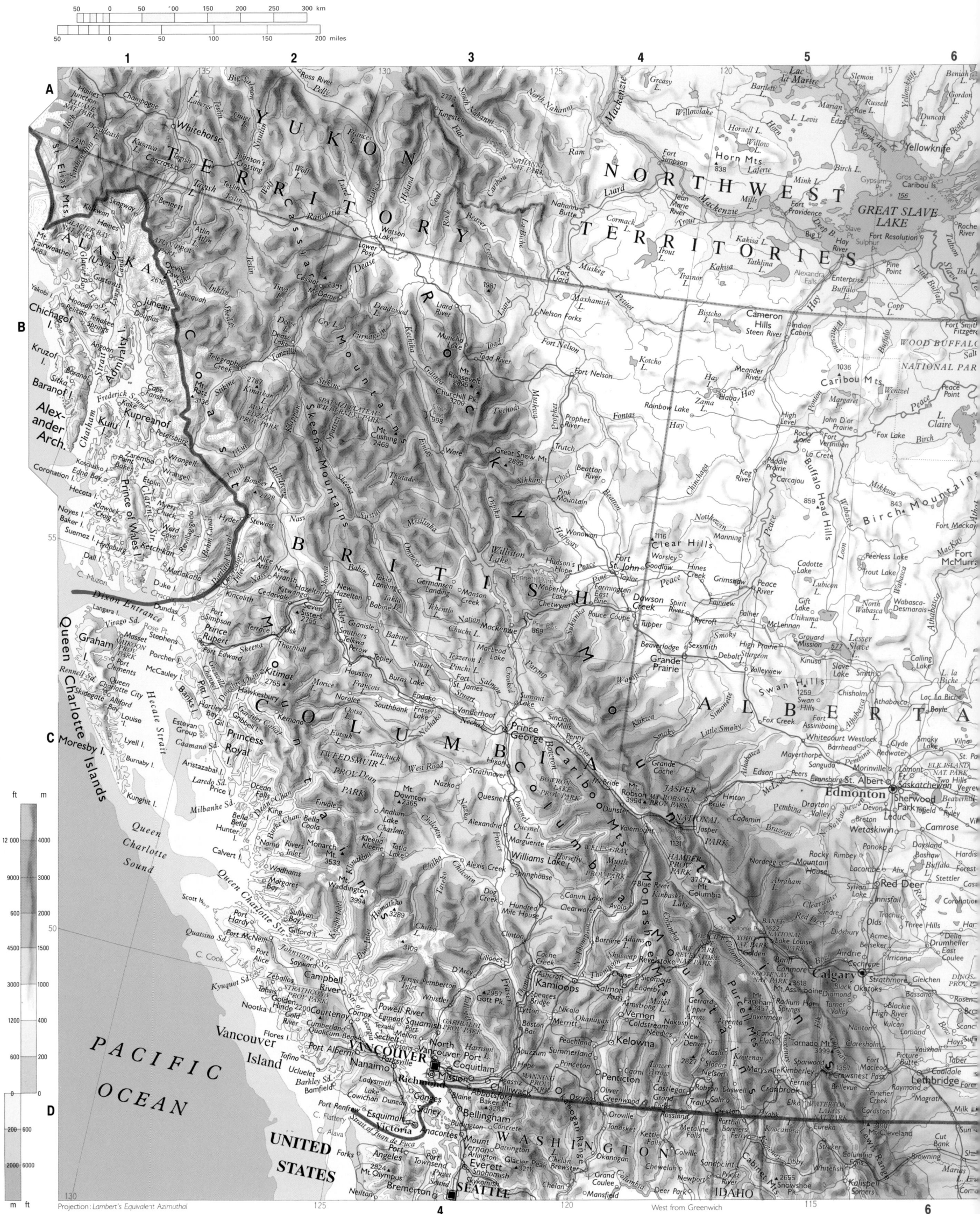

100
102
114
112

7
8
9
10
11
A
B
C
D
NUNAVUT
HUDSON BAY
MANITOBA
SASKATCHEWAN
ONTARIO
NORTH DAKOTA
MINNESOTA
MONTANA
Lake Athabasca
Wollaston L.
Reindeer Lake
Southern Indian L.
Cedar Lake
Lake Winnipegosis
LAKE WINNIPEG
Lake Manitoba
Lake of the Woods
Lac Seul
Churchill
Thompson
Flin Flon
The Pas
Prince Albert
Saskatoon
North Battleford
Lloydminster
Regina
Moose Jaw
Swift Current
Medicine Hat
Yorkton
Brandon
Winnipeg
Kenora
Dryden
Fort Frances
International Falls
Grand Forks
Minot
Williston
Bemidji
Duluth
Superior
Arviat
Whale Cove
Dawson Inlet
Fort Chipewyan
Uranium City
La Ronge
Cypress Hills
Estevan
Weyburn
Portage la Prairie
Gillam
Norway House
Grand Rapids
COPYRIGHT GEORGE PHILIP LTD.

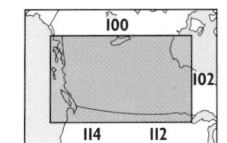

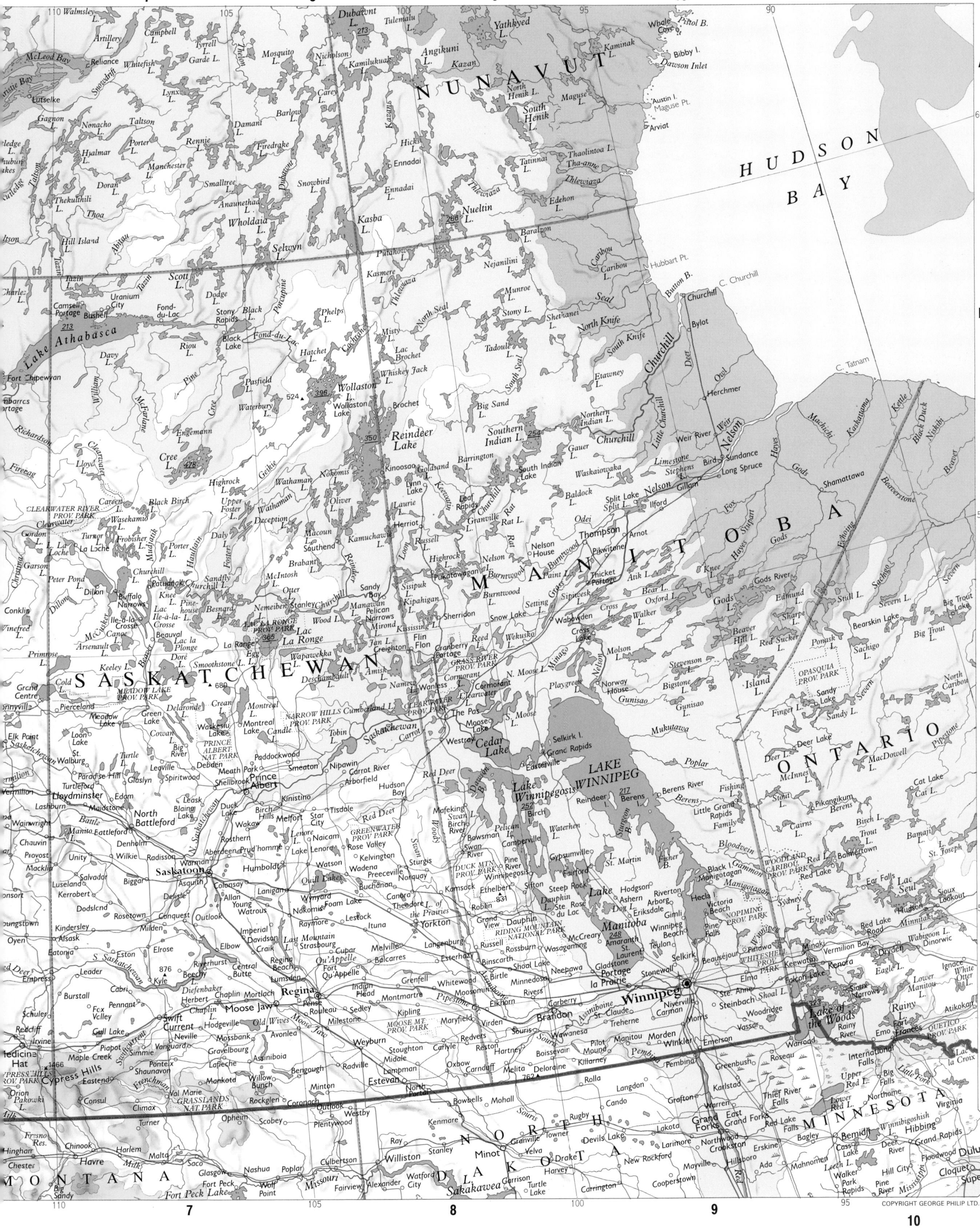

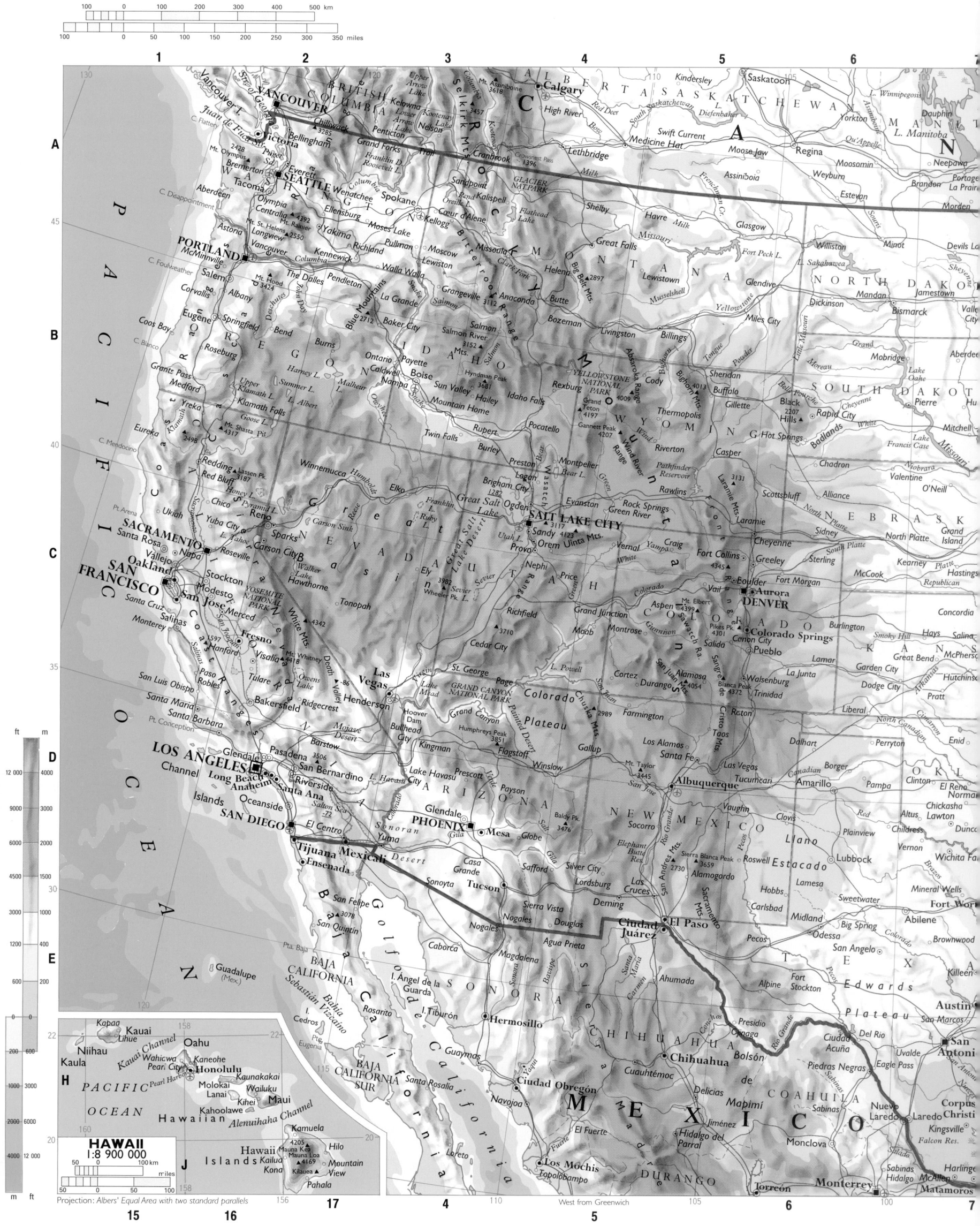

Projection: Albers' Equal Area with two standard parallels

West from Greenwich

HAWAII 1:8 900 000

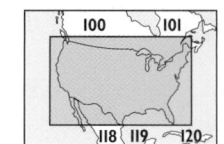

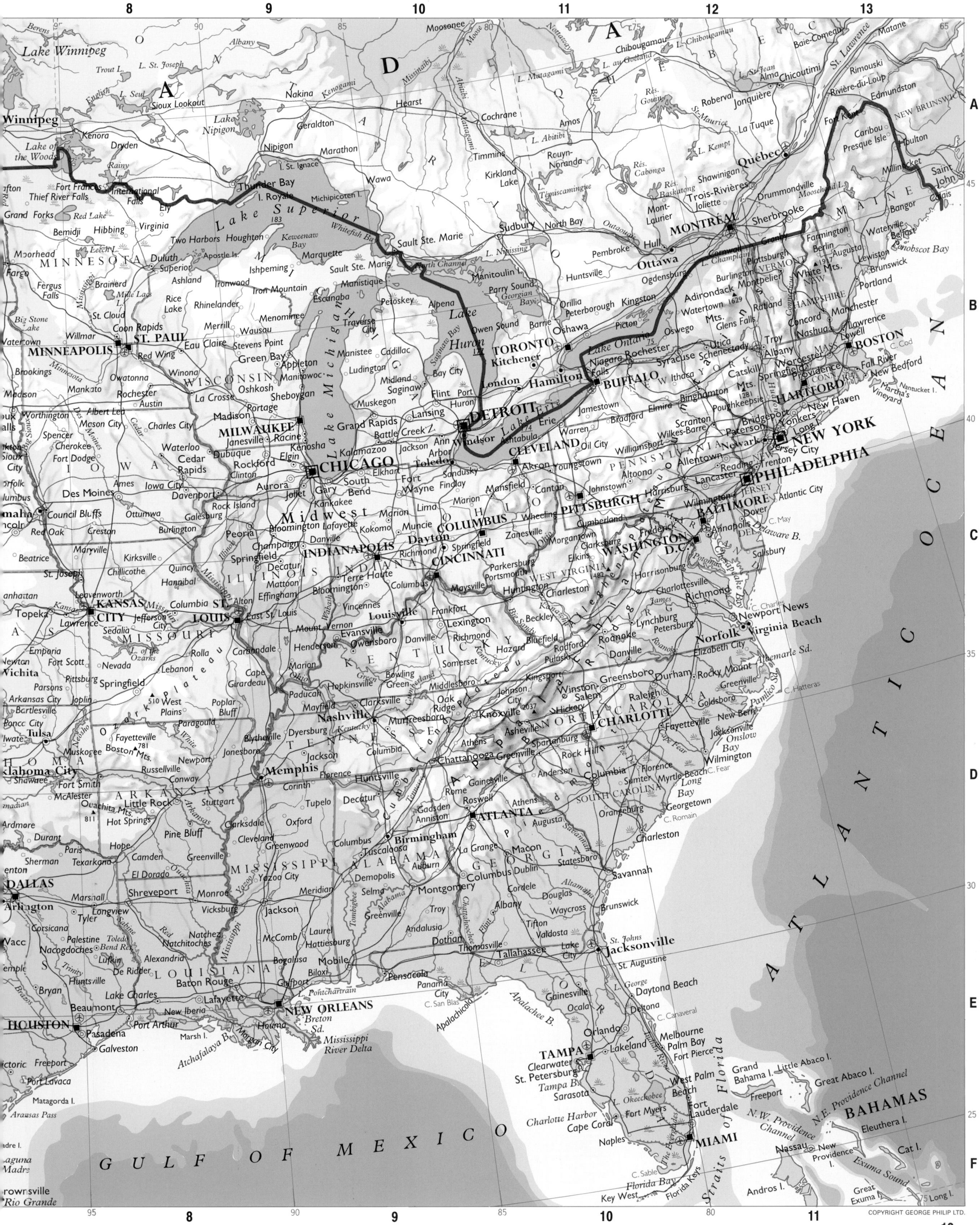

50 0 50 100 150 200 km
50 0 50 100 150 miles

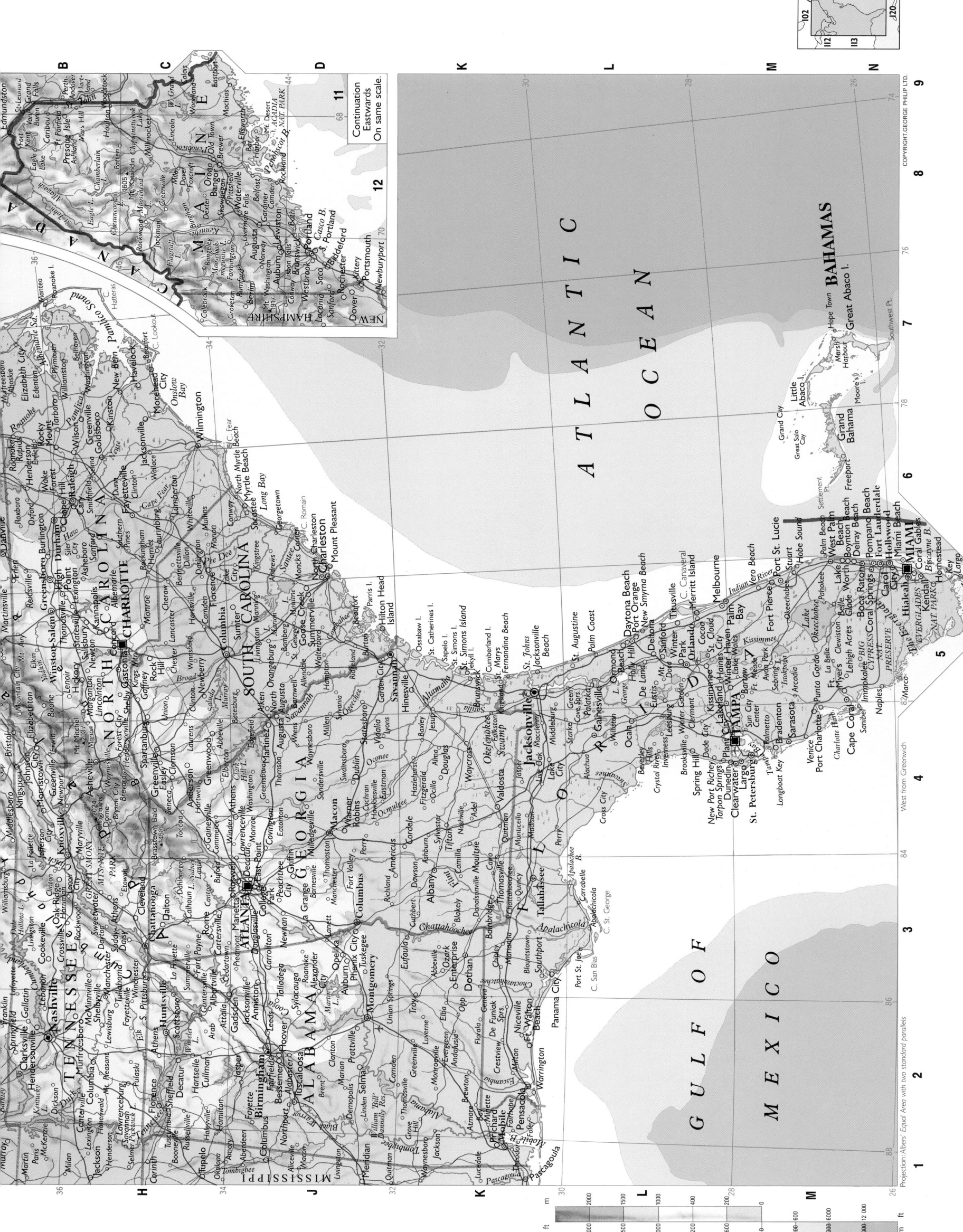

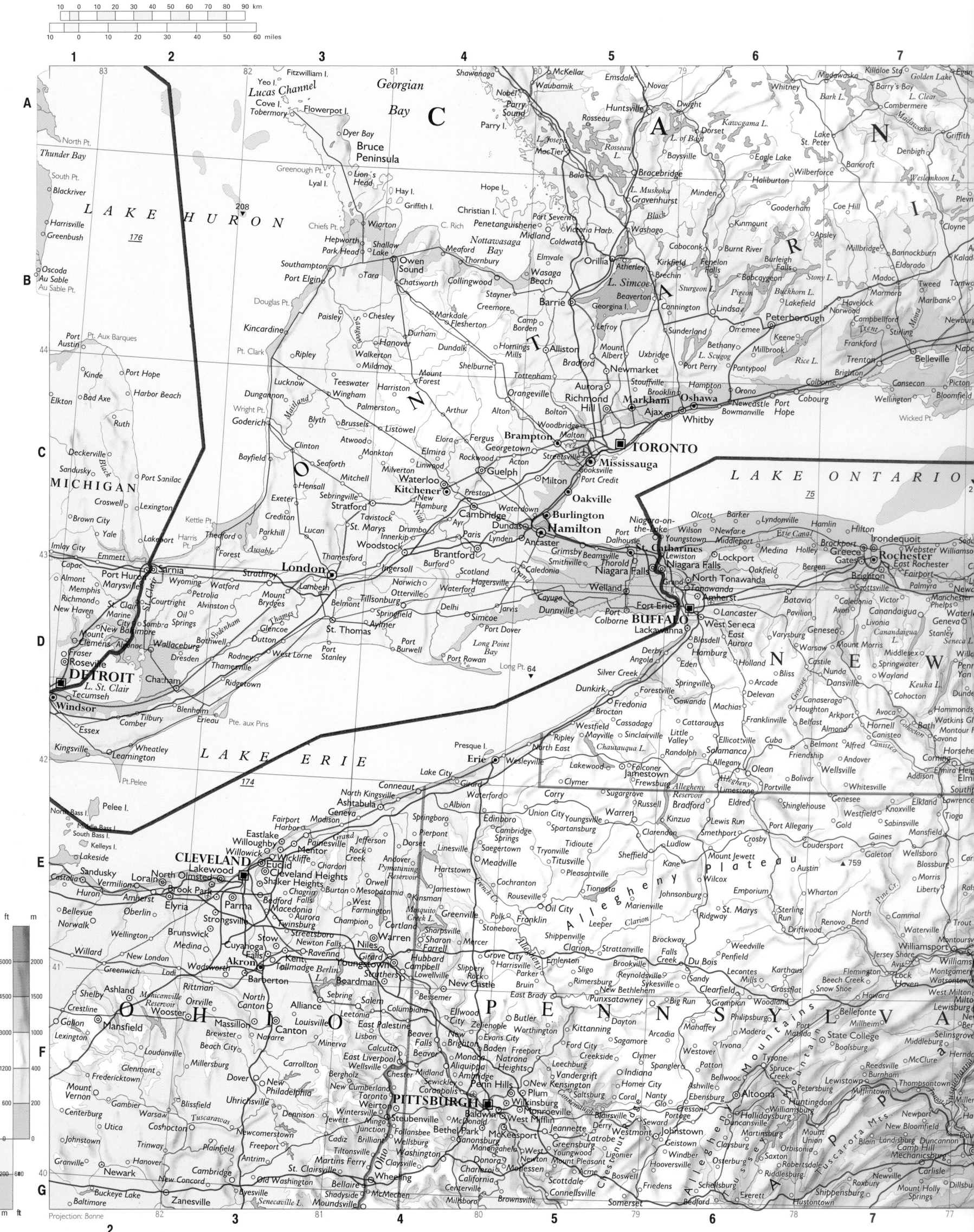

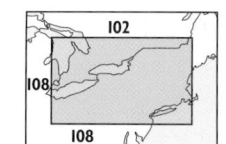

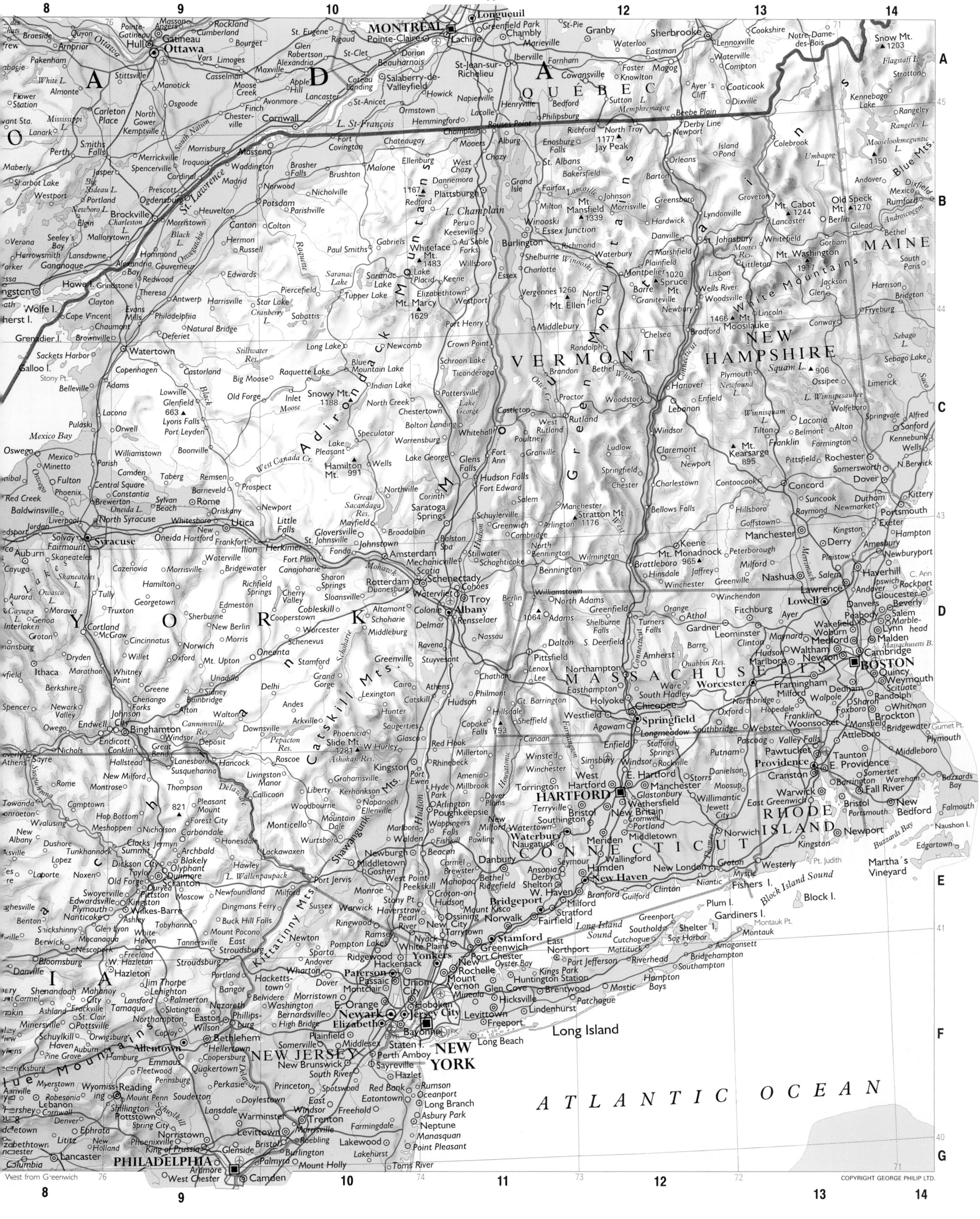

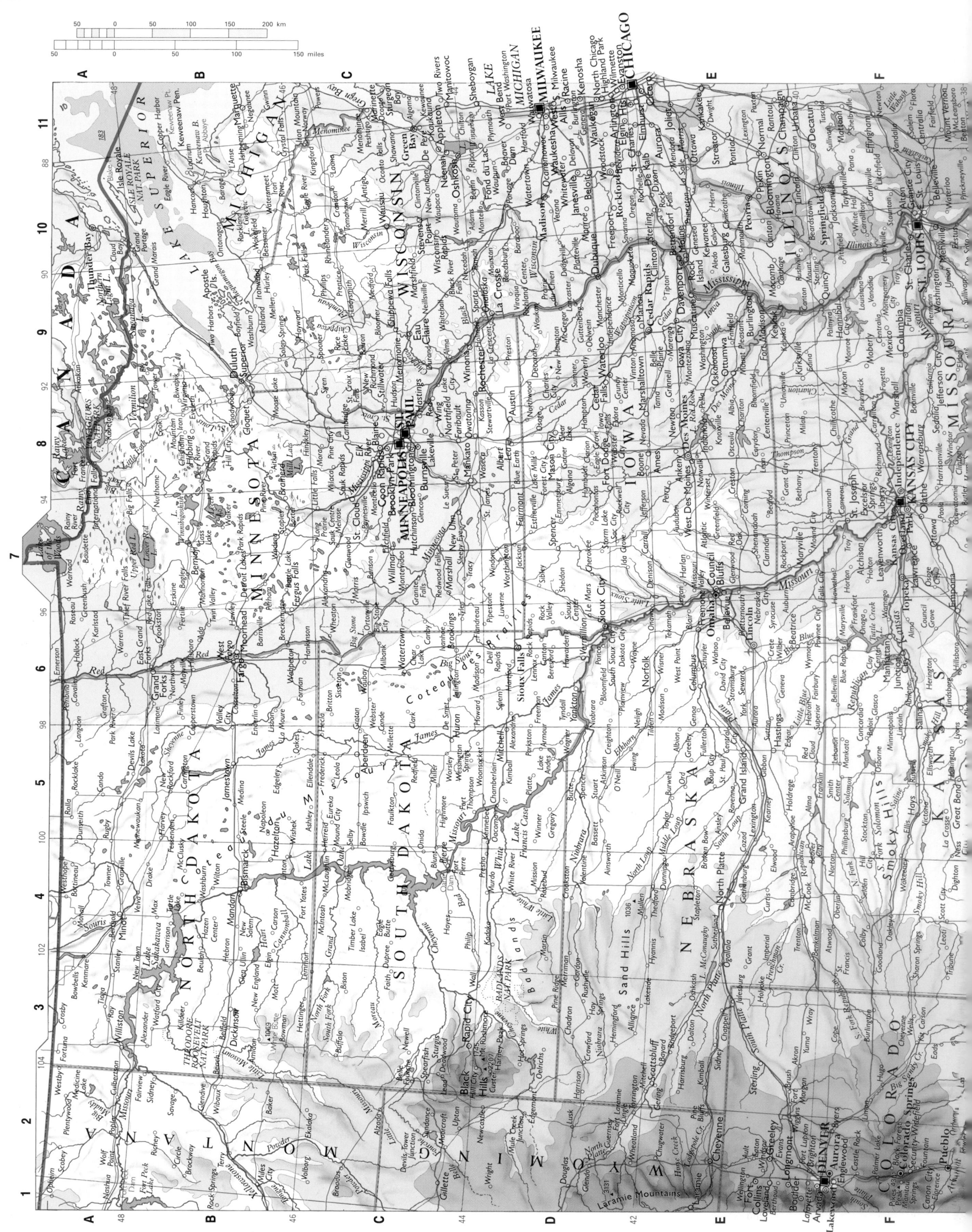

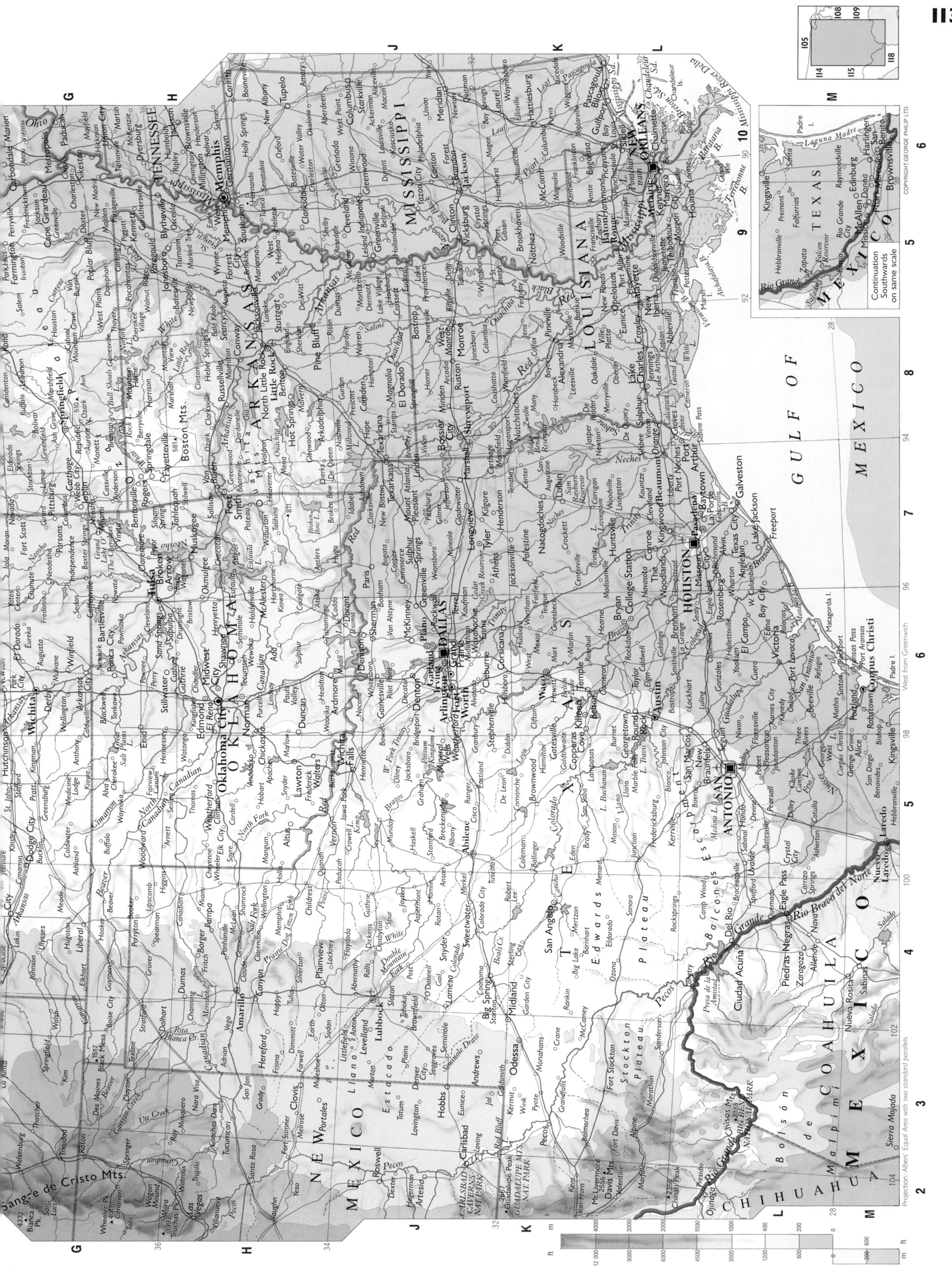

Continuation
Southwards
on same scale

Projection: Albers' Equal Area with two standard parallels

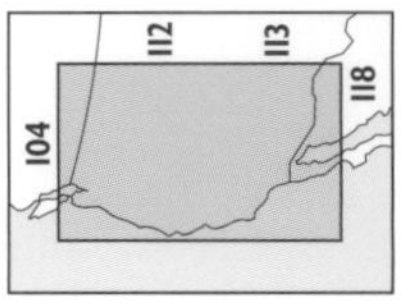

50 0 50 100 150 200 km
50 0 50 100 150 miles

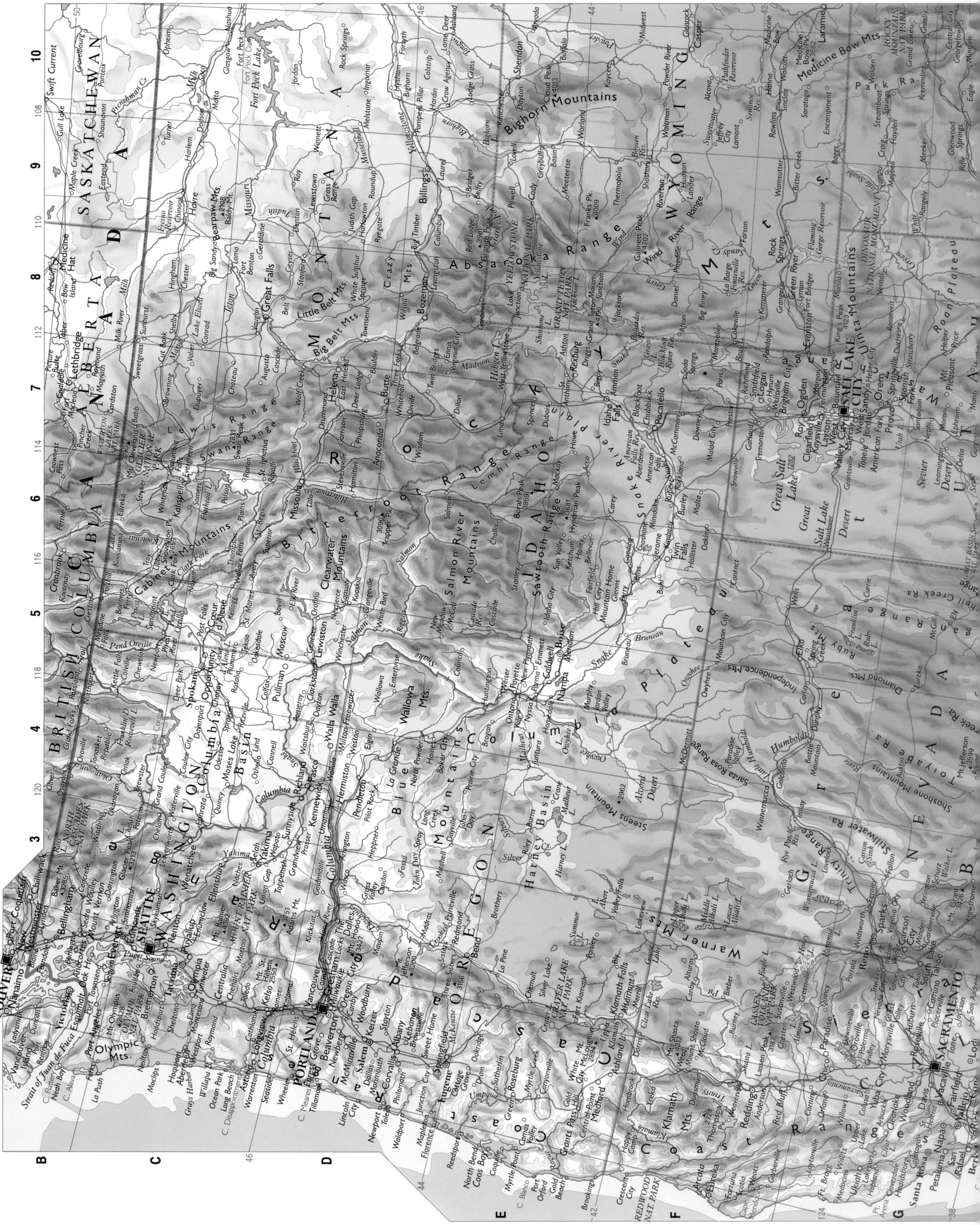

SASKATCHEWAN

ALBERTA

BRITISH COLUMBIA

MONTANA

WYOMING

WASHINGTON

OREGON

IDAHO

NEVADA

UTAH

VANCOUVER

SEATTLE

PORTLAND

SALT LAKE CITY

SACRAMENTO

Rocky Mountains

Bighorn Mountains

Absaroka Range

Salmon River Mountains

Snake River

Columbia Plateau

Blue Mountains

Great Salt Lake

Great Salt Lake Desert

Uinta Mountains

Cascade Range

Olympic Mts.

Bitterroot Mountains

Cabinet Mountains

Lewis Range

Great Falls

Helena

Butte

Bozeman

Billings

Sheridan

Casper

Spokane

Yakima

Boise

Pocatello

Idaho Falls

Ogden

Provo

Reno

Coeur d'Alene

Lewiston

Pullman

Walla Walla

Pendleton

Eugene

Salem

Medford

Klamath Falls

Warner Mts.

Harney Basin

Steens Mountain

Coast Range

REDWOOD NAT. PARK

CRATER LAKE NAT. PARK

LASSEN VOLCANIC NAT. PARK

Strait of Juan de Fuca

Puget Sound

Columbia River

Missouri River

Yellowstone

YELLOWSTONE NATIONAL PARK

GRAND TETON NAT. PARK

GLACIER NATIONAL PARK

MOUNT RAINIER NAT. PARK

NORTH CASCADES NAT. PARK

DINOSAUR NATIONAL MONUMENT

Medicine Bow Mts.

ROCKY MOUNTAIN NAT. PARK

Roan Plateau

Humboldt River

Ruby Mts.

Shoshone Mountains

Stillwater Ra.

Santa Rosa Range

Toiyabe Ra.

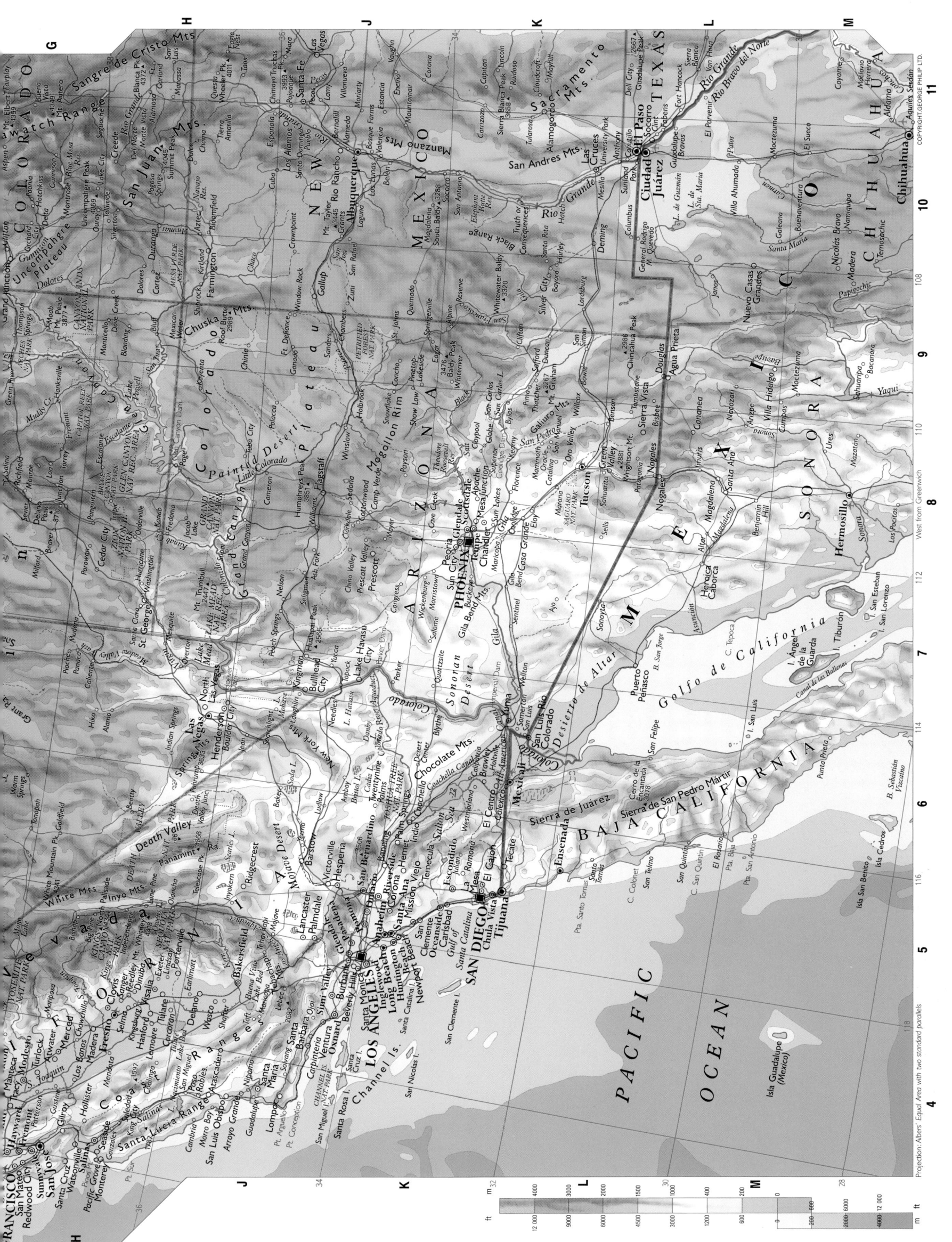

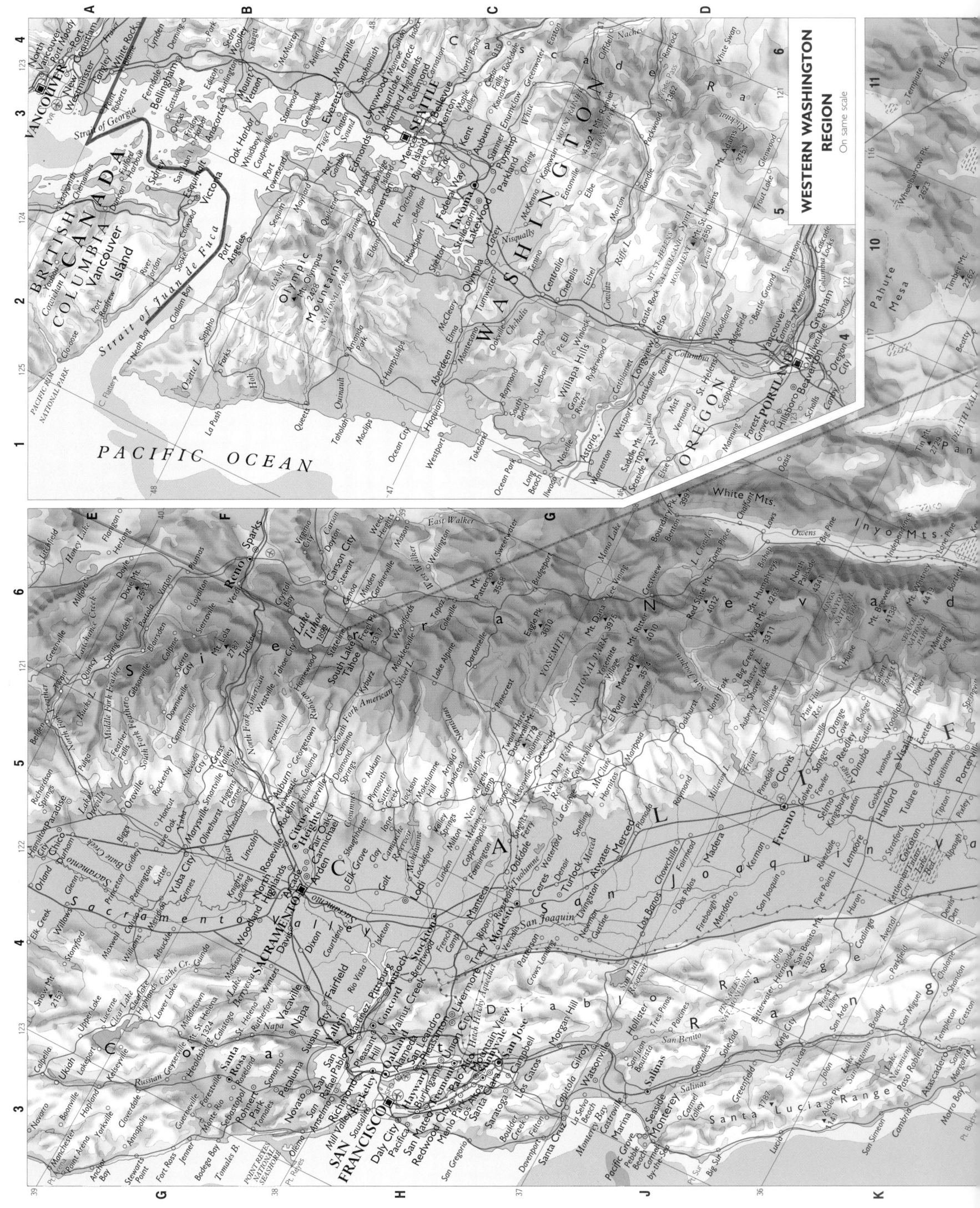

WESTERN WASHINGTON REGION
On same scale

PACIFIC OCEAN

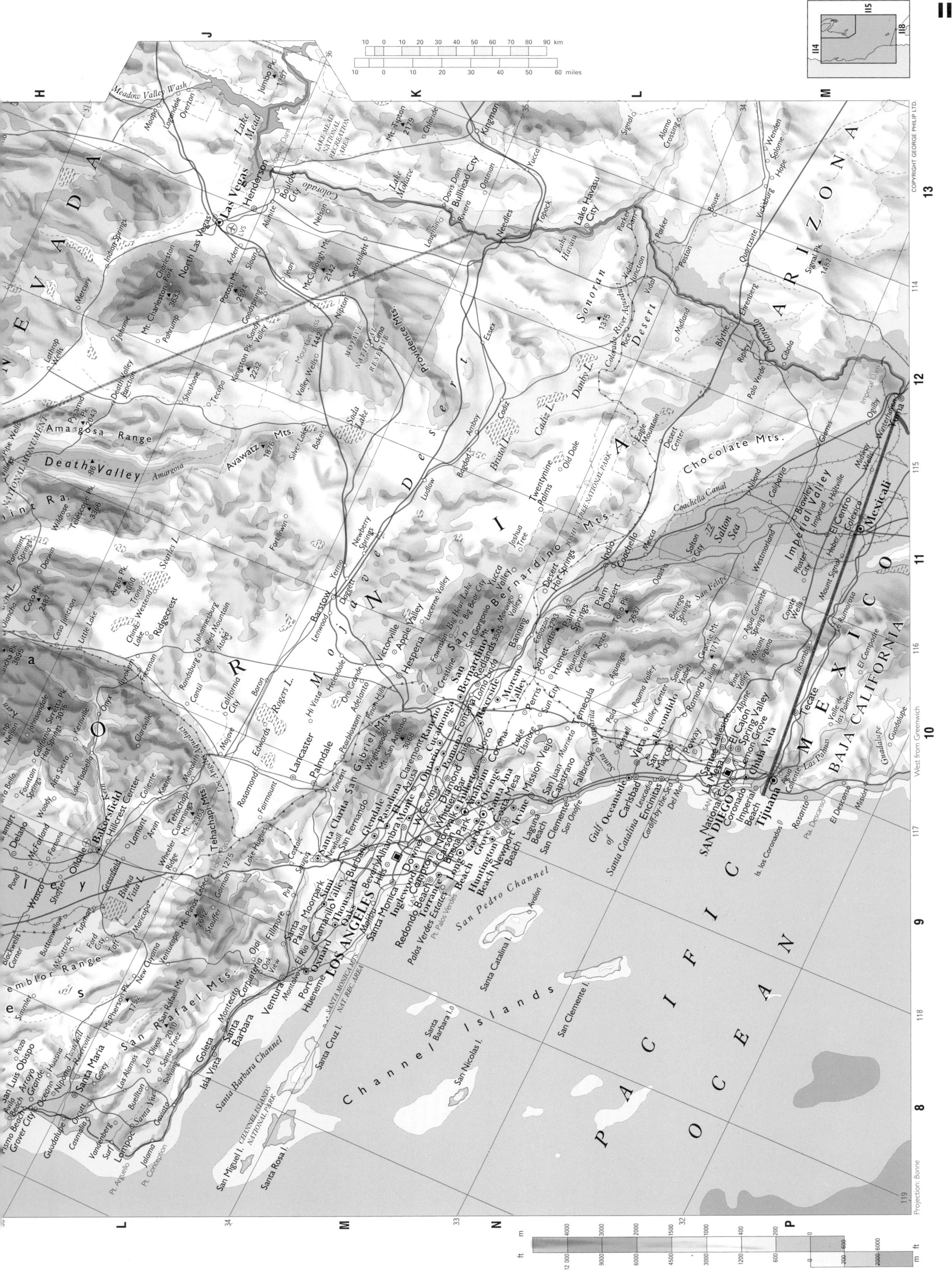

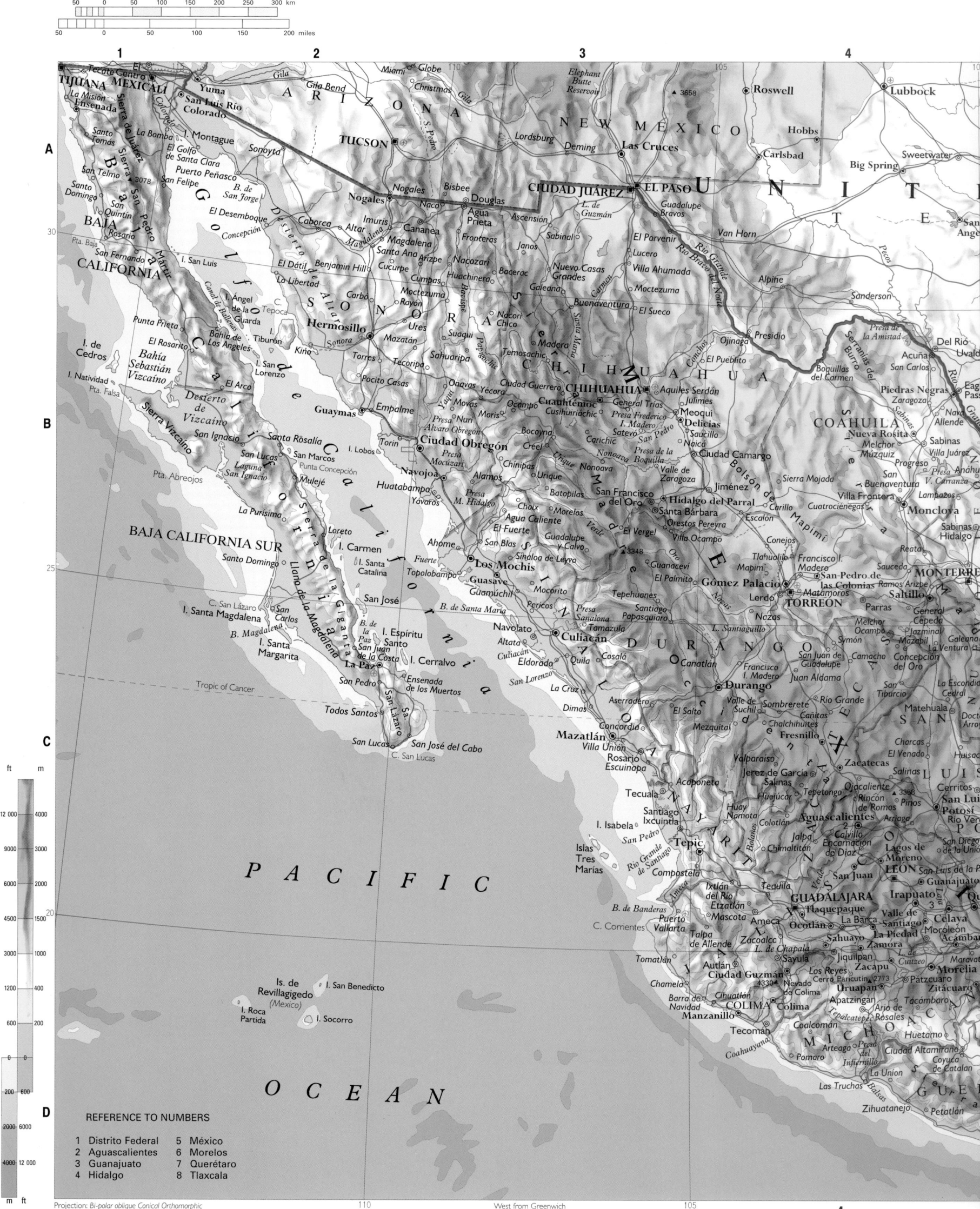

50   0   50   100   150   200   250   300 km
50   0   50   100   150   200 miles

REFERENCE TO NUMBERS

1 Distrito Federal   5 México
2 Aguascalientes   6 Morelos
3 Guanajuato   7 Querétaro
4 Hidalgo   8 Tlaxcala

Projection: Bi-polar oblique Conical Orthomorphic

West from Greenwich

106
107
120

5
6
7
8
A
B
C
D
E
Wichita Falls
Denison
Sherman
Paris
Red
Hope
Camden
ARKANSAS
Texarkana
El Dorado
Greenville
MISSISSIPPI
Tombigbee
Tuscaloosa
Coosa
Opelika
Phenix City
Columbus
Ocmulgee
McRae
Possum Kingdom Res.
Brazos
Denton
Greenville
FORT WORTH
DALLAS
Marshall
Monroe
Vicksburg
Meridian
ALABAMA
Selma
Montgomery
Troy
Americus
Cordele
Albany
GEORGIA
Tifton
Abilene
Ranger
Cleburne
Longview
Tyler
Shreveport
LOUISIANA
Tallulah
Jackson
UNITED STATES
Alabama
Chattahoochee
Waycross
Hillsboro
Corsicana
Palestine
Toledo Bend Res.
Mississippi
Natchez
Pearl
Laurel
Hattiesburg
Dothan
Jim Woodruff Res.
Valdosta
Flomaton
Chattahoochee
Tallahassee
TEXAS
Brownwood
Waco
Nacogdoches
Lufkin
Sam Rayburn Reservoir
Jewett
Alexandria
Sabine
McComb
MOBILE
Pensacola
FLORIDA
Panama City
Lake City
Temple
Colorado
Trinity
Baton Rouge
Hammond
Bogalusa
Biloxi
Gulfport
Mobile Bay
Apalachee Bay
Huntsville
Bryan
L. Pontchartrain
NEW ORLEANS
Breton Sd.
C. San Blas
Suwannee
Austin
Navasota
Beaumont
Lake Charles
Lafayette
Port Arthur
HOUSTON
Atchafalaya Bay
Terrebonne Bay
Mississippi River Delta
Galveston
Rosenberg
SAN ANTONIO
Guadalupe
Victoria
Clearwater
Dilley
Nueces
Alice
Corpus Christi
Laredo
Nuevo Laredo
Kingsville
Zapata
GULF OF MEXICO
Laguna Madre
Presa Falcón
Camargo
McAllen
Harlingen
Brownsville
Reynosa
Matamoros
Presa M. R. Gomez
China
Valle Hermoso
Santa Teresa
Montemorelos
Conchos
Mendez
Laguna Madre
San Fernando
Linares
Villagrán
Hidalgo
Santander Jiménez
TAMAULIPAS
La Pesca
Soto la Marina
Tropic of Cancer
Zaragoza
Ciudad Victoria
Sierra de Tamaulipas
Llera
Calles
Aldama
Pta. Jerez
I. Desterrada
I. Pérez (Mexico)
La Esperanza
CUBA
Guane
La Fe
C. Corrientes
C. San Antonio
Canal de Yucatán
Ocampo
Ciudad Mante
Altamira
Ciudad Madero
Tampico
Ciudad de Valles
Cárdenas
Pánuco
L. de Tamiahua
C. Rojo
Ozuluama
Tempoal
Tantoyuca
Tamazunchale
Chicontepec
Pta. Yalkubul
Rio Lagartos
C. Catoche
Cancún
Puerto Juárez
Dzilam de Bravo
El Cuyo
Tizimín
Progreso
Motul
Temax
Izamal
Espita
DZIBILCHALTUN
Mérida
YUCATAN
Valladolid
Puerto Morelos
MAYAPAN
Sotuta
CHICHEN ITZA
Cozumel
Isla Cozumel
Maxcanú
Ticul
Peto
Tuxpan
Zimapán
Zacualtipán
Poza Rica
Papantla
UXMAL
Tenabo
Tekax
Vigía Chico
B. de la Ascensión
Bolonchenticul
Felipe Carrillo Puerto
B. del Espíritu Santo
San Juan del Rio
Huichapan
Pachuca
Huauchinango
Nautla
Misantla
Golfo de Campeche
Campeche
Hopelchén
EDZNA
QUINTANA ROO
Tulancingo
Teziutlán
Jalapa Enríquez
Champotón
Chenkán
Bacalar
Chetumal
B. de Chetumal
Banco Chinchorro
MÉXICO
Zumpango
Tlaxcala
Apizaco
4282
ZEMPOALA
Veracruz
Ciudad del Carmen
L. de Términos
Matamoros
CAMPECHE
Corozal
Toluca
Amecameca
Tenango
PUEBLA
Citlaltépetl
5700
Coatepec
Córdoba
Alvarado
Tlacotalpan
San Andrés Tuxtla
1879
Paraiso
Frontera
Orange Walk
Ambergris Cay
Popocatépetl
5452
Orizaba
Cosamaloapan
Comalcalco
TABASCO
Palizada
Concepción
Hondo
Cuernavaca
Jojutla
Izúcar de Matamoros
Tehuacán
Ajalpan
Tres Valles
Coatzacoalcos
LA VENTA
Villahermosa
Balancán
Belize City
Turneffe Is.
Iguala
Chiautla
Acatlán
Chilac
Huautla de Jiménez
Presa Miguel Alemán
Acayucan
Minatitlán
Cárdenas
Macuspana
Uaxactún
San Ignacio
Belmopan
BELIZE
Huajuapan de León
Asunción Nochixtlán
San Juan Bautista Valle Nacional
Istmo de Tehuantepec
Raudales de Malpaso
Teapa
Tenosique
PALENQUE
TIKAL
Benque Viejo
Dangriga
Is. de la Bahía
Mixteca
Silacayoapan
Jesús Carranza
Presa Netzahualcóyotl
Simojovel
Ocosingo
L. Petén Itzá
La Libertad
Flores
Golfo de Honduras
Roatán
Puerto Castilla
Chilapa
Chilpancingo
Sierra Madre del Sur
Tlaxiaco
Oaxaca
MONTE ALBAN
Tlacolula
Tehuantepec
Tuxtla Gutiérrez
Chiapa de Corzo
San Cristóbal de las Casas
La Independencia
Usumacinta
Maya Mts.
Monkey River
Iriona
Tierra Colorada
OAXACA
Trinidad
Matías Romero
CHIAPAS
Comitán
Lacantún
San Luis
San Antonio
Trujillo
Ayutla
Ometepec
San Jerónimo Taviche
Ixtepec
Salinas
Punta Gorda
Puerto Barrios
Tela
Balfate
Savá
Acapulco
Ocotlán
Ejutla
Juchitán
Sebol
Livingston
San Pedro Sula
El Progreso
Arenal
Olanchito
Pinotepa Nacional
Tehuantepec
Arriaga
Tonalá
Sierra de los Cuchumatanes
GUATEMALA
L. de Izabal
HONDURAS
Papagayo
Miahuatlán
Salina Cruz
Sierra Madre
La Concordia
Cobán
Motagua
Yoro
Punta Maldonado
Jamiltepec
Tututepec
3139
Puerto Arista
Motozintla
3993
Huehuetenango
Sierra de las Minas
Gualán
Santa Barbara
Sulaco
Juticalpa
Catacamas
San Pedro Mixtepec
Pochutla
Golfo de Tehuantepec
Mar Muerto
Pijijiapan
Mapastepec
Cuilco
4220
UTATLAN
Totonicapán
Zacapa
Santa Rosa de Copán
L. de Yojoa
Comayagua
Patuca
Verde
Puerto Escondido
Puerto Ángel
Huixtla
San Marcos
Sololá
Jalapa
Chiquimula
COPÁN
Tegucigalpa
Tapachula
Coatepeque
Antigua
Mazatenango
GUATEMALA
Amatitlán
La Esperanza
La Paz
Danlí
Retalhuleu
Yuscarán
25
20
15
30
100
95
90
85

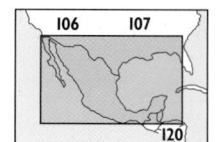

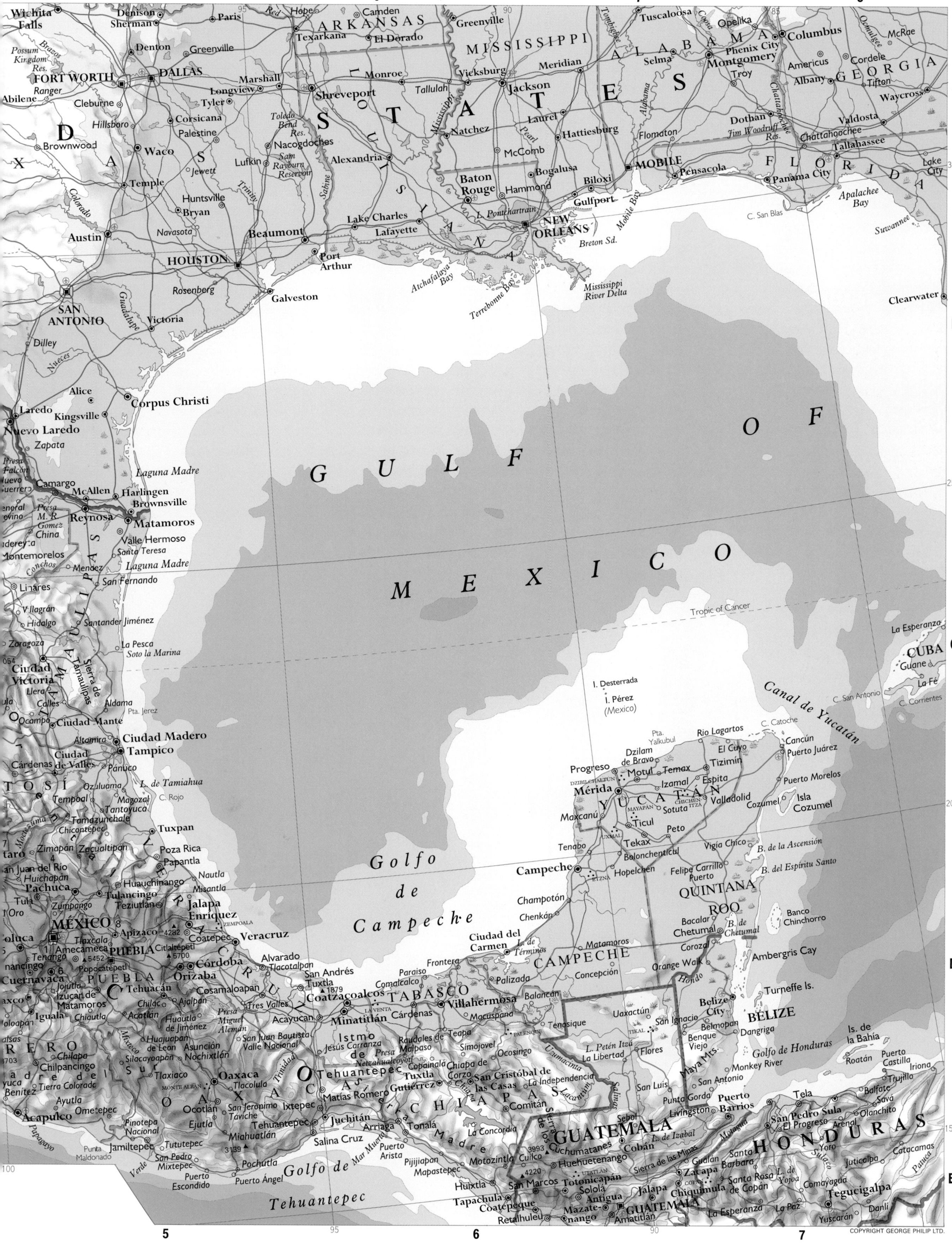

GULF OF MEXICO

PACIFIC OCEAN

MEXICO

GUATEMALA

BELIZE

HONDURAS

EL SALVADOR

NICARAGUA

COSTA RICA

PANAMA

CUBA

JAMAICA

U.S.A.

BAH...

CARIB...

Straits of Florida

Florida Keys

Canal de Yucatán

YUCATÁN

CAMPECHE

QUINTANA ROO

Mosquitia

Projection: Conical with two standard parallels

Miami · Fort Lauderdale · West Palm Beach · Naples · Key West · Dry Tortugas (U.S.A.) · La Habana (Havana) · MARIANAO · Matanzas · Cárdenas · Cienfuegos · Santa Clara · Sancti Spíritus · Ciego de Ávila · Camagüey · Holguín · SANTIAGO DE CUBA · Georgetown · Grand Cayman · Cayman Islands (U.K.) · Montego Bay · KINGSTON · Spanish Town

Mérida · Progreso · Motul · Campeche · Ciudad del Carmen · Chetumal · Belize City · BELMOPAN · Flores · GUATEMALA · Quetzaltenango · San Salvador · SAN SALVADOR · Santa Ana · TEGUCIGALPA · San Pedro Sula · La Ceiba · Trujillo · Comayagua · Juticalpa · Choluteca · Puerto Cabezas · MANAGUA · Masaya · Granada · León · Chinandega · Matagalpa · Bluefields · Lago de Nicaragua · Liberia · Puntarenas · SAN JOSÉ · Cartago · Limón · PANAMÁ · Colón · David · Santiago

Isla Cozumel · Cozumel · Cancún · Isla de la Juventud · Cayman Brac · Little Cayman · Swan Islands (U.S.A. & Honduras) · Is. de la Bahía · Cayos Miskitos (Nicaragua) · I. de Providencia (Colombia) · Cayos Roncador (U.S.A. & Colombia) · I. de San Andrés (Colombia) · Cayos de Albuquerque (Colombia) · Is. del Maíz (Nicaragua, U.S.A.) · Archipiélago de San Blas · Golfo del Darién · Golfo de Panamá

ATLANTIC

OCEAN

Tropic of Cancer

ft m

12 000 · 4000

9000 · 3000

6000 · 2000

4500 · 1500

3000 · 1000

1200 · 400

600 · 200

0 · 0

200 · 600

2000 · 6000

4000 · 12 000

6000 · 18 000

8000 · 24 000

m ft

MAS

rthur's Town

The Bight

Cat I.

San Salvador I.

Conception I.

Rum Cay

Long I.

Clarence

Town   Samana Cay

Crooked I. Passage

Albert   Crooked I.

Town Snug   Plana Cays

Corner   Mayaguana I.

Acklins I.

Cay Verde   Mira por vos Cay

Hogsty Reef

Little Inagua I.

Lake Rosa   Turks & Caicos

Matthew   Great   Caicos Is. (U.K.)

Town   Inagua I.   Turks Is.

Turks Island Passage

Caicos Passage

Puerto Rico Trench

Milwaukee
Deep ▾
9200

Baracoa

Moa

Mayari

Maisi   Pta. de Maisi

Î. de la Tortue

Monte   LA ISABELA

Cristi

Guantánamo   Paso de los Vientos   Cap-   Port-de-   Puerto   Santiago de los Cabelleros

(Windward Passage)   Haïtien   Paix   Plata

Jean Rabel   Fort Liberté   La Vega   San Francisco de Macorís

Cap-à-   Gonaïves   Cord.   Nagua   Samaná

Foux   G. de la Gonâve   Hinche   Central   Sabana de la Mar   San Juan   Bayamón   SAN JUAN

3175   Sánchez   Hato Mayor   Arecibo   Carolina

Jérémie   Î. de la Gonâve   PORT   DOMINICAN   San Pedro   C. Engaño   Aguadilla   1538   Virgin Is.   St. Thomas   Road Town   Anegada   Sombrero (U.K.)

HAITI   AU-PRINCE   San Juan   REP   de Macorís   Ponce   Fajardo   Virgin Gorda   Anegada   Passage

avassa I.   L. Enriquillo   SANTO   Higüey   B. de   Caguas   Virgin Is.   Charlotte   Anguilla (U.K.)

(U.S.A.)   Dame   Petit   2280   Barahona   Agua de   DOMINGO   Yuma   Mayagüez   Amalie   (U.S.A.)   St.-Martin (Fr.)

Marie   Massif de la Hotte   Gôave   Jacmel   Compostela   San Cristóbal   I. Saona   Isla   Guayama   Christiansted   St. Maarten   St.-Barthélemy (Fr.)

Les Cayes   Aquín   Baní   Mona   (Neth.)   Saba (Neth.)   Barbuda

Carcasse   Î. à Vache   Pedernales   PUERTO   (U.S.A.)   Frederiksted   St. Croix   St. Eustatius   ST. KITTS   ANTIGUA

Pointe-à-Gravois   RICO   (Neth.)   & NEVIS   & BARBUDA

Hispaniola   (U.S.A.)   Basseterre   St. John's

Nevis   Antigua

Redonda

A n t i l l e s   Montserrat   Guadeloupe Passage

(U.K.)   Ste.-Rose   Le Moule   La Désirade

I. Beata   C. Beata   GUADELOUPE   Pointe-à-Pitre

(Fr.)   Marie-Galante (Fr.)

Basse-Terre   Grand-Bourg

I. des Saintes   Dominica Passage

(Fr.)

I. de Aves   Portsmouth   DOMINICA

(Venezuela)   Roseau

L e s s e r   A n t i l l e s   Martinique Passage

Mt. Pelée   Ste.-Marie

B E A N   S E A   1397   Le François

Fort-de-   Rivière-Pilote

France   MARTINIQUE

(Fr.)

St. Lucia Channel

Castries

Soufrière   ST. LUCIA

St. Vincent Passage

La Soufrière 1234   ST. VINCENT

Speightstown

Kingstown   Bridgetown

& THE   BARBADOS

Hillsborough   GRENADINES

Grenadines

St. George's   GRENADA

Aruba   Curaçao   Bonaire

(Neth.)   L e s s e r   A n t i l l e s

Pta. Gallinas   C. San Román   Willemstad   NETH.   I. Blanquilla (Ven.)

Pen. de la   Pta.   Pen. de   ANTILLES   Is. Las Aves   I. Orchila   I. Los Hermanos   Tobago

Guajira   Espada   Paraguaná   Punto Fijo   (Ven.)   (Ven.)   Scarborough

SANTA   Ríohacha   Uribia   Punta   Puerto   Is. Los Roques   I. Los Testigos   Galera

MARTA   GUAJIRA   Golfo de   Cardón   Cumarebo   (Ven.)   I. de Margarita   (Ven.)   Port of   Point

ARRAN-   Cienaga   Venezuela   Altagracia   Cord. La Vela de Coro   La Asunción   Spain

QUILLA   Sierra Nevada de   San   FALCÓN   Tucacas   Maiquetía   NUEVA   Porlamar   Trinidad

Baranca   Santa Marta   Rafael   Mene de Mauroa   Puerto   Maracay   La Guaira   ESPARTA   Arima

TLÁNTICO   Soledad   5800   La Concepción   Baragua   Tocuyo   Cabello   CARACAS   La Tortuga   Río   Carúpano   Rio Claro

Sabanalarga   Cabimas   Carora   San Felipe   CARABOBO   DISTRITO FEDERAL   (Ven.)   Caribe   Güiria

Fundación   La Sierra de   Villa del   LARA   Valencia   MIRANDA   Cumaná   Cariaco   San Fernando   TRINIDAD

MAGDALENA   Agustín   Rosario   Ojeda   Maracay   Higuerote   SUCRE   & TOBAGO

Codazzi   Machiques   BARQUISIMETO   Yaritagua   Villa   Río Chico   Puerto   Serpent's Mouth

ince   Plato   CÉSAR   ZULIA   Mene Grande   El Tocuyo   de Cura   los Morros   Ocumare del Tuy   La Cruz   Barcelona   Caicara   Maturín

Zambrano   Lago de   TRUJILLO   Acarigua   San Carlos   San Juan   Araqua de   Anaco   MONAGAS   DELTA

Carmen   Maracaibo   Betijoque   COJEDES   de los Morros   Barcelona   Cantaura   Tucupita

ince   Mompós   El Banco   Valera   PORTUGUESA   El Baúl   GUÁRICO   Valle de   El Tigre   AMACURO

Sahagún   Magangué   San Carlos   Guanare   Portuguesa   la Pascua   Santa María   Los Barrancos

San   NORTE   del Zulia   TRUJILLO   Calabozo   de Ipire   ANZOÁTEGUI   Ciudad Guayana

Marcos   DE OCAÑA   MÉRIDA   BARINAS   El Pao   Sierra Imataca

Planeta   Agustín   Cord. de Mérida   Barinas   Libertad   San Fernando   Soledad   Ciudad Bolívar

OBA   BOLÍVAR   Simiti   MÉRIDA   Ciudad   Bruzual   Puerto de Nutrias   de Apure   El Pao   Guasipati   El Callao

Caucasia   SANTANDER   TÁCHIRA   Bolivia   BARINAS   San Fernando   Embalse de Guri   Tumeremo

Cúcuta   V E N E Z U E L A   Achaguas   Apure   Caicara   Orinoco   Upata

West from Greenwich   COPYRIGHT GEORGE PHILIP LTD

100 0 200 400 600 800 1000 1200 1400 km

100 0 200 400 600 800 1000 miles

NORTH ATLANTIC OCEAN

Tropic of Cancer

Yucatan Channel
Gulf of Campeche
Yucatán Peninsula
Isthmus of Tehuantepec
Guatemala Trench
G. de Honduras
Coco
L. Nicaragua
C. Gracias a Dios
Panama Canal
Gulf of Panamá
Gulf of Darién

Cuba
Greater Antilles
Jamaica
Hispaniola
Turks & Caicos Is.
Puerto Rico 9200
Lesser Antilles
Guadeloupe
Dominica
Martinique
St. Lucia
St. Vincent
Barbados
Grenada
Tobago
Trinidad
I. Margarita

Caribbean Sea

C. de la Aguja
Sierra Nevada de Santa Marta 5800
Maracaibo
Cord. de Merida

Orinoco
Meta

Cordillera Occidental
Cordillera Central
Cordillera Oriental
C. de San Francisco
Cotopaxi 5897
Chimborazo 6267
G. of Guayaquil
Pta. Pariñas
Pta. Negra
Huascarán 6768

Llanos
Guaviare
Caquetá
Putumayo
Napo
Marañón
Ucayali

Guiana Highlands
Mt. Roraima 2810
Sierra Pacaraima
Serra Tumucumaque
Branco
Negro
Japurá
Amazon
Amazon
Juruá
Purus
Madre de Dios
Mamoré
Guaporé

C. Orange
Equator
Marajó I.
Tocantins
Tapajós
Xingu
Araguaia
Arinos
Teles Pires
Aripuanã
Roosevelt
Juruena

C. de São Roque
Plat. of Borborema
São Francisco

Selvas

PACIFIC OCEAN

Galapagos Is.
Chincha Alta

L. Titicaca
Nevada Ancohuma 6550
Bolivian Plateau
L. de Poopó

Plateau of Mato Grosso
Paraguay

Brazilian Highlands
Serra da Mantiqueira 2890
Pico da Bandeira
Serra do Mar
Abrolhos Bank
C. Frio

Tropic of Capricorn
San Félix
San Ambrosio
8050
Cerro Ojos del Salado 6863
Atacama Desert
Salinas Grandes
Chile Peru Trench

Andes
Gran Chaco
Pilcomayo
Paraná
Salado
Paraguay
Uruguay
Iguaçu Falls
Entre Ríos
L. dos Patos

Arch. de Juan Fernández
Mt. Aconcagua 6960
Sierra de Córdoba
L. Mar Chiquita
Pampas
Río de la Plata

Chile Rise
Chiloé I.
Chonos Archipelago
Taitao Peninsula
Gulf of Penas
Wellington I.
Madre de Dios I.
Mte. San Valentín 4058
Patagonia
Negro
Colorado
Bahía Blanca
G. San Matías
Valdés Peninsula
Chubut
G. San Jorge

SOUTH ATLANTIC OCEAN

Argentine Basin
6212

Magellan's Str.
Santa Inés I.
Canal Cockburn
Canal Beagle
Tierra del Fuego
Staten I.
C. Horn
West Falkland
East Falkland
Falkland Is.
South Georgia

ft m
12000 4000
9000 3000
6000 2000
3000 1000
1500 500
600 200
0 0
200 600
1000 3000
2000 6000
4000 12000
6000 18000
8000 24000
m ft

Projection: Lambert's Azimuthal Equal Area

30 CARTOGRAPHY BY PHILIP'S.

West from Greenwich

100 0 200 400 600 800 1000 1200 1400 km
100 0 200 400 600 800 1000 miles

1 2 3 4 5 6 7

Tropic of Cancer

A Havana CUBA BAHAMAS Turks & Caicos Is. (U.K.) NORTH **A** 20 20

HAITI DOMINICAN REP. Virgin Is. (U.K.) ATLANTIC
JAMAICA Port-au-Prince San Juan ANTIGUA & BARBUDA
MEXICO Kingston PUERTO RICO (U.S.A.) ST. KITTS & NEVIS GUADELOUPE (Fr.)
BELIZE Basse-Terre DOMINICA OCEAN
B GUATEMALA HONDURAS Caribbean Sea Fort-de-France MARTINIQUE (Fr.) **B**
Guatemala Tegucigalpa Castries ST. LUCIA
San Salvador EL SALVADOR NICARAGUA ST. VINCENT BARBADOS
Managua Kingstown Bridgetown
COSTA RICA San José Aruba Curaçao GRENADA St. George's TRINIDAD & TOBAGO
Panamá C. de la Aguja Barranquilla Maracaibo Caracas Port of Spain
PANAMA G. of Darién Cartagena Barquisimeto Valencia
C Gulf of Panamá Medellín Cúcuta San Cristóbal Orinoco Ciudad Guayana Georgetown Paramaribo **C**
Bucaramanga VENEZUELA GUYANA SURINAM Cayenne
Cali Bogotá C. Orange
COLOMBIA RORAIMA FRENCH GUIANA
AMAPÁ
Galapagos Is. (Ecuador) Quito Branco Equator
ECUADOR Napo Putumayo Japurá Amazon Marajó I. Belém
Guayaquil Iquitos Manaus Santarém PARÁ São Luís Fortaleza
G. of Guayaquil Marañón Amazon MARANHÃO C. de São Roque
D AMAZONAS Juruá Madeira Tapajós Xingu Teresina CEARÁ Natal **D**
Chiclayo Purus RIO G. DO NORTE
Trujillo Ucayali PIAUÍ PARAÍBA Campina Grande
Chimbote ACRE Pôrto Velho PERNAMBUCO Recife
10 PERU RONDÔNIA BRAZIL ALAGOAS Maceió 10
Callao LIMA Madre de Dios TOCANTINS São Francisco SERGIPE Aracaju
Cuzco Mamoré MATO GROSSO BAHÍA Salvador
L. Titicaca GOIÁS
BOLIVIA DIS. FED. Brasília
Arequipa La Paz Cochabamba
Iquique Santa Cruz Cuiabá Goiânia MINAS GERAIS
E Sucre Belo Horizonte ESPÍRITO **E**
Paraguay MATO GROSSO Ribeirão SANTO
20 Antofagasta DO SUL Prêto Juiz de Fora Vitória 20
PARAGUAY Paraná SÃO PAULO Campos
Salta PARANÁ Campinas R. DE J.
Asunción SÃO PAULO RIO DE
San Miguel de Tucumán Pilcomayo Curitiba NITERÓI JANEIRO
F Resistencia SANTA CATARINA **F**
Tropic of Capricorn Corrientes Uruguay
San Félix (Chile) San Ambrosio (Chile) RIO GRANDE
DO SUL Pôrto Alegre
Córdoba Santa Fe
Arch. de Juan Fernández (Chile) Viña del Mar San Juan Paraná Pelotas
30 Valparaíso Mendoza Rosario URUGUAY 30
SANTIAGO ARGENTINA BUENOS AIRES Montevideo
Talca La Plata Río de la Plata
G Concepción Bahía Colorado Mar del Plata SOUTH **G**
Blanca
Valdivia Negro Viedma ATLANTIC
Puerto Montt
40 Chubut OCEAN 40
Comodoro Rivadavia
Gulf of San Jorge
H Gulf of Penas West Falkland FALKLAND IS. (U.K.) **H**
Magellan's Str. Stanley
Punta Arenas East Falkland
Tierra del Fuego South Georgia (U.K.)
C. Horn

PACIFIC OCEAN

Projection: Lambert's Azimuthal Equal Area
CARTOGRAPHY BY PHILIP'S
West from Greenwich

■ LIMA Capital Cities

1 2 3 4 5 6 7

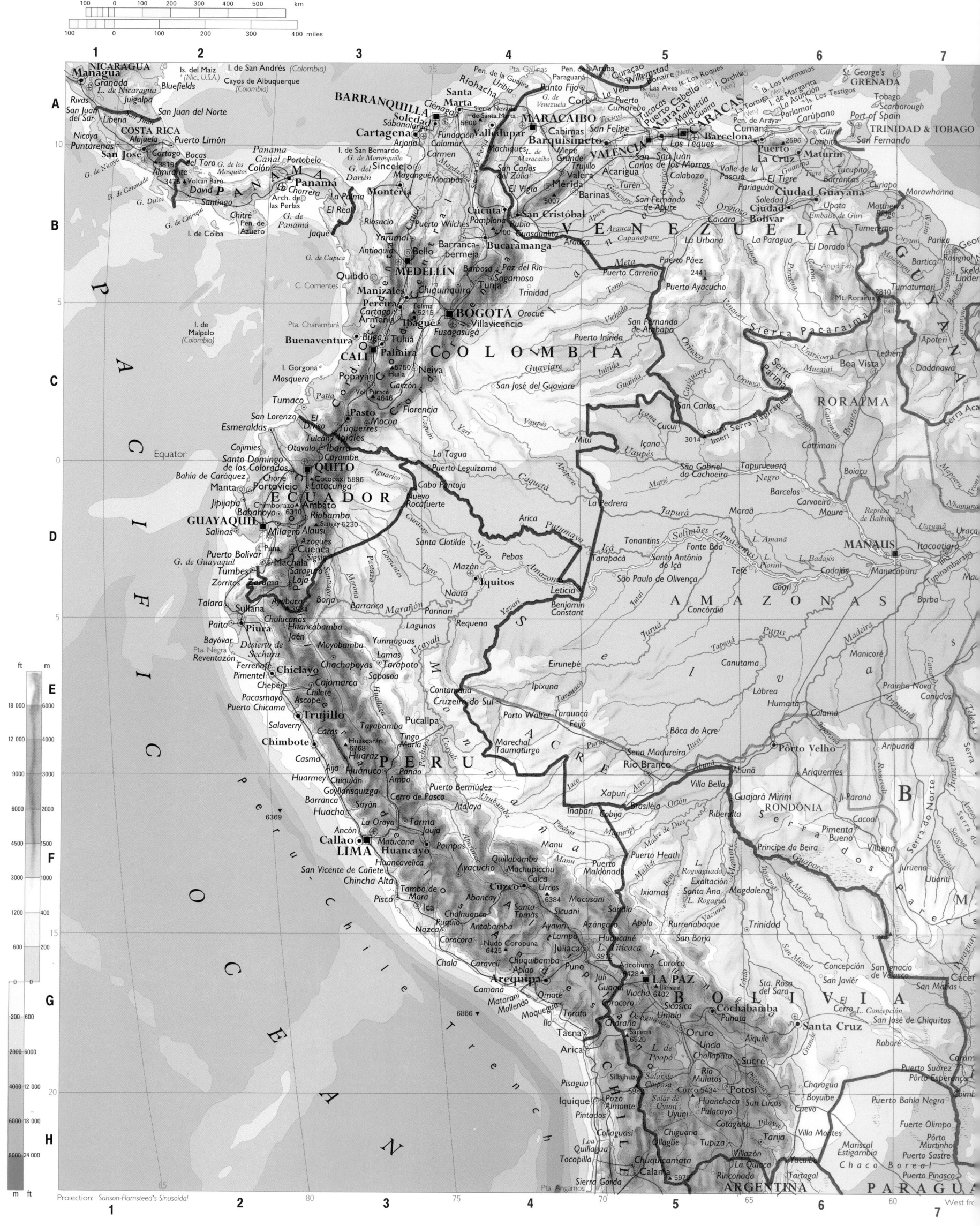

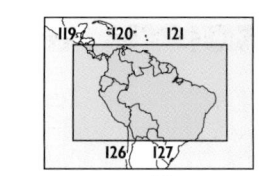

8   9   10   11   12   13

A

B

$A T L A N T I C$

$O C E A N$

Equator

C

D

FRENCH
GUIANA

SURINAM

Paramaribo

Nieuw Amsterdam

Cayenne

AMAPÁ

Macapá

I. de Maracá

I. Caviana
I. Mexiana

Marajó BELÉM

PARÁ

Santarém

Altamira

MARANHÃO

Imperatriz

Teresina

CEARÁ

FORTALEZA

São Luís

Parnaíba

Sobral

Mossoró

RIO GRANDE
DO NORTE

Natal

PIAUÍ

PARAÍBA

João Pessoa

Campina
Grande

Olinda

RECIFE

PERNAMBUCO

Jaboatão

Caruaru

Fernando de Noronha
(Braz.)

São Paulo
(Braz.)

TOCANTINS

Palmas

BAHIA

Maceió

ALAGOAS

SERGIPE

Aracaju

Feira de
Santana

SALVADOR

MATO GROSSO

Planalto do
Mato Grosso

GOIÁS

BRASÍLIA

Goiânia

DISTR.
FED.

Formosa

Anápolis

E

F

G

H

MINAS GERAIS

Belo Horizonte

Uberlândia

MATO GROSSO
DO SUL

Campo
Grande

SÃO PAULO

Ribeirão Prêto

Campinas

Vitória
Vila Velha

RIO DE JANEIRO

Niterói

Petrópolis

Trindade
(Braz.)

55   50   45   40   35   30

8   9   10   11   12   13

COPYRIGHT GEORGE PHILIP LTD.

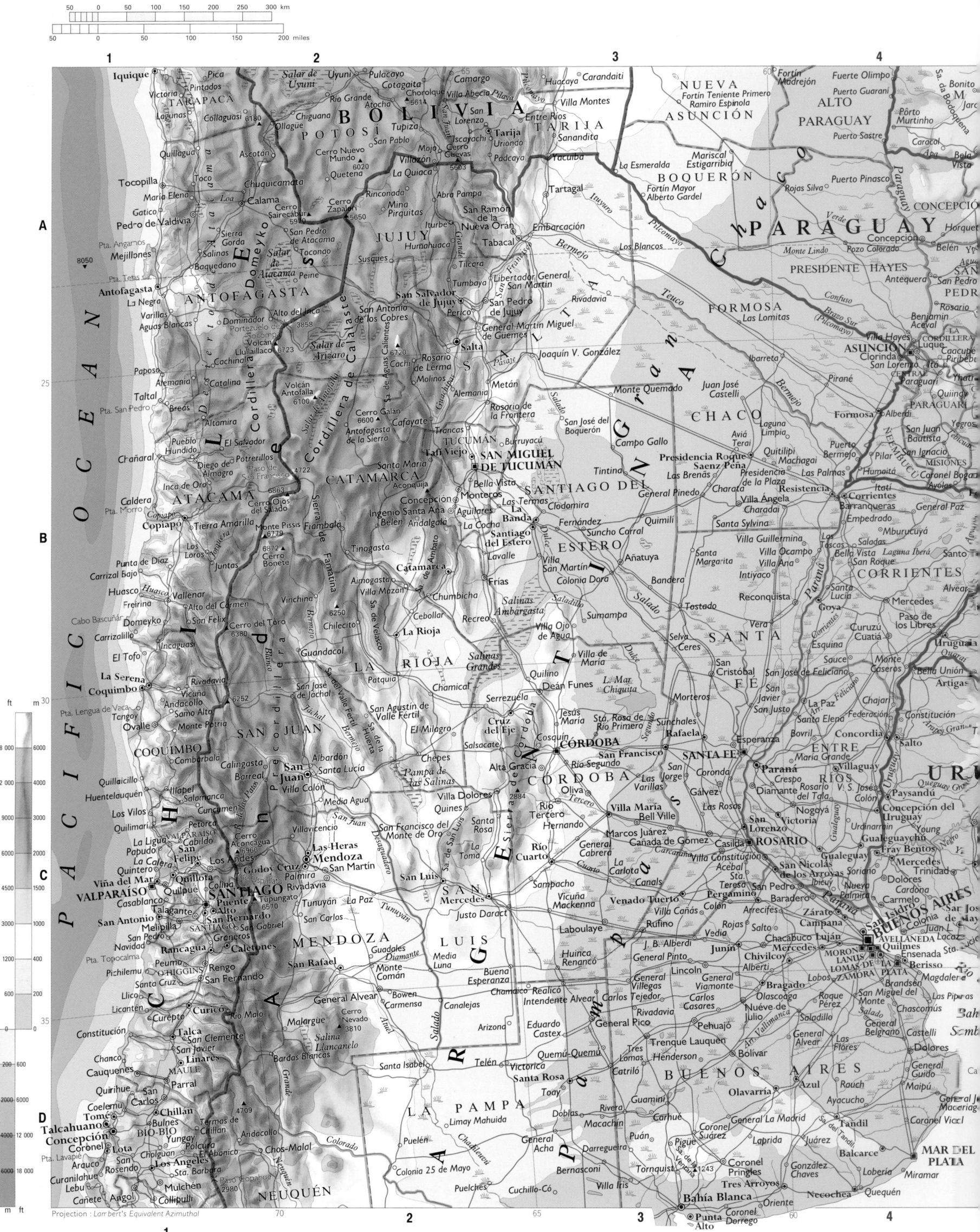

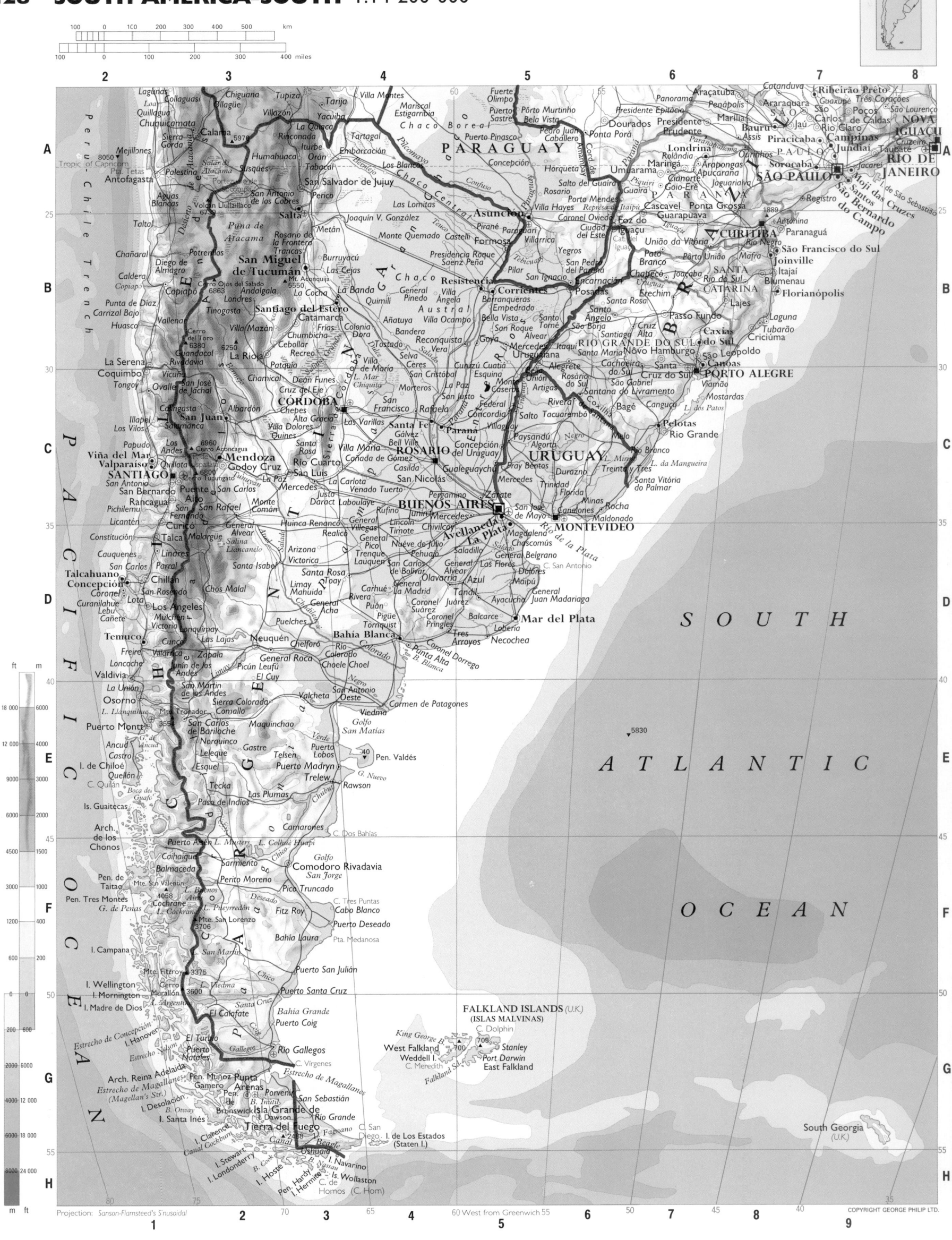

INDEX

The index contains the names of all the principal places and features shown on the World Maps. Each name is followed by an additional entry in italics giving the country or region within which it is located. The alphabetical order of names composed of two or more words is governed primarily by the first word and then by the second. This is an example of the rule:

Mīr Kūh, *Iran*. **71**   **E8**
Mīr Shahdād, *Iran* **71**   **E8**
Mira, *Italy* **29**   **C9**
Mira por vos Cay, *Bahamas* . . **121**   **B5**
Miraj, *India* **66**   **L9**

Physical features composed of a proper name (Erie) and a description (Lake) are positioned alphabetically by the proper name. The description is positioned after the proper name and is usually abbreviated:

Erie, L., *N. Amer.* **110**   **D4**

Where a description forms part of a settlement or administrative name however, it is always written in full and put in its true alphabetic position:

Mount Morris, *U.S.A.* **110**   **D7**

Names beginning with M' and Mc are indexed as if they were spelled Mac. Names beginning St. are alphabetised under Saint, but Sankt, Sint, Sant', Santa and San are all spelt in full and are alphabetised accordingly. If the same place name occurs two or more times in the index and all are in the same country, each is followed by the name of the administrative subdivision in which it is located. The names are placed in the alphabetical order of the subdivisions. For example:

Jackson, *Ky., U.S.A.* **108**   **G4**
Jackson, *Mich., U.S.A.* **108**   **D3**
Jackson, *Minn., U.S.A.* **112**   **D7**

The number in bold type which follows each name in the index refers to the number of the map page where that feature or place will be found. This is usually the largest scale at which the place or feature appears.

The letter and figure which are in bold type immediately after the page number give the grid square on the map page, within which the feature is situated. The letter represents the latitude and the figure the longitude.

In some cases the feature itself may fall within the specified square, while the name is outside. This is usually the case only with features which are larger than a grid square.

Rivers are indexed to their mouths or confluences, and carry the symbol → after their names. A solid square ■ follows the name of a country, while an open square □ refers to a first order administrative area.

ABBREVIATIONS USED IN THE INDEX

A.C.T. – Australian Capital Territory
Afghan. – Afghanistan
Ala. – Alabama
Alta. – Alberta
Amer. – America(n)
Arch. – Archipelago
Ariz. – Arizona
Ark. – Arkansas
Atl. Oc. – Atlantic Ocean
B. – Baie, Bahía, Bay, Bucht, Bugt
B.C. – British Columbia
Bangla. – Bangladesh
Barr. – Barrage
Bos.-H. – Bosnia-Herzegovina
C. – Cabo, Cap, Cape, Coast
C.A.R. – Central African Republic
C. Prov. – Cape Province
Calif. – California
Cent. – Central
Chan. – Channel
Colo. – Colorado
Conn. – Connecticut
Cord. – Cordillera
Cr. – Creek
Czech. – Czech Republic
D.C. – District of Columbia
Del. – Delaware
Dep. – Dependency
Des. – Desert
Dist. – District
Dj. – Djebel
Domin. – Dominica
Dom. Rep. – Dominican Republic
E. – East

E. Salv. – El Salvador
Eq. Guin. – Equatorial Guinea
Fla. – Florida
Falk. Is. – Falkland Is.
G. – Golfe, Golfo, Gulf, Guba, Gebel
Ga. – Georgia
Gt. – Great, Greater
Guinea-Biss. – Guinea-Bissau
H.K. – Hong Kong
H.P. – Himachal Pradesh
Hants. – Hampshire
Harb. – Harbor, Harbour
Hd. – Head
Hts. – Heights
I.(s). – Île, Ilha, Insel, Isla, Island, Isle
Ill. – Illinois
Ind. – Indiana
Ind. Oc. – Indian Ocean
Ivory C. – Ivory Coast
J. – Jabal, Jebel, Jazira
Junc. – Junction
K. – Kap, Kapp
Kans. – Kansas
Kep. – Kepulauan
Ky. – Kentucky
L. – Lac, Lacul, Lago, Lagoa, Lake, Limni, Loch, Lough
La. – Louisiana
Liech. – Liechtenstein
Lux. – Luxembourg
Mad. P. – Madhya Pradesh
Madag. – Madagascar
Man. – Manitoba
Mass. – Massachusetts

Md. – Maryland
Me. – Maine
Medit. S. – Mediterranean Sea
Mich. – Michigan
Minn. – Minnesota
Miss. – Mississippi
Mo. – Missouri
Mont. – Montana
Mozam. – Mozambique
Mt.(e) – Mont, Monte, Monti, Montaña, Mountain
N. – Nord, Norte, North, Northern, Nouveau
N.B. – New Brunswick
N.C. – North Carolina
N. Cal. – New Caledonia
N. Dak. – North Dakota
N.H. – New Hampshire
N.I. – North Island
N.J. – New Jersey
N. Mex. – New Mexico
N.S. – Nova Scotia
N.S.W. – New South Wales
N.W.T. – North West Territory
N.Y. – New York
N.Z. – New Zealand
Nebr. – Nebraska
Neths. – Netherlands
Nev. – Nevada
Nfld. – Newfoundland
Nic. – Nicaragua
O. – Oued, Ouadi
Occ. – Occidentale
Okla. – Oklahoma
Ont. – Ontario
Or. – Orientale

Oreg. – Oregon
Os. – Ostrov
Oz. – Ozero
P. – Pass, Passo, Pasul, Pulau
P.E.I. – Prince Edward Island
Pa. – Pennsylvania
Pac. Oc. – Pacific Ocean
Papua N.G. – Papua New Guinea
Pass. – Passage
Pen. – Peninsula, Péninsule
Phil. – Philippines
Pk. – Park, Peak
Plat. – Plateau
Prov. – Province, Provincial
Pt. – Point
Pta. – Ponta, Punta
Pte. – Pointe
Qué. – Québec
Queens. – Queensland
R. – Rio, River
R.I. – Rhode Island
Ra.(s). – Range(s)
Raj. – Rajasthan
Reg. – Region
Rep. – Republic
Res. – Reserve, Reservoir
S. – San, South, Sea
Si. Arabia – Saudi Arabia
S.C. – South Carolina
S. Dak. – South Dakota
S.I. – South Island
S. Leone – Sierra Leone
Sa. – Serra, Sierra
Sask. – Saskatchewan
Scot. – Scotland
Sd. – Sound

Sev. – Severnaya
Sib. – Siberia
Sprs. – Springs
St. – Saint
Sta. – Santa, Station
Ste. – Sainte
Sto. – Santo
Str. – Strait, Stretto
Switz. – Switzerland
Tas. – Tasmania
Tenn. – Tennessee
Tex. – Texas
Tg. – Tanjung
Trin. & Tob. – Trinidad & Tobago
U.A.E. – United Arab Emirates
U.K. – United Kingdom
U.S.A. – United States of America
Ut. P. – Uttar Pradesh
Va. – Virginia
Vdkhr. – Vodokhranilishche
Vf. – Vîrful
Vic. – Victoria
Vol. – Volcano
Vt. – Vermont
W. – Wadi, West
W. Va. – West Virginia
Wash. – Washington
Wis. – Wisconsin
Wlkp. – Wielkopolski
Wyo. – Wyoming
Yorks. – Yorkshire
Yug. – Yugoslavia

A Baña

A

A Baña, *Spain* 34 C2
A Cañiza, *Spain* 34 C2
A Coruña, *Spain* 34 B2
A Estrada, *Spain* 34 C2
A Fonsagrada, *Spain* 34 B3
A Guarda, *Spain* 34 D2
A Gudiña, *Spain* 34 C3
A Rúa, *Spain* 34 C3
Aachen, *Germany* 24 E2
Aalborg = Ålborg, *Denmark* 11 G3
Aalen, *Germany* 25 G6
A'âli an Nîl □, *Sudan* 81 F3
Aalst, *Belgium* 17 D4
Aalten, *Neths.* 17 C6
Aalter, *Belgium* 17 C3
Äänekoski, *Finland* 9 E21
Aarau, *Switz.* 25 H4
Aarberg, *Switz.* 25 H3
Aare →, *Switz.* 25 H4
Aargau □, *Switz.* 25 H4
Aarhus = Århus, *Denmark* 11 H4
Aarschot, *Belgium* 17 D4
Aba, *China* 58 A3
Aba, *Dem. Rep. of the Congo* 86 B3
Aba, *Nigeria* 83 D6
Âbâ, Jazîrat, *Sudan* 81 E3
Abadab, J., *Sudan* 80 D4
Ābādān, *Iran* 71 D6
Abade, *Ethiopia* 81 F4
Ābādeh, *Iran* 71 D7
Abadin, *Spain* 34 B3
Abadla, *Algeria* 78 B5
Abaetetuba, *Brazil* 125 D9
Abagnar Qi, *China* 56 C9
Abai, *Paraguay* 127 B4
Abak, *Nigeria* 83 E6
Abakaliki, *Nigeria* 83 D6
Abakan, *Russia* 51 D10
Abala, *Niger* 83 C5
Abalak, *Niger* 83 B6
Abalemma, *Niger* 83 B6
Abana, *Turkey* 72 B6
Abancay, *Peru* 124 F4
Abano Terme, *Italy* 29 C8
Abarán, *Spain* 33 G3
Abariringa, *Kiribati* 96 H10
Abarqū, *Iran* 71 D7
Abashiri, *Japan* 54 C12
Abashiri-Wan, *Japan* 54 C12
Abaújszántó, *Hungary* 42 B6
Abava →, *Latvia* 44 A8
Ābay = Nîl el Azraq →, *Sudan* 81 D3
Abay, *Kazakstan* 50 E8
Abaya, L., *Ethiopia* 81 F4
Abaza, *Russia* 50 D10
Abbadia San Salvatore, *Italy* 29 F8
'Abbāsābād, *Iran* 71 C8
Abbay = Nîl el Azraq →, *Sudan* 81 D3
Abbaye, Pt., *U.S.A.* 108 B1
Abbé, L., *Ethiopia* 81 E5
Abbeville, *France* 19 B8
Abbeville, *Ala., U.S.A.* 109 K3
Abbeville, *La., U.S.A.* 113 L8
Abbeville, *S.C., U.S.A.* 109 H4
Abbiategrasso, *Italy* 28 C5
Abbot Ice Shelf, *Antarctica* 5 D16
Abbottabad, *Pakistan* 68 B5
Abd al Kūrī, *Ind. Oc.* 74 E5
Ābdar, *Iran* 71 D7
'Abdolābād, *Iran* 71 C8
Abdulpur, *Bangla.* 69 G13
Abéché, *Chad* 79 F10
Abejar, *Spain* 32 D2
Abekr, *Sudan* 81 E2
Abengourou, *Ivory C.* 82 D4
Abenójar, *Spain* 35 G6
Åbenrå, *Denmark* 11 J3
Abensberg, *Germany* 25 G7
Abeokuta, *Nigeria* 83 D5
Aber, *Uganda* 86 B3
Aberaeron, *U.K.* 13 E3
Aberayron = Aberaeron, *U.K.* 13 E3
Aberchirder, *U.K.* 14 D6
Abercorn = Mbala, *Zambia* 87 D3
Abercorn, *Australia* 95 D5
Aberdare, *U.K.* 13 F4
Aberdare Ra., *Kenya* 86 C4
Aberdeen, *Australia* 95 E5
Aberdeen, *Canada* 105 C7
Aberdeen, *S. Africa* 88 E3
Aberdeen, *U.K.* 14 D6
Aberdeen, *Ala., U.S.A.* 109 J1
Aberdeen, *Idaho, U.S.A.* 114 E7
Aberdeen, *Md., U.S.A.* 108 F7
Aberdeen, *S. Dak., U.S.A.* 112 C5
Aberdeen, *Wash., U.S.A.* 116 D3
Aberdeen, City of □, *U.K.* 14 D6
Aberdeenshire □, *U.K.* 14 D6
Aberdovey = Aberdyfi, *U.K.* 13 E3
Aberdyfi, *U.K.* 13 E3
Aberfeldy, *U.K.* 14 E5
Abergavenny, *U.K.* 13 F4
Abergele, *U.K.* 12 D4
Abernathy, *U.S.A.* 113 J4
Abert, L., *U.S.A.* 114 E3
Aberystwyth, *U.K.* 13 E3
Abhā, *Si. Arabia* 74 D3
Abhar, *Iran* 71 B6
Abhayapuri, *India* 69 F14
Abia □, *Nigeria* 83 D6
Abide, *Turkey* 39 C11
Abidiya, *Sudan* 80 D3
Abidjan, *Ivory C.* 82 D4
Abilene, *Kans., U.S.A.* 112 F6
Abilene, *Tex., U.S.A.* 113 J5
Abingdon, *U.K.* 13 F6
Abingdon, *U.S.A.* 109 G5
Abington Reef, *Australia* 94 B4
Abitau →, *Canada* 105 B7
Abitibi →, *Canada* 102 B3
Abitibi, L., *Canada* 102 C4
Abiy Adi, *Ethiopia* 81 E4
Abkhaz Republic = Abkhazia □, *Georgia* 49 J5
Abkhazia □, *Georgia* 49 J5
Abminga, *Australia* 95 D1
Abnûb, *Egypt* 80 B3
Åbo = Turku, *Finland* 9 F20
Abocho, *Nigeria* 83 D6
Abohar, *India* 68 D6
Aboisso, *Ivory C.* 82 D4
Abomey, *Benin* 83 D5
Abong-Mbang, *Cameroon* 84 D2
Abonnema, *Nigeria* 83 E6
Abony, *Hungary* 42 C5
Aboso, *Ghana* 82 D4
Abou-Deïa, *Chad* 79 F9
Aboyne, *U.K.* 14 D6
Abra Pampa, *Argentina* 126 A2
Abraham L., *Canada* 104 C5
Abrantes, *Portugal* 35 F2
Abreojos, Pta., *Mexico* 118 B2
Abri, *Esh Shamâliya, Sudan* 80 C3
Abri, *Janub Kordofân, Sudan* 81 E3
Abrud, *Romania* 42 D8
Abruzzo □, *Italy* 29 F10
Absaroka Range, *U.S.A.* 114 D9
Abtenau, *Austria* 26 D6
Abu, *India* 68 G5
Abū al Abyad, *U.A.E.* 71 E7
Abū al Khaşīb, *Iraq* 71 D6
Abū 'Alī, *Si. Arabia* 71 E6
Abū 'Alī →, *Lebanon* 75 A4
Abu Ballas, *Egypt* 80 C2
Abu Deleiq, *Sudan* 81 D3
Abu Dhabi = Abū Ẓāby, *U.A.E.* 71 E7
Abu Dis, *Sudan* 80 D3
Abu Dom, *Sudan* 81 D3
Abū Du'ān, *Syria* 70 B3
Abu el Gairi, W. →, *Egypt* 75 F2
Abu Fatma, Ras, *Sudan* 80 C4
Abu Gabra, *Sudan* 81 E2
Abu Ga'da, W. →, *Egypt* 75 F1
Abu Gelba, *Sudan* 81 E3
Abu Gubeiha, *Sudan* 81 E3
Abu Habl, Khawr →, *Sudan* 81 E3
Abū Ḥadrīyah, *Si. Arabia* 71 E6
Abu Hamed, *Sudan* 80 D3
Abu Haraz, *An Nîl el Azraq, Sudan* 80 D3
Abu Haraz, *El Gezira, Sudan* 81 E3
Abu Haraz, *Esh Shamâliya, Sudan* 80 D3
Abu Higar, *Sudan* 81 E3
Abū Kamāl, *Syria* 70 C4
Abu Kuleiwat, *Sudan* 81 E2
Abū Madd, Ra's, *Si. Arabia* 70 E3
Abu Matariq, *Sudan* 81 E2
Abu Mendi, *Ethiopia* 81 E4
Abū Mūsā, *U.A.E.* 71 E7
Abu Qir, *Egypt* 80 H7
Abu Qireiya, *Egypt* 80 C4
Abu Qurqâs, *Egypt* 80 B3
Abu Şafāt, W. →, *Jordan* 75 E5
Abu Shagara, Ras, *Sudan* 80 C4
Abu Shanab, *Sudan* 81 E2
Abu Simbel, *Egypt* 80 C3
Abū Şukhayr, *Iraq* 70 D5
Abu Sultân, *Egypt* 80 H8
Abu Tabari, *Sudan* 80 D2
Abu Tig, *Egypt* 80 B3
Abu Tiga, *Sudan* 81 E3
Abu Tineitin, *Sudan* 81 E3
Abu Uruq, *Sudan* 81 D3
Abu Zabad, *Sudan* 81 E2
Abū Ẓāby, *U.A.E.* 71 E7
Abū Zeydābād, *Iran* 71 C6
Abuja, *Nigeria* 83 D6
Abukuma-Gawa →, *Japan* 54 E10
Abukuma-Sammyaku, *Japan* 54 F10
Abunã, *Brazil* 124 E5
Abunã →, *Brazil* 124 E5
Abune Yosef, *Ethiopia* 81 E4
Aburo, *Dem. Rep. of the Congo* 86 B3
Abut Hd., *N.Z.* 91 K3
Abuye Meda, *Ethiopia* 81 E4
Abwong, *Sudan* 81 F3
Åby, *Sweden* 11 F10
Aby, Lagune, *Ivory C.* 82 D4
Abyad, *Sudan* 81 E2
Åbybro, *Denmark* 11 G3
Acadia National Park, *U.S.A.* 109 C11
Açailândia, *Brazil* 125 D9
Acajutla, *El Salv.* 120 D2
Acámbaro, *Mexico* 118 D4
Acanthus, *Greece* 40 F7
Acaponeta, *Mexico* 118 C3
Acapulco, *Mexico* 119 D5
Acarai, Serra, *Brazil* 124 C7
Acarigua, *Venezuela* 124 B5
Acatlán, *Mexico* 119 D5
Acayucan, *Mexico* 119 D6
Accéglio, *Italy* 28 D4
Accomac, *U.S.A.* 108 G8
Accous, *France* 20 E3
Accra, *Ghana* 83 D4
Accrington, *U.K.* 12 D5
Acebal, *Argentina* 126 C3
Aceh □, *Indonesia* 62 D1
Acerra, *Italy* 31 B7
Aceuchal, *Spain* 35 G4
Achalpur, *India* 66 J10
Acheng, *China* 57 B14
Achenkirch, *Austria* 26 D4
Achensee, *Austria* 26 D4
Acher, *India* 68 H5
Achern, *Germany* 25 G4
Achill Hd., *Ireland* 15 C1
Achill I., *Ireland* 15 C1
Achim, *Germany* 24 B5
Achinsk, *Russia* 51 D10
Acıgöl, *Turkey* 39 D11
Acıpayam, *Turkey* 39 D11
Acireale, *Italy* 31 E8
Ackerman, *U.S.A.* 113 J10
Acklins I., *Bahamas* 121 B5
Acme, *Canada* 104 C6
Acme, *U.S.A.* 110 F5
Aconcagua, Cerro, *Argentina* 126 C2
Aconquija, Mt., *Argentina* 126 B2
Açores, Is. dos = Azores, *Atl. Oc.* 78 A1
Acornhoek, *S. Africa* 89 C5
Acquapendente, *Italy* 29 F8
Acquasanta Terme, *Italy* 29 F10
Acquasparta, *Italy* 29 F9
Acquaviva delle Fonti, *Italy* 31 B9
Ácqui Terme, *Italy* 28 D5
Acraman, L., *Australia* 95 E2
Acre = 'Akko, *Israel* 75 C4
Acre □, *Brazil* 124 E4
Acre →, *Brazil* 124 E5
Acri, *Italy* 31 C9
Acs, *Hungary* 42 C3
Actium, *Greece* 38 C2
Acton, *Canada* 110 C4
Acuña, *Mexico* 118 B4
Ad Dammām, *Si. Arabia* 71 E6
Ad Dāmūr, *Lebanon* 75 B4
Ad Dawādimī, *Si. Arabia* 70 E5
Ad Dawḥah, *Qatar* 71 E6
Ad Dawr, *Iraq* 70 C4
Ad Dir'īyah, *Si. Arabia* 70 E5
Ad Dīwānīyah, *Iraq* 70 D5
Ad Dujayl, *Iraq* 70 C5
Ad Duwayd, *Si. Arabia* 70 D4
Ada, *Ghana* 83 D5
Ada, *Serbia, Yug.* 42 E5
Ada, *Minn., U.S.A.* 112 B6
Ada, *Okla., U.S.A.* 113 H6
Adabiya, *Egypt* 75 F1
Adair, C., *Canada* 101 A12
Adaja →, *Spain* 34 D6
Adak I., *U.S.A.* 100 C2
Adamaoua, Massif de l', *Cameroon* 83 D7
Adamawa □, *Nigeria* 83 D7
Adamawa Highlands = Adamaoua, Massif de l', *Cameroon* 83 D7
Adamello, Mte., *Italy* 28 B7
Adami Tulu, *Ethiopia* 81 F4
Adaminaby, *Australia* 95 F4
Adams, *Mass., U.S.A.* 111 D11
Adams, *N.Y., U.S.A.* 111 C8
Adams, *Wis., U.S.A.* 112 D10
Adam's Bridge, *Sri Lanka* 66 Q11
Adams L., *Canada* 104 C5
Adams Mt., *U.S.A.* 116 D5
Adam's Peak, *Sri Lanka* 66 R12
Adamuz, *Spain* 35 G6
Adana, *Turkey* 70 B2
Adanero, *Spain* 34 E6
Adapazarı = Sakarya, *Turkey* 72 B4
Adar Gwagwa, J., *Sudan* 80 C4
Adarama, *Sudan* 81 D3
Adare, C., *Antarctica* 5 D11
Adarte, *Eritrea* 81 E5
Adaut, *Indonesia* 63 F8
Adavale, *Australia* 95 D3
Adda →, *Italy* 28 C6
Addis Ababa = Addis Abeba, *Ethiopia* 81 F4
Addis Abeba, *Ethiopia* 81 F4
Addis Alem, *Ethiopia* 81 F4
Addis Zemen, *Ethiopia* 81 E4
Addison, *U.S.A.* 110 D7
Addo, *S. Africa* 88 E4
Adebour, *Niger* 83 C7
Ādeh, *Iran* 70 B5
Adel, *U.S.A.* 109 K4
Adelaide, *Australia* 95 E2
Adelaide, *Bahamas* 120 A4
Adelaide, *S. Africa* 88 E4
Adelaide I., *Antarctica* 5 C17
Adelaide Pen., *Canada* 100 B10
Adelaide River, *Australia* 92 B5
Adelanto, *U.S.A.* 117 L9
Adele I., *Australia* 92 C3
Adélie, Terre, *Antarctica* 5 C10
Adélie Land = Adélie, Terre, *Antarctica* 5 C10
Ademuz, *Spain* 32 E3
Aden = Al 'Adan, *Yemen* 74 E4
Aden, G. of, *Asia* 74 E4
Adendorp, *S. Africa* 88 E3
Aderbissinat, *Niger* 83 B6
Adh Dhayd, *U.A.E.* 71 E7
Adhoi, *India* 68 H4
Adi, *Indonesia* 63 E8
Adi Arkai, *Ethiopia* 81 E4
Adi Daro, *Ethiopia* 81 E4
Adi Keyih, *Eritrea* 81 E4
Adi Kwala, *Eritrea* 81 E4
Adi Ugri, *Eritrea* 81 E4
Adieu, C., *Australia* 93 F5
Adieu Pt., *Australia* 92 C3
Adigala, *Ethiopia* 81 E5
Adige →, *Italy* 29 C9
Adigrat, *Ethiopia* 81 E4
Adıgüzel Barajı, *Turkey* 39 C11
Adilabad, *India* 66 K11
Adilcevaz, *Turkey* 73 C10
Adin Khel, *Afghan.* 66 C6
Adirondack Mts., *U.S.A.* 111 C10
Adıyaman, *Turkey* 73 D8
Adjohon, *Benin* 83 D5
Adjud, *Romania* 43 D12
Adjumani, *Uganda* 86 B3
Adlavik Is., *Canada* 103 A8
Adler, *Russia* 49 J4
Admer, *Algeria* 83 A6
Admiralty G., *Australia* 92 B4
Admiralty I., *U.S.A.* 104 B2
Admiralty Is., *Papua N. G.* 96 H6
Ado, *Nigeria* 83 D5
Ado-Ekiti, *Nigeria* 83 D6
Adok, *Sudan* 81 F3
Adola, *Ethiopia* 81 E5
Adonara, *Indonesia* 63 F6
Adoni, *India* 66 M10
Adony, *Hungary* 42 C3
Adour →, *France* 20 E2
Adra, *India* 69 H12
Adra, *Spain* 35 J7
Adrano, *Italy* 31 E7
Adrar, *Mauritania* 78 D3
Adrar des Iforas, *Algeria* 76 D4
Ádria, *Italy* 29 C9
Adrian, *Mich., U.S.A.* 108 E3
Adrian, *Tex., U.S.A.* 113 H3
Adriatic Sea, *Medit. S.* 6 G9
Adua, *Indonesia* 63 E7
Adwa, *Ethiopia* 81 E4
Adygea □, *Russia* 49 H5
Adzhar Republic = Ajaria □, *Georgia* 49 K6
Adzopé, *Ivory C.* 82 D4
Ægean Sea, *Medit. S.* 39 C7
Aerhtai Shan, *Mongolia* 60 B4
Ærø, *Denmark* 11 K4
Ærøskøbing, *Denmark* 11 K4
Aëtós, *Greece* 38 D3
'Afak, *Iraq* 70 C5
Afándou, *Greece* 36 C10
Afghanistan ■, *Asia* 66 C4
Afikpo, *Nigeria* 83 D6
Aflou, *Algeria* 78 B6
Afragóla, *Italy* 31 B7
Afram →, *Ghana* 83 D4
Afrera, *Ethiopia* 81 E5
Africa 76 E6
'Afrīn, *Syria* 70 B3
Afşin, *Turkey* 72 C7
Afton, *N.Y., U.S.A.* 111 D9
Afton, *Wyo., U.S.A.* 114 E8
Afuá, *Brazil* 125 D8
'Afula, *Israel* 75 C4
Afyon, *Turkey* 39 C12
Afyon □, *Turkey* 39 C12
Afyonkarahisar = Afyon, *Turkey* 39 C12
Aga, *Egypt* 80 H7
Agadès = Agadez, *Niger* 83 B6
Agadez, *Niger* 83 B6
Agadir, *Morocco* 78 B4
Agaete, *Canary Is.* 37 F4
Agaie, *Nigeria* 83 D6
Again, *Sudan* 81 F2
Ağapınar, *Turkey* 39 B12
Agar, *India* 68 H7
Agaro, *Ethiopia* 81 F4
Agartala, *India* 67 H17
Agăş, *Romania* 43 D11
Agassiz, *Canada* 104 D4
Agats, *Indonesia* 63 F9
Agawam, *U.S.A.* 111 D12
Agbélouvé, *Togo* 83 D5
Agboville, *Ivory C.* 82 D4
Ağcabädi, *Azerbaijan* 49 K8
Ağdam, *Azerbaijan* 49 L8
Ağdaş, *Azerbaijan* 49 K8
Agde, *France* 20 E7
Agde, C. d', *France* 20 E7
Agdzhabedi = Ağcabädi, *Azerbaijan* 49 K8
Agen, *France* 20 D4
Agerbæk, *Denmark* 11 J2
Agersø, *Denmark* 11 J5
Ageyevo, *Russia* 46 E9
Āgh Kand, *Iran* 71 B6
Aghireşu, *Romania* 43 D8
Aginskoye, *Russia* 51 D12
Ağlasun, *Turkey* 39 D12
Agly →, *France* 20 F7
Agnew, *Australia* 93 E3
Agnibilékrou, *Ivory C.* 82 D4
Agnita, *Romania* 43 E9
Agnone, *Italy* 29 G11
Agofie, *Ghana* 83 D5
Agogna →, *Italy* 28 C5
Agogo, *Sudan* 81 F2
Agön, *Sweden* 10 C11
Agon Coutainville, *France* 18 C5
Ágordo, *Italy* 29 B9
Agori, *India* 69 G10
Agouna, *Benin* 83 D5
Agout →, *France* 20 E5
Agra, *India* 68 F7
Agrakhanskiy Poluostrov, *Russia* 49 J8
Agramunt, *Spain* 32 D6
Agreda, *Spain* 32 D3
Ağri, *Turkey* 73 C10
Agri →, *Italy* 31 B9
Ağrı Dağı, *Turkey* 70 B5
Agriá, *Greece* 38 B5
Agrigento, *Italy* 30 E6
Agrínion, *Greece* 38 C3
Agrópoli, *Italy* 31 B7
Ağstafa, *Azerbaijan* 49 K7
Agua Caliente, *Baja Calif., Mexico* 117 N10
Agua Caliente, *Sinaloa, Mexico* 118 B3
Agua Caliente Springs, *U.S.A.* 117 N10
Água Clara, *Brazil* 125 H8
Agua Hechicero, *Mexico* 117 N10
Agua Prieta, *Mexico* 118 A3
Aguadilla, *Puerto Rico* 121 C6
Aguadulce, *Panama* 120 E3
Aguanga, *U.S.A.* 117 M10
Aguanish, *Canada* 103 B7
Aguanus →, *Canada* 103 B7
Aguapey →, *Argentina* 126 B4
Aguaray Guazú →, *Paraguay* 126 A4
Aguarico →, *Ecuador* 124 D3
Aguas →, *Spain* 32 D4
Aguas Blancas, *Chile* 126 A2
Aguas Calientes, Sierra de, *Argentina* 126 B2
Aguascalientes, *Mexico* 118 C4
Aguascalientes □, *Mexico* 118 C4
Agudo, *Spain* 35 G6
Águeda, *Portugal* 34 E2
Agueda →, *Spain* 34 D4
Aguelhok, *Mali* 83 B5
Aguié, *Niger* 83 C6
Aguilafuente, *Spain* 34 D6
Aguilar, *Spain* 35 H6
Aguilar de Campóo, *Spain* 34 C6
Aguilares, *Argentina* 126 B2
Aguilas, *Spain* 33 H3
Agüimes, *Canary Is.* 37 G4
Aguja, C. de la, *Colombia* 122 B3
Agulaa, *Ethiopia* 81 E4
Agulhas, C., *S. Africa* 88 E3
Agulo, *Canary Is.* 37 F2
Agung, *Indonesia* 62 F5
Agur, *Uganda* 86 B3
Agusan →, *Phil.* 61 G6
Ağva, *Turkey* 41 E13
Agvali, *Russia* 49 J8
Aha Mts., *Botswana* 88 B3
Ahaggar, *Algeria* 78 D7
Ahamansu, *Ghana* 83 D5
Ahar, *Iran* 70 B5
Ahat, *Turkey* 39 C11
Ahaus, *Germany* 24 C2
Ahipara B., *N.Z.* 91 F4
Ahir Dağı, *Turkey* 39 C12
Ahiri, *India* 66 K12
Ahlat, *Turkey* 73 C10
Ahlen, *Germany* 24 D3
Ahmad Wal, *Pakistan* 68 E1
Ahmadabad, *India* 68 H5
Aḩmadābād, *Khorāsān, Iran* 71 C9
Aḩmadābād, *Khorāsān, Iran* 71 C8
Aḩmadī, *Iran* 71 E8
Ahmadnagar, *India* 66 K9
Ahmadpur, *Pakistan* 68 E4
Ahmadpur Lamma, *Pakistan* 68 E4
Ahmar, *Ethiopia* 81 F5
Ahmedabad = Ahmadabad, *India* 68 H5
Ahmednagar = Ahmadnagar, *India* 66 K9
Ahmetbey, *Turkey* 41 E11
Ahmetler, *Turkey* 39 C11
Ahmetli, *Turkey* 39 C9
Ahoada, *Nigeria* 83 D6
Ahome, *Mexico* 118 B3
Ahoskie, *U.S.A.* 109 G7
Ahr →, *Germany* 24 E3
Ahram, *Iran* 71 D6
Ahrax Pt., *Malta* 36 D1
Ahrensbök, *Germany* 24 A6
Ahrensburg, *Germany* 24 B6
Āhū, *Iran* 71 C6
Ahuachapán, *El Salv.* 120 D2
Ahun, *France* 19 F9
Åhus, *Sweden* 11 J8
Ahvāz, *Iran* 71 D6
Ahvenanmaa = Åland, *Finland* 9 F19
Aḩwar, *Yemen* 74 E4
Ahzar →, *Mali* 83 B5
Ai →, *India* 69 F14
Ai-Ais, *Namibia* 88 D2
Aichach, *Germany* 25 G7
Aichi □, *Japan* 55 G8
Aigle, *Switz.* 25 J2
Aignay-le-Duc, *France* 19 E11
Aigoual, Mt., *France* 20 D7
Aigre, *France* 20 C4
Aigua, *Uruguay* 127 C5
Aigueperse, *France* 19 F10
Aigues →, *France* 21 D8
Aigues-Mortes, *France* 21 E8
Aigues-Mortes, G. d', *France* 21 E8
Aiguilles, *France* 21 D10
Aiguillon, *France* 20 D4
Aigurande, *France* 19 F8
Aihui, *China* 60 A7
Aija, *Peru* 124 E3
Aikawa, *Japan* 54 E9
Aiken, *U.S.A.* 109 J5
Ailao Shan, *China* 58 F3
Aileron, *Australia* 94 C1
Aillant-sur-Tholon, *France* 19 E10
Aillik, *Canada* 103 A8
Ailsa Craig, *U.K.* 14 F3
'Ailūn, *Jordan* 75 C4
Aim, *Russia* 51 D14
Aimere, *Indonesia* 63 F6
Aimogasta, *Argentina* 126 B2
Ain □, *France* 19 F12
Ain →, *France* 21 C9
Aïn Ben Tili, *Mauritania* 78 C4

Name	Page	Grid
Ain Dalla, *Egypt*	80	B2
Ain el Mafki, *Egypt*	80	B2
Ain Girba, *Egypt*	80	B2
Ain Murr, *Sudan*	80	C2
Ain Qeiqab, *Egypt*	80	B1
Aïn-Sefra, *Algeria*	78	B5
Ain Sheikh Murzûk, *Egypt*	80	B2
Ain Sudr, *Egypt*	75	F2
Ain Sukhna, *Egypt*	80	J8
Ain Zeitûn, *Egypt*	80	B2
Ainaži, *Latvia*	9	H21
Aínos Óros, *Greece*	38	C2
Ainsworth, *U.S.A.*	112	D5
Aiquile, *Bolivia*	124	G5
Aïr, *Niger*	83	B6
Air Force I., *Canada*	101	B12
Air Hitam, *Malaysia*	65	M4
Airaines, *France*	19	C8
Airdrie, *Canada*	104	C6
Airdrie, *U.K.*	14	F5
Aire →, *France*	19	C11
Aire →, *U.K.*	12	D7
Aire, I. de l', *Spain*	37	B11
Aire-sur-la-Lys, *France*	19	B9
Aire-sur-l'Adour, *France*	20	E3
Airlie Beach, *Australia*	94	C4
Airvault, *France*	18	F6
Aisch →, *Germany*	25	F6
Aisne □, *France*	19	C10
Aisne →, *France*	19	C9
Ait, *India*	69	G8
Aitana, Sierra de, *Spain*	33	G4
Aitkin, *U.S.A.*	112	B8
Aitolía Kai Akarnanía □, *Greece*	38	C3
Aitolikón, *Greece*	38	C3
Aiud, *Romania*	43	D8
Aix-en-Provence. *France*	21	E9
Aix-la-Chapelle = Aachen, *Germany*	24	E2
Aix-les-Bains, *France*	21	C9
Aixe-sur-Vienne, *France*	20	C5
Áíyina, *Greece*	38	D5
Aiyínion, *Greece*	40	F6
Aíyion, *Greece*	38	C4
Aizawl, *India*	67	H18
Aizenay, *France*	18	F5
Aizkraukle, *Latvia*	9	H21
Aizpute, *Latvia*	9	H19
Aizuwakamatsu, *Japan*	54	F9
Ajaccio, *France*	21	G12
Ajaccio, G. d', *France*	21	G12
Ajaigarh, *India*	69	G9
Ajalpan, *Mexico*	119	D5
Ajanta Ra., *India*	66	J9
Ajari Rep. = Ajaria □, *Georgia*	49	K6
Ajaria □, *Georgia*	49	K6
Ajax, *Canada*	110	C5
Ajdâbiyah, *Libya*	79	B10
Ajdovščina, *Slovenia*	29	C10
Ajibar, *Ethiopia*	81	E4
Ajka, *Hungary*	42	C2
'Ajmān, *U.A.E.*	71	E7
Ajmer, *India*	68	F6
Ajnala, *India*	68	D6
Ajo, *U.S.A.*	115	K7
Ajo, C. de, *Spain*	34	B7
Ajok, *Sudan*	81	F2
Ajuy, *Phil.*	61	F5
Ak Dağ, *Turkey*	39	E11
Ak Dağları, *Muğla, Turkey*	39	E11
Ak Dağları, *Sivas, Turkey*	72	C7
Akaba, *Togo*	83	D5
Akabira, *Japan*	54	C11
Akaki Beseka, *Ethiopia*	81	F4
Akala, *Sudan*	81	D4
Akamas □, *Cyprus*	36	D11
Akanthou, *Cyprus*	36	D12
Akarca, *Turkey*	39	C11
Akaroa, *N.Z.*	91	K4
Akasha, *Sudan*	80	C3
Akashi, *Japan*	55	G7
Akbarpur, *Bihar, India*	69	G10
Akbarpur, *Ut. P., India*	69	F10
Açaabat, *Turkey*	73	B8
Açadağ, *Turkey*	72	C7
Açakale, *Turkey*	73	D8
Açakoca, *Turkey*	72	B4
Açaova, *Turkey*	41	E13
Açcay, *Turkey*	39	E11
Açcay →, *Turkey*	39	D10
Akdağ, *Turkey*	39	C8
Akdağmadeni, *Turkey*	72	C6
Akelamo, *Indonesia*	63	D7
Åkers styckebruk, *Sweden*	10	E11
Åkersberga, *Sweden*	10	E12
Aketi, *Dem. Rep. of the Congo*	84	D4
Akhaïa □, *Greece*	38	C3
Akhalkalaki, *Georgia*	49	K6
Akhaltsikhe, *Georgia*	49	K6
Akharnaí, *Greece*	38	C5
Akhelóös →, *Greece*	38	C3
Akhendriá, *Greece*	39	G7
Akhisar, *Turkey*	39	C9
Akhladhókambos, *Greece*	38	D4
Akhmîm, *Egypt*	80	B3
Akhnur, *India*	69	C6
Akhtopol, *Bulgaria*	41	D11
Akhtuba →, *Russia*	49	G8
Akhtubinsk, *Russia*	49	F8
Akhty, *Russia*	49	K8
Akhtyrka = Okhtyrka, *Ukraine*	47	G8
Aki, *Japan*	55	H6
Akimiski I., *Canada*	102	B3
Akimovka, *Ukraine*	47	J8
Åkirkeby, *Denmark*	11	J8
Akita, *Japan*	54	E10
Akita □, *Japan*	54	E10
Akjoujt, *Mauritania*	82	B2
Akka, *Mali*	82	B4
Akkaya Tepesi, *Turkey*	39	D11
Akkeshi, *Japan*	54	C12
'Akko, *Israel*	75	C4
Akköy, *Turkey*	39	D9
Aklampa, *Benin*	83	D5
Aklavik, *Canada*	100	B6
Aklera, *India*	68	G7
Akmenė, *Lithuania*	44	B9
Akmenrags, *Latvia*	44	B8
Akmolinsk = Astana, *Kazakhstan*	50	D8
Akmonte = Almonte, *Spain*	35	H4
Akö, *Japan*	55	G7
Ako, *Nigeria*	83	C7
Akôbô →, *Sudan*	81	F3
Akobo →, *Ethiopia*	81	F3
Akola, *India*	66	J10
Akonolinga, *Cameroon*	83	E7
Akor, *Mali*	82	C3
Akordat, *Eritrea*	81	D4
Akosombo Dam, *Ghana*	83	D5
Akot, *Sudan*	81	F3
Akoupé, *Ivory C.*	82	D4
Akpatok I., *Canada*	101	B13
Åkrahamn, *Norway*	9	G11
Akranes, *Iceland*	8	D2
Akreïjit, *Mauritania*	82	B3
Akrítas Venétiko, Ákra, *Greece*	38	E3
Akron, *Colo., U.S.A.*	112	E3
Akron, *Ohio, U.S.A.*	110	E3
Akrotiri, *Cyprus*	36	E11
Akrotíri, Ákra, *Greece*	41	F9
Akrotiri Bay, *Cyprus*	36	E12
Aksai Chin, *India*	69	B8
Aksaray, *Turkey*	70	B2
Aksay, *Kazakstan*	50	D6
Akşehir, *Turkey*	70	B1
Akşehir Gölü, *Turkey*	72	C4
Akstafa = Ağstafa, *Azerbaijan*	49	K7
Aksu, *China*	60	B3
Aksu →, *Turkey*	72	D4
Aksum, *Ethiopia*	81	E4
Aktash, *Russia*	48	C11
Aktogay, *Kazakstan*	50	E8
Aktsyabrski, *Belarus*	47	F5
Aktyubinsk = Aqtöbe, *Kazakstan*	50	D6
Aku, *Nigeria*	83	D6
Akure, *Nigeria*	83	D6
Akureyri, *Iceland*	8	D4
Akuseki-Shima, *Japan*	55	K4
Akusha, *Russia*	49	J8
Akwa-Ibom □, *Nigeria*	83	E6
Akyab = Sittwe, *Burma*	67	J18
Akyazı, *Turkey*	72	B4
Al 'Adan, *Yemen*	74	E4
Al Aḩsā = Hasa □, *Si. Arabia*	71	E6
Al Ajfar, *Si. Arabia*	70	E4
Al Amādīyah, *Iraq*	70	B4
Al 'Amārah, *Iraq*	70	D5
Al 'Aqabah, *Jordan*	75	F4
Al Arak, *Syria*	70	C3
Al 'Aramah, *Si. Arabia*	70	E5
Al Arṭāwīyah, *Si. Arabia*	70	E5
Al 'Āṣimah = 'Ammān □, *Jordan*	75	D5
Al 'Assāfīyah, *Si. Arabia*	70	D3
Al 'Ayn, *Oman*	71	E7
Al 'Ayn, *Si. Arabia*	70	E3
Al 'Azamīyah, *Iraq*	70	C5
Al 'Azīzīyah, *Iraq*	70	C5
Al Bāb, *Syria*	70	B3
Al Bad', *Si. Arabia*	70	D2
Al Bādī, *Iraq*	70	C4
Al Baḩrah, *Kuwait*	70	D5
Al Baḩral Mayyit = Dead Sea, *Asia*	75	D4
Al Balqā' □, *Jordan*	75	C4
Al Bārūk, J., *Lebanon*	75	B4
Al Başrah, *Iraq*	70	D5
Al Batḩā, *Iraq*	70	D5
Al Batrūn, *Lebanon*	75	A4
Al Baydā, *Libya*	79	B10
Al Biqā, *Lebanon*	75	A5
Al Bi'r, *Si. Arabia*	70	D3
Al Burayj, *Syria*	75	A5
Al Faḍilī, *Si. Arabia*	71	E6
Al Fallūjah, *Iraq*	70	C4
Al Fāw, *Iraq*	71	D6
Al Fujayrah, *U.A.E.*	71	E8
Al Ghadaf, W. →, *Jordan*	75	D5
Al Ghammās, *Iraq*	70	D5
Al Ghazālah, *Si. Arabia*	70	E4
Al Ḩābah, *Si. Arabia*	70	E5
Al Ḩadīthah, *Iraq*	70	C4
Al Ḩadīthah, *Si. Arabia*	70	D6
Al Ḩadr, *Iraq*	70	C4
Al Ḩājānah, *Syria*	75	B5
Al Hajar al Gharbi, *Oman*	71	E8
Al Ḩāmad, *Si. Arabia*	70	D3
Al Hamdāniyah, *Syria*	70	C3
Al Ḩamīdīyah, *Syria*	75	A4
Al Ḩammār, *Iraq*	70	D5
Al Ḩanākīyah, *Si. Arabia*	70	E4
Al Ḩarīr, W. →, *Jordan*	75	C4
Al Ḩasā, W. →, *Jordan*	75	D4
Al Ḩayy, *Iraq*	70	C5
Al Ḩijarah, *Asia*	70	D4
Al Ḩillah, *Iraq*	70	C5
Al Hindīyah, *Iraq*	70	C5
Al Hirmil, *Lebanon*	75	A5
Al Hoceïma, *Morocco*	78	A5
Al Ḩudaydah, *Yemen*	74	E3
Al Hufūf, *Si. Arabia*	71	E6
Al Ḩumaydah, *Si. Arabia*	70	D2
Al Ḩunayy, *Si. Arabia*	71	E6
Al Ḩunayy, *Si. Arabia*	70	D3
Al Jafr, *Jordan*	75	E5
Al Jaghbūb, *Libya*	79	C10
Al Jahrah, *Kuwait*	70	D5
Al Jalāmīd, *Si. Arabia*	70	D3
Al Jamalīyah, *Qatar*	71	E6
Al Janūb □, *Lebanon*	75	B4
Al Jawf, *Libya*	79	D10
Al Jawf, *Si. Arabia*	70	D3
Al Jazirah, *Iraq*	70	C5
Al Jithāmīyah, *Si. Arabia*	70	E4
Al Jubayl, *Si. Arabia*	71	E6
Al Jubaylah, *Si. Arabia*	70	E5
Al Jubb, *Si. Arabia*	70	E4
Al Junaynah, *Sudan*	79	F10
Al Kabā'ish, *Iraq*	70	D5
Al Karak, *Jordan*	75	D4
Al Karak □, *Jordan*	75	E5
Al Kāzim Tyah, *Iraq*	70	C5
Al Khābūra, *Oman*	71	F8
Al Khafjī, *Si. Arabia*	71	E6
Al Khalīl, *West Bank*	75	D4
Al Khāliş, *Iraq*	70	C5
Al Kharsānīyah, *Si. Arabia*	71	E6
Al Khaşab, *Oman*	71	E8
Al Khawr, *Qatar*	71	E6
Al Khiḍr, *Iraq*	70	D5
Al Khiyām, *Lebanon*	75	B4
Al Khums, *Libya*	79	B8
Al Kiswah, *Syria*	75	B5
Al Kūfah, *Iraq*	70	C5
Al Kufrah, *Libya*	79	D10
Al Kuhayfīyah, *Si. Arabia*	70	E4
Al Kūt, *Iraq*	70	C5
Al Kuwayt, *Kuwait*	70	D5
Al Labwah, *Lebanon*	75	A5
Al Lādhiqīyah, *Syria*	70	C2
Al Līth, *Si. Arabia*	74	C3
Al Liwā', *Oman*	71	E8
Al Luḩayyah, *Yemen*	74	D3
Al Madīnah, *Iraq*	70	D5
Al Madīnah, *Si. Arabia*	70	E3
Al Mafraq, *Jordan*	75	C5
Al Maḩmūdīyah, *Iraq*	70	C5
Al Majma'ah, *Si. Arabia*	70	E5
Al Makhruq, W. →, *Jordan*	75	D6
Al Makhūl, *Si. Arabia*	70	E4
Al Manāmah, *Bahrain*	71	E6
Al Maqwa', *Kuwait*	70	D5
Al Marj, *Libya*	79	B10
Al Maṭlā, *Kuwait*	70	D5
Al Mawjib, W. →, *Jordan*	75	D4
Al Mawşil, *Iraq*	70	B4
Al Mayādin, *Syria*	70	C4
Al Mazār, *Jordan*	75	D4
Al Midhnab, *Si. Arabia*	70	E5
Al Minā', *Lebanon*	75	A4
Al Miqdādīyah, *Iraq*	70	C5
Al Mubarraz, *Si. Arabia*	71	E6
Al Mudawwarah, *Jordan*	75	F5
Al Mughayrā', *U.A.E.*	71	E7
Al Muḩarraq, *Bahrain*	71	E6
Al Mukallā, *Yemen*	74	E4
Al Mukhā, *Yemen*	74	E3
Al Musayjīd, *Si. Arabia*	70	E3
Al Musayyib, *Iraq*	70	C5
Al Muwayḩ, *Si. Arabia*	80	C5
Al Muwayliḩ, *Si. Arabia*	70	E2
Al Owuho = Otukpa, *Nigeria*	83	D6
Al Qā'im, *Iraq*	70	C4
Al Qalībah, *Si. Arabia*	70	D3
Al Qāmishlī, *Syria*	70	B4
Al Qaryatayn, *Syria*	70	A6
Al Qaşīm, *Si. Arabia*	70	E4
Al Qaţ'ā, *Syria*	70	C4
Al Qaţīf, *Si. Arabia*	71	E6
Al Qaţrānah, *Jordan*	75	D5
Al Qaţrūn, *Libya*	79	D9
Al Qayşūmah, *Si. Arabia*	70	D5
Al Quds = Jerusalem, *Israel*	75	D4
Al Qunayţirah, *Syria*	75	C4
Al Qunfudhah, *Si. Arabia*	80	D5
Al Qurnah, *Iraq*	70	D5
Al Quşayr, *Iraq*	70	D5
Al Quşayr, *Syria*	75	A5
Al Qutayfah, *Syria*	75	B5
Al 'Ubaylah, *Si. Arabia*	74	C5
Al 'Uḍaylīyah, *Si. Arabia*	71	E6
Al 'Ulā, *Si. Arabia*	70	E3
Al 'Uqayr, *Si. Arabia*	71	E6
Al 'Uthmānīyah, *Si. Arabia*	71	E6
Al 'Uwaynid, *Si. Arabia*	70	E5
Al 'Uwayqīlah, *Si. Arabia*	70	D4
Al 'Uyūn, *Ḩijāz, Si. Arabia*	70	E3
Al 'Uyūn, *Najd, Si. Arabia*	70	E4
Al 'Uzayr, *Iraq*	70	D5
Al Wajh, *Si. Arabia*	70	E3
Al Wakrah, *Qatar*	71	E6
Al Wannān, *Si. Arabia*	70	E6
Al Waqbah, *Si. Arabia*	70	D5
Al Wusayl, *Qatar*	71	E6
Ala, *Italy*	28	C8
Ala Dağ, *Turkey*	73	C10
Alabama □, *U.S.A.*	109	J2
Alabama →, *U.S.A.*	109	J2
Alabaster, *U.S.A.*	109	J2
Alaca, *Turkey*	72	B6
Alaçam, *Turkey*	39	B10
Alaçam Dağları, *Turkey*	39	B10
Alaçatı, *Turkey*	39	C8
Alachua, *U.S.A.*	109	L4
Alaejos, *Spain*	34	D5
Alaérma, *Greece*	36	C9
Alagir, *Russia*	49	J7
Alagna Valsésia, *Italy*	28	C4
Alagoa Grande, *Brazil*	125	E11
Alagoas □, *Brazil*	125	E11
Alagoinhas, *Brazil*	125	F11
Alagón, *Spain*	32	D3
Alagón →, *Spain*	34	F4
Alaior, *Spain*	37	B11
Alajero, *Canary Is.*	37	F2
Alajuela, *Costa Rica*	120	D3
Alakamisy, *Madag.*	89	C8
Alaknanda →, *India*	69	D8
Alamarvdasht, *Iran*	71	E7
Alamata, *Ethiopia*	81	E4
Alameda, *Calif., U.S.A.*	116	H4
Alameda, *N. Mex., U.S.A.*	115	J10
Alaminos, *Phil.*	61	C3
Alamo, *U.S.A.*	117	J11
Alamo Crossing, *U.S.A.*	117	L13
Alamogordo, *U.S.A.*	115	K11
Alamos, *Mexico*	118	B3
Alamosa, *U.S.A.*	115	H11
Åland, *Finland*	9	F19
Alandroal, *Portugal*	35	G3
Ålands hav, *Sweden*	9	F18
Alandur, *India*	66	N12
Alange, Presa de, *Spain*	35	G4
Alania = North Ossetia □, *Russia*	49	J7
Alanís, *Spain*	35	G5
Alanya, *Turkey*	70	B1
Alaotra, Farihin', *Madag.*	89	B8
Alapayevsk, *Russia*	50	D7
Alar del Rey, *Spain*	34	C6
Alaraz, *Spain*	34	E5
Alarcón, Embalse de, *Spain*	32	F2
Alaşehir, *Turkey*	39	C10
Alaska □, *U.S.A.*	100	B5
Alaska, G. of, *Pac. Oc.*	100	C5
Alaska Peninsula, *U.S.A.*	100	C4
Alaska Range, *U.S.A.*	100	B4
Alássio, *Italy*	28	E5
Ålåt, *Azerbaijan*	49	L9
Alatri, *Italy*	29	G10
Alatyr, *Russia*	48	C8
Alatyr →, *Russia*	48	C8
Alausi, *Ecuador*	124	D3
Álava □, *Spain*	32	C2
Álava, C., *U.S.A.*	114	B1
Alaverdi, *Armenia*	49	K7
Alavus, *Finland*	9	E20
Alawoona, *Australia*	95	E3
'Alayh, *Lebanon*	75	B4
Alazani →, *Azerbaijan*	49	K8
Alba, *Italy*	28	D5
Alba □, *Romania*	43	D8
Alba Adriática, *Italy*	29	F10
Alba de Tormes, *Spain*	34	E5
Alba-Iulia, *Romania*	43	D8
Albac, *Romania*	42	D7
Albacete, *Spain*	33	F3
Albacete □, *Spain*	33	G3
Albacutya, L., *Australia*	95	F3
Ålbæk, *Denmark*	11	G4
Ålbæk Bugt, *Denmark*	11	G4
Albaida, *Spain*	33	G4
Albalate de las Nogueras, *Spain*	32	E2
Albalate del Arzobispo, *Spain*	32	D4
Alban, *France*	20	E6
Albanel, L., *Canada*	102	B5
Albania ■, *Europe*	40	E4
Albano Laziale, *Italy*	29	G9
Albany, *Australia*	93	G2
Albany, *Ga., U.S.A.*	109	K3
Albany, *N.Y., U.S.A.*	111	D11
Albany, *Oreg., U.S.A.*	114	D2
Albany, *Tex., U.S.A.*	113	J5
Albany →, *Canada*	102	B3
Albardón, *Argentina*	126	C2
Albarracín, *Spain*	32	E3
Albarracín, Sierra de, *Spain*	32	E3
Albatera, *Spain*	33	G4
Albatross B., *Australia*	94	A3
Albegna →, *Italy*	29	F8
Albemarle, *U.S.A.*	109	H5
Albemarle Sd., *U.S.A.*	109	H7
Albenga, *Italy*	28	D5
Alberche →, *Spain*	34	F6
Alberdi, *Paraguay*	126	B4
Alberes, Mts., *France*	20	F6
Ålborga, *Sweden*	11	F10
Albersdorf, *Germany*	24	A5
Albert, *France*	19	C9
Albert, L., *Australia*	95	F2
Albert Edward Ra., *Australia*	92	C4
Albert L., *Africa*	86	B3
Albert Lea, *U.S.A.*	112	D8
Albert Nile →, *Uganda*	86	B3
Albert Town, *Bahamas*	121	B5
Alberta □, *Canada*	104	C6
Alberti, *Argentina*	126	C3
Albertínia, *S. Africa*	88	E3
Albertirsa, *Hungary*	42	C4
Alberton, *Canada*	103	C7
Albertville = Kalemie, *Dem. Rep. of the Congo*	86	D2
Albertville, *France*	21	C10
Albertville, *U.S.A.*	109	H2
Albi, *France*	20	E6
Albia, *U.S.A.*	112	E8
Albina, *Surinam*	125	B8
Albina, Ponta, *Angola*	88	B1
Albino, *Italy*	28	C6
Albion, *Mich., U.S.A.*	108	D3
Albion, *Nebr., U.S.A.*	112	E6
Albion, *Pa., U.S.A.*	110	E4
Albocácer, *Spain*	32	E5
Albolote, *Spain*	35	H7
Alborán, *Medit. S.*	35	K7
Alborea, *Spain*	33	F3
Ålborg, *Denmark*	11	G3
Ålborg Bugt, *Denmark*	11	H4
Alborz, Reshteh-ye Kūhhā-ye, *Iran*	71	C7
Albox, *Spain*	33	H2
Albufeira, *Portugal*	35	H2
Albula →, *Switz.*	25	J5
Albuñol, *Spain*	35	J7
Albuquerque, *U.S.A.*	115	J10
Albuquerque, Cayos de, *Caribbean*	120	D3
Alburg, *U.S.A.*	111	B11
Alburno, Mte., *Italy*	31	B8
Alburquerque, *Spain*	35	F4
Albury-Wodonga, *Australia*	95	F4
Alcácer do Sal, *Portugal*	35	G2
Alcáçovas, *Portugal*	35	G2
Alcalá de Chivert, *Spain*	32	E5
Alcalá de Guadaira, *Spain*	35	H5
Alcalá de Henares, *Spain*	34	E7
Alcalá de los Gazules, *Spain*	35	J5
Alcalá del Júcar, *Spain*	33	F3
Alcalá del Río, *Spain*	35	H5
Alcalá del Valle, *Spain*	35	J5
Alcalá la Real, *Spain*	35	H7
Álcamo, *Italy*	30	E5
Alcanadre, *Spain*	32	C2
Alcanadre →, *Spain*	32	D4
Alcanar, *Spain*	32	E5
Alcanede, *Portugal*	35	F2
Alcanena, *Portugal*	35	F2
Alcañices, *Spain*	34	D4
Alcañiz, *Spain*	32	D4
Alcântara, *Brazil*	125	D10
Alcántara, *Spain*	34	F4
Alcántara, Embalse de, *Spain*	34	F4
Alcantarilla, *Spain*	33	H3
Alcaracejos, *Spain*	35	G6
Alcaraz, *Spain*	33	G2
Alcaraz, Sierra de, *Spain*	33	G2
Alcaudete, *Spain*	35	H6
Alcázar de San Juan, *Spain*	35	F7
Alchevsk, *Ukraine*	47	H10
Alcira = Alzira, *Spain*	33	F4
Alcobaça, *Portugal*	35	F2
Alcobendas, *Spain*	34	E7
Alcolea del Pinar, *Spain*	32	D2
Alcora, *Spain*	32	E4
Alcorcón, *Spain*	34	E7
Alcoutim, *Portugal*	35	H3
Alcova, *U.S.A.*	114	E10
Alcoy, *Spain*	33	G4
Alcubierre, Sierra de, *Spain*	32	D4
Alcublas, *Spain*	32	F4
Alcúdia, *Spain*	37	B10
Alcudia, B. d', *Spain*	37	B10
Alcudia, Sierra de la, *Spain*	35	G6
Aldabra Is., *Seychelles*	77	G8
Aldama, *Mexico*	119	C5
Aldan, *Russia*	51	D13
Aldan →, *Russia*	51	C13
Aldea, Pta. de la, *Canary Is.*	37	G4
Aldeburgh, *U.K.*	13	E9
Alder Pk., *U.S.A.*	116	K5
Alderney, *U.K.*	13	H5
Aldershot, *U.K.*	13	F7
Åled, *Sweden*	11	H6
Aledo, *U.S.A.*	112	E9
Alefa, *Ethiopia*	81	E4
Aleg, *Mauritania*	82	B2
Alegranza, *Canary Is.*	37	E6
Alegranza, I., *Canary Is.*	37	E6
Alegre, *Brazil*	127	A7
Alegrete, *Brazil*	127	B4
Aleisk, *Russia*	50	D9
Aleksandriya = Oleksandriya, *Kirovohrad, Ukraine*	47	H7
Aleksandriya = Oleksandriya, *Rivne, Ukraine*	47	G4
Aleksandriyskaya, *Russia*	49	J8
Aleksandrov, *Russia*	46	D10
Aleksandrov Gay, *Russia*	48	E9
Aleksandrovac, *Serbia, Yug.*	40	C5
Aleksandrovac, *Serbia, Yug.*	40	B5
Aleksandrovka = Oleksandrovka, *Ukraine*	47	H7
Aleksandrovo, *Bulgaria*	41	C8
Aleksandrovsk-Sakhalinskiy, *Russia*	51	D15
Aleksandrów Kujawski, *Poland*	45	F5
Aleksandrów Łódzki, *Poland*	45	G6
Alekseyevka, *Samara, Russia*	48	D10
Alekseyevka, *Voronezh, Russia*	47	G10
Aleksin, *Russia*	46	E9
Aleksinac, *Serbia, Yug.*	40	C5
Além Paraíba, *Brazil*	127	A7
Alemania, *Argentina*	126	B2
Alemania, *Chile*	126	B2
Alençon, *France*	18	D7
Alenquer, *Portugal*	35	F2
Alenuihaha Channel, *U.S.A.*	106	H17
Alépé, *Ivory C.*	82	D4
Aleppo = Ḩalab, *Syria*	70	B3
Aléria, *France*	21	F13
Alès, *France*	21	D8
Aleşd, *Romania*	42	C7
Alessándria, *Italy*	28	D5
Alestrup, *Denmark*	11	H3
Ålesund, *Norway*	9	E12
Alet-les-Bains, *France*	20	F6
Aletschhorn, *Switz.*	25	J4
Aleutian Is., *Pac. Oc.*	100	C1
Aleutian Trench, *Pac. Oc.*	96	C10

Alexander, U.S.A. 112 B3
Alexander, Mt., Australia .. 93 E3
Alexander Arch., U.S.A. .. 100 C6
Alexander Bay, S. Africa .. 88 D2
Alexander City, U.S.A. .. 109 J3
Alexander I., Antarctica .. 5 C17
Alexandra, Australia 95 F4
Alexandra, N.Z. 91 L2
Alexandra Falls, Canada .. 104 A5
Alexandria = El Iskandarîya,
  Egypt 80 H7
Alexandria, B.C., Canada . 104 C4
Alexandria, Ont., Canada . 102 C5
Alexandria, Romania 43 G10
Alexandria, S. Africa 88 E4
Alexandria, U.K. 14 F4
Alexandria, La., U.S.A. .. 113 K8
Alexandria, Minn., U.S.A. 112 C7
Alexandria, S. Dak., U.S.A. 112 D6
Alexandria, Va., U.S.A. .. 108 F7
Alexandria Bay, U.S.A. .. 111 B9
Alexandroúpolis, Greece .. 41 F9
Alexis →, Canada 103 B8
Alexis Creek, Canada 104 C4
Alfabia, Spain 37 B9
Alfambra, Spain 32 E3
Alfândega da Fé, Portugal . 34 D4
Alfaro, Spain 32 C3
Alfatar, Bulgaria 41 C11
Alfaz del Pi, Spain 33 G4
Alfeld, Germany 24 D5
Alfenas, Brazil 127 A6
Alfiós →, Greece 38 D3
Alföld, Hungary 42 D5
Alfonsine, Italy 29 D9
Alford, Aberds., U.K. 14 D6
Alford, Lincs., U.K. 12 D8
Alfred, Maine, U.S.A. .. 111 C14
Alfred, N.Y., U.S.A. 110 D7
Alfreton, U.K. 12 D6
Alfta, Sweden 10 C10
Alga, Kazakstan 50 E6
Algaida, Spain 37 B9
Algar, Spain 35 J5
Ålgård, Norway 9 G11
Algarinejo, Spain 35 H6
Algarve, Portugal 35 J2
Algeciras, Spain 35 J5
Algemesí, Spain 33 F4
Alger, Algeria 78 A6
Algeria ■, Africa 78 C6
Alghero, Italy 30 B1
Älghult, Sweden 11 G9
Algiers = Alger, Algeria .. 78 A6
Algoa B., S. Africa 88 E4
Algodonales, Spain 35 J5
Algodor →, Spain 34 F7
Algoma, U.S.A. 108 C2
Algona, U.S.A. 112 D7
Algonac, U.S.A. 110 D2
Algonquin Prov. Park,
  Canada 102 C4
Algorta, Uruguay 128 C5
Alhama de Almería, Spain . 35 J8
Alhama de Aragón, Spain . 32 D3
Alhama de Granada, Spain . 35 H7
Alhama de Murcia, Spain . 33 H3
Alhambra, U.S.A. 117 L8
Alhaurín el Grande, Spain . 35 J6
Alhucemas = Al Hoceïma,
  Morocco 78 A5
'Alī al Gharbī, Iraq 70 C5
'Alī ash Sharqī, Iraq 70 C5
Äli Bayramlı, Azerbaijan .. 49 L9
'Alī Khēl, Afghan. 68 C3
Ali Sahîh, Djibouti 81 E5
Alī Shāh, Iran 70 B5
Ália, Italy 30 E6
'Alīābād, Khorāsān, Iran . 71 C8
'Alīābād, Kordestān, Iran . 70 C5
'Alīābād, Yazd, Iran 71 D7
Aliaga, Spain 32 E4
Aliağa, Turkey 39 C8
Aliákmon →, Greece 40 F6
Alibo, Ethiopia 81 F4
Alibori →, Benin 83 C5
Alibunar, Serbia, Yug. .. 42 E5
Alicante, Spain 33 G4
Alicante □, Spain 33 G4
Alice, S. Africa 88 E4
Alice, U.S.A. 113 M5
Alice →, Queens., Australia 94 C3
Alice →, Queens., Australia 94 B3
Alice, Punta, Italy 31 C10
Alice Arm, Canada 104 B3
Alice Springs, Australia .. 94 C1
Alicedale, S. Africa 88 E4
Aliceville, U.S.A. 109 J1
Alicudi, Italy 31 D7
Aliganj, India 69 F8
Aligarh, Raj., India 68 G7
Aligarh, Ut. P., India 68 F8
Alīgūdarz, Iran 71 C6
Alijó, Portugal 34 D3
Alimnía, Greece 36 C9
Alingsås, Sweden 11 G6
Alipur, Pakistan 68 E4
Alipur Duar, India 67 F16
Aliquippa, U.S.A. 110 F4
Alishan, Taiwan 59 F13
Aliste →, Spain 34 D5
Alitus = Alytus, Lithuania . 9 J21
Alivérion, Greece 38 C6
Aliwal North, S. Africa .. 88 E4
Alix, Canada 104 C6
Aljezur, Portugal 35 H2
Aljustrel, Portugal 35 H2
Alkamari, Niger 83 C7
Alkmaar, Neths. 17 B4
All American Canal, U.S.A. 115 K6

Allada, Benin 83 D5
Allagash →, U.S.A. 109 B11
Allah Dad, Pakistan 68 G2
Allahabad, India 69 G9
Allan, Canada 105 C7
Allanche, France 20 C6
Allanmyo, Burma 67 K19
Allanridge, S. Africa 88 D4
Allaqi, Wadi →, Egypt ... 80 C3
Allariz, Spain 34 C3
Allassac, France 20 C5
Ålleberg, Sweden 11 F7
Allegany, U.S.A. 110 D6
Allegheny →, U.S.A. 110 F5
Allegheny Mts., U.S.A. .. 108 G6
Allegheny Reservoir, U.S.A. 110 E6
Allègre, France 20 C7
Allen, Bog of, Ireland 15 C5
Allen, L., Ireland 15 B3
Allendale, U.S.A. 109 J5
Allende, Mexico 118 B4
Allentown, U.S.A. 111 F9
Allentsteig, Austria 26 C8
Alleppey, India 66 Q10
Allepuz, Spain 32 E4
Aller →, Germany 24 C5
Alliance, Nebr., U.S.A. .. 112 D3
Alliance, Ohio, U.S.A. .. 110 F3
Allier □, France 19 F9
Allier →, France 19 F10
Alliford Bay, Canada 104 C2
Allinge, Denmark 11 J8
Alliston, Canada 102 D4
Alloa, U.K. 14 E5
Allones, France 18 D8
Allora, Australia 95 D5
Allos, France 21 D10
Alluitsup Paa, Greenland .. 4 C5
Alma, Canada 103 C5
Alma, Ga., U.S.A. 109 K4
Alma, Kans., U.S.A. 112 F6
Alma, Mich., U.S.A. 108 D3
Alma, Nebr., U.S.A. 112 E5
Alma Ata = Almaty,
  Kazakstan 50 E8
Almacelles, Spain 32 D5
Almada, Portugal 35 G1
Almaden, Australia 94 B3
Almadén, Spain 35 G6
Almanor, L., U.S.A. 114 F3
Almansa, Spain 33 G3
Almanza, Spain 34 C5
Almanzor, Pico, Spain .. 34 E5
Almanzora →, Spain 33 H3
Almaş, Munţii, Romania . 42 F7
Almassora, Spain 32 F4
Almaty, Kazakstan 50 E8
Almazán, Spain 32 D2
Almeirim, Brazil 125 D8
Almeirim, Portugal 35 F2
Almelo, Neths. 17 B6
Almenar de Soria, Spain . 32 D2
Almenara, Spain 32 F4
Almenara, Sierra de la,
  Spain 33 H3
Almendra, Embalse de,
  Spain 34 D4
Almendralejo, Spain 35 G4
Almere-Stad, Neths. 17 B5
Almería, Spain 35 J8
Almería □, Spain 33 H2
Almería, G. de, Spain 33 J2
Almetyevsk, Russia 48 C11
Älmhult, Sweden 11 H8
Almirante, Panama 120 E3
Almiropótamos, Greece .. 38 C6
Almirós, Greece 38 B4
Almirou, Kólpos, Greece .. 36 D6
Almodôvar, Portugal 35 H2
Almodóvar del Campo,
  Spain 35 G6
Almodóvar del Río, Spain . 35 H5
Almond, U.S.A. 110 D7
Almont, U.S.A. 110 D1
Almonte, Canada 111 A8
Almonte, Spain 35 H4
Almora, India 69 E8
Almoradí, Spain 33 G4
Almorox, Spain 34 E6
Almoustarat, Mali 83 B5
Älmsta, Sweden 10 E12
Almudévar, Spain 32 C4
Almuñécar, Spain 35 J7
Almunge, Sweden 10 E12
Almuradiel, Spain 35 G7
Alness, U.K. 14 D4
Alnmouth, U.K. 12 B6
Alnwick, U.K. 12 B6
Aloi, Uganda 86 B3
Alon, Burma 67 H19
Alor, Indonesia 63 F6
Alor Setar, Malaysia 65 J3
Álora, Spain 35 J6
Alosno, Spain 35 H3
Alot, India 68 H6
Aloysius, Mt., Australia .. 93 E4
Alpaugh, U.S.A. 116 K7
Alpedrinha, Portugal 34 E3
Alpena, U.S.A. 108 C4
Alpes-de-Haute-Provence □,
  France 21 D10
Alpes-Maritimes □, France . 21 E11
Alpha, Australia 94 C4
Alphen aan den Rijn, Neths. 17 B4
Alpiarça, Portugal 35 F2
Alpine, Ariz., U.S.A. 115 K9
Alpine, Calif., U.S.A. .. 117 N10
Alpine, Tex., U.S.A. 113 K3
Alps, Europe 6 F7
Alpu, Turkey 72 C4

Alqueta, Barragem do,
  Portugal 35 G3
Alrø, Denmark 11 J4
Als, Denmark 11 K3
Alsace, France 19 D14
Alsask, Canada 105 C7
Alsasua, Spain 32 C2
Alsek →, U.S.A. 104 B1
Alsfeld, Germany 24 E5
Alsten, Norway 8 D15
Alstermo, Sweden 11 H9
Alston, U.K. 12 C5
Alta, Norway 8 B20
Alta, Sierra, Spain 32 E3
Alta Gracia, Argentina .. 126 C3
Alta Sierra, U.S.A. 117 K8
Altaelva →, Norway 8 B20
Altafjorden, Norway 8 A20
Altai = Aerhtai Shan,
  Mongolia 60 B4
Altamaha →, U.S.A. 109 K5
Altamira, Brazil 125 D8
Altamira, Chile 126 B2
Altamira, Mexico 119 C5
Altamira, Cuevas de, Spain . 34 B6
Altamont, U.S.A. 111 D10
Altamura, Italy 31 B9
Altanbulag, Mongolia .. 60 A5
Altar, Mexico 118 A2
Altar, Desierto de, Mexico . 118 B2
Altata, Mexico 118 C3
Altavista, U.S.A. 108 G6
Altay, China 60 B3
Altdorf, Switz. 25 J4
Alte Mellum, Germany .. 24 B4
Altea, Spain 33 G4
Altenberg, Germany 24 E9
Altenbruch, Germany .. 24 B4
Altenburg, Germany 24 E8
Altenkirchen,
  Mecklenburg-Vorpommern,
  Germany 24 A9
Altenkirchen, Rhld.-Pfz.,
  Germany 24 E3
Altenmarkt, Austria 26 D7
Alter do Chão, Portugal .. 35 F3
Altınoluk, Turkey 39 B8
Altınova, Turkey 39 B8
Altıntaş, Turkey 39 B12
Altınyaka, Turkey 39 E12
Altınyayla, Turkey 39 D11
Altiplano = Bolivian
  Plateau, S. Amer. 122 E4
Altkirch, France 19 E14
Altmark, Germany 24 C7
Altmühl →, Germany .. 25 G7
Altmunster, Austria 26 D6
Alto Adige = Trentino-Alto
  Adige □, Italy 29 B8
Alto Araguaia, Brazil 125 G8
Alto Cuchumatanes =
  Cuchumatanes, Sierra de
  los, Guatemala 120 C1
Alto del Carmen, Chile .. 126 B1
Alto del Inca, Chile 126 A2
Alto Ligonha, Mozam. .. 87 F4
Alto Molocue, Mozam. .. 87 F4
Alto Paraguay □, Paraguay 126 A4
Alto Paraná □, Paraguay . 127 B5
Alton, Canada 110 C4
Alton, U.K. 13 F7
Alton, Ill., U.S.A. 112 F9
Alton, N.H., U.S.A. 111 C13
Altoona, U.S.A. 110 F6
Altötting, Germany 25 G8
Altstätten, Switz. 25 H5
Altūn Kūprī, Iraq 70 C5
Altun Shan, China 60 C3
Alturas, U.S.A. 114 F3
Altus, U.S.A. 113 H5
Alubijid, Phil. 61 G6
Alucra, Turkey 73 B8
Aluk, Sudan 81 F2
Alūksne, Latvia 9 H22
Alunda, Sweden 10 D12
Alunite, U.S.A. 117 K12
Aluoro →, Ethiopia 81 F3
Alupka, Ukraine 47 K8
Alushta, Ukraine 47 K8
Alusi, Indonesia 63 F8
Alustante, Spain 32 E3
Alva, U.S.A. 113 G5
Alvaiázere, Portugal 34 F2
Älvängen, Sweden 11 G6
Alvarado, Mexico 119 D5
Alvarado, U.S.A. 113 J6
Alvaro Obregón, Presa,
  Mexico 118 B3
Älvdalen, Sweden 10 C8
Alvear, Argentina 126 B4
Alverca, Portugal 35 G1
Alvesta, Sweden 11 H8
Alvin, U.S.A. 113 L7
Alvinston, Canada 110 D3
Alvito, Portugal 35 G3
Älvkarleby, Sweden 10 D11
Alvord Desert, U.S.A. .. 114 E4
Älvros, Sweden 10 B8
Älvsbyn, Sweden 8 D19
Alwar, India 68 F7
Alxa Zuoqi, China 56 E3
Alyangula, Australia 94 A2
Alyata = Älät, Azerbaijan . 49 L9
Alyth, U.K. 14 E5
Alytus, Lithuania 9 J21
Alzada, U.S.A. 112 C2
Alzey, Germany 25 F4
Alzira, Spain 33 F4
Am-Timan, Chad 79 F10
Amadeus, L., Australia .. 93 D5

Amadi,
  Dem. Rep. of the Congo . 86 B2
Amâdi, Sudan 81 F3
Amadjuak L., Canada .. 101 B12
Amadora, Portugal 35 G1
Amagansett, U.S.A. 111 F12
Amagasaki, Japan 55 G7
Amager, Denmark 11 J6
Amagunze, Nigeria 83 D6
Amahai, Indonesia 63 E7
Amakusa-Shotō, Japan .. 55 H5
Åmål, Sweden 10 E6
Amalfi, Italy 31 B7
Amaliás, Greece 38 D3
Amalner, India 66 J9
Amamapare, Indonesia .. 63 E9
Amambaí, Brazil 127 A4
Amambaí →, Brazil 127 A5
Amambay □, Paraguay .. 127 A4
Amambay, Cordillera de,
  S. Amer. 127 A4
Amami-Guntō, Japan .. 55 L4
Amami-Ō-Shima, Japan . 55 L4
Amaná →, Brazil 124 D6
Amanat →, India 69 G11
Amanda Park, U.S.A. .. 116 C3
Amangeldy, Kazakstan .. 50 D7
Amantea, Italy 31 C9
Amapá, Brazil 125 C8
Amapá □, Brazil 125 C8
Amara, Sudan 81 E3
Amarante, Brazil 125 E10
Amarante, Portugal 34 D2
Amaranth, Canada 105 C9
Amareleja, Portugal 35 G3
Amargosa →, U.S.A. .. 117 J10
Amargosa Range, U.S.A. . 117 J10
Amári, Greece 36 D6
Amarillo, U.S.A. 113 H4
Amarkantak, India 69 H9
Amârna, Tell el', Sudan .. 80 B3
Amaro, Mte., Italy 29 F11
Amarpur, India 69 G12
Amarti, Eritrea 81 E5
Amarwara, India 69 H8
Amasra, Turkey 72 B5
Amassama, Nigeria 83 D6
Amasya, Turkey 72 B6
Amata, Australia 93 E5
Amatikulu, S. Africa 89 D5
Amatitlán, Guatemala .. 120 D1
Amatrice, Italy 29 F10
Amay, Belgium 17 D5
Amazon = Amazonas →,
  S. Amer. 122 D5
Amazonas □, Brazil 124 E6
Amazonas □, S. Amer. .. 122 D5
Amba Ferit, Ethiopia 81 E4
Ambah, India 68 F8
Ambahakily, Madag. 89 C7
Ambahita, Madag. 89 C8
Ambala, India 68 D7
Ambalavao, Madag. 89 C8
Ambanja, Madag. 89 A8
Ambararata, Madag. 89 B8
Ambarchik, Russia 51 C17
Ambarijeby, Madag. 89 A8
Ambaro, Helodranon',
  Madag. 89 A8
Ambato, Ecuador 124 D3
Ambato, Sierra de,
  Argentina 126 B2
Ambato Boeny, Madag. .. 89 B8
Ambatofinandrahana,
  Madag. 89 C8
Ambatolampy, Madag. .. 89 B8
Ambatomainty, Madag. .. 89 B8
Ambatomanoina, Madag. . 89 B8
Ambatondrazaka, Madag. . 89 B8
Ambatosoratra, Madag. .. 89 B8
Ambelón, Greece 38 B4
Ambenja, Madag. 89 B8
Ambergris Cay, Belize .. 119 D7
Ambérieu-en-Bugey, France 21 C9
Amberley, N.Z. 91 K4
Ambert, France 20 C7
Ambidédi, Mali 82 C2
Ambikapur, India 69 H10
Ambikol, Sudan 80 C3
Ambilobé, Madag. 89 A8
Ambinanindrano, Madag. . 89 C8
Ambinanitelo, Madag. .. 89 B8
Ambinda, Madag. 89 B8
Amble, U.K. 12 B6
Ambleside, U.K. 12 C5
Ambo, Peru 124 F3
Amboahangy, Madag. .. 89 C8
Ambodifototra, Madag. .. 89 B8
Ambodilazana, Madag. .. 89 B8
Ambodiriana, Madag. .. 89 B8
Ambohidratrimo, Madag. . 89 B8
Ambohidray, Madag. .. 89 B8
Ambohimahamasina, Madag. 89 C8
Ambohimahasoa, Madag. . 89 C8
Ambohimanga, Madag. .. 89 C8
Ambohimitombo, Madag. . 89 C8
Ambohitra, Madag. 89 A8
Amboise, France 18 E8
Ambon, Indonesia 63 E7
Amboseli, L., Kenya 86 C4
Ambositra, Madag. 89 C8
Ambovombe, Madag. .. 89 D8
Amboy, U.S.A. 117 L11
Amboyna Cay, S. China Sea 62 C4
Ambridge, U.S.A. 110 F4
Ambriz, Angola 84 F2
Amchitka I., U.S.A. 100 C1
Amderma, Russia 50 C7

Amdhi, India 69 H9
Ameca, Mexico 118 C4
Ameca →, Mexico 118 C3
Amecameca, Mexico 119 D5
Ameland, Neths. 17 A5
Amélia, Italy 29 F9
Amendolara, Italy 31 C9
Amenia, U.S.A. 111 E11
American Falls, U.S.A. .. 114 E7
American Falls Reservoir,
  U.S.A. 114 E7
American Fork, U.S.A. .. 114 F8
American Highland,
  Antarctica 5 D6
American Samoa ■,
  Pac. Oc. 91 B13
Americana, Brazil 127 A6
Americus, U.S.A. 109 K3
Amersfoort, Neths. 17 B5
Amersfoort, S. Africa 89 D4
Ames, Spain 34 C2
Ames, U.S.A. 112 E8
Amesbury, U.S.A. 111 D14
Amet, India 68 G5
Amfíklia, Greece 38 C4
Amfilokhía, Greece 38 C3
Amfissa, Greece 38 C4
Amga, Russia 51 C14
Amga →, Russia 51 C14
Amgu, Russia 51 E14
Amgun →, Russia 51 D14
Amherst, Burma 67 L20
Amherst, Canada 103 C7
Amherst, Mass., U.S.A. . 111 D12
Amherst, N.Y., U.S.A. .. 110 D6
Amherst, Ohio, U.S.A. .. 110 E2
Amherst I., Canada 111 B8
Amherstburg, Canada .. 102 D3
Amiata, Mte., Italy 29 F8
Amidon, U.S.A. 112 B3
Amiens, France 19 C9
Amindaion, Greece 40 F5
Åminne, Sweden 11 G7
Amino, Ethiopia 81 G5
Aminuis, Namibia 88 C2
Amīrābād, Iran 70 C5
Amirante Is., Seychelles .. 52 K9
Amisk L., Canada 105 C8
Amistad, Presa de la, Mexico 118 B4
Amite, U.S.A. 113 K9
Amla, India 68 J8
Amlia I., U.S.A. 100 C2
Amlwch, U.K. 12 D3
Amm Adam, Sudan 81 D4
'Ammān, Jordan 75 D4
'Ammān □, Jordan 75 D5
Ammanford, U.K. 13 F4
Ammassalik = Tasiilaq,
  Greenland 4 C6
Ammerån →, Sweden .. 10 A10
Ammersee, Germany 25 G7
Ammon, U.S.A. 114 E8
Amnat Charoen, Thailand . 64 E5
Amnura, Bangla. 69 G13
Amo Jiang →, China 58 F3
Åmol, Iran 71 B7
Amorgós, Greece 39 E7
Amory, U.S.A. 109 J1
Amos, Canada 102 C4
Åmot, Norway 9 G13
Åmotfors, Sweden 10 E6
Amoy = Xiamen, China .. 59 E12
Ampanavoana, Madag. .. 89 B9
Ampang, Malaysia 65 L3
Ampangalana,
  Lakandranon', Madag. . 89 C8
Ampanihy, Madag. 89 C7
Amparafaravola, Madag. . 89 B8
Ampasinambo, Madag. .. 89 C8
Ampasindava, Helodranon',
  Madag. 89 A8
Ampasindava, Saikanosy,
  Madag. 89 A8
Ampenan, Indonesia 62 F5
Amper, Nigeria 83 D6
Amper →, Germany 25 G7
Ampezzo, Italy 29 B9
Ampitsikinana, Réunion . 89 A8
Ampombiantambo, Madag. 89 A8
Amposta, Spain 32 E5
Ampotaka, Madag. 89 D7
Ampoza, Madag. 89 C7
Amqui, Canada 103 C6
Amravati, India 66 J10
Amreli, India 68 J4
Amritsar, India 68 D6
Amroha, India 69 E8
Amrum, Germany 24 A4
Amstelveen, Neths. 17 B5
Amsterdam, U.S.A. 111 D10
Amsterdam, I. = Nouvelle-
  Amsterdam, I., Ind. Oc. . 3 F13
Amstetten, Austria 26 C7
Amudarya →, Uzbekistan 50 E6
Amundsen Gulf, Canada . 100 A7
Amundsen Sea, Antarctica . 5 D15
Amungen, Sweden 10 C9
Amur →, Russia 51 D15
Amur, W. →, Sudan 80 D3
Amurang, Indonesia 63 D6
Amuri Pass, N.Z. 91 K4
Amursk, Russia 51 D14
Amusco, Spain 34 C6
Amvrakikós Kólpos, Greece 38 C2
Amvrosiyivka, Ukraine .. 47 J9
Amyderya = Amudarya →,
  Uzbekistan 50 E6

Aragona

An Bien, *Vietnam* 65 H5
An Hoa, *Vietnam* 64 E7
An Nabatīyah at Tahta, *Lebanon* 75 B4
An Nabk, *Si. Arabia* 70 D3
An Nabk, *Syria* 75 A5
An Nabk Abū Qaşr, *Si. Arabia* 70 D3
An Nafūd, *Si. Arabia* 70 D4
An Najaf, *Iraq* 70 C5
An Nāşirīyah, *Iraq* 70 D5
An Nhon, *Vietnam* 64 F7
An Nîl □, *Sudan* 80 D3
An Nîl el Abyad □, *Sudan* 81 E3
An Nîl el Azraq □, *Sudan* 81 E3
An Nu'ayrīyah, *Si. Arabia* 71 E6
An Nu'mānīyah, *Iraq* 73 F11
An Nuwayb'ī, W. →, *Si. Arabia* 75 F3
An Thoi, Dao, *Vietnam* 65 H4
An Uaimh, *Ireland* 15 C5
Anabar →, *Russia* 51 B12
'Anabtā, *West Bank* 75 C4
Anaconda, *U.S.A.* 114 C7
Anacortes, *U.S.A.* 116 B4
Anacuao, Mt., *Phil.* 61 C4
Anadarko, *U.S.A.* 113 H5
Anadia, *Portugal* 34 E2
Anadolu, *Turkey* 72 C5
Anadyr, *Russia* 51 C18
Anadyr →, *Russia* 51 C18
Anadyrskiy Zaliv, *Russia* 51 C19
Anáfi, *Greece* 39 E7
Anafópoulo, *Greece* 39 E7
Anaga, Pta. de, *Canary Is.* 37 F3
Anagni, *Italy* 29 G10
'Ānah, *Iraq* 70 C4
Anaheim, *U.S.A.* 117 M9
Anahim Lake, *Canada* 104 C3
Anáhuac, *Mexico* 118 B4
Anakapalle, *India* 67 L13
Anakie, *Australia* 94 C4
Anaklia, *Georgia* 49 J5
Analalava, *Madag.* 89 A8
Analavoka, *Madag.* 89 C8
Análipsis, *Greece* 36 A3
Anambar →, *Pakistan* 68 D3
Anambas, Kepulauan, *Indonesia* 65 L6
Anambas Is. = Anambas, Kepulauan, *Indonesia* 65 L6
Anambra □, *Nigeria* 83 D6
Anamosa, *U.S.A.* 112 D9
Anamur, *Turkey* 70 B2
Anamur Burnu, *Turkey* 72 D5
Anan, *Japan* 55 H7
Anand, *India* 68 H5
Anánes, *Greece* 38 E6
Anantnag, *India* 69 C6
Ananyiv, *Ukraine* 47 J5
Anapa, *Russia* 47 K9
Anapodháris →, *Greece* 36 E7
Anápolis, *Brazil* 125 G9
Anapu →, *Brazil* 125 D8
Anār, *Iran* 71 D7
Anārak, *Iran* 71 C7
Anarisfjällen, *Sweden* 10 A7
Anas →, *India* 68 H5
Anatolia = Anadolu, *Turkey* 72 C5
Anatsogno, *Madag.* 89 C7
Añatuya, *Argentina* 126 B3
Anaunethad L., *Canada* 105 A8
Anbyŏn, *N. Korea* 57 E14
Ancares, Sierra de, *Spain* 34 C4
Ancaster, *Canada* 110 C5
Ancenis, *France* 18 E5
Anchor Bay, *U.S.A.* 116 G3
Anchorage, *U.S.A.* 100 B5
Anci, *China* 56 E9
Ancohuma, Nevada, *Bolivia* 122 E4
Ancón, *Peru* 124 F3
Ancona, *Italy* 29 E10
Ancud, *Chile* 128 E2
Ancud, G. de, *Chile* 128 E2
Ancy-le-Franc, *France* 19 E11
Andacollo, *Argentina* 126 D1
Andacollo, *Chile* 126 C1
Andaingo, *Madag.* 89 B8
Andalgalá, *Argentina* 126 B2
Åndalsnes, *Norway* 9 E12
Andalucía □, *Spain* 35 H6
Andalusia = Andalucía □, *Spain* 35 H6
Andalusia, *U.S.A.* 109 K2
Andaman Is., *Ind. Oc.* 52 H13
Andaman Sea, *Ind. Oc.* 62 B1
Andamooka Opal Fields, *Australia* 95 E2
Andapa, *Madag.* 89 A8
Andara, *Namibia* 88 B3
Andelot-Blancheville, *France* 19 D12
Andenes, *Norway* 8 B17
Andenne, *Belgium* 17 D5
Andéranboukane, *Mali* 83 B5
Andermatt, *Switz.* 25 J4
Andernach, *Germany* 24 E3
Andernos-les-Bains, *France* 20 D2
Anderslöv, *Sweden* 11 J7
Anderson, *Alaska, U.S.A.* 100 B5
Anderson, *Calif., U.S.A.* 114 F2
Anderson, *Ind., U.S.A.* 108 E3
Anderson, *Mo., U.S.A.* 113 G7
Anderson, *S.C., U.S.A.* 109 H4
Anderson →, *Canada* 100 B7
Anderstorp, *Sweden* 11 G7
Andes, *U.S.A.* 111 D10
Andes, Cord. de los, *S. Amer.* 122 F4
Andfjorden, *Norway* 8 B17
Andhra Pradesh □, *India* 66 L11
Andijon, *Uzbekistan* 50 E8
Andikíthira, *Greece* 38 F5
Andilamena, *Madag.* 89 B8
Andīmeshk, *Iran* 71 C6
Andímilos, *Greece* 38 E6
Andíparos, *Greece* 39 D7
Andípaxoi, *Greece* 38 B2
Andípsara, *Greece* 39 C7
Andírrion, *Greece* 38 C3
Andizhan = Andijon, *Uzbekistan* 50 E8
Andoain, *Spain* 32 B2
Andoany, *Madag.* 89 A8
Andong, *S. Korea* 57 F15
Andongwei, *China* 57 G10
Andoom, *Australia* 94 A3
Andorra, *Spain* 32 E4
Andorra ■, *Europe* 20 F5
Andorra La Vella, *Andorra* 20 F5
Andover, *U.K.* 13 F6
Andover, *Maine, U.S.A.* 111 B14
Andover, *Mass., U.S.A.* 111 D13
Andover, *N.J., U.S.A.* 111 F10
Andover, *N.Y., U.S.A.* 110 D7
Andover, *Ohio, U.S.A.* 110 E4
Andøya, *Norway* 8 B16
Andradina, *Brazil* 125 H8
Andrahary, Mt., *Madag.* 89 A8
Andramasina, *Madag.* 89 B8
Andranopasy, *Madag.* 89 C7
Andranovory, *Madag.* 89 C7
Andratx, *Spain* 37 B9
Andreanof Is., *U.S.A.* 100 C2
Andreapol, *Russia* 46 D7
Andrews, *S.C., U.S.A.* 109 J6
Andrews, *Tex., U.S.A.* 113 J3
Andreyevka, *Russia* 48 D10
Ándria, *Italy* 31 A9
Andriamena, *Madag.* 89 B8
Andriandampy, *Madag.* 89 C8
Andriba, *Madag.* 89 B8
Andrijevica, *Montenegro, Yug.* 40 D3
Andrítsaina, *Greece* 38 D3
Androka, *Madag.* 89 C7
Andropov = Rybinsk, *Russia* 46 C10
Ándros, *Greece* 38 D6
Andros I., *Bahamas* 120 B4
Andros Town, *Bahamas* 120 B4
Androscoggin →, *U.S.A.* 111 C14
Andrychów, *Poland* 45 J6
Andselv, *Norway* 8 B18
Andújar, *Spain* 35 G6
Andulo, *Angola* 84 G3
Aneby, *Sweden* 11 G8
Anegada I., *Virgin Is.* 121 C7
Anegada Passage, *W. Indies* 121 C7
Aného, *Togo* 83 D5
Anenni-Noi, *Moldova* 43 D14
Aneto, Pico de, *Spain* 32 C5
Anfu, *China* 59 D10
Ang Thong, *Thailand* 64 E3
Angamos, Punta, *Chile* 126 A1
Angara →, *Russia* 51 D10
Angara-Débou, *Benin* 83 C5
Angarab, *Ethiopia* 81 E4
Angarbaka, *Sudan* 81 F1
Angarsk, *Russia* 51 D11
Angas Hills, *Australia* 92 D4
Angaston, *Australia* 95 E2
Angaur I., *Pac. Oc.* 63 C8
Ånge, *Sweden* 10 B9
Ángel, Salto = Angel Falls, *Venezuela* 124 B6
Ángel de la Guarda, I., *Mexico* 118 B2
Angel Falls, *Venezuela* 124 B6
Angeles, *Phil.* 61 D4
Ängelholm, *Sweden* 11 H6
Angels Camp, *U.S.A.* 116 G6
Ängelsberg, *Sweden* 10 E10
Anger →, *Ethiopia* 81 F4
Angereb →, *Ethiopia* 81 E4
Ångermanälven →, *Sweden* 10 B11
Ångermanland, *Sweden* 8 E18
Angermünde, *Germany* 24 B9
Angers, *Canada* 111 A9
Angers, *France* 18 E6
Angerville, *France* 19 D9
Ängesån →, *Sweden* 8 C20
Angikuni L., *Canada* 105 A9
Angkor, *Cambodia* 64 F4
Anglès, *Spain* 32 D7
Anglesey, Isle of □, *U.K.* 12 D3
Anglet, *France* 20 E2
Angleton, *U.S.A.* 113 L7
Anglin →, *France* 20 B4
Anglisidhes, *Cyprus* 36 E12
Anglure, *France* 19 D10
Angmagssalik = Tasiilaq, *Greenland* 4 C6
Ango, *Dem. Rep. of the Congo* 86 B2
Angoche, *Mozam.* 87 F4
Angoche, I., *Mozam.* 87 F4
Angol, *Chile* 126 D1
Angola, *Ind., U.S.A.* 108 E3
Angola, *N.Y., U.S.A.* 110 D5
Angola ■, *Africa* 85 G3
Angoulême, *France* 20 C4
Angoumois, *France* 20 C4
Angra dos Reis, *Brazil* 127 A7
Angren, *Uzbekistan* 50 E8
Angtassom, *Cambodia* 65 G5
Angu, *Dem. Rep. of the Congo* 86 B1
Anguang, *China* 57 B12
Anguilla ■, *W. Indies* 121 C7
Anguo, *China* 56 E8
Angurugu, *Australia* 94 A2
Angus □, *U.K.* 14 E6
Angwa →, *Zimbabwe* 89 B5
Anhanduí →, *Brazil* 127 A5
Anholt, *Denmark* 11 H5
Anhua, *China* 59 C8
Anhui □, *China* 59 B11
Anhwei = Anhui □, *China* 59 B11
Anichab, *Namibia* 88 C1
Ánidhros, *Greece* 39 E7
Anié, *Togo* 83 D5
Animas →, *U.S.A.* 115 H9
Anina, *Romania* 42 E6
Aninoasa, *Romania* 43 F9
Anivorano, *Madag.* 89 B8
Anjalankoski, *Finland* 9 F22
Anjar, *India* 68 H4
Anji, *China* 59 B12
Anjidiv I., *India* 66 M9
Anjou, *France* 18 E6
Anjozorobe, *Madag.* 89 B8
Anju, *N. Korea* 57 E13
Anka, *Nigeria* 83 C6
Ankaboa, Tanjona, *Madag.* 89 C7
Ankang, *China* 56 H5
Ankara, *Turkey* 72 C5
Ankaramena, *Madag.* 89 C8
Ankaratra, *Madag.* 85 H9
Ankarsrum, *Sweden* 11 G10
Ankasakasa, *Madag.* 89 B7
Ankavandra, *Madag.* 89 B8
Ankazoabo, *Madag.* 89 C7
Ankazobe, *Madag.* 89 B8
Ankeny, *U.S.A.* 112 E8
Ankilimalinika, *Madag.* 89 C7
Ankilizato, *Madag.* 89 C8
Ankisabe, *Madag.* 89 B8
Anklam, *Germany* 24 B9
Ankober, *Ethiopia* 81 F4
Ankoro, *Dem. Rep. of the Congo* 86 D2
Ankororoka, *Madag.* 89 D8
Anlong, *China* 58 E5
Anlu, *China* 59 B9
Anmyŏn-do, *S. Korea* 57 F14
Ånn, *Sweden* 10 A6
Ann, C., *U.S.A.* 111 D14
Ann Arbor, *U.S.A.* 108 D4
Anna, *Russia* 48 E5
Anna, *U.S.A.* 113 G10
Annaba, *Algeria* 78 A7
Annaberg-Buchholz, *Germany* 24 E9
Annalee →, *Ireland* 15 B4
Annam, *Vietnam* 64 E7
Annamitique, Chaîne, *Asia* 64 D6
Annan, *U.K.* 14 G5
Annan →, *U.K.* 14 G5
Annapolis, *U.S.A.* 108 F7
Annapolis Royal, *Canada* 103 D6
Annapurna, *Nepal* 69 E10
Annean, L., *Australia* 93 E2
Anneberg, *Sweden* 11 G8
Annecy, *France* 21 C10
Annecy, Lac d', *France* 21 C10
Annemasse, *France* 19 F13
Annenskiy Most, *Russia* 46 B9
Anning, *China* 58 E4
Anniston, *U.S.A.* 109 J3
Annobón, *Atl. Oc.* 77 G4
Annonay, *France* 21 C8
Annot, *France* 21 E10
Annotto Bay, *Jamaica* 120 C4
Ånnsjön, *Sweden* 10 A6
Annville, *U.S.A.* 111 F8
Annweiler, *Germany* 25 F3
Áno Arkhánai, *Greece* 39 F7
Áno Porróia, *Greece* 40 E7
Áno Síros, *Greece* 38 D6
Áno Viánnos, *Greece* 36 D7
Anorotsangana, *Madag.* 89 A8
Anosibe, *Madag.* 89 B8
Anou Mellene, *Mali* 83 B5
Anoumaba, *Ivory C.* 82 D4
Anóyia, *Greece* 36 D6
Anping, *Hebei, China* 56 E8
Anping, *Liaoning, China* 57 D12
Anpu Gang, *China* 58 G7
Anqing, *China* 59 B11
Anqiu, *China* 57 F10
Anren, *China* 59 D9
Ansager, *Denmark* 11 J2
Ansai, *China* 56 F5
Ansbach, *Germany* 25 F6
Anseba →, *Eritrea* 81 D4
Ansfelden, *Austria* 26 C7
Anshan, *China* 57 D12
Anshun, *China* 58 D5
Ansião, *Portugal* 34 F2
Ansley, *U.S.A.* 112 E5
Ansó, *Spain* 32 C4
Ansoain, *Spain* 32 C3
Anson, *U.S.A.* 113 J5
Anson B., *Australia* 92 B5
Ansongo, *Mali* 83 B5
Ansonia, *U.S.A.* 111 E11
Anstruther, *U.K.* 14 E6
Ansudu, *Indonesia* 63 E9
Antabamba, *Peru* 124 F4
Antakya, *Turkey* 70 B3
Antalaha, *Madag.* 89 A9
Antalya, *Turkey* 72 D4
Antalya □, *Turkey* 39 E12
Antalya Körfezi, *Turkey* 72 D4
Antambohobe, *Madag.* 89 C8
Antanambao-Manampotsy, *Madag.* 89 B8
Antanambe, *Madag.* 89 B8
Antananarivo, *Madag.* 89 B8
Antananarivo □, *Madag.* 89 B8
Antanifotsy, *Madag.* 89 B8
Antanimbaribe, *Madag.* 89 C7
Antanimora, *Madag.* 89 C8
Antarctic Pen., *Antarctica* 5 C18
Antarctica 5 E3
Antelope, *Zimbabwe* 87 G2
Antequera, *Paraguay* 126 A4
Antequera, *Spain* 35 H6
Antero, Mt., *U.S.A.* 115 G10
Antevamena, *Madag.* 89 C7
Anthemoús, *Greece* 40 F7
Anthony, *Kans., U.S.A.* 113 G5
Anthony, *N. Mex., U.S.A.* 115 K10
Anti Atlas, *Morocco* 78 C4
Anti-Lebanon = Ash Sharqi, Al Jabal, *Lebanon* 75 B5
Antibes, *France* 21 E11
Antibes, C. d', *France* 21 E11
Anticosti, Î. d', *Canada* 103 C7
Antifer, C. d', *France* 18 C7
Antigo, *U.S.A.* 112 C10
Antigonish, *Canada* 103 C7
Antigua, *Canary Is.* 37 F5
Antigua, *W. Indies* 121 C7
Antigua & Barbuda ■, *W. Indies* 121 C7
Antigua Guatemala, *Guatemala* 120 D1
Antilla, *Cuba* 120 B4
Antilles = West Indies, *Cent. Amer.* 121 D7
Antioch, *U.S.A.* 116 G5
Antioche, Pertuis d', *France* 20 B2
Antioquia, *Colombia* 124 B3
Antipodes Is., *Pac. Oc.* 96 M9
Antlers, *U.S.A.* 113 H7
Antoetra, *Madag.* 89 C8
Antofagasta, *Chile* 126 A1
Antofagasta □, *Chile* 126 A2
Antofagasta de la Sierra, *Argentina* 126 B2
Antofalla, *Argentina* 126 B2
Antofalla, Salar de, *Argentina* 126 B2
Anton, *U.S.A.* 113 J3
Antongila, Helodrano, *Madag.* 89 B8
Antonibé, *Madag.* 89 B8
Antonibé, Presqu'île d', *Madag.* 89 A8
Antonina, *Brazil* 127 B6
Antrain, *France* 18 D5
Antrim, *U.K.* 15 B5
Antrim, *U.S.A.* 110 F3
Antrim □, *U.K.* 15 B5
Antrim, Mts. of, *U.K.* 15 A5
Antrim Plateau, *Australia* 92 C4
Antrodoco, *Italy* 29 F10
Antropovo, *Russia* 48 A6
Antsakabary, *Madag.* 89 B8
Antsalova, *Madag.* 89 B7
Antsenavolo, *Madag.* 89 C8
Antsiafabositra, *Madag.* 89 B8
Antsirabe, *Antananarivo, Madag.* 89 B8
Antsirabe, *Antsiranana, Madag.* 89 A8
Antsirabe, *Mahajanga, Madag.* 89 B8
Antsiranana, *Madag.* 89 A8
Antsiranana □, *Madag.* 89 A8
Antsohihy, *Madag.* 89 A8
Antsohimbondrona Seranana, *Madag.* 89 A8
Antu, *China* 57 C15
Antwerp = Antwerpen, *Belgium* 17 C4
Antwerp, *U.S.A.* 111 B9
Antwerpen, *Belgium* 17 C4
Antwerpen □, *Belgium* 17 C4
Anupgarh, *India* 68 E5
Anuppur, *India* 69 H9
Anuradhapura, *Sri Lanka* 66 Q12
Anveh, *Iran* 71 E7
Anvers = Antwerpen, *Belgium* 17 C4
Anvers I., *Antarctica* 5 C17
Anwen, *China* 59 C13
Anxi, *Fujian, China* 59 E12
Anxi, *Gansu, China* 60 B4
Anxian, *China* 58 B5
Anxiang, *China* 59 C9
Anxious B., *Australia* 95 E1
Anyama, *Ivory C.* 82 D4
Anyang, *China* 56 F8
Anyer-Kidul, *Indonesia* 63 G11
Anyi, *Jiangxi, China* 59 C10
Anyi, *Shanxi, China* 56 G6
Anyuan, *China* 59 E10
Anyue, *China* 58 B5
Anza, *U.S.A.* 117 M10
Anze, *China* 56 F7
Anzhero-Sudzhensk, *Russia* 50 D9
Ánzio, *Italy* 30 A5
Aoga-Shima, *Japan* 55 H9
Aoiz, *Spain* 32 C3
Aomen = Macau, *Asia* 59 F9
Aomori, *Japan* 54 D10
Aomori □, *Japan* 54 D10
Aonla, *India* 69 E8
Aosta, *Italy* 28 C4
Aoudéras, *Niger* 83 B6
Aoukâr, *Mauritania* 82 B3
Aozou, *Chad* 79 D9
Apa →, *S. Amer.* 126 A4
Apache, *U.S.A.* 113 H5
Apache Junction, *U.S.A.* 115 K8
Apalachee B., *U.S.A.* 109 L4
Apalachicola, *U.S.A.* 109 L3
Apalachicola →, *U.S.A.* 109 L3
Apam, *Ghana* 83 D4
Apapa, *Nigeria* 83 D5
Apaporis →, *Colombia* 124 D5
Aparri, *Phil.* 61 B4
Apateu, *Romania* 42 D6
Apatin, *Serbia, Yug.* 42 E4
Apatity, *Russia* 50 C4
Apatzingán, *Mexico* 118 D4
Apeldoorn, *Neths.* 17 B5
Apen, *Germany* 24 B3
Apennines = Appennini, *Italy* 28 E7
Aphrodisias, *Turkey* 39 D10
Apia, *W. Samoa* 91 A13
Apiacás, Serra dos, *Brazil* 124 E7
Apies →, *S. Africa* 89 D4
Apizaco, *Mexico* 119 D5
Aplao, *Peru* 124 G4
Apo, Mt., *Phil.* 63 C7
Apolakkiá, *Greece* 36 C9
Apolakkiá, Órmos, *Greece* 36 C9
Apolda, *Germany* 24 D7
Apollo Bay, *Australia* 95 F3
Apollonia, *Greece* 38 E6
Apolo, *Bolivia* 124 F5
Aporé →, *Brazil* 125 G8
Apostle Is., *U.S.A.* 112 B9
Apóstoles, *Argentina* 127 B4
Apostolos Andreas, C., *Cyprus* 36 D13
Apostolovo, *Ukraine* 47 J7
Apoteri, *Guyana* 124 C7
Appalachian Mts., *U.S.A.* 108 G6
Äppelbo, *Sweden* 10 D8
Appennini, *Italy* 28 E7
Appennino Ligure, *Italy* 28 D6
Appenzell-Ausser Rhoden □, *Switz.* 25 H5
Appenzell-Inner Rhoden □, *Switz.* 25 H5
Appiano, *Italy* 29 B8
Apple Hill, *Canada* 111 A10
Apple Valley, *U.S.A.* 117 L9
Appleby-in-Westmorland, *U.K.* 12 C5
Appleton, *U.S.A.* 108 C1
Approuague →, *Fr. Guiana* 125 C8
Apricena, *Italy* 29 G12
Aprília, *Italy* 30 A5
Apsheronsk, *Russia* 49 H4
Apsley, *Canada* 110 B6
Apt, *France* 21 E9
Apuane, Alpi, *Italy* 28 D7
Apucarana, *Brazil* 127 A5
Apulia = Púglia □, *Italy* 31 A9
Apure →, *Venezuela* 124 B5
Apurimac →, *Peru* 124 F4
Apuseni, Munţii, *Romania* 42 D7
Āqā Jarī, *Iran* 71 D6
Aqaba = Al 'Aqabah, *Jordan* 75 F4
Aqaba, G. of, *Red Sea* 70 D2
'Aqabah, Khalīj al = Aqaba, G. of, *Red Sea* 70 D2
'Aqdā, *Iran* 71 C7
Aqîq, *Sudan* 80 D4
Aqîq, Khalîg, *Sudan* 80 D4
Aqmola = Astana, *Kazakstan* 50 D8
Aqrah, *Iraq* 70 B4
Aqtaū, *Kazakstan* 50 E6
Aqtöbe, *Kazakstan* 50 D6
Aquidauana, *Brazil* 125 H7
Aquiles Serdán, *Mexico* 118 B3
Aquin, *Haiti* 121 C5
Aquitaine □, *France* 20 D3
Ar Rachidiya, *Morocco* 78 B5
Ar Rafīd, *Syria* 75 C4
Ar Raḥḥālīyah, *Iraq* 70 C4
Ar Ramādī, *Iraq* 70 C4
Ar Ramthā, *Jordan* 75 C5
Ar Raqqah, *Syria* 70 C3
Ar Rass, *Si. Arabia* 70 E4
Ar Rawshān, *Si. Arabia* 80 C5
Ar Rifā'ī, *Iraq* 70 D5
Ar Riyāḍ, *Si. Arabia* 70 E5
Ar Ru'ays, *Qatar* 71 E6
Ar Rukhaymīyah, *Iraq* 70 D5
Ar Ruqayyidah, *Si. Arabia* 71 E6
Ar Ruşāfah, *Syria* 70 C3
Ar Ruţbah, *Iraq* 70 C4
Ara, *India* 69 G11
Ara Goro, *Ethiopia* 81 F5
Ara Tera, *Ethiopia* 81 F5
Arab, *U.S.A.* 109 H2
'Arab, Bahr el →, *Sudan* 81 F2
Arab, Khalîg el, *Egypt* 80 A2
'Araba, W. →, *Egypt* 80 J8
'Arabābād, *Iran* 71 C8
Araban, *Turkey* 72 D7
Arabatskaya Strelka, *Ukraine* 47 K8
Arabba, *Italy* 29 B8
Arabia, *Asia* 52 G8
Arabian Desert = Es Sahrâ' Esh Sharqîya, *Egypt* 80 B3
Arabian Gulf = Gulf, The, *Asia* 71 E6
Arabian Sea, *Ind. Oc.* 52 H10
Araç, *Turkey* 72 B5
Aracaju, *Brazil* 125 F11
Aracati, *Brazil* 125 D11
Araçatuba, *Brazil* 127 A5
Aracena, *Spain* 35 H4
Aracena, Sierra de, *Spain* 35 H4
Aračinovo, *Macedonia* 40 D5
Araçuaí, *Brazil* 125 G10
'Arad, *Israel* 75 D4
Arad, *Romania* 42 D6
Arad □, *Romania* 42 D6
Arādān, *Iran* 71 C7
Aradhippou, *Cyprus* 36 E12
Arafura Sea, *E. Indies* 52 K17
Aragats, *Armenia* 49 K7
Aragón □, *Spain* 32 D4
Aragón →, *Spain* 32 C3
Aragona, *Italy* 30 E6

Araguacema, Brazil 125 E9
Araguaia →, Brazil 122 D6
Araguaína, Brazil 125 E9
Araguari, Brazil 125 G9
Araguari →, Brazil 125 C9
Arain, India 68 F6
Arak, Algeria 78 C6
Arāk, Iran 71 C6
Araka, Sudan 81 G3
Arakan Coast, Burma 67 K19
Arakan Yoma, Burma 67 K19
Arákhova, Greece 38 C4
Arakli, Turkey 73 B8
Araks = Aras, Rūd-e →, Azerbaijan 49 K9
Aral, Kazakstan 50 E7
Aral Sea, Asia 50 E7
Aral Tengizi = Aral Sea, Asia 50 E7
Aralsk = Aral, Kazakstan .. 50 E7
Aralskoye More = Aral Sea, Asia 50 E7
Aralsor, Ozero, Kazakstan . 49 F9
Aramac, Australia 94 C4
Aran, Ireland 15 A3
Aran Is., Ireland 15 C2
Aranda de Duero, Spain .. 34 D7
Arandān, Iran 70 C5
Arandelovac, Serbia, Yug. . 40 B4
Aranjuez, Spain 34 E7
Aranos, Namibia 88 C2
Aransas Pass, U.S.A. 113 M6
Aranyaprathet, Thailand .. 64 F4
Araouane, Mali 82 B4
Arapahoe, U.S.A. 112 E5
Arapey Grande →, Uruguay 126 C4
Arapgir, Turkey 70 B3
Arapiraca, Brazil 125 E11
Arapongas, Brazil 127 A5
Ar'ar, Si. Arabia 70 D4
Araranguá, Brazil 127 B6
Araraquara, Brazil 125 H9
Ararás, Serra das, Brazil . 127 B5
Ararat, Armenia 73 C11
Ararat, Australia 95 F3
Ararat, Mt. = Ağrı Dağı, Turkey 70 B5
Araria, India 69 F12
Araripe, Chapada do, Brazil 125 E11
Araruama, L. de, Brazil ... 127 A7
Aras, Rūd-e →, Azerbaijan 49 K9
Aratāne, Mauritania 82 B3
Arauca, Colombia 124 B4
Arauca →, Venezuela 124 B5
Arauco, Chile 126 D1
Arawa, Ethiopia 81 F5
Araxá, Brazil 125 G9
Araya, Pen. de, Venezuela . 124 A6
Arba Gugu, Ethiopia 81 F5
Arba Minch, Ethiopia 81 F4
Arbat, Iraq 70 C5
Árbatax, Italy 30 C2
Arbi, Ethiopia 81 F4
Arbīl, Iraq 70 B5
Arboga, Sweden 10 E9
Arbois, France 19 F12
Arbore, Ethiopia 81 F4
Arboréa, Italy 30 C1
Arborfield, Canada 105 C8
Arborg, Canada 105 C9
Arbre du Ténéré, Niger .. 83 B7
Arbroath, U.K. 14 E6
Arbuckle, U.S.A. 116 F4
Arbus, Italy 30 C1
Arc →, France 21 C10
Arc-lès-Gray, France 19 E12
Arcachon, France 20 D2
Arcachon, Bassin d', France 20 D2
Arcade, Calif., U.S.A. 117 L8
Arcade, N.Y., U.S.A. 110 D6
Arcadia, Fla., U.S.A. 109 M5
Arcadia, La., U.S.A. 113 J8
Arcadia, Pa., U.S.A. 110 F6
Arcata, U.S.A. 114 F1
Arcévia, Italy 29 E9
Archangel = Arkhangelsk, Russia 50 C5
Archar, Bulgaria 40 C6
Archbald, U.S.A. 111 E9
Archena, Spain 33 G3
Archer →, Australia 94 A3
Archer B., Australia 94 A3
Archers Post, Kenya 86 B4
Arches National Park, U.S.A. 115 G9
Archidona, Spain 35 H6
Arci, Mte., Italy 30 C1
Arcidosso, Italy 29 F8
Arcis-sur-Aube, France ... 19 D11
Arckaringa Cr. →, Australia 95 D2
Arco, Italy 28 C7
Arco, U.S.A. 114 E7
Arcos = Arcos de Jalón, Spain 32 D2
Arcos de Jalón, Spain ... 32 D2
Arcos de la Frontera, Spain 35 J5
Arcos de Valdevez, Portugal 34 D2
Arcot, India 66 N11
Arcozelo, Portugal 34 D2
Arctic Bay, Canada 101 A11
Arctic Ocean, Arctic 4 B18
Arctic Red River = Tsiigehtchic, Canada .. 100 B6
Arda →, Bulgaria 41 E10
Arda →, Italy 28 C7
Ardabīl, Iran 71 B6
Ardahan, Turkey 73 B10
Ardakān = Sepīdān, Iran . 71 D7
Ardakān, Iran 71 C7
Ardala, Sweden 11 F7
Ardales, Spain 35 J6

Ardèche □, France 21 D8
Ardèche →, France 21 D8
Ardee, Ireland 15 C5
Arden, Canada 110 B8
Arden, Denmark 11 H3
Arden, Calif., U.S.A. 116 G5
Arden, Nev., U.S.A. 117 J11
Ardenne, Belgium 6 F7
Ardennes = Ardenne, Belgium 6 F7
Ardennes □, France 19 C11
Ardentes, France 19 F8
Arderin, Ireland 15 C4
Ardeşen, Turkey 73 B9
Ardestān, Iran 71 C7
Árdhas →, Greece 41 E10
Ardhéa, Greece 40 F6
Ardila →, Portugal 35 G3
Ardino, Bulgaria 41 E9
Ardivachar Pt., U.K. 14 D1
Ardlethan, Australia 95 E4
Ardmore, Okla., U.S.A. 113 H6
Ardmore, Pa., U.S.A. 111 G9
Ardnamurchan, Pt. of, U.K. 14 E2
Ardnave Pt., U.K. 14 F2
Ardon, Russia 49 J7
Ardore, Italy 31 D9
Ardres, France 19 B8
Ardrossan, Australia 95 E2
Ardrossan, U.K. 14 F4
Ards Pen., U.K. 15 B6
Arduan, Sudan 80 D3
Ardud, Romania 42 C7
Åre, Sweden 10 A7
Arecibo, Puerto Rico 121 C6
Areia Branca, Brazil 125 E11
Arena, Pt., U.S.A. 116 G3
Arenal, Honduras 120 C2
Arenas = Las Arenas, Spain 34 B6
Arenas de San Pedro, Spain 34 E5
Arendal, Norway 9 G13
Arendsee, Germany 24 C7
Arenys de Mar, Spain 32 D7
Areópolis, Greece 38 E4
Arequipa, Peru 124 G4
Arero, Ethiopia 81 G4
Arès, France 20 D2
Arévalo, Spain 34 D6
Arezzo, Italy 29 E8
Arga, Turkey 70 B3
Arga →, Spain 32 C3
Argalastí, Greece 38 B5
Argamasilla de Alba, Spain 35 F7
Argamasilla de Calatrava, Spain 35 G6
Arganda, Spain 34 E7
Arganil, Portugal 34 E2
Argedeb, Ethiopia 81 F5
Argelès-Gazost, France ... 20 E3
Argelès-sur-Mer, France ... 20 F7
Argens →, France 21 E10
Argent-sur-Sauldre, France 19 E9
Argenta, Canada 104 C5
Argenta, Italy 29 D8
Argentan, France 18 D6
Argentário, Mte., Italy 29 F8
Argentat, France 20 C5
Argentera, Italy 28 D4
Argenteuil, France 19 D9
Argentia, Canada 103 C9
Argentiera, C. dell', Italy .. 30 B1
Argentina ■, S. Amer. 128 D3
Argentina Is., Antarctica .. 5 C17
Argentino, L., Argentina .. 128 G2
Argenton-Château, France . 18 F6
Argenton-sur-Creuse, France 19 F8
Argeş □, Romania 43 F9
Argeş →, Romania 43 F11
Arghandab →, Afghan. ... 68 D1
Argheile, Ethiopia 81 F5
Argo, Sudan 80 D3
Argolikós Kólpos, Greece .. 38 D4
Argolís □, Greece 38 D4
Argonne, France 19 C12
Árgos, Greece 38 D4
Árgos Orestikón, Greece .. 40 F5
Argostólion, Greece 38 C2
Arguedas, Spain 32 C3
Arguello, Pt., U.S.A. 117 L6
Arguineguín, Canary Is. ... 37 G4
Argun, Russia 49 J7
Argun →, Russia 51 D13
Argungu, Nigeria 83 C5
Argus Pk., U.S.A. 117 K9
Argyle, L., Australia 92 C4
Argyll & Bute □, U.K. 14 E3
Arhavi, Turkey 73 B9
Århus, Denmark 11 H4
Århus Amtskommune □, Denmark 11 H4
Ariadnoye, Russia 54 B7
Ariamsvlei, Namibia 88 D2
Ariana, Tunisia 79 A7
Ariano Irpino, Italy 31 A8
Aribinda, Burkina Faso 83 C4
Arica, Chile 124 G4
Arica, Colombia 124 D4
Arico, Canary Is. 37 F3
Arid, C., Australia 93 F3
Arida, Japan 55 G7
Ariège □, France 20 F5
Ariège →, France 20 E5
Arieş →, Romania 43 D8
Arīhā, Israel 80 A4
Arilje, Serbia, Yug. 40 C4
Arílla, Ákra, Greece 36 A3
Arima, Trin. & Tob. 121 D7
Arinos →, Brazil 122 E6
Ario de Rosales, Mexico .. 118 D4
Ariogala, Lithuania 44 C10

Aripuanã, Brazil 124 E6
Aripuanã →, Brazil 122 D4
Ariquemes, Brazil 124 E6
Arisaig, U.K. 14 E3
Arîsh, W. el →, Egypt 80 A3
Arissa, Ethiopia 81 E5
Aristazabal I., Canada 104 C3
Arivonimamo, Madag. 89 B8
Ariza, Spain 32 D2
Arizaro, Salar de, Argentina 126 A2
Arizona, Argentina 126 D2
Arizona □, U.S.A. 115 J8
Arizpe, Mexico 118 A2
Arjäng, Sweden 10 E6
Arjeplog, Sweden 8 D18
Arjona, Colombia 124 A3
Arjona, Spain 35 H6
Arjuna, Indonesia 63 G15
Arka, Russia 51 C15
Arkadak, Russia 48 E6
Arkadelphia, U.S.A. 113 H8
Arkadhía □, Greece 38 D4
Arkaig, L., U.K. 14 E3
Arkalyk = Arqalyq, Kazakstan 50 D7
Arkansas □, U.S.A. 113 H8
Arkansas →, U.S.A. 113 J9
Arkansas City, U.S.A. 113 G6
Arkaroola, Australia 95 E2
Arkathos →, Greece 38 B3
Arkhángelos, Greece 36 C10
Arkhangelsk, Russia 50 C5
Arkhangelskoye, Russia ... 48 E5
Arki, India 68 D7
Arklow, Ireland 15 D5
Arkona, Kap, Germany 24 A9
Arkösund, Sweden 11 F10
Arkoúdhi, Greece 38 C2
Arkport, U.S.A. 110 D7
Arktícheskiy, Mys, Russia . 51 A10
Arkul, Russia 48 B10
Arkville, U.S.A. 111 D10
Ärla, Sweden 10 E10
Arlanza →, Spain 34 C6
Arlanzón →, Spain 34 C6
Arlberg P., Austria 26 D3
Arles, France 21 E8
Arlington, S. Africa 89 D4
Arlington, N.Y., U.S.A. 111 E11
Arlington, Oreg., U.S.A. ... 114 D3
Arlington, S. Dak., U.S.A. . 112 C6
Arlington, Tex., U.S.A. 113 J6
Arlington, Va., U.S.A. 108 F7
Arlington, Vt., U.S.A. 111 C11
Arlington, Wash., U.S.A. .. 116 B4
Arlington Heights, U.S.A. .. 108 D2
Arlit, Niger 78 E7
Arlon, Belgium 17 E5
Arltunga, Australia 94 C1
Arly, Burkina Faso 83 C5
Armagh, U.K. 15 B5
Armagh □, U.K. 15 B5
Armagnac, France 20 E4
Armançon →, France 19 E10
Armavir, Russia 49 H5
Armenia, Colombia 124 C3
Armenia ■, Asia 49 K7
Armeniş, Romania 42 E7
Armenistís, Ákra, Greece .. 36 C9
Armentières, France 19 B9
Armidale, Australia 95 E5
Armilla, Spain 35 H7
Armour, U.S.A. 112 D5
Armstrong, B.C., Canada .. 104 C5
Armstrong, Ont., Canada .. 102 B2
Armutlu, Bursa, Turkey ... 41 F12
Armutlu, İzmir, Turkey 39 C9
Arnaía, Greece 40 F7
Arnarfjörður, Iceland 8 D2
Arnaud →, Canada 101 B12
Arnauti, C., Cyprus 36 D11
Arnay-le-Duc, France 19 E11
Arnedillo, Spain 32 C2
Arnedo, Spain 32 C2
Arnett, U.S.A. 113 G5
Arnhem, Neths. 17 C5
Arnhem, C., Australia 94 A2
Arnhem B., Australia 94 A2
Arnhem Land, Australia ... 94 A1
Arnissa, Greece 40 F5
Arno →, Italy 28 E7
Arno Bay, Australia 95 E2
Arnold, U.K. 12 D6
Arnold, U.S.A. 116 G6
Arnoldstein, Austria 26 E6
Arnon →, France 19 E9
Arnot, Canada 105 B9
Arnøy, Norway 8 A19
Arnprior, Canada 102 C4
Arnsberg, Germany 24 D4
Arnstadt, Germany 24 E6
Aroab, Namibia 88 D2
Aroánia Óri, Greece 38 D4
Aroche, Spain 35 H4
Arochuku, Nigeria 83 D6
Arolsen, Germany 24 D5
Aron, India 68 G6
Aron →, France 19 F10
Arona, Italy 28 C5
Aroroy, Phil. 61 E5
Arosa, Ría de, Spain 34 C2
Arpajon, France 19 D9
Arpajon-sur-Cère, France . 20 D6
Arpaşu de Jos, Romania .. 43 E9
Arqalyk, Kazakstan 50 D7
Arrabury, Australia 95 D3
Arrah = Ara, India 69 G11
Arrah, Ivory Coast 82 D4
Arraiolos, Portugal 35 G3
Arran, U.K. 14 F3

Arras, France 19 B9
Arrasate, Spain 32 B2
Arrats →, France 20 D4
Arreau, France 20 F4
Arrecife, Canary Is. 37 F6
Arrecifes, Argentina 126 C3
Arrée, Mts. d', France 18 D3
Arresø, Denmark 11 J6
Arriaga, Chiapas, Mexico . 119 D6
Arriaga, San Luis Potosí, Mexico 118 C4
Arrilalah, Australia 94 C3
Arrino, Australia 93 E2
Arriondas, Spain 34 B5
Arromanches-les-Bains, France 18 C6
Arronches, Portugal 35 F3
Arros →, France 20 E3
Arrow, L., Ireland 15 B3
Arrowhead, L., U.S.A. 117 L9
Arrowtown, N.Z. 91 L2
Arroyo de la Luz, Spain ... 35 F4
Arroyo Grande, U.S.A. 117 K6
Ars, Denmark 11 H3
Ars, Iran 70 B5
Ars-sur-Moselle, France ... 19 C13
Arsenault L., Canada 105 B7
Arsenev, Russia 54 B6
Arsi □, Ethiopia 81 F4
Arsiero, Italy 29 C8
Arsin, Turkey 73 B8
Arsk, Russia 48 B9
Ársunda, Sweden 10 D10
Árta, Greece 38 B3
Artà, Spain 37 B10
Árta □, Greece 38 B3
Arteaga, Mexico 118 D4
Arteche, Phil. 61 E6
Arteijo = Arteixo, Spain .. 34 B2
Arteixo, Spain 34 B2
Artem = Artyom, Azerbaijan 49 K10
Artem, Russia 54 C6
Artemovsk, Russia 51 D10
Artemovsk, Ukraine 47 H9
Artemovskiy, Russia 49 G5
Artenay, France 19 D8
Artern, Germany 24 D7
Artesa de Segre, Spain 32 D6
Artesia = Mosomane, Botswana 88 C4
Artesia, U.S.A. 113 J2
Arthington, Liberia 82 D2
Arthur, Canada 110 C4
Arthur →, Australia 94 G3
Arthur Cr. →, Australia ... 94 C2
Arthur Pt., Australia 94 C5
Arthur River, Australia ... 93 F2
Arthur's Pass, N.Z. 91 K3
Arthur's Town, Bahamas .. 121 B4
Artigas, Uruguay 126 C4
Artik, Armenia 49 K6
Artillery L., Canada 105 A7
Artois, France 19 B9
Artotína, Greece 38 C4
Artrutx, C. de, Spain 37 B10
Artsyz, Ukraine 47 J5
Artvin, Turkey 73 B9
Artyom, Azerbaijan 49 K10
Aru, Kepulauan, Indonesia . 63 F8
Aru Is. = Aru, Kepulauan, Indonesia 63 F8
Arua, Uganda 86 B3
Aruanã, Brazil 125 F8
Aruba ■, W. Indies 121 D6
Arucas, Canary Is. 37 F4
Arudy, France 20 E3
Arun →, Nepal 69 F12
Arun →, U.K. 13 G7
Arunachal Pradesh □, India 67 F19
Arusha, Tanzania 86 C4
Arusha □, Tanzania 86 C4
Arusha Chini, Tanzania ... 86 C4
Aruwimi →, Dem. Rep. of the Congo . 86 B1
Arvada, Colo., U.S.A. 112 F2
Arvada, Wyo., U.S.A. 114 D10
Arve →, France 19 F13
Árvi, Greece 36 E7
Arviat, Canada 105 A10
Arvidsjaur, Sweden 8 D18
Arvika, Sweden 10 E6
Arvin, U.S.A. 117 K8
Arwal, India 69 G11
Arxan, China 60 B6
Aryd, Sweden 11 H8
Aryirádhes, Greece 36 B3
Aryiroúpolis, Greece 36 D6
Arys, Kazakstan 50 E7
Arzachena, Italy 30 A2
Arzamas, Russia 48 C6
Arzgir, Russia 49 H7
Arzignano, Italy 29 C8
Arzúa, Spain 34 C2
Aš, Czech Rep. 26 A5
Ås, Sweden 10 A8
As Pontes de García Rodríguez, Spain 34 B3
Aş Şafā, Syria 75 B6
As Safḩ, U.A.E. 71 E7
Aş Şāfīyah, Si. Arabia 71 E6
Aş Şafīrah, Syria 70 B3
Aş Şaḩm, Oman 71 E8
As Sājir, Si. Arabia 70 E5
As Salamīyah, Syria 70 C3
As Salmān, Iraq 70 D5
As Salţ, Jordan 75 C4
As Sal'w'a, Qatar 71 E6
As Samāwah, Iraq 70 D5
As Sanamayn, Syria 75 B5
As Sohar = Şuḩār, Oman . 71 E8

As Sukhnah, Syria 70 C3
As Sulaymānīyah, Iraq 70 C5
As Sulaymī, Si. Arabia 70 E4
As Sulayyil, Si. Arabia 74 C4
As Summān, Si. Arabia ... 70 E5
As Suwaydā', Syria 75 C5
As Suwaydā' □, Syria 75 C5
As Suwayq, Oman 71 F8
As Şuwayrah, Iraq 70 C5
Åsa, Sweden 11 G6
Asab, Namibia 88 D2
Asaba, Nigeria 83 D6
Asad, Buḩayrat al, Syria .. 70 C3
Asadābād, Iran 73 E13
Asafo, Ghana 82 D4
Asahi-Gawa →, Japan 55 G7
Asahigawa, Japan 54 C11
Asale, L., Ethiopia 81 E5
Asamankese, Ghana 83 D4
Asan →, India 69 F8
Asansol, India 69 H12
Åsarna, Sweden 10 B8
Asayita, Ethiopia 81 E5
Asbe Teferi, Ethiopia 81 F5
Asbesberg, S. Africa 88 D3
Asbestos, Canada 103 C5
Asbury Park, U.S.A. 111 F10
Ascea, Italy 31 B8
Ascension, Mexico 118 A3
Ascensión, B. de la, Mexico 119 D7
Ascension I., Atl. Oc. 77 G2
Aschach an der Donau, Austria 26 C7
Aschaffenburg, Germany .. 25 F5
Aschendorf, Germany 24 B3
Aschersleben, Germany ... 24 D7
Asciano, Italy 29 E8
 Áscoli Piceno, Italy 29 F10
 Áscoli Satriano, Italy 31 A8
Ascope, Peru 124 E3
Ascotán, Chile 126 A2
Aseb, Eritrea 81 E5
Åseda, Sweden 11 G9
Asela, Ethiopia 81 F4
Åsen, Sweden 10 C7
Asenovgrad, Bulgaria 41 D8
Aşfeld, France 19 C11
Asfûn el Matâ'na, Egypt .. 80 B3
Asgata, Cyprus 36 E12
Ash Fork, U.S.A. 115 J7
Ash Grove, U.S.A. 113 G8
Ash Shabakah, Iraq 70 D4
Ash Shamāl □, Lebanon .. 75 A5
Ash Shāmīyah, Iraq 70 D5
Ash Shāriqah, U.A.E. 71 E7
Ash Sharmah, Si. Arabia .. 70 D2
Ash Sharqāt, Iraq 70 C4
Ash Sharqi, Al Jabal, Lebanon 75 B5
Ash Shaṭrah, Iraq 70 D5
Ash Shawbak, Jordan 70 D2
Ash Shawmari, J., Jordan . 75 E5
Ash Shināfīyah, Iraq 70 D5
Ash Shu'bah, Si. Arabia ... 70 D5
Ash Shumlūl, Si. Arabia ... 70 E5
Ash Shūr'a, Iraq 70 C4
Ash Shurayf, Si. Arabia ... 70 E4
Ash Shuwayfāt, Lebanon .. 75 B4
Ashanti □, Ghana 83 D4
Ashau, Vietnam 64 D6
Ashbourne, U.K. 12 D6
Ashburn, U.S.A. 109 K4
Ashburton, N.Z. 91 K3
Ashburton →, Australia ... 92 D1
Ashcroft, Canada 104 C4
Ashdod, Israel 75 D3
Ashdown, U.S.A. 113 J7
Asheboro, U.S.A. 109 H6
Ashern, Canada 105 C9
Asherton, U.S.A. 113 L5
Asheville, U.S.A. 109 H4
Ashewat, Pakistan 68 D3
Asheweig →, Canada 102 B2
Ashford, Australia 95 D5
Ashford, U.K. 13 F8
Ashgabat, Turkmenistan .. 50 F6
Ashibetsu, Japan 54 C11
Ashikaga, Japan 55 F9
Ashington, U.K. 12 B6
Ashizuri-Zaki, Japan 55 H6
Ashkarkot, Afghan. 68 C2
Ashkhabad = Ashgabat, Turkmenistan 50 F6
Åshkhāneh, Iran 71 B8
Ashland, Kans., U.S.A. ... 113 G5
Ashland, Ky., U.S.A. 108 F4
Ashland, Mont., U.S.A. ... 114 D10
Ashland, Ohio, U.S.A. 110 F2
Ashland, Oreg., U.S.A. 114 E2
Ashland, Pa., U.S.A. 111 F8
Ashland, Va., U.S.A. 108 G7
Ashland, Wis., U.S.A. 112 B9
Ashley, N. Dak., U.S.A. ... 112 B5
Ashley, Pa., U.S.A. 111 E9
Ashmore Reef, Australia .. 92 B3
Ashmûn, Egypt 80 H7
Ashmyany, Belarus 9 J21
Ashokan Reservoir, U.S.A. 111 E10
Ashqelon, Israel 75 D3
Ashta, India 68 H7
Ashtabula, U.S.A. 110 E4
Ashton, S. Africa 88 E3
Ashton, U.S.A. 114 D8
Ashuanipi, L., Canada 103 B6
Ashville, U.S.A. 110 F6
'Āṣī →, Asia 72 E11
Asia, Kepulauan, Indonesia 63 D8
Asia Bak, Iran 71 C6
Asiago, Italy 29 C8

Asifabad, India ... 66 K11
Asinara, Italy ... 30 A1
Asinara, G. dell', Italy ... 30 A1
Asino, Russia ... 50 D9
Asipovichy, Belarus ... 46 F5
'Asīr □, Si. Arabia ... 74 D3
Asir, Ras, Somali Rep. ... 74 E5
Aşkale, Turkey ... 73 C9
Askersund, Sweden ... 11 F8
Askham, S. Africa ... 88 D3
Askim, Norway ... 9 G14
Askja, Iceland ... 8 D5
Askøy, Norway ... 9 F11
Asl, Egypt ... 80 B3
Aslan Burnu, Turkey ... 39 C8
Aslanapa, Eritrea ... 39 B11
Asmara = Asmera, Eritrea ... 81 D4
Asmera, Eritrea ... 81 D4
Asnæs, Denmark ... 11 J4
Åsnen, Sweden ... 11 H8
Asola, Italy ... 28 C7
Asosa, Ethiopia ... 81 E3
Asoteriba, Jebel, Sudan ... 80 C4
Aspe, Spain ... 33 G4
Aspen, U.S.A. ... 115 G10
Aspendos, Turkey ... 72 D4
Aspermont, U.S.A. ... 113 J4
Aspet, France ... 20 E4
Aspiring, Mt., N.Z. ... 91 L2
Aspres-sur-Buëch, France ... 21 D9
Asprókavos, Ákra, Greece ... 36 B4
Aspromonte, Italy ... 31 D9
Aspur, India ... 68 H6
Asquith, Canada ... 105 C7
Assâba, Massif de l', Mauritania ... 82 B2
Assaikio, Nigeria ... 83 D6
Assal, L., Djibouti ... 81 E5
Assam □, India ... 67 G18
Assamakka, Niger ... 83 B6
Asse, Belgium ... 17 D4
Assémini, Italy ... 30 C1
Assen, Neths. ... 17 A6
Assens, Denmark ... 11 J3
Assini, Ivory C. ... 82 D4
Assiniboia, Canada ... 105 D7
Assiniboine →, Canada ... 105 D9
Assiniboine, Mt., Canada ... 104 C5
Assis, Brazil ... 127 A5
Assisi, Italy ... 29 E9
Ássos, Greece ... 38 C2
Assynt, L., U.K. ... 14 C3
Astaffort, France ... 20 D4
Astakidha, Greece ... 39 F8
Astakós, Greece ... 38 C3
Astana, Kazakstan ... 50 D8
Āstāneh, Iran ... 71 B6
Astara, Azerbaijan ... 71 B6
Āstārā, Iran ... 73 C13
Asterousía, Greece ... 36 E7
Asti, Italy ... 28 D5
Astipálaia, Greece ... 39 E8
Astorga, Spain ... 34 C4
Astoria, U.S.A. ... 116 D3
Åstorp, Sweden ... 11 H6
Astrakhan, Russia ... 49 G9
Astudillo, Spain ... 34 C6
Asturias □, Spain ... 34 B5
Asunción, Paraguay ... 126 B4
Asunción Nochixtlán, Mexico ... 119 D5
Åsunden, Sweden ... 11 F9
Asutri, Sudan ... 81 D4
Aswa →, Uganda ... 86 B3
Aswad, Ra's al, Si. Arabia ... 80 C4
Aswân, Egypt ... 80 C3
Aswân High Dam = Sadd el Aali, Egypt ... 80 C3
Asyût, Egypt ... 80 B3
Asyûti, Wadi →, Egypt ... 80 B3
Aszód, Hungary ... 42 C4
At Ţafīlah, Jordan ... 75 E4
Aţ Ţā'if, Si. Arabia ... 74 C3
Aţ Ţirāq, Si. Arabia ... 70 E5
Aţ Tubayq, Si. Arabia ... 70 D3
Atabey, Turkey ... 39 D12
Atacama □, Chile ... 126 B2
Atacama, Desierto de, Chile ... 126 A2
Atacama, Salar de, Chile ... 126 A2
Atakpamé, Togo ... 83 D5
Atalándi, Greece ... 38 C4
Atalaya, Peru ... 124 F4
Atalaya de Femes, Canary Is. ... 37 F6
Atami, Japan ... 55 G9
Atapupu, Indonesia ... 63 F6
Atâr, Mauritania ... 78 D3
Atarfe, Spain ... 35 H7
Atari, Pakistan ... 68 D6
Atascadero, U.S.A. ... 116 K6
Atasu, Kazakstan ... 50 E8
Atatürk Baraji, Turkey ... 73 D8
Atauro, Indonesia ... 63 F7
Atbara, Sudan ... 80 D3
'Atbara →, Sudan ... 80 D3
Atbasar, Kazakstan ... 50 D7
Atça, Turkey ... 39 D10
Atchafalaya B., U.S.A. ... 113 L9
Atchison, U.S.A. ... 112 F7
Atebubu, Ghana ... 83 D4
Ateca, Spain ... 32 D3
Aterno →, Italy ... 29 F10
Āteshān, Iran ... 71 C7
Atesine, Alpi, Italy ... 29 B8
Atessa, Italy ... 29 F11
Atfih, Egypt ... 80 J7
Ath, Belgium ... 17 D3
Athabasca, Canada ... 104 C6
Athabasca →, Canada ... 105 B6
Athabasca, L., Canada ... 105 B7
Athboy, Ireland ... 15 C5
Athenry, Ireland ... 15 C3

Athens = Athínai, Greece ... 38 D5
Athens, Ala., U.S.A. ... 109 H2
Athens, Ga., U.S.A. ... 109 J4
Athens, N.Y., U.S.A. ... 111 D11
Athens, Ohio, U.S.A. ... 108 F4
Athens, Pa., U.S.A. ... 111 E8
Athens, Tenn., U.S.A. ... 109 H3
Athens, Tex., U.S.A. ... 113 J7
Atherley, Canada ... 110 B5
Atherton, Australia ... 94 B4
Athiéme, Benin ... 83 D5
Athienou, Cyprus ... 36 D12
Athínai, Greece ... 38 D5
Athlone, Ireland ... 15 C4
Athna, Cyprus ... 36 D12
Athol, U.S.A. ... 111 D12
Atholl, Forest of, U.K. ... 14 E5
Atholville, Canada ... 103 C6
Áthos, Greece ... 41 F8
Athy, Ireland ... 15 C5
Ati, Chad ... 79 F9
Ati, Sudan ... 81 E2
Atiak, Uganda ... 86 B3
Atienza, Spain ... 32 D2
Atiit, Sudan ... 81 F3
Atik L., Canada ... 105 B9
Atikameg →, Canada ... 102 B3
Atikokan, Canada ... 102 C1
Atikonak L., Canada ... 103 B7
Atimonan, Phil. ... 61 E4
Atka, Russia ... 51 C16
Atka I., U.S.A. ... 100 C2
Atkarsk, Russia ... 48 E7
Atkinson, U.S.A. ... 112 D5
Atlanta, Ga., U.S.A. ... 109 J3
Atlanta, Tex., U.S.A. ... 113 J7
Atlantic, U.S.A. ... 112 E7
Atlantic City, U.S.A. ... 108 F8
Atlantic Ocean ... 2 E9
Atlas Mts. = Haut Atlas, Morocco ... 78 B4
Atlin, Canada ... 104 B2
Atlin, L., Canada ... 104 B2
Atlin Prov. Park, Canada ... 104 B2
Atmore, U.S.A. ... 109 K2
Atoka, U.S.A. ... 113 H6
Átokos, Greece ... 38 C2
Atolia, U.S.A. ... 117 K9
Atrai →, Bangla. ... 69 G13
Atrak = Atrek →, Turkmenistan ... 71 B8
Åtran, Sweden ... 11 G6
Åtran →, Sweden ... 11 H6
Atrauli, India ... 68 E8
Atrek →, Turkmenistan ... 71 B8
Atri, Italy ... 29 F10
Atsiki, Greece ... 39 B7
Atsoum, Mts., Cameroon ... 83 D7
Atsuta, Japan ... 54 C10
Attalla, U.S.A. ... 109 H2
Attapu, Laos ... 64 E6
Attávíros, Greece ... 36 C9
Attawapiskat, Canada ... 102 B3
Attawapiskat →, Canada ... 102 B3
Attawapiskat L., Canada ... 102 B2
Attersee, Austria ... 26 D6
Attica, Ind., U.S.A. ... 108 E2
Attica, Ohio, U.S.A. ... 110 E2
Attichy, France ... 19 C10
Attigny, France ... 19 C11
Attikamagen L., Canada ... 103 B6
Attikí □, Greece ... 38 D5
Attleboro, U.S.A. ... 111 E13
Attock, Pakistan ... 68 C5
Attopeu = Attapu, Laos ... 64 E6
Attu I., U.S.A. ... 100 C1
Attur, India ... 66 P11
Atuel →, Argentina ... 126 D2
Åtvidaberg, Sweden ... 11 F10
Atwater, U.S.A. ... 116 H6
Atwood, Canada ... 110 C3
Atwood, U.S.A. ... 112 F4
Atyraū, Kazakstan ... 50 E6
Au Sable →, U.S.A. ... 110 B1
Au Sable →, U.S.A. ... 108 C4
Au Sable Forks, U.S.A. ... 111 B11
Au Sable Pt., U.S.A. ... 110 B1
Aubagne, France ... 21 E9
Aubarca, C. d', Spain ... 37 B7
Aube □, France ... 19 D11
Aube →, France ... 19 D10
Aubenas, France ... 21 D8
Aubenton, France ... 19 C11
Auberry, U.S.A. ... 116 H7
Aubigny-sur-Nère, France ... 19 E9
Aubin, France ... 20 D6
Aubrac, Mts. d', France ... 20 D7
Auburn, Ala., U.S.A. ... 109 J3
Auburn, Calif., U.S.A. ... 116 G5
Auburn, Ind., U.S.A. ... 108 E3
Auburn, Maine, U.S.A. ... 109 C10
Auburn, N.Y., U.S.A. ... 111 D8
Auburn, Nebr., U.S.A. ... 112 E7
Auburn, Pa., U.S.A. ... 111 F8
Auburn, Wash., U.S.A. ... 116 C4
Auburn Ra., Australia ... 95 D5
Aubusson, France ... 20 C6
Auce, Latvia ... 44 B9
Auch, France ... 20 E4
Auchi, Nigeria ... 83 D6
Auckland, N.Z. ... 91 G5
Auckland Is., Pac. Oc. ... 96 N8
Aude □, France ... 20 E6
Aude →, France ... 20 E7
Auden, Canada ... 102 B2
Auderville, France ... 18 C5
Audierne, France ... 18 D2
Audincourt, France ... 19 E13
Audo, Ethiopia ... 81 F5
Audubon, U.S.A. ... 112 E7
Aue, Germany ... 24 E8

Auerbach, Germany ... 24 E8
Augathella, Australia ... 95 D4
Aughnacloy, U.K. ... 15 B5
Augrabies Falls, S. Africa ... 88 D3
Augsburg, Germany ... 25 G6
Augusta, Australia ... 93 F2
Augusta, Italy ... 31 E8
Augusta, Ark., U.S.A. ... 113 H9
Augusta, Ga., U.S.A. ... 109 J5
Augusta, Kans., U.S.A. ... 113 G6
Augusta, Maine, U.S.A. ... 101 D13
Augusta, Mont., U.S.A. ... 114 C7
Augustenborg, Denmark ... 11 K3
Augustów, Poland ... 44 E9
Augustus, Mt., Australia ... 93 D2
Augustus I., Australia ... 92 C3
Aukan, Eritrea ... 81 D5
Aukum, U.S.A. ... 116 G6
Auld, L., Australia ... 92 D3
Aulla, Italy ... 28 D6
Aulnay, France ... 20 B3
Aulne →, France ... 18 D2
Aulnoye-Aymeries, France ... 19 B10
Ault, France ... 18 B8
Ault, U.S.A. ... 112 E2
Aulus-les-Bains, France ... 20 F5
Aumale, France ... 19 C8
Aumont-Aubrac, France ... 20 D7
Auna, Nigeria ... 83 C5
Auning, Denmark ... 11 H4
Aunis, France ... 20 B3
Auponhia, Indonesia ... 63 E7
Aur, Pulau, Malaysia ... 65 L5
Auraiya, India ... 69 F8
Aurangabad, Bihar, India ... 69 G11
Aurangabad, Maharashtra, India ... 66 K9
Auray, France ... 18 E4
Aurich, Germany ... 24 B3
Aurillac, France ... 20 D6
Auronzo di Cadore, Italy ... 29 B9
Aurora, Canada ... 110 C5
Aurora, S. Africa ... 88 E2
Aurora, Colo., U.S.A. ... 112 F2
Aurora, Ill., U.S.A. ... 108 E1
Aurora, Mo., U.S.A. ... 113 G8
Aurora, N.Y., U.S.A. ... 111 D8
Aurora, Nebr., U.S.A. ... 112 E6
Aurora, Ohio, U.S.A. ... 110 E3
Aurukun, Australia ... 94 A3
Aus, Namibia ... 88 D2
Ausable →, Canada ... 110 C3
Auschwitz = Oświęcim, Poland ... 45 H6
Austerlitz = Slavkov u Brna, Czech Rep. ... 27 B9
Austin, Minn., U.S.A. ... 112 D8
Austin, Nev., U.S.A. ... 114 G5
Austin, Pa., U.S.A. ... 110 E6
Austin, Tex., U.S.A. ... 113 K6
Austin, L., Australia ... 93 E2
Austin I., Canada ... 105 A10
Austra, Norway ... 8 D14
Austral Is. = Tubai Is., Pac. Oc. ... 97 K13
Austral Seamount Chain, Pac. Oc. ... 97 K13
Australia ■, Oceania ... 96 K5
Australian Capital Territory □, Australia ... 95 F4
Australind, Australia ... 93 F2
Austria ■, Europe ... 26 E7
Austvågøy, Norway ... 8 B16
Auterive, France ... 20 E5
Authie →, France ... 19 B8
Authon-du-Perche, France ... 18 D7
Autlán, Mexico ... 118 D4
Autun, France ... 19 F11
Auvergne, France ... 20 C7
Auvergne, Mts. d', France ... 20 C6
Auvézère →, France ... 20 C4
Auxerre, France ... 19 E10
Auxi-le-Château, France ... 19 B9
Auxonne, France ... 19 E12
Auzances, France ... 20 B6
Ava, U.S.A. ... 113 G8
Avallon, France ... 19 E10
Avalon, U.S.A. ... 117 M8
Avalon Pen., Canada ... 103 C9
Avanos, Turkey ... 70 B2
Avaré, Brazil ... 127 A6
Ávas, Greece ... 41 F9
Avawatz Mts., U.S.A. ... 117 K10
Avdan Dağı, Turkey ... 41 F13
Aveiro, Brazil ... 125 D7
Aveiro, Portugal ... 34 E2
Aveiro □, Portugal ... 34 E2
Āvej, Iran ... 71 C6
Avellaneda, Argentina ... 126 C4
Avellino, Italy ... 31 B7
Avenal, U.S.A. ... 116 K6
Aversa, Italy ... 31 B7
Avery, U.S.A. ... 114 C6
Aves, Is. las, Venezuela ... 121 D6
Avesnes-sur-Helpe, France ... 19 B10
Avesta, Sweden ... 10 D10
Aveyron □, France ... 20 D6
Aveyron →, France ... 20 D5
Avezzano, Italy ... 29 F10
Avgó, Greece ... 39 F7
Aviá Terai, Argentina ... 126 B3
Aviano, Italy ... 29 B9
Aviemore, U.K. ... 14 D5
Avigliana, Italy ... 28 C4
Avigliano, Italy ... 31 B8
Avignon, France ... 21 E8
Ávila, Spain ... 34 E6
Ávila □, Spain ... 34 E6
Ávila, Sierra de, Spain ... 34 E5
Avila Beach, U.S.A. ... 117 K6

Avilés, Spain ... 34 B5
Avintes, Portugal ... 34 D2
Avionárion, Greece ... 38 C6
Avis, Portugal ... 35 F3
Avis, U.S.A. ... 110 E7
Avísio →, Italy ... 28 B8
Aviz = Avis, Portugal ... 35 F3
Avize, France ... 19 D11
Avlum, Denmark ... 11 H2
Avoca, U.S.A. ... 110 D7
Avoca →, Australia ... 95 F3
Avoca →, Ireland ... 15 D5
Avola, Canada ... 104 C5
Avola, Italy ... 31 F8
Avon, U.S.A. ... 110 D7
Avon →, Australia ... 93 F2
Avon →, Bristol, U.K. ... 13 F5
Avon →, Dorset, U.K. ... 13 G6
Avon →, Warks., U.K. ... 13 E5
Avon Park, U.S.A. ... 109 M5
Avondale, Zimbabwe ... 87 F3
Avonlea, Canada ... 105 D8
Avonmore, Canada ... 111 A10
Avramov, Bulgaria ... 41 D10
Avranches, France ... 18 D5
Avre →, France ... 18 D8
Avrig, Romania ... 43 E9
Avrillé, France ... 18 E6
Avtovac, Bos.-H. ... 40 C2
Awag el Baqar, Sudan ... 81 E3
A'waj →, Syria ... 75 B5
Awaji-Shima, Japan ... 55 G7
'Awālī, Bahrain ... 71 E6
Awantipur, India ... 69 C6
Awasa, Ethiopia ... 81 F4
Awasa, L., Ethiopia ... 81 F4
Awash, Ethiopia ... 81 F5
Awash →, Ethiopia ... 81 E5
Awaso, Ghana ... 82 D4
Awatere →, N.Z. ... 91 J5
Awbārī, Libya ... 79 C8
Awe, L., U.K. ... 14 E3
Aweil, Sudan ... 81 F2
Awgu, Nigeria ... 83 D6
Awjilah, Libya ... 79 C10
Awka, Nigeria ... 83 D6
Ax-les-Thermes, France ... 20 F5
Axat, France ... 20 F6
Axe →, U.K. ... 13 F5
Axel Heiberg I., Canada ... 4 B3
Axim, Ghana ... 82 E4
Axintele, Romania ... 43 F11
Axiós →, Greece ... 40 F6
Axminster, U.K. ... 13 G4
Ay, France ... 19 C11
Ayabaca, Peru ... 124 D3
Ayabe, Japan ... 55 G7
Ayacucho, Argentina ... 126 D4
Ayacucho, Peru ... 124 F4
Ayaguz, Kazakstan ... 50 E9
Ayamé, Ivory C. ... 82 D4
Ayamonte, Spain ... 35 H3
Ayan, Russia ... 51 D14
Ayancık, Turkey ... 72 B6
Ayas, Turkey ... 72 B5
Ayaviri, Peru ... 124 F4
Aybastı, Turkey ... 72 B7
Aydın, Turkey ... 72 D2
Aydın □, Turkey ... 39 D9
Aydın Dağları, Turkey ... 39 D10
Ayelu, Ethiopia ... 81 E5
Ayenngré, Togo ... 83 D5
Ayer, U.S.A. ... 111 D13
Ayerbe, Spain ... 32 C4
Ayer's Cliff, Canada ... 111 A12
Ayers Rock, Australia ... 93 E5
Ayiá, Greece ... 38 B4
Ayia Aikateríni, Ákra, Greece ... 36 A3
Ayía Dhéka, Greece ... 36 D6
Ayía Gálini, Greece ... 36 D6
Ayía Marína, Kásos, Greece ... 39 F8
Ayía Marína, Léros, Greece ... 39 D8
Ayía Napa, Cyprus ... 36 E13
Ayía Paraskeví, Greece ... 39 B8
Ayía Phyla, Cyprus ... 36 E12
Ayía Rouméli, Greece ... 38 F5
Ayía Varvára, Greece ... 36 D6
Ayiássos, Greece ... 39 B8
Áyioi Theódhoroi, Greece ... 38 D5
Áyion Óros, Greece ... 41 F8
Áyios Amvrósios, Cyprus ... 36 D12
Áyios Andréas, Greece ... 38 D4
Áyios Evstrátios, Greece ... 38 B6
Áyios Ioánnis, Ákra, Greece ... 36 D7
Áyios Isídhoros, Greece ... 36 C9
Áyios Kírikos, Greece ... 39 D8
Áyios Matthaíos, Greece ... 36 B3
Áyios Mírono, Greece ... 39 F7
Áyios Pétros, Greece ... 38 C2
Áyios Seryios, Cyprus ... 36 D12
Áyios Theodhoros, Cyprus ... 36 D13
Áyios Yeóryios, Greece ... 38 D5
Aykhal, Russia ... 51 C12
Aykirikçi, Turkey ... 39 B12
Aylesbury, U.K. ... 13 F7
Aylmer, Canada ... 110 D4
Aylmer, L., Canada ... 100 B8
'Ayn, Wādī al, Oman ... 71 F7
Ayn Dār, Si. Arabia ... 71 E7
Ayn Zālah, Iraq ... 70 B4
Ayna, Spain ... 33 G2
Ayod, Sudan ... 81 F3
Ayolas, Paraguay ... 126 B4
Ayom, Sudan ... 81 F2
Ayon, Ostrov, Russia ... 51 C17
Ayora, Spain ... 33 F3
Ayorou, Niger ... 83 C5

Ayr, Australia ... 94 B4
Ayr, Canada ... 110 C4
Ayr, U.K. ... 14 F4
Ayr →, U.K. ... 14 F4
Ayrancı, Turkey ... 72 D5
Ayranclar, Turkey ... 39 C9
Ayre, Pt. of, U.K. ... 12 C3
Aysha, Ethiopia ... 81 E5
Ayton, Australia ... 94 B4
Aytos, Bulgaria ... 41 D11
Aytoska Planina, Bulgaria ... 41 D11
Ayu, Kepulauan, Indonesia ... 63 D8
Ayutla, Guatemala ... 120 D1
Ayutla, Mexico ... 119 D5
Ayvacık, Turkey ... 72 C2
Ayvalık, Turkey ... 39 B8
Az Zabadānī, Syria ... 75 B5
Az Ẓāhirīyah, West Bank ... 75 D3
Az Zahrān, Si. Arabia ... 71 E6
Az Zarqā, Jordan ... 75 C5
Az Zarqā', U.A.E. ... 71 E7
Az Zāwiyah, Libya ... 79 B8
Az Zibār, Iraq ... 70 B5
Az Zilfī, Si. Arabia ... 70 E5
Az Zubayr, Iraq ... 70 D5
Az Zuwaytīnah, Yemen ... 81 E5
Azambuja, Portugal ... 35 F2
Azamgarh, India ... 69 F10
Azangaro, Peru ... 124 F4
Azaouad, Mali ... 82 B5
Azaouak, Vallée de l', Mali ... 83 B5
Āzar Shahr, Iran ... 70 B5
Azara, Nigeria ... 83 D6
Azarán, Iran ... 70 B5
Āzarbāyjān = Azerbaijan ■, Asia ... 49 K9
Āzarbāyjān-e Gharbī □, Iran ... 70 B5
Āzarbāyjān-e Sharqī □, Iran ... 70 B5
Azare, Nigeria ... 83 C7
Azay-le-Rideau, France ... 18 E7
A'zāz, Syria ... 70 B3
Azbine = Aïr, Niger ... 83 B6
Azerbaijan ■, Asia ... 49 K9
Azerbaijchan = Azerbaijan ■, Asia ... 49 K9
Azezo, Ethiopia ... 81 E4
Azimganj, India ... 69 G13
Aznalcóllar, Spain ... 35 H4
Azogues, Ecuador ... 124 D3
Azores, Atl. Oc. ... 78 A1
Azov, Russia ... 47 J10
Azov, Sea of, Europe ... 47 J9
Azovskoye More = Azov, Sea of, Europe ... 47 J9
Azpeitia, Spain ... 32 B2
Azraq ash Shīshān, Jordan ... 75 D5
Aztec, U.S.A. ... 115 H10
Azúa de Compostela, Dom. Rep. ... 121 C5
Azuaga, Spain ... 35 G5
Azuara, Spain ... 32 D4
Azuer →, Spain ... 35 F7
Azuero, Pen. de, Panama ... 120 E3
Azuga, Romania ... 43 E10
Azul, Argentina ... 126 D4
Azusa, U.S.A. ... 117 L9
Azzano Décimo, Italy ... 29 C9

B

Ba Don, Vietnam ... 64 D6
Ba Dong, Vietnam ... 65 H6
Ba Ngoi = Cam Lam, Vietnam ... 65 G7
Ba Tri, Vietnam ... 65 G6
Ba Xian = Bazhou, China ... 56 E9
Baa, Indonesia ... 63 F6
Baamonde, Spain ... 34 B3
Baarle-Nassau, Belgium ... 17 C4
Bab el Mandeb, Red Sea ... 74 E3
Baba, Bulgaria ... 40 D7
Baba Burnu, Turkey ... 39 B8
Baba dag, Azerbaijan ... 49 K9
Bābā Kalū, Iran ... 71 D6
Babadag, Romania ... 43 F13
Babadağ, Turkey ... 39 D10
Babadayhan, Turkmenistan ... 50 F7
Babaeski, Turkey ... 41 E11
Babahoyo, Ecuador ... 124 D3
Babai = Sarju →, India ... 69 F9
Babana, Nigeria ... 83 C5
Babanusa, Sudan ... 81 E2
Babar, Indonesia ... 63 F7
Babar, Pakistan ... 68 D3
Babarkach, Pakistan ... 68 E3
Babayevo, Russia ... 46 C8
Babb, U.S.A. ... 114 C7
Babelthuap, Pac. Oc. ... 63 C8
Băbeni, Romania ... 43 F9
Baberu, India ... 69 G9
Babi Besar, Pulau, Malaysia ... 65 L4
Babia Gora, Europe ... 45 J6
Babian Jiang →, China ... 58 F3
Babile, Ethiopia ... 81 F5
Babimost, Poland ... 45 F2
Babinda, Australia ... 94 B4
Babine, Canada ... 104 B3
Babine →, Canada ... 104 B3
Babine L., Canada ... 104 C3
Babo, Indonesia ... 63 E8
Babócsa, Hungary ... 42 D2
Bābol, Iran ... 71 B7
Bābol Sar, Iran ... 71 B7
Baborów, Poland ... 45 H5

Babruysk, *Belarus* 47 F5
Babuhri, *India* 68 F3
Babuna, *Macedonia* 40 E5
Babura, *Nigeria* 83 C6
Babusar Pass, *Pakistan* 69 B5
Babuyan Chan., *Phil.* 61 B4
Babylon, *Iraq* 70 C5
Bač, *Serbia, Yug.* 42 E4
Bâc →, *Moldova* 43 D14
Bac Can, *Vietnam* 58 F5
Bac Giang, *Vietnam* 58 G6
Bac Lieu, *Vietnam* 65 H5
Bac Ninh, *Vietnam* 58 G6
Bac Phan, *Vietnam* 64 B5
Bac Quang, *Vietnam* 58 F5
Bacabal, *Brazil* 125 D10
Bacalar, *Mexico* 119 D7
Bacan, Kepulauan, *Indonesia* 63 E7
Bacarra, *Phil.* 61 B4
Bacău, *Romania* 43 D11
Bacău □, *Romania* 43 D11
Baccarat, *France* 19 D13
Bacerac, *Mexico* 118 A3
Băceşti, *Romania* 43 D12
Bach Long Vi, Dao, *Vietnam* 64 B6
Bacharach, *Germany* 25 E3
Bachelina, *Russia* 50 D7
Bachhwara, *India* 69 G11
Bachuma, *Ethiopia* 81 F4
Bačina, *Serbia, Yug.* 40 C5
Back →, *Canada* 100 B9
Bačka Palanka, *Serbia, Yug.* 42 E4
Bačka Topola, *Serbia, Yug.* 42 E4
Bäckaby, *Sweden* 11 H10
Bäckefors, *Sweden* 11 F6
Bäckhammar, *Sweden* 10 E8
Bački Petrovac, *Serbia, Yug.* 42 E4
Backnang, *Germany* 25 G5
Baco, Mt., *Phil.* 61 E4
Bacolod, *Phil.* 61 F5
Bacqueville-en-Caux, *France* 18 C8
Bács-Kiskun □, *Hungary* 42 D4
Bácsalmás, *Hungary* 42 D4
Bacuag = Placer, *Phil.* 61 G6
Bacuk, *Malaysia* 65 J4
Bād, *Iran* 71 C7
Bad →, *U.S.A.* 112 C4
Bad Aussee, *Austria* 26 D6
Bad Axe, *U.S.A.* 110 C2
Bad Bergzabern, *Germany* 25 F3
Bad Berleburg, *Germany* 24 D4
Bad Bevensen, *Germany* 24 B6
Bad Bramstedt, *Germany* 24 B5
Bad Brückenau, *Germany* 25 E5
Bad Doberan, *Germany* 24 A7
Bad Driburg, *Germany* 24 D5
Bad Ems, *Germany* 25 E3
Bad Frankenhausen, *Germany* 24 D7
Bad Freienwalde, *Germany* 24 C10
Bad Goisern, *Austria* 26 D6
Bad Harzburg, *Germany* 24 D6
Bad Hersfeld, *Germany* 24 E5
Bad Hofgastein, *Austria* 26 D6
Bad Homburg, *Germany* 25 E4
Bad Honnef, *Germany* 24 E3
Bad Iburg, *Germany* 24 C4
Bad Ischl, *Austria* 26 D6
Bad Kissingen, *Germany* 25 E6
Bad Königshofen, *Germany* 25 E6
Bad Kreuznach, *Germany* 25 F3
Bad Krozingen, *Germany* 25 H3
Bad Laasphe, *Germany* 24 E4
Bad Lands, *U.S.A.* 112 D3
Bad Langensalza, *Germany* 24 D6
Bad Lauterberg, *Germany* 24 D6
Bad Leonfelden, *Austria* 26 C7
Bad Liebenwerda, *Germany* 24 D9
Bad Mergentheim, *Germany* 25 F5
Bad Münstereifel, *Germany* 24 E2
Bad Nauheim, *Germany* 25 E4
Bad Neuenahr-Ahrweiler, *Germany* 24 E3
Bad Neustadt, *Germany* 25 E6
Bad Oeynhausen, *Germany* 24 C4
Bad Oldesloe, *Germany* 24 B6
Bad Orb, *Germany* 25 E5
Bad Pyrmont, *Germany* 24 D5
Bad Reichenhall, *Germany* 25 H8
Bad Säckingen, *Germany* 25 H3
Bad Salzuflen, *Germany* 24 C4
Bad Salzungen, *Germany* 24 E6
Bad Schwartau, *Germany* 24 B6
Bad Segeberg, *Germany* 24 B6
Bad St. Leonhard, *Austria* 26 E7
Bad Tölz, *Germany* 25 H7
Bad Urach, *Germany* 25 G5
Bad Vöslau, *Austria* 27 D9
Bad Waldsee, *Germany* 25 H5
Bad Wildungen, *Germany* 24 D5
Bad Wimpfen, *Germany* 25 F5
Bad Windsheim, *Germany* 25 F6
Bad Zwischenahn, *Germany* 24 B4
Bada Barabil, *India* 69 H11
Badagara, *India* 66 P9
Badagri, *Nigeria* 83 D5
Badajós, L., *Brazil* 124 D6
Badajoz, *Spain* 35 G4
Badajoz □, *Spain* 35 G4
Badalona, *Spain* 32 D7
Badalzai, *Afghan.* 68 E1
Badampahar, *India* 67 H15
Badanah, *Si. Arabia* 70 D4
Badarinath, *India* 69 D8
Badas, Kepulauan, *Indonesia* 62 D3
Baddo →, *Pakistan* 66 F4
Bade, *Indonesia* 63 F9
Badeggi, *Nigeria* 83 D6
Badéguichéri, *Niger* 83 C6
Baden, *Austria* 27 C9

Baden, *Switz.* 25 H4
Baden, *U.S.A.* 110 F4
Baden-Baden, *Germany* 25 G4
Baden-Württemberg □, *Germany* 25 G4
Badgastein, *Austria* 26 D6
Badger, *Canada* 103 C8
Badger, *U.S.A.* 116 J7
Bādghīsāt □, *Afghan.* 66 B3
Badgom, *India* 69 B6
Badia Polésine, *Italy* 29 C8
Badin, *Pakistan* 68 G3
Badlands National Park, *U.S.A.* 112 D3
Badogo, *Mali* 82 C3
Badoumbé, *Mali* 82 C2
Badrah, *Iraq* 70 C5
Badrinath, *India* 69 D8
Badulla, *Sri Lanka* 66 R12
Baena, *Spain* 35 H6
Baeza, *Spain* 35 H7
Bafang, *Cameroon* 83 D7
Bafatá, *Guinea-Biss.* 82 C2
Baffin B., *Canada* 4 B4
Baffin I., *Canada* 101 B12
Bafia, *Cameroon* 83 E7
Bafilo, *Togo* 83 D5
Bafing →, *Mali* 82 C2
Bafliyūn, *Syria* 70 B3
Bafoulabé, *Mali* 82 C2
Bafoussam, *Cameroon* 83 D7
Bāfq, *Iran* 71 D7
Bafra, *Turkey* 72 B6
Bafra Burnu, *Turkey* 72 B7
Bāft, *Iran* 71 D8
Bafut, *Cameroon* 83 D7
Bafwasende, *Dem. Rep. of the Congo* 86 B2
Bagam, *Niger* 83 B6
Bagamoyo, *Tanzania* 86 D4
Bagan Datoh, *Malaysia* 65 L3
Bagan Serai, *Malaysia* 65 K3
Baganga, *Phil.* 61 H7
Bagani, *Namibia* 88 B3
Bagansiapiapi, *Indonesia* 62 D2
Bagasra, *India* 68 J4
Bagaud, *India* 68 H6
Bagawi, *Sudan* 81 E3
Bagbag, *Sudan* 81 D3
Bagdad, *U.S.A.* 117 L11
Bagdarin, *Russia* 51 D12
Bagé, *Brazil* 127 C5
Bagenalstown = Muine Bheag, *Ireland* 15 D5
Baggs, *U.S.A.* 114 F10
Bagh, *Pakistan* 69 C5
Baghain →, *India* 69 G9
Baghdād, *Iraq* 70 C5
Bagheria, *Italy* 30 D6
Baghlān, *Afghan.* 66 A6
Bagley, *U.S.A.* 112 B7
Bagnara Cálabra, *Italy* 31 D8
Bagnasco, *Italy* 28 D5
Bagnères-de-Bigorre, *France* 20 E4
Bagnères-de-Luchon, *France* 20 F4
Bagni di Lucca, *Italy* 28 D7
Bagno di Romagna, *Italy* 29 E8
Bagnoles-de-l'Orne, *France* 18 D6
Bagnols-sur-Cèze, *France* 21 D8
Bagnorégio, *Italy* 29 F9
Bago = Pegu, *Burma* 67 L20
Bagodar, *India* 69 G11
Bagrationovsk, *Russia* 9 J19
Bagrdan, *Serbia, Yug.* 40 B5
Baguio, *Phil.* 61 C4
Bağyurdu, *Turkey* 39 C9
Bagzane, Monts, *Niger* 83 B6
Bah, *India* 69 F8
Bahabón de Esgueva, *Spain* 34 D7
Bahadurganj, *India* 69 F12
Bahadurgarh, *India* 68 E7
Bahama, Canal Viejo de, *W. Indies* 120 B4
Bahamas ■, *N. Amer.* 121 B5
Bahār, *Iran* 73 E13
Baharampur, *India* 69 G13
Baharîya, El Wâhât al, *Egypt* 80 B2
Bahawalnagar, *Pakistan* 68 E5
Bahawalpur, *Pakistan* 68 E4
Bahçe, *Turkey* 72 D7
Bahçecik, *Turkey* 41 F13
Baheri, *India* 69 E8
Bahgul →, *India* 69 F8
Bahi, *Tanzania* 86 D4
Bahi Swamp, *Tanzania* 86 D4
Bahía = Salvador, *Brazil* 125 F11
Bahía □, *Brazil* 125 F10
Bahía, Is. de la, *Honduras* 120 C2
Bahía Blanca, *Argentina* 126 D3
Bahía de Caráquez, *Ecuador* 124 D2
Bahía Honda, *Cuba* 120 B3
Bahía Laura, *Argentina* 128 F3
Bahía Negra, *Paraguay* 124 H7
Bahir Dar, *Ethiopia* 81 E4
Bahmanzād, *Iran* 71 D6
Bahr el Ahmar □, *Sudan* 80 D4
Bahr el Ghazâl □, *Sudan* 81 F2
Bahr el Jabal □, *Sudan* 81 G3
Bahr Yûsef →, *Egypt* 80 B3
Bahraich, *India* 69 F9
Bahrain ■, *Asia* 71 E6
Bahror, *India* 68 F7
Bāhū Kalāt, *Iran* 71 E9
Bai, *Mali* 82 C4
Bai Bung, Mui = Ca Mau, Mui, *Vietnam* 65 H5
Bai Duc, *Vietnam* 64 C5
Bai Thuong, *Vietnam* 64 C5
Baia de Aramă, *Romania* 42 E7
Baia Mare, *Romania* 43 C8
Baia-Sprie, *Romania* 43 C8

Baião, *Brazil* 125 D9
Baïbokoum, *Chad* 79 G9
Baicheng, *China* 57 B12
Băicoi, *Romania* 43 E10
Baidoa, *Somali Rep.* 74 G3
Baie Comeau, *Canada* 103 C6
Baie-St-Paul, *Canada* 103 C5
Baie Trinité, *Canada* 103 C6
Baie Verte, *Canada* 103 C8
Baignes-Ste-Radegonde, *France* 20 C3
Baigneux-les-Juifs, *France* 19 E11
Baihar, *India* 69 H9
Baihe, *China* 56 H6
Ba'ījī, *Iraq* 70 C4
Baijnath, *India* 69 E8
Baikal, L. = Baykal, Oz., *Russia* 51 D11
Baikunthpur, *India* 69 H10
Baile Atha Cliath = Dublin, *Ireland* 15 C5
Băile Govora, *Romania* 43 E9
Băile Herculane, *Romania* 42 F7
Băile Olăneşti, *Romania* 43 E9
Băile Tuşnad, *Romania* 43 D10
Bailén, *Spain* 35 G7
Băileşti, *Romania* 43 F8
Baima, *China* 58 A3
Bain-de-Bretagne, *France* 18 E5
Bainbridge, Ga., *U.S.A.* 109 K3
Bainbridge, N.Y., *U.S.A.* 111 D9
Baing, *Indonesia* 63 F6
Bainiu, *China* 56 H7
Baiona, *Spain* 34 C2
Bā'ir, *Jordan* 75 E5
Bairin Youqi, *China* 57 C10
Bairin Zuoqi, *China* 57 C10
Bairnsdale, *Australia* 95 F4
Bais, *Phil.* 61 G5
Baisha, *China* 56 G7
Baissa, *Nigeria* 83 D7
Baitadi, *Nepal* 69 E9
Baiyin, *China* 56 F3
Baiyü, *China* 58 B2
Baiyu Shan, *China* 56 F4
Baiyuda, *Sudan* 80 D3
Baj Baj, *India* 69 H13
Baja, *Hungary* 42 D3
Baja, Pta., *Mexico* 118 B1
Baja California, *Mexico* 118 A1
Baja California □, *Mexico* 118 B2
Baja California Sur □, *Mexico* 118 B2
Bajag, *India* 69 H9
Bajamar, *Canary Is.* 37 F3
Bajana, *India* 68 H4
Bājgīrān, *Iran* 71 B8
Bajimba, Mt., *Australia* 95 D5
Bajmok, *Serbia, Yug.* 42 E4
Bajo Nuevo, *Caribbean* 120 C4
Bajoga, *Nigeria* 83 C7
Bajool, *Australia* 94 C5
Bak, *Hungary* 42 D1
Bakar, *Croatia* 29 C11
Bakel, *Senegal* 82 C2
Baker, Calif., *U.S.A.* 117 K10
Baker, Mont., *U.S.A.* 112 B2
Baker, L., *Canada* 100 B10
Baker City, *U.S.A.* 114 D5
Baker I., *Pac. Oc.* 96 G10
Baker I., *U.S.A.* 104 B2
Baker L., *Australia* 93 E4
Baker Lake, *Canada* 100 B10
Baker Mt., *U.S.A.* 114 B3
Bakers Creek, *Australia* 94 C4
Baker's Dozen Is., *Canada* 102 A4
Bakersfield, Calif., *U.S.A.* 117 K8
Bakersfield, Vt., *U.S.A.* 111 B12
Bakhchysaray, *Ukraine* 47 K7
Bakhmach, *Ukraine* 47 G7
Bākhtarān, *Iran* 70 C5
Bākhtarān □, *Iran* 70 C5
Bakı, *Azerbaijan* 49 K9
Bakır →, *Turkey* 39 C9
Bakırdağı, *Turkey* 72 C6
Bakkafjörður, *Iceland* 8 C6
Baklan, *Turkey* 39 C11
Bako, *Ethiopia* 81 F4
Bako, *Ivory C.* 82 D3
Bakony, *Hungary* 42 C2
Bakony Forest = Bakony, *Hungary* 42 C2
Bakori, *Nigeria* 83 C6
Bakouma, *C.A.R.* 84 C4
Baksan, *Russia* 49 J6
Bakswaho, *India* 69 G8
Baku = Bakı, *Azerbaijan* 49 K9
Bakutis Coast, *Antarctica* 5 D15
Baky = Bakı, *Azerbaijan* 49 K9
Bala, *Canada* 110 A5
Bala, *Senegal* 82 C2
Bâla, *Turkey* 72 C5
Bala, *U.K.* 12 E4
Bala, L., *U.K.* 12 E4
Balabac I., *Phil.* 62 C5
Balabac Str., *E. Indies* 62 C5
Balabagh, *Afghan.* 68 B4
Balabalangan, Kepulauan, *Indonesia* 62 E5
Bălăciţa, *Romania* 43 F8
Balad, *Iraq* 70 C5
Balad Rūz, *Iraq* 70 C5
Bālādeh, Fārs, *Iran* 71 D6
Bālādeh, Māzandaran, *Iran* 71 B6
Balaghat, *India* 69 J12
Balaghat Ra., *India* 66 K10
Balaguer, *Spain* 32 D5
Balakhna, *Russia* 48 B6

Balaklava, *Ukraine* 47 K7
Balakliya, *Ukraine* 47 H9
Balakovo, *Russia* 48 D8
Balamau, *India* 69 F9
Bălan, *Romania* 43 D10
Balancán, *Mexico* 119 D6
Balashov, *Russia* 48 E6
Balasinor, *India* 68 H5
Balasore = Baleshwar, *India* 67 J15
Balassagyarmat, *Hungary* 42 B4
Balât, *Egypt* 80 B2
Balaton, *Hungary* 42 D2
Balatonboglár, *Hungary* 42 D2
Balatonfüred, *Hungary* 42 D2
Balatonszentgyörgy, *Hungary* 42 D2
Balayan, *Phil.* 61 E4
Balazote, *Spain* 33 G2
Balbieriškis, *Lithuania* 44 D10
Balbigny, *France* 21 C8
Balbina, Reprêsa de, *Brazil* 124 D7
Balboa, *Panama* 120 E4
Balbriggan, *Ireland* 15 C5
Balcarce, *Argentina* 126 D4
Balcarres, *Canada* 105 C8
Bălceşti, *Romania* 43 F8
Balchik, *Bulgaria* 41 C12
Balclutha, *N.Z.* 91 M2
Balcones Escarpment, *U.S.A.* 113 L5
Balça, *Turkey* 39 C9
Bald Hd., *Australia* 93 G2
Bald I., *Australia* 93 F2
Bald Knob, *U.S.A.* 113 H9
Baldock L., *Canada* 105 B9
Baldwin, Mich., *U.S.A.* 108 D3
Baldwin, Pa., *U.S.A.* 110 F5
Baldwinsville, *U.S.A.* 111 C8
Baldy Mt., *U.S.A.* 114 B9
Baldy Peak, *U.S.A.* 115 K9
Bale, *Croatia* 29 C10
Bale, *Ethiopia* 81 F5
Bale □, *Ethiopia* 81 F5
Baleares, Is., *Spain* 37 B10
Balearic Is. = Baleares, Is., *Spain* 37 B10
Baleine = Whale →, *Canada* 103 A6
Băleni, *Romania* 43 E12
Baler, *Phil.* 61 D4
Baler Bay, *Phil.* 61 D4
Baleshare, *U.K.* 14 D1
Baleshwar, *India* 67 J15
Balezino, *Russia* 48 B11
Balfate, *Honduras* 120 C2
Bali, *Cameroon* 83 D7
Balí, *Greece* 36 D6
Bali, *India* 68 G5
Bali □, *Indonesia* 62 F5
Bali, Selat, *Indonesia* 63 H16
Balia, *S. Leone* 82 D2
Baliapal, *India* 69 J12
Baligród, *Poland* 45 J9
Balikeşir, *Turkey* 39 B9
Balikeşir □, *Turkey* 39 B9
Balıklıçeşme, *Turkey* 41 F11
Balikpapan, *Indonesia* 62 E5
Balimbing, *Phil.* 63 C5
Balingen, *Germany* 25 G4
Baling, *Malaysia* 65 K3
Balint, *Romania* 42 E6
Balintang Channel, *Phil.* 61 B4
Balipara, *India* 67 F18
Balkan Mts. = Stara Planina, *Bulgaria* 40 C7
Balkhash = Balqash, *Kazakstan* 50 E8
Balkhash, Ozero = Balqash Köl, *Kazakstan* 50 E8
Balla, *Bangla.* 67 G17
Ballachulish, *U.K.* 14 E3
Balladonia, *Australia* 93 F3
Ballaghaderreen, *Ireland* 15 C3
Ballarat, *Australia* 95 F3
Ballard, L., *Australia* 93 E3
Ballater, *U.K.* 14 D5
Ballé, *Mali* 82 B3
Ballenas, Canal de, *Mexico* 118 B2
Balleny Is., *Antarctica* 5 C11
Balleroy, *France* 18 C6
Ballerup, *Denmark* 11 J6
Ballı, *Turkey* 41 F11
Ballia, *India* 69 G11
Ballina, *Australia* 95 D5
Ballina, *Ireland* 15 C2
Ballinasloe, *Ireland* 15 C3
Ballinger, *U.S.A.* 113 K5
Ballinrobe, *Ireland* 15 C2
Ballinskelligs B., *Ireland* 15 E1
Ballon, *France* 18 D7
Ballston Spa, *U.S.A.* 111 D11
Ballycastle, *U.K.* 15 A5
Ballyclare, *U.K.* 15 B5
Ballyhaunis, *Ireland* 15 C3
Ballymena, *U.K.* 15 B5
Ballymoney, *U.K.* 15 A5
Ballynahinch, *U.K.* 15 B6
Ballyquintin Pt., *U.K.* 15 B6
Ballyshannon, *Ireland* 15 B3
Balmaceda, *Chile* 128 F2
Balmaseda, *Spain* 32 B1
Balmazújváros, *Hungary* 42 C6
Balmertown, *Canada* 105 C10
Balmoral, *Australia* 95 F3
Balmorhea, *U.S.A.* 113 K3
Balonne →, *Australia* 95 D4
Balotra, *India* 68 G5
Balqash, *Kazakstan* 50 E8
Balqash Köl, *Kazakstan* 50 E8
Balrampur, *India* 69 F10

Balranald, *Australia* 95 E3
Balş, *Romania* 43 F9
Balsas, *Mexico* 119 D5
Balsas →, *Brazil* 125 E9
Balsas →, *Mexico* 118 D4
Bålsta, *Sweden* 10 E11
Balston Spa, *U.S.A.* 111 D11
Balta, *Romania* 42 F7
Balta, *Ukraine* 47 H5
Baltanás, *Spain* 34 D6
Bălţi, *Moldova* 43 C12
Baltic Sea, *Europe* 9 H18
Baltîm, *Egypt* 80 H7
Baltimore, *Ireland* 15 E2
Baltimore, Md., *U.S.A.* 108 F7
Baltimore, Ohio, *U.S.A.* 110 G2
Baltit, *Pakistan* 69 A6
Baltiysk, *Russia* 9 J18
Baltrum, *Germany* 24 B3
Baluchistan □, *Pakistan* 66 F4
Balurghat, *India* 69 G13
Balvi, *Latvia* 9 H22
Balya, *Turkey* 39 B9
Bam, *Iran* 71 D8
Bama, *China* 58 E6
Bama, *Nigeria* 83 C7
Bamaga, *Australia* 94 A3
Bamaji L., *Canada* 102 B1
Bamako, *Mali* 82 C3
Bamba, *Mali* 83 B4
Bambara Maoundé, *Mali* 82 B4
Bambari, *C.A.R.* 84 C4
Bambaroo, *Australia* 94 B4
Bambaya, *Guinea* 82 D2
Bamberg, *Germany* 25 F6
Bamberg, *U.S.A.* 109 J5
Bambesi, *Ethiopia* 81 F3
Bambey, *Senegal* 82 C1
Bambili, *Dem. Rep. of the Congo* 86 B2
Bamboi, *Ghana* 82 D4
Bamenda, *Cameroon* 83 D7
Bamfield, *Canada* 104 D3
Bāmiān □, *Afghan.* 66 B5
Bamiancheng, *China* 57 C13
Bamkin, *Cameroon* 83 D7
Bampūr, *Iran* 71 E9
Ban, *Burkina Faso* 82 C4
Ban Ban, *Laos* 64 C4
Ban Bang Hin, *Thailand* 65 H2
Ban Chiang Klang, *Thailand* 64 C3
Ban Chik, *Laos* 64 D4
Ban Choho, *Thailand* 64 E4
Ban Dan Lan Hoi, *Thailand* 64 D2
Ban Don = Surat Thani, *Thailand* 65 H2
Ban Don, *Vietnam* 64 F6
Ban Don, Ao →, *Thailand* 65 H2
Ban Dong, *Thailand* 64 C3
Ban Hong, *Thailand* 64 C2
Ban Kaeng, *Thailand* 64 D3
Ban Kantang, *Thailand* 65 J2
Ban Keun, *Laos* 64 C4
Ban Khai, *Thailand* 64 F3
Ban Kheun, *Laos* 64 B3
Ban Khlong Kua, *Thailand* 65 J3
Ban Khuan Mao, *Thailand* 65 J2
Ban Ko Yai Chim, *Thailand* 65 G2
Ban Kok, *Thailand* 64 D4
Ban Laem, *Thailand* 64 F2
Ban Lao Ngam, *Laos* 64 E6
Ban Le Kathe, *Thailand* 64 E2
Ban Mae Chedi, *Thailand* 64 C2
Ban Mae Laeng, *Thailand* 64 B2
Ban Mae Sariang, *Thailand* 64 C1
Ban Mê Thuot = Buon Ma Thuot, *Vietnam* 64 F7
Ban Mi, *Thailand* 64 E3
Ban Muong Mo, *Laos* 64 C4
Ban Na Mo, *Laos* 64 D5
Ban Na San, *Thailand* 65 H2
Ban Na Tong, *Laos* 64 B3
Ban Nam Bac, *Laos* 64 B4
Ban Nam Ma, *Laos* 64 A3
Ban Ngang, *Laos* 64 E6
Ban Nong Bok, *Laos* 64 D5
Ban Nong Boua, *Laos* 64 E6
Ban Nong Pling, *Thailand* 64 E3
Ban Pak Chan, *Thailand* 65 G2
Ban Phai, *Thailand* 64 D4
Ban Pong, *Thailand* 64 F2
Ban Ron Phibun, *Thailand* 65 H2
Ban Sanam Chai, *Thailand* 65 J3
Ban Sangkha, *Thailand* 64 E4
Ban Tak, *Thailand* 64 D2
Ban Tha Dua, *Thailand* 64 D2
Ban Tha Li, *Thailand* 64 D3
Ban Tha Nun, *Thailand* 65 H2
Ban Thahine, *Laos* 64 E5
Ban Xien Kok, *Laos* 64 B3
Ban Yen Nhan, *Vietnam* 64 B6
Banaba, *Kiribati* 96 H8
Banalia, *Dem. Rep. of the Congo* 86 B2
Banam, *Cambodia* 65 G5
Banamba, *Mali* 82 C3
Banana Is., *S. Leone* 82 D2
Bananal, I. do, *Brazil* 125 F8
Banaras = Varanasi, *India* 69 G10
Banas →, Gujarat, *India* 68 H4
Banas →, Mad. P., *India* 69 G9
Banâs, Ras, *Egypt* 80 C4
Banaz, *Turkey* 39 C11
Banaz →, *Turkey* 39 C11
Banbān, *Si. Arabia* 70 E5
Banbridge, *U.K.* 15 B5
Banbury, *U.K.* 13 E6
Banchory, *U.K.* 14 D6
Banco, *Ethiopia* 81 F4

Bancroft, *Canada* 102 C4
Band, *Romania* 43 D9
Band Bonī, *Iran* 71 E8
Band Qīr, *Iran* 71 D6
Banda, *Mad. P., India* 69 G8
Banda, *Ut. P., India* 69 G9
Banda, Kepulauan, *Indonesia* 63 E7
Banda Aceh, *Indonesia* 62 C1
Banda Banda, Mt., *Australia* 95 E5
Banda Elat, *Indonesia* 63 F8
Banda Is. = Banda, Kepulauan, *Indonesia* 63 E7
Banda Sea, *Indonesia* 63 F7
Bandai-San, *Japan* 54 F10
Bandama →, *Ivory C.* 82 D3
Bandama Blanc →, *Ivory C.* 82 D3
Bandama Rouge →, *Ivory C.* 82 D4
Bandān, *Iran* 71 D9
Bandanaira, *Indonesia* 63 E7
Bandanwara, *India* 68 F6
Bandar = Machilipatnam, *India* 67 L12
Bandar 'Abbās, *Iran* 71 E8
Bandar-e Anzalī, *Iran* 71 B6
Bandar-e Bushehr = Büshehr, *Iran* 71 D6
Bandar-e Chārak, *Iran* 71 E7
Bandar-e Deylam, *Iran* 71 D6
Bandar-e Khomeynī, *Iran* .. 71 D6
Bandar-e Lengeh, *Iran* 71 E7
Bandar-e Maqām, *Iran* 71 E7
Bandar-e Ma'shur, *Iran* ... 71 D6
Bandar-e Nakhīlū, *Iran* ... 71 E7
Bandar-e Rīg, *Iran* 71 D6
Bandar-e Torkeman, *Iran* .. 71 B7
Bandar Maharani = Muar, *Malaysia* 65 L4
Bandar Penggaram = Batu Pahat, *Malaysia* 65 M4
Bandar Seri Begawan, *Brunei* 62 C4
Bandar Sri Aman, *Malaysia* 62 D4
Bandawe, *Malawi* 87 E3
Bande, *Spain* 34 C3
Bandeira, Pico da, *Brazil* . 127 A7
Bandera, *Argentina* 126 B3
Banderas, B. de, *Mexico* ... 118 C3
Bandhogarh, *India* 69 H9
Bandi →, *India* 68 F6
Bandiagara, *Mali* 82 C4
Bandikui, *India* 68 F7
Bandırma, *Turkey* 41 F11
Bandol, *France* 21 E9
Bandon, *Ireland* 15 E3
Bandon →, *Ireland* 15 E3
Bandula, *Mozam.* 87 F3
Bandundu, *Dem. Rep. of the Congo* . 84 E3
Bandung, *Indonesia* 63 G12
Bané, *Burkina Faso* 83 C4
Băneasa, *Romania* 43 E12
Bañeh, *Iran* 70 C5
Bañeres, *Spain* 33 G4
Banes, *Cuba* 121 B4
Banff, *Canada* 104 C5
Banff, *U.K.* 14 D6
Banff Nat. Park, *Canada* .. 104 C5
Banfora, *Burkina Faso* 82 C4
Bang Fai →, *Laos* 64 D5
Bang Hieng →, *Laos* 64 D5
Bang Krathum, *Thailand* .. 64 D3
Bang Lamung, *Thailand* .. 64 F3
Bang Mun Nak, *Thailand* . 64 D3
Bang Pa In, *Thailand* 64 E3
Bang Rakam, *Thailand* ... 64 D3
Bang Saphan, *Thailand* ... 65 G2
Bangaduni I., *India* 69 J13
Bangala Dam, *Zimbabwe* .. 87 G3
Bangalore, *India* 66 N10
Banganga →, *India* 68 F6
Bangangté, *Cameroon* 83 D7
Bangaon, *India* 69 H13
Bangassou, *C.A.R.* 84 D4
Banggai, *Indonesia* 63 E6
Banggai, Kepulauan, *Indonesia* 63 E6
Banggai Arch. = Banggai, Kepulauan, *Indonesia* .. 63 E6
Banggi, *Malaysia* 62 C5
Banghāzī, *Libya* 79 B10
Bangjang, *Sudan* 81 E3
Bangka, *Sulawesi, Indonesia* 63 D7
Bangka, *Sumatera, Indonesia* 62 E3
Bangka, Selat, *Indonesia* .. 62 E3
Bangkalan, *Indonesia* 63 G15
Bangkinang, *Indonesia* 62 D2
Bangko, *Indonesia* 62 E2
Bangkok, *Thailand* 64 F3
Bangladesh ■, *Asia* 67 H17
Bangolo, *Ivory C.* 82 D3
Bangong Co, *India* 69 B8
Bangor, *Down, U.K.* 15 B6
Bangor, *Gwynedd, U.K.* .. 12 D3
Bangor, *Maine, U.S.A.* ... 101 D13
Bangor, *Pa., U.S.A.* 111 F9
Bangued, *Phil.* 61 C4
Bangui, *C.A.R.* 84 D3
Bangui, *Phil.* 61 B4
Banguru, *Dem. Rep. of the Congo* . 86 B2
Bangweulu, L., *Zambia* ... 87 E3
Bangweulu Swamp, *Zambia* 87 E3
Bani, *Dom. Rep.* 121 C5
Bani →, *Mali* 82 C4
Bani Bangou, *Niger* 83 B5
Bania, *Ivory C.* 82 D4
Banihal Pass, *India* 69 C6
Banikoara, *Benin* 83 C5
Bāniyās, *Syria* 70 C3

Banja Luka, *Bos.-H.* 42 F2
Banjar, *India* 68 D7
Banjar →, *India* 69 H9
Banjarmasin, *Indonesia* ... 62 E4
Banjul, *Gambia* 82 C1
Banka, *India* 69 G12
Bankas, *Mali* 82 C4
Bankeryd, *Sweden* 11 G8
Banket, *Zimbabwe* 87 F3
Bankilaré, *Niger* 83 C5
Bankipore, *India* 67 G14
Banks I., *B.C., Canada* ... 104 C3
Banks I., *N.W.T., Canada* . 100 A7
Banks Pen., *N.Z.* 91 K4
Banks Str., *Australia* 94 G4
Bankura, *India* 69 H12
Bankya, *Bulgaria* 40 D7
Banmankhi, *India* 69 G12
Bann →, *Arm., U.K.* 15 B5
Bann →, *L'derry., U.K.* .. 15 A5
Bannalec, *France* 18 E3
Bannang Sata, *Thailand* ... 65 J3
Banning, *U.S.A.* 117 M10
Banningville = Bandundu, *Dem. Rep. of the Congo* . 84 E3
Banno, *Ethiopia* 81 G4
Bannockburn, *Canada* 110 B7
Bannockburn, *U.K.* 14 E5
Bannockburn, *Zimbabwe* .. 87 G2
Bannu, *Pakistan* 66 C7
Bano, *India* 69 H11
Bañolas = Banyoles, *Spain* . 32 C7
Banon, *France* 21 D9
Baños de la Encina, *Spain* . 35 G7
Baños de Molgas, *Spain* .. 34 C3
Bánovce nad Bebravou, *Slovak Rep.* 27 C11
Banovići, *Bos.-H.* 42 F3
Bansgaon, *India* 69 F10
Banská Bystrica, *Slovak Rep.* 27 C12
Banská Štiavnica, *Slovak Rep.* 27 C11
Bansko, *Bulgaria* 40 E7
Banskobystrický □, *Slovak Rep.* 27 C12
Banswara, *India* 68 H6
Bantaeng, *Indonesia* 63 F5
Bantaji, *Nigeria* 83 D7
Bantayan, *Phil.* 61 F5
Bantry, *Ireland* 15 E2
Bantry B., *Ireland* 15 E2
Bantul, *Indonesia* 63 G14
Bantva, *India* 68 J4
Banu, *Afghan.* 66 B6
Banya, *Bulgaria* 41 D8
Banyak, Kepulauan, *Indonesia* 62 D1
Banyalbufar, *Spain* 37 B9
Banyo, *Cameroon* 83 D7
Banyoles, *Spain* 32 C7
Banyuls-sur-Mer, *France* .. 20 F7
Banyumas, *Indonesia* 63 G13
Banyuwangi, *Indonesia* ... 63 H16
Banzare Coast, *Antarctica* .. 5 C9
Banzyville = Mobayi, *Dem. Rep. of the Congo* . 84 D4
Bao Ha, *Vietnam* 58 F5
Bao Lac, *Vietnam* 64 A5
Bao Loc, *Vietnam* 65 G6
Bao'an = Shenzhen, *China* . 59 F10
Baocheng, *China* 56 H4
Baode, *China* 56 E6
Baodi, *China* 57 E9
Baoding, *China* 56 E8
Baoji, *China* 56 G4
Baojing, *China* 58 C7
Baokang, *China* 59 B8
Baoshan, *Shanghai, China* . 59 B13
Baoshan, *Yunnan, China* .. 58 E2
Baotou, *China* 56 D6
Baoxing, *China* 58 B4
Baoying, *China* 57 H10
Bap, *India* 68 F5
Bapatla, *India* 67 M12
Bapaume, *France* 19 B9
Bāqerābād, *Iran* 71 C6
Ba'qūbah, *Iraq* 70 C5
Baquedano, *Chile* 126 A2
Bar, *Montenegro, Yug.* ... 40 D3
Bar, *Ukraine* 47 H4
Bar Bigha, *India* 69 G11
Bar Harbor, *U.S.A.* 109 C11
Bar-le-Duc, *France* 19 D12
Bar-sur-Aube, *France* 19 D11
Bar-sur-Seine, *France* 19 D11
Bara, *India* 69 G9
Bâra, *Romania* 43 C12
Bara Banki, *India* 69 F9
Barabai, *Indonesia* 62 E5
Baraboo, *U.S.A.* 112 D10
Baracoa, *Cuba* 121 B5
Baradā →, *Syria* 75 B5
Baradero, *Argentina* 126 C4
Baradine, *Australia* 95 E4
Baraga, *U.S.A.* 112 B10
Bărăganul, *Romania* 43 F12
Barah →, *India* 68 F6
Barahona, *Dom. Rep.* 121 C5
Barahona, *Spain* 32 D2
Barail Range, *India* 67 G18
Baraka, *Sudan* 81 E2
Baraka →, *Sudan* 80 D4
Barakaldo, *Spain* 32 B2
Barakar →, *India* 69 G12
Barakhola, *India* 67 G18
Barakot, *India* 69 J11
Barakpur, *India* 69 H13
Baralaba, *Australia* 94 C4
Baralla, *Spain* 34 C3
Baralzon L., *Canada* 105 B9
Barameiya, *Sudan* 80 D4

Baramula, *India* 69 B6
Baran, *India* 68 G7
Baran →, *Pakistan* 68 G3
Barañain, *Spain* 32 C3
Baranavichy, *Belarus* 47 F4
Barani, *Burkina Faso* 82 C4
Baranof, *U.S.A.* 104 B2
Baranof I., *U.S.A.* 100 C6
Baranów Sandomierski, *Poland* 45 H8
Baranya □, *Hungary* 42 E3
Baraolt, *Romania* 43 D10
Barapasi, *Indonesia* 63 E9
Barasat, *India* 69 H13
Barat Daya, Kepulauan, *Indonesia* 63 F7
Barataria B., *U.S.A.* 113 L10
Barauda, *India* 68 H6
Baraut, *India* 68 E7
Barbacena, *Brazil* 127 A7
Barban, *Croatia* 29 C11
Bàrbara, C. de, *Spain* 37 C7
Barbaros, *Turkey* 41 F11
Barbastro, *Spain* 32 C5
Barbate = Barbate de Franco, *Spain* 35 J5
Barbate de Franco, *Spain* . 35 J5
Barberino di Mugello, *Italy* . 29 E8
Barberton, *S. Africa* 89 D5
Barberton, *U.S.A.* 110 E3
Barbezieux-St-Hilaire, *France* 20 C3
Barbourville, *U.S.A.* 109 G4
Barbuda, *W. Indies* 121 C7
Bârca, *Romania* 43 G8
Barcaldine, *Australia* 94 C4
Barcarrota, *Spain* 35 G4
Barcellona Pozzo di Gotto, *Italy* 31 D8
Barcelona, *Spain* 32 D7
Barcelona, *Venezuela* 124 A6
Barcelona □, *Spain* 32 D7
Barcelonette, *France* 21 D10
Barcelos, *Brazil* 124 D6
Barcin, *Poland* 45 F4
Barclayville, *Liberia* 82 E3
Barcoo →, *Australia* 94 D3
Barcs, *Hungary* 42 E2
Barczewo, *Poland* 44 E7
Bärdä, *Azerbaijan* 49 K8
Bardaï, *Chad* 79 D9
Bardas Blancas, *Argentina* . 126 D2
Barddhaman, *India* 69 H12
Bardejov, *Slovak Rep.* 27 B14
Bardera, *Somali Rep.* 74 G3
Bardi, *Italy* 28 D6
Bardīyah, *Libya* 79 B10
Bardolino, *Italy* 28 C7
Bardonécchia, *Italy* 28 C3
Bardsey I., *U.K.* 12 E3
Bardstown, *U.S.A.* 108 G3
Bareilly, *India* 69 E8
Barela, *India* 69 H9
Barentin, *France* 18 C7
Barenton, *France* 18 D6
Barents Sea, *Arctic* 4 B9
Barentu, *Eritrea* 81 D4
Barfleur, *France* 18 C5
Barfleur, Pte. de, *France* .. 18 C5
Barga, *Italy* 28 D7
Bargara, *Australia* 94 C5
Bargas, *Spain* 34 F6
Barge, *Italy* 28 D4
Bârgăului Bistriţa, *Romania* 43 C9
Barge, *Italy* 28 D4
Bargnop, *Sudan* 81 F2
Bargteheide, *Germany* 24 B6
Barguzin, *Russia* 51 D11
Barh, *India* 69 G11
Barhaj, *India* 69 F10
Barham, *Australia* 95 F3
Barharwa, *India* 69 G12
Barhi, *India* 69 G11
Bari, *India* 68 F7
Bari, *Italy* 31 A9
Bari Doab, *Pakistan* 68 D5
Bari Sadri, *India* 68 G6
Bari Sardo, *Italy* 30 C2
Barīdī, Ra's, *Si. Arabia* .. 70 E3
Barīm, *Yemen* 76 E8
Barinas, *Venezuela* 124 B4
Baring, C., *Canada* 100 B8
Baringo, *Kenya* 86 B4
Baringo, L., *Kenya* 86 B4
Barito →, *Indonesia* 62 E4
Barjac, *France* 21 D8
Barjols, *France* 21 E10
Bark L., *Canada* 110 A7
Barka = Baraka →, *Sudan* 80 D4
Barkakana, *India* 69 H11
Barkam, *China* 58 B4
Barker, *U.S.A.* 110 C6
Barkley, L., *U.S.A.* 109 G2
Barkley Sound, *Canada* ... 104 D3
Barkly East, *S. Africa* 88 E4
Barkly Roadhouse, *Australia* 94 B2
Barkly Tableland, *Australia* 94 B2
Barkly West, *S. Africa* 88 D3
Barkol, Wadi →, *Sudan* . 80 D3
Barla Dağı, *Turkey* 39 C12
Bârlad, *Romania* 43 D12
Bârlad →, *Romania* 43 E12
Barlee, L., *Australia* 93 E2
Barlee, Mt., *Australia* 93 D4
Barletta, *Italy* 31 A9
Barlinek, *Poland* 45 F2
Barlovento, *Canary Is.* ... 37 F2
Barlow L., *Canada* 105 A8

Barmedman, *Australia* 95 E4
Barmer, *India* 68 G4
Barmera, *Australia* 95 E3
Barmouth, *U.K.* 12 E3
Barmstedt, *Germany* 24 B5
Barna →, *India* 69 G10
Barnagar, *India* 68 H6
Barnala, *India* 68 D6
Barnard Castle, *U.K.* 12 C6
Barnaul, *Russia* 50 D9
Barnesville, *U.S.A.* 109 J3
Barnet, *U.K.* 13 F7
Barneveld, *Neths.* 17 B5
Barneveld, *U.S.A.* 111 C9
Barneville-Cartevert, *France* 18 C5
Barnhart, *U.S.A.* 113 K4
Barnsley, *U.K.* 12 D6
Barnstable, *U.S.A.* 13 F3
Barnstaple, *U.K.* 13 F3
Barnstaple Bay = Bideford Bay, *U.K.* 13 F3
Barnsville, *U.S.A.* 112 B6
Barnwell, *U.S.A.* 109 J5
Baro →, *Ethiopia* 81 F3
Baro →, *Nigeria* 83 D6
Baroda = Vadodara, *India* . 68 H5
Baroda, *India* 68 G7
Baroe, *S. Africa* 88 E3
Baron Ra., *Australia* 92 D4
Barong, *China* 58 B2
Barotseland, *Zambia* 85 H4
Barouéli, *Mali* 82 C3
Barpeta, *India* 67 F17
Barques, Pt. Aux, *U.S.A.* . 110 B2
Barquísimeto, *Venezuela* .. 124 A5
Barr, *France* 19 D14
Barr, Ras el, *Egypt* 80 H7
Barr Smith Range, *Australia* 93 E3
Barra, *Brazil* 125 F10
Barra, *U.K.* 14 E1
Barra, Sd. of, *U.K.* 14 D1
Barra de Navidad, *Mexico* . 118 D4
Barra do Corda, *Brazil* ... 125 E9
Barra do Piraí, *Brazil* 127 A7
Barra Falsa, Pta. da, *Mozam.* 89 C6
Barra Hd., *U.K.* 14 E1
Barra Mansa, *Brazil* 127 A7
Barraba, *Australia* 95 E5
Barrackpur = Barakpur, *India* 69 H13
Barradale Roadhouse, *Australia* 92 D1
Barrafranca, *Italy* 31 E7
Barraigh = Barra, *U.K.* .. 14 E1
Barranca, *Lima, Peru* 124 F3
Barranca, *Loreto, Peru* ... 124 D3
Barrancabermeja, *Colombia* 124 B4
Barrancas, *Venezuela* 124 B6
Barrancos, *Portugal* 35 G4
Barranqueras, *Argentina* .. 126 B4
Barranquilla, *Colombia* ... 124 A4
Barraute, *Canada* 102 C4
Barre, *Mass., U.S.A.* 111 D12
Barre, *Vt., U.S.A.* 111 B12
Barreal, *Argentina* 126 C2
Barreiras, *Brazil* 125 F10
Barreiro, *Portugal* 35 G1
Barreirinhas, *Brazil* 125 D10
Barrême, *France* 21 E10
Barren, Nosy, *Madag.* 89 B7
Barretos, *Brazil* 125 H9
Barrhead, *Canada* 104 C6
Barrie, *Canada* 102 D4
Barrier Ra., *Australia* 95 E3
Barrière, *Canada* 104 C4
Barrington, *U.S.A.* 111 E13
Barrington L., *Canada* 105 B8
Barrington Tops, *Australia* . 95 E5
Barringun, *Australia* 95 D4
Barro do Garças, *Brazil* .. 125 G8
Barron, *U.S.A.* 112 C9
Barrow, *U.S.A.* 100 A4
Barrow →, *Ireland* 15 D5
Barrow Creek, *Australia* .. 94 C1
Barrow I., *Australia* 92 D2
Barrow-in-Furness, *U.K.* .. 12 C4
Barrow Pt., *Australia* 94 A3
Barrow Pt., *U.S.A.* 98 B4
Barrow Ra., *Australia* 93 E4
Barrow Str., *Canada* 4 B3
Barruecomedio, *Spain* 34 D6
Barruelo de Santullán, *Spain* 34 C6
Barry, *U.K.* 13 F4
Barry's Bay, *Canada* 102 C4
Barsalogho, *Burkina Faso* . 83 C4
Barsat, *Pakistan* 69 A5
Barsham, *Syria* 70 C4
Barsi, *India* 66 K9
Barsinghausen, *Germany* .. 24 C5
Barsoi, *India* 67 G15
Barstow, *U.S.A.* 117 L9
Barth, *Germany* 24 A8
Barthélemy, Col, *Vietnam* . 64 C5
Bartica, *Guyana* 124 B7
Bartin, *Turkey* 72 B5
Bartlesville, *U.S.A.* 113 G7
Bartlett, *U.S.A.* 116 J8
Bartlett, L., *Canada* 104 A5
Bartolomeu Dias, *Mozam.* . 87 G4
Barton, *U.S.A.* 111 B12
Barton upon Humber, *U.K.* 12 D7
Bartoszyce, *Poland* 44 D8
Bartow, *U.S.A.* 109 M5
Barú, Volcan, *Panama* 120 E3
Barumba, *Dem. Rep. of the Congo* . 86 B1
Baruth, *Germany* 24 C9
Baruunsuu, *Mongolia* 56 C3
Barvinkove, *Ukraine* 47 H9
Barwani, *India* 68 H6
Barwice, *Poland* 44 E3
Barycz →, *Poland* 45 G3

Barysaw, *Belarus* 46 E5
Barysh, *Russia* 48 D8
Bârzava, *Romania* 42 D6
Bas-Rhin □, *France* 19 D14
Bašaid, *Serbia, Yug.* 42 E5
Bāsa'idū, *Iran* 71 E7
Basal, *Pakistan* 68 C5
Basankusa, *Dem. Rep. of the Congo* . 84 D3
Basarabeasca, *Moldova* ... 43 D13
Basarabi, *Romania* 43 F13
Basauri, *Spain* 32 B2
Basawa, *Afghan.* 68 B4
Bascuñán, C., *Chile* 126 B1
Basel, *Switz.* 25 H3
Basel-Landschaft □, *Switz.* . 25 H3
Basento →, *Italy* 31 B9
Bashäkerd, Kühhä-ye, *Iran* . 71 E8
Bashaw, *Canada* 104 C6
Bāshī, *Iran* 71 D6
Bashkir Republic = Bashkortostan □, *Russia* . 50 D6
Bashkortostan □, *Russia* ... 50 D6
Basibasy, *Madag.* 89 C7
Basilan I., *Phil.* 61 H5
Basilan Str., *Phil.* 61 H5
Basildon, *U.K.* 13 F8
Basilé, *Eq. Guin.* 83 E6
Basilicata □, *Italy* 31 B9
Basim = Washim, *India* ... 66 J10
Basin, *U.S.A.* 114 D9
Basingstoke, *U.K.* 13 F6
Baška, *Croatia* 29 D11
Başkale, *Turkey* 73 C10
Baskatong, Rés., *Canada* .. 102 C4
Basle = Basel, *Switz.* 25 H3
Başmakçı, *Turkey* 39 D12
Basoda, *India* 68 H7
Basoka, *Dem. Rep. of the Congo* . 86 B1
Basque, Pays, *France* 20 E2
Basque Provinces = País Vasco □, *Spain* 32 C2
Basra = Al Baṣrah, *Iraq* ... 70 D5
Bass Str., *Australia* 94 F4
Bassano, *Canada* 104 C6
Bassano del Grappa, *Italy* . 29 C8
Bassar, *Togo* 83 D5
Bassas da India, *Ind. Oc.* . 85 J7
Basse-Normandie □, *France* 18 D6
Basse Santa-Su, *Gambia* .. 82 C2
Basse-Terre, *Guadeloupe* .. 121 C7
Bassein, *Burma* 67 L19
Basseterre, *St. Kitts & Nevis* 121 C7
Bassett, *U.S.A.* 112 D5
Bassi, *India* 68 D7
Bassigny, *France* 19 E12
Bassikounou, *Mauritania* .. 82 B3
Bassila, *Benin* 83 D5
Bassum, *Germany* 24 C4
Båstad, *Sweden* 11 H6
Bastak, *Iran* 71 E7
Baştām, *Iran* 71 B7
Bastar, *India* 67 K12
Bastelica, *France* 21 F13
Basti, *India* 69 F10
Bastia, *France* 21 F13
Bastogne, *Belgium* 17 D5
Bastrop, *La., U.S.A.* 113 J9
Bastrop, *Tex., U.S.A.* 113 K6
Bat Yam, *Israel* 75 C3
Bata, *Eq. Guin.* 84 D1
Bata, *Romania* 42 D7
Bataan □, *Phil.* 61 D4
Batabanó, *Cuba* 120 B3
Batabanó, G. de, *Cuba* ... 120 B3
Batac, *Phil.* 61 B4
Batagai, *Russia* 51 C14
Batajnica, *Serbia, Yug.* ... 40 B4
Batak, *Bulgaria* 41 E8
Batala, *India* 68 D6
Batalha, *Portugal* 34 F2
Batama, *Dem. Rep. of the Congo* . 86 B2
Batamay, *Russia* 51 C13
Batang, *China* 58 B2
Batang, *Indonesia* 63 G13
Batangas, *Phil.* 61 E4
Batanta, *Indonesia* 63 E8
Batatais, *Brazil* 127 A6
Batavia, *U.S.A.* 110 D6
Bataysk, *Russia* 47 J10
Batchelor, *Australia* 92 B5
Batdambang, *Cambodia* ... 64 F4
Bateman's B., *Australia* ... 95 F5
Batemans Bay, *Australia* .. 95 F5
Bates Ra., *Australia* 93 E3
Batesburg, *U.S.A.* 109 J5
Batesville, *Ark., U.S.A.* .. 113 H9
Batesville, *Miss., U.S.A.* .. 113 H10
Batesville, *Tex., U.S.A.* ... 113 L5
Bath, *Canada* 111 B8
Bath, *U.K.* 13 F5
Bath, *Maine, U.S.A.* 109 D11
Bath, *N.Y., U.S.A.* 110 D7
Bath & North East Somerset □, *U.K.* 13 F5
Batheay, *Cambodia* 65 G5
Bathurst = Banjul, *Gambia* 82 C1
Bathurst, *Australia* 95 E4
Bathurst, *Canada* 103 C6
Bathurst, *S. Africa* 88 E4
Bathurst, C., *Canada* 100 A7
Bathurst B., *Australia* 94 A3
Bathurst Harb., *Australia* .. 94 G4
Bathurst I., *Australia* 92 B5
Bathurst I., *Canada* 4 B2
Bathurst Inlet, *Canada* ... 100 B9
Bati, *Ethiopia* 81 E5
Batie, *Burkina Faso* 82 D4

Batlow, *Australia* 95 F4
Batman, *Turkey* 70 B4
Baṭn al Ghūl, *Jordan* 75 F4
Batna, *Algeria* 78 A4
Batobato = San Isidro, *Phil.* 61 H7
Batočina, *Serbia, Yug.* 40 B5
Batoka, *Zambia* 87 F2
Baton Rouge, *U.S.A.* 113 K9
Batong, Ko, *Thailand* 65 J2
Bátonyterenye, *Hungary* .. 42 C4
Batopilas, *Mexico* 118 B3
Batouri, *Cameroon* 84 D2
Båtsfjord, *Norway* 8 A23
Battambang = Batdambang, *Cambodia* 64 F4
Batticaloa, *Sri Lanka* ... 66 R12
Battipáglia, *Italy* 31 B7
Battle, *U.K.* 13 G8
Battle →, *Canada* 105 C7
Battle Creek, *U.S.A.* 108 D3
Battle Ground, *U.S.A.* 116 E4
Battle Harbour, *Canada* .. 103 B8
Battle Lake, *U.S.A.* 112 B7
Battle Mountain, *U.S.A.* .. 114 F5
Battlefields, *Zimbabwe* ... 87 F2
Battleford, *Canada* 105 C7
Battonya, *Hungary* 42 D6
Batu, *Ethiopia* 81 F4
Batu, Kepulauan, *Indonesia* 62 E1
Batu Caves, *Malaysia* 65 L3
Batu Gajah, *Malaysia* 65 K3
Batu Is. = Batu, Kepulauan, *Indonesia* 62 E1
Batu Pahat, *Malaysia* 65 M4
Batuata, *Indonesia* 63 F6
Batumi, *Georgia* 49 K5
Baturaja, *Indonesia* 62 E2
Baturité, *Brazil* 125 D11
Bau, *Malaysia* 62 D4
Baubau, *Indonesia* 63 F6
Bauchi, *Nigeria* 83 C6
Bauchi □, *Nigeria* 83 C7
Baud, *France* 18 E3
Baudette, *U.S.A.* 112 A7
Bauer, C., *Australia* 95 E1
Bauhinia, *Australia* 94 C4
Baukau, *Indonesia* 63 F7
Bauld, C., *Canada* 101 C14
Baume-les-Dames, *France* . 19 E13
Baunatal, *Germany* 24 D5
Baunei, *Italy* 30 B2
Baure, *Nigeria* 83 C6
Bauru, *Brazil* 127 A6
Bausi, *India* 69 G12
Bauska, *Latvia* 9 H21
Bautino, *Kazakstan* 49 H10
Bautzen, *Germany* 24 D10
Bauya, *S. Leone* 82 D2
Bavānāt, *Iran* 71 D7
Bavanište, *Serbia, Yug.* ... 42 F5
Bavaria = Bayern □, *Germany* 25 G7
Båven, *Sweden* 10 E10
Bavispe →, *Mexico* 118 B3
Bawdwin, *Burma* 67 H20
Bawean, *Indonesia* 62 F4
Bawku, *Ghana* 83 C4
Bawlake, *Burma* 67 K20
Bawolung, *China* 58 C3
Baxley, *U.S.A.* 109 K4
Baxoi, *China* 58 B1
Baxter, *U.S.A.* 112 B7
Baxter Springs, *U.S.A.* ... 113 G7
Bay, L. de, *Phil.* 61 D4
Bay City, Mich., *U.S.A.* .. 108 D4
Bay City, Tex., *U.S.A.* ... 113 L7
Bay Minette, *U.S.A.* 109 K2
Bay Roberts, *Canada* 103 C9
Bay St. Louis, *U.S.A.* 113 K10
Bay Springs, *U.S.A.* 113 K10
Bay View, *N.Z.* 91 H6
Baya, *Dem. Rep. of the Congo* . 87 E2
Bayamo, *Cuba* 120 B4
Bayamón, *Puerto Rico* ... 121 C6
Bayan Har Shan, *China* ... 60 C4
Bayan Hot = Alxa Zuoqi, *China* 56 E3
Bayan Obo, *China* 56 D5
Bayan-Ovoo = Erdenetsogt, *Mongolia* 56 C4
Bayana, *India* 68 F7
Bayanaūyl, *Kazakstan* 50 D8
Bayandalay, *Mongolia* 56 C2
Bayanhongor, *Mongolia* ... 60 B5
Bayard, N. Mex., *U.S.A.* .. 115 K9
Bayard, Nebr., *U.S.A.* 112 E3
Bayawan, *Phil.* 61 G5
Baybay, *Phil.* 61 F6
Bayburt, *Turkey* 73 B9
Bayelsa □, *Nigeria* 83 E6
Bayerische Alpen, *Germany* 25 H7
Bayerischer Wald, *Germany* 25 G8
Bayern □, *Germany* 25 G7
Bayeux, *France* 18 C6
Bayfield, *Canada* 110 C3
Bayfield, *U.S.A.* 112 B9
Bayındır, *Turkey* 39 C9
Baykal, Oz., *Russia* 51 D11
Baykan, *Turkey* 70 B4
Baykonur = Bayqongyr, *Kazakstan* 50 E7
Baynes Mts., *Namibia* 88 B1
Bayombong, *Phil.* 61 C4
Bayon, *France* 19 D13
Bayona = Baiona, *Spain* .. 34 C2
Bayonne, *France* 20 E2
Bayonne, *U.S.A.* 111 F10
Bayovar, *Peru* 124 E2
Bayqongyr, *Kazakstan* 50 E7

Bayram-Ali = Bayramaly, *Turkmenistan* 50 F7
Bayramaly, *Turkmenistan* . 50 F7
Bayramiç, *Turkey* 39 B8
Bayreuth, *Germany* 25 F7
Bayrischzell, *Germany* 25 H8
Bayrūt, *Lebanon* 75 B4
Bays, L. of, *Canada* 110 A5
Baysville, *Canada* 110 A5
Bayt Laḥm, *West Bank* ... 75 D4
Baytown, *U.S.A.* 113 L7
Bayzo, *Niger* 83 C5
Baza, *Spain* 35 H8
Bazar Dyuzi, *Russia* 49 K8
Bazardüzü = Bazar Dyuzi, *Russia* 49 K8
Bazarny Karabulak, *Russia* . 48 D8
Bazarnyy Syzgan, *Russia* .. 48 D8
Bazaruto, I. do, *Mozam.* ... 89 C6
Bazas, *France* 20 D3
Bazhong, *China* 58 B6
Bazhou, *China* 56 E9
Bāzmān, Kūh-e, *Iran* 71 D9
Beach, *U.S.A.* 112 B3
Beach City, *U.S.A.* 110 F3
Beachport, *Australia* 95 F3
Beachy Hd., *U.K.* 13 G8
Beacon, *Australia* 93 F2
Beacon, *U.S.A.* 111 E11
Beaconsfield, *Australia* 94 G4
Beagle, Canal, *S. Amer.* 122 J4
Beagle Bay, *Australia* 92 C3
Bealanana, *Madag.* 89 A8
Beals Cr. →, *U.S.A.* 113 J4
Beamsville, *Canada* 110 C5
Bear →, Calif., *U.S.A.* 116 G5
Bear →, Utah, *U.S.A.* 106 B4
Béar, C., *France* 20 F7
Bear I., *Ireland* 15 E2
Bear L., *Canada* 105 B9
Bear L., *U.S.A.* 114 F8
Beardmore, *Canada* 102 C2
Beardmore Glacier, *Antarctica* 5 E11
Beardstown, *U.S.A.* 112 F9
Bearma →, *India* 69 G8
Béarn, *France* 20 E3
Bearpaw Mts., *U.S.A.* 114 B9
Bearskin Lake, *Canada* ... 102 B1
Beas →, *India* 68 D6
Beas de Segura, *Spain* 35 G8
Beasain, *Spain* 32 B2
Beata, C., *Dom. Rep.* 121 C5
Beata, I., *Dom. Rep.* 121 C5
Beatrice, *U.S.A.* 112 E6
Beatrice, *Zimbabwe* 87 F3
Beatrice, C., *Australia* 94 A2
Beatton →, *Canada* 104 B4
Beatton River, *Canada* 104 B4
Beatty, *U.S.A.* 116 J10
Beaucaire, *France* 21 E8
Beauce, Plaine de la, *France* 19 D8
Beauceville, *Canada* 103 C5
Beaudesert, *Australia* 95 D5
Beaufort, *France* 21 C10
Beaufort, *Malaysia* 62 C5
Beaufort, N.C., *U.S.A.* 109 H7
Beaufort, S.C., *U.S.A.* 109 J5
Beaufort Sea, *Arctic* 4 B1
Beaufort West, *S. Africa* .. 88 E3
Beaugency, *France* 19 E8
Beauharnois, *Canada* 111 A11
Beaujeu, *France* 19 F11
Beaujolais, *France* 19 F11
Beaulieu →, *Canada* 104 A6
Beaulieu-sur-Dordogne, *France* 20 D5
Beaulieu-sur-Mer, *France* . 21 E11
Beauly, *U.K.* 14 D4
Beauly →, *U.K.* 14 D4
Beaumaris, *U.K.* 12 D3
Beaumont, *Belgium* 17 D4
Beaumont, *France* 20 D4
Beaumont, *U.S.A.* 113 K7
Beaumont-de-Lomagne, *France* 20 E5
Beaumont-le-Roger, *France* 18 C7
Beaumont-sur-Sarthe, *France* 18 D7
Beaune, *France* 19 E11
Beaune-la-Rolande, *France* . 19 D9
Beaupré, *Canada* 103 C5
Beaupréau, *France* 18 E6
Beauraing, *Belgium* 17 D4
Beaurepaire, *France* 21 C9
Beauséjour, *Canada* 105 C9
Beauvais, *France* 19 C9
Beauval, *Canada* 105 B7
Beauvoir-sur-Mer, *France* . 18 F4
Beauvoir-sur-Niort, *France* . 20 B3
Beaver, Okla., *U.S.A.* 113 G4
Beaver, Pa., *U.S.A.* 110 F4
Beaver, Utah, *U.S.A.* 115 G7
Beaver →, B.C., *Canada* .. 104 B4
Beaver →, Ont., *Canada* .. 102 A2
Beaver →, Sask., *Canada* . 105 B7
Beaver →, *U.S.A.* 113 G5
Beaver City, *U.S.A.* 112 E5
Beaver Creek, *Canada* 100 B5
Beaver Dam, *U.S.A.* 112 D10
Beaver Falls, *U.S.A.* 110 F4
Beaver Hill L., *Canada* 105 C10
Beaver I., *U.S.A.* 108 C3
Beaverhill L., *Canada* 104 C6
Beaverlodge, *Canada* 104 B5
Beaverstone →, *Canada* .. 102 B2
Beaverton, *Canada* 110 B5
Beaverton, *U.S.A.* 116 E4
Beawar, *India* 68 F6
Bebedouro, *Brazil* 127 A6
Beboa, *Madag.* 89 B7
Bebra, *Germany* 24 E5

Beccles, *U.K.* 13 E9
Bečej, *Serbia, Yug.* 42 E5
Beceni, *Romania* 43 E11
Becerreá, *Spain* 34 C3
Béchar, *Algeria* 78 B5
Bechyně, *Czech Rep.* 26 B7
Beckley, *U.S.A.* 108 G5
Beckum, *Germany* 24 D4
Beclean, *Romania* 43 C9
Bečov nad Teplou, *Czech Rep.* 26 A5
Bečva →, *Czech Rep.* 27 B10
Bédar, *Spain* 33 H3
Bédarieux, *France* 20 E7
Beddouza, Ras, *Morocco* .. 78 B4
Bedele, *Ethiopia* 81 F4
Bederkesa, *Germany* 24 B4
Bedeso, *Ethiopia* 81 F5
Bedford, *Canada* 111 A12
Bedford, *S. Africa* 88 E4
Bedford, *U.K.* 13 E7
Bedford, Ind., *U.S.A.* 108 F2
Bedford, Iowa, *U.S.A.* 112 E7
Bedford, Ohio, *U.S.A.* 110 E3
Bedford, Pa., *U.S.A.* 110 F6
Bedford, Va., *U.S.A.* 108 G6
Bedford, C., *Australia* 94 B4
Bedfordshire □, *U.K.* 13 E7
Będków, *Poland* 45 G6
Bednja →, *Croatia* 29 B13
Bednodemyanovsk, *Russia* . 48 D6
Bednódia, *Italy* 28 D6
Bedourie, *Australia* 94 C2
Bedum, *Neths.* 17 A6
Będzin, *Poland* 45 H6
Beebe Plain, *Canada* 111 A12
Beech Creek, *U.S.A.* 110 E7
Beelitz, *Germany* 24 C8
Beenleigh, *Australia* 95 D5
Be'er Menuḥa, *Israel* 70 D2
Be'er Sheva, *Israel* 75 D3
Beersheba = Be'er Sheva, *Israel* 75 D3
Beeskow, *Germany* 24 C10
Beestekraal, *S. Africa* 89 D4
Beeston, *U.K.* 12 E6
Beetzendorf, *Germany* 24 C7
Beeville, *U.S.A.* 113 L6
Befale, *Dem. Rep. of the Congo* . 84 D4
Befandriana, Mahajanga, *Madag.* 89 B8
Befandriana, Toliara, *Madag.* 89 C7
Befasy, *Madag.* 89 C7
Béfotaka, Antsiranana, *Madag.* 89 A8
Befotaka, Fianarantsoa, *Madag.* 89 C8
Bega, *Australia* 95 F4
Bega, Canalul, *Romania* ... 42 E5
Bégard, *France* 18 D3
Beğendik, *Turkey* 41 F10
Begoro, *Ghana* 83 D4
Begusarai, *India* 69 G12
Behābād, *Iran* 71 C8
Behala, *India* 69 H13
Behara, *Madag.* 89 C8
Behbehān, *Iran* 71 D6
Behm Canal, *U.S.A.* 104 B2
Behshahr, *Iran* 71 B7
Bei Jiang →, *China* 59 F9
Bei'an, *China* 60 B7
Beibei, *China* 58 C6
Beichuan, *China* 58 B5
Beihai, *China* 58 G7
Beijing, *China* 56 E9
Beijing □, *China* 56 E9
Beilen, *Neths.* 17 B6
Beiliu, *China* 59 F8
Beilngries, *Germany* 25 F7
Beilpajah, *Australia* 95 E3
Beilul, *Eritrea* 81 E5
Beinn na Faoghla = Benbecula, *U.K.* 14 D1
Beipan Jiang →, *China* 58 E5
Beipiao, *China* 57 D11
Beira, *Mozam.* 87 F3
Beirut = Bayrūt, *Lebanon* . 75 B4
Beiseker, *Canada* 104 C6
Beitaolaizhao, *China* 57 B13
Beitbridge, *Zimbabwe* 87 G3
Beiuş, *Romania* 42 D7
Beizhen = Binzhou, *China* . 57 F10
Beizhen, *China* 57 D11
Beizhengzhen, *China* 57 B12
Beja, *Portugal* 35 G3
Béja, *Tunisia* 79 A7
Beja □, *Portugal* 35 H3
Bejaia, *Algeria* 78 A7
Béjar, *Spain* 34 E5
Bejestān, *Iran* 71 C8
Bekçiler, *Turkey* 39 E11
Békés, *Hungary* 42 D6
Békés □, *Hungary* 42 D6
Békéscsaba, *Hungary* 42 D6
Bekily, *Madag.* 89 C8
Bekitro, *Madag.* 89 C8
Bekodoka, *Madag.* 89 B8
Bekoji, *Ethiopia* 81 F4
Bekopaka, *Madag.* 89 B7
Bekwai, *Ghana* 83 D4
Bela, *India* 69 G10
Bela, *Pakistan* 68 F2
Bela Crkva, *Serbia, Yug.* .. 42 F6
Bela Palanka, *Serbia, Yug.* . 40 C6
Bela Vista, *Brazil* 126 A4
Bela Vista, *Mozam.* 89 D5

Bélâbre, *France* 20 B5
Belalcázar, *Spain* 35 G5
Belan →, *India* 69 G9
Belanovica, *Serbia, Yug.* ... 40 B4
Belarus ■, *Europe* 46 F4
Belau = Palau ■, *Pac. Oc.* . 52 J17
Belavenona, *Madag.* 89 C8
Belawan, *Indonesia* 62 D1
Belaya, *Ethiopia* 81 E4
Belaya →, *Russia* 49 C9
Belaya Glina, *Russia* 49 G5
Belaya Kalitva, *Russia* 49 F5
Belaya Tserkov = Bila Tserkva, *Ukraine* 47 H6
Belcești, *Romania* 43 C12
Bełchatów, *Poland* 45 G6
Belcher Is., *Canada* 102 A3
Belchite, *Spain* 32 D4
Belden, *U.S.A.* 116 E5
Belém, *Brazil* 125 D9
Belén, *Argentina* 126 B2
Belén, *Paraguay* 126 A4
Belen, *U.S.A.* 115 J10
Belene, *Bulgaria* 41 C9
Beleni, *Turkey* 72 D7
Bélesta, *France* 20 F5
Belet Uen, *Somali Rep.* ... 74 G4
Belev, *Russia* 46 F9
Belevi, *Turkey* 39 C9
Belfair, *U.S.A.* 116 C4
Belfast, *S. Africa* 89 D5
Belfast, *U.K.* 15 B6
Belfast, Maine, *U.S.A.* 109 C11
Belfast, N.Y., *U.S.A.* 110 D6
Belfast L., *U.K.* 15 B6
Belfield, *U.S.A.* 112 B3
Belfort, *France* 19 E13
Belfort, Territoire de □, *France* 19 E13
Belfry, *U.S.A.* 114 D9
Belgaum, *India* 66 M9
Belgioioso, *Italy* 28 C6
Belgium ■, *Europe* 17 D4
Belgodère, *France* 21 F13
Belgorod, *Russia* 47 G9
Belgorod-Dnestrovskiy = Bilhorod-Dnistrovskyy, *Ukraine* 47 J6
Belgrade = Beograd, *Serbia, Yug.* 40 B4
Belgrade, *U.S.A.* 114 D8
Belhaven, *U.S.A.* 109 H7
Beli Drim →, *Europe* 40 D4
Beli Manastir, *Croatia* 42 E3
Beli Timok →, *Serbia, Yug.* 40 C6
Bélice →, *Italy* 30 E5
Belinskiy, *Russia* 48 D6
Belinyu, *Indonesia* 62 E3
Beliton Is. = Belitung, *Indonesia* 62 E3
Belitung, *Indonesia* 62 E3
Beliu, *Romania* 42 D6
Belize ■, *Cent. Amer.* 119 D7
Belize City, *Belize* 119 D7
Beljakovci, *Macedonia* 40 D5
Beljanica, *Serbia, Yug.* 40 B5
Belkovskiy, Ostrov, *Russia* . 51 B14
Bell →, *Canada* 102 C4
Bell I., *Canada* 103 B8
Bell-Irving →, *Canada* 104 B3
Bell Peninsula, *Canada* ... 101 B11
Bell Ville, *Argentina* 126 C3
Bella, *Italy* 31 B8
Bella Bella, *Canada* 104 C3
Bella Coola, *Canada* 104 C3
Bella Unión, *Uruguay* 126 C4
Bella Vista, Corrientes, *Argentina* 126 B4
Bella Vista, Tucuman, *Argentina* 126 B2
Bellac, *France* 20 B5
Bellágio, *Italy* 28 C6
Bellaire, *U.S.A.* 110 F4
Bellária, *Italy* 29 D9
Bellata, *Australia* 95 D4
Belle-Chasse, *U.S.A.* 113 L10
Belle Fourche, *U.S.A.* 112 C3
Belle Fourche →, *U.S.A.* . 112 C3
Belle Glade, *U.S.A.* 109 M5
Belle-Île, *France* 18 E3
Belle Isle, *Canada* 103 B8
Belle Isle, Str. of, *Canada* . 103 B8
Belle Plaine, *U.S.A.* 112 E8
Belle Yella, *Liberia* 82 D3
Belledonne, *France* 21 C10
Bellefontaine, *U.S.A.* 108 E4
Bellefonte, *U.S.A.* 110 F7
Bellegarde, *France* 19 E9
Bellegarde-en-Marche, *France* 20 C6
Bellegarde-sur-Valserine, *France* 19 F12
Bellême, *France* 18 D7
Belleoram, *Canada* 103 C8
Belleville, *Canada* 102 D4
Belleville, *France* 19 F11
Belleville, Ill., *U.S.A.* 112 F10
Belleville, Kans., *U.S.A.* ... 112 F6
Belleville, N.Y., *U.S.A.* 111 C8
Belleville-sur-Vie, *France* .. 18 F5
Bellevue, *Canada* 104 D6
Bellevue, Idaho, *U.S.A.* ... 114 E6
Bellevue, Nebr., *U.S.A.* ... 112 E7
Bellevue, Ohio, *U.S.A.* 110 E2
Bellevue, Wash., *U.S.A.* ... 116 C4
Belley, *France* 21 C9
Bellin = Kangirsuk, *Canada* 101 B13
Bellingen, *Australia* 95 E5
Bellingham, *U.S.A.* 100 D7

Bellingshausen Sea, *Antarctica* 5 C17
Bellinzona, *Switz.* 25 J5
Bello, *Colombia* 124 B3
Bellows Falls, *U.S.A.* 111 C12
Bellpat, *Pakistan* 68 E3
Bellpuig d'Urgell, *Spain* ... 32 D6
Belluno, *Italy* 29 B9
Bellwood, *U.S.A.* 110 F6
Bélmez, *Spain* 35 G5
Belmont, *Canada* 110 D3
Belmont, *S. Africa* 88 D3
Belmont, *U.S.A.* 110 D6
Belmonte, *Brazil* 125 G11
Belmonte, *Portugal* 34 E3
Belmonte, *Spain* 33 F2
Belmopan, *Belize* 119 D7
Belmullet, *Ireland* 15 B2
Belo Horizonte, *Brazil* 125 G10
Belo-sur-Mer, *Madag.* 89 C7
Belo-Tsiribihina, *Madag.* .. 89 B7
Belogorsk = Bilohirsk, *Ukraine* 47 K8
Belogorsk, *Russia* 51 D13
Belogradchik, *Bulgaria* 40 C6
Belogradets, *Bulgaria* 41 C11
Beloha, *Madag.* 89 D8
Beloit, Kans., *U.S.A.* 112 F5
Beloit, Wis., *U.S.A.* 112 D10
Belokorovichi, *Ukraine* 47 G5
Belomorsk, *Russia* 50 C4
Belonia, *India* 67 H17
Belopolye = Bilopillya, *Ukraine* 47 G8
Beloretchensk, *Russia* 49 H4
Belorussia = Belarus ■, *Europe* 46 F4
Beloslav, *Bulgaria* 41 C11
Belovo, *Bulgaria* 41 D8
Belovo, *Russia* 50 D9
Belovodsk, *Ukraine* 47 H10
Beloye, Ozero, *Russia* 46 B9
Beloye More, *Russia* 50 C4
Belozem, *Bulgaria* 41 D9
Belozersk, *Russia* 46 B9
Belpasso, *Italy* 31 E7
Belpre, *U.S.A.* 108 F5
Belrain, *India* 69 E9
Belt, *U.S.A.* 114 C8
Beltana, *Australia* 95 E2
Belterra, *Brazil* 125 D8
Belton, *U.S.A.* 113 K6
Belton L., *U.S.A.* 113 K6
Beltsy = Bălți, *Moldova* ... 43 C12
Belturbet, *Ireland* 15 B4
Belukha, *Russia* 50 E9
Beluran, *Malaysia* 62 C5
Beluša, *Slovak Rep.* 27 B11
Belušić, *Serbia, Yug.* 40 C5
Belvédère Maríttimo, *Italy* . 31 C8
Belvès, *France* 20 D5
Belvidere, Ill., *U.S.A.* 112 D10
Belvidere, N.J., *U.S.A.* 111 F9
Belvis de la Jara, *Spain* ... 34 F6
Belyando →, *Australia* 94 C4
Belyy, *Russia* 46 E7
Belyy, Ostrov, *Russia* 50 B8
Belyy Yar, *Russia* 50 D9
Belżec, *Poland* 45 H10
Belzig, *Germany* 24 C8
Belzoni, *U.S.A.* 113 J9
Bełżyce, *Poland* 45 G9
Bemaraha, Lembalemban' i, *Madag.* 89 B7
Bemarivo, *Madag.* 89 C7
Bemarivo →, Antsiranana, *Madag.* 89 A9
Bemarivo →, Mahajanga, *Madag.* 89 B8
Bemavo, *Madag.* 89 C8
Bembéréke, *Benin* 83 C5
Bembesi, *Zimbabwe* 87 G2
Bembesi →, *Zimbabwe* ... 87 F2
Bembézar →, *Spain* 35 H5
Bembibre, *Spain* 34 C4
Bemetara, *India* 69 J9
Bemidji, *U.S.A.* 112 B7
Bemolanga, *Madag.* 89 B8
Ben, *Iran* 71 C6
Ben Cruachan, *U.K.* 14 E3
Ben Dearg, *U.K.* 14 D4
Ben Hope, *U.K.* 14 C4
Ben Lawers, *U.K.* 14 E4
Ben Lomond, N.S.W., *Australia* 95 E5
Ben Lomond, Tas., *Australia* 94 G4
Ben Lomond, *U.K.* 14 E4
Ben Luc, *Vietnam* 65 G6
Ben Macdhui, *U.K.* 14 D5
Ben Mhor, *U.K.* 14 D1
Ben More, Arg. & Bute, *U.K.* 14 E2
Ben More, Stirl., *U.K.* 14 E4
Ben More Assynt, *U.K.* 14 C4
Ben Nevis, *U.K.* 14 E3
Ben Quang, *Vietnam* 64 D6
Ben Vorlich, *U.K.* 14 E4
Ben Wyvis, *U.K.* 14 D4
Bena, *Nigeria* 83 C6
Benāb, *Iran* 73 D12
Benalla, *Australia* 95 F4
Benalmádena, *Spain* 35 J6
Benares = Varanasi, *India* . 69 G10
Bénat, C., *France* 21 E10
Benavente, *Portugal* 35 G2
Benavente, *Spain* 34 C5
Benavides, *U.S.A.* 113 M5
Benavides de Órbigo, *Spain* 34 C5
Benbecula, *U.K.* 14 D1
Benbonyathe, *Australia* 95 E2

Bend, *U.S.A.* 114 D3
Bendemeer, *Australia* 95 E5
Bender Beila, *Somali Rep.* 74 F5
Bendery = Tighina, *Moldova* 43 D14
Bendigo, *Australia* 95 F3
Bendorf, *Germany* 24 E3
Benē Beraq, *Israel* 75 C3
Bénéna, *Mali* 82 C4
Benenitra, *Madag.* 89 C8
Benevento, *Italy* 31 A7
Benfeld, *France* 19 D14
Benga, *Mozam.* 87 F3
Bengal, Bay of, *Ind. Oc.* 67 M17
Bengbis, *Cameroon* 83 E7
Bengbu, *China* 57 H9
Benghazi = Banghāzī, *Libya* 79 B10
Bengkalis, *Indonesia* 62 D2
Bengkulu, *Indonesia* 62 E2
Bengkulu □, *Indonesia* 62 E2
Bengough, *Canada* 105 D7
Bengtsfors, *Sweden* 10 E6
Benguela, *Angola* 85 G2
Benguérua, I., *Mozam.* 89 C6
Benha, *Egypt* 80 H7
Beni,
Dem. Rep. of the Congo 86 B2
Beni →, *Bolivia* 124 F5
Beni Mazâr, *Egypt* 80 B3
Beni Mellal, *Morocco* 78 B4
Beni Suef, *Egypt* 80 J7
Beniah L., *Canada* 104 A6
Benicarló, *Spain* 32 E5
Benicàssim, *Spain* 32 E5
Benicia, *U.S.A.* 116 G4
Benidorm, *Spain* 33 G4
Benin ■, *Africa* 83 D5
Benin →, *Nigeria* 83 D6
Benin, Bight of, *W. Afr.* 83 E5
Benin City, *Nigeria* 83 D6
Benisa, *Spain* 33 G5
Benitses, *Greece* 36 A3
Benjamin Aceval, *Paraguay* 126 A4
Benjamin Constant, *Brazil* 124 D4
Benjamin Hill, *Mexico* 118 A2
Benkelman, *U.S.A.* 112 E4
Benkovac, *Croatia* 29 D12
Bennett, *Canada* 104 B2
Bennett, *Australia* 92 D5
Bennetta, Ostrov, *Russia* 51 B15
Bennettsville, *U.S.A.* 109 H6
Bennichchâb, *Mauritania* 82 B1
Bennington, N.H., *U.S.A.* 111 D11
Bennington, Vt., *U.S.A.* 111 D11
Bénodet, *France* 18 E2
Benoni, *S. Africa* 89 D4
Benque Viejo, *Belize* 119 D7
Bensheim, *Germany* 25 F4
Benson, Ariz., *U.S.A.* 115 L8
Benson, Minn., *U.S.A.* 112 C7
Bent, *Iran* 71 E8
Benteng, *Indonesia* 63 F6
Bentinck I., *Australia* 94 B2
Bentiu, *Sudan* 81 F2
Bento Gonçalves, *Brazil* 127 B5
Benton, Ark., *U.S.A.* 113 H8
Benton, Calif., *U.S.A.* 116 H8
Benton, Ill., *U.S.A.* 112 G10
Benton, Pa., *U.S.A.* 111 E8
Benton Harbor, *U.S.A.* 108 D2
Bentonville, *U.S.A.* 113 G7
Bentu Liben, *Ethiopia* 81 F4
Bentung, *Malaysia* 65 L3
Benue □, *Nigeria* 83 D6
Benue →, *Nigeria* 83 D6
Benxi, *China* 57 D12
Beo, *Indonesia* 63 D7
Beograd, *Serbia, Yug.* 40 B4
Beoumi, *Ivory C.* 82 D3
Bepan Jiang →, *China* 58 E6
Beppu, *Japan* 55 H5
Beqaa Valley = Al Biqā,
Lebanon 75 A5
Ber Mota, *India* 68 H3
Berach →, *India* 68 G6
Beraketa, *Madag.* 89 C7
Berane, *Montenegro, Yug.* 40 D3
Berat, *Albania* 40 F3
Berau, Teluk, *Indonesia* 63 E8
Beravina, *Madag.* 89 B8
Berber, *Sudan* 80 D3
Berbera, *Somali Rep.* 74 E4
Berbérati, *C.A.R.* 84 D3
Berbice →, *Guyana* 124 B7
Berceto, *Italy* 28 D6
Berchidda, *Italy* 30 B2
Berchtesgaden, *Germany* 25 H8
Berck, *France* 19 B8
Berdichev = Berdychiv,
Ukraine 47 H5
Berdsk, *Russia* 50 D9
Berdyansk, *Ukraine* 47 J9
Berdychiv, *Ukraine* 47 H5
Berea, *U.S.A.* 108 G3
Berebere, *Indonesia* 63 D7
Bereda, *Somali Rep.* 74 E5
Berehove, *Ukraine* 47 H2
Berekum, *Ghana* 82 D4
Berenice, *Egypt* 80 C4
Berens →, *Canada* 105 C9
Berens I., *Canada* 105 C9
Berens River, *Canada* 105 C9
Beresford, *U.S.A.* 112 D6
Berestechko, *Ukraine* 47 G3
Berești, *Romania* 43 D12
Beretău →, *Romania* 42 C6
Berettyó →, *Hungary* 42 D6
Berettyóújfalu, *Hungary* 42 C6
Berevo, Mahajanga, *Madag.* 89 B7
Berevo, Toliara, *Madag.* 89 B7
Bereza, *Belarus* 47 F3

Berezhany, *Ukraine* 47 H3
Berezina = Byarezina →,
Belarus 47 F6
Berezivka, *Ukraine* 47 J6
Berezna, *Ukraine* 47 G6
Berezniki, *Russia* 50 C5
Berezniki, *Russia* 50 D6
Berezovo, *Russia* 50 C7
Berga, *Spain* 32 C6
Berga, *Sweden* 11 G10
Bergama, *Turkey* 39 B9
Bérgamo, *Italy* 28 C6
Bergara, *Spain* 32 B2
Bergby, *Sweden* 10 D11
Bergen,
Mecklenburg-Vorpommern,
Germany 24 A9
Bergen, *Niedersachsen,*
Germany 24 C5
Bergen, *Neths.* 17 B4
Bergen, *Norway* 9 F11
Bergen, *U.S.A.* 110 C7
Bergen op Zoom, *Neths.* 17 C4
Bergerac, *France* 20 D4
Bergheim, *Germany* 24 E2
Bergholz, *U.S.A.* 110 F4
Bergisch Gladbach, *Germany* 17 D7
Bergkamen, *Germany* 24 D3
Bergkvara, *Sweden* 11 H10
Bergshamra, *Sweden* 10 E12
Bergsjö, *Sweden* 10 C11
Bergues, *France* 19 B9
Bergviken, *Sweden* 10 C10
Berhala, Selat, *Indonesia* 62 E2
Berhampore = Baharampur,
India 69 G13
Berhampur = Brahmapur,
India 67 K14
Berheci →, *Romania* 43 E12
Bering Sea, *Pac. Oc.* 100 C1
Bering Strait, *Pac. Oc.* 100 B3
Beringovskiy, *Russia* 51 C18
Berisso, *Argentina* 126 C4
Berja, *Spain* 35 J8
Berkeley, *U.S.A.* 116 H4
Berkner I., *Antarctica* 5 D18
Berkovitsa, *Bulgaria* 40 C7
Berkshire, *U.S.A.* 111 D8
Berkshire Downs, *U.K.* 13 F6
Berlanga, *Spain* 35 G5
Berlenga, I., *Portugal* 35 F1
Berlin, *Germany* 24 C9
Berlin, Md., *U.S.A.* 108 F8
Berlin, N.H., *U.S.A.* 111 B13
Berlin, N.Y., *U.S.A.* 111 D11
Berlin, Wis., *U.S.A.* 108 D1
Berlin □, *Germany* 24 C9
Berlin L., *U.S.A.* 110 E4
Bermeja, Sierra, *Spain* 35 J5
Bermejo →, *Formosa,*
Argentina 126 B4
Bermejo →, *San Juan,*
Argentina 126 C2
Bermen, L., *Canada* 103 B6
Bermeo, *Spain* 32 B2
Bermillo de Sayago, *Spain* 34 D4
Bermuda ■, *Atl. Oc.* 98 F13
Bern, *Switz.* 25 J3
Bern □, *Switz.* 25 J3
Bernalda, *Italy* 31 B9
Bernalillo, *U.S.A.* 115 J10
Bernardo de Irigoyen,
Argentina 127 B5
Bernardo O'Higgins □, *Chile* 126 C1
Bernardsville, *U.S.A.* 111 F10
Bernasconi, *Argentina* 126 D3
Bernau, *Bayern, Germany* 25 H8
Bernau, *Brandenburg,*
Germany 24 C9
Bernay, *France* 18 C7
Bernburg, *Germany* 24 D7
Berndorf, *Austria* 26 D9
Berne = Bern, *Switz.* 25 J3
Berne □, *Switz.* 25 J3
Berner Alpen, *Switz.* 25 J3
Berneray, *U.K.* 14 D1
Bernier I., *Australia* 93 D1
Bernina, Piz, *Switz.* 25 J5
Bernkastel-Kues, *Germany* 25 F3
Beroroha, *Madag.* 89 C8
Béroubouay, *Benin* 83 D5
Beroun, *Czech Rep.* 26 B7
Berounka →, *Czech Rep.* 26 B7
Berovo, *Macedonia* 40 E6
Berre, Étang de, *France* 21 E9
Berre-l'Étang, *France* 21 E9
Berri, *Australia* 95 E3
Berriane, *Algeria* 78 B6
Berrigan, *Australia* 95 F4
Berry, *Australia* 95 E5
Berry, *France* 19 F8
Berry Is., *Bahamas* 120 A4
Berryessa L., *U.S.A.* 116 G4
Berryville, *U.S.A.* 113 G8
Berseba, *Namibia* 88 D2
Bersenbrück, *Germany* 24 C3
Bershad, *Ukraine* 47 H5
Berthold, *U.S.A.* 112 A4
Berthoud, *U.S.A.* 112 E2
Bertincourt, *France* 19 B9
Bertoua, *Cameroon* 84 D2
Bertraghboy B., *Ireland* 15 C2
Berwick, *U.S.A.* 111 E8
Berwick-upon-Tweed, *U.K.* 12 B6
Berwyn Mts., *U.K.* 12 E4
Beryslav, *Ukraine* 47 J7
Berzasca, *Romania* 42 F6
Berzence, *Hungary* 42 D2

Besal, *Pakistan* 69 B5
Besalampy, *Madag.* 89 B7
Besançon, *France* 19 E13
Besar, *Indonesia* 62 E5
Beshenkovichi, *Belarus* 46 E5
Beška, *Serbia, Yug.* 42 E5
Beslan, *Russia* 49 J7
Besna Kobila, *Serbia, Yug.* 40 D6
Besnard L., *Canada* 105 B7
Besni, *Turkey* 70 B3
Besor, N. →, *Egypt* 75 D3
Bessarabiya, *Moldova* 47 J5
Bessarabka = Basarabeasca,
Moldova 43 D13
Bessèges, *France* 21 D8
Bessemer, Ala., *U.S.A.* 109 J2
Bessemer, Mich., *U.S.A.* 112 B9
Bessemer, Pa., *U.S.A.* 110 F4
Bessin, *France* 18 C6
Bessines-sur-Gartempe,
France 20 B5
Beswick, *Australia* 92 B5
Bet She'an, *Israel* 75 C4
Bet Shemesh, *Israel* 75 D4
Betafo, *Madag.* 89 B8
Betancuria, *Canary Is.* 37 F5
Betanzos, *Spain* 34 B2
Bétaré Oya, *Cameroon* 84 C2
Betatao, *Madag.* 89 B8
Bétera, *Spain* 33 F4
Bétérou, *Benin* 83 D5
Bethal, *S. Africa* 89 D4
Bethanien, *Namibia* 88 D2
Bethany, *Canada* 110 B6
Bethany, *U.S.A.* 112 E7
Bethel, Alaska, *U.S.A.* 100 B3
Bethel, Conn., *U.S.A.* 111 E11
Bethel, Maine, *U.S.A.* 111 B13
Bethel, Vt., *U.S.A.* 111 C12
Bethel Park, *U.S.A.* 110 F4
Bethlehem = Bayt Laḥm,
West Bank 75 D4
Bethlehem, *S. Africa* 89 D4
Bethlehem, *U.S.A.* 111 F9
Bethulie, *S. Africa* 88 E4
Béthune, *France* 19 B9
Béthune →, *France* 18 C8
Betioky, *Madag.* 89 C7
Betong, *Thailand* 65 K3
Betoota, *Australia* 94 D3
Betor, *Ethiopia* 81 E4
Betroka, *Madag.* 89 C8
Betsiamites, *Canada* 103 C6
Betsiamites →, *Canada* 103 C6
Betsiboka →, *Madag.* 89 B8
Bettendorf, *U.S.A.* 112 E9
Bettiah, *India* 69 F11
Bettna, *Sweden* 11 F10
Béttola, *Italy* 28 D6
Betul, *India* 66 J10
Betung, *Malaysia* 62 D4
Betws-y-Coed, *U.K.* 12 D4
Betxi, *Spain* 32 F4
Betzdorf, *Germany* 24 E3
Beuil, *France* 21 D10
Beulah, Mich., *U.S.A.* 108 C2
Beulah, N. Dak., *U.S.A.* 112 B4
Beuvron →, *France* 18 E8
Beveren, *Belgium* 17 C4
Beverley, *Australia* 93 F2
Beverley, *U.K.* 12 D7
Beverley Hills, *U.S.A.* 109 L4
Beverly, *U.S.A.* 111 D14
Beverly Hills, *U.S.A.* 117 L8
Beverungen, *Germany* 24 D5
Bevoalavo, *Madag.* 89 D7
Bewas →, *India* 69 H8
Bex, *Switz.* 25 J3
Bexhill, *U.K.* 13 G8
Bey Dağları, *Turkey* 39 E12
Beyānlū, *Iran* 70 C5
Beyazköy, *Turkey* 41 E11
Beyçayır, *Turkey* 41 F10
Beydağ, *Turkey* 39 D10
Beyeğaç, *Turkey* 39 D10
Beyin, *Ghana* 82 D4
Beykoz, *Turkey* 41 E13
Beyla, *Guinea* 82 D3
Beynat, *France* 20 C5
Beyneu, *Kazakstan* 50 E6
Beyoba, *Turkey* 39 C9
Beypazarı, *Turkey* 72 B4
Beyşehir, *Turkey* 72 D4
Beyşehir Gölü, *Turkey* 70 B1
Beytüşşebap, *Turkey* 73 D10
Bezdan, *Serbia, Yug.* 42 E3
Bezhetsk, *Russia* 46 D9
Béziers, *France* 20 E7
Bezwada = Vijayawada,
India 67 L12
Bhabua, *India* 69 G10
Bhachau, *India* 66 H7
Bhadar →, *Gujarat, India* 68 H5
Bhadar →, *Gujarat, India* 68 J3
Bhadarwah, *India* 69 C6
Bhadohi, *India* 69 G10
Bhadra, *India* 68 E6
Bhadrakh, *India* 67 J15
Bhadran, *India* 68 H5
Bhadravati, *India* 66 N9
Bhag, *Pakistan* 68 E2
Bhagalpur, *India* 69 G12
Bhagirathi →, *Ut. P., India* 69 D8
Bhagirathi →, *W. Bengal,*
India 69 H13
Bhakkar, *Pakistan* 68 D4
Bhakra Dam, *India* 68 D7
Bhamo, *Burma* 67 G20
Bhandara, *India* 66 J11

Bhanpura, *India* 68 G6
Bhanrer Ra., *India* 69 H8
Bhaptiahi, *India* 69 F12
Bharat = India ■, *Asia* 66 K11
Bharatpur, *Mad. P., India* 69 H9
Bharatpur, *Raj., India* 68 F7
Bharno, *India* 69 H11
Bhatpara, *India* 69 H13
Bhattu, *India* 68 E6
Bhaun, *Pakistan* 68 C5
Bhaunagar = Bhavnagar,
India 66 J8
Bhavnagar, *India* 66 J8
Bhawanipatna, *India* 67 K12
Bhawari, *India* 68 G5
Bhayavadar, *India* 68 J4
Bhera, *Pakistan* 68 C5
Bhikangaon, *India* 68 J6
Bhilsa = Vidisha, *India* 68 H7
Bhilwara, *India* 68 G6
Bhima →, *India* 66 L10
Bhimavaram, *India* 67 L12
Bhimbar, *Pakistan* 69 C6
Bhind, *India* 69 F8
Bhinga, *India* 69 F9
Bhinmal, *India* 68 G5
Bhiwandi, *India* 66 K8
Bhiwani, *India* 68 E7
Bhogava →, *India* 68 H5
Bhola, *Bangla.* 67 H17
Bholari, *Pakistan* 68 G3
Bhopal, *India* 68 H7
Bhubaneshwar, *India* 67 J14
Bhuj, *India* 68 H3
Bhusaval, *India* 66 J9
Bhutan ■, *Asia* 67 F17
Biafra, B. of = Bonny, Bight
of, *Africa* 83 E6
Biak, *Indonesia* 63 E9
Biała, *Poland* 45 H4
Biała →, *Poland* 45 H7
Biała Piska, *Poland* 44 E9
Biała Podlaska, *Poland* 45 F10
Biała Rawska, *Poland* 45 G7
Białobrzegi, *Poland* 45 G7
Białogard, *Poland* 44 D2
Białowieża, *Poland* 45 F10
Biały Bór, *Poland* 44 E3
Białystok, *Poland* 45 E10
Biancavilla, *Italy* 31 E7
Bianco, *Italy* 31 D9
Biankouma, *Ivory C.* 82 D3
Biaora, *India* 68 H7
Bīārjmand, *Iran* 71 B7
Biaro, *Indonesia* 63 D7
Biarritz, *France* 20 E2
Biasca, *Switz.* 25 J4
Biba, *Egypt* 80 J7
Bibai, *Japan* 54 C10
Bibala, *Angola* 85 G2
Bibbiena, *Italy* 29 E8
Bibby I., *Canada* 105 A10
Bibel →, *Spain* 34 C3
Biberach, *Germany* 25 G5
Bibiani, *Ghana* 82 D4
Bibungwa,
Dem. Rep. of the Congo 86 C2
Bic, *Canada* 103 C6
Bicaj, *Albania* 40 E4
Bicaz, *Romania* 43 D10
Bicazu Ardelean, *Romania* 43 D10
Bíccari, *Italy* 31 A8
Bicester, *U.K.* 13 F6
Bichena, *Ethiopia* 81 E4
Bicheno, *Australia* 94 G4
Bichia, *India* 69 H9
Bichvinta, *Georgia* 49 J5
Bickerton I., *Australia* 94 A2
Bicske, *Hungary* 42 C3
Bida, *Nigeria* 83 D6
Bidar, *India* 66 L10
Biddeford, *U.S.A.* 109 D10
Biddwara, *Ethiopia* 81 F4
Bideford, *U.K.* 13 F3
Bideford Bay, *U.K.* 13 F3
Bidhuna, *India* 69 F8
Bidor, *Malaysia* 65 K3
Bie, *Sweden* 10 E10
Bié, Planalto de, *Angola* 85 G3
Bieber, *U.S.A.* 114 F3
Biebrza →, *Poland* 45 E9
Biecz, *Poland* 45 J8
Biel, *Switz.* 25 H3
Bielawa, *Poland* 45 H3
Bielefeld, *Germany* 24 C4
Bielersee, *Switz.* 25 H3
Biella, *Italy* 28 C5
Bielsk Podlaski, *Poland* 45 F10
Bielsko-Biała, *Poland* 45 J6
Bien Hoa, *Vietnam* 65 G6
Bienne = Biel, *Switz.* 25 H3
Bienvenida, *Spain* 35 G4
Bienville, L., *Canada* 102 A5
Bierné, *France* 18 E6
Bierun, *Poland* 45 H6
Bierutów, *Poland* 45 G4
Biese →, *Germany* 24 C7
Biesiesfontein, *S. Africa* 88 E2
Bietigheim-Bissingen,
Germany 25 G5
Bieżuń, *Poland* 45 E6
Biferno →, *Italy* 29 G12
Big →, *Canada* 103 B8
Big B., *Canada* 103 A7
Big Bear City, *U.S.A.* 117 L10
Big Bear Lake, *U.S.A.* 117 L10
Big Belt Mts., *U.S.A.* 114 C8
Big Bend, *Swaziland* 89 D5
Big Bend National Park,
U.S.A. 113 L3

Big Black →, *U.S.A.* 113 K9
Big Blue →, *U.S.A.* 112 F6
Big Creek, *U.S.A.* 116 H7
Big Cypress National
Preserve, *U.S.A.* 109 M5
Big Cypress Swamp, *U.S.A.* 109 M5
Big Falls, *U.S.A.* 112 A8
Big Fork →, *U.S.A.* 112 A8
Big Horn Mts. = Bighorn
Mts., *U.S.A.* 114 D10
Big I., *Canada* 104 A5
Big Lake, *U.S.A.* 113 K4
Big Moose, *U.S.A.* 111 C10
Big Muddy Cr. →, *U.S.A.* 112 A2
Big Pine, *U.S.A.* 116 H8
Big Piney, *U.S.A.* 114 E8
Big Rapids, *U.S.A.* 108 D3
Big Rideau L., *Canada* 111 B8
Big River, *Canada* 105 C7
Big Run, *U.S.A.* 110 F6
Big Sable Pt., *U.S.A.* 108 C2
Big Salmon →, *Canada* 104 A2
Big Sand L., *Canada* 105 B9
Big Sandy, *U.S.A.* 114 B8
Big Sandy →, *U.S.A.* 108 F4
Big Sandy Cr. →, *U.S.A.* 112 F3
Big Sioux →, *U.S.A.* 112 D6
Big Spring, *U.S.A.* 113 J4
Big Stone City, *U.S.A.* 112 C6
Big Stone Gap, *U.S.A.* 109 G4
Big Stone L., *U.S.A.* 112 C6
Big Sur, *U.S.A.* 116 J5
Big Timber, *U.S.A.* 114 D9
Big Trout L., *Canada* 102 B2
Big Trout Lake, *Canada* 102 B2
Biğa, *Turkey* 41 F11
Biga →, *Turkey* 41 F11
Bigadiç, *Turkey* 39 B10
Biganos, *France* 20 D3
Biggar, *Canada* 105 C7
Biggar, *U.K.* 14 F5
Bigge I., *Australia* 92 B4
Biggenden, *Australia* 95 D5
Biggleswade, *U.K.* 13 E7
Biggs, *U.S.A.* 116 F5
Bighorn, *U.S.A.* 114 C10
Bighorn →, *U.S.A.* 114 C10
Bighorn L., *U.S.A.* 114 D9
Bighorn Mts., *U.S.A.* 114 D10
Bignona, *Senegal* 82 C1
Bigorre, *France* 20 E4
Bigstone L., *Canada* 105 C9
Biguglia, Étang de, *France* 21 F13
Bigwa, *Tanzania* 86 D4
Bihać, *Bos.-H.* 29 D12
Bihar, *India* 69 G11
Bihar □, *India* 69 G12
Biharamulo, *Tanzania* 86 C3
Bihariganj, *India* 69 G12
Biharkeresztes, *Hungary* 42 C6
Bihor □, *Romania* 42 D7
Bihor, Munții, *Romania* 42 D7
Bijagós, Arquipélago dos,
Guinea-Biss. 82 C1
Bijainagar, *India* 68 G6
Bijapur, *Karnataka, India* 66 L9
Bijapur, *Mad. P., India* 67 K12
Bījār, *Iran* 70 C5
Bijawar, *India* 69 G8
Bijeljina, *Bos.-H.* 42 F4
Bijelo Polje,
Montenegro, Yug. 40 C3
Bijie, *China* 58 D5
Bijnor, *India* 68 E8
Bikaner, *India* 68 E5
Bikapur, *India* 69 F10
Bikeqi, *China* 56 D6
Bikfayyā, *Lebanon* 75 B4
Bikin, *Russia* 51 E14
Bikin →, *Russia* 54 A7
Bikini Atoll, *Marshall Is.* 96 F8
Bikita, *Zimbabwe* 89 C5
Bikoué, *Cameroon* 83 E7
Bila Tserkva, *Ukraine* 47 H6
Bilanga, *Burkina Faso* 83 C4
Bilara, *India* 68 F5
Bilaspur, *Mad. P., India* 69 H10
Bilaspur, *Punjab, India* 68 D7
Biläsuvar, *Azerbaijan* 73 C13
Bilauk Taungdan, *Thailand* 64 F2
Bilbao, *Spain* 32 B2
Bilbeis, *Egypt* 80 H7
Bilbo = Bilbao, *Spain* 32 B2
Bilbor, *Romania* 43 C10
Bilciurești, *Romania* 43 F10
Bíldudalur, *Iceland* 8 D2
Bílé Karpaty, *Europe* 27 B11
Bileća, *Bos.-H.* 40 D2
Bilecik, *Turkey* 72 B4
Biłgoraj, *Poland* 45 H9
Bilgram, *India* 69 F9
Bilhaur, *India* 69 F9
Bilhorod-Dnistrovskyy,
Ukraine 47 J6
Bilibino, *Russia* 51 C17
Bilibiza, *Mozam.* 87 E5
Bilishti, *Albania* 40 F5
Billabalong Roadhouse,
Australia 93 E2
Billdal, *Sweden* 11 G5
Billiluna, *Australia* 92 C4
Billings, *U.S.A.* 114 D9
Billiton Is. = Belitung,
Indonesia 62 E3
Billsta, *Sweden* 10 A12
Billund, *Denmark* 11 J3
Bilma, *Niger* 79 E8
Bilo Gora, *Croatia* 42 E2
Biloela, *Australia* 94 C5
Bilohirsk, *Ukraine* 47 K8
Bilopillya, *Ukraine* 47 G8

Biloxi, *U.S.A.* 113 K10
Bilpa Morea Claypan,
  Australia 94 D3
Biltine, *Chad* 79 F10
Bilyarsk, *Russia* 48 C10
Bima, *Indonesia* 63 F5
Bimban, *Egypt* 80 C3
Bimbila, *Ghana* 83 D5
Bimini Is., *Bahamas* 120 A4
Bin Xian, *Heilongjiang,*
  China 57 B14
Bin Xian, *Shaanxi, China* .. 56 G5
Bin Yauri, *Nigeria* 83 C5
Bina-Etawah, *India* 68 G8
Bināb, *Iran* 71 B6
Binalbagan, *Phil.* 61 F5
Binalong, *Australia* 95 E4
Bīnālūd, Kūh-e, *Iran* 71 B8
Binatang = Bintangor,
  Malaysia 62 D4
Binche, *Belgium* 17 D4
Binchuan, *China* 58 E3
Binder, *Chad* 83 D7
Bindki, *India* 69 F9
Bindslev, *Denmark* 11 G4
Bindura, *Zimbabwe* 87 F3
Binefar, *Spain* 32 D5
Bingara, *Australia* 95 D5
Bingen, *Germany* 25 F3
Bingerville, *Ivory C.* 83 D4
Bingham, *U.S.A.* 109 C11
Binghamton, *U.S.A.* 111 D9
Bingöl, *Turkey* 70 B4
Bingöl Dağları, *Turkey* 73 C9
Bingsjö, *Sweden* 10 C9
Binh Dinh = An Nhon,
  Vietnam 64 F7
Binh Khe, *Vietnam* 64 F7
Binh Son, *Vietnam* 64 E7
Binhai, *China* 57 G10
Binic, *France* 18 D4
Binisatua, *Spain* 37 B11
Binjai, *Indonesia* 62 D3
Binji, *Nigeria* 83 C5
Binnaway, *Australia* 95 E4
Binongko, *Indonesia* 63 F6
Binscarth, *Canada* 105 C8
Bint Goda, *Sudan* 81 E3
Bintan, *Indonesia* 62 D2
Bintangor, *Malaysia* 62 D4
Bintulu, *Malaysia* 62 D4
Bintuni, *Indonesia* 63 E8
Binyang, *China* 58 F7
Binz, *Germany* 24 A9
Binzert = Bizerte, *Tunisia* . 79 A7
Binzhou, *China* 57 F10
Bío Bío □, *Chile* 126 D1
Biograd na Moru, *Croatia* .. 29 E12
Bioko, *Eq. Guin.* 83 E6
Biokovo, *Croatia* 29 E14
Bipindi, *Cameroon* 83 E7
Bir, *India* 66 K9
Bir, Ras, *Djibouti* 81 E5
Bîr Abu Hashim, *Egypt* 80 C3
Bîr Abu Minqar, *Egypt* 80 B2
Bîr Abu Muḥammad, *Egypt* ... 75 F3
Bi'r ad Dabbāghāt, *Jordan* . 75 E4
Bi'r Adal Deib, *Sudan* 80 C4
Bi'r al Butayyiḥāt, *Jordan* . 75 F4
Bi'r al Mārī, *Jordan* 75 E4
Bi'r al Qattār, *Jordan* 75 F4
Bīr 'Asal, *Egypt* 80 B3
Bir Atrun, *Sudan* 80 D2
Bîr Beida, *Egypt* 75 E3
Bîr Diqnash, *Egypt* 80 A2
Bîr el 'Abd, *Egypt* 75 D2
Bîr el Basur, *Egypt* 80 B2
Bîr el Biarât, *Egypt* 75 F3
Bîr el Duweidar, *Egypt* 75 E1
Bîr el Garârât, *Egypt* 75 D2
Bîr el Gellaz, *Egypt* 80 A2
Bîr el Heisi, *Egypt* 75 F3
Bîr el Jafir, *Egypt* 75 E1
Bîr el Mâlḥi, *Egypt* 75 E2
Bîr el Shaqqa, *Egypt* 80 A2
Bîr el Thamâda, *Egypt* 75 E2
Bîr Fuad, *Egypt* 80 A2
Bîr Gebeil Ḥiṣn, *Egypt* 75 E2
Bi'r Ghadir, *Syria* 75 A6
Bîr Haimur, *Egypt* 80 C3
Bîr Ḥasana, *Egypt* 75 E2
Bîr Hōōker, *Egypt* 80 H7
Bîr Kanayis, *Egypt* 80 C3
Bîr Kaseiba, *Egypt* 75 E2
Bîr Kerawein, *Egypt* 80 B2
Bîr Lahfân, *Egypt* 75 E2
Bîr Madkûr, *Egypt* 75 E1
Bîr Maql, *Egypt* 80 C3
Bîr Mineiga, *Sudan* 80 C4
Bîr Misaha, *Egypt* 80 C2
Bîr Murr, *Egypt* 80 C3
Bi'r Muṭribah, *Kuwait* 70 D5
Bîr Nakheila, *Egypt* 80 C3
Bîr Qaṭia, *Egypt* 75 E1
Bîr Qatrani, *Egypt* 80 A2
Bîr Ranga, *Egypt* 80 C3
Bîr Sahara, *Egypt* 80 C2
Bîr Seiyâla, *Egypt* 80 B3
Bîr Shalatein, *Egypt* 80 C4
Bîr Shebb, *Egypt* 80 C2
Bîr Shût, *Egypt* 80 C3
Bîr Terfawi, *Egypt* 80 C2
Bîr Umm Qubûr, *Egypt* 80 C3
Bîr Za'farâna, *Egypt* 80 J8
Bîr Zeidûn, *Egypt* 80 B3
Biramféro, *Guinea* 82 C3
Biratnagar, *Nepal* 69 F12
Birawa,
  Dem. Rep. of the Congo . 86 C2

Birch →, *Canada* 104 B6
Birch Hills, *Canada* 105 C7
Birch I., *Canada* 105 C9
Birch L., *N.W.T., Canada* .. 104 A5
Birch L., *Ont., Canada* 102 B1
Birch Mts., *Canada* 104 B6
Birch River, *Canada* 105 C8
Birchip, *Australia* 95 F3
Birchiş, *Romania* 42 E7
Bird, *Canada* 105 B10
Bird I. = Las Aves, Is.,
  W. Indies 121 C7
Birdsville, *Australia* 94 D2
Birdum Cr., *Australia* 92 C5
Birecik, *Turkey* 70 B3
Birein, *Israel* 75 E3
Bireuen, *Indonesia* 62 C1
Biri →, *Sudan* 81 F2
Birifo, *Gambia* 82 C2
Birigui, *Brazil* 127 A5
Birjand, *Iran* 71 C8
Birkenfeld, *Germany* 25 F3
Birkenhead, *U.K.* 12 D4
Birkerød, *Denmark* 11 J6
Birket Qârûn, *Egypt* 80 J7
Birkfeld, *Austria* 26 D8
Bîrlad = Bârlad, *Romania* .. 43 D12
Birmingham, *U.K.* 13 E6
Birmingham, *U.S.A.* 109 J2
Birmitrapur, *India* 67 H14
Birni Ngaouré, *Niger* 83 C5
Birni Nkonni, *Niger* 83 C6
Birnin Gwari, *Nigeria* 83 C6
Birnin Kebbi, *Nigeria* 83 C5
Birnin Kudu, *Nigeria* 83 C6
Birobidzhan, *Russia* 51 E14
Birr, *Ireland* 15 C4
Birrie →, *Australia* 95 D4
Birsilpur, *India* 68 E5
Birsk, *Russia* 50 D6
Birštonas, *Lithuania* 44 D11
Birtle, *Canada* 105 C8
Birur, *India* 66 N9
Biryuchiy, *Ukraine* 47 J8
Biržai, *Lithuania* 9 H21
Birzebbugga, *Malta* 36 D2
Bisa, *Indonesia* 63 E7
Bisáccia, *Italy* 31 A8
Bisacquino, *Italy* 30 E6
Bisalpur, *India* 69 E8
Bisbee, *U.S.A.* 115 L9
Biscarrosse, *France* 20 D2
Biscarrosse et de Parentis,
  Étang de, *France* 20 D2
Biscay, B. of, *Atl. Oc.* ... 6 F5
Biscayne B., *U.S.A.* 109 N5
Biscéglie, *Italy* 31 A9
Bischheim, *France* 19 D14
Bischofshofen, *Austria* 26 D6
Bischofswerda, *Germany* 24 D10
Bischwiller, *France* 19 D14
Biscoe Bay, *Antarctica* 5 D13
Biscoe Is., *Antarctica* 5 C17
Biscostasing, *Canada* 102 C3
Biševo, *Croatia* 29 F13
Bisha, *Eritrea* 81 D4
Bishah, W. →, *Si. Arabia* .. 80 C5
Bishan, *China* 58 C6
Bishkek, *Kyrgyzstan* 50 E8
Bishnupur, *India* 69 H12
Bisho, *S. Africa* 89 E4
Bishop, *Calif., U.S.A.* 116 H8
Bishop, *Tex., U.S.A.* 113 M6
Bishop Auckland, *U.K.* 12 C6
Bishop's Falls, *Canada* 103 C8
Bishop's Stortford, *U.K.* .. 13 F8
Bisignano, *Italy* 31 C9
Bisina, L., *Uganda* 86 B3
Biskra, *Algeria* 78 B7
Biskupiec, *Poland* 44 E7
Bismarck, *U.S.A.* 112 B4
Bismarck Arch.,
  Papua N. G. 96 H7
Bismark, *Germany* 24 C7
Bismil, *Turkey* 73 D9
Biso, *Uganda* 86 B3
Bison, *U.S.A.* 112 C3
Bīsotūn, *Iran* 70 C5
Bispgården, *Sweden* 10 A10
Bissagos = Bijagós,
  Arquipélago dos,
  Guinea-Biss. 82 C1
Bissau, *Guinea-Biss.* 82 C1
Bissaula, *Nigeria* 83 D7
Bissikrima, *Guinea* 82 C2
Bissorã, *Guinea-Biss.* 82 C1
Bistcho L., *Canada* 104 B5
Bistreţ, *Romania* 43 G8
Bistrica = Ilirska-Bistrica,
  Slovenia 29 C11
Bistriţa, *Romania* 43 C9
Bistriţa →, *Romania* 43 D11
Bistriţa Năsăud □, *Romania* . 43 C9
Bistriţei, Munţii, *Romania* . 43 C10
Biswan, *India* 69 F9
Bisztynek, *Poland* 44 D7
Bitburg, *Germany* 25 F2
Bitche, *France* 19 C14
Bithynia, *Turkey* 72 B4
Bitlis, *Turkey* 70 B4
Bitola, *Macedonia* 40 E5
Bitolj = Bitola, *Macedonia* . 40 E5
Bitonto, *Italy* 31 A9
Bitter Creek, *U.S.A.* 114 F9
Bitter L. = Buheirat-Murrat-
  el-Kubra, *Egypt* 80 H8
Bitterfeld, *Germany* 24 D8
Bitterfontein, *S. Africa* .. 88 E2
Bitterroot →, *U.S.A.* 114 C6
Bitterroot Range, *U.S.A.* .. 114 D6
Bitterwater, *U.S.A.* 116 J6

Bitti, *Italy* 30 B2
Bittou, *Burkina Faso* 83 C4
Biu, *Nigeria* 83 C7
Bivolari, *Romania* 43 C12
Bivolu, Vf., *Romania* 43 C10
Biwa-Ko, *Japan* 55 G8
Biwabik, *U.S.A.* 112 B8
Bixad, *Romania* 43 C8
Bixby, *U.S.A.* 113 H7
Biyang, *China* 56 H7
Biysk, *Russia* 50 D9
Bizana, *S. Africa* 89 E4
Bizen, *Japan* 55 G7
Bizerte, *Tunisia* 79 A7
Bjargtangar, *Iceland* 8 D1
Bjärnum, *Sweden* 11 H7
Bjästa, *Sweden* 10 A12
Bjelasica, *Montenegro, Yug.* . 40 D3
Bjelašnica, *Bos.-H.* 42 G3
Bjelovar, *Croatia* 29 C13
Bjerringbro, *Denmark* 11 H3
Bjørbo, *Sweden* 10 D8
Björklinge, *Sweden* 10 D11
Björneborg, *Sweden* 10 E8
Bjørnevatn, *Norway* 8 B23
Bjørnøya, *Arctic* 4 B8
Bjursås, *Sweden* 10 D9
Bjuv, *Sweden* 11 H6
Bla, *Mali* 82 C3
Blace, *Serbia, Yug.* 40 C5
Blachownia, *Poland* 45 H5
Black = Da →, *Vietnam* 58 G5
Black →, *Canada* 110 B5
Black →, *Ariz., U.S.A.* 115 K8
Black →, *Ark., U.S.A.* 113 H9
Black →, *Mich., U.S.A.* 110 D2
Black →, *N.Y., U.S.A.* 111 C8
Black →, *Wis., U.S.A.* 112 D9
Black Bay Pen., *Canada* 102 C2
Black Birch L., *Canada* 105 B7
Black Diamond, *Canada* 104 C6
Black Duck →, *Canada* 102 A2
Black Forest = Schwarzwald,
  Germany 25 G4
Black Forest, *U.S.A.* 112 F2
Black Hd., *Ireland* 15 C2
Black Hills, *U.S.A.* 112 D3
Black I., *Canada* 105 C9
Black L., *Canada* 105 B7
Black L., *Mich., U.S.A.* ... 108 C3
Black L., *N.Y., U.S.A.* 111 B9
Black Lake, *Canada* 105 B7
Black Mesa, *U.S.A.* 113 G3
Black Mt. = Mynydd Du,
  U.K. 13 F4
Black Mts., *U.K.* 13 F4
Black Range, *U.S.A.* 115 K10
Black River, *Jamaica* 120 C4
Black River Falls, *U.S.A.* . 112 C9
Black Sea, *Eurasia* 6 G12
Black Tickle, *Canada* 103 B8
Black Volta →, *Africa* 82 D4
Black Warrior →, *U.S.A.* ... 109 J2
Blackall, *Australia* 94 C4
Blackball, *N.Z.* 91 K3
Blackbull, *Australia* 94 B3
Blackburn, *U.K.* 12 D5
Blackburn with Darwen □,
  U.K. 12 D5
Blackfoot, *U.S.A.* 114 E7
Blackfoot →, *U.S.A.* 114 C7
Blackfoot River Reservoir,
  U.S.A. 114 E8
Blackie, *Canada* 104 C6
Blackpool, *U.K.* 12 D4
Blackpool □, *U.K.* 12 D4
Blackriver, *U.S.A.* 110 B1
Blacks Harbour, *Canada* 103 C6
Blacksburg, *U.S.A.* 108 G5
Blacksod B., *Ireland* 15 B1
Blackstone, *U.S.A.* 108 G7
Blackstone Ra., *Australia* . 93 E4
Blackwater, *Australia* 94 C4
Blackwater →, *Meath,*
  Ireland 15 C4
Blackwater →, *Waterford,*
  Ireland 15 D4
Blackwater →, *U.K.* 15 B5
Blackwell, *U.S.A.* 113 G6
Blackwells Corner, *U.S.A.* . 117 K7
Blaenau Ffestiniog, *U.K.* .. 12 E4
Blaenau Gwent □, *U.K.* 13 F4
Blagaj, *Bos.-H.* 40 C1
Blagodarnoye =
  Blagodarnyy, *Russia* 49 H6
Blagodarnyy, *Russia* 49 H6
Blagoevgrad, *Bulgaria* 40 D7
Blagoveshchensk, *Russia* ... 51 D13
Blain, *France* 18 E5
Blain, *U.S.A.* 110 F7
Blaine, *Minn., U.S.A.* 112 C8
Blaine, *Wash., U.S.A.* 116 B4
Blaine Lake, *Canada* 105 C7
Blair, *U.S.A.* 112 E6
Blair Athol, *Australia* 94 C4
Blair Atholl, *U.K.* 14 E5
Blairgowrie, *U.K.* 14 E5
Blairsville, *U.S.A.* 110 F5
Blaj, *Romania* 43 D8
Blake Pt., *U.S.A.* 112 A10
Blakely, *Ga., U.S.A.* 109 K3
Blakely, *Pa., U.S.A.* 111 E9
Blâmont, *France* 19 D13
Blanc, Mont, *Alps* 21 C10
Blanc-Sablon, *Canada* 103 B8
Blanca, B., *Argentina* 122 G4
Blanca Peak, *U.S.A.* 115 H11
Blanche, C., *Australia* 95 E1

Blanche, L., *S. Austral.,*
  Australia 95 D2
Blanche, L., *W. Austral.,*
  Australia 92 D3
Blanco, *S. Africa* 88 E3
Blanco, *U.S.A.* 113 K5
Blanco →, *Argentina* 126 C2
Blanco, C., *Costa Rica* 120 E2
Blanco, C., *U.S.A.* 114 E1
Blanda →, *Iceland* 8 D3
Blandford Forum, *U.K.* 13 G5
Blanding, *U.S.A.* 115 H9
Blanes, *Spain* 32 D7
Blangy-sur-Bresle, *France* . 19 C8
Blanice →, *Czech Rep.* 26 B7
Blankaholm, *Sweden* 11 G10
Blankenberge, *Belgium* 17 C3
Blankenburg, *Germany* 24 D6
Blanquefort, *France* 20 D3
Blanquilla, I., *Venezuela* . 121 D7
Blanquillo, *Uruguay* 127 C4
Blansko, *Czech Rep.* 27 B9
Blantyre, *Malawi* 87 F4
Blarney, *Ireland* 15 E3
Blasdell, *U.S.A.* 110 D6
Błaszki, *Poland* 45 G5
Blato, *Croatia* 29 F13
Blatná, *Czech Rep.* 26 B6
Blatnica, *Bos.-H.* 42 F2
Błażowa, *Poland* 45 J9
Bleckede, *Germany* 24 B6
Bled, *Slovenia* 29 B11
Bleiburg, *Austria* 26 E7
Blejeşti, *Romania* 43 F10
Blekinge, *Sweden* 9 H16
Blekinge län □, *Sweden* 11 H9
Blenheim, *Canada* 110 D3
Blenheim, *N.Z.* 91 J4
Bléone →, *France* 21 D10
Blérancourt, *France* 19 C10
Bletchley, *U.K.* 13 F7
Blida, *Algeria* 78 A6
Blidö, *Sweden* 10 E12
Blidsberg, *Sweden* 11 G7
Blieskastel, *Germany* 25 F3
Bligh Sound, *N.Z.* 91 L1
Blind River, *Canada* 102 C3
Blinisht, *Albania* 40 E3
Bliss, *Idaho, U.S.A.* 114 E6
Bliss, *N.Y., U.S.A.* 110 D6
Blissfield, *U.S.A.* 110 F3
Blitar, *Indonesia* 63 H15
Blitta, *Togo* 83 D5
Block I., *U.S.A.* 111 E13
Block Island Sd., *U.S.A.* .. 111 E13
Blodgett Iceberg Tongue,
  Antarctica 5 C9
Bloemfontein, *S. Africa* ... 88 D4
Bloemhof, *S. Africa* 88 D4
Blois, *France* 18 E8
Blomskog, *Sweden* 10 E6
Blomstermåla, *Sweden* 11 H10
Blönduós, *Iceland* 8 D3
Błonie, *Poland* 45 F7
Bloodvein →, *Canada* 105 C9
Bloody Foreland, *Ireland* .. 15 A3
Bloomer, *U.S.A.* 112 C9
Bloomfield, *Canada* 110 C7
Bloomfield, *Iowa, U.S.A.* .. 112 E8
Bloomfield, *N. Mex., U.S.A.* 115 H10
Bloomfield, *Nebr., U.S.A.* . 112 D6
Bloomington, *Ill., U.S.A.* . 112 E10
Bloomington, *Ind., U.S.A.* . 108 F2
Bloomington, *Minn., U.S.A.* 112 C8
Bloomsburg, *U.S.A.* 111 F8
Blora, *Indonesia* 63 G14
Blossburg, *U.S.A.* 110 E7
Blouberg, *S. Africa* 89 C4
Blountstown, *U.S.A.* 109 K3
Bludenz, *Austria* 26 D2
Blue Earth, *U.S.A.* 112 D8
Blue Mesa Reservoir, *U.S.A.* 115 G10
Blue Mountain Lake, *U.S.A.* 111 C10
Blue Mts., *Maine, U.S.A.* .. 111 B14
Blue Mts., *Oreg., U.S.A.* .. 114 D4
Blue Mts., *Pa., U.S.A.* 111 F8
Blue Mud B., *Australia* 94 A2
Blue Nile = Nîl el
  Azraq →, *Sudan* 81 D3
Blue Rapids, *U.S.A.* 112 F6
Blue Ridge Mts., *U.S.A.* ... 109 G5
Blue River, *Canada* 104 C5
Bluefield, *U.S.A.* 108 G5
Bluefields, *Nic.* 120 D3
Bluff, *Australia* 94 C4
Bluff, *N.Z.* 91 M2
Bluff, *U.S.A.* 115 H9
Bluff Knoll, *Australia* 93 F2
Bluff Pt., *Australia* 93 E1
Bluffton, *U.S.A.* 108 E3
Blumenau, *Brazil* 127 B6
Blunt, *U.S.A.* 112 C5
Bly, *U.S.A.* 114 E3
Blyth, *Canada* 110 C3
Blyth, *U.K.* 12 B6
Blythe, *U.S.A.* 117 M12
Blytheville, *U.S.A.* 113 H10
Bo, *S. Leone* 82 D2
Bo Duc, *Vietnam* 65 G6
Bo Hai, *China* 57 E10
Bo Xian = Bozhou, *China* ... 56 H8
Boa Vista, *Brazil* 124 C6
Boac, *Phil.* 61 E4
Boaco, *Nic.* 120 D2

Bo'ai, *China* 56 G7
Boal, *Spain* 34 B4
Boalsburg, *U.S.A.* 110 F7
Boane, *Mozam.* 89 D5
Boardman, *U.S.A.* 110 E4
Bobadah, *Australia* 95 E4
Bobai, *China* 58 F7
Bóbbio, *Italy* 28 D6
Bobcaygeon, *Canada* 102 D4
Böblingen, *Germany* 25 G5
Bobo-Dioulasso,
  Burkina Faso 82 C4
Bobolice, *Poland* 44 E3
Boboshevo, *Bulgaria* 40 D7
Bobov Dol, *Bulgaria* 40 D6
Bóbr →, *Poland* 45 F2
Bobraomby, Tanjon' i,
  Madag. 89 A8
Bobrinets, *Ukraine* 47 H7
Bobrov, *Russia* 48 E5
Bobrovitsa, *Ukraine* 47 G6
Bobruysk = Babruysk,
  Belarus 47 F5
Boby, Pic, *Madag.* 85 J9
Bôca do Acre, *Brazil* 124 E5
Boca Raton, *U.S.A.* 109 M5
Bocanda, *Ivory C.* 82 D4
Bocas del Toro, *Panama* ... 120 E3
Boceguillas, *Spain* 34 D7
Bochnia, *Poland* 45 J7
Bocholt, *Germany* 24 D2
Bochum, *Germany* 24 D3
Bockenem, *Germany* 24 C6
Bočki, *Poland* 45 F10
Bocognano, *France* 21 F13
Bocoyna, *Mexico* 118 B3
Bocşa, *Romania* 42 E6
Böda, *Kalmar, Sweden* 11 G11
Boda, *Kopparberg, Sweden* . 10 C9
Boda, *Västernorrland,*
  Sweden 10 B10
Bodafors, *Sweden* 11 G8
Bodaybo, *Russia* 51 D12
Boddam, *U.K.* 14 B7
Boddington, *Australia* 93 F2
Bode Sadu, *Nigeria* 83 D5
Bodega Bay, *U.S.A.* 116 G3
Boden, *Sweden* 8 D19
Bodensee, *Europe* 25 H5
Bodenteich, *Germany* 24 C6
Bodhan, *India* 66 K10
Bodinga, *Nigeria* 83 C6
Bodmin, *U.K.* 13 G3
Bodmin Moor, *U.K.* 13 G3
Bodø, *Norway* 8 C16
Bodrog →, *Hungary* 42 D6
Bodrum, *Turkey* 39 D9
Bódva →, *Hungary* 42 C5
Boën, *France* 21 C8
Boende,
  Dem. Rep. of the Congo . 84 E4
Boerne, *U.S.A.* 113 L5
Boesmans →, *S. Africa* 88 E4
Boffa, *Guinea* 82 C2
Bogalusa, *U.S.A.* 113 K10
Bogan →, *Australia* 95 D4
Bogan Gate, *Australia* 83 C4
Bogandé, *Burkina Faso* 95 E4
Bogantungan, *Australia* 94 C4
Bogata, *U.S.A.* 113 J7
Bogatić, *Serbia, Yug.* 40 B3
Boğazkale, *Turkey* 72 B6
Boğazlıyan, *Turkey* 72 C6
Bogen, *Sweden* 10 D6
Bogense, *Denmark* 11 J4
Boggabilla, *Australia* 95 D5
Boggabri, *Australia* 95 E5
Boggeragh Mts., *Ireland* ... 15 D3
Boglan = Solhan, *Turkey* ... 70 B4
Bognor Regis, *U.K.* 13 G7
Bogo, *Phil.* 61 F6
Bogodukhov = Bohodukhiv,
  Ukraine 47 G8
Bogol Manya, *Ethiopia* 81 G5
Bogong, Mt., *Australia* 95 F4
Bogor, *Indonesia* 63 G12
Bogoroditsk, *Russia* 46 F10
Bogorodsk, *Russia* 48 B6
Bogoso, *Ghana* 82 D4
Bogotá, *Colombia* 124 C4
Bogotol, *Russia* 50 D9
Bogou, *Togo* 83 C5
Bogra, *Bangla.* 69 G16
Boguchany, *Russia* 51 D10
Boguchar, *Russia* 48 F5
Bogué, *Mauritania* 82 B2
Boguslav, *Ukraine* 47 H6
Boguszów-Gorce, *Poland* 45 H3
Bohain-en-Vermandois,
  France 19 C10
Bohemian Forest =
  Böhmerwald, *Germany* 25 F9
Bohinjska Bistrica, *Slovenia* 29 B11
Böhmerwald, *Germany* 25 F9
Bohmte, *Germany* 24 C4
Bohodukhiv, *Ukraine* 47 G8
Bohol □, *Phil.* 61 G6
Bohol Sea, *Phil.* 63 C6
Bohongou, *Burkina Faso* 83 C5
Böhönye, *Hungary* 42 D2
Boi, *Nigeria* 83 D6
Boi, Pta. de, *Brazil* 127 A6
Boiaçu, *Brazil* 124 D6
Boileau, C., *Australia* 92 C3
Boing'o, *Sudan* 81 F3
Boiro, *Spain* 34 C2
Boise, *U.S.A.* 114 E5
Boise City, *U.S.A.* 113 G3

Brakel

Boissevain, *Canada* 105 D8
Bóite →, *Italy* 29 B9
Boitzenburg, *Germany* 24 B9
Boizenburg, *Germany* 24 B6
Bojador C., *W. Sahara* 78 C3
Bojana →, *Albania* 40 E3
Bojano, *Italy* 31 A7
Bojanowo, *Poland* 45 G3
Bøjden, *Denmark* 11 J4
Bojnūrd, *Iran* 71 B8
Bojonegoro, *Indonesia* 63 G14
Boju, *Nigeria* 83 D6
Boka, *Serbia, Yug.* 42 E5
Boka Kotorska, *Montenegro, Yug.* 40 D2
Bokala, *Ivory C.* 82 D4
Bokani, *Nigeria* 83 D6
Bokaro, *India* 69 H11
Boké, *Guinea* 82 C2
Bokhara →, *Australia* 95 D4
Bokkos, *Nigeria* 83 D6
Boknafjorden, *Norway* 9 G11
Bokoro, *Chad* 79 F9
Bokpyin, *Burma* 65 G2
Boksitogorsk, *Russia* 46 C7
Bol, *Croatia* 29 E13
Bolama, *Guinea-Biss.* 82 C1
Bolan →, *Pakistan* 68 E2
Bolan Pass, *Pakistan* 66 E5
Bolaños →, *Mexico* 118 C4
Bolaños de Calatrava, *Spain* 35 G7
Bolayır, *Turkey* 41 F10
Bolbec, *France* 18 C7
Boldājī, *Iran* 71 D6
Boldeşti-Scăeni, *Romania* 43 E11
Bole, *China* 60 B3
Bole, *Ethiopia* 81 F4
Bole, *Ghana* 82 D4
Bolekhiv, *Ukraine* 47 H2
Bolesławiec, *Poland* 45 G2
Bolgatanga, *Ghana* 83 C4
Bolgrad = Bolhrad, *Ukraine* 47 K5
Bolhrad, *Ukraine* 47 K5
Bolinao, *Phil.* 61 C3
Bolintin-Vale, *Romania* 43 F10
Bolívar, *Argentina* 126 D3
Bolivar, *Mo., U.S.A.* 113 G8
Bolivar, *N.Y., U.S.A.* 110 D6
Bolivar, *Tenn., U.S.A.* 113 H10
Bolivia ■, *S. Amer.* 124 G6
Bolivian Plateau, *S. Amer.* 122 E4
Boljevac, *Serbia, Yug.* 40 C5
Bolkhov, *Russia* 46 F9
Bolków, *Poland* 45 H3
Bollebygd, *Sweden* 11 G6
Bollène, *France* 21 D8
Bollnäs, *Sweden* 10 C10
Bollon, *Australia* 95 D4
Bollstabruk, *Sweden* 10 B11
Bolmen, *Sweden* 11 H7
Bolobo, *Dem. Rep. of the Congo* 84 E3
Bologna, *Italy* 29 D8
Bologoye, *Russia* 46 D8
Bolonchenticul, *Mexico* 119 D7
Bolótana, *Italy* 30 B1
Boloven, Cao Nguyen, *Laos* 64 E6
Bolpur, *India* 69 H12
Bolsena, *Italy* 29 F8
Bolsena, L. di, *Italy* 29 F8
Bolshaya Chernigovka, *Russia* 48 D10
Bolshaya Glushitsa, *Russia* 48 D10
Bolshaya Martynovka, *Russia* 49 G5
Bolshaya Vradiyevka, *Ukraine* 47 J6
Bolshevik, Ostrov, *Russia* 51 B11
Bolshoi Kavkas = Caucasus Mountains, *Eurasia* 49 J7
Bolshoy Anyuy →, *Russia* 51 C17
Bolshoy Begichev, Ostrov, *Russia* 51 B12
Bolshoy Lyakhovskiy, Ostrov, *Russia* 51 B15
Bolshoy Tokmak = Tokmak, *Ukraine* 47 J8
Bolshoy Tyuters, Ostrov, *Russia* 9 G22
Bolsward, *Neths.* 17 A5
Bolt Head, *U.K.* 13 G4
Boltaña, *Spain* 32 C5
Boltigen, *Switz.* 25 J3
Bolton, *Canada* 110 C5
Bolton, *U.K.* 12 D5
Bolton Landing, *U.S.A.* 111 C11
Bolu, *Turkey* 72 B4
Bolungavík, *Iceland* 8 C2
Boluo, *China* 59 F10
Bolvadin, *Turkey* 70 B1
Bolzano, *Italy* 29 B8
Bom Jesus da Lapa, *Brazil* 125 F10
Boma, *Dem. Rep. of the Congo* 84 F2
Bombala, *Australia* 95 F4
Bombarral, *Portugal* 35 F1
Bombay = Mumbai, *India* 66 K8
Bomboma, *Dem. Rep. of the Congo* 84 D3
Bombombwa, *Dem. Rep. of the Congo* 86 B2
Bomi Hills, *Liberia* 82 D2
Bomili, *Dem. Rep. of the Congo* 86 B2
Bømlo, *Norway* 9 G11
Bomokandi →, *Dem. Rep. of the Congo* 86 B2
Bomu →, *C.A.R.* 84 D4
Bon, C., *Tunisia* 76 C5
Bon Sar Pa, *Vietnam* 64 F6
Bonaigarh, *India* 69 J11
Bonaire, *Neth. Ant.* 121 D6
Bonang, *Australia* 95 F4
Bonanza, *Nic.* 120 D3
Bonaparte Arch., *Australia* 92 B3
Boñar, *Spain* 34 C5
Bonaventure, *Canada* 103 C6
Bonavista, *Canada* 103 C9
Bonavista, C., *Canada* 103 C9
Bonavista B., *Canada* 103 C9
Bondeno, *Italy* 29 D8
Bondo, *Dem. Rep. of the Congo* 86 B1
Bondoukou, *Ivory C.* 82 D4
Bondowoso, *Indonesia* 63 G15
Bone, Teluk, *Indonesia* 63 E6
Bonerate, *Indonesia* 63 F6
Bonerate, Kepulauan, *Indonesia* 63 F6
Bo'ness, *U.K.* 14 E5
Bonete, Cerro, *Argentina* 126 B2
Bong Son = Hoai Nhon, *Vietnam* 64 E7
Bonga, *Ethiopia* 81 F4
Bongabong, *Phil.* 61 E4
Bongor, *Chad* 79 F9
Bongouanou, *Ivory C.* 82 D4
Bonham, *U.S.A.* 113 J6
Boni, *Mali* 82 B4
Bonifacio, *France* 21 G13
Bonifacio, Bouches de, *Medit. S.* 30 A2
Bonin Is. = Ogasawara Gunto, *Pac. Oc.* 52 G18
Bonke, *Ethiopia* 81 F4
Bonkoukou, *Niger* 83 C5
Bonn, *Germany* 24 E3
Bonnat, *France* 19 F8
Bonne Terre, *U.S.A.* 113 G9
Bonners Ferry, *U.S.A.* 114 B5
Bonnétable, *France* 18 D7
Bonneval, *Eure-et-Loir, France* 18 D8
Bonneval, *Savoie, France* 21 C11
Bonneville, *France* 19 F13
Bonney, L., *Australia* 95 F3
Bonnie Rock, *Australia* 93 F2
Bonny, *Nigeria* 83 E6
Bonny →, *Nigeria* 83 E6
Bonny, Bight of, *Africa* 83 E6
Bonny-sur-Loire, *France* 19 E9
Bonnyrigg, *U.K.* 14 F5
Bonnyville, *Canada* 105 C6
Bono, *Italy* 30 B2
Bonoi, *Indonesia* 63 E9
Bonorva, *Italy* 30 B1
Bonsall, *U.S.A.* 117 M9
Bontang, *Indonesia* 62 D5
Bonthe, *S. Leone* 82 D2
Bontoc, *Phil.* 61 C4
Bonyeri, *Ghana* 82 D4
Bonyhád, *Hungary* 42 D3
Bonython Ra., *Australia* 92 D4
Bookabie, *Australia* 93 F5
Booker, *U.S.A.* 113 G4
Boola, *Guinea* 82 D3
Booligal, *Australia* 95 E3
Boonah, *Australia* 95 D5
Boone, *Iowa, U.S.A.* 112 D8
Boone, *N.C., U.S.A.* 109 G5
Booneville, *Ark., U.S.A.* 113 H8
Booneville, *Miss., U.S.A.* 109 H1
Boonville, *Calif., U.S.A.* 116 F3
Boonville, *Ind., U.S.A.* 108 F2
Boonville, *Mo., U.S.A.* 112 F8
Boonville, *N.Y., U.S.A.* 111 C9
Boorindal, *Australia* 95 E4
Boorowa, *Australia* 95 E4
Boothia, Gulf of, *Canada* 101 A11
Boothia Pen., *Canada* 100 A10
Bootle, *U.K.* 12 D4
Booué, *Gabon* 84 E2
Boppard, *Germany* 25 E3
Boquete, *Panama* 120 E3
Boquilla, Presa de la, *Mexico* 118 B3
Boquillas del Carmen, *Mexico* 118 B4
Bor, *Czech Rep.* 26 B5
Bor, *Russia* 48 B7
Bor, *Serbia, Yug.* 40 B6
Bôr, *Sudan* 81 F3
Bor, *Sweden* 11 G8
Bor, *Turkey* 72 D6
Bor Mashash, *Israel* 75 D3
Borah Peak, *U.S.A.* 114 D7
Borang, *Sudan* 81 G3
Borås, *Sweden* 11 G6
Borāzjān, *Iran* 71 D6
Borba, *Brazil* 124 D7
Borba, *Portugal* 35 G3
Borborema, Planalto da, *Brazil* 122 D7
Borcea, *Romania* 43 F12
Borçka, *Turkey* 73 B9
Bord Khūn-e Now, *Iran* 71 D6
Borda, C., *Australia* 95 F2
Bordeaux, *France* 20 D3
Borden, *Australia* 93 F2
Borden, *Canada* 103 C7
Borden I., *Canada* 4 B2
Borden Pen., *Canada* 101 A11
Borders = Scottish Borders □, *U.K.* 14 F6
Bordertown, *Australia* 95 F3
Borðeyri, *Iceland* 8 D3
Bordighera, *Italy* 28 E4
Bordj Fly Ste. Marie, *Algeria* 78 C5
Bordj-in-Eker, *Algeria* 78 D7
Bordj Omar Driss, *Algeria* 78 C7
Bore, *Ethiopia* 81 G4
Borehamwood, *U.K.* 13 F7
Borek Wielkopolski, *Poland* 45 G4
Borensberg, *Sweden* 11 F9
Borgå = Porvoo, *Finland* 9 F21
Borgarfjörður, *Iceland* 8 D7
Borgarnes, *Iceland* 8 D3
Børgefjellet, *Norway* 8 D15
Borger, *Neths.* 17 B6
Borger, *U.S.A.* 113 H4
Borgholm, *Sweden* 11 H10
Bórgia, *Italy* 31 D9
Borgo San Dalmazzo, *Italy* 28 D4
Borgo San Lorenzo, *Italy* 29 E8
Borgo Val di Taro, *Italy* 28 D6
Borgo Valsugana, *Italy* 29 B8
Borgomanero, *Italy* 28 C5
Borgorose, *Italy* 29 F10
Borgosésia, *Italy* 28 C5
Borhoyn Tal, *Mongolia* 56 C6
Bori, *Nigeria* 83 E6
Borikhane, *Laos* 64 C4
Borisoglebsk, *Russia* 48 E6
Borisov = Barysaw, *Belarus* 46 E5
Borisovka, *Russia* 47 G9
Borja, *Peru* 124 D3
Borja, *Spain* 32 D3
Borjas Blancas = Les Borges Blanques, *Spain* 32 D5
Borjomi, *Georgia* 49 K6
Borken, *Germany* 24 D2
Børkop, *Denmark* 11 J3
Borkou, *Chad* 79 E9
Borkum, *Germany* 24 B2
Borlänge, *Sweden* 10 D9
Borley, C., *Antarctica* 5 C5
Borlu, *Turkey* 39 C10
Bormida →, *Italy* 28 D5
Bórmio, *Italy* 28 B7
Borna, *Germany* 24 D8
Borne Sulinowo, *Poland* 44 E3
Borneo, *E. Indies* 62 D5
Bornholm, *Denmark* 11 J8
Bornholms Amtskommune □, *Denmark* 11 J8
Bornholmsgattet, *Europe* 11 J8
Borno □, *Nigeria* 83 C7
Bornos, *Spain* 35 J5
Bornova, *Turkey* 39 C9
Bornu Yassa, *Nigeria* 83 C7
Boro →, *Sudan* 81 F2
Borodino, *Russia* 46 E8
Borogontsy, *Russia* 51 C14
Boromo, *Burkina Faso* 82 C4
Boron, *U.S.A.* 117 L9
Borongan, *Phil.* 61 F6
Borotangba Mts., *C.A.R.* 81 F2
Borotou, *Ivory C.* 82 D3
Borovan, *Bulgaria* 40 C7
Borovichi, *Russia* 46 C7
Borovsk, *Russia* 46 E9
Borrby, *Sweden* 11 J8
Borrego Springs, *U.S.A.* 117 M10
Borriol, *Spain* 32 E4
Borroloola, *Australia* 94 B2
Borşa, *Cluj, Romania* 43 D8
Borşa, *Maramureş, Romania* 43 C9
Borsad, *India* 68 H5
Borsec, *Romania* 43 D10
Borsod-Abaúj-Zemplén □, *Hungary* 42 B6
Bort-les-Orgues, *France* 20 C6
Borth, *U.K.* 13 E3
Börtnan, *Sweden* 10 B7
Borūjerd, *Iran* 71 C6
Boryslav, *Ukraine* 47 H2
Boryspil, *Ukraine* 47 G6
Borzhomi = Borjomi, *Georgia* 49 K6
Borzna, *Ukraine* 47 G7
Borzya, *Russia* 51 D12
Bosa, *Italy* 30 B1
Bosanska Dubica, *Bos.-H.* 29 C13
Bosanska Gradiška, *Bos.-H.* 42 E2
Bosanska Kostajnica, *Bos.-H.* 29 C13
Bosanska Krupa, *Bos.-H.* 29 D13
Bosanski Brod, *Bos.-H.* 42 E2
Bosanski Novi, *Bos.-H.* 29 C13
Bosanski Petrovac, *Bos.-H.* 29 D13
Bosanski Šamac, *Bos.-H.* 42 E3
Bosansko Grahovo, *Bos.-H.* 29 D13
Bosaso, *Somali Rep.* 74 E4
Boscastle, *U.K.* 13 G3
Bose, *China* 58 F6
Boshan, *China* 57 F9
Boshof, *S. Africa* 88 D4
Boshrūyeh, *Iran* 71 C8
Bosilegrad, *Serbia, Yug.* 40 D6
Boskovice, *Czech Rep.* 27 B9
Bosna →, *Bos.-H.* 42 E3
Bosna i Hercegovina = Bosnia-Herzegovina ■, *Europe* 42 G2
Bosnia-Herzegovina ■, *Europe* 42 G2
Bosnik, *Indonesia* 63 E9
Bosobolo, *Dem. Rep. of the Congo* 84 D3
Bosporus = İstanbul Boğazı, *Turkey* 41 E13
Bosque Farms, *U.S.A.* 115 J10
Bossangoa, *C.A.R.* 84 C3
Bossé Bangou, *Niger* 83 C5
Bossier City, *U.S.A.* 113 J8
Bosso, *Niger* 83 C7
Bosso, Dallol →, *Niger* 83 C5
Bostan, *Pakistan* 68 D2
Bostānābād, *Iran* 70 B5
Bosten Hu, *China* 60 B3
Boston, *U.K.* 12 E7
Boston, *U.S.A.* 111 D13
Boston Bar, *Canada* 104 D4
Boston Mts., *U.S.A.* 113 H8
Bosut →, *Croatia* 42 E3
Boswell, *Canada* 104 D5
Boswell, *U.S.A.* 110 F5
Botad, *India* 68 H4
Botan →, *Turkey* 73 D10
Botene, *Laos* 64 D3
Botev, *Bulgaria* 41 D8
Botevgrad, *Bulgaria* 40 D7
Bothaville, *S. Africa* 88 D4
Bothnia, G. of, *Europe* 8 E19
Bothwell, *Australia* 94 G4
Bothwell, *Canada* 110 D3
Boticas, *Portugal* 34 D3
Botletle →, *Botswana* 88 C3
Botlikh, *Russia* 49 J8
Botna →, *Moldova* 43 D14
Botoroaga, *Romania* 43 F10
Botoşani, *Romania* 43 C11
Botoşani □, *Romania* 43 C11
Botou, *Burkina Faso* 83 C5
Botricello, *Italy* 31 D9
Botro, *Ivory C.* 82 D3
Botswana ■, *Africa* 88 C3
Bottineau, *U.S.A.* 112 A4
Bottnaryd, *Sweden* 11 G7
Bottrop, *Germany* 17 C6
Botucatu, *Brazil* 127 A6
Botwood, *Canada* 103 C8
Bou Djébéha, *Mali* 82 B4
Bou Rjeïmât, *Mauritania* 82 B1
Bouaflé, *Ivory C.* 82 D3
Bouaké, *Ivory C.* 82 D3
Bouar, *C.A.R.* 84 C3
Bouârfa, *Morocco* 78 B5
Boucaut B., *Australia* 94 A1
Bouches-du-Rhône □, *France* 21 E9
Bougainville, C., *Australia* 92 B4
Bougainville I., *Papua N. G.* 96 H7
Bougainville Reef, *Australia* 94 B4
Bougie = Bejaia, *Algeria* 78 A7
Bougouni, *Mali* 82 C3
Bouillon, *Belgium* 17 E5
Boukombé, *Benin* 83 C5
Boulal, *Mali* 82 B3
Boulazac, *France* 20 C4
Boulder, *Colo., U.S.A.* 112 E2
Boulder, *Mont., U.S.A.* 114 C7
Boulder City, *U.S.A.* 117 K12
Boulder Creek, *U.S.A.* 116 H4
Boulder Dam = Hoover Dam, *U.S.A.* 117 K12
Bouli, *Mauritania* 82 B2
Boulia, *Australia* 94 C2
Bouligny, *France* 19 C12
Boulogne →, *France* 18 E5
Boulogne-sur-Gesse, *France* 20 E4
Boulogne-sur-Mer, *France* 19 B8
Bouloire, *France* 18 E7
Boulouli, *Mali* 82 B3
Boulsa, *Burkina Faso* 83 C4
Boultoum, *Niger* 83 C7
Boûmdeïd, *Mauritania* 82 B2
Boun Neua, *Laos* 64 B3
Boun Tai, *Laos* 64 B3
Bouna, *Ivory C.* 82 D4
Boundary Peak, *U.S.A.* 116 H8
Boundiali, *Ivory C.* 82 D3
Bountiful, *U.S.A.* 114 F8
Bounty Is., *Pac. Oc.* 96 M9
Boura, *Mali* 82 C4
Bourbon-Lancy, *France* 19 F10
Bourbon-l'Archambault, *France* 19 F10
Bourbonnais, *France* 19 F10
Bourbonne-les-Bains, *France* 19 E12
Bourbourg, *France* 19 B9
Bourdel L., *Canada* 102 A5
Bourem, *Mali* 83 B4
Bourg, *France* 20 C3
Bourg-Argental, *France* 21 C8
Bourg-de-Péage, *France* 21 C9
Bourg-en-Bresse, *France* 19 F12
Bourg-Lastic, *France* 20 C6
Bourg-Madame, *France* 20 F5
Bourg-St-Andéol, *France* 21 D8
Bourg-St-Maurice, *France* 21 C10
Bourganeuf, *France* 20 C5
Bourges, *France* 19 E9
Bourget, *Canada* 111 A9
Bourget, Lac du, *France* 21 C9
Bourgneuf, B. de, *France* 18 E4
Bourgneuf-en-Retz, *France* 18 E5
Bourgogne, *France* 19 F11
Bourgoin-Jallieu, *France* 21 C9
Bourgueil, *France* 18 E7
Bourke, *Australia* 95 E4
Bourne, *U.K.* 12 E7
Bournemouth, *U.K.* 13 G6
Bournemouth □, *U.K.* 13 G6
Bouroum, *Burkina Faso* 83 C4
Bouse, *U.S.A.* 117 M13
Boussac, *France* 19 F9
Boussé, *Burkina Faso* 83 C4
Boussouma, *Burkina Faso* 83 C4
Boutilimit, *Mauritania* 82 B2
Boutonne →, *France* 20 C3
Bouvet I. = Bouvetøya, *Antarctica* 3 G10
Bouvetøya, *Antarctica* 3 G10
Bouxwiller, *France* 19 D14
Bouza, *Niger* 83 C6
Bouzonville, *France* 19 C13
Bova Marina, *Italy* 31 E8
Bovalino Marina, *Italy* 31 D9
Bovec, *Slovenia* 29 B10
Bovill, *U.S.A.* 114 C5
Bovino, *Italy* 31 A8
Bovril, *Argentina* 126 C4
Bow →, *Canada* 104 C6
Bow Island, *Canada* 104 D6
Bowbells, *U.S.A.* 112 A3
Bowdle, *U.S.A.* 112 C5
Bowelling, *Australia* 93 F2
Bowen, *Argentina* 126 D2
Bowen, *Australia* 94 C4
Bowen Mts., *Australia* 95 F4
Bowie, *Ariz., U.S.A.* 115 K9
Bowie, *Tex., U.S.A.* 113 J6
Bowkān, *Iran* 70 B5
Bowland, Forest of, *U.K.* 12 D5
Bowling Green, *Ky., U.S.A.* 108 G2
Bowling Green, *Ohio, U.S.A.* 108 E4
Bowling Green, C., *Australia* 94 B4
Bowman, *U.S.A.* 112 B3
Bowman I., *Antarctica* 5 C8
Bowmanville, *Canada* 110 C6
Bowmore, *U.K.* 14 F2
Bowral, *Australia* 95 E5
Bowraville, *Australia* 95 E5
Bowron →, *Canada* 104 C4
Bowron Lake Prov. Park, *Canada* 104 C4
Bowser L., *Canada* 104 B3
Bowsman, *Canada* 105 C8
Bowwood, *Zambia* 87 F2
Box Cr. →, *Australia* 95 E3
Boxholm, *Sweden* 11 F9
Boxmeer, *Neths.* 17 C5
Boxtel, *Neths.* 17 C5
Boyabat, *Turkey* 72 B6
Boyalıca, *Turkey* 41 F13
Boyang, *China* 59 C11
Boyce, *U.S.A.* 113 K8
Boyd L., *Canada* 102 B4
Boyle, *Canada* 104 C6
Boyle, *Ireland* 15 C3
Boyne →, *Ireland* 15 C5
Boyne City, *U.S.A.* 108 C3
Boynitsa, *Bulgaria* 40 C6
Boynton Beach, *U.S.A.* 109 M5
Boyolali, *Indonesia* 63 G14
Boyoma, Chutes, *Dem. Rep. of the Congo* 86 B2
Boysen Reservoir, *U.S.A.* 114 E9
Boyuibe, *Bolivia* 124 G6
Boyup Brook, *Australia* 93 F2
Boz Burun, *Turkey* 41 F12
Boz Dağ, *Turkey* 39 D11
Boz Dağları, *Turkey* 39 C10
Bozburun, *Turkey* 39 E10
Bozcaada, *Turkey* 72 C2
Bozdoğan, *Turkey* 39 D10
Bozeman, *U.S.A.* 114 D8
Bozen = Bolzano, *Italy* 29 B8
Boževac, *Serbia, Yug.* 40 B5
Bozhou, *China* 56 H8
Bozkır, *Turkey* 72 D5
Bozkurt, *Turkey* 39 D11
Bozouls, *France* 20 D6
Bozoum, *C.A.R.* 84 C3
Bozova, *Antalya, Turkey* 39 D12
Bozova, *Sanliurfa, Turkey* 73 D8
Bozovici, *Romania* 42 F7
Bozüyük, *Turkey* 39 B12
Bra, *Italy* 28 D4
Braås, *Sweden* 11 G9
Brabant □, *Belgium* 17 D4
Brabant L., *Canada* 105 B8
Brabrand, *Denmark* 11 H4
Brač, *Croatia* 29 E13
Bracadale, L., *U.K.* 14 D2
Bracciano, *Italy* 29 F9
Bracciano, L. di, *Italy* 29 F9
Bracebridge, *Canada* 102 C4
Brach, *Libya* 79 C8
Bracieux, *France* 18 E8
Bräcke, *Sweden* 10 B9
Brackettville, *U.S.A.* 113 L4
Bracki Kanal, *Croatia* 29 E13
Bracknell, *U.K.* 13 F7
Bracknell Forest □, *U.K.* 13 F7
Brad, *Romania* 42 D7
Brádano →, *Italy* 31 B9
Bradenton, *U.S.A.* 109 M4
Bradford, *Canada* 110 B5
Bradford, *U.K.* 12 D6
Bradford, *Pa., U.S.A.* 110 E6
Bradford, *Vt., U.S.A.* 111 C12
Bradley, *Ark., U.S.A.* 113 J8
Bradley, *Calif., U.S.A.* 116 K6
Bradley Institute, *Zimbabwe* 87 F3
Brady, *U.S.A.* 113 K5
Brædstrup, *Denmark* 11 J3
Braemar, *U.K.* 14 D5
Braeside, *Canada* 111 A8
Braga, *Portugal* 34 D2
Braga □, *Portugal* 34 D2
Bragadiru, *Romania* 43 G10
Bragado, *Argentina* 126 D3
Bragança, *Brazil* 125 D9
Bragança, *Portugal* 34 D4
Bragança □, *Portugal* 34 D4
Bragança Paulista, *Brazil* 127 A6
Brahmanbaria, *Bangla.* 67 H17
Brahmani →, *India* 67 J15
Brahmapur, *India* 67 K14
Brahmaputra →, *India* 69 H13
Braich-y-pwll, *U.K.* 12 E3
Braidwood, *Australia* 95 F4
Brăila, *Romania* 43 E12
Brăila □, *Romania* 43 E12
Brainerd, *U.S.A.* 112 B7
Braintree, *U.K.* 13 F8
Braintree, *U.S.A.* 111 D14
Brak →, *S. Africa* 88 D3
Brake, *Germany* 24 B4
Brakel, *Germany* 24 D5

Bräkne-Hoby, *Sweden* 11 H9
Brakwater, *Namibia* 88 C2
Brålanda, *Sweden* 11 F6
Bramberg, *Germany* 25 E6
Bramdrupdam, *Denmark* .. 11 J3
Bramming, *Denmark* 11 J2
Brämön, *Sweden* 10 B11
Brampton, *Canada* 102 D4
Brampton, *U.K.* 12 C5
Bramsche, *Germany* 24 C3
Branco →, *Brazil* 122 D4
Brandberg, *Namibia* 88 B2
Brande, *Denmark* 11 J3
Brandenburg = Neubrandenburg, *Germany* 24 B9
Brandenburg, *Germany* 24 C8
Brandenburg □, *Germany* .. 24 C9
Brandfort, *S. Africa* 88 D4
Brando, *France* 21 F13
Brandon, *Canada* 105 D9
Brandon, *U.S.A.* 111 C11
Brandon B., *Ireland* 15 D1
Brandon Mt., *Ireland* 15 D1
Brandsen, *Argentina* 126 D4
Brandvlei, *S. Africa* 88 E3
Brandýs nad Labem, *Czech Rep.* 26 A7
Brănești, *Romania* 43 F11
Branford, *U.S.A.* 111 E12
Braniewo, *Poland* 44 D6
Bransfield Str., *Antarctica* . 5 C18
Brańsk, *Poland* 45 F9
Branson, *U.S.A.* 113 G8
Brantford, *Canada* 102 D3
Brantôme, *France* 20 C4
Branzi, *Italy* 28 B6
Bras d'Or L., *Canada* 103 C7
Brasher Falls, *U.S.A.* 111 B10
Brasil, Planalto, *Brazil* 122 E6
Brasiléia, *Brazil* 124 F5
Brasília, *Brazil* 125 G9
Brasília Legal, *Brazil* 125 D7
Braslaw, *Belarus* 9 J22
Braslovče, *Slovenia* 29 B12
Brașov, *Romania* 43 E10
Brașov □, *Romania* 43 E10
Brass, *Nigeria* 83 E6
Brass →, *Nigeria* 83 E6
Brassac-les-Mines, *France* . 20 C7
Brasschaat, *Belgium* 17 C4
Brassey, Banjaran, *Malaysia* 62 D5
Brassey Ra., *Australia* 93 E3
Brasstown Bald, *U.S.A.* ... 109 H4
Brastad, *Sweden* 11 F5
Brastavățu, *Romania* 43 G9
Bratan = Morozov, *Bulgaria* 41 D9
Brateș, *Romania* 43 E11
Bratislava, *Slovak Rep.* ... 27 C10
Bratislavský □, *Slovak Rep.* 27 C10
Bratsigovo, *Bulgaria* 41 D8
Bratsk, *Russia* 51 D11
Brattleboro, *U.S.A.* 111 D12
Bratunac, *Bos.-H.* 42 F4
Braunau, *Austria* 26 C6
Braunschweig, *Germany* ... 24 C6
Braunton, *U.K.* 13 F3
Bravicea, *Moldova* 43 C13
Bråviken, *Sweden* 11 F10
Bravo del Norte, Rio = Grande, Rio →, *U.S.A.* . 113 N6
Brawley, *U.S.A.* 117 N11
Bray, *Ireland* 15 C5
Bray, Mt., *Australia* 94 A1
Bray-sur-Seine, *France* 19 D10
Brazeau →, *Canada* 104 C5
Brazil, *U.S.A.* 108 F2
Brazil ■, *S. Amer.* 125 F9
Brazilian Highlands = Brasil, Planalto, *Brazil* ... 122 E6
Brazo Sur →, *S. Amer.* ... 126 B4
Brazos →, *U.S.A.* 113 L7
Brazzaville, *Congo* 84 E3
Brčko, *Bos.-H.* 42 F3
Brda →, *Poland* 45 E5
Brdy, *Czech Rep.* 26 B6
Breaden, L., *Australia* 93 E4
Breaksea Sd., *N.Z.* 91 L1
Bream B., *N.Z.* 91 F5
Bream Hd., *N.Z.* 91 F5
Breas, *Chile* 126 B1
Breaza, *Romania* 43 E10
Brebes, *Indonesia* 63 G13
Brechin, *Canada* 110 B5
Brechin, *U.K.* 14 E6
Brecht, *Belgium* 17 C4
Breckenridge, *Colo., U.S.A.* 114 G10
Breckenridge, *Minn., U.S.A.* 112 B6
Breckenridge, *Tex., U.S.A.* 113 J5
Breckland, *U.K.* 13 E8
Břeclav, *Czech Rep.* 27 C9
Brecon, *U.K.* 13 F4
Brecon Beacons, *U.K.* 13 F4
Breda, *Neths.* 17 C4
Bredaryd, *Sweden* 11 G7
Bredasdorp, *S. Africa* 88 E3
Bredebro, *Denmark* 11 J2
Bredstedt, *Germany* 24 A4
Bree, *Belgium* 17 C5
Bregalnica →, *Macedonia* . 40 E6
Bregenz, *Austria* 26 D2
Bregovo, *Bulgaria* 40 B6
Bréhal, *France* 18 D4
Bréhat, Î. de, *France* 18 D4
Breiðafjörður, *Iceland* 8 D2
Breil-sur-Roya, *France* 21 E11
Breisach, *Germany* 25 G3
Brejo, *Brazil* 125 D10
Bremen, *Germany* 24 B4
Bremen □, *Germany* 24 B4
Bremer Bay, *Australia* 93 F2

Bremer I., *Australia* 94 A2
Bremerhaven, *Germany* ... 24 B4
Bremerton, *U.S.A.* 116 C4
Bremervörde, *Germany* ... 24 B5
Brenes, *Spain* 35 H5
Brenham, *U.S.A.* 113 K6
Brenne, *France* 20 B5
Brennerpass, *Austria* 26 D4
Breno, *Italy* 28 C7
Brent, *U.S.A.* 109 J2
Brenta →, *Italy* 29 C9
Brentwood, *U.K.* 13 F8
Brentwood, *Calif., U.S.A.* . 116 H5
Brentwood, *N.Y., U.S.A.* . 111 F11
Bréscia, *Italy* 28 C7
Breskens, *Neths.* 17 C3
Breslau = Wrocław, *Poland* 45 G4
Bresle →, *France* 18 B8
Bressanone, *Italy* 29 B8
Bressay, *U.K.* 14 A7
Bresse, *France* 19 F12
Bressuire, *France* 18 F6
Brest, *Belarus* 47 F2
Brest, *France* 18 D2
Brest-Litovsk = Brest, *Belarus* 47 F2
Bretagne, *France* 18 D3
Bretçu, *Romania* 43 D11
Bretenoux, *France* 20 D5
Breteuil, *Eure, France* 18 D7
Breteuil, *Oise, France* 19 C9
Breton, *Canada* 104 C6
Breton, Pertuis, *France* ... 20 B2
Breton Sd., *U.S.A.* 113 L10
Brett, C., *N.Z.* 91 F5
Bretten, *Germany* 25 F4
Breuil-Cervínia, *Italy* 28 C4
Brevard, *U.S.A.* 109 H4
Breves, *Brazil* 125 D8
Brewarrina, *Australia* 95 E4
Brewer, *U.S.A.* 109 C11
Brewer, Mt., *U.S.A.* 116 J8
Brewerville, *Liberia* 82 D2
Brewster, *N.Y., U.S.A.* ... 111 E11
Brewster, *Ohio, U.S.A.* ... 110 F3
Brewster, *Wash., U.S.A.* . 114 B4
Brewster, Kap = Kangikajik, *Greenland* 4 B6
Brewton, *U.S.A.* 109 K2
Breyten, *S. Africa* 89 D5
Breza, *Bos.-H.* 42 F3
Brezhnev = Naberezhnyye Chelny, *Russia* 48 C11
Brežice, *Slovenia* 29 C12
Březnice, *Czech Rep.* 26 B6
Breznik, *Bulgaria* 40 D6
Brezno, *Slovak Rep.* 27 C12
Brezoi, *Romania* 43 E9
Brezovica, *Kosovo, Yug.* .. 40 D5
Brezovo, *Bulgaria* 41 D9
Briançon, *France* 21 D10
Briare, *France* 19 E9
Briático, *Italy* 31 D9
Bribie I., *Australia* 95 D5
Bribri, *Costa Rica* 120 E3
Bricquebec, *France* 18 C5
Bridgehampton, *U.S.A.* ... 111 F12
Bridgend, *U.K.* 13 F4
Bridgend □, *U.K.* 13 F4
Bridgeport, *Calif., U.S.A.* . 116 G7
Bridgeport, *Conn., U.S.A.* . 111 E11
Bridgeport, *Nebr., U.S.A.* . 112 E3
Bridger, *U.S.A.* 114 D9
Bridgeton, *U.S.A.* 108 F8
Bridgetown, *Australia* 93 F2
Bridgetown, *Barbados* 121 D8
Bridgetown, *Canada* 103 D6
Bridgewater, *Canada* 103 D7
Bridgewater, *Mass., U.S.A.* 111 E14
Bridgewater, *N.Y., U.S.A.* . 111 D9
Bridgewater, C., *Australia* . 95 F3
Bridgewater-Gagebrook, *Australia* 94 G4
Bridgnorth, *U.K.* 13 E5
Bridgton, *U.S.A.* 111 B14
Bridgwater, *U.K.* 13 F5
Bridgwater B., *U.K.* 13 F4
Bridlington, *U.K.* 12 C7
Bridlington B., *U.K.* 12 C7
Bridport, *Australia* 94 G4
Bridport, *U.K.* 13 G5
Briec, *France* 18 D2
Brienne-le-Château, *France* 19 D11
Brienon-sur-Armançon, *France* 19 E10
Brienz, *Switz.* 25 J4
Brienzersee, *Switz.* 25 J3
Brig, *Switz.* 25 J3
Brigg, *U.K.* 12 D7
Brigham City, *U.S.A.* 114 F7
Bright, *Australia* 95 F4
Brighton, *Australia* 95 F2
Brighton, *Canada* 110 B7
Brighton, *U.K.* 13 G7
Brighton, *Colo., U.S.A.* ... 112 F2
Brighton, *N.Y., U.S.A.* ... 110 C7
Brignogan-Plage, *France* .. 18 D2
Brignoles, *France* 21 E10
Brihuega, *Spain* 32 E2
Brikama, *Gambia* 82 C1
Brilliant, *U.S.A.* 110 F4
Brilon, *Germany* 24 D4
Bríndisi, *Italy* 31 B10
Brinje, *Croatia* 29 D12
Brinkley, *U.S.A.* 113 H9
Brinnon, *U.S.A.* 116 C4
Brion, I., *Canada* 103 C7
Brionne, *France* 18 C7

Brionski, *Croatia* 29 D10
Brioude, *France* 20 C7
Briouze, *France* 18 D6
Brisbane, *Australia* 95 D5
Brisbane →, *Australia* 95 D5
Brisighella, *Italy* 29 D8
Bristol, *U.K.* 13 F5
Bristol, *Conn., U.S.A.* 111 E12
Bristol, *Pa., U.S.A.* 111 F10
Bristol, *R.I., U.S.A.* 111 E13
Bristol, *Tenn., U.S.A.* 109 G4
Bristol, City of □, *U.K.* ... 13 F5
Bristol B., *U.S.A.* 100 C4
Bristol Channel, *U.K.* 13 F3
Bristol I., *Antarctica* 5 B1
Bristol L., *U.S.A.* 115 J5
Bristow, *U.S.A.* 113 H6
Britain = Great Britain, *Europe* 6 E5
British Columbia □, *Canada* 104 C3
British Indian Ocean Terr. = Chagos Arch., *Ind. Oc.* .. 52 K11
British Isles, *Europe* 6 E5
Brits, *S. Africa* 89 D4
Britstown, *S. Africa* 88 E3
Britt, *Canada* 102 C3
Brittany = Bretagne, *France* 18 D3
Britton, *U.S.A.* 112 C6
Brive-la-Gaillarde, *France* . 20 C5
Briviesca, *Spain* 34 C7
Brixen = Bressanone, *Italy* . 29 B8
Brixham, *U.K.* 13 G4
Brnaze, *Croatia* 29 E13
Brno, *Czech Rep.* 27 B9
Broad →, *U.S.A.* 109 J5
Broad Arrow, *Australia* ... 93 F3
Broad B., *U.K.* 14 C2
Broad Haven, *Ireland* 15 B2
Broad Law, *U.K.* 14 F5
Broad Sd., *Australia* 94 C4
Broadalbin, *U.S.A.* 111 C10
Broadback →, *Canada* 102 B4
Broadford, *Australia* 95 F4
Broadhurst Ra., *Australia* . 92 D3
Broads, The, *U.K.* 12 E9
Broadus, *U.S.A.* 112 C2
Broager, *Denmark* 11 K3
Broby, *Sweden* 11 H8
Broceni, *Latvia* 44 B9
Brochet, *Canada* 105 B8
Brochet, L., *Canada* 105 B8
Brocken, *Germany* 24 D6
Brockport, *U.S.A.* 110 C7
Brockton, *U.S.A.* 111 D13
Brockville, *Canada* 102 D4
Brockway, *Mont., U.S.A.* . 112 B2
Brockway, *Pa., U.S.A.* ... 110 E6
Brocton, *U.S.A.* 110 D5
Brod, *Macedonia* 40 E5
Brodarevo, *Serbia, Yug.* .. 40 C3
Brodeur Pen., *Canada* ... 101 A11
Brodhead, Mt., *U.S.A.* ... 110 E7
Brodick, *U.K.* 14 F3
Brodnica, *Poland* 45 E6
Brody, *Ukraine* 47 G3
Brogan, *U.S.A.* 114 D5
Broglie, *France* 18 C7
Brok, *Poland* 45 F8
Broken Arrow, *U.S.A.* 113 G7
Broken Bow, *Nebr., U.S.A.* 112 E5
Broken Bow, *Okla., U.S.A.* 113 H7
Broken Bow Lake, *U.S.A.* . 113 H7
Broken Hill = Kabwe, *Zambia* 87 E2
Broken Hill, *Australia* 95 E3
Brokind, *Sweden* 11 F9
Bromley, *U.K.* 13 F8
Bromölla, *Sweden* 11 H8
Bromsgrove, *U.K.* 13 E5
Brønderslev, *Denmark* ... 11 G3
Brong-Ahafo □, *Ghana* ... 82 D4
Broni, *Italy* 28 C6
Bronkhorstspruit, *S. Africa* 89 D4
Brønnøysund, *Norway* ... 8 D15
Bronte, *Italy* 31 E7
Brook Park, *U.S.A.* 110 E4
Brookhaven, *U.S.A.* 113 K9
Brookings, *Oreg., U.S.A.* . 114 E1
Brookings, *S. Dak., U.S.A.* 112 C6
Brooklin, *Canada* 110 C6
Brooklyn Park, *U.S.A.* ... 112 C8
Brooks, *Canada* 104 C6
Brooks Range, *U.S.A.* 100 B5
Brooksville, *U.S.A.* 109 L4
Brookton, *Australia* 93 F2
Brookville, *U.S.A.* 110 E5
Broom, L., *Australia* 14 D3
Broome, *Australia* 92 C3
Broons, *France* 18 D4
Brora, *U.K.* 14 C5
Brora →, *U.K.* 14 C5
Brørup, *Denmark* 11 J2
Brösarp, *Sweden* 11 J8
Brosna →, *Ireland* 15 C4
Broșteni, *Mehedinți, Romania* 42 F7
Broșteni, *Suceava, Romania* 43 C10
Brothers, *U.S.A.* 114 E3
Brou, *France* 18 D8
Brouage, *France* 20 C2
Brough, *U.K.* 12 C5
Brough Hd., *U.K.* 14 B5
Broughton Island = Qikiqtarjuaq, *Canada* ... 101 B13
Broumov, *Czech Rep.* 27 A9
Brovary, *Ukraine* 47 G6
Brovst, *Denmark* 11 G3
Brown, L., *Australia* 93 F2
Brown, Pt., *Australia* 95 E1
Brown City, *U.S.A.* 110 C2

Brown Willy, *U.K.* 13 G3
Brownfield, *U.S.A.* 113 J3
Browning, *U.S.A.* 114 B7
Brownsville, *Oreg., U.S.A.* . 114 D2
Brownsville, *Pa., U.S.A.* .. 110 F5
Brownsville, *Tenn., U.S.A.* 113 H10
Brownsville, *Tex., U.S.A.* . 113 N6
Brownville, *U.S.A.* 111 C9
Brownwood, *U.S.A.* 113 K5
Browse I., *Australia* 92 B3
Bruas, *Malaysia* 65 K3
Bruay-la-Buissière, *France* . 19 B9
Bruce, Mt., *Australia* 92 D2
Bruce Pen., *Canada* 110 B3
Bruce Rock, *Australia* 93 F2
Bruche →, *France* 19 D14
Bruchsal, *Germany* 25 F4
Bruck an der Leitha, *Austria* 27 C9
Bruck an der Mur, *Austria* . 26 D8
Brue →, *U.K.* 13 F5
Bruges = Brugge, *Belgium* . 17 C3
Brugg, *Switz.* 25 H4
Brugge, *Belgium* 17 C3
Bruin, *U.S.A.* 110 E5
Brûlé, *Canada* 104 C5
Brûlon, *France* 18 E6
Brumado, *Brazil* 125 F10
Brumath, *France* 19 D14
Brumunddal, *Norway* 9 F14
Bruneau, *U.S.A.* 114 E6
Bruneau →, *U.S.A.* 114 E6
Bruneck = Brunico, *Italy* .. 29 B8
Brunei = Bandar Seri Begawan, *Brunei* 62 C4
Brunei ■, *Asia* 62 D4
Brunflo, *Sweden* 10 A8
Brunico, *Italy* 29 B8
Brunna, *Sweden* 10 E11
Brunnen, *Switz.* 25 J4
Brunner, L., *N.Z.* 91 K3
Brunsbüttel, *Germany* ... 24 B5
Brunssum, *Neths.* 17 D5
Brunswick = Braunschweig, *Germany* 24 C6
Brunswick, *Ga., U.S.A.* ... 109 K5
Brunswick, *Maine, U.S.A.* . 109 D11
Brunswick, *Md., U.S.A.* .. 108 F7
Brunswick, *Mo., U.S.A.* .. 112 F8
Brunswick, *Ohio, U.S.A.* .. 110 E3
Brunswick, Pen. de, *Chile* . 128 G2
Brunswick B., *Australia* ... 92 C3
Brunswick Junction, *Australia* 93 F2
Bruntál, *Czech Rep.* 27 B10
Bruny I., *Australia* 94 G4
Brus Laguna, *Honduras* ... 120 C3
Brusartsi, *Bulgaria* 40 C7
Brush, *U.S.A.* 112 E3
Brushton, *U.S.A.* 111 B10
Brusio, *Switz.* 25 J6
Brusque, *Brazil* 127 B6
Brussel, *Belgium* 17 D4
Brussels = Brussel, *Belgium* 17 D4
Brussels, *Canada* 110 C3
Brusy, *Poland* 44 E4
Bruthen, *Australia* 95 F4
Bruxelles = Brussel, *Belgium* 17 D4
Bruyères, *France* 19 D13
Bruz, *France* 18 D5
Brwinów, *Poland* 45 F7
Bryagovo, *Bulgaria* 41 E9
Bryan, *Ohio, U.S.A.* 108 E3
Bryan, *Tex., U.S.A.* 113 K6
Bryan, Mt., *Australia* 95 E2
Bryanka, *Ukraine* 47 H10
Bryansk, *Bryansk, Russia* .. 47 F8
Bryansk, *Dagestan, Russia* . 49 H8
Bryanskoye = Bryansk, *Russia* 49 H8
Bryce Canyon National Park, *U.S.A.* 115 H7
Bryne, *Norway* 9 G11
Bryson City, *U.S.A.* 109 H4
Bryukhovetskaya, *Russia* .. 47 K10
Brza Palanka, *Serbia, Yug.* . 40 B6
Brzeg, *Poland* 45 H4
Brzeg Dolny, *Poland* 45 G3
Brześć Kujawski, *Poland* .. 45 F5
Brzesko, *Poland* 45 J7
Brzeziny, *Poland* 45 G6
Brzozów, *Poland* 45 J9
Bsharri, *Lebanon* 75 A5
Bū Baqarah, *U.A.E.* 71 E8
Bu Craa, *W. Sahara* 78 C3
Bū Ḥasā, *U.A.E.* 71 F7
Bua, *Sweden* 11 G6
Bua Yai, *Thailand* 64 E4
Buapinang, *Indonesia* ... 63 E6
Buba, *Guinea-Biss.* 82 C2
Bubanza, *Burundi* 86 C2
Bubaque, *Guinea-Biss.* ... 82 C1
Bube, *Ethiopia* 81 F4
Būbiyān, *Kuwait* 71 D6
Buca, *Turkey* 39 C9
Bucak, *Turkey* 39 D12
Bucaramanga, *Colombia* .. 124 B4
Bucas Grande I., *Phil.* 61 G6
Bucasia, *Australia* 94 C4
Buccaneer Arch., *Australia* . 92 C3
Buccino, *Italy* 31 B8
Bucecea, *Romania* 43 C11
Buchach, *Ukraine* 47 H3
Buchan, *U.K.* 14 D6
Buchan Ness, *U.K.* 14 D7
Buchanan, *Canada* 105 C8
Buchanan, *Liberia* 82 D2
Buchanan, L., *Queens., Australia* 94 C4
Buchanan, L., *W. Austral., Australia* 93 E3

Buchanan, L., *U.S.A.* 113 K5
Buchanan Cr. →, *Australia* 94 B2
Buchans, *Canada* 103 C8
Bucharest = București, *Romania* 43 F11
Buchen, *Germany* 25 F5
Buchholz, *Germany* 24 B5
Buchloe, *Germany* 25 G6
Buchon, Pt., *U.S.A.* 116 K6
Buciumi, *Romania* 42 C8
Buck Hill Falls, *U.S.A.* ... 111 E9
Bückeburg, *Germany* 24 C5
Buckeye, *U.S.A.* 115 K7
Buckeye Lake, *U.S.A.* 110 F2
Buckhannon, *U.S.A.* 108 F5
Buckhaven, *U.K.* 14 E5
Buckhorn L., *Canada* 110 B6
Buckie, *U.K.* 14 D6
Buckingham, *Canada* 102 C4
Buckingham, *U.K.* 13 F7
Buckingham B., *Australia* . 94 A2
Buckinghamshire □, *U.K.* . 13 F7
Buckle Hd., *Australia* 92 B4
Buckleboo, *Australia* 95 E2
Buckley, *U.K.* 12 D4
Buckley →, *Australia* 94 C2
Bucklin, *U.S.A.* 113 G5
Bucks L., *U.S.A.* 116 F5
Bucquoy, *France* 19 B9
Buctouche, *Canada* 103 C7
București, *Romania* 43 F11
Bucyrus, *U.S.A.* 108 E4
Budacu, Vf., *Romania* ... 43 C10
Budalin, *Burma* 67 H19
Budapest, *Hungary* 42 C4
Budapest □, *Hungary* 42 C4
Budaun, *India* 69 E8
Budd Coast, *Antarctica* .. 5 C8
Buddusò, *Italy* 30 B2
Bude, *U.K.* 13 G3
Budennovsk, *Russia* 49 H7
Budești, *Romania* 43 F11
Budge Budge = Baj Baj, *India* 69 H13
Budgewoi, *Australia* 95 E5
Budia, *Spain* 32 E2
Büdingen, *Germany* 25 E5
Budjala, *Dem. Rep. of the Congo* . 84 D3
Budoni, *Italy* 30 B2
Búdrio, *Italy* 29 D8
Budva, *Montenegro, Yug.* . 40 D2
Budzyń, *Poland* 45 F3
Buea, *Cameroon* 83 E6
Buellton, *U.S.A.* 117 L6
Buena Esperanza, *Argentina* 126 C2
Buena Park, *U.S.A.* 117 M9
Buena Vista, *Colo., U.S.A.* 115 G10
Buena Vista, *Va., U.S.A.* . 108 G6
Buena Vista Lake Bed, *U.S.A.* 117 K7
Buenaventura, *Colombia* . 124 C3
Buenaventura, *Mexico* ... 118 B3
Buendía, Embalse de, *Spain* 32 E2
Buenos Aires, *Argentina* . 126 C4
Buenos Aires, *Costa Rica* . 120 E3
Buenos Aires □, *Argentina* 126 D4
Buenos Aires, L., *Chile* ... 128 F2
Buffalo, *Mo., U.S.A.* 113 G8
Buffalo, *N.Y., U.S.A.* 110 D6
Buffalo, *Okla., U.S.A.* ... 113 G5
Buffalo, *S. Dak., U.S.A.* .. 112 C3
Buffalo, *Wyo., U.S.A.* ... 114 D10
Buffalo →, *Canada* 104 A5
Buffalo →, *S. Africa* 89 D5
Buffalo Head Hills, *Canada* 104 B5
Buffalo L., *Alta., Canada* . 104 C6
Buffalo L., *N.W.T., Canada* 104 A5
Buffalo Narrows, *Canada* . 105 B7
Buffels →, *S. Africa* 88 D2
Buford, *U.S.A.* 109 H4
Bug →, *Poland* 45 F8
Bug →, *Ukraine* 47 J6
Buga, *Colombia* 124 C3
Buganda, *Uganda* 86 C3
Buganga, *Uganda* 86 C3
Bugasong, *Phil.* 61 F5
Bugel, Tanjung, *Indonesia* . 63 G14
Bugibba, *Malta* 36 D1
Bugojno, *Bos.-H.* 42 F2
Bugsuk, *Phil.* 62 C5
Buguma, *Nigeria* 83 E6
Bugun Shara, *Mongolia* .. 60 B5
Buguruslan, *Russia* 50 D6
Buh →, *Ukraine* 47 J6
Buharkent, *Turkey* 39 D10
Buheirat-Murrat-el-Kubra, *Egypt* 80 H8
Buhera, *Zimbabwe* 89 B5
Bühl, *Germany* 25 G4
Buhl, *U.S.A.* 114 E6
Buhuși, *Romania* 43 D11
Builth Wells, *U.K.* 13 E4
Buinsk, *Russia* 48 C9
Buir Nur, *Mongolia* 60 B6
Buis-les-Baronnies, *France* . 21 D9
Buitrago = Buitrago del Lozoya, *Spain* 34 E7
Buitrago del Lozoya, *Spain* . 34 E7
Bujalance, *Spain* 35 H6
Bujaraloz, *Spain* 32 D4
Buje, *Croatia* 29 C10
Bujumbura, *Burundi* 86 C2
Bük, *Hungary* 42 C1
Buk, *Poland* 45 F3
Bukachacha, *Russia* 51 D12
Bukama, *Dem. Rep. of the Congo* . 87 D2

Bukavu,
  Dem. Rep. of the Congo . 86 C2
Bukene, Tanzania 86 C3
Bukhara = Bukhoro,
  Uzbekistan 50 F7
Bukhoro, Uzbekistan 50 F7
Bukima, Tanzania 86 C3
Bukit Mertajam, Malaysia .. 65 K3
Bukittinggi, Indonesia 62 E2
Bükk, Hungary 42 B5
Bukoba, Tanzania 86 C3
Bukuru, Nigeria 83 D6
Bukuya, Uganda 86 B3
Būl, Kuh-e, Iran 71 D7
Bula, Guinea-Biss. 82 C1
Bula, Indonesia 63 E8
Bülach, Switz. 25 H4
Bulahdelah, Australia 95 E5
Bulan, Phil. 61 E5
Bulancak, Turkey 73 B8
Bulandshahr, India 68 E7
Bulanık, Turkey 73 C10
Būlâq, Egypt 80 B3
Bulawayo, Zimbabwe 87 G2
Buldan, Turkey 39 C10
Bulgar, Russia 48 C9
Bulgaria ■, Europe 41 D9
Bulgheria, Monte, Italy ... 31 B8
Bulgurca, Turkey 39 C9
Buli, Teluk, Indonesia 63 D7
Buliluyan, C., Phil. 61 G2
Bulki, Ethiopia 81 F4
Bulkley →, Canada 104 B3
Bull Shoals L., U.S.A. 113 G8
Bullaque →, Spain 35 G6
Bullas, Spain 33 G3
Bulle, Switz. 25 J3
Bullhead City, U.S.A. 117 K12
Büllingen, Belgium 17 D6
Bulloo →, Australia 95 D3
Bulloo L., Australia 95 D3
Bulls, N.Z. 91 J5
Bully-les-Mines, France ... 19 B9
Bulnes, Chile 126 D1
Bulqiza, Albania 40 E4
Bulsar = Valsad, India ... 66 J8
Bultfontein, S. Africa 88 D4
Bulukumba, Indonesia 63 F6
Bulun, Russia 51 B13
Bumba,
  Dem. Rep. of the Congo . 84 D4
Bumbești-Jiu, Romania ... 43 E8
Bumbiri I., Tanzania 86 C3
Bumbuna, S. Leone 82 D2
Bumhpa Bum, Burma 67 F20
Bumi →, Zimbabwe 87 F2
Buna, Kenya 86 B4
Bunawan, Phil. 61 G6
Bunazi, Tanzania 86 C3
Bunbury, Australia 93 F2
Bunclody, Ireland 15 D5
Buncrana, Ireland 15 A4
Bundaberg, Australia 95 C5
Bünde, Germany 24 C4
Bundey →, Australia 94 C2
Bundi, India 68 G6
Bundoran, Ireland 15 B3
Bundukia, Sudan 81 F3
Bung Kan, Thailand 64 C4
Bunga →, Nigeria 83 C6
Bungatakada, Japan 55 H5
Bungay, U.K. 13 E9
Bungil Cr. →, Australia .. 95 D4
Bungo-Suidō, Japan 55 H6
Bungoma, Kenya 86 B3
Bungu, Tanzania 86 D4
Bunia,
  Dem. Rep. of the Congo . 86 B3
Bunji, Pakistan 69 B6
Bunkie, U.S.A. 113 K8
Buñol, Spain 33 F4
Bunsuru, Nigeria 83 C5
Buntok, Indonesia 62 E4
Bununu Dass, Nigeria ... 83 C6
Bununu Kasa, Nigeria ... 83 D6
Bünyan, Turkey 72 C6
Bunyu, Indonesia 62 D5
Bunza, Nigeria 83 C5
Buol, Indonesia 63 D6
Buon Brieng, Vietnam ... 64 F7
Buon Ma Thuot, Vietnam . 64 F7
Buong Long, Cambodia ... 64 F6
Buorkhaya, Mys, Russia .. 51 B14
Buqayq, Si. Arabia 71 E6
Buqbuq, Egypt 80 A2
Bur Acaba, Somali Rep. .. 74 G3
Bûr Fuad, Egypt 80 H8
Bûr Safâga, Egypt 70 E2
Bûr Sa'îd, Egypt 80 H8
Bûr Sûdân, Sudan 80 D4
Bûr Taufiq, Egypt 80 J8
Bura, Kenya 86 C4
Burakin, Australia 93 F2
Buram, Sudan 81 E3
Burao, Somali Rep. 74 F4
Burāq, Syria 75 B5
Burbank, U.S.A. 117 L8
Burda, India 68 G6
Burdekin →, Australia ... 94 B4
Burdur, Turkey 39 D12
Burdur □, Turkey 39 D12
Burdur Gölü, Turkey 39 D12
Burdwan = Barddhaman,
  India 69 H12
Bure, Gojam, Ethiopia ... 81 E4
Bure, Ilubabor, Ethiopia .. 81 F4
Bure →, U.K. 12 E9
Büren, Germany 24 D4
Bureya →, Russia 51 E13

Burford, Canada 110 C4
Burg, Germany 24 C7
Burg auf Fehmarn, Germany 24 A7
Burg el Arab, Egypt 80 H6
Burg et Tuyur, Sudan 80 C2
Burg Stargard, Germany .. 24 B9
Burgas, Bulgaria 41 D11
Burgas □, Bulgaria 41 D10
Burgaski Zaliv, Bulgaria .. 41 D11
Burgdorf, Germany 24 C6
Burgdorf, Switz. 25 H3
Burgenland □, Austria ... 27 D9
Burgeo, Canada 103 C8
Burgersdorp, S. Africa ... 88 E4
Burges, Mt., Australia ... 93 F3
Burghausen, Germany ... 25 G8
Búrgio, Italy 30 E6
Burglengenfeld, Germany . 25 F8
Burgohondo, Spain 34 E6
Burgos, Spain 34 C7
Burgos □, Spain 34 C7
Burgstädt, Germany 24 E8
Burgsvik, Sweden 11 G12
Burguillos del Cerro, Spain . 35 G4
Burgundy = Bourgogne,
  France 19 F11
Burhaniye, Turkey 39 B8
Burhanpur, India 66 J10
Burhi Gandak →, India .. 69 G12
Burhner →, India 69 H9
Buri Pen., Eritrea 81 D4
Burias I., Phil. 61 E5
Burica, Pta., Costa Rica .. 120 E3
Burien, U.S.A. 116 C4
Burigi, L., Tanzania 86 C3
Burin, Canada 103 C8
Buriram, Thailand 64 E4
Burj Sāfītā, Syria 70 C3
Burji, Ethiopia 81 F4
Burkburnett, U.S.A. 113 H5
Burke →, Australia 94 C2
Burke Chan., Canada 104 C3
Burketown, Australia 94 B2
Burkina Faso ■, Africa ... 82 C4
Burk's Falls, Canada 102 C4
Burlada, Spain 32 C3
Burleigh Falls, Canada ... 110 B6
Burley, U.S.A. 114 E7
Burlingame, U.S.A. 116 H4
Burlington, Canada 102 D4
Burlington, Colo., U.S.A. . 112 F3
Burlington, Iowa, U.S.A. .. 112 E9
Burlington, Kans., U.S.A. . 112 F7
Burlington, N.C., U.S.A. .. 109 G6
Burlington, N.J., U.S.A. .. 111 F10
Burlington, Vt., U.S.A. ... 111 B11
Burlington, Wash., U.S.A. . 116 B4
Burlington, Wis., U.S.A. .. 108 D1
Burlyu-Tyube, Kazakhstan .. 50 E8
Burma ■, Asia 67 J20
Burnaby I., Canada 104 C2
Burnet, U.S.A. 113 K5
Burney, U.S.A. 114 F3
Burnham, U.S.A. 110 F7
Burnham-on-Sea, U.K. ... 13 F5
Burnie, Australia 94 G4
Burnley, U.K. 12 D5
Burns, U.S.A. 114 E4
Burns Lake, Canada 104 C3
Burnside →, Canada 100 B9
Burnside, L., Australia ... 93 E3
Burnsville, U.S.A. 112 C8
Burnt L., Canada 103 B7
Burnt River, Canada 110 B6
Burntwood →, Canada .. 105 B9
Burntwood L., Canada ... 105 B8
Burqān, Kuwait 70 D5
Burra, Australia 95 E2
Burra, Nigeria 83 C6
Burray, U.K. 14 C6
Burreli, Albania 40 E4
Burren Junction, Australia . 95 E4
Burriana, Spain 32 F4
Burrinjuck Res., Australia . 95 F4
Burro, Serranías del, Mexico 118 B4
Burrow Hd., U.K. 14 G4
Burruyacú, Argentina 126 B3
Burry Port, U.K. 13 F3
Bursa, Turkey 41 F13
Burseryd, Sweden 11 G7
Burstall, Canada 105 C7
Burton, Ohio, U.S.A. 110 E3
Burton, S.C., U.S.A. 109 J5
Burton, L., Canada 102 B4
Burton upon Trent, U.K. .. 12 E6
Burullus, Bahra el, Egypt . 80 H7
Burûn, Râs, Egypt 75 D7
Burundi ■, Africa 86 C3
Bururi, Burundi 86 C2
Burutu, Nigeria 83 D6
Burwell, U.S.A. 112 E5
Burwick, U.K. 14 C5
Bury, U.K. 12 D5
Bury St. Edmunds, U.K. .. 13 E8
Buryatia □, Russia 51 D11
Buryn, Ukraine 47 G7
Burzenin, Poland 45 G5
Busalla, Italy 28 D5
Busango Swamp, Zambia . 87 E2
Buşayrah, Syria 70 C4
Busca, Italy 28 D4
Bushati, Albania 40 E3
Büshehr, Iran 71 D6
Büshehr □, Iran 71 D6
Bushell, Canada 105 B7
Bushenyi, Uganda 86 C3
Bushire = Büshehr, Iran .. 71 D6
Busie, Ghana 82 C4
Businga,
  Dem. Rep. of the Congo . 84 D4

Busko-Zdrój, Poland 45 H7
Busovača, Bos.-H. 42 F2
Buşra ash Shām, Syria ... 75 C5
Busselton, Australia 93 F2
Busseri →, Sudan 81 F2
Bussière-Badil, France ... 20 C4
Bussolengo, Italy 28 C7
Bussum, Neths. 17 B5
Busto Arsízio, Italy 28 C5
Busu-Djanoa,
  Dem. Rep. of the Congo . 84 D4
Busuanga I., Phil. 61 E3
Buta,
  Dem. Rep. of the Congo . 86 B1
Butare, Rwanda 86 C2
Butaritari, Kiribati 96 G9
Bute, U.K. 14 F3
Bute Inlet, Canada 104 C4
Butemba, Uganda 86 B3
Butembo,
  Dem. Rep. of the Congo . 86 B2
Buteni, Romania 42 D7
Butera, Italy 31 E7
Butha Qi, China 60 B7
Butiaba, Uganda 86 B3
Butler, Mo., U.S.A. 112 F7
Butler, Pa., U.S.A. 110 F5
Buton, Indonesia 63 E6
Butte, Mont., U.S.A. 114 C7
Butte, Nebr., U.S.A. 112 D5
Butte Creek →, U.S.A. .. 116 F5
Butterworth = Gcuwa,
  S. Africa 89 E4
Butterworth, Malaysia ... 65 K3
Buttevant, Ireland 15 D3
Buttfield, Mt., Australia .. 93 D4
Button B., Canada 105 B10
Buttonwillow, U.S.A. 117 K7
Butty Hd., Australia 93 F3
Butuan, Phil. 61 G6
Butuku-Luba, Eq. Guin. .. 83 E6
Butung = Buton, Indonesia 63 E6
Buturlinovka, Russia 48 E5
Butzbach, Germany 25 E4
Bützow, Germany 24 B7
Buxa Duar, India 69 F13
Buxar, India 69 G10
Buxtehude, Germany 24 B5
Buxton, U.K. 12 D6
Buxy, France 19 F11
Buy, Russia 48 A5
Buynaksk, Russia 49 J8
Buyo, Ivory C. 82 D3
Buyo, L. de, Ivory C. 82 D3
Büyük Menderes →, Turkey 39 D9
Büyükçekmece, Turkey ... 41 E12
Büyükkarıştiran, Turkey .. 41 E11
Büyükkemikli Burnu, Turkey 41 F10
Büyükkorhan, Turkey 39 B10
Büyükyoncalı, Turkey 41 E11
Buzançais, France 18 F8
Buzău, Romania 43 E11
Buzău □, Romania 43 E11
Buzău →, Romania 43 E12
Buzău, Pasul, Romania .. 43 E11
Buzen, Japan 55 H5
Buzet, Croatia 29 C10
Buzi →, Mozam. 87 F3
Buziaş, Romania 42 E6
Buzuluk, Russia 50 D6
Buzuluk →, Russia 48 E6
Buzzards B., U.S.A. 111 E14
Buzzards Bay, U.S.A. 111 E14
Bwana Mkubwe,
  Dem. Rep. of the Congo . 87 E2
Byala, Ruse, Bulgaria 41 C9
Byala, Varna, Bulgaria ... 41 D11
Byala Slatina, Bulgaria ... 40 C7
Byarezina →, Belarus ... 47 F6
Bychawa, Poland 45 G9
Byczyna, Poland 45 G5
Bydgoszcz, Poland 45 E5
Byelarus = Belarus ■,
  Europe 46 F4
Byelorussia = Belarus ■,
  Europe 46 F4
Byers, U.S.A. 112 F2
Byesville, U.S.A. 110 G3
Byford, Australia 93 F2
Bykhaw, Belarus 46 F6
Bykhov = Bykhaw, Belarus 46 F6
Bykovo, Russia 48 E7
Bylas, U.S.A. 115 K8
Bylot, Canada 105 B8
Bylot I., Canada 101 A12
Byrd, C., Antarctica 5 C17
Byrock, Australia 95 E4
Byron Bay, Australia 95 D5
Byrranga, Gory, Russia .. 51 B11
Byrranga Mts. = Byrranga,
  Gory, Russia 51 B11
Byrum, Denmark 11 G5
Byske, Sweden 8 D19
Byske älv →, Sweden ... 8 D19
Bystrzyca →, Dolnośląskie,
  Poland 45 G3
Bystrzyca →, Lubelskie,
  Poland 45 G9
Bystrzyca Kłodzka, Poland . 45 H3
Bytča, Slovak Rep. 27 B11
Bytom, Poland 45 H5
Bytom Odrzański, Poland . 45 G2
Bytów, Poland 44 D4
Byumba, Rwanda 86 C3
Bzenec, Czech Rep. 27 C10
Bzura →, Poland 45 F7

C

Ca →, Vietnam 64 C5
Ca Mau, Vietnam 65 H5
Ca Mau, Mui, Vietnam ... 65 H5
Ca Na, Vietnam 65 G7
Caacupé, Paraguay 126 B4
Caála, Angola 85 G3
Caamano Sd., Canada ... 104 C3
Caazapá, Paraguay 126 B4
Caazapá □, Paraguay ... 127 B4
Cabadbaran, Phil. 61 G6
Cabalian = San Juan, Phil. . 61 F6
Cabanaquinta, Spain 34 B5
Cabanatuan, Phil. 61 D4
Cabanes, Spain 32 E5
Cabano, Canada 103 C6
Čabar, Croatia 29 C11
Cabazon, U.S.A. 117 M10
Cabedelo, Brazil 125 E12
Cabeza del Buey, Spain .. 35 G5
Cabezón de la Sal, Spain .. 34 B6
Cabildo, Chile 126 C1
Cabimas, Venezuela 124 A4
Cabinda, Angola 84 F2
Cabinda □, Angola 84 F2
Cabinet Mts., U.S.A. 114 C6
Cabo Blanco, Argentina .. 128 F3
Cabo Frio, Brazil 127 A7
Cabo Pantoja, Peru 124 D3
Cabonga, Réservoir, Canada 102 C4
Cabool, U.S.A. 113 G8
Caboolture, Australia 95 D5
Cabora Bassa Dam =
  Cahora Bassa, Reprêsa de,
  Mozam. 87 F3
Caborca, Mexico 118 A2
Cabot, Mt., U.S.A. 111 B13
Cabot Hd., Canada 110 A3
Cabot Str., Canada 103 C8
Cabra, Spain 35 H6
Cabra del Santo Cristo,
  Spain 35 H7
Cábras, Italy 30 C1
Cabrera, Spain 37 B9
Cabrera, Sierra, Spain ... 34 C4
Cabri, Canada 105 C7
Cabriel →, Spain 33 F3
Cabugao, Phil. 61 C4
Cacabelos, Spain 34 C4
Çaçador, Brazil 127 B5
Čačak, Serbia, Yug. 40 C4
Caçapava do Sul, Brazil .. 127 C5
Cáccamo, Italy 30 E6
Cáceres, Brazil 124 G7
Cáceres, Spain 35 F4
Cáceres □, Spain 34 F5
Cache Bay, Canada 102 C4
Cache Cr. →, U.S.A. ... 116 G5
Cache Creek, Canada 104 C4
Cacheu, Guinea-Biss. 82 C1
Cachi, Argentina 126 B2
Cachimbo, Serra do, Brazil 125 E7
Cachinal de la Sierra, Chile 126 A2
Cachoeira, Brazil 125 F11
Cachoeira de Itapemirim,
  Brazil 127 A7
Cachoeira do Sul, Brazil .. 127 C5
Cachopo, Portugal 35 H3
Cacine, Guinea-Biss. 82 C1
Cacoal, Brazil 124 F6
Cacólo, Angola 84 G3
Caconda, Angola 85 G3
Čadca, Slovak Rep. 27 B11
Caddo, U.S.A. 113 H6
Cader Idris, U.K. 13 E4
Cadereyta, Mexico 118 B5
Cadí, Sierra del, Spain ... 32 C6
Cadibarrawirracanna, L.,
  Australia 95 D2
Cadillac, France 20 D3
Cadillac, U.S.A. 108 C3
Cádiz, Phil. 61 F5
Cádiz, Spain 35 J4
Cadiz, Calif., U.S.A. 117 L11
Cadiz, Ohio, U.S.A. 110 F4
Cádiz □, Spain 35 J5
Cádiz, G. de, Spain 35 J3
Cadiz L., U.S.A. 115 J6
Cadney Park, Australia ... 95 D1
Cadomin, Canada 104 C5
Cadotte Lake, Canada ... 104 B5
Cadours, France 20 E5
Cadoux, Australia 93 F2
Caen, France 18 C6
Caernarfon, U.K. 12 D3
Caernarfon B., U.K. 12 D3
Caernarvon = Caernarfon,
  U.K. 12 D3
Caerphilly, U.K. 13 F4
Caerphilly □, U.K. 13 F4
Caesarea, Israel 75 C3
Cafayate, Argentina 126 B2
Cafu, Angola 88 B2
Cagayan →, Phil. 61 B4
Cagayan de Oro, Phil. ... 61 G6
Cagayan Is., Phil. 61 G4
Cagayan Sulu I., Phil. 61 H3
Cágliari, Italy 30 C2
Cágliari, G. di, Italy 30 C2
Cagnano Varano, Italy ... 29 G12
Cagnes-sur-Mer, France .. 21 E11
Caguán →, Colombia ... 124 D4
Caguas, Puerto Rico 121 C6
Caha Mts., Ireland 15 E2
Cahama, Angola 88 B1

Caher, Ireland 15 D4
Cahersiveen, Ireland 15 E1
Cahora Bassa, Reprêsa de,
  Mozam. 87 F3
Cahore Pt., Ireland 15 D5
Cahors, France 20 D5
Cahul, Moldova 43 E13
Cai Bau, Dao, Vietnam ... 58 G6
Cai Nuoc, Vietnam 65 H5
Caia, Mozam. 87 F4
Caianda, Angola 87 E1
Caibarién, Cuba 120 B4
Caibiran, Phil. 61 F6
Caicara, Venezuela 124 B5
Caicó, Brazil 125 E11
Caicos Is., W. Indies 121 B5
Caicos Passage, W. Indies . 121 B5
Caidian, China 59 B10
Căinari, Moldova 43 D14
Caird Coast, Antarctica .. 5 D1
Cairn Gorm, U.K. 14 D5
Cairngorm Mts., U.K. ... 14 D5
Cairnryan, U.K. 14 G3
Cairns, Australia 94 B4
Cairns L., Canada 105 C10
Cairo = El Qâhira, Egypt . 80 H7
Cairo, Ga., U.S.A. 109 K3
Cairo, Ill., U.S.A. 113 G10
Cairo, N.Y., U.S.A. 111 D11
Cairo Montenotte, Italy .. 28 D5
Caithness, Ord of, U.K. .. 14 C5
Cajamarca, Peru 124 E3
Cajarc, France 20 D5
Çajàzeiras, Brazil 125 E11
Čajetina, Serbia, Yug. ... 40 C3
Çakirgol, Turkey 73 B8
Çakmak, Turkey 39 C11
Čakovec, Croatia 29 B13
Çal, Turkey 39 C11
Cala, Spain 35 H4
Cala →, Spain 35 H4
Cala Cadolar, Punta de =
  Rotja, Pta., Spain 33 G4
Cala d'Or, Spain 37 B10
Cala en Porter, Spain 37 B11
Cala Figuera, C. de, Spain . 37 B9
Cala Forcat, Spain 37 B10
Cala Major, Spain 37 B9
Cala Mezquida = Sa
  Mesquida, Spain 37 B11
Cala Millor, Spain 37 B10
Cala Ratjada, Spain 37 B10
Cala Santa Galdana, Spain . 37 B10
Calabanga, Phil. 61 E5
Calabar, Nigeria 83 E6
Calabogie, Canada 111 A8
Calabozo, Venezuela 124 B5
Calábria □, Italy 31 C9
Calaburras, Pta. de, Spain . 35 J6
Calaceite, Spain 32 D5
Calacuccia, France 21 F13
Calafat, Romania 42 G7
Calafate, Argentina 128 G2
Calahorra, Spain 32 C3
Calais, France 19 B8
Calais, U.S.A. 109 C12
Calalaste, Cord. de,
  Argentina 126 B2
Calama, Brazil 124 E6
Calama, Chile 126 A2
Calamar, Colombia 124 A4
Calamian Group, Phil. ... 61 F3
Calamocha, Spain 32 E3
Calamonte, Spain 35 G4
Călan, Romania 42 E7
Calañas, Spain 35 H4
Calanda, Spain 32 E4
Calang, Indonesia 62 D1
Calangiánus, Italy 30 B2
Calapan, Phil. 61 E4
Călărasi, Moldova 43 C13
Călăraşi, Romania 43 F12
Călăraşi □, Romania 43 F12
Calasparra, Spain 33 G3
Calatafimi, Italy 30 E5
Calatayud, Spain 32 D3
Călătele, Romania 42 D7
Calato = Kálathos, Greece . 39 E10
Calauag, Phil. 61 E5
Calavà, C., Italy 31 D7
Calavite, C., Phil. 61 E4
Calayan, Phil. 61 B4
Calbayog, Phil. 61 E6
Calca, Peru 124 F4
Calcasieu L., U.S.A. 113 L8
Calcutta, India 69 H13
Caldaro, Italy 29 B8
Caldas da Rainha, Portugal 35 F1
Caldas de Reis, Spain ... 34 C2
Calder →, U.K. 12 D6
Caldera, Chile 126 B1
Caldwell, Idaho, U.S.A. .. 114 E5
Caldwell, Kans., U.S.A. .. 113 G6
Caldwell, Tex., U.S.A. ... 113 K6
Caledon, S. Africa 88 E2
Caledon →, S. Africa ... 88 E4
Caledon B., Australia ... 94 A2
Caledonia, Canada 110 C5
Caledonia, U.S.A. 110 D7
Calella, Spain 32 D7
Calemba, Angola 88 B2
Calen, Australia 94 C4
Calenzana, France 21 F12
Caletones, Chile 126 C1
Calf of Man, U.K. 12 C3
Calgary, Canada 104 C6
Calheta, Madeira 37 D2
Calhoun, U.S.A. 109 H3

Cali

Cali, *Colombia* 124 C3
Calicut, *India* 66 P9
Caliente, *U.S.A.* 115 H6
California, *Mo., U.S.A.* . . . 112 F8
California, *Pa., U.S.A.* . . . 110 F5
California □, *U.S.A.* 116 H7
California, Baja, *Mexico* . . 118 A1
California, Baja, T.N. =
   Baja California □, *Mexico* 118 B2
California, Baja, T.S. = Baja
   California □, *Mexico* . . 118 B2
California, G. de, *Mexico* . . 118 B2
California Sur □, *U.S.A.* . . 117 K9
California City, *U.S.A.* . . . 117 K9
California Hot Springs,
   U.S.A. 117 K8
Călimăneşti, *Romania* 43 E9
Călimani, Munţii, *Romania* . 43 C10
Calingasta, *Argentina* 126 C2
Calipatria, *U.S.A.* 117 M11
Calistoga, *U.S.A.* 116 G4
Calitri, *Italy* 31 B8
Calitzdorp, *S. Africa* 88 E3
Callabonna, L., *Australia* . . 95 D3
Callac, *France* 18 D3
Callan, *Ireland* 15 D4
Callander, *U.K.* 14 E4
Callao, *Peru* 124 F3
Calles, *Mexico* 119 C5
Callicoon, *U.S.A.* 111 E9
Calling Lake, *Canada* 104 B6
Calliope, *Australia* 94 C5
Callosa de Ensarriá, *Spain* . 33 G4
Callosa de Segura, *Spain* . . 33 G4
Calne, *U.K.* 13 F6
Calola, *Angola* 88 B2
Calolbon = San Andres,
   Phil. 61 E6
Calonge, *Spain* 32 D8
Caloocan, *Phil.* 61 D4
Calore →, *Italy* 31 A7
Caloundra, *Australia* 95 D5
Calpe, *Spain* 33 G5
Calpella, *U.S.A.* 116 F3
Calpine, *U.S.A.* 116 F6
Calstock, *Canada* 102 C3
Caltabellotta, *Italy* 30 E6
Caltagirone, *Italy* 31 E7
Caltanissetta, *Italy* 31 E7
Çaltılıbük, *Turkey* 41 G12
Caluire-et-Cuire, *France* . . 19 G11
Calulo, *Angola* 84 G2
Caluso, *Italy* 28 C4
Calvados □, *France* 18 C6
Calvert →, *Australia* 94 B2
Calvert I., *Canada* 104 C3
Calvert Ra., *Australia* 92 D3
Calvi, *France* 21 F12
Calviá, *Spain* 33 F7
Calvillo, *Mexico* 118 C4
Calvinia, *S. Africa* 88 E2
Calvo, Mte. = Calvo, Mte., *Italy* . 29 G12
Calvo, Mte., *Italy* 29 G12
Calwa, *U.S.A.* 116 J7
Calzada Almuradiel =
   Almuradiel, *Spain* 35 G7
Calzada de Calatrava, *Spain* 35 G7
Cam →, *U.K.* 13 E8
Cam Lam, *Vietnam* 65 G7
Cam Pha, *Vietnam* 58 G6
Cam Ranh, *Vietnam* 65 G7
Cam Xuyen, *Vietnam* 64 C6
Camabatela, *Angola* 84 F3
Camacha, *Madeira* 37 D3
Camacho, *Mexico* 118 C4
Camacupa, *Angola* 85 G3
Camagüey, *Cuba* 120 B4
Camaiore, *Italy* 28 E7
Camaná, *Peru* 124 G4
Camanche Reservoir, *U.S.A.* 116 G6
Camaquã, *Brazil* 127 C5
Camaquã →, *Brazil* 127 C5
Câmara de Lobos, *Madeira* . 37 D3
Camarat, C., *France* 21 E10
Camarès, *France* 20 E6
Camaret-sur-Mer, *France* . . 18 D2
Camargo, *Mexico* 119 B5
Camargue, *France* 21 E8
Camarillo, *U.S.A.* 117 L7
Camariñas, *Spain* 34 B1
Camarón, C., *Honduras* . . 120 C2
Camarones, *Argentina* . . . 128 E3
Camas, *Spain* 35 H4
Camas, *U.S.A.* 116 E4
Camas Valley, *U.S.A.* 114 E2
Camballin, *Australia* 92 C3
Cambará, *Brazil* 127 A5
Cambay = Khambhat, *India* 68 H5
Cambay, G. of = Khambhat,
   G. of, *India* 66 J8
Cambil, *Spain* 35 H7
Cambo-les-Bains, *France* . . 20 E2
Cambodia ■, *Asia* 64 F5
Camborne, *U.K.* 13 G2
Cambrai, *France* 19 B10
Cambre, *Spain* 34 B2
Cambria, *U.S.A.* 116 K5
Cambrian Mts., *U.K.* 13 E4
Cambridge, *Canada* 102 D3
Cambridge, *Jamaica* 120 C4
Cambridge, *N.Z.* 91 G5
Cambridge, *U.K.* 13 E8
Cambridge, *Mass., U.S.A.* . 111 D13
Cambridge, *Minn., U.S.A.* . 112 C8
Cambridge, *N.Y., U.S.A.* . . 111 C11
Cambridge, *Nebr., U.S.A.* . 112 E4
Cambridge, *Ohio, U.S.A.* . . 110 F3
Cambridge Bay =
   Ikaluktutiak, *Canada* . . 100 B9
Cambridge G., *Australia* . . 92 B4
Cambridge Springs, *U.S.A.* 110 E4
Cambridgeshire □, *U.K.* . . 13 E7

Cambrils, *Spain* 32 D6
Cambuci, *Brazil* 127 A7
Cambundi-Catembo, *Angola* 84 G3
Camden, *Ala., U.S.A.* 109 K2
Camden, *Ark., U.S.A.* 113 J8
Camden, *Maine, U.S.A.* . . . 109 C11
Camden, *N.J., U.S.A.* 111 G9
Camden, *N.Y., U.S.A.* 111 C9
Camden, *S.C., U.S.A.* 109 H5
Camden Sd., *Australia* . . . 92 C3
Camdenton, *U.S.A.* 113 F8
Çameli, *Turkey* 39 D11
Camenca, *Moldova* 43 B13
Camerino, *Italy* 29 E10
Cameron, *Ariz., U.S.A.* . . . 115 J8
Cameron, *La., U.S.A.* 113 L8
Cameron, *Mo., U.S.A.* . . . 112 F7
Cameron, *Tex., U.S.A.* . . . 113 K6
Cameron Highlands,
   Malaysia 65 K3
Cameron Hills, *Canada* . . . 104 B5
Cameroon ■, *Africa* 84 C2
Camerota, *Italy* 31 B8
Cameroun →, *Cameroon* . . 83 E6
Cameroun, Mt., *Cameroon* . 83 E6
Cametá, *Brazil* 125 D9
Çamiçi Gölü, *Turkey* 39 D9
Camiguin □, *Phil.* 61 G6
Camiguin I., *Phil.* 61 B4
Camiling, *Phil.* 61 D4
Camilla, *U.S.A.* 109 K3
Caminha, *Portugal* 34 D2
Camino, *U.S.A.* 116 G6
Camira Creek, *Australia* . . 95 D5
Cammal, *U.S.A.* 110 E7
Cammarata, *Italy* 30 E6
Camocim, *Brazil* 125 D10
Camooweal, *Australia* . . . 94 B2
Camopi, *Fr. Guiana* 125 C8
Camotes Is., *Phil.* 61 F6
Camotes Sea, *Phil.* 61 F6
Camp Borden, *Canada* . . . 110 B5
Camp Hill, *U.S.A.* 110 F8
Camp Nelson, *U.S.A.* 117 J8
Camp Pendleton, *U.S.A.* . . 117 M9
Camp Verde, *U.S.A.* 115 J8
Camp Wood, *U.S.A.* 113 L5
Campagna, *Italy* 31 B8
Campana, *Argentina* 126 C4
Campana, I., *Chile* 128 F1
Campanário, *Madeira* 37 D2
Campanario, *Spain* 35 G5
Campánia □, *Italy* 31 B7
Campbell, *S. Africa* 88 D3
Campbell, *Calif., U.S.A.* . . 116 H5
Campbell, *Ohio, U.S.A.* . . . 110 E4
Campbell I., *Pac. Oc.* 96 N8
Campbell L., *Canada* 105 A7
Campbell River, *Canada* . . 104 C3
Campbell Town, *Australia* . 94 G4
Campbellford, *Canada* . . . 110 B7
Campbellpur, *Pakistan* . . . 68 C5
Campbellsville, *U.S.A.* . . . 108 G3
Campbellton, *Canada* 103 C6
Campbeltown, *U.K.* 14 F3
Campbelltown, *Australia* . . 95 E5
Campeche, *Mexico* 119 D6
Campeche □, *Mexico* 119 D6
Campeche, Golfo de, *Mexico* 119 D6
Campello, *Spain* 33 G4
Câmpeni, *Romania* 42 D8
Camperdown, *Australia* . . 95 F3
Camperville, *Canada* 105 C8
Campi Salentina, *Italy* . . . 31 B11
Câmpia Turzii, *Romania* . . 43 D8
Campidano, *Italy* 30 C1
Campíglia Maríttima, *Italy* . 28 E7
Campillo de Altobuey, *Spain* 33 F3
Campillos, *Spain* 35 H6
Câmpina, *Romania* 43 E10
Campina Grande, *Brazil* . . 125 E11
Campinas, *Brazil* 127 A6
Campli, *Italy* 29 F10
Campo, *Spain* 32 C5
Campo de Criptana, *Spain* . 35 F7
Campo de Gibraltar, *Spain* . 35 J5
Campo Grande, *Brazil* . . . 125 H8
Campo Maíor, *Brazil* 125 D10
Campo Maior, *Portugal* . . 35 F3
Campo Mourão, *Brazil* . . . 127 A5
Campo Túres, *Italy* 29 B8
Campobasso, *Italy* 31 A7
Campobello di Licata, *Italy* . 30 E6
Campobello di Mazara, *Italy* 30 E5
Campofelice di Roccella,
   Italy 30 E6
Campomarino, *Italy* 29 G12
Camporeale, *Italy* 30 E6
Camporrobles, *Spain* 32 F3
Campos, *Brazil* 127 A7
Campos Belos, *Brazil* 125 F9
Campos del Puerto, *Spain* . 37 B10
Campos Novos, *Brazil* . . . 127 B5
Camprodón, *Spain* 32 C7
Camptonville, *U.S.A.* 116 F5
Camptown, *U.S.A.* 111 E8
Câmpulung, *Argeş, Romania* 43 E10
Câmpulung, *Suceava,
   Romania* 43 C10
Câmpuri, *Romania* 43 D11
Camrose, *Canada* 104 C6
Camsell Portage, *Canada* . 105 B7
Çamyuva, *Turkey* 39 E12
Çan, *Turkey* 41 F11
Can Clavo, *Spain* 37 C7
Can Creu, *Spain* 37 C7
Can Gio, *Vietnam* 65 G6
Can Tho, *Vietnam* 65 G5
Canaan, *U.S.A.* 111 D11
Canada ■, *N. Amer.* 100 C10
Cañada de Gómez, *Argentina* 126 C3

Canadian, *U.S.A.* 113 H4
Canadian →, *U.S.A.* 113 H7
Canajoharie, *U.S.A.* 111 D10
Çanakkale, *Turkey* 41 F10
Çanakkale □, *Turkey* 41 F10
Çanakkale Boğazı, *Turkey* . 41 F10
Canal Flats, *Canada* 104 C5
Canalejas, *Argentina* 126 D2
Canals, *Argentina* 126 C3
Canals, *Spain* 33 G4
Canandaigua, *U.S.A.* 110 D7
Canandaigua L., *U.S.A.* . . . 110 D7
Cananea, *Mexico* 118 A2
Canarias, Is., *Atl. Oc.* 37 F4
Canarreos, Arch. de los,
   Cuba 120 B3
Canary Is. = Canarias, Is.,
   Atl. Oc. 37 F4
Canaseraga, *U.S.A.* 110 D7
Canatlán, *Mexico* 118 C4
Canaveral, C., *U.S.A.* 109 L5
Cañaverales, *Spain* 32 E2
Canavieiras, *Brazil* 125 G11
Canberra, *Australia* 95 F4
Canby, *Calif., U.S.A.* 114 F3
Canby, *Minn., U.S.A.* 112 C6
Canby, *Oreg., U.S.A.* 116 E4
Cancale, *France* 18 D5
Canche →, *France* 19 B8
Cancún, *Mexico* 119 C7
Candanchu, *Spain* 32 C4
Çandarlı, *Turkey* 39 C8
Çandarlı Körfezi, *Turkey* . . 39 C8
Çandas, *Spain* 34 B5
Candé, *France* 18 E5
Candela, *Italy* 31 A8
Candelaria, *Argentina* . . . 127 B4
Candelaria, *Canary Is.* . . . 37 F3
Candeleda, *Spain* 34 E5
Candelo, *Australia* 95 F4
Candia = Iráklion, *Greece* . 36 D7
Candia, Sea of = Crete, Sea
   of, *Greece* 39 E7
Candle L., *Canada* 105 C7
Candlemas I., *Antarctica* . . 5 B1
Candon, *Phil.* 61 C4
Canea = Khaniá, *Greece* . . 36 D6
Canelli, *Italy* 28 D5
Canelones, *Uruguay* 127 C4
Canet-Plage, *France* 20 F7
Canete, *Chile* 126 D1
Cañete, *Peru* 124 F3
Cañete, *Spain* 32 E3
Cañete de las Torres, *Spain* 35 H6
Cangas, *Spain* 34 C2
Cangas de Narcea, *Spain* . 34 B4
Cangas de Onís, *Spain* . . . 34 B5
Cangnan, *China* 59 D13
Canguaretama, *Brazil* . . . 125 E11
Canguçu, *Brazil* 127 C5
Canguçu, Serra do, *Brazil* . 127 C5
Cangwu, *China* 59 F8
Cangxi, *China* 58 B5
Cangzhou, *China* 56 E9
Caniapiscau →, *Canada* . . 103 A6
Caniapiscau Rés. de, *Canada* 103 B6
Canicattì, *Italy* 30 E6
Canicattini Bagni, *Italy* . . 31 E8
Caniles, *Spain* 35 H8
Canim Lake, *Canada* 104 C4
Canindeyu □, *Paraguay* . . 127 A5
Canino, *Italy* 29 F8
Canisteo, *U.S.A.* 110 D7
Canisteo →, *U.S.A.* 110 D7
Cañitas, *Mexico* 118 C4
Cañizal, *Spain* 34 D5
Canjáyar, *Spain* 35 H8
Çankırı, *Turkey* 72 B5
Cankuzo, *Burundi* 86 C3
Canmore, *Canada* 104 C5
Cann River, *Australia* 95 F4
Canna, *U.K.* 14 D2
Cannanore, *India* 66 P9
Cannes, *France* 21 E11
Canning Town = Port
   Canning, *India* 69 H13
Cannington, *Canada* 110 B5
Cannóbio, *Italy* 28 B5
Cannock, *U.K.* 13 E5
Cannon Ball →, *U.S.A.* . . . 112 B4
Cannondale Mt., *Australia* . 94 D4
Cannonsville Reservoir,
   U.S.A. 111 D9
Cannonvale, *Australia* . . . 94 C4
Canoas, *Brazil* 127 B5
Canoe L., *Canada* 105 B7
Canon City, *U.S.A.* 112 F2
Canora, *Canada* 105 C8
Canosa di Púglia, *Italy* . . . 31 A9
Canowindra, *Australia* . . . 95 E4
Canso, *Canada* 103 C7
Cantabria □, *Spain* 34 B7
Cantabria, Sierra de, *Spain* . 32 C2
Cantabrian Mts. =
   Cantábrica, Cordillera,
   Spain 34 C5
Cantábrica, Cordillera, *Spain* 34 C5
Cantal □, *France* 20 C6
Cantal, Plomb du, *France* . 20 C6
Cantanhede, *Portugal* . . . 34 E2
Cantavieja, *Spain* 32 E4
Čantavir, *Serbia, Yug.* . . . 42 E4
Cantemir, *Moldova* 43 D13
Canterbury, *Australia* 94 D3
Canterbury, *U.K.* 13 F9
Canterbury □, *N.Z.* 91 K3
Canterbury Bight, *N.Z.* . . . 91 L3
Canterbury Plains, *N.Z.* . . 91 K3
Cantil, *U.S.A.* 117 K9

Cantillana, *Spain* 35 H5
Canton = Guangzhou, *China* 59 F9
Canton, *Ga., U.S.A.* 109 H3
Canton, *Ill., U.S.A.* 112 E9
Canton, *Miss., U.S.A.* 113 J9
Canton, *Mo., U.S.A.* 112 E9
Canton, *N.Y., U.S.A.* 111 B9
Canton, *Ohio, U.S.A.* 110 F3
Canton, *Pa., U.S.A.* 110 E8
Canton, *S. Dak., U.S.A.* . . 112 D6
Canton L., *U.S.A.* 113 G5
Cantù, *Italy* 28 C6
Canudos, *Brazil* 124 E7
Canumã →, *Brazil* 124 D7
Canutama, *Brazil* 124 E6
Canutillo, *U.S.A.* 115 L10
Canvey, *U.K.* 13 F8
Canyon, *U.S.A.* 113 H4
Canyonlands National Park,
   U.S.A. 115 G9
Canyonville, *U.S.A.* 114 E2
Cao Bang, *Vietnam* 58 F6
Cao He →, *China* 57 D13
Cao Lanh, *Vietnam* 65 G5
Cao Xian, *China* 56 G8
Cáorle, *Italy* 29 C9
Cap-aux-Meules, *Canada* . . 103 C7
Cap-Chat, *Canada* 103 C6
Cap-de-la-Madeleine,
   Canada 102 C5
Cap-Haïtien, *Haiti* 121 C5
Capac, *U.S.A.* 110 D2
Capáccio, *Italy* 31 B8
Capanaparo →, *Venezuela* . 124 B5
Capánnori, *Italy* 28 E7
Capbreton, *France* 20 E2
Capdenac, *France* 20 D6
Capdepera, *Spain* 32 F8
Cape →, *Australia* 94 C4
Cape Barren I., *Australia* . . 94 G4
Cape Breton Highlands Nat.
   Park, *Canada* 103 C7
Cape Breton I., *Canada* . . . 103 C7
Cape Charles, *U.S.A.* 108 G8
Cape Coast, *Ghana* 83 D4
Cape Coral, *U.S.A.* 109 M5
Cape Dorset, *Canada* 101 B12
Cape Fear →, *U.S.A.* 109 H6
Cape Girardeau, *U.S.A.* . . . 113 G10
Cape May, *U.S.A.* 108 F8
Cape May Point, *U.S.A.* . . 108 F8
Cape Province, *S. Africa* . . 85 L3
Cape Tormentine, *Canada* . 103 C7
Cape Town, *S. Africa* 88 E2
Cape Verde Is. ■, *Atl. Oc.* . 77 E1
Cape Vincent, *U.S.A.* 111 B8
Cape York Peninsula,
   Australia 94 A3
Capela, *Brazil* 125 F11
Capella, *Australia* 94 C4
Capendu, *France* 20 E6
Capestang, *France* 20 E7
Capim →, *Brazil* 125 D9
Capistrello, *Italy* 29 G10
Capitan, *U.S.A.* 115 K11
Capitol Reef National Park,
   U.S.A. 115 G8
Capitola, *U.S.A.* 116 J5
Capizzi, *Italy* 31 E7
Capoche →, *Mozam.* 87 F3
Capoterra, *Italy* 30 C1
Cappadocia, *Turkey* 72 C6
Capraia, *Italy* 28 E6
Caprara, Pta., *Italy* 30 A1
Caprarola, *Italy* 29 F9
Capreol, *Canada* 102 C3
Caprera, *Italy* 30 A2
Capri, *Italy* 31 B7
Capricorn Group, *Australia* 94 C5
Capricorn Ra., *Australia* . . 92 D2
Caprino Veronese, *Italy* . . 28 C7
Caprivi Strip, *Namibia* . . . 88 B3
Captain's Flat, *Australia* . . 95 F4
Captieux, *France* 20 D3
Caquetá →, *Colombia* . . . 122 D4
Caracal, *Romania* 43 F9
Caracas, *Venezuela* 124 A5
Caracol,
   *Mato Grosso do Sul,
   Brazil* 126 A4
Caracol, *Piauí, Brazil* 125 E10
Caráglio, *Italy* 28 D4
Carajas, *Brazil* 125 E8
Carajás, Serra dos, *Brazil* . 125 E8
Carangola, *Brazil* 127 A7
Caransebeş, *Romania* . . . 42 E7
Carantec, *France* 18 D3
Caraquet, *Canada* 103 C6
Caras, *Peru* 124 E3
Caraş Severin □, *Romania* . 42 E7
Caraşova, *Romania* 42 E6
Caratasca, L., *Honduras* . . 120 C3
Caratinga, *Brazil* 125 G10
Caraúbas, *Brazil* 125 E11
Caravaca = Caravaca de la
   Cruz, *Spain* 33 G3
Caravaca de la Cruz, *Spain* . 33 G3
Caravággio, *Italy* 28 C6
Caravela, *Guinea-Biss.* . . . 82 C1
Caravelas, *Brazil* 125 G11
Caraveli, *Peru* 124 G4
Caràzinho, *Brazil* 127 B5
Carballino = O Carballiño,
   Spain 34 C2
Carballo, *Spain* 34 B2
Carberry, *Canada* 105 D9
Carbó, *Mexico* 118 B2
Carbonara, C., *Italy* 30 C2
Carbondale, *Colo., U.S.A.* . 114 G10
Carbondale, *Ill., U.S.A.* . . . 113 G10

Carbondale, *Pa., U.S.A.* . . 111 E9
Carbonear, *Canada* 103 C9
Carboneras, *Spain* 33 J3
Carboneras de Guadazón,
   Spain 32 F3
Carbónia, *Italy* 30 C1
Carcabuey, *Spain* 35 H6
Carcagente = Carcaixent,
   Spain 33 F4
Carcaixent, *Spain* 33 F4
Carcajou, *Canada* 104 B5
Carcar, *Phil.* 61 F5
Carcarana →, *Argentina* . . 126 C3
Carcasse, C., *Haiti* 121 C5
Carcassonne, *France* 20 E6
Carcross, *Canada* 104 A2
Çardak, *Çanakkale, Turkey* . 41 F10
Çardak, *Denizli, Turkey* . . 39 D11
Cardamon Hills, *India* . . . 66 Q10
Cardeña, *Spain* 35 G6
Cárdenas, *Cuba* 120 B3
Cárdenas, *San Luis Potosí,
   Mexico* 119 C5
Cárdenas, *Tabasco, Mexico* 119 D6
Cardenete, *Spain* 32 F3
Cardiff, *U.K.* 13 F4
Cardiff □, *U.K.* 13 F4
Cardiff-by-the-Sea, *U.S.A.* . 117 M9
Cardigan, *U.K.* 13 E3
Cardigan B., *U.K.* 13 E3
Cardinal, *Canada* 111 B9
Cardona, *Spain* 32 D6
Cardona, *Uruguay* 126 C4
Cardoner →, *Spain* 32 D6
Cardoso, Ilha do, *Brazil* . . 127 B5
Cardston, *Canada* 104 D6
Cardwell, *Australia* 94 B4
Careen L., *Canada* 105 B7
Carei, *Romania* 42 C7
Careme = Ciremai,
   Indonesia 63 G13
Carentan, *France* 18 C5
Carey, *U.S.A.* 114 E7
Carey, L., *Australia* 93 E3
Carey L., *Canada* 105 A8
Careysburg, *Liberia* 82 D2
Cargèse, *France* 21 F12
Carhaix-Plouguer, *France* . 18 D3
Carhué, *Argentina* 126 D3
Caria, *Turkey* 39 D10
Cariacica, *Brazil* 125 H10
Cariati, *Italy* 31 C9
Caribbean Sea, *W. Indies* . 121 D5
Cariboo Mts., *Canada* 104 C4
Caribou, *U.S.A.* 109 B12
Caribou →, *Man., Canada* . 105 B10
Caribou →, *N.W.T.,
   Canada* 104 A3
Caribou I., *Canada* 102 C2
Caribou Is., *Canada* 104 A6
Caribou L., *Man., Canada* . 105 B9
Caribou L., *Ont., Canada* . 102 B2
Caribou Mts., *Canada* . . . 104 B5
Carichic, *Mexico* 118 B3
Carigara, *Phil.* 61 F6
Carignan, *France* 19 C12
Carignano, *Italy* 28 D4
Carillo, *Mexico* 118 B4
Carinda, *Australia* 95 E4
Cariñena, *Spain* 32 D3
Carinhanha, *Brazil* 125 F10
Carinhanha →, *Brazil* 125 F10
Carini, *Italy* 30 D6
Cariño, *Spain* 34 B3
Carínola, *Italy* 30 A6
Carinthia = Kärnten □,
   Austria 26 E6
Caripito, *Venezuela* 124 A6
Carlet, *Spain* 33 F4
Carleton, Mt., *Canada* . . . 103 C6
Carleton Place, *Canada* . . 102 C4
Carletonville, *S. Africa* . . . 88 D4
Cârlibaba, *Romania* 43 C10
Carlin, *U.S.A.* 114 F5
Carlingford L., *U.K.* 15 B5
Carlinville, *U.S.A.* 112 F10
Carlisle, *U.K.* 12 C5
Carlisle, *U.S.A.* 110 F7
Carlit, Pic, *France* 20 F5
Carloforte, *Italy* 30 C1
Carlos Casares, *Argentina* . 126 D3
Carlos Tejedor, *Argentina* . 126 D3
Carlow, *Ireland* 15 D5
Carlow □, *Ireland* 15 D5
Carlsbad, *Calif., U.S.A.* . . . 117 M9
Carlsbad, *N. Mex., U.S.A.* . 113 J2
Carlsbad Caverns National
   Park, *U.S.A.* 113 J2
Carluke, *U.K.* 14 F5
Carlyle, *Canada* 105 D8
Carmacks, *Canada* 100 B6
Carmagnola, *Italy* 28 D4
Carman, *Canada* 105 D9
Carmarthen, *U.K.* 13 F3
Carmarthen B., *U.K.* 13 F3
Carmarthenshire □, *U.K.* . 13 F3
Carmaux, *France* 20 D6
Carmel, *U.S.A.* 111 E11
Carmel-by-the-Sea, *U.S.A.* . 116 J5
Carmel Valley, *U.S.A.* 116 J5
Carmelo, *Uruguay* 126 C4
Carmen, *Colombia* 124 B3
Carmen, *Paraguay* 127 B4
Carmen →, *Mexico* 118 A3
Carmen, I., *Mexico* 118 B2
Carmen de Patagones,
   Argentina 128 E4
Cármenes, *Spain* 34 C5
Carmensa, *Argentina* 126 D2

Carmi, Canada 104 D5
Carmi, U.S.A. 108 F1
Carmichael, U.S.A. 116 G5
Carmila, Australia 94 C4
Carmona, Costa Rica 120 E2
Carmona, Spain 35 H5
Carn Ban, U.K. 14 D4
Carn Eige, U.K. 14 D3
Carnamah, Australia 93 E2
Carnarvon, Australia 93 D1
Carnarvon, S. Africa 88 E3
Carnarvon Ra., Queens., Australia 94 D4
Carnarvon Ra., W. Austral., Australia 93 E3
Carnation, U.S.A. 116 C5
Carndonagh, Ireland 15 A4
Carnduff, Canada 105 D8
Carnegie, U.S.A. 110 C4
Carnegie, L., Australia 93 E3
Carnic Alps = Karnische Alpen, Europe 26 E6
Carniche Alpi = Karnische Alpen, Europe 26 E6
Carnot, C.A.R. 84 D3
Carnot, C., Australia 95 E2
Carnot B., Australia 92 C3
Carnoustie, U.K. 14 E5
Carnsore Pt., Ireland 15 D5
Caro, U.S.A. 108 D4
Carol City, U.S.A. 109 N5
Carolina, Brazil 125 E9
Carolina, Puerto Rico 121 C6
Carolina, S. Africa 89 D5
Caroline I., Kiribati 97 H12
Caroline Is., Micronesia 52 J17
Caroni →, Venezuela 124 B6
Caronie = Nébrodi, Monti, Italy 31 E7
Caroona, Australia 95 E5
Carpathians, Europe 6 F10
Carpații Meridionali, Romania 43 E9
Carpentaria, G. of, Australia 94 A2
Carpentras, France 21 D9
Carpi, Italy 28 D7
Cărpineni, Moldova 43 D13
Carpinteria, U.S.A. 117 L7
Carpio, Spain 34 D5
Carr Boyd Ra., Australia 92 C4
Carrabelle, U.S.A. 109 L3
Carral, Spain 34 B2
Carranza, Presa V., Mexico 118 B4
Carrara, Italy 28 D7
Carrascal, Phil. 61 G6
Carrascosa del Campo, Spain 32 E2
Carrauntoohill, Ireland 15 D2
Carrick-on-Shannon, Ireland 15 C3
Carrick-on-Suir, Ireland 15 D4
Carrickfergus, U.K. 15 B6
Carrickmacross, Ireland 15 B5
Carrieton, Australia 95 E2
Carrington, U.S.A. 112 B5
Carrión →, Spain 34 D6
Carrión de los Condes, Spain 34 C6
Carrizal Bajo, Chile 126 B1
Carrizalillo, Chile 126 B1
Carrizo Cr. →, U.S.A. 113 G3
Carrizo Springs, U.S.A. 113 L5
Carrizozo, U.S.A. 115 K11
Carroll, U.S.A. 112 D7
Carrollton, Ga., U.S.A. 109 J3
Carrollton, Ill., U.S.A. 112 F9
Carrollton, Ky., U.S.A. 108 F3
Carrollton, Mo., U.S.A. 112 F8
Carrollton, Ohio, U.S.A. 110 F3
Carron →, U.K. 14 D4
Carron, L., U.K. 14 D3
Carrot →, Canada 105 C8
Carrot River, Canada 105 C8
Carrouges, France 18 D6
Carrù, Italy 28 D4
Carruthers, Canada 105 C7
Carsa Dek, Ethiopia 81 F4
Çarşamba, Turkey 72 B7
Carsóli, Italy 29 F10
Carson, Calif., U.S.A. 117 M8
Carson, N. Dak., U.S.A. 112 B4
Carson →, U.S.A. 116 F8
Carson City, U.S.A. 116 F7
Carson Sink, U.S.A. 114 G4
Cartagena, Colombia 124 A3
Cartagena, Spain 33 H4
Cartago, Colombia 124 C3
Cartago, Costa Rica 120 E3
Cártama, Spain 35 J6
Cartaxo, Portugal 35 F2
Cartaya, Spain 35 H3
Carterton, N.Z. 91 J5
Carthage, Tunisia 30 F4
Carthage, Ill., U.S.A. 112 E9
Carthage, Mo., U.S.A. 113 G7
Carthage, N.Y., U.S.A. 108 D8
Carthage, Tex., U.S.A. 113 J7
Cartier I., Australia 92 B3
Cartwright, Canada 103 B8
Caruaru, Brazil 125 E11
Carúpano, Venezuela 124 A6
Caruthersville, U.S.A. 113 G10
Carvin, France 19 B9
Carvoeiro, Brazil 124 D6
Carvoeiro, C., Portugal 35 F1
Cary, U.S.A. 109 H6
Casa Branca, Portugal 35 G2
Casa Grande, U.S.A. 115 K8
Casablanca, Chile 126 C1
Casablanca, Morocco 78 B4
Casacalenda, Italy 29 G11
Casalbordino, Italy 29 F11
Casale Monferrato, Italy 28 C5

Casalmaggiore, Italy 28 D7
Casalpusterlengo, Italy 28 C6
Casamance →, Senegal 82 C1
Casarano, Italy 31 B11
Casares, Spain 35 J5
Casas Ibáñez, Spain 33 F3
Casasimarro, Spain 33 F2
Casatejada, Spain 34 F5
Casavieja, Spain 34 E6
Cascade, Idaho, U.S.A. 114 D5
Cascade, Mont., U.S.A. 114 C8
Cascade Locks, U.S.A. 116 E5
Cascade Ra., U.S.A. 116 D5
Cascade Reservoir, U.S.A. 114 D5
Cascais, Portugal 35 G1
Cascavel, Brazil 127 A5
Cáscina, Italy 28 E7
Casco B., U.S.A. 109 D10
Caselle Torinese, Italy 28 C4
Caserta, Italy 31 A7
Cashel, Ireland 15 D4
Casiguran, Phil. 61 C5
Casilda, Argentina 126 C3
Casimcea, Romania 43 F13
Casino, Australia 95 D5
Casiquiare →, Venezuela 124 C5
Čáslav, Czech Rep. 26 B8
Casma, Peru 124 E3
Casmalia, U.S.A. 117 L6
Cásola Valsénio, Italy 29 D8
Cásoli, Italy 29 F11
Caspe, Spain 32 D4
Casper, U.S.A. 114 E10
Caspian Depression, Eurasia 49 G9
Caspian Sea, Eurasia 50 E6
Cass Lake, U.S.A. 112 B7
Cassà de la Selva, Spain 32 D7
Cassadaga, U.S.A. 110 D5
Cassano allo Iónio, Italy 31 C9
Casse, Grande, France 21 C10
Cassel, France 19 B9
Casselman, Canada 111 A9
Casselton, U.S.A. 112 B6
Cassiar, Canada 104 B3
Cassiar Mts., Canada 104 B2
Cassino, Italy 30 A6
Cassis, France 21 E9
Cassville, U.S.A. 113 G8
Castagneto Carducci, Italy 28 E7
Castaic, U.S.A. 117 L8
Castalia, U.S.A. 110 E2
Castanhal, Brazil 125 D9
Castéggio, Italy 28 C6
Castejón de Monegros, Spain 32 D4
Castèl di Sangro, Italy 29 G11
Castèl San Giovanni, Italy 28 C6
Castèl San Pietro Terme, Italy 29 D8
Castelbuono, Italy 31 E7
Castelfidardo, Italy 29 E10
Castelfiorentino, Italy 28 E7
Castelfranco Emília, Italy 28 D8
Castelfranco Véneto, Italy 29 C8
Casteljaloux, France 20 D4
Castellabate, Italy 31 B7
Castellammare, G. di, Italy 30 D5
Castellammare del Golfo, Italy 30 D5
Castellammare di Stábia, Italy 31 B7
Castellamonte, Italy 28 C4
Castellane, France 21 E10
Castellaneta, Italy 31 B9
Castelli, Argentina 126 D4
Castelló de la Plana, Spain 32 F4
Castellote, Spain 32 E4
Castelmáuro, Italy 29 G11
Castelnau-de-Médoc, France 20 C3
Castelnau-Magnoac, France 20 E4
Castelnaudary, France 20 E5
Castelnovo ne' Monti, Italy 28 D7
Castelnuovo di Val di Cécina, Italy 28 E7
Castelo, Brazil 127 A7
Castelo Branco, Portugal 34 F3
Castelo Branco □, Portugal 34 F3
Castelo de Paiva, Portugal 34 D2
Castelo de Vide, Portugal 35 F3
Castelsardo, Italy 30 B1
Castelsarrasin, France 20 D5
Casteltérmini, Italy 30 E6
Castelvetrano, Italy 30 E5
Casterton, Australia 95 F3
Castets, France 20 E2
Castiglion Fiorentino, Italy 29 E8
Castiglione del Lago, Italy 29 E9
Castiglione della Pescáia, Italy 28 F7
Castiglione delle Stiviere, Italy 28 C7
Castilblanco, Spain 35 F5
Castile, U.S.A. 110 D6
Castilla, Playa de, Spain 35 J4
Castilla y Leon □, Spain 34 D6
Castillo de Locubín, Spain 35 H7
Castillon-en-Couserans, France 20 F5
Castillonès, France 20 D4
Castillos, Uruguay 127 C5
Castle Dale, U.S.A. 114 G8
Castle Douglas, U.K. 14 G5
Castle Rock, Colo., U.S.A. 112 F2
Castle Rock, Wash., U.S.A. 116 D4
Castlebar, Ireland 15 C2
Castleblaney, Ireland 15 B5
Castlederg, U.K. 15 B4
Castleford, U.K. 12 D6
Castlegar, Canada 104 D5

Castlemaine, Australia 95 F3
Castlepollard, Ireland 15 C4
Castlerea, Ireland 15 C3
Castlereagh →, Australia 95 E4
Castlereagh B., Australia 94 A2
Castleton, U.S.A. 111 C11
Castletown, U.K. 12 C3
Castletown Bearhaven, Ireland 15 E2
Castor, Canada 104 C6
Castor →, Canada 102 B4
Castorland, U.S.A. 111 C9
Castres, France 20 E6
Castricum, Neths. 17 B4
Castril, Spain 35 H8
Castro, Brazil 127 A6
Castro, Chile 128 E2
Castro Alves, Brazil 125 F11
Castro del Río, Spain 35 H6
Castro-Urdiales, Spain 34 B7
Castro Verde, Portugal 35 H2
Castrojeriz, Spain 34 C6
Castropol, Spain 34 B4
Castroreale, Italy 31 D8
Castrovíllari, Italy 31 C9
Castroville, U.S.A. 116 J5
Castuera, Spain 35 G5
Çat, Turkey 73 C9
Cat Ba, Dao, Vietnam 64 B6
Cat I., Bahamas 121 B4
Cat L., Canada 102 B1
Cat Lake, Canada 102 B1
Čata, Slovak Rep. 27 D11
Catacamas, Honduras 120 D2
Cataguases, Brazil 127 A7
Çatak, Turkey 73 C10
Catalão, Brazil 125 G9
Çatalca, Turkey 41 E12
Catalina, Canada 103 C9
Catalina, Chile 126 B2
Catalina, U.S.A. 115 K8
Catalonia = Cataluña □, Spain 32 D6
Cataluña □, Spain 32 D6
Çatalzeytin, Turkey 72 B6
Catamarca, Argentina 126 B2
Catamarca □, Argentina 126 B2
Catanauan, Phil. 61 E5
Catanduanes □, Phil. 61 E6
Catanduva, Brazil 127 A6
Catánia, Italy 31 E8
Catánia, G. di, Italy 31 E8
Catanzaro, Italy 31 D9
Catarman, Phil. 61 E6
Catbalogan, Phil. 61 F6
Cateel, Phil. 61 H7
Catembe, Mozam. 89 D5
Caterham, U.K. 13 F7
Cathcart, S. Africa 88 E4
Cathlamet, U.S.A. 116 D3
Catio, Guinea-Biss. 82 C1
Catlettsburg, U.S.A. 108 F4
Çatma Daği, Turkey 39 C11
Catoche, C., Mexico 119 C7
Cátria, Mte., Italy 29 E9
Catriló, Argentina 126 D3
Catrimani, Brazil 124 C6
Catrimani →, Brazil 124 C6
Catskill, U.S.A. 111 D11
Catskill Mts., U.S.A. 111 D10
Catt, Mt., Australia 94 A1
Cattaraugus, U.S.A. 110 D6
Cattólica, Italy 29 E9
Cattólica Eraclea, Italy 30 E6
Catuala, Angola 88 B2
Catuane, Mozam. 89 D5
Catur, Mozam. 87 E4
Catwick Is., Vietnam 65 G7
Cauca →, Colombia 124 B4
Caucaia, Brazil 125 D11
Caucasus Mountains, Eurasia 49 J7
Caudry, France 19 B10
Caulnes, France 18 D4
Caulónia, Italy 31 D9
Caungula, Angola 84 F3
Cauquenes, Chile 126 D1
Caura →, Venezuela 124 B6
Cauresi →, Mozam. 87 F3
Cauterets, France 20 F3
Cauvery →, India 66 P11
Caux, Pays de, France 18 C7
Cava de' Tirreni, Italy 31 B7
Cávado →, Portugal 34 D2
Cavaillon, France 21 E9
Cavalaire-sur-Mer, France 21 E10
Cavalese, Italy 29 B8
Cavalier, U.S.A. 112 A6
Cavalla = Cavally →, Africa 82 E3
Cavalleria, C. de, Spain 37 A11
Cavallo, I. de, France 21 G13
Cavan, Ireland 15 B4
Cavan □, Ireland 15 C4
Cavárzere, Italy 29 C9
Çavdarhisar, Turkey 39 B11
Çavdır, Turkey 39 D11
Cave Creek, U.S.A. 115 K7
Cavenagh Ra., Australia 93 E4
Cavendish, Australia 95 F3
Caviana, I., Brazil 125 C8
Cavite, Phil. 61 D4
Cavnic, Romania 43 C8
Cavour, Italy 28 D4
Cavtat, Croatia 40 D7
Cawndilla L., Australia 95 E3

Cawnpore = Kanpur, India 69 F9
Caxias, Brazil 125 D10
Caxias do Sul, Brazil 127 B5
Çay, Turkey 72 C4
Cay Sal Bank, Bahamas 120 B4
Cayambe, Ecuador 124 C3
Çaycuma, Turkey 72 B5
Çayeli, Turkey 73 B9
Cayenne, Fr. Guiana 125 B8
Caygören Baraji, Turkey 39 B10
Cayiralan, Turkey 72 C6
Caylus, France 20 D5
Cayman Brac, Cayman Is. 120 C4
Cayman Is. ■, W. Indies 120 C3
Cayo Romano, Cuba 120 B4
Cayres, France 20 D7
Cazalla de la Sierra, Spain 35 H5
Căzănești, Romania 43 F12
Cazaubon, France 20 E3
Cazaux et de Sanguinet, Étang de, France 20 D2
Cazenovia, U.S.A. 111 D9
Cazères, France 20 E5
Cazin, Bos.-H. 29 D12
Cazombo, Angola 85 G4
Cazorla, Spain 35 H7
Cazorla, Sierra de, Spain 35 G8
Cea →, Spain 34 C5
Ceamurlia de Jos, Romania 43 F13
Ceanannus Mor, Ireland 15 C5
Ceará = Fortaleza, Brazil 125 D11
Ceará □, Brazil 125 E11
Ceará Mirim, Brazil 125 E11
Ceauru, L., Romania 43 F8
Cebaco, I. de, Panama 120 E3
Cebollar, Argentina 126 B2
Cebollera, Sierra de, Spain 32 C2
Cebreros, Spain 34 E6
Cebu, Phil. 61 F5
Čečava, Bos.-H. 42 F2
Ceccano, Italy 30 A6
Cece, Hungary 42 D3
Cechi, Ivory C. 82 D4
Cécina, Italy 28 E7
Cécina →, Italy 28 E7
Ceclavín, Spain 34 F4
Cedar →, U.S.A. 112 E9
Cedar City, U.S.A. 115 H7
Cedar Creek Reservoir, U.S.A. 113 J6
Cedar Falls, Iowa, U.S.A. 112 D8
Cedar Falls, Wash., U.S.A. 116 C5
Cedar L., Canada 105 C9
Cedar Rapids, U.S.A. 112 E9
Cedartown, U.S.A. 109 H3
Cedarvale, Canada 104 B3
Cedarville, S. Africa 89 E4
Cedeira, Spain 34 B2
Cedral, Mexico 118 C4
Cedrino →, Italy 30 B2
Cedro, Brazil 125 E11
Cedros, I. de, Mexico 118 B1
Ceduna, Australia 95 E1
Cefalù, Italy 31 D7
Cega →, Spain 34 D6
Cegléd, Hungary 42 C4
Céglie Messápico, Italy 31 B10
Cehegín, Spain 33 G3
Cehu-Silvaniei, Romania 43 C8
Ceica, Romania 42 D7
Ceira →, Portugal 34 E2
Čelákovice, Czech Rep. 26 A7
Celano, Italy 29 F10
Celanova, Spain 34 C3
Čelić, Bos.-H. 42 F3
Celina, U.S.A. 108 E3
Celinac, Bos.-H. 42 F2
Celje, Slovenia 29 B12
Celldömölk, Hungary 42 C2
Celle, Germany 24 C6
Celorico da Beira, Portugal 34 E3
Çeltikçi, Turkey 39 D12
Çemişgezek, Turkey 73 C8
Cenderwasih, Teluk, Indonesia 63 E9
Cengong, China 58 D7
Ceno →, Italy 28 D7
Centallo, Italy 28 D4
Centelles, Spain 32 D7
Center, N. Dak., U.S.A. 112 B4
Center, Tex., U.S.A. 113 K7
Centerburg, U.S.A. 110 F2
Centerville, Calif., U.S.A. 116 J7
Centerville, Iowa, U.S.A. 112 E8
Centerville, Pa., U.S.A. 110 F5
Centerville, Tenn., U.S.A. 109 H2
Centerville, Tex., U.S.A. 113 K7
Cento, Italy 29 D8
Central □, Ghana 83 D4
Central □, Kenya 86 C4
Central □, Malawi 87 E3
Central □, Zambia 87 E2
Central, Cordillera, Colombia 122 C3
Central, Cordillera, Costa Rica 120 D3
Central, Cordillera, Dom. Rep. 121 C5
Central, Cordillera, Phil. 61 C4
Central African Rep. ■, Africa 84 C4

Central America, America 98 H11
Central Butte, Canada 105 C7
Central City, Colo., U.S.A. 114 G11
Central City, Ky., U.S.A. 108 G2
Central City, Nebr., U.S.A. 112 E6
Central I., Kenya 86 B4
Central Makran Range, Pakistan 66 F4
Central Patricia, Canada 102 B1
Central Point, U.S.A. 114 E2
Central Russian Uplands, Europe 6 E13
Central Siberian Plateau, Russia 52 C14
Central Square, U.S.A. 111 C8
Centralia, Ill., U.S.A. 112 F10
Centralia, Mo., U.S.A. 112 F8
Centralia, Wash., U.S.A. 116 D4
Cenxi, China 59 F8
Ceotina →, Bos.-H. 40 C2
Cephalonia = Kefalliniá, Greece 38 C2
Čepin, Croatia 42 E3
Ceprano, Italy 30 A6
Ceptura, Romania 43 E11
Cepu, Indonesia 63 G14
Ceram = Seram, Indonesia 63 E7
Ceram Sea = Seram Sea, Indonesia 63 E7
Cerbère, France 20 F7
Cerbicales, Is., France 21 G13
Cercal, Portugal 35 H2
Cerdaña, Spain 32 C6
Cère →, France 20 D5
Cerea, Italy 29 C8
Ceredigion □, U.K. 13 E3
Ceres, Argentina 126 B3
Ceres, S. Africa 88 E2
Ceres, U.S.A. 116 H6
Céret, France 20 F6
Cergy, France 19 C9
Cerignola, Italy 31 A8
Cerigo = Kíthira, Greece 38 E5
Cérilly, France 19 F9
Cerisiers, France 19 D10
Cerizay, France 18 F6
Çerkeş, Turkey 72 B5
Çerkezköy, Turkey 41 E12
Cerknica, Slovenia 29 C11
Cerkovica, Bulgaria 41 C8
Cermenika, Serbia, Yug. 40 C4
Çermik, Turkey 73 C8
Cerna, Romania 43 E13
Cerna →, Romania 43 F8
Cernavodă, Romania 43 F13
Cernay, France 19 E14
Cernik, Croatia 42 E2
Cerralvo, I., Mexico 118 C3
Cërrik, Albania 40 E3
Cerritos, Mexico 118 C4
Cerro Chato, Uruguay 127 C4
Certaldo, Italy 28 E8
Cervaro →, Italy 31 A8
Cervati, Monte, Italy 31 B8
Cervantes, Australia 93 F2
Cervera, Spain 32 D6
Cervera de Pisuerga, Spain 34 C6
Cervera del Río Alhama, Spain 32 C3
Cervéteri, Italy 29 F9
Cérvia, Italy 29 D9
Cervignano del Friuli, Italy 29 C10
Cervinara, Italy 31 A7
Cervione, France 21 F13
Cervo, Spain 34 B3
Cesena, Italy 29 D9
Cesenático, Italy 29 D9
Cēsis, Latvia 9 H21
Česká Lípa, Czech Rep. 26 A7
Česká Třebová, Czech Rep. 27 B9
České Budějovice, Czech Rep. 26 C7
České Velenice, Czech Rep. 26 C7
Českomoravská Vrchovina, Czech Rep. 26 B8
Český Brod, Czech Rep. 26 A7
Český Krumlov, Czech Rep. 26 C7
Český Těšín, Czech Rep. 27 B11
Česma →, Croatia 29 C13
Çeşme, Turkey 39 C8
Cessnock, Australia 95 E5
Cesson-Sévigné, France 18 D5
Cestas, France 20 D3
Cestos →, Liberia 82 D3
Cetate, Romania 42 F8
Cetin Grad, Croatia 29 C12
Cetina →, Croatia 29 E13
Cetinje, Montenegro, Yug. 40 D2
Cetraro, Italy 31 C8
Ceuta, N. Afr. 78 A4
Ceva, Italy 28 D5
Cévennes, France 20 D7
Ceyhan, Turkey 70 B2
Ceyhan →, Turkey 72 D6
Ceylânpinar, Turkey 73 D9
Ceylon = Sri Lanka ■, Asia 66 R12
Cèze →, France 21 D8
Cha-am, Thailand 64 F2
Cha Pa, Vietnam 64 A4
Chabanais, France 20 C4
Chabeuil, France 21 D9
Chablais, France 19 F13
Chablis, France 19 E10
Chacabuco, Argentina 126 C3
Chachapoyas, Peru 124 E3
Chachoengsao, Thailand 64 F3
Chachran, Pakistan 66 E7
Chachro, Pakistan 68 G4
Chaco □, Argentina 126 B3
Chaco □, Paraguay 126 B4

Chaco →, U.S.A. 115 H9
Chaco Austral, S. Amer. ... 128 B4
Chaco Boreal, S. Amer. ... 124 H6
Chaco Central, S. Amer. ... 128 A4
Chacon, C., U.S.A. 104 C2
Chad ■, Africa 79 E9
Chad, L. = Tchad, L., Chad 79 F8
Chadan, Russia 51 D10
Chadileuvú →, Argentina .. 126 D2
Chadiza, Zambia 87 E3
Chadron, U.S.A. 112 D3
Chadyr-Lunga = Ciadâr-
Lunga, Moldova 43 D13
Chae Hom, Thailand 64 C2
Chaem →, Thailand 64 C2
Chaeryŏng, N. Korea 57 E13
Chagai Hills, Afghan. 66 E3
Chagda, Russia 51 D14
Chagny, France 19 F11
Chagoda, Russia 46 C8
Chagos Arch., Ind. Oc 52 K11
Chagrin Falls, U.S.A. 110 E3
Chāh Ākhvor, Iran 71 C8
Chāh Bahār, Iran 71 E9
Chāh-e Kavīr, Iran 71 C8
Chahar Burjak, Afghan. ... 66 D3
Chahār Maḥāll va
Bakhtīarī □, Iran 71 C6
Chaibasa, India 67 H14
Chaillé-les-Marais, France .. 20 B2
Chainat, Thailand 64 E3
Chaiya, Thailand 65 H2
Chaj Doab, Pakistan 68 C5
Chajari, Argentina 126 C4
Chak Amru, Pakistan 68 C6
Chaka, Sudan 81 G3
Chakar →, Pakistan 68 E3
Chakari, Zimbabwe 89 B4
Chake Chake, Tanzania ... 86 D4
Chakhānsūr, Afghan. 66 D3
Chakonipau, L., Canada ... 103 A6
Chakradharpur, India 69 H11
Chakrata, India 68 D7
Chakwal, Pakistan 68 C5
Chala, Peru 124 G4
Chalais, France 20 C4
Chalchihuites, Mexico 118 C4
Chalcis = Khalkís, Greece . 38 C5
Châlette-sur-Loing, France . 19 D9
Chaleur B., Canada 103 C6
Chalfant, U.S.A. 116 H8
Chalhuanca, Peru 124 F4
Chalindrey, France 19 E12
Chaling, China 59 D9
Chalisgaon, India 66 J9
Chalk River, Canada 102 C4
Chalky Inlet, N.Z. 91 M1
Challans, France 18 F5
Challapata, Bolivia 124 G5
Challis, U.S.A. 114 D6
Chalmette, U.S.A. 113 L10
Chalon-sur-Saône, France . 19 F11
Chalonnes-sur-Loire, France 18 E6
Châlons-en-Champagne,
France 19 D11
Châlus, France 20 C4
Chalyaphum, Thailand 64 E4
Cham, Germany 25 F8
Cham, Cu Lao, Vietnam ... 64 E7
Chama, U.S.A. 115 H10
Chamaicó, Argentina 126 D3
Chaman, Pakistan 66 D5
Chamba, India 68 C7
Chamba, Tanzania 87 E4
Chambal →, India 69 F8
Chamberlain, U.S.A. 112 D5
Chamberlain →, Australia . 92 C4
Chamberlain L., U.S.A. ... 109 B11
Chambers, U.S.A. 115 J9
Chambersburg, U.S.A. 108 F7
Chambéry, France 21 C9
Chambeshi →, Zambia ... 84 G6
Chambly, Canada 111 A11
Chambord, Canada 103 C5
Chamboulive, France 20 C5
Chamchamal, Iraq 70 C5
Chamela, Mexico 118 D3
Chamical, Argentina 126 C2
Chamkar Luong, Cambodia 65 G4
Chamoli, India 69 D8
Chamonix-Mont Blanc,
France 21 C10
Chamouchouane →, Canada 102 C5
Champa, India 69 H10
Champagne, Canada 104 A1
Champagne, France 19 D11
Champagnole, France 19 F12
Champaign, U.S.A. 108 E1
Champassak, Laos 64 E5
Champaubert, France 19 D10
Champawat, India 69 E9
Champdeniers-St-Denis,
France 20 B3
Champdoré, L., Canada ... 103 A6
Champeix, France 20 C7
Champion, U.S.A. 110 E4
Champlain, U.S.A. 111 B11
Champlain, L., U.S.A. 111 B11
Champlitte, France 19 E12
Champotón, Mexico 119 D6
Champua, India 69 H11
Chamusca, Portugal 35 F2
Chana, Thailand 65 J3
Chañaral, Chile 126 B1
Chanārān, Iran 71 B8
Chanasma, India 68 H5
Chanco, Chile 126 D1
Chand, India 69 J8
Chandan, India 69 G12
Chandan Chauki, India ... 69 E9
Chandannagar, India 69 H13

Chandausi, India 69 E8
Chandeleur Is., U.S.A. 113 L10
Chandeleur Sd., U.S.A. ... 113 L10
Chandigarh, India 68 D7
Chandil, India 69 H12
Chandler, Australia 95 D1
Chandler, Canada 103 C7
Chandler, Ariz., U.S.A. ... 115 K8
Chandler, Okla., U.S.A. ... 113 H6
Chandod, India 68 J5
Chandpur, Bangla. 67 H17
Chandrapur, India 66 K11
Chānf, Iran 71 E9
Chang, Pakistan 68 F3
Chang, Ko, Thailand 65 F4
Ch'ang Chiang = Chang
Jiang →, China 59 B13
Chang Jiang →, China ... 59 B13
Changa, India 69 C7
Changanacheri, India 66 Q10
Changane →, Mozam. ... 89 C5
Changbai, China 57 D15
Changbai Shan, China ... 57 C15
Changchiak'ou =
Zhangjiakou, China 56 D8
Ch'angchou = Changzhou,
China 59 B12
Changchun, China 57 B13
Changchunling, China 57 B13
Changde, China 59 C8
Changdo-ri, N. Korea 57 E14
Changfeng, China 59 A11
Changhai = Shanghai, China 59 B13
Changhua, China 59 B12
Changhua, Taiwan 59 E13
Changhŭng, S. Korea 57 G14
Changhŭngni, N. Korea ... 57 D15
Changjiang, China 64 C7
Changjin, N. Korea 57 D14
Changjin-chŏsuji, N. Korea 57 D14
Changle, China 59 E12
Changli, China 57 E10
Changling, China 57 B12
Changlun, Malaysia 65 J3
Changning, Hunan, China . 59 D9
Changning, Sichuan, China 58 C5
Changning, Yunnan, China 58 E2
Changping, China 56 D9
Changsha, China 59 C9
Changshan, China 59 C12
Changshu, China 59 B13
Changshun, China 58 D6
Changtai, China 59 E11
Changting, China 59 E11
Changwu, China 56 G4
Changxing, China 59 B12
Changyang, China 59 B8
Changyi, China 57 F10
Changyŏn, N. Korea 57 E13
Changyuan, China 56 G8
Changzhi, China 56 F7
Changzhou, China 59 B12
Chanhanga, Angola 88 B1
Chanlar = Xanlar,
Azerbaijan 49 K8
Channapatna, India 66 N10
Channel Is., U.K. 13 H5
Channel Is., U.S.A. 117 M7
Channel Islands National
Park, U.S.A. 117 M8
Channel-Port aux Basques,
Canada 103 C8
Channel Tunnel, Europe .. 13 F9
Channing, U.S.A. 113 H3
Chantada, Spain 34 C3
Chanthaburi, Thailand ... 64 F4
Chantilly, France 19 C9
Chantonnay, France 18 F5
Chantrey Inlet, Canada ... 100 B10
Chanute, U.S.A. 113 G7
Chanza →, Spain 35 H3
Chao Hu, China 59 B11
Chao Phraya →, Thailand 64 F3
Chao Phraya Lowlands,
Thailand 64 E3
Chaocheng, China 56 F8
Chaohu, China 59 B11
Chaoyang, Guangdong,
China 59 F11
Chaoyang, Liaoning, China 57 D11
Chaozhou, China 59 F11
Chapais, Canada 102 C5
Chapala, Mozam. 87 F4
Chapala, L. de, Mexico ... 118 C4
Chapayev, Kazakstan 48 E10
Chapayevsk, Russia 48 D9
Chapecó, Brazil 127 B5
Chapel Hill, U.S.A. 109 H6
Chapleau, Canada 102 C3
Chaplin, Canada 105 C7
Chaplin L., Canada 105 C7
Chaplino, Ukraine 47 H9
Chaplygin, Russia 46 F11
Chappell, U.S.A. 112 E3
Chara, Russia 51 D12
Charadai, Argentina 126 B4
Charagua, Bolivia 124 G6
Charambirá, Punta,
Colombia 124 C3
Charaña, Bolivia 124 G5
Charantsavan, Armenia ... 49 K7
Charanwala, India 68 F5
Charcas, Argentina 126 B3
Charcas, Mexico 118 C4
Chard, U.K. 13 G5
Chardon, U.S.A. 110 E3
Chardzhou = Chärjew,
Turkmenistan 50 F7
Charente □, France 20 C4
Charente →, France 20 C2

Charente-Maritime □,
France 20 C3
Charente-du-Cher, France . 19 F9
Chari →, Chad 79 F8
Chārīkār, Afghan. 66 B6
Chariton →, U.S.A. 112 F8
Chārjew, Turkmenistan ... 50 F7
Charkhari, India 69 G8
Charkhi Dadri, India 68 E7
Charleroi, Belgium 17 D4
Charleroi, U.S.A. 110 F5
Charles, C., U.S.A. 108 G8
Charles City, U.S.A. 112 D8
Charles L., Canada 105 B6
Charles Town, U.S.A. 108 F7
Charleston, Ill., U.S.A. ... 108 F1
Charleston, Miss., U.S.A. . 113 H9
Charleston, Mo., U.S.A. .. 113 G10
Charleston, S.C., U.S.A. . 109 J6
Charleston, W. Va., U.S.A. 108 F5
Charleston L., Canada 111 B9
Charleston Peak, U.S.A. .. 117 J11
Charlestown, Ireland 15 C3
Charlestown, S. Africa ... 89 D4
Charlestown, Ind., U.S.A. 108 F3
Charlestown, N.H., U.S.A. 111 C12
Charleville = Rath Luirc,
Ireland 15 D3
Charleville, Australia 95 D4
Charleville-Mézières, France 19 C11
Charlevoix, U.S.A. 108 C3
Charlieu, France 19 F11
Charlotte, Mich., U.S.A. . 108 D3
Charlotte, N.C., U.S.A. .. 109 H5
Charlotte, Vt., U.S.A. ... 111 B11
Charlotte Amalie, Virgin Is. 121 C7
Charlotte Harbor, U.S.A. . 109 M4
Charlotte L., Canada 104 C3
Charlottenberg, Sweden .. 10 E6
Charlottesville, U.S.A. ... 108 F6
Charlottetown, Nfld.,
Canada 103 B8
Charlottetown, P.E.I.,
Canada 103 C7
Charlton, Australia 95 F3
Charlton, U.S.A. 112 E7
Charlton I., Canada 102 B4
Charmes, France 19 D13
Charny, Canada 103 C5
Charolles, France 19 F11
Charouine, Algeria 78 C5
Charre, Mozam. 87 F4
Charroux, France 20 B4
Charsadda, Pakistan 68 B4
Charters Towers, Australia 94 C4
Chartres, France 18 D8
Chascomús, Argentina ... 126 D4
Chasefu, Zambia 87 E3
Chashma Barrage, Pakistan 68 C4
Chasseneuil-sur-Bonnieure,
France 20 C4
Chât, Iran 71 B7
Chatal Balkan = Udvoy
Balkan, Bulgaria 41 D10
Château-Arnoux, France .. 21 D10
Château-Chinon, France .. 19 E10
Château-d'Olonne, France . 20 B2
Château-du-Loir, France .. 18 E7
Château-la-Vallière, France 18 E7
Château-Landon, France .. 19 D9
Château-Renault, France .. 18 E7
Château-Salins, France ... 19 D13
Château-Thierry, France .. 19 C10
Châteaubourg, France 18 D5
Châteaubriant, France 18 E5
Châteaudun, France 18 D8
Chateaugay, U.S.A. 111 B10
Châteauguay, France 18 D2
Châteauguay, L., Canada . 103 A5
Châteaulin, France 18 D2
Châteaumeillant, France .. 19 F9
Châteauneuf-du-Faou,
France 18 D3
Châteauneuf-sur-Charente,
France 20 C3
Châteauneuf-sur-Cher,
France 19 F9
Châteauneuf-sur-Loire,
France 19 E9
Châteaurenard,
Bouches-du-Rhône, France 21 E8
Châteaurenard, Loiret,
France 19 E9
Châteauroux, France 19 F8
Châteauvillain, France ... 19 D11
Châtelaillon-Plage, France 20 B2
Châtelguyon, France 20 C7
Châtellerault, France 18 F7
Châtelus-Malvaleix, France 19 F9
Chatham = Miramichi,
Canada 103 C6
Chatham, Canada 102 D3
Chatham, U.K. 13 F8
Chatham, U.S.A. 111 D11
Chatham Is., Pac. Oc. ... 96 M10
Chatmohar, Bangla. 69 G13
Chatra, India 69 G11
Chatrapur, India 67 K14
Chats, L. des, Canada ... 111 A8
Chatsu, India 68 F6
Chatsworth, Canada 110 B4
Chatsworth, Zimbabwe ... 87 F3
Chattahoochee, U.S.A. ... 109 K3
Chattahoochee →, U.S.A. 109 K3

Chattanooga, U.S.A. 109 H3
Chatteris, U.K. 13 E8
Chaturat, Thailand 64 E3
Chau Doc, Vietnam 65 G5
Chaudes-Aigues, France .. 20 D7
Chauffailles, France 19 F11
Chauk, Burma 67 J19
Chaukan La, Burma 67 F20
Chaumont, U.S.A. 111 D12
Chaumont, France 19 D12
Chaumont-en-Vexin, France 19 C8
Chaumont-sur-Loire, France 18 E8
Chaunay, France 20 B4
Chauny, France 19 C10
Chausey, Îs., France 18 D5
Chaussin, France 19 F12
Chautauqua L., U.S.A. ... 110 D5
Chauvigny, France 18 F7
Chauvin, Canada 105 C6
Chavanges, France 19 D11
Chaves, Brazil 125 D9
Chaves, Portugal 34 D3
Chawang, Thailand 65 H2
Chazelles-sur-Lyon, France 21 C8
Chazy, U.S.A. 111 B11
Cheb, Czech Rep. 26 A5
Cheboksarskoye Vdkhr.,
Russia 48 B8
Cheboksary, Russia 48 B8
Cheboygan, U.S.A. 108 C3
Chebsara, Russia 46 C10
Chech, Erg, Africa 78 D5
Chechen, Ostrov, Russia . 49 H8
Chechenia □, Russia 49 J7
Checheno-Ingush Republic =
Chechenia □, Russia ... 49 J7
Chechnya = Chechenia □,
Russia 49 J7
Chech'ŏn, S. Korea 57 F15
Chęciny, Poland 45 H7
Checotah, U.S.A. 113 H7
Chedabucto B., Canada ... 103 C7
Cheduba I., Burma 67 K18
Cheepie, Australia 95 D4
Chef-Boutonne, France ... 20 B3
Chegdomyn, Russia 51 D14
Chegga, Mauritania 78 C4
Chegutu, Zimbabwe 87 F3
Chehalis, U.S.A. 116 D4
Chehalis →, U.S.A. 116 D3
Cheiron, Mt., France 21 E10
Cheju do, S. Korea 57 H14
Chekalin, Russia 46 E9
Chekiang = Zhejiang □,
China 59 C13
Chel = Kuru, Bahr el →,
Sudan 81 F2
Chela, Sa. da, Angola 88 B1
Chelan, U.S.A. 114 C4
Chelan, L., U.S.A. 114 B3
Cheleken, Turkmenistan .. 50 F6
Cheleken Yarymadasy,
Turkmenistan 71 B7
Chelforó, Argentina 128 D3
Chelkar = Shalqar,
Kazakstan 50 E6
Chelkar Tengiz, Solonchak,
Kazakstan 50 E7
Chella, Ethiopia 81 F4
Chelles, France 19 D9
Chełm, Poland 45 G10
Chełmno, Poland 45 B5
Chelmsford, U.K. 13 F8
Chełmża, Poland 45 B5
Chelsea, U.S.A. 111 C12
Cheltenham, U.K. 13 F5
Chelva, Spain 32 F4
Chelyabinsk, Russia 50 D7
Chelyuskin, C., Russia ... 52 B14
Chemainus, Canada 116 B3
Chemba, Mozam. 85 H6
Chembar = Belinskiy, Russia 48 D6
Chemillé, France 18 E6
Chemnitz, Germany 24 E8
Chemult, U.S.A. 114 E3
Chen, Gora, Russia 51 C15
Chenab →, Pakistan 68 D4
Chenango Forks, U.S.A. .. 111 D9
Chencha, Ethiopia 81 F4
Chenchiang = Zhenjiang,
China 59 A12
Chengbu, China 59 D8
Chengcheng, China 56 G5
Chengchou = Zhengzhou,
China 56 G7
Chengde, China 57 D9
Chengdong Hu, China ... 59 A11
Chengdu, China 58 B5
Chenggong, China 58 E4
Chenggu, China 56 H4
Chenghai, China 59 F11
Chengjiang, China 58 E4
Chengkou, China 58 B7
Ch'engmai, China 64 C7
Ch'engtu = Chengdu, China 58 B5
Chengwu, China 56 G8
Chengyang, China 57 F11
Chengjiang, China 57 G10
Chenkán, Mexico 119 D6
Chennai, India 66 N12
Chenôve, France 19 E12
Chenxi, China 59 C8
Chenzhou, China 59 E9
Cheo Reo, Vietnam 62 B3
Cheom Ksan, Cambodia . 64 E5
Chepelare, Bulgaria 41 E8
Chepén, Peru 124 E3
Chepes, Argentina 126 C2

Chepo, Panama 120 E4
Chepstow, U.K. 13 F5
Cheptulil, Mt., Kenya 86 B4
Chequamegon B., U.S.A. . 112 B9
Cher □, France 19 E9
Cher →, France 18 E7
Chérادi, Italy 31 B10
Cherasco, Italy 28 D4
Cheraw, U.S.A. 109 H6
Cherbourg, France 18 C5
Cherdakly, Russia 48 C9
Cherdyn, Russia 50 C6
Cheremkhovo, Russia 51 D11
Cherepanovo, Russia 50 D9
Cherepovets, Russia 46 C9
Chergui, Chott ech, Algeria 78 B6
Cherikov = Cherykaw,
Belarus 46 F6
Cherkasy, Ukraine 47 H7
Cherkessk, Russia 49 H6
Cherlak, Russia 50 D8
Cherni, Bulgaria 40 D7
Chernaya, Russia 51 B9
Chernigov = Chernihiv,
Ukraine 47 G6
Chernihiv, Ukraine 47 G6
Chernivtsi, Ukraine 47 H3
Chernobyl = Chornobyl,
Ukraine 47 G6
Chernogorsk, Russia 51 D10
Chernomorskoye =
Chornomorske, Ukraine . 47 K7
Chernovtsy = Chernivtsi,
Ukraine 47 H3
Chernyakhovsk, Russia ... 9 J19
Chernyanka, Russia 47 G9
Chernysheyskiy, Russia .. 51 C12
Chernyye Zemli, Russia .. 49 H8
Cherokee, Iowa, U.S.A. .. 112 D7
Cherokee, Okla., U.S.A. .. 113 G5
Cherokee Village, U.S.A. . 113 G9
Cherokees, Grand Lake O'
The, U.S.A. 113 G7
Cherrapunji, India 67 G17
Cherry Valley, Calif., U.S.A. 117 M10
Cherry Valley, N.Y., U.S.A. 111 D10
Cherskiy, Russia 51 C17
Cherskogo Khrebet, Russia 51 C15
Chertkovo, Russia 47 H11
Cherven, Belarus 46 F5
Cherven-Bryag, Bulgaria . 41 C8
Chervonohrad, Ukraine .. 47 G3
Cherwell →, U.K. 13 F6
Cherykaw, Belarus 46 F6
Chesapeake, U.S.A. 108 G7
Chesapeake B., U.S.A. ... 108 G7
Cheshire □, U.K. 12 D5
Cheshskaya Guba, Russia . 50 C5
Cheshunt, U.K. 13 F7
Chesil Beach, U.K. 13 G5
Chesley, Canada 110 B3
Cheste, Spain 33 F4
Chester, U.K. 12 D5
Chester, Calif., U.S.A. ... 114 F3
Chester, Ill., U.S.A. 113 G10
Chester, Mont., U.S.A. .. 114 B8
Chester, Pa., U.S.A. 108 F8
Chester, S.C., U.S.A. 109 H5
Chester, Vt., U.S.A. 111 C12
Chester, W. Va., U.S.A. .. 110 F4
Chester-le-Street, U.K. .. 12 C6
Chesterfield, U.K. 12 D6
Chesterfield, Is., N. Cal. . 96 J7
Chesterfield Inlet, Canada 100 B10
Chesterton Ra., Australia . 95 D4
Chestertown, U.S.A. 111 C11
Chesterville, Canada 111 A9
Chestnut Ridge, U.S.A. .. 110 F5
Chesuncook L., U.S.A. ... 109 C11
Chéticamp, Canada 103 C7
Chetrosu, Moldova 43 B12
Chetumal, Mexico 119 D7
Chetumal, B. de, Mexico . 119 D7
Chetwynd, Canada 104 B4
Chevanceaux, France 20 C3
Cheviot, The, U.K. 12 B5
Cheviot Ra., Australia ... 94 D3
Cheviot Hills, U.K. 12 B5
Chew Bahir, Ethiopia 81 G4
Chewelah, U.S.A. 114 B5
Cheyenne, Okla., U.S.A. . 113 H5
Cheyenne, Wyo., U.S.A. . 112 E2
Cheyenne →, U.S.A. 112 C4
Cheyenne Wells, U.S.A. . 112 F3
Cheyne B., Australia 93 F2
Chhabra, India 68 G7
Chhaktala, India 68 H6
Chhapra, India 69 G11
Chhata, India 68 F7
Chhatarpur, Bihar, India . 69 G11
Chhatarpur, Mad. P., India 69 G8
Chhep, Cambodia 64 F5
Chhindwara, Mad. P., India 69 H8
Chhindwara, Mad. P., India 69 H8
Chhlong, Cambodia 65 F5
Chhota Tawa →, India .. 68 H7
Chhoti Kali Sindh →, India 68 G6
Chhuikhadan, India 69 J9
Chhuk, Cambodia 65 G5
Chi →, Thailand 64 E5
Chiai, Taiwan 59 F13
Chiali, Taiwan 59 F13
Chiamboni, Somali Rep. . 84 E8
Chiamussu = Jiamusi, China 60 B8
Chianciano Terme, Italy . 29 E8
Chiang Dao, Thailand ... 64 C2
Chiang Kham, Thailand .. 64 C3
Chiang Khan, Thailand .. 64 D3
Chiang Khong, Thailand . 58 G3
Chiang Mai, Thailand ... 64 C2
Chiang Rai, Thailand ... 58 H2

Chiang Saen, Thailand 58 G3
Chiapa →, Mexico 119 D6
Chiapa de Corzo, Mexico .. 119 D6
Chiapas □, Mexico 119 D6
Chiaramonte Gulfi, Italy .. 31 E7
Chiaravalle, Italy 29 E10
Chiaravalle Centrale, Italy . 31 D9
Chiari, Italy 28 C6
Chiatura, Georgia 49 J6
Chiautla, Mexico 119 D5
Chiávari, Italy 28 D6
Chiavenna, Italy 28 B6
Chiba, Japan 55 G10
Chiba □, Japan 55 G10
Chibabava, Mozam. 89 C5
Chibemba, Cunene, Angola . 85 H2
Chibemba, Huila, Angola .. 88 B2
Chibi, Zimbabwe 89 C5
Chibia, Angola 85 H2
Chibougamau, Canada 102 C5
Chibougamau, L., Canada . 102 C5
Chibuk, Nigeria 83 C7
Chibuto, Mozam. 89 C5
Chic-Chocs, Mts., Canada . 103 C6
Chicacole = Srikakulam,
  India 67 K13
Chicago, U.S.A. 108 E2
Chicago Heights, U.S.A. ... 108 E2
Chichagof I., U.S.A. 100 C6
Chichén-Itzá, Mexico 119 C7
Chicheng, China 56 D8
Chichester, U.K. 13 G7
Chichester Ra., Australia .. 92 D2
Chichibu, Japan 55 F9
Ch'ich'ihaerh = Qiqihar,
  China 51 E13
Chicholi, India 68 H8
Chickasha, U.S.A. 113 H6
Chiclana de la Frontera,
  Spain 35 J4
Chiclayo, Peru 124 E3
Chico, U.S.A. 116 F5
Chico →, Chubut, Argentina 128 G3
Chico →, Santa Cruz,
  Argentina 128 G3
Chicomo, Mozam. 89 C5
Chicontepec, Mexico 119 C5
Chicopee, U.S.A. 111 D12
Chicoutimi, Canada 103 C5
Chicualacuala, Mozam. ... 89 C5
Chidambaram, India 66 P11
Chidenguele, Mozam. 89 C5
Chidley, C., Canada 101 B13
Chiducuane, Mozam. 89 C5
Chiede, Angola 88 B2
Chiefs Pt., Canada 110 B3
Chiem Hoa, Vietnam 64 A5
Chiemsee, Germany 25 H8
Chiengi, Zambia 87 D2
Chiengmai = Chiang Mai,
  Thailand 64 C2
Chienti →, Italy 29 E10
Chieri, Italy 28 C4
Chiers →, France 19 C11
Chiesa in Valmalenco, Italy 28 B6
Chiese →, Italy 28 C7
Chieti, Italy 29 F11
Chifeng, China 57 C10
Chigirin, Ukraine 47 H7
Chignecto B., Canada 103 C7
Chiguana, Bolivia 126 A2
Chigwell, U.K. 13 F8
Chiha-ri, N. Korea 57 E14
Chihli, G. of = Bo Hai,
  China 57 E10
Chihuahua, Mexico 118 B3
Chihuahua □, Mexico 118 B3
Chiili, Kazakstan 50 E7
Chik Bollapur, India 66 N10
Chikmagalur, India 66 N9
Chikwawa, Malawi 87 F3
Chilac, Mexico 119 D5
Chilam Chavki, Pakistan . 69 B6
Chilanga, Zambia 87 F2
Chilapa, Mexico 119 D5
Chilas, Pakistan 69 B6
Chilaw, Sri Lanka 66 R11
Chilcotin →, Canada 104 C4
Childers, Australia 95 D5
Childress, U.S.A. 113 H4
Chile ■, S. Amer. 128 D2
Chile Rise, Pac. Oc. 97 L18
Chilecito, Argentina 126 B2
Chilete, Peru 124 E3
Chilia, Brațul →, Romania 43 E14
Chililabombwe, Zambia ... 87 E2
Chilin = Jilin, China 57 C14
Chilka L., India 67 K14
Chilko →, Canada 104 C4
Chilko L., Canada 104 C4
Chillagoe, Australia 94 B3
Chillán, Chile 126 D1
Chillicothe, Ill., U.S.A. ... 112 E10
Chillicothe, Mo., U.S.A. .. 112 F8
Chillicothe, Ohio, U.S.A. . 108 F4
Chilliwack, Canada 104 D4
Chilo, India 68 F5
Chiloane, I., Mozam. 89 C5
Chiloé, I. de, Chile 122 H3
Chilpancingo, Mexico 119 D5
Chiltern Hills, U.K. 13 F7
Chilton, U.S.A. 108 C1
Chilubi, Zambia 87 E3
Chilubula, Zambia 87 E3
Chilumba, Malawi 87 E3
Chilung, Taiwan 59 E13
Chilwa, L., Malawi 87 F4
Chimaltitán, Mexico 118 C4
Chimán, Panama 120 E4
Chimanimani, Zimbabwe .. 89 B5
Chimay, Belgium 17 D4

Chimayo, U.S.A. 115 H11
Chimbay, Uzbekistan 50 E6
Chimborazo, Ecuador 122 D3
Chimbote, Peru 124 E3
Chimkent = Shymkent,
  Kazakhstan 50 E7
Chimoio, Mozam. 87 F3
Chimpembe, Zambia 87 D2
Chin □, Burma 67 J18
Chin Ling Shan = Qinling
  Shandi, China 56 H5
China, Mexico 119 B5
China ■, Asia 60 D6
China Lake, U.S.A. 117 K9
Chinan = Jinan, China ... 56 F9
Chinandega, Nic. 120 D2
Chinati Peak, U.S.A. 113 L2
Chincha Alta, Peru 122 F3
Chinchaga →, Canada ... 104 B5
Chinchilla, Australia 95 D5
Chinchilla de Monte Aragón,
  Spain 33 G3
Chinchorro, Banco, Mexico 119 D7
Chinchou = Jinzhou, China 57 D11
Chincoteague, U.S.A. 108 G8
Chinde, Mozam. 87 F4
Chindo, S. Korea 57 G14
Chindwin →, Burma 67 J19
Chineni, India 69 C6
Chinga, Mozam. 87 F4
Chingola, Zambia 87 E2
Chingole, Malawi 87 E3
Ch'ingtao = Qingdao, China 57 F11
Chinguetti, Mauritania ... 78 D3
Chingune, Mozam. 89 C5
Chinhae, S. Korea 57 G15
Chinhanguanine, Mozam. . 89 D5
Chinhoyi, Zimbabwe 87 F3
Chini, India 68 D8
Chiniot, Pakistan 68 D5
Chínipas, Mexico 118 B3
Chinji, Pakistan 68 C5
Chinju, S. Korea 57 G15
Chinle, U.S.A. 115 H9
Chinmen, Taiwan 59 E13
Chinmen Tao, Taiwan 59 E12
Chinnampo = Namp'o,
  N. Korea 57 E13
Chino, Japan 55 G9
Chino, U.S.A. 117 L9
Chino Valley, U.S.A. 115 J7
Chinon, France 18 E4
Chinook, U.S.A. 114 B9
Chinsali, Zambia 87 E3
Chióggia, Italy 29 C9
Chíos = Khíos, Greece ... 39 C8
Chipata, Zambia 87 E3
Chipceni, Moldova 43 C13
Chipinge, Zimbabwe 87 G3
Chipiona, Spain 35 J4
Chipley, U.S.A. 109 K3
Chipman, Canada 103 C6
Chipoka, Malawi 87 E3
Chippenham, U.K. 13 F5
Chippewa →, U.S.A. 112 C8
Chippewa Falls, U.S.A. ... 112 C9
Chipping Norton, U.K. ... 13 F6
Chiprovtsi, Bulgaria 40 C6
Chiputneticook Lakes,
  U.S.A. 109 C11
Chiquián, Peru 124 F3
Chiquimula, Guatemala .. 120 D2
Chiquinquira, Colombia .. 124 B4
Chir →, Russia 49 F6
Chirala, India 66 M12
Chiramba, Mozam. 87 F3
Chirawa, India 68 E6
Chirchiq, Uzbekistan 50 E7
Chiredzi, Zimbabwe 89 C5
Chirfa, Niger 79 D8
Chiricahua Peak, U.S.A. .. 115 L9
Chiriquí, G. de, Panama .. 120 E3
Chiriquí, L. de, Panama .. 120 E3
Chirivira Falls, Zimbabwe . 87 G3
Chirmiri, India 67 H13
Chirnogi, Romania 43 F11
Chirpan, Bulgaria 41 D9
Chirripó Grande, Cerro,
  Costa Rica 120 E3
Chirundu, Zimbabwe 89 B4
Chisamba, Zambia 87 E2
Chisapani Garhi, Nepal .. 67 F14
Chisasibi, Canada 102 B4
Ch'ishan, Taiwan 59 F13
Chisholm, Canada 104 C6
Chisholm, U.S.A. 112 B8
Chishtian Mandi, Pakistan . 68 E5
Chishui, China 58 C5
Chishui He →, China 58 C5
Chisimaio, Somali Rep. ... 77 G8
Chisimba Falls, Zambia .. 87 E3
Chișinău, Moldova 43 C13
Chișineu Criș, Romania .. 42 D6
Chisone →, Italy 28 D4
Chisos Mts., U.S.A. 113 L3
Chistopol, Russia 48 C10
Chita, Russia 51 D12
Chitipa, Malawi 87 D3
Chitose, Japan 54 C10
Chitral, Pakistan 66 B7
Chitré, Panama 120 E3
Chittagong, Bangla. 67 H17
Chittagong □, Bangla. 67 G17
Chittaurgarh, India 68 G6
Chittoor, India 66 N11
Chitungwiza, Zimbabwe .. 87 F3
Chiusi, Italy 29 E8
Chiva, Spain 33 F4
Chivasso, Italy 28 C4
Chivhu, Zimbabwe 87 F3
Chivilcoy, Argentina 126 C4

Chiwanda, Tanzania 87 E3
Chixi, China 59 G9
Chizera, Zambia 87 E2
Chkalov = Orenburg, Russia 50 D6
Chkolovsk, Russia 48 B6
Chloride, U.S.A. 117 K12
Chlumec nad Cidlinou,
  Czech Rep. 26 A8
Chmielnik, Poland 45 H7
Cho Bo, Vietnam 58 G5
Cho-do, N. Korea 57 E13
Cho Phuoc Hai, Vietnam . 65 G6
Choba, Kenya 86 B4
Chobe National Park,
  Botswana 88 B4
Choch'iwŏn, S. Korea 57 F14
Chocianów, Poland 45 G2
Chociwel, Poland 44 E2
Chocolate Mts., U.S.A. ... 117 M11
Choctawatchee →, U.S.A. . 109 K3
Chodecz, Poland 45 F6
Chodov, Czech Rep. 26 A5
Chodziez, Poland 45 F3
Choele Choel, Argentina . 128 D3
Choix, Mexico 118 B3
Chojna, Poland 45 F1
Chojnice, Poland 44 E4
Chojnów, Poland 45 G2
Chōkai-San, Japan 54 E10
Choke, Ethiopia 81 E4
Choke Canyon L., U.S.A. . 113 L5
Chokurdakh, Russia 51 B15
Cholame, U.S.A. 116 K6
Cholet, France 18 E6
Cholguan, Chile 126 D1
Choluteca, Honduras 120 D2
Choluteca →, Honduras .. 120 D2
Chom Bung, Thailand ... 64 F2
Chom Thong, Thailand .. 64 C2
Choma, Zambia 87 F2
Chomen Swamp, Ethiopia . 81 F4
Chomun, India 68 F6
Chomutov, Czech Rep. ... 26 A6
Chon Buri, Thailand 64 F3
Chon Thanh, Vietnam ... 65 G6
Ch'onan, S. Korea 57 F14
Chone, Ecuador 124 D3
Chong Kai, Cambodia ... 64 F4
Chong Mek, Thailand ... 64 E5
Chongde, China 59 B13
Chŏngdo, S. Korea 57 G15
Chŏngha, S. Korea 57 F15
Chŏngjin, N. Korea 57 D15
Chŏngju, S. Korea 57 F14
Chŏngju, N. Korea 57 E13
Chongli, China 56 D8
Chongming, China 59 B13
Chongming Dao, China .. 59 B13
Chongqing, Chongqing,
  China 58 C6
Chongqing, Sichuan, China . 58 B4
Chongqing □, China 60 C5
Chongqing Shi □, China .. 58 C6
Chongren, China 59 D11
Chonguene, Mozam. 89 C5
Chŏngŭp, S. Korea 57 G14
Chongyi, China 59 E10
Chongzuo, China 58 F6
Chŏnju, S. Korea 57 G14
Chonos, Arch. de los, Chile 122 H3
Chop, Ukraine 47 H2
Chopim →, Brazil 127 B5
Chor, Pakistan 68 G3
Chorbat La, India 69 B7
Chorley, U.K. 12 D5
Chornobyl, Ukraine 47 G6
Chornomorske, Ukraine .. 47 K7
Chorolque, Cerro, Bolivia . 126 A2
Choroszcz, Poland 45 E9
Chorregon, Australia 94 C3
Chortkiv, Ukraine 47 H3
Ch'ŏrwŏn, S. Korea 57 E14
Chorzele, Poland 45 E7
Chorzów, Poland 45 H5
Chos-Malal, Argentina .. 126 D1
Ch'osan, N. Korea 57 D13
Choszczno, Poland 45 E2
Choteau, U.S.A. 114 C7
Chotěboř, Czech Rep. ... 26 B8
Chotila, India 68 H4
Chotta Udepur, India 68 H6
Chowchilla, U.S.A. 116 H6
Choybalsan, Mongolia ... 60 B6
Christchurch, N.Z. 91 K4
Christchurch, U.K. 13 G6
Christian I., Canada 110 B4
Christiana, S. Africa 88 D4
Christiansfeld, Denmark . 11 J3
Christiansted, Virgin Is. .. 121 C7
Christie B., Canada 105 A6
Christina →, Canada 105 B6
Christmas Cr. →, Australia 92 C4
Christmas I. = Kiritimati,
  Kiribati 97 G12
Christmas I., Ind. Oc. ... 96 J2
Christopher L., Australia . 93 D4
Chrudim, Czech Rep. 26 B8
Chrzanów, Poland 45 H6
Chtimba, Malawi 87 E3
Chu = Shu, Kazakhstan . 50 E8
Chu →= Shu →, Kazakhstan . 52 E10
Chu Lai, Vietnam 64 E7
Ch'uanchou = Quanzhou,
  China 59 E12
Chuankou, China 56 G6
Chubbuck, U.S.A. 114 E7
Chūbu □, Japan 55 F8
Chubut →, Argentina ... 122 H4
Chuchi L., Canada 104 B4
Chuda, India 68 H4

Chudovo, Russia 46 C6
Chudskoye, Ozero, Russia . 9 G22
Chūgoku □, Japan 55 G6
Chūgoku-Sanchi, Japan .. 55 G6
Chuguyev = Chuhuyiv,
  Ukraine 47 H9
Chuhuyiv, Ukraine 47 H9
Chukchi Sea, Russia 51 C19
Chukotskoye Nagorye,
  Russia 51 C18
Chula Vista, U.S.A. 117 N9
Chulman, Russia 51 D14
Chulucanas, Peru 124 E2
Chulym →, Russia 50 D9
Chum Phae, Thailand ... 64 D4
Chum Saeng, Thailand .. 64 E3
Chumar, India 69 C8
Chumbicha, Argentina .. 126 B2
Chumerna, Bulgaria 41 D9
Chumikan, Russia 51 D14
Chumphon, Thailand ... 65 G2
Chumuare, Mozam. 87 E3
Chumunjin, S. Korea 57 F15
Chuna →, Russia 51 D10
Chun'an, China 59 C12
Chunchura, India 69 H13
Chunga, Zambia 87 F2
Chunggang-ŭp, N. Korea . 57 D14
Chunghwa, N. Korea 57 E13
Ch'ungju, S. Korea 57 F14
Chungking = Chongqing,
  China 58 C6
Chungli, Taiwan 59 E13
Ch'ungmu, S. Korea 57 G15
Chungt'iaoshan = Zhongtiao
  Shan, China 56 G6
Chungyang Shanmo, Taiwan 59 F13
Chunian, Pakistan 68 D6
Chunya, Tanzania 87 D3
Chunyang, China 57 C15
Chuquibamba, Peru 124 G4
Chuquicamata, Chile 126 A2
Chur, Switz. 25 J5
Churachandpur, India ... 67 G18
Churchill, Canada 105 B10
Churchill →, Man., Canada 105 B10
Churchill →, Nfld., Canada 103 B7
Churchill, C., Canada 105 B10
Churchill Falls, Canada .. 103 B7
Churchill L., Canada 105 B7
Churchill Pk., Canada ... 104 B3
Churki, India 69 H10
Churu, India 68 E6
Churún Merú = Angel Falls,
  Venezuela 124 B6
Chushal, India 69 C8
Chuska Mts., U.S.A. 115 H9
Chusovoy, Russia 50 D6
Chute-aux-Outardes, Canada 103 C6
Chuuronjang, N. Korea .. 57 D15
Chuvash Republic =
  Chuvashia □, Russia .. 48 C8
Chuvashia □, Russia 48 C8
Chuwārtah, Iraq 70 C5
Chuxiong, China 58 E3
Chuy, Uruguay 127 C5
Chuzhou, China 59 A12
Ci Xian, China 56 F8
Ciacova, Romania 42 E6
Ciadâr-Lunga, Moldova .. 43 D13
Ciamis, Indonesia 63 G13
Cianjur, Indonesia 63 G12
Cianorte, Brazil 127 A5
Cibola, U.S.A. 117 M12
Cicero, U.S.A. 108 E2
Cidacos →, Spain 32 C3
Cide, Turkey 72 B5
Ciechanów, Poland 45 F7
Ciechanowiec, Poland ... 45 F9
Ciechocinek, Poland 45 F5
Ciego de Avila, Cuba 120 B4
Ciénaga, Colombia 124 A4
Cienfuegos, Cuba 120 B3
Cieplice Śląskie Zdrój,
  Poland 45 H2
Cierp, France 20 F4
Cíes, Is., Spain 34 C2
Cieszanów, Poland 45 H10
Cieszyn, Poland 45 J5
Cieza, Spain 33 G3
Çifteler, Turkey 72 C4
Cifuentes, Spain 32 E2
Cihanbeyli, Turkey 72 C5
Cihuatlán, Mexico 118 D4
Cijara, Embalse de, Spain . 35 F6
Cijulang, Indonesia 63 G13
Cilacap, Indonesia 63 G13
Çıldır, Turkey 73 B10
Çıldır Gölü, Turkey 73 B10
Cili, China 59 C8
Cilibia, Romania 43 E12
Cilicia, Turkey 72 D5
Cill Chainnigh = Kilkenny,
  Ireland 15 D4
Cilo Dağı, Turkey 73 D10
Cimarron, Kans., U.S.A. . 113 G4
Cimarron, N. Mex., U.S.A. 113 G2
Cimarron →, U.S.A. 113 G6
Cimișlia, Moldova 43 D13
Cimone, Mte., Italy 28 D7
Çınar, Turkey 73 D9
Çinarcık, Turkey 41 F13
Cinca →, Spain 32 D5
Cincar, Bos.-H. 29 E7
Cincinnati, U.S.A. 108 F3
Cincinnatus, U.S.A. 111 D9
Çine, Turkey 39 D10
Ciney, Belgium 17 D5
Cíngoli, Italy 29 E10
Cinigiano, Italy 29 F8
Cinto, Mte., France 21 F12

Cintruénigo, Spain 32 C3
Ciocile, Romania 43 F12
Ciolănești din Deal, Romania 43 F10
Ciorani, Romania 43 F11
Čiovo, Croatia 29 E13
Circeo, Mte., Italy 30 A6
Çirçir, Turkey 72 C7
Circle, Alaska, U.S.A. ... 100 B5
Circle, Mont., U.S.A. 112 B2
Circleville, U.S.A. 108 F4
Cirebon, Indonesia 63 G13
Ciremai, Indonesia 63 G13
Cirencester, U.K. 13 F6
Cireșu, Romania 42 F7
Cirey-sur-Vezouze, France 19 D13
Ciriè, Italy 28 C4
Cirò, Italy 31 C10
Cirò Marina, Italy 31 C10
Ciron →, France 20 D3
Cisco, U.S.A. 113 J5
Cislău, Romania 43 E11
Cisna, Poland 45 J9
Cisnădie, Romania 43 E9
Cisterna di Latina, Italy .. 30 A5
Cisternino, Italy 31 B10
Cistierna, Spain 34 C5
Citeli-Ckaro = Tsiteli-
  Tsqaro, Georgia 49 K8
Citlaltépetl, Mexico 119 D5
Citrus Heights, U.S.A. ... 116 G5
Citrusdal, S. Africa 88 E2
Città della Pieve, Italy ... 29 F9
Città di Castello, Italy ... 29 E9
Città Sant' Angelo, Italy . 29 F11
Cittadella, Italy 29 C8
Cittaducale, Italy 29 F9
Cittanova, Italy 31 D9
Ciuc, Munții, Romania .. 43 D11
Ciucaș, Vf., Romania 43 E10
Ciucea, Romania 42 D7
Ciuciulea, Moldova 43 C12
Ciuciuleni, Moldova 43 C13
Ciudad Altamirano, Mexico 118 D4
Ciudad Bolívar, Venezuela 124 B6
Ciudad Camargo, Mexico 118 B3
Ciudad de Valles, Mexico 119 C5
Ciudad del Carmen, Mexico 119 D6
Ciudad del Este, Paraguay 127 B5
Ciudad Delicias = Delicias,
  Mexico 118 B3
Ciudad Guayana, Venezuela 124 B6
Ciudad Guerrero, Mexico 118 B3
Ciudad Guzmán, Mexico 118 D4
Ciudad Juárez, Mexico ... 118 A3
Ciudad Madero, Mexico . 119 C5
Ciudad Mante, Mexico .. 119 C5
Ciudad Obregón, Mexico 118 B3
Ciudad Real, Spain 35 G7
Ciudad Real □, Spain ... 35 G7
Ciudad Rodrigo, Spain .. 34 E4
Ciudad Trujillo = Santo
  Domingo, Dom. Rep. . 121 C6
Ciudad Victoria, Mexico . 119 C5
Ciudadela, Spain 37 B10
Ciulnița, Romania 43 F12
Ciumeghiu, Romania ... 42 D6
Ciuperceni, Romania ... 42 F8
Civa Burnu, Turkey 72 B7
Cividale del Friuli, Italy . 29 B10
Cívita Castellana, Italy .. 29 F9
Civitanova Marche, Italy . 29 E10
Civitavécchia, Italy 29 F8
Civray, France 20 B4
Çivril, Turkey 39 C11
Cixerri →, Italy 30 C1
Cixi, China 59 B13
Cizre, Turkey 70 B4
Cizur Mayor, Spain 32 C3
Clackmannanshire □, U.K. 14 E5
Clacton-on-Sea, U.K. ... 13 F9
Clain →, France 18 F7
Claire, L., Canada 104 B6
Clairton, U.S.A. 110 F5
Clairvaux-les-Lacs, France 19 F12
Claise →, France 20 B5
Callam Bay, U.S.A. 116 B2
Clamecy, France 19 E10
Clanton, U.S.A. 109 J2
Clanwilliam, S. Africa ... 88 E2
Clara, Ireland 15 C4
Claraville, U.S.A. 117 K8
Clare, Australia 95 E2
Clare, U.S.A. 108 D3
Clare □, Ireland 15 D3
Clare →, Ireland 15 C2
Clare I., Ireland 15 C1
Claremont, Calif., U.S.A. 117 L9
Claremont, N.H., U.S.A. 111 C12
Claremont Pt., Australia . 94 A3
Claremore, U.S.A. 113 G7
Claremorris, Ireland 15 C3
Clarence →, Australia .. 95 D5
Clarence →, N.Z. 91 K4
Clarence, I., Chile 128 G2
Clarence I., Antarctica .. 5 C18
Clarence Str., Australia . 92 B5
Clarence Town, Bahamas 121 B5
Clarendon, Pa., U.S.A. .. 110 E5
Clarendon, Tex., U.S.A. . 113 H4
Clarenville, Canada 103 C9
Claresholm, Canada 104 D6
Clarie Coast, Antarctica . 5 C9
Clarinda, U.S.A. 112 E7
Clarion, Iowa, U.S.A. ... 112 D8
Clarion, Pa., U.S.A. 110 E5
Clarion →, U.S.A. 110 E5
Clark, U.S.A. 112 C6
Clark, Pt., Canada 110 B3
Clark Fork, U.S.A. 114 B5
Clark Fork →, U.S.A. ... 114 B5

Clark Hill L., *U.S.A.* 109 J4
Clarkdale, *U.S.A.* 115 J7
Clarke City, *Canada* 103 B6
Clarke I., *Australia* 94 G4
Clarke Ra., *Australia* 94 C4
Clark's Fork →, *U.S.A.* 114 D9
Clark's Harbour, *Canada* 103 D6
Clarks Summit, *U.S.A.* 111 E9
Clarksburg, *U.S.A.* 108 F5
Clarksdale, *U.S.A.* 113 H9
Clarksville, *Ark., U.S.A.* 113 H8
Clarksville, *Tenn., U.S.A.* 109 G2
Clarksville, *Tex., U.S.A.* 113 J7
Clatskanie, *U.S.A.* 116 D3
Claude, *U.S.A.* 113 H4
Claveria, *Phil.* 61 B4
Clay, *U.S.A.* 116 G5
Clay Center, *U.S.A.* 112 F6
Claypool, *U.S.A.* 115 K8
Claysburg, *U.S.A.* 110 F6
Claysville, *U.S.A.* 110 F4
Clayton, *N. Mex., U.S.A.* 113 G3
Clayton, *N.Y., U.S.A.* 111 B8
Clear, C., *Ireland* 15 E2
Clear, L., *Canada* 110 A7
Clear Hills, *Canada* 104 B5
Clear I., *Ireland* 15 E2
Clear L., *U.S.A.* 116 F4
Clear Lake, *Iowa, U.S.A.* 112 D8
Clear Lake, *S. Dak., U.S.A.* 112 C6
Clear Lake Reservoir,
 U.S.A. 114 F3
Clearfield, *Pa., U.S.A.* 110 E6
Clearfield, *Utah, U.S.A.* 114 F8
Clearlake, *U.S.A.* 114 G2
Clearlake Highlands, *U.S.A.* 116 G4
Clearwater, *Canada* 104 C4
Clearwater, *U.S.A.* 109 M4
Clearwater →, *Alta.,
 Canada* 104 C6
Clearwater →, *Alta.,
 Canada* 105 B6
Clearwater L., *Canada* 105 C9
Clearwater Mts., *Canada* 114 C6
Clearwater Prov. Park,
 Canada 105 C8
Clearwater River Prov. Park,
 Canada 105 B7
Cleburne, *U.S.A.* 113 J6
Clee Hills, *U.K.* 13 E5
Cleethorpes, *U.K.* 12 D7
Cleeve Cloud, *U.K.* 13 F6
Clelles, *France* 21 D9
Clemson, *U.S.A.* 109 H4
Clerke Reef, *Australia* 92 C2
Clermont, *Australia* 94 C4
Clermont, *France* 19 C9
Clermont, *U.S.A.* 109 L5
Clermont-en-Argonne,
 France 19 C12
Clermont-Ferrand, *France* 20 C7
Clermont-l'Hérault, *France* 20 E7
Clerval, *France* 19 E13
Clervaux, *Lux.* 17 D6
Cles, *Italy* 28 B8
Cleve, *Australia* 95 E2
Clevedon, *U.K.* 13 F5
Cleveland, *Miss., U.S.A.* 113 J9
Cleveland, *Ohio, U.S.A.* 110 E3
Cleveland, *Okla., U.S.A.* 113 G6
Cleveland, *Tenn., U.S.A.* 109 H3
Cleveland, *Tex., U.S.A.* 113 K7
Cleveland, *Mt., U.S.A.* 114 B7
Cleveland, C., *Australia* 94 B4
Cleveland Heights, *U.S.A.* 110 E3
Clevelândia, *Brazil* 127 B5
Clew B., *Ireland* 15 C2
Clewiston, *U.S.A.* 109 M5
Clifden, *Ireland* 15 C1
Clifden, *N.Z.* 91 M1
Cliffdell, *U.S.A.* 116 D5
Cliffy Hd., *Australia* 93 G2
Clifton, *Australia* 95 D5
Clifton, *Ariz., U.S.A.* 115 K9
Clifton, *Colo., U.S.A.* 115 G9
Clifton, *Tex., U.S.A.* 113 K6
Clifton Beach, *Australia* 94 B4
Climax, *Canada* 105 D7
Clinch →, *U.S.A.* 109 H3
Clingmans Dome, *U.S.A.* 109 H4
Clint, *U.S.A.* 115 L10
Clinton, *B.C., Canada* 104 C4
Clinton, *Ont., Canada* 102 D3
Clinton, *N.Z.* 91 M2
Clinton, *Ark., U.S.A.* 113 H8
Clinton, *Conn., U.S.A.* 111 E12
Clinton, *Ill., U.S.A.* 112 E10
Clinton, *Ind., U.S.A.* 108 F2
Clinton, *Iowa, U.S.A.* 112 E9
Clinton, *Mass., U.S.A.* 111 D13
Clinton, *Miss., U.S.A.* 113 J9
Clinton, *Mo., U.S.A.* 112 F8
Clinton, *N.C., U.S.A.* 109 H6
Clinton, *Okla., U.S.A.* 113 H5
Clinton, *S.C., U.S.A.* 109 H5
Clinton, *Tenn., U.S.A.* 109 G3
Clinton, *Wash., U.S.A.* 116 C4
Clinton C., *Australia* 94 C5
Clinton Colden L., *Canada* 100 B9
Clintonville, *U.S.A.* 112 C10
Clipperton, I., *Pac. Oc.* 97 F17
Clisham, *U.K.* 14 D2
Clisson, *France* 18 E5
Clitheroe, *U.K.* 12 D5
Clo-oose, *Canada* 116 B2
Cloates, Pt., *Australia* 92 D1
Clocolan, *S. Africa* 89 D4
Clodomira, *Argentina* 126 B3
Clogher Hd., *Ireland* 15 C5
Clonakilty, *Ireland* 15 E3
Clonakilty B., *Ireland* 15 E3

Cloncurry, *Australia* 94 C3
Cloncurry →, *Australia* 94 B3
Clondalkin, *Ireland* 15 C5
Clones, *Ireland* 15 B4
Clonmel, *Ireland* 15 D4
Cloppenburg, *Germany* 24 C4
Cloquet, *U.S.A.* 112 B8
Clorinda, *Argentina* 126 B4
Cloud Bay, *Canada* 102 C2
Cloud Peak, *U.S.A.* 114 D10
Cloudcroft, *U.S.A.* 115 K11
Cloverdale, *U.S.A.* 116 G4
Clovis, *Calif., U.S.A.* 116 J7
Clovis, *N. Mex., U.S.A.* 113 H3
Cloyes-sur-le-Loir, *France* 18 E8
Cloyne, *Canada* 110 B7
Cluj □, *Romania* 43 D8
Cluj-Napoca, *Romania* 43 D8
Clunes, *Australia* 95 F3
Cluny, *France* 19 F11
Cluses, *France* 19 F13
Clusone, *Italy* 28 C6
Clutha →, *N.Z.* 91 M2
Clwyd □, *U.K.* 12 D4
Clwyd →, *U.K.* 12 D4
Clyde, *Canada* 104 C6
Clyde, *N.Z.* 91 L2
Clyde, *U.S.A.* 110 C8
Clyde →, *U.K.* 14 F4
Clyde, Firth of, *U.K.* 14 F3
Clyde River, *Canada* 101 A13
Clydebank, *U.K.* 14 F4
Clymer, *N.Y., U.S.A.* 110 D5
Clymer, *Pa., U.S.A.* 110 D5
Ćmielów, *Poland* 45 H8
Côa →, *Portugal* 34 D3
Coachella, *U.S.A.* 117 M10
Coachella Canal, *U.S.A.* 117 N12
Coahoma, *U.S.A.* 113 J4
Coahuayana →, *Mexico* 118 D4
Coahuila □, *Mexico* 118 B4
Coal →, *Canada* 104 B3
Coalane, *Mozam.* 87 F4
Coalcomán, *Mexico* 118 D4
Coaldale, *Canada* 104 D6
Coalgate, *U.S.A.* 113 H6
Coalinga, *U.S.A.* 116 J6
Coalisland, *U.K.* 15 B5
Coalville, *U.K.* 12 E6
Coalville, *U.S.A.* 114 F8
Coari, *Brazil* 124 D6
Coast □, *Kenya* 86 C4
Coast Mts., *Canada* 104 C3
Coast Ranges, *U.S.A.* 116 G4
Coatbridge, *U.K.* 14 F4
Coatepec, *Mexico* 119 D5
Coatepeque, *Guatemala* 120 D1
Coatesville, *U.S.A.* 108 F8
Coaticook, *Canada* 103 C5
Coats I., *Canada* 101 B11
Coats Land, *Antarctica* 5 D1
Coatzacoalcos, *Mexico* 119 D6
Cobadin, *Romania* 43 F13
Cobalt, *Canada* 102 C4
Cobán, *Guatemala* 120 C1
Çobanlar, *Turkey* 39 C12
Cobar, *Australia* 95 E4
Cobargo, *Australia* 95 F4
Cóbh, *Ireland* 15 E3
Cobija, *Bolivia* 124 F5
Cobleskill, *U.S.A.* 111 D10
Coboconk, *Canada* 110 B6
Cobourg, *Canada* 102 D4
Cobourg Pen., *Australia* 92 B5
Cobram, *Australia* 95 F4
Cóbué, *Mozam.* 87 E3
Coburg, *Germany* 25 E6
Coca, *Spain* 34 D6
Cocanada = Kakinada, *India* 67 L13
Cocentaina, *Spain* 33 G4
Cochabamba, *Bolivia* 124 G5
Cochem, *Germany* 25 E3
Cochemane, *Mozam.* 87 F3
Cochin, *India* 66 Q10
Cochin China, *Vietnam* 65 G6
Cochran, *U.S.A.* 109 J4
Cochrane, *Alta., Canada* 104 C6
Cochrane, *Chile* 128 F2
Cochrane →, *Canada* 105 B8
Cochrane, L., *Chile* 128 F2
Cochranton, *U.S.A.* 110 E4
Cockburn, *Australia* 95 E3
Cockburn, Canal, *Chile* 122 J3
Cockburn I., *Canada* 102 C3
Cockburn Ra., *Australia* 92 C4
Cockermouth, *U.K.* 12 C4
Cocklebiddy, *Australia* 93 F4
Coco →, *Cent. Amer.* 120 D3
Coco, I. del, *Pac. Oc.* 97 G19
Cocoa, *U.S.A.* 109 L5
Cocobeach, *Gabon* 84 D1
Cocora, *Romania* 43 F12
Cocos Is., *Ind. Oc.* 96 J1
Cod, C., *U.S.A.* 108 D10
Codajás, *Brazil* 124 D6
Codigoro, *Italy* 29 D9
Codlea, *Romania* 43 E10
Codó, *Brazil* 125 D10
Codogno, *Italy* 28 C6
Codróipo, *Italy* 29 C10
Codru, Munții, *Romania* 42 D7
Cody, *U.S.A.* 114 D9
Coe Hill, *Canada* 110 B7
Coelemu, *Chile* 126 D1
Coen, *Australia* 94 A3
Coesfeld, *Germany* 24 D3
Cœur d'Alene, *U.S.A.* 114 C5
Cœur d'Alene L., *U.S.A.* 114 C5
Coevorden, *Neths.* 17 B6
Cofete, *Canary Is.* 37 F5
Coffeyville, *U.S.A.* 113 G7

Coffin B., *Australia* 95 E2
Coffin Bay, *Australia* 95 E2
Coffin Bay Peninsula,
 Australia 95 E2
Coffs Harbour, *Australia* 95 E5
Cofrentes, *Spain* 33 F3
Cogalnic →, *Moldova* 43 E14
Cogealac, *Romania* 43 F13
Coghinas →, *Italy* 30 B1
Coghinas, L. del, *Italy* 30 B2
Cognac, *France* 20 C3
Cogne, *Italy* 28 C4
Cogolin, *France* 21 E10
Cogolludo, *Spain* 32 E1
Cohocton, *U.S.A.* 110 D7
Cohocton →, *U.S.A.* 110 D7
Cohoes, *U.S.A.* 111 D11
Cohuna, *Australia* 95 F3
Coiba, I., *Panama* 120 E3
Coig →, *Argentina* 128 G3
Coigeach, Rubha, *U.K.* 14 C3
Coihaique, *Chile* 128 F2
Coimbatore, *India* 66 P10
Coimbra, *Brazil* 124 G7
Coimbra, *Portugal* 34 E2
Coimbra □, *Portugal* 34 E2
Coín, *Spain* 35 J6
Coipasa, Salar de, *Bolivia* 124 G5
Cojimies, *Ecuador* 124 C3
Cojocna, *Romania* 43 D8
Cojutepequé, *El Salv.* 120 D2
Çoka, *Serbia, Yug.* 42 E5
Cokeville, *U.S.A.* 114 E8
Colac, *Australia* 95 F3
Colatina, *Brazil* 125 G10
Colbeck, C., *Antarctica* 5 D13
Colborne, *Canada* 110 C7
Colby, *U.S.A.* 112 F4
Colchester, *U.K.* 13 F8
Cold L., *Canada* 105 C7
Coldstream, *Canada* 104 C5
Coldstream, *U.K.* 14 F6
Coldwater, *Canada* 110 B5
Coldwater, *Kans., U.S.A.* 113 G5
Coldwater, *Mich., U.S.A.* 108 E3
Coleambally, *Australia* 95 E4
Colebrook, *U.S.A.* 111 B13
Coleman, *U.S.A.* 113 K5
Coleman →, *Australia* 94 B3
Colenso, *S. Africa* 89 D4
Coleraine, *Australia* 95 F3
Coleraine, *U.K.* 15 A5
Coleridge, L., *N.Z.* 91 K3
Colesberg, *S. Africa* 88 E4
Coleville, *U.S.A.* 116 G7
Colfax, *Calif., U.S.A.* 116 F6
Colfax, *La., U.S.A.* 113 K8
Colfax, *Wash., U.S.A.* 114 C5
Colhué Huapi, L., *Argentina* 128 F3
Colibași, *Moldova* 43 E13
Colibași, *Romania* 43 F9
Cólico, *Italy* 28 B6
Coligny, *France* 19 F12
Coligny, *S. Africa* 89 D4
Colima, *Mexico* 118 D4
Colima □, *Mexico* 118 D4
Colima, Nevado de, *Mexico* 118 D4
Colina, *Chile* 126 C1
Colina do Norte,
 Guinea-Biss. 82 C2
Colinas, *Brazil* 125 E10
Colindres, *Spain* 34 B7
Coll, *U.K.* 14 E2
Collaguasi, *Chile* 126 A2
Collarada, Peña, *Spain* 32 C4
Collarenebri, *Australia* 95 D4
Colle di Val d'Elsa, *Italy* 28 E8
Collécchio, *Italy* 28 D7
Colleen Bawn, *Zimbabwe* 87 G2
College Park, *U.S.A.* 109 J3
College Station, *U.S.A.* 113 K6
Collesalvetti, *Italy* 28 E7
Collie, *Australia* 93 F2
Collier B., *Australia* 92 C3
Collier Ra., *Australia* 93 D2
Collina, Passo di, *Italy* 28 D7
Collingwood, *Canada* 102 D3
Collingwood, *N.Z.* 91 J4
Collins, *Canada* 102 B2
Collinsville, *Australia* 94 C4
Collipulli, *Chile* 126 D1
Collooney, *Ireland* 15 B3
Colmar, *France* 19 D14
Colmenar, *Spain* 35 J6
Colmenar de Oreja, *Spain* 34 E7
Colmenar Viejo, *Spain* 34 E7
Colo →, *Australia* 95 E5
Cologne = Köln, *Germany* 24 E2
Colom, I. d'en, *Spain* 37 B11
Coloma, *U.S.A.* 116 G6
Colomb-Béchar = Béchar,
 Algeria 78 B5
Colombey-les-Belles, *France* 19 D12
Colombey-les-Deux-Églises,
 France 19 D11
Colombia ■, *S. Amer.* 124 C4
Colombian Basin, *S. Amer.* 98 H12
Colombo, *Sri Lanka* 66 R11
Colómiers, *France* 20 E5
Colón, *Buenos Aires,
 Argentina* 126 C3
Colón, *Entre Ríos, Argentina* 126 C4
Colón, *Cuba* 120 B3
Colón, *Panama* 120 E4
Colona de Sant Jordi, *Spain* 37 B9
Colonia del Sacramento,
 Uruguay 126 C4
Colonia Dora, *Argentina* 126 B3
Colonial Beach, *U.S.A.* 108 F7
Colonie, *U.S.A.* 111 D11

Colonna, C., *Italy* 31 C10
Colonsay, *Canada* 105 C7
Colonsay, *U.K.* 14 E2
Colorado □, *U.S.A.* 115 G10
Colorado →, *Argentina* 128 D4
Colorado →, *N. Amer.* 115 L6
Colorado →, *U.S.A.* 113 L7
Colorado City, *U.S.A.* 113 J4
Colorado Plateau, *U.S.A.* 115 H8
Colorado River Aqueduct,
 U.S.A. 117 L12
Colorado Springs, *U.S.A.* 112 F2
Colorno, *Italy* 28 D7
Colotlán, *Mexico* 118 C4
Colstrip, *U.S.A.* 114 D10
Colton, *U.S.A.* 111 B10
Columbia, *Ky., U.S.A.* 108 G3
Columbia, *La., U.S.A.* 113 J8
Columbia, *Miss., U.S.A.* 113 K10
Columbia, *Mo., U.S.A.* 112 F8
Columbia, *Pa., U.S.A.* 111 F8
Columbia, *S.C., U.S.A.* 109 J5
Columbia, *Tenn., U.S.A.* 109 H2
Columbia →, *N. Amer.* 116 D2
Columbia, C., *Canada* 4 A4
Columbia, District of □,
 U.S.A. 108 F7
Columbia, Mt., *Canada* 104 C5
Columbia Basin, *U.S.A.* 114 C4
Columbia Falls, *U.S.A.* 114 B6
Columbia Mts., *Canada* 104 C5
Columbia Plateau, *U.S.A.* 114 D5
Columbiana, *U.S.A.* 110 F4
Columbretes, Is., *Spain* 32 F5
Columbus, *Ga., U.S.A.* 109 J3
Columbus, *Ind., U.S.A.* 108 F3
Columbus, *Kans., U.S.A.* 113 G7
Columbus, *Miss., U.S.A.* 109 J1
Columbus, *Mont., U.S.A.* 114 D9
Columbus, *N. Mex., U.S.A.* 115 L10
Columbus, *Nebr., U.S.A.* 112 E6
Columbus, *Ohio, U.S.A.* 108 F4
Columbus, *Tex., U.S.A.* 113 L6
Colunga, *Spain* 34 B5
Colusa, *U.S.A.* 116 F4
Colville, *U.S.A.* 114 B5
Colville →, *U.S.A.* 100 A4
Colville, C., *N.Z.* 91 G5
Colwood, *Canada* 116 B3
Colwyn Bay, *U.K.* 12 D4
Coma, *Ethiopia* 81 F4
Comácchio, *Italy* 29 D9
Comalcalco, *Mexico* 119 D6
Comallo, *Argentina* 128 E2
Comana, *Romania* 43 F11
Comanche, *U.S.A.* 113 K5
Comănești, *Romania* 43 D11
Comarnic, *Romania* 43 E10
Comayagua, *Honduras* 120 D2
Combahee →, *U.S.A.* 109 J5
Combarbalá, *Chile* 126 C1
Combeaufontaine, *France* 19 E12
Comber, *Canada* 110 D2
Comber, *U.K.* 15 B6
Combermere, *Canada* 110 A7
Comblain-au-Pont, *Belgium* 17 D5
Combourg, *France* 18 D5
Combrailles, *France* 19 F9
Combronde, *France* 20 C7
Comeragh Mts., *Ireland* 15 D4
Comet, *Australia* 94 C4
Comilla, *Bangla.* 67 H17
Comino, *Malta* 36 C1
Comino, C., *Italy* 30 B2
Cómiso, *Italy* 31 F7
Comitán, *Mexico* 119 D6
Commentry, *France* 19 F9
Commerce, *Ga., U.S.A.* 109 H4
Commerce, *Tex., U.S.A.* 113 J7
Commercy, *France* 19 D12
Committee B., *Canada* 101 B11
Commonwealth B.,
 Antarctica 5 C10
Commoron Cr. →, *Australia* 95 D5
Communism Pk. =
 Kommunizma, Pik,
 Tajikistan 50 F8
Como, *Italy* 28 C6
Como, Lago di, *Italy* 28 B6
Comodoro Rivadavia,
 Argentina 128 F3
Comorâște, *Romania* 42 E6
Comorin, C., *India* 66 Q10
Comoro Is. = Comoros ■,
 Ind. Oc. 77 H8
Comoros ■, *Ind. Oc.* 77 H8
Comox, *Canada* 104 D4
Compiègne, *France* 19 C9
Comporta, *Portugal* 35 G2
Compostela, *Mexico* 118 C4
Comprida, I., *Brazil* 127 A6
Compton, *Canada* 111 A13
Compton, *U.S.A.* 117 M8
Comrat, *Moldova* 43 D13
Con Cuong, *Vietnam* 64 C5
Con Son, *Vietnam* 65 H6
Conakry, *Guinea* 82 D2
Conara, *Australia* 94 G4
Concarneau, *France* 18 E3
Conceição, *Mozam.* 87 F4
Conceição da Barra, *Brazil* 125 G11
Conceição do Araguaia,
 Brazil 125 E9

Concepción, L., *Bolivia* 124 G6
Concepción, Punta, *Mexico* 118 B2
Concepción del Oro, *Mexico* 118 C4
Concepción del Uruguay,
 Argentina 126 C4
Conception, Pt., *U.S.A.* 117 L6
Conception B., *Canada* 103 C9
Conception B., *Namibia* 88 C1
Conception I., *Bahamas* 121 B4
Concession, *Zimbabwe* 87 F3
Conchas Dam, *U.S.A.* 113 H2
Conches-en-Ouche, *France* 18 D7
Concho, *U.S.A.* 115 J9
Concho →, *U.S.A.* 113 K5
Conchos →, *Chihuahua,
 Mexico* 118 B4
Conchos →, *Tamaulipas,
 Mexico* 119 B5
Concord, *Calif., U.S.A.* 116 H4
Concord, *N.C., U.S.A.* 109 H5
Concord, *N.H., U.S.A.* 111 C13
Concordia, *Argentina* 126 C4
Concórdia, *Brazil* 124 D5
Concordia, *Mexico* 118 C3
Concordia, *U.S.A.* 112 F6
Concrete, *U.S.A.* 114 B3
Condamine, *Australia* 95 D5
Condat, *France* 20 C6
Conde, *U.S.A.* 112 C5
Condé-sur-Noireau, *France* 18 D6
Condeúba, *Brazil* 125 F10
Condobolin, *Australia* 95 E4
Condom, *France* 20 E4
Condon, *U.S.A.* 114 D3
Conegliano, *Italy* 29 C9
Conejera, I. = Conills, I.
 des, *Spain* 37 B9
Conejos, *Mexico* 118 B4
Confolens, *France* 20 B4
Confuso →, *Paraguay* 126 B4
Congaz, *Moldova* 43 D13
Conghua, *China* 59 F9
Congjiang, *China* 58 E7
Congleton, *U.K.* 12 D5
Congo (Kinshasa) = Congo,
 Dem. Rep. of the ■,
 Africa 84 E4
Congo ■, *Africa* 84 E3
Congo →, *Africa* 84 F2
Congo, Dem. Rep. of the ■,
 Africa 84 E4
Congo Basin, *Africa* 84 E4
Congonhas, *Brazil* 127 A7
Congress, *U.S.A.* 115 J7
Conil = Conil de la
 Frontera, *Spain* 35 J4
Conil de la Frontera, *Spain* 35 J4
Conills, I. des, *Spain* 37 B9
Coniston, *Canada* 102 C3
Conjeeveram =
 Kanchipuram, *India* 66 N11
Conklin, *Canada* 105 B6
Conklin, *U.S.A.* 111 D9
Conn, L., *Ireland* 15 B2
Connacht □, *Ireland* 15 C2
Conneaut, *U.S.A.* 110 E4
Connecticut □, *U.S.A.* 111 E12
Connecticut →, *U.S.A.* 111 E12
Connell, *U.S.A.* 114 C4
Connellsville, *U.S.A.* 110 F5
Connemara, *Ireland* 15 C2
Connemaugh →, *U.S.A.* 110 F5
Conner, *France* 18 D7
Connersville, *U.S.A.* 108 F3
Connors Ra., *Australia* 94 C4
Conques, *France* 20 D6
Conquest, *Canada* 105 C7
Conrad, *U.S.A.* 114 B8
Conran, C., *Australia* 95 F4
Conroe, *U.S.A.* 113 K7
Consecon, *Canada* 110 C7
Conselheiro Lafaiete, *Brazil* 127 A7
Conselve, *Italy* 29 C9
Consett, *U.K.* 12 C6
Consort, *Canada* 105 C6
Constance = Konstanz,
 Germany 25 H5
Constance, L. = Bodensee,
 Europe 25 H5
Constanța, *Romania* 43 F13
Constanța □, *Romania* 43 F13
Constantia, *U.S.A.* 111 C8
Constantina, *Spain* 35 H5
Constantine, *Algeria* 78 A7
Constitución, *Chile* 126 D1
Constitución, *Uruguay* 126 C4
Consuegra, *Spain* 34 F7
Consul, *Canada* 105 D7
Contact, *U.S.A.* 114 F6
Contai, *India* 69 J12
Contamana, *Peru* 124 E4
Contarina, *Italy* 29 C9
Contas →, *Brazil* 125 F11
Contes, *France* 21 E11
Contoocook, *U.S.A.* 111 C13
Contra Costa, *Mozam.* 89 D5
Contres, *France* 18 E8
Contrexéville, *France* 19 D12
Contwoyto L., *Canada* 100 B8
Conversano, *Italy* 31 B10
Conway = Conwy, *U.K.* 12 D4
Conway = Conwy →, *U.K.* 12 D4
Conway, *Ark., U.S.A.* 113 H8
Conway, *N.H., U.S.A.* 111 C13
Conway, *S.C., U.S.A.* 109 J6
Conway, L., *Australia* 95 D2
Conwy, *U.K.* 12 D4
Conwy □, *U.K.* 12 D4
Conwy →, *U.K.* 12 D4
Coober Pedy, *Australia* 95 D1

Cooch Behar = Koch Bihar, India 67 F16
Cooinda, Australia 92 B5
Cook, Australia 93 F5
Cook, U.S.A. 112 B8
Cook, B., Chile 128 H3
Cook, C., Canada 104 C3
Cook Inlet, U.S.A. 100 C4
Cook, Mt., N.Z. 91 K3
Cook Strait, N.Z. 91 J5
Cook Is., Pac. Oc. 97 J12
Cookeville, U.S.A. 109 G3
Cookhouse, S. Africa 88 E4
Cookshire, Canada 111 A13
Cookstown, U.K. 15 B5
Cooksville, Canada 110 C5
Cooktown, Australia 94 B4
Coolabah, Australia 95 E4
Cooladdi, Australia 95 D4
Coolah, Australia 95 E4
Coolamon, Australia 95 E4
Coolgardie, Australia 93 F3
Coolidge, U.S.A. 115 K8
Coolidge Dam, U.S.A. 115 K8
Cooma, Australia 95 F4
Coon Rapids, U.S.A. 112 C8
Coonabarabran, Australia 95 E4
Coonalpyn, Australia 95 F2
Coonamble, Australia 95 E4
Coonana, Australia 93 F3
Coondapoor, India 66 N9
Cooninie, L., Australia 95 D2
Cooper, U.S.A. 113 J7
Cooper Cr. →, Australia 95 D2
Cooperstown, N. Dak., U.S.A. 112 B5
Cooperstown, N.Y., U.S.A. 111 D10
Coorabie, Australia 93 F5
Coorow, Australia 93 E2
Cooroy, Australia 95 D5
Coos Bay, U.S.A. 114 E1
Coosa →, U.S.A. 109 J2
Cootamundra, Australia 95 E4
Cootehill, Ireland 15 B4
Copahue Paso, Argentina 126 D1
Copainalá, Mexico 119 D6
Copake Falls, U.S.A. 111 D11
Copalnic Mănăştur, Romania 43 C8
Copán, Honduras 120 D2
Cope, U.S.A. 112 F3
Cope, C., Spain 33 H3
Copenhagen = København, Denmark 11 J6
Copenhagen, U.S.A. 111 C9
Copertino, Italy 31 B11
Copiapó, Chile 126 B1
Copiapó →, Chile 126 B1
Coplay, U.S.A. 111 F9
Copp L., Canada 104 A6
Copparo, Italy 29 D8
Coppename →, Surinam 125 B7
Copper Harbor, U.S.A. 108 B2
Copper Queen, Zimbabwe 87 F2
Copperas Cove, U.S.A. 113 K6
Copperbelt □, Zambia 87 E2
Coppermine = Kugluktuk, Canada 100 B8
Coppermine →, Canada 100 B8
Copperopolis, U.S.A. 116 H6
Copşa Mică, Romania 43 D9
Coquet →, U.K. 12 B6
Coquilhatville = Mbandaka, Dem. Rep. of the Congo 84 D3
Coquille, U.S.A. 114 E1
Coquimbo, Chile 126 C1
Coquimbo □, Chile 126 C1
Corabia, Romania 43 G9
Coracora, Peru 124 G4
Coraki, Australia 95 D5
Coral, U.S.A. 110 F5
Coral Gables, U.S.A. 109 N5
Coral Harbour = Salliq, Canada 101 B11
Coral Sea, Pac. Oc. 96 J7
Coral Springs, U.S.A. 109 M5
Coraopolis, U.S.A. 110 F4
Corato, Italy 31 A9
Corbeil-Essonnes, France 19 D9
Corbie, France 19 C9
Corbières, France 20 F6
Corbigny, France 19 E10
Corbin, U.S.A. 108 G3
Corbones →, Spain 35 H5
Corbu, Romania 43 F13
Corby, U.K. 13 E7
Corcaigh = Cork, Ireland 15 E3
Corcoran, U.S.A. 116 J7
Cordele, U.S.A. 109 K4
Cordell, U.S.A. 113 H5
Cordenòns, Italy 29 C9
Cordes, France 20 D5
Córdoba, Argentina 126 C3
Córdoba, Mexico 119 D5
Córdoba, Spain 35 H6
Córdoba □, Argentina 126 C3
Córdoba □, Spain 35 G6
Córdoba, Sierra de, Argentina 126 C3
Cordon, Phil. 61 C4
Cordova, U.S.A. 100 B5
Corella, Spain 32 C3
Corella →, Australia 94 B3
Corfield, Australia 94 C3
Corfu = Kérkira, Greece 36 A3
Corfu, Str. of, Greece 36 A4
Corgo = O Corgo, Spain 34 C3
Cori, Italy 30 A5
Coria, Spain 34 F4
Coria del Río, Spain 35 H4
Corigliano Cálabro, Italy 31 C9
Coringa Is., Australia 94 B4

Corinth = Kórinthos, Greece 38 D4
Corinth, Miss., U.S.A. 109 H1
Corinth, N.Y., U.S.A. 111 C11
Corinth, N.Y., U.S.A. 111 C11
Corinth, G. of = Korinthiakós Kólpos, Greece 38 C4
Corinth Canal, Greece 38 D4
Corinto, Brazil 125 G10
Corinto, Nic. 120 D2
Cork, Ireland 15 E3
Cork □, Ireland 15 E3
Cork Harbour, Ireland 15 E3
Corlay, France 18 D3
Corleone, Italy 30 E6
Corleto Perticara, Italy 31 B9
Çorlu, Turkey 41 E11
Cormack L., Canada 104 A4
Cormòns, Italy 29 C10
Cormorant, Canada 105 C8
Cormorant L., Canada 105 C8
Corn Is. = Maiz, Is. del, Nic. 120 D3
Cornélio Procópio, Brazil 127 A5
Corner Brook, Canada 103 C8
Corneşti, Moldova 43 C13
Corníglio, Italy 28 D7
Corning, Ark., U.S.A. 113 G9
Corning, Calif., U.S.A. 114 G2
Corning, Iowa, U.S.A. 112 E7
Corning, N.Y., U.S.A. 110 D7
Corno Grande, Italy 29 F10
Cornwall, Canada 102 C5
Cornwall, U.S.A. 111 F8
Cornwall □, U.K. 13 G3
Cornwall I., Canada 109 B3
Corny Pt., Australia 95 E2
Coro, Venezuela 124 A5
Coroatá, Brazil 125 D10
Corocoro, Bolivia 124 G5
Coroico, Bolivia 124 G5
Coromandel, N.Z. 91 G5
Coromandel Coast, India 66 N12
Corona, Calif., U.S.A. 117 M9
Corona, N. Mex., U.S.A. 115 J11
Coronach, Canada 105 D7
Coronado, U.S.A. 117 N9
Coronado, B. de, Costa Rica 120 E3
Coronados, Is. los, U.S.A. 117 N9
Coronation, Canada 104 C6
Coronation Gulf, Canada 100 B8
Coronation I., Antarctica 5 C18
Coronation Is., Australia 92 B3
Coronda, Argentina 126 C3
Coronel, Chile 126 D1
Coronel Bogado, Paraguay 126 B4
Coronel Dorrego, Argentina 126 D3
Coronel Oviedo, Paraguay 126 B4
Coronel Pringles, Argentina 126 D3
Coronel Suárez, Argentina 126 D3
Coronel Vidal, Argentina 126 D4
Coropuna, Nevado, Peru 124 G4
Çorovoda, Albania 40 F4
Corowa, Australia 95 F4
Corozal, Belize 119 D7
Corps, France 21 D9
Corpus, Argentina 127 B4
Corpus Christi, U.S.A. 113 M6
Corpus Christi, L., U.S.A. 113 L6
Corral de Almaguer, Spain 34 F7
Corralejo, Canary Is. 37 F6
Corréggio, Italy 28 D7
Correntes, C. das, Mozam. 89 C6
Corrèze □, France 20 C5
Corrèze →, France 20 C5
Corrib, L., Ireland 15 C2
Corridónia, Italy 29 E10
Corrientes, Argentina 126 B4
Corrientes □, Argentina 126 B4
Corrientes →, Argentina 126 C4
Corrientes →, Peru 124 D4
Corrientes, C., Colombia 124 B3
Corrientes, C., Cuba 120 B3
Corrientes, C., Mexico 118 C3
Corrigan, U.S.A. 113 K7
Corrigin, Australia 93 F2
Corry, U.S.A. 110 E5
Corryong, Australia 95 F4
Corse, C., France 21 E13
Corse, C., France 21 E13
Corse-du-Sud □, France 21 G13
Corsica = Corse, France 21 G13
Corsicana, U.S.A. 113 J6
Corte, France 21 F13
Corte Pinto, Portugal 35 H3
Cortegana, Spain 35 H4
Cortez, U.S.A. 115 H9
Cortina d'Ampezzo, Italy 29 B9
Cortland, N.Y., U.S.A. 111 D8
Cortland, Ohio, U.S.A. 110 E4
Cortona, Italy 29 E8
Corubal →, Guinea-Biss. 82 C2
Coruche, Portugal 35 G2
Çoruh →, Turkey 49 K5
Çorum, Turkey 72 B6
Corumbá, Brazil 124 G7
Corund, Romania 43 D10
Corunna = A Coruña, Spain 34 B1
Corvallis, U.S.A. 114 D2
Corvette, L. de la, Canada 102 B5
Corydon, U.S.A. 112 E8
Cosalá, Mexico 118 C3
Cosamaloapan, Mexico 119 D5
Cosenza, Italy 31 C9
Coşereni, Romania 43 F11
Cosmo Newberry, Australia 93 E3
Cosne-Cours-sur-Loire, France 19 E9
Coso Junction, U.S.A. 117 J9
Coso Pk., U.S.A. 117 J9

Cospeito, Spain 34 B3
Cosquín, Argentina 126 C3
Cossato, Italy 28 C5
Cossé-le-Vivien, France 18 E6
Cosson →, France 18 E8
Costa Blanca, Spain 33 G4
Costa Brava, Spain 32 D8
Costa del Sol, Spain 35 J6
Costa Dorada, Spain 32 D6
Costa Mesa, U.S.A. 117 M9
Costa Rica ■, Cent. Amer. 120 E3
Costa Smeralda, Italy 30 A2
Costeşti, Romania 43 F9
Costigliole d'Asti, Italy 28 D5
Cosumnes →, U.S.A. 116 G5
Coswig, Sachsen, Germany 24 D9
Coswig, Sachsen-Anhalt, Germany 24 D8
Cotabato, Phil. 61 H6
Cotagaita, Bolivia 126 A2
Côte d'Azur, France 21 E11
Côte-d'Ivoire = Ivory Coast ■, Africa 82 D4
Côte d'Or, France 19 E11
Côte-d'Or □, France 19 E11
Coteau des Prairies, U.S.A. 112 C6
Coteau du Missouri, U.S.A. 112 B4
Coteau Landing, Canada 111 A10
Cotentin, France 18 C5
Côtes-d'Armor □, France 18 D4
Côtes de Meuse, France 19 C12
Côtes-du-Nord = Côtes-d'Armor □, France 18 D4
Cotiella, Spain 32 C5
Cotillo, Canary Is. 37 F5
Cotijueni, Moldova 43 C13
Cotonou, Benin 83 D5
Cotopaxi, Ecuador 122 D3
Cotronei, Italy 31 C9
Cotswold Hills, U.K. 13 F5
Cottage Grove, U.S.A. 114 E2
Cottbus, Germany 24 D10
Cottonwood, U.S.A. 115 J7
Cotulla, U.S.A. 113 L5
Coubre, Pte. de la, France 20 C2
Couches, France 19 F11
Couço, Portugal 35 G2
Coudersport, U.S.A. 110 E6
Couedic, C. du, Australia 95 F2
Couëron, France 18 E5
Couesnon →, France 18 D5
Couhé, France 20 B4
Coulanges-sur-Yonne, France 19 E10
Coulee City, U.S.A. 114 C4
Coulman I., Antarctica 5 D11
Coulommiers, France 19 D10
Coulon →, France 21 E9
Coulonge →, Canada 102 C4
Coulonges-sur-l'Autize, France 20 B3
Coulounieix-Chamiers, France 20 C4
Coulterville, U.S.A. 116 H6
Council, U.S.A. 114 D5
Council Bluffs, U.S.A. 112 E7
Council Grove, U.S.A. 112 F6
Coupeville, U.S.A. 116 B4
Courantyne →, S. Amer. 122 C5
Courcelles, Belgium 17 D4
Courçon, France 20 B3
Courmayeur, Italy 28 C3
Couronne, C. de, France 21 E9
Cours-la-Ville, France 19 F11
Coursan, France 20 E7
Courseulles-sur-Mer, France 18 C6
Courtenay, Canada 104 D3
Courtenay, France 19 D10
Courtland, U.S.A. 116 G5
Courtrai = Kortrijk, Belgium 17 D3
Courtright, Canada 110 D2
Coushatta, U.S.A. 113 J8
Coutances, France 18 C5
Coutras, France 20 C3
Coutts Crossing, Australia 95 D5
Couvin, Belgium 17 D4
Covarrubias, Spain 34 C7
Covasna, Romania 43 E11
Covasna □, Romania 43 E11
Cove I., Canada 110 A3
Coventry, U.K. 13 E6
Covilhã, Portugal 34 E3
Covington, Ga., U.S.A. 109 J4
Covington, Ky., U.S.A. 108 F3
Covington, Okla., U.S.A. 113 G6
Covington, Tenn., U.S.A. 113 H10
Covington, Va., U.S.A. 108 G5
Cowal, L., Australia 95 E4
Cowan, L., Australia 93 F3
Cowan L., Canada 105 C7
Cowangie, Australia 95 F3
Cowansville, Canada 102 C5
Coward Springs, Australia 95 D2
Cowcowing Lakes, Australia 93 F2
Cowdenbeath, U.K. 14 E5
Cowell, Australia 95 E2
Cowes, U.K. 13 G6
Cowichan L., Canada 116 D4
Cowlitz →, U.S.A. 116 D4
Cowra, Australia 95 E4
Cox, Spain 33 G4
Coxilha Grande, Brazil 127 B5
Cox's Bazar, Bangla. 67 J17
Coyote Wells, U.S.A. 117 N11
Coyuca de Benítez, Mexico 119 D4
Coyuca de Catalan, Mexico 118 D4
Cozad, U.S.A. 112 E5
Cozes, France 20 C3
Cozumel, Mexico 119 C7
Cozumel, Isla, Mexico 119 C7
Cracow = Kraków, Poland 45 H6

Cracow, Australia 95 D5
Cradock, Australia 95 E2
Cradock, S. Africa 88 E4
Craig, U.S.A. 114 F10
Craigavon, U.K. 15 B5
Craigmore, Zimbabwe 87 G3
Craik, Canada 105 C7
Crailsheim, Germany 25 F6
Craiova, Romania 43 F8
Cramsie, Australia 94 C3
Cranberry L., U.S.A. 111 B10
Cranberry Portage, Canada 105 C8
Cranbrook, Australia 93 F2
Cranbrook, Canada 104 D5
Crandon, U.S.A. 112 C10
Crane, Oreg., U.S.A. 114 E4
Crane, Tex., U.S.A. 113 K3
Cranston, U.S.A. 111 E13
Craon, France 18 E6
Craonne, France 19 C10
Craponne-sur-Arzon, France 20 C7
Crasna, Romania 43 D12
Crasna →, Romania 42 C7
Crasnei, Munţii, Romania 43 C8
Crater L., U.S.A. 114 E2
Crater Lake National Park, U.S.A. 114 E2
Crateús, Brazil 125 E10
Crati →, Italy 31 C9
Crato, Brazil 125 E11
Crato, Portugal 35 F3
Craven, L., Canada 102 B4
Crawford, U.S.A. 112 D3
Crawfordsville, U.S.A. 108 E2
Crawley, U.K. 13 F7
Crazy Mts., U.S.A. 114 C8
Crean L., Canada 105 C7
Crécy-en-Ponthieu, France 19 B8
Crediton, Canada 110 C3
Cree →, Canada 105 B7
Cree →, U.K. 14 G4
Cree L., Canada 105 B7
Creede, U.S.A. 115 H10
Creekside, U.S.A. 110 F5
Creel, Mexico 118 B3
Creemore, Canada 110 B4
Creighton, Canada 105 C8
Creighton, U.S.A. 112 D6
Creil, France 19 C9
Crema, Italy 28 C6
Cremona, Italy 28 C7
Crepaja, Serbia, Yug. 42 E5
Crépy, France 19 C10
Crépy-en-Valois, France 19 C9
Cres, Croatia 29 D11
Crescent City, U.S.A. 114 F1
Crescentino, Italy 28 C5
Cresco, U.S.A. 112 D8
Crespino, Italy 29 D8
Crespo, Argentina 126 C3
Cresson, U.S.A. 110 F6
Crest, France 21 D9
Cresta, Mt., Phil. 61 C5
Crestline, Calif., U.S.A. 117 L9
Crestline, Ohio, U.S.A. 110 F2
Creston, Canada 104 D5
Creston, Calif., U.S.A. 116 K6
Creston, Iowa, U.S.A. 112 E7
Crestview, Calif., U.S.A. 116 H8
Crestview, Fla., U.S.A. 109 K2
Creswick, Australia 95 F3
Crete = Kríti, Greece 36 D7
Crete, U.S.A. 112 E6
Crete, Sea of, Greece 39 E7
Créteil, France 19 D9
Creus, C. de, Spain 32 C8
Creuse □, France 19 F9
Creuse →, France 20 B4
Creutzwald, France 19 C13
Creuzburg, Germany 24 D6
Crèvecœur-le-Grand, France 19 C9
Crevillente, Spain 33 G4
Crewe, U.K. 12 D5
Crewkerne, U.K. 13 G5
Criciúma, Brazil 127 B6
Cricova, Moldova 43 C13
Crieff, U.K. 14 E5
Crikvenica, Croatia 29 C11
Crimea □, Ukraine 47 K8
Crimean Pen. = Krymskyy Pivostriv, Ukraine 47 K8
Crimmitschau, Germany 24 E8
Cristuru Secuiesc, Romania 43 D10
Crişul Alb →, Romania 42 D6
Crişul Negru →, Romania 42 D6
Crişul Repede →, Romania 42 D5
Criuleni, Moldova 43 C14
Crivitz, Germany 24 B7
Crna →, Macedonia 40 E5
Crna Gora = Montenegro □, Yugoslavia 40 D3
Crna Gora, Macedonia 40 D5
Crna Reka = Crna →, Macedonia 40 E5
Crna Trava, Serbia, Yug. 40 D6
Crni Drim →, Macedonia 40 E4
Crni Timok →, Serbia, Yug. 40 C6
Crnoljeva Planina, Kosovo, Yug. 40 D5
Črnomelj, Slovenia 29 C12
Croagh Patrick, Ireland 15 C2
Croatia ■, Europe 29 C13
Crocker, Banjaran, Malaysia 62 C5
Crockett, U.S.A. 113 K7
Crocodile = Krokodil →, Mozam. 89 D5
Crocodile Is., Australia 94 A1
Crocq, France 20 C6
Crodo, Italy 28 B4
Crohy Hd., Ireland 15 B3
Croisette, Pte. du, France 21 E11
Croisic, Pte. du, France 18 E4
Croix, L. La, Canada 102 C1

Croker, C., Australia 92 B5
Croker, C., Canada 110 B4
Croker I., Australia 92 B5
Cromarty, U.K. 14 D4
Cromer, U.K. 12 E9
Cromwell, N.Z. 91 L2
Cromwell, U.S.A. 111 E12
Cronat, France 19 F10
Crook, U.K. 12 C6
Crooked →, Canada 104 C4
Crooked →, U.S.A. 114 D3
Crooked I., Bahamas 121 B5
Crooked Island Passage, Bahamas 121 B5
Crookston, Minn., U.S.A. 112 B6
Crookston, Nebr., U.S.A. 112 D4
Crookwell, Australia 95 E4
Crosby, U.K. 12 D4
Crosby, N. Dak., U.S.A. 112 A3
Crosby, Pa., U.S.A. 110 E6
Crosbyton, U.S.A. 113 J4
Crosía, Italy 31 C9
Cross →, Nigeria 83 E6
Cross City, U.S.A. 109 L4
Cross Fell, U.K. 12 C5
Cross L., Canada 105 C9
Cross Lake, Canada 105 C9
Cross River □, Nigeria 83 D6
Cross Sound, U.S.A. 100 C6
Crossett, U.S.A. 113 J9
Crosshaven, Ireland 15 E3
Crossville, U.S.A. 109 G3
Croswell, U.S.A. 110 C2
Croton-on-Hudson, U.S.A. 111 E11
Crotone, Italy 31 C10
Crow →, Canada 104 B4
Crow Agency, U.S.A. 114 D10
Crow Hd., Ireland 15 E1
Crowell, U.S.A. 113 J5
Crowley, U.S.A. 113 K8
Crowley, L., U.S.A. 116 H8
Crown Point, Ind., U.S.A. 108 E2
Crown Point, N.Y., U.S.A. 111 C11
Crownpoint, U.S.A. 115 J9
Crows Landing, U.S.A. 116 H5
Crows Nest, Australia 95 D5
Crowsnest Pass, Canada 104 D6
Croydon, Australia 94 B3
Croydon, U.K. 13 F7
Crozet, Is., Ind. Oc. 3 G12
Crozon, France 18 D2
Cruz, C., Cuba 120 C4
Cruz Alta, Brazil 127 B5
Cruz de Incio, Spain 34 C3
Cruz del Eje, Argentina 126 C3
Cruzeiro, Brazil 127 A7
Cruzeiro do Oeste, Brazil 127 A5
Cruzeiro do Sul, Brazil 124 E4
Cry L., Canada 104 B3
Crystal Bay, U.S.A. 116 F7
Crystal Brook, Australia 95 E2
Crystal City, U.S.A. 113 L5
Crystal Falls, U.S.A. 108 B1
Crystal River, U.S.A. 109 L4
Crystal Springs, U.S.A. 113 K9
Csenger, Hungary 42 C7
Csongrád, Hungary 42 D5
Csongrád □, Hungary 42 D5
Csorna, Hungary 42 C2
Csurgo, Hungary 42 D2
Cu Lao Hon, Vietnam 65 G7
Cua Rao, Vietnam 64 C5
Cuácua →, Mozam. 87 F4
Cuamato, Angola 88 B2
Cuamba, Mozam. 87 E4
Cuando →, Angola 85 H4
Cuando Cubango □, Angola 88 B3
Cuangar, Angola 88 B2
Cuanza →, Angola 76 G5
Cuarto →, Argentina 126 C3
Cuatrociénegas, Mexico 118 B4
Cuauhtémoc, Mexico 118 B3
Cuba, Portugal 35 G3
Cuba, N. Mex., U.S.A. 115 J10
Cuba, N.Y., U.S.A. 110 D6
Cuba ■, W. Indies 120 B4
Çubuk, Turkey 72 B5
Cuchumatanes, Sierra de los, Guatemala 120 C1
Cuckfield, U.K. 13 F7
Cucuí, Brazil 124 C5
Cucurpe, Mexico 118 A2
Cúcuta, Colombia 124 B4
Cudalbi, Romania 43 E12
Cuddalore, India 66 P11
Cuddapah, India 66 M11
Cuddapan, L., Australia 94 D3
Cudillero, Spain 34 B4
Cue, Australia 93 E2
Cuéllar, Spain 34 D6
Cuenca, Ecuador 124 D3
Cuenca, Spain 32 E2
Cuenca □, Spain 32 F3
Cuenca, Serranía de, Spain 32 F3
Cuerdo del Pozo, Embalse de la, Spain 32 D2
Cuernavaca, Mexico 119 D5
Cuero, U.S.A. 113 L6
Cuers, France 21 E10
Cuevas del Almanzora, Spain 33 H3
Cuevo, Bolivia 124 H6
Cugir, Romania 43 E8
Cuhai-Bakony →, Hungary 42 C2
Cuiabá, Brazil 125 G7
Cuiabá →, Brazil 125 G7
Cuijk, Neths. 17 C5
Cuilco, Guatemala 120 C1
Cuillin Hills, U.K. 14 D2
Cuillin Sd., U.K. 14 D2

Cuiseaux

Cuiseaux, France 19 F12
Cuito →, Angola 88 B3
Cuitzeo, L. de, Mexico 118 D4
Cujmir, Romania 42 F7
Cukai, Malaysia 65 K4
Culbertson, U.S.A. 112 A2
Culcairn, Australia 95 F4
Culebra, Sierra de la, Spain 34 D4
Culfa, Azerbaijan 73 C11
Culgoa →, Australia 95 D4
Culiacán, Mexico 118 C3
Culiacán →, Mexico 118 C3
Culion, Phil. 61 F4
Cúllar, Spain 35 H8
Cullarin Ra., Australia 95 E4
Cullen, U.K. 14 D6
Cullen Pt., Australia 94 A3
Cullera, Spain 33 F4
Cullman, U.S.A. 109 H2
Culoz, France 21 C9
Culpeper, U.S.A. 108 F7
Culuene →, Brazil 125 F8
Culver, Pt., Australia 93 F3
Culverden, N.Z. 91 K4
Cumaná, Venezuela 124 A6
Cumaovası, Turkey 39 C9
Cumberland, B.C., Canada 104 D4
Cumberland, Ont., Canada 111 A9
Cumberland, U.S.A. 108 F6
Cumberland →, U.S.A. 109 G2
Cumberland, L., U.S.A. 109 G3
Cumberland I., U.S.A. 109 K5
Cumberland Is., Australia 94 C4
Cumberland L., Canada 105 C8
Cumberland Pen., Canada 101 B13
Cumberland Plateau, U.S.A. 109 H3
Cumberland Sd., Canada 101 B13
Cumbernauld, U.K. 14 F5
Cumborah, Australia 95 D4
Cumbres Mayores, Spain 35 G4
Cumbria □, U.K. 12 C5
Cumbrian Mts., U.K. 12 C5
Cumbum, India 66 M11
Cuminá →, Brazil 125 D7
Cummings Mt., U.S.A. 117 K8
Cummins, Australia 95 E2
Cumnock, Australia 95 E4
Cumnock, U.K. 14 F4
Cumpas, Mexico 118 B3
Cumplida, Pta., Canary Is. 37 F2
Çumra, Turkey 72 D5
Cunco, Chile 128 D2
Cuncumén, Chile 126 C1
Cunderdin, Australia 93 F2
Cunene →, Angola 88 B1
Cúneo, Italy 28 D4
Çüngüş, Turkey 70 B3
Cunillera, I. = Sa Conillera, Spain 37 C7
Cunlhat, France 20 C7
Cunnamulla, Australia 95 D4
Cuorgnè, Italy 28 C4
Cupar, Canada 105 C8
Cupar, U.K. 14 E5
Cupcini, Moldova 43 B12
Cupica, G. de, Colombia 124 B3
Ćuprija, Serbia, Yug. 40 C5
Curaçao, Neth. Ant. 121 D6
Curanilahue, Chile 126 D1
Curaray →, Peru 124 D4
Cure →, France 19 E10
Curepto, Chile 126 D1
Curiapo, Venezuela 124 B6
Curicó, Chile 126 C1
Curinga, Italy 31 D9
Curitiba, Brazil 127 B6
Curitibanos, Brazil 127 B5
Currabubula, Australia 95 E5
Currais Novos, Brazil 125 E11
Curralinho, Brazil 125 D9
Currant, U.S.A. 114 G6
Current →, U.S.A. 113 G9
Currie, Australia 94 F3
Currie, U.S.A. 114 F6
Curtea de Argeş, Romania 43 E9
Curtici, Romania 42 D6
Curtis, U.S.A. 112 E4
Curtis Group, Australia 94 F4
Curtis I., Australia 94 C5
Curuápanema →, Brazil 125 D7
Curuçá, Brazil 125 D9
Curuguaty, Paraguay 127 A4
Curup, Indonesia 62 E2
Cururupu, Brazil 125 D10
Curuzú Cuatiá, Argentina 126 B4
Curvelo, Brazil 125 G10
Cushing, U.S.A. 113 H6
Cushing, Mt., Canada 104 B3
Cusihuiriáchic, Mexico 118 B3
Cusna, Mte., Italy 28 D7
Cusset, France 19 F10
Custer, U.S.A. 112 D3
Cut Bank, U.S.A. 114 B7
Cutchogue, U.S.A. 111 E12
Cuthbert, U.S.A. 109 K3
Cutler, U.S.A. 116 J7
Cutro, Italy 31 C9
Cuttaburra →, Australia 95 D3
Cuttack, India 67 J14
Cuvier, C., Australia 93 D1
Cuvier I., N.Z. 91 G5
Cuxhaven, Germany 24 B4
Cuyahoga Falls, U.S.A. 110 E3
Cuyapo, Phil. 61 D4
Cuyo, Phil. 61 F4
Cuyo East Pass, Phil. 61 F4
Cuyo West Pass, Phil. 61 F4
Cuyuni →, Guyana 124 B7
Cuzco, Bolivia 124 H5
Cuzco, Peru 124 F4
Čvrsnica, Bos.-H. 42 G2
Cwmbran, U.K. 13 F4
Cyangugu, Rwanda 86 C2
Cybinka, Poland 45 F1
Cyclades = Kikládhes, Greece 38 E6
Cygnet, Australia 94 G4
Cynthiana, U.S.A. 108 F3
Cypress Hills, Canada 105 D7
Cypress Hills Prov. Park, Canada 105 D7
Cyprus ■, Asia 36 E12
Cyrenaica, Libya 79 C10
Czaplinek, Poland 44 E3
Czar, Canada 105 C6
Czarna →, Łódzkie, Poland 45 G6
Czarna →, Świętokrzyskie, Poland 45 H8
Czarna Białostocka, Poland 45 E10
Czarna Woda, Poland 44 E5
Czarne, Poland 44 E3
Czarnków, Poland 45 F3
Czech Rep. ■, Europe 26 B8
Czechowice-Dziedzice, Poland 45 J5
Czempiń, Poland 45 F3
Czeremcha, Poland 45 F10
Czerniejewo, Poland 45 F4
Czersk, Poland 44 E4
Czerwieńsk, Poland 45 F2
Czerwionka-Leszczyny, Poland 45 H5
Częstochowa, Poland 45 H6
Człopa, Poland 45 E3
Człuchów, Poland 44 E4
Czyżew-Osada, Poland 45 F9

D

Da →, Vietnam 58 G5
Da Hinggan Ling, China 60 B7
Da Lat, Vietnam 65 G7
Da Nang, Vietnam 64 D7
Da Qaidam, China 60 C4
Da Yunhe →, China 57 G11
Da'an, China 57 B13
Dab'a, Ras el, Egypt 80 H6
Daba Shan, China 58 B7
Dabai, Nigeria 83 C6
Dabakala, Ivory C. 82 D4
Dabas, Hungary 42 C4
Dabat, Ethiopia 81 E4
Dabbagh, Jabal, Si. Arabia 70 E2
Dabhoi, India 68 H5
Dąbie, Poland 45 F5
Dabie Shan, China 59 B10
Dabilda, Cameroon 83 C7
Dabnou, Niger 83 C6
Dabo = Pasirkuning, Indonesia 62 E2
Dabola, Guinea 82 C2
Dabou, Ivory C. 82 D4
Daboya, Ghana 83 D4
Dąbrowa Białostocka, Poland 44 E10
Dąbrowa Górnicza, Poland 45 H6
Dąbrowa Tarnowska, Poland 45 H7
Dabu, China 59 E11
Dabung, Malaysia 65 K4
Dabus →, Ethiopia 81 E4
Dacato →, Ethiopia 81 F5
Dacca = Dhaka, Bangla. 69 H14
Dacca = Dhaka □, Bangla. 69 G14
Dachau, Germany 25 G7
Dachstein, Hoher, Austria 26 D6
Dačice, Czech Rep. 26 B8
Dadanawa, Guyana 124 C7
Daday, Turkey 72 B5
Dade City, U.S.A. 109 L4
Dadhar, Pakistan 68 E2
Dadiya, Nigeria 83 D7
Dadra & Nagar Haveli □, India 66 J8
Dadri = Charkhi Dadri, India 68 E7
Dadu, Pakistan 68 F2
Dadu He →, China 58 C4
Daet, Phil. 61 D5
Dafang, China 58 D5
Dağ, Turkey 39 D12
Dagana, Senegal 82 B1
Dagash, Sudan 80 D3
Dagestan □, Russia 49 J8
Dagestanskiye Ogni, Russia 49 J9
Daggett, U.S.A. 117 L10
Daghestan Republic = Dagestan □, Russia 49 J8
Daghfeli, Sudan 80 D3
Dağlıq Qarabağ = Nagorno-Karabakh, Azerbaijan 70 B5
Dagö = Hiiumaa, Estonia 9 G20
Dagu, China 57 E9
Daguan, China 58 D4
Dagupan, Phil. 61 C4
Daguragu, Australia 92 C5
Dahab, Egypt 80 B3
Dahlak Kebir, Eritrea 81 D5
Dahlenburg, Germany 24 B6
Dahlonega, U.S.A. 109 H4
Dahme, Germany 24 D9
Dahod, India 68 H6
Dahomey = Benin ■, Africa 83 D5
Dahong Shan, China 59 B9
Dahra, Senegal 82 B1
Dahshûr, Egypt 80 J7
Dahūk, Iraq 70 B3
Dai Hao, Vietnam 64 C6
Dai-Sen, Japan 55 G6
Dai Shan, China 59 B14
Dai Xian, China 56 E7
Daicheng, China 56 E9
Daimiel, Spain 35 F7
Daingean, Ireland 15 C4
Dainkog, China 58 A1
Daintree, Australia 94 B4
Daiō-Misaki, Japan 55 G8
Dair, J. ed, Sudan 81 E3
Dairût, Egypt 80 B3
Daisetsu-Zan, Japan 54 C11
Dajarra, Australia 94 C2
Dajin Chuan →, China 58 B3
Dak Dam, Cambodia 64 F6
Dak Nhe, Vietnam 64 E6
Dak Pek, Vietnam 64 E6
Dak Song, Vietnam 65 F6
Dak Sui, Vietnam 64 E6
Dakar, Senegal 82 C1
Dakhla, W. Sahara 78 D2
Dakhla, El Wâhât el-, Egypt 80 B2
Dakingari, Nigeria 83 C5
Dakor, India 68 H5
Dakoro, Niger 83 C6
Dakota City, U.S.A. 112 D6
Đakovica, Kosovo, Yug. 40 D4
Đakovo, Croatia 42 E3
Dalaba, Guinea 82 C2
Dalachi, China 56 F3
Dalai Nur, China 56 C9
Dālakī, Iran 71 D6
Dalälven, Sweden 10 D10
Dalaman, Turkey 39 E10
Dalaman →, Turkey 39 E10
Dalandzadgad, Mongolia 56 C3
Dalap-Uliga-Darrit, Marshall Is. 96 G9
Dalarna, Sweden 10 D8
Dālbandīn, Pakistan 66 E4
Dalbeattie, U.K. 14 G5
Dalbeg, Australia 94 C4
Dalbosjön, Sweden 11 F6
Dalby, Australia 95 D5
Dalby, Sweden 11 J7
Dale City, U.S.A. 108 F7
Dale Hollow L., U.S.A. 109 G3
Dalga, Egypt 80 B3
Dalgān, Iran 71 E8
Dalhart, U.S.A. 113 G3
Dalhousie, Canada 103 C6
Dalhousie, India 68 C6
Dali, Shaanxi, China 56 G5
Dali, Yunnan, China 58 E3
Dalian, China 57 E11
Daliang Shan, China 58 D4
Daling He →, China 57 D11
Dāliyat el Karmel, Israel 75 C4
Dalj, Croatia 42 E3
Dalkeith, U.K. 14 F5
Dallas, Oreg., U.S.A. 114 D2
Dallas, Tex., U.S.A. 113 J6
Dallol, Ethiopia 81 E5
Dalmā, U.A.E. 71 E7
Dalmacija, Croatia 29 E13
Dalmas, L., Canada 103 B5
Dalmatia = Dalmacija, Croatia 29 E13
Dalmau, India 69 F9
Dalmellington, U.K. 14 F4
Dalnegorsk, Russia 51 E14
Dalnerechensk, Russia 51 E14
Daloa, Ivory C. 82 D3
Dalou Shan, China 58 C6
Dalry, U.K. 14 F4
Dalrymple, L., Australia 94 C4
Dals Långed, Sweden 11 F6
Dalsjöfors, Sweden 11 G7
Dalsland, Sweden 11 F6
Daltenganj, India 69 H11
Dalton, Ga., U.S.A. 109 H3
Dalton, Mass., U.S.A. 111 D11
Dalton, Nebr., U.S.A. 112 E3
Dalton Iceberg Tongue, Antarctica 5 C9
Dalton-in-Furness, U.K. 12 C4
Dalupiri I., Phil. 61 B4
Dalvík, Iceland 8 D4
Dalwallinu, Australia 93 F2
Daly →, Australia 92 B5
Daly City, U.S.A. 116 H4
Daly L., Canada 105 B7
Daly River, Australia 92 B5
Daly Waters, Australia 94 B1
Dalyan, Turkey 39 E10
Dam Doi, Vietnam 65 H5
Dam Ha, Vietnam 64 B6
Daman, India 66 J8
Dāmaneh, Iran 71 C6
Damanhûr, Egypt 80 H7
Damant L., Canada 105 A7
Damanzhuang, China 56 E9
Damar, Indonesia 63 F7
Damaraland, Namibia 88 C2
Damascus = Dimashq, Syria 75 B5
Damaturu, Nigeria 83 C7
Damāvand, Iran 71 C7
Damāvand, Qolleh-ye, Iran 71 C7
Damba, Angola 84 F3
Dâmboviţa □, Romania 43 F10
Dâmboviţa →, Romania 43 F11
Dâmbovnic →, Romania 43 F10
Dame Marie, Haiti 121 C5
Dāmghān, Iran 71 B7
Dămienesti, Romania 43 D11
Damietta = Dumyât, Egypt 80 H7
Daming, China 56 F8
Damīr Qābū, Syria 70 B4
Dammam = Ad Dammām, Si. Arabia 71 E6
Dammarie-les-Lys, France 19 D9
Dammartin-en-Goële, France 19 C9
Damme, Germany 24 C4
Damodar →, India 69 H12
Damoh, India 69 H8
Dampier, Australia 92 D2
Dampier, Selat, Indonesia 63 E8
Dampier Arch., Australia 92 D2
Damrei, Chuor Phnum, Cambodia 65 G4
Damvillers, France 19 C12
Dan-Gulbi, Nigeria 83 C6
Dan Xian, China 64 C7
Dana, Indonesia 63 F6
Dana, L., Canada 102 B4
Dana, Mt., U.S.A. 116 H7
Danakil Depression, Ethiopia 81 E5
Danakil Desert, Ethiopia 81 E5
Danané, Ivory C. 82 D3
Danao, Phil. 61 F6
Danau Poso, Indonesia 63 E6
Danba, China 58 B3
Danbury, U.S.A. 111 E11
Danby L., U.S.A. 115 J6
Dand, Afghan. 68 D1
Dandeldhura, Nepal 69 E9
Dandeli, India 66 M9
Dandenong, Australia 95 F4
Dandîl, Egypt 80 J7
Dandong, China 57 D13
Danfeng, China 56 H6
Dangan Liedao, China 59 F10
Dangé-St-Roman, France 20 B4
Dângeni, Romania 43 C11
Danger Is. = Pukapuka, Cook Is. 97 J11
Danger Pt., S. Africa 88 E2
Dangla, Ethiopia 81 E4
Dangla Shan = Tanggula Shan, China 60 C4
Dangora, Nigeria 83 C6
Dangouadougou, Burkina Faso 82 D4
Dangrek, Phnom, Thailand 64 E5
Dangriga, Belize 119 D7
Dangshan, China 56 G9
Dangtu, China 59 B12
Dangyang, China 59 B8
Dani, Burkina Faso 83 C4
Daniel, U.S.A. 114 E8
Daniel's Harbour, Canada 103 B8
Danielskuil, S. Africa 88 D3
Danielson, U.S.A. 111 E13
Danilov, Russia 46 C11
Danilovgrad, Montenegro, Yug. 40 D3
Danilovka, Russia 48 E7
Daning, China 56 F6
Danissa, Kenya 86 B5
Danja, Nigeria 83 C6
Danjiangkou, China 59 A8
Danjiangkou Shuiku, China 59 A8
Dank, Oman 71 F8
Dankalwa, Nigeria 83 C7
Dankama, Nigeria 83 C6
Dankhar Gompa, India 66 C11
Dankov, Russia 46 F10
Danleng, China 58 B4
Danlí, Honduras 120 D2
Dannemora, U.S.A. 111 B11
Dannenberg, Germany 24 B7
Dannevirke, N.Z. 91 J6
Dannhauser, S. Africa 89 D5
Dansville, U.S.A. 110 D7
Danta, India 68 G5
Dantan, India 69 J12
Dante, Somali Rep. 74 E5
Danube = Dunărea →, Europe 43 E14
Danvers, U.S.A. 111 D14
Danville, Ill., U.S.A. 108 E2
Danville, Ky., U.S.A. 108 G3
Danville, Pa., U.S.A. 111 F8
Danville, Va., U.S.A. 109 G6
Danville, Vt., U.S.A. 111 B12
Danyang, China 59 B12
Danzhai, China 58 D6
Danzig = Gdańsk, Poland 44 D5
Dão →, Portugal 34 E2
Dao Xian, China 59 E8
Daocheng, China 58 C3
Daoukro, Ivory C. 82 D4
Dapaong, Togo 83 C5
Dapchi, Nigeria 83 C7
Dapitan, Phil. 61 G5
Daqing Shan, China 56 D6
Daqu Shan, China 59 B14
Dar Banda, Africa 76 F6
Dar el Beida = Casablanca, Morocco 78 B4
Dar es Salaam, Tanzania 86 D4
Dar Mazār, Iran 71 D8
Dar'ā, Syria 75 C5
Dar'ā □, Syria 75 C5
Dārāb, Iran 71 D7
Daraban, Pakistan 68 D4
Darabani, Romania 43 B11
Daraina, Madag. 89 A8
Daraj, Libya 79 B8
Dārān, Iran 71 C6
Daravica, Kosovo, Yug. 40 D4
Daraw, Egypt 80 C3
Dārayyā, Syria 75 B5
Darazo, Nigeria 83 C7
Darband, Pakistan 68 B5
Darband, Kūh-e, Iran 71 D8
Darbhanga, India 69 F11
D'Arcy, Canada 104 C4
Darda, Croatia 42 E3
Dardanelle, Ark., U.S.A. 113 H8
Dardanelle, Calif., U.S.A. 116 G7
Dardanelles = Çanakkale Boğazı, Turkey 41 F10
Dare →, Ethiopia 81 F5
Darende, Turkey 72 C7
Dārestān, Iran 71 D8
Darfo, Italy 28 C7
Dârfûr, Sudan 79 F10
Dargai, Pakistan 68 B4
Dargan Ata, Uzbekistan 50 E7
Dargaville, N.Z. 91 F4
Dargol, Niger 83 C5
Darhan Muminggan Lianheqi, China 56 D6
Dari, Sudan 81 F3
Darıca, Turkey 72 B3
Darién, G. del, Colombia 122 C3
Dariganga = Ovoot, Mongolia 56 B7
Darinskoye, Kazakstan 48 E10
Darjeeling = Darjiling, India 69 F13
Darjiling, India 69 F13
Darkan, Australia 93 F2
Darkhana, Pakistan 68 D5
Darkhazīneh, Iran 71 D6
Darkot Pass, Pakistan 69 A5
Darling →, Australia 95 E3
Darling Downs, Australia 95 D5
Darling Ra., Australia 93 F2
Darlington, U.K. 12 C6
Darlington, U.S.A. 109 H6
Darlington □, U.K. 12 C6
Darlington, L., S. Africa 88 E4
Darlington Point, Australia 95 E4
Darlot, L., Australia 93 E3
Darłowo, Poland 44 D3
Dărmăneşti, Bacău, Romania 43 D11
Dărmăneşti, Suceava, Romania 43 C11
Darmstadt, Germany 25 F4
Darnah, Libya 79 B10
Darnall, S. Africa 89 D5
Darney, France 19 D13
Darnley, C., Antarctica 5 C6
Darnley B., Canada 100 B7
Daroca, Spain 32 D3
Darou-Mousti, Senegal 82 B1
Darr →, Australia 94 C3
Darra Pezu, Pakistan 68 C4
Darrequeira, Argentina 126 D3
Darrington, U.S.A. 114 B3
Darsser Ort, Germany 24 A8
Dart →, U.K. 13 G4
Dart, C., Antarctica 5 D14
Dartford, U.K. 13 F8
Dartmoor, U.K. 13 G4
Dartmouth, Canada 103 D7
Dartmouth, U.K. 13 G4
Dartmouth, L., Australia 95 D4
Dartuch, C. = Artrutx, C. de, Spain 37 B10
Daruvar, Croatia 42 E2
Darvaza, Turkmenistan 50 E6
Darvel, Teluk = Lahad Datu, Teluk, Malaysia 63 D5
Darwen, U.K. 12 D5
Darwendale, Zimbabwe 89 B5
Darwha, India 66 J10
Darwin, Australia 92 B5
Darwin, U.S.A. 117 J9
Darya Khan, Pakistan 68 D4
Daryoi Amu = Amudarya →, Uzbekistan 50 E6
Dās, U.A.E. 71 E7
Dashen, Ras, Ethiopia 81 E4
Dashetai, China 56 D5
Dashhowuz, Turkmenistan 50 E6
Dashkesan = Daşkäsän, Azerbaijan 49 K7
Dashköpri, Turkmenistan 71 B9
Dasht, Iran 71 B8
Dasht →, Pakistan 66 G2
Daska, Pakistan 68 C6
Daşkäsän, Azerbaijan 49 K7
Dassa, Benin 83 D5
Dasuya, India 68 D6
Datça, Turkey 39 E9
Datia, India 69 G8
Datian, China 59 E11
Datong, Anhui, China 59 B11
Datong, Shanxi, China 56 D7
Dattakhel, Pakistan 68 C3
Datteln, Germany 24 D3
Datu, Tanjung, Indonesia 62 D3
Datu Piang, Phil. 61 H6
Daud Khel, Pakistan 68 C4
Daudnagar, India 69 G11
Daugava →, Latvia 9 H21
Daugavpils, Latvia 9 J22
Daulpur, India 68 F7
Daun, Germany 25 E2
Dauphin, Canada 105 C8
Dauphin, U.S.A. 110 F8
Dauphin L., Canada 105 C9
Dauphiné, France 21 C9
Daura, Borno, Nigeria 83 C7
Daura, Katsina, Nigeria 83 C6
Dausa, India 68 F7
Däväçi, Azerbaijan 49 K9
Davangere, India 66 M9
Davao, Phil. 61 H6
Davao G., Phil. 61 H6
Dāvar Panāh, Iran 71 E9
Davenport, Calif., U.S.A. 116 H4
Davenport, Iowa, U.S.A. 112 E9
Davenport, Wash., U.S.A. 114 C4
Davenport Ra., Australia 94 C1
Daventry, U.K. 13 E6
David, Panama 120 E3
David City, U.S.A. 112 E6
David Gorodok = Davyd Haradok, Belarus 47 F4
Davidson, Canada 105 C7
Davis, U.S.A. 116 G5
Davis Dam, U.S.A. 117 K12

Davis Inlet, Canada 103 A7
Davis Mts., U.S.A. 113 K2
Davis Sea, Antarctica 5 C7
Davis Str., N. Amer. 101 B14
Davo →, Ivory C. 82 D3
Davos, Switz. 25 J5
Davutlar, Turkey 39 D9
Davy L., Canada 105 B7
Davyd Haradok, Belarus ... 47 F4
Dawa →, Ethiopia 81 G5
Dawaki, Bauchi, Nigeria ... 83 D6
Dawaki, Kano, Nigeria ... 83 C6
Dawei, Burma 64 E2
Dawes Ra., Australia 94 C5
Dawlish, U.K. 13 G4
Dawros Hd., Ireland 15 B3
Dawson, Canada 100 B6
Dawson, U.S.A. 109 K3
Dawson, I., Chile 128 G2
Dawson B., Canada 105 C8
Dawson Creek, Canada ... 104 B4
Dawson Inlet, Canada 105 A10
Dawson Ra., Australia 94 C4
Dawu, Hubei, China 59 B9
Dawu, Sichuan, China 58 B3
Dax, France 20 E2
Daxian, China 58 B6
Daxin, China 58 F6
Daxindian, China 57 F11
Daxinggou, China 57 C15
Daxue Shan, Sichuan, China 58 B3
Daxue Shan, Yunnan, China 58 F2
Dayao, China 58 E3
Daye, China 59 B10
Dayet en Naharat, Mali ... 82 B4
Dayi, China 58 B4
Daylesford, Australia 95 F3
Dayong, China 59 C8
Dayr az Zawr, Syria 70 C4
Daysland, Canada 104 C6
Dayton, Nev., U.S.A. 116 F7
Dayton, Ohio, U.S.A. 108 F3
Dayton, Pa., U.S.A. 110 F5
Dayton, Tenn., U.S.A. 109 H3
Dayton, Wash., U.S.A. ... 114 C4
Dayton, Wyo., U.S.A. 114 D10
Daytona Beach, U.S.A. ... 109 L5
Dayu, China 59 E10
Dayville, U.S.A. 114 D4
Dazhu, China 58 B6
Dazkırı, Turkey 39 D11
Dazu, China 58 C5
De Aar, S. Africa 88 E3
De Funiak Springs, U.S.A. 109 K2
De Grey →, Australia 92 D2
De Haan, Belgium 17 C3
De Kalb, U.S.A. 112 E10
De Land, U.S.A. 109 L5
De Leon, U.S.A. 113 J5
De Panne, Belgium 17 C2
De Pere, U.S.A. 108 C1
De Queen, U.S.A. 113 H7
De Quincy, U.S.A. 113 K8
De Ridder, U.S.A. 113 K8
De Smet, U.S.A. 112 C6
De Soto, U.S.A. 112 F9
De Tour Village, U.S.A. ... 108 C4
De Witt, U.S.A. 113 H9
Dead Sea, Asia 75 D4
Deadwood, U.S.A. 112 C3
Deadwood L., Canada 104 B3
Deal, U.K. 13 F9
Deal I., Australia 94 F4
Dealesville, S Africa 88 D4
De'an, China 59 C10
Dean →, Canada 104 C3
Dean, Forest of, U.K. 13 F5
Dean Chan., Canada 104 C3
Deán Funes, Argentina ... 126 C3
Dease →, Canada 104 B3
Dease L., Canada 104 B2
Dease Lake, Canada 104 B2
Death Valley, U.S.A. 117 J10
Death Valley Junction,
 U.S.A. 117 J10
Death Valley National Park,
 U.S.A. 117 J10
Deauville, France 18 C7
Deba, Spain 32 B2
Deba Habe, Nigeria 83 C7
Debaltsevo, Ukraine 47 H10
Debao, China 58 F6
Debar, Macedonia 40 E4
Debden, Canada 105 C7
Dębica, Poland 45 H8
Dęblin, Poland 45 G8
Dębno, Poland 45 F1
Débo, L., Mali 82 B4
Debolt, Canada 104 B5
Deborah East, L., Australia 93 F2
Deborah West, L., Australia 93 F2
Debrc, Serbia, Yug. 40 B3
Debre Birhan, Ethiopia ... 81 F4
Debre Markos, Ethiopia ... 81 E4
Debre May, Ethiopia 81 E4
Debre Sina, Ethiopia 81 F4
Debre Tabor, Ethiopia 81 E4
Debre Zevit, Ethiopia 81 F4
Debre Zeyit, Ethiopia 81 F4
Debrecen, Hungary 42 C6
Debrzno, Poland 44 E4
Dečani, Kosovo, Yug. 40 D4
Decatur, Ala., U.S.A. 109 H2
Decatur, Ga., U.S.A. 109 J3
Decatur, Ill., U.S.A. 112 F10
Decatur, Ind., U.S.A. 108 E3
Decatur, Tex., U.S.A. 113 J6
Decazeville, France 20 D6
Deccan, India 66 L11
Deception Bay, Australia .. 95 D5
Deception L., Canada 105 B8

Dechang, China 58 D4
Dechhu, India 68 F5
Děčín, Czech Rep. 26 A7
Decize, France 19 F10
Deckerville, U.S.A. 110 C2
Decollatura, Italy 31 C9
Decorah, U.S.A. 112 D9
Deda, Romania 43 D9
Dedéagach =
 Alexandroúpolis, Greece . 41 F9
Deder, Ethiopia 81 F5
Dedham, U.S.A. 111 D13
Dédougou, Burkina Faso . 82 C4
Dedovichi, Russia 46 D5
Dedza, Malawi 87 E3
Dee →, Aberds., U.K. ... 14 D6
Dee →, Dumf. & Gall.,
 U.K. 14 G4
Dee →, Wales, U.K. 12 D4
Deep B., Canada 104 A5
Deepwater, Australia 95 D5
Deer →, Canada 105 B10
Deer L., Canada 105 C10
Deer Lake, Nfld., Canada . 103 C8
Deer Lake, Ont., Canada .. 105 C10
Deer Lodge, U.S.A. 114 C7
Deer Park, U.S.A. 114 C5
Deer River, U.S.A. 112 B8
Deeragun, Australia 94 B4
Deerdepoort, S. Africa ... 88 C4
Deferiet, U.S.A. 111 B9
Defiance, U.S.A. 108 E3
Degana, India 68 F6
Dêgê, China 58 B2
Degebe →, Portugal 35 G3
Degeberga, Sweden 11 J8
Dégelis, Canada 103 C6
Degema, Nigeria 83 E6
Degerfors, Sweden 10 E8
Degerhamn, Sweden 11 H10
Deggendorf, Germany 25 G8
Degh →, Pakistan 68 D5
Degloor, India 66 K10
Değirmendere, Turkey ... 41 F13
Deh Bīd, Iran 71 D7
Deh-e Shīr, Iran 71 D7
Dehaj, Iran 71 D7
Dehak, Iran 71 E9
Dehdez, Iran 71 D6
Dehej, India 68 J5
Dehestān, Iran 71 D7
Dehgolān, Iran 70 C5
Dehi Titan, Afghan. 66 C3
Dehibat, Tunisia 79 B8
Dehloran, Iran 70 C5
Dehnow-e Kūhestān, Iran .. 71 E8
Dehra Dun, India 68 D8
Dehri, India 69 G11
Dehua, China 59 E12
Dehui, China 57 B13
Deim Zubeir, Sudan 81 F2
Deinze, Belgium 17 D3
Dej, Romania 43 C8
Deje, Sweden 10 E7
Dejiang, China 58 C7
Deka →, S. Africa 88 B4
Dekemhare, Eritrea 81 D4
Dekese,
 Dem. Rep. of the Congo . 84 E4
Del Mar, U.S.A. 117 N9
Del Norte, U.S.A. 115 H10
Del Rio, U.S.A. 113 L4
Delai, Sudan 80 D4
Delambre I., Australia ... 92 D2
Delano, U.S.A. 117 K7
Delano Peak, U.S.A. 115 G7
Delareyville, S. Africa ... 88 D4
Delaronde L., Canada 105 C7
Delavan, U.S.A. 112 D10
Delaware, U.S.A. 108 E4
Delaware □, U.S.A. 108 F8
Delaware →, U.S.A. 111 G9
Delaware B., U.S.A. 108 F8
Delay →, Canada 103 A5
Delbrück, Germany 24 D4
Delčevo, Macedonia 40 E6
Delegate, Australia 95 F4
Delémont, Switz. 25 H3
Delevan, U.S.A. 110 D6
Delft, Neths. 17 B4
Delfzijl, Neths. 17 A6
Delgado, C., Mozam. 87 E5
Delgerhet, Mongolia 56 B6
Delgo, Sudan 80 C3
Delhi, Canada 110 D4
Delhi, India 68 E7
Delhi, La., U.S.A. 113 J9
Delhi, N.Y., U.S.A. 111 D10
Deli Jovan, Serbia, Yug. .. 40 B6
Delia, Canada 104 C6
Delice, Turkey 72 C6
Delicias, Mexico 118 B3
Delījān, Iran 71 C6
Déline, Canada 100 B7
Delisle, Canada 105 C7
Delitzsch, Germany 24 D8
Dell City, U.S.A. 115 L11
Dell Rapids, U.S.A. 112 D6
Delle, France 19 E14
Delmar, U.S.A. 111 D11
Delmenhorst, Germany 24 B4
Delnice, Croatia 29 C11
Delong, Ostrova, Russia .. 51 B15
Deloraine, Australia 94 G4
Deloraine, Canada 105 D8
Delphi, Greece 38 C4
Delphi, U.S.A. 108 E2
Delphos, U.S.A. 108 E3
Delportshoop, S. Africa ... 88 D3
Delray Beach, U.S.A. ... 109 M5
Delsbo, Sweden 10 C10

Delta, Colo., U.S.A. 115 G9
Delta, Utah, U.S.A. 114 G7
Delta □, Nigeria 83 D6
Delta Junction, U.S.A. ... 100 B5
Deltona, U.S.A. 109 L5
Delungra, Australia 95 D5
Delvada, India 68 J4
Delvinë, Albania 40 G4
Demak, Indonesia 63 G14
Demanda, Sierra de la, Spain 32 C2
Demavand = Damāvand,
 Iran 71 C7
Dembecha, Ethiopia 81 E4
Dembi, Ethiopia 81 F4
Dembia,
 Dem. Rep. of the Congo . 86 B2
Dembidolo, Ethiopia 81 F3
Demchok, India 69 C8
Demer →, Belgium 17 D4
Demetrias, Greece 38 B5
Demidov, Russia 46 E6
Deming, N. Mex., U.S.A. . 115 K10
Deming, Wash., U.S.A. ... 116 B4
Demini →, Brazil 124 D6
Demirci, Turkey 39 B10
Demirköprü Barajı, Turkey 39 C10
Demirköy, Turkey 41 E11
Demmin, Germany 24 B9
Demonte, Italy 28 D4
Demopolis, U.S.A. 109 J2
Dempo, Indonesia 62 E2
Demyansk, Russia 46 D7
Den Burg, Neths. 17 A4
Den Chai, Thailand 64 D3
Den Haag = 's-Gravenhage,
 Neths. 17 B4
Den Helder, Neths. 17 B4
Den Oever, Neths. 17 B5
Denain, France 19 B10
Denair, U.S.A. 116 H6
Denau, Uzbekistan 50 F7
Denbigh, Canada 110 A7
Denbigh, U.K. 12 D4
Denbighshire □, U.K. ... 12 D4
Dendang, Indonesia 62 E3
Dendermonde, Belgium ... 17 C4
Deneba, Ethiopia 81 F4
Denge, Nigeria 83 C6
Dengchuan, China 58 E3
Dengfeng, China 56 G7
Dengi, Nigeria 83 D6
Dengkou, China 56 D4
Dengzhou, China 59 A9
Denham, Australia 93 E1
Denham Ra., Australia ... 94 C4
Denham Sd., Australia ... 93 E1
Denholm, Canada 105 C7
Denia, Spain 33 G5
Denial B., Australia 95 E1
Deniliquin, Australia ... 95 F3
Denison, Iowa, U.S.A. ... 112 E7
Denison, Tex., U.S.A. ... 113 J6
Denison Plains, Australia . 92 C4
Denizli, Turkey 39 D11
Denizli □, Turkey 39 D11
Denman Glacier, Antarctica 5 C7
Denmark, Australia 93 F2
Denmark ■, Europe 11 J3
Denmark Str., Atl. Oc. ... 4 C6
Dennison, U.S.A. 110 F3
Denny, U.K. 14 E5
Denpasar, Indonesia ... 62 F5
Denton, Mont., U.S.A. ... 114 C9
Denton, Tex., U.S.A. 113 J6
D'Entrecasteaux, Pt.,
 Australia 93 F2
Denu, Ghana 83 D5
Denver, Colo., U.S.A. ... 112 F2
Denver, Pa., U.S.A. 111 F8
Denver City, U.S.A. 113 J3
Deoband, India 68 E7
Deogarh, India 68 G5
Deoghar, India 69 G12
Deolali, India 66 K8
Deoli = Devli, India 68 G6
Deoli, India 69 J10
Deora, India 68 F4
Deori, India 69 H8
Deoria, India 69 F10
Deosai Mts., Pakistan ... 69 B6
Deosri, India 69 F14
Depalpur, India 68 H6
Deping, China 57 F9
Deposit, U.S.A. 111 D9
Depuch I., Australia ... 92 D2
Deputatskiy, Russia 51 C14
Dêqên, China 58 C2
Deqing, China 59 F8
Dera Ghazi Khan, Pakistan 68 D4
Dera Ismail Khan, Pakistan 68 D4
Derabugti, Pakistan 68 E3
Derawar Fort, Pakistan .. 68 E4
Derbent, Russia 49 J9
Derbent, Turkey 39 C10
Derby, Australia 92 C3
Derby, U.K. 12 E6
Derby, Conn., U.S.A. ... 111 E11
Derby, Kans., U.S.A. ... 113 G6
Derby, N.Y., U.S.A. 110 D6
Derby City □, U.K. 12 E6
Derby Line, U.S.A. 111 B12
Derbyshire □, U.K. 12 E6
Derecske, Hungary 42 C6
Dereköy, Turkey 41 E11
Dereli, Turkey 73 B8
Derg →, U.K. 15 B4
Derg, L., Ireland 15 D3
Dergachi = Derhaci, Ukraine 47 G9
Dergaon, India 67 F19
Derhaci, Ukraine 47 G9
Dhamási, Greece 38 B4

Derik, Turkey 73 D9
Derinkuyu, Turkey 72 C6
Dermantsi, Bulgaria 41 C8
Dermott, U.S.A. 113 J9
Dêrong, China 58 C2
Derry = Londonderry, U.K. 15 B4
Derry = Londonderry □,
 U.K. 15 B4
Derry, N.H., U.S.A. 111 D13
Derry, Pa., U.S.A. 110 F5
Derryveagh Mts., Ireland . 15 B3
Derudub, Sudan 80 D4
Derval, France 18 E5
Dervéni, Greece 38 C4
Derventa, Bos.-H. 42 F2
Derwent →, Derby, U.K. . 12 E6
Derwent →, N. Yorks.,
 U.K. 12 D7
Derwent Water, U.K. ... 12 C4
Des Moines, Iowa, U.S.A. . 112 E8
Des Moines, N. Mex.,
 U.S.A. 113 G3
Des Moines →, U.S.A. ... 112 E9
Desa, Romania 42 G8
Desaguadero →, Argentina 126 C2
Desaguadero →, Bolivia .. 124 G5
Descanso, Pta., Mexico ... 117 N9
Descartes, France 20 B4
Deschaillons, Canada ... 103 C5
Deschambault L., Canada . 105 C8
Deschutes →, U.S.A. ... 114 D3
Dese, Ethiopia 81 E4
Deseado →, Argentina ... 128 F3
Desenzano del Garda, Italy 28 C7
Desert Center, U.S.A. ... 117 M11
Desert Hot Springs, U.S.A. 117 M10
Deshnok, India 68 F5
Desna →, Ukraine 47 G6
Desnățui →, Romania ... 43 G8
Desolación, I., Chile 128 G2
Despeñaperros, Paso, Spain 35 G7
Despotovac, Serbia, Yug. . 40 B5
Dessau, Germany 24 D8
Dessye = Dese, Ethiopia .. 81 E4
Desuri, India 68 G5
Desvres, France 19 B8
Det Udom, Thailand 64 E5
Deta, Romania 42 E6
Dete, S. Africa 88 B4
Dete, Zimbabwe 87 F2
Đetinja →, Serbia, Yug. .. 40 C4
Detmold, Germany 24 D4
Detour, Pt., U.S.A. 108 C2
Detroit, U.S.A. 110 D1
Detroit Lakes, U.S.A. ... 112 B7
Detva, Slovak Rep. 27 C12
Deurne, Neths. 17 C5
Deutsche Bucht, Germany . 24 A4
Deutschlandsberg, Austria . 26 E8
Deux-Sèvres □, France ... 18 F6
Deva, Romania 42 E7
Devakottai, India 66 Q11
Devaprayag, India 69 D8
Dévaványa, Hungary 42 C5
Deveci Dağları, Turkey ... 72 B7
Devecikonağı, Turkey ... 41 G12
Devecser, Hungary 42 C2
Develi, Turkey 72 C6
Deventer, Neths. 17 B6
Deveron →, U.K. 14 D6
Devesel, Romania 42 F7
Devgadh Bariya, India ... 68 H5
Devikot, India 68 F4
Devils Den, U.S.A. 116 K7
Devils Lake, U.S.A. 112 A5
Devils Paw, Canada 104 B2
Devils Tower Junction,
 U.S.A. 112 C2
Devin, Bulgaria 41 E8
Devine, U.S.A. 113 L5
Devizes, U.K. 13 F6
Devli, India 68 G6
Devolii →, Albania 40 F4
Devon, Canada 104 C6
Devon □, U.K. 13 G4
Devon I., Canada 4 B3
Devonport, Australia ... 94 G4
Devonport, N.Z. 91 G5
Devrek, Turkey 72 B5
Devrekâni, Turkey 72 B5
Devrez →, Turkey 72 B6
Dewas, India 68 H7
Dewetsdorp, S. Africa ... 88 D4
Dexing, China 59 C11
Dexter, Maine, U.S.A. ... 109 C11
Dexter, Mo., U.S.A. 113 G10
Dexter, N. Mex., U.S.A. .. 113 J2
Deyang, China 58 B5
Deyhūk, Iran 71 C8
Deyyer, Iran 71 E6
Dezadeash L., Canada ... 104 A1
Dezfūl, Iran 71 C6
Dezhneva, Mys, Russia .. 51 C19
Dezhou, China 56 F9
Dhadhar →, India 69 G11
Dhahiriya = Aẕ Ẕāhiriyah,
 West Bank 75 D3
Dhahran = Aẓ Ẓahrān,
 Si. Arabia 71 E6
Dhak, Pakistan 68 C5
Dhaka, Bangla. 69 H14
Dhaka □, Bangla. 69 G14
Dhali, Cyprus 36 D12

Dhampur, India 69 E8
Dhamtari, India 67 J12
Dhanbad, India 69 H12
Dhangarhi, Nepal 67 E12
Dhankuta, Nepal 69 F12
Dhar, India 68 H6
Dharamsala = Dharmsala,
 India 68 C7
Dhariwal, India 68 D6
Dharla →, Bangla. 69 G13
Dharmapuri, India 66 N11
Dharmjaygarh, India ... 69 H10
Dharmsala, India 68 C7
Dharni, India 68 J7
Dhasan →, India 69 G8
Dhaulagiri, Nepal 69 E10
Dhebar, L., India 68 G6
Dheftera, Cyprus 36 D12
Dhenkanal, India 67 J14
Dhenoúsa, Greece 39 D7
Dherinia, Cyprus 36 D12
Dheskáti, Greece 40 G5
Dhespotikó, Greece 38 E6
Dhestina, Greece 38 C4
Dhiarrizos →, Cyprus ... 36 E11
Dhībān, Jordan 75 D4
Dhidhimótikhon, Greece .. 41 E10
Dhíkti Óros, Greece 36 D7
Dhilianáta, Greece 38 C2
Dhílos, Greece 39 D7
Dhilwan, India 68 D6
Dhimarkhera, India 69 H9
Dhimitsána, Greece 38 D4
Dhírfis = Dhírfis Óros,
 Greece 38 C5
Dhírfis Óros, Greece ... 38 C5
Dhodhekánisos, Greece .. 39 E8
Dhodhekánisos □, Greece 39 E8
Dhokós, Greece 38 D5
Dholiana, Greece 38 B2
Dholka, India 68 H5
Dhomokós, Greece 38 B4
Dhoraji, India 68 J4
Dhoxáton, Greece 41 E8
Dhragonísi, Greece 39 D7
Dhráhstis, Ákra, Greece .. 36 A3
Dhrangadhra, India 68 H4
Dhrápanon, Ákra, Greece 36 D6
Dhriopís, Greece 38 D6
Dhrol, India 68 H4
Dhuburi, India 67 F16
Dhule, India 66 J9
Di-ib, W. →, Sudan 80 D4
Di Linh, Vietnam 65 G7
Di Linh, Cao Nguyen,
 Vietnam 65 G7
Día, Greece 36 D7
Diabakania, Guinea 82 C2
Diablo, Mt., U.S.A. 116 H5
Diablo Range, U.S.A. ... 116 J5
Diafarabé, Mali 82 C4
Diala, Mali 82 C3
Dialakoro, Mali 82 C3
Dialakoto, Senegal 82 C2
Diallassagou, Mali 82 C4
Diamante, Argentina ... 126 C3
Diamante, Italy 31 C8
Diamante →, Argentina .. 126 C2
Diamantina, Brazil 125 G10
Diamantina →, Australia .. 95 D2
Diamantino, Brazil 125 F7
Diamond Bar, U.S.A. ... 117 L9
Diamond Harbour, India . 69 H13
Diamond Is., Australia ... 94 B5
Diamond Mts., U.S.A. ... 114 G6
Diamond Springs, U.S.A. . 116 G6
Dian Chi, China 58 E4
Dianalund, Denmark ... 11 J5
Dianbai, China 59 G8
Diancheng, China 59 G8
Dianjiang, China 58 B6
Diano Marina, Italy 28 E5
Dianra, Ivory C. 82 D3
Diapaga, Burkina Faso .. 83 C5
Diapangou, Burkina Faso 83 C5
Diariguila, Guinea 82 C2
Dībā, Oman 71 E8
Dibai, India 68 E8
Dibaya-Lubue,
 Dem. Rep. of the Congo . 84 E3
Dibete, Botswana 88 C4
Dibrugarh, India 67 F19
Dickens, U.S.A. 113 J4
Dickinson, U.S.A. 112 B3
Dickson = Dikson, Russia . 50 B9
Dickson, U.S.A. 109 G2
Dickson City, U.S.A. ... 111 E9
Dicle Nehri →, Turkey .. 73 D9
Dicomano, Italy 29 E8
Didesa, W. →, Ethiopia .. 81 E4
Didi, Sudan 81 F3
Didiéni, Mali 82 C3
Didsbury, Canada 104 C6
Die, France 21 D9
Diébougou, Burkina Faso . 82 C4
Diecke, Guinea 82 D3
Diefenbaker, L., Canada .. 105 C7
Diego de Almagro, Chile . 126 B1
Diekirch, Lux. 17 E6
Diéma, Mali 82 C3
Diembéring, Senegal ... 82 C1
Dien Ban, Vietnam 64 E7
Dien Bien, Vietnam 58 G4
Dien Khanh, Vietnam ... 65 F7
Diepholz, Germany 24 C4
Dieppe, France 18 C4
Dierks, U.S.A. 113 H8
Diest, Belgium 17 D5

Dietikon, *Switz.* 25 H4
Dieulefit, *France* 21 D9
Dieuze, *France* 19 D13
Dif, *Somali Rep.* 74 G3
Differdange, *Lux.* 17 E5
Dig, *India* 68 F7
Digba,
  Dem. Rep. of the Congo . 86 B2
Digby, *Canada* 103 D6
Diggi, *India* 68 F6
Dighinala, *Bangla.* 67 H18
Dighton, *U.S.A.* 112 F4
Digna, *Mali* 82 C3
Digne-les-Bains, *France* 21 D10
Digoin, *France* 19 F11
Digor, *Turkey* 73 B10
Digos, *Phil.* 61 H6
Digranes, *Iceland* 8 C6
Digul →, *Indonesia* 63 F9
Dihang →, *India* 67 F19
Dijlah, Nahr →, *Asia* 70 D5
Dijon, *France* 19 E12
Dikhil, *Djibouti* 81 E5
Dikili, *Turkey* 39 B8
Dikirnis, *Egypt* 80 H7
Dikkil = Dikhil, *Djibouti* .. 81 E5
Dikodougou, *Ivory C.* 82 D3
Diksmuide, *Belgium* 17 C2
Dikson, *Russia* 50 B9
Dikwa, *Nigeria* 83 C7
Dila, *Ethiopia* 81 F4
Dili, *Indonesia* 63 F7
Dilijan, *Armenia* 49 K7
Dilizhan = Dilijan, *Armenia* 49 K7
Dilj, *Croatia* 42 E3
Dillenburg, *Germany* 24 E4
Dilley, *U.S.A.* 113 L5
Dilling, *Sudan* 81 E2
Dillingen, *Bayern, Germany* 25 G6
Dillingen, *Saarland,*
  Germany 25 F2
Dillingham, *U.S.A.* 100 C4
Dillon, *Canada* 105 B7
Dillon, *Mont., U.S.A.* 114 D7
Dillon, *S.C., U.S.A.* 109 H6
Dillon →, *Canada* 105 B7
Dillsburg, *U.S.A.* 110 F7
Dilly, *Mali* 82 C3
Dilolo,
  Dem. Rep. of the Congo . 84 G4
Dimas, *Mexico* 118 C3
Dimashq, *Syria* 75 B5
Dimashq □, *Syria* 75 B5
Dimbaza, *S. Africa* 89 E4
Dimbokro, *Ivory C.* 82 D4
Dimboola, *Australia* 95 F3
Dîmbovița = Dâmbovița →,
  Romania 43 F11
Dimbulah, *Australia* 94 B4
Dimitrovgrad, *Bulgaria* .. 41 D9
Dimitrovgrad, *Russia* 48 C9
Dimitrovgrad, *Serbia, Yug.* . 40 C6
Dimitrovo = Pernik,
  Bulgaria 40 D7
Dimmitt, *U.S.A.* 113 H3
Dimo, *Sudan* 81 F2
Dimona, *Israel* 75 D4
Dimovo, *Bulgaria* 40 C6
Dinagat, *Phil.* 61 F6
Dinajpur, *Bangla.* 67 G16
Dinan, *France* 18 D4
Dīnān Āb, *Iran* 71 C8
Dinant, *Belgium* 17 D4
Dinapur, *India* 69 G11
Dinar, *Turkey* 39 C12
Dīnār, Kūh-e, *Iran* 71 D6
Dinara Planina, *Croatia* .. 29 D13
Dinard, *France* 18 D4
Dinaric Alps = Dinara
  Planina, *Croatia* 29 D13
Dindanko, *Mali* 82 C3
Dinder, Nahr ed →, *Sudan* . 81 E3
Dindigul, *India* 66 P11
Dindori, *India* 69 H9
Ding Xian = Dingzhou,
  China 56 E8
Dinga, *Pakistan* 68 G2
Dingalan, *Phil.* 61 D4
Dingbian, *China* 56 F4
Dingelstädt, *Germany* 24 D6
Dingle, *Ireland* 15 D1
Dingle, *Sweden* 11 F5
Dingle B., *Ireland* 15 D1
Dingmans Ferry, *U.S.A.* ... 111 E10
Dingnan, *China* 59 E10
Dingo, *Australia* 94 C4
Dingolfing, *Germany* 25 G8
Dingtao, *China* 56 G8
Dinguira, *Mali* 82 C2
Dinguiraye, *Guinea* 82 C2
Dingwall, *U.K.* 14 D4
Dingxi, *China* 56 G3
Dingxiang, *China* 56 E7
Dingyuan, *China* 59 A11
Dingzhou, *China* 56 E8
Dinh, Mui, *Vietnam* 65 G7
Dinh Lap, *Vietnam* 58 G6
Dinokwe, *Botswana* 88 C4
Dinorwic, *Canada* 105 D10
Dinosaur National
  Monument, *U.S.A.* 114 F9
Dinosaur Prov. Park, *Canada* 104 C6
Dinuba, *U.S.A.* 116 J7
Diö, *Sweden* 11 H8
Dioïla, *Mali* 82 C3
Dioka, *Mali* 82 C2
Diongoï, *Mali* 82 C3
Diósgyör, *Hungary* 42 B5
Diosig, *Romania* 42 C7
Diougani, *Mali* 82 C4
Diouloulou, *Senegal* . 82 C1

Dioura, *Mali* 82 C3
Diourbel, *Senegal* 82 C1
Dipalpur, *Pakistan* 68 D5
Diplo, *Pakistan* 68 G3
Dipolog, *Phil.* 61 G5
Dir, *Pakistan* 66 B7
Diré, *Mali* 82 B4
Dire Dawa, *Ethiopia* 81 F5
Diriamba, *Nic.* 120 D2
Dirk Hartog I., *Australia* .. 93 E1
Dirranbandi, *Australia* 95 D4
Disa, *India* 68 G5
Disa, *Sudan* 81 E3
Disappointment, C., *U.S.A.* 114 C2
Disappointment, L.,
  Australia 92 D3
Disaster B., *Australia* 95 F4
Discovery B., *Australia* 95 F3
Disentis Muster, *Switz.* 25 J4
Dishna, *Egypt* 80 B3
Disina, *Nigeria* 83 C6
Disko = Qeqertarsuaq,
  Greenland 4 C5
Disko Bugt, *Greenland* 4 C5
Disna = Dzisna →, *Belarus* 46 E5
Diss, *U.K.* 13 E9
Disteghil Sar, *Pakistan* .. 69 A6
Distrito Federal □, *Brazil* . 125 G9
Distrito Federal □, *Mexico* . 119 D5
Disûq, *Egypt* 80 H7
Diu, *India* 68 J4
Dīvāndarreh, *Iran* 70 C5
Dives →, *France* 18 C6
Dives-sur-Mer, *France* 18 C6
Divichi = Dāvāçi, *Azerbaijan* 49 K9
Divide, *U.S.A.* 114 D7
Dividing Ra., *Australia* .. 93 E2
Divinópolis, *Brazil* 125 H10
Divjake, *Albania* 40 F3
Divnoye, *Russia* 49 H6
Divo, *Ivory C.* 82 D3
Divriği, *Turkey* 73 C8
Dīwāl Kol, *Afghan.* 68 B2
Dixie Mt., *U.S.A.* 116 F6
Dixon, *Calif., U.S.A.* 116 G5
Dixon, *Ill., U.S.A.* 112 E10
Dixon Entrance, *U.S.A.* .. 100 C6
Dixville, *Canada* 111 A13
Diyadin, *Turkey* 73 C10
Diyālā →, *Iraq* 70 C5
Diyarbakır, *Turkey* 70 B4
Diyodar, *India* 68 G4
Djakarta = Jakarta,
  Indonesia 63 G12
Djamba, *Angola* 88 B1
Djambala, *Congo* 84 E2
Djanet, *Algeria* 78 D7
Djawa = Jawa, *Indonesia* . 63 G14
Djelfa, *Algeria* 78 B6
Djema, *C.A.R.* 86 A2
Djenné, *Mali* 82 C4
Djerba, I. de, *Tunisia* 79 B8
Djerid, Chott, *Tunisia* 78 B7
Djibo, *Burkina Faso* 83 C4
Djibouti, *Djibouti* 81 E5
Djibouti ■, *Africa* 81 E5
Djolu,
  Dem. Rep. of the Congo . 84 D4
Djougou, *Benin* 83 D5
Djoum, *Cameroon* 84 D2
Djourab, Erg du, *Chad* 79 E9
Djugu,
  Dem. Rep. of the Congo . 86 B3
Djúpivogur, *Iceland* 8 D6
Djursland, *Denmark* 11 H4
Dmitriya Lapteva, Proliv,
  Russia 51 B15
Dmitriyev Lgovskiy, *Russia* 47 F8
Dmitrov, *Russia* 46 D9
Dmitrovsk-Orlovskiy, *Russia* 47 F8
Dnepr →= Dnipro →,
  Ukraine 47 J7
Dneprodzerzhinsk =
  Dniprodzerzhynsk,
  Ukraine 47 H8
Dneprodzerzhinskoye
  Vdkhr. =
  Dniprodzerzhynske
  Vdskh., *Ukraine* 47 H8
Dnepropetrovsk =
  Dnipropetrovsk, *Ukraine* . 47 H8
Dneprorudnoye =
  Dniprorudne, *Ukraine* ... 47 J8
Dnestr →= Dnister →,
  Europe 47 J6
Dnestrovski = Belgorod,
  Russia 47 G9
Dnieper = Dnipro →,
  Ukraine 47 J7
Dniester = Dnister →,
  Europe 47 J6
Dnipro →, *Ukraine* 47 J7
Dniprodzerzhynsk, *Ukraine* 47 H8
Dniprodzerzhynske Vdskh.,
  Ukraine 47 H8
Dnipropetrovsk, *Ukraine* .. 47 H8
Dniprorudne, *Ukraine* 47 J8
Dnister →, *Europe* 47 J6
Dnistrovskyy Lyman,
  Ukraine 47 J6
Dno, *Russia* 46 D5
Dnyapro = Dnipro →,
  Ukraine 47 J7
Doaktown, *Canada* 103 C6
Doan Hung, *Vietnam* 58 G5
Doany, *Madag.* 89 A8
Doba, *Chad* 79 G9
Dobandi, *Pakistan* 68 D2
Dobbiaco, *Italy* 29 B9
Dobbyn, *Australia* 94 B3

Dobczyce, *Poland* 45 J7
Dobele, *Latvia* 9 H20
Dobele □, *Latvia* 44 B10
Döbeln, *Germany* 24 D9
Doberai, Jazirah, *Indonesia* 63 E8
Dobiegniew, *Poland* 45 F2
Doblas, *Argentina* 126 D3
Dobo, *Indonesia* 63 F8
Doboj, *Bos.-H.* 42 F3
Dobra, Wielkopolskie,
  Poland 45 G5
Dobra,
  Zachodnio-Pomorskie,
  Poland 44 E2
Dobra, Dîmbovița, *Romania* 43 F10
Dobra, Hunedoara, *Romania* 42 E7
Dobre Miasto, *Poland* 44 E7
Dobrești, *Romania* 42 D7
Dobrich, *Bulgaria* 41 C11
Dobrinishta, *Bulgaria* 40 E7
Dobříš, *Czech Rep.* 26 B7
Dobrodzień, *Poland* 45 H5
Dobropole, *Ukraine* 47 H9
Dobruja, *Europe* 43 F13
Dobrush, *Belarus* 47 F6
Dobrzany, *Poland* 44 E2
Dobrzyń nad Wisłą, *Poland* 45 F6
Doc, Mui, *Vietnam* 64 D6
Docker River, *Australia* .. 93 D4
Docksta, *Sweden* 10 A12
Doctor Arroyo, *Mexico* ... 118 C4
Doda, *India* 69 C6
Doda, L., *Canada* 102 C4
Dodecanese =
  Dhodhekánisos, *Greece* . 39 E8
Dodge City, *U.S.A.* 113 G5
Dodge L., *Canada* 105 B7
Dodgeville, *U.S.A.* 112 D9
Dodo, *Cameroon* 83 D7
Dodo, *Sudan* 81 F2
Dodola, *Ethiopia* 81 F4
Dodoma, *Tanzania* 86 D4
Dodoma □, *Tanzania* 86 D4
Dodona, *Greece* 38 B2
Dodsland, *Canada* 105 C7
Dodson, *U.S.A.* 114 B9
Dodurga, *Turkey* 39 B11
Doesburg, *Neths.* 17 B6
Doetinchem, *Neths.* 17 C6
Dog Creek, *Canada* 104 C4
Dog L., *Man., Canada* 105 C9
Dog L., *Ont., Canada* 102 C2
Doğanşehir, *Turkey* 72 C7
Dogi, *Afghan.* 66 C3
Dogliani, *Italy* 28 D4
Dogondoutchi, *Niger* 83 C5
Dogran, *Pakistan* 68 D5
Doğubayazıt, *Turkey* 70 B5
Doguéraoua, *Niger* 83 C6
Doha = Ad Dawḥah, *Qatar* 71 E6
Dohazari, *Bangla.* 67 H18
Dohrighat, *India* 69 F10
Doi, *Indonesia* 63 D7
Doi Luang, *Thailand* 64 C3
Doi Saket, *Thailand* 64 C2
Dois Irmãos, Sa., *Brazil* ... 125 E10
Dojransko Jezero,
  Macedonia 40 E6
Dokkum, *Neths.* 17 A5
Dokri, *Pakistan* 68 F3
Dokuchayevsk, *Ukraine* ... 47 J9
Dol-de-Bretagne, *France* .. 18 D5
Dolac, *Kosovo, Yug.* 40 D4
Dolak, Pulau, *Indonesia* .. 63 F9
Dolbeau, *Canada* 103 C5
Dole, *France* 19 E12
Doleib, Wadi →, *Sudan* .. 81 E3
Dolenji Logatec, *Slovenia* . 29 C11
Dolgellau, *U.K.* 12 E4
Dolgelley = Dolgellau, *U.K.* 12 E4
Dolhasca, *Romania* 43 C11
Dolianova, *Italy* 30 C2
Dolinskaya = Dolynska,
  Ukraine 47 H7
Dolj □, *Romania* 43 F8
Dolla Banya, *Bulgaria* 40 D7
Dolni Chiflik, *Bulgaria* .. 41 D11
Dolni Dŭbnik, *Bulgaria* .. 41 C8
Dolnośląskie □, *Poland* ... 45 G3
Dolný Kubín, *Slovak Rep.* . 27 B12
Dolo, *Ethiopia* 81 G5
Dolo, *Italy* 29 C9
Dolomites = Dolomiti, *Italy* 29 B8
Dolomiti, *Italy* 29 B8
Dolores, *Argentina* 126 D4
Dolores, *Uruguay* 126 C4
Dolores, *U.S.A.* 115 H9
Dolores →, *U.S.A.* 115 G9
Dolovo, *Serbia, Yug.* 42 F5
Dolphin, C., *Falk. Is.* 128 G5
Dolphin and Union Str.,
  Canada 100 B8
Dolsk, *Poland* 45 G4
Dolynska, *Ukraine* 47 H7
Dolzhanskaya, *Russia* 47 J9
Dom Pedrito, *Brazil* 127 C5
Doma, *Nigeria* 83 D6
Domaniç, *Turkey* 39 B11
Domariaganj →, *India* 69 F10
Domasi, *Malawi* 87 F4
Dombarovskiy, *Russia* 50 D6
Dombås, *Norway* 9 E13
Dombasle-sur-Meurthe,
  France 19 D13
Dombes, *France* 21 C9
Dombóvár, *Hungary* 42 D3
Dombrád, *Hungary* 42 B6

Domel I. = Letsôk-aw Kyun,
  Burma 65 G2
Domérat, *France* 19 F9
Domeyko, *Chile* 126 B1
Domeyko, Cordillera, *Chile* 126 A2
Domfront, *France* 18 D6
Dominador, *Chile* 126 A2
Dominica ■, *W. Indies* 121 C7
Dominica Passage, *W. Indies* 121 C7
Dominican Rep. ■,
  W. Indies 121 C5
Dömitz, *Germany* 24 B7
Domme, *France* 20 D5
Domnești, *Romania* 43 E9
Domodóssola, *Italy* 28 B5
Dompaire, *France* 19 D13
Dompim, *Ghana* 82 D4
Domrémy-la-Pucelle, *France* 19 D12
Domville, Mt., *Australia* .. 95 D5
Domvraína, *Greece* 38 C4
Domžale, *Slovenia* 29 B11
Don →, *Russia* 47 J10
Don →, *Aberds., U.K.* 14 D6
Don →, *S. Yorks., U.K.* .. 12 D7
Don, C., *Australia* 92 B5
Don Benito, *Spain* 35 G5
Dona Ana = Nhamaabué,
  Mozam. 87 F4
Doña Mencía, *Spain* 35 H6
Donaghadee, *U.K.* 15 B6
Donald, *Australia* 95 F3
Donaldsonville, *U.S.A.* .. 113 K9
Donalsonville, *U.S.A.* .. 109 K3
Donau = Dunărea →,
  Europe 43 E14
Donau →, *Austria* 17 D3
Donaueschingen, *Germany* . 25 H4
Donauwörth, *Germany* 25 G6
Doncaster, *U.K.* 12 D6
Dondo, *Mozam.* 87 F3
Dondo, Teluk, *Indonesia* ... 63 D6
Dondra Head, *Sri Lanka* .. 66 S12
Donduşeni, *Moldova* 43 B12
Donegal, *Ireland* 15 B3
Donegal □, *Ireland* 15 B4
Donegal B., *Ireland* 15 B3
Donets →, *Russia* 49 G5
Donetsk, *Ukraine* 47 J9
Dong Ba Thin, *Vietnam* .. 65 F7
Dong Dang, *Vietnam* 58 G6
Dong Giam, *Vietnam* 64 C5
Dong Ha, *Vietnam* 64 D6
Dong Hene, *Laos* 64 D5
Dong Hoi, *Vietnam* 64 D6
Dong Jiang →, *China* 59 F10
Dong Khe, *Vietnam* 64 A6
Dong Ujimqin Qi, *China* .. 56 B9
Dong Van, *Vietnam* 64 A5
Dong Xoai, *Vietnam* 65 G6
Donga, *Nigeria* 83 D7
Donga →, *Nigeria* 83 D7
Dong'an, *China* 59 D8
Dongara, *Australia* 93 E1
Dongbei, *China* 57 D13
Dongchuan, *China* 58 D4
Donges, *France* 18 E4
Dongfang, *China* 64 C7
Dongfeng, *China* 57 C13
Donggala, *Indonesia* 63 E5
Donggan, *China* 58 F5
Donggou, *China* 57 E13
Dongguan, *China* 59 F9
Dongguang, *China* 56 F9
Donghai Dao, *China* 59 G8
Dongjingcheng, *China* 57 B15
Dongkou, *China* 59 D8
Donglan, *China* 58 E6
Dongliu, *China* 59 B11
Dongmen, *China* 58 F6
Dongning, *China* 57 B16
Dongnyi, *China* 58 C3
Dongola, *Sudan* 80 D3
Dongping, *China* 56 G9
Dongshan, *China* 59 F11
Dongsheng, *China* 56 E6
Dongtai, *China* 57 H11
Dongting Hu, *China* 59 C9
Dongtou, *China* 59 D13
Dongxiang, *China* 59 C11
Dongxing, *China* 58 G7
Dongyang, *China* 59 C13
Dongzhi, *China* 59 B11
Donington, C., *Australia* .. 95 E2
Doniphan, *U.S.A.* 113 G9
Donja Stubica, *Croatia* ... 29 C12
Donji Dušnik, *Serbia, Yug.* 40 C5
Donji Miholjac, *Croatia* 42 E3
Donji Milanovac,
  Serbia, Yug. 40 B6
Donji Vakuf, *Bos.-H.* 42 F2
Dønna, *Norway* 8 C15
Donna, *U.S.A.* 113 M5
Donnaconna, *Canada* 103 C5
Donnelly's Crossing, *N.Z.* . 91 F4
Donnybrook, *Australia* 93 F2
Donnybrook, *S. Africa* 89 D4
Donora, *U.S.A.* 110 F5
Donostia = Donostia-San
  Sebastián, *Spain* 32 B3
Donostia-San Sebastián,
  Spain 32 B3
Donskoy, *Russia* 46 F10
Donsol, *Phil.* 61 E5
Donzère, *France* 21 D8
Donzy, *France* 19 E10
Doon →, *U.K.* 14 F4
Dora, L., *Australia* 92 D3
Dora Báltea →, *Italy* 28 C5
Dora Ripária →, *Italy* 28 C4

Domel I. = Letsôk-aw Kyun,
Doran L., *Canada* 105 A7
Dorchester, *U.K.* 13 G5
Dorchester, C., *Canada* 101 B12
Dordabis, *Namibia* 88 C2
Dordogne □, *France* 20 C4
Dordogne →, *France* 20 C3
Dordrecht, *Neths.* 17 C4
Dordrecht, *S. Africa* 88 E4
Dore, Mts., *France* 20 C7
Doré L., *Canada* 105 C7
Doré Lake, *Canada* 105 C7
Dorfen, *Germany* 25 G8
Dorgali, *Italy* 30 B2
Dori, *Burkina Faso* 83 C4
Doring →, *S. Africa* 88 E2
Doringbos, *S. Africa* 88 E2
Dorion, *Canada* 111 A10
Dormaa-Ahenkro, *Ghana* . 82 D4
Dormans, *France* 19 C10
Dormo, Ras, *Eritrea* 81 E5
Dornbirn, *Austria* 26 D2
Dornes, *France* 19 F10
Dornești, *Romania* 43 C11
Dornie, *U.K.* 14 D3
Dornoch, *U.K.* 14 D4
Dornoch Firth, *U.K.* 14 D4
Dornogovĭ □, *Mongolia* .. 56 C6
Doro, *Mali* 83 B4
Dorog, *Hungary* 42 C3
Dorogobuzh, *Russia* 46 E7
Dorohoi, *Romania* 43 C11
Döröö Nuur, *Mongolia* 60 B4
Dorr, *Iran* 71 C6
Dorre I., *Australia* 93 E1
Dorrigo, *Australia* 95 E5
Dorris, *U.S.A.* 114 F3
Dorset, *Canada* 110 A6
Dorset, *U.S.A.* 110 E4
Dorset □, *U.K.* 13 G5
Dorsten, *Germany* 24 D2
Dortmund, *Germany* 24 D3
Dortmund-Ems-Kanal →,
  Germany 24 D3
Dörtyol, *Turkey* 72 D7
Dorum, *Germany* 24 B4
Doruma,
  Dem. Rep. of the Congo . 86 B2
Dorūneh, *Iran* 71 C8
Dos Bahías, C., *Argentina* . 128 E3
Dos Hermanas, *Spain* 35 H5
Dos Palos, *U.S.A.* 116 J6
Döşemealtı, *Turkey* 39 D12
Dosso, *Niger* 83 C5
Dothan, *U.S.A.* 109 K3
Doty, *U.S.A.* 116 D3
Douai, *France* 19 B10
Douako, *Guinea* 82 D2
Douala, *Cameroon* 83 D6
Douarnenez, *France* 18 D2
Doubabougou, *Mali* 82 C3
Double Island Pt., *Australia* 95 D5
Double Mountain Fork →,
  U.S.A. 113 J4
Doubrava →, *Czech Rep.* . 26 A8
Doubs □, *France* 19 E13
Doubs →, *France* 19 F12
Doubtful Sd., *N.Z.* 91 L1
Doubtless B., *N.Z.* 91 F4
Doudeville, *France* 18 E6
Doué-la-Fontaine, *France* .. 18 E6
Douentza, *Mali* 82 C4
Douglas, *S. Africa* 88 D3
Douglas, *U.K.* 12 C3
Douglas, *Ariz., U.S.A.* 115 L9
Douglas, *Ga., U.S.A.* 109 K4
Douglas, *Wyo., U.S.A.* .. 112 D2
Douglas Chan., *Canada* ... 104 C3
Douglasville, *U.S.A.* 109 J3
Doukáton, Ákra, *Greece* .. 38 C2
Doulevant-le-Château,
  France 19 D11
Doullens, *France* 19 B9
Doumen, *China* 59 F9
Douna, *Mali* 82 C3
Dounreay, *U.K.* 14 C5
Dourada, Serra, *Brazil* 125 F9
Dourados, *Brazil* 127 A5
Dourados, *Brazil* 127 A5
Dourados, Serra dos, *Brazil* 127 A5
Dourdan, *France* 19 D9
Douro →, *Europe* 34 D2
Douvaine, *France* 19 F13
Douvres-la-Délivrande,
  France 18 C6
Douze →, *France* 20 E3
Dove →, *U.K.* 12 E6
Dove Creek, *U.S.A.* 115 H9
Dover, *Australia* 94 G4
Dover, *U.K.* 13 F9
Dover, *Del., U.S.A.* 108 F8
Dover, *N.H., U.S.A.* 111 C14
Dover, *N.J., U.S.A.* 111 F10
Dover, *Ohio, U.S.A.* 110 F3
Dover, Pt., *Australia* 93 F4
Dover, Str. of, *Europe* 13 G9
Dover-Foxcroft, *U.S.A.* .. 109 C11
Dover Plains, *U.S.A.* 111 E11
Dovey = Dyfi →, *U.K.* 12 E3
Dovrefjell, *Norway* 9 E13
Dow Rūd, *Iran* 71 C6
Dowa, *Malawi* 87 E3
Dowagiac, *U.S.A.* 108 E2
Dowerin, *Australia* 93 F2
Dowgha'i, *Iran* 71 B8
Dowlatābād, *Iran* 71 D8
Down □, *U.K.* 15 B5
Downey, *Calif., U.S.A.* .. 117 M8
Downey, *Idaho, U.S.A.* .. 114 E7

Downham Market, U.K. ... 13 E8
Downieville, U.S.A. 116 F6
Downpatrick, U.K. 15 B6
Downpatrick Hd., Ireland . 15 B2
Downsville, U.S.A. 111 D10
Downton, Mt., Canada ... 104 C4
Dowsārī, Iran 71 D8
Doyle, U.S.A. 116 E6
Doylestown, U.S.A. 111 F9
Dozois, Rés., Canada 102 C4
Dra Khel, Pakistan 68 F2
Drac →, France 21 C9
Dračevo, Macedonia 40 E5
Drachten, Neths. 17 A6
Drăgănești, Moldova 43 C13
Drăgănești-Olt, Romania . 43 F9
Drăgănești-Vlașca, Romania 43 F10
Dragaš, Kosovo, Yug. 40 D4
Dragocvet, Serbia, Yug. ... 40 C5
Dragovishtitsa, Bulgaria .. 40 D6
Draguignan, France 21 E10
Drain, U.S.A. 114 E2
Drake, U.S.A. 112 B4
Drake Passage, S. Ocean . 5 B17
Drakensberg, S. Africa ... 89 D4
Dráma, Greece 41 E8
Dráma □, Greece 41 E8
Drammen, Norway 9 G14
Drangajökull, Iceland 8 C2
Dranov, Ostrov, Romania . 43 F14
Dras, India 69 B6
Drau = Drava →, Croatia . 42 E3
Drava →, Croatia 42 E3
Dravograd, Slovenia 29 B12
Drawa →, Poland 45 F2
Drawno, Poland 45 E2
Drawsko Pomorskie, Poland 44 E2
Drayton Valley, Canada .. 104 C6
Dreieich, Germany 25 E4
Dren, Kosovo, Yug. 40 C4
Drenthe □, Neths. 17 B6
Drepanum, C., Cyprus ... 36 E11
Dresden, Canada 110 D2
Dresden, Germany 24 D9
Dreux, France 18 D8
Drezdenko, Poland 45 F2
Driffield, U.K. 12 C7
Driftwood, U.S.A. 110 E6
Driggs, U.S.A. 114 E8
Drin i Zi →, Albania 40 E4
Drina →, Bos.-H. 40 B3
Drincea →, Romania 42 F7
Drini →, Albania 40 D3
Drinjača →, Bos.-H. 42 F4
Drissa = Vyerkhnyadzvinsk,
 Belarus 46 E4
Drniš, Croatia 29 E13
Drøbak, Norway 9 G14
Drobin, Poland 45 F6
Drochia, Moldova 43 B12
Drogheda, Ireland 15 C5
Drogichin = Dragichyn,
 Belarus 47 F3
Drogobych = Drohobych,
 Ukraine 47 H2
Drohiczyn, Poland 45 F9
Drohobych, Ukraine 47 H2
Droichead Atha =
 Drogheda, Ireland 15 C5
Droichead Nua, Ireland .. 15 C5
Droitwich, U.K. 13 E5
Drôme □, France 21 D9
Drôme →, France 21 D8
Dromedary, C., Australia .. 95 F5
Dromore, U.K. 15 B4
Dromore West, Ireland .. 15 B3
Dronero, Italy 28 D4
Dronfield, U.K. 12 D6
Dronne →, France 20 C4
Dronninglund, Denmark .. 11 G4
Dronten, Neths. 17 B5
Dropt →, France 20 D3
Drosendorf, Austria 26 C8
Droué, France 18 D8
Drumbo, Canada 110 C4
Drumheller, Canada 104 C6
Drummond, U.S.A. 114 C7
Drummond I., U.S.A. 108 C4
Drummond Pt., Australia .. 95 E2
Drummond Ra., Australia . 94 C4
Drummondville, Canada .. 102 C5
Drumright, U.S.A. 113 H6
Druskininkai, Lithuania .. 9 J20
Drut →, Belarus 47 F6
Druya, Belarus 46 E4
Druzhba, Bulgaria 41 C12
Druzhina, Russia 51 C15
Drvar, Bos.-H. 29 D13
Drvenik, Croatia 29 E13
Drwęca →, Poland 45 E5
Dry Tortugas, U.S.A. 120 B3
Dryanovo, Bulgaria 41 D9
Dryden, Canada 105 D10
Dryden, U.S.A. 111 D8
Drygalski I., Antarctica .. 5 C7
Drysdale →, Australia .. 92 B4
Drysdale I., Australia ... 94 A2
Drzewica, Poland 45 G7
Drzewiczka →, Poland ... 45 G7
Dschang, Cameroon 83 D7
Du Bois, U.S.A. 110 E6
Du Gué →, Canada 102 A5
Du He, China 59 A8
Du Quoin, U.S.A. 112 G10
Du'an, China 58 F7
Duanesburg, U.S.A. 111 D10
Duaringa, Australia 94 C4
Dubā, Si. Arabia 70 E3
Dubai = Dubayy, U.A.E. .. 71 E7

Dubăsari, Moldova 43 C14
Dubăsari Vdkhr., Moldova . 43 C13
Dubawnt →, Canada 105 A8
Dubawnt, L., Canada 105 A8
Dubayy, U.A.E. 71 E7
Dubbo, Australia 95 E4
Dubele,
 Dem. Rep. of the Congo . 86 B2
Dübendorf, Switz. 25 H4
Dubica, Croatia 29 C13
Dublin, Ireland 15 C5
Dublin, Ga., U.S.A. 109 J4
Dublin, Tex., U.S.A. 113 J5
Dublin □, Ireland 15 C5
Dubna, Russia 46 D9
Dubnica nad Váhom,
 Slovak Rep. 27 C11
Dubno, Ukraine 47 G3
Dubois, U.S.A. 114 D7
Dubossary = Dubăsari,
 Moldova 43 C14
Dubossary Vdkhr. =
 Dubăsari Vdkhr., Moldova 43 C13
Dubovka, Russia 49 F7
Dubovskoye, Russia 49 G6
Dubrajpur, India 69 H12
Dubréka, Guinea 82 D2
Dubrovitsa = Dubrovytsya,
 Ukraine 47 G4
Dubrovnik, Croatia 40 D2
Dubrovytsya, Ukraine 47 G4
Dubuque, U.S.A. 112 D9
Dubysa →, Lithuania 44 C10
Duchang, China 59 C11
Duchesne, U.S.A. 114 F8
Duchess, Australia 94 C2
Ducie I., Pac. Oc. 97 K15
Duck →, U.S.A. 109 G2
Duck Cr. →, Australia ... 92 D2
Duck Lake, Canada 105 C7
Duck Mountain Prov. Park,
 Canada 105 C8
Duckwall, Mt., U.S.A. ... 116 H6
Duderstadt, Germany 24 D6
Dudhi, India 67 G13
Dudinka, Russia 51 C9
Dudley, U.K. 13 E5
Dudwa, India 69 E9
Duékoué, Ivory C. 82 D3
Dueñas, Spain 34 D6
Duero = Douro →, Europe 34 D2
Dufftown, U.K. 14 D5
Dufourspitz, Switz. 25 K3
Dugi Otok, Croatia 29 D11
Dugo Selo, Croatia 29 C13
Duifken Pt., Australia 94 A3
Duisburg, Germany 24 D2
Duiwelskloof, S. Africa ... 89 C5
Dujiangyan, China 58 B4
Duk Fadiat, Sudan 81 F3
Duk Faiwil, Sudan 81 F3
Dukati, Albania 40 F3
Dūkdamīn, Iran 71 C8
Dukelský Průsmyk,
 Slovak Rep. 27 B14
Dukhān, Qatar 71 E6
Dukhovshchina, Russia ... 46 E7
Duki, Pakistan 66 D6
Dukla, Poland 45 J8
Duku, Bauchi, Nigeria ... 83 C7
Duku, Sokoto, Nigeria ... 83 C5
Dulag, Phil. 61 F6
Dulce, U.S.A. 115 H10
Dulce →, Argentina 126 C3
Dulce, G., Costa Rica 120 E3
Dulf, Iraq 70 C5
Dŭlgopol, Bulgaria 41 C11
Dulit, Banjaran, Malaysia . 62 D4
Duliu, China 56 E9
Dullewala, Pakistan 68 D4
Dullstroom, S. Africa 89 D5
Dülmen, Germany 24 D3
Dulovo, Bulgaria 41 C11
Dulq Maghār, Syria 70 B3
Duluth, U.S.A. 112 B8
Dum Dum, India 69 H13
Dum Duma, India 67 F19
Dūmā, Syria 75 B5
Dumaguete, Phil. 61 G5
Dumai, Indonesia 62 D2
Dumaran, Phil. 61 F3
Dumas, Ark., U.S.A. 113 J9
Dumas, Tex., U.S.A. 113 H4
Dumayr, Syria 75 B5
Dumbarton, U.K. 14 F4
Dumbier, Slovak Rep. ... 27 C12
Dumbleyung, Australia ... 93 F2
Dumboa, Nigeria 83 C7
Dumbrăveni, Romania ... 43 D9
Dumfries, U.K. 14 F5
Dumfries & Galloway □,
 U.K. 14 F5
Dumitrești, Romania 43 E11
Dumka, India 69 G12
Dumlupınar, Turkey 39 C12
Dümmer, Germany 24 C4
Dumoine →, Canada ... 102 C4
Dumoine, L., Canada ... 102 C4
Dumraon, India 69 G11
Dumyât, Egypt 80 H7
Dumyât, Masabb, Egypt .. 80 H7
Dún Dealgan = Dundalk,
 Ireland 15 B5
Dun Laoghaire, Ireland .. 15 C5
Dun-le-Palestel, France .. 19 F8
Dun-sur-Auron, France .. 19 F9
Dun-sur-Meuse, France .. 19 C12
Duna = Dunărea →,
 Europe 43 E14
Duna →, Hungary 42 E3
Duna-völgyi-főcsatorna,
 Hungary 42 D4

Dunaföldvár, Hungary 42 D3
Dunagiri, India 69 D8
Dunaj = Dunărea →,
 Europe 43 E14
Dunaj →, Slovak Rep. ... 27 D11
Dunajec →, Poland 45 H7
Dunajská Streda,
 Slovak Rep. 27 C10
Dunakeszi, Hungary 42 C4
Dunapataj, Hungary 42 D4
Dunărea →, Europe 43 E14
Dunaszekcső, Hungary ... 42 D3
Dunaújváros, Hungary ... 42 D3
Dunav = Dunărea →,
 Europe 43 E14
Dunavăț de Jos, Romania . 43 F14
Dunavtsi, Bulgaria 40 C6
Dunay, Russia 54 C6
Dunback, N.Z. 91 L3
Dunbar, U.K. 14 E6
Dunblane, U.K. 14 E5
Duncan, Canada 104 D4
Duncan, Ariz., U.S.A. ... 115 K9
Duncan, Okla., U.S.A. ... 113 H6
Duncan, L., Canada 102 B4
Duncan L., Canada 104 A6
Duncan Town, Bahamas . 120 B4
Duncannon, U.S.A. 110 F7
Duncansby Head, U.K. .. 14 C5
Duncanville, U.S.A. 110 F6
Dundaga, Latvia 44 A9
Dundalk, Canada 110 B4
Dundalk, Ireland 15 B5
Dundalk, U.S.A. 108 F7
Dundalk Bay, Ireland ... 15 C5
Dundas, Canada 110 C5
Dundas, L., Australia 93 F3
Dundas I., Canada 104 C2
Dundas Str., Australia ... 92 B5
Dundee, S. Africa 89 D5
Dundee, U.K. 14 E6
Dundee, U.S.A. 110 D8
Dundee City □, U.K. ... 14 E6
Dundgovĭ □, Mongolia .. 56 B4
Dundrum, U.K. 15 B6
Dundrum B., U.K. 15 B6
Dunedin, N.Z. 91 L3
Dunedin, U.S.A. 109 L4
Dunedoo, Australia 95 E4
Dunfermline, U.K. 14 E5
Dungannon, Canada 110 C3
Dungannon, U.K. 15 B5
Dungarpur, India 68 H5
Dungarvan, Ireland 15 D4
Dungarvan Harbour, Ireland 15 D4
Dungeness, U.K. 13 G8
Dungo, L. do, Angola ... 88 B2
Dungog, Australia 95 E5
Dungu,
 Dem. Rep. of the Congo . 86 B2
Dungun, Malaysia 65 K4
Dungunâb, Sudan 80 C4
Dungunâb, Khalij, Sudan . 80 C4
Dunhua, China 57 C15
Dunhuang, China 60 B4
Dunk I., Australia 94 B4
Dunkassa, Benin 83 C5
Dunkeld, Australia 95 E4
Dunkeld, U.K. 14 E5
Dunkerque, France 19 A9
Dunkery Beacon, U.K. .. 13 F4
Dunkirk = Dunkerque,
 France 19 A9
Dunkirk, U.S.A. 110 D5
Dunkuj, Sudan 81 E3
Dunkwa, Central, Ghana . 82 D4
Dunkwa, Central, Ghana . 83 D4
Dúnleary = Dun Laoghaire,
 Ireland 15 C5
Dunleer, Ireland 15 C5
Dunmanus B., Ireland .. 15 E2
Dunmanway, Ireland ... 15 E2
Dunmara, Australia 94 B1
Dunmore, U.S.A. 111 E9
Dunmore Hd., Ireland .. 15 D1
Dunmore Town, Bahamas . 120 A4
Dunn, U.S.A. 109 H6
Dunnet Hd., U.K. 14 C5
Dunning, U.S.A. 112 E4
Dunnville, Canada 110 D5
Dunolly, Australia 95 F3
Dunoon, U.K. 14 F4
Dunphy, U.S.A. 114 F5
Dunqul, Egypt 80 C3
Duns, U.K. 14 F6
Dunseith, U.S.A. 112 A4
Dunsmuir, U.S.A. 114 F2
Dunstable, U.K. 13 F7
Dunstan Mts., N.Z. 91 L2
Dunster, Canada 104 C5
Dunvegan L., Canada .. 105 A7
Duolun, China 56 C9
Duong Dong, Vietnam .. 65 G4
Dupree, U.S.A. 112 C4
Dupuyer, U.S.A. 114 B7
Duque de Caxias, Brazil . 127 A7
Durack →, Australia ... 92 C4
Durack Ra., Australia ... 92 C4
Durağan, Turkey 72 B6
Durak, Turkey 39 B10
Đurakovac, Kosovo, Yug. . 40 D4
Durance →, France 21 E9
Durand, U.S.A. 112 C9
Durango, Mexico 118 C4
Durango □, Mexico 118 C4
Durango, U.S.A. 115 H10
Durankulak, Bulgaria ... 41 C12
Durant, Miss., U.S.A. ... 113 J10
Durant, Okla., U.S.A. ... 113 J6
Duratón →, Spain 34 D6
Durazno, Uruguay 126 C4

Durazzo = Durrësi, Albania 40 E3
Durban, France 20 F6
Durban, S. Africa 89 D5
Durbuy, Belgium 17 D5
Dúrcal, Spain 35 J7
Đurđevac, Croatia 42 D2
Düren, Germany 24 E2
Durg, India 67 J12
Durgapur, India 69 H12
Durham, Canada 102 D3
Durham, U.K. 12 C6
Durham, Calif., U.S.A. .. 116 F5
Durham, N.C., U.S.A. .. 109 H6
Durham, N.H., U.S.A. .. 111 C14
Durham □, U.K. 12 C6
Durlești, Moldova 43 C13
Durmā, Si. Arabia 70 E5
Durmitor, Montenegro, Yug. 40 C4
Durness, U.K. 14 C4
Durrësi, Albania 40 E3
Durrow, Ireland 15 D4
Dursey I., Ireland 15 E1
Dursunbey, Turkey 39 B10
Durtal, France 18 E6
Duru,
 Dem. Rep. of the Congo . 86 B2
Duru Gölü, Turkey 41 E12
Durusu, Turkey 41 E12
Durūz, Jabal ad, Jordan . 75 C5
D'Urville, Tanjung,
 Indonesia 63 E9
D'Urville I., N.Z. 91 J4
Dûsh, Egypt 80 C3
Dushak, Turkmenistan .. 50 F7
Dushan, China 58 E6
Dushanbe, Tajikistan ... 50 F7
Dusheti, Georgia 49 J7
Dushore, U.S.A. 111 E8
Dusky Sd., N.Z. 91 L1
Dussejour, C., Australia .. 92 B4
Düsseldorf, Germany ... 24 D2
Duszniki-Zdrój, Poland .. 45 H3
Dutch Harbor, U.S.A. .. 100 C3
Dutlwe, Botswana 88 C3
Dutsan Wai, Nigeria ... 83 C6
Dutton, Canada 110 D3
Dutton →, Australia ... 94 C3
Duved, Sweden 10 A6
Düvertepe, Turkey 39 B10
Duwayhin, Khawr, U.A.E. . 71 E6
Duyun, China 58 D6
Düzağaç, Turkey 39 C12
Düzce, Turkey 72 B4
Duzdab = Zāhedān, Iran . 71 D9
Dve Mogili, Bulgaria ... 41 C9
Dvina, Severnaya →, Russia 50 C5
Dvinsk = Daugavpils, Latvia 9 J22
Dvor, Croatia 29 C13
Dvůr Králové nad Labem,
 Czech Rep. 26 A8
Dwarka, India 68 H3
Dwellingup, Australia .. 93 F2
Dwight, Canada 110 A5
Dwight, U.S.A. 108 E1
Dyatkovo, Russia 46 F8
Dyatlovo = Dzyatlava,
 Belarus 46 F3
Dyce, U.K. 14 D6
Dyer, U.S.A. 112 G9
Dyer Bay, Canada 110 A3
Dyer Plateau, Antarctica . 5 D17
Dyersburg, U.S.A. 113 G10
Dyfi →, U.K. 13 E3
Dyje →, Czech Rep. ... 27 C9
Dymer, Ukraine 47 G6
Dynów, Poland 45 J9
Dysart, Australia 94 C4
Dzamin Üüd = Borhoyn Tal,
 Mongolia 56 C6
Dzerzhinsk, Russia 48 B6
Dzhalinda, Russia 51 D13
Dzhambul = Zhambyl,
 Kazakstan 50 E8
Dzhankoy, Ukraine 47 K8
Dzhanybek, Kazakstan . 48 F8
Dzharylhach, Ostriv, Ukraine 47 J7
Dzhezkazgan =
 Zhezqazghan, Kazakstan . 50 E7
Dzhizak = Jizzakh,
 Uzbekistan 50 E7
Dzhugdzur, Khrebet, Russia 51 D14
Dzhvari = Jvari, Georgia . 49 J6
Działdowo, Poland 45 E7
Działoszyce, Poland 45 H7
Działoszyn, Poland 45 G5
Dzibilchaltun, Mexico .. 119 C7
Dzierzgoń, Poland 44 E6
Dzierżoniów, Poland ... 45 H3
Dzilam de Bravo, Mexico . 119 C7
Dzisna, Belarus 46 E5
Dzisna →, Belarus 46 E5
Dziwnów, Poland 44 D1
Dzungaria = Junggar Pendi,
 China 60 B3
Dzuumod, Mongolia ... 60 B5
Dzyarzhynsk, Belarus .. 46 F4
Dzyatlava, Belarus 46 F3

E

Eabamet L., Canada 102 B2
Eads, U.S.A. 112 F3
Eagar, U.S.A. 115 J9
Eagle, Alaska, U.S.A. ... 100 B5
Eagle, Colo., U.S.A. 114 G10
Eagle →, Canada 103 B8
Eagle Butte, U.S.A. 112 C4

Eagle Grove, U.S.A. 112 D8
Eagle L., Canada 105 D10
Eagle L., Calif., U.S.A. ... 114 F3
Eagle L., Maine, U.S.A. .. 109 B11
Eagle Lake, Canada 110 A6
Eagle Lake, Maine, U.S.A. . 109 B11
Eagle Lake, Tex., U.S.A. .. 113 L6
Eagle Mountain, U.S.A. .. 117 M11
Eagle Nest, U.S.A. 115 H11
Eagle Pass, U.S.A. 113 L4
Eagle Pk., U.S.A. 116 G7
Eagle Pt., Australia 92 C3
Eagle River, Mich., U.S.A. . 108 B1
Eagle River, Wis., U.S.A. . 112 C10
Eaglehawk, Australia 95 F3
Eagles Mere, U.S.A. 111 E8
Ealing, U.K. 13 F7
Ear Falls, Canada 105 C10
Earle, U.S.A. 113 H9
Earlimart, U.S.A. 117 K7
Earn →, U.K. 14 E5
Earn, L., U.K. 14 E4
Earnslaw, Mt., N.Z. 91 L2
Earth, U.S.A. 113 H3
Easley, U.S.A. 109 H4
East Anglia, U.K. 12 E9
East Angus, Canada 103 C5
East Aurora, U.S.A. 110 D6
East Ayrshire □, U.K. ... 14 F4
East Bengal, Bangla. 67 H17
East Beskids = Vychodné
 Beskydy, Europe 27 B15
East Brady, U.S.A. 110 F5
East C., N.Z. 91 G7
East Chicago, U.S.A. ... 108 E2
East China Sea, Asia ... 60 C7
East Coulee, Canada ... 104 C6
East Dereham, U.K. 13 E8
East Dunbartonshire □,
 U.K. 14 F4
East Falkland, Falk. Is. .. 122 J5
East Grand Forks, U.S.A. . 112 B6
East Greenwich, U.S.A. .. 111 E13
East Grinstead, U.K. 13 F8
East Hartford, U.S.A. ... 111 E12
East Helena, U.S.A. 114 C8
East Indies, Asia 52 K15
East Kilbride, U.K. 14 F4
East Lansing, U.S.A. 108 D3
East Liverpool, U.S.A. .. 110 F4
East London, S. Africa .. 89 E4
East Lothian □, U.K. ... 14 F6
East Main = Eastmain,
 Canada 102 B4
East Northport, U.S.A. .. 111 F11
East Orange, U.S.A. 111 F10
East Pacific Ridge, Pac. Oc. 97 J17
East Palestine, U.S.A. ... 110 F4
East Pine, Canada 104 B4
East Point, U.S.A. 109 J3
East Providence, U.S.A. . 111 E13
East Pt., Canada 103 C7
East Renfrewshire □, U.K. 14 F4
East Retford = Retford,
 U.K. 12 D7
East Riding of Yorkshire □,
 U.K. 12 D7
East Rochester, U.S.A. .. 110 D7
East St. Louis, U.S.A. ... 112 F9
East Schelde =
 Oosterschelde →, Neths. 17 C4
East Siberian Sea, Russia . 51 B17
East Stroudsburg, U.S.A. . 111 E9
East Sussex □, U.K. 13 G8
East Tawas, U.S.A. 108 C4
East Timor = Timor
 Timur □, Indonesia ... 63 F7
East Toorale, Australia .. 95 E4
East Walker →, U.S.A. .. 116 G7
East Windsor, U.S.A. ... 111 F10
Eastbourne, N.Z. 91 J5
Eastbourne, U.K. 13 G8
Eastend, Canada 105 D7
Easter I. = Pascua, I. de,
 Pac. Oc. 97 K17
Eastern □, Ghana 83 D4
Eastern □, Kenya 86 C4
Eastern □, Uganda 86 B3
Eastern Cape □, S. Africa . 88 E4
Eastern Cr. →, Australia . 94 C3
Eastern Ghats, India ... 66 N11
Eastern Group = Lau
 Group, Fiji 91 C9
Eastern Group, Australia . 93 F3
Eastern Province □,
 S. Leone 82 D2
Eastern Transvaal =
 Mpumalanga □, S. Africa 89 B5
Easterville, Canada 105 C9
Easthampton, U.S.A. ... 111 D12
Eastlake, U.S.A. 110 E3
Eastland, U.S.A. 113 J5
Eastleigh, U.K. 13 G6
Eastmain, Canada 102 B4
Eastmain →, Canada .. 102 B4
Eastman, Canada 111 A12
Eastman, U.S.A. 109 J4
Easton, Md., U.S.A. ... 108 F7
Easton, Pa., U.S.A. 111 F9
Easton, Wash., U.S.A. .. 116 C5
Eastpointe, U.S.A. 110 D2
Eastport, U.S.A. 109 C12
Eastsound, U.S.A. 116 B4
Eaton, U.S.A. 112 C3
Eatonia, Canada 105 C7
Eatonton, U.S.A. 109 J4
Eatontown, U.S.A. 111 F10
Eatonville, U.S.A. 116 D4
Eau Claire, U.S.A. 112 C9
Eau Claire, L. à l', Canada . 102 A5
Eauze, France 20 E4

Eban, *Nigeria* 83 D5
Ebbw Vale, *U.K.* 13 F4
Ebeltoft, *Denmark* 11 H4
Ebeltoft Vig, *Denmark* 11 H4
Ebensburg, *U.S.A.* 110 F6
Ebensee, *Austria* 26 D6
Eber Gölü, *Turkey* 72 C4
Eberbach, *Germany* 25 F4
Eberswalde-Finow, *Germany* 24 C9
Ebetsu, *Japan* 54 C10
Ebian, *China* 58 C4
Ebingen, *Germany* 25 G5
Éboli, *Italy* 31 B8
Ebolowa, *Cameroon* 83 E7
Ebonyi □, *Nigeria* 83 D6
Ebrach, *Germany* 25 F6
Ébrié, Lagune, *Ivory C.* ... 82 D4
Ebro →, *Spain* 32 E5
Ebro, Embalse del, *Spain* . 34 C7
Ebstorf, *Germany* 24 B6
Eccaba, *Turkey* 41 F10
Ech Cheliff, *Algeria* 78 A6
Echigo-Sammyaku, *Japan* .. 55 F9
Échirolles, *France* 21 C9
Echizen-Misaki, *Japan* 55 G7
Echmiadzin = Yejmiadzin, *Armenia* 49 K7
Echo Bay, *N.W.T., Canada* 100 B8
Echo Bay, *Ont., Canada* .. 102 C3
Echoing →, *Canada* 102 B1
Echternach, *Lux.* 17 E6
Echuca, *Australia* 95 F3
Ecija, *Spain* 35 H5
Eckental, *Germany* 25 F7
Eckernförde, *Germany* 24 A5
Eclipse Is., *Australia* 92 B4
Eclipse Sd., *Canada* 101 A11
Écommoy, *France* 18 E7
Écouché, *France* 18 D6
Ecuador ■, *S. Amer.* 124 D3
Écueillé, *France* 18 E8
Ed, *Sweden* 11 F5
Ed Dabbura, *Sudan* 80 D3
Ed Da'ein, *Sudan* 81 E2
Ed Damazin, *Sudan* 79 F12
Ed Dâmer, *Sudan* 80 D3
Ed Debba, *Sudan* 80 D3
Ed-Déffa, *Egypt* 80 A2
Ed Deim, *Sudan* 81 E2
Ed Dueim, *Sudan* 81 E3
Edam, *Canada* 105 C7
Edam, *Neths.* 17 B5
Edane, *Sweden* 10 E6
Eday, *U.K.* 14 B6
Edd, *Eritrea* 81 E5
Eddrachillis B., *U.K.* 14 C3
Eddystone Pt., *Australia* ... 94 G4
Ede, *Neths.* 17 B5
Ede, *Nigeria* 83 D5
Edéa, *Cameroon* 83 E7
Edebäck, *Sweden* 10 D7
Edehon L., *Canada* 105 A9
Edelény, *Hungary* 42 B5
Eden, *Australia* 95 F4
Eden, *N.C., U.S.A.* 109 G6
Eden, *N.Y., U.S.A.* 110 D6
Eden, *Tex., U.S.A.* 113 K5
Eden →, *U.K.* 12 C4
Edenburg, *S. Africa* 88 D4
Edendale, *S. Africa* 89 D5
Edenderry, *Ireland* 15 C4
Edenhope, *Australia* 95 F3
Edenton, *U.S.A.* 109 G7
Edenville, *S. Africa* 89 D4
Eder →, *Germany* 24 D5
Eder-Stausee, *Germany* ... 24 D4
Edewecht, *Germany* 24 B3
Edgar, *U.S.A.* 112 E6
Edgartown, *U.S.A.* 111 E14
Edge Hill, *U.K.* 13 E6
Edgefield, *U.S.A.* 109 J5
Edgeley, *U.S.A.* 112 B5
Edgemont, *U.S.A.* 112 D3
Edgeøya, *Svalbard* 4 B9
Édhessa, *Greece* 40 F6
Edievale, *N.Z.* 91 L2
Edina, *Liberia* 82 D2
Edina, *U.S.A.* 112 E8
Edinboro, *U.S.A.* 110 E4
Edinburg, *U.S.A.* 113 M5
Edinburgh, *U.K.* 14 F5
Edinburgh, City of □, *U.K.* 14 F5
Edinet, *Moldova* 43 B12
Edirne, *Turkey* 41 E10
Edirne □, *Turkey* 41 E10
Edison, *U.S.A.* 116 B4
Edithburgh, *Australia* 95 F2
Edmeston, *U.S.A.* 111 D9
Edmond, *U.S.A.* 113 H6
Edmonds, *U.S.A.* 116 C4
Edmonton, *Australia* 94 B4
Edmonton, *Canada* 104 C6
Edmund L., *Canada* 102 B1
Edmundston, *Canada* 103 C6
Edna, *U.S.A.* 113 L6
Edo □, *Nigeria* 83 D6
Edolo, *Italy* 28 B7
Edremit, *Turkey* 39 B9
Edremit Körfezi, *Turkey* ... 39 B8
Edsbro, *Sweden* 10 E12
Edsbyn, *Sweden* 10 C9
Edson, *Canada* 104 C5
Eduardo Castex, *Argentina* 126 D3
Edward →, *Australia* 95 F3
Edward, L., *Africa* 86 C2
Edward River, *Australia* ... 94 A3
Edward VII Land, *Antarctica* 5 E13
Edwards, *Calif., U.S.A.* ... 117 L9
Edwards, *N.Y., U.S.A.* ... 111 B9
Edwards Air Force Base, *U.S.A.* 117 L9

Edwards Plateau, *U.S.A.* .. 113 K4
Edwardsville, *U.S.A.* 111 E9
Edzo, *Canada* 104 A5
Eeklo, *Belgium* 17 C3
Eferding, *Austria* 26 C7
Effingham, *U.S.A.* 108 F1
Eforie, *Romania* 43 F13
Ega →, *Spain* 32 C3
Égadi, Ísole, *Italy* 30 E5
Egan Range, *U.S.A.* 114 G6
Eganville, *Canada* 102 C4
Eger = Cheb, *Czech Rep.* . 26 A5
Eger, *Hungary* 42 C5
Eger →, *Hungary* 42 C5
Egersund, *Norway* 9 G12
Egg L., *Canada* 105 B7
Eggenburg, *Austria* 26 C8
Eggenfelden, *Germany* 25 G8
Éghezée, *Belgium* 17 D4
Égletons, *France* 20 C5
Egmont, *Canada* 104 D4
Egmont, C., *N.Z.* 91 H4
Egmont, Mt., *N.Z.* 91 H5
Egra, *India* 69 J12
Eğridir, *Turkey* 72 D4
Eğridir Gölü, *Turkey* 70 B1
Egtved, *Denmark* 11 J3
Egume, *Nigeria* 83 D6
Éguzon-Chantôme, *France* . 19 F8
Egvekinot, *Russia* 51 C19
Egyek, *Hungary* 42 C5
Egypt ■, *Africa* 80 B3
Eha Amufu, *Nigeria* 83 D6
Ehime □, *Japan* 55 H6
Ehingen, *Germany* 25 G5
Ehrenberg, *U.S.A.* 117 M12
Ehrwald, *Austria* 25 H4
Eibar, *Spain* 32 B2
Eichstätt, *Germany* 25 G7
Eider →, *Germany* 24 A4
Eidsvold, *Australia* 95 D5
Eidsvoll, *Norway* 9 F14
Eifel, *Germany* 25 E2
Eiffel Flats, *Zimbabwe* 87 F3
Eiger, *Switz.* 28 B5
Eigg, *U.K.* 14 E2
Eighty Mile Beach, *Australia* 92 C3
Eil, *Somali Rep.* 74 F4
Eil, L., *U.K.* 14 E3
Eildon, *Australia* 95 F4
Eildon, L., *Australia* 95 F4
Eilenburg, *Germany* 24 D8
Ein el Luweiqa, *Sudan* 81 E3
Einasleigh, *Australia* 94 B3
Einasleigh →, *Australia* ... 94 B3
Einbeck, *Germany* 24 D5
Eindhoven, *Neths.* 17 C5
Einsiedeln, *Switz.* 25 H4
Eire = Ireland ■, *Europe* . 15 C4
Eiríksjökull, *Iceland* 8 D3
Eirunepé, *Brazil* 124 E5
Eiseb →, *Namibia* 88 C2
Eisenach, *Germany* 24 E6
Eisenberg, *Germany* 24 E7
Eisenerz, *Austria* 26 D7
Eisenhüttenstadt, *Germany* . 24 C10
Eisenkappel, *Austria* 26 E7
Eisenstadt, *Austria* 27 D9
Eisfeld, *Germany* 25 E6
Eisleben, *Germany* 24 D7
Eislingen, *Germany* 25 G5
Eivissa, *Spain* 37 C7
Eixe, Serra do, *Spain* 34 C4
Ejea de los Caballeros, *Spain* 32 C3
Ejeda, *Madag.* 89 C7
Ejura, *Ghana* 83 D4
Ejutla, *Mexico* 119 D5
Ekalaka, *U.S.A.* 112 C2
Ekenässjön, *Sweden* 11 G9
Ekerö, *Sweden* 10 E11
Eket, *Nigeria* 83 E6
Eketahuna, *N.Z.* 91 J5
Ekhínos, *Greece* 41 E9
Ekibastuz, *Kazakstan* 50 D8
Ekiti □, *Nigeria* 83 D6
Ekoli, *Dem. Rep. of the Congo* . 86 C1
Ekoln, *Sweden* 10 E11
Ekshärad, *Sweden* 10 D7
Eksjö, *Sweden* 11 G8
Ekuma →, *Namibia* 88 B2
Ekwan →, *Canada* 102 B3
Ekwan Pt., *Canada* 102 B3
El Aaiún, *W. Sahara* 78 C3
El Abanico, *Chile* 126 D1
El Abbasia, *Sudan* 81 E3
El 'Agrûd, *Egypt* 75 E3
El Ait, *Sudan* 81 E3
El 'Aiyat, *Egypt* 80 J7
El Alamein, *Egypt* 80 A2
El 'Aqaba, W. →, *Egypt* . 75 E2
El 'Arag, *Egypt* 80 B2
El Arahal, *Spain* 35 H5
El Arîḥâ, *West Bank* 75 D4
El 'Arîsh, *Egypt* 75 D2
El 'Arîsh, W. →, *Egypt* .. 75 D2
El Asnam = Ech Cheliff, *Algeria* 78 A6
El Astillero, *Spain* 34 B7
El Badâri, *Egypt* 80 B3
El Bahrein, *Egypt* 80 B2
El Ballâs, *Egypt* 80 B3
El Balyana, *Egypt* 80 B3
El Baqeir, *Sudan* 80 D3
El Barco de Ávila, *Spain* . 34 E5
El Barco de Valdeorras = O Barco, *Spain* 34 C4
El Bauga, *Sudan* 80 D3
El Bawiti, *Egypt* 80 B2
El Bayadh, *Algeria* 78 B6
El Bierzo, *Spain* 34 C4

El Bluff, *Nic.* 120 D3
El Bonillo, *Spain* 33 G2
El Brûk, W. →, *Egypt* ... 75 E2
El Buheirat □, *Sudan* 81 F3
El Burgo de Osma, *Spain* . 32 D1
El Cajon, *U.S.A.* 117 N10
El Campo, *U.S.A.* 113 L6
El Centro, *U.S.A.* 117 N11
El Cerro, *Bolivia* 124 G6
El Cerro de Andévalo, *Spain* 35 H4
El Compadre, *Mexico* 117 N10
El Coronil, *Spain* 35 H5
El Cuy, *Argentina* 128 D3
El Cuyo, *Mexico* 119 C7
El Dab'a, *Egypt* 80 H6
El Daheir, *Egypt* 75 D3
El Dátil, *Mexico* 118 B2
El Deir, *Egypt* 80 B3
El Dere, *Somali Rep.* 74 G4
El Descanso, *Mexico* 117 N10
El Desemboque, *Mexico* .. 118 A2
El Dilingat, *Egypt* 80 H7
El Diviso, *Colombia* 124 C3
El Djouf, *Mauritania* 78 D4
El Dorado, *Ark., U.S.A.* . 113 J8
El Dorado, *Kans., U.S.A.* 113 G6
El Dorado, *Venezuela* ... 124 B6
El 'Ein, *Sudan* 81 D2
El Ejido, *Spain* 35 J8
El Escorial, *Spain* 34 E6
El Espinar, *Spain* 34 D6
El Faiyûm, *Egypt* 80 J7
El Fâsher, *Sudan* 81 E2
El Fashn, *Egypt* 80 J7
El Ferrol = Ferrol, *Spain* . 34 B2
El Fifi, *Sudan* 81 E2
El Fuerte, *Mexico* 118 B3
El Ga'a, *Sudan* 81 E3
El Gal, *Somali Rep.* 74 E5
El Garef, *Sudan* 81 E3
El Gebir, *Sudan* 81 E2
El Gedida, *Egypt* 80 B2
El Geneina = Al Junaynah, *Sudan* 79 F10
El Geteina, *Sudan* 81 E3
El Gir, *Sudan* 80 D2
El Gîza, *Egypt* 80 J7
El Goléa, *Algeria* 78 B6
El Grau, *Spain* 33 G4
El Hagiz, *Sudan* 81 D4
El Hâi, *Egypt* 80 J7
El Hammam, *Egypt* 80 A2
El Hawata, *Sudan* 81 E3
El Heiz, *Egypt* 80 B2
El Hideib, *Sudan* 81 E3
El Hilla, *Sudan* 81 E2
El 'Idisât, *Egypt* 80 B3
El Iskandarîya, *Egypt* 80 H7
El Istiwa'iya, *Sudan* 79 G11
El Jadida, *Morocco* 78 B4
El Jardal, *Honduras* 120 D2
El Jebelein, *Sudan* 81 E3
El Kab, *Sudan* 80 D3
El Kabrît, G., *Egypt* 75 E2
El Kafr el Sharqi, *Egypt* .. 80 H7
El Kamlin, *Sudan* 81 D3
El Karaba, *Sudan* 80 D3
El Kere, *Ethiopia* 81 F5
El Khandaq, *Sudan* 80 D3
El Khârga, *Egypt* 80 B3
El Khartûm, *Sudan* 81 D3
El Khartûm □, *Sudan* 81 D3
El Khartûm Bahrî, *Sudan* . 81 D3
El Kuntilla, *Egypt* 75 E3
El Laqâwa, *Sudan* 81 E2
El Laqeita, *Egypt* 80 B3
El Leh, *Ethiopia* 81 G4
El Leiya, *Sudan* 81 D4
El Maestrazgo, *Spain* 32 E4
El Mafâza, *Sudan* 81 E3
El Maghra, *Egypt* 80 A2
El Mahalla el Kubra, *Egypt* 80 H7
El Mahâriq, *Egypt* 80 B3
El Maîmûn, *Egypt* 80 J7
El Maks el Bahari, *Egypt* . 80 C3
El Manshâh, *Egypt* 80 B3
El Mansûra, *Egypt* 80 H7
El Manzala, *Egypt* 80 H7
El Marâgha, *Egypt* 80 B3
El Masid, *Sudan* 81 D3
El Masnou, *Spain* 32 D7
El Matariya, *Egypt* 80 H8
El Meda, *Ethiopia* 81 F5
El Medano, *Canary Is.* ... 37 F3
El Metemma, *Sudan* 81 D3
El Milagro, *Argentina* 126 C2
El Minyâ, *Egypt* 80 B3
El Monte, *U.S.A.* 117 L8
El Montseny, *Spain* 32 D7
El Mreyye, *Mauritania* 82 B3
El Niybo, *Ethiopia* 81 G4
El Obeid, *Sudan* 81 E2
El Odaiya, *Sudan* 81 E2
El Oro, *Mexico* 119 D4
El Oued, *Algeria* 78 B7
El Palmito, Presa, *Mexico* 118 B3
El Paso, *U.S.A.* 115 L10
El Paso Robles, *U.S.A.* .. 116 K6
El Pedernoso, *Spain* 33 F2
El Pedroso, *Spain* 35 H5
El Pobo de Dueñas, *Spain* . 32 E3
El Portal, *U.S.A.* 116 H7
El Porvenir, *Mexico* 118 A3
El Prat de Llobregat, *Spain* 33 D7
El Progreso, *Honduras* ... 120 C2
El Pueblito, *Mexico* 118 B3
El Pueblo, *Canary Is.* 37 F2
El Puente del Arzobispo, *Spain* 34 F5

El Puerto de Santa María, *Spain* 35 J4
El Qâhira, *Egypt* 80 H7
El Qantara, *Egypt* 75 E1
El Qasr, *Egypt* 80 B2
El Qubâbât, *Egypt* 80 J7
El Quseima, *Egypt* 75 E3
El Qusîya, *Egypt* 80 B3
El Râshda, *Egypt* 80 B2
El Real, *Panama* 124 B3
El Reno, *U.S.A.* 113 H6
El Rîdisiya, *Egypt* 80 C3
El Rio, *U.S.A.* 117 L7
El Ronquillo, *Spain* 35 H4
El Roque, Pta., *Canary Is.* 37 F4
El Rosarito, *Mexico* 118 B2
El Rubio, *Spain* 35 H5
El Saff, *Egypt* 80 J7
El Saheira, W. →, *Egypt* . 75 E2
El Salto, *Mexico* 118 C3
El Salvador ■, *Cent. Amer.* 120 D2
El Sauce, *Nic.* 120 D2
El Saucejo, *Spain* 35 H5
El Shallal, *Egypt* 80 C3
El Simbillawein, *Egypt* 80 H7
El Sueco, *Mexico* 118 B3
El Suweis, *Egypt* 80 J8
El Tabbîn, *Egypt* 80 J7
El Tamarâni, W. →, *Egypt* 75 E3
El Thamad, *Egypt* 75 F3
El Tigre, *Venezuela* 124 B6
El Tîh, Gebal, *Egypt* 75 F2
El Tîna, *Egypt* 80 H8
El Tîna, Khalîg, *Egypt* ... 75 D1
El Tofo, *Chile* 126 B1
El Tránsito, *Chile* 126 B1
El Tûr, *Egypt* 70 D2
El Turbio, *Argentina* 128 G2
El Uqsur, *Egypt* 80 B3
El Venado, *Mexico* 118 C4
El Vendrell, *Spain* 32 D6
El Vergel, *Mexico* 118 B3
El Vigía, *Venezuela* 124 B4
El Viso del Alcor, *Spain* .. 35 H5
El Wabeira, *Egypt* 75 F2
El Wak, *Kenya* 86 B5
El Waqf, *Egypt* 80 B3
El Weguet, *Ethiopia* 81 F5
El Wuz, *Sudan* 81 D3
Elafónisos, *Greece* 38 E4
Élancourt, *France* 19 D8
Élassa, *Greece* 39 F8
Elassón, *Greece* 38 B4
Elat, *Israel* 75 F3
Eláthia, *Greece* 38 C4
Elâzığ, *Turkey* 70 B3
Elba, *Italy* 28 F7
Elba, *U.S.A.* 109 K2
Elbasani, *Albania* 40 E4
Elbe, *U.S.A.* 116 D4
Elbe →, *Europe* 24 B4
Elbe-Seitenkanal, *Germany* . 24 C6
Elbert, Mt., *U.S.A.* 115 G10
Elberton, *U.S.A.* 109 H4
Elbeuf, *France* 18 C8
Elbidtan, *Turkey* 70 B3
Elbing = Elbląg, *Poland* .. 44 D6
Elbistan, *Turkey* 72 C7
Elbląg, *Poland* 44 D6
Elbow, *Canada* 105 C7
Elbrus, *Asia* 49 J6
Elburz Mts. = Alborz, Reshteh-ye Kûhhâ-ye, *Iran* 71 C7
Elche, *Spain* 33 G4
Elche de la Sierra, *Spain* . 33 G2
Elcho I., *Australia* 94 A2
Elda, *Spain* 33 G4
Eldon, *Mo., U.S.A.* 112 F8
Eldon, *Wash., U.S.A.* ... 116 C3
Eldora, *U.S.A.* 112 D8
Eldorado, *Argentina* 127 B5
Eldorado, *Canada* 105 B7
Eldorado, *Mexico* 118 C3
Eldorado, *Ill., U.S.A.* ... 108 G1
Eldorado, *Tex., U.S.A.* .. 113 K4
Eldorado Springs, *U.S.A.* 113 G8
Eldoret, *Kenya* 86 B4
Eldred, *U.S.A.* 110 E6
Elea, C., *Cyprus* 36 D13
Eleanora, Pk., *Australia* .. 93 F3
Elefantes →, *Mozam.* ... 89 C5
Elektrogorsk, *Russia* 46 E10
Elektrostal, *Russia* 46 E10
Elele, *Nigeria* 83 D6
Elena, *Bulgaria* 41 D9
Elephant Butte Reservoir, *U.S.A.* 115 K10
Elephant I., *Antarctica* ... 5 C18
Eleshnitsa, *Bulgaria* 40 E7
Eleşkirt, *Turkey* 73 C10
Eleuthera, *Bahamas* 120 B4
Elevsís, *Greece* 38 C5
Elevtheroúpolis, *Greece* .. 41 F8
Elgin, *Canada* 111 B8
Elgin, *U.K.* 14 D5
Elgin, *Ill., U.S.A.* 108 D1
Elgin, *N. Dak., U.S.A.* .. 112 B4
Elgin, *Oreg., U.S.A.* 114 D5
Elgin, *Tex., U.S.A.* 113 K6
Elgoibar, *Spain* 32 B2
Elgon, Mt., *Africa* 86 B3
Eliase, *Indonesia* 63 F8
Elikón, *Greece* 38 C4
Elim, *Namibia* 88 B2
Elim, *S. Africa* 88 E2
Elin Pelin, *Bulgaria* 40 D4
Elisabethville = Lubumbashi, *Dem. Rep. of the Congo* . 87 E2
Elista, *Russia* 49 G7

Elizabeth, *Australia* 95 E2
Elizabeth, *N.J., U.S.A.* .. 111 F10
Elizabeth, *N.J., U.S.A.* .. 111 F10
Elizabeth City, *U.S.A.* ... 109 G7
Elizabethton, *U.S.A.* 109 G4
Elizabethtown, *Ky., U.S.A.* 108 G3
Elizabethtown, *N.Y., U.S.A.* 111 B11
Elizabethtown, *Pa., U.S.A.* 111 F8
Elizondo, *Spain* 32 B3
Elk, *Poland* 44 E9
Elk →, *Canada* 104 C5
Elk →, *Poland* 44 E9
Elk →, *U.S.A.* 109 H2
Elk City, *U.S.A.* 113 H5
Elk Creek, *U.S.A.* 116 F4
Elk Grove, *U.S.A.* 116 G5
Elk Island Nat. Park, *Canada* 104 C6
Elk Lake, *Canada* 102 C3
Elk Point, *Canada* 105 C6
Elk River, *Idaho, U.S.A.* 114 C5
Elk River, *Minn., U.S.A.* 112 C8
Elkedra →, *Australia* ... 94 C2
Elkhart, *Ind., U.S.A.* .. 108 E3
Elkhart, *Kans., U.S.A.* . 113 G4
Elkhorn, *Canada* 105 D8
Elkhorn →, *U.S.A.* ... 112 E6
Elkhovo, *Bulgaria* 41 D10
Elkin, *U.S.A.* 109 G5
Elkins, *U.S.A.* 108 F6
Elkland, *U.S.A.* 110 E7
Elko, *Canada* 104 D5
Elko, *U.S.A.* 114 F6
Elkton, *U.S.A.* 110 C1
Ell, L., *Australia* 93 E4
Ellef Ringnes I. *Canada* . 4 B2
Ellen, Mt., *U.S.A.* 111 B12
Ellenburg, *U.S.A.* 111 B11
Ellendale, *U.S.A.* 112 B5
Ellensburg, *U.S.A.* ... 114 C3
Ellenville, *U.S.A.* 111 E10
Ellery, Mt., *Australia* .. 95 F4
Ellesmere, L., *N.Z.* ... 91 M4
Ellesmere I., *Canada* .. 4 B4
Ellesmere Port, *U.K.* .. 12 D5
Ellice Is. = Tuvalu ■, *Pac. Oc.* 96 H9
Ellicottville, *U.S.A.* ... 110 D6
Elliot, *Australia* 94 B1
Elliot, *S. Africa* 89 E4
Elliot Lake, *Canada* ... 102 C3
Elliotdale = Xhora, *S. Africa* 89 E4
Ellis, *U.S.A.* 112 F5
Elliston, *Austria* 95 E1
Ellisville, *U.S.A.* 113 K10
Ellon, *U.K.* 14 D6
Ellore = Eluru, *India* .. 67 L12
Ellsworth, *Kans., U.S.A.* 112 F5
Ellsworth, *Maine, U.S.A.* 109 C11
Ellsworth Land *Antarctica* . 5 D16
Ellsworth Mts., *Antarctica* . 5 D16
Ellwangen, *Germany* ... 25 G6
Ellwood City, *U.S.A.* .. 110 F4
Elm, *Switz.* 25 C8
Elma, *Canada* 105 D9
Elma, *U.S.A.* 116 D3
Elmadağ, *Turkey* 72 C5
Elmalı, *Turkey* 39 E11
Elmhurst, *U.S.A.* 108 E2
Elmina, *Ghana* 83 D4
Elmira, *Canada* 110 C4
Elmira, *U.S.A.* 110 D8
Elmira Heights, *U.S.A.* . 110 D8
Elmore, *Australia* 95 F3
Elmore, *U.S.A.* 117 M11
Elmshorn, *Germany* ... 24 B5
Elmvale, *Canada* 110 B5
Elne, *France* 20 F7
Elora, *Canada* 110 C4
Elos, *Greece* 38 E4
Eloúnda, *Greece* 36 D7
Eloy, *U.S.A.* 115 K8
Éloyes, *France* 19 D13
Elrose, *Canada* 105 C7
Elsdorf, *Germany* 24 E2
Elsie, *U.S.A.* 116 E3
Elsinore = Helsingør, *Denmark* 11 H6
Elster →, *Germany* ... 24 D7
Elsterwerda, *Germany* . 24 D9
Eltham, *N.Z.* 91 H5
Elton, *Russia* 49 F8
Elton, Ozero, *Russia* .. 49 F8
Eltville, *Germany* 25 E4
Eluru, *India* 67 L12
Elvas, *Portugal* 35 G3
Elven, *France* 18 E4
Elverum, *Norway* 9 F14
Elvire →, *Australia* ... 92 C4
Elvire, Mt., *Australia* . 93 E2
Elvo →, *Italy* 28 C5
Elwell, L., *U.S.A.* ... 114 B8
Elwood, *Ind., U.S.A.* . 108 E3
Elwood, *Nebr., U.S.A.* 112 E5
Elx = Elche, *Spain* ... 33 G4
Ely, *U.K.* 13 E8
Ely, *Minn., U.S.A.* .. 112 B9
Ely, *Nev., U.S.A.* .. 114 G6
Elyria, *U.S.A.* 110 E2
Elyrus, *Greece* 38 F5
Elz →, *Germany* 25 G3
Emådalen, *Sweden* ... 10 C8
Emâmrûd, *Iran* 71 B7
Emån →, *Sweden* ... 11 G10
Emba, *Kazakstan* 50 E6
Emba →, *Kazakstan* . 50 E6
Embarcación, *Argentina* 126 A3
Embarras Portage, *Canada* . 105 B6
Embetsu, *Japan* 54 B10
Embi = Emba, *Kazakstan* 50 E6

Embi = Emba →,
　Kazakstan 50 E6
Embóna, Greece 36 C9
Embrun, France 21 D10
Embu, Kenya 86 C4
Emden, Germany 24 B3
Emecik, Turkey 39 E9
Emerald, Australia 94 C4
Emerson, Canada 105 D9
Emet, Turkey 39 B11
Emi Koussi, Chad 79 E9
Emília-Romagna □, Italy .. 28 D8
Emilius, Mte., Italy 28 C4
Eminabad, Pakistan 68 C6
Emine, Nos, Bulgaria 41 D11
Emirdağ, Turkey 72 C4
Emlenton, U.S.A. 110 E5
Emlichheim, Germany 24 C2
Emmaboda, Sweden 11 H9
Emmaus, S. Africa 88 D4
Emmaus, U.S.A. 111 F9
Emme →, Switz. 25 H3
Emmeloord, Neths. 17 B5
Emmen, Neths. 17 B6
Emmen, Switz. 25 H3
Emmendingen, Germany ... 25 G3
Emmental, Switz. 25 J3
Emmerich, Germany 24 D2
Emmet, Australia 94 C3
Emmetsburg, U.S.A. 112 D7
Emmett, Idaho, U.S.A. ... 114 E5
Emmett, Mich., U.S.A. .. 110 D2
Emmonak, U.S.A. 100 B3
Emo, Canada 105 D10
Emőd, Hungary 42 C5
Emona, Bulgaria 41 D11
Empalme, Mexico 118 B2
Empangeni, S. Africa 89 D5
Empedrado, Argentina .. 126 B4
Emperor Seamount Chain,
　Pac. Oc. 96 D9
Empoli, Italy 28 E7
Emporia, Kans., U.S.A. .. 112 F6
Emporia, Va., U.S.A. ... 109 G7
Emporium, U.S.A. 110 E6
Empress, Canada 105 C7
Empty Quarter = Rub' al
　Khālī, Si. Arabia 74 D4
Ems →, Germany 24 B3
Emsdale, Canada 110 A5
Emsdetten, Germany 24 C3
Emu, China 57 C15
Emu Park, Australia 94 C5
'En 'Avrona, Israel 75 F4
En Nahud, Sudan 81 E2
En Nofalab, Sudan 81 D3
Ena, Japan 55 G8
Enana, Namibia 88 B2
Enånger, Sweden 10 C11
Enaratoli, Indonesia 63 E9
Enard B., U.K. 14 C3
Enare = Inarijärvi, Finland . 8 B22
Encampment, U.S.A. ... 114 F10
Encantadas, Serra, Brazil . 127 C5
Encarnación, Paraguay ... 127 B4
Encarnación de Díaz, Mexico 118 C4
Enchi, Ghana 82 D4
Encinitas, U.S.A. 117 M9
Encino, U.S.A. 115 J11
Encounter B., Australia .. 95 F2
Encs, Hungary 42 B6
Endako, Canada 104 C3
Ende, Indonesia 63 F6
Endeavour Str., Australia .. 94 A3
Endelave, Denmark 11 J4
Enderbury I., Kiribati ... 96 H10
Enderby, Canada 104 C5
Enderby I., Australia 92 D2
Enderby Land, Antarctica . 5 C5
Enderlin, U.S.A. 112 B6
Endicott, U.S.A. 111 D8
Endwell, U.S.A. 111 D8
Endyalgout I., Australia .. 92 B5
Eneabba, Australia 93 E2
Enewetak Atoll, Marshall Is. 96 F8
Enez, Turkey 41 F10
Enfield, Canada 103 D7
Enfield, Conn., U.S.A. . 111 E12
Enfield, N.H., U.S.A. .. 111 C12
Engadin, Switz. 25 J6
Engaño, C., Dom. Rep. .. 121 C6
Engaño, C., Phil. 63 A6
Engaru, Japan 54 B11
Engcobo, S. Africa 89 E4
Engelberg, Switz. 25 J4
Engels, Russia 48 E8
Engemann L., Canada ... 105 B7
Engershatu, Eritrea 81 D4
Enggano, Indonesia 62 F2
England, U.S.A. 113 H9
England □, U.K. 12 D7
Englee, Canada 103 B8
Englehart, Canada 102 C4
Englewood, U.S.A. 112 F2
English →, Canada 105 C10
English Bazar = Ingraj
　Bazar, India 69 G13
English Channel, Europe .. 13 G6
English River, Canada 102 C1
Engures ezers, Latvia 44 A10
Enguri →, Georgia 49 J5
Enid, U.S.A. 113 G6
Enipévs →, Greece 38 E4
Enkhuizen, Neths. 17 B5
Enköping, Sweden 10 E11
Enle, China 58 F3
Enna, Italy 31 E7
Ennadai, Canada 105 A8
Ennadai L., Canada 105 A8
Ennedi, Chad 79 E10
Enngonia, Australia 95 D4

Ennigerloh, Germany 24 D4
Ennis, Ireland 15 D3
Ennis, Mont., U.S.A. ... 114 D8
Ennis, Tex., U.S.A. 113 J6
Enniscorthy, Ireland 15 D5
Enniskillen, U.K. 15 B4
Ennistimon, Ireland 15 D2
Enns, Austria 26 C7
Enns →, Austria 26 C7
Enontekiö, Finland 8 B20
Enosburg Falls, U.S.A. .. 111 B11
Enriquillo, L., Dom. Rep. . 121 C5
Enschede, Neths. 17 B6
Ensenada, Argentina ... 126 C4
Ensenada, Mexico 118 A1
Ensenada de los Muertos,
　Mexico 118 C2
Enshi, China 58 B7
Ensiola, Pta. de n', Spain .. 37 B9
Ensisheim, France 19 E14
Entebbe, Uganda 86 B3
Enterprise, Canada 104 A5
Enterprise, Ala., U.S.A. . 109 K3
Enterprise, Oreg., U.S.A. .. 114 D5
Entraygues-sur-Truyère,
　France 20 D6
Entre Ríos, Bolivia 126 A3
Entre Ríos □, Argentina . 126 C4
Entrepeñas, Embalse de,
　Spain 32 E2
Entroncamento, Portugal .. 35 F2
Enugu, Nigeria 83 D6
Enugu □, Nigeria 83 D6
Enugu Ezike, Nigeria 83 D6
Enumclaw, U.S.A. 116 C5
Envermeu, France 18 C8
Enviken, Sweden 10 D9
Enying, Hungary 42 D3
Enza →, Italy 28 D7
Eólie, Ís., Italy 31 D7
Epanomí, Greece 40 F6
Epe, Neths. 17 B5
Epe, Nigeria 83 D5
Épernay, France 19 C10
Épernon, France 19 D8
Ephesus, Turkey 39 D9
Ephraim, U.S.A. 114 G8
Ephrata, Pa., U.S.A. ... 111 F8
Ephrata, Wash., U.S.A. .. 114 C4
Epidaurus Limera, Greece . 38 E5
Épila, Spain 32 D3
Épinac, France 19 F11
Épinal, France 19 D13
Episkopi, Cyprus 36 E11
Episkopí, Greece 36 D6
Episkopi Bay, Cyprus 36 E11
Epitálion, Greece 38 D3
Eppan = Appiano, Italy .. 29 B8
Eppingen, Germany 25 F4
Epsom, U.K. 13 F7
Epukiro, Namibia 88 C2
Equatorial Guinea ■, Africa 84 D1
Er Hai, China 58 E3
Er Rahad, Sudan 81 E3
Er Rif, Morocco 78 A5
Er Rogel, Sudan 80 D4
Er Roseires, Sudan 81 E3
Er Rua'at, Sudan 81 E3
Eraclea, Italy 29 C9
Erāwadī Myit =
　Irrawaddy →, Burma .. 67 M19
Erba, Italy 28 C6
Erba, Sudan 80 D4
Erba, J., Sudan 80 C4
Erbaa, Turkey 72 B7
Erbeskopf, Germany 25 F3
Erbu, Ethiopia 81 E3
Erçek, Turkey 70 B4
Erciş, Turkey 73 C10
Erciyaş Dağı, Turkey ... 70 B2
Érd, Hungary 42 C3
Erdao Jiang →, China .. 57 C14
Erdek, Turkey 41 F11
Erdemli, Turkey 72 D6
Erdene = Ulaan-Uul,
　Mongolia 56 B6
Erdenetsogt, Mongolia .. 56 C4
Erding, Germany 25 G7
Erebus, Mt., Antarctica .. 5 D11
Erechim, Brazil 127 B5
Ereğli, Konya, Turkey .. 70 D6
Ereğli, Zonguldak, Turkey .. 72 B4
Erei, Monti, Italy 31 E7
Erenhot, China 56 C7
Eresma →, Spain 34 D6
Eressós, Greece 39 B7
Erewadi Myitwanya, Burma 67 M19
Erfenisdam, S. Africa ... 88 D4
Erfjord, Norway 11 E3
Erft →, Germany 24 D2
Erfurt, Germany 24 E7
Erg Iguidi, Africa 78 C4
Ergani, Turkey 70 B3
Ergel, Mongolia 56 C5
Ergene →, Turkey 41 E10
Ergeni Vozvyshennost,
　Russia 49 G7
Ērgļi, Latvia 9 H21
Erhlin, Taiwan 59 F13
Eria →, Spain 34 C5
Eriba, Sudan 81 D4
Eriboll, L., U.K. 14 C4
Érice, Italy 30 D5
Erie, U.S.A. 110 D4
Erie, L., N. Amer. 110 D4
Erie Canal, U.S.A. 110 C7
Erieau, Canada 110 D3
Erigavo, Somali Rep. 74 E4

Erikoúsa, Greece 36 A3
Eriksdale, Canada 105 C9
Erímanthos, Greece 38 D3
Erimo-misaki, Japan 54 D11
Erinpura, India 68 G5
Eriskay, U.K. 14 D1
Eritrea ■, Africa 81 E4
Erjas →, Portugal 34 F3
Erkelenz, Germany 24 D2
Erkner, Germany 24 C9
Erlangen, Germany 25 F6
Erldunda, Australia 94 D1
Ermelo, Neths. 17 B5
Ermelo, S. Africa 89 D4
Ermenek, Turkey 70 B2
Ermil, Sudan 81 E2
Ermióni, Greece 38 D5
Ermones, Greece 36 A3
Ermoúpolis = Síros, Greece 38 D6
Ernakulam = Cochin, India 66 Q10
Erne →, Ireland 15 B3
Erne, Lower L., U.K. 15 B4
Erne, Upper L., U.K. 15 B4
Ernée, France 18 D6
Ernest Giles Ra., Australia . 93 E3
Ernstberg, Germany 25 E2
Erode, India 66 P10
Eromanga, Australia 95 D3
Erongo, Namibia 88 C2
Erquy, France 18 D4
Erramala Hills, India 66 M11
Errer →, Ethiopia 81 F5
Errigal, Ireland 15 A3
Erris Hd., Ireland 15 B1
Erseka, Albania 40 F4
Erskine, U.S.A. 112 B7
Erstein, France 19 D14
Ertholmene, Denmark ... 11 J9
Ertil, Russia 48 E5
Ertis = Irtysh →, Russia .. 50 C7
Eruh, Turkey 73 D10
Eruwa, Nigeria 83 D5
Ervy-le-Châtel, France ... 19 D10
Erwin, U.S.A. 109 G4
Erzgebirge, Germany ... 24 E8
Erzin, Russia 51 D10
Erzincan, Turkey 70 B3
Erzurum, Turkey 70 B4
Es Caló, Spain 37 C8
Es Canar, Spain 37 B8
Es Mercadal, Spain 37 B11
Es Migjorn Gran, Spain .. 37 B11
Es Safiya, Sudan 81 D3
Es Sahrâ' Esh Sharqîya,
　Egypt 80 B3
Es Sînâ', Egypt 75 F3
Es Sûkî, Sudan 81 E3
Es Vedrà, Spain 37 C7
Esambo,
　Dem. Rep. of the Congo . 86 C1
Esan-Misaki, Japan 54 D10
Esashi, Hokkaidō, Japan .. 54 B11
Esashi, Hokkaidō, Japan .. 54 D10
Esbjerg, Denmark 11 J2
Escalante, U.S.A. 115 H8
Escalante →, U.S.A. ... 115 H8
Escalón, Mexico 118 B4
Escambia →, U.S.A. ... 109 K2
Escanaba, U.S.A. 108 C2
Esch-sur-Alzette, Lux. ... 17 E6
Eschede, Germany 24 C6
Eschwege, Germany 24 D6
Eschweiler, Germany ... 24 E2
Escondido, U.S.A. 117 M9
Escravos →, Nigeria 83 D6
Escuinapa, Mexico 118 C3
Escuintla, Guatemala ... 120 D1
Eséka, Cameroon 83 E7
Eşen →, Turkey 39 E11
Esenguly, Turkmenistan .. 50 F6
Esens, Germany 24 B3
Esenyurt, Turkey 41 E12
Esera →, Spain 32 C5
Esfahān, Iran 71 C6
Esfahān □, Iran 71 C6
Esfarāyen, Iran 71 B8
Esfideh, Iran 71 C8
Esgueva →, Spain 34 D6
Esh Sham = Dimashq, Syria 75 B5
Esh Shamâlîya □, Sudan .. 80 D2
Esha Ness, U.K. 14 A7
Eshan, China 58 E4
Esher, U.K. 13 F7
Eshowe, S. Africa 89 D5
Esiama, Ghana 82 E4
Esigodini, Zimbabwe 89 C4
Esil = Ishim →, Russia .. 50 D7
Esino →, Italy 29 E10
Esira, Madag. 89 C8
Esk →, Cumb., U.K. 14 G5
Esk →, N. Yorks., U.K. .. 12 C7
Eskān, Iran 71 E9
Esker, Canada 103 B6
Eskifjörður, Iceland 8 D7
Eskilstuna, Sweden 11 F10
Eskimalatya, Turkey 73 C8
Eskimo Pt., Canada 100 B10
Eskişehir, Turkey 39 B12
Eskişehir □, Turkey 39 B12
Esla →, Spain 34 D4
Eslāmābād-e Gharb, Iran .. 70 C5
Eslāmshahr, Iran 71 C6
Eslöv, Sweden 11 J7
Eşme, Turkey 39 C10
Esmeraldas, Ecuador ... 124 C3
Esnagi L., Canada 102 C3
Espalion, France 20 D6

Espanola, Canada 102 C3
Espanola, U.S.A. 115 H10
Esparreguera, Spain 32 D6
Esparta, Costa Rica 120 E3
Espelkamp, Germany ... 24 C4
Esperance, Australia 93 F3
Esperance B., Australia .. 93 F3
Esperanza, Argentina .. 126 C3
Esperanza, Phil. 61 G6
Espéraza, France 20 F6
Espichel, C., Portugal ... 35 G1
Espiel, Spain 35 G5
Espigão, Serra do, Brazil .. 127 B5
Espinazo, Sierra del =
　Espinhaço, Serra do,
　Brazil 125 G10
Espinhaço, Serra do, Brazil 125 G10
Espinho, Portugal 34 D2
Espinilho, Serra do, Brazil . 127 B5
Espinosa de los Monteros,
　Spain 34 B7
Espírito Santo □, Brazil ... 125 H10
Espíritu Santo, Vanuatu 96 J8
Espíritu Santo, B. del,
　Mexico 119 D7
Espíritu Santo, I., Mexico . 118 C2
Espita, Mexico 119 C7
Espiye, Turkey 73 B8
Espluga de Francolí, Spain . 32 D6
Espoo, Finland 9 F21
Espuña, Sierra de, Spain .. 33 H3
Esquel, Argentina 128 E2
Esquimalt, Canada 104 D4
Esquina, Argentina ... 126 C4
Essaouira, Morocco 78 B4
Essebie,
　Dem. Rep. of the Congo . 86 B3
Essen, Belgium 17 C4
Essen, Germany 24 D3
Essendon, Mt., Australia . 93 E3
Essequibo →, Guyana .. 122 C5
Essex →, Canada 110 D2
Essex, Calif., U.S.A. ... 117 L11
Essex, N.Y., U.S.A. ... 111 B11
Essex □, U.K. 13 F8
Essex Junction, U.S.A. .. 111 B11
Esslingen, Germany 25 G5
Essonne □, France 19 D9
Estaca de Bares, C. de,
　Spain 34 B3
Estadilla, Spain 32 C5
Estados, I. de Los, Argentina 122 J4
Estagel, France 20 F6
Eştahbānāt, Iran 71 D7
Estância, Brazil 125 F11
Estancia, U.S.A. 115 J10
Estārm, Iran 71 D8
Estarreja, Portugal 34 E2
Estats, Pic d', Spain 32 C6
Estcourt, S. Africa 89 D4
Este, Italy 29 C8
Estelí, Nic. 120 D2
Estella, Spain 32 C2
Estellencs, Spain 37 B9
Estena →, Spain 35 F6
Estepa, Spain 35 H6
Estepona, Spain 35 J5
Esterhazy, Canada 105 C8
Esternay, France 19 D10
Esterri d'Aneu, Spain ... 32 C6
Estevan, Canada 105 D8
Estevan Group, Canada . 104 C3
Estherville, U.S.A. 112 D7
Estissac, France 19 D10
Eston, Canada 105 C7
Estonia ■, Europe 9 G21
Estoril, Portugal 35 G1
Estouk, Mali 83 B5
Estreito, Brazil 125 E9
Estrela, Serra da, Portugal . 34 E3
Estrella, Spain 35 G7
Estremoz, Portugal 35 G3
Estrondo, Serra do, Brazil . 125 E9
Esztergom, Hungary ... 42 C3
Et Tîdra, Mauritania ... 82 B1
Etah, India 69 F8
Étain, France 19 C12
Étampes, France 19 D9
Etanga, Namibia 88 B1
Étaples, France 19 B8
Etawah, India 69 F8
Etawney L., Canada ... 105 B9
Ete, Nigeria 83 D6
Ethel, U.S.A. 116 D4
Ethelbert, Canada 105 C8
Ethiopia ■, Africa 74 F3
Ethiopian Highlands,
　Ethiopia 52 J7
Etili, Turkey 41 G10
Etive, L., U.K. 14 E3
Etna, Italy 31 E7
Etoile,
　Dem. Rep. of the Congo . 87 E2
Etosha Nat. Park, Namibia . 88 B2
Etosha Pan, Namibia 88 B2
Etowah, U.S.A. 109 H3
Étréchy, France 19 D9
Étrépagny, France 19 C8
Étretat, France 18 C7
Etropole, Bulgaria 41 D8
Ettelbruck, Lux. 17 E6
Ettlingen, Germany 25 G4
Ettrick Water →, U.K. .. 14 F6
Etuku,
　Dem. Rep. of the Congo . 86 C2
Etulia, Moldova 43 E13
Etzatlán, Mexico 118 C4
Etzná, Mexico 119 D6
Eu, France 18 B8

Euboea = Évvoia, Greece .. 38 C6
Eucla, Australia 93 F4
Euclid, U.S.A. 110 E3
Eucumbene, L., Australia .. 95 F4
Eudora, U.S.A. 113 J9
Eufaula, Ala., U.S.A. .. 109 K3
Eufaula, Okla., U.S.A. . 113 H7
Eufaula L., U.S.A. 113 H7
Eugene, U.S.A. 114 E2
Eugowra, Australia 95 E4
Eulo, Australia 95 D4
Eunice, La., U.S.A. ... 113 K8
Eunice, N. Mex., U.S.A. . 113 J3
Eupen, Belgium 17 D6
Euphrates = Furāt, Nahr
　al →, Asia 70 D5
Eure □, France 18 C8
Eure →, France 18 C8
Eure-et-Loir □, France ... 18 D8
Eureka, Canada 4 B3
Eureka, Calif., U.S.A. .. 114 F1
Eureka, Kans., U.S.A. .. 113 G6
Eureka, Mont., U.S.A. .. 114 B6
Eureka, Nev., U.S.A. ... 114 G5
Eureka, S. Dak., U.S.A. . 112 C5
Eureka, Mt., Australia ... 93 E3
Euroa, Australia 95 F4
Europa, Île, Ind. Oc. ... 85 J8
Europa, Picos de, Spain .. 34 B6
Europa, Pta. de, Gib. 35 J5
Europe 6 E10
Europoort, Neths. 17 C4
Euskirchen, Germany ... 24 E2
Eustis, U.S.A. 109 L5
Euston, Australia 95 E3
Eutin, Germany 24 A6
Eutsuk L., Canada 104 C3
Evale, Angola 88 B2
Evans, U.S.A. 112 E2
Evans, L., Canada 102 B4
Evans City, U.S.A. 110 F4
Evans Head, Australia ... 95 D5
Evans Mills, U.S.A. 111 B9
Evansburg, Canada 104 C5
Evanston, Ill., U.S.A. .. 108 E2
Evanston, Wyo., U.S.A. . 114 F8
Évaux-les-Bains, France .. 19 F9
Evaz, Iran 71 E7
Eveleth, U.S.A. 112 B8
Evensk, Russia 51 C16
Everard, L., Australia ... 95 E2
Everard Ranges, Australia . 93 E5
Everest, Mt., Nepal 69 E12
Everett, Pa., U.S.A. ... 110 F6
Everett, Wash., U.S.A. . 116 C4
Everglades, The, U.S.A. . 109 N5
Everglades National Park,
　U.S.A. 109 N5
Evergreen, Ala., U.S.A. . 109 K2
Evergreen, Mont., U.S.A. . 114 B6
Everöd, Sweden 11 J8
Evertsberg, Sweden 10 C7
Evesham, U.K. 13 E6
Évian-les-Bains, France .. 19 F13
Évinos →, Greece 38 C3
Évisa, France 21 F12
Evje, Norway 9 G12
Évora, Portugal 35 G3
Évora □, Portugal 35 G3
Evowghlī, Iran 70 B5
Évreux, France 18 C8
Évritanía □, Greece 38 B3
Évron, France 18 D6
Évros □, Bulgaria 72 B2
Evrótas →, Greece 38 E4
Évry, France 19 D9
Évvoia, Greece 38 C6
Evvoia □, Greece 38 C5
Ewe, L., U.K. 14 D3
Ewing, U.S.A. 112 D5
Ewo, Congo 84 E2
Exaltación, Bolivia 124 F5
Excelsior Springs, U.S.A. . 112 F7
Excideuil, France 20 C5
Exe →, U.K. 13 G4
Exeter, Canada 110 C3
Exeter, U.K. 13 G4
Exeter, Calif., U.S.A. .. 116 J7
Exeter, N.H., U.S.A. .. 111 D14
Exmoor, U.K. 13 F4
Exmouth, Australia 92 D1
Exmouth, U.K. 13 G4
Exmouth G., Australia ... 92 D1
Expedition Ra., Australia .. 94 C4
Extremadura □, Spain ... 35 F4
Exuma Sound, Bahamas . 120 B4
Eyasi, L., Tanzania 86 C4
Eye Pen., U.K. 14 C2
Eyemouth, U.K. 14 F6
Eyjafjörður, Iceland 8 C4
Eymet, France 20 D4
Eymoutiers, France 20 C5
Eynsil, Turkey 73 B8
Eyre (North), L., Australia . 95 D2
Eyre (South), L., Australia . 95 D2
Eyre Mts., N.Z. 91 L2
Eyre Pen., Australia 95 E2
Eyvānkī, Iran 71 C6
Ez Zeidab, Sudan 80 D3
Ezcaray, Spain 32 C1
Ezere, Latvia 9 H20
Ezerělis, Lithuania 44 D10
Ezhou, China 59 B10
Ezine, Turkey 39 B8
Ezouza →, Cyprus 36 E11

F

F.Y.R.O.M. =
Macedonia ■, Europe ... 40 E5
Fabala, Guinea 82 D3
Fabens, U.S.A. 115 L10
Fabero, Spain 34 C4
Fåborg, Denmark 11 J4
Fabriano, Italy 29 E9
Făcăeni, Romania 43 F12
Fachi, Niger 79 E8
Fada, Chad 79 E10
Fada-n-Gourma,
Burkina Faso 83 C5
Fadd, Hungary 42 D3
Faddeyevskiy, Ostrov, Russia 51 B15
Faddor, Sudan 81 F3
Fadghāmī, Syria 70 C4
Fadlab, Sudan 80 D3
Faenza, Italy 29 D8
Færoe Is. = Føroyar,
Atl. Oc. 8 F9
Fafa, Mali 83 B5
Fafe, Portugal 34 D2
Fagam, Nigeria 83 C7
Făgăraş, Romania 43 E9
Făgăraş, Munţii, Romania . 43 E9
Fagelmara, Sweden 11 H9
Fagerhult, Sweden 11 G5
Fagersta, Sweden 10 D9
Făget, Romania 42 E7
Făget, Munţii, Romania .. 43 C8
Fagnano, L., Argentina ... 128 G3
Fagnières, France 19 D11
Faguibine, L., Mali 82 B4
Fahlīān, Iran 71 D6
Fahraj, Kermān, Iran ... 71 D8
Fahraj, Yazd, Iran 71 D7
Fai Tsi Long Archipelago,
Vietnam 58 G6
Faial, Madeira 37 D3
Fair Haven, U.S.A. 108 D9
Fair Hd., U.K. 15 A5
Fair Oaks, U.S.A. 116 G5
Fairbanks, U.S.A. 100 B5
Fairbury, U.S.A. 112 E6
Fairfax, U.S.A. 111 B11
Fairfield, Ala., U.S.A. . 109 J2
Fairfield, Calif., U.S.A. 116 G4
Fairfield, Conn., U.S.A. . 111 E11
Fairfield, Idaho, U.S.A. . 114 E6
Fairfield, Ill., U.S.A. . 108 F1
Fairfield, Iowa, U.S.A. . 112 E9
Fairfield, Tex., U.S.A. . 113 K7
Fairford, Canada 105 C9
Fairhope, U.S.A. 109 K2
Fairlie, N.Z. 91 L3
Fairmead, U.S.A. 116 H6
Fairmont, Minn., U.S.A. . 112 D7
Fairmont, W. Va., U.S.A. 108 F5
Fairmount, Calif., U.S.A. 117 L8
Fairmount, N.Y., U.S.A. . 111 C8
Fairplay, U.S.A. 115 G11
Fairport, U.S.A. 110 C7
Fairport Harbor, U.S.A. . 110 E3
Fairview, Canada 104 B5
Fairview, Mont., U.S.A. . 112 B2
Fairview, Okla., U.S.A. . 113 G5
Fairweather, Mt., U.S.A. 104 B1
Faisalabad, Pakistan ... 68 D5
Faith, U.S.A. 112 C3
Faizabad, India 69 F10
Fajardo, Puerto Rico ... 121 C6
Fajr, W. →, Si. Arabia . 70 D4
Fakenham, U.K. 12 E8
Fåker, Sweden 10 A8
Fakfak, Indonesia 63 E8
Fakiya, Bulgaria 41 D11
Fakobli, Ivory C. 82 D3
Fakse, Denmark 11 J6
Fakse Bugt, Denmark 11 J6
Fakse Ladeplads, Denmark 11 J6
Faku, China 57 C12
Falaba, S. Leone 82 D2
Falaise, France 18 D6
Falaise, Mui, Vietnam .. 64 C5
Falakrón Óros, Greece ... 40 E7
Falam, Burma 67 H18
Falces, Spain 32 C3
Fălciu, Romania 43 D13
Falcó, C. des, Spain ... 37 C7
Falcón, Presa, Mexico .. 119 B5
Falcon Lake, Canada 105 D9
Falcon Reservoir, U.S.A. 113 M5
Falconara Maríttima, Italy 29 E10
Falcone, C. del, Italy .. 30 B1
Falconer, U.S.A. 110 D5
Faléa, Mali 82 C2
Falémé →, Senegal 82 C2
Falerum, Sweden 11 F10
Faleshty = Fălești, Moldova 43 C12
Fălești, Moldova 43 C12
Falfurrias, U.S.A. 113 M5
Falher, Canada 104 B5
Falirakí, Greece 36 C10
Falkenberg, Germany 24 D9
Falkenberg, Sweden 11 H6
Falkensee, Germany 24 C9
Falkirk, U.K. 14 F5
Falkirk □, U.K. 14 F5
Falkland, U.K. 14 E5
Falkland Is. □, Atl. Oc. 128 G5
Falkland Sd., Falk. Is. . 128 G5
Falkonéra, Greece 38 E5
Falköping, Sweden 11 F7
Fall River, U.S.A. 111 E13
Fallbrook, U.S.A. 117 M9
Fallon, U.S.A. 114 G4
Falls City, U.S.A. 112 E7
Falls Creek, U.S.A. 110 E6

Falmouth, Jamaica 120 C4
Falmouth, U.K. 13 G2
Falmouth, U.S.A. 111 E14
Falsa, Pta., Mexico 118 B1
False B., S. Africa 88 E2
Falso, C., Honduras 120 C3
Falster, Denmark 11 K5
Falsterbo, Sweden 9 J15
Fălticeni, Romania 43 C11
Falun, Sweden 10 D9
Famagusta, Cyprus 36 D12
Famagusta Bay, Cyprus .. 36 D13
Famalé, Niger 78 F6
Famatina, Sierra de,
Argentina 126 B2
Family L., Canada 105 C9
Famoso, U.S.A. 117 K7
Fan Xian, China 56 G8
Fana, Mali 82 C3
Fanad Hd., Ireland 15 A4
Fanárion, Greece 38 B3
Fandriana, Madag. 89 C8
Fang, Thailand 58 H2
Fang Xian, China 59 A8
Fangaga, Sudan 80 D4
Fangak, Sudan 81 F3
Fangchang, China 59 B12
Fangcheng, China 56 H7
Fangchenggang, China ... 58 G7
Fangliao, Taiwan 59 F13
Fangshan, China 56 E6
Fangzi, China 57 F10
Fani i Madh →, Albania . 40 E4
Fanjakana, Madag. 89 C8
Fanjiatun, China 57 C13
Fannich, L., U.K. 14 D4
Fannūj, Iran 71 E8
Fanø, Denmark 11 J2
Fano, Italy 29 E10
Fanshi, China 56 E7
Fao = Al Fāw, Iraq 71 D6
Faqirwali, Pakistan 68 E5
Fâqûs, Egypt 80 H7
Fara in Sabina, Italy .. 29 F9
Faradje,
Dem. Rep. of the Congo 86 B2
Farafangana, Madag. 89 C8
Faráfra, El Wâhât el-, Egypt 80 B2
Farāh, Afghan. 66 C3
Farāh □, Afghan. 66 C3
Farahalana, Madag. 89 A9
Faraid, Gebel, Egypt ... 80 C4
Farako, Ivory C. 82 D4
Faramana, Burkina Faso . 82 C4
Faranah, Guinea 82 C2
Farasān, Jazā'ir, Si. Arabia 74 D3
Farasān Is. = Farasān,
Jazā'ir, Si. Arabia 74 D3
Faratsiho, Madag. 89 B8
Fardes →, Spain 35 H7
Fareham, U.K. 13 G6
Farewell, C., N.Z. 91 J4
Farewell C. = Nunap Isua,
Greenland 4 D5
Färgelanda, Sweden 11 F5
Farghona, Uzbekistan ... 50 E8
Fargo, U.S.A. 112 B6
Fār'iah, W. al →,
West Bank 75 C4
Faribault, U.S.A. 112 C8
Faridabad, India 68 E6
Faridkot, India 68 D6
Faridpur, Bangla. 69 H13
Faridpur, India 69 E8
Färila, Sweden 10 C9
Farim, Guinea-Biss. 82 C1
Farīmān, Iran 71 C8
Farina, Australia 95 E2
Fariones, Pta., Canary Is. 37 E6
Fârliug, Romania 42 E6
Farmakonisi, Greece 39 D9
Farmerville, U.S.A. 113 J8
Farmingdale, U.S.A. 111 F10
Farmington, Canada 104 B4
Farmington, Calif., U.S.A. 116 H6
Farmington, Maine, U.S.A. 109 C10
Farmington, Mo., U.S.A. 113 G9
Farmington, N.H., U.S.A. 111 C13
Farmington, N. Mex.,
U.S.A. 115 H9
Farmington, Utah, U.S.A. 114 F8
Farmington →, U.S.A. ... 111 E12
Farmville, U.S.A. 108 G6
Färnäs, Sweden 10 D8
Farne Is., U.K. 12 B6
Farnham, Canada 111 A12
Farnham, Mt., Canada ... 104 C5
Faro, Brazil 125 D7
Faro, Canada 100 B6
Faro, Portugal 35 H3
Fårö, Sweden 9 H18
Faro □, Portugal 35 H3
Fårösund, Sweden 11 G13
Farquhar, C., Australia . 93 D1
Farrars Cr. →, Australia 94 D3
Farrāshband, Iran 71 D7
Farrell, U.S.A. 110 E4
Farrokhī, Iran 71 C8
Farruch, C. = Ferrutx, C.,
Spain 37 B10
Farrukhabad-cum-Fatehgarh,
India 66 F11
Fārs □, Iran 71 D7
Fársala, Greece 38 B4
Farsø, Denmark 11 H3
Farson, U.S.A. 114 E9
Farsund, Norway 9 G12
Fartak, Râs, Si. Arabia . 70 D2
Fartak, Ra's, Yemen 74 D5

Fârţăneşti, Romania 43 E12
Fartura, Serra da, Brazil 127 B5
Faru, Nigeria 83 C6
Fārūj, Iran 71 B8
Fårup, Denmark 11 H3
Farvel, Kap = Nunap Isua,
Greenland 4 D5
Farwell, U.S.A. 113 H3
Fasā, Iran 71 D7
Fasano, Italy 31 B10
Fashoda, Sudan 81 F3
Fassa, Mali 82 C3
Fastiv, Ukraine 47 G5
Fastov = Fastiv, Ukraine 47 G5
Fatagar, Tanjung, Indonesia 63 E8
Fatehabad, Haryana, India 68 E6
Fatehabad, Ut. P., India 68 F8
Fatehgarh, India 69 F8
Fatehpur, Bihar, India .. 69 G11
Fatehpur, Raj., India .. 68 F6
Fatehpur, Ut. P., India 69 G9
Fatehpur, Ut. P., India 69 F9
Fatehpur Sikri, India .. 68 F6
Fatesh, Russia 47 F8
Fathai, Sudan 81 F3
Fatick, Senegal 82 C1
Fátima, Canada 103 C7
Fátima, Portugal 35 F2
Fatoya, Guinea 82 C3
Fatsa, Turkey 72 B7
Faucille, Col de la, France 19 F13
Faulkton, U.S.A. 112 C5
Faulquemont, France 19 C13
Faure I., Australia 93 E1
Fauresmith, S. Africa .. 88 D4
Fauske, Norway 8 C16
Favara, Italy 30 E6
Faváritx, C. de, Spain . 37 B11
Faverges, France 21 C10
Favignana, Italy 30 E5
Favignana, I., Italy ... 30 E5
Fawcett, Pt., Australia . 92 B5
Fawn →, Canada 102 A3
Fawnskin, U.S.A. 117 L10
Faxaflói, Iceland 8 D2
Faxälven →, Sweden 10 A10
Faya-Largeau, Chad 79 E9
Fayd, Si. Arabia 70 E4
Fayence, France 21 E10
Fayette, Ala., U.S.A. .. 109 J2
Fayette, Mo., U.S.A. ... 112 F8
Fayetteville, Ark., U.S.A. 113 G7
Fayetteville, N.C., U.S.A. 109 H6
Fayetteville, Tenn., U.S.A. 109 H2
Fayied, Egypt 80 H8
Fayón, Spain 32 D5
Fazilka, India 68 D6
Fazilpur, Pakistan 68 E4
Fdérik, Mauritania 78 D3
Feale →, Ireland 15 D2
Fear, C., U.S.A. 109 J7
Feather →, U.S.A. 114 G3
Feather Falls, U.S.A. .. 116 F5
Featherston, N.Z. 91 J5
Featherstone, Zimbabwe . 87 F3
Fécamp, France 18 C7
Fedala = Mohammedia,
Morocco 78 B4
Federación, Argentina .. 126 C4
Féderal, Argentina 128 C5
Federal Capital Terr. □,
Nigeria 83 D6
Federal Way, U.S.A. 116 C4
Fedeshkūh, Iran 71 D7
Fehérgyarmat, Hungary .. 42 C7
Fehmarn, Germany 24 A7
Fehmarn Bælt, Europe ... 11 K5
Fehmarn Belt = Fehmarn
Bælt, Europe 11 K5
Fei Xian, China 57 G9
Feijó, Brazil 124 E4
Feilding, N.Z. 91 J5
Feira de Santana, Brazil 125 D11
Feixi, China 59 B11
Feixiang, China 56 F8
Fejér □, Hungary 42 C3
Fejø, Denmark 11 K5
Feke, Turkey 72 D6
Fekete →, Hungary 42 E3
Felanitx, Spain 37 B10
Feldbach, Austria 26 E8
Feldberg, Baden-W.,
Germany 25 H3
Feldberg,
Mecklenburg-Vorpommern,
Germany 24 B9
Feldkirch, Austria 26 D2
Feldkirchen, Austria ... 26 E7
Felipe Carrillo Puerto,
Mexico 119 D7
Felixburg, Zimbabwe 89 B5
Felixstowe, U.K. 13 F9
Felletin, France 20 C6
Fellingsbro, Sweden 10 E9
Felton, U.S.A. 116 H4
Feltre, Italy 29 B8
Femer Bælt = Fehmarn
Bælt, Europe 11 K5
Femø, Denmark 11 K5
Femunden, Norway 9 E14
Fen He →, China 56 G6
Fene, Spain 34 B2
Fenelon Falls, Canada .. 110 B6
Fener Burnu, Turkey 39 E9
Feneroa, Ethiopia 81 E4
Feng Xian, Jiangsu, China 56 G9
Feng Xian, Shaanxi, China 56 H4
Fengári, Greece 41 F9
Fengcheng, Jiangxi, China 59 C10
Fengcheng, Liaoning, China 57 D13

Fengfeng, China 56 F8
Fenggang, China 58 D6
Fenghua, China 59 C13
Fenghuang, China 58 D7
Fengkai, China 59 F8
Fengkang, Taiwan 59 F13
Fengle, China 59 B9
Fenglin, Taiwan 59 F13
Fengning, China 56 D9
Fengqing, China 58 E2
Fengqiu, China 56 G8
Fengrun, China 57 E10
Fengshan,
Guangxi Zhuangzu, China 58 E7
Fengshan,
Guangxi Zhuangzu, China 58 E6
Fengshan, Taiwan 59 F13
Fengshun, China 59 F11
Fengtai, Anhui, China .. 59 A11
Fengtai, Beijing, China 56 E9
Fengxiang, China 56 G4
Fengxin, China 59 C10
Fengyang, China 57 H9
Fengyi, China 58 E3
Fengyüan, Taiwan 59 E13
Fengzhen, China 56 D7
Feno, C. de, France 21 G12
Fenoarivo, Fianarantsoa,
Madag. 89 C8
Fenoarivo, Fianarantsoa,
Madag. 89 C8
Fenoarivo Afovoany, Madag. 89 B8
Fenoarivo Atsinanana,
Madag. 89 B8
Fens, The, U.K. 12 E7
Fensmark, Denmark 11 J5
Fenton, U.S.A. 108 D4
Fenxi, China 56 F6
Fenyang, China 56 F6
Fenyi, China 59 D10
Feodosiya, Ukraine 47 K8
Ferdows, Iran 71 C8
Fère-Champenoise, France 19 D10
Fère-en-Tardenois, France 19 C10
Ferentino, Italy 29 G10
Ferfer, Somali Rep. 74 F4
Fergana = Farghona,
Uzbekistan 50 E8
Fergus, Canada 110 C4
Fergus Falls, U.S.A. ... 112 B6
Feričanci, Croatia 42 E2
Ferkéssédougou, Ivory C. 82 D3
Ferlach, Austria 26 E7
Ferland, Canada 102 B2
Ferlo, Vallée du, Senegal 82 B2
Fermanagh □, U.K. 15 B4
Fermo, Italy 29 E10
Fermont, Canada 103 B6
Fermoselle, Spain 34 D4
Fermoy, Ireland 15 D3
Fernán Núñez, Spain 35 H6
Fernández, Argentina ... 126 B3
Fernandina Beach, U.S.A. 109 K5
Fernando de Noronha, Brazil 125 D12
Fernando Póo = Bioko,
Eq. Guin. 83 E6
Ferndale, U.S.A. 116 B4
Fernie, Canada 104 D5
Fernlees, Australia 94 C4
Fernley, U.S.A. 114 G4
Ferozepore = Firozpur,
India 68 D6
Férrai, Greece 41 F10
Ferrara, Italy 29 D8
Ferrato, C., Italy 30 C2
Ferreira do Alentejo,
Portugal 35 G2
Ferreñafe, Peru 124 E3
Ferrerías, Spain 37 B11
Ferret, C., France 20 D2
Ferrette, France 19 E14
Ferriday, U.S.A. 113 K9
Ferriere, Italy 28 D6
Ferrières, France 19 D9
Ferro, Capo, Italy 30 A2
Ferrol, Spain 34 B2
Ferron, U.S.A. 115 G8
Ferrutx, C., Spain 37 B10
Ferryland, Canada 103 C9
Fertile, U.S.A. 112 B6
Fertőszentmiklós, Hungary 42 C1
Fès, Morocco 78 B5
Fessenden, U.S.A. 112 B5
Festus, U.S.A. 112 F9
Feté Bowé, Senegal 82 C2
Fetești, Romania 43 F12
Fethiye, Turkey 39 E11
Fethiye Körfezi, Turkey 39 E10
Fetlar, U.K. 14 A8
Feuilles →, Canada 101 C12
Feurs, France 21 C8
Fez = Fès, Morocco 78 B5
Fezzan, Libya 79 C8
Fiambalá, Argentina 126 B2
Fianarantsoa, Madag. ... 89 C8
Fianarantsoa □, Madag. . 89 B8
Fiche, Ethiopia 81 F4
Fichtelgebirge, Germany 25 E7
Ficksburg, S. Africa ... 89 D4
Fidenza, Italy 28 D7
Field →, Australia 94 C2
Field I., Australia 92 B5
Fier, Romania 43 E10
Fieri, Albania 40 F3
Fierzë, Albania 40 D4
Fife □, U.K. 14 E5
Fife Ness, U.K. 14 E6
Fifth Cataract, Sudan .. 80 D3

Figari, France 21 G13
Figeac, France 20 D6
Figeholm, Sweden 11 G10
Figline Valdarno, Italy 29 E8
Figtree, Zimbabwe 87 G2
Figueira Castelo Rodrigo,
Portugal 34 E4
Figueira da Foz, Portugal 34 E2
Figueiró dos Vinhos,
Portugal 34 F2
Figueres, Spain 32 C7
Figuig, Morocco 78 B5
Fihaonana, Madag. 89 B8
Fiherenana, Madag. 89 B8
Fiherenana →, Madag. ... 89 C7
Fiji ■, Pac. Oc. 91 C8
Fik, Ethiopia 81 F5
Fika, Nigeria 83 C7
Filabres, Sierra de los, Spain 35 H8
Filabusi, Zimbabwe 89 C4
Filadélfia, Italy 31 D9
Fil'akovo, Slovak Rep. . 27 C12
Filey, U.K. 12 C7
Filey B., U.K. 12 C7
Filfla, Malta 36 D1
Filiaşi, Romania 43 F8
Filiátes, Greece 38 B2
Filiatrá, Greece 38 D3
Filicudi, Italy 31 D7
Filingué, Niger 83 C5
Filipstad, Sweden 10 E8
Filisur, Switz. 25 J5
Fillmore, Calif., U.S.A. 117 L8
Fillmore, Utah, U.S.A. . 115 G7
Filótion, Greece 39 D7
Filottrano, Italy 29 E10
Filtu, Ethiopia 81 F5
Finale Emília, Italy ... 29 D8
Finale Lígure, Italy ... 28 D5
Fiñana, Spain 35 H8
Finch, Canada 111 A9
Findhorn →, U.K. 14 D5
Findlay, U.S.A. 108 E4
Finger L., Canada 102 B1
Finger Lakes, U.S.A. ... 111 D8
Fíngoè, Mozam. 87 E3
Finike, Turkey 39 E12
Finike Körfezi, Turkey . 39 E12
Finiq, Albania 40 G4
Finistère □, France 18 D3
Finisterre = Fisterra, Spain 34 C1
Finisterre, C. = Fisterra, C.,
Spain 34 C1
Finke, Australia 94 D1
Finland ■, Europe 8 E22
Finland, G. of, Europe . 9 G21
Finlay →, Canada 104 B3
Finley, Australia 95 F4
Finley, U.S.A. 112 B6
Finn →, Ireland 15 B4
Finnerödja, Sweden 11 F8
Finnigan, Mt., Australia 94 B4
Finniss, C., Australia . 95 E1
Finnmark, Norway 8 B20
Finnsnes, Norway 8 B18
Finspång, Sweden 11 F9
Finsteraarhorn, Switz. . 25 J4
Finsterwalde, Germany .. 24 D9
Fiora →, Italy 29 F8
Fiorenzuola d'Arda, Italy 28 D6
Fiq, Syria 75 C4
Firat = Furāt, Nahr al →,
Asia 70 D5
Firebag →, Canada 105 B6
Firebaugh, U.S.A. 116 J6
Firedrake L., Canada ... 105 A8
Firenze, Italy 29 E8
Firenzuola, Italy 29 D8
Firk →, Iraq 70 D5
Firmi, France 20 D6
Firminy, France 21 C8
Firozabad, India 69 F8
Firozpur, India 68 D6
Firozpur-Jhirka, India . 68 F7
Fīrūzābād, Iran 71 D7
Fīrūzkūh, Iran 71 C7
Firvale, Canada 104 C3
Fish →, Namibia 88 D2
Fish →, S. Africa 88 E3
Fish River Canyon, Namibia 88 D2
Fisher, Australia 93 F5
Fisher B., Canada 105 C9
Fishers I., U.S.A. 111 E13
Fishguard, U.K. 13 E3
Fishing L., Canada 105 C9
Fishkill, U.S.A. 111 E11
Fismes, France 19 C10
Fisterra, Spain 34 C1
Fisterra, C., Spain 34 C1
Fitchburg, U.S.A. 111 D13
Fitz Roy, Argentina 128 F3
Fitzgerald, Canada 104 B6
Fitzgerald, U.S.A. 109 K4
Fitzmaurice →, Australia 92 B5
Fitzroy →, Queens.,
Australia 94 C5
Fitzroy →, W. Austral.,
Australia 92 C3
Fitzroy, Mte., Argentina 128 F2
Fitzroy Crossing, Australia 92 C4
Fitzwilliam I., Canada . 110 A3
Fiuggi, Italy 29 G10
Fiume = Rijeka, Croatia 29 C11
Five Points, U.S.A. 116 J6
Fivizzano, Italy 28 D7
Fizi, Dem. Rep. of the Congo 86 C2
Fjällbacka, Sweden 11 F5
Fjärdhundra, Sweden 10 E10
Fjellerup, Denmark 11 H4
Fjerritslev, Denmark ... 11 G3

Fritch

Fjugesta, *Sweden* 10 E8
Flagstaff, *U.S.A.* 115 J8
Flagstaff L., *U.S.A.* 109 C10
Flaherty I., *Canada* 102 A4
Flåm, *Norway* 9 F12
Flambeau →, *U.S.A.* 112 C9
Flamborough Hd., *U.K.* 12 C7
Fläming, *Germany* 24 C8
Flaming Gorge Reservoir, *U.S.A.* 114 F9
Flamingo, Teluk, *Indonesia* 63 F9
Flanders = Flandre, *Europe* 19 B9
Flandre, *Europe* 19 B9
Flandre Occidentale = West-Vlaanderen □, *Belgium* 17 D2
Flandre Orientale = Oost-Vlaanderen □, *Belgium* 17 C3
Flandreau, *U.S.A.* 112 C6
Flanigan, *U.S.A.* 116 E7
Flannan Is., *U.K.* 14 C1
Flåsjön, *Sweden* 8 D16
Flat →, *Canada* 104 A3
Flathead L., *U.S.A.* 114 C7
Flattery, C., *Australia* 94 A4
Flattery, C., *U.S.A.* 116 B2
Flatwoods, *U.S.A.* 108 F4
Fleetwood, *U.K.* 12 D4
Fleetwood, *U.S.A.* 111 F9
Flekkefjord, *Norway* 9 G12
Flemington, *U.S.A.* 110 E7
Flen, *Sweden* 10 E10
Flensburg, *Germany* 24 A5
Flers, *France* 18 D6
Flesherton, *Canada* 110 B4
Flesko, Tanjung, *Indonesia* 63 D6
Fleurance, *France* 20 E4
Fleurier, *Switz.* 25 J2
Fleurieu Pen., *Australia* 95 F2
Flevoland □, *Neths.* 17 B5
Flin Flon, *Canada* 105 C8
Flinders →, *Australia* 94 B3
Flinders B., *Australia* 93 F2
Flinders Group, *Australia* 94 A3
Flinders I., *S. Austral., Australia* 95 E1
Flinders I., *Tas., Australia* 94 G4
Flinders Ranges, *Australia* 95 E2
Flinders Reefs, *Australia* 94 B4
Flint, *U.K.* 12 D4
Flint, *U.S.A.* 108 D4
Flint →, *U.S.A.* 109 K3
Flint I., *Kiribati* 97 J12
Flintshire □, *U.K.* 12 D4
Fliseryd, *Sweden* 11 G10
Flix, *Spain* 32 D5
Flixecourt, *France* 19 B9
Floby, *Sweden* 11 F7
Floda, *Sweden* 11 G6
Flodden, *U.K.* 12 B5
Flogny-la-Chapelle, *France* 19 E10
Floodwood, *U.S.A.* 112 B8
Flora, *U.S.A.* 108 F1
Florac, *France* 20 D7
Florala, *U.S.A.* 109 K2
Florence = Firenze, *Italy* 29 E8
Florence, *Ala., U.S.A.* 109 H2
Florence, *Ariz., U.S.A.* 115 K8
Florence, *Colo., U.S.A.* 112 F2
Florence, *Oreg., U.S.A.* 114 E1
Florence, *S.C., U.S.A.* 109 H6
Florence, L., *Australia* 95 D2
Florencia, *Colombia* 124
Florennes, *Belgium* 17 D4
Florensac, *France* 20 E7
Florenville, *Belgium* 17 E5
Flores, *Guatemala* 120 C2
Flores, *Indonesia* 63 F6
Flores I., *Canada* 104 D3
Flores Sea, *Indonesia* 63 F6
Florești, *Moldova* 43 C13
Floresville, *U.S.A.* 113 L5
Floriano, *Brazil* 125 E10
Florianópolis, *Brazil* 127 B6
Florida, *Cuba* 120 B4
Florida, *Uruguay* 127 C4
Florida □, *U.S.A.* 109 L5
Florida, Straits of, *U.S.A.* 120 B4
Florida B., *U.S.A.* 120 B3
Florida Keys, *U.S.A.* 109 N5
Florídia, *Italy* 31 E8
Flórina, *Greece* 40 F5
Flórina □, *Greece* 40 F5
Florø, *Norway* 9 F11
Flower Station, *Canada* 111 A8
Flowerpot I., *Canada* 110 A3
Floydada, *U.S.A.* 113 J4
Fluk, *Indonesia* 63 E7
Flúmen →, *Spain* 32 D4
Flumendosa →, *Italy* 30 C2
Fluminimaggiore, *Italy* 30 C1
Flushing = Vlissingen, *Neths.* 17 C3
Fluvià →, *Spain* 32 C8
Flying Fish, C., *Antarctica* 5 D15
Foam Lake, *Canada* 105 C8
Foča, *Bos.-H.* 40 C2
Foça, *Turkey* 39 C8
Focșani, *Romania* 43 E12
Fodécontéa, *Guinea* 82 C2
Fogang, *China* 59 F9
Fóggia, *Italy* 31 A8
Foggo, *Nigeria* 83 C6
Foglia →, *Italy* 29 E9
Fogo, *Canada* 103 C9
Fogo I., *Canada* 103 C9
Fohnsdorf, *Austria* 26 D7
Föhr, *Germany* 24 A4
Foia, *Portugal* 35 H2
Foix, *France* 20 F5
Fojnica, *Bos.-H.* 42 G2
Fokino, *Russia* 46 F8
Fokís □, *Greece* 38 C4
Fokku, *Nigeria* 83 C5
Folda, *Nord-Trøndelag, Norway* 8 D14
Folda, *Nordland, Norway* 8 C16
Földeák, *Hungary* 42 D5
Folégandros, *Greece* 38 E6
Foley, *Botswana* 88 C4
Foley, *U.S.A.* 109 K2
Foleyet, *Canada* 102 C3
Folgefonni, *Norway* 9 F12
Foligno, *Italy* 29 F9
Folkestone, *U.K.* 13 F9
Folkston, *U.S.A.* 109 K5
Follansbee, *U.S.A.* 110 F4
Follónica, *Italy* 28 F7
Follónica, G. di, *Italy* 28 F7
Folsom L., *U.S.A.* 116 G5
Foltești, *Romania* 43 E13
Fond-du-Lac, *Canada* 105 B7
Fond du Lac, *U.S.A.* 112 D10
Fond-du-Lac →, *Canada* 105 B7
Fonda, *U.S.A.* 111 D10
Fondi, *Italy* 30 A6
Fonfría, *Spain* 34 D4
Fongafale, *Tuvalu* 96 H9
Fonni, *Italy* 30 B2
Fonsagrada = A Fonsagrada, *Spain* 34 B3
Fonseca, G. de, *Cent. Amer.* 120 D2
Font-Romeu, *France* 20 F5
Fontaine-Française, *France* 19 E12
Fontainebleau, *France* 19 D9
Fontana, *U.S.A.* 117 L9
Fontas →, *Canada* 104 B4
Fonte Boa, *Brazil* 124 D5
Fontem, *Cameroon* 83 D6
Fontenay-le-Comte, *France* 20 B3
Fontenelle Reservoir, *U.S.A.* 114 E8
Fontur, *Iceland* 8 C6
Fonyód, *Hungary* 42 D2
Foochow = Fuzhou, *China* 59 D12
Foping, *China* 56 H5
Forbach, *France* 19 C13
Forbes, *Australia* 95 E4
Forbesganj, *India* 69 F12
Forcados, *Nigeria* 83 D6
Forcados →, *Nigeria* 83 D6
Forcalquier, *France* 21 E9
Forchheim, *Germany* 25 F7
Ford City, *Calif., U.S.A.* 117 K7
Ford City, *Pa., U.S.A.* 110 F5
Førde, *Norway* 9 F11
Ford's Bridge, *Australia* 95 D4
Fordyce, *U.S.A.* 113 J8
Forécariah, *Guinea* 82 D2
Forel, Mt., *Greenland* 4 C6
Foremost, *Canada* 104 D6
Forest, *Canada* 110 C3
Forest, *U.S.A.* 113 J10
Forest City, *Iowa, U.S.A.* 112 D8
Forest City, *N.C., U.S.A.* 109 H5
Forest City, *Pa., U.S.A.* 111 E9
Forest Grove, *U.S.A.* 116 E3
Forestburg, *Canada* 104 C6
Foresthill, *U.S.A.* 116 F6
Forestier Pen., *Australia* 94 G4
Forestville, *Canada* 103 C6
Forestville, *Calif., U.S.A.* 116 G4
Forestville, *N.Y., U.S.A.* 110 D5
Forez, Mts. du, *France* 20 C7
Forfar, *U.K.* 14 E6
Forks, *U.S.A.* 116 C2
Forksville, *U.S.A.* 111 E8
Forlì, *Italy* 29 D9
Forman, *U.S.A.* 112 B6
Formazza, *Italy* 28 B5
Formby Pt., *U.K.* 12 D4
Formentera, *Spain* 37 C7
Formentor, C. de, *Spain* 37 B10
Former Yugoslav Republic of Macedonia = Macedonia ■, *Europe* 40 E5
Fórmia, *Italy* 30 A6
Formígine, *Italy* 28 D7
Formosa = Taiwan ■, *Asia* 59 F13
Formosa, *Argentina* 126 B4
Formosa, *Brazil* 125 G9
Formosa □, *Argentina* 126 B3
Formosa, Serra, *Brazil* 125 F8
Formosa Bay, *Kenya* 86 C5
Formosa Strait = Taiwan Strait, *Asia* 59 E12
Fornells, *Spain* 37 A11
Fornos de Algodres, *Portugal* 34 E3
Fornovo di Taro, *Italy* 28 D7
Føroyar, *Atl. Oc.* 8 F9
Forres, *U.K.* 14 D5
Forrest, *Australia* 93 F4
Forrest, Mt., *Australia* 93 D4
Forrest City, *U.S.A.* 113 H9
Fors, *Sweden* 10 D10
Forsayth, *Australia* 94 B3
Forshaga, *Sweden* 10 E7
Förslöv, *Sweden* 11 H6
Forsmo, *Sweden* 10 A11
Forssa, *Finland* 9 F20
Forst, *Germany* 24 D10
Forsvik, *Sweden* 11 F8
Forsyth, *U.S.A.* 114 C10
Fort Abbas, *Pakistan* 68 E5
Fort Albany, *Canada* 102 B3
Fort Ann, *U.S.A.* 111 C11
Fort Assiniboine, *Canada* 104 C6
Fort Augustus, *U.K.* 14 D4
Fort Beaufort, *S. Africa* 88 E4
Fort Benton, *U.S.A.* 114 C8
Fort Bragg, *U.S.A.* 114 G2
Fort Bridger, *U.S.A.* 114 F8
Fort Chipewyan, *Canada* 105 B6
Fort Collins, *U.S.A.* 112 E2
Fort-Coulonge, *Canada* 102 C4
Fort Covington, *U.S.A.* 111 B10
Fort Davis, *U.S.A.* 113 K3
Fort-de-France, *Martinique* 121 D7
Fort Defiance, *U.S.A.* 115 J9
Fort Dodge, *U.S.A.* 112 D7
Fort Edward, *U.S.A.* 111 C11
Fort Erie, *Canada* 110 D6
Fort Fairfield, *U.S.A.* 109 B12
Fort Frances, *Canada* 105 D10
Fort Garland, *U.S.A.* 115 H11
Fort George = Chisasibi, *Canada* 102 B4
Fort Good-Hope, *Canada* 100 B7
Fort Hancock, *U.S.A.* 115 L11
Fort Hertz = Putao, *Burma* 67 F20
Fort Hope, *Canada* 102 B2
Fort Irwin, *U.S.A.* 117 K10
Fort Jameson = Chipata, *Zambia* 87 E3
Fort Kent, *U.S.A.* 109 B11
Fort Klamath, *U.S.A.* 114 E3
Fort-Lamy = Ndjamena, *Chad* 79 F8
Fort Laramie, *U.S.A.* 112 D2
Fort Lauderdale, *U.S.A.* 109 M5
Fort Liard, *Canada* 104 A4
Fort Liberté, *Haiti* 121 C5
Fort Lupton, *U.S.A.* 112 E2
Fort Mackay, *Canada* 104 B6
Fort Macleod, *Canada* 104 D6
Fort McMurray, *Canada* 104 B6
Fort McPherson, *Canada* 100 B6
Fort Madison, *U.S.A.* 112 E9
Fort Meade, *U.S.A.* 109 M5
Fort Morgan, *U.S.A.* 112 E3
Fort Munro, *Pakistan* 68 E3
Fort Myers, *U.S.A.* 109 M5
Fort Nelson, *Canada* 104 B4
Fort Nelson →, *Canada* 104 B4
Fort Norman = Tulita, *Canada* 100 B7
Fort Payne, *U.S.A.* 109 H3
Fort Peck, *U.S.A.* 114 B10
Fort Peck Dam, *U.S.A.* 114 C10
Fort Peck L., *U.S.A.* 114 C10
Fort Pierce, *U.S.A.* 109 M5
Fort Pierre, *U.S.A.* 112 C4
Fort Plain, *U.S.A.* 111 D10
Fort Portal, *Uganda* 86 B3
Fort Providence, *Canada* 104 A5
Fort Qu'Appelle, *Canada* 105 C8
Fort Resolution, *Canada* 104 A6
Fort Rixon, *Zimbabwe* 87 G2
Fort Rosebery = Mansa, *Zambia* 87 E2
Fort Ross, *U.S.A.* 116 G3
Fort Rupert = Waskaganish, *Canada* 102 B4
Fort St. James, *Canada* 104 C4
Fort St. John, *Canada* 104 B4
Fort Sandeman = Zhob, *Pakistan* 68 D3
Fort Saskatchewan, *Canada* 104 C6
Fort Scott, *U.S.A.* 113 G7
Fort Severn, *Canada* 102 A2
Fort Shevchenko, *Kazakstan* 49 H10
Fort Simpson, *Canada* 104 A4
Fort Smith, *Canada* 104 B6
Fort Smith, *U.S.A.* 113 H7
Fort Stockton, *U.S.A.* 113 K3
Fort Sumner, *U.S.A.* 113 H2
Fort Thompson, *U.S.A.* 112 C5
Fort Trinquet = Bir Mogreïn, *Mauritania* 78 C3
Fort Valley, *U.S.A.* 109 J4
Fort Vermilion, *Canada* 104 B5
Fort Walton Beach, *U.S.A.* 109 K2
Fort Wayne, *U.S.A.* 108 E3
Fort William, *U.K.* 14 E3
Fort Worth, *U.S.A.* 113 J6
Fort Yates, *U.S.A.* 112 B4
Fort Yukon, *U.S.A.* 100 B5
Fortaleza, *Brazil* 125 D11
Forteau, *Canada* 103 B8
Fortescue →, *Australia* 92 D2
Forth →, *U.K.* 14 E5
Forth, Firth of, *U.K.* 14 E6
Fortore →, *Italy* 29 G12
Fortrose, *U.K.* 14 D4
Fortuna, *Spain* 33 G3
Fortuna, *Calif., U.S.A.* 114 F1
Fortuna, *N. Dak., U.S.A.* 112 A3
Fortune, *Canada* 103 C8
Fortune B., *Canada* 103 C8
Forūr, *Iran* 71 E7
Fos-sur-Mer, *France* 21 E8
Foshan, *China* 59 F9
Fosna, *Norway* 8 E14
Fosnavåg, *Norway* 9 E11
Foso, *Ghana* 83 D4
Fossano, *Italy* 28 D4
Fossil, *U.S.A.* 114 D3
Fossombrone, *Italy* 29 E9
Foster, *Australia* 95 F4
Foster, *Canada* 111 A12
Foster →, *Canada* 105 B7
Fosters Ra., *Australia* 94 C1
Fostoria, *U.S.A.* 108 E4
Fotadrevo, *Madag.* 89 C8
Fouesnant, *France* 18 E2
Fougères, *France* 18 D5
Foul Pt., *Sri Lanka* 66 Q12
Foula, *U.K.* 14 A6
Foulalaba, *Mali* 82 C3
Foulness I., *U.K.* 13 F8
Foulpointe, *Madag.* 89 B8
Foulweather, C., *U.S.A.* 106 B2
Foumban, *Cameroon* 83 D7
Foumbot, *Cameroon* 83 D7
Foundiougne, *Senegal* 82 C1
Fountain, *U.S.A.* 112 F2
Fountain Springs, *U.S.A.* 117 K8
Fourchambault, *France* 19 E10
Fouriesburg, *S. Africa* 88 D4
Fourmies, *France* 19 B11
Fournás, *Greece* 38 B3
Foúrnoi, *Greece* 39 D8
Fours, *France* 19 F10
Fourth Cataract, *Sudan* 80 D3
Fouta Djalon, *Guinea* 82 C2
Foux, Cap-à-, *Haiti* 121 C5
Foveaux Str., *N.Z.* 91 M2
Fowey, *U.K.* 13 G3
Fowler, *Calif., U.S.A.* 116 J7
Fowler, *Colo., U.S.A.* 112 F3
Fowlers B., *Australia* 93 F5
Fowman, *Iran* 71 B6
Fox →, *Canada* 105 B10
Fox Creek, *Canada* 104 C5
Fox Lake, *Canada* 104 B6
Fox Valley, *Canada* 105 C7
Foxboro, *U.S.A.* 111 D13
Foxe Basin, *Canada* 101 B12
Foxe Chan., *Canada* 101 B11
Foxe Pen., *Canada* 101 B12
Foxen, *Sweden* 10 E5
Foxton, *N.Z.* 91 J5
Foyle, Lough, *U.K.* 15 A4
Foynes, *Ireland* 15 D2
Foz, *Spain* 34 B3
Fóz do Cunene, *Angola* 88 B1
Foz do Iguaçu, *Brazil* 127 B5
Frackville, *U.S.A.* 111 F8
Fraga, *Spain* 32 D5
Fraile Muerto, *Uruguay* 127 C5
Framingham, *U.S.A.* 111 D13
Frampol, *Poland* 45 H9
Franca, *Brazil* 125 H9
Francavilla al Mare, *Italy* 29 F11
Francavilla Fontana, *Italy* 31 B10
France ■, *Europe* 7 F6
Frances, *Australia* 95 F3
Frances →, *Canada* 104 A3
Frances L., *Canada* 104 A3
Franceville, *Gabon* 84 E2
Franche-Comté, *France* 19 F12
Francis Case, L., *U.S.A.* 112 D5
Francisco Beltrão, *Brazil* 127 B5
Francisco I. Madero, *Coahuila, Mexico* 118 B4
Francisco I. Madero, *Durango, Mexico* 118 C4
Francistown, *Botswana* 89 C4
Francofonte, *Italy* 31 E7
François, *Canada* 103 C8
François L., *Canada* 104 C3
Franeker, *Neths.* 17 A5
Frankado, *Djibouti* 81 E5
Frankenberg, *Germany* 24 D4
Frankenwald, *Germany* 25 E7
Frankford, *Canada* 110 B7
Frankfort, *S. Africa* 89 D4
Frankfort, *Ind., U.S.A.* 108 E2
Frankfort, *Kans., U.S.A.* 112 F6
Frankfort, *Ky., U.S.A.* 108 F3
Frankfort, *N.Y., U.S.A.* 111 C9
Frankfurt, *Brandenburg, Germany* 24 C10
Frankfurt, *Hessen, Germany* 25 E4
Fränkische Alb, *Germany* 25 F7
Fränkische Rezat →, *Germany* 25 F7
Fränkische Saale →, *Germany* 25 E5
Fränkische Schweiz, *Germany* 25 F7
Frankland →, *Australia* 93 G2
Franklin, *Ky., U.S.A.* 109 G2
Franklin, *La., U.S.A.* 113 L9
Franklin, *Mass., U.S.A.* 111 D13
Franklin, *N.H., U.S.A.* 111 C13
Franklin, *Nebr., U.S.A.* 112 E5
Franklin, *Pa., U.S.A.* 110 E5
Franklin, *Va., U.S.A.* 109 G7
Franklin, *W. Va., U.S.A.* 108 F6
Franklin B., *Canada* 100 B7
Franklin D. Roosevelt L., *U.S.A.* 114 B4
Franklin I., *Antarctica* 5 D11
Franklin L., *U.S.A.* 114 F6
Franklin Mts., *Canada* 100 B7
Franklin Str., *Canada* 100 A10
Franklinton, *U.S.A.* 113 K9
Franklinville, *U.S.A.* 110 D6
Franks Pk., *U.S.A.* 114 E9
Frankston, *Australia* 95 F4
Fränö, *Sweden* 10 B11
Fransfontein, *Namibia* 88 C2
Fränsta, *Sweden* 10 B10
Frantsa Iosifa, Zemlya, *Russia* 50 A6
Franz, *Canada* 102 C3
Franz Josef Land = Frantsa Iosifa, Zemlya, *Russia* 50 A6
Franzburg, *Germany* 24 A8
Frascati, *Italy* 29 G9
Fraser, *U.S.A.* 110 D2
Fraser →, *B.C., Canada* 104 D4
Fraser →, *Nfld., Canada* 103 A7
Fraser, Mt., *Australia* 93 E2
Fraser I., *Australia* 95 D5
Fraser Lake, *Canada* 104 C4
Fraserburg, *S. Africa* 88 E3
Fraserburgh, *U.K.* 14 D6
Fraserdale, *Canada* 102 C3
Frashëri, *Albania* 40 F4
Frasne, *France* 19 F13
Frătești, *Romania* 43 G10
Frauenfeld, *Switz.* 25 H4
Fray Bentos, *Uruguay* 126 C4
Frechilla, *Spain* 34 C6
Fredericia, *Denmark* 11 J3
Frederick, *Md., U.S.A.* 108 F7
Frederick, *Okla., U.S.A.* 113 H5
Frederick, *S. Dak., U.S.A.* 112 C5
Fredericksburg, *Pa., U.S.A.* 111 F8
Fredericksburg, *Tex., U.S.A.* 113 K5
Fredericksburg, *Va., U.S.A.* 108 F7
Fredericktown, *Mo., U.S.A.* 113 G9
Fredericktown, *Ohio, U.S.A.* 110 F2
Frederico I. Madero, Presa, *Mexico* 118 B3
Frederico Westphalen, *Brazil* 127 B5
Fredericton, *Canada* 103 C6
Fredericton Junction, *Canada* 103 C6
Frederiksborg Amtskommune □, *Denmark* 11 J6
Frederikshåb = Paamiut, *Greenland* 4 C5
Frederikshavn, *Denmark* 11 G4
Frederikssund, *Denmark* 11 J6
Frederiksted, *Virgin Is.* 121 C7
Frederiksværk, *Denmark* 11 J6
Fredonia, *Ariz., U.S.A.* 115 H7
Fredonia, *Kans., U.S.A.* 113 G7
Fredonia, *N.Y., U.S.A.* 110 D5
Fredriksberg, *Sweden* 10 D8
Fredrikstad, *Norway* 9 G14
Free State □, *S. Africa* 88 D4
Freehold, *U.S.A.* 111 F10
Freel Peak, *U.S.A.* 116 G7
Freeland, *U.S.A.* 111 E9
Freels, C., *Canada* 103 C9
Freeman, *Calif., U.S.A.* 117 K9
Freeman, *S. Dak., U.S.A.* 112 D6
Freeport, *Bahamas* 120 A4
Freeport, *Ill., U.S.A.* 112 D10
Freeport, *N.Y., U.S.A.* 111 F11
Freeport, *Ohio, U.S.A.* 110 F3
Freeport, *Pa., U.S.A.* 110 F5
Freeport, *Tex., U.S.A.* 113 L7
Freetown, *S. Leone* 82 D2
Frégate, L., *Canada* 102 B5
Fregenal de la Sierra, *Spain* 35 G4
Fregene, *Italy* 29 G9
Fréhel, C., *France* 18 D4
Freiberg, *Germany* 24 E9
Freibourg = Fribourg, *Switz.* 25 J3
Freiburg, *Baden-W., Germany* 25 H3
Freiburg, *Niedersachsen, Germany* 24 B5
Freilassing, *Germany* 25 H8
Freire, *Chile* 128 D2
Freirina, *Chile* 126 B1
Freising, *Germany* 25 G7
Freistadt, *Austria* 26 C7
Freital, *Germany* 24 D9
Fréjus, *France* 21 E10
Fremantle, *Australia* 93 F2
Fremont, *Calif., U.S.A.* 116 H4
Fremont, *Mich., U.S.A.* 108 D3
Fremont, *Nebr., U.S.A.* 112 E6
Fremont, *Ohio, U.S.A.* 108 E4
Fremont →, *U.S.A.* 115 G8
French Camp, *U.S.A.* 116 H5
French Creek →, *U.S.A.* 110 E5
French Guiana ■, *S. Amer.* 125 C8
French Pass, *N.Z.* 91 J4
French Polynesia ■, *Pac. Oc.* 97 K13
Frenchman Cr. →, *N. Amer.* 114 B10
Frenchman Cr. →, *U.S.A.* 112 E4
Frenštát pod Radhoštěm, *Czech Rep.* 27 B11
Fresco, *Ivory C.* 82 D3
Fresco →, *Brazil* 125 E8
Freshfield, C., *Antarctica* 5 C10
Fresnay-sur-Sarthe, *France* 18 D7
Fresnillo, *Mexico* 118 C4
Fresno, *U.S.A.* 116 J7
Fresno Alhandiga, *Spain* 34 E5
Fresno Reservoir, *U.S.A.* 114 B9
Freudenstadt, *Germany* 25 G4
Frévent, *France* 19 B9
Frew →, *Australia* 94 C2
Frewsburg, *U.S.A.* 110 D5
Freycinet Pen., *Australia* 94 G4
Freyming-Merlebach, *France* 19 C13
Freyung, *Germany* 25 G9
Fria, *Guinea* 82 C2
Fria, C., *Namibia* 88 B1
Friant, *U.S.A.* 116 J7
Frías, *Argentina* 126 B2
Fribourg, *Switz.* 25 J3
Fribourg □, *Switz.* 25 J3
Fridafors, *Sweden* 11 H8
Friday Harbor, *U.S.A.* 116 B3
Friedberg, *Bayern, Germany* 25 G6
Friedberg, *Hessen, Germany* 25 E4
Friedens, *U.S.A.* 110 F6
Friedland, *Germany* 24 B9
Friedrichshafen, *Germany* 25 H5
Friedrichskoog, *Germany* 24 A4
Friedrichstadt, *Germany* 24 A5
Friendly Is. = Tonga ■, *Pac. Oc.* 91 D11
Friendship, *U.S.A.* 110 D6
Friesach, *Austria* 26 E7
Friesack, *Germany* 24 C8
Friesland □, *Neths.* 17 A5
Friesoythe, *Germany* 24 B3
Friggesund, *Sweden* 10 C10
Frillesås, *Sweden* 11 G6
Frinnaryd, *Sweden* 11 G8
Frio →, *U.S.A.* 113 L5
Frio, C., *Brazil* 122 F6
Friol, *Spain* 34 B3
Friona, *U.S.A.* 113 H3
Fristad, *Sweden* 11 G6
Fritch, *U.S.A.* 113 H4

Fritsla, Sweden 11 G6
Fritzlar, Germany 24 D5
Friuli-Venézia Giulia □, Italy 29 B9
Frobisher B., Canada 101 B13
Frobisher Bay = Iqaluit, Canada 101 B13
Frobisher L., Canada 105 B7
Frohavet, Norway 8 E13
Frohnleiten, Austria 26 D6
Frolovo, Russia 48 F6
Frombork, Poland 44 D6
Frome, U.K. 13 F5
Frome →, U.K. 13 G5
Frome, L., Australia 95 E2
Frómista, Spain 34 C6
Front Range, U.S.A. 106 C5
Front Royal, U.S.A. 108 F6
Fronteira, Portugal 35 F3
Frontera, Canary Is. 37 G2
Frontera, Mexico 119 D6
Fronteras, Mexico 118 A3
Frontignan, France 20 E7
Frosinone, Italy 30 A6
Frostburg, U.S.A. 108 F6
Frostisen, Norway 8 B17
Frouard, France 19 D13
Frövi, Sweden 10 E9
Frøya, Norway 8 E13
Frumoasa, Romania 43 D10
Frunze = Bishkek, Kyrgyzstan 50 E8
Fruška Gora, Serbia, Yug. . 42 E4
Frutal, Brazil 125 H9
Frutigen, Switz. 25 J3
Frýdek-Místek, Czech Rep. 27 B11
Frýdlant, Czech Rep. 26 A8
Fryeburg, U.S.A. 111 B14
Fryvaldov = Jeseník, Czech Rep. 27 A10
Fthiótis □, Greece 38 C4
Fu Jiang →, China 58 C6
Fu Xian = Wafangdian, China 57 E11
Fu Xian, China 56 G5
Fu'an, China 59 D12
Fubian, China 58 B4
Fucheng, China 56 F9
Fuchou = Fuzhou, China . 59 D12
Fuchū, Japan 55 G6
Fuchuan, China 59 E8
Fuchun Jiang →, China .. 59 B13
Fúcino, Piana del, Italy .. 29 F10
Fuding, China 59 D13
Fuencaliente, Canary Is. .. 37 F2
Fuencaliente, Spain 35 G6
Fuencaliente, Pta., Canary Is. 37 F2
Fuengirola, Spain 35 J6
Fuenlabrada, Spain 34 E7
Fuensalida, Spain 34 E6
Fuente-Álamo, Spain 33 G3
Fuente-Álamo de Murcia, Spain 33 H3
Fuente de Cantos, Spain .. 35 G4
Fuente del Maestre, Spain . 35 G4
Fuente el Fresno, Spain .. 35 F7
Fuente Obejuna, Spain ... 35 G5
Fuente Palmera, Spain ... 35 H5
Fuentes de Andalucía, Spain 35 H5
Fuentes de Ebro, Spain ... 32 D4
Fuentes de León, Spain ... 35 G4
Fuentes de Oñoro, Spain .. 34 E4
Fuentesaúco, Spain 34 D5
Fuerte →, Mexico 118 B3
Fuerte Olimpo, Paraguay . 126 A4
Fuerteventura, Canary Is. . 37 F6
Fufeng, China 56 G5
Fuga I., Phil. 61 B4
Fugong, China 58 D2
Fugou, China 56 G8
Fugu, China 56 E6
Fuhai, China 60 B3
Fuḥaymī, Iraq 70 C4
Fuji, Japan 55 G9
Fuji-San, Japan 55 G9
Fuji-yoshida, Japan 55 G9
Fujian □, China 59 E12
Fujinomiya, Japan 55 G9
Fujisawa, Japan 55 G9
Fujiyama, Mt. = Fuji-San, Japan 55 G9
Fukien = Fujian □, China 59 E12
Fukuchiyama, Japan 55 G7
Fukue-Shima, Japan 55 H4
Fukui, Japan 55 F8
Fukui □, Japan 55 G8
Fukuoka, Japan 55 H5
Fukuoka □, Japan 55 H5
Fukushima, Japan 54 F10
Fukushima □, Japan 54 F10
Fukuyama, Japan 55 G6
Fulacunda, Guinea-Biss. .. 82 C1
Fulda, Germany 24 E5
Fulda →, Germany 24 D5
Fulford Harbour, Canada . 116 B3
Fuliang, China 59 C11
Fullerton, Calif., U.S.A. . 117 M9
Fullerton, Nebr., U.S.A. . 112 E6
Fulongquan, China 57 B13
Fülöpszállás, Hungary ... 42 D4
Fulton, Mo., U.S.A. 112 F9
Fulton, N.Y., U.S.A. 111 C8
Fuluälven →, Sweden 10 C7
Fulufjället, Sweden 10 C6
Fumay, France 19 C11
Fumel, France 20 D4
Fumin, China 58 E4
Funabashi, Japan 55 G10
Funäsdalen, Sweden 10 B6
Funchal, Madeira 37 D13

Fundación, Colombia 124 A4
Fundão, Portugal 34 E3
Fundu Moldovei, Romania . 43 C10
Fundulea, Romania 43 F11
Fundy, B. of, Canada 103 D6
Funhalouro, Mozam. 89 C5
Funing, Hebei, China 57 E10
Funing, Jiangsu, China ... 57 H10
Funing, Yunnan, China ... 58 F5
Funiu Shan, China 56 H7
Funsi, Ghana 82 C4
Funtua, Nigeria 83 C6
Fuping, Hebei, China 56 E8
Fuping, Shaanxi, China ... 56 G5
Fuqing, China 59 E12
Fuquan, China 58 D6
Furano, Japan 54 C11
Furāt, Nahr al →, Asia ... 70 D5
Fürg, Iran 71 D7
Furmanov, Russia 48 B5
Furmanovo, Kazakstan ... 48 F9
Furnás, Spain 37 B8
Furnas, Reprêsa de, Brazil . 127 A6
Furneaux Group, Australia . 94 G4
Furqlus, Syria 75 A6
Fürstenau, Germany 24 C3
Fürstenberg, Germany 24 B9
Fürstenfeld, Austria 26 D9
Fürstenfeldbruck, Germany 25 G7
Fürstenwalde, Germany ... 24 C10
Fürth, Germany 25 F6
Furth im Wald, Germany . 25 F8
Furtwangen, Germany 25 G4
Furudal, Sweden 10 C9
Furukawa, Japan 54 E10
Furulund, Sweden 11 J7
Fury and Hecla Str., Canada 101 B11
Fusagasuga, Colombia 124 C4
Fuscaldo, Italy 31 C9
Fushan, Shandong, China . 57 F11
Fushan, Shanxi, China ... 56 G6
Fushë Arrëzi, Albania 40 D4
Fushë-Krujë, Albania 40 E3
Fushun, Liaoning, China . 57 D12
Fushun, Sichuan, China .. 58 C5
Fusong, China 57 C14
Füssen, Germany 25 H6
Fusui, China 58 F6
Futog, Yugoslavia 42 E4
Futuna, Wall. & F. Is. ... 91 B8
Fuwa, Egypt 80 H7
Fuxian Hu, China 58 E4
Fuxin, China 57 C11
Fuyang, Anhui, China ... 56 H8
Fuyang, Zhejiang, China . 59 B12
Fuyang He →, China 56 E9
Fuying Dao, China 59 D13
Fuyu, China 57 B13
Fuyuan, China 58 E5
Füzesgyarmat, Hungary .. 42 C6
Fuzhou, China 59 D12
Fylde, U.K. 12 D5
Fyn, Denmark 11 J4
Fyne, L., U.K. 14 F3
Fyns Amtskommune □, Denmark 11 J4
Fynshav, Denmark 11 K3

G

Ga, Ghana 82 D4
Gaanda, Nigeria 83 C7
Gabarin, Nigeria 83 C7
Gabas →, France 20 E3
Gabela, Angola 84 G2
Gabès, Tunisia 79 B8
Gabès, G. de, Tunisia 79 B8
Gabgaba, W. →, Egypt ... 80 C3
Gabin, Poland 45 F6
Gabon ■, Africa 84 E2
Gaborone, Botswana 88 C4
Gabriels, U.S.A. 111 B10
Gābrīk, Iran 71 E8
Gabrovo, Bulgaria 41 D9
Gacé, France 18 D7
Gāch Sār, Iran 71 B6
Gachsārān, Iran 71 D6
Gacko, Bos.-H. 40 C2
Gadag, India 66 M9
Gadamai, Sudan 81 D4
Gadap, Pakistan 68 G2
Gadarwara, India 69 H8
Gadebusch, Germany 24 B7
Gadein, Sudan 81 F2
Gadhada, India 68 J4
Gádor, Sierra de, Spain .. 35 J8
Gadra, Pakistan 68 G4
Gadsden, U.S.A. 109 H3
Gadwal, India 66 L10
Gadyach = Hadyach, Ukraine 47 G8
Găeşti, Romania 43 F10
Gaeta, Italy 30 A6
Gaeta, G. di, Italy 30 A6
Gaffney, U.S.A. 109 H5
Gafsa, Tunisia 78 B7
Gagarawa, Nigeria 83 C6
Gagaria, India 68 G4
Gagarin, Russia 46 E8
Gaggenau, Germany 25 G4
Gaghamni, Sudan 81 E2
Gagino, Russia 48 C7
Gagliano del Capo, Italy .. 31 C11
Gagnef, Sweden 10 D9
Gagnoa, Ivory C. 82 D3
Gagnon, Canada 103 B6
Gagnon, L., Canada 105 A6
Gagra, Georgia 49 J5

Gahini, Rwanda 86 C3
Gahmar, India 69 G10
Gai Xian = Gaizhou, China 57 D12
Gaïdhouronísi, Greece 36 E7
Gail, U.S.A. 113 J4
Gail →, Austria 26 E6
Gaillac, France 20 E5
Gaillimh = Galway, Ireland 15 C2
Gaillon, France 18 C8
Gaines, U.S.A. 110 E7
Gainesville, Fla., U.S.A. . 109 L4
Gainesville, Ga., U.S.A. . 109 H4
Gainesville, Mo., U.S.A. . 113 G8
Gainesville, Tex., U.S.A. . 113 J6
Gainsborough, U.K. 12 D7
Gairdner, L., Australia ... 95 E2
Gairloch, L., U.K. 14 D3
Gaizhou, China 57 D12
Gaj, Croatia 42 E2
Gaj →, Pakistan 68 F2
Gakuch, Pakistan 69 A5
Galala, Gebel el, Egypt ... 80 J8
Galán, Cerro, Argentina .. 126 B2
Galana →, Kenya 86 C5
Galanta, Slovak Rep. 27 C10
Galápagar, Spain 34 E7
Galápagos, Pac. Oc. 122 D1
Galashiels, U.K. 14 F6
Galați, Romania 43 E13
Galați □, Romania 43 E12
Galatia, Turkey 72 C5
Galatina, Italy 31 B11
Galátone, Italy 31 B11
Galax, U.S.A. 109 G5
Galaxídhion, Greece 38 C4
Galcaio, Somali Rep. 74 F4
Galdhøpiggen, Norway ... 9 F12
Galeana, Chihuahua, Mexico 118 A3
Galeana, Nuevo León, Mexico 118 A3
Galegu, Sudan 81 E4
Galela, Indonesia 63 D7
Galena, U.S.A. 100 B4
Galera, Spain 33 H2
Galera Point, Trin. & Tob. . 121 D7
Galesburg, U.S.A. 112 E9
Galeton, U.S.A. 110 E7
Galga, Ethiopia 81 F4
Gali, Georgia 49 J5
Galicea Mare, Romania ... 43 F8
Galich, Russia 48 A6
Galiche, Bulgaria 40 C7
Galicia □, Spain 34 C3
Galilee = Hagalil, Israel .. 75 C4
Galilee, L., Australia 94 C4
Galilee, Sea of = Yam Kinneret, Israel 75 C4
Galim, Cameroon 83 D7
Galinoporni, Cyprus 36 D13
Galion, U.S.A. 110 F2
Galiuro Mts., U.S.A. 115 K8
Galiwinku, Australia 94 A2
Gallabat, Sudan 81 E4
Gallan Hd., U.K. 14 C1
Gallarate, Italy 28 C5
Gallatin, U.S.A. 109 G2
Galle, Sri Lanka 66 R12
Gállego →, Spain 32 D4
Gallegos →, Argentina ... 128 G3
Galletti →, Ethiopia 81 F5
Galley Hd., Ireland 15 E3
Galliate, Italy 28 C5
Gallinas, Pta., Colombia .. 124 A4
Gallipoli = Gelibolu, Turkey 41 F10
Gallípoli, Italy 31 B10
Gallipolis, U.S.A. 108 F4
Gällivare, Sweden 8 C19
Gällneukirchen, Austria .. 26 C7
Gällö, Sweden 10 B9
Gallo, C., Italy 30 D6
Gallocanta, L. de, Spain .. 32 E3
Galloo I., U.S.A. 111 C8
Galloway, U.K. 14 F4
Galloway, Mull of, U.K. .. 14 G4
Gallup, U.S.A. 115 J9
Gallur, Spain 32 D3
Galoya, Sri Lanka 66 Q12
Galt, U.S.A. 116 G5
Galten, Denmark 11 H3
Galtür, Austria 26 E3
Galty Mts., Ireland 15 D3
Galtymore, Ireland 15 D3
Galva, U.S.A. 112 E9
Galve de Sorbe, Spain ... 32 D1
Galveston, U.S.A. 113 L7
Galveston B., U.S.A. 113 L7
Gálvez, Argentina 126 C3
Galway, Ireland 15 C2
Galway □, Ireland 15 C2
Galway B., Ireland 15 C2
Gam →, Vietnam 64 B5
Gamagori, Japan 55 G8
Gamari, L., Ethiopia 81 E5
Gamawa, Nigeria 83 C7
Gamay, Phil. 61 E6
Gambaga, Ghana 83 C4
Gambat, Pakistan 68 F3
Gambela, Ethiopia 81 F3
Gambhir →, India 68 F6
Gambia ■, W. Afr. 82 C1
Gambia →, W. Afr. 82 C1
Gambier, C., Australia ... 92 B5
Gambier Is., Australia ... 95 F2
Gambo, Canada 103 C9
Gamboli, Pakistan 68 E3
Gambomba, Congo 84 E3
Gamka →, S. Africa 88 E3
Gamkab →, Namibia 88 D2
Gamla Uppsala, Sweden .. 10 E11

Gamlakarleby = Kokkola, Finland 8 E20
Gamleby, Sweden 11 G10
Gammon →, Canada 105 C9
Gamo-Gofa □, Ethiopia .. 81 F4
Gamou, Niger 83 C6
Gamtoos →, S. Africa ... 88 E4
Gan, France 20 E3
Gan Jiang →, China 59 C11
Gan Goriama, Mts., Cameroon 83 D7
Ganado, U.S.A. 115 J9
Gananita, Sudan 80 D3
Gananoque, Canada 102 D4
Ganāveh, Iran 71 D6
Gäncä, Azerbaijan 49 K8
Gancheng, China 64 C7
Gand = Gent, Belgium ... 17 C3
Ganda, Angola 85 G2
Gandajika, Dem. Rep. of the Congo . 84 F4
Gandak →, India 69 G11
Gandava, Pakistan 68 E2
Gander, Canada 103 C9
Ganderkesee, Germany ... 24 B4
Ganderowe Falls, Zimbabwe 87 F2
Gandesa, Spain 32 D5
Gandhi Sagar, India 68 G6
Gandhinagar, India 68 H5
Gandi, Nigeria 83 C6
Gandía, Spain 33 G4
Gando, Pta., Canary Is. .. 37 G4
Gandole, Nigeria 83 D7
Gâneb, Mauritania 82 B2
Ganedidalem = Gani, Indonesia 63 E7
Ganetti, Sudan 80 D3
Ganga →, India 69 H14
Ganga Sagar, India 69 J13
Gangafani, Mali 82 C4
Gangan →, India 69 E8
Ganganagar, India 68 E5
Gangapur, India 68 F7
Gangara, Niger 83 C6
Gangaw, Burma 67 H19
Gangdisê Shan, China ... 67 D12
Ganges = Ganga →, India 69 H14
Ganges, Canada 104 D4
Ganges, France 20 E7
Ganges, Mouths of the, India 69 J14
Gånghester, Sweden 11 G7
Gangi, Italy 31 E7
Gângiova, Romania 43 G8
Gangoh, India 68 E7
Gangroti, India 69 D8
Gangtok, India 67 F16
Gangu, China 56 G3
Gangyao, China 57 B14
Gani, Indonesia 63 E7
Ganj, India 69 F8
Ganluc, China 58 C4
Ganquan, China 56 F5
Gänserdorf, Austria 27 C9
Ganshui, China 58 C6
Gansu □, China 56 G3
Ganta, Liberia 82 D3
Gantheaume, C., Australia . 95 F2
Gantheaume B., Australia . 93 E1
Gantsevichi = Hantsavichy, Belarus 47 F4
Ganye, Nigeria 83 D7
Ganyem = Genyem, Indonesia 63 E10
Ganyu, China 57 G10
Ganzhou, China 59 E10
Gao, Mali 83 B5
Gao Xian, China 58 C5
Gao'an, China 59 C10
Gaochun, China 59 B12
Gaohe, China 59 F9
Gaohebu, China 59 B11
Gaokeng, China 59 D9
Gaolan Dao, China 59 G10
Gaoligong Shan, China .. 58 E2
Gaomi, China 57 F10
Gaoming, China 59 F9
Gaoping, China 56 G7
Gaotang, China 56 F9
Gaoua, Burkina Faso 82 C4
Gaoual, Guinea 82 C2
Gaoxiong = Kaohsiung, Taiwan 59 F13
Gaoyang, China 56 E8
Gaoyao, China 59 F9
Gaoyou, China 59 A12
Gaoyou Hu, China 57 H10
Gaoyuan, China 57 F9
Gaozhou, China 59 F8
Gap, France 21 D10
Gapat →, India 69 G10
Gapuwiyak, Australia ... 94 A2
Gar, China 60 C2
Garabogazköl Aylagy, Turkmenistan 50 E6
Garachico, Canary Is. 37 F3
Garachiné, Panama 120 E4
Garafia, Canary Is. 37 F2
Garah, Australia 95 D4
Garajonay, Canary Is. ... 37 F2
Garanhuns, Brazil 125 E11
Garango, Burkina Faso ... 83 C4
Garara, Papua N. G. 95 A5

Garberville, U.S.A. 114 F2
Garbiyang, India 69 D9
Garbsen, Germany 24 C5
Gard □, France 21 D8
Gard →, France 21 E8
Garda, L. di, Italy 28 C7
Gardanne, France 21 E9
Gårdby, Sweden 11 H10
Garde L., Canada 105 A7
Gardelegen, Germany ... 24 C7
Garden City, Ga., U.S.A. . 109 J5
Garden City, Kans., U.S.A. 113 K4
Garden City, Tex., U.S.A. 113 K4
Garden Grove, U.S.A. ... 117 M9
Gardēz, Afghan. 68 C3
Gardhíki, Greece 38 C3
Gardiner, Maine, U.S.A. . 109 C11
Gardiner, Mont., U.S.A. . 114 D8
Gardiners I., U.S.A. 111 E12
Gardner, U.S.A. 111 D13
Gardner Canal, Canada .. 104 C3
Gardnerville, U.S.A. 116 G7
Gardno, Jezioro, Poland .. 44 D4
Gardo, Somali Rep. 74 F4
Gardone Val Trómpia, Italy 28 C7
Gárdony, Hungary 42 C3
Garešnica, Croatia 29 C13
Garéssio, Italy 28 D5
Garey, U.S.A. 117 L6
Garfield, U.S.A. 114 C5
Garforth, U.K. 12 D6
Gargaliánoi, Greece 38 D3
Gargan, Mt., France 20 C5
Gargouna, Mali 83 B5
Gargždai, Lithuania 44 C8
Garibaldi Prov. Park, Canada 104 D4
Gariep, L., S. Africa 88 E4
Garies, S. Africa 88 E2
Garigliano →, Italy 30 A6
Garissa, Kenya 86 C4
Garkida, Nigeria 83 C7
Garko, Nigeria 83 C6
Garland, Tex., U.S.A. ... 113 J6
Garland, Utah, U.S.A. ... 114 F7
Garlasco, Italy 28 C5
Garliava, Lithuania 44 D10
Garlin, France 20 E3
Garm, Tajikistan 50 F8
Garmāb, Iran 71 C8
Garmisch-Partenkirchen, Germany 25 H7
Garmsār, Iran 71 C7
Garner, U.S.A. 112 D8
Garnett, U.S.A. 112 F7
Garo Hills, India 69 G14
Garoe, Somali Rep. 74 F4
Garonne →, France 20 C3
Garonne, Canal Latéral à la, France 20 D4
Garot, India 68 G6
Garoua, Cameroon 83 D7
Garpenberg, Sweden 10 D10
Garphyttan, Sweden 10 E8
Garrauli, India 69 G8
Garrel, Germany 24 C4
Garrigue = Garrigues, France 20 E7
Garrigues, France 20 E7
Garrison, Mont., U.S.A. . 114 C7
Garrison, N. Dak., U.S.A. 112 B4
Garrison Res. = Sakakawea, L., U.S.A. 112 B4
Garron Pt., U.K. 15 A6
Garrovillas, Spain 35 F4
Garrucha, Spain 33 H3
Garry →, U.K. 14 E5
Garry, L., Canada 100 B9
Garsen, Kenya 86 C5
Gärsnäs, Sweden 11 J8
Garson L., Canada 105 B6
Gartempe →, France ... 20 B4
Gartz, Germany 24 B10
Garu, Ghana 83 C4
Garub, Namibia 88 D2
Garut, Indonesia 63 G12
Garvão, Portugal 35 H2
Garvie Mts., N.Z. 91 L2
Garwa = Garoua, Cameroon 83 D7
Garwa, India 69 G10
Garwolin, Poland 45 G8
Gary, U.S.A. 108 E2
Garz, Germany 24 A9
Garzê, China 58 B3
Garzón, Colombia 124 C3
Gas-San, Japan 54 E10
Gasan Kuli = Esenguly, Turkmenistan 50 F6
Gascogne, France 20 E4
Gascogne, G. de, Europe . 20 E2
Gascony = Gascogne, France 20 E4
Gascoyne →, Australia .. 93 D1
Gascoyne Junction, Australia 93 E2
Gascueña, Spain 32 E2
Gash, Wadi →, Ethiopia .. 81 D4
Gashagar, Nigeria 83 C7
Gasherbrum, Pakistan ... 69 B7
Gashua, Nigeria 83 C7
Gaspé, Canada 103 C7
Gaspé, C. de, Canada ... 103 C7
Gaspé, Pén. de, Canada .. 103 C6
Gaspésie, Parc de Conservation de la, Canada 103 C6
Gassan, Burkina Faso ... 82 C4
Gassol, Nigeria 83 D7
Gasteiz = Vitoria-Gasteiz, Spain 32 C2
Gastonia, U.S.A. 109 H5

Gastoúni, Greece 38 D3
Gastoúni, Greece 38 B1
Gastre, Argentina 128 E3
Gästrikland, Sweden 10 D10
Gata, C., Cyprus 36 E12
Gata, C. de, Spain 33 J2
Gata, Sierra de. Spain 34 E4
Gataga →, Canada 104 B3
Gătaia, Romania 42 E6
Gatchina, Russia 46 C6
Gatehouse of Fleet, U.K. .. 14 G4
Gates, U.S.A. 110 C7
Gateshead, U.K. 12 C6
Gatesville, U.S.A. 113 K6
Gaths, Zimbabwe 87 G3
Gatico, Chile 126 A1
Gâtinais, France 19 D9
Gâtine, Hauteurs de, France 20 B3
Gatineau, Canada 111 A9
Gatineau →, Canada 102 C4
Gatineau, Parc Nat. de la,
  Canada 102 C4
Gattaran, Phil. 61 B4
Gattinara, Italy 28 C5
Gatton, Australia 95 D5
Gatun, L., Panama 120 C4
Gatyana, S. Africa 89 E4
Gau, Fiji 91 D8
Gaucín, Spain 35 J5
Gauer L., Canada 105 B9
Gauhati, India 67 F17
Gauja →, Latvia 9 H21
Gaula →, Norway 8 E14
Gauri Phanta, India 69 E9
Gausta, Norway 9 G13
Gauteng □, S. Africa 89 D4
Gāv Koshī, Iran 71 D8
Gāvakān, Iran 71 D7
Gavarnie, France 20 F3
Gavāter, Iran 71 E9
Gāvbandī, Iran 71 E7
Gavdhopoúla, Greece 36 E6
Gávdhos, Greece 36 E6
Gavi, Italy 28 D5
Gavião, Portugal 35 F3
Gaviota, U.S.A. 117 L6
Gāvkhūnī, Bāţlāq-e, Iran . 71 C7
Gävle, Sweden 10 D11
Gävleborgs län □, Sweden . 10 C10
Gävlebukten, Sweden 10 D11
Gavorrano, Italy 28 F7
Gavray, France 18 D5
Gavrilov Yam, Russia 46 D10
Gávrion, Greece 38 D6
Gawachab, Namibia 88 D2
Gawilgarh Hills, India ... 66 J10
Gawler, Australia 95 E2
Gawu, Nigeria 83 D6
Gaxun Nur, China 60 B5
Gaya, India 69 G11
Gaya, Niger 83 C5
Gaya, Nigeria 83 C6
Gayéri, Burkina Faso 83 C5
Gaylord, U.S.A. 108 C3
Gayndah, Australia 95 D5
Gaysin = Haysyn, Ukraine . 47 H5
Gayvoron = Hayvoron,
  Ukraine 47 H5
Gaza, Gaza Strip 75 D3
Gaza □, Mozam. 89 C5
Gaza Strip □, Asia 75 D3
Gazanjyk, Turkmenistan ... 71 B7
Gazaoua, Niger 83 C6
Gāzbor, Iran 71 D8
Gazi,
  Dem. Rep. of the Congo . 86 B1
Gaziantep, Turkey 70 B3
Gazipaşa, Turkey 72 D5
Gbarnga, Liberia 82 D3
Gbekebo, Nigeria 83 D5
Gboko, Nigeria 83 D6
Gbongan, Nigeria 83 D5
Gcoverega, Botswana 88 B3
Gcuwa, S. Africa 89 E4
Gdańsk, Poland 44 D5
Gdańska, Zatoka, Poland .. 44 D6
Gdov, Russia 9 G22
Gdynia, Poland 44 D5
Geba →, Guinea-Biss. 82 C1
Gebe, Indonesia 63 D7
Gebeciler, Turkey 39 C12
Gebeit Mine, Sudan 80 C4
Gebel Abyad, Sudan 80 D2
Gebel Iweibid, Egypt 80 H8
Gebze, Turkey 41 F13
Gecha, Ethiopia 81 F4
Gedaref, Sudan 81 E4
Gedaref □, Sudan 81 E4
Gediz, Turkey 39 B11
Gediz →, Turkey 39 C8
Gedo, Ethiopia 81 F4
Gèdre, France 20 F4
Gedser, Denmark 11 K5
Geegully Cr. →, Australia . 92 C3
Geel, Belgium 17 C4
Geelong, Australia 95 F3
Geelvink B. = Cenderwasih,
  Teluk, Indonesia 63 E9
Geelvink Chan., Australia . 93 E1
Geesthacht, Germany 24 B6
Geidam, Nigeria 83 C7
Geikie →, Canada 105 B8
Geilenkirchen, Germany .. 24 E2
Geili, Sudan 81 D3
Geisingen, Germany 25 H4
Geislingen, Germany 25 G5
Geistown, U.S.A. 110 F6
Geita, Tanzania 86 C3
Gejiu, China 58 F4
Gel →, Sudan 81 F2
Gel, Meydān-e, Iran 71 D7

Gel River, Sudan 81 F2
Gela, Italy 31 E7
Gela, G. di, Italy 31 F7
Gelahun, Liberia 82 D2
Gelderland □, Neths. 17 B6
Geldern, Germany 24 D2
Geldrop, Neths. 17 C5
Geleen, Neths. 17 D5
Gelehun, S. Leone 82 D2
Gelembe, Turkey 39 B9
Gelemso, Ethiopia 81 F5
Gelendost, Turkey 72 C4
Gelendzhik, Russia 47 K10
Gelibolu, Turkey 41 F10
Gelibolu Yarımadası, Turkey 41 F10
Gelidonya Burnu, Turkey . 72 D4
Gelnhausen, Germany ... 25 E5
Gelnica, Slovak Rep. 27 C13
Gelsenkirchen, Germany .. 24 D3
Gelting, Germany 24 A5
Gemas, Malaysia 65 L4
Gembloux, Belgium 17 D4
Gembu, Nigeria 83 D7
Gemena,
  Dem. Rep. of the Congo . 84 D3
Gemerek, Turkey 70 B3
Gemla, Sweden 11 H8
Gemlik, Turkey 41 F13
Gemlik Körfezi, Turkey .. 41 F12
Gemona del Friuli, Italy .. 29 B10
Gemsa, Egypt 80 B3
Gemünden, Germany 25 E5
Genale →, Ethiopia 81 F4
Genç, Turkey 73 C9
Gençay, France 20 B4
Geneina, Gebel, Egypt ... 80 B3
General Acha, Argentina .. 126 D3
General Alvear,
  Buenos Aires, Argentina . 126 D13
General Alvear, Mendoza,
  Argentina 126 D2
General Artigas, Paraguay . 126 B4
General Belgrano, Argentina 126 D4
General Cabrera, Argentina 126 C3
General Cepeda, Mexico ... 118 B4
General Guido, Argentina . 126 D4
General Juan Madariaga,
  Argentina 126 D4
General La Madrid,
  Argentina 126 D3
General MacArthur, Phil. .. 61 F6
General Martin Miguel de
  Güemes, Argentina 126 A3
General Paz, Argentina ... 126 B4
General Pico, Argentina ... 126 D3
General Pinedo, Argentina . 126 B3
General Pinto, Argentina .. 126 C3
General Roca, Argentina .. 128 D3
General Santos, Phil. 61 H6
General Toshevo, Bulgaria . 41 C12
General Trevino, Mexico ... 119 B5
General Trías, Mexico 118 B3
General Viamonte, Argentina 126 D3
General Villegas, Argentina 126 D3
Genesee, Idaho, U.S.A. ... 114 C5
Genesee, Pa., U.S.A. 110 E7
Genesee →, U.S.A. 110 C7
Geneseo, Ill., U.S.A. 112 E9
Geneseo, N.Y., U.S.A. 110 D7
Geneva = Genève, Switz. .. 25 J2
Geneva, Ala., U.S.A. 109 K3
Geneva, N.Y., U.S.A. 110 D7
Geneva, Nebr., U.S.A. 112 E6
Geneva, Ohio, U.S.A. 110 E4
Geneva, L. = Léman, L.,
  Europe 19 F13
Geneva, L., U.S.A. 108 D1
Genève, Switz. 25 J2
Gengenbach, Germany ... 25 G4
Genichesk = Henichesk,
  Ukraine 47 J8
Genil →, Spain 35 H5
Genk, Belgium 17 D5
Genlis, France 19 E12
Gennargentu, Mti. del, Italy 30 B2
Gennes, France 18 E6
Genoa = Génova, Italy ... 28 D5
Genoa, Australia 95 F4
Genoa, N.Y., U.S.A. 111 D8
Genoa, Nebr., U.S.A. 112 E6
Genoa, Nev., U.S.A. 116 F7
Génova, Italy 28 D5
Génova, G. di, Italy 28 E6
Genriyetty, Ostrov, Russia . 51 B16
Gent, Belgium 17 C3
Genteng, Indonesia 63 G12
Genthin, Germany 24 C8
Genyem, Indonesia 63 E10
Genzano di Lucánia, Italy . 31 B9
Genzano di Roma, Italy ... 29 G9
Geoagiu, Romania 43 E8
Geographe B., Australia .. 93 F2
Geographe Chan., Australia 93 D1
Geokchay = Göyçay,
  Azerbaijan 49 K8
Georga, Zemlya, Russia ... 50 A5
George, S. Africa 88 E3
George →, Canada 103 A6
George, L., N.S.W.,
  Australia 95 F4
George, L., S. Austral.,
  Australia 95 F3
George, L., W. Austral.,
  Australia 92 D3
George, L., Uganda 86 B3
George, L., Fla., U.S.A. ... 109 L5
George, L., N.Y., U.S.A. .. 111 C11
George Gill Ra., Australia . 92 D5
George River =
  Kangiqsualujjuaq, Canada 101 C13

George Sound, N.Z. 91 L1
George Town, Australia ... 94 G4
George Town, Bahamas ... 120 B4
George Town, Malaysia ... 65 K3
George V Land, Antarctica . 5 C10
George VI Sound, Antarctica 5 D17
George West, U.S.A. 113 L5
Georgetown, Australia ... 94 B3
Georgetown, Ont., Canada . 102 D4
Georgetown, P.E.I., Canada 103 C7
Georgetown, Cayman Is. .. 120 C3
Georgetown, Gambia 82 C2
Georgetown, Guyana 124 B7
Georgetown, Calif., U.S.A. 116 G6
Georgetown, Colo., U.S.A. 114 G11
Georgetown, Ky., U.S.A. . 108 F3
Georgetown, N.Y., U.S.A. . 111 D9
Georgetown, Ohio, U.S.A. 108 F4
Georgetown, S.C., U.S.A. . 109 J6
Georgetown, Tex., U.S.A. . 113 K6
Georgia □, U.S.A. 109 K5
Georgia ■, Asia 49 J6
Georgia, Str. of, Canada .. 104 D4
Georgian B., Canada 102 C3
Georgina →, Australia ... 94 C2
Georgina I., Canada 110 B5
Georgiu-Dezh = Liski,
  Russia 47 G10
Georgiyevsk, Russia 49 H6
Georgsmarienhütte,
  Germany 24 C4
Gera, Germany 24 E8
Geraardsbergen, Belgium . 17 D3
Geral, Serra, Brazil 127 B6
Geral de Goiás, Serra, Brazil 125 F9
Geraldine, U.S.A. 114 C8
Geraldton, Australia 93 E1
Geraldton, Canada 102 C2
Gérardmer, France 19 D13
Gercüş, Turkey 73 D9
Gerede, Turkey 72 B5
Gerês, Sierra do, Portugal . 34 D3
Gereshk, Afghan. 66 D4
Geretsried, Germany 25 H7
Gérgal, Spain 33 H2
Gerik, Malaysia 65 K3
Gering, U.S.A. 112 E3
Gerlach, U.S.A. 114 F4
Gerlachovský štít,
  Slovak Rep. 27 B13
German Planina, Macedonia 40 D6
Germansen Landing, Canada 104 B4
Germantown, U.S.A. 113 M10
Germany ■, Europe 24 E6
Germencik, Turkey 39 D9
Germering, Germany 25 G7
Germersheim, Germany .. 25 F4
Germī, Iran 71 B6
Germiston, S. Africa 89 D4
Gernika-Lumo, Spain 32 B2
Gernsheim, Germany 25 F4
Gero, Japan 55 G8
Gerolzhofen, Germany ... 25 F6
Gerona = Girona, Spain ... 32 D7
Gerrard, Canada 104 C5
Gers □, France 20 E4
Gers →, France 20 D4
Gersfeld, Germany 24 E5
Gersthofen, Germany 25 G6
Gerzat, France 20 C7
Gerze, Turkey 72 B6
Geseke, Germany 24 D4
Geser, Indonesia 63 E8
Gesso →, Italy 28 D4
Gestro, Wabi →, Ethiopia . 81 G5
Getafe, Spain 34 E7
Getinge, Sweden 11 H6
Gettysburg, Pa., U.S.A. .. 108 F7
Gettysburg, S. Dak., U.S.A. 112 C5
Getxo, Spain 32 B2
Getz Ice Shelf, Antarctica . 5 D14
Gevaş, Turkey 73 C10
Gévaudan, France 20 D7
Gevgelija, Macedonia 40 E6
Gévora →, Spain 35 G4
Gewani, Ethiopia 81 E5
Gex, France 19 F13
Geyikli, Turkey 39 B8
Geyser, U.S.A. 114 C8
Geyserville, U.S.A. 116 G4
Geyve, Turkey 72 B4
Ghâbat el Arab = Wang
  Kai, Sudan 81 F2
Ghabeish, Sudan 81 E2
Ghaggar →, India 68 E6
Ghaghara →, India 69 G11
Ghaghat →, Bangla. 69 G13
Ghagra, India 69 H11
Ghalla, Wadi el →, Sudan . 81 E2
Ghana ■, W. Afr. 83 D4
Ghansor, India 69 H9
Ghanzi, Botswana 88 C3
Gharb el Istiwa'iya □, Sudan 81 F2
Gharb Kordofân □, Sudan . 81 E2
Gharbîya, Es Sahrâ el, Egypt 80 B2
Ghardaïa, Algeria 78 B6
Ghârib, G., Egypt 80 B3
Gharig, Sudan 81 E2
Gharyân, Libya 79 B8
Ghat, Libya 79 D8
Ghatal, India 69 H12
Ghatampur, India 69 F9
Ghatsila, India 69 H12
Ghaţţī, Si. Arabia 70 D3
Ghawdex = Gozo, Malta . 36 C1
Ghazal, Bahr el →, Chad . 79 F9
Ghazâl, Bahr el →, Sudan . 81 F3
Ghaziabad, India 68 E7
Ghazipur, India 69 G10
Ghaznī, Afghan. 68 C3

Ghazni □, Afghan. 66 C6
Ghedi, Italy 28 C7
Ghelari, Romania 42 E7
Ghent = Gent, Belgium .. 17 C3
Gheorghe Gheorghiu-Dej =
  Oneşti, Romania 43 D11
Gheorgheni, Romania ... 43 D10
Gherla, Romania 43 C8
Ghidigeni, Romania 43 D12
Ghilarza, Italy 30 B1
Ghīnah, Wādī al, Si. Arabia 70 D3
Ghīnah, Wādī al →,
  Si. Arabia 80 B4
Ghisonaccia, France 21 F13
Ghisoni, France 21 F13
Ghizao, Afghan. 68 C1
Ghizar →, Pakistan 69 A5
Ghot Ogrein, Egypt 80 A2
Ghotaru, India 68 F4
Ghotki, Pakistan 68 E3
Ghowr □, Afghan. 66 C4
Ghudaf, W. al →, Iraq ... 70 C4
Ghughri, India 69 H9
Ghugus, India 66 K11
Ghulam Mohammad
  Barrage, Pakistan 68 G3
Ghūrīān, Afghan. 66 B2
Gia Dinh, Vietnam 65 G6
Gia Lai = Plei Ku, Vietnam 64 F7
Gia Nghia, Vietnam 65 G6
Gia Ngoc, Vietnam 64 E7
Gia Vuc, Vietnam 64 E7
Giannutri, Italy 28 F8
Giant Forest, U.S.A. 116 J8
Giant Mts. = Krkonoše,
  Czech Rep. 26 A8
Giants Causeway, U.K. .. 15 A5
Giarabub = Al Jaghbūb,
  Libya 79 C10
Giarre, Italy 31 E8
Giaveno, Italy 28 C4
Gibara, Cuba 120 B4
Gibb River, Australia ... 92 C4
Gibbon, U.S.A. 112 E5
Gibe →, Ethiopia 81 F4
Gibellina Nuova, Italy ... 30 E5
Gibeon, Namibia 88 D2
Gibraléon, Spain 35 H4
Gibraltar ■, Europe 35 J5
Gibraltar, Str. of, Medit. S. 35 K5
Gibson Desert, Australia . 92 D4
Gibsons, Canada 104 D4
Gibsonville, U.S.A. 116 F6
Giddings, U.S.A. 113 K6
Gidole, Ethiopia 81 F4
Gien, France 19 E9
Giengen, Germany 25 G6
Giessen, Germany 24 E4
Gīfān, Iran 71 B8
Gifatin, Geziret, Egypt .. 80 B3
Gifhorn, Germany 24 C6
Gift Lake, Canada 104 B5
Gifu, Japan 55 G8
Gifu □, Japan 55 G8
Gigant, Russia 49 G5
Giganta, Sa. de la, Mexico . 118 B2
Gigen, Bulgaria 41 C8
Gigha, U.K. 14 F3
Gíglio, Italy 28 F7
Gignac, France 20 E7
Gigüela →, Spain 35 F7
Gijón, Spain 34 B5
Gil I., Canada 104 C3
Gila →, U.S.A. 115 K6
Gila Bend, U.S.A. 115 K7
Gila Bend Mts., U.S.A. .. 115 K7
Gīlān □, Iran 71 B6
Gīlău, Romania 43 D8
Gilbert →, Australia 94 B3
Gilbert Is., Kiribati 96 G9
Gilbert River, Australia .. 94 B3
Gilead, U.S.A. 111 B14
Gilf el Kebîr, Hadabat el,
  Egypt 80 C2
Gilford I., Canada 104 C3
Gilgandra, Australia 95 E4
Gilgil, Kenya 86 C4
Gilgit, India 69 B6
Gilgit →, Pakistan 69 B6
Gilgunnia, Australia 95 E4
Giljeva Planina, Serbia, Yug. 40 C3
Gillam, Canada 105 B10
Gilleleje, Denmark 11 H6
Gillen, L., Australia 93 E3
Gilles, L., Australia 95 E2
Gillette, U.S.A. 112 C2
Gilliat, Australia 94 C3
Gillingham, U.K. 13 F8
Gilmer, U.S.A. 113 J7
Gilmore, Australia 95 F4
Gilmore, L., Australia ... 93 F3
Gilo →, Ethiopia 81 F3
Gilort →, Romania 43 F8
Gilroy, U.S.A. 116 H5
Gimbi, Ethiopia 81 F4
Gimli, Canada 105 C9
Gimo, Sweden 10 D12
Gimone →, France 20 E4
Gimont, France 20 E4
Gin Gin, Australia 95 D5
Gīnāh, Egypt 80 B3
Gineifa, Egypt 80 H8
Gingin, Australia 93 F2
Gingindlovu, S. Africa .. 89 D5
Ginir, Ethiopia 81 F5
Ginosa, Italy 31 B9
Ginzo de Limia = Xinzo de
  Limia, Spain 34 C3
Gióia, G. di, Italy 31 D8

Gióia del Colle, Italy 31 B9
Gióia Táuro, Italy 31 D8
Gioiosa Iónica, Italy 31 D9
Gioiosa Marea, Italy 31 D7
Gióna, Óros, Greece 38 C4
Giovi, Passo dei, Italy 28 D5
Giovinazzo, Italy 31 A9
Gippsland, Australia 95 F4
Gir Hills, India 68 J4
Girab, India 68 F4
Girâfi, W. →, Egypt 75 F3
Giraltovce, Slovak Rep. ... 27 B14
Girard, Kans., U.S.A. 113 G7
Girard, Ohio, U.S.A. 110 E4
Girard, Pa., U.S.A. 110 D4
Girard, Pa., U.S.A. 110 E4
Girdle Ness, U.K. 14 D6
Giresun, Turkey 73 B8
Girga, Egypt 80 B3
Giri →, India 68 D7
Giridih, India 69 G12
Girifalco, Italy 31 D9
Girne = Kyrenia, Cyprus . 36 D12
Giro, Nigeria 83 C5
Giromagny, France 19 E13
Girona, Spain 32 D7
Girona □, Spain 32 C7
Gironde □, France 20 D3
Gironde →, France 20 C2
Gironella, Spain 32 C6
Giru, Australia 94 B4
Girvan, U.K. 14 F4
Gisborne, N.Z. 91 H7
Gisenyi, Rwanda 86 C2
Gislaved, Sweden 11 G7
Gisors, France 19 C8
Gitega, Burundi 86 C2
Giuba →, Somali Rep. ... 74 G3
Giugliano in Campania, Italy 31 B7
Giulianova, Italy 29 F10
Giurgeni, Romania 43 F12
Giurgiu, Romania 43 G10
Giurgiu □, Romania 43 F10
Giurgiuleşti, Moldova ... 43 E13
Give, Denmark 11 J3
Givet, France 19 B11
Givors, France 21 C8
Giyon, Ethiopia 81 F4
Giza = El Gîza, Egypt 80 J7
Gizhiga, Russia 51 C17
Gizhiginskaya Guba, Russia 51 C16
Giżycko, Poland 44 D8
Gizzeria, Italy 31 D9
Gjalicës e Lumës, Mal,
  Albania 40 D4
Gjegjani, Albania 40 E4
Gjirokastra, Albania 40 F4
Gjoa Haven, Canada 100 B10
Gjøvik, Norway 9 F14
Gjuhës, Kep i, Albania ... 40 F3
Glace Bay, Canada 103 C8
Glacier Bay National Park
  and Preserve, U.S.A. ... 104 B1
Glacier National Park,
  Canada 104 C5
Glacier National Park,
  U.S.A. 114 B7
Glacier Peak, U.S.A. 114 B3
Gladewater, U.S.A. 113 J7
Gladstone, Queens.,
  Australia 94 C5
Gladstone, S. Austral.,
  Australia 95 E2
Gladstone, Canada 105 C9
Gladstone, U.S.A. 108 C2
Gladwin, U.S.A. 108 D3
Glafsfjorden, Sweden ... 10 E6
Głogów Małopolski, Poland 45 H8
Glåma = Glomma →,
  Norway 9 G14
Gláma, Iceland 8 D2
Glamoč, Bos.-H. 29 D13
Glamsbjerg, Denmark ... 11 J4
Glarus, Switz. 25 H5
Glarus □, Switz. 25 J5
Glasco, Kans., U.S.A. ... 112 F6
Glasco, N.Y., U.S.A. 111 D11
Glasgow, U.K. 14 F4
Glasgow, Ky., U.S.A. ... 108 G3
Glasgow, Mont., U.S.A. . 114 B10
Glasgow, City of □, U.K. . 14 F4
Glaslyn, Canada 105 C7
Glastonbury, U.K. 13 F5
Glastonbury, U.S.A. 111 E12
Glauchau, Germany 24 E8
Glava, Sweden 10 E6
Glavice, Croatia 29 E13
Glazov, Russia 48 A11
Gleichen, Canada 104 C6
Gleisdorf, Austria 26 D8
Gleiwitz = Gliwice, Poland 45 H5
Glen, U.S.A. 111 B13
Glen Affric, U.K. 14 D4
Glen Canyon, U.S.A. ... 115 H8
Glen Canyon Dam, U.S.A. 115 H8
Glen Canyon National
  Recreation Area, U.S.A. 115 H8
Glen Coe, U.K. 14 E4
Glen Cove, U.S.A. 111 F11
Glen Garry, U.K. 14 D3
Glen Innes, Australia ... 95 D5
Glen Lyon, U.S.A. 111 E8
Glen Mor, U.K. 14 D4
Glen Moriston, U.K. ... 14 D4
Glen Robertson, Canada . 111 A10
Glen Spean, U.K. 14 E4
Glen Ullin, U.S.A. 112 B4
Glénan, Îs. de, France ... 18 E3

Name	Page	Grid
Glencoe, *Canada*	110	D3
Glencoe, *S. Africa*	89	D5
Glencoe, *U.S.A.*	112	C7
Glendale, *Ariz., U.S.A.*	115	K7
Glendale, *Calif., U.S.A.*	117	L8
Glendale, *Zimbabwe*	87	F3
Glendive, *U.S.A.*	112	B2
Glendo, *U.S.A.*	112	D2
Glenelg ➤, *Australia*	95	F3
Glenfield, *U.S.A.*	111	C9
Glengarriff, *Ireland*	15	E2
Glenmont, *U.S.A.*	110	F2
Glenmorgan, *Australia*	95	D4
Glenn, *U.S.A.*	116	F4
Glennallen, *U.S.A.*	100	B5
Glennamaddy, *Ireland*	15	C3
Glenns Ferry, *U.S.A.*	114	E6
Glenore, *Australia*	94	B3
Glenreagh, *Australia*	95	E5
Glenrock, *U.S.A.*	114	E11
Glenrothes, *U.K.*	14	E5
Glens Falls, *U.S.A.*	111	C11
Glenside, *U.S.A.*	111	F9
Glenties, *Ireland*	15	B3
Glenville, *U.S.A.*	108	F5
Glenwood, *Canada*	103	C9
Glenwood, *Ark., U.S.A.*	113	H8
Glenwood, *Hawaii, U.S.A.*	106	J17
Glenwood, *Iowa, U.S.A.*	112	E7
Glenwood, *Minn., U.S.A.*	112	C7
Glenwood, *Wash., U.S.A.*	116	D5
Glenwood Springs, *U.S.A.*	114	G10
Glettinganes, *Iceland*	8	D7
Glifádha, *Greece*	38	D5
Glimåkra, *Sweden*	11	H8
Glina, *Croatia*	29	C13
Glinojeck, *Poland*	45	F7
Gliwice, *Poland*	45	H5
Globe, *U.S.A.*	115	K8
Glodeanu Siliştea, *Romania*	43	F11
Glodeni, *Moldova*	43	C12
Glödnitz, *Austria*	26	E7
Gloggnitz, *Austria*	26	D8
Głogów, *Poland*	45	G3
Głogówek, *Poland*	45	H4
Glomma ➤, *Norway*	9	G14
Glorieuses, Is., *Ind. Oc.*	89	A8
Glóssa, *Greece*	38	B5
Glossop, *U.K.*	12	D6
Gloucester, *Australia*	95	E5
Gloucester, *U.K.*	13	F5
Gloucester, *U.S.A.*	111	D14
Gloucester I., *Australia*	94	C4
Gloucester Point, *U.S.A.*	108	G7
Gloucestershire □, *U.K.*	13	F5
Gloversville, *U.S.A.*	111	C10
Glovertown, *Canada*	103	C9
Głowno, *Poland*	45	G6
Głubczyce, *Poland*	45	H4
Glubokiy, *Russia*	49	F5
Glubokoye = Hlybokaye, *Belarus*	46	E4
Głuchołazy, *Poland*	45	H4
Glücksburg, *Germany*	24	A5
Glückstadt, *Germany*	24	B5
Glukhov = Hlukhiv, *Ukraine*	47	G7
Glusk, *Belarus*	47	F5
Głuszyca, *Poland*	45	H3
Glyngøre, *Denmark*	11	H2
Gmünd, *Kärnten, Austria*	26	E6
Gmünd, *Niederösterreich, Austria*	26	C8
Gmunden, *Austria*	26	D6
Gnarp, *Sweden*	10	B11
Gnesta, *Sweden*	10	E11
Gniew, *Poland*	44	E5
Gniewkowo, *Poland*	45	F5
Gniezno, *Poland*	45	F4
Gnjilane, *Kosovo, Yug.*	40	D5
Gnoien, *Germany*	24	B8
Gnosjö, *Sweden*	11	G7
Gnowangerup, *Australia*	93	F2
Go Cong, *Vietnam*	65	G6
Gō-no-ura, *Japan*	55	H4
Goa, *India*	66	M8
Goa □, *India*	66	M8
Goalen Hd., *Australia*	95	F5
Goalpara, *India*	67	F17
Goaltor, *India*	69	H12
Goalundo Ghat, *Bangla.*	69	H13
Goaso, *Ghana*	82	D4
Goat Fell, *U.K.*	14	F3
Goba, *Ethiopia*	81	F4
Goba, *Mozam.*	89	D5
Gobabis, *Namibia*	88	C2
Göbel, *Turkey*	41	F12
Gobi, *Asia*	56	C6
Gobō, *Japan*	55	H7
Gobo, *Sudan*	81	F3
Göçbeyli, *Turkey*	39	B9
Goch, *Germany*	24	D2
Gochas, *Namibia*	88	C2
Godavari ➤, *India*	67	L13
Godavari Pt., *India*	67	L13
Godbout, *Canada*	103	C6
Godda, *India*	69	G12
Godech, *Bulgaria*	40	C7
Goderich, *Canada*	102	D3
Goderville, *France*	18	C7
Godfrey Ra., *Australia*	93	D2
Godhavn = Qeqertarsuaq, *Greenland*	4	C5
Godhra, *India*	68	H5
Gödöllő, *Hungary*	42	C4
Godoy Cruz, *Argentina*	126	C2
Gods ➤, *Canada*	102	A1
Gods L., *Canada*	102	B1
Gods River, *Canada*	105	C10
Godthåb = Nuuk, *Greenland*	101	B14
Godwin Austen = K2, *Pakistan*	69	B7

Goeie Hoop, Kaap die = Good Hope, C. of, *S. Africa*	88	E2
Goéland, L. au, *Canada*	102	C4
Goeree, *Neths.*	17	C3
Goes, *Neths.*	17	C3
Goffstown, *U.S.A.*	111	C13
Gogama, *Canada*	102	C3
Gogebic, L., *U.S.A.*	112	B10
Goggetti, *Ethiopia*	81	F4
Gogolin, *Poland*	45	H5
Gogonou, *Benin*	83	C5
Gogra = Ghaghara ➤, *India*	69	G11
Gogriâl, *Sudan*	81	F2
Gogti, *Ethiopia*	81	E5
Gohana, *India*	68	E7
Goharganj, *India*	68	H7
Goi ➤, *India*	68	H6
Goiânia, *Brazil*	125	G9
Goiás, *Brazil*	125	G8
Goiás □, *Brazil*	125	F9
Goio-Ere, *Brazil*	127	A5
Góis, *Portugal*	34	E2
Gojam □, *Ethiopia*	81	E4
Gojeb, Wabi ➤, *Ethiopia*	81	F4
Gojō, *Japan*	55	G7
Gojra, *Pakistan*	68	D5
Gökçeada, *Turkey*	41	F9
Gökçedağ, *Turkey*	39	B10
Gökçen, *Turkey*	39	C9
Gökçeören, *Turkey*	39	C10
Gökçeyazı, *Turkey*	39	B9
Gökırmak ➤, *Turkey*	72	B6
Gökova, *Turkey*	39	D10
Gökova Körfezi, *Turkey*	39	E9
Göksu ➤, *Turkey*	72	D6
Göksun, *Turkey*	72	C7
Gokteik, *Burma*	67	H20
Göktepe, *Turkey*	39	D10
Gokurt, *Pakistan*	68	E2
Gokwe, *Zimbabwe*	89	B4
Gol Gol, *Australia*	95	E3
Gola, *India*	69	E9
Golakganj, *India*	69	F13
Golan Heights = Hagolan, *Syria*	75	C4
Gołańcz, *Poland*	45	F4
Goläshkerd, *Iran*	71	E8
Golaya Pristen = Hola Pristan, *Ukraine*	47	J7
Gölbaşı, *Adiyaman, Turkey*	72	D7
Gölbaşı, *Ankara, Turkey*	72	C5
Golchikha, *Russia*	4	B12
Golconda, *U.S.A.*	114	F5
Gölcük, *Kocaeli, Turkey*	41	F13
Gölcük, *Niğde, Turkey*	72	C6
Gold, *U.S.A.*	110	E7
Gold Beach, *U.S.A.*	114	E1
Gold Coast, *W. Afr.*	83	E4
Gold Hill, *U.S.A.*	114	E2
Gold River, *Canada*	104	D3
Gołdap, *Poland*	44	D9
Goldberg, *Germany*	24	B8
Golden, *Canada*	104	C5
Golden B., *N.Z.*	91	J4
Golden Gate, *U.S.A.*	114	H2
Golden Hinde, *Canada*	104	D3
Golden Lake, *Canada*	110	A7
Golden Vale, *Ireland*	15	D3
Goldendale, *U.S.A.*	114	D3
Goldfield, *U.S.A.*	115	H5
Goldsand L., *Canada*	105	B8
Goldsboro, *U.S.A.*	109	H7
Goldsmith, *Australia*	92	D2
Goldsmith, *U.S.A.*	113	K3
Goldsworthy, *Australia*	92	D2
Goldthwaite, *U.S.A.*	113	K5
Golegã, *Portugal*	35	F2
Goleniów, *Poland*	44	E1
Golestānak, *Iran*	71	D7
Goleta, *U.S.A.*	117	L7
Golfito, *Costa Rica*	120	E3
Golfo Aranci, *Italy*	30	B2
Gölgeli Dağları, *Turkey*	39	D10
Goliad, *U.S.A.*	113	L6
Golija, *Montenegro, Yug.*	40	C2
Golija, *Serbia, Yug.*	40	C4
Golina, *Poland*	45	F5
Gölköy, *Turkey*	72	B7
Göllersdorf, *Austria*	26	C9
Gölmarmara, *Turkey*	39	C9
Golo ➤, *France*	21	F13
Gölova, *Turkey*	39	E12
Golpāyegān, *Iran*	71	C6
Gölpazarı, *Turkey*	72	B4
Golra, *Pakistan*	68	C5
Golspie, *U.K.*	14	D5
Golub-Dobrzyń, *Poland*	45	E6
Golubac, *Serbia, Yug.*	40	B5
Golyam Perelik, *Bulgaria*	41	E8
Golyama Kamchiya ➤, *Bulgaria*	41	C11
Goma, *Dem. Rep. of the Congo*	86	C2
Gomal Pass, *Pakistan*	68	D3
Gomati ➤, *India*	69	G10
Gombari, *Dem. Rep. of the Congo*	86	B2
Gombe, *Nigeria*	83	C7
Gömbe, *Turkey*	39	E11
Gombe □, *Nigeria*	83	C7
Gombe ➤, *Tanzania*	86	C3
Gombi, *Nigeria*	83	C7
Gomel = Homyel, *Belarus*	47	F6
Gomera, *Canary Is.*	37	F2
Gómez Palacio, *Mexico*	118	B4
Gomīshān, *Iran*	71	B7
Gommern, *Germany*	24	C7
Gomogomo, *Indonesia*	63	F8
Gomoh, *India*	67	H15

Gomotartsi, *Bulgaria*	40	B6
Gompa = Ganta, *Liberia*	82	D3
Gomphi, *Greece*	38	B3
Gonābād, *Iran*	71	C8
Gonaïves, *Haiti*	121	C5
Gonâve, G. de la, *Haiti*	121	C5
Gonâve, I. de la, *Haiti*	121	C5
Gonbad-e Kāvūs, *Iran*	71	B7
Gönc, *Hungary*	42	B6
Gonda, *India*	69	F9
Gondal, *India*	68	J4
Gonder, *Ethiopia*	81	E4
Gonder □, *Ethiopia*	81	E4
Gondia, *India*	66	J12
Gondola, *Mozam.*	87	F3
Gondomar, *Portugal*	34	D2
Gondrecourt-le-Château, *France*	19	D12
Gönen, *Balıkesir, Turkey*	41	F11
Gönen, *Isparta, Turkey*	39	D12
Gönen ➤, *Turkey*	41	F11
Gong Xian, *China*	58	C5
Gong'an, *China*	59	B9
Gongcheng, *China*	59	E8
Gongga Shan, *China*	58	C3
Gonggar, *China*	58	G7
Gonghe, *China*	60	C5
Gongola ➤, *Nigeria*	83	D7
Gongolgon, *Australia*	95	E4
Gongshan, *China*	58	D2
Gongtan, *China*	58	C7
Gongzhuling, *China*	57	C13
Goniadz, *Poland*	44	E9
Goniri, *Nigeria*	83	C7
Gonjo, *China*	58	B2
Gonnesa, *Italy*	30	C1
Gonnosfanàdiga, *Italy*	30	C1
Gonzales, *Calif., U.S.A.*	116	J5
Gonzales, *Tex., U.S.A.*	113	L6
González Chaves, *Argentina*	126	D3
Good Hope, C. of, *S. Africa*	88	E2
Gooderham, *Canada*	110	B6
Goodhouse, *S. Africa*	88	D2
Gooding, *U.S.A.*	114	E6
Goodland, *U.S.A.*	112	F4
Goodlow, *Canada*	104	B4
Goodooga, *Australia*	95	D4
Goodsprings, *U.S.A.*	117	K11
Goole, *U.K.*	12	D7
Goolgowi, *Australia*	95	E4
Goolwa, *Australia*	95	F2
Goomalling, *Australia*	93	F2
Goomeri, *Australia*	95	D5
Goondiwindi, *Australia*	95	D5
Goongarrie, L., *Australia*	93	F3
Goonyella, *Australia*	94	C4
Goose ➤, *Canada*	103	B7
Goose Creek, *U.S.A.*	109	J5
Goose L., *U.S.A.*	114	F3
Gop, *India*	66	H6
Gopalganj, *India*	69	F11
Göppingen, *Germany*	25	G5
Gor, *Spain*	35	H8
Góra, *Dolnośląsk, Poland*	45	G3
Góra, *Mazowieckie, Poland*	45	F7
Góra Kalwaria, *Poland*	45	G8
Gorakhpur, *India*	69	F10
Goražde, *Bos.-H.*	42	G3
Gorbatov, *Russia*	48	B6
Gorbea, Peña, *Spain*	32	B2
Gorda, *U.S.A.*	116	K5
Gorda, Pta., *Canary Is.*	37	F2
Gorda, Pta., *Nic.*	120	D3
Gordan B., *Australia*	92	B5
Gördes, *Turkey*	39	C10
Gordon, *U.S.A.*	112	D3
Gordon ➤, *Australia*	94	G4
Gordon L., *Alta., Canada*	105	B6
Gordon L., *N.W.T., Canada*	104	A6
Gordonvale, *Australia*	94	B4
Gore, *Ethiopia*	81	F4
Gore, *N.Z.*	91	M2
Gore Bay, *Canada*	102	C3
Görele, *Turkey*	73	B8
Goreme, *Turkey*	72	C6
Gorey, *Ireland*	15	D5
Gorg, *Iran*	71	D8
Gorgān, *Iran*	71	B7
Gorgona, *Italy*	28	E6
Gorgona, I., *Colombia*	124	C3
Gorgora, *Ethiopia*	81	E4
Gorgoram, *Nigeria*	83	C7
Gorham, *U.S.A.*	111	B13
Gori, *Georgia*	49	J7
Goriganga ➤, *India*	69	E9
Gorinchem, *Neths.*	17	C4
Goris, *Armenia*	73	C12
Goritsy, *Russia*	46	D9
Gorízia, *Italy*	29	C10
Gorj □, *Romania*	43	E8
Gorki = Horki, *Belarus*	46	E6
Gorkiy = Nizhniy Novgorod, *Russia*	48	B7
Gorkovskoye Vdkhr., *Russia*	48	B6
Gorlice, *Poland*	45	J8
Görlitz, *Germany*	24	D10
Gorlovka = Horlivka, *Ukraine*	47	H10
Gorna Dzhumayo = Blagoevgrad, *Bulgaria*	40	D7
Gorna Oryakhovitsa, *Bulgaria*	41	C9
Gornja Radgona, *Slovenia*	29	B13
Gornja Tuzla, *Bos.-H.*	42	F3
Gornji Grad, *Slovenia*	29	B11

Gornji Milanovac, *Serbia, Yug.*	40	B4
Gornji Vakuf, *Bos.-H.*	42	G2
Gorno Ablanovo, *Bulgaria*	41	C9
Gorno-Altay □, *Russia*	50	D9
Gorno-Altaysk, *Russia*	50	D9
Gornyatskiy, *Russia*	49	F5
Gornyy, *Saratov, Russia*	48	E9
Gornyy, *Sib., Russia*	54	B6
Gorodenka = Horodenka, *Ukraine*	47	H3
Gorodets, *Russia*	48	B6
Gorodishche = Horodyshche, *Ukraine*	47	H6
Gorodishche, *Russia*	48	D7
Gorodnya = Horodnya, *Ukraine*	47	G6
Gorodok = Haradok, *Belarus*	46	E6
Gorodok = Horodok, *Ukraine*	47	H2
Gorodovikovsk, *Russia*	49	G5
Gorokhov = Horokhiv, *Ukraine*	47	G3
Gorokhovets, *Russia*	48	B6
Gorom Gorom, *Burkina Faso*	83	C4
Goromonzi, *Zimbabwe*	87	F3
Gorong, Kepulauan, *Indonesia*	63	E8
Gorongose ➤, *Mozam.*	89	C5
Gorongoza, *Mozam.*	87	F3
Gorongoza, Sa. da, *Mozam.*	87	F3
Gorontalo, *Indonesia*	63	D6
Goronyo, *Nigeria*	83	C6
Górowo Iławeckie, *Poland*	44	D7
Gorron, *France*	18	D6
Gorshechnoye, *Russia*	47	G10
Gort, *Ireland*	15	C3
Gortis, *Greece*	36	D6
Góry Bystrzyckie, *Poland*	45	H3
Gorzkowice, *Poland*	45	G6
Górzno, *Poland*	45	E6
Gorzów Śląski, *Poland*	45	G5
Gorzów Wielkopolski, *Poland*	45	F2
Gosford, *Australia*	95	E5
Goshen, *Calif., U.S.A.*	116	J7
Goshen, *Ind., U.S.A.*	108	E3
Goshen, *N.Y., U.S.A.*	111	E10
Goshogawara, *Japan*	54	D10
Goslar, *Germany*	24	D6
Gospič, *Croatia*	29	D12
Gosport, *U.K.*	13	G6
Gossas, *Senegal*	82	C1
Gosse ➤, *Australia*	94	B1
Gossi, *Mali*	83	B4
Gossinga, *Sudan*	81	F2
Gostivar, *Macedonia*	40	E4
Gostyń, *Poland*	45	G4
Gostynin, *Poland*	45	F6
Göta älv ➤, *Sweden*	11	G5
Göta kanal, *Sweden*	11	F9
Götaland, *Sweden*	11	G8
Göteborg, *Sweden*	11	G5
Göteborgs och Bohus län □, *Sweden*	11	F5
Götene, *Sweden*	11	F7
Goteşti, *Moldova*	43	D13
Gotha, *Germany*	24	E6
Gothenburg = Göteborg, *Sweden*	11	G5
Gothenburg, *U.S.A.*	112	E4
Göthèye, *Niger*	83	C5
Gotland, *Sweden*	11	G12
Gotlands län □, *Sweden*	11	G12
Gotō-Rettō, *Japan*	55	H4
Gotse Delchev, *Bulgaria*	40	E7
Gotska Sandön, *Sweden*	9	G18
Götsu, *Japan*	55	G6
Gott Pk., *Canada*	104	C4
Góttero, Monte, *Italy*	28	D6
Göttingen, *Germany*	24	D5
Gottwald = Zmiyev, *Ukraine*	47	H9
Gottwaldov = Zlín, *Czech Rep.*	27	B10
Goubangzi, *China*	57	D11
Gouda, *Neths.*	17	B4
Goúdhoura, Ákra, *Greece*	36	E8
Goudiry, *Senegal*	82	C2
Goudoumaria, *Niger*	83	C7
Gouéké, *Guinea*	82	D3
Gough I., *Atl. Oc.*	2	G9
Gouin, Rés., *Canada*	102	C5
Gouitafla, *Ivory C.*	82	D3
Goulburn, *Australia*	95	E4
Goulburn Is., *Australia*	94	A1
Goulia, *Ivory C.*	82	C3
Goulimine, *Morocco*	78	C3
Goumbou, *Mali*	82	B3
Gouménissa, *Greece*	40	F6
Goundam, *Mali*	82	B4
Goúra, *Greece*	38	D4
Gourbassi, *Mali*	82	C2
Gourdon, *France*	20	D5
Gouré, *Niger*	83	C7
Gourin, *France*	18	D3
Gourits ➤, *S. Africa*	88	E3
Gourma-Rharous, *Mali*	83	B4
Goúrnais, *Greece*	36	D7
Gournay-en-Bray, *France*	19	C8
Goursi, *Burkina Faso*	82	C4
Gouverneur, *U.S.A.*	111	B9
Gouviá, *Greece*	36	A3
Gouzon, *France*	19	F9
Governador Valadares, *Brazil*	125	G10
Governor's Harbour, *Bahamas*	120	A4
Govindgarh, *India*	69	G9

Gowan Ra., *Australia*	94	D4
Gowanda, *U.S.A.*	110	D6
Gowd-e Zirreh, *Afghan.*	66	E3
Gower, *U.K.*	13	F3
Gowna, L., *Ireland*	15	C4
Goya, *Argentina*	126	B4
Göyçay, *Azerbaijan*	49	K8
Goyder Lagoon, *Australia*	95	D2
Goyllarisquisga, *Peru*	124	F3
Göynük, *Antalya, Turkey*	39	E12
Göynük, *Bolu, Turkey*	72	B4
Goz Beïda, *Chad*	79	F10
Goz Regeb, *Sudan*	81	D4
Gozo, *Malta*	36	C1
Gozdnica, *Poland*	45	G2
Graaff-Reinet, *S. Africa*	88	E3
Grabo, *Ivory C.*	82	D3
Grabow, *Germany*	24	B7
Grabów nad Prosną, *Poland*	45	G5
Gračac, *Croatia*	29	D12
Gračanica, *Bos.-H.*	42	F3
Graçay, *France*	19	E8
Gracias a Dios, C., *Honduras*	120	D3
Graciosa, I., *Canary Is.*	37	F6
Grad Sofiya □, *Bulgaria*	40	D7
Gradac, *Montenegro, Yug.*	40	C3
Gradačac, *Bos.-H.*	42	F3
Gradeška Planina, *Macedonia*	40	E6
Gradets, *Bulgaria*	41	D10
Gradište, *Croatia*	29	B12
Grădiştea de Munte, *Romania*	43	E8
Grado, *Italy*	29	C10
Grado, *Spain*	34	B4
Grady, *U.S.A.*	113	H3
Graeca, Lacul, *Romania*	43	F11
Grafenau, *Germany*	25	G9
Gräfenberg, *Germany*	25	F7
Grafham Water, *U.K.*	13	E7
Grafton, *Australia*	95	D5
Grafton, *N. Dak., U.S.A.*	112	A6
Grafton, *W. Va., U.S.A.*	108	F5
Graham, *Canada*	102	C1
Graham, *U.S.A.*	113	J5
Graham, Mt., *U.S.A.*	115	K9
Graham Bell, Ostrov = Greem-Bell, Ostrov, *Russia*	50	A7
Graham I., *B.C., Canada*	104	C2
Graham I., *N.W.T., Canada*	100	C6
Graham Land, *Antarctica*	5	C17
Grahamstown, *S. Africa*	88	E4
Grahamsville, *U.S.A.*	111	E10
Grahovo, *Montenegro, Yug.*	40	D2
Graie, Alpi, *Europe*	21	C11
Grain Coast, *W. Afr.*	82	E3
Grajaú, *Brazil*	125	E9
Grajaú ➤, *Brazil*	125	D10
Grajewo, *Poland*	44	E9
Gramada, *Bulgaria*	40	C6
Gramat, *France*	20	D5
Grammichele, *Italy*	31	E7
Grámmos, Óros, *Greece*	40	F4
Grampian Highlands = Grampian Mts., *U.K.*	14	E5
Grampian Mts., *U.K.*	14	E5
Grampians, The, *Australia*	95	F3
Gramsh, *Albania*	40	F4
Gran Canaria, *Canary Is.*	37	G4
Gran Chaco, *S. Amer.*	126	B3
Gran Paradiso, *Italy*	28	C4
Gran Sasso d'Itália, *Italy*	29	F10
Granada, *Nic.*	120	D2
Granada, *Spain*	35	H7
Granada, *U.S.A.*	113	F3
Granada □, *Spain*	35	H7
Granadilla de Abona, *Canary Is.*	37	F3
Granard, *Ireland*	15	C4
Granbury, *U.S.A.*	113	J6
Granby, *Canada*	102	C5
Granby, *U.S.A.*	114	F11
Grand ➤, *Canada*	110	D5
Grand ➤, *Mo., U.S.A.*	112	F8
Grand ➤, *S. Dak., U.S.A.*	112	C4
Grand Bahama, *Bahamas*	120	A4
Grand Bank, *Canada*	103	C8
Grand Bassam, *Ivory C.*	82	D4
Grand Béréby, *Ivory C.*	82	E3
Grand-Bourg, *Guadeloupe*	121	C7
Grand Canal = Yun Ho ➤, *China*	57	E9
Grand Canyon, *U.S.A.*	115	H7
Grand Canyon National Park, *U.S.A.*	115	H7
Grand Cayman, *Cayman Is.*	120	C3
Grand Centre, *Canada*	105	C6
Grand Coulee, *U.S.A.*	114	C4
Grand Coulee Dam, *U.S.A.*	114	C4
Grand Erg du Bilma, *Niger*	79	D8
Grand Erg Occidental, *Algeria*	78	B6
Grand Erg Oriental, *Algeria*	78	B7
Grand Falls, *Canada*	103	C6
Grand Falls-Windsor, *Canada*	103	C8
Grand Forks, *Canada*	104	D5
Grand Forks, *U.S.A.*	112	B6
Grand Gorge, *U.S.A.*	111	D10
Grand Haven, *U.S.A.*	108	D2
Grand I., *Mich., U.S.A.*	108	B2
Grand I., *N.Y., U.S.A.*	110	D6
Grand Island, *U.S.A.*	112	E5
Grand Isle, *La., U.S.A.*	113	L9
Grand Isle, *Vt., U.S.A.*	111	B11
Grand Junction, *U.S.A.*	115	G9
Grand L., *N.B., Canada*	103	C6

Grand L., Nfld., Canada 103 C8
Grand L., Nfld., Canada 103 B7
Grand L., U.S.A. 113 L8
Grand Lahou, Ivory C. 82 D3
Grand Lake, U.S.A. 114 F11
Grand-Lieu, L. de, France 18 E5
Grand Manan I., Canada 103 D6
Grand Marais, Canada 112 B9
Grand Marais, U.S.A. 108 B3
Grand-Mère, Canada 102 C5
Grand Popo, Benin 83 D5
Grand Portage, U.S.A. 112 B10
Grand Prairie, U.S.A. 113 J6
Grand Rapids, Canada 105 C9
Grand Rapids, Mich., U.S.A. 108 D2
Grand Rapids, Minn., U.S.A. 112 B8
Grand St-Bernard, Col du, Europe 25 K3
Grand Teton, U.S.A. 114 E8
Grand Teton National Park, U.S.A. 114 D8
Grand Union Canal, U.K. 13 E7
Grand View, Canada 105 C8
Grandas de Salime, Spain 34 B4
Grande →, Jujuy, Argentina 126 A2
Grande →, Mendoza, Argentina 126 D2
Grande →, Bolivia 124 G6
Grande →, Bahia, Brazil 125 F10
Grande →, Minas Gerais, Brazil 125 H8
Grande, B., Argentina 128 G3
Grande, Rio →, U.S.A. 113 N6
Grande Baleine, R. de la →, Canada 102 A4
Grande Cache, Canada 104 C5
Grande-Entrée, Canada 103 C7
Grande Prairie, Canada 104 B5
Grande-Rivière, Canada 103 C7
Grande-Vallée, Canada 103 C6
Grandfalls, U.S.A. 113 K3
Grândola, Portugal 35 G2
Grandpré, France 19 C11
Grandview, U.S.A. 114 C4
Grandvilliers, France 19 C8
Graneros, Chile 126 C1
Grangemouth, U.K. 14 E5
Granger, U.S.A. 114 F9
Grängesberg, Sweden 10 D9
Grangeville, U.S.A. 114 D5
Granisle, Canada 104 C3
Granite City, U.S.A. 112 F9
Granite Falls, U.S.A. 112 C7
Granite L., Canada 103 C8
Granite Mt., U.S.A. 117 M10
Granite Pk., U.S.A. 114 D9
Graniteville, U.S.A. 111 B12
Granitola, C., Italy 30 E5
Granity, N.Z. 91 J3
Granja, Brazil 125 D10
Granja de Moreruela, Spain 34 D5
Granja de Torrehermosa, Spain 35 G5
Gränna, Sweden 11 F8
Granollers, Spain 32 D7
Gransee, Germany 24 B9
Grant, U.S.A. 112 E4
Grant, Mt., U.S.A. 114 G4
Grant City, U.S.A. 112 E7
Grant I., Australia 92 B5
Grant Range, U.S.A. 115 G6
Grantham, U.K. 12 E7
Grantown-on-Spey, U.K. 14 D5
Grants, U.S.A. 115 J10
Grants Pass, U.S.A. 114 E2
Grantsville, U.S.A. 114 F7
Granville, France 18 D5
Granville, N. Dak., U.S.A. 112 A4
Granville, N.Y., U.S.A. 111 C11
Granville, Ohio, U.S.A. 110 F2
Granville L., Canada 105 B8
Graskop, S. Africa 89 C5
Gräsö, Sweden 10 D12
Grass →, Canada 105 B9
Grass Range, U.S.A. 114 C9
Grass River Prov. Park, Canada 105 C8
Grass Valley, Calif., U.S.A. 116 F6
Grass Valley, Oreg., U.S.A. 114 D3
Grassano, Italy 31 B9
Grasse, France 21 E10
Grassflat, U.S.A. 110 F6
Grasslands Nat. Park, Canada 105 D7
Grassy, Australia 94 G3
Gråsten, Denmark 11 K3
Grästorp, Sweden 11 F6
Gratkorn, Austria 26 D8
Graubünden □, Switz. 25 J5
Graulhet, France 20 E5
Graus, Spain 32 C5
Grave, Pte. de, France 20 C2
Gravelbourg, Canada 105 D7
Gravelines, France 19 A9
's-Gravenhage, Neths. 17 B4
Gravenhurst, Canada 102 D4
Gravesend, Australia 95 D5
Gravesend, U.K. 13 F8
Gravina in Púglia, Italy 31 B9
Gravois, Pointe-à-, Haiti 121 C5
Gravone →, France 21 G12
Gray, France 19 E12
Grayling, U.S.A. 108 C3
Grays Harbor, U.S.A. 114 C1
Grays L., U.S.A. 114 E8
Grays River, U.S.A. 116 D3
Grayvoron, Russia 47 G8
Graz, Austria 26 D8
Grdelica, Serbia, Yug. 40 D6
Greasy L., Canada 104 A4
Great Abaco I., Bahamas 120 A4
Great Artesian Basin, Australia 94 C3
Great Australian Bight, Australia 93 F5
Great Bahama Bank, Bahamas 120 B4
Great Barrier I., N.Z. 91 G5
Great Barrier Reef, Australia 94 B4
Great Barrington, U.S.A. 111 D11
Great Basin, U.S.A. 114 G5
Great Basin Nat. Park, U.S.A. 114 G6
Great Bear →, Canada 100 B7
Great Bear L., Canada 100 B7
Great Belt = Store Bælt, Denmark 11 J4
Great Bend, Kans., U.S.A. 112 F5
Great Bend, Pa., U.S.A. 111 E9
Great Blasket I., Ireland 15 D1
Great Britain, Europe 6 E5
Great Codroy, Canada 103 C8
Great Dividing Ra., Australia 94 C4
Great Driffield = Driffield, U.K. 12 C7
Great Exuma I., Bahamas 120 B4
Great Falls, U.S.A. 114 C8
Great Fish = Groot Vis →, S. Africa 88 E4
Great Guana Cay, Bahamas 120 B4
Great Inagua I., Bahamas 121 B5
Great Indian Desert = Thar Desert, India 68 F5
Great Karoo, S. Africa 88 E3
Great Lake, Australia 94 G4
Great Lakes, N. Amer. 98 E11
Great Malvern, U.K. 13 E5
Great Miami →, U.S.A. 108 F3
Great Ormes Head, U.K. 12 D4
Great Ouse →, U.K. 12 E8
Great Palm I., Australia 94 B4
Great Plains, N. Amer. 106 A6
Great Ruaha →, Tanzania 86 D4
Great Sacandaga Res., U.S.A. 111 C10
Great Saint Bernard Pass = Grand St-Bernard, Col du, Europe 25 K3
Great Salt L., U.S.A. 114 F7
Great Salt Lake Desert, U.S.A. 114 F7
Great Salt Plains L., U.S.A. 113 G5
Great Sandy Desert, Australia 92 D3
Great Sangi = Sangihe, Pulau, Indonesia 63 D7
Great Scarcies →, S. Leone 82 D2
Great Skellig, Ireland 15 E1
Great Slave L., Canada 104 A5
Great Smoky Mts. Nat. Park, U.S.A. 109 H4
Great Snow Mt., Canada 104 B4
Great Stour = Stour →, U.K. 13 F9
Great Victoria Desert, Australia 93 E4
Great Wall, China 56 E5
Great Whernside, U.K. 12 C6
Great Yarmouth, U.K. 13 E9
Greater Antilles, W. Indies 121 C5
Greater London □, U.K. 13 F7
Greater Manchester □, U.K. 12 D5
Greater Sunda Is., Indonesia 62 F4
Grebbestad, Sweden 11 F5
Grebenka = Hrebenka, Ukraine 47 G7
Greco, C., Cyprus 36 E13
Greco, Mte., Italy 29 G10
Gredos, Sierra de, Spain 34 E6
Greece, U.S.A. 110 C7
Greece ■, Europe 38 B3
Greeley, Colo., U.S.A. 112 E2
Greeley, Nebr., U.S.A. 112 E5
Greem-Bell, Ostrov, Russia 50 A7
Green, U.S.A. 114 E2
Green →, Ky., U.S.A. 108 G2
Green →, Utah, U.S.A. 115 G9
Green B., U.S.A. 108 C2
Green Bay, U.S.A. 108 C2
Green C., Australia 95 F5
Green Cove Springs, U.S.A. 109 L5
Green Lake, Canada 105 C7
Green Mts., U.S.A. 111 C12
Green River, Utah, U.S.A. 115 G8
Green River, Wyo., U.S.A. 114 F9
Green Valley, U.S.A. 115 L8
Greenbank, U.S.A. 116 B4
Greenbush, Mich., U.S.A. 110 B1
Greenbush, Minn., U.S.A. 112 A6
Greencastle, U.S.A. 108 F2
Greene, U.S.A. 111 D9
Greenfield, Calif., U.S.A. 116 J5
Greenfield, Calif., U.S.A. 117 K8
Greenfield, Ind., U.S.A. 108 F3
Greenfield, Iowa, U.S.A. 112 E7
Greenfield, Mass., U.S.A. 111 D12
Greenfield, Mo., U.S.A. 113 G8
Greenfield Park, Canada 111 A11
Greenland ■, N. Amer. 4 C5
Greenland Sea, Arctic 4 B7
Greenock, U.K. 14 F4
Greenore, Ireland 15 B5
Greenore Pt., Ireland 15 D5
Greenough, Australia 93 E1
Greenough →, Australia 93 E1
Greenough Pt., Canada 110 B3
Greenport, U.S.A. 111 E12
Greensboro, Ga., U.S.A. 109 J4
Greensboro, N.C., U.S.A. 109 G6
Greensboro, Vt., U.S.A. 111 B12
Greensburg, Ind., U.S.A. 108 F3
Greensburg, Kans., U.S.A. 113 G5
Greensburg, Pa., U.S.A. 110 F5
Greenstone Pt., U.K. 14 D3
Greenvale, Australia 94 B4
Greenville, Liberia 82 D3
Greenville, Ala., U.S.A. 109 K2
Greenville, Calif., U.S.A. 116 E6
Greenville, Maine, U.S.A. 109 C11
Greenville, Mich., U.S.A. 108 D3
Greenville, Miss., U.S.A. 113 J9
Greenville, Mo., U.S.A. 113 G9
Greenville, N.C., U.S.A. 109 H7
Greenville, N.H., U.S.A. 111 D13
Greenville, N.Y., U.S.A. 111 D10
Greenville, Ohio, U.S.A. 108 E3
Greenville, Pa., U.S.A. 110 E4
Greenville, S.C., U.S.A. 109 H4
Greenville, Tenn., U.S.A. 109 G4
Greenville, Tex., U.S.A. 113 J6
Greenwater Lake Prov. Park, Canada 105 C8
Greenwich, U.K. 13 F8
Greenwich, Conn., U.S.A. 111 E11
Greenwich, N.Y., U.S.A. 111 C11
Greenwich, Ohio, U.S.A. 110 E2
Greenwood, Canada 104 D5
Greenwood, Ark., U.S.A. 113 H7
Greenwood, Ind., U.S.A. 108 F2
Greenwood, Miss., U.S.A. 113 J9
Greenwood, S.C., U.S.A. 109 H4
Greenwood, Mt., Australia 92 B5
Gregbe, Ivory C. 82 D3
Gregory, U.S.A. 112 D5
Gregory →, Australia 94 B2
Gregory, L., S. Austral., Australia 95 D2
Gregory, L., W. Austral., Australia 93 E2
Gregory Downs, Australia 94 B2
Gregory L., Australia 92 D4
Gregory Ra., Queens., Australia 94 B3
Gregory Ra., W. Austral., Australia 92 D3
Greiffenberg, Germany 24 B9
Greifswald, Germany 24 A9
Greifswalder Bodden, Germany 24 A9
Grein, Austria 26 C7
Greiz, Germany 24 E8
Gremikha, Russia 50 C4
Grenå, Denmark 11 H4
Grenada, U.S.A. 113 J10
Grenada ■, W. Indies 121 D7
Grenade, France 20 E5
Grenadier I., U.S.A. 111 B8
Grenadines, W. Indies 121 D7
Grenchen, Switz. 25 H3
Grenen, Denmark 11 G4
Grenfell, Australia 95 E4
Grenfell, Canada 105 C8
Grenoble, France 21 C9
Grenville, C., Australia 94 A3
Grenville Chan., Canada 104 C3
Gréoux-les-Bains, France 21 E9
Gresham, U.S.A. 116 E4
Gresik, Indonesia 63 G15
Gretna, U.K. 14 F5
Greven, Germany 24 C3
Grevená, Greece 40 F5
Grevená □, Greece 40 F5
Grevenbroich, Germany 24 D2
Grevenmacher, Lux. 17 E6
Grevesmühlen, Germany 24 B7
Grevestrand, Denmark 11 J6
Grey →, Canada 103 C8
Grey →, N.Z. 91 K3
Grey, C., Australia 94 A2
Grey Ra., Australia 95 D3
Greybull, U.S.A. 114 D9
Greymouth, N.Z. 91 K3
Greystones, Ireland 15 C5
Greytown, N.Z. 91 J5
Greytown, S. Africa 89 D5
Gribanovskiy, Russia 48 E5
Gribbell I., Canada 104 C3
Gribës, Mal i, Albania 40 F3
Gridley, U.S.A. 116 F5
Griekwastad, S. Africa 88 D3
Griesheim, Germany 25 F4
Grieskirchen, Austria 26 C6
Griffin, U.S.A. 109 J3
Griffith, Australia 95 E4
Griffith, Canada 110 A7
Griffith I., Canada 110 B4
Grignols, France 20 D3
Grigoriopol, Moldova 43 C14
Grimaylov = Hrymayliv, Ukraine 47 H4
Grimes, U.S.A. 116 F5
Grimma, Germany 24 D8
Grimmen, Germany 24 A9
Grimsay, U.K. 14 D1
Grimsby, Canada 110 C5
Grimsby, U.K. 12 D7
Grímsey, Iceland 8 C5
Grimshaw, Canada 104 B5
Grimslöv, Sweden 11 H8
Grimstad, Norway 9 G13
Grindelwald, Switz. 25 J4
Grindsted, Denmark 11 J2
Grindstone I., Canada 111 B8
Grindu, Romania 43 F11
Grinnell, U.S.A. 112 E8
Grintavec, Slovenia 29 B11
Gris-Nez, C., France 19 B8
Grisolles, France 20 E5
Grisons = Graubünden □, Switz. 25 J5
Grisslehamn, Sweden 10 D12
Grmeč Planina, Bos.-H. 29 D13
Groais I., Canada 103 B8
Grobiņa, Latvia 44 B8
Groblersdal, S. Africa 89 D4
Grobming, Austria 26 D6
Grocka, Serbia, Yug. 40 B4
Gródek, Poland 45 E10
Grodków, Poland 45 H4
Grodno = Hrodna, Belarus 46 F2
Grodzisk Mazowiecki, Poland 45 F7
Grodzisk Wielkopolski, Poland 45 F3
Grodzyanka = Hrodzyanka, Belarus 46 F5
Groesbeck, U.S.A. 113 K6
Groix, France 18 E3
Groix, Î. de, France 18 E3
Grójec, Poland 45 G7
Gronau, Niedersachsen, Germany 24 C5
Gronau, Nordrhein-Westfalen, Germany 24 C3
Grong, Norway 8 D15
Grönhögen, Sweden 11 H10
Groningen, Neths. 17 A6
Groningen □, Neths. 17 A6
Groom, U.S.A. 113 H4
Groot →, S. Africa 88 E3
Groot Berg →, S. Africa 88 E2
Groot-Brakrivier, S. Africa 88 E3
Groot Karasberge, Namibia 88 D2
Groot-Kei →, S. Africa 89 E4
Groot Vis →, S. Africa 88 E4
Grootdrink, S. Africa 88 D3
Groote Eylandt, Australia 94 A2
Grootfontein, Namibia 88 B2
Grootlaagte →, Africa 88 C3
Grootvloer →, S. Africa 88 E3
Gros C., Canada 104 A6
Gros Morne Nat. Park, Canada 103 C8
Grósio, Italy 28 B7
Grosne →, France 19 F11
Grossa, Pta., Spain 37 B8
Grossenbrode, Germany 24 A7
Grossenhain, Germany 24 D9
Grosser Arber, Germany 25 F9
Grosser Plöner See, Germany 24 A6
Grosseto, Italy 29 F8
Grossgerungs, Austria 26 C7
Grossglockner, Austria 26 D5
Groswater B., Canada 103 B8
Groton, Conn., U.S.A. 111 E12
Groton, N.Y., U.S.A. 111 D8
Groton, S. Dak., U.S.A. 112 C5
Grottáglie, Italy 31 B10
Grottaminarda, Italy 31 A8
Grottammare, Italy 29 F10
Grouard Mission, Canada 104 B5
Grouin, Pte. du, France 18 D5
Groundhog →, Canada 102 C3
Grouw, Neths. 17 A5
Grove City, U.S.A. 110 E4
Grove Hill, U.S.A. 109 K2
Groveland, U.S.A. 116 H6
Grover City, U.S.A. 117 K6
Groves, U.S.A. 113 L8
Groveton, U.S.A. 111 B13
Grožnjan, Croatia 29 C10
Groznyy, Russia 49 J7
Grubišno Polje, Croatia 42 E2
Grudovo, Bulgaria 41 D11
Grudusk, Poland 45 E7
Grudziądz, Poland 44 E5
Gruinard B., U.K. 14 D3
Gruissan, France 20 E7
Grumo Áppula, Italy 31 A9
Grums, Sweden 10 E7
Grünberg, Germany 24 E4
Gründau, Germany 25 E5
Grundy Center, U.S.A. 112 D8
Grünstadt, Germany 25 F4
Gruvberget, Sweden 10 C10
Gruver, U.S.A. 113 G4
Gruyères, Switz. 25 J3
Gruža, Serbia, Yug. 40 C4
Gryazi, Russia 47 F10
Gryazovets, Russia 46 C11
Grybów, Poland 45 J7
Grycksbo, Sweden 10 D9
Gryfice, Poland 44 E2
Gryfino, Poland 45 E1
Gryfów Śląski, Poland 45 G2
Grythyttan, Sweden 10 E8
Gstaad, Switz. 25 J3
Gua, India 67 H14
Gua Musang, Malaysia 65 K3
Guacanayabo, G. de, Cuba 120 B4
Guachípas →, Argentina 126 B2
Guadajoz →, Spain 35 H6
Guadalajara, Mexico 118 C4
Guadalajara, Spain 32 E1
Guadalajara □, Spain 32 E2
Guadalcanal, Solomon Is. 96 H8
Guadalcanal, Spain 35 G5
Guadalén →, Spain 35 G7
Guadales, Argentina 126 C2
Guadalete →, Spain 35 J4
Guadalimar →, Spain 35 G7
Guadalmena →, Spain 35 G8
Guadalmez →, Spain 35 G5
Guadalope →, Spain 32 D4
Guadalquivir →, Spain 35 J4
Guadalupe = Guadeloupe ■, W. Indies 121 C7
Guadalupe, Mexico 117 N10
Guadalupe, Spain 35 F5
Guadalupe, U.S.A. 117 L6
Guadalupe →, Mexico 117 N10
Guadalupe →, U.S.A. 113 L6
Guadalupe, Sierra de, Spain 35 F5
Guadalupe Bravos, Mexico 118 A3
Guadalupe I., Pac. Oc. 98 G8
Guadalupe Mts. Nat. Park, U.S.A. 113 K2
Guadalupe Peak, U.S.A. 113 K2
Guadalupe y Calvo, Mexico 118 B3
Guadarrama, Sierra de, Spain 34 E7
Guadauta, Georgia 49 J5
Guadeloupe ■, W. Indies 121 C7
Guadeloupe Passage, W. Indies 121 C7
Guadiamar →, Spain 35 J4
Guadiana →, Portugal 35 H3
Guadiana Menor →, Spain 35 H7
Guadiaro →, Spain 35 J5
Guadiato →, Spain 35 H5
Guadiela →, Spain 32 E2
Guadix, Spain 35 H7
Guafo, Boca del, Chile 128 E2
Guainía →, Colombia 124 C5
Guaíra, Brazil 127 A5
Guaíra □, Paraguay 126 B4
Guaitecas, Is., Chile 128 E2
Guajará-Mirim, Brazil 124 F5
Guajira, Pen. de la, Colombia 124 A4
Gualán, Guatemala 120 C2
Gualdo Tadino, Italy 29 E9
Gualeguay, Argentina 126 C4
Gualeguaychú, Argentina 126 C4
Gualequay →, Argentina 126 C4
Guam ■, Pac. Oc. 96 F6
Guaminí, Argentina 126 D3
Guamúchil, Mexico 118 B3
Guanabacoa, Cuba 120 B3
Guanacaste, Cordillera del, Costa Rica 120 D2
Guanaceví, Mexico 118 B3
Guanahani = San Salvador I., Bahamas 121 B5
Guanajay, Cuba 120 B3
Guanajuato, Mexico 118 C4
Guanajuato □, Mexico 118 C4
Guandacol, Argentina 126 B2
Guane, Cuba 120 B3
Guang'an, China 58 B6
Guangchang, China 59 D11
Guangde, China 59 B12
Guangdong □, China 59 F9
Guangfeng, China 59 C12
Guanghan, China 58 B5
Guangling, China 56 E8
Guangnan, China 58 E5
Guangning, China 59 F9
Guangrao, China 57 F10
Guangshui, China 59 B9
Guangshun, China 58 D6
Guangwu, China 56 F3
Guangxi Zhuangzu Zizhiqu □, China 58 F7
Guangyuan, China 58 A5
Guangze, China 59 D11
Guangzhou, China 59 F9
Guanipa →, Venezuela 124 B6
Guanling, China 58 E5
Guannan, China 57 G10
Guantánamo, Cuba 121 B4
Guantao, China 56 F8
Guanyang, China 59 E8
Guanyun, China 57 G10
Guápiles, Costa Rica 120 D3
Guaporé, Brazil 127 B5
Guaporé →, Brazil 122 E4
Guaqui, Bolivia 124 G5
Guara, Sierra de, Spain 32 C4
Guarapari, Brazil 127 A7
Guarapuava, Brazil 127 B5
Guaratinguetá, Brazil 127 A6
Guaratuba, Brazil 127 B6
Guarda, Portugal 34 E3
Guarda □, Portugal 34 E3
Guardafui, C. = Asir, Ras, Somali Rep. 74 E5
Guardamar del Segura, Spain 33 G4
Guardavalle, Italy 31 D9
Guárdia Sanframondi, Italy 31 A7
Guardiagrele, Italy 29 F11
Guardo, Spain 34 C6
Guareña, Spain 35 G4
Guareña →, Spain 34 D5
Guárico □, Venezuela 124 B5
Guarujá, Brazil 127 A6
Guarus, Brazil 127 A7
Guasave, Mexico 118 B3
Guasdualito, Venezuela 124 B4
Guastalla, Italy 28 D7
Guatemala, Guatemala 120 D1
Guatemala ■, Cent. Amer. 120 C1
Guaviare →, Colombia 122 C4
Guaxupé, Brazil 127 A6
Guayama, Puerto Rico 121 C6
Guayaquil, Ecuador 124 D3
Guayaquil, G. de, Ecuador 122 D2
Guaymas, Mexico 118 B2
Guazhou, China 59 A12
Guba, Dem. Rep. of the Congo 87 E2
Guba, Ethiopia 81 E4
Gûbâl, Madîq, Egypt 80 B3
Gubat, Phil. 61 E6
Gúbbio, Italy 29 E9
Guben, Germany 24 D10
Gubin, Poland 45 G1
Gubio, Nigeria 83 C7
Gubkin, Russia 47 G9
Guča, Serbia, Yug. 40 C4

Gucheng, *China* 59 A8
Gudata = Guadauta, *Georgia* 49 J5
Gudbrandsdalen, *Norway* .. 9 F14
Guddu Barrage, *Pakistan* . 66 E6
Gudenå →, *Denmark* 11 H4
Gudermes, *Russia* 49 J8
Gudhjem, *Denmark* 11 J8
Gudivada, *India* 67 L12
Gudur, *India* 66 M11
Guebwiller, *France* 19 E14
Guecho = Getxo, *Spain* .. 32 B2
Guékédou, *Guinea* 82 D2
Guéle Mendouka, *Cameroon* 83 E7
Guelph, *Canada* 102 D3
Guémené-Penfao, *France* . 18 E5
Guémené-sur-Scorff, *France* 18 D3
Guéné, *Benin* 83 C5
Guer, *France* 18 E4
Guérande, *France* 18 E4
Guéret, *France* 19 F8
Guérigny, *France* 19 E10
Guerneville, *U.S.A.* 116 G4
Guernica = Gernika-Lumo, *Spain* 32 B2
Guernsey, *U.K.* 13 H5
Guernsey, *U.S.A.* 112 D2
Guerrero □, *Mexico* 119 D5
Guessou-Sud, *Benin* 83 C5
Gueugnon, *France* 19 F11
Guéyo, *Ivory C.* 82 D3
Gughe, *Ethiopia* 81 F4
Gügher, *Iran* 71 D8
Guglionesi, *Italy* 29 G11
Guhakolak, Tanjung, *Indonesia* 63 G11
Gui Jiang →, *China* 59 F8
Guia, *Canary Is.* 37 F4
Guia de Isora, *Canary Is.* .. 37 F3
Guia Lopes da Laguna, *Brazil* 127 A4
Guiana, *S. Amer.* 122 C4
Guibéroua, *Ivory C.* 82 D3
Guichi, *China* 59 B11
Guider, *Cameroon* 83 D7
Guidiguir, *Niger* 83 C6
Guidimouni, *Niger* 83 C6
Guiding, *China* 58 D6
Guidong, *China* 59 D9
Guidónia-Montecélio, *Italy* . 29 F9
Guiers, L. de, *Senegal* 82 B1
Guigang, *China* 58 F7
Guiglo, *Ivory C.* 82 D3
Guihulñgan, *Phil.* 61 F5
Guijá, *Mozam.* 89 C5
Guijuelo, *Spain* 34 E5
Guildford, *U.K.* 13 F7
Guilford, *U.S.A.* 111 E12
Guilin, *China* 59 E8
Guillaume-Delisle L., *Canada* 102 A4
Guillaumes, *France* 21 D10
Guillestre, *France* 21 D10
Guilvinec, *France* 18 E2
Güimar, *Canary Is.* 37 F3
Guimarães, *Portugal* 34 D2
Guimaras □, *Phil.* 61 F5
Guinda, *U.S.A.* 116 G4
Guinea, *Africa* 76 F4
Guinea ■, *W. Afr.* 82 C2
Guinea, Gulf of, *Atl. Oc.* .. 83 E5
Guinea-Bissau ■, *Africa* .. 82 C2
Güines, *Cuba* 120 B3
Guingamp, *France* 18 D3
Guinguinéo, *Senegal* 82 C1
Guipavas, *France* 18 D2
Guiping, *China* 59 F8
Guipúzcoa □, *Spain* 32 B2
Guir, *Mali* 82 B4
Guirel, *Mauritania* 82 B3
Güiria, *Venezuela* 124 A6
Guiscard, *France* 19 C10
Guise, *France* 19 C10
Guitiriz, *Spain* 34 B3
Guitri, *Ivory C.* 82 D3
Guiuan, *Phil.* 61 F6
Guixi, *China* 59 C11
Guiyang, *Guizhou, China* .. 58 D6
Guiyang, *Hunan, China* ... 59 E9
Guizhou □, *China* 58 D6
Gujan-Mestras, *France* ... 20 D2
Gujar Khan, *Pakistan* 68 C5
Gujarat □, *India* 68 H4
Gujiang, *China* 59 D10
Gujranwala, *Pakistan* 68 C6
Gujrat, *Pakistan* 68 C6
Gukovo, *Russia* 49 F5
Gulargambone, *Australia* .. 95 E4
Gulbarga, *India* 66 L10
Gulbene, *Latvia* 9 H22
Gulf, The, *Asia* 71 E6
Gulfport, *U.S.A.* 113 K10
Gulgong, *Australia* 95 E4
Gulin, *China* 58 C5
Gulistan, *Pakistan* 68 D2
Gull Lake, *Canada* 105 C7
Gullringen, *Sweden* 11 H6
Gullspång, *Sweden* 11 F8
Güllük, *Turkey* 39 D9
Güllük Korfezi, *Turkey* ... 39 D9
Gulma, *Nigeria* 83 C5
Gulmarg, *India* 69 B6
Gülnar, *Turkey* 72 D5
Gülpınar, *Turkey* 39 B8
Gülşehir, *Turkey* 72 C6
Gulshad, *Kazakstan* 50 E8
Gulu, *Uganda* 86 B3
Gülübovo, *Bulgaria* 41 D9
Gulud, J., *Sudan* 81 E2
Gulwe, *Tanzania* 86 D4

Gulyaypole = Hulyaypole, *Ukraine* 47 J9
Gumal →, *Pakistan* 68 D4
Gumbaz, *Pakistan* 68 D3
Gumel, *Nigeria* 83 C6
Gumiel de Hizán, *Spain* ... 34 D7
Gumla, *India* 69 H11
Gumlu, *Australia* 94 B4
Gumma □, *Japan* 55 F9
Gummersbach, *Germany* .. 24 D3
Gummi, *Nigeria* 83 C6
Gümüldür, *Turkey* 39 C9
Gümüşçay, *Turkey* 41 F11
Gümüşhacıköy, *Turkey* ... 72 B6
Gümüşhane, *Turkey* 73 B8
Gümüşsu, *Turkey* 39 C11
Gumzai, *Indonesia* 63 F8
Guna, *Ethiopia* 81 F4
Guna, *India* 68 G7
Gundelfingen, *Germany* .. 25 G6
Güney, *Burdur, Turkey* ... 39 D11
Güney, *Denizli, Turkey* ... 39 C11
Güneydoğu Toroslar, *Turkey* 73 C9
Gunisao →, *Canada* 105 C9
Gunisao L., *Canada* 105 C9
Gunjyal, *Pakistan* 68 C4
Günlüce, *Turkey* 39 E10
Gunnarskog, *Sweden* 10 E6
Gunnbjørn Fjeld, *Greenland* 4 C6
Gunnebo, *Sweden* 11 G10
Gunnedah, *Australia* 95 E5
Gunnewin, *Australia* 95 D4
Gunningbar Cr. →, *Australia* 95 E4
Gunnison, *Colo., U.S.A.* .. 115 G10
Gunnison, *Utah, U.S.A.* .. 114 G8
Gunnison →, *U.S.A.* 115 G9
Gunpowder, *Australia* 94 B2
Guntakal, *India* 66 M10
Guntersville, *U.S.A.* 109 H2
Guntong, *Malaysia* 65 K3
Guntur, *India* 67 L12
Gunungapi, *Indonesia* 63 F7
Gunungsitoli, *Indonesia* .. 62 D1
Günz →, *Germany* 25 G6
Gunza, *Angola* 84 G2
Günzburg, *Germany* 25 G6
Gunzenhausen, *Germany* . 25 F6
Guo He →, *China* 57 H9
Guoyang, *China* 56 H9
Gupis, *Pakistan* 69 A5
Gura Humorului, *Romania* . 43 C10
Gura-Teghii, *Romania* 43 E11
Gurag, *Ethiopia* 81 F4
Gurahonţ, *Romania* 42 D7
Gurdaspur, *India* 68 C6
Gurdon, *U.S.A.* 113 J8
Güre, *Balıkesir, Turkey* ... 39 B8
Güre, *Uşak, Turkey* 39 C11
Gurgaon, *India* 68 E7
Gürgentepe, *Turkey* 72 B7
Gurghiu, Munţii, *Romania* . 43 D10
Gurgueia →, *Brazil* 125 E10
Gurha, *India* 68 G4
Guri, Embalse de, *Venezuela* 124 B6
Gurin, *Nigeria* 83 D7
Gurjaani, *Georgia* 49 K7
Gurk →, *Austria* 26 E7
Gurkha, *Nepal* 69 E11
Gurley, *Australia* 95 D4
Gurnet Point, *U.S.A.* 111 D14
Gürpınar, *İst., Turkey* 41 F12
Gürpınar, *Van, Turkey* ... 73 C10
Gürsu, *Turkey* 41 F13
Gurué, *Mozam.* 87 F4
Gurun, *Malaysia* 65 K3
Gürün, *Turkey* 72 C7
Gurupá, *Brazil* 125 D8
Gurupá, I. Grande de, *Brazil* 125 D8
Gurupi, *Brazil* 125 F9
Gurupi →, *Brazil* 125 D9
Guruwe, *Zimbabwe* 89 B5
Guryev = Atyraū, *Kazakstan* 50 E6
Gusau, *Nigeria* 83 C6
Gusev, *Russia* 9 J20
Gushan, *China* 57 E12
Gushgy, *Turkmenistan* 50 F7
Gushi, *China* 59 A10
Gushiago, *Ghana* 83 D4
Gusinje, *Montenegro, Yug.* . 40 D3
Gusinoozersk, *Russia* 51 D11
Gúspini, *Italy* 30 C1
Güssing, *Austria* 27 D9
Gustavsberg, *Sweden* 10 E12
Gustavus, *U.S.A.* 104 B1
Gustine, *U.S.A.* 116 H6
Güstrow, *Germany* 24 B8
Gusum, *Sweden* 11 F10
Guta = Kolárovo, *Slovak Rep.* 27 D10
Gütersloh, *Germany* 24 D4
Gutha, *Australia* 93 E2
Guthalungra, *Australia* ... 94 B4
Guthrie, *Okla., U.S.A.* 113 H6
Guthrie, *Tex., U.S.A.* 113 J4
Gutian, *China* 59 D12
Gutu, *Zimbabwe* 89 B5
Guyana ■, *S. Amer.* 124 C7
Guyane française = French Guiana □, *S. Amer.* 125 C8
Guyang, *China* 56 D6
Guyenne, *France* 20 D4
Guymon, *U.S.A.* 113 G4
Guyra, *Australia* 95 E5
Guyuan, *Hebei, China* 56 D8
Guyuan, *Ningxia Huizu, China* 56 G4
Güzelbahçe, *Turkey* 39 C8
Guzhang, *China* 58 C7

Guzhen, *China* 57 H9
Guzmán, L. de, *Mexico* ... 118 A3
Gvardeysk, *Russia* 9 J19
Gvardeyskoye, *Ukraine* ... 47 K8
Gwa, *Burma* 67 L19
Gwaai, *Zimbabwe* 87 F2
Gwabegar, *Australia* 95 E4
Gwadabawa, *Nigeria* 83 C6
Gwādar, *Pakistan* 66 G3
Gwagwada, *Nigeria* 83 C6
Gwalior, *India* 68 F8
Gwanara, *Nigeria* 83 D5
Gwanda, *Zimbabwe* 87 G2
Gwandu, *Nigeria* 83 C5
Gwane, *Dem. Rep. of the Congo* . 86 B2
Gwaram, *Nigeria* 83 C7
Gwarzo, *Nigeria* 83 C6
Gwasero, *Nigeria* 83 D5
Gwda →, *Poland* 45 E3
Gweebarra B., *Ireland* 15 B3
Gweedore, *Ireland* 15 A3
Gweru, *Zimbabwe* 87 F2
Gwi, *Nigeria* 83 D6
Gwinn, *U.S.A.* 108 B2
Gwio Kura, *Nigeria* 83 C7
Gwoza, *Nigeria* 83 C7
Gwydir →, *Australia* 95 D4
Gwynedd □, *U.K.* 12 E3
Gyandzha = Gäncä, *Azerbaijan* 49 K8
Gyaring Hu, *China* 60 C4
Gydanskiy Poluostrov, *Russia* 50 C8
Gympie, *Australia* 95 D5
Gyomaendrőd, *Hungary* .. 42 D5
Gyöngyös, *Hungary* 42 C4
Győr, *Hungary* 42 C2
Győr-Moson-Sopron □, *Hungary* 42 C2
Gypsum Pt., *Canada* 104 A6
Gypsumville, *Canada* 105 C9
Gyueshevo, *Bulgaria* 40 D6
Gyula, *Hungary* 42 D6
Gyumri, *Armenia* 49 K6
Gyzylarbat, *Turkmenistan* . 50 F6
Gyzyletrek, *Turkmenistan* . 71 B7
Gzhatsk = Gagarin, *Russia* . 46 E8

H

Ha 'Arava →, *Israel* 75 E4
Ha Coi, *Vietnam* 58 G6
Ha Dong, *Vietnam* 58 G5
Ha Giang, *Vietnam* 58 F5
Ha Tien, *Vietnam* 65 G5
Ha Tinh, *Vietnam* 64 C5
Ha Trung, *Vietnam* 64 C5
Haaksbergen, *Neths.* 17 B6
Haapsalu, *Estonia* 9 G20
Haarlem, *Neths.* 17 B4
Haast →, *N.Z.* 91 K2
Haast Bluff, *Australia* 92 D5
Hab →, *Pakistan* 68 G3
Hab Nadi Chauki, *Pakistan* . 68 G2
Habaswein, *Kenya* 86 B4
Habay, *Canada* 104 B5
Ḥabbānīyah, *Iraq* 70 C4
Ḥabbānīyah, Hawr al, *Iraq* . 73 F10
Habo, *Sweden* 11 G8
Haboro, *Japan* 54 B10
Ḥabshān, *U.A.E.* 71 F7
Hachenburg, *Germany* ... 24 E3
Hachijō-Jima, *Japan* 55 H9
Hachinohe, *Japan* 54 D10
Hachiōji, *Japan* 55 G9
Hachŏn, *N. Korea* 57 D15
Hacıbektaş, *Turkey* 72 C6
Hacılar, *Turkey* 72 C6
Hackås, *Sweden* 10 B8
Hackensack, *U.S.A.* 111 F10
Hackettstown, *U.S.A.* 111 F10
Hadali, *Pakistan* 68 C5
Hadarba, Ras, *Sudan* 80 C4
Hadarom □, *Israel* 75 E4
Hadd, Ra's al, *Oman* 74 C6
Hadejia, *Nigeria* 83 C7
Hadejia →, *Nigeria* 83 C7
Hadera, *Israel* 75 C3
Hadera, N. →, *Israel* 75 C3
Haderslev, *Denmark* 11 J3
Hadhramaut = Ḥaḍramawt, *Yemen* 74 D4
Hadibu, *Yemen* 74 E5
Hadım, *Turkey* 72 D5
Hadong, *S. Korea* 57 G14
Ḥaḍramawt, *Yemen* 74 D4
Ḥadrānīyah, *Iraq* 70 C4
Hadrian's Wall, *U.K.* 12 B5
Hadsten, *Denmark* 11 H4
Hadsund, *Denmark* 11 H4
Hadyach, *Ukraine* 47 G8
Haeju, *N. Korea* 57 E13
Haenam, *S. Korea* 57 G14
Haerhpin = Harbin, *China* . 57 B14
Hafar al Bāṭin, *Si. Arabia* .. 70 D5
Hafik, *Turkey* 72 C7
Ḥafirat al 'Aydā, *Si. Arabia* . 70 E3
Ḥafit, *Oman* 71 F7
Ḥafit, Jabal, *Oman* 71 E7
Hafizabad, *Pakistan* 68 C5
Haflong, *India* 67 G18
Hafnarfjörður, *Iceland* 8 D3
Haft Gel, *Iran* 71 D6
Hafun, Ras, *Somali Rep.* .. 74 E5
Hagalil, *Israel* 75 C4
Hagby, *Sweden* 11 H10

Hagen, *Germany* 24 D3
Hagenow, *Germany* 24 B7
Hagerman, *U.S.A.* 113 J2
Hagerstown, *U.S.A.* 108 F7
Hagersville, *Canada* 110 D4
Hagetmau, *France* 20 E3
Hagfors, *Sweden* 10 D7
Hagi, *Japan* 55 G5
Hagolan, *Syria* 75 C4
Hagondange, *France* 19 C13
Hags Hd., *Ireland* 15 D2
Hague, C. de la, *France* ... 18 C5
Hague, The = 's-Gravenhage, *Neths.* 17 B4
Haguenau, *France* 19 D14
Hai Duong, *Vietnam* 58 G6
Hai'an, *Guangdong, China* . 59 G8
Hai'an, *Jiangsu, China* ... 59 A13
Haicheng, *Fujian, China* .. 59 E11
Haicheng, *Liaoning, China* . 57 D12
Haidar Khel, *Afghan.* 68 C3
Haidargarh, *India* 69 F9
Haifa = Ḥefa, *Israel* 75 C4
Haifeng, *China* 59 F10
Haiger, *Germany* 24 E4
Haikou, *China* 60 D6
Ḥā'il, *Si. Arabia* 70 E4
Hailar, *China* 60 B6
Hailey, *U.S.A.* 114 E6
Haileybury, *Canada* 102 C4
Hailin, *China* 57 B15
Hailing Dao, *China* 59 G8
Hailong, *China* 57 C13
Hailuoto, *Finland* 8 D21
Haimen, *Guangdong, China* 59 F11
Haimen, *Jiangsu, China* ... 59 B13
Hainan □, *China* 60 E5
Hainaut □, *Belgium* 17 D4
Hainburg, *Austria* 27 C9
Haines, *Alaska, U.S.A.* ... 104 B1
Haines, *Oreg., U.S.A.* 114 D5
Haines City, *U.S.A.* 109 L5
Haines Junction, *Canada* .. 104 A1
Hainfeld, *Austria* 26 C8
Haining, *China* 59 B13
Haiphong, *Vietnam* 58 G6
Haitan Dao, *China* 59 E12
Haiti ■, *W. Indies* 121 C5
Haiya, *Sudan* 80 D4
Haiyan, *China* 59 B13
Haiyang, *China* 57 F11
Haiyuan, *Guangxi Zhuangzu, China* 58 F6
Haiyuan, *Ningxia Huizu, China* 56 F3
Ḥamḏ, W. al →, *Si. Arabia* 70 E3
Hamden, *U.S.A.* 111 E12
Hamdibey, *Turkey* 39 B9
Häme, *Finland* 9 F21
Hämeenlinna, *Finland* 9 F21
Hamélé, *Ghana* 82 C4
Hamelin Pool, *Australia* .. 93 E1
Hameln, *Germany* 24 C5
Hamerkaz □, *Israel* 75 C3
Hamersley Ra., *Australia* .. 92 D2
Hamhung, *N. Korea* 57 E14
Hami, *China* 60 B4
Hamilton, *Australia* 95 F3
Hamilton, *Canada* 102 D4
Hamilton, *N.Z.* 91 G5
Hamilton, *U.K.* 14 F4
Hamilton, *Ala., U.S.A.* ... 109 H1
Hamilton, *Mont., U.S.A.* .. 114 C6
Hamilton, *N.Y., U.S.A.* ... 111 D9
Hamilton, *Ohio, U.S.A.* ... 108 F3
Hamilton, *Tex., U.S.A.* ... 113 K5
Hamilton →, *Australia* ... 94 C2
Hamilton City, *U.S.A.* 116 F4
Hamilton Inlet, *Canada* ... 103 B8
Hamilton Mt., *U.S.A.* 111 C10
Hamina, *Finland* 9 F22
Hamirpur, *H.P., India* 68 D7
Hamirpur, *Ut. P., India* ... 69 G9
Hamitabat, *Turkey* 41 E11
Hamlet, *U.S.A.* 109 H6
Hamley Bridge, *Australia* . 95 E2
Hamlin = Hameln, *Germany* 24 C5
Hamlin, *N.Y., U.S.A.* 110 C7
Hamlin, *Tex., U.S.A.* 113 J4
Hamm, *Germany* 24 D3
Ḥammār, Hawr al, *Iraq* ... 70 D5
Hammarstrand, *Sweden* .. 10 A10
Hammelburg, *Germany* ... 25 E5
Hammeren, *Denmark* 11 J8
Hammerfest, *Norway* 8 A20
Hammerum, *Denmark* ... 11 H3
Hamminkeln, *Germany* ... 24 D2
Hammond, *Ind., U.S.A.* .. 108 E2
Hammond, *La., U.S.A.* ... 113 K9
Hammond, *N.Y., U.S.A.* .. 111 B9
Hammondsport, *U.S.A.* .. 110 D7
Hammonton, *U.S.A.* 108 F8
Hamneda, *Sweden* 11 H7
Hamoyet, Jebel, *Sudan* ... 80 D4
Hampden, *N.Z.* 91 L3
Hampshire □, *U.K.* 13 F6
Hampshire Downs, *U.K.* .. 13 F6
Hampton, *N.B., Canada* .. 103 C6
Hampton, *Ont., Canada* .. 110 C6
Hampton, *Ark., U.S.A.* ... 113 J8
Hampton, *Iowa, U.S.A.* ... 112 D8
Hampton, *N.H., U.S.A.* ... 111 D14
Hampton, *S.C., U.S.A.* ... 109 J5
Hampton, *Va., U.S.A.* 108 G7
Hampton Bays, *U.S.A.* ... 111 F12
Hampton Tableland, *Australia* 93 F4
Hamra, *Sweden* 10 C8
Hamrat esh Sheikh, *Sudan* . 81 E2
Hamur, *Turkey* 73 C10
Hamyang, *S. Korea* 57 G14
Han Jiang →, *China* 59 F11

Halle, *Nordrhein-Westfalen, Germany* 24 C4
Halle, *Sachsen-Anhalt, Germany* 24 D7
Hällefors, *Sweden* 10 E8
Hälleforsnäs, *Sweden* ... 10 E10
Hallein, *Austria* 26 D6
Hällekis, *Sweden* 11 F7
Hallen, *Sweden* 10 A8
Hallett, *Australia* 95 E2
Hallettsville, *U.S.A.* 113 L6
Hallim, *S. Korea* 57 H14
Hallingdalselvi →, *Norway* 9 F13
Hallock, *U.S.A.* 112 A6
Halls Creek, *Australia* 92 C4
Hallsberg, *Sweden* 10 E8
Hallstahammar, *Sweden* .. 10 E10
Hallstatt, *Austria* 26 D6
Hallstavik, *Sweden* 10 D12
Halmahera, *Indonesia* 63 D7
Halmeu, *Romania* 42 C8
Halmstad, *Sweden* 11 H6
Hals, *Denmark* 11 H4
Hälsingborg = Helsingborg, *Sweden* 11 H6
Hälsingland, *Sweden* 10 C10
Halstead, *U.K.* 13 F8
Haltern, *Germany* 24 D3
Halti, *Finland* 8 B19
Halton □, *U.K.* 12 D5
Haltwhistle, *U.K.* 12 C5
Halul, *Qatar* 71 E7
Halvad, *India* 68 H4
Halvān, *Iran* 71 C8
Ham, *France* 19 C10
Ham Tan, *Vietnam* 65 G6
Ham Yen, *Vietnam* 64 A5
Hamab, *Namibia* 88 D2
Hamad, *Sudan* 81 D3
Hamada, *Japan* 55 G6
Hamadān, *Iran* 71 C6
Hamadān □, *Iran* 71 C6
Ḥamāh, *Syria* 70 C3
Hamamatsu, *Japan* 55 G8
Hamar, *Norway* 9 F14
Hamâta, Gebel, *Egypt* ... 70 E2
Hambantota, *Sri Lanka* .. 66 R12
Hamber Prov. Park, *Canada* 104 C5
Hamburg, *Germany* 24 B5
Hamburg, *Ark., U.S.A.* ... 113 J9
Hamburg, *N.Y., U.S.A.* ... 110 D6
Hamburg, *Pa., U.S.A.* ... 111 F9
Hamburg □, *Germany* 24 B5

Han Shui, *China* 58 A7
Han Shui, *China* 59 B10
Hana, *U.S.A.* 106 H17
Hanak, *Si. Arabia* 70 E3
Hanamaki, *Japan* 54 E10
Hanau, *Germany* 25 E4
Hanbogd = Ihbulag, *Mongolia* 56 C4
Hançalar, *Turkey* 39 C11
Hânceşti, *Moldova* 43 D13
Hancheng, *China* 56 G6
Hanchuan, *China* 59 B9
Hancock, *Mich., U.S.A.* 112 B10
Hancock, *N.Y., U.S.A.* 111 E9
Handa, *Japan* 55 G8
Handan, *China* 56 F8
Handeni, *Tanzania* 86 D4
Handlová, *Slovak Rep.* 27 C11
Handub, *Sudan* 80 D4
Handwara, *India* 69 B6
Hanegev, *Israel* 75 E4
Hanford, *U.S.A.* 116 J7
Hang Chat, *Thailand* 64 C2
Hang Dong, *Thailand* 64 C2
Hangang →, *S. Korea* 57 F14
Hangayn Nuruu, *Mongolia* 60 B4
Hangchou = Hangzhou, *China* 59 B13
Hanggin Houqi, *China* 56 D4
Hanggin Qi, *China* 56 E5
Hangu, *China* 57 E9
Hangzhou, *China* 59 B13
Hangzhou Wan, *China* 59 B13
Hanhongor, *Mongolia* 56 C3
Hanīdh, *Si. Arabia* 71 E6
Hanīsh, *Yemen* 74 E3
Haniska, *Slovak Rep.* 27 C14
Hanjiang, *China* 59 E12
Hankinson, *U.S.A.* 112 B6
Hanko, *Finland* 9 G20
Hankou, *China* 59 B10
Hanksville, *U.S.A.* 115 G8
Hanle, *India* 69 C8
Hanmer Springs, *N.Z.* 91 K4
Hann →, *Australia* 92 C4
Hann, Mt., *Australia* 92 C4
Hanna, *Canada* 104 C6
Hanna, *U.S.A.* 114 F10
Hannah B., *Canada* 102 B4
Hannibal, *Mo., U.S.A.* 112 F9
Hannibal, *N.Y., U.S.A.* 111 C8
Hannik, *Sudan* 80 D3
Hannover, *Germany* 24 C5
Hanö, *Sweden* 11 H8
Hanöbukten, *Sweden* 11 J8
Hanoi, *Vietnam* 58 G5
Hanover = Hannover, *Germany* 24 C5
Hanover, *Canada* 102 D3
Hanover, *S. Africa* 88 E3
Hanover, *N.H., U.S.A.* 111 C12
Hanover, *Ohio, U.S.A.* 110 F2
Hanover, *Pa., U.S.A.* 108 F7
Hanover, I., *Chile* 128 G2
Hansdiha, *India* 69 G12
Hanshou, *China* 59 C8
Hansi, *India* 68 E6
Hanson, L., *Australia* 95 E2
Hanstholm, *Denmark* 11 G2
Hantsavichy, *Belarus* 47 F4
Hanumangarh, *India* 68 E6
Hanyin, *China* 58 A7
Hanyuan, *China* 58 C4
Hanzhong, *China* 56 H4
Hanzhuang, *China* 57 G9
Haora, *India* 69 H13
Haoxue, *China* 59 B9
Haparanda, *Sweden* 8 D21
Happy, *U.S.A.* 113 H4
Happy Camp, *U.S.A.* 114 F2
Happy Valley-Goose Bay, *Canada* 103 B7
Hapsu, *N. Korea* 57 D15
Hapur, *India* 68 E7
Haql, *Si. Arabia* 75 F3
Har, *Indonesia* 63 F8
Har-Ayrag, *Mongolia* 56 B5
Har Hu, *China* 60 C4
Har Us Nuur, *Mongolia* 60 B4
Har Yehuda, *Israel* 75 D3
Haraḍ, *Si. Arabia* 74 C4
Haradok, *Belarus* 46 E6
Häradsbäck, *Sweden* 11 H8
Haranomachi, *Japan* 54 F10
Harare, *Zimbabwe* 87 F3
Harat, *Eritrea* 81 D4
Harbin, *China* 57 B14
Harbiye, *Turkey* 72 D7
Harbo, *Sweden* 10 D11
Harboør, *Denmark* 11 H2
Harbor Beach, *U.S.A.* 110 C2
Harbour Breton, *Canada* 103 C8
Harbour Deep, *Canada* 103 B8
Harburg, *Germany* 24 B5
Hårby, *Denmark* 11 J4
Harda, *India* 68 H7
Hardangerfjorden, *Norway* 9 F12
Hardangervidda, *Norway* 9 F12
Hardap Dam, *Namibia* 88 C2
Hardenberg, *Neths.* 17 B6
Harderwijk, *Neths.* 17 B5
Hardey →, *Australia* 92 D2
Hardin, *U.S.A.* 114 D10
Harding, *S. Africa* 89 E4
Harding Ra., *Australia* 92 C3
Hardisty, *Canada* 104 C6
Hardoi, *India* 69 F9
Hardwar = Haridwar, *India* 68 E8
Hardwick, *U.S.A.* 111 B12
Hardy, Pen., *Chile* 128 H3

Hare B., *Canada* 103 B8
Hareid, *Norway* 9 E12
Haren, *Germany* 24 C3
Harer, *Ethiopia* 81 F5
Harerge □, *Ethiopia* 81 F5
Hareto, *Ethiopia* 81 F4
Harfleur, *France* 18 C7
Hargeisa, *Somali Rep.* 74 F3
Harghita □, *Romania* 43 D10
Harghita, Munții, *Romania* 43 D10
Hargshamn, *Sweden* 10 D12
Hari →, *Indonesia* 62 E2
Haria, *Canary Is.* 37 E6
Haridwar, *India* 68 E8
Harim, Jabal al, *Oman* 71 E8
Haringhata →, *Bangla.* 67 J16
Härjedalen, *Sweden* 10 B7
Harīrūd →, *Asia* 66 A2
Harlan, *Iowa, U.S.A.* 112 E7
Harlan, *Ky., U.S.A.* 109 G4
Hârlău, *Romania* 43 C11
Harlech, *U.K.* 12 E3
Harlem, *U.S.A.* 114 B9
Hårlev, *Denmark* 11 J6
Harlingen, *Neths.* 17 A5
Harlingen, *U.S.A.* 113 M6
Harlow, *U.K.* 13 F8
Harlowton, *U.S.A.* 114 C9
Harmancık, *Turkey* 39 B11
Harmånger, *Sweden* 10 C11
Harmil, *Eritrea* 81 D5
Harnai, *Pakistan* 68 D2
Harney Basin, *U.S.A.* 114 E4
Harney L., *U.S.A.* 114 E4
Harney Peak, *U.S.A.* 112 D3
Härnön, *Sweden* 10 B12
Härnösand, *Sweden* 10 B11
Haro, *Spain* 32 C2
Haroldswick, *U.K.* 14 A8
Harp L., *Canada* 103 A7
Harplinge, *Sweden* 11 H6
Harr, *Mauritania* 82 B2
Harrai, *India* 69 H8
Harrand, *Pakistan* 68 E4
Harricana →, *Canada* 102 B4
Harriman, *U.S.A.* 109 H3
Harrington Harbour, *Canada* 103 B8
Harris, *U.K.* 14 D2
Harris, Sd. of, *U.K.* 14 D1
Harris, L., *Australia* 95 E2
Harris Pt., *Canada* 110 C2
Harrisburg, *Ill., U.S.A.* 113 G10
Harrisburg, *Nebr., U.S.A.* 112 E3
Harrisburg, *Pa., U.S.A.* 110 F8
Harrismith, *S. Africa* 89 D4
Harrison, *Ark., U.S.A.* 113 G8
Harrison, *Maine, U.S.A.* 111 B14
Harrison, *Nebr., U.S.A.* 112 D3
Harrison, C., *Canada* 103 B8
Harrison L., *Canada* 104 D4
Harrisonburg, *U.S.A.* 108 F6
Harrisonville, *U.S.A.* 112 F7
Harriston, *Canada* 110 C4
Harrisville, *Mich., U.S.A.* 110 B1
Harrisville, *N.Y., U.S.A.* 111 B9
Harrisville, *Pa., U.S.A.* 110 E5
Harrodsburg, *U.S.A.* 108 G3
Harrogate, *U.K.* 12 C6
Harrow, *U.K.* 13 F7
Harrowsmith, *Canada* 111 B8
Harry S. Truman Reservoir, *U.S.A.* 112 F7
Harsefeld, *Germany* 24 B5
Harsewinkel, *Germany* 24 D4
Harsīn, *Iran* 70 C5
Hârşova, *Romania* 43 F12
Harstad, *Norway* 8 B17
Harsud, *India* 68 H7
Hart, *U.S.A.* 108 D2
Hart, L., *Australia* 95 E2
Hartbees →, *S. Africa* 88 D3
Hartberg, *Austria* 26 D8
Hartford, *Conn., U.S.A.* 111 E12
Hartford, *Ky., U.S.A.* 108 G2
Hartford, *S. Dak., U.S.A.* 112 D6
Hartford, *Wis., U.S.A.* 112 D10
Hartford City, *U.S.A.* 108 E3
Hartland, *Canada* 103 C6
Hartland Pt., *U.K.* 13 F3
Hartlepool, *U.K.* 12 C6
Hartlepool □, *U.K.* 12 C6
Hartley Bay, *Canada* 104 C3
Hartmannberge, *Namibia* 88 B1
Hartney, *Canada* 105 D8
Hârtop, *Moldova* 43 D13
Harts →, *S. Africa* 88 D3
Hartselle, *U.S.A.* 109 H2
Hartshorne, *U.S.A.* 113 H7
Hartstown, *U.S.A.* 110 E4
Hartsville, *U.S.A.* 109 H5
Hartswater, *S. Africa* 88 D3
Hartwell, *U.S.A.* 109 H4
Harunabad, *Pakistan* 68 E5
Harvand, *Iran* 71 D7
Harvey, *Australia* 93 F2
Harvey, *Ill., U.S.A.* 108 E2
Harvey, *N. Dak., U.S.A.* 112 B5
Harwich, *U.K.* 13 F9
Haryana □, *India* 68 E7
Haryn →, *Belarus* 47 F4
Harz, *Germany* 24 D6
Harzgerode, *Germany* 24 D7
Hasa □, *Si. Arabia* 71 E6
Hasaheisa, *Sudan* 81 E3
Ḥasanābād, *Iran* 71 C7
Hasdo →, *India* 69 J10
Haselünne, *Germany* 24 C3
Hashimoto, *Japan* 55 G7

Hashtjerd, *Iran* 71 C6
Haskell, *U.S.A.* 113 J5
Hasköy, *Turkey* 41 E10
Haslach, *Germany* 25 G4
Hasle, *Denmark* 11 J8
Haslemere, *U.K.* 13 F7
Haslev, *Denmark* 11 J5
Hasparren, *France* 20 E2
Hassa, *Turkey* 72 D7
Hassela, *Sweden* 10 B10
Hasselt, *Belgium* 17 D5
Hassfurt, *Germany* 25 E6
Hassi Messaoud, *Algeria* 78 B7
Hässleholm, *Sweden* 11 H7
Hassloch, *Germany* 25 F4
Hästholmen, *Sweden* 11 F8
Hastings, *N.Z.* 91 H6
Hastings, *U.K.* 13 G8
Hastings, *Mich., U.S.A.* 108 D3
Hastings, *Minn., U.S.A.* 112 C8
Hastings, *Nebr., U.S.A.* 112 E5
Hastings Ra., *Australia* 95 E5
Hästveda, *Sweden* 11 H7
Hat Yai, *Thailand* 65 J3
Hatanbulag = Ergel, *Mongolia* 56 C5
Hatay = Antalya, *Turkey* 72 D4
Hatch, *U.S.A.* 115 K10
Hatchet L., *Canada* 105 B8
Hațeg, *Romania* 42 E7
Hateruma-Shima, *Japan* 55 M1
Hatfield P.O., *Australia* 95 E3
Hatgal, *Mongolia* 60 A5
Hathras, *India* 68 F8
Hatia, *Bangla.* 67 H17
Ḥātibah, Ra's, *Si. Arabia* 80 C4
Hato Mayor, *Dom. Rep.* 121 C6
Hatta, *India* 69 G8
Hattah, *Australia* 95 E3
Hatteras, C., *U.S.A.* 109 H8
Hattiesburg, *U.S.A.* 113 K10
Hatvan, *Hungary* 42 C4
Hau Bon = Cheo Reo, *Vietnam* 62 B3
Hau Duc, *Vietnam* 64 E7
Haugesund, *Norway* 9 G11
Haukipudas, *Finland* 8 D21
Haultain →, *Canada* 105 B7
Hauraki G., *N.Z.* 91 G5
Hausruck, *Austria* 26 C6
Haut Atlas, *Morocco* 78 B4
Haut-Rhin □, *France* 19 E14
Haut-Zaïre = Orientale □, *Dem. Rep. of the Congo* 86 B2
Haute-Corse □, *France* 21 F13
Haute-Garonne □, *France* 20 E5
Haute-Loire □, *France* 20 C7
Haute-Marne □, *France* 19 D12
Haute-Normandie □, *France* 18 C7
Haute-Saône □, *France* 19 E13
Haute-Savoie □, *France* 21 C10
Haute-Vienne □, *France* 20 C5
Hautes-Alpes □, *France* 21 D10
Hautes Fagnes = Hohe Venn, *Belgium* 17 D6
Hautes-Pyrénées □, *France* 20 F4
Hauteville-Lompnès, *France* 21 C9
Hautmont, *France* 19 B10
Hauts-de-Seine □, *France* 19 D9
Hauts Plateaux, *Algeria* 76 C4
Hauzenberg, *Germany* 25 G9
Havana = La Habana, *Cuba* 120 B3
Havana, *U.S.A.* 112 E9
Havant, *U.K.* 13 G7
Havârna, *Romania* 43 B11
Havasu, L., *U.S.A.* 117 L12
Havdhem, *Sweden* 11 G12
Havel →, *Germany* 24 C8
Havelian, *Pakistan* 68 B5
Havelock, *Canada* 102 D4
Havelock, *N.Z.* 91 J4
Havelock, *U.S.A.* 109 H7
Haverfordwest, *U.K.* 13 F3
Haverhill, *U.S.A.* 111 D13
Haverstraw, *U.S.A.* 111 E11
Håverud, *Sweden* 11 F6
Havirga, *Mongolia* 56 B7
Havířov, *Czech.* 27 B11
Havlíčkův Brod, *Czech Rep.* 26 B8
Havneby, *Denmark* 11 J2
Havran, *Turkey* 39 B9
Havre, *U.S.A.* 114 B9
Havre-Aubert, *Canada* 103 C7
Havre-St.-Pierre, *Canada* 103 B7
Havsa, *Turkey* 41 E10
Havza, *Turkey* 72 B6
Haw →, *U.S.A.* 109 H6
Hawaii □, *U.S.A.* 106 H16
Hawaii I., *Pac. Oc.* 106 J17
Hawaiian Is., *Pac. Oc.* 106 H17
Hawaiian Ridge, *Pac. Oc.* 97 E11
Hawarden, *U.S.A.* 112 D6
Hawea, L., *N.Z.* 91 L2
Hawera, *N.Z.* 91 H5
Hawick, *U.K.* 14 F6
Hawk Junction, *Canada* 102 C3
Hawke B., *N.Z.* 91 H6
Hawker, *Australia* 95 E2
Hawkesbury, *Canada* 102 C5
Hawkesbury I., *Canada* 104 C3
Hawkesbury Pt., *Australia* 94 A1
Hawkinsville, *U.S.A.* 109 J4
Hawley, *Minn., U.S.A.* 112 B6
Hawley, *Pa., U.S.A.* 111 E9
Ḥawrān, W. →, *Iraq* 70 C4
Hawsh Mūssá, *Lebanon* 75 B4
Hawthorne, *U.S.A.* 114 G4
Hay, *Australia* 95 E3
Hay →, *Australia* 94 C2
Hay →, *Canada* 104 A5
Hay, C., *Australia* 92 B4

Hay I., *Canada* 110 B4
Hay L., *Canada* 104 B5
Hay-on-Wye, *U.K.* 13 E4
Hay River, *Canada* 104 A5
Hay Springs, *U.S.A.* 112 D3
Haya = Tehoru, *Indonesia* 63 E7
Hayachine-San, *Japan* 54 E10
Hayange, *France* 19 C13
Haydarlı, *Turkey* 39 C12
Hayden, *U.S.A.* 114 F10
Haydon, *Australia* 94 B3
Hayes, *U.S.A.* 112 C4
Hayes →, *Canada* 102 A1
Hayes Creek, *Australia* 92 B5
Hayle, *U.K.* 13 G2
Hayling I., *U.K.* 13 G7
Haymana, *Turkey* 72 C5
Hayrabolu, *Turkey* 41 E11
Hays, *Canada* 104 C6
Hays, *U.S.A.* 112 F5
Haysyn, *Ukraine* 47 H5
Hayvoron, *Ukraine* 47 H5
Hayward, *Calif., U.S.A.* 116 H4
Hayward, *Wis., U.S.A.* 112 B9
Haywards Heath, *U.K.* 13 G7
Hazafon □, *Israel* 75 C4
Hazārān, Kūh-e, *Iran* 71 D8
Hazard, *U.S.A.* 108 G4
Hazaribag, *India* 69 H11
Hazaribag Road, *India* 69 G11
Hazebrouck, *France* 19 B9
Hazelton, *Canada* 104 B3
Hazelton, *U.S.A.* 112 B4
Hazen, *U.S.A.* 112 B4
Hazlehurst, *Ga., U.S.A.* 109 K4
Hazlehurst, *Miss., U.S.A.* 113 K9
Hazlet, *U.S.A.* 111 F10
Hazleton, *U.S.A.* 111 F9
Hazlett, L., *Australia* 92 D4
Hazro, *Turkey* 70 B4
He Xian, *Anhui, China* 59 B12
He Xian, *Guangxi Zhuangzu, China* 59 E8
Head of Bight, *Australia* 93 F5
Headlands, *Zimbabwe* 87 F3
Healdsburg, *U.S.A.* 116 G4
Healdton, *U.S.A.* 113 H6
Healesville, *Australia* 95 F4
Heany Junction, *Zimbabwe* 89 C4
Heard I., *Ind. Oc.* 3 G13
Hearne, *U.S.A.* 113 K6
Hearst, *Canada* 102 C3
Heart →, *U.S.A.* 112 B4
Heart's Content, *Canada* 103 C9
Heath Pt., *Canada* 103 C7
Heavener, *U.S.A.* 113 H7
Hebbronville, *U.S.A.* 113 M5
Hebei □, *China* 56 E9
Hebel, *Australia* 95 D4
Heber, *U.S.A.* 117 N11
Heber City, *U.S.A.* 114 F8
Heber Springs, *U.S.A.* 113 H9
Hebert, *Canada* 105 C7
Hebgen L., *U.S.A.* 114 D8
Hebi, *China* 56 G8
Hebrides, *U.K.* 6 D4
Hebron = Al Khalīl, *West Bank* 75 D4
Hebron, *Canada* 101 C13
Hebron, *N. Dak., U.S.A.* 112 B3
Hebron, *Nebr., U.S.A.* 112 E6
Heby, *Sweden* 10 E10
Hecate Str., *Canada* 104 C2
Heceta I., *U.S.A.* 104 B2
Hechi, *China* 58 E7
Hechingen, *Germany* 25 G4
Hechuan, *China* 58 B6
Hecla, *U.S.A.* 112 C5
Hecla I., *Canada* 105 C9
Hédé, *France* 18 D5
Hede, *Sweden* 10 B7
Hedemora, *Sweden* 10 D9
Hedensted, *Denmark* 11 J3
Hedesunda, *Sweden* 10 D10
Heerde, *Neths.* 17 B6
Heerenveen, *Neths.* 17 B5
Heerhugowaard, *Neths.* 17 B4
Heerlen, *Neths.* 17 D5
Hefa, *Israel* 75 C4
Hefa □, *Israel* 75 C4
Hefei, *China* 59 B11
Hefeng, *China* 59 C8
Hegalig, *Sudan* 81 E3
Hegang, *China* 60 B8
Heiban, *Sudan* 81 E3
Heichengzhen, *China* 56 F4
Heide, *Germany* 24 A5
Heidelberg, *Germany* 25 F4
Heidelberg, *S. Africa* 88 E3
Heidenau, *Germany* 24 D9
Heidenheim, *Germany* 25 G6
Heijing, *China* 58 E3
Heilbad Heiligenstadt, *Germany* 24 D6
Heilbron, *S. Africa* 89 D4
Heilbronn, *Germany* 25 F5
Heiligenhafen, *Germany* 24 A6
Heilongjiang □, *China* 60 B7
Heilunkiang = Heilongjiang □, *China* 60 B7
Heimaey, *Iceland* 8 E3
Heinola, *Finland* 9 F22
Heinsberg, *Germany* 24 C2
Heinze Is., *Burma* 67 M20
Heishan, *China* 57 D12
Heishui, *Liaoning, China* 57 C10
Heishui, *Sichuan, China* 58 A4
Hejaz = Ḥijāz □, *Si. Arabia* 70 E3
Hejian, *China* 56 E9
Hejiang, *China* 58 C5

Hejin, *China* 56 G6
Hekimhan, *Turkey* 70 B3
Hekla, *Iceland* 8 E4
Hekou, *Guangdong, China* 59 F9
Hekou, *Yunnan, China* 58 F4
Hel, *Poland* 44 D5
Helagsfjället, *Sweden* 10 B6
Helan Shan, *China* 56 E3
Helechosa, *Spain* 35 F6
Helen Atoll, *Pac. Oc.* 63 D8
Helena, *Ark., U.S.A.* 113 H9
Helena, *Mont., U.S.A.* 114 C7
Helendale, *U.S.A.* 117 L9
Helensburgh, *U.K.* 14 E4
Helensville, *N.Z.* 91 G5
Helenvale, *Australia* 94 B4
Helgasjön, *Sweden* 11 H8
Helgeland, *Norway* 8 C15
Helgoland, *Germany* 24 A3
Heligoland = Helgoland, *Germany* 24 A3
Heligoland B. = Deutsche Bucht, *Germany* 24 A4
Heliopolis, *Egypt* 80 H7
Hella, *Iceland* 8 E3
Hellertown, *U.S.A.* 111 F9
Hellespont = Çanakkale Boğazı, *Turkey* 41 F10
Hellevoetsluis, *Neths.* 17 C4
Hellín, *Spain* 33 G3
Helmand □, *Afghan.* 66 D4
Helmand →, *Afghan.* 66 D2
Helme →, *Germany* 24 D7
Helmeringhausen, *Namibia* 88 D2
Helmond, *Neths.* 17 C5
Helmsdale, *U.K.* 14 C5
Helmsdale →, *U.K.* 14 C5
Helmstedt, *Germany* 24 C7
Helong, *China* 57 C15
Helper, *U.S.A.* 114 G8
Helsingborg, *Sweden* 11 H6
Helsinge, *Denmark* 11 H6
Helsingfors = Helsinki, *Finland* 9 F21
Helsingør, *Denmark* 11 H6
Helsinki, *Finland* 9 F21
Helska, Mierzeja, *Poland* 44 D5
Helston, *U.K.* 13 G2
Helvellyn, *U.K.* 12 C4
Helwân, *Egypt* 80 J7
Hemel Hempstead, *U.K.* 13 F7
Hemet, *U.S.A.* 117 M10
Hemingford, *U.S.A.* 112 D3
Hemmingford, *Canada* 111 A11
Hempstead, *U.S.A.* 113 K6
Hemse, *Sweden* 11 G12
Hemsön, *Sweden* 10 B12
Henån, *Sweden* 11 F5
Henan □, *China* 56 H8
Henares →, *Spain* 34 E7
Henashi-Misaki, *Japan* 54 D9
Hendaye, *France* 20 E2
Hendek, *Turkey* 72 B4
Henderson, *Argentina* 126 D3
Henderson, *Ky., U.S.A.* 108 G2
Henderson, *N.C., U.S.A.* 109 G6
Henderson, *Nev., U.S.A.* 117 J12
Henderson, *Tenn., U.S.A.* 109 H1
Henderson, *Tex., U.S.A.* 113 J7
Hendersonville, *N.C., U.S.A.* 109 H4
Hendersonville, *Tenn., U.S.A.* 109 G2
Hendījān, *Iran* 71 D6
Hendorābī, *Iran* 71 E7
Heng Jiang, *China* 58 C5
Heng Xian, *China* 58 F7
Hengcheng, *China* 56 E4
Hengchun, *Taiwan* 59 F13
Hengdaohezi, *China* 57 B15
Hengelo, *Neths.* 17 B6
Hengshan, *Hunan, China* 59 D9
Hengshan, *Shaanxi, China* 56 F5
Hengshui, *China* 56 F8
Hengyang, *Hunan, China* 59 D9
Hengyang, *Hunan, China* 59 D9
Henichesk, *Ukraine* 47 J8
Hénin-Beaumont, *France* 19 B9
Henlopen, C., *U.S.A.* 108 F8
Hennan, *Sweden* 10 B9
Hennebont, *France* 18 E3
Hennenman, *S. Africa* 88 D4
Hennessey, *U.S.A.* 113 G6
Hennigsdorf, *Germany* 24 C9
Henrietta, *U.S.A.* 113 J5
Henrietta, Ostrov = Genriyetty, Ostrov, *Russia* 51 B16
Henrietta Maria, C., *Canada* 102 A3
Henry, *U.S.A.* 112 E10
Henryetta, *U.S.A.* 113 H7
Henryville, *Canada* 111 A11
Hensall, *Canada* 110 C3
Henstedt-Ulzburg, *Germany* 24 B6
Hentiesbaai, *Namibia* 88 C1
Hentiyn Nuruu, *Mongolia* 60 B5
Henty, *Australia* 95 F4
Henzada, *Burma* 67 L19
Hephaestia, *Greece* 39 B7
Heppner, *U.S.A.* 114 D4
Hepu, *China* 58 G7
Hepworth, *Canada* 110 B3
Hequ, *China* 56 E6
Heraðsflói, *Iceland* 8 D6
Heraðsvötn →, *Iceland* 8 D4
Herald Cays, *Australia* 94 B4
Herāt, *Afghan.* 66 B3
Herāt □, *Afghan.* 66 B3
Hérault □, *France* 20 E7

Hérault →, France 20 E7
Herbault, France 18 E8
Herbert →, Australia 94 B4
Herberton, Australia 94 B4
Herbertsdale, S. Africa ... 88 E3
Herbignac, France 18 E4
Herborn, Germany 24 E4
Herby, Poland 45 H5
Herceg-Novi,
  Montenegro, Yug. 40 D2
Herchmer, Canada 105 B10
Herðubreið, Iceland 8 D5
Hereford, U.K. 13 E5
Hereford, U.S.A. 113 H3
Herefordshire □, U.K. 13 E5
Hereke, Turkey 41 F13
Herencia, Spain 35 F7
Herentals, Belgium 17 C4
Herford, Germany 24 C4
Héricourt, France 19 E13
Herington, U.S.A. 112 F6
Herisau, Switz. 25 H5
Hérisson, France 19 F9
Herkimer, U.S.A. 111 D10
Herlong, U.S.A. 116 E6
Herm, U.K. 13 H5
Hermann, U.S.A. 112 F9
Hermannsburg, Australia . 92 D5
Hermannsburg, Germany . 24 C6
Hermanus, S. Africa 88 E2
Herment, France 20 C6
Hermidale, Australia 95 E4
Hermiston, U.S.A. 114 D4
Hermitage, N.Z. 91 K3
Hermite, I., Chile 128 H3
Hermon, U.S.A. 111 B9
Hermon, Mt. = Shaykh, J.
  ash, Lebanon 75 B4
Hermosillo, Mexico 118 B2
Hernád →, Hungary 42 C6
Hernandarias, Paraguay . 127 B5
Hernandez, U.S.A. 116 J6
Hernando, Argentina 126 C3
Hernando, U.S.A. 113 H10
Hernani, Spain 32 B3
Herndon, U.S.A. 110 F8
Herne, Germany 17 C7
Herne Bay, U.K. 13 F9
Herning, Denmark 11 H2
Heroica = Caborca, Mexico 118 A2
Heroica Nogales = Nogales,
  Mexico 118 A2
Heron Bay, Canada 102 C2
Herradura, Pta. de la,
  Canary Is. 37 F5
Herreid, U.S.A. 112 C4
Herrenberg, Germany 25 G4
Herrera, Spain 35 H6
Herrera de Alcántara, Spain 35 F3
Herrera de Pisuerga, Spain 34 C6
Herrera del Duque, Spain . 35 F5
Herrestad, Sweden 11 F5
Herrin, U.S.A. 113 G10
Herriot, Canada 105 B8
Herrljunga, Sweden 11 F7
Hersbruck, Germany 25 F7
Hershey, U.S.A. 111 F8
Hersonissos, Greece 36 D7
Herstal, Belgium 17 D5
Hertford, U.K. 13 F7
Hertfordshire □, U.K. 13 F7
's-Hertogenbosch, Neths. . 17 C5
Hertzogville, S. Africa ... 88 D4
Hervás, Spain 34 E5
Hervey B., Australia 94 C5
Herzberg, Brandenburg,
  Germany 24 D9
Herzberg, Niedersachsen,
  Germany 24 D6
Herzliyya, Israel 75 C3
Herzogenburg, Austria ... 26 C8
Heşār, Fārs, Iran 71 D6
Heşār, Markazī, Iran 71 C6
Hesdin, France 19 B9
Heshan, China 58 F7
Heshui, China 56 G5
Heshun, China 56 F7
Hesperia, U.S.A. 117 L9
Hesse = Hessen □, Germany 24 E4
Hessen □, Germany 24 E4
Hestra, Sweden 11 G7
Hetch Hetchy Aqueduct,
  U.S.A. 116 H5
Hettinger, U.S.A. 112 C3
Hettstedt, Germany 24 D7
Heuvelton, U.S.A. 111 B9
Heves, Hungary 42 C5
Heves □, Hungary 42 C5
Hewitt, U.S.A. 113 K6
Hexham, U.K. 12 C5
Hexi, Yunnan, China 58 E4
Hexi, Zhejiang, China ... 59 D12
Hexigten Qi, China 57 C9
Heydarābād, Iran 71 D7
Heysham, U.K. 12 C5
Heyuan, China 59 F10
Heywood, Australia 95 F3
Heze, China 56 G8
Hezhang, China 58 D5
Hi Vista, U.S.A. 117 L9
Hialeah, U.S.A. 109 N5
Hiawatha, U.S.A. 112 F7
Hibbing, U.S.A. 112 B8
Hibbs B., Australia 94 G4
Hibernia Reef, Australia . 92 B3
Hickman, U.S.A. 113 G10
Hickory, U.S.A. 109 H5
Hicks, Pt., Australia 95 F4
Hicks L., Canada 105 A9
Hicksville, U.S.A. 111 F11
Hida, Romania 43 C8

Hida-Gawa →, Japan 55 G8
Hida-Sammyaku, Japan .. 55 F8
Hidaka-Sammyaku, Japan . 54 C11
Hidalgo, Mexico 119 C5
Hidalgo □, Mexico 119 C5
Hidalgo, Presa M., Mexico 118 B3
Hidalgo, Pta. del, Canary Is. 37 F3
Hidalgo del Parral, Mexico . 118 B3
Hiddensee, Germany 24 A9
Hieflau, Austria 26 D7
Hiendelaencina, Spain ... 32 D2
Hierro, Canary Is. 37 G1
Higashiajima-San, Japan . 54 F10
Higashiōsaka, Japan 55 G7
Higgins, U.S.A. 113 G4
Higgins Corner, U.S.A. .. 116 F5
High Atlas = Haut Atlas,
  Morocco 78 B4
High Bridge, U.S.A. 111 F10
High Level, Canada 104 B5
High Point, U.S.A. 109 H6
High Prairie, Canada 104 B5
High River, Canada 104 C6
High Tatra = Tatry,
  Slovak Rep. 27 B13
High Veld, Africa 76 J6
High Wycombe, U.K. 13 F7
Highland □, U.K. 14 D4
Highland Park, U.S.A. ... 108 D2
Highmore, U.S.A. 112 C5
Highrock L., Man., Canada 105 B8
Highrock L., Sask., Canada 105 B7
Higüey, Dom. Rep. 121 C6
Hiiumaa, Estonia 9 G20
Híjar, Spain 32 D4
Ḥijāz □, Si. Arabia 70 E3
Hijo = Tagum, Phil. 61 H6
Hikari, Japan 55 H5
Hikmak, Ras el, Egypt ... 80 A2
Hiko, U.S.A. 116 H11
Hikone, Japan 55 G8
Hikurangi, N.Z. 91 F5
Hikurangi, Mt., N.Z. 91 H6
Hildburghausen, Germany . 24 E6
Hildesheim, Germany ... 24 C5
Hill →, Australia 93 F2
Hill City, Idaho, U.S.A. .. 114 E6
Hill City, Kans., U.S.A. .. 112 F5
Hill City, S. Dak., U.S.A. . 112 D3
Hill Island L., Canada ... 105 A7
Hillared, Sweden 11 G7
Hillcrest Center, U.S.A. .. 117 K8
Hillegom, Neths. 17 B4
Hillerød, Denmark 11 J6
Hillerstorp, Sweden 11 G7
Hillsboro, Kans., U.S.A. . 112 F6
Hillsboro, N. Dak., U.S.A. 112 B6
Hillsboro, N.H., U.S.A. .. 111 C13
Hillsboro, Ohio, U.S.A. .. 108 F4
Hillsboro, Oreg., U.S.A. . 116 E4
Hillsboro, Tex., U.S.A. .. 113 J6
Hillsborough, Grenada ... 121 D7
Hillsdale, Mich., U.S.A. . 108 E3
Hillsdale, N.Y., U.S.A. .. 111 D11
Hillsport, Canada 102 C2
Hillston, Australia 95 E4
Hilo, U.S.A. 106 J17
Hilton, U.S.A. 110 C7
Hilton Head Island, U.S.A. 109 J5
Hilvan, Turkey 73 D8
Hilversum, Neths. 17 B5
Himachal Pradesh □, India . 68 D7
Himalaya, Asia 69 E11
Himamaylan, Phil. 61 F5
Himara, Albania 40 F3
Himatnagar, India 66 H8
Himeji, Japan 55 G7
Himi, Japan 55 F8
Himmerland, Denmark .. 11 H3
Ḥimş, Syria 75 A5
Ḥimş □, Syria 75 A6
Hinche, Haiti 121 C5
Hinchinbrook I., Australia . 94 B4
Hinckley, U.K. 13 E6
Hinckley, U.S.A. 112 B8
Hindaun, India 68 F7
Hindmarsh, L., Australia . 95 F3
Hindsholm, Denmark ... 11 J4
Hindu Bagh, Pakistan ... 68 D2
Hindu Kush, Asia 66 B7
Hindubagh, Pakistan 66 D5
Hindupur, India 66 N10
Hines Creek, Canada 104 B5
Hinesville, U.S.A. 109 K5
Hinganghat, India 66 J11
Hingham, U.S.A. 114 B8
Hingir, India 69 J10
Hingoli, India 66 K10
Hinigaran, Phil. 61 F5
Hinis, Turkey 73 C9
Hinna = Imi, Ethiopia ... 81 F5
Hinna, Nigeria 83 C7
Hinnerup, Denmark 11 H4
Hinnøya, Norway 8 B16
Hinojosa del Duque, Spain . 35 G5
Hinsdale, U.S.A. 111 D12
Hinterrhein →, Switz. ... 25 J5
Hinton, Canada 104 C5
Hinton, U.S.A. 108 G5
Hinzir Burnu, Turkey ... 72 D6
Hirado, Japan 55 H4
Hirakud Dam, India 67 J13
Hiran →, India 69 H8
Hirapur, India 69 G8
Hiratsuka, Japan 55 G9
Hirfanlı Baraji, Turkey ... 72 C5
Hiroo, Japan 54 C11
Hirosaki, Japan 54 D10
Hiroshima, Japan 55 G6
Hiroshima □, Japan 55 G6

Hirson, France 19 C11
Hirtshals, Denmark 11 G3
Hisar, India 68 E6
Hisarcık, Turkey 39 B11
Hisaria, Bulgaria 41 D8
Ḩişn, Iraq 70 D5
Hispaniola, W. Indies ... 121 C5
Hita, Japan 55 H5
Hitachi, Japan 55 F10
Hitchin, U.K. 13 F7
Hitoyoshi, Japan 55 H5
Hitra, Norway 8 E13
Hitzacker, Germany 24 B7
Hixon, Canada 104 C4
Ḥiyyon, N. →, Israel ... 75 E4
Hjalmar L., Canada 105 A7
Hjälmaren, Sweden 10 E9
Hjältevad, Sweden 11 G9
Hjo, Sweden 11 F8
Hjørring, Denmark 11 G3
Hjortkvarn, Sweden 11 F9
Hlinsko, Czech Rep. 26 B8
Hlobane, S. Africa 89 D5
Hlohovec, Slovak Rep. .. 27 C10
Hlučín, Czech Rep. 27 B11
Hluhluwe, S. Africa 89 D5
Hlukhiv, Ukraine 47 G7
Hlyboka, Ukraine 47 H3
Hlybokaye, Belarus 46 E4
Hnúšťa, Slovak Rep. 27 C12
Ho, Ghana 83 D5
Ho Chi Minh City = Phanh
  Bho Ho Chi Minh,
  Vietnam 65 G6
Ho Thuong, Vietnam ... 64 C5
Hoa Binh, Vietnam 58 G5
Hoa Da, Vietnam 65 G7
Hoa Hiep, Vietnam 65 G5
Hoai Nhon, Vietnam 64 E7
Hoang Lien Son, Vietnam . 58 F4
Hoanib →, Namibia 88 B2
Hoare B., Canada 101 B13
Hoarusib →, Namibia .. 88 B2
Hobart, Australia 94 G4
Hobart, U.S.A. 113 H5
Hobbs, U.S.A. 113 J3
Hobbs Coast, Antarctica . 5 D14
Hobe Sound, U.S.A. 109 M5
Hoboken, U.S.A. 111 F10
Hobro, Denmark 11 H3
Hoburgen, Sweden 11 H12
Hocalar, Turkey 39 C11
Hochfeld, Namibia 88 C2
Hochschwab, Austria ... 26 D8
Höchstadt, Germany 25 F6
Hockenheim, Germany .. 25 F4
Hodaka-Dake, Japan 55 F8
Hodgeville, Canada 105 C7
Hodgson, Canada 105 C9
Hódmezővásárhely, Hungary . 42 D5
Hodna, Chott el, Algeria . 78 A6
Hodonín, Czech Rep. ... 27 C10
Hoeamdong, N. Korea .. 57 C16
Hœdic, Î. de, France 18 E4
Hoek van Holland, Neths. . 17 C4
Hoengsŏng, S. Korea ... 57 F14
Hoeryong, N. Korea 57 C15
Hoeyang, N. Korea 57 E14
Hof, Germany 25 E7
Hofgeismar, Germany ... 24 D5
Hofheim, Germany 25 E4
Hofmeyr, S. Africa 88 E4
Höfn, Iceland 8 D6
Hofors, Sweden 10 D10
Hofsjökull, Iceland 8 D4
Höfu, Japan 55 G5
Hogan Group, Australia . 95 F4
Höganäs, Sweden 11 H6
Hogarth, Mt., Australia . 94 C2
Hoggar = Ahaggar, Algeria 78 D7
Högsäter, Sweden 11 F5
Högsby, Sweden 11 G10
Högsjö, Sweden 10 E9
Hogsty Reef, Bahamas .. 121 B5
Hoh →, U.S.A. 116 C2
Hohe Acht, Germany ... 25 E3
Hohe Tauern, Austria ... 26 D5
Hohe Venn, Belgium 17 D6
Hohenau, Austria 27 C9
Hohenems, Austria 26 D2
Hohenloher Ebene, Germany 25 F5
Hohenwald, U.S.A. 109 H2
Hohenwestedt, Germany . 24 A5
Hoher Rhön = Rhön,
  Germany 24 E5
Hohhot, China 56 D6
Hóhlakas, Greece 36 D9
Hohoe, Ghana 83 D5
Hoi An, Vietnam 64 E7
Hoi Xuan, Vietnam 58 G5
Hoisington, U.S.A. 112 F5
Højer, Denmark 11 K2
Hōjō, Japan 55 H6
Hok, U.S.A. 113 H12
Hökensås, Sweden 11 F8
Hökerum, Sweden 11 G7
Hokianga Harbour, N.Z. . 91 F4
Hokitika, N.Z. 91 K3
Hokkaidō □, Japan 54 C11
Hol-Hol, Djibouti 81 E5
Hola Pristan, Ukraine ... 47 J7
Holbæk, Denmark 11 J5
Holbrook, Australia 95 F4
Holbrook, U.S.A. 115 J8
Holden, U.S.A. 114 G7
Holdenville, U.S.A. 113 H6
Holdrege, U.S.A. 112 E5
Holešov, Czech Rep. ... 27 B10
Holguín, Cuba 120 B4

Holíč, Slovak Rep. 27 C10
Holice, Czech Rep. 26 A8
Höljes, Sweden 10 D6
Hollabrunn, Austria 26 C9
Hollams Bird I., Namibia . 88 C1
Holland, Mich., U.S.A. .. 108 D2
Holland, N.Y., U.S.A. ... 110 D6
Hollandale, U.S.A. 113 J9
Hollandia = Jayapura,
  Indonesia 63 E10
Holley, U.S.A. 110 C6
Hollfeld, Germany 25 F7
Hollidaysburg, U.S.A. ... 110 F6
Hollis, U.S.A. 113 H5
Hollister, Calif., U.S.A. . 116 J5
Hollister, Idaho, U.S.A. . 114 E6
Höllviken, Sweden 11 J6
Holly Hill, U.S.A. 109 L5
Holly Springs, U.S.A. ... 113 H10
Hollywood, Calif., U.S.A. 106 D3
Hollywood, Fla., U.S.A. . 109 N5
Holman, Canada 100 A8
Hólmavík, Iceland 8 D3
Holmen, U.S.A. 112 D9
Holmes Reefs, Australia . 94 B4
Holmsjö, Sweden 11 H9
Holmsjön, Västernorrland,
  Sweden 10 B10
Holmsjön, Västernorrland,
  Sweden 10 B9
Holmsland Klit, Denmark . 11 J2
Holmsund, Sweden 8 E19
Holod, Romania 42 D7
Holroyd →, Australia ... 94 A3
Holstebro, Denmark 11 H2
Holsworthy, U.K. 13 G3
Holton, Canada 103 B8
Holton, U.S.A. 112 F7
Holtville, U.S.A. 117 N11
Holwerd, Neths. 17 A5
Holy I., Angl., U.K. 12 D3
Holy I., Northumb., U.K. . 12 B6
Holyhead, U.K. 12 D3
Holyoke, Colo., U.S.A. .. 112 E3
Holyoke, Mass., U.S.A. . 111 D12
Holyrood, Canada 103 C9
Holzkirchen, Germany .. 25 H7
Holzminden, Germany .. 24 D5
Homa Bay, Kenya 86 C3
Homalin, Burma 67 G19
Homand, Iran 71 C8
Homathko →, Canada .. 104 C4
Homberg, Germany 24 D5
Hombori, Mali 83 B4
Home B., Canada 101 B13
Home Hill, Australia ... 94 B4
Homedale, U.S.A. 114 E5
Homer, Alaska, U.S.A. .. 100 C4
Homer, La., U.S.A. 113 J8
Homer City, U.S.A. 110 F5
Homestead, Australia ... 94 C4
Homestead, U.S.A. 109 N5
Homewood, U.S.A. 116 F6
Homoine, Mozam. 89 C6
Homolijske Planina,
  Serbia, Yug. 40 B5
Homorod, Romania 43 D10
Homs = Ḩimş, Syria 75 A5
Homyel, Belarus 47 F6
Hon Chong, Vietnam ... 65 G5
Hon Me, Vietnam 64 C5
Honan = Henan □, China . 56 H8
Honan, Turkey 39 D11
Honbetsu, Japan 54 C11
Honcut, U.S.A. 116 F5
Honda Bay, Phil. 61 G3
Hondarribia, Spain 32 B3
Hondeklipbaai, S. Africa . 88 E2
Hondo, Japan 55 H5
Hondo, U.S.A. 113 L5
Hondo →, Belize 119 D7
Honduras ■, Cent. Amer. . 120 D2
Honduras, G. de, Caribbean 120 C2
Hønefoss, Norway 9 F14
Honesdale, U.S.A. 111 E9
Honey L., U.S.A. 116 F6
Honfleur, France 18 C7
Høng, Denmark 11 J5
Hong →, Vietnam 58 F5
Hong Gai, Vietnam 58 G6
Hong He →, China 56 H8
Hong Hu, China 59 C9
Hong Kong □, China ... 59 F10
Hong'an, China 59 B10
Honghai Wan, China ... 59 F10
Honghe, China 58 F4
Honghu, China 59 C9
Hongjiang, China 58 D7
Hongliu He →, China .. 56 F5
Hongor, Mongolia 56 B7
Hongsa, Laos 64 C3
Hongshui He →, China . 58 F7
Hongsŏng, S. Korea 57 F14
Hongtong, China 56 F6
Honguedo, Détroit d',
  Canada 103 C7
Hongwon, N. Korea 57 E14
Hongya, China 58 C4
Hongyuan, China 58 A4
Hongze Hu, China 57 H10
Honiara, Solomon Is. ... 96 H7
Honiton, U.K. 13 G4
Honkorâb, Ras, Egypt .. 80 C4
Honningsvåg, Norway .. 8 A21
Hönö, Sweden 11 G5
Honolulu, U.S.A. 106 H16
Honshū, Japan 55 G9
Hontoria del Pinar, Spain . 32 D1

Hood, Mt., U.S.A. 114 D3
Hood, Pt., Australia 93 F2
Hood River, U.S.A. 114 D3
Hoodsport, U.S.A. 116 C3
Hooge, Germany 24 A4
Hoogeveen, Neths. 17 B6
Hoogezand-Sappemeer,
  Neths. 17 A6
Hooghly = Hugli →, India 69 J13
Hooghly-Chinsura =
  Chunchura, India 69 H13
Hook Hd., Ireland 15 D5
Hook I., Australia 94 C4
Hook of Holland = Hoek
  van Holland, Neths. ... 17 C4
Hooker, U.S.A. 113 G4
Hooker Creek, Australia . 92 C5
Hoonah, U.S.A. 104 B1
Hooper Bay, U.S.A. 100 B3
Hoopeston, U.S.A. 108 E2
Hoopstad, S. Africa 88 D4
Höör, Sweden 11 J7
Hoorn, Neths. 17 B5
Hoover, U.S.A. 109 J2
Hoover Dam, U.S.A. ... 117 K12
Hooversville, U.S.A. ... 110 F6
Hop Bottom, U.S.A. ... 111 E9
Hopa, Turkey 73 B9
Hope, Canada 104 D4
Hope, Ariz., U.S.A. 117 M13
Hope, Ark., U.S.A. 113 J8
Hope, L., S. Austral.,
  Australia 95 D2
Hope, L., W. Austral.,
  Australia 93 F3
Hope I., Canada 110 B4
Hope Town, Bahamas .. 120 A4
Hopedale, Canada 103 A7
Hopedale, U.S.A. 111 D13
Hopefield, S. Africa 88 E2
Hopei = Hebei □, China . 56 E9
Hopelchén, Mexico 119 D7
Hopetoun, Vic., Australia . 95 F3
Hopetoun, W. Austral.,
  Australia 93 F3
Hopetown, S. Africa 88 D3
Hopevale, Australia 94 B4
Hopewell, U.S.A. 108 G7
Hopfgarten, Austria 26 D5
Hopkins, L., Australia .. 93 D4
Hopkinsville, U.S.A. ... 109 G2
Hopland, U.S.A. 116 G3
Hoquiam, U.S.A. 116 C2
Horasan, Turkey 73 B10
Horažďovice, Czech Rep. . 26 B6
Horb, Germany 25 G4
Hörby, Sweden 11 J7
Horcajo de Santiago, Spain 32 F1
Horden Hills, Australia . 92 D5
Horezu, Romania 43 E8
Horgen, Switz. 25 H4
Horgoš, Serbia, Yug. ... 42 D4
Hořice, Czech Rep. 26 A8
Horinger, China 56 D6
Horki, Belarus 46 E6
Horlick Mts., Antarctica . 5 E11
Horlivka, Ukraine 47 H10
Hormak, Iran 71 D9
Hormoz, Iran 71 E7
Hormoz, Jaz.-ye, Iran ... 71 E8
Hormozgān □, Iran 71 E8
Hormuz, Kūh-e, Iran 71 E7
Hormuz, Str. of, The Gulf . 71 E8
Horn, Austria 26 C8
Horn, Iceland 8 C2
Horn →, Canada 104 A5
Horn, Cape = Hornos, C.
  de, Chile 122 J4
Horn Head, Ireland 15 A3
Horn I., Australia 94 A3
Horn Mts., Canada 104 A5
Hornachuelos, Spain ... 35 H5
Hornavan, Sweden 8 C17
Hornbeck, U.S.A. 113 K8
Hornbrook, U.S.A. 114 F2
Hornburg, Germany 24 C6
Horncastle, U.K. 12 D7
Horndal, Sweden 10 D10
Hornell, U.S.A. 110 D7
Hornell L., Canada 104 A5
Hornepayne, Canada ... 102 C3
Horní Planá, Czech Rep. . 26 C7
Hornings Mills, Canada . 110 B4
Hornitos, U.S.A. 116 H6
Hornos, C. de, Chile 122 J4
Hornoy-le-Bourg, France . 19 C8
Hornsea, U.K. 12 D7
Hornslandet, Sweden ... 10 C11
Hörnum, Germany 24 A4
Horobetsu, Japan 54 C10
Horodenka, Ukraine 47 H3
Horodnya, Ukraine 47 G6
Horodok, Khmelnytskyy,
  Ukraine 47 H4
Horodok, Lviv, Ukraine . 47 H2
Horodyshche, Ukraine .. 47 H6
Horokhiv, Ukraine 47 G3
Horovice, Czech Rep. ... 26 B6
Horqin Youyi Qianqi, China 57 A12
Horqueta, Paraguay 126 A4
Horred, Sweden 11 G6
Horse Creek, U.S.A. ... 112 E2
Horse Is., Canada 103 B8
Horsefly L., Canada 104 C4
Horseheads, U.S.A. 110 D8
Horsens, Denmark 11 J3
Horsham, Australia 95 F3
Horsham, U.K. 13 F7
Horšovský Týn, Czech Rep. 26 B5
Horten, Norway 9 G14

Hortobágy →, Hungary	42	C6
Horton, U.S.A.	112	F7
Horton →, Canada	100	B7
Horwood L., Canada	102	C3
Hosaina, Ethiopia	81	F4
Hose, Gunung-Gunung, Malaysia	62	D4
Ḥoseynābād, Khuzestān, Iran	71	C6
Ḥoseynābād, Kordestān, Iran	70	C5
Hoshangabad, India	68	H7
Hoshiarpur, India	68	D6
Hospet, India	66	M10
Hoste, I., Chile	128	H3
Hostens, France	20	D3
Hot, Thailand	64	C2
Hot Creek Range, U.S.A.	114	G6
Hot Springs, Ark., U.S.A.	113	H8
Hot Springs, S. Dak., U.S.A.	112	D3
Hotagen, Sweden	8	E16
Hotan, China	60	C2
Hotazel, S. Africa	88	D3
Hotchkiss, U.S.A.	115	G10
Hotham, C., Australia	92	B5
Hoting, Sweden	8	D17
Hotolishti, Albania	40	E4
Hotte, Massif de la, Haiti	121	C5
Hottentotsbaai, Namibia	88	D1
Houat, Î. de, France	18	E4
Houdan, France	19	D8
Houei Sai, Laos	58	G3
Houeillès, France	20	D4
Houffalize, Belgium	17	D5
Houghton, Mich., U.S.A.	112	B10
Houghton, N.Y., U.S.A.	110	D6
Houghton L., U.S.A.	108	C3
Houhora Heads, N.Z.	91	F4
Houlton, U.S.A.	109	B12
Houma, U.S.A.	113	L9
Houndé, Burkina Faso	82	C4
Hourtin, France	20	C2
Hourtin-Carcans, Étang d', France	20	C2
Housatonic →, U.S.A.	111	E11
Houston, Canada	104	C3
Houston, Mo., U.S.A.	113	G9
Houston, Tex., U.S.A.	113	L7
Hout →, S. Africa	89	C4
Houtkraal, S. Africa	88	E3
Houtman Abrolhos, Australia	93	E1
Hovd, Mongolia	60	B4
Hove, U.K.	13	G7
Hovmantorp, Sweden	11	H9
Hövsgöl, Mongolia	56	C5
Hövsgöl Nuur, Mongolia	60	A5
Hovsta, Sweden	10	E9
Howakil, Eritrea	81	D5
Howar, Wadi →, Sudan	81	D2
Howard, Australia	95	D5
Howard, Pa., U.S.A.	110	F7
Howard, S. Dak., U.S.A.	112	C6
Howe, U.S.A.	114	E7
Howe, C., Australia	95	F5
Howe I., Canada	111	B8
Howell, U.S.A.	108	D4
Howick, Canada	111	A11
Howick, S. Africa	89	D5
Howick Group, Australia	94	A4
Howitt, L., Australia	95	D2
Howland I., Pac. Oc.	96	G10
Howrah = Haora, India	69	H13
Howth Hd., Ireland	15	C5
Höxter, Germany	24	D5
Hoy, U.K.	14	C5
Hoya, Germany	24	C5
Høyanger, Norway	9	F12
Hoyerswerda, Germany	24	D10
Hoylake, U.K.	12	D4
Hoyos, Spain	34	E4
Hpa-an = Pa-an, Burma	67	L20
Hpungan Pass, Burma	67	F20
Hradec Králové, Czech Rep.	26	A8
Hrádek, Czech Rep.	27	C9
Hranice, Czech Rep.	27	B10
Hrazdan, Armenia	49	K7
Hrebenka, Ukraine	47	G7
Hrodna, Belarus	46	F2
Hrodzyanka, Belarus	46	F5
Hron →, Slovak Rep.	27	D11
Hrubieszów, Poland	45	H10
Hrubý Jeseník, Czech Rep.	27	A10
Hrvatska = Croatia ■, Europe	29	C13
Hrymayliv, Ukraine	47	H4
Hsenwi, Burma	67	H20
Hsiamen = Xiamen, China	59	E12
Hsian = Xi'an, China	56	G5
Hsinchu, Taiwan	59	E13
Hsinhailien = Lianyungang, China	57	G10
Hsinying, Taiwan	59	F13
Hsopket, Burma	58	F2
Hsüchou = Xuzhou, China	57	G9
Hu Jian, China	56	G5
Hua Hin, Thailand	64	F2
Hua Xian, Henan, China	56	G8
Hua Xian, Shaanxi, China	56	G5
Hua'an, China	59	E11
Huab →, Namibia	88	B2
Huacheng, China	59	E10
Huachinera, Mexico	118	A3
Huacho, Peru	124	F3
Huade, China	56	D7
Huadian, China	57	C14
Huadu, China	59	F9
Huai He →, China	59	A12
Huai Yot, Thailand	65	J2
Huai'an, Hebei, China	56	D8
Huai'an, Jiangsu, China	57	H10
Huaibei, China	56	G9
Huaibin, China	59	A10
Huaide = Gongzhuling, China	57	C13
Huaidezhen, China	57	C13
Huaihua, China	58	D7
Huaiji, China	59	F9
Huainan, China	59	A11
Huaining, China	59	B11
Huairen, China	56	E7
Huairou, China	56	D9
Huaiyang, China	56	H8
Huaiyin, China	57	H10
Huaiyuan, Anhui, China	57	H9
Huaiyuan, Guangxi Zhuangzu, China	58	E7
Huajianzi, China	57	D13
Huajuapan de Leon, Mexico	119	D5
Hualapai Peak, U.S.A.	115	J7
Hualien, Taiwan	59	E13
Huallaga →, Peru	124	E3
Huambo, Angola	85	G3
Huan Jiang →, China	56	G5
Huancabamba, Peru	124	E3
Huancane, Peru	124	G5
Huancavelica, Peru	124	F3
Huancayo, Peru	124	F3
Huanchaca, Bolivia	124	H5
Huang Hai = Yellow Sea, China	57	G12
Huang He →, China	57	F10
Huang Xian, China	57	F11
Huangchuan, China	59	A10
Huanggang, China	59	B10
Huangguoshu, China	58	E5
Huangling, China	56	G5
Huanglong, China	56	G5
Huanglongtan, China	59	A8
Huangmei, China	59	B10
Huangpi, China	59	B10
Huangping, China	58	D6
Huangshan, China	59	C12
Huangshi, China	59	B10
Huangsongdian, China	57	C14
Huangyan, China	59	C13
Huangyangsi, China	59	D8
Huaning, China	58	E4
Huanjiang, China	58	E7
Huantai, China	57	F9
Huánuco, Peru	124	E3
Huaping, China	58	D3
Huaraz, Peru	124	E3
Huarmey, Peru	124	F3
Huarong, China	59	C9
Huascarán, Peru	122	D3
Huasco, Chile	126	B1
Huasco →, Chile	126	B1
Huasna, U.S.A.	117	K6
Huatabampo, Mexico	118	B3
Huauchinango, Mexico	119	C5
Huautla de Jiménez, Mexico	119	D5
Huaxi, China	58	D6
Huay Namota, Mexico	118	C4
Huayin, China	56	G6
Huayuan, China	58	C7
Huayun, China	58	B6
Huazhou, China	59	G8
Hubbard, Ohio, U.S.A.	110	E4
Hubbard, Tex., U.S.A.	113	K6
Hubbart Pt., Canada	105	B10
Hubei □, China	59	B9
Hubli, India	66	M9
Huch'ang, N. Korea	57	D14
Hucknall, U.K.	12	D6
Huddersfield, U.K.	12	D6
Hude, Germany	24	B4
Hudi, Sudan	80	D3
Hudiksvall, Sweden	10	C11
Hudson, Canada	102	B1
Hudson, Mass., U.S.A.	111	D13
Hudson, N.Y., U.S.A.	111	D11
Hudson, Wis., U.S.A.	112	C8
Hudson, Wyo., U.S.A.	114	E9
Hudson →, U.S.A.	111	F10
Hudson Bay, N.W.T., Canada	101	C11
Hudson Bay, Sask., Canada	105	C8
Hudson Falls, U.S.A.	111	C11
Hudson Mts., Antarctica	5	D16
Hudson Str., Canada	101	B13
Hudson's Hope, Canada	104	B4
Hue, Vietnam	64	D6
Huebra →, Spain	34	D4
Huedin, Romania	42	D8
Huehuetenango, Guatemala	120	C1
Huejúcar, Mexico	118	C4
Huélamo, Spain	32	E3
Huelgoat, France	18	D3
Huelma, Spain	35	H7
Huelva, Spain	35	H4
Huelva □, Spain	35	H4
Huelva →, Spain	35	H5
Huentelauquén, Chile	126	C1
Huércal-Overa, Spain	33	H3
Huerta, Sa. de la, Argentina	126	C2
Huertas, C. de las, Spain	33	G4
Huerva →, Spain	32	D4
Huesca, Spain	32	D4
Huesca □, Spain	32	D5
Huéscar, Spain	33	H2
Huetamo, Mexico	118	D4
Huete, Spain	32	E2
Hugh →, Australia	94	D1
Hughenden, Australia	94	C3
Hughes, Australia	93	F4
Hughesville, U.S.A.	111	E8
Hugli →, India	69	J13
Hugo, Colo., U.S.A.	112	F3
Hugo, Okla., U.S.A.	113	H7
Hugoton, U.S.A.	113	G4
Hui Xian = Huixian, China	56	G7
Hui Xian, China	56	H4
Hui'an, China	59	E12
Hui'anbu, China	56	F4
Huichang, China	59	E10
Huichapán, Mexico	119	C5
Huidong, Guangdong, China	59	F10
Huidong, Sichuan, China	58	D4
Huifa He →, China	57	C14
Huila, Nevado del, Colombia	124	C3
Huilai, China	59	F11
Huili, China	58	D4
Huimin, China	57	F9
Huinan, China	57	C14
Huinca Renancó, Argentina	126	C3
Huining, China	56	G3
Huinong, China	56	E4
Huisache, Mexico	118	C4
Huishui, China	58	D6
Huisne →, France	18	E7
Huiting, China	56	G9
Huitong, China	58	D7
Huixian, China	56	G7
Huixtla, Mexico	119	D6
Huize, China	58	D4
Huizhou, China	59	F10
Hukawng Valley, Burma	67	F20
Hukou, China	59	C11
Hukuntsi, Botswana	88	C3
Ḥulayfāʾ, Si. Arabia	70	E4
Huld = Ulaanjirem, Mongolia	56	B3
Hulin He →, China	57	B12
Hull = Kingston upon Hull, U.K.	12	D7
Hull, Canada	102	C4
Hull →, U.K.	12	D7
Hulst, Neths.	17	C4
Hultsfred, Sweden	11	G9
Hulun Nur, China	60	B6
Hulyaypole, Ukraine	47	J9
Humahuaca, Argentina	126	A2
Humaitá, Brazil	124	E6
Humaitá, Paraguay	126	B4
Humansdorp, S. Africa	88	E3
Humara, J., Sudan	81	D3
Humbe, Angola	88	B1
Humber →, U.K.	12	D7
Humboldt, Canada	105	C7
Humboldt, Iowa, U.S.A.	112	D7
Humboldt, Tenn., U.S.A.	113	H10
Humboldt →, U.S.A.	114	F4
Humboldt Gletscher, Greenland	4	B4
Hume, U.S.A.	116	J8
Hume, L., Australia	95	F4
Humenné, Slovak Rep.	27	C14
Hummelsta, Sweden	10	E10
Humphreys, Mt., U.S.A.	116	H8
Humphreys Peak, U.S.A.	115	J8
Humpolec, Czech Rep.	26	B8
Humptulips, U.S.A.	116	C3
Hūn, Libya	79	C9
Hun Jiang →, China	57	D13
Húnaflói, Iceland	8	D3
Hunan □, China	59	D9
Hunchun, China	57	C16
Hundested, Denmark	11	J5
Hundewali, Pakistan	68	D5
Hundred Mile House, Canada	104	C4
Hunedoara, Romania	42	E7
Hunedoara □, Romania	42	E7
Hünfeld, Germany	24	E5
Hung Yen, Vietnam	58	G6
Hungary ■, Europe	27	D12
Hungary, Plain of, Europe	6	F10
Hungerford, Australia	95	D3
Hŭngnam, N. Korea	57	E14
Hungt'ou Hsü, Taiwan	59	F13
Huni Valley, Ghana	82	D4
Hunneberg, Sweden	11	F6
Hunnebostrand, Sweden	11	F5
Hunsberge, Namibia	88	D2
Hunsrück, Germany	25	F3
Hunstanton, U.K.	12	E8
Hunte →, Germany	24	B4
Hunter, U.S.A.	111	D10
Hunter I., Australia	94	G3
Hunter I., Canada	104	C3
Hunter Ra., Australia	95	E5
Hunters Road, Zimbabwe	87	F2
Hunterville, N.Z.	91	H5
Huntingburg, U.S.A.	108	F2
Huntingdon, Canada	102	C5
Huntingdon, U.K.	13	E7
Huntington, Ind., U.S.A.	108	E3
Huntington, Oreg., U.S.A.	114	D5
Huntington, Utah, U.S.A.	114	G8
Huntington, W. Va., U.S.A.	108	F4
Huntington Beach, U.S.A.	117	M9
Huntington Station, U.S.A.	111	F11
Huntly, N.Z.	91	G5
Huntly, U.K.	14	D6
Huntsville, Canada	102	C4
Huntsville, Ala., U.S.A.	109	H2
Huntsville, Tex., U.S.A.	113	K7
Hunyani →, Zimbabwe	87	F3
Hunyuan, China	56	E7
Hunza →, India	69	B6
Huo Xian = Huozhou, China	56	F6
Huong Hoa, Vietnam	64	D6
Huong Khe, Vietnam	64	C5
Huonville, Australia	94	G4
Huoqiu, China	59	A11
Huoshan, Anhui, China	59	A12
Huoshan, Anhui, China	59	B11
Huoshao Dao = Lü-Tao, Taiwan	59	F13
Huozhou, China	56	F6
Hupeh = Hubei □, China	59	B9
Ḥūr, Iran	71	D8
Hurbanovo, Slovak Rep.	27	D11
Hurd, C., Canada	110	A3
Hure Qi, China	57	C11
Hurezani, Romania	43	F8
Hurghada, Egypt	80	B3
Hurley, N. Mex., U.S.A.	115	K9
Hurley, Wis., U.S.A.	112	B9
Huron, Calif., U.S.A.	116	J6
Huron, Ohio, U.S.A.	110	E2
Huron, S. Dak., U.S.A.	112	C5
Huron, L., U.S.A.	110	B2
Hurricane, U.S.A.	115	H7
Hurso, Ethiopia	81	F5
Hurunui →, N.Z.	91	K4
Hurup, Denmark	11	H2
Húsavík, Iceland	8	C5
Huşi, Romania	43	D13
Huskvarna, Sweden	11	G8
Hustadvika, Norway	8	E12
Hustontown, U.S.A.	110	F6
Hustopeče, Czech Rep.	27	C9
Husum, Germany	24	A5
Husum, Sweden	10	A13
Hutchinson, Kans., U.S.A.	113	F6
Hutchinson, Minn., U.S.A.	112	C7
Hutte Sauvage, L. de la, Canada	103	A7
Hüttenberg, Austria	26	E7
Hutton, Mt., Australia	95	D4
Huwun, Ethiopia	81	G5
Huy, Belgium	17	D5
Huzhou, China	59	B13
Hvalpsund, Denmark	11	H3
Hvammstangi, Iceland	8	D3
Hvar, Croatia	29	E13
Hvarski Kanal, Croatia	29	E13
Hvítá →, Iceland	8	D3
Hwachŏn-chŏsuji, S. Korea	57	E14
Hwang Ho = Huang He →, China	57	F10
Hwange, Zimbabwe	87	F2
Hwange Nat. Park, Zimbabwe	88	B4
Hyannis, Mass., U.S.A.	108	E14
Hyannis, Nebr., U.S.A.	112	E4
Hyargas Nuur, Mongolia	60	B4
Hybo, Sweden	10	C10
Hydaburg, U.S.A.	104	B2
Hyde Park, U.S.A.	111	E11
Hyden, Australia	93	F2
Hyderabad, India	66	L11
Hyderabad, Pakistan	68	G3
Hyères, France	21	E10
Hyères, Îs. d', France	21	F10
Hyesan, N. Korea	57	D15
Hyland →, Canada	104	B3
Hyltebruk, Sweden	11	H7
Hymia, India	69	C8
Hyndman Peak, U.S.A.	114	E6
Hyōgo □, Japan	55	G7
Hyrum, U.S.A.	114	F8
Hysham, U.S.A.	114	C10
Hythe, U.K.	13	F9
Hyūga, Japan	55	H5
Hyvinge = Hyvinkää, Finland	9	F21
Hyvinkää, Finland	9	F21

I

I-n-Gall, Niger	83	B6
I-n-Oudad, Algeria	83	A5
I-n-Ouzzal, Algeria	83	A5
I-n-Tadrest, Niger	83	B6
Iablaniţa, Romania	42	F7
Iaco →, Brazil	124	E5
Iacobeni, Romania	43	C10
Iakora, Madag.	89	C8
Ialomiţa □, Romania	43	F12
Ialomiţa →, Romania	43	F12
Ialoveni, Moldova	43	D13
Ialpug →, Moldova	43	E13
Ianca, Romania	43	E12
Iara, Romania	43	D8
Iarda, Ethiopia	81	E4
Iargara, Moldova	43	D13
Iaşi, Romania	43	C12
Iaşi □, Romania	43	C12
Íasmos, Greece	41	E9
Ib →, India	69	J10
Iba, Phil.	61	D3
Ibadan, Nigeria	83	D5
Ibagué, Colombia	124	C3
Ibăneşti, Botoşani, Romania	43	B11
Ibăneşti, Mureş, Romania	43	D9
Ibar →, Serbia, Yug.	40	C4
Ibaraki □, Japan	55	F10
Ibarra, Ecuador	124	C3
Ibba, Sudan	81	G2
Ibba →, Sudan	81	F2
Ibbenbüren, Germany	24	C3
Ibembo, Dem. Rep. of the Congo	86	B1
Ibera, L., Argentina	126	B4
Iberian Peninsula, Europe	6	H5
Iberville, Canada	102	C5
Iberville, Lac d', Canada	102	A5
Ibi, Nigeria	83	D6
Ibi, Spain	33	G4
Ibiá, Brazil	125	G9
Ibicaraí, Brazil	125	F11
Ibicuí →, Brazil	127	B4
Ibicuy, Argentina	126	C4
Ibioapaba, Sa. da, Brazil	125	D10
Ibiza = Eivissa, Spain	37	C7
Íblei, Monti, Italy	31	E7
Ibo, Mozam.	87	E5
Ibonma, Indonesia	63	E8
Ibotirama, Brazil	125	F10
Ibrāhīm →, Lebanon	75	A4
ʿIbrī, Oman	71	F8
Ibriktepe, Turkey	41	E10
Ibshawâi, Egypt	80	J7
Ibu, Indonesia	63	D7
Ibusuki, Japan	55	J5
Ica, Peru	124	F3
Ica →, Brazil	124	D5
Içana, Brazil	124	C5
Içana →, Brazil	124	C5
İçel = Mersin, Turkey	70	B2
Iceland ■, Europe	8	D4
Ich'ang = Yichang, China	59	B8
Ichchapuram, India	67	K14
Ichhawar, India	68	H7
Ichihara, Japan	55	G10
Ichikawa, Japan	55	G9
Ichilo →, Bolivia	124	G6
Ichinohe, Japan	54	D10
Ichinomiya, Japan	55	G8
Ichinoseki, Japan	54	E10
Ichnya, Ukraine	47	G7
Ichŏn, S. Korea	57	F14
Icod, Canary Is.	37	F3
Ida Grove, U.S.A.	112	D7
Idabel, U.S.A.	113	J7
Idaga Hamus, Ethiopia	81	E4
Idah, Nigeria	83	D6
Idaho □, U.S.A.	114	D7
Idaho City, U.S.A.	114	E6
Idaho Falls, U.S.A.	114	E7
Idanha-a-Nova, Portugal	34	F3
Idar-Oberstein, Germany	25	F3
Idfû, Egypt	80	C3
Ídhi Óros, Greece	36	D6
Ídhra, Greece	38	D5
Idi, Indonesia	62	C1
Idiofa, Dem. Rep. of the Congo	84	E3
Idkerberget, Sweden	10	D9
Idku, Bahra el, Egypt	80	H7
Idlib, Syria	70	C3
Idre, Sweden	10	C6
Idria, U.S.A.	116	J6
Idrija, Slovenia	29	C11
Idritsa, Russia	46	D5
Idutywa, S. Africa	89	E4
Ieper, Belgium	17	D2
Ierápetra, Greece	36	E7
Ierissós, Greece	40	F7
Ierissoú Kólpos, Greece	40	F7
Iernut, Romania	43	D9
Iesi, Italy	29	E10
Iésolo, Italy	29	C9
Ifach, Peñón de, Spain	33	G5
Ifakara, Tanzania	84	F7
'Ifal, W. al →, Si. Arabia	70	D2
Ifanadiana, Madag.	89	C8
Ife, Nigeria	83	D5
Iférouâne, Niger	83	B6
Iffley, Australia	94	B3
Ifni, Morocco	78	C3
Ifon, Nigeria	83	D6
Iforas, Adrar des, Mali	83	B5
Ifould, L., Australia	93	F5
Iganga, Uganda	86	B3
Igarapava, Brazil	125	H9
Igarka, Russia	50	C9
Igatimi, Paraguay	127	A4
Igbetti, Nigeria	83	D5
Igbo-Ora, Nigeria	83	D5
Igboho, Nigeria	83	D5
Igbor, Nigeria	83	D6
Iğdır, Turkey	73	C11
Igelfors, Sweden	11	F9
Iggesund, Sweden	10	C11
Iglésias, Italy	30	C1
Igloolik, Canada	101	B11
Igluligaarjuk, Canada	101	B10
Igma, Gebel el, Egypt	80	B3
Ignace, Canada	102	C1
Iğneada, Turkey	41	E11
Iğneada Burnu, Turkey	41	E12
Igoumenítsa, Greece	38	B2
Igra, Russia	48	B11
Iguaçu →, Brazil	127	B5
Iguaçu, Cat. del, Brazil	127	B5
Iguaçu Falls = Iguaçu, Cat. del, Brazil	127	B5
Iguala, Mexico	119	D5
Igualada, Spain	32	D6
Iguassu = Iguaçu →, Brazil	127	B5
Iguatu, Brazil	125	E11
Iharana, Madag.	89	A9
Ihbulag, Mongolia	56	C4
Iheya-Shima, Japan	55	L3
Ihiala, Nigeria	83	D6
Ihosy, Madag.	89	C8
Ihotry, Farihy, Madag.	89	C7
Ihugh, Nigeria	83	D6
Ii, Finland	8	D21
Ii-Shima, Japan	55	L3
Iijoki →, Finland	8	D21
Iisalmi, Finland	8	E22
Iiyama, Japan	55	F9
Iizuka, Japan	55	H5
Ijebu-Igbo, Nigeria	83	D5
Ijebu-Ode, Nigeria	83	D5
IJmuiden, Neths.	17	B4
IJssel →, Neths.	17	B5
IJsselmeer, Neths.	17	B5
Ijuí, Brazil	127	B5
Ijuí →, Brazil	127	B4
Ikalamavony, Madag.	89	C8
Ikale, Nigeria	83	D6
Ikaluktutiak, Canada	100	B9

Ikang, *Nigeria* ... 83 E6
Ikara, *Nigeria* ... 83 C6
Ikare, *Nigeria* ... 83 D6
Ikaría, *Greece* ... 39 D8
Ikast, *Denmark* ... 11 H3
Ikeda, *Japan* ... 55 G6
Ikeja, *Nigeria* ... 83 D5
Ikela, *Dem. Rep. of the Congo* . 84 E4
Ikerre-Ekiti, *Nigeria* ... 83 D6
Ikhtiman, *Bulgaria* ... 40 D7
Iki, *Japan* ... 55 H4
Ikimba L., *Tanzania* ... 86 C3
Ikire, *Nigeria* ... 83 D5
Ikizdere, *Turkey* ... 73 B9
Ikom, *Nigeria* ... 83 D6
Ikongo, *Madag.* ... 89 C8
Ikopa →, *Madag.* ... 89 B8
Ikot Ekpene, *Nigeria* ... 83 D6
Ikungu, *Tanzania* ... 86 C3
Ikurun, *Nigeria* ... 83 D5
Ila, *Nigeria* ... 83 D5
Ilagan, *Phil.* ... 61 C4
Ilaka, *Madag.* ... 89 B8
Īlām, *Iran* ... 70 C5
Ilam, *Nepal* ... 69 F12
Ilam □, *Iran* ... 70 C5
Ilan, *Taiwan* ... 59 E13
Ilanskiy, *Russia* ... 51 D10
Ilaro, *Nigeria* ... 83 D5
Ilatane, *Niger* ... 83 B5
Iława, *Poland* ... 44 E6
Ile-à-la-Crosse, *Canada* ... 105 B7
Ile-à-la-Crosse, Lac, *Canada* 105 B7
Île-de-France □, *France* ... 19 D9
Ileanda, *Romania* ... 43 C8
Ilebo, *Dem. Rep. of the Congo* . 84 E4
Ilek, *Russia* ... 50 D6
Ilero, *Nigeria* ... 83 D5
Ilesha, *Kwara, Nigeria* ... 83 D5
Ilesha, *Oyo, Nigeria* ... 83 D5
Ilford, *Canada* ... 105 B9
Ilfracombe, *Australia* ... 94 C3
Ilfracombe, *U.K.* ... 13 F3
Ilgaz, *Turkey* ... 72 B5
Ilgaz Dağları, *Turkey* ... 72 B5
Ilgın, *Turkey* ... 72 C4
Ílhavo, *Portugal* ... 34 E2
Ilhéus, *Brazil* ... 125 F11
Ili →, *Kazakstan* ... 50 E8
Ilia, *Romania* ... 42 E7
Ilía □, *Greece* ... 38 D3
Iliamna L., *U.S.A.* ... 100 C4
Iliç, *Turkey* ... 73 C8
Ilıca, *Turkey* ... 39 B9
Ilichevsk, *Azerbaijan* ... 73 C11
Iligan, *Phil.* ... 61 G6
Iligan Bay, *Phil.* ... 61 G6
Ilíki, L., *Greece* ... 38 C5
Ilin I., *Phil.* ... 61 E4
Iliodhrómia, *Greece* ... 38 B5
Ilion, *U.S.A.* ... 111 D9
Ilirska-Bistrica, *Slovenia* ... 29 C11
Ilkeston, *U.K.* ... 12 E6
Ilkley, *U.K.* ... 12 D6
Illampu = Ancohuma, *Nevada, Bolivia* ... 122 E4
Illana B., *Phil.* ... 61 H5
Illapel, *Chile* ... 126 C1
Ille-et-Vilaine □, *France* ... 18 D5
Ille-sur-Têt, *France* ... 20 F6
Illéla, *Niger* ... 83 C6
Iller →, *Germany* ... 25 G5
Illertissen, *Germany* ... 25 G6
Illescas, *Spain* ... 34 E7
Illetas, *Spain* ... 37 B9
Illichivsk, *Ukraine* ... 47 J6
Illiers-Combray, *France* ... 18 D8
Illimani, Nevado, *Bolivia* ... 124 G5
Illinois □, *U.S.A.* ... 112 E10
Illinois →, *U.S.A.* ... 107 C8
Illium = Troy, *Turkey* ... 39 B8
Illizi, *Algeria* ... 78 C7
Illkirch-Graffenstaden, *France* ... 19 D14
Illoqqortoormiit, *Greenland* ... 4 B6
Íllora, *Spain* ... 35 H7
Ilm →, *Germany* ... 24 D7
Ilmajoki, *Finland* ... 9 E20
Ilmen, Ozero, *Russia* ... 46 C6
Ilmenau, *Germany* ... 24 E6
Ilo, *Peru* ... 124 G4
Ilobu, *Nigeria* ... 83 D5
Iloilo, *Phil.* ... 61 F5
Ilora, *Nigeria* ... 83 D5
Ilorin, *Nigeria* ... 83 D5
Ilovatka, *Russia* ... 48 E7
Ilovlya, *Russia* ... 49 F7
Ilovlya →, *Russia* ... 49 F7
Iłowa, *Poland* ... 45 G2
Ilubabor □, *Ethiopia* ... 81 F4
Ilva Mică, *Romania* ... 43 C9
Ilwaco, *U.S.A.* ... 116 D2
Ilwaki, *Indonesia* ... 63 F7
Ilyichevsk = Illichivsk, *Ukraine* ... 47 J6
Iłża, *Poland* ... 45 G8
Iłzanka →, *Poland* ... 45 G8
Imabari, *Japan* ... 55 G6
Imaloto →, *Madag.* ... 89 C8
Imamoğlu, *Turkey* ... 72 D6
Imandra, Ozero, *Russia* ... 50 C4
Imanombo, *Madag.* ... 89 C8
Imari, *Japan* ... 55 H4
Imasa, *Sudan* ... 80 D4
Imathía □, *Greece* ... 40 F6
Imatra, *Finland* ... 46 B5
Imbil, *Australia* ... 95 D5
Iménas, *Mali* ... 83 B5

imeni 26 Bakinskikh Komissarov = Neftçala, *Azerbaijan* ... 71 B6
imeni 26 Bakinskikh Komissarov, *Turkmenistan* 71 B7
Imeri, Serra, *Brazil* ... 124 C5
Imerimandroso, *Madag.* ... 89 B8
Imi, *Ethiopia* ... 81 F5
Imishly = Imişli, *Azerbaijan* 49 L9
Imişli, *Azerbaijan* ... 49 L9
Imlay, *U.S.A.* ... 114 F4
Imlay City, *U.S.A.* ... 110 D1
Immaseri, *Sudan* ... 81 D2
Immenstadt, *Germany* ... 25 H6
Immingham, *U.K.* ... 12 D7
Immokalee, *U.S.A.* ... 109 M5
Imo □, *Nigeria* ... 83 D6
Imo →, *Nigeria* ... 83 E6
Ímola, *Italy* ... 29 D8
Imotski, *Croatia* ... 29 E14
Imperatriz, *Brazil* ... 125 E9
Impéria, *Italy* ... 28 E5
Imperial, *Canada* ... 105 C7
Imperial, *Calif., U.S.A.* ... 117 N11
Imperial, *Nebr., U.S.A.* ... 112 E4
Imperial Beach, *U.S.A.* ... 117 N9
Imperial Dam, *U.S.A.* ... 117 N12
Imperial Reservoir, *U.S.A.* 117 N12
Imperial Valley, *U.S.A.* ... 117 N11
Imperieuse Reef, *Australia* .. 92 C2
Impfondo, *Congo* ... 84 D3
Imphal, *India* ... 67 G18
Imphy, *France* ... 19 F10
İmranlı, *Turkey* ... 73 C8
İmroz = Gökçeada, *Turkey* 41 F9
İmroz, *Turkey* ... 41 F9
Imst, *Austria* ... 26 D3
Imuris, *Mexico* ... 118 A2
Imuruan B., *Phil.* ... 63 B5
In Akhmed, *Mali* ... 83 B4
In-Aleï, *Mali* ... 82 B4
In Delimane, *Mali* ... 83 B5
In-Guezzam, *Niger* ... 83 B6
In Koufi, *Mali* ... 83 B5
In Salah, *Algeria* ... 78 C6
In Tallak, *Mali* ... 83 B5
In Tebezas, *Mali* ... 83 B5
Ina, *Japan* ... 55 G8
Inangahua Junction, *N.Z.* .. 91 J3
Inanwatan, *Indonesia* ... 63 E8
Iñapari, *Peru* ... 124 F5
Inari, *Finland* ... 8 B22
Inarijärvi, *Finland* ... 8 B22
Inawashiro-Ko, *Japan* ... 54 F10
Inca, *Spain* ... 37 B9
Inca de Oro, *Chile* ... 126 B2
Incaguasi, *Chile* ... 126 B1
Ince Burun, *Turkey* ... 72 A4
Incekum Burnu, *Turkey* ... 72 D5
Incesu, *Turkey* ... 70 B2
Inch'ŏn, *S. Korea* ... 57 F14
Incio = Cruz de Incio, *Spain* 34 C3
Incirliova, *Turkey* ... 39 D9
Incline Village, *U.S.A.* ... 114 G4
Incomáti →, *Mozam.* ... 89 D5
Inda Silase, *Ethiopia* ... 81 E4
Indal, *Sweden* ... 10 B11
Indalsälven →, *Sweden* ... 10 B11
Indaw, *Burma* ... 67 G20
Indbir, *Ethiopia* ... 81 F4
Independence, *Calif., U.S.A.* 116 J8
Independence, *Iowa, U.S.A.* 112 D9
Independence, *Kans., U.S.A.* 113 G7
Independence, *Ky., U.S.A.* 108 F3
Independence, *Mo., U.S.A.* 112 F7
Independence Fjord, *Greenland* ... 4 A6
Independence Mts., *U.S.A.* 114 F5
Independenţa, *Romania* ... 43 E12
Index, *U.S.A.* ... 116 C5
India ■, *Asia* ... 66 K11
Indian →, *U.S.A.* ... 109 M5
Indian Cabins, *Canada* ... 104 B5
Indian Harbour, *Canada* ... 103 B8
Indian Head, *Canada* ... 105 C8
Indian Lake, *U.S.A.* ... 111 C10
Indian Ocean, ... 52 K11
Indian Springs, *U.S.A.* ... 117 J11
Indiana, *U.S.A.* ... 110 F5
Indiana □, *U.S.A.* ... 108 F3
Indianapolis, *U.S.A.* ... 108 F2
Indianola, *Iowa, U.S.A.* ... 112 E8
Indianola, *Miss., U.S.A.* ... 113 J9
Indigirka →, *Russia* ... 51 B15
Indija, *Serbia, Yug.* ... 42 E5
Indio, *U.S.A.* ... 117 M10
Indo-China, *Asia* ... 52 H14
Indonesia ■, *Asia* ... 62 F5
Indore, *India* ... 68 H6
Indramayu, *Indonesia* ... 63 G13
Indravati →, *India* ... 67 K12
Indre □, *France* ... 19 F8
Indre →, *France* ... 18 E7
Indre-et-Loire □, *France* .. 18 E7
Indulkana, *Australia* ... 95 D1
Indus →, *Pakistan* ... 68 G2
Indus, Mouth of the, *Pakistan* ... 68 H3
İnebolu, *Turkey* ... 72 B5
İnecik, *Turkey* ... 41 F11
İnegöl, *Turkey* ... 41 F13
Ineu, *Romania* ... 42 D6
Infantes = Villanueva de los Infantes, *Spain* ... 35 G7
Infiernillo, Presa del, *Mexico* 118 D4
Infiesto, *Spain* ... 34 B5
Ingatestad, *Sweden* ... 11 H8
Ingenio, *Canary Is.* ... 37 G4
Ingenio Santa Ana, *Argentina* ... 126 B2
Ingersoll, *Canada* ... 102 D3

Ingham, *Australia* ... 94 B4
Ingleborough, *U.K.* ... 12 C5
Inglewood, *Queens., Australia* ... 95 D5
Inglewood, *Vic., Australia* .. 95 F3
Inglewood, *N.Z.* ... 91 H5
Inglewood, *U.S.A.* ... 117 M8
Ingólfshöfði, *Iceland* ... 8 E5
Ingolstadt, *Germany* ... 25 G7
Ingomar, *U.S.A.* ... 114 C10
Ingonish, *Canada* ... 103 C7
Ingore, *Guinea-Biss.* ... 82 C1
Ingraj Bazar, *India* ... 69 G13
Ingrid Christensen Coast, *Antarctica* ... 5 C6
Ingul = Inhul →, *Ukraine* ... 47 J7
Ingulec = Inhulec →, *Ukraine* ... 47 J7
Ingulets → = Inhulets →, *Ukraine* ... 47 J7
Inguri → = Enguri →, *Georgia* ... 49 J5
Ingushetia □, *Russia* ... 49 J7
Ingwavuma, *S. Africa* ... 89 D5
Inhaca, *Mozam.* ... 89 D5
Inhafenga, *Mozam.* ... 89 C5
Inhambane, *Mozam.* ... 89 C6
Inhambane □, *Mozam.* ... 89 C5
Inhaminga, *Mozam.* ... 87 F4
Inharrime, *Mozam.* ... 89 C6
Inharrime →, *Mozam.* ... 89 C6
Inhisar, *Turkey* ... 39 A12
Inhul →, *Ukraine* ... 47 J7
Inhulec →, *Ukraine* ... 47 J7
Inhulets →, *Ukraine* ... 47 J7
Iniesta, *Spain* ... 33 F3
Ining = Yining, *China* ... 50 E9
Inírida →, *Colombia* ... 124 C5
Inishbofin, *Ireland* ... 15 C1
Inisheer, *Ireland* ... 15 C2
Inishfree B., *Ireland* ... 15 A3
Inishkea North, *Ireland* ... 15 B1
Inishkea South, *Ireland* ... 15 B1
Inishmaan, *Ireland* ... 15 C2
Inishmore, *Ireland* ... 15 C2
Inishowen Pen., *Ireland* ... 15 A4
Inishshark, *Ireland* ... 15 C1
Inishturk, *Ireland* ... 15 C1
Inishvickillane, *Ireland* ... 15 D1
Injibara, *Ethiopia* ... 81 E4
Injune, *Australia* ... 95 D4
Inklin →, *Canada* ... 104 B2
Inle L., *Burma* ... 67 J20
Inlet, *U.S.A.* ... 111 C10
Inn →, *Austria* ... 26 C6
Innamincka, *Australia* ... 95 D3
Inner Hebrides, *U.K.* ... 14 E2
Inner Mongolia = Nei Mongol Zizhiqu □, *China* 56 D7
Inner Sound, *U.K.* ... 14 D3
Innerkip, *Canada* ... 110 C4
Innetalling I., *Canada* ... 102 A4
Innisfail, *Australia* ... 94 B4
Innisfail, *Canada* ... 104 C6
In'no-shima, *Japan* ... 55 G6
Innsbruck, *Austria* ... 26 D4
Innviertel, *Austria* ... 26 C6
Inny →, *Ireland* ... 15 C4
Inongo, *Dem. Rep. of the Congo* . 84 E3
İnönü, *Turkey* ... 39 B12
Inoucdjouac = Inukjuak, *Canada* ... 101 C12
Inowrocław, *Poland* ... 45 F5
Inpundong, *N. Korea* ... 57 D14
Inscription, C., *Australia* ... 93 E1
Insein, *Burma* ... 67 L20
Insjön, *Sweden* ... 10 D9
Ińsko, *Poland* ... 44 E2
Însurăţei, *Romania* ... 43 F12
Inta, *Russia* ... 50 C6
Intendente Alvear, *Argentina* 126 D3
Întorsura Buzăului, *Romania* 43 E11
Intiyaco, *Argentina* ... 126 B3
Inukjuak, *Canada* ... 101 C12
Inútil, B., *Chile* ... 128 G2
Inuvik, *Canada* ... 100 B6
Inveraray, *U.K.* ... 14 E3
Inverbervie, *U.K.* ... 14 E6
Invercargill, *N.Z.* ... 91 M2
Inverclyde □, *U.K.* ... 14 F4
Inverell, *Australia* ... 95 D5
Invergordon, *U.K.* ... 14 D4
Inverloch, *Australia* ... 95 F4
Invermere, *Canada* ... 104 C5
Inverness, *Canada* ... 103 C7
Inverness, *U.K.* ... 14 D4
Inverness, *U.S.A.* ... 109 L4
Inverurie, *U.K.* ... 14 D6
Investigator Group, *Australia* 95 E1
Investigator Str., *Australia* .. 95 F2
Inya, *Russia* ... 50 D9
Inyanga, *Zimbabwe* ... 87 F3
Inyangani, *Zimbabwe* ... 87 F3
Inyantue, *Zimbabwe* ... 88 B4
Inyo Mts., *U.S.A.* ... 116 J9
Inyokern, *U.S.A.* ... 117 K9
Inza, *Russia* ... 48 D8
Inzhavino, *Russia* ... 48 D6
Iō-Jima, *Japan* ... 55 J5
Ioánnina, *Greece* ... 38 B2
Ioánnina □, *Greece* ... 38 B2
Iola, *U.S.A.* ... 113 G7
Ion Corvin, *Romania* ... 43 F12
Iona, *U.K.* ... 14 E2
Ione, *U.S.A.* ... 116 G6
Ionia, *U.S.A.* ... 108 D3

Ionian Is. = Iónioi Nísoi, *Greece* ... 38 C2
Ionian Sea, *Medit. S.* ... 6 H9
Iónioi Nísoi, *Greece* ... 38 C2
Iónioi Nísoi □, *Greece* ... 38 C2
Íos, *Greece* ... 39 E7
Iowa □, *U.S.A.* ... 112 D8
Iowa →, *U.S.A.* ... 112 E9
Iowa City, *U.S.A.* ... 112 E9
Iowa Falls, *U.S.A.* ... 112 D8
Iowa Park, *U.S.A.* ... 113 J5
Ipala, *Tanzania* ... 86 C3
Ipameri, *Brazil* ... 125 G9
Ipáti, *Greece* ... 38 C4
Ipatinga, *Brazil* ... 125 G10
Ipatovo, *Russia* ... 49 H6
Ipel' →, *Europe* ... 27 D11
Ipiales, *Colombia* ... 124 C3
Ipin = Yibin, *China* ... 58 C5
Ipixuna, *Brazil* ... 124 E4
Ipoh, *Malaysia* ... 65 K3
Ippy, *C.A.R.* ... 84 C4
Ipsala, *Turkey* ... 41 F10
Ipsárion, Óros, *Greece* ... 41 F8
Ipswich, *Australia* ... 95 D5
Ipswich, *U.K.* ... 13 E9
Ipswich, *Mass., U.S.A.* ... 111 D14
Ipswich, *S. Dak., U.S.A.* ... 112 C5
Ipu, *Brazil* ... 125 D10
Iqaluit, *Canada* ... 101 B13
Iquique, *Chile* ... 124 H4
Iquitos, *Peru* ... 124 D4
Irabu-Jima, *Japan* ... 55 M2
Iracoubo, *Fr. Guiana* ... 125 B8
Irafshān, *Iran* ... 71 E9
Irahuan, *Phil.* ... 61 G3
Iráklia, *Kikládhes, Greece* .. 39 E7
Iráklia, *Sérrai, Greece* ... 40 E7
Iráklion, *Greece* ... 36 D7
Iráklion □, *Greece* ... 36 D7
Irala, *Paraguay* ... 127 B5
Iran ■, *Asia* ... 71 C7
Iran, Gunung-Gunung, *Malaysia* ... 62 D4
Iran, Plateau of, *Asia* ... 52 F9
Iran Ra. = Iran, Gunung-Gunung, *Malaysia* ... 62 D4
Īrānshahr, *Iran* ... 71 E9
Irapuato, *Mexico* ... 118 C4
Iraq ■, *Asia* ... 70 C5
Irati, *Brazil* ... 127 B5
Irbes saurums, *Latvia* ... 44 A9
Irbid, *Jordan* ... 75 C4
Irbid □, *Jordan* ... 75 C5
Iregua →, *Spain* ... 32 C2
Ireland ■, *Europe* ... 15 C4
Irele, *Nigeria* ... 83 D6
Irgiz, Bolshaya →, *Russia* .. 48 D9
Irhyangdong, *N. Korea* ... 57 D15
Iri, *S. Korea* ... 57 G14
Irian Jaya □, *Indonesia* ... 63 E9
Irié, *Guinea* ... 82 D3
Iriga, *Phil.* ... 61 E5
Iringa, *Tanzania* ... 86 D4
Iringa □, *Tanzania* ... 86 D4
Iriomote-Jima, *Japan* ... 55 M1
Iriona, *Honduras* ... 120 C2
Iriri →, *Brazil* ... 125 D8
Irish Republic ■, *Europe* .. 15 C3
Irish Sea, *U.K.* ... 12 D3
Irkutsk, *Russia* ... 51 D11
Irlğanlı, *Turkey* ... 39 D11
Irma, *Canada* ... 105 C6
Irō-Zaki, *Japan* ... 55 G9
Iroise, Mer d', *France* ... 18 D2
Iron Baron, *Australia* ... 95 E2
Iron Gate = Portile de Fier, *Europe* ... 42 F7
Iron Knob, *Australia* ... 95 E2
Iron Mountain, *U.S.A.* ... 108 C1
Iron River, *U.S.A.* ... 112 B10
Irondequoit, *U.S.A.* ... 110 C7
Ironton, *Mo., U.S.A.* ... 113 G9
Ironton, *Ohio, U.S.A.* ... 108 F4
Ironwood, *U.S.A.* ... 112 B9
Iroquois, *Canada* ... 111 B9
Iroquois Falls, *Canada* ... 102 C3
Irosin, *Phil.* ... 61 E6
Irpin, *Ukraine* ... 47 G6
Irrara Cr. →, *Australia* ... 95 D4
Irrawaddy □, *Burma* ... 67 L19
Irrawaddy →, *Burma* ... 67 M19
Irricana, *Canada* ... 104 C6
Irsina, *Italy* ... 31 B9
Irtysh →, *Russia* ... 50 C7
Irumu, *Dem. Rep. of the Congo* . 86 B2
Irún, *Spain* ... 32 B3
Irunea = Pamplona, *Spain* .. 32 C3
Irurzun, *Spain* ... 32 C3
Irvine, *Canada* ... 105 D6
Irvine, *U.K.* ... 14 F4
Irvine, *Calif., U.S.A.* ... 117 M9
Irvine, *Ky., U.S.A.* ... 108 G4
Irvinestown, *U.K.* ... 15 B4
Irving, *U.S.A.* ... 113 J6
Irvona, *U.S.A.* ... 110 F6
Irwin →, *Australia* ... 93 E1
Irymple, *Australia* ... 95 E3
Is, Jebel, *Sudan* ... 80 C4
Is-sur-Tille, *France* ... 19 E12
Isa, *Nigeria* ... 83 C6
Isa Khel, *Pakistan* ... 68 C4
Isaac →, *Australia* ... 94 C4
Isabel, *U.S.A.* ... 112 C4
Isabela, *Phil.* ... 61 H5
Isabela, I., *Mexico* ... 118 C3
Isabela, Cord., *Nic.* ... 120 D2
Isabella Ra., *Australia* ... 92 D3

Isaccea, *Romania* ... 43 E13
Ísafjarðardjúp, *Iceland* ... 8 C2
Ísafjörður, *Iceland* ... 8 C2
Isagarh, *India* ... 68 G7
Isahaya, *Japan* ... 55 H5
Isaka, *Tanzania* ... 86 C3
Isakly, *Russia* ... 48 C10
Işalniţa, *Romania* ... 43 F8
Isan = Içana →, *Brazil* .. 124 C5
Isanlu Makutu, *Nigeria* ... 83 D6
Isar →, *Germany* ... 25 G8
Ísarco →, *Italy* ... 29 B8
Ísari, *Greece* ... 38 D3
Íscar, *Spain* ... 34 D6
Iscehisar, *Turkey* ... 39 C12
Íschia, *Italy* ... 30 B6
Isdell →, *Australia* ... 92 C3
Ise, *Japan* ... 55 G8
Ise-Wan, *Japan* ... 55 G8
Isefjord, *Denmark* ... 11 J5
Isel →, *Austria* ... 26 E5
Iseo, *Italy* ... 28 C7
Iseo, L. d', *Italy* ... 28 C7
Iseramagazi, *Tanzania* ... 86 C3
Isère □, *France* ... 21 C9
Isère →, *France* ... 21 D8
Iserlohn, *Germany* ... 24 D3
Isérnia, *Italy* ... 31 A7
Iseyin, *Nigeria* ... 83 D5
Isfahan = Eşfahān, *Iran* ... 71 C6
Ishigaki-Shima, *Japan* ... 55 M2
Ishikari-Gawa →, *Japan* ... 54 C10
Ishikari-Sammyaku, *Japan* . 54 C11
Ishikari-Wan, *Japan* ... 54 C10
Ishikawa □, *Japan* ... 55 F8
Ishim, *Russia* ... 50 D7
Ishim →, *Russia* ... 50 D8
Ishinomaki, *Japan* ... 54 E10
Ishioka, *Japan* ... 55 F10
Ishkuman, *Pakistan* ... 69 A5
Ishmi, *Albania* ... 40 E3
Ishpeming, *U.S.A.* ... 108 B2
Isigny-sur-Mer, *France* ... 18 C5
Işıklar Dağı, *Turkey* ... 41 F11
Işıklı, *Turkey* ... 39 C11
Isil Kul, *Russia* ... 50 D8
Ísili, *Italy* ... 30 C2
Isiolo, *Kenya* ... 86 B4
Isiro, *Dem. Rep. of the Congo* . 86 B2
Isisford, *Australia* ... 94 C3
Iskenderun, *Turkey* ... 70 B3
İskenderun Körfezi, *Turkey* 70 D6
İskilip, *Turkey* ... 72 B5
Iskür →, *Bulgaria* ... 41 C8
Iskür, Yazovir, *Bulgaria* ... 40 D8
Iskut →, *Canada* ... 104 B2
Isla →, *U.K.* ... 14 E5
Isla Cristina, *Spain* ... 35 H3
Isla Vista, *U.S.A.* ... 117 L7
Islâhiye, *Turkey* ... 72 D7
Islam Headworks, *Pakistan* .. 68 E5
Islamabad, *Pakistan* ... 68 C5
Islamgarh, *Pakistan* ... 68 F4
Islamkot, *Pakistan* ... 68 G4
Islampur, *India* ... 69 G11
Island L., *Canada* ... 105 C10
Island Lagoon, *Australia* ... 95 E2
Island Pond, *U.S.A.* ... 111 B13
Islands, B. of, *Canada* ... 103 C8
Islay, *U.K.* ... 14 F2
Isle →, *France* ... 20 D3
Isle aux Morts, *Canada* ... 103 C8
Isle of Wight □, *U.K.* ... 13 G6
Isle Royale, *U.S.A.* ... 112 B10
Isle Royale National Park, *U.S.A.* ... 112 B10
Isleton, *U.S.A.* ... 116 G5
Ismail = Izmayil, *Ukraine* .. 47 K5
Smâ'ilîya, *Egypt* ... 80 H7
Ismaning, *Germany* ... 25 G7
Isna, *Egypt* ... 80 B3
Isoanala, *Madag.* ... 89 C8
Isogstalo, *India* ... 69 B8
Ísola del Liri, *Italy* ... 29 G10
Ísola della Scala, *Italy* ... 28 C7
Ísola di Capo Rizzuto, *Italy* 31 D10
Isparta, *Turkey* ... 39 D12
Isperikh, *Bulgaria* ... 41 C10
Íspica, *Italy* ... 31 F7
Israel ■, *Asia* ... 75 D3
Isratu, *Eritrea* ... 81 D4
Issia, *Ivory C.* ... 82 D3
Issoire, *France* ... 20 C7
Issoudun, *France* ... 19 F8
Issyk-Kul, Ozero = Ysyk-Köl, Ozero, *Kyrgyzstan* .. 50 E8
Ist, *Croatia* ... 29 D11
Istállós-kő, *Hungary* ... 42 D5
Istanbul, *Turkey* ... 41 E12
İstanbul □, *Turkey* ... 41 E12
İstanbul Boğazı, *Turkey* ... 41 E13
Istiaía, *Greece* ... 38 C5
Istok, *Kosovo, Yug.* ... 40 D4
Istokpoga, L., *U.S.A.* ... 109 M5
Istra, *Croatia* ... 29 C10
Istres, *France* ... 21 E8
Istria = Istra, *Croatia* ... 29 C10
Itá, *Paraguay* ... 126 B4
Itaberaba, *Brazil* ... 125 F10
Itabira, *Brazil* ... 125 G10
Itabirito, *Brazil* ... 127 A7
Itabuna, *Brazil* ... 125 F11
Itacaunas →, *Brazil* ... 125 E9
Itacoatiara, *Brazil* ... 124 D7
Itaipú, Reprêsa de, *Brazil* .. 127 B5
Itaituba, *Brazil* ... 125 D7
Itajaí, *Brazil* ... 127 B6
Itajubá, *Brazil* ... 127 A6

Jiangling

Itaka, *Tanzania* 87 D3
Italy ■, *Europe* 7 G8
Itamaraju, *Brazil* 125 G11
Itampolo, *Madag.* 89 C7
Itandrano, *Madag.* 89 C8
Itapecuru-Mirim, *Brazil* 125 D10
Itaperuna, *Brazil* 127 A7
Itapetininga, *Brazil* 127 A6
Itapeva, *Brazil* 127 A6
Itapicuru →, *Bahia, Brazil* 125 F11
Itapicuru →, *Maranhão, Brazil* 125 D10
Itapipoca, *Brazil* 125 D11
Itapuá □, *Paraguay* 127 B4
Itaquari, *Brazil* 127 A7
Itaquí, *Brazil* 126 B4
Itararé, *Brazil* 127 A6
Itarsi, *India* 68 H7
Itatí, *Argentina* 126 B4
Itbayat, *Phil.* 61 A4
Itchen →, *U.K.* 13 G6
Itéa, *Greece* 38 C4
Itezhi Tezhi, L., *Zambia* 87 F2
Ithaca = Itháki, *Greece* 38 C2
Ithaca, *U.S.A.* 111 D8
Itháki, *Greece* 38 C2
Itiquira →, *Brazil* 125 G7
Ito, *Japan* 55 G9
Ito Aba I., *S. China Sea* 62 B4
Itoigawa, *Japan* 55 F8
Iton →, *France* 18 C8
Itonamas →, *Bolivia* 124 F6
Itri, *Italy* 30 A6
Itsa, *Egypt* 80 J7
Íttiri, *Italy* 30 B1
Itu, *Brazil* 127 A6
Itu, *Nigeria* 83 D6
Ituiutaba, *Brazil* 125 G9
Itumbiara, *Brazil* 125 G9
Ituna, *Canada* 105 C8
Itunge Port, *Tanzania* 87 D3
Iturbe, *Argentina* 126 A2
Ituri →, *Dem. Rep. of the Congo* 86 B2
Iturup, Ostrov, *Russia* 51 E15
Ituxi →, *Brazil* 124 E6
Ituyuro →, *Argentina* 126 A3
Itzehoe, *Germany* 24 B5
Ivahona, *Madag.* 89 C8
Ivaí →, *Brazil* 127 A5
Ivalo, *Finland* 8 B22
Ivalojoki →, *Finland* 8 B22
Ivanava, *Belarus* 47 F3
Ivančice, *Czech Rep.* 27 B9
Ivăneşti, *Romania* 43 D12
Ivangorod, *Russia* 46 C5
Ivanhoe, *Australia* 95 E3
Ivanhoe, *Calif., U.S.A.* 116 J7
Ivanhoe, *Minn., U.S.A.* 112 C6
Ivanić Grad, *Croatia* 29 C13
Ivanjica, *Serbia, Yug.* 40 C4
Ivanjska, *Bos.-H.* 42 F2
Ivankoyskoye Vdkhr., *Russia* 46 D9
Ivano-Frankivsk, *Ukraine* 47 H3
Ivano-Frankovsk = Ivano-Frankivsk, *Ukraine* 47 H3
Ivanovo = Ivanava, *Belarus* 47 F3
Ivanovo, *Russia* 46 D11
Ivanšćica, *Croatia* 29 B13
Ivato, *Madag.* 89 C8
Ivatsevichy, *Belarus* 47 F3
Ivaylovgrad, *Bulgaria* 41 E10
Ivinheima →, *Brazil* 127 A5
Ivinhema, *Brazil* 127 A5
Ivohibe, *Madag.* 89 C8
Ivory Coast, *W. Afr.* 82 E4
Ivory Coast ■, *Africa* 82 D4
Ivösjön, *Sweden* 11 H8
Ivrea, *Italy* 28 C4
İvrindi, *Turkey* 39 B9
Ivujivik, *Canada* 101 B12
Ivybridge, *U.K.* 13 G4
Iwaizumi, *Japan* 54 E10
Iwaki, *Japan* 55 F10
Iwakuni, *Japan* 55 G6
Iwamizawa, *Japan* 54 C10
Iwanai, *Japan* 54 C10
Iwata, *Japan* 55 G8
Iwate □, *Japan* 54 E10
Iwate-San, *Japan* 54 E10
Iwo, *Nigeria* 83 D5
Iwonicz-Zdrój, *Poland* 45 J8
Ixiamas, *Bolivia* 124 F5
Ixopo, *S. Africa* 89 E5
Ixtepec, *Mexico* 119 D5
Ixtlán del Río, *Mexico* 118 C4
Iyal Bakhit, *Sudan* 81 E2
Iyo, *Japan* 55 H6
Izabal, L. de, *Guatemala* 120 C2
Izamal, *Mexico* 119 C7
Izberbash, *Russia* 49 J8
Izbica, *Poland* 45 H10
Izbica Kujawska, *Poland* 45 F5
Izbiceni, *Romania* 43 G9
Izena-Shima, *Japan* 55 L3
Izgrev, *Bulgaria* 41 C10
Izhevsk, *Russia* 50 D6
Izmayil, *Ukraine* 47 K5
İzmir, *Turkey* 39 C9
İzmir □, *Turkey* 39 C9
İzmir Körfezi, *Turkey* 39 C8
İzmit = Kocaeli, *Turkey* 41 F13
Iznájar, *Spain* 35 H6
Iznalloz, *Spain* 35 H7
İznik, *Turkey* 72 B3
İznik Gölü, *Turkey* 41 F13
Izobil'nyy, *Russia* 49 H5
Izola, *Slovenia* 29 C10
Izra, *Syria* 75 C5
Iztochni Rodopi, *Bulgaria* 41 E9
Izu-Shotō, *Japan* 55 G10
Izúcar de Matamoros, *Mexico* 119 D5
Izumi-sano, *Japan* 55 G7
Izumo, *Japan* 55 G6
Izyaslav, *Ukraine* 47 G4
Izyum, *Ukraine* 47 H9

J

Jaba, *Ethiopia* 81 F4
Jabal al Awliyā, *Sudan* 81 D3
Jabal at Ta'ir, *Eritrea* 81 D5
Jabalón →, *Spain* 35 G6
Jabalpur, *India* 69 H8
Jabbūl, *Syria* 70 B3
Jabiru, *Australia* 92 B5
Jablah, *Syria* 70 C3
Jablanac, *Croatia* 29 D11
Jablanica, *Bos.-H.* 42 G2
Jablonec nad Nisou, *Czech Rep.* 26 A8
Jablonica, *Slovak Rep.* 27 C10
Jabłonowo Pomorskie, *Poland* 44 E6
Jablunkov, *Czech Rep.* 27 B11
Jaboatão, *Brazil* 125 E11
Jaboticabal, *Brazil* 127 A6
Jabukovac, *Serbia, Yug.* 40 B6
Jaca, *Spain* 32 C4
Jacareí, *Brazil* 127 A6
Jacarèzinho, *Brazil* 127 A6
Jackman, *U.S.A.* 109 C10
Jacksboro, *U.S.A.* 113 J5
Jackson, *Ala., U.S.A.* 109 K2
Jackson, *Calif., U.S.A.* 116 G6
Jackson, *Ky., U.S.A.* 108 G4
Jackson, *Mich., U.S.A.* 108 D3
Jackson, *Minn., U.S.A.* 112 D7
Jackson, *Miss., U.S.A.* 113 J9
Jackson, *Mo., U.S.A.* 113 G10
Jackson, *N.H., U.S.A.* 111 B13
Jackson, *Ohio, U.S.A.* 108 F4
Jackson, *Tenn., U.S.A.* 109 H1
Jackson, *Wyo., U.S.A.* 114 E8
Jackson B., *N.Z.* 91 K2
Jackson L., *U.S.A.* 114 E8
Jacksons, *N.Z.* 91 K3
Jackson's Arm, *Canada* 103 C8
Jacksonville, *Ala., U.S.A.* 109 J3
Jacksonville, *Ark., U.S.A.* 113 H8
Jacksonville, *Calif., U.S.A.* 116 H6
Jacksonville, *Fla., U.S.A.* 109 K5
Jacksonville, *Ill., U.S.A.* 112 F9
Jacksonville, *N.C., U.S.A.* 109 H7
Jacksonville, *Tex., U.S.A.* 113 K7
Jacksonville Beach, *U.S.A.* 109 K5
Jacmel, *Haiti* 121 C5
Jacob Lake, *U.S.A.* 115 H7
Jacobabad, *Pakistan* 68 E3
Jacobina, *Brazil* 125 F10
Jacques Cartier, Dét. de, *Canada* 103 C7
Jacques-Cartier, Mt., *Canada* 103 C6
Jacques Cartier, Parc Prov., *Canada* 103 C5
Jacqueville, *Ivory C.* 82 D4
Jacuí →, *Brazil* 127 C5
Jacumba, *U.S.A.* 117 N10
Jacundá →, *Brazil* 125 D8
Jade, *Germany* 24 B4
Jadebusen, *Germany* 24 B4
Jadotville = Likasi, *Dem. Rep. of the Congo* 87 E2
Jadovnik, *Serbia, Yug.* 40 C3
Jadraque, *Spain* 32 E2
Jaén, *Peru* 124 E3
Jaén, *Spain* 35 H7
Jaén □, *Spain* 35 H7
Jafarabad, *India* 68 J4
Jaffa = Tel Aviv-Yafo, *Israel* 75 C3
Jaffa, C., *Australia* 95 F2
Jaffna, *Sri Lanka* 66 Q12
Jaffrey, *U.S.A.* 111 D12
Jagadhri, *India* 68 D7
Jagadishpur, *India* 69 G11
Jagdalpur, *India* 67 K13
Jagersfontein, *S. Africa* 88 D4
Jaghīn →, *Iran* 71 E8
Jagodina, *Serbia, Yug.* 40 B5
Jagraon, *India* 66 D9
Jagst →, *Germany* 25 F5
Jagtial, *India* 66 K11
Jaguariaíva, *Brazil* 127 A6
Jaguaribe →, *Brazil* 125 D11
Jagüey Grande, *Cuba* 120 B3
Jahanabad, *India* 69 G11
Jahazpur, *India* 68 G6
Jahrom, *Iran* 71 D7
Jaijon, *India* 68 D7
Jailolo, *Indonesia* 63 D7
Jailolo, Selat, *Indonesia* 63 D7
Jaipur, *India* 68 F6
Jais, *India* 69 F9
Jaisalmer, *India* 68 F4
Jaisinghnagar, *India* 69 H8
Jaitaran, *India* 68 F5
Jaithari, *India* 69 H8
Jājarm, *Iran* 71 B8
Jajce, *Bos.-H.* 42 F2
Jakam →, *India* 68 H6
Jakarta, *Indonesia* 63 G12
Jakhal, *India* 68 E6
Jakhau, *India* 68 H3
Jakobstad = Pietarsaari, *Finland* 8 E20
Jakupica, *Macedonia* 40 E5
Jal, *U.S.A.* 113 J3
Jalalabad, *Afghan.* 68 B4
Jalalabad, *India* 69 F8
Jalalpur Jattan, *Pakistan* 68 C6
Jalama, *U.S.A.* 117 L6
Jalapa, *Guatemala* 120 D2
Jalapa Enríquez, *Mexico* 119 D5
Jalasjärvi, *Finland* 9 E20
Jalaun, *India* 69 F8
Jaldhaka →, *Bangla.* 69 F13
Jalesar, *India* 68 F8
Jaleswar, *Nepal* 69 F11
Jalgaon, *Maharashtra, India* 66 J10
Jalgaon, *Maharashtra, India* 66 J9
Jalībah, *Iraq* 70 D5
Jalingo, *Nigeria* 83 D7
Jalisco □, *Mexico* 118 D4
Jalkot, *Pakistan* 69 B5
Jallas →, *Spain* 34 C1
Jalna, *India* 66 K9
Jalón →, *Spain* 32 D3
Jalor, *India* 68 G5
Jalpa, *Mexico* 118 C4
Jalpaiguri, *India* 67 F16
Jaluit I., *Marshall Is.* 96 G8
Jalūlā, *Iraq* 70 C5
Jamaari, *Nigeria* 83 C6
Jamaica ■, *W. Indies* 120 C4
Jamalpur, *Bangla.* 67 G16
Jamalpur, *India* 69 G12
Jamalpurganj, *India* 69 H13
Jamanxim →, *Brazil* 125 D7
Jambi, *Indonesia* 62 E2
Jambi □, *Indonesia* 62 E2
Jambusar, *India* 68 H5
James →, *S. Dak., U.S.A.* 112 D6
James →, *Va., U.S.A.* 108 G7
James B., *Canada* 102 B3
James Ranges, *Australia* 92 D5
James Ross I., *Antarctica* 5 C18
Jamesabad, *Pakistan* 68 G3
Jamestown, *Australia* 95 E2
Jamestown, *S. Africa* 88 E4
Jamestown, *N. Dak., U.S.A.* 112 B5
Jamestown, *N.Y., U.S.A.* 110 D5
Jamestown, *Pa., U.S.A.* 110 E4
Jamīlābād, *Iran* 71 C6
Jamiltepec, *Mexico* 119 D5
Jamira →, *India* 69 J13
Jämjö, *Sweden* 11 H9
Jamkhandi, *India* 66 L9
Jammerbugt, *Denmark* 11 G3
Jammu, *India* 68 C6
Jammu & Kashmir □, *India* 69 B7
Jamnagar, *India* 68 H4
Jamni →, *India* 69 G8
Jampur, *Pakistan* 68 E4
Jamrud, *Pakistan* 68 C4
Jämsä, *Finland* 9 F21
Jamshedpur, *India* 69 H12
Jamtara, *India* 69 H12
Jämtland, *Sweden* 8 E15
Jämtlands län □, *Sweden* 10 B7
Jan L., *Canada* 105 C8
Jan Mayen, *Arctic* 4 B7
Janakkala, *Finland* 9 F21
Janaúba, *Brazil* 125 G10
Jand, *Pakistan* 68 C5
Jandaq, *Iran* 71 C7
Jandia, *Canary Is.* 37 F5
Jandia, Pta. de, *Canary Is.* 37 F5
Jandola, *Pakistan* 68 C4
Jandowae, *Australia* 95 D5
Jándula →, *Spain* 35 G6
Janesville, *U.S.A.* 112 D10
Janga, *Ghana* 83 C4
Jangamo, *Mozam.* 89 C6
Janghai, *India* 69 G10
Janikowo, *Poland* 45 F5
Janīn, *West Bank* 75 C4
Janinà = Ioánnina □, *Greece* 38 B2
Janja, *Bos.-H.* 42 F4
Janjevo, *Kosovo, Yug.* 40 D5
Janjgir, *India* 69 J10
Janjina, *Croatia* 29 F14
Janjina, *Madag.* 89 C8
Janos, *Mexico* 118 A3
Jánoshalma, *Hungary* 42 D4
Jánosháza, *Hungary* 42 C2
Jánossomorja, *Hungary* 42 C2
Janów, *Poland* 45 H6
Janów Lubelski, *Poland* 45 H9
Janów Podlaski, *Poland* 45 F10
Janowiec Wielkopolski, *Poland* 45 F4
Januária, *Brazil* 125 G10
Janub Dârfûr □, *Sudan* 81 E2
Janub Kordofân □, *Sudan* 81 E3
Janubio, *Canary Is.* 37 F6
Janville, *France* 19 D8
Janzé, *France* 18 E5
Jaora, *India* 68 H6
Japan ■, *Asia* 55 G8
Japan, Sea of, *Asia* 54 E7
Japan Trench, *Pac. Oc.* 52 F18
Japen = Yapen, *Indonesia* 63 E9
Japla, *India* 69 G11
Japurá →, *Brazil* 122 D4
Jaquarão, *Brazil* 127 C5
Jaqué, *Panama* 120 E4
Jarābulus, *Syria* 70 B3
Jaraicejo, *Spain* 35 F5
Jaraíz de la Vera, *Spain* 34 E5
Jarama →, *Spain* 34 E7
Jaramānah, *Syria* 72 F7
Jarandilla, *Spain* 34 E5
Jaranwala, *Pakistan* 68 D5
Jarash, *Jordan* 75 C4
Järbo, *Sweden* 10 D10
Jardim, *Brazil* 126 A4
Jardín →, *Spain* 33 G2
Jardines de la Reina, Arch. de los, *Cuba* 120 B4
Jargalang, *China* 57 C12
Jargalant = Hovd, *Mongolia* 60 B4
Jari →, *Brazil* 125 D8
Jarīr, W. al →, *Si. Arabia* 70 E4
Järlåsa, *Sweden* 10 E11
Jarmen, *Germany* 24 B9
Järna, *Kopparberg, Sweden* 10 D8
Järna, *Stockholm, Sweden* 10 E11
Jarnac, *France* 20 C3
Jarny, *France* 19 C12
Jarocin, *Poland* 45 G4
Jaroměř, *Czech Rep.* 26 A8
Jarosław, *Poland* 45 H9
Järpås, *Sweden* 11 F6
Järpen, *Sweden* 10 A7
Jarrahdale, *Australia* 93 F2
Jarrahi →, *Iran* 71 D6
Jarres, Plaine des, *Laos* 64 C4
Jarso, *Ethiopia* 81 F4
Jartai, *China* 56 E3
Jarud Qi, *China* 57 B11
Järvenpää, *Finland* 9 F21
Jarvis, *Canada* 110 D4
Jarvis I., *Pac. Oc.* 97 H12
Jarvorník, *Czech Rep.* 27 A10
Järvsö, *Sweden* 10 C10
Jarwa, *India* 69 F10
Jaša Tomić, *Serbia, Yug.* 42 E5
Jasdan, *India* 68 H4
Jashpurnagar, *India* 69 H11
Jasidih, *India* 69 G12
Jasień, *Poland* 45 G2
Jāsimīyah, *Iraq* 70 C5
Jasin, *Malaysia* 65 L4
Jāsk, *Iran* 71 E8
Jasło, *Poland* 45 J8
Jasmund, *Germany* 24 A9
Jaso, *India* 69 G9
Jasper, *Alta., Canada* 104 C5
Jasper, *Ont., Canada* 111 B9
Jasper, *Ala., U.S.A.* 109 J2
Jasper, *Fla., U.S.A.* 109 K4
Jasper, *Ind., U.S.A.* 108 F2
Jasper, *Tex., U.S.A.* 113 K8
Jasper Nat. Park, *Canada* 104 C5
Jasrasar, *India* 68 F5
Jastarnia, *Poland* 44 D5
Jastrebarsko, *Croatia* 29 C12
Jastrowie, *Poland* 44 E3
Jastrzębie Zdrój, *Poland* 45 J5
Jász-Nagykun-Szolnok □, *Hungary* 42 C5
Jászapáti, *Hungary* 42 C5
Jászárokszállás, *Hungary* 42 C4
Jászberény, *Hungary* 42 C4
Jászkisér, *Hungary* 42 C5
Jászladány, *Hungary* 42 C5
Jataí, *Brazil* 125 G8
Jati, *Pakistan* 68 G3
Jatibarang, *Indonesia* 63 G13
Jatinegara, *Indonesia* 63 G12
Játiva = Xátiva, *Spain* 33 G4
Jättendal, *Sweden* 10 C11
Jaú, *Brazil* 127 A6
Jauja, *Peru* 124 F3
Jaunpur, *India* 69 G10
Java = Jawa, *Indonesia* 63 G14
Java Barat □, *Indonesia* 63 G12
Java Sea, *Indonesia* 62 E3
Java Tengah □, *Indonesia* 63 G14
Java Timur □, *Indonesia* 63 G15
Java Trench, *Ind. Oc.* 62 F3
Javalambre, Sa. de, *Spain* 32 E4
Jávea, *Spain* 33 G5
Javhlant = Uliastay, *Mongolia* 60 B4
Jawa, *Indonesia* 63 G14
Jawad, *India* 68 G6
Jawor, *Poland* 45 G3
Jaworzno, *Poland* 45 H6
Jaworzyna Śląska, *Poland* 45 H3
Jay Peak, *U.S.A.* 111 B12
Jaya, Puncak, *Indonesia* 63 E9
Jayanti, *India* 67 F16
Jayapura, *Indonesia* 63 E10
Jayawijaya, Pegunungan, *Indonesia* 63 E9
Jaynagar, *India* 67 F15
Jayrūd, *Syria* 70 C3
Jayton, *U.S.A.* 113 J4
Jāz Mūrīān, Hāmūn-e, *Iran* 71 E8
Jazīreh-ye Shīf, *Iran* 71 D6
Jazminal, *Mexico* 118 C4
Jazzīn, *Lebanon* 75 B4
Jean, *U.S.A.* 117 K11
Jean Marie River, *Canada* 104 A4
Jean Rabel, *Haiti* 121 C5
Jeanerette, *U.S.A.* 113 L9
Jeanette, Ostrov = Zhannetty, Ostrov, *Russia* 51 B16
Jeannette, *U.S.A.* 110 F5
Jebāl Bārez, Kūh-e, *Iran* 71 D8
Jebba, *Nigeria* 83 D5
Jebel, Bahr el →, *Sudan* 81 F3
Jebel Dud, *Sudan* 81 E3
Jebel Qerri, *Sudan* 81 D3
Jedburgh, *U.K.* 14 F6
Jedda = Jiddah, *Si. Arabia* 74 C2
Jeddore L., *Canada* 103 C8
Jedlicze, *Poland* 45 J8
Jędrzejów, *Poland* 45 H7
Jedwabne, *Poland* 45 E9
Jeetzel →, *Germany* 24 B7
Jefferson, *Iowa, U.S.A.* 112 D7
Jefferson, *Ohio, U.S.A.* 110 E4
Jefferson, *Tex., U.S.A.* 113 J7
Jefferson, Mt., *Nev., U.S.A.* 114 G5
Jefferson, Mt., *Oreg., U.S.A.* 114 D3
Jefferson City, *Mo., U.S.A.* 112 F8
Jefferson City, *Tenn., U.S.A.* 109 G4
Jeffersontown, *U.S.A.* 108 F3
Jeffersonville, *U.S.A.* 108 F3
Jeffrey City, *U.S.A.* 114 E10
Jega, *Nigeria* 83 C5
Jēkabpils, *Latvia* 9 H21
Jekyll I., *U.S.A.* 109 K5
Jelcz-Laskowice, *Poland* 45 G4
Jelenia Góra, *Poland* 45 H2
Jelgava, *Latvia* 9 H20
Jelgava □, *Latvia* 44 B10
Jelica, *Serbia, Yug.* 40 C4
Jelli, *Sudan* 81 F3
Jelšava, *Slovak Rep.* 27 C13
Jemaja, *Indonesia* 65 L5
Jemaluang, *Malaysia* 65 L4
Jember, *Indonesia* 63 H15
Jembongan, *Malaysia* 62 C5
Jena, *Germany* 24 E7
Jena, *U.S.A.* 113 K8
Jenbach, *Austria* 26 D4
Jenkins, *U.S.A.* 108 G4
Jenner, *U.S.A.* 116 G3
Jennings, *U.S.A.* 113 K8
Jepara, *Indonesia* 63 G14
Jeparit, *Australia* 95 F3
Jequié, *Brazil* 125 F10
Jequitinhonha, *Brazil* 125 G10
Jequitinhonha →, *Brazil* 125 G11
Jerantut, *Malaysia* 65 L4
Jérémie, *Haiti* 121 C5
Jerez, Punta, *Mexico* 119 C5
Jerez de García Salinas, *Mexico* 118 C4
Jerez de la Frontera, *Spain* 35 J4
Jerez de los Caballeros, *Spain* 35 G4
Jericho = El Arīḥā, *West Bank* 75 D4
Jericho, *Australia* 94 C4
Jerichow, *Germany* 24 C8
Jerilderie, *Australia* 95 F4
Jermyn, *U.S.A.* 111 E9
Jerome, *U.S.A.* 114 E6
Jerramungup, *Australia* 93 F2
Jersey, *U.K.* 13 H5
Jersey City, *U.S.A.* 111 F10
Jersey Shore, *U.S.A.* 110 E7
Jerseyville, *U.S.A.* 112 F9
Jerusalem, *Israel* 75 D4
Jervis B., *Australia* 95 F5
Jervis Inlet, *Canada* 104 C4
Jerzu, *Italy* 30 C2
Jesenice, *Slovenia* 29 B11
Jeseník, *Czech Rep.* 27 A10
Jesenké, *Slovak Rep.* 27 C13
Jesselton = Kota Kinabalu, *Malaysia* 62 C5
Jessnitz, *Germany* 24 D8
Jessore, *Bangla.* 67 H16
Jesup, *U.S.A.* 109 K5
Jesús Carranza, *Mexico* 119 D5
Jesús María, *Argentina* 126 C3
Jetmore, *U.S.A.* 113 F5
Jetpur, *India* 68 J4
Jeumont, *France* 19 B11
Jevnaker, *Norway* 9 F14
Jewett, *U.S.A.* 110 F3
Jewett City, *U.S.A.* 111 E13
Jeyḥūnābād, *Iran* 71 C6
Jeypore, *India* 67 K13
Jeziorak, Jezioro, *Poland* 44 E6
Jeziorany, *Poland* 44 E7
Jeziorka →, *Poland* 45 F8
Jha Jha, *India* 69 G12
Jhabua, *India* 68 H6
Jhajjar, *India* 68 E7
Jhal, *Pakistan* 68 E2
Jhal Jhao, *Pakistan* 66 F4
Jhalawar, *India* 68 G7
Jhalida, *India* 69 H11
Jhalrapatan, *India* 68 G7
Jhang Maghiana, *Pakistan* 68 D5
Jhansi, *India* 69 G8
Jhargram, *India* 69 H12
Jharia, *India* 69 H12
Jharsuguda, *India* 67 J14
Jhelum, *Pakistan* 68 C5
Jhelum →, *Pakistan* 68 D5
Jhilmilli, *India* 69 H10
Jhudo, *Pakistan* 68 G3
Jhunjhunu, *India* 68 E6
Ji-Paraná, *Brazil* 124 F6
Ji Xian, *Hebei, China* 56 F8
Ji Xian, *Henan, China* 56 G8
Ji Xian, *Shanxi, China* 56 F6
Jia Xian, *Henan, China* 56 H7
Jia Xian, *Shaanxi, China* 56 E6
Jiading, *China* 59 B13
Jiahe, *China* 59 E9
Jialing Jiang →, *China* 58 C6
Jiamusi, *China* 60 B8
Ji'an, *Jiangxi, China* 59 D10
Ji'an, *Jilin, China* 57 D14
Jianchang, *China* 57 D11
Jianchangying, *China* 57 D10
Jianchuan, *China* 58 D2
Jiande, *China* 59 C12
Jiang'an, *China* 58 C5
Jiangbei, *China* 58 C6
Jiangcheng, *China* 58 F3
Jiangchuan, *China* 58 E4
Jiangdi, *China* 58 D4
Jiangdu, *China* 59 A12
Jiange, *China* 58 A5
Jianghua, *China* 59 E8
Jiangjin, *China* 58 C6
Jiangkou, *China* 58 D7
Jiangle, *China* 59 D11
Jiangling, *China* 59 B9

Jiangmen, *China* 59 F9
Jiangning, *China* 59 B12
Jiangshan, *China* 59 C12
Jiangsu □, *China* 57 H11
Jiangxi □, *China* 59 D11
Jiangyan, *China* 59 A13
Jiangyin, *China* 59 B13
Jiangyong, *China* 59 E8
Jiangyou, *China* 58 B5
Jianhe, *China* 58 D7
Jianli, *China* 59 C9
Jianning, *China* 59 D11
Jian'ou, *China* 59 D12
Jianshi, *China* 58 B7
Jianshui, *China* 58 F4
Jianyang, *Fujian, China* . 59 D12
Jianyang, *Sichuan, China* .. 58 B5
Jiao Xian = Jiaozhou, *China* 57 F11
Jiaohe, *Hebei, China* 56 E9
Jiaohe, *Jilin, China* 57 C14
Jiaojiang, *China* 59 C13
Jiaoling, *China* 59 E11
Jiaozhou, *China* 57 F11
Jiaozhou Wan, *China* 57 F11
Jiaozuo, *China* 56 G7
Jiashan, *China* 59 B13
Jiawang, *China* 57 G9
Jiaxiang, *China* 56 G9
Jiaxing, *China* 59 B13
Jiayi = Chiai, *Taiwan* 59 F13
Jiayu, *China* 59 C6
Jibiya, *Nigeria* 83 C6
Jibou, *Romania* 43 C8
Jibuti = Djibouti ■, *Africa* . 81 E5
Jicarón, I., *Panama* 120 E3
Jičín, *Czech Rep.* 26 A8
Jiddah, *Si. Arabia* 74 C2
Jido, *India* 67 E19
Jieshou, *China* 56 H8
Jiexiu, *China* 56 F6
Jieyang, *China* 59 F11
Jigawa □, *Nigeria* 83 C6
Jiggalong, *Australia* ... 92 D3
Jigni, *India* 69 G8
Jihlava, *Czech Rep.* 26 B8
Jihlava →, *Czech Rep.* ... 27 C9
Jihočeský □, *Czech Rep.* ... 26 B7
Jihomoravský □, *Czech Rep.* 27 B9
Jijiga, *Ethiopia* 74 F3
Jikamshi, *Nigeria* 83 C6
Jikau, *Sudan* 81 F3
Jilin, *China* 57 C14
Jilin □, *China* 57 C14
Jiloca →, *Spain* 32 D3
Jilong = Chilung, *Taiwan* . 59 E13
Jim Thorpe, *U.S.A.* 111 F9
Jima, *Ethiopia* 81 F4
Jimbolia, *Romania* 42 E5
Jimena de la Frontera, *Spain* 35 J5
Jiménez, *Mexico* 118 B4
Jimo, *China* 57 F11
Jin Jiang →, *China* 59 C10
Jin Xian = Jinzhou, *China* . 56 E8
Jin Xian, *China* 57 E11
Jinan, *China* 56 F9
Jincheng, *China* 56 G7
Jinchuan, *China* 58 B4
Jind, *India* 68 E7
Jindabyne, *Australia* ... 95 F4
Jindřichův Hradec,
  Czech Rep. 26 B8
Jing He →, *China* 56 G5
Jing Shan, *China* 59 B8
Jing Xian, *China* 59 B12
Jing'an, *China* 59 C10
Jingbian, *China* 56 F5
Jingchuan, *China* 56 G4
Jingde, *China* 59 B12
Jingdezhen, *China* 59 C11
Jingdong, *China* 58 E3
Jinggangshan, *China* ... 59 D10
Jinggu, *China* 58 F3
Jinghai, *China* 56 E9
Jinghong, *China* 58 G3
Jingjiang, *China* 59 A13
Jingle, *China* 56 E6
Jingmen, *China* 59 B9
Jingning, *China* 56 G3
Jingpo Hu, *China* 57 C15
Jingshan, *China* 59 B9
Jingtai, *China* 56 F3
Jingxi, *China* 58 F6
Jingxing, *China* 56 E8
Jingyang, *China* 56 G5
Jingyu, *China* 57 C14
Jingyuan, *China* 56 F3
Jingzhou, *China* 58 D7
Jingziguan, *China* 56 H6
Jinhua, *China* 59 C12
Jining, *Nei Mongol Zizhiqu,
  China* 56 D7
Jining, *Shandong, China* .. 56 G9
Jinja, *Uganda* 86 B3
Jinjang, *Malaysia* 65 L3
Jinji, *China* 56 F4
Jinjiang, *Fujian, China* .. 59 E12
Jinjiang, *Yunnan, China* . 58 D3
Jinjie, *China* 58 F6
Jinjini, *Ghana* 82 D4
Jinkou, *China* 59 B10
Jinkouhe, *China* 58 C5
Jinmen Dao, *China* 59 E12
Jinnah Barrage, *Pakistan* . 66 C7
Jinning, *China* 58 E4
Jinotega, *Nic.* 120 D2
Jinotepe, *Nic.* 120 D2
Jinping, *Guizhou, China* ... 58 D7
Jinping, *Yunnan, China* .. 58 F4
Jinsha, *China* 58 D6
Jinsha Jiang →, *China* .. 58 C5
Jinshan, *China* 59 B13

Jinshi, *China* 59 C8
Jintan, *China* 59 B12
Jinxi, *Jiangxi, China* ... 59 D11
Jinxi, *Liaoning, China* ... 57 D11
Jinxian, *China* 59 C11
Jinxiang, *China* 56 G9
Jinyang, *China* 58 D4
Jinyun, *China* 59 C13
Jinzhai, *China* 59 B10
Jinzhou, *Hebei, China* ... 56 E8
Jinzhou, *Liaoning, China* . 57 D11
Jiparaná →, *Brazil* 124 E6
Jipijapa, *Ecuador* 124 D2
Jiquilpan, *Mexico* 118 D4
Jishan, *China* 56 G6
Jishou, *China* 58 C7
Jishui, *China* 59 D10
Jisr ash Shughūr, *Syria* .. 70 C3
Jitarning, *Australia* ... 93 F2
Jitra, *Malaysia* 65 J3
Jiu →, *Romania* 43 G8
Jiudengkou, *China* 56 E4
Jiujiang, *Guangdong, China* 59 F9
Jiujiang, *Jiangxi, China* . 59 C10
Jiuling Shan, *China* 59 C10
Jiulong, *China* 58 C3
Jiutai, *China* 57 B13
Jiuxiangcheng, *China* ... 56 H8
Jiuxincheng, *China* 56 E8
Jiuyuhang, *China* 59 B12
Jixi, *Anhui, China* 59 B12
Jixi, *Heilongjiang, China* . 57 B16
Jiyang, *China* 57 F9
Jiyuan, *China* 56 G7
Jīzān, *Si. Arabia* 74 D3
Jize, *China* 56 F8
Jizera →, *Czech Rep.* ... 26 A7
Jizl, W. →, *Si. Arabia* ... 80 B4
Jizl, Wādī al, *Si. Arabia* . 70 E3
Jizō-Zaki, *Japan* 55 G6
Jizzakh, *Uzbekistan* 50 E7
Joaçaba, *Brazil* 127 B5
Joal Fadiout, *Senegal* .. 82 C1
João Pessoa, *Brazil* 125 E12
Joaquín V. González,
  Argentina 126 B3
Jobat, *India* 68 H6
Jobourg, Nez de, *France* . 18 C5
Jódar, *Spain* 35 H7
Jodhpur, *India* 68 F5
Jodiya, *India* 68 H4
Jōetsu, *Japan* 55 F9
Jœuf, *France* 19 C12
Jofane, *Mozam.* 89 C5
Jogbani, *India* 69 F12
Jōgeva, *Estonia* 9 G22
Jogjakarta = Yogyakarta,
  Indonesia 63 G14
Johannesburg, *S. Africa* .. 89 D4
Johannesburg, *U.S.A.* ... 117 K9
Johansfors, *Sweden* 11 H9
Johilla →, *India* 69 H9
John Day, *U.S.A.* 114 D4
John Day →, *U.S.A.* 114 D3
John D'Or Prairie, *Canada* 104 B5
John H. Kerr Reservoir,
  U.S.A. 109 G6
John o' Groats, *U.K.* 14 C5
Johnnie, *U.S.A.* 117 J10
John's Ra., *Australia* ... 94 C1
Johnson, *Kans., U.S.A.* .. 113 G4
Johnson, *Vt., U.S.A.* 111 B12
Johnson City, *N.Y., U.S.A.* 111 D9
Johnson City, *Tenn., U.S.A.* 109 G4
Johnson City, *Tex., U.S.A.* 113 K5
Johnsonburg, *U.S.A.* ... 110 E6
Johnsondale, *U.S.A.* ... 117 K8
Johnson's Crossing, *Canada* 104 A2
Johnston, L., *Australia* .. 93 F3
Johnston Falls = Mambilima
  Falls, *Zambia* 87 E2
Johnston I., *Pac. Oc.* ... 97 F11
Johnstone Str., *Canada* .. 104 C3
Johnstown, *N.Y., U.S.A.* . 111 C10
Johnstown, *Ohio, U.S.A.* . 110 F2
Johnstown, *Pa., U.S.A.* .. 110 F6
Johor Baharu, *Malaysia* . 65 M4
Jõhvi, *Estonia* 9 G22
Joigny, *France* 19 E10
Joinville, *Brazil* 127 B6
Joinville, *France* 19 D12
Joinville I., *Antarctica* . 5 C18
Jojutla, *Mexico* 119 D5
Jokkmokk, *Sweden* 8 C18
Jökulsá á Bru →, *Iceland* 8 D6
Jökulsá á Fjöllum →,
  Iceland 8 C5
Jolfà, *Āzarbāyjān-e Sharqī,
  Iran* 70 B5
Jolfà, *Esfahan, Iran* 71 C6
Joliet, *U.S.A.* 108 E1
Joliette, *Canada* 102 C5
Jolo, *Phil.* 61 J4
Jolon, *U.S.A.* 116 K5
Jomalig I., *Phil.* 61 D5
Jombang, *Indonesia* 63 G15
Jomda, *China* 58 B2
Jonava, *Lithuania* 9 J21
Jones Sound, *Canada* ... 4 B3
Jonesboro, *Ark., U.S.A.* . 113 H9
Jonesboro, *La., U.S.A.* .. 113 J8
Jong →, *S. Leone* 82 D2
Jonglei, *Sudan* 81 F3
Jonglei □, *Sudan* 81 F3
Joniškis, *Lithuania* 9 H20
Jönköping, *Sweden* 11 G8
Jönköpings län □, *Sweden* 11 G8
Jonquière, *Canada* 103 C5
Jonsered, *Sweden* 11 G6
Jonzac, *France* 20 C3
Joplin, *U.S.A.* 113 G7

Jora, *India* 68 F6
Jordan, *Mont., U.S.A.* .. 114 C10
Jordan, *N.Y., U.S.A.* ... 111 C8
Jordan ■, *Asia* 75 E5
Jordan →, *Asia* 75 D4
Jordan Valley, *U.S.A.* .. 114 E5
Jordanów, *Poland* 45 J6
Jorhat, *India* 67 F19
Jörn, *Sweden* 8 D19
Jorong, *Indonesia* 62 E4
Jørpeland, *Norway* 9 G11
Jorquera →, *Chile* 126 B2
Jos, *Nigeria* 83 D6
Jos Plateau, *Nigeria* ... 83 D6
Jošanička Banja,
  Serbia, Yug. 40 C4
José Batle y Ordóñez,
  Uruguay 127 C4
Joseni, *Romania* 43 D10
Joseph, L., *Nfld., Canada* . 103 B6
Joseph, L., *Ont., Canada* . 110 A5
Joseph Bonaparte G.,
  Australia 92 B4
Joshinath, *India* 69 D8
Joshua Tree, *U.S.A.* 117 L10
Joshua Tree National Park,
  U.S.A. 117 M10
Josselin, *France* 18 E4
Jostedalsbreen, *Norway* . 9 F12
Jotunheimen, *Norway* ... 9 F13
Joubertberge, *Namibia* .. 88 B1
Joué-lès-Tours, *France* . 18 E7
Jourdanton, *U.S.A.* 113 L5
Joutseno, *Finland* 46 B5
Jovellanos, *Cuba* 120 B3
Joyeuse, *France* 21 D8
Józefów, *Lubelskie, Poland* 45 H10
Józefów, *Mazowieckie,
  Poland* 45 F8
Ju Xian, *China* 57 F10
Juan Aldama, *Mexico* ... 118 C4
Juan Bautista Alberdi,
  Argentina 126 C3
Juan de Fuca Str., *Canada* . 116 B3
Juan de Nova, *Ind. Oc.* .. 89 B7
Juan Fernández, Arch. de,
  Pac. Oc. 122 G2
Juan José Castelli, *Argentina* 126 B3
Juan L. Lacaze, *Uruguay* . 126 C4
Juankoski, *Finland* 8 E23
Juárez, *Argentina* 126 D4
Juárez, *Mexico* 117 N11
Juárez, Sierra de, *Mexico* . 118 A1
Juàzeiro, *Brazil* 125 E10
Juàzeiro do Norte, *Brazil* . 125 E11
Juba, *Sudan* 81 G3
Jubayl, *Lebanon* 75 A4
Jubbah, *Si. Arabia* 70 D4
Jubbal, *India* 68 D7
Jubbulpore = Jabalpur, *India* 69 H8
Jübek, *Germany* 24 A5
Jubga, *Russia* 49 H4
Jubilee L., *Australia* ... 93 E4
Juby, C., *Morocco* 78 C3
Júcar = Xúquer →, *Spain* . 33 F4
Júcaro, *Cuba* 120 B4
Juchitán, *Mexico* 119 D5
Judaea = Har Yehuda, *Israel* 75 D3
Judenburg, *Austria* 26 D7
Judith →, *U.S.A.* 114 C9
Judith, Pt., *U.S.A.* 111 E13
Judith Gap, *U.S.A.* 114 C9
Juelsminde, *Denmark* ... 11 J4
Jugoslavia = Yugoslavia ■,
  Europe 40 C4
Juigalpa, *Nic.* 120 D2
Juillac, *France* 20 C5
Juist, *Germany* 24 B2
Juiz de Fora, *Brazil* ... 127 A7
Jujuy □, *Argentina* 126 A2
Julesburg, *U.S.A.* 112 E3
Juli, *Peru* 124 G5
Julia Cr. →, *Australia* .. 94 C3
Julia Creek, *Australia* .. 94 C3
Juliaca, *Peru* 124 G4
Julian, *U.S.A.* 117 M10
Julian Alps = Julijske Alpe,
  Slovenia 29 B11
Julian L., *Canada* 102 B4
Julianatop, *Surinam* ... 125 C7
Julianehåb = Qaqortoq,
  Greenland 4 C5
Jülich, *Germany* 24 E2
Julijske Alpe, *Slovenia* . 29 B11
Julimes, *Mexico* 118 B3
Jullundur, *India* 68 D6
Julu, *China* 56 F8
Jumbo, *Zimbabwe* 87 F3
Jumbo Pk., *U.S.A.* 117 J12
Jumentos Cays, *Bahamas* . 120 B4
Jumilla, *Spain* 33 G3
Jumla, *Nepal* 69 E10
Jumna = Yamuna →, *India* 69 G9
Junagadh, *India* 68 J4
Junction, *Tex., U.S.A.* .. 113 K5
Junction, *Utah, U.S.A.* .. 115 G7
Junction B., *Australia* .. 94 A1
Junction City, *Kans., U.S.A.* 112 F6
Junction City, *Oreg., U.S.A.* 114 D2
Junction Pt., *Australia* .. 94 A1
Jundah, *Australia* 94 C3
Jundiaí, *Brazil* 127 A6
Juneau, *U.S.A.* 104 B2
Junee, *Australia* 95 E4
Junggar Pendi, *China* .. 60 B3
Jungshahi, *Pakistan* ... 68 G2
Junín, *Argentina* 126 C3
Junín de los Andes,
  Argentina 128 D2

Jūniyah, *Lebanon* 75 B4
Junlian, *China* 58 C5
Juntas, *Chile* 126 B2
Juntura, *U.S.A.* 114 E4
Jur, Nahr el →, *Sudan* .. 81 F2
Jura = Jura, Mts. du,
  Europe 19 F13
Jura = Schwäbische Alb,
  Germany 25 G5
Jura, *U.K.* 14 F3
Jura □, *France* 19 F12
Jura □, *Switz.* 25 H3
Jūra →, *Lithuania* 44 C9
Jura, Mts. du, *Europe* .. 19 F13
Jura, Sd. of, *U.K.* 14 F3
Jurbarkas, *Lithuania* ... 9 J20
Jurien, *Australia* 93 F2
Jurilovca, *Romania* 43 F13
Jūrmala, *Latvia* 9 H20
Jurong, *China* 59 B12
Juruá →, *Brazil* 122 D4
Juruena, *Brazil* 124 F7
Juruena →, *Brazil* 124 E7
Juruti, *Brazil* 125 D7
Jussey, *France* 19 E12
Justo Daract, *Argentina* . 126 C2
Jutaí →, *Brazil* 124 D5
Jüterbog, *Germany* 24 D9
Juticalpa, *Honduras* ... 120 D2
Jutland = Jylland, *Denmark* 11 H3
Juventud, I. de la, *Cuba* . 120 B3
Juvigny-sous-Andaine,
  France 18 D6
Juwain, *Afghan.* 66 D2
Jūy Zar, *Iran* 70 C5
Juye, *China* 56 G9
Juzennecourt, *France* .. 19 D11
Jvari, *Georgia* 49 J6
Jwaneng, *Botswana* 85 J4
Jyderup, *Denmark* 11 J5
Jylland, *Denmark* 11 H3
Jyväskylä, *Finland* 9 E21

K

K2, *Pakistan* 69 B7
Ka →, *Nigeria* 83 C5
Kaap Plateau, *S. Africa* . 88 D3
Kaapkruis, *Namibia* 88 C1
Kaapstad = Cape Town,
  S. Africa 88 E2
Kaba, *Guinea* 82 C2
Kabaena, *Indonesia* 63 F6
Kabala, *S. Leone* 82 D2
Kabale, *Uganda* 86 C3
Kabalo,
  Dem. Rep. of the Congo . 86 D2
Kabambare,
  Dem. Rep. of the Congo . 86 C2
Kabango,
  Dem. Rep. of the Congo . 87 D2
Kabanjahe, *Indonesia* .. 62 D1
Kabankalan, *Phil.* 61 G5
Kabara, *Mali* 82 B4
Kabardinka, *Russia* 47 K10
Kabardino-Balkar
  Republic = Kabardino-
  Balkaria □, *Russia* ... 49 J6
Kabardino-Balkaria □,
  Russia 49 J6
Kabarega Falls = Murchison
  Falls, *Uganda* 86 B3
Kabasalan, *Phil.* 61 H5
Kabba, *Nigeria* 83 D6
Kabetogama, *U.S.A.* ... 112 A8
Kabi, *Niger* 83 C7
Kabin Buri, *Thailand* .. 64 F3
Kabinakagami L., *Canada* 102 C3
Kabinda,
  Dem. Rep. of the Congo . 84 F4
Kabna, *Sudan* 80 D3
Kabompo, *Zambia* 87 E1
Kabompo →, *Zambia* ... 85 G4
Kabondo,
  Dem. Rep. of the Congo . 87 D2
Kabongo,
  Dem. Rep. of the Congo . 86 D2
Kabot, *Guinea* 82 C2
Kabou, *Togo* 83 D5
Kabr, *Sudan* 81 E2
Kabūd Gonbad, *Iran* ... 71 B8
Kabugao, *Phil.* 61 B4
Kābul, *Afghan.* 68 B3
Kābul □, *Afghan.* 68 B3
Kabul →, *Pakistan* 68 C5
Kabunga,
  Dem. Rep. of the Congo . 86 C2
Kaburuang, *Indonesia* .. 63 D7
Kabushiya, *Sudan* 81 D3
Kabwe, *Zambia* 87 E2
Kačanik, *Kosovo, Yug.* . 40 D5
Kačerginė, *Lithuania* .. 44 D10
Kachchh, Gulf of, *India* . 68 H3
Kachchh, Rann of, *India* . 68 H4
Kachchhidhana, *India* .. 69 J8
Kachebera, *Zambia* 87 E3
Kachia, *Nigeria* 83 D6
Kachin □, *Burma* 58 D1
Kachira, L., *Uganda* ... 86 C3
Kachiry, *Kazakstan* 50 D8
Kachnara, *India* 68 H6
Kachot, *Cambodia* 65 G4
Kaçkar, *Turkey* 73 B9
Kadan, *Czech Rep.* 26 A6
Kadan Kyun, *Burma* ... 64 F2
Kadanai →, *Afghan.* ... 68 D1

Kadarkút, *Hungary* 42 D2
Kade, *Ghana* 83 D4
Kadi, *India* 68 H5
Kadina, *Australia* 95 E2
Kadınhanı, *Turkey* 72 C5
Kadiolo, *Mali* 82 C3
Kadipur, *India* 69 F10
Kadirli, *Turkey* 70 B3
Kadiyevka = Stakhanov,
  Ukraine 47 H10
Kadodo, *Sudan* 81 E2
Kadoka, *U.S.A.* 112 D4
Kadom, *Russia* 48 C6
Kadoma, *Zimbabwe* 87 F2
Kâdugli, *Sudan* 81 E2
Kaduna, *Nigeria* 83 C6
Kaduna □, *Nigeria* 83 C6
Kaduy, *Russia* 46 C9
Kaédi, *Mauritania* 82 B2
Kaélé, *Cameroon* 83 C7
Kaeng Khoï, *Thailand* . 64 E3
Kaesŏng, *N. Korea* 57 F14
Kāf, *Si. Arabia* 70 D3
Kafan = Kapan, *Armenia* . 70 B5
Kafanchan, *Nigeria* ... 83 D6
Kafareti, *Nigeria* 83 C7
Kaffrine, *Senegal* 82 C1
Kafin, *Nigeria* 83 D6
Kafin Madaki, *Nigeria* . 83 C6
Kafinda, *Zambia* 87 E3
Kafirévs, Ákra, *Greece* . 38 C6
Kafr el Battikh, *Egypt* . 80 H7
Kafr el Dauwâr, *Egypt* . 80 H7
Kafr el Sheikh, *Egypt* .. 80 H7
Kafue, *Zambia* 87 F2
Kafue →, *Zambia* 85 H5
Kafue Flats, *Zambia* ... 87 F2
Kafue Nat. Park, *Zambia* . 87 F2
Kafulwe, *Zambia* 87 D2
Kaga, *Afghan.* 68 B4
Kaga Bandoro, *C.A.R.* .. 84 C3
Kagawa □, *Japan* 55 G7
Kagera □, *Tanzania* ... 86 C3
Kagera →, *Tanzania* ... 86 C3
Kağızman, *Turkey* 70 B4
Kagmar, *Sudan* 81 E3
Kagoshima, *Japan* 55 J5
Kagoshima □, *Japan* ... 55 J5
Kagul = Cahul, *Moldova* . 43 E13
Kahak, *Iran* 71 B6
Kahama, *Tanzania* 86 C3
Kahan, *Pakistan* 68 E3
Kahang, *Malaysia* 65 L4
Kahayan →, *Indonesia* . 62 E4
Kahe, *Tanzania* 86 C4
Kahnūj, *Iran* 71 E8
Kahoka, *U.S.A.* 112 E9
Kahoolawe, *U.S.A.* 106 H16
Kahramanmaraş, *Turkey* . 70 B3
Kâhta, *Turkey* 73 D8
Kahuta, *Pakistan* 68 C5
Kai, Kepulauan, *Indonesia* 63 F8
Kai Besar, *Indonesia* .. 63 F8
Kai Is. = Kai, Kepulauan,
  Indonesia 63 F8
Kai Kecil, *Indonesia* .. 63 F8
Kai Xian, *China* 58 B7
Kaiama, *Nigeria* 83 D5
Kaiapoi, *N.Z.* 91 K4
Kaieteur Falls, *Guyana* . 124 B7
Kaifeng, *China* 56 G8
Kaihua, *China* 59 C12
Kaijiang, *China* 58 B6
Kaikohe, *N.Z.* 91 F4
Kaikoura, *N.Z.* 91 K4
Kaikoura Ra., *N.Z.* 91 J4
Kailahun, *S. Leone* ... 82 D2
Kaili, *China* 58 D6
Kailu, *China* 57 C11
Kailua Kona, *U.S.A.* ... 106 J17
Kaimana, *Indonesia* ... 63 E8
Kaimanawa Mts., *N.Z.* . 91 H5
Kaimganj, *India* 69 F8
Kaimur Hills, *India* ... 69 G10
Kainab →, *Namibia* ... 88 D2
Kaingaroa Forest, *N.Z.* . 91 H6
Kainji Dam, *Nigeria* .. 83 D5
Kainji Res., *Nigeria* .. 83 C5
Kainuu, *Finland* 8 D23
Kaipara Harbour, *N.Z.* . 91 G5
Kaiping, *China* 59 F9
Kaipokok B., *Canada* .. 103 B8
Kaira, *India* 68 H5
Kairana, *India* 68 E7
Kaironi, *Indonesia* ... 63 E8
Kairouan, *Tunisia* 79 A8
Kaiserstuhl, *Germany* . 25 G3
Kaitaia, *N.Z.* 91 F4
Kaitangata, *N.Z.* 91 M2
Kaithal, *India* 68 E7
Kaitu →, *Pakistan* 68 C4
Kaiwi Channel, *U.S.A.* . 106 H16
Kaiyang, *China* 58 D6
Kaiyuan, *Liaoning, China* 57 C13
Kaiyuan, *Yunnan, China* . 58 F4
Kajaani, *Finland* 8 D22
Kajabbi, *Australia* ... 94 C3
Kajana = Kajaani, *Finland* 8 D22
Kajang, *Malaysia* 65 L3
Kajaran, *Armenia* 73 C12
Kajiado, *Kenya* 86 C4
Kajo Kaji, *Sudan* 81 G3
Kajuru, *Nigeria* 83 C6
Kaka, *Sudan* 81 E3
Kakabeka Falls, *Canada* . 102 C2
Kakadu Nat. Park, *Australia* 92 B5
Kakamas, *S. Africa* ... 88 D3
Kakamega, *Kenya* 86 B3

Kakanj, Bos.-H.	42	F3
Kakanui Mts., N.Z.	91	L3
Kakata, Liberia	82	D2
Kakdwip, India	69	J13
Kake, Japan	55	G6
Kake, U.S.A.	104	B2
Kakegawa, Japan	55	G9
Kakeroma-Jima, Japan	55	K4
Kakhib, Russia	49	J8
Kakhovka, Ukraine	47	J7
Kakhovske Vdskh., Ukraine	47	J7
Kakinada, India	67	L13
Kakisa →, Canada	104	A5
Kakisa L., Canada	104	A5
Kakogawa, Japan	55	G7
Kakwa →, Canada	104	C5
Kāl Gūsheh, Iran	71	D8
Kal Safīd, Iran	70	C5
Kala, Nigeria	83	C7
Kalaallit Nunaat = Greenland ■, N. Amer.	4	C5
Kalabagh, Pakistan	68	C4
Kalabahi, Indonesia	63	F6
Kalabáka, Greece	38	B3
Kalabana, Mali	82	C3
Kalach, Russia	48	E5
Kalach na Donu, Russia	49	F6
Kaladan →, Burma	67	J18
Kaladar, Canada	102	D4
Kalahari, Africa	88	C3
Kalahari Gemsbok Nat. Park, S. Africa	88	D3
Kalajoki, Finland	8	D20
Kālak, Iran	71	E8
Kalakamati, Botswana	89	C4
Kalakan, Russia	51	D12
K'alak'unlun Shank'ou = Karakoram Pass, Pakistan	69	B7
Kalam, Pakistan	69	B5
Kalama, Dem. Rep. of the Congo	86	C2
Kalama, U.S.A.	116	E4
Kalámai, Greece	38	D4
Kalamariá, Greece	40	F6
Kalamata = Kalámai, Greece	38	D4
Kalamazoo, U.S.A.	108	D3
Kalamazoo →, U.S.A.	108	D2
Kalambo Falls, Tanzania	87	D3
Kálamos, Attikí, Greece	38	C5
Kálamos, Iónioi Nísoi, Greece	38	C2
Kalan, Turkey	70	B3
Kalankalan, Guinea	82	C3
Kalannie, Australia	93	F2
Kalántarī, Iran	71	C7
Kalao, Indonesia	63	F6
Kalaotoa, Indonesia	63	F6
Kälarne, Sweden	10	B10
Kalasin, Thailand	64	D4
Kalat, Pakistan	66	E5
Kalāteh, Iran	71	B7
Kalāteh-ye Ganj, Iran	71	E8
Kálathos, Greece	39	E10
Kalaus →, Russia	49	H7
Kalávrita, Greece	38	C4
Kalbarri, Australia	93	E1
Kale, Antalya, Turkey	39	E12
Kale, Denizli, Turkey	39	D10
Kalecik, Turkey	72	B5
Kalegauk Kyun, Burma	67	M20
Kalehe, Dem. Rep. of the Congo	86	C2
Kalema, Tanzania	86	C3
Kalemie, Dem. Rep. of the Congo	86	D2
Kalety, Poland	45	H5
Kalewa, Burma	67	H19
Kaleybar, Iran	70	B5
Kalgan = Zhangjiakou, China	56	D8
Kalgoorlie-Boulder, Australia	93	F3
Kali →, India	69	F8
Kali Sindh →, India	68	G6
Kaliakra, Nos, Bulgaria	41	C12
Kalianda, Indonesia	62	F3
Kalibo, Phil.	61	F5
Kalima, Dem. Rep. of the Congo	86	C2
Kalimantan □, Indonesia	62	E4
Kalimantan Barat □, Indonesia	62	E4
Kalimantan Selatan □, Indonesia	62	E5
Kalimantan Tengah □, Indonesia	62	E4
Kalimantan Timur □, Indonesia	62	D5
Kálimnos, Greece	39	D8
Kalimpong, India	69	F13
Kalinin = Tver, Russia	46	D8
Kaliningrad, Russia	9	J19
Kalininsk, Russia	48	E7
Kalinkavichy, Belarus	47	F5
Kalinkovichi = Kalinkavichy, Belarus	47	F5
Kalinovik, Bos.-H.	40	C2
Kalipetrovo, Bulgaria	41	B11
Kaliro, Uganda	86	B3
Kalirrákhi, Greece	41	F8
Kalispell, U.S.A.	114	B6
Kalisz, Poland	45	G5
Kalisz Pomorski, Poland	45	E2
Kaliua, Tanzania	86	D3
Kalívia Thorikoú, Greece	38	D5
Kalix, Sweden	8	D20
Kalix →, Sweden	8	D20
Kalka, India	68	D7
Kalkan, Turkey	39	E11
Kalkarindji, Australia	92	C5
Kalkaska, U.S.A.	108	C3
Kalkfeld, Namibia	88	C2
Kalkfontein, Botswana	88	C3
Kalkım, Turkey	39	B9
Kalkrand, Namibia	88	C2
Kållandsö, Sweden	11	F7
Kallavesi, Finland	8	E22
Källby, Sweden	11	F7
Källered, Sweden	11	G6
Kallimasiá, Greece	39	C8
Kallinge, Sweden	11	H9
Kallithéa, Greece	38	D5
Kallmeti, Albania	40	E3
Kallóni, Greece	39	B8
Kallonís, Kólpos, Greece	39	B8
Kallsjön, Sweden	8	E15
Kalmalo, Nigeria	83	C6
Kalmar, Sweden	11	H10
Kalmar län □, Sweden	11	G10
Kalmar sund, Sweden	11	H10
Kalmyk Republic = Kalmykia □, Russia	49	G8
Kalmykia □, Russia	49	G8
Kalmykovo, Kazakhstan	50	E6
Kalna, India	69	H13
Kalnai, India	69	H10
Kalocsa, Hungary	42	D4
Kalofer, Bulgaria	41	D8
Kalokhorio, Cyprus	36	E12
Kaloko, Dem. Rep. of the Congo	86	D2
Kalol, Gujarat, India	68	H5
Kalol, Gujarat, India	68	H5
Kalolímnos, Greece	39	D9
Kalomo, Zambia	87	F2
Kalonerón, Greece	38	D3
Kalpi, India	69	F8
Kaltern = Caldaro, Italy	29	B8
Kaltungo, Nigeria	83	D7
Kalu, Pakistan	68	G2
Kaluga, Russia	46	E9
Kalulushi, Zambia	87	E2
Kalundborg, Denmark	11	J5
Kalush, Ukraine	47	H3
Kałuszyn, Poland	45	F8
Kalutara, Sri Lanka	66	R12
Kalvarija, Lithuania	44	D10
Kalyazin, Russia	46	D9
Kam →, Nigeria	83	D7
Kama, Dem. Rep. of the Congo	86	C2
Kama →, Russia	6	D16
Kamachumu, Tanzania	86	C3
Kamaishi, Japan	54	E10
Kamalia, Pakistan	68	D5
Kaman, India	68	F6
Kaman, Turkey	72	C5
Kamanjab, Namibia	88	B2
Kamapanda, Zambia	87	E1
Kamaran, Yemen	74	D3
Kamativi, Zimbabwe	88	B4
Kamba, Nigeria	83	C5
Kambalda, Australia	93	F3
Kambar, Pakistan	68	F3
Kambia, S. Leone	82	D2
Kambolé, Togo	83	D5
Kambolé, Zambia	87	D3
Kambos, Cyprus	36	D11
Kambove, Dem. Rep. of the Congo	87	E2
Kamchatka, Poluostrov, Russia	51	D16
Kamchatka Pen. = Kamchatka, Poluostrov, Russia	51	D16
Kamchiya →, Bulgaria	41	C11
Kamen, Russia	50	D9
Kamen-Rybolov, Russia	54	B6
Kamenica, Serbia, Yug.	40	C6
Kamenica, Serbia, Yug.	40	B3
Kamenice nad Lipou, Czech Rep.	26	B8
Kamenjak, Rt., Croatia	29	D10
Kamenka = Kaminka, Ukraine	47	H7
Kamenka, Kazakhstan	48	E10
Kamenka, Penza, Russia	48	D6
Kamenka, Voronezh, Russia	47	G10
Kamenka Bugskaya = Kamyanka-Buzka, Ukraine	47	G3
Kamenka Dneprovskaya = Kamyanka-Dniprovska, Ukraine	47	J8
Kamennomostskiy, Russia	49	H5
Kameno, Bulgaria	41	D11
Kamenolomni, Russia	49	G5
Kamensk-Shakhtinskiy, Russia	49	F5
Kamensk Uralskiy, Russia	50	D7
Kamenskiy, Russia	48	E7
Kamenskoye, Russia	51	C17
Kamenyak, Bulgaria	41	C10
Kamenz, Germany	24	D10
Kameoka, Japan	55	G7
Kami, Albania	40	D4
Kamiah, U.S.A.	114	C5
Kamień Krajeński, Poland	44	E4
Kamień Pomorski, Poland	44	E1
Kamienna →, Poland	45	G8
Kamienna Góra, Poland	45	H3
Kamieńsk, Poland	45	G6
Kamieskroon, S. Africa	88	E2
Kamilukuak, L., Canada	105	A8
Kamin-Kashyrskyy, Ukraine	47	G3
Kamina, Dem. Rep. of the Congo	86	D2
Kaminak L., Canada	105	A10
Kaministiquia, Canada	102	C1
Kaminka, Ukraine	47	H7
Kaminoyama, Japan	54	E10
Kamiros, Greece	36	C9
Kamituga, Dem. Rep. of the Congo	86	C2
Kamla →, India	69	G12
Kamloops, Canada	104	C4
Kamnik, Slovenia	29	B11
Kamo, Armenia	49	K7
Kamo, Japan	54	F9
Kamoke, Pakistan	68	C6
Kamp →, Austria	26	C6
Kampala, Uganda	86	B3
Kampang Chhnang, Cambodia	65	F5
Kampar, Malaysia	65	K3
Kampar →, Indonesia	62	D2
Kampen, Neths.	17	B5
Kampene, Dem. Rep. of the Congo	84	E5
Kamphaeng Phet, Thailand	64	D2
Kampolombo, L., Zambia	87	E2
Kampong Saom, Cambodia	65	G4
Kampong Saom, Chaak, Cambodia	65	G4
Kampong To, Thailand	65	J3
Kampot, Cambodia	65	G5
Kampti, Burkina Faso	82	C4
Kampuchea = Cambodia ■, Asia	64	F5
Kampung Air Putih, Malaysia	65	K4
Kampung Jerangau, Malaysia	65	K4
Kampung Raja, Malaysia	65	K4
Kampungbaru = Tolitoli, Indonesia	63	D6
Kamrau, Teluk, Indonesia	63	E8
Kamsack, Canada	105	C8
Kamsai, Guinea	82	C2
Kamskoye Ustye, Russia	48	C9
Kamuchawie L., Canada	105	B8
Kamuela, U.S.A.	106	H17
Kamui-Misaki, Japan	54	C10
Kamyanets-Podilskyy, Ukraine	47	H4
Kamyanka-Buzka, Ukraine	47	G3
Kamyanka-Dniprovska, Ukraine	47	J8
Kāmyārān, Iran	70	C5
Kamyshin, Russia	48	E7
Kamyzyak, Russia	49	G9
Kan, Sudan	81	F3
Kanaaupscow, Canada	102	B4
Kanaaupscow →, Canada	101	C12
Kanab, U.S.A.	115	H7
Kanab →, U.S.A.	115	H7
Kanagi, Japan	54	D10
Kanairiktok →, Canada	103	A7
Kanália, Greece	38	B4
Kananga, Dem. Rep. of the Congo	84	F4
Kanash, Russia	48	C8
Kanaskat, U.S.A.	116	C5
Kanastraíon, Ákra = Palioúrion, Ákra, Greece	40	G7
Kanawha →, U.S.A.	108	F4
Kanazawa, Japan	55	F8
Kanchanaburi, Thailand	64	E2
Kanchenjunga, Nepal	69	F13
Kanchipuram, India	66	N11
Kańczuga, Poland	45	J9
Kandaghat, India	68	D7
Kandahar = Qandahār, Afghan.	66	D4
Kandalaksha, Russia	50	C4
Kandalu, Afghan.	66	E3
Kandangan, Indonesia	62	E5
Kandanghaur, Indonesia	63	G13
Kandanos, Greece	36	D5
Kandava, Latvia	44	A9
Kandhíla, Greece	38	D4
Kandhkot, Pakistan	68	E3
Kandhla, India	68	E7
Kandi, Benin	83	C5
Kandi, India	69	H13
Kandiaro, Pakistan	68	F3
Kandıra, Turkey	72	B4
Kandla, India	68	H4
Kandos, Australia	95	E4
Kandreho, Madag.	89	B8
Kandy, Sri Lanka	66	R12
Kane, U.S.A.	110	E6
Kane Basin, Greenland	4	B4
Kanel, Senegal	82	B2
Kaneohe, U.S.A.	106	H16
Kanevskaya, Russia	49	G4
Kanfanar, Croatia	29	C10
Kang, Botswana	88	C3
Kangaba, Mali	82	C3
Kangal, Turkey	72	C7
Kangān, Fārs, Iran	71	E7
Kangān, Hormozgān, Iran	71	E8
Kangar, Malaysia	65	J3
Kangaré, Mali	82	C3
Kangaroo I., Australia	95	F2
Kangaroo Mts., Australia	94	C3
Kangasala, Finland	9	F21
Kangāvar, Iran	71	C6
Kangding, China	58	B3
Kangean, Kepulauan, Indonesia	62	F5
Kangean Is. = Kangean, Kepulauan, Indonesia	62	F5
Kangen →, Sudan	81	F3
Kanggye, N. Korea	57	D14
Kanggyŏng, S. Korea	57	F14
Kanghwa, S. Korea	57	F14
Kangikajik, Greenland	4	B6
Kangiqsualujjuaq, Canada	101	C13
Kangiqsujuaq, Canada	101	B12
Kangirsuk, Canada	101	B13
Kangnŭng, S. Korea	57	F15
Kangping, China	57	C12
Kangra, India	68	C7
Kangto, India	67	F18
Kanhar →, India	69	G10
Kani, Ivory C.	82	D3
Kaniama, Dem. Rep. of the Congo	86	D1
Kaniapiskau = Caniapiscau →, Canada	103	A6
Kaniapiskau, Res. = Caniapiscau Rés. de, Canada	103	B6
Kanin, Poluostrov, Russia	50	C5
Kanin Nos, Mys, Russia	50	C5
Kanin Pen. = Kanin, Poluostrov, Russia	50	C5
Kanina, Albania	40	F3
Kaniva, Australia	95	F3
Kanjiža, Serbia, Yug.	42	D5
Kankaanpää, Finland	9	F20
Kankakee, U.S.A.	108	E2
Kankakee →, U.S.A.	108	E1
Kankan, Guinea	82	C3
Kankendy = Xankändi, Azerbaijan	70	B5
Kanker, India	67	J12
Kankossa, Mauritania	82	B2
Kankroli, India	68	G5
Kannapolis, U.S.A.	109	H5
Kannauj, India	69	F8
Kannod, India	66	H10
Kano, Nigeria	83	C6
Kano □, Nigeria	83	C6
Kan'onji, Japan	55	G6
Kanoroba, Ivory C.	82	D3
Kanowit, Malaysia	62	D4
Kanoya, Japan	55	J5
Kanpetlet, Burma	67	J18
Kanpur, India	69	F9
Kansas □, U.S.A.	112	F6
Kansas →, U.S.A.	112	F7
Kansas City, Kans., U.S.A.	112	F7
Kansas City, Mo., U.S.A.	112	F7
Kansenia, Dem. Rep. of the Congo	87	E2
Kansk, Russia	51	D10
Kansŏng, S. Korea	57	E15
Kansu = Gansu □, China	56	G3
Kantaphor, India	68	H7
Kantchari, Burkina Faso	83	C5
Kantché, Niger	83	C6
Kantemirovka, Russia	47	H10
Kantharalak, Thailand	64	E5
Kantli →, India	68	E6
Kantō □, Japan	55	F9
Kantō-Sanchi, Japan	55	G9
Kanturk, Ireland	15	D3
Kanuma, Japan	55	F9
Kanus, Namibia	88	D2
Kanye, Botswana	88	C4
Kanzenze, Dem. Rep. of the Congo	87	E2
Kanzi, Ras, Tanzania	86	D4
Kaohsiung, Taiwan	59	F13
Kaokoveld, Namibia	88	B1
Kaolack, Senegal	82	C1
Kaoshan, China	57	B13
Kapaa, U.S.A.	106	G15
Kapadvanj, India	68	H5
Kapan, Armenia	70	B5
Kapanga, Dem. Rep. of the Congo	84	F4
Kapchagai = Qapshaghay, Kazakhstan	50	E8
Kapela = Velika Kapela, Croatia	29	C12
Kapéllo, Ákra, Greece	38	E5
Kapema, Dem. Rep. of the Congo	87	E2
Kapfenberg, Austria	26	D8
Kapı Dağı, Turkey	41	F11
Kapiri Mposhi, Zambia	87	E2
Kapiskau →, Canada	102	B3
Kapit, Malaysia	62	D4
Kapiti I., N.Z.	91	J5
Kaplan, U.S.A.	113	K8
Kaplice, Czech Rep.	26	C7
Kapoe, Thailand	65	H2
Kapoeta, Sudan	81	G3
Kápolnásnyék, Hungary	42	C3
Kapos →, Hungary	42	D3
Kaposvár, Hungary	42	D2
Kapowsin, U.S.A.	116	D4
Kappeln, Germany	24	A5
Kappelshamn, Sweden	11	G12
Kapps, Namibia	88	C2
Kaprije, Croatia	29	E12
Kapsan, N. Korea	57	D15
Kapsukas = Marijampolė, Lithuania	9	J20
Kapuas →, Indonesia	62	E3
Kapuas Hulu, Pegunungan, Malaysia	62	D4
Kapuas Hulu Ra. = Kapuas Hulu, Pegunungan, Indonesia	62	D4
Kapulo, Dem. Rep. of the Congo	87	D2
Kapunda, Australia	95	E2
Kapuni, N.Z.	91	H5
Kapurthala, India	68	D6
Kapuskasing, Canada	102	C3
Kapuskasing →, Canada	102	C3
Kapustin Yar, Russia	49	F7
Kaputar, Australia	95	E5
Kaputir, Kenya	86	B4
Kapuvár, Hungary	42	C2
Kara →, Russia	50	C7
Kara Ada, Turkey	39	E9
Kara Bogaz Gol, Zaliv = Garabogazköl Aylagy, Turkmenistan	50	E6
Kara Burun, Turkey	39	E9
Kara Kalpak Republic = Karakalpakstan □, Uzbekistan	50	E6
Kara Kum, Turkmenistan	50	F6
Kara Sea, Russia	50	B7
Karaadilli, Turkey	39	C12
Karabiğa, Turkey	41	F11
Karabük, Turkey	72	B5
Karaburun, Turkey	39	C8
Karaburuni, Albania	40	F3
Karabutak = Qarabutaq, Kazakhstan	50	E7
Karacabey, Turkey	41	F12
Karacakılavuz, Turkey	41	E11
Karacaköy, Turkey	41	E12
Karacasu, Turkey	39	D10
Karachala = Qaraçala, Azerbaijan	49	L9
Karachayevsk, Russia	49	J5
Karachev, Russia	47	F8
Karachey-Cherkessia □, Russia	49	J5
Karachi, Pakistan	68	G2
Karad, India	66	L9
Karadirek, Turkey	39	C12
Karaga, Ghana	83	D4
Karaganda = Qaraghandy, Kazakhstan	50	E8
Karagayly, Kazakhstan	50	E8
Karaginskiy, Ostrov, Russia	51	D17
Karagola Road, India	69	G12
Karagüney Dağları, Turkey	72	B6
Karahallı, Turkey	39	C11
Karaikal, India	66	P11
Karaikkudi, India	66	P11
Karaisalı, Turkey	72	D6
Karaj, Iran	71	C6
Karak, Malaysia	65	L4
Karakalpakstan □, Uzbekistan	50	E6
Karakelong, Indonesia	63	D7
Karakitang, Indonesia	63	D7
Karaklis = Vanadzor, Armenia	49	K7
Karakoçan, Turkey	73	C9
Karakoram Pass, Pakistan	69	B7
Karakoram Ra., Pakistan	69	B7
Karakurt, Turkey	73	B10
Karakuwisa, Namibia	88	B2
Karalon, Russia	51	D12
Karama, Jordan	75	D4
Karaman, Balıkesir, Turkey	39	B9
Karaman, Konya, Turkey	70	B2
Karamanlı, Turkey	39	D11
Karamay, China	60	B3
Karambu, Indonesia	62	E5
Karamea Bight, N.Z.	91	J3
Karamnasa →, India	69	G10
Karamürsel, Turkey	41	F13
Karand, Iran	70	C5
Karangana, Mali	82	C3
Karanganyar, Indonesia	63	G13
Karanjia, India	69	J11
Karankasso, Burkina Faso	82	C4
Karaova, Turkey	39	D9
Karapınar, Turkey	72	D5
Karasburg, Namibia	88	D2
Karasino, Russia	50	C9
Karasjok, Norway	8	B21
Karasu, Turkey	72	B4
Karasu →, Turkey	39	E12
Karasuk, Russia	50	D8
Karasuyama, Japan	55	F10
Karataş, Adana, Turkey	72	D6
Karataş, Manisa, Turkey	39	C10
Karataş Burnu, Turkey	72	D6
Karatau = Qarataū, Kazakhstan	50	E8
Karatau, Khrebet, Kazakhstan	50	E7
Karatoprak, Turkey	39	D9
Karatsu, Japan	55	H5
Karaul, Russia	50	B9
Karauli, India	68	F7
Karavastasë, L. e, Albania	40	F3
Karávi, Greece	38	E5
Karavostasi, Cyprus	36	D11
Karawang, Indonesia	63	G12
Karawanken, Europe	26	E7
Karazhal, Kazakhstan	50	E8
Karbalā', Iraq	70	C5
Kårböle, Sweden	10	C9
Karcag, Hungary	42	C5
Karcha →, Pakistan	69	B7
Karchana, India	69	G9
Karczew, Poland	45	F8
Kardam, Bulgaria	41	C12
Kardeljovo = Ploče, Croatia	29	E14
Kardhámila, Greece	39	C8
Kardhamíli, Greece	38	E4
Kárdhitsa, Greece	38	B3
Kárdhitsa □, Greece	38	B3
Kärdla, Estonia	9	G20
Kareeberge, S. Africa	88	E3
Kareha →, India	69	G12
Karelia, Sudan	80	D3
Karelia □, Russia	50	C4
Karelian Republic = Karelia □, Russia	50	C4
Kärevändar, Iran	71	E9
Kargasok, Russia	50	D9
Kargı, Turkey	72	B6
Kargil, India	69	B7
Kargopol, Russia	46	B10
Kargowa, Poland	45	F2

Karguéri, *Niger* 83 C7
Karhal, *India* 69 F8
Kariá, *Greece* 38 C2
Kariaí, *Greece* 41 F8
Karīān, *Iran* 71 E8
Karianga, *Madag.* 89 C8
Kariba, *Zimbabwe* 87 F2
Kariba, L., *Zimbabwe* 87 F2
Kariba Dam, *Zimbabwe* ... 87 F2
Kariba Gorge, *Zambia* 87 F2
Karibib, *Namibia* 88 C2
Karimata, Kepulauan,
  Indonesia 62 E3
Karimata, Selat, *Indonesia* . 62 E3
Karimata Is. = Karimata,
  Kepulauan, *Indonesia* ... 62 E3
Karimnagar, *India* 66 K11
Karimunjawa, Kepulauan,
  Indonesia 62 F4
Karin, *Somali Rep.* 74 E4
Káristos, *Greece* 38 C6
Karīt, *Iran* 71 C8
Kariya, *Japan* 55 G8
Kariyangwe, *Zimbabwe* 89 B4
Karjala, *Finland* 46 A5
Karkaralinsk = Qarqaraly,
  Kazakstan 50 E8
Karkheh →, *Iran* 70 D5
Karkinitska Zatoka, *Ukraine* 47 K7
Karkinitskiy Zaliv =
  Karkinitska Zatoka,
  Ukraine 47 K7
Karkur Tohl, *Egypt* 80 C2
Karl Liebknecht, *Russia* .. 47 G8
Karl-Marx-Stadt =
  Chemnitz, *Germany* 24 E8
Karlholmsbruk, *Sweden* .. 10 D11
Karlino, *Poland* 44 D2
Karlivka, *Ukraine* 47 H8
Karlobag, *Croatia* 29 D12
Karlovac, *Croatia* 29 C12
Karlovka = Karlivka,
  Ukraine 47 H8
Karlovo, *Bulgaria* 41 D8
Karlovy Vary, *Czech Rep.* . 26 A5
Karlsbad = Karlovy Vary,
  Czech Rep. 26 A5
Karlsborg, *Sweden* 11 F8
Karlshamn, *Sweden* 11 H8
Karlskoga, *Sweden* 10 E8
Karlskrona, *Sweden* 11 H9
Karlsruhe, *Germany* 25 F4
Karlstad, *Sweden* 10 E7
Karlstad, *U.S.A.* 112 A6
Karlstadt, *Germany* 25 F5
Karma, *Niger* 83 C5
Karmélava, *Lithuania* 44 D11
Karmi'el, *Israel* 75 C4
Karnak, *Egypt* 79 C12
Karnal, *India* 68 E7
Karnali →, *Nepal* 69 E9
Karnaphuli Res., *Bangla.* . 67 H18
Karnaprayag, *India* 69 D8
Karnataka □, *India* 66 N10
Karnes City, *U.S.A.* 113 L6
Karnische Alpen, *Europe* . 26 E6
Karnobat, *Bulgaria* 41 D10
Kärnten □, *Austria* 26 E6
Karo, *Mali* 82 C4
Karoi, *Zimbabwe* 87 F2
Karonga, *Malawi* 87 D3
Karoonda, *Australia* 95 F2
Karor, *Pakistan* 68 D4
Karora, *Sudan* 80 D4
Káros, *Greece* 39 E7
Karousádhes, *Greece* 38 B1
Karpacz, *Poland* 45 H2
Karpasia □, *Cyprus* 36 D13
Kárpathos, *Greece* 39 F9
Kárpathos, Stenón, *Greece* . 39 F9
Karpenísion, *Greece* 38 C3
Karpuz Burnu = Apostolos
  Andreas, C., *Cyprus* 36 D13
Karpuzlu, *Turkey* 39 D9
Karratha, *Australia* 92 D2
Kars, *Turkey* 73 B10
Karsakpay, *Kazakstan* 50 E7
Karsha, *Kazakstan* 48 F10
Karshi = Qarshi, *Uzbekistan* 50 F7
Karsiyang, *India* 69 F13
Karsog, *India* 68 D7
Karst = Kras, *Croatia* 29 C10
Kartal, *Turkey* 41 F13
Kartál Óros, *Greece* 41 E9
Kartaly, *Russia* 50 D7
Kartapur, *India* 68 D6
Karthaus, *U.S.A.* 110 E6
Kartuzy, *Poland* 44 D5
Karufa, *Indonesia* 63 E8
Karumba, *Australia* 94 B3
Karumo, *Tanzania* 86 C3
Karumwa, *Tanzania* 86 C3
Kārūn →, *Iran* 71 D6
Karungu, *Kenya* 86 C3
Karup, *Denmark* 11 H3
Karviná, *Czech Rep.* 27 B11
Karwan →, *India* 68 F8
Karwar, *India* 66 M9
Karwi, *India* 69 G9
Kaş, *Turkey* 39 E11
Kasaba, *Turkey* 39 E11
Kasache, *Malawi* 87 E3
Kasai →,
  Dem. Rep. of the Congo . 84 E3
Kasaï-Oriental □,
  Dem. Rep. of the Congo . 86 D1
Kasaji,
  Dem. Rep. of the Congo . 87 E1
Kasama, *Zambia* 87 E3
Kasan-dong, *N. Korea* 57 D14

Kasane, *Namibia* 88 B3
Kasanga, *Tanzania* 87 D3
Kasar, Ras, *Sudan* 80 D4
Kasaragod, *India* 66 N9
Kasba L., *Canada* 105 A8
Käseh Garān, *Iran* 70 C5
Kasempa, *Zambia* 87 E2
Kasenga,
  Dem. Rep. of the Congo . 87 E2
Kasese, *Uganda* 86 B3
Kasewa, *Zambia* 87 E2
Kasganj, *India* 69 F8
Kashabowie, *Canada* 102 C1
Kashaf, *Iran* 71 C9
Kāshān, *Iran* 71 C6
Kashechewan, *Canada* 102 B3
Kashi, *China* 60 C2
Kashimbo,
  Dem. Rep. of the Congo . 87 E2
Kashin, *Russia* 46 D9
Kashipur, *India* 69 E8
Kashira, *Russia* 46 E10
Kashiwazaki, *Japan* 55 F9
Kashk-e Kohneh, *Afghan.* . 66 B3
Kashkū'īyeh, *Iran* 71 D7
Kāshmar, *Iran* 71 C8
Kashmir, *Asia* 69 C7
Kashmor, *Pakistan* 68 E3
Kashpirovka, *Russia* 48 D9
Kashun Noerh = Gaxun
  Nur, *China* 60 B5
Kasiari, *India* 69 H12
Kasimov, *Russia* 48 C5
Kasinge,
  Dem. Rep. of the Congo . 86 D2
Kasiruta, *Indonesia* 63 E7
Kaskaskia →, *U.S.A.* 112 G10
Kaskattama →, *Canada* .. 105 B10
Kaskinen, *Finland* 9 E19
Kaslo, *Canada* 104 D5
Kasmere L., *Canada* 105 B8
Kasongo,
  Dem. Rep. of the Congo . 86 C2
Kasongo Lunda,
  Dem. Rep. of the Congo . 84 F3
Kásos, *Greece* 39 F8
Kásos, Stenón, *Greece* 39 F8
Kaspi, *Georgia* 49 K7
Kaspichan, *Bulgaria* 41 C11
Kaspiysk, *Russia* 49 J8
Kaspiyskiy, *Russia* 49 H8
Kassab ed Doleib, *Sudan* . 81 E3
Kassaba, *Egypt* 80 C2
Kassalâ, *Sudan* 81 D4
Kassalâ □, *Sudan* 81 D4
Kassándra, *Greece* 40 F7
Kassándrinon, *Greece* 40 F7
Kassel, *Germany* 24 D5
Kassinger, *Sudan* 80 D3
Kassiópi, *Greece* 36 A3
Kasson, *U.S.A.* 112 C8
Kastamonu, *Turkey* 72 B5
Kastav, *Croatia* 29 C11
Kastélli, *Greece* 36 D5
Kastéllion, *Greece* 36 D7
Kastellórizon = Megiste,
  Greece 39 E11
Kástellos, *Greece* 39 E9
Kastellou, Ákra, *Greece* .. 39 F9
Kasterlee, *Belgium* 17 C4
Kastlösa, *Sweden* 11 H10
Kastóri, *Greece* 38 D4
Kastoría, *Greece* 40 F5
Kastoría □, *Greece* 40 F5
Kastorías, Límni, *Greece* .. 40 F5
Kastornoye, *Russia* 47 G10
Kastós, *Greece* 38 C2
Kastrosikiá, *Greece* 38 B2
Kastsyukovichy, *Belarus* .. 46 F7
Kasulu, *Tanzania* 86 C3
Kasumi, *Japan* 55 G7
Kasumkent, *Russia* 49 K9
Kasungu, *Malawi* 87 E3
Kasur, *Pakistan* 68 D6
Kataba, *Zambia* 87 F2
Katagum, *Nigeria* 83 C7
Katahdin, Mt., *U.S.A.* 109 C11
Katako Kombe,
  Dem. Rep. of the Congo . 86 C1
Katákolon, *Greece* 38 D3
Katale, *Tanzania* 86 C3
Katanda, Katanga,
  Dem. Rep. of the Congo . 86 D1
Katanda, Nord-Kivu,
  Dem. Rep. of the Congo . 86 C2
Katanga □,
  Dem. Rep. of the Congo . 86 D2
Katangi, *India* 66 J11
Katanning, *Australia* 93 F2
Katastári, *Greece* 38 D2
Katavi Swamp, *Tanzania* .. 86 D3
Kateríni, *Greece* 40 F6
Katghora, *India* 69 H10
Katha, *Burma* 67 G20
Katherîna, Gebel, *Egypt* .. 70 D2
Katherine, *Australia* 92 B5
Katherine Gorge, *Australia* . 92 B5
Kathi, *India* 68 J6
Kathiawar, *India* 68 H4
Kathikas, *Cyprus* 36 E11
Kathua, *India* 68 C6
Kati, *Mali* 82 C3
Katihar, *India* 69 G12
Katima Mulilo, *Zambia* ... 88 B3
Katimbira, *Malawi* 87 E3
Katingan = Mendawai →,
  Indonesia 62 E4
Katiola, *Ivory C.* 82 D3
Katlanovo, *Macedonia* 40 E5
Katmandu, *Nepal* 69 F11
Katni, *India* 69 H9

Kato Akhaïa, *Greece* 38 C3
Káto Arkhánai, *Greece* ... 36 D7
Kato Pyrgos, *Cyprus* 36 D11
Káto Khorió, *Greece* 36 D7
Káto Stavros, *Greece* 40 F7
Katokhí, *Greece* 38 C3
Katompe,
  Dem. Rep. of the Congo . 86 D2
Katonga →, *Uganda* 86 B3
Katoomba, *Australia* 95 E5
Katoúna, *Greece* 38 C3
Katowice, *Poland* 45 H6
Katrancı Dağı, *Turkey* 39 D12
Katrine, L., *U.K.* 14 E4
Katrineholm, *Sweden* 11 E10
Katsepe, *Madag.* 89 B8
Katsina, *Nigeria* 83 C6
Katsina □, *Nigeria* 83 C6
Katsina Ala, *Nigeria* 83 D6
Katsina Ala →, *Nigeria* .. 83 D6
Katsumoto, *Japan* 55 H4
Katsuura, *Japan* 55 G10
Katsuyama, *Japan* 55 F8
Kattaviá, *Greece* 36 D9
Kattegat, *Denmark* 11 H5
Katthammarsvik, *Sweden* . 11 G12
Katul, J., *Sudan* 81 E2
Katumba,
  Dem. Rep. of the Congo . 86 D2
Katungu, *Kenya* 86 C5
Katwa, *India* 69 H13
Katwijk, *Neths.* 17 B4
Kaub, *Germany* 25 E3
Kaufbeuren, *Germany* 25 H6
Kaufman, *U.S.A.* 113 J6
Kauhajoki, *Finland* 9 E20
Kaukauna, *U.S.A.* 108 C1
Kaukauveld, *Namibia* 88 C3
Kaunakakai, *U.S.A.* 106 H16
Kaunas, *Lithuania* 9 J20
Kaunia, *Bangla.* 69 G13
Kaunos, *Turkey* 39 E10
Kaura Namoda, *Nigeria* ... 83 C6
Kauru, *Nigeria* 83 C6
Kautokeino, *Norway* 8 B20
Kauwapur, *India* 69 F10
Kavacha, *Russia* 51 C17
Kavadarci, *Macedonia* 40 E5
Kavaja, *Albania* 40 E3
Kavak, *Turkey* 72 B7
Kavak Dağı, *Turkey* 39 D10
Kavaklı, *Turkey* 41 E11
Kavaklıdere, *Turkey* 39 D10
Kavalerovo, *Russia* 54 B7
Kavali, *India* 66 M12
Kaválla, *Greece* 41 E8
Kaválla □, *Greece* 41 E8
Kaválla Kólpos, *Greece* ... 41 F8
Kavār, *Iran* 71 D7
Kavarna, *Bulgaria* 41 C12
Kavi, *India* 68 H5
Kavimba, *Botswana* 88 B3
Kavīr, Dasht-e, *Iran* 71 C7
Kavkaz, *Russia* 47 K9
Kävlinge, *Sweden* 11 J7
Kavos, *Greece* 36 B4
Kavoúsi, *Greece* 39 F7
Kaw, *Fr. Guiana* 125 C8
Kawa, *Sudan* 81 E3
Kawagama L., *Canada* ... 110 A6
Kawagoe, *Japan* 55 G9
Kawaguchi, *Japan* 55 G9
Kawaihae, *U.S.A.* 106 H17
Kawambwa, *Zambia* 87 D2
Kawanoe, *Japan* 55 G6
Kawardha, *India* 69 J9
Kawasaki, *Japan* 55 G9
Kawasi, *Indonesia* 63 E7
Kawerau, *N.Z.* 91 H6
Kawhia Harbour, *N.Z.* 91 H5
Kawio, Kepulauan, *Indonesia* 63 D7
Kawnro, *Burma* 67 H21
Kawthaung, *Burma* 65 H2
Kawthoolei = Kawthule □,
  Burma 67 L20
Kawthule □, *Burma* 67 L20
Kaxholmen, *Sweden* 11 G8
Kaya, *Burkina Faso* 83 C4
Kayah □, *Burma* 67 K20
Kayalıköy Barajı, *Turkey* .. 41 E11
Kayan →, *Indonesia* 62 D5
Kaycee, *U.S.A.* 114 E10
Kayeli, *Indonesia* 63 E7
Kayenta, *U.S.A.* 115 H8
Kayes, *Mali* 82 C2
Kayı, *Turkey* 39 B12
Kayima, *S. Leone* 82 D2
Kayin = Kawthule □, *Burma* 67 L20
Kaymakçı, *Turkey* 39 C10
Kayoa, *Indonesia* 63 D7
Kayomba, *Zambia* 87 E1
Kaysatskoye, *Russia* 48 F8
Kayseri, *Turkey* 70 B3
Kaysville, *U.S.A.* 114 F8
Kaz Dağı, *Turkey* 39 B8
Kazachye, *Russia* 51 B14
Kazakstan ■, *Asia* 50 E7
Kazan →, *Canada* 105 A9
Kazan-Rettō, *Pac. Oc.* ... 96 E6
Kazanlůk, *Bulgaria* 41 D9
Kazanskaya, *Russia* 48 F5
Kazatin = Kozyatyn,
  Ukraine 47 H5
Kazaure, *Nigeria* 83 C6
Kazbek, *Russia* 49 J7
Kāzerūn, *Iran* 71 D6

Kazi Magomed =
  Qazimämmäd, *Azerbaijan* 49 K9
Kazimierz Dolny, *Poland* .. 45 G8
Kazimierza Wielka, *Poland* . 45 H7
Kazincbarcika, *Hungary* ... 42 B5
Kazlų Rūda, *Lithuania* 44 D10
Kaztalovka, *Kazakstan* 48 F9
Kazuno, *Japan* 54 D10
Kazym →, *Russia* 50 C7
Kcynia, *Poland* 45 F4
Ké-Macina, *Mali* 82 C3
Kéa, *Greece* 38 D6
Keady, *U.K.* 15 B5
Kearney, *U.S.A.* 112 E5
Kearny, *U.S.A.* 115 K8
Kearsarge, Mt., *U.S.A.* ... 111 C13
Keban, *Turkey* 73 C8
Keban Baraji, *Turkey* 70 B3
Kebbi □, *Nigeria* 83 C5
Kébi, *Ivory C.* 82 D3
Kebnekaise, *Sweden* 8 C18
Kebri Dehar, *Ethiopia* 74 F3
Kebumen, *Indonesia* 63 G13
Kecel, *Hungary* 42 D4
Kechika →, *Canada* 104 B3
Keçiborlu, *Turkey* 39 D12
Kecskemét, *Hungary* 42 D4
Kedada, *Ethiopia* 81 F4
Kédainiai, *Lithuania* 9 J21
Kedarnath, *India* 69 D8
Kedgwick, *Canada* 103 C6
Kédhros Óros, *Greece* 36 D6
Kediri, *Indonesia* 63 G15
Kedjebi, *Ghana* 83 D5
Kédougou, *Senegal* 82 C2
Kędzierzyn-Koźle, *Poland* . 45 H5
Keeler, *U.S.A.* 116 J9
Keeley L., *Canada* 105 C7
Keeling Is. = Cocos Is.,
  Ind. Oc. 96 J1
Keelung = Chilung, *Taiwan* 59 E13
Keene, *Canada* 110 B6
Keene, *Calif., U.S.A.* 117 K8
Keene, *N.H., U.S.A.* 111 D12
Keene, *N.Y., U.S.A.* 111 B11
Keeper Hill, *Ireland* 15 D3
Keer-Weer, C., *Australia* .. 94 A3
Keeseville, *U.S.A.* 111 B11
Keetmanshoop, *Namibia* .. 88 D2
Keewatin, *Canada* 102 A1
Keewatin →, *Canada* 105 B8
Kefa □, *Ethiopia* 81 F4
Kefallinía, *Greece* 38 C2
Kefallinía □, *Greece* 38 C2
Kefalos, *Greece* 39 E8
Kefamenanu, *Indonesia* .. 63 F6
Kefar Sava, *Israel* 75 C3
Keffi, *Nigeria* 83 D6
Keffin Hausa, *Nigeria* 83 C6
Keflavík, *Iceland* 8 D2
Keftya, *Ethiopia* 81 E4
Keg River, *Canada* 104 B5
Kegaska, *Canada* 103 B7
Keheili, *Sudan* 80 D3
Kehl, *Germany* 25 G3
Keighley, *U.K.* 12 D6
Keila, *Estonia* 9 G21
Keimoes, *S. Africa* 88 D3
Keita, *Niger* 83 C6
Keitele, *Finland* 8 E22
Keith, *Australia* 95 F3
Keith, *U.K.* 14 D6
Keizer, *U.S.A.* 114 D2
Kejimkujik Nat. Park,
  Canada 103 D6
Kejser Franz Joseph Fd.,
  Greenland 4 B6
Kekri, *India* 68 G6
Kelam, *Ethiopia* 81 G4
Kelamet, *Eritrea* 81 D4
Kelan, *China* 56 E6
Kelang, *Malaysia* 65 L3
Kelantan □, *Malaysia* 65 J4
Kelcyra, *Albania* 40 F4
Kelekçi, *Turkey* 39 D11
Keles, *Turkey* 41 G13
Kelheim, *Germany* 25 G7
Kelibia, *Tunisia* 53 A7
Kelkit, *Turkey* 73 B8
Kelkit →, *Turkey* 72 B7
Kellerberrin, *Australia* ... 93 F2
Kellett, C., *Canada* 4 B1
Kelleys I., *U.S.A.* 110 E2
Kellogg, *U.S.A.* 114 C5
Kells = Ceanannus Mor,
  Ireland 15 C5
Kelmė, *Lithuania* 44 D10
Kelokedhara, *Cyprus* 36 E11
Kelowna, *Canada* 104 D5
Kelseyville, *U.S.A.* 116 G4
Kelso, *N.Z.* 91 L2
Kelso, *U.K.* 14 F6
Kelso, *U.S.A.* 116 D4
Keluang, *Malaysia* 65 L4
Kelvington, *Canada* 105 C8
Kem, *Russia* 50 C4
Kem →, *Russia* 50 C4
Kema, *Indonesia* 63 D7
Kemah, *Turkey* 70 B3
Kemaliye, *Erzincan, Turkey* 73 C8
Kemaliye, *Manisa, Turkey* . 39 C10
Kemalpaşa, *Turkey* 39 C9
Kemaman, *Malaysia* 62 D2
Kemano, *Canada* 104 C3
Kemasik, *Malaysia* 65 K4
Kembolcha, *Ethiopia* 81 E4
Kemer, *Burdur, Turkey* ... 39 E12
Kemer, *Muğla, Turkey* ... 39 E11
Kemer, *Muğla, Turkey* ... 39 D10
Kemerovo, *Russia* 50 D9
Kemi, *Finland* 8 D21

Kemi älv = Kemijoki →,
  Finland 8 D21
Kemijärvi, *Finland* 8 C22
Kemijoki →, *Finland* 8 D21
Kemmerer, *U.S.A.* 114 F8
Kemmuna = Comino, *Malta* 36 C1
Kemp, L., *U.S.A.* 113 J5
Kemp Land, *Antarctica* ... 5 C5
Kempsey, *Australia* 95 E5
Kempt, L., *Canada* 102 C5
Kempten, *Germany* 25 H6
Kempton, *Australia* 94 G4
Kemptville, *Canada* 102 D4
Ken →, *India* 69 G9
Kenai, *U.S.A.* 100 B4
Kendai, *India* 69 H10
Kendal, *Indonesia* 63 G14
Kendal, *U.K.* 12 C5
Kendall, *Australia* 95 E5
Kendall, *U.S.A.* 109 N5
Kendall →, *Australia* 94 A3
Kendallville, *U.S.A.* 108 E3
Kendari, *Indonesia* 63 E6
Kendawangan, *Indonesia* . 62 E4
Kende, *Nigeria* 83 C5
Kendrapara, *India* 67 J15
Kéndrevičes, Maja e,
  Albania 40 F3
Kendrew, *S. Africa* 88 E3
Kene Thao, *Laos* 64 D3
Kenedy, *U.S.A.* 113 L6
Kenema, *S. Leone* 82 D2
Keng Kok, *Laos* 64 D5
Keng Tawng, *Burma* 67 J21
Keng Tung, *Burma* 58 G2
Kengeja, *Tanzania* 86 D4
Kenhardt, *S. Africa* 88 D3
Kéniéba, *Mali* 82 C2
Kenitra, *Morocco* 78 B4
Kenli, *China* 57 F10
Kenmare, *Ireland* 15 E2
Kenmare, *U.S.A.* 112 A3
Kenmare River, *Ireland* .. 15 E2
Kennebago Lake, *U.S.A.* .. 111 A14
Kennebec, *U.S.A.* 112 D5
Kennebec →, *U.S.A.* 109 D11
Kennebunk, *U.S.A.* 111 C14
Kennedy, *Zimbabwe* 88 B4
Kennedy Ra., *Australia* ... 93 D2
Kennedy Taungdeik, *Burma* 67 H18
Kenner, *U.S.A.* 113 L9
Kennet →, *U.K.* 13 F7
Kenneth Ra., *Australia* ... 93 D2
Kennett, *U.S.A.* 113 G9
Kennewick, *U.S.A.* 114 C4
Kenogami →, *Canada* ... 102 B3
Kenora, *Canada* 105 D10
Kenosha, *U.S.A.* 108 D2
Kensington, *Canada* 103 C7
Kent, *Ohio, U.S.A.* 110 E3
Kent, *Tex., U.S.A.* 113 K2
Kent, *Wash., U.S.A.* 116 C4
Kent □, *U.K.* 13 F8
Kent Group, *Australia* 94 F4
Kent Pen., *Canada* 100 B9
Kentau, *Kazakstan* 50 E7
Kentland, *U.S.A.* 108 E2
Kenton, *U.S.A.* 108 E4
Kentucky □, *U.S.A.* 108 G3
Kentucky →, *U.S.A.* 108 F3
Kentucky L., *U.S.A.* 109 G2
Kentville, *Canada* 103 C7
Kentwood, *U.S.A.* 113 K9
Kenya ■, *Africa* 86 B4
Kenya, Mt., *Kenya* 86 C4
Keo Neua, Deo, *Vietnam* . 64 C5
Keokuk, *U.S.A.* 112 E9
Keonjhargarh, *India* 69 J11
Kep, *Cambodia* 65 G5
Kep, *Vietnam* 64 B6
Kepez, *Turkey* 41 F10
Kepi, *Indonesia* 63 F9
Kępice, *Poland* 44 D3
Kepno, *Poland* 45 G4
Kepsut, *Turkey* 39 B10
Kerala □, *India* 66 P10
Kerama-Rettō, *Japan* 55 L3
Keran, *Pakistan* 69 B5
Kerang, *Australia* 95 F3
Keranyo, *Ethiopia* 81 F4
Kerao →, *Sudan* 81 E3
Keratéa, *Greece* 38 D5
Keraudren, C., *Australia* .. 92 D2
Kerava, *Finland* 9 F21
Kerch, *Ukraine* 47 K9
Kerchenskiy Proliv,
  Black Sea 47 K9
Kerchoual, *Mali* 83 B5
Kerema, Burnu, *Turkey* ... 72 A5
Keren, *Eritrea* 81 D4
Kerewan, *Gambia* 82 C1
Kerguelen, *Ind. Oc.* 3 G13
Keri, *Greece* 38 D2
Keri Kera, *Sudan* 81 E3
Kerinci, *Indonesia* 62 E2
Kerki, *Turkmenistan* 50 F7
Kerkinítis, Límni, *Greece* . 40 E7
Kérkira, *Greece* 36 A3
Kérkira □, *Greece* 38 B1
Kerkrade, *Neths.* 17 D6
Kerma, *Sudan* 80 D3
Kermadec Is., *Pac. Oc.* ... 96 L10
Kermadec Trench, *Pac. Oc.* 96 L10
Kermān, *Iran* 71 D8
Kermān □, *Iran* 71 D8
Kermān, Bābān-e, *Iran* ... 71 D8
Kermānshāh = Bākhtarān,
  Iran 70 C5
Kermen, *Bulgaria* 41 D10

Kermit, *U.S.A.* 113 K3
Kern →, *U.S.A.* 117 K7
Kernhof, *Austria* 26 D8
Kernville, *U.S.A.* 117 K8
Kéroh, *Malaysia* 65 K3
Kérou, *Benin* 83 C5
Kérouane, *Guinea* 82 D3
Kerpen, *Germany* 24 E2
Kerrera, *U.K.* 14 E3
Kerrobert, *Canada* 105 C7
Kerrville, *U.S.A.* 113 K5
Kerry □, *Ireland* 15 D2
Kerry Hd., *Ireland* 15 D2
Kersa, *Ethiopia* 81 F5
Kerulen →, *Asia* 60 B6
Kerzaz, *Algeria* 78 C5
Kesagami →, *Canada* 102 B4
Kesagami L., *Canada* 102 B3
Keşan, *Turkey* 41 F10
Kesennuma, *Japan* 54 E10
Keshit, *Iran* 71 D8
Keşiş Dağ, *Turkey* 73 C8
Keskin, *Turkey* 72 C5
Kestell, *S. Africa* 89 D4
Kestenga, *Russia* 50 C4
Keswick, *U.K.* 12 C4
Keszthely, *Hungary* 42 D2
Ket →, *Russia* 50 D9
Keta, *Ghana* 83 D5
Keta Lagoon, *Ghana* 83 D5
Ketapang, *Indonesia* 62 E4
Ketchikan, *U.S.A.* 104 B2
Ketchum, *U.S.A.* 114 E6
Kete Krachi, *Ghana* 83 D4
Ketef, Khalîg Umm el, *Egypt* 70 F2
Keti Bandar, *Pakistan* 68 G2
Kétou, *Benin* 83 D5
Ketri, *India* 68 E6
Kętrzyn, *Poland* 44 D8
Kettering, *U.K.* 13 E7
Kettering, *U.S.A.* 108 F3
Kettle →, *Canada* 105 B11
Kettle Falls, *U.S.A.* 114 B4
Kettle Pt., *Canada* 110 C2
Kettleman City, *U.S.A.* 116 J7
Kęty, *Poland* 45 J6
Keuka L., *U.S.A.* 110 D7
Keuruu, *Finland* 9 E21
Kevelaer, *Germany* 24 D2
Kewanee, *U.S.A.* 112 E10
Kewaunee, *U.S.A.* 108 C2
Keweenaw B., *U.S.A.* 108 B1
Keweenaw Pen., *U.S.A.* 108 B2
Keweenaw Pt., *U.S.A.* 108 B2
Key Largo, *U.S.A.* 109 N5
Key West, *U.S.A.* 107 F10
Keyala, *Sudan* 81 G3
Keynsham, *U.K.* 13 F5
Keyser, *U.S.A.* 108 F6
Kezhma, *Russia* 51 D11
Kezi, *Zimbabwe* 89 C4
Kežmarok, *Slovak Rep.* 27 B13
Khabarovsk, *Russia* 51 E14
Khabr, *Iran* 71 D8
Khābūr →, *Syria* 70 C4
Khachmas = Xaçmaz,
  Azerbaijan 49 K9
Khachrod, *India* 68 H6
Khadari, W. el →, *Sudan* 81 E2
Khadro, *Pakistan* 68 F3
Khadyzhensk, *Russia* 49 H4
Khadzhilyangar, *India* 69 B8
Khaga, *India* 69 G9
Khagaria, *India* 69 G12
Khaipur, *Pakistan* 68 E5
Khair, *India* 68 F7
Khairabad, *India* 69 F9
Khairagarh, *India* 69 J9
Khairpur, *Pakistan* 68 F3
Khairpur Nathan Shah,
  Pakistan 68 F2
Khairwara, *India* 68 H5
Khaisor →, *Pakistan* 68 D3
Khajuri Kach, *Pakistan* 68 C3
Khakassia □, *Russia* 50 D9
Khakhea, *Botswana* 88 C3
Khalafâbad, *Iran* 71 D6
Khalilabad, *India* 69 F10
Khalîlî, *Iran* 71 E7
Khalkhāl, *Iran* 71 B6
Khálki, *Dhodhekánisos,
  Greece* 39 E9
Khálki, *Thessalía, Greece* 38 B4
Khalkidhikí □, *Greece* 40 F7
Khalkís, *Greece* 38 C5
Khalmer-Sede = Tazovskiy,
  Russia 50 C8
Khalmer Yu, *Russia* 50 C7
Khalûf, *Oman* 74 C6
Kham Keut, *Laos* 64 C5
Khamaria, *India* 69 H9
Khambhaliya, *India* 68 H3
Khambhat, *India* 68 H5
Khambhat, G. of, *India* 66 J8
Khamilonísion, *Greece* 39 F8
Khamîr, *Iran* 71 E7
Khamir, *Yemen* 74 D3
Khamsa, *Egypt* 75 E1
Khan →, *Namibia* 88 C2
Khān Abū Shāmat, *Syria* 75 B5
Khān Azād, *Iraq* 70 C5
Khān Mujiddah, *Iraq* 70 C4
Khān Shaykhūn, *Syria* 70 C3
Khān Yūnis, *Gaza Strip* 75 D3
Khanai, *Pakistan* 68 D2
Khānaqīn, *Iraq* 70 C5
Khānbāghī, *Iran* 71 B7
Khandrá, *Greece* 39 F8
Khandwa, *India* 66 J10
Khandyga, *Russia* 51 C14
Khāneh, *Iran* 70 B5

Khanewal, *Pakistan* 68 D4
Khangah Dogran, *Pakistan* 68 D5
Khanh Duong, *Vietnam* 64 F7
Khaniá, *Greece* 36 D6
Khaniá □, *Greece* 36 D6
Khaniadhana, *India* 68 G8
Khaníon, Kólpos, *Greece* 36 D5
Khanka, L., *Asia* 51 E14
Khankendy = Xankändi,
  Azerbaijan 70 B5
Khanna, *India* 68 D7
Khanozai, *Pakistan* 68 D2
Khanpur, *Pakistan* 68 E4
Khanty-Mansiysk, *Russia* 50 C7
Khapalu, *Pakistan* 69 B7
Khapcheranga, *Russia* 51 E12
Kharabali, *Russia* 49 G8
Kharaghoda, *India* 68 H4
Kharagpur, *India* 69 H12
Khárakas, *Greece* 36 D7
Kharan Kalat, *Pakistan* 66 E4
Kharānaq, *Iran* 71 C7
Kharda, *India* 66 K9
Khardung La, *India* 69 B7
Khârga, El Wâhât-el, *Egypt* 80 B3
Khargon, *India* 66 J9
Khari →, *India* 68 G6
Kharian, *Pakistan* 68 C5
Kharit, Wadi el →, *Egypt* 80 C3
Khārk, Jazīreh-ye, *Iran* 71 D6
Kharkiv, *Ukraine* 47 H9
Kharkov = Kharkiv, *Ukraine* 47 H9
Kharmanli, *Bulgaria* 41 E9
Kharovsk, *Russia* 46 C11
Kharsawangarh, *India* 69 H11
Kharta, *Turkey* 72 B3
Khartoum = El Khartûm,
  Sudan 81 D3
Khasan, *Russia* 54 C5
Khasavyurt, *Russia* 49 J8
Khāsh, *Iran* 66 E2
Khashm el Girba, *Sudan* 81 E4
Khashum, *Sudan* 81 E2
Khashuri, *Georgia* 49 J6
Khaskovo, *Bulgaria* 41 E9
Khaskovo □, *Bulgaria* 41 E9
Khatanga, *Russia* 51 B11
Khatanga →, *Russia* 51 B11
Khatauli, *India* 68 E7
Khatra, *India* 69 H12
Khātūnābād, *Iran* 71 D7
Khatyrka, *Russia* 51 C18
Khavda, *India* 68 H3
Khaybar, Harrat, *Si. Arabia* 70 E4
Khayelitsha, *S. Africa* 85 L3
Khāzimiyah, *Iraq* 70 C4
Khazzān Jabal al Awliyā,
  Sudan 81 D3
Khe Bo, *Vietnam* 64 C5
Khe Long, *Vietnam* 64 B5
Khed Brahma, *India* 66 G4
Khekra, *India* 68 E7
Khemarak Phouminville,
  Cambodia 65 G4
Khemisset, *Morocco* 78 B4
Khemmarat, *Thailand* 64 D5
Khenāmān, *Iran* 71 D8
Khenchela, *Algeria* 78 A7
Khersán →, *Iran* 71 D6
Khérson, *Greece* 40 E6
Kherson, *Ukraine* 47 J7
Khersónisos Akrotíri, *Greece* 36 D6
Kheta →, *Russia* 51 B11
Khewari, *Pakistan* 68 F3
Khilchipur, *India* 68 G7
Khiliomódhion, *Greece* 38 D4
Khilok, *Russia* 51 D12
Khimki, *Russia* 46 E9
Khíos, *Greece* 39 C8
Khíos □, *Greece* 39 C8
Khirsadoh, *India* 69 H8
Khiuma = Hiiumaa, *Estonia* 9 G20
Khiva, *Uzbekistan* 50 E7
Khīyāv, *Iran* 70 B5
Khlebarovo, *Bulgaria* 41 C10
Khlong Khlung, *Thailand* 64 D2
Khmelnik, *Ukraine* 47 H4
Khmelnitskiy =
  Khmelnytskyy, *Ukraine* 47 H4
Khmelnytskyy, *Ukraine* 47 H4
Khmer Rep. = Cambodia ■,
  Asia 64 F5
Khoai, Hon, *Vietnam* 65 H5
Khodoriv, *Ukraine* 47 H3
Khodzent = Khudzhand,
  Tajikistan 50 E7
Khojak Pass, *Afghan.* 68 D2
Khok Kloi, *Thailand* 65 H2
Khok Pho, *Thailand* 65 J3
Kholm, *Russia* 46 D6
Kholmsk, *Russia* 51 E15
Khomas Hochland, *Namibia* 88 C2
Khombole, *Senegal* 82 C1
Khomeyn, *Iran* 71 C6
Khomeynī Shahr, *Iran* 71 C6
Khomodino, *Botswana* 88 C3
Khon Kaen, *Thailand* 64 D4
Khong →, *Cambodia* 64 F5
Khong Sedone, *Laos* 64 E5
Khonuu, *Russia* 51 C15
Khoper →, *Russia* 48 F6
Khor 'Atash, *Sudan* 81 E3
Khóra, *Greece* 38 D3
Khóra Sfakíon, *Greece* 36 D6
Khorāsān □, *Iran* 71 C8
Khorat = Nakhon
  Ratchasima, *Thailand* 64 E4
Khorat, Cao Nguyen,
  Thailand 64 E4
Khorixas, *Namibia* 88 C1
Khorol, *Ukraine* 47 H7

Khorramābād, *Khorāsān,
  Iran* 71 C8
Khorramābād, *Lorestān, Iran* 71 C6
Khorrāmshahr, *Iran* 71 D6
Khorugh, *Tajikistan* 50 F8
Khosravī, *Iran* 71 D6
Khosrowābād, *Khuzestān,
  Iran* 71 D6
Khosrowābād, *Kordestān,
  Iran* 70 C5
Khost, *Pakistan* 68 D2
Khosūyeh, *Iran* 71 D7
Khotyn, *Ukraine* 47 H4
Khouribga, *Morocco* 78 B4
Khowai, *Bangla.* 67 G17
Khowst, *Afghan.* 68 C3
Khoyniki, *Belarus* 47 G5
Khrami →, *Georgia* 49 K7
Khrenovoye, *Russia* 48 E5
Khrisoúpolis, *Greece* 41 F8
Khristianá, *Greece* 39 E7
Khrysokhou B., *Cyprus* 36 D11
Khtapodhiá, *Greece* 39 D7
Khu Khan, *Thailand* 64 E5
Khudzhand, *Tajikistan* 50 E7
Khuff, *Si. Arabia* 70 E5
Khūgīānī, *Afghan.* 68 D1
Khuis, *Botswana* 88 D3
Khuiyala, *India* 68 F4
Khujner, *India* 68 H7
Khulna, *Bangla.* 67 H16
Khulna □, *Bangla.* 67 H16
Khulo, *Georgia* 49 K6
Khumago, *Botswana* 88 C3
Khūnsorkh, *Iran* 71 E8
Khunti, *India* 69 H11
Khūr, *Iran* 71 C8
Khurai, *India* 68 G8
Khurayş, *Si. Arabia* 71 E6
Khureit, *Sudan* 81 E2
Khurīyā Murīyā, Jazā 'ir,
  Oman 74 D6
Khurja, *India* 68 E7
Khūrmāl, *Iraq* 70 C5
Khurr, Wādī al, *Iraq* 70 C4
Khūsf, *Iran* 71 C8
Khush, *Afghan.* 66 C3
Khushab, *Pakistan* 68 C5
Khust, *Ukraine* 47 H2
Khuzdar, *Pakistan* 68 F2
Khūzestān □, *Iran* 71 D6
Khvāf, *Iran* 71 C9
Khvājeh, *Iran* 70 B5
Khvalynsk, *Russia* 48 D9
Khvānsār, *Iran* 71 D7
Khvatovka, *Russia* 48 D8
Khvor, *Iran* 71 C7
Khvorgū, *Iran* 71 E8
Khvormūj, *Iran* 71 D6
Khvoy, *Iran* 70 B5
Khvoynaya, *Russia* 46 C8
Khyber Pass, *Afghan.* 68 B4
Kiabukwa,
  Dem. Rep. of the Congo 87 D1
Kiama, *Australia* 95 E5
Kiamba, *Phil.* 61 H6
Kiambi,
  Dem. Rep. of the Congo 86 D2
Kiambu, *Kenya* 86 C4
Kiangara, *Madag.* 89 B8
Kiangsi = Jiangxi □, *China* 59 D11
Kiangsu = Jiangsu □, *China* 57 H11
Kiáton, *Greece* 38 C4
Kibæk, *Denmark* 11 H2
Kibanga Port, *Uganda* 86 B3
Kibara, *Tanzania* 86 C3
Kibare, Mts.,
  Dem. Rep. of the Congo 86 D2
Kibombo,
  Dem. Rep. of the Congo 86 C2
Kibondo, *Tanzania* 86 C3
Kibre Mengist, *Ethiopia* 81 F4
Kibumbu, *Burundi* 86 C2
Kibungo, *Rwanda* 86 C3
Kibuye, *Burundi* 86 C2
Kibuye, *Rwanda* 86 C2
Kibwesa, *Tanzania* 86 D2
Kibwezi, *Kenya* 86 C4
Kicasları, *Turkey* 41 E10
Kičevo, *Macedonia* 40 E4
Kichha, *India* 69 E8
Kichha →, *India* 69 E8
Kicking Horse Pass, *Canada* 104 C5
Kidal, *Mali* 83 B5
Kidderminster, *U.K.* 13 E5
Kidete, *Tanzania* 86 D4
Kidira, *Senegal* 82 C2
Kidnappers, C., *N.Z.* 91 H6
Kidsgrove, *U.K.* 12 D5
Kidston, *Australia* 94 B3
Kidugallo, *Tanzania* 86 D4
Kiel, *Germany* 24 A6
Kiel Canal = Nord-Ostsee-
  Kanal, *Germany* 24 A5
Kielce, *Poland* 45 H7
Kielder Water, *U.K.* 12 B5
Kieler Bucht, *Germany* 24 A6
Kiembara, *Burkina Faso* 82 C4
Kien Binh, *Vietnam* 65 H5
Kien Tan, *Vietnam* 65 G5
Kienge,
  Dem. Rep. of the Congo 87 E2
Kiessé, *Niger* 83 C5
Kiev = Kyyiv, *Ukraine* 47 G6
Kifaya, *Guinea* 82 C2
Kiffa, *Mauritania* 82 B2
Kifissós →, *Greece* 38 C5
Kifrī, *Iraq* 70 C5
Kigali, *Rwanda* 86 C3
King George B., *Falk. Is.* 128 G4

Kigelle, *Sudan* 81 F3
Kigoma □, *Tanzania* 86 D3
Kigoma-Ujiji, *Tanzania* 86 C2
Kigomasha, Ras, *Tanzania* 86 C4
Kiǧzı, *Turkey* 70 B4
Kihei, *U.S.A.* 106 H16
Kihnu, *Estonia* 9 G21
Kii-Sanchi, *Japan* 55 G8
Kii-Suidō, *Japan* 55 H7
Kikaiga-Shima, *Japan* 55 K4
Kikinda, *Serbia, Yug.* 42 E5
Kikládhes, *Greece* 38 E6
Kikládhes □, *Greece* 38 D6
Kikwit,
  Dem. Rep. of the Congo 84 E3
Kil, *Sweden* 10 E7
Kilafors, *Sweden* 10 C10
Kilar, *India* 68 C7
Kilauea, *U.S.A.* 106 J14
Kilauea Crater, *U.S.A.* 106 J17
Kilchu, *N. Korea* 57 D15
Kilcoy, *Australia* 95 D5
Kildare, *Ireland* 15 C5
Kildare □, *Ireland* 15 C5
Kileikli, *Sudan* 81 E2
Kilfinnane, *Ireland* 15 D3
Kilgore, *U.S.A.* 113 J7
Kilibo, *Benin* 83 D5
Kilifi, *Kenya* 86 C4
Kilimanjaro, *Tanzania* 86 C4
Kilimanjaro □, *Tanzania* 86 C4
Kilimli, *Turkey* 72 B4
Kilindini, *Kenya* 86 C4
Kilis, *Turkey* 70 B3
Kiliya, *Ukraine* 47 K5
Kilkee, *Ireland* 15 D2
Kilkeel, *U.K.* 15 B5
Kilkenny, *Ireland* 15 D4
Kilkenny □, *Ireland* 15 D4
Kilkieran B., *Ireland* 15 C2
Kilkís, *Greece* 40 F6
Kilkís □, *Greece* 40 E6
Killala, *Ireland* 15 B2
Killala B., *Ireland* 15 B2
Killaloe, *Ireland* 15 D3
Killaloe Sta., *Canada* 110 A7
Killarney, *Australia* 95 D5
Killarney, *Canada* 105 D9
Killarney, *Ireland* 15 D2
Killary Harbour, *Ireland* 15 C2
Killdeer, *Canada* 112 B3
Killeberg, *Sweden* 11 H8
Killeen, *U.S.A.* 113 K6
Killin, *U.K.* 14 E4
Killíni, *Ilía, Greece* 38 D3
Killíni, *Korinthía, Greece* 38 D4
Killorglin, *Ireland* 15 D2
Killybegs, *Ireland* 15 B3
Kilmarnock, *U.K.* 14 F4
Kilmez, *Russia* 48 B10
Kilmez →, *Russia* 48 B10
Kilmore, *Australia* 95 F3
Kilondo, *Tanzania* 87 D3
Kilosa, *Tanzania* 86 D4
Kilrush, *Ireland* 15 D2
Kilwa Kisiwani, *Tanzania* 87 D4
Kilwa Kivinje, *Tanzania* 87 D4
Kilwa Masoko, *Tanzania* 87 D4
Kilwinning, *U.K.* 14 F4
Kim, *U.S.A.* 113 G3
Kim →, *Cameroon* 83 D7
Kimaam, *Indonesia* 63 F9
Kimamba, *Tanzania* 86 D4
Kimba, *Australia* 95 E2
Kimball, *Nebr., U.S.A.* 112 E3
Kimball, *S. Dak., U.S.A.* 112 D5
Kimberley, *Australia* 92 C4
Kimberley, *Canada* 104 D5
Kimberley, *S. Africa* 88 D3
Kimberly, *U.S.A.* 114 E6
Kimch'aek, *N. Korea* 57 D15
Kimch'ŏn, *S. Korea* 57 F15
Kími, *Greece* 38 C6
Kimje, *S. Korea* 57 G14
Kimmirut, *Canada* 101 B13
Kímolos, *Greece* 38 E6
Kimovsk, *Moskva, Russia* 46 E9
Kimovsk, *Tula, Russia* 46 E10
Kimparana, *Mali* 82 C4
Kimpese,
  Dem. Rep. of the Congo 84 F2
Kimry, *Russia* 46 D9
Kimstad, *Sweden* 11 F9
Kinabalu, Gunong, *Malaysia* 62 C5
Kínaros, *Greece* 39 E8
Kinaskan L., *Canada* 104 B2
Kinbasket L., *Canada* 104 C5
Kincardine, *Canada* 102 D3
Kincolith, *Canada* 104 C3
Kinda,
  Dem. Rep. of the Congo 87 D2
Kindberg, *Austria* 26 D8
Kinde, *U.S.A.* 110 C2
Kinder Scout, *U.K.* 12 D6
Kindersley, *Canada* 105 C7
Kindia, *Guinea* 82 D2
Kindu,
  Dem. Rep. of the Congo 86 C2
Kinel, *Russia* 48 D10
Kineshma, *Russia* 48 B6
Kinesi, *Tanzania* 86 C3
King, L., *Australia* 93 F2
King, Mt., *Australia* 94 D4
King City, *U.S.A.* 116 J5
King Cr. →, *Australia* 94 C2
King Edward →, *Australia* 92 B4
King Frederick VI Land =
  Kong Frederik VI Kyst,
  Greenland 4 C5

King George I., *Antarctica* 5 C18
King George Is., *Canada* 101 C11
King I. = Kadan Kyun,
  Burma 64 F2
King I., *Australia* 94 F3
King I., *Canada* 104 C3
King Leopold Ranges,
  Australia 92 C4
King of Prussia, *U.S.A.* 111 F9
King Sd., *Australia* 92 C3
King William I., *Canada* 100 B10
King William's Town,
  S. Africa 88 E4
Kingaroy, *Australia* 95 D5
Kingfisher, *U.S.A.* 113 H6
Kingirbān, *Iraq* 70 C5
Kingisepp = Kuressaare,
  Estonia 9 G20
Kingisepp, *Russia* 46 C5
Kingman, *Ariz., U.S.A.* 117 K12
Kingman, *Kans., U.S.A.* 113 G5
Kingoonya, *Australia* 95 E2
Kingri, *Pakistan* 68 D3
Kings →, *U.S.A.* 116 J7
Kings Canyon National Park,
  U.S.A. 116 J8
King's Lynn, *U.K.* 12 E8
Kings Mountain, *U.S.A.* 109 H5
Kings Park, *U.S.A.* 111 F11
King's Peak, *U.S.A.* 114 F8
Kingsbridge, *U.K.* 13 G4
Kingsburg, *U.S.A.* 116 J7
Kingscote, *Australia* 95 F2
Kingscourt, *Ireland* 15 C5
Kingsford, *U.S.A.* 108 C1
Kingsland, *U.S.A.* 109 K5
Kingsley, *U.S.A.* 112 D7
Kingston, *Canada* 102 D4
Kingston, *Jamaica* 120 C4
Kingston, *N.Z.* 91 L2
Kingston, *N.H., U.S.A.* 111 D13
Kingston, *N.Y., U.S.A.* 111 E11
Kingston, *Pa., U.S.A.* 111 E9
Kingston, *R.I., U.S.A.* 111 E13
Kingston Pk., *U.S.A.* 117 K11
Kingston South East,
  Australia 95 F2
Kingston upon Hull, *U.K.* 12 D7
Kingston upon Hull □, *U.K.* 12 D7
Kingston-upon-Thames, *U.K.* 13 F7
Kingstown, *St. Vincent* 121 D7
Kingstree, *U.S.A.* 109 J6
Kingsville, *Canada* 102 D3
Kingsville, *U.S.A.* 113 M6
Kingussie, *U.K.* 14 D4
Kingwood, *U.S.A.* 113 K7
Kınık, *Antalya, Turkey* 39 E11
Kınık, *İzmir, Turkey* 39 B9
Kinistino, *Canada* 105 C7
Kinkala, *Congo* 84 E2
Kinki □, *Japan* 55 H8
Kinleith, *N.Z.* 91 H5
Kinna, *Sweden* 11 G6
Kinnairds Hd., *U.K.* 14 D6
Kinnared, *Sweden* 11 G7
Kinnarodden, *Norway* 6 A11
Kinnarp, *Sweden* 11 F7
Kinneviken, *Sweden* 11 F7
Kino, *Mexico* 118 B2
Kinoje →, *Canada* 102 B3
Kinomoto, *Japan* 55 G8
Kinoni, *Uganda* 86 C3
Kinoosao, *Canada* 105 B8
Kinross, *U.K.* 14 E5
Kinsale, *Ireland* 15 E3
Kinsale, Old Hd. of, *Ireland* 15 E3
Kinsha = Chang Jiang →,
  China 59 B13
Kinshasa,
  Dem. Rep. of the Congo 84 E3
Kinsley, *U.S.A.* 113 G5
Kinsman, *U.S.A.* 110 E4
Kinston, *U.S.A.* 109 H7
Kintampo, *Ghana* 83 D4
Kintore Ra., *Australia* 92 D4
Kintyre, *U.K.* 14 F3
Kintyre, Mull of, *U.K.* 14 F3
Kinushseo →, *Canada* 102 A3
Kinuso, *Canada* 104 B5
Kinyangiri, *Tanzania* 86 C3
Kinyeti, *Sudan* 81 G3
Kinzig →, *Germany* 25 G4
Kinzua, *U.S.A.* 110 E6
Kinzua Dam, *U.S.A.* 110 E6
Kióni, *Greece* 38 C2
Kiosk, *Canada* 102 C4
Kiowa, *Kans., U.S.A.* 113 G5
Kiowa, *Okla., U.S.A.* 113 H7
Kipahigan L., *Canada* 105 B8
Kipanga, *Tanzania* 86 D4
Kiparissía, *Greece* 38 D3
Kiparissiakós Kólpos, *Greece* 38 D3
Kipembawe, *Tanzania* 86 D3
Kipengere Ra., *Tanzania* 87 D3
Kipili, *Tanzania* 86 D3
Kipini, *Kenya* 86 C5
Kipling, *Canada* 105 C8
Kippure, *Ireland* 15 C5
Kipushi,
  Dem. Rep. of the Congo 87 E2
Kirane, *Mali* 82 B2
Kiranomena, *Madag.* 89 B8
Kiraz, *Turkey* 39 C10
Kırazlı, *Turkey* 41 F10
Kirchhain, *Germany* 24 E4
Kirchheim, *Germany* 25 G5
Kirchheimbolanden,
  Germany 25 F3

Kirchschlag, *Austria* 27 D9
Kireç, *Turkey* 39 B10
Kirensk, *Russia* 51 D11
Kirghizia = Kyrgyzstan ■,
  Asia 50 E8
Kirghizstan = Kyrgyzstan ■,
  Asia 50 E8
Kiribati ■, *Pac. Oc.* 96 H10
Kırıkhan, *Turkey* 72 D7
Kırıkkale, *Turkey* 72 C5
Kirillov, *Russia* 46 C10
Kirin = Jilin, *China* 57 C14
Kirishi, *Russia* 46 C7
Kiritimati, *Kiribati* 97 G12
Kırka, *Turkey* 39 B12
Kırkağaç, *Turkey* 39 B9
Kirkby, *U.K.* 12 D5
Kirkby Lonsdale, *U.K.* 12 C5
Kirkcaldy, *U.K.* 14 E5
Kirkcudbright, *U.K.* 14 G4
Kirkee, *India* 66 K8
Kirkenes, *Norway* 8 B23
Kirkfield, *Canada* 110 B6
Kirkkonummi, *Finland* 9 F21
Kirkland Lake, *Canada* 102 C3
Kırklareli, *Turkey* 41 E11
Kırklareli □, *Turkey* 41 E11
Kirksville, *U.S.A.* 112 E8
Kirkūk, *Iraq* 70 C5
Kirkwall, *U.K.* 14 C6
Kirkwood, *S. Africa* 88 E4
Kirn, *Germany* 25 F3
Kirov, *Kaluga, Russia* 46 E8
Kirov, *Kirov, Russia* 50 D5
Kirovabad = Gäncä,
  Azerbaijan 49 K8
Kirovakan = Vanadzor,
  Armenia 49 K7
Kirovograd = Kirovohrad,
  Ukraine 47 H7
Kirovohrad, *Ukraine* 47 H7
Kirovsk = Babadayhan,
  Turkmenistan 50 F7
Kirovskiy, *Astrakhan, Russia* 49 H9
Kirovskiy, *Kamchatka,
  Russia* 51 D16
Kirovskiy, *Primorsk, Russia* 54 B6
Kirriemuir, *U.K.* 14 E5
Kirsanov, *Russia* 48 D6
Kırşehir, *Turkey* 70 B2
Kirtachi, *Niger* 83 C5
Kirthar Range, *Pakistan* .. 68 F2
Kirtland, *U.S.A.* 115 H9
Kiruna, *Sweden* 8 C19
Kirundu,
  Dem. Rep. of the Congo . 86 C2
Kirya, *Russia* 48 C8
Kiryū, *Japan* 55 F9
Kisa, *Sweden* 11 G9
Kisaga, *Tanzania* 86 C3
Kisalaya, *Nic.* 120 D3
Kisalföld, *Hungary* 42 C2
Kisámou, Kólpos, *Greece* .. 36 D5
Kisanga,
  Dem. Rep. of the Congo . 86 B2
Kisangani,
  Dem. Rep. of the Congo . 86 B2
Kisar, *Indonesia* 63 F7
Kisarawe, *Tanzania* 86 D4
Kisarazu, *Japan* 55 G9
Kisbér, *Hungary* 42 C3
Kishanganga ➝, *Pakistan* .. 69 B5
Kishanganj, *India* 69 F13
Kishangarh, *Raj., India* ... 68 F6
Kishangarh, *Raj., India* ... 68 F4
Kishi, *Nigeria* 83 D5
Kishinev = Chişinău,
  Moldova 43 C13
Kishiwada, *Japan* 55 G7
Kishtwar, *India* 69 C6
Kisielice, *Poland* 44 E6
Kisii, *Kenya* 86 C3
Kisiju, *Tanzania* 86 D4
Kisir, *Turkey* 73 B10
Kisizi, *Uganda* 86 C2
Kiskomárom = Zalakomár,
  Hungary 42 D2
Kiskörei-víztároló, *Hungary* 42 C5
Kiskőrös, *Hungary* 42 D4
Kiskundorozsma, *Hungary* . 42 D5
Kiskunfélegyháza, *Hungary* 42 D4
Kiskunhalas, *Hungary* 42 D4
Kiskunmajsa, *Hungary* 42 D4
Kislovodsk, *Russia* 49 J6
Kismayu = Chisimaio,
  Somali Rep. 77 G8
Kiso-Gawa ➝, *Japan* 55 G8
Kiso-Sammyaku, *Japan* 55 G8
Kisofukushima, *Japan* 55 G8
Kisoro, *Uganda* 86 C2
Kissidougou, *Guinea* 82 D2
Kissimmee, *U.S.A.* 109 L5
Kissimmee ➝, *U.S.A.* 109 M5
Kississing L., *Canada* 105 B8
Kissónerga, *Cyprus* 36 E11
Kissu, J., *Sudan* 80 C2
Kistanje, *Croatia* 29 E12
Kisújszállás, *Hungary* 42 C5
Kisumu, *Kenya* 86 C3
Kisvárda, *Hungary* 42 B7
Kiswani, *Tanzania* 86 C4
Kiswere, *Tanzania* 87 D4
Kit Carson, *U.S.A.* 112 F3
Kita, *Mali* 82 C3
Kitaibaraki, *Japan* 55 F10
Kitakami, *Japan* 54 E10
Kitakami-Gawa ➝, *Japan* .. 54 E10
Kitakami-Sammyaku, *Japan* 54 E10
Kitakata, *Japan* 54 F9
Kitakyūshū, *Japan* 55 H5

Kitale, *Kenya* 86 B4
Kitami, *Japan* 54 C11
Kitami-Sammyaku, *Japan* .. 54 B11
Kitangiri, L., *Tanzania* 86 C3
Kitaya, *Tanzania* 87 E5
Kitchener, *Canada* 102 D3
Kitee, *Finland* 46 A6
Kitega = Gitega, *Burundi* .. 86 C2
Kitengo,
  Dem. Rep. of the Congo . 86 D1
Kitgum, *Uganda* 86 B3
Kíthira, *Greece* 38 E5
Kíthnos, *Greece* 38 D6
Kiti, *Cyprus* 36 E12
Kiti, C., *Cyprus* 36 E12
Kitimat, *Canada* 104 C3
Kitinen ➝, *Finland* 8 C22
Kitiyab, *Sudan* 81 D3
Kítros, *Greece* 40 F6
Kitsuki, *Japan* 55 H5
Kittakittaooloo, L., *Australia* 95 D2
Kittanning, *U.S.A.* 110 F5
Kittatinny Mts., *U.S.A.* 111 F10
Kittery, *U.S.A.* 109 D10
Kittilä, *Finland* 8 C21
Kitui, *Kenya* 86 C4
Kitwanga, *Canada* 104 B3
Kitwe, *Zambia* 87 E2
Kitzbühel, *Austria* 26 D5
Kitzbühler Alpen, *Austria* .. 26 D5
Kitzingen, *Germany* 25 F6
Kivarli, *India* 68 G5
Kivertsi, *Ukraine* 47 G3
Kividhes, *Cyprus* 36 E11
Kivik, *Sweden* 11 J8
Kivotós, *Greece* 40 F5
Kivu, L.,
  Dem. Rep. of the Congo . 86 C2
Kiyev = Kyyiv, *Ukraine* ... 47 G6
Kiyevskoye Vdkhr. =
  Kyyivske Vdskh., *Ukraine* 47 G6
Kıyıköy, *Turkey* 41 E12
Kızıl Adalar, *Turkey* 41 F13
Kizil Irmak ➝, *Turkey* 72 B6
Kizil Jilga, *India* 69 B8
Kizil Yurt, *Russia* 49 J8
Kızılcabölük, *Turkey* 39 D11
Kızılcadağ, *Turkey* 39 D11
Kızılcahamam, *Turkey* 72 B5
Kızılhisar, *Turkey* 72 D3
Kızılırmak, *Turkey* 72 B5
Kızılkaya, *Turkey* 39 D12
Kızılören, *Turkey* 39 C12
Kızıltepe, *Turkey* 70 B4
Kizimkazi, *Tanzania* 86 D4
Kizlyar, *Russia* 49 J8
Kizyl-Arvat = Gyzylarbat,
  Turkmenistan 50 F6
Kjellerup, *Denmark* 11 H3
Kjölur, *Iceland* 8 D4
Kladanj, *Bos.-H.* 42 F3
Kladnica, *Serbia, Yug.* 40 C4
Kladno, *Czech Rep.* 26 A7
Kladovo, *Serbia, Yug.* 40 B6
Klaeng, *Thailand* 64 F3
Klagenfurt, *Austria* 26 E7
Klaipėda, *Lithuania* 9 J19
Klaipėda □, *Lithuania* 44 C8
Klaksvík, *Færoe Is.* 8 E9
Klamath ➝, *U.S.A.* 114 F1
Klamath Falls, *U.S.A.* 114 E3
Klamath Mts., *U.S.A.* 114 F2
Klamono, *Indonesia* 63 E8
Klanjec, *Croatia* 29 B12
Klappan ➝, *Canada* 104 B3
Klarälven ➝, *Sweden* 10 E7
Klässbol, *Sweden* 10 E6
Klatovy, *Czech Rep.* 26 B6
Klawer, *S. Africa* 88 E2
Klazienaveen, *Neths.* 17 B6
Klé, *Mali* 82 C3
Klecko, *Poland* 45 F4
Kleczew, *Poland* 45 F5
Kleena Kleene, *Canada* 104 C4
Klein-Karas, *Namibia* 88 D2
Klekovača, *Bos.-H.* 29 D13
Klenoec, *Macedonia* 40 E4
Klenovec, *Slovak Rep.* 27 C12
Klerksdorp, *S. Africa* 88 D4
Kleszczele, *Poland* 45 F10
Kletnya, *Russia* 46 F7
Kletsk = Klyetsk, *Belarus* . 47 F4
Kletskiy, *Russia* 49 F6
Kleve, *Germany* 24 D2
Klickitat, *U.S.A.* 114 D3
Klickitat ➝, *U.S.A.* 116 E5
Klidhes, *Cyprus* 36 D13
Klimovichi, *Belarus* 46 F6
Klin, *Russia* 46 D9
Klina, *Kosovo, Yug.* 40 D4
Klinaklini ➝, *Canada* 104 C3
Klintehamn, *Sweden* 11 G12
Klintsy, *Russia* 47 F7
Klip ➝, *S. Africa* 89 D4
Klipdale, *S. Africa* 88 E2
Klippan, *Sweden* 11 H7
Klipplaat, *S. Africa* 88 E3
Klisura, *Bulgaria* 41 D8
Kljajićevo, *Serbia, Yug.* 42 E4
Ključ, *Bos.-H.* 29 D13
Kłobuck, *Poland* 45 H5
Kłodawa, *Poland* 45 F5
Kłodzko, *Poland* 45 H3
Klosi, *Albania* 40 E4
Klosterneuburg, *Austria* ... 27 C9
Klosters, *Switz.* 25 J5
Klötze, *Germany* 24 C7
Klouto, *Togo* 83 D5
Kluane L., *Canada* 100 B6

Kluane Nat. Park, *Canada* . 104 A1
Kluczbork, *Poland* 45 H5
Klukwan, *U.S.A.* 104 B1
Klyetsk, *Belarus* 47 F4
Klyuchevskaya, Gora, *Russia* 51 D17
Knäred, *Sweden* 11 H7
Knaresborough, *U.K.* 12 C6
Knee L., *Man., Canada* 102 A1
Knee L., *Sask., Canada* 105 B7
Knezha, *Bulgaria* 41 C8
Knić, *Serbia, Yug.* 40 C4
Knight Inlet, *Canada* 104 C3
Knighton, *U.K.* 13 E4
Knights Ferry, *U.S.A.* 116 H6
Knights Landing, *U.S.A.* ... 116 G5
Knin, *Croatia* 29 D13
Knislinge, *Sweden* 11 H8
Knittelfeld, *Austria* 26 D7
Knivsta, *Sweden* 10 E11
Knjaževac, *Serbia, Yug.* 40 C6
Knob, C., *Australia* 93 F2
Knock, *Ireland* 15 C3
Knockmealdown Mts.,
  Ireland 15 D4
Knokke-Heist, *Belgium* 17 C3
Knossós, *Greece* 36 D7
Knowlton, *Canada* 111 A12
Knox, *U.S.A.* 108 E2
Knox Coast, *Antarctica* 5 C8
Knoxville, *Iowa, U.S.A.* 112 E8
Knoxville, *Pa., U.S.A.* 110 E7
Knoxville, *Tenn., U.S.A.* ... 109 H4
Knysna, *S. Africa* 88 E3
Knyszyn, *Poland* 44 E9
Ko Kha, *Thailand* 64 C2
Koartac = Quaqtaq, *Canada* 101 B13
Koba, *Indonesia* 63 F9
Kobarid, *Slovenia* 29 B10
Kobayashi, *Japan* 55 J5
Kobdo = Hovd, *Mongolia* .. 60 B4
Kōbe, *Japan* 55 G7
Kobelyaky, *Ukraine* 47 H8
København, *Denmark* 11 J6
Københavns
  Amtskommune □,
  Denmark 11 J6
Kobenni, *Mauritania* 82 B3
Kōbi-Sho, *Japan* 55 M1
Koblenz, *Germany* 25 E3
Kobo, *Ethiopia* 81 E4
Kobryn, *Belarus* 47 F3
Kobuleti, *Georgia* 49 K5
Kobylin, *Poland* 45 G4
Kobyłka, *Poland* 45 F8
Kobylkino, *Russia* 48 C6
Koca ➝, *Turkey* 41 F11
Kocaeli, *Turkey* 41 F13
Kocaeli □, *Turkey* 41 F13
Kočane, *Serbia, Yug.* 40 C5
Kočani, *Macedonia* 40 E6
Koçarlı, *Turkey* 39 D9
Koceljevo, *Serbia, Yug.* 40 B3
Kočevje, *Slovenia* 29 C11
Koch Bihar, *India* 67 F16
Kochang, *S. Korea* 57 G14
Kochas, *India* 69 G10
Kocher ➝, *Germany* 25 F5
Kōchi, *Japan* 55 H6
Kōchi □, *Japan* 55 H6
Kochiu = Gejiu, *China* 58 F4
Kock, *Poland* 45 G9
Kodarma, *India* 69 G11
Kode, *Sweden* 11 G5
Kodiak, *U.S.A.* 100 C4
Kodiak I., *U.S.A.* 100 C4
Kodinar, *India* 68 J4
Kodok, *Sudan* 81 F3
Kodori ➝, *Georgia* 49 J5
Koedoesberge, *S. Africa* ... 88 E3
Koes, *Namibia* 88 D2
Kofçaz, *Turkey* 41 E11
Koffiefontein, *S. Africa* 88 D4
Kofiau, *Indonesia* 63 E7
Köflach, *Austria* 26 D8
Koforidua, *Ghana* 83 D4
Kōfu, *Japan* 55 G9
Koga, *Japan* 55 F9
Kogaluk ➝, *Canada* 103 A7
Køge, *Denmark* 11 J6
Køge Bugt, *Denmark* 11 J6
Kogi □, *Nigeria* 83 D6
Kogin Baba, *Nigeria* 83 D7
Koh-i-Bābā, *Afghan.* 66 B5
Koh-i-Khurd, *Afghan.* 66 C1
Koh-i-Maran, *Pakistan* 68 E2
Kohat, *Pakistan* 68 C4
Kohima, *India* 67 G19
Kohkīlūyeh va Būyer
  Aḥmadi □, *Iran* 71 D6
Kohler Ra., *Antarctica* 5 D15
Kohlu, *Pakistan* 68 E3
Kohtla-Järve, *Estonia* 9 G22
Koillismaa, *Finland* 8 D23
Koin-dong, *N. Korea* 57 D14
Koinare, *Bulgaria* 41 C8
Kojetín, *Czech Rep.* 27 B10
Kŏjŏ, *N. Korea* 57 E14
Kojonup, *Australia* 93 F2
Kojūr, *Iran* 71 B6
Koka, *Sudan* 80 C3
Kokand = Qūqon,
  Uzbekistan 50 E8
Kokas, *Indonesia* 63 E8
Kokava, *Slovak Rep.* 27 C12
Kokchetav = Kökshetaü,
  Kazakstan 50 D7
Kokemäenjoki ➝, *Finland* . 9 F19
Kokhma, *Russia* 48 B5
Koki, *Senegal* 82 B1

Kokkola, *Finland* 8 E20
Koko, *Nigeria* 83 C5
Koko Kyunzu, *Burma* 67 M18
Kokolopozo, *Ivory C.* 82 D3
Kokomo, *U.S.A.* 108 E2
Kokoro, *Niger* 83 C5
Koksan, *N. Korea* 57 E14
Kökshetaü, *Kazakstan* 50 D7
Koksoak ➝, *Canada* 101 C13
Kokstad, *S. Africa* 89 E4
Kokubu, *Japan* 55 J5
Kola, *Indonesia* 63 F8
Kola Pen. = Kolskiy
  Poluostrov, *Russia* 50 C4
Kolachi ➝, *Pakistan* 68 F2
Kolahoi, *India* 69 B6
Kolaka, *Indonesia* 63 E6
Kolar, *India* 66 N11
Kolar Gold Fields, *India* 66 N11
Kolaras, *India* 68 G6
Kolari, *Finland* 8 C20
Kolárovo, *Slovak Rep.* 27 D10
Kolašin, *Montenegro, Yug.* . 40 D3
Kolayat, *India* 66 F8
Kolbäck, *Sweden* 10 E10
Kolbäcksån ➝, *Sweden* 10 E10
Kolbermoor, *Germany* 25 H8
Kolbuszowa, *Poland* 45 H8
Kolchugino = Leninsk-
  Kuznetskiy, *Russia* 50 D9
Kolchugino, *Russia* 46 D10
Kolda, *Senegal* 82 C2
Koldegi, *Sudan* 81 E3
Kolding, *Denmark* 11 J3
Kolepom = Dolak, Pulau,
  Indonesia 63 F9
Kolguyev, Ostrov, *Russia* .. 50 C5
Kolhapur, *India* 66 L9
Kolia, *Ivory C.* 82 D3
Kolín, *Czech Rep.* 26 A8
Kolind, *Denmark* 11 H4
Kolkas rags, *Latvia* 9 H20
Kölleda, *Germany* 24 D7
Kollum, *Neths.* 17 A6
Kolmanskop, *Namibia* 88 D2
Köln, *Germany* 24 E2
Kolno, *Poland* 44 E8
Koło, *Poland* 45 F5
Kołobrzeg, *Poland* 44 D2
Kolokani, *Mali* 82 C3
Koloko, *Burkina Faso* 82 C3
Kololo, *Ethiopia* 81 F5
Kolomna, *Russia* 46 E10
Kolomyya, *Ukraine* 47 H3
Kolondiéba, *Mali* 82 C3
Kolonodale, *Indonesia* 63 E6
Kolonowskie, *Poland* 45 H5
Kolosib, *India* 67 G18
Kolpashevo, *Russia* 50 D9
Kolpino, *Russia* 46 C6
Kolpny, *Russia* 47 F9
Kolskiy Poluostrov, *Russia* . 50 C4
Kolsva, *Sweden* 10 E9
Kolubara ➝, *Serbia, Yug.* .. 40 B4
Koluszki, *Poland* 45 G6
Kolwezi,
  Dem. Rep. of the Congo . 87 E2
Kolyma ➝, *Russia* 51 C17
Kolymskoye Nagorye, *Russia* 51 C16
Kôm Hamâda, *Egypt* 80 H7
Kôm Ombo, *Egypt* 80 C3
Komadugu Gana ➝, *Nigeria* 83 C7
Komandorskiye Is. =
  Komandorskiye Ostrova,
  Russia 51 D17
Komandorskiye Ostrova,
  Russia 51 D17
Komárno, *Slovak Rep.* 27 D11
Komárom, *Hungary* 42 C3
Komárom-Esztergom □,
  Hungary 42 C3
Komatipoort, *S. Africa* 89 D5
Komatou Yialou, *Cyprus* ... 36 D13
Komatsu, *Japan* 55 F8
Komatsujima, *Japan* 55 H7
Kombissiri, *Burkina Faso* ... 83 C4
Kombori, *Burkina Faso* 82 C4
Kombóti, *Greece* 38 B3
Komen, *Slovenia* 29 C10
Komenda, *Ghana* 83 D4
Komi □, *Russia* 50 C6
Komiža, *Croatia* 29 E13
Komló, *Hungary* 42 D3
Kommunarsk = Alchevsk,
  Ukraine 47 H10
Kommunizma, Pik,
  Tajikistan 50 F8
Komodo, *Indonesia* 63 F5
Komoé ➝, *Ivory C.* 82 D4
Komoran, Pulau, *Indonesia* 63 F9
Komoro, *Japan* 55 F9
Komotini, *Greece* 41 E9
Komovi, *Montenegro, Yug.* . 40 D3
Kompasberg, *S. Africa* 88 E3
Kompong Bang, *Cambodia* . 65 F5
Kompong Cham, *Cambodia* 65 F5
Kompong Chhnang =
  Kampong Chhnang,
  Cambodia 65 F5
Kompong Chikreng,
  Cambodia 64 F5
Kompong Kleang, *Cambodia* 64 F5
Kompong Luong, *Cambodia* 65 G5
Kompong Pranak, *Cambodia* 64 F5
Kompong Som = Kampong
  Saom, *Cambodia* 65 G4
Kompong Som, Chhung =
  Kampong Saom, Chaak,
  Cambodia 65 G4
Kompong Speu, *Cambodia* . 65 G5

Kompong Sralao, *Cambodia* 64 E5
Kompong Thom, *Cambodia* 64 F5
Kompong Trabeck,
  Cambodia 64 F5
Kompong Trabeck,
  Cambodia 65 G5
Kompong Trach, *Cambodia* 65 G5
Kompong Tralach, *Cambodia* 65 G5
Komrat = Comrat, *Moldova* 43 D13
Komsberg, *S. Africa* 88 E3
Komsomolets, Ostrov, *Russia* 51 A10
Komsomolsk, *Amur, Russia* 51 D14
Komsomolsk, *Ivanovo,
  Russia* 46 D11
Komsomolskiy, *Russia* 48 C7
Kömür Burnu, *Turkey* 39 C8
Kon Tum, *Vietnam* 64 E7
Kon Tum, Plateau du,
  Vietnam 64 E7
Kona, *Mali* 82 C4
Konakovo, *Russia* 46 D9
Konarhā □, *Afghan.* 66 B7
Konārī, *Iran* 71 D6
Konch, *India* 69 G8
Konde, *Tanzania* 86 C4
Kondiá, *Greece* 39 B7
Kondinin, *Australia* 93 F2
Kondoa, *Tanzania* 86 C4
Kondókali, *Greece* 36 A3
Kondopaga, *Russia* 46 A8
Kondratyevo, *Russia* 51 D10
Kondrovo, *Russia* 46 E8
Konduga, *Nigeria* 83 C7
Köneürgench, *Turkmenistan* 50 E6
Konevo, *Russia* 46 A10
Kong = Khong ➝,
  Cambodia 64 F5
Kong, *Ivory C.* 82 D4
Kong, Koh, *Cambodia* 65 G4
Kong Christian IX Land,
  Greenland 4 C6
Kong Christian X Land,
  Greenland 4 B6
Kong Frederik IX Land,
  Greenland 4 C5
Kong Frederik VI Kyst,
  Greenland 4 C5
Kong Frederik VIII Land,
  Greenland 4 B6
Kong Oscar Fjord,
  Greenland 4 B6
Kongeå ➝, *Denmark* 11 J2
Kongerslev, *Denmark* 11 H4
Kongju, *S. Korea* 57 F14
Konglu, *Burma* 67 F20
Kongola, *Namibia* 88 B3
Kongolo, *Kasai-Or.,
  Dem. Rep. of the Congo* . 86 D1
Kongolo, *Katanga,
  Dem. Rep. of the Congo* . 86 D2
Kongor, *Sudan* 81 F3
Kongoussi, *Burkina Faso* ... 83 C4
Kongsberg, *Norway* 9 G13
Kongsvinger, *Norway* 9 F15
Kongwa, *Tanzania* 86 D4
Koni,
  Dem. Rep. of the Congo . 87 E2
Koni, Mts.,
  Dem. Rep. of the Congo . 87 E2
Koniakari, *Mali* 82 C2
Koniecpol, *Poland* 45 H6
Königs Wusterhausen,
  Germany 24 C9
Königsberg = Kaliningrad,
  Russia 9 J19
Königsbrunn, *Germany* 25 G6
Königslutter, *Germany* 24 C6
Konin, *Poland* 45 F5
Konispoli, *Albania* 40 G4
Kónitsa, *Greece* 38 A2
Konjic, *Bos.-H.* 42 G2
Konkiep, *Namibia* 88 D2
Konkouré ➝, *Guinea* 82 D2
Könnern, *Germany* 24 D7
Kono, *S. Leone* 82 D2
Konongo, *Ghana* 83 D4
Konosha, *Russia* 46 B11
Kōnosu, *Japan* 55 F9
Konotop, *Ukraine* 47 G7
Konsankoro, *Guinea* 82 D3
Końskie, *Poland* 45 G7
Konstancin-Jeziorna, *Poland* 45 F8
Konstantinovka =
  Kostyantynivka, *Ukraine* . 47 H9
Konstantinovsk, *Russia* 49 G5
Konstantynów Łódzki,
  Poland 45 G6
Konstanz, *Germany* 25 H5
Kont, *Iran* 71 E9
Kontagora, *Nigeria* 83 C6
Kontcha, *Cameroon* 83 D7
Konya, *Turkey* 70 B2
Konya □, *Germany* 72 C5
Konya Ovası, *Turkey* 72 C5
Konza, *Kenya* 86 C4
Koocanusa, L., *Canada* 114 B6
Kookynie, *Australia* 93 E3
Koolyanobbing, *Australia* ... 93 F2
Koonibba, *Australia* 95 E1
Koorawatha, *Australia* 95 E4
Koorda, *Australia* 93 F2
Kooskia, *U.S.A.* 114 C6
Kootenay ➝, *U.S.A.* 104 D5
Kootenay Nat. Park, *Canada* 104 C5
Kootjieskolk, *S. Africa* 88 E3
Kopaonik, *Yugoslavia* 40 C4
Kópavogur, *Iceland* 8 D3
Koper, *Slovenia* 29 C10
Kopervik, *Norway* 9 G11

Kopet Dagh, Asia 71 B8
Kopi, Australia 95 E2
Köping, Sweden 10 E10
Köpingsvik, Sweden 11 H10
Kopište, Croatia 29 F13
Kopliku, Albania 40 D3
Köpmanholmen, Sweden ... 10 A12
Kopparberg, Sweden 10 E9
Kopparbergs län □, Sweden . 10 C8
Koppeh Dãgh = Kopet
  Dagh, Asia 71 B8
Koppies, S. Africa 89 D4
Koppom, Sweden 10 E6
Koprivlen, Bulgaria 40 E7
Koprivnica, Croatia 29 B13
Kopřivnice, Czech Rep. ... 27 B11
Koprivshtitsa, Bulgaria ... 41 D8
Köprübaşı, Turkey 39 C10
Kopychyntsi, Ukraine 47 H3
Korab, Macedonia 40 E4
Korakiána, Greece 36 A3
Koral, India 68 J5
Korarou, L., Mali 82 B4
Korba, India 69 H10
Korbach, Germany 24 D4
Korbu, G., Malaysia 65 K3
Korça, Albania 40 F4
Korce = Korça, Albania ... 40 F4
Korčula, Croatia 29 F13
Korčulanski Kanal, Croatia . 29 E13
Kord Kūy, Iran 71 B7
Kord Sheykh, Iran 71 D7
Kordestãn □, Iran 70 C5
Kordofãn, Sudan 79 F11
Koré Mayroua, Niger 83 C5
Korea, North ■, Asia 57 E14
Korea, South ■, Asia 57 G15
Korea Bay, Korea 57 E13
Korea Strait, Asia 57 H15
Korem, Ethiopia 81 E4
Korenevo, Russia 47 G8
Korenovsk, Russia 49 H4
Korets, Ukraine 47 G4
Korfantów, Poland 45 H4
Korgan, Turkey 72 B7
Korgus, Sudan 80 D3
Korhogo, Ivory C. 82 D3
Koribundu, S. Leone 82 D2
Korienzé, Mali 82 B4
Korinthía □, Greece 38 D4
Korinthiakós Kólpos, Greece . 38 C4
Kórinthos, Greece 38 D4
Korioumé, Mali 82 B4
Koríssa, Límni, Greece ... 36 B3
Kõriyama, Japan 54 F10
Korkuteli, Turkey 39 D12
Kormakiti, C., Cyprus ... 36 D11
Körmend, Hungary 42 C1
Kornat, Croatia 29 E12
Korneshty = Cornești,
  Moldova 43 C13
Korneuburg, Austria 27 C9
Kórnik, Poland 45 F4
Koro, Fiji 91 C8
Koro, Ivory C. 82 D3
Koro, Mali 82 C4
Koro Sea, Fiji 91 C9
Korocha, Russia 47 G9
Köroğlu Dağları, Turkey ... 72 B5
Korogwe, Tanzania 86 D4
Koronadal, Phil. 61 H6
Koróni, Greece 38 E3
Korónia, Limni, Greece ... 40 F7
Koronís, Greece 39 D7
Koronowo, Poland 45 E4
Koror, Palau 63 C8
Körös →, Hungary 42 D5
Köröstarcsa, Hungary 42 D6
Korosten, Ukraine 47 G5
Korostyshev, Ukraine 47 G5
Korotoyak, Russia 47 G10
Korraraika, Helodranon' i,
  Madag. 89 B7
Korsakov, Russia 51 E15
Korsberga, Sweden 11 G9
Korshunovo, Russia 51 D12
Korsør, Denmark 11 J5
Korsun Shevchenkovskiy,
  Ukraine 47 H6
Korsze, Poland 44 D8
Korti, Sudan 80 D3
Kortrijk, Belgium 17 D3
Korucu, Turkey 39 B9
Korwai, India 68 G8
Koryakskoye Nagorye,
  Russia 51 C18
Koryŏng, S. Korea 57 G15
Koryukovka, Ukraine 47 G7
Kos, Greece 39 E9
Kosa, Ethiopia 81 F4
Kosaya Gora, Russia 46 E9
Kościan, Poland 45 F3
Kościerzyna, Poland 44 D4
Kosciusko, U.S.A. 113 J10
Kosciusko, Mt., Australia . 95 F4
Kösély →, Hungary 42 C6
Kosha, Sudan 80 C3
Koshava, Bulgaria 40 B7
K'oshih = Kashi, China .. 60 C2
Koshiki-Rettō, Japan 55 J4
Kosi, India 68 F7
Kosi →, India 69 E8
Košice, Slovak Rep. 27 C14
Košický □, Slovak Rep. ... 27 C14
Kosjerić, Serbia, Yug. ... 40 B3
Köşk, Turkey 39 D10
Koskhinoú, Greece 36 C10
Koslan, Russia 50 C5
Košöngs, N Korea 57 E15
Kosovo □, Yugoslavia ... 40 D4
Kosovo Polje, Kosovo, Yug. . 40 D5

Kosovska Kamenica,
  Kosovo, Yug. 40 D5
Kosovska Mitrovica,
  Kosovo, Yug. 40 D4
Kossou, L. de, Ivory C. 82 D3
Kosta, Sweden 11 H9
Kostajnica, Croatia 29 C13
Kostanjevica, Slovenia ... 29 C12
Kostenets, Bulgaria 40 D7
Koster, S. Africa 88 D4
Kôstî, Sudan 81 E3
Kostinbrod, Bulgaria 40 D7
Kostolac, Serbia, Yug. 40 B5
Kostopil, Ukraine 47 G4
Kostroma, Russia 46 D11
Kostromskoye Vdkhr.,
  Russia 46 D11
Kostrzyn, Lubuskie, Poland . 45 F1
Kostrzyn, Wielkopolskie,
  Poland 45 F4
Kostyantynivka, Ukraine .. 47 H9
Kostyukovichi =
  Kastsyukovichy, Belarus . 46 F7
Koszalin, Poland 44 D3
Kőszeg, Hungary 42 C1
Kot Addu, Pakistan 68 D4
Kot Kapura, India 68 D6
Kot Moman, Pakistan ... 68 C5
Kot Sultan, Pakistan 68 D4
Kota, India 68 G6
Kota Baharu, Malaysia ... 65 J4
Kota Barrage, India 68 G6
Kota Belud, Malaysia 62 C5
Kota Kinabalu, Malaysia .. 62 C5
Kota Kubu Baharu, Malaysia . 65 L4
Kota Tinggi, Malaysia ... 65 M4
Kotaagung, Indonesia 62 F2
Kotabaru, Indonesia 62 E5
Kotabumi, Indonesia 62 E2
Kotamobagu, Indonesia ... 63 D6
Kotcho L., Canada 104 B4
Kotdwara, India 69 E8
Kotelnich, Russia 48 A9
Kotel, Bulgaria 41 D10
Kotelnikovo, Russia 49 G6
Kotelnyy, Ostrov, Russia ... 51 B14
Kothari →, India 68 G6
Köthen, Germany 24 D7
Kothi, Mad. P., India ... 69 H10
Kothi, Mad. P., India ... 69 G9
Kotiro, Pakistan 68 F2
Kotka, Finland 9 F22
Kotlas, Russia 50 C5
Kotlenska Planina, Bulgaria . 41 D10
Kotli, Pakistan 68 C5
Kotma, India 69 H9
Kotmul, Pakistan 69 B6
Koton-Karifi, Nigeria ... 83 D6
Kotonkoro, Nigeria 83 C6
Kotor, Montenegro, Yug. .. 40 D2
Kotor Varoš, Bos.-H. 42 F2
Kotoriba, Croatia 29 B13
Kotovo, Russia 48 E7
Kotovsk, Russia 48 D5
Kotovsk, Ukraine 47 J5
Kotputli, India 68 F7
Kotri, Pakistan 68 G3
Kótronas, Greece 38 E4
Kötschach-Mauthen, Austria . 26 E6
Kottayam, India 66 Q10
Kotturu, India 66 M10
Kotuy →, Russia 51 B11
Kotzebue, U.S.A. 100 B3
Koudougou, Burkina Faso . 82 C4
Koufonísi, Greece 36 E8
Koufonísia, Greece 39 E7
Kougaberge, S. Africa ... 88 E3
Kouibli, Ivory C. 82 D3
Kouilou →, Congo 84 E2
Koula Moutou, Gabon ... 84 E2
Koulen = Kulen, Cambodia . 64 F5
Koulikoro, Mali 82 C3
Kouloúra, Greece 36 A3
Koúm-bournoú, Ákra,
  Greece 36 C10
Koumala, Australia 94 C4
Koumankou, Mali 82 C3
Koumbia, Burkina Faso .. 82 C4
Koumbia, Guinea 82 C2
Koumboum, Guinea 82 C2
Koumpenntoum, Senegal .. 82 C2
Koumra, Chad 79 G9
Koun-Fao, Ivory C. 82 D4
Koundara, Guinea 82 C2
Koundian, Guinea 82 C3
Koungheul, Senegal 82 C2
Kounradskiy, Kazakstan .. 50 E8
Kountze, U.S.A. 113 K7
Koupéla, Burkina Faso ... 83 C4
Kouris →, Cyprus 36 E11
Kourou, Fr. Guiana 125 B8
Kourouba, Mali 82 C2
Kouroukoto, Mali 82 C2
Kourouma, Burkina Faso . 82 C4
Kourouninkoto, Mali 82 C2
Kouroussa, Guinea 82 C2
Koussanar, Senegal 82 C2
Koussané, Mali 82 C2
Kousseri, Cameroon 79 F8
Koutiala, Mali 82 C3
Kouto, Ivory C. 82 D3
Kouvé, Togo 83 D5
Kouvola, Finland 9 F22
Kovačica, Serbia, Yug. ... 42 E5
Kovel, Ukraine 47 G3
Kovin, Serbia, Yug. 42 F5
Kovrov, Russia 48 B5
Kowal, Poland 45 F6

Kowalewo Pomorskie,
  Poland 45 E5
Kowanyama, Australia ... 94 B3
Kowloon, H.K. 59 F10
Kowŏn, N. Korea 57 E14
Köyceğiz, Turkey 39 E10
Köyceğiz Gölü, Turkey ... 39 E10
Koyulhisar, Turkey 72 B7
Koyunyeri, Turkey 41 F10
Koza, Japan 55 L3
Kozak, Turkey 39 B9
Kozan, Turkey 70 B2
Kozáni, Greece 40 F5
Kozara, Bos.-H. 29 D14
Kozarac, Bos.-H. 29 D13
Kozelets, Ukraine 47 G6
Kozelsk, Russia 46 E8
Kozhikode = Calicut, India . 66 P9
Koziegłowy, Poland 45 H6
Kozienice, Poland 45 G8
Kozje, Slovenia 29 B12
Kozloduy, Bulgaria 40 C7
Kozlovets, Bulgaria 41 C9
Kozlovka, Russia 48 C9
Kozlu, Turkey 72 B4
Kozluk, Turkey 73 C9
Kozmin, Poland 45 G4
Kozmodemyansk, Russia .. 48 B8
Kożuchów, Poland 45 G2
Kozyatyn, Ukraine 47 H5
Kpabia, Ghana 83 D4
Kpalimé, Togo 83 D5
Kpandae, Ghana 83 D5
Kpessi, Togo 83 D5
Kra, Isthmus of = Kra, Kho
  Khot, Thailand 65 G2
Kra, Kho Khot, Thailand .. 65 G2
Kra Buri, Thailand 65 G2
Kraai →, S. Africa 88 E4
Krabi, Thailand 65 H2
Kracheh, Cambodia 64 F6
Kragan, Indonesia 63 G14
Kragerø, Norway 9 G13
Kragujevac, Serbia, Yug. .. 40 B4
Krajenka, Poland 45 E3
Krajina, Bos.-H. 29 D13
Krakatau = Rakata, Pulau,
  Indonesia 62 F3
Krakatoa = Rakata, Pulau,
  Indonesia 62 F3
Krakor, Cambodia 64 F5
Kraków, Poland 45 H6
Kralanh, Cambodia 64 F4
Králíky, Czech Rep. 27 A9
Kraljevo, Serbia, Yug. ... 40 C4
Královský Chlmec,
  Slovak Rep. 27 C14
Kralupy nad Vltavou,
  Czech Rep. 26 A7
Kramatorsk, Ukraine 47 H9
Kramfors, Sweden 10 B11
Kraniá, Greece 40 G5
Kranía Elassónas, Greece . 38 B4
Kranídhion, Greece 38 D5
Kranj, Slovenia 29 B11
Kranjska Gora, Slovenia .. 29 B10
Krankskop, S. Africa 89 D5
Krapina, Croatia 29 B12
Krapina →, Croatia 29 C12
Krapkowice, Poland 45 H4
Kras, Croatia 29 C10
Kraskino, Russia 51 E14
Kräslava, Latvia 46 E4
Kraslice, Czech Rep. 26 A5
Krasnaya Gorbatka, Russia . 48 C5
Krasnaya Polyana, Russia .. 49 J5
Kraśnik, Poland 45 H9
Krasnoarmeisk, Ukraine .. 47 H9
Krasnoarmeysk, Russia ... 48 E7
Krasnoarmeyskiy, Russia .. 49 G6
Krasnobrod, Poland 45 H10
Krasnodar, Russia 49 H4
Krasnodon, Ukraine 47 H10
Krasnogorskiy, Russia ... 48 B9
Krasnograd = Krasnohrad,
  Ukraine 47 H8
Krasnogvardeyskoye, Russia . 49 H5
Krasnogvardeysk, Ukraine .. 47 K8
Krasnohrad, Ukraine 47 H8
Krasnokamsk, Ukraine ... 47 G8
Krasnolesnyy, Russia 47 G10
Krasnoperekopsk, Ukraine . 47 J7
Krasnorechenskiy, Russia .. 54 B7
Krasnoselkup, Russia 50 C9
Krasnoslobodsk, Mordvinia,
  Russia 48 C6
Krasnoslobodsk, Volgograd,
  Russia 49 F7
Krasnoturinsk, Russia ... 50 D7
Krasnovodsk =
  Türkmenbashi,
  Turkmenistan 50 E6
Krasnoyarsk, Russia 51 D10
Krasnoye = Krasnyy, Russia . 46 E6
Krasny Sulin, Russia 47 J11
Krasnystaw, Poland 45 H10
Krasnyy, Russia 46 E6
Krasnyy Kholm, Russia ... 46 C9
Krasnyy Kut, Russia 48 E8
Krasnyy Liman, Ukraine .. 47 H9
Krasnyy Luch, Ukraine ... 47 H10
Krasnyy Profintern, Russia . 46 D11
Krasnyy Yar, Astrakhan,
  Russia 49 G9
Krasnyy Yar, Samara, Russia . 48 D10
Krasnyy Yar, Volgograd,
  Russia 48 E7
Krasnyye Baki, Russia ... 48 B7

Krasnyyoskolske Vdskh.,
  Ukraine 47 H9
Kraszna →, Hungary 42 B7
Kratie = Kracheh, Cambodia . 64 F6
Kratovo, Macedonia 40 D6
Krau, Indonesia 63 E10
Kravanh, Chuor Phnum,
  Cambodia 65 G4
Krefeld, Germany 24 D2
Krémaston, Límni, Greece . 38 C3
Kremenchug = Kremenchuk,
  Ukraine 47 H7
Kremenchuk, Ukraine ... 47 H7
Kremenchuksk Vdskh.,
  Ukraine 47 H7
Kremenets, Ukraine 47 G3
Kremennaya, Ukraine ... 47 H10
Kremges = Svitlovodsk,
  Ukraine 47 H7
Kremmen, Germany 24 C9
Kremmling, U.S.A. 114 F10
Kremnica, Slovak Rep. ... 27 C11
Krems, Austria 26 C8
Kremsmünster, Austria ... 26 C7
Kretinga, Lithuania 9 J19
Krettsy, Russia 46 C7
Kreuzberg, Germany 25 E5
Kreuztal, Germany 24 E4
Kría Vrísi, Greece 40 F6
Kribi, Cameroon 83 E6
Krichem, Bulgaria 41 D8
Krichev = Krychaw, Belarus . 46 F6
Krim, Slovenia 29 C11
Kriós, Ákra, Greece 36 D5
Krishna →, India 67 M12
Krishnanagar, India 69 H13
Kristalla, Sweden 11 G10
Kristiansand, Norway ... 9 G13
Kristianstad, Sweden 11 H8
Kristiansund, Norway ... 8 E12
Kristiinankaupunki, Finland . 9 E19
Kristinehamn, Sweden ... 10 E8
Kristinestad =
  Kristiinankaupunki,
  Finland 9 E19
Kríti, Greece 36 D7
Kritsá, Greece 36 D7
Kriva →, Macedonia 40 D5
Kriva Palanka, Macedonia . 40 D6
Krivaja →, Bos.-H. 42 F3
Krivelj, Serbia, Yug. 40 B6
Krivoy Rog = Kryvyy Rih,
  Ukraine 47 J7
Križevci, Croatia 29 B13
Krk, Croatia 29 C11
Krka →, Slovenia 29 C12
Krkonoše, Czech Rep. ... 26 A8
Krnov, Czech Rep. 27 A10
Krobia, Poland 45 G3
Krokeaí, Greece 38 E4
Krokek, Sweden 11 F10
Krokodil →, Mozam. ... 89 D5
Krokom, Sweden 10 A8
Krokowa, Poland 44 D5
Krolevets, Ukraine 47 G7
Kroměříž, Czech Rep. ... 27 B13
Kromy, Russia 47 F8
Kronach, Germany 25 E7
Krong Kaoh Kong,
  Cambodia 62 B2
Kronobergs län □, Sweden . 11 H8
Kronprins Olav Kyst,
  Antarctica 5 C5
Kronshtadt, Russia 46 C5
Kroonstad, S. Africa 88 D4
Kröpelin, Germany 24 A7
Kropotkin, Russia 49 H5
Kropp, Germany 24 A5
Krosna, Lithuania 44 D10
Krośniewice, Poland 45 F6
Krosno, Poland 45 J8
Krosno Odrzańskie, Poland . 45 F2
Krotoszyn, Poland 45 G4
Krotz Springs, U.S.A. ... 113 K9
Kroussón, Greece 36 D6
Krraba, Albania 40 E3
Krško, Slovenia 29 C12
Krstača, Serbia, Yug. 40 D3
Kruger Nat. Park, S. Africa . 89 C5
Krugersdorp, S. Africa ... 89 D4
Kruisfontein, S. Africa ... 88 E3
Kruja, Albania 40 E3
Krulevshchina =
  Krulyewshchyna, Belarus . 46 E4
Krulyewshchyna, Belarus .. 46 E4
Kruma, Albania 40 D4
Krumbach, Germany 25 G6
Krumovgrad, Bulgaria ... 41 E9
Krung Thep = Bangkok,
  Thailand 64 F3
Krupanj, Serbia, Yug. 40 B3
Krupina, Slovak Rep. 27 C12
Krupinica →, Slovak Rep. . 27 C11
Krupki, Belarus 46 E5
Kruševac, Macedonia 40 E5
Kruševo, Macedonia 40 E5
Kruszwica, Poland 45 F5
Krychaw, Belarus 46 F6
Krymsk, Russia 47 K10
Krymskiy Poluostrov =
  Krymskyy Pivostriv,
  Ukraine 47 K8
Krymskyy Pivostriv, Ukraine . 47 K8
Krynica, Poland 45 J7
Krynica Morska, Poland .. 44 D6
Krynki, Poland 45 E10
Kryvyy Rih, Ukraine 47 J7
Krzepice, Poland 45 H5
Krzeszów, Poland 45 H9

Krzna →, Poland 45 F10
Krzywiń, Poland 45 G3
Krzyż Wielkopolski, Poland . 45 F2
Ksar el Kebir, Morocco ... 78 B4
Ksar es Souk = Ar
  Rachidiya, Morocco ... 78 B5
Ksiąz Wielkopolski, Poland . 45 F4
Kstovo, Russia 48 B7
Ku, W. el →, Sudan 81 E2
Kuala Belait, Malaysia ... 62 D4
Kuala Berang, Malaysia .. 65 K4
Kuala Dungun = Dungun,
  Malaysia 65 K4
Kuala Kangsar, Malaysia . 65 K3
Kuala Kelawang, Malaysia . 65 L4
Kuala Kerai, Malaysia ... 65 K4
Kuala Lipis, Malaysia ... 65 K4
Kuala Lumpur, Malaysia . 65 L4
Kuala Nerang, Malaysia .. 65 J3
Kuala Pilah, Malaysia ... 65 L4
Kuala Rompin, Malaysia . 65 L4
Kuala Selangor, Malaysia . 65 L3
Kuala Sepetang, Malaysia . 65 K3
Kuala Terengganu, Malaysia . 65 K4
Kualajelai, Indonesia 62 E4
Kualakapuas, Indonesia .. 62 E4
Kualakurun, Indonesia ... 62 E4
Kualapembuang, Indonesia . 62 E4
Kualasimpang, Indonesia . 62 D1
Kuancheng, China 57 D10
Kuandang, Indonesia ... 63 D6
Kuandian, China 57 D13
Kuangchou = Guangzhou,
  China 59 F9
Kuanshan, Taiwan 59 F13
Kuantan, Malaysia 65 L4
Kuba = Quba, Azerbaijan . 49 K9
Kuban →, Russia 47 K9
Kubenskoye, Ozero, Russia . 46 C10
Kubokawa, Japan 55 H6
Kubrat, Bulgaria 41 C10
Kučevo, Serbia, Yug. 40 B5
Kucha Gompa, India 69 B7
Kuchaman, India 68 F6
Kuchenspitze, Austria ... 26 D3
Kuchinda, India 69 J11
Kuching, Malaysia 62 D4
Kuchino-eruba-Jima, Japan . 55 J5
Kuchino-Shima, Japan ... 55 K4
Kuchinotsu, Japan 55 H5
Kuchl, Austria 26 D6
Kucing = Kuching, Malaysia . 62 D4
Kuçovë, Albania 40 F3
Küçükbahçe, Turkey 39 C8
Küçükköy, Turkey 39 B8
Küçükkuyu, Turkey 39 B8
Küçükmenderes →, Turkey . 39 D9
Kud →, Pakistan 68 F2
Kuda, India 66 H7
Kudat, Malaysia 62 C5
Kudirkos Naumiestis,
  Lithuania 44 D9
Kudowa-Zdrój, Poland ... 45 H3
Kudus, Indonesia 63 G14
Kudymkar, Russia 50 D6
Kueiyang = Guiyang, China . 58 D6
Kufra Oasis = Al Kufrah,
  Libya 79 D10
Kufstein, Austria 26 D5
Kugluktuk, Canada 100 B8
Kugong I., Canada 102 A4
Kūhak, Iran 66 F3
Kuhan, Pakistan 68 E2
Kühbonãn, Iran 71 D8
Kühestak, Iran 71 E8
Kuhin, Iran 71 B6
Kührī, Iran 71 E9
Kuhnsdorf, Austria 26 E7
Kühpãyeh, Eşfahan, Iran .. 71 C7
Kühpãyeh, Kermãn, Iran .. 71 D8
Kührãn, Küh-e, Iran 71 E8
Kui Buri, Thailand 65 F2
Kuiseb →, Namibia 88 B2
Kuito, Angola 85 G3
Kuiu I., U.S.A. 104 B2
Kujang, N. Korea 57 E14
Kujawsko-Pomorskie □,
  Poland 44 E5
Kuji, Japan 54 D10
Kuju-San, Japan 55 H5
Kukavica, Serbia, Yug. ... 40 D5
Kukawa, Nigeria 83 C7
Kukësi, Albania 40 D4
Kukmor, Russia 48 B10
Kukup, Malaysia 65 M4
Kukvidze, Russia 48 E6
Kula, Bulgaria 40 C6
Kula, Serbia, Yug. 42 E4
Kula, Turkey 39 C10
Kulachi, Pakistan 68 D3
Kulai, Malaysia 65 M4
Kulal, Mt., Kenya 86 B4
Kulaly, Ostrov, Kazakstan . 49 H10
Kulasekarappattinam, India . 66 Q11
Kulautuva, Lithuania ... 44 D10
Kuldīga, Latvia 9 H19
Kuldja = Yining, China .. 50 E9
Kulgam, India 69 C6
Kulgera, Australia 94 D1
Kuli, Russia 49 J8
Kulim, Malaysia 65 K3
Kulin, Australia 93 F2
Kullen, Sweden 11 H6
Kulmbach, Germany ... 25 E7
Kŭlob, Tajikistan 50 F7
Kulp, Turkey 73 C9
Kulpawn →, Ghana 83 D4

Kulsary, *Kazakstan* 50 E6
Kulti, *India* 69 H12
Kulu, *India* 68 D7
Kulu, *Turkey* 72 C5
Kulumbura, *Australia* 92 B4
Kulunda, *Russia* 50 D8
Kulungar, *Afghan.* 68 C3
Kūlvand, *Iran* 71 D7
Kulwin, *Australia* 95 F3
Kulyab = Kŭlob, *Tajikistan* 50 F7
Kuma →, *Russia* 49 H8
Kumafşarı, *Turkey* 39 D11
Kumaganum, *Nigeria* 83 C7
Kumagaya, *Japan* 55 F9
Kumai, *Indonesia* 62 E4
Kumalar Dağı, *Turkey* 39 C12
Kumamba, Kepulauan,
  Indonesia 63 E9
Kumamoto, *Japan* 55 H5
Kumamoto □, *Japan* 55 H5
Kumanovo, *Macedonia* 40 D5
Kumara, *N.Z.* 91 K3
Kumarina, *Australia* 93 D2
Kumasi, *Ghana* 82 D4
Kumayri = Gyumri, *Armenia* 49 K6
Kumba, *Cameroon* 83 E6
Kumbağ, *Turkey* 41 F11
Kumbakonam, *India* 66 P11
Kumbarilla, *Australia* 95 D5
Kumbhraj, *India* 68 G7
Kumbia, *Australia* 95 D5
Kumbo, *Cameroon* 83 D7
Kŭmch'ŏn, *N. Korea* 57 E14
Kumdok, *India* 69 C8
Kume-Shima, *Japan* 55 L3
Kumeny, *Russia* 48 A9
Kumharsain, *India* 68 D7
Kŭmhwa, *S. Korea* 57 E14
Kumi, *Uganda* 86 B3
Kumkale, *Turkey* 41 G10
Kumla, *Sweden* 10 E9
Kumluca, *Turkey* 39 E12
Kummerower See, *Germany* 24 B8
Kumo, *Nigeria* 83 C7
Kumon Bum, *Burma* 67 F20
Kumylzhenskaya, *Russia* .. 48 F6
Kunágota, *Hungary* 42 D6
Kunashir, Ostrov, *Russia* .. 51 E15
Kunda, *Estonia* 9 G22
Kunda, *India* 69 G9
Kundar →, *Pakistan* 68 D3
Kundian, *Pakistan* 68 C4
Kundla, *India* 68 J4
Kunga →, *Bangla.* 69 J13
Kungälv, *Sweden* 11 G5
Kunghit I., *Canada* 104 C2
Kungrad = Qŭnghirot,
  Uzbekistan 50 E6
Kungsängen, *Sweden* 10 E11
Kungsbacka, *Sweden* 11 G6
Kungsgården, *Sweden* 10 D10
Kungshamn, *Sweden* 11 F5
Kungsör, *Sweden* 10 E10
Kungur, *Russia* 50 D6
Kunhar →, *Pakistan* 69 B5
Kunhegyes, *Hungary* 42 C5
Kuningan, *Indonesia* 63 G13
Kunlong, *Burma* 58 F2
Kunlun Shan, *Asia* 60 C3
Kunmadaras, *Hungary* 42 C5
Kunming, *China* 58 E4
Kunów, *Poland* 45 H8
Kunsan, *S. Korea* 57 G14
Kunshan, *China* 59 B13
Kunszentmárton, *Hungary* . 42 D5
Kunszentmiklós, *Hungary* . 42 C4
Kuntaur, *Senegal* 82 C2
Kununurra, *Australia* 92 C4
Kunwari →, *India* 69 F8
Kunya-Urgench =
  Köneürgench,
  Turkmenistan 50 E6
Künzelsau, *Germany* 25 F5
Kuopio, *Finland* 8 E22
Kupa →, *Croatia* 29 C13
Kupang, *Indonesia* 63 F6
Kupreanof I., *U.S.A.* 104 B2
Kupres, *Bos.-H.* 42 G2
Kupyansk, *Ukraine* 47 H9
Kupyansk-Uzlovoi, *Ukraine* 47 H9
Kuqa, *China* 60 B3
Kür →, *Azerbaijan* 73 C13
Kür Dili, *Azerbaijan* 71 B6
Kura = Kür →, *Azerbaijan* 73 C13
Kuranda, *Australia* 94 B4
Kuranga, *India* 68 H3
Kurashiki, *Japan* 55 G6
Kurayoshi, *Japan* 55 G6
Kürdämir, *Azerbaijan* 49 K9
Kurdistan, *Asia* 73 D10
Kŭrdzhali, *Bulgaria* 41 E9
Kure, *Japan* 55 G6
Küre, *Turkey* 72 B5
Küre Dağları, *Turkey* 72 B6
Kuressaare, *Estonia* 9 G20
Kurgan, *Russia* 50 D7
Kurganinsk, *Russia* 49 H5
Kurgannaya = Kurganinsk,
  Russia 49 H5
Kuri, *India* 68 F4
Kuria Maria Is. = Khurīyā
  Murīyā, Jazā ʾir, *Oman* . 74 D6
Kuridala, *Australia* 94 C3
Kurigram, *Bangla.* 67 G16
Kurikka, *Finland* 9 E20
Kuril Is. = Kurilskiye
  Ostrova, *Russia* 51 E15
Kuril Trench, *Pac. Oc.* ... 52 E19
Kurilsk, *Russia* 51 E15
Kurilskiye Ostrova, *Russia* 51 E15
Kurino, *Japan* 55 J5

Kurinskaya Kosa = Kür Dili,
  Azerbaijan 71 B6
Kurkur, *Egypt* 80 C3
Kurlovskiy, *Russia* 48 C5
Kurmuk, *Sudan* 81 E3
Kurnool, *India* 66 M11
Kuro-Shima, *Kagoshima,*
  Japan 55 J4
Kuro-Shima, *Okinawa, Japan* 55 M2
Kuror, J., *Sudan* 80 C3
Kurow, *N.Z.* 91 L3
Kurów, *Poland* 45 G9
Kurram →, *Pakistan* 68 C4
Kurri Kurri, *Australia* 95 E5
Kurrimine, *Australia* 94 B4
Kursavka, *Russia* 49 H6
Kuršėnai, *Lithuania* 44 B9
Kurshskiy Zaliv, *Russia* ... 9 J19
Kursk, *Russia* 47 G9
Kuršumlija, *Serbia, Yug.* .. 40 C5
Kuršumlijska Banja,
  Serbia, Yug. 40 C5
Kurşunlu, *Bursa, Turkey* .. 41 F13
Kurşunlu, *Çankırı, Turkey* . 72 B5
Kurtalan, *Turkey* 73 D9
Kurtbey, *Turkey* 41 E10
Kuru, *Turkey* 81 F2
Kuru, Bahr el →, *Sudan* .. 81 F2
Kurucaşile, *Turkey* 72 B5
Kuruçay, *Turkey* 70 B3
Kuruktag, *China* 60 B3
Kuruman, *S. Africa* 88 D3
Kuruman →, *S. Africa* ... 88 D3
Kurume, *Japan* 55 H5
Kurun →, *Sudan* 81 F3
Kurunegala, *Sri Lanka* 66 R12
Kurya, *Russia* 50 C6
Kuş Gölü, *Turkey* 41 F11
Kuşadası, *Turkey* 72 D2
Kuşadası Körfezi, *Turkey* . 39 D8
Kusatsu, *Japan* 55 F9
Kusawa L., *Canada* 104 A1
Kusel, *Germany* 25 F3
Kushaka, *Nigeria* 83 C6
Kushalgarh, *India* 68 H6
Kushchevskaya, *Russia* ... 49 G4
Kusheriki, *Nigeria* 83 C6
Kushikino, *Japan* 55 J5
Kushima, *Japan* 55 J5
Kushimoto, *Japan* 55 H7
Kushiro, *Japan* 54 C12
Kushiro-Gawa →, *Japan* . 54 C12
Kūshk, *Iran* 71 D8
Kushka = Gushgy,
  Turkmenistan 50 F7
Kūshkī, *Iran* 70 C5
Kushol, *India* 69 C7
Kushtia, *Bangla.* 67 H16
Kushum →, *Kazakstan* ... 48 F10
Kuskokwim B., *U.S.A.* ... 100 C3
Kusmi, *India* 69 H10
Kussharo-Ko, *Japan* 54 C12
Kustanay = Qostanay,
  Kazakstan 50 D7
Kut, Ko, *Thailand* 65 G4
Kütahya, *Turkey* 39 B12
Kütahya □, *Turkey* 39 B11
Kutaisi, *Georgia* 49 J6
Kutaraja = Banda Aceh,
  Indonesia 62 C1
Kutch, Gulf of = Kachchh,
  Gulf of, *India* 68 H3
Kutch, Rann of = Kachchh,
  Rann of, *India* 68 H4
Kutina, *Croatia* 29 C13
Kutiyana, *India* 68 J4
Kutjevo, *Croatia* 42 E2
Kutkashen, *Azerbaijan* ... 49 K8
Kutná Hora, *Czech Rep.* . 26 B8
Kutno, *Poland* 45 F6
Kutse, *Botswana* 88 C3
Kutu,
  Dem. Rep. of the Congo . 84 E3
Kutum, *Sudan* 81 E1
Kúty, *Slovak Rep.* 27 C10
Kuujjuaq, *Canada* 101 C13
Kuujjuarapik, *Canada* 102 A4
Kŭup-tong, *N. Korea* 57 D14
Kuusamo, *Finland* 8 D23
Kuusankoski, *Finland* 9 F22
Kuvshinovo, *Russia* 46 D8
Kuwait = Al Kuwayt,
  Kuwait 70 D5
Kuwait ■, *Asia* 70 D5
Kuwana, *Japan* 55 G8
Kuwana →, *India* 69 F10
Kuybyshev = Samara, *Russia* 48 D10
Kuybyshev, *Russia* 50 D8
Kuybyshevo, *Ukraine* 47 J9
Kuybyshevskoye Vdkhr.,
  Russia 48 C9
Kuye He →, *China* 56 E6
Kūyeh, *Iran* 70 B5
Kūysanjaq, *Iraq* 70 B5
Kuyucak, *Turkey* 39 D10
Kuyumba, *Russia* 51 C10
Kuzey Anadolu Dağları,
  Turkey 72 B7
Kuzmin, *Serbia, Yug.* 42 E4
Kuznetsk, *Russia* 48 D8
Kuzomen, *Russia* 50 C4
Kvænangen, *Norway* 8 A19
Kværndrup, *Denmark* 11 J4
Kvæventi →, *Norway* 8 B18
Kvareli = Qvareli, *Georgia* . 49 K7
Kvarner, *Croatia* 29 D11
Kvarnerič, *Croatia* 29 D11
Kvicksund, *Sweden* 10 E10
Kvillsfors, *Sweden* 11 G9
Kvinesdal, *Norway* 11 F7
Kv1num, *Sweden* 11 F7
Kvismare kanal, *Sweden* .. 10 E9

Kvissleby, *Sweden* 10 B11
Kwa-Nobuhle, *S. Africa* .. 85 L5
Kwabhaca, *S. Africa* 89 E4
Kwakhanai, *Botswana* 88 C3
Kwakoegron, *Surinam* 125 B7
Kwale, *Kenya* 86 C4
Kwale, *Nigeria* 83 D6
KwaMashu, *S. Africa* 89 D5
Kwando →, *Africa* 88 B3
Kwangdaeri, *N. Korea* ... 57 D14
Kwangju, *S. Korea* 57 G14
Kwango →,
  Dem. Rep. of the Congo . 77 G5
Kwangsi-Chuang = Guangxi
  Zhuangzu Zizhiqu □,
  China 58 F7
Kwangtung = Guangdong □,
  China 59 F9
Kwara □, *Nigeria* 83 D6
Kwataboahegan →, *Canada* 102 B3
Kwatisore, *Indonesia* 63 E8
KwaZulu Natal □, *S. Africa* 89 D5
Kweichow = Guizhou □,
  China 58 D6
Kwekwe, *Zimbabwe* 87 F2
Kwidzyn, *Poland* 44 E5
Kwiha, *Ethiopia* 81 E4
Kwinana New Town,
  Australia 93 F2
Kwisa →, *Poland* 45 G2
Kwoka, *Indonesia* 63 E8
Kwolla, *Nigeria* 83 D6
Kyabra Cr. →, *Australia* . 95 D3
Kyabram, *Australia* 95 F4
Kyaikto, *Burma* 64 D1
Kyakhta, *Russia* 51 D11
Kyancutta, *Australia* 95 E2
Kyangin, *Burma* 67 K19
Kyaukpadaung, *Burma* ... 67 J19
Kyaukpyu, *Burma* 67 K18
Kyaukse, *Burma* 67 J20
Kybartai, *Lithuania* 44 D9
Kyburz, *U.S.A.* 116 G6
Kyelang, *India* 68 C7
Kyenjojo, *Uganda* 86 B3
Kyle, *Canada* 105 C7
Kyle Dam, *Zimbabwe* 87 G3
Kyle of Lochalsh, *U.K.* ... 14 D3
Kyll →, *Germany* 25 F2
Kyllburg, *Germany* 25 E2
Kymijoki →, *Finland* 9 F22
Kyneton, *Australia* 95 F3
Kynuna, *Australia* 94 C3
Kyō-ga-Saki, *Japan* 55 G7
Kyoga, L., *Uganda* 86 B3
Kyogle, *Australia* 95 D5
Kyom →, *Sudan* 81 F2
Kyongju, *S. Korea* 57 G15
Kyongpyaw, *Burma* 67 L19
Kyŏngsŏng, *N. Korea* 57 D15
Kyōto, *Japan* 55 G7
Kyōto □, *Japan* 55 G7
Kyparissovouno, *Cyprus* .. 36 D12
Kyperounda, *Cyprus* 36 E11
Kyrenia, *Cyprus* 36 D12
Kyrgyzstan ■, *Asia* 50 E8
Kyritz, *Germany* 24 C8
Kyrkhult, *Sweden* 11 H8
Kyrönjoki →, *Finland* 8 E19
Kystatyam, *Russia* 51 C13
Kysucké Nové Mesto,
  Slovak Rep. 27 B11
Kythréa, *Cyprus* 36 D12
Kyunhla, *Burma* 67 H19
Kyuquot Sound, *Canada* . 104 D3
Kyurdamir = Kürdämir,
  Azerbaijan 49 K9
Kyūshū, *Japan* 55 H5
Kyūshū □, *Japan* 55 H5
Kyūshū-Sanchi, *Japan* 55 H5
Kyustendil, *Bulgaria* 40 D6
Kyusyur, *Russia* 51 B13
Kyyiv, *Ukraine* 47 G6
Kyyivske Vdskh., *Ukraine* . 47 G6
Kyzyl, *Russia* 51 D10
Kyzyl Kum, *Uzbekistan* .. 50 E7
Kyzyl-Kyya, *Kyrgyzstan* .. 50 E8
Kyzyl-Orda = Qyzylorda,
  Kazakstan 50 E7

L

La Albuera, *Spain* 35 G4
La Alcarria, *Spain* 32 E2
La Almarcha, *Spain* 32 F2
La Almunia de Doña
  Godina, *Spain* 32 D3
La Asunción, *Venezuela* .. 124 A6
La Baie, *Canada* 103 C5
La Banda, *Argentina* 126 B3
La Bañeza, *Spain* 34 C5
La Barca, *Mexico* 118 C4
La Barge, *U.S.A.* 114 E8
La Bastide-Puylaurent,
  France 20 D7
La Baule-Escoublac, *France* 18 E4
La Belle, *U.S.A.* 109 M5
La Biche →, *Canada* 104 B4
La Biche, L., *Canada* 104 C6
La Bisbal d'Empordà, *Spain* 32 D8
La Bomba, *Mexico* 118 A1
La Bresse, *France* 19 D13
La Bureba, *Spain* 34 C7
La Calera, *Chile* 126 C1
La Campiña, *Spain* 35 H6
La Canal = Sa Canal, *Spain* 37 C7

La Cañiza = A Cañiza,
  Spain 34 C2
La Canourgue, *France* 20 D7
La Capelle, *France* 19 C10
La Carlota, *Argentina* 126 C3
La Carlota, *Phil.* 61 F5
La Carlota, *Spain* 35 H6
La Carolina, *Spain* 35 G7
La Cavalerie, *France* 20 D7
La Ceiba, *Honduras* 120 C2
La Chaise-Dieu, *France* ... 20 C7
La Chapelle d'Angillon,
  France 19 E9
La Chapelle-St-Luc, *France* 19 D11
La Chapelle-sur-Erdre,
  France 18 E5
La Charité-sur-Loire, *France* 19 E10
La Chartre-sur-le-Loir,
  France 18 E7
La Châtaigneraie, *France* .. 20 B3
La Châtre, *France* 19 F9
La Chaux-de-Fonds, *Switz.* 25 H2
La Chorrera, *Panama* 120 E4
La Ciotat, *France* 21 E9
La Clayette, *France* 19 F11
La Cocha, *Argentina* 126 B2
La Concepción = Ri-Aba,
  Eq. Guin. 83 E6
La Concepción, *Panama* .. 120 E3
La Concordia, *Mexico* 119 D6
La Coruña = A Coruña,
  Spain 34 B2
La Coruña □, *Spain* 34 B2
La Côte-St-André, *France* . 21 C9
La Courtine-le-Trucq, *France* 20 C6
La Crau, *Bouches-du-Rhône,*
  France 21 E8
La Crau, *Var, France* 21 E10
La Crescent, *U.S.A.* 112 D9
La Crete, *Canada* 104 B5
La Crosse, *Kans., U.S.A.* . 112 F5
La Crosse, *Wis., U.S.A.* .. 112 D9
La Cruz, *Costa Rica* 120 D2
La Cruz, *Mexico* 118 C3
La Désirade, *Guadeloupe* . 121 C7
La Escondida, *Mexico* 118 C5
La Esmeralda, *Paraguay* .. 126 A3
La Esperanza, *Cuba* 120 B3
La Esperanza, *Honduras* .. 120 D2
La Estrada = A Estrada,
  Spain 34 C2
La Faouët, *France* 18 D3
La Fayette, *U.S.A.* 109 H3
La Fé, *Cuba* 120 B3
La Fère, *France* 19 C10
La Ferté-Bernard, *France* . 18 D7
La Ferté-Gaucher, *France* . 19 D10
La Ferté-Macé, *France* ... 18 D6
La Ferté-St-Aubin, *France* . 19 E8
La Ferté-sous-Jouarre,
  France 19 D10
La Ferté-Vidame, *France* .. 18 D7
La Flèche, *France* 18 E6
La Follette, *U.S.A.* 109 G3
La Fregeneda, *Spain* 34 E4
La Fuente de San Esteban,
  Spain 34 E4
La Gacilly, *France* 18 E4
La Gineta, *Spain* 33 F2
La Grand-Combe, *France* . 21 D8
La Grande, *U.S.A.* 114 D4
La Grande →, *Canada* ... 102 B5
La Grande Deux, Rés.,
  Canada 102 B4
La Grande-Motte, *France* . 21 E8
La Grande Quatre, Rés.,
  Canada 102 B5
La Grande Trois, Rés.,
  Canada 102 B4
La Grange, *Calif., U.S.A.* . 116 H6
La Grange, *Ga., U.S.A.* .. 109 J3
La Grange, *Ky., U.S.A.* .. 108 F3
La Grange, *Tex., U.S.A.* . 113 L6
La Grave, *France* 21 C10
La Guaira, *Venezuela* 124 A5
La Guardia = A Guarda,
  Spain 34 D2
La Gudiña = A Gudiña,
  Spain 34 C3
La Guerche-de-Bretagne,
  France 18 E5
La Guerche-sur-l'Aubois,
  France 19 F9
La Habana, *Cuba* 120 B3
La Haye-du-Puits, *France* . 18 C5
La Horra, *Spain* 34 D7
La Independencia, *Mexico* . 119 D6
La Isabela, *Dom. Rep.* ... 121 C5
La Junta, *U.S.A.* 113 F3
La Laguna, *Canary Is.* ... 37 F3
La Libertad, *Guatemala* .. 120 C1
La Libertad, *Mexico* 118 B2
La Ligua, *Chile* 126 C1
La Línea de la Concepción,
  Spain 35 J5
La Loche, *Canada* 105 B7
La Londe-les-Maures, *France* 21 E10
La Lora, *Spain* 34 C7
La Loupe, *France* 18 D8
La Louvière, *Belgium* 17 D4
La Machine, *France* 19 F10
La Maddalena, *Italy* 30 A2
La Malbaie, *Canada* 103 C5
La Mancha, *Spain* 33 F2
La Mariña, *Spain* 34 B3
La Martre, L., *Canada* ... 104 A5
La Mesa, *U.S.A.* 117 N9
La Misión, *Mexico* 118 A1
La Mothe-Achard, *France* . 18 F5
La Motte, *France* 21 D10

La Motte-Chalançon, *France* 21 D9
La Motte-Servolex, *France* . 21 C9
La Moure, *U.S.A.* 112 B5
La Muela, *Spain* 32 D3
La Mure, *France* 21 D9
La Negra, *Chile* 126 A1
La Oliva, *Canary Is.* 37 F6
La Orotava, *Canary Is.* ... 37 F3
La Oroya, *Peru* 124
La Pacaudière, *France* 19 F10
La Palma, *Canary Is.* 37 F2
La Palma, *Panama* 120 E4
La Palma del Condado,
  Spain 35 H4
La Paloma, *Chile* 126 C1
La Pampa □, *Argentina* .. 126 D2
La Paragua, *Venezuela* ... 124 B6
La Paz, *Entre Ríos,*
  Argentina 126 C4
La Paz, *San Luis, Argentina* 126 C2
La Paz, *Bolivia* 124 G5
La Paz, *Honduras* 120 D2
La Paz, *Mexico* 118 C2
La Paz, *Phil.* 61 D4
La Paz Centro, *Nic.* 120 D2
La Pedrera, *Colombia* 124 D5
La Pérade, *Canada* 103 C5
La Perouse Str., *Asia* 54 B11
La Pesca, *Mexico* 119 C5
La Piedad, *Mexico* 118 C4
La Pine, *U.S.A.* 114 E3
La Plata, *Argentina* 126 D4
La Pobla de Lillet, *Spain* .. 32 C6
La Pocatière, *Canada* 103 C5
La Pola de Gordón, *Spain* . 34 C5
La Porta, *France* 21 F13
La Porte, *Ind., U.S.A.* ... 108 E2
La Porte, *Tex., U.S.A.* ... 113 L7
La Presanella, *Italy* 28 B7
La Puebla = Sa Pobla, *Spain* 32 F8
La Puebla de Cazalla, *Spain* 35 H5
La Puebla de los Infantes,
  Spain 35 H5
La Puebla de Montalbán,
  Spain 34 F6
La Puebla del Río, *Spain* .. 35 H4
La Puerta de Segura, *Spain* 35 G8
La Purísima, *Mexico* 118 B2
La Push, *U.S.A.* 116 C2
La Quiaca, *Argentina* 126 A2
La Réole, *France* 20 D3
La Restinga, *Canary Is.* ... 37 G2
La Rioja, *Argentina* 126 B2
La Rioja □, *Argentina* ... 126 B2
La Rioja □, *Spain* 32 C2
La Robla, *Spain* 34 C5
La Roche-Bernard, *France* . 18 E4
La Roche-Canillac, *France* . 20 C5
La Roche-en-Ardenne,
  Belgium 17 D5
La Roche-sur-Foron, *France* 19 F13
La Roche-sur-Yon, *France* . 18 F5
La Rochefoucauld, *France* . 20 C4
La Rochelle, *France* 20 B2
La Roda, *Spain* 33 F2
La Roda de Andalucía,
  Spain 35 H6
La Romana, *Dom. Rep.* .. 121 C6
La Ronge, *Canada* 105 B7
La Rumorosa, *Mexico* ... 117 N10
La Sabina = Sa Savina,
  Spain 37 C7
La Sagra, *Spain* 33 H2
La Salle, *U.S.A.* 112 E10
La Sanabria, *Spain* 34 C4
La Santa, *Canary Is.* 37 E6
La Sarre, *Canada* 102 C4
La Scie, *Canada* 103 C8
La Selva, *Spain* 32 C7
La Selva Beach, *U.S.A.* ... 116 J5
La Selva del Camp, *Spain* . 32 D6
La Serena, *Chile* 126 B1
La Serena, *Spain* 35 G5
La Seu d'Urgell, *Spain* ... 32 C6
La Seyne-sur-Mer, *France* . 21 E9
La Sila, *Italy* 31 C9
La Solana, *Spain* 35 G7
La Souterraine, *France* 19 F8
La Spézia, *Italy* 28 D6
La Suze-sur-Sarthe, *France* 18 E7
La Tagua, *Colombia* 124 C4
La Teste, *France* 20 D2
La Tortuga, *Venezuela* ... 121 D6
La Tour-du-Pin, *France* ... 21 C9
La Tranche-sur-Mer, *France* 18 F5
La Tremblade, *France* 20 C2
La Tuque, *Canada* 102 C5
La Unión, *Chile* 128 C2
La Unión, *El Salv.* 120 D2
La Unión, *Mexico* 118 D4
La Unión, *Spain* 33 H4
La Urbana, *Venezuela* 124 B5
La Vall d'Uixó, *Spain* 32 F4
La Vecilla de Curveño, *Spain* 34 C5
La Vega, *Dom. Rep.* 121 C5
La Vela de Coro, *Venezuela* 124 A5
La Veleta, *Spain* 35 H7
La Ventura, *Mexico* 118 C4
La Voulte-sur-Rhône, *France* 21 D8
Laa an der Thaya, *Austria* . 27 C9
Laaber, Grosse →,
  Germany 25 G8
Laatzen, *Germany* 24 C5
Laba →, *Russia* 49 H4
Labason, *Phil.* 61 G5
Labastide-Murat, *France* .. 20 D5
Labastide-Rouairoux, *France* 20 E6
Labbézenga, *Mali* 83 B5

Labe = Elbe →, Europe . . 24 B4
Labé, Guinea 82 C2
Laberge, L., Canada 104 A1
Labin, Croatia 29 C11
Labis, Malaysia 65 L4
Łabiszyn, Poland 45 F4
Labo, Phil. 61 D5
Laboe, Germany 24 A6
Laborec →, Slovak Rep. .. 27 C14
Labouheyre, France 20 D3
Laboulaye, Argentina 126 C3
Labrador, Canada 103 B7
Labrador City, Canada ... 103 B6
Labrador Sea, Atl. Oc. ... 101 C14
Lábrea, Brazil 124 E6
Labrède, France 20 D3
Labruguière, France 20 E6
Labuan, Malaysia 62 C5
Labuan, Pulau, Malaysia .. 62 C5
Labuha, Indonesia 63 E7
Labuhan, Indonesia 63 G11
Labuhanbajo, Indonesia .. 63 F6
Labuk, Telok, Malaysia ... 62 C5
Labyrinth, L., Australia ... 95 E2
Labytnangi, Russia 50 C7
Laç, Albania 40 E3
Lac Bouchette, Canada ... 103 C5
Lac Édouard, Canada 102 C5
Lac la Biche, Canada 104 C6
Lac la Martre = Wha Ti,
  Canada 100 B8
Lac La Ronge Prov. Park,
  Canada 105 B7
Lac-Mégantic, Canada 103 C5
Lac Seul, Res., Canada ... 102 B1
Lac Thien, Vietnam 64 F7
Lacanau, France 20 D2
Lacanau, Étang de, France . 20 D2
Lacantúm →, Mexico 119 D6
Lacara →, Spain 35 G4
Lacaune, France 20 E6
Lacaune, Mts. de, France . 20 E6
Laccadive Is. =
  Lakshadweep Is., Ind. Oc. 52 H11
Lacepede B., Australia 95 F2
Lacepede Is., Australia 92 C3
Lacerdónia, Mozam. 87 F4
Lacey, U.S.A. 116 C4
Lachhmangarh, India 68 F6
Lachi, Pakistan 68 C4
Lachine, Canada 102 C5
Lachlan →, Australia 95 E3
Lachute, Canada 102 C5
Lackawanna, U.S.A. 110 D6
Lackawaxen, U.S.A. 111 E10
Lacolle, Canada 111 A11
Lacombe, Canada 104 C6
Lacona, U.S.A. 111 C8
Láconi, Italy 30 C2
Laconia, U.S.A. 111 C13
Lacq, France 20 E3
Ladakh Ra., India 69 C8
Lądek-Zdrój, Poland 45 H3
Ládhon →, Greece 38 D3
Ladik, Turkey 72 B6
Ladismith, S. Africa 88 E3
Ladíspoli, Italy 29 G9
Lādīz, Iran 71 D9
Ladnun, India 68 F6
Ladoga, L. = Ladozhskoye
  Ozero, Russia 46 B6
Ladozhskoye Ozero, Russia 46 B6
Lady Elliott I., Australia .. 94 C5
Lady Grey, S. Africa 88 E4
Ladybrand, S. Africa 88 D4
Ladysmith, Canada 104 D4
Ladysmith, S. Africa 89 D4
Ladysmith, U.S.A. 112 C9
Lae, Papua N. G. 96 H6
Laem Ngop, Thailand 65 F4
Laem Pho, Thailand 65 J3
Læsø, Denmark 11 G5
Læsø Rende, Denmark ... 11 G4
Lafayette, Colo., U.S.A. .. 112 F2
Lafayette, Ind., U.S.A. ... 108 E2
Lafayette, La., U.S.A. 113 K9
Lafayette, Tenn., U.S.A. .. 109 G2
Laferte →, Canada 104 A5
Lafia, Nigeria 83 D6
Lafiagi, Nigeria 83 D6
Lafleche, Canada 105 D7
Lafon, Sudan 81 F3
Lagan, Sweden 11 H7
Lagan →, Sweden 11 H6
Lagan →, U.K. 15 B6
Lagarfljót →, Iceland 8 D6
Lage, Germany 24 D4
Lågen →, Oppland, Norway 9 F14
Lågen →, Vestfold, Norway 9 G14
Lägerdorf, Germany 24 B5
Laghouat, Algeria 78 B6
Lagnieu, France 21 C9
Lagny-sur-Marne, France . 19 D9
Lago, Italy 31 C9
Lagôa, Portugal 35 H2
Lagoa Vermelha, Brazil .. 127 B5
Lagoaça, Portugal 34 D4
Lagodekhi, Georgia 49 K8
Lagónegro, Italy 31 B8
Lagonoy G., Phil. 61 E5
Lagos, Nigeria 83 D5
Lagos, Portugal 35 H2
Lagos →, Nigeria 83 D5
Lagos de Moreno, Mexico 118 C4
Lagrange, Australia 92 C3
Lagrange B., Australia ... 92 C3
Laguardia, Spain 32 C2
Laguépie, France 20 D5
Laguna, Brazil 127 B6
Laguna, U.S.A. 115 J10

Laguna Beach, U.S.A. 117 M9
Laguna de Duera, Spain .. 34 D6
Laguna Limpia, Argentina . 126 B4
Laguna Madre, U.S.A. ... 119 B5
Lagunas, Chile 126 A2
Lagunas, Peru 124 E3
Lahad Datu, Malaysia 63 C5
Lahad Datu, Teluk, Malaysia 63 D5
Lahan Sai, Thailand 64 E4
Lahanam, Laos 64 D5
Lahar, India 69 F8
Laharpur, India 69 F9
Lahat, Indonesia 62 E2
Lahewa, Indonesia 62 D1
Lāhījān, Iran 71 B6
Lahn →, Germany 25 E3
Lahnstein, Germany 25 E3
Laholm, Sweden 11 H7
Laholmsbukten, Sweden .. 11 H6
Lahore, Pakistan 68 D6
Lahr, Germany 25 G3
Lahri, Pakistan 68 E3
Lahti, Finland 9 F21
Lahtis = Lahti, Finland ... 9 F21
Laï, Chad 79 G9
Lai Chau, Vietnam 58 F4
Lai'an, China 59 A12
Laibin, China 58 F7
Laifeng, China 58 C7
L'Aigle, France 18 D7
Laignes, France 19 E11
L'Aiguillon-sur-Mer, France 20 B2
Laila = Laylá, Si. Arabia .. 74 C4
Laingsburg, S. Africa 88 E3
Lainio älv →, Sweden 8 C20
Lairg, U.K. 14 C4
Laishui, China 56 E8
Laissac, France 20 D6
Láives, Italy 29 B8
Laiwu, China 57 F9
Laixi, China 57 F11
Laiyang, China 57 F11
Laiyuan, China 56 E8
Laizhou, China 57 F10
Laizhou Wan, China 57 F10
Laja →, Mexico 118 C4
Lajere, Nigeria 83 C7
Lajes, Brazil 127 B5
Lajkovac, Serbia, Yug. ... 40 B4
Lak Sao, Laos 64 C5
Lakaband, Pakistan 68 D3
Lakamané, Mali 82 C3
Lake Alpine, U.S.A. 116 G7
Lake Andes, U.S.A. 112 D5
Lake Arthur, U.S.A. 113 K8
Lake Cargelligo, Australia . 95 E4
Lake Charles, U.S.A. 113 K8
Lake City, Colo., U.S.A. .. 115 G10
Lake City, Fla., U.S.A. ... 109 K4
Lake City, Mich., U.S.A. .. 108 C3
Lake City, Minn., U.S.A. .. 112 C8
Lake City, Pa., U.S.A. 110 D4
Lake City, S.C., U.S.A. ... 109 J6
Lake Cowichan, Canada .. 104 D4
Lake District, U.K. 12 C4
Lake Elsinore, U.S.A. 117 M9
Lake George, U.S.A. 111 C11
Lake Grace, Australia 93 F2
Lake Harbour = Kimmirut,
  Canada 101 B13
Lake Havasu City, U.S.A. . 117 L12
Lake Hughes, U.S.A. 117 L8
Lake Isabella, U.S.A. 117 K8
Lake Jackson, U.S.A. 113 L7
Lake Junction, U.S.A. ... 114 D8
Lake King, Australia 93 F2
Lake Lenore, Canada 105 C8
Lake Louise, Canada 104 C5
Lake Mead National
  Recreation Area, U.S.A. 117 K12
Lake Mills, U.S.A. 112 D8
Lake Placid, U.S.A. 111 B11
Lake Pleasant, U.S.A. ... 111 C10
Lake Providence, U.S.A. . 113 J9
Lake St. Peter, Canada ... 110 A6
Lake Superior Prov. Park,
  Canada 102 C3
Lake Village, U.S.A. 113 J9
Lake Wales, U.S.A. 109 M5
Lake Worth, U.S.A. 109 M5
Lakefield, Canada 102 D4
Lakehurst, U.S.A. 111 F10
Lakeland, Australia 94 B3
Lakeland, U.S.A. 109 M5
Lakemba, Fiji 91 D9
Lakeport, Calif., U.S.A. .. 116 F4
Lakeport, Mich., U.S.A. .. 110 C2
Lakes Entrance, Australia . 95 F4
Lakeside, Ariz., U.S.A. ... 115 J9
Lakeside, Calif., U.S.A. .. 117 N10
Lakeside, Ohio, U.S.A. ... 112 D3
Lakeside, Ohio, U.S.A. ... 110 E2
Lakeview, U.S.A. 114 E3
Lakeville, U.S.A. 112 C8
Lakewood, Colo., U.S.A. . 112 F2
Lakewood, N.J., U.S.A. .. 111 F10
Lakewood, N.Y., U.S.A. .. 110 D5
Lakewood, Ohio, U.S.A. .. 110 E3
Lakewood, Wash., U.S.A. . 116 C4
Lakha, India 68 F4
Lakhania, Greece 36 D9
Lakhimpur, India 69 F9
Lakhnadon, India 69 H8
Lakhpat, India 68 H3
Lakhonpheng, Laos 64 E5
Läki, Azerbaijan 49 K8
Lakin, U.S.A. 113 G4
Lakitusaki →, Canada ... 102 B3
Lakki, Pakistan 68 C4
Lákkoi, Greece 36 D5

Lakonía □, Greece 38 E4
Lakonikós Kólpos, Greece . 38 E4
Lakor, Indonesia 63 F7
Lakota, Ivory C. 82 D3
Lakota, U.S.A. 112 A5
Laksar, India 68 E8
Laksefjorden, Norway ... 8 A22
Lakselv, Norway 8 A21
Lakshadweep Is., Ind. Oc. . 52 H11
Lakshmanpur, India 69 H10
Lakshmikantapur, India .. 69 H13
Lala Ghat, India 67 G18
Lala Musa, Pakistan 68 C5
Lalago, Tanzania 86 C3
Lalapanzi, Zimbabwe ... 87 F3
Lalapaşa, Turkey 41 E10
Lalbenque, France 20 D5
L'Albufera, Spain 33 F4
Lalganj, India 69 G11
Lalgola, India 69 G13
Lālī, Iran 71 C6
Lalibela, Ethiopia 81 E4
Lalin, China 57 B14
Lalín, Spain 34 C2
Lalin He →, China 57 B13
Lalinde, France 20 D4
Lalitapur = Patan, Nepal . 67 F14
Lalitpur, India 69 G8
Lalkua, India 69 E8
Lalsot, India 68 F7
Lam, Vietnam 64 B6
Lam Pao Res., Thailand .. 64 D4
Lama Kara, Togo 83 D5
Lamaing, Burma 67 M20
Lamar, Colo., U.S.A. 112 F3
Lamar, Mo., U.S.A. 113 G7
Lamas, Peru 124 E3
Lamastre, France 21 D8
Lambach, Austria 26 C6
Lamballe, France 18 D4
Lambaréné, Gabon 84 E2
Lambasa, Fiji 91 C8
Lambay I., Ireland 15 C5
Lambert Glacier, Antarctica 5 D6
Lambert's Bay, S. Africa .. 88 E2
Lambesc, France 21 E9
Lambeth, Canada 110 D3
Lambi Kyun, Burma 65 G2
Lámbia, Greece 38 D3
Lambomakondro, Madag. 89 C7
Lambro →, Italy 28 C6
Lame, Nigeria 83 C6
Lame Deer, U.S.A. 114 D10
Lamego, Portugal 34 D3
Lamèque, Canada 103 C7
Lameroo, Australia 95 F3
Lamesa, U.S.A. 113 J4
Lamía, Greece 38 C4
Lamitan, Phil. 61 H5
Lamon B., Phil. 61 D5
Lamont, Canada 104 C6
Lamont, Calif., U.S.A. ... 117 K8
Lamont, Wyo., U.S.A. ... 114 E10
Lamotte-Beuvron, France 19 E9
Lampa, Peru 124 G4
Lampang, Thailand 64 C2
Lampasas, U.S.A. 113 K5
Lampazos de Naranjo,
  Mexico 118 B4
Lampedusa, Italy 30 G5
Lampeter, U.K. 13 E3
Lampman, Canada 105 D8
Lamprechtshausen, Austria . 26 D5
Lampung □, Indonesia ... 62 F2
Lamta, India 69 H9
Lamu, Kenya 86 C5
Lamy, U.S.A. 115 J11
Lan Xian, China 56 E6
Lan Yu = Hungt'ou Hsü,
  Taiwan 59 F13
Lanai, U.S.A. 106 H16
Lanak La, India 69 B8
Lanak'o Shank'ou = Lanak
  La, India 69 B8
Lanao, L., Phil. 61 H6
Lanark, Canada 111 A8
Lanark, U.K. 14 F5
Lancang, China 58 F2
Lancang Jiang →, China . 58 G3
Lancashire □, U.K. 12 D5
Lancaster, Canada 111 A10
Lancaster, U.K. 12 C5
Lancaster, Calif., U.S.A. .. 117 L8
Lancaster, Ky., U.S.A. ... 108 G3
Lancaster, N.H., U.S.A. .. 111 B13
Lancaster, N.Y., U.S.A. .. 110 D6
Lancaster, Ohio, U.S.A. .. 108 F4
Lancaster, Pa., U.S.A. ... 111 F8
Lancaster, S.C., U.S.A. ... 109 H5
Lancaster, Wis., U.S.A. .. 112 D9
Lancaster Sd., Canada ... 101 A11
Lancelin, Australia 93 F2
Lanchow = Lanzhou, China 56 F2
Lanciano, Italy 29 F11
Lancun, China 57 F11
Łańcut, Poland 45 H9
Landau, Bayern, Germany 25 G8
Landau, Rhld.-Pfz., Germany 25 F4
Landeck, Austria 26 D3
Lander, U.S.A. 114 E9
Lander →, Australia 92 D5
Landerneau, France 18 D2
Landeryd, Sweden 11 G7
Landes □, France 20 D3
Landes □, France 20 E3
Landete, Spain 32 F3
Landi Kotal, Pakistan ... 68 B4
Landisburg, U.S.A. 110 F7

Landivisiau, France 18 D2
Landquart, Switz. 25 J5
Landrecies, France 19 B10
Land's End, U.K. 13 G2
Landsberg, Germany 25 G6
Landsborough Cr. →,
  Australia 94 C3
Landsbro, Sweden 11 G8
Landshut, Germany 25 G8
Landskrona, Sweden 11 J6
Landstuhl, Germany 25 F3
Landvetter, Sweden 11 G6
Lanesboro, U.S.A. 111 E9
Lanester, France 18 E3
Lanett, U.S.A. 109 J3
Lang Qua, Vietnam 64 A5
Lang Shan, China 56 D4
Lang Son, Vietnam 58 G6
Lang Suan, Thailand 65 H2
Langå, Denmark 11 H3
La'nga Co, China 67 D12
Lángádhás, Greece 40 F7
Langádhia, Greece 38 D4
Langano, L., Ethiopia ... 81 F4
Langar, Iran 71 C9
Langara I., Canada 104 C2
Långås, Sweden 11 H6
Langdai, China 58 D5
Langdon, U.S.A. 112 A5
Länge Jan = Ölands södra
  udde, Sweden 11 H10
Langeac, France 20 C7
Langeais, France 18 E7
Langeb Baraka →, Sudan 80 D4
Langeberg, S. Africa 88 E3
Langeberge, S. Africa ... 88 D3
Langeland, Denmark 11 K4
Langelands Bælt, Denmark . 11 K4
Langen, Hessen, Germany . 25 F4
Langen, Niedersachsen,
  Germany 24 B4
Langenburg, Canada 105 C8
Langeneß, Germany 24 A4
Langenlois, Austria 26 C8
Langeoog, Germany 24 B3
Langeskov, Denmark ... 11 J4
Länghem, Sweden 11 G7
Langhirano, Italy 28 D7
Langholm, U.K. 14 F5
Langjökull, Iceland 8 D3
Langkawi, Pulau, Malaysia 65 J2
Langklip, S. Africa 88 D3
Langkon, Malaysia 62 C5
Langlade, St.- P. & M. ... 103 C8
Langley, Canada 116 A4
Langnau, Switz. 25 J3
Langogne, France 20 D7
Langon, France 20 D3
Langøya, Norway 8 B16
Langreo, Spain 34 B5
Langres, France 19 E12
Langres, Plateau de, France 19 E12
Langsa, Indonesia 62 D1
Långsele, Sweden 10 A11
Långshyttan, Sweden ... 10 D10
Langtang, Nigeria 83 D6
Langtry, U.S.A. 113 L4
Langu, Thailand 65 J2
Languedoc, France 20 E7
Languedoc-Roussillon □,
  France 20 E6
Langxi, China 59 B12
Langxiangzhen, China .. 56 E9
Langzhong, China 58 B5
Lanigan, Canada 105 C7
Lankao, China 56 G8
Länkäran, Azerbaijan ... 71 B6
Lanmeur, France 18 D3
Lannemezan, France ... 20 E4
Lannilis, France 18 D2
Lannion, France 18 D3
L'Annonciation, Canada . 102 C5
Lanping, China 58 D2
Lansdale, U.S.A. 111 F9
Lansdowne, Australia ... 95 E5
Lansdowne, Canada 111 B8
Lansdowne, India 69 E8
Lansdowne House, Canada 102 B2
L'Anse, Mich., U.S.A. ... 108 B1
L'Anse, U.S.A. 112 B10
L'Anse au Loup, Canada . 103 B8
L'Anse aux Meadows,
  Canada 103 B8
Lansford, U.S.A. 111 F9
Lanshan, China 59 E9
Lansing, U.S.A. 108 D3
Lanslebourg-Mont-Cenis,
  France 21 C10
Lanta Yai, Ko, Thailand .. 65 J2
Lantewa, Nigeria 83 C7
Lantian, China 56 G5
Lanus, Argentina 126 C4
Lanusei, Italy 30 C2
Lanuza, Phil. 61 G7
Lanxi, China 59 C12
Lanzarote, Canary Is. ... 37 F6
Lanzhou, China 56 F2
Lao →, Italy 31 C8
Lao Bao, Laos 64 D6
Lao Cai, Vietnam 58 F4
Laoag, Phil. 61 B4
Laoang, Phil. 61 E6
Laoha He →, China 57 C11
Laohekou, China 59 A8
Laois □, Ireland 15 D4
Laon, France 19 C10
Laona, U.S.A. 108 C1
Laos ■, Asia 64 D5
Lapa, Brazil 127 B6

Lapai, Nigeria 83 D6
Lapalisse, France 19 F10
Lapeer, U.S.A. 108 D4
Lapeyrade, France 20 D3
Lapithos, Cyprus 36 D12
Lapland = Lappland, Europe 8 B21
Laporte, U.S.A. 111 E8
Lapovo, Serbia, Yug. 40 B5
Lappeenranta, Finland .. 9 F23
Lappland, Europe 8 B21
Laprida, Argentina 126 D3
Lapseki, Turkey 41 F10
Laptev Sea, Russia 51 B13
Lapua, Finland 8 E20
Lăpuş →, Romania 43 C8
Lăpuş, Munţii, Romania . 43 C8
Lăpuşna, Moldova 43 D13
Łapy, Poland 45 F9
Laqiya Arba'in, Sudan .. 80 C2
Laqiya Umran, Sudan ... 80 D2
L'Aquila, Italy 29 F10
Lār, Āzarbājān-e Sharqī,
  Iran 70 B5
Lār, Fārs, Iran 71 E7
Larabanga, Ghana 82 D4
Laragne-Montéglin, France 21 D9
Laramie, U.S.A. 112 E2
Laramie →, U.S.A. 114 F11
Laramie Mts., U.S.A. ... 112 E2
Laranjeiras do Sul, Brazil . 127 B5
Larantuka, Indonesia ... 63 F6
Larat, Indonesia 63 F8
L'Arbresle, France 21 C8
Lärbro, Sweden 11 G12
Larde, Mozam. 87 F4
Larder Lake, Canada ... 102 C4
Lardhos, Ákra = Líndhos,
  Ákra, Greece 36 C10
Lardhos, Órmos, Greece . 36 C10
Laredo, Spain 34 B7
Laredo, U.S.A. 113 M5
Laredo Sd., Canada 104 C3
Largentière, France 21 D8
L'Argentière-la-Bessée,
  France 21 D10
Largo, U.S.A. 109 M4
Largs, U.K. 14 F4
Lari, Italy 28 E7
Lariang, Indonesia 63 E5
Larimore, U.S.A. 112 B6
Lārīn, Iran 71 C7
Larino, Italy 29 G11
Lárisa, Greece 38 B4
Lárisa □, Greece 38 B4
Larkana, Pakistan 68 F3
Larnaca, Cyprus 36 E12
Larnaca Bay, Cyprus ... 36 E12
Larne, U.K. 15 B6
Larned, U.S.A. 112 F5
Laroquebrou, France ... 20 D6
Larose, U.S.A. 113 L9
Larrimah, Australia 92 C5
Larsen Ice Shelf, Antarctica 5 C17
Laruns, France 20 F3
Larvik, Norway 9 G14
Larzac, Causse du, France 20 E7
Las Alpujarras, Spain ... 33 J1
Las Animas, U.S.A. 112 F3
Las Anod, Somali Rep. . 74 F4
Las Arenas, Spain 34 B6
Las Aves, Is., W. Indies . 121 C7
Las Brenãs, Argentina .. 126 B3
Las Cabezas de San Juan,
  Spain 35 J5
Las Cejas, Argentina ... 128 B4
Las Chimeneas, Mexico . 117 N10
Las Cruces, U.S.A. 115 K10
Las Flores, Argentina ... 126 D4
Las Heras, Argentina ... 126 C2
Las Lajas, Argentina ... 128 D2
Las Lomitas, Argentina . 126 A3
Las Marismas, Spain ... 35 H4
Las Minas, Spain 33 G3
Las Navas de la Concepción,
  Spain 35 H5
Las Navas del Marqués,
  Spain 34 E6
Las Palmas, Argentina .. 126 B4
Las Palmas, Canary Is. .. 37 F4
Las Palmas →, Mexico .. 117 N10
Las Pedroñeras, Spain .. 33 F2
Las Piedras, Uruguay ... 127 C4
Las Pipinas, Argentina .. 126 D4
Las Plumas, Argentina .. 128 E3
Las Rosas, Argentina ... 126 C3
Las Rozas, Spain 34 E7
Las Tablas, Panama 120 E3
Las Termas, Argentina .. 126 B3
Las Toscas, Argentina .. 126 B4
Las Truchas, Argentina .. 118 D4
Las Varillas, Argentina .. 126 C3
Las Vegas, N. Mex., U.S.A. 115 J11
Las Vegas, Nev., U.S.A. . 117 J11
Lasarte, Spain 32 B2
Lashburn, Canada 105 C7
Lashio, Burma 67 H20
Lashkar, India 68 F8
Lasín, Poland 44 E6
Lasíthi, Greece 36 D7
Lasíthi □, Greece 36 D7
Lāsjerd, Iran 71 C7
Lask, Poland 45 G6
Łaskarzew, Poland 45 G8
Laško, Slovenia 29 B12
Lassay-les-Châteaux, France 18 D6
Lassen Pk., U.S.A. 114 F3
Lassen Volcanic National
  Park, U.S.A. 114 F3
Last Mountain L., Canada 105 C7
Lastchance Cr. →, U.S.A. 116 E5

Lastoursville, *Gabon* ... 84 E2
Lastovo, *Croatia* ... 29 F13
Lastovski Kanal, *Croatia* ... 29 F14
Lat Yao, *Thailand* ... 64 E2
Latacunga, *Ecuador* ... 124 D3
Latakia = Al Lādhiqīyah, *Syria* ... 70 C2
Latchford, *Canada* ... 102 C4
Latehar, *India* ... 69 H11
Laterza, *Italy* ... 31 B9
Latham, *Australia* ... 93 E2
Lathen, *Germany* ... 24 C3
Lathi, *India* ... 68 F4
Lathrop Wells, *U.S.A.* ... 117 J10
Latiano, *Italy* ... 31 B10
Latina, *Italy* ... 30 A5
Latisana, *Italy* ... 29 C10
Latium = Lazio □, *Italy* ... 29 F9
Laton, *U.S.A.* ... 116 J7
Latorytsya →, *Slovak Rep.* ... 27 C14
Latouche Treville, C., *Australia* ... 92 C3
Latrobe, *Australia* ... 94 G4
Latrobe, *U.S.A.* ... 110 F5
Latrónico, *Italy* ... 31 B9
Latvia ■, *Europe* ... 9 H20
Lau, *Nigeria* ... 83 D7
Lau Group, *Fiji* ... 91 C9
Lauchhammer, *Germany* ... 24 D9
Lauda-Königshofen, *Germany* ... 25 F5
Lauenburg, *Germany* ... 24 B6
Lauf, *Germany* ... 25 F7
Laughlin, *U.S.A.* ... 115 J6
Laujar de Andarax, *Spain* ... 33 H2
Laukaa, *Finland* ... 9 E21
Launceston, *Australia* ... 94 G4
Launceston, *U.K.* ... 13 G3
Laune →, *Ireland* ... 15 D2
Launglon Bok, *Burma* ... 64 F1
Laupheim, *Germany* ... 25 G5
Laura, *Australia* ... 94 B3
Laureana di Borrello, *Italy* ... 31 D9
Laurel, *Miss., U.S.A.* ... 113 K10
Laurel, *Mont., U.S.A.* ... 114 D9
Laurencekirk, *U.K.* ... 14 E6
Laurens, *U.S.A.* ... 109 H4
Laurentian Plateau, *Canada* ... 103 B6
Lauria, *Italy* ... 31 B8
Laurie L., *Canada* ... 105 B8
Laurinburg, *U.S.A.* ... 109 H6
Laurium, *U.S.A.* ... 108 B1
Lausanne, *Switz.* ... 25 J2
Laut, *Indonesia* ... 65 K6
Laut, Pulau, *Indonesia* ... 62 E5
Laut Kecil, Kepulauan, *Indonesia* ... 62 E5
Lauterbach, *Germany* ... 24 E5
Lauterecken, *Germany* ... 25 F3
Lautoka, *Fiji* ... 91 C7
Lauzès, *France* ... 20 D5
Laval, *France* ... 18 D6
Lavalle, *Argentina* ... 126 B2
Lavant Station, *Canada* ... 111 A8
Lāvar Meydān, *Iran* ... 71 D7
Lávara, *Greece* ... 41 E10
Lavardac, *France* ... 20 D4
Lavaur, *France* ... 20 E5
Lavelanet, *France* ... 20 F5
Lavello, *Italy* ... 31 A8
Laverton, *Australia* ... 93 E3
Lavis, *Italy* ... 28 B8
Lávkos, *Greece* ... 38 B5
Lavos, *Portugal* ... 34 E2
Lavradio, *Portugal* ... 35 G1
Lavras, *Brazil* ... 127 A7
Lavre, *Portugal* ... 35 G2
Lávrion, *Greece* ... 38 D6
Lávris, *Greece* ... 36 D6
Lavumisa, *Swaziland* ... 89 D5
Lawas, *Malaysia* ... 62 D5
Lawele, *Indonesia* ... 63 F6
Lawng Pit, *Burma* ... 67 G20
Lawqah, *Si. Arabia* ... 70 D4
Lawra, *Ghana* ... 82 C4
Lawrence, *N.Z.* ... 91 L2
Lawrence, *Kans., U.S.A.* ... 112 F7
Lawrence, *Mass., U.S.A.* ... 111 D13
Lawrenceburg, *Ind., U.S.A.* ... 108 F3
Lawrenceburg, *Tenn., U.S.A.* ... 109 H2
Lawrenceville, *Ga., U.S.A.* ... 109 J4
Lawrenceville, *Pa., U.S.A.* ... 110 E7
Laws, *U.S.A.* ... 116 H8
Lawton, *U.S.A.* ... 113 H5
Lawu, *Indonesia* ... 63 G14
Lawz, J. al, *Si. Arabia* ... 80 B4
Laxá, *Sweden* ... 11 F8
Laxford, L., *U.K.* ... 14 C3
Laxou, *France* ... 19 D13
Lay →, *France* ... 20 B2
Laylá, *Si. Arabia* ... 74 C4
Laylān, *Iraq* ... 70 C5
Layon →, *France* ... 18 E6
Layton, *U.S.A.* ... 114 F7
Laytonville, *U.S.A.* ... 114 G2
Lazarevac, *Serbia, Yug.* ... 40 B4
Lazarevskoye, *Russia* ... 49 J4
Lazarivo, *Madag.* ... 89 C8
Lazdijai, *Lithuania* ... 9 J20
Lazio □, *Italy* ... 29 F9
Lazo, *Moldova* ... 43 C13
Lazo, *Russia* ... 54 C6
Le Beausset, *France* ... 21 E9
Le Blanc, *France* ... 20 B5
Le Bleymard, *France* ... 20 D7
Le Bourgneuf-la-Fôret, *France* ... 18 D6
Le Bugue, *France* ... 20 D4

Le Canourgue = La Canourgue, *France* ... 20 D7
Le Cateau Cambrésis, *France* ... 19 B10
Le Caylar, *France* ... 20 E7
Le Chambon-Feugerolles, *France* ... 21 C8
Le Châtelet, *France* ... 19 F9
Le Chesne, *France* ... 19 C11
Le Cheylard, *France* ... 21 D8
Le Conquet, *France* ... 18 D2
Le Creusot, *France* ... 19 F11
Le Croisic, *France* ... 18 E4
Le Donjon, *France* ... 19 F10
Le Dorat, *France* ... 20 B5
Le François, *Martinique* ... 121 D7
Le Grand-Lucé, *France* ... 18 E7
Le Grand-Pressigny, *France* ... 18 F7
Le Grand-Quevilly, *France* ... 18 C8
Le Havre, *France* ... 18 C7
Le Lavandou, *France* ... 21 E10
Le Lion-d'Angers, *France* ... 18 E6
Le Louroux-Béconnais, *France* ... 18 E6
Le Luc, *France* ... 21 E10
Le Lude, *France* ... 18 E7
Le Mans, *France* ... 18 E7
Le Mars, *U.S.A.* ... 112 D6
Le Mayet-de-Montagne, *France* ... 19 F10
Le Mêle-sur-Sarthe, *France* ... 18 D7
Le Monastier-sur-Gazeille, *France* ... 20 D7
Le Monêtier-les-Bains, *France* ... 21 D10
Le Mont-Dore, *France* ... 20 C6
Le Mont-St-Michel, *France* ... 18 D5
Le Moule, *Guadeloupe* ... 121 C7
Le Muy, *France* ... 21 E10
Le Palais, *France* ... 18 E3
Le Perthus, *France* ... 20 F6
Le Puy-en-Velay, *France* ... 20 C7
Le Sueur, *U.S.A.* ... 112 C8
Le Teil, *France* ... 21 D8
Le Teilleul, *France* ... 18 D6
Le Theil, *France* ... 18 D7
Le Thillot, *France* ... 19 E13
Le Thuy, *Vietnam* ... 64 D6
Le Touquet-Paris-Plage, *France* ... 19 B8
Le Tréport, *France* ... 18 B8
Le Val-d'Ajol, *France* ... 19 E13
Le Verdon-sur-Mer, *France* ... 20 C2
Le Vigan, *France* ... 20 E7
Lea →, *U.K.* ... 13 F8
Leach, *Cambodia* ... 65 F4
Lead, *U.S.A.* ... 112 C3
Leader, *Canada* ... 105 C7
Leadville, *U.S.A.* ... 115 G10
Leaf →, *U.S.A.* ... 113 K10
Leaf Rapids, *Canada* ... 105 B9
Leamington, *Canada* ... 102 D3
Leamington, *U.S.A.* ... 114 G7
Leamington Spa = Royal Leamington Spa, *U.K.* ... 13 E6
Le'an, *China* ... 59 D10
Leandro Norte Alem, *Argentina* ... 127 B4
Leane, L., *Ireland* ... 15 D2
Learmonth, *Australia* ... 92 D1
Leask, *Canada* ... 105 C7
Leatherhead, *U.K.* ... 13 F7
Leavenworth, *Kans., U.S.A.* ... 112 F7
Leavenworth, *Wash., U.S.A.* ... 114 C3
Łeba, *Poland* ... 44 D4
Łeba →, *Poland* ... 44 D4
Lebach, *Germany* ... 25 F2
Lebak, *Phil.* ... 61 H6
Lebam, *U.S.A.* ... 116 D3
Lebane, *Serbia, Yug.* ... 40 D5
Lebanon, *Ind., U.S.A.* ... 108 E2
Lebanon, *Kans., U.S.A.* ... 112 F5
Lebanon, *Ky., U.S.A.* ... 108 G3
Lebanon, *Mo., U.S.A.* ... 113 G8
Lebanon, *N.H., U.S.A.* ... 111 C12
Lebanon, *Oreg., U.S.A.* ... 114 D2
Lebanon, *Pa., U.S.A.* ... 111 F8
Lebanon, *Tenn., U.S.A.* ... 109 G2
Lebanon ■, *Asia* ... 75 B5
Lebec, *U.S.A.* ... 117 L8
Lebedyan, *Russia* ... 47 F10
Lebedyn, *Ukraine* ... 47 G8
Lebel-sur-Quévillon, *Canada* ... 102 C4
Lebomboberge, *S. Africa* ... 89 C5
Łebork, *Poland* ... 44 D4
Lebrija, *Spain* ... 35 J4
Łebsko, Jezioro, *Poland* ... 44 D4
Lebu, *Chile* ... 126 D1
Leca da Palmeira, *Portugal* ... 34 D2
Lecce, *Italy* ... 31 B11
Lecco, *Italy* ... 28 C6
Lecco, L. di, *Italy* ... 28 C6
Lécera, *Spain* ... 32 D4
Lech, *Austria* ... 26 D3
Lech →, *Germany* ... 25 G6
Lechang, *China* ... 59 E9
Lechtaler Alpen, *Austria* ... 26 D3
Lecontes Mills, *U.S.A.* ... 110 E6
Lectoure, *France* ... 20 E4
Łęczna, *Poland* ... 45 G9
Łęczyca, *Poland* ... 45 F6
Ledesma, *Spain* ... 34 D5
Ledong, *China* ... 64 C7
Leduc, *Canada* ... 104 C6
Lee, *U.S.A.* ... 111 D11
Lee →, *Ireland* ... 15 E3
Lee Vining, *U.S.A.* ... 116 H7
Leech L., *U.S.A.* ... 112 B7
Leechburg, *U.S.A.* ... 110 F5
Leeds, *U.K.* ... 12 D6
Leeds, *U.S.A.* ... 109 J2
Leek, *Neths.* ... 17 A6

Leek, *U.K.* ... 12 D5
Leeman, *Australia* ... 93 E1
Leeper, *U.S.A.* ... 110 E5
Leer, *Germany* ... 24 B3
Leesburg, *U.S.A.* ... 109 L5
Leesville, *U.S.A.* ... 113 K8
Leeton, *Australia* ... 95 E4
Leetonia, *U.S.A.* ... 110 F4
Leeu Gamka, *S. Africa* ... 88 E3
Leeuwarden, *Neths.* ... 17 A5
Leeuwin, C., *Australia* ... 93 F2
Leeward Is., *Atl. Oc.* ... 121 C7
Lefka, *Cyprus* ... 36 D11
Lefkoniko, *Cyprus* ... 36 D12
Lefroy, *Canada* ... 110 B5
Lefroy, L., *Australia* ... 93 F3
Łeg →, *Poland* ... 45 H8
Leganés, *Spain* ... 34 E7
Legazpi, *Phil.* ... 61 E5
Lège, *France* ... 20 D2
Lège Hida, *Ethiopia* ... 81 F5
Legendre I., *Australia* ... 92 D2
Leghorn = Livorno, *Italy* ... 28 E7
Legionowo, *Poland* ... 45 F7
Legnago, *Italy* ... 29 C8
Legnano, *Italy* ... 28 C5
Legnica, *Poland* ... 45 G3
Legrad, *Croatia* ... 29 B13
Leh, *India* ... 69 B7
Lehigh Acres, *U.S.A.* ... 109 M5
Lehighton, *U.S.A.* ... 111 F9
Lehliu, *Romania* ... 43 F11
Leho, *Sudan* ... 81 F3
Lehrte, *Germany* ... 24 C5
Lehututu, *Botswana* ... 88 C3
Lei Shui →, *China* ... 59 D9
Leiah, *Pakistan* ... 68 D4
Leibnitz, *Austria* ... 26 E8
Leibo, *China* ... 58 C4
Leicester, *U.K.* ... 13 E6
Leicester City □, *U.K.* ... 13 E6
Leicestershire □, *U.K.* ... 13 E6
Leichhardt →, *Australia* ... 94 B2
Leichhardt Ra., *Australia* ... 94 C4
Leiden, *Neths.* ... 17 B4
Leie →, *Belgium* ... 17 C3
Leifers = Láives, *Italy* ... 29 B8
Leigh Creek, *Australia* ... 95 E2
Leimen, *Germany* ... 25 F4
Leine →, *Germany* ... 24 C5
Leinefelde, *Germany* ... 24 D6
Leinster, *Australia* ... 93 E3
Leinster □, *Ireland* ... 15 C4
Leinster, Mt., *Ireland* ... 15 D5
Leipalingis, *Lithuania* ... 44 D10
Leipzig, *Germany* ... 24 D8
Leiria, *Portugal* ... 34 F2
Leiria □, *Portugal* ... 34 F2
Leirvik, *Norway* ... 9 G11
Leishan, *China* ... 58 D7
Leisler, Mt., *Australia* ... 92 D4
Leith, *U.K.* ... 14 F5
Leith Hill, *U.K.* ... 13 F7
Leitha →, *Europe* ... 27 D10
Leitrim, *Ireland* ... 15 B3
Leitrim □, *Ireland* ... 15 B4
Leitza, *Spain* ... 32 B3
Leiyang, *China* ... 59 D9
Leizhou, *China* ... 59 G8
Leizhou Bandao, *China* ... 58 G7
Leizhou Wan, *China* ... 59 G8
Lek →, *Neths.* ... 17 C4
Leka, *Norway* ... 8 D14
Lekáni, *Greece* ... 41 E8
Lekbibaj, *Albania* ... 40 D3
Lekeitio, *Spain* ... 32 B2
Lekhainá, *Greece* ... 38 D3
Lekoui, *Burkina Faso* ... 82 C4
Leksand, *Sweden* ... 10 D9
Lékva Óros, *Greece* ... 36 D6
Leland, *Mich., U.S.A.* ... 108 C3
Leland, *Miss., U.S.A.* ... 113 J9
Lelâng, *Sweden* ... 10 E6
Leleque, *Argentina* ... 128 E2
Lelystad, *Neths.* ... 17 B5
Lem, *Denmark* ... 11 H2
Lema, *Nigeria* ... 83 C5
Lema Shilindi, *Ethiopia* ... 81 G5
Léman, L., *Europe* ... 19 F13
Lemera, *Dem. Rep. of the Congo* ... 86 C2
Lemery, *Phil.* ... 61 E4
Lemhi Ra., *U.S.A.* ... 114 D7
Lemmer, *Neths.* ... 17 B5
Lemmon, *U.S.A.* ... 112 C3
Lemon Grove, *U.S.A.* ... 117 N9
Lemoore, *U.S.A.* ... 116 J7
Lempdes, *France* ... 20 C7
Lemvig, *Denmark* ... 11 H2
Lena →, *Russia* ... 51 B13
Lenart, *Slovenia* ... 29 B12
Lenartovce, *Slovak Rep.* ... 27 C13
Lencloître, *France* ... 18 F7
Léndas, *Greece* ... 36 E6
Lendava, *Slovenia* ... 29 B13
Lendeh, *Iran* ... 71 D6
Lengerich, *Germany* ... 24 C3
Lenggong, *Malaysia* ... 65 K3
Lenggries, *Germany* ... 25 H7
Lengshuijiang, *China* ... 59 D8
Lengshuitan, *China* ... 59 D8
Lengua de Vaca, Pta., *Chile* ... 126 C1
Lengyeltóti, *Hungary* ... 42 D2
Lenhovda, *Sweden* ... 11 G9
Lenina, Kanal →, *Russia* ... 49 J7

Leninabad = Khudzhand, *Tajikistan* ... 50 E7
Leninakan = Gyumri, *Armenia* ... 49 K6

Leningrad = Sankt-Peterburg, *Russia* ... 46 C6
Lenino, *Ukraine* ... 47 K8
Leninogorsk, *Kazakstan* ... 50 D9
Leninsk, *Russia* ... 49 F7
Leninsk-Kuznetskiy, *Russia* ... 50 D9
Leninskoye, *Russia* ... 48 A8
Lenk, *Switz.* ... 25 J3
Lenkoran = Länkäran, *Azerbaijan* ... 71 B6
Lenmalu, *Indonesia* ... 63 E8
Lenne →, *Germany* ... 24 D3
Lennestadt, *Germany* ... 24 D4
Lennox, *U.S.A.* ... 112 D6
Lennoxville, *Canada* ... 111 A13
Leno, *Italy* ... 28 C7
Lenoir, *U.S.A.* ... 109 H5
Lenoir City, *U.S.A.* ... 109 H3
Lenore L., *Canada* ... 105 C8
Lenox, *U.S.A.* ... 111 D11
Lens, *France* ... 19 B9
Lensahn, *Germany* ... 24 A6
Lensk, *Russia* ... 51 C12
Lentekhi, *Georgia* ... 49 J6
Lenti, *Hungary* ... 42 D1
Lentini, *Italy* ... 31 E8
Lenwood, *U.S.A.* ... 117 L9
Lenya, *Burma* ... 62 B1
Lenzen, *Germany* ... 24 B7
Léo, *Burkina Faso* ... 82 C4
Leoben, *Austria* ... 26 D8
Leodhas = Lewis, *U.K.* ... 14 C2
Leola, *U.S.A.* ... 112 C5
Leominster, *U.K.* ... 13 E5
Leominster, *U.S.A.* ... 111 D13
León, *France* ... 20 E2
León, *Mexico* ... 118 C4
León, *Nic.* ... 120 D2
León, *Spain* ... 34 C5
León, *U.S.A.* ... 112 E8
León □, *Spain* ... 34 C5
León →, *U.S.A.* ... 113 K6
León, Montes de, *Spain* ... 34 C4
Leonardtown, *U.S.A.* ... 108 F7
Leonardville, *Namibia* ... 88 C2
Leonberg, *Germany* ... 25 G5
Leonding, *Austria* ... 26 C7
Leonessa, *Italy* ... 29 F9
Leonforte, *Italy* ... 31 E7
Leongatha, *Australia* ... 95 F4
Leonídhion, *Greece* ... 38 D4
Leonora, *Australia* ... 93 E3
Léopold II, Lac = Mai-Ndombe, L., *Dem. Rep. of the Congo* ... 84 E3
Leopoldina, *Brazil* ... 127 A7
Leopoldsburg, *Belgium* ... 17 C5
Léopoldville = Kinshasa, *Dem. Rep. of the Congo* ... 84 E3
Leoti, *U.S.A.* ... 112 F4
Leova, *Moldova* ... 43 D13
Leoville, *Canada* ... 105 C7
Lepe, *Spain* ... 35 H3
Lepel = Lyepyel, *Belarus* ... 46 E5
Lepenou, *Greece* ... 38 C3
Leping, *China* ... 59 C11
Lépo, L. do, *Angola* ... 88 B2
Lepontine, Alpi, *Italy* ... 25 B5
Leppävirta, *Finland* ... 9 E22
Lepsény, *Hungary* ... 42 D3
Lequeitio = Lekeitio, *Spain* ... 32 B2
Lercara Friddi, *Italy* ... 30 E6
Lerdo, *Mexico* ... 118 B4
Léré, *Chad* ... 83 D7
Léré, *Mali* ... 82 B4
Lere, *Bauchi, Nigeria* ... 83 D6
Lere, *Kaduna, Nigeria* ... 83 C6
Leribe, *Lesotho* ... 89 D4
Lérici, *Italy* ... 28 D6
Lérida = Lleida, *Spain* ... 32 D5
Lérins, Îs. de, *France* ... 21 E11
Lerma, *Spain* ... 34 C7
Léros, *Greece* ... 39 D8
Lérouville, *France* ... 19 D12
Lerum, *Sweden* ... 11 G6
Lerwick, *U.K.* ... 14 A7
Leş, *Romania* ... 42 D6
Les Abrets, *France* ... 21 C9
Les Andelys, *France* ... 18 C8
Les Borges Blanques, *Spain* ... 32 D5
Les Cayes, *Haiti* ... 121 C5
Les Essarts, *France* ... 18 F5
Les Herbiers, *France* ... 18 F5
Les Minquiers, Plateau des, *Chan. Is.* ... 18 D4
Les Pieux, *France* ... 18 C5
Les Ponts-de-Cé, *France* ... 18 E6
Les Riceys, *France* ... 19 E11
Les Sables-d'Olonne, *France* ... 18 F5
Les Vans, *France* ... 21 D8
Lesbos = Lésvos, *Greece* ... 39 B8
L'Escala, *Spain* ... 32 C8
Leshan, *China* ... 58 C4
Lésina, *Italy* ... 29 G12
Lésina, L. di, *Italy* ... 29 G12
Lesjöfors, *Sweden* ... 10 E8
Lesko, *Poland* ... 45 J9
Leskov I., *Antarctica* ... 5 B1
Leskovac, *Serbia, Yug.* ... 40 C5
Leskoviku, *Albania* ... 40 F4
Leśna, *Poland* ... 45 G2
Lesnoye, *Russia* ... 46 C9
Leśnica, *Poland* ... 45 H5
Lešnica, *Serbia, Yug.* ... 40 B3
Lesosibirsk, *Russia* ... 51 D10
Lesotho ■, *Africa* ... 89 D4
Lesozavodsk, *Russia* ... 51 E14
Lesparre-Médoc, *France* ... 20 C3
Lessay, *France* ... 18 C5
Lesse →, *Belgium* ... 17 D4

Lessebo, *Sweden* ... 11 H9
Lesser Antilles, *W. Indies* ... 121 D7
Lesser Slave L., *Canada* ... 104 B5
Lesser Sunda Is., *Indonesia* ... 63 F6
Lessines, *Belgium* ... 17 D3
Lester, *U.S.A.* ... 116 C5
Lestock, *Canada* ... 105 C8
Lesuer I., *Australia* ... 92 B4
Lésvos, *Greece* ... 39 B8
Leszno, *Poland* ... 45 G3
Letaba, *S. Africa* ... 89 C5
Letälven, *Sweden* ... 10 E8
Létavértes, *Hungary* ... 42 C6
Letchworth, *U.K.* ... 13 F7
Letea, Ostrov, *Romania* ... 43 E14
Lethbridge, *Canada* ... 104 D6
Lethem, *Guyana* ... 124 C7
Leti, Kepulauan, *Indonesia* ... 63 F7
Leti Is. = Leti, Kepulauan, *Indonesia* ... 63 F7
Letiahau →, *Botswana* ... 88 C3
Leticia, *Colombia* ... 124 D5
Leting, *China* ... 57 E10
Letjiesbos, *S. Africa* ... 88 E3
Letlhakane, *Botswana* ... 88 C4
Letlhakeng, *Botswana* ... 88 C3
Letong, *Indonesia* ... 62 D3
Letpadan, *Burma* ... 67 L19
Letpan, *Burma* ... 67 K19
Letsôk-aw Kyun, *Burma* ... 65 G2
Letterkenny, *Ireland* ... 15 B4
Leu, *Romania* ... 43 F9
Leucadia, *U.S.A.* ... 117 M9
Leucate, *France* ... 20 F7
Leucate, Étang de, *France* ... 20 F7
Leuk, *Switz.* ... 25 J3
Leuşeni, *Moldova* ... 43 D13
Leuser, G., *Indonesia* ... 62 D1
Leutkirch, *Germany* ... 25 H6
Leuven, *Belgium* ... 17 D4
Leuze-en-Hainaut, *Belgium* ... 17 D3
Lev Tolstoy, *Russia* ... 46 F10
Levádhia, *Greece* ... 38 C4
Levanger, *Norway* ... 8 E14
Levani, *Albania* ... 40 F3
Levant, Î. du, *France* ... 21 E10
Lévanto, *Italy* ... 28 D6
Lévanzo, *Italy* ... 30 D5
Levelland, *U.S.A.* ... 113 J3
Leven, *U.K.* ... 14 E6
Leven, L., *U.K.* ... 14 E5
Leven, Toraka, *Madag.* ... 89 A8
Leveque C., *Australia* ... 92 C3
Leverano, *Italy* ... 31 B10
Leverkusen, *Germany* ... 24 D2
Levice, *Slovak Rep.* ... 27 C11
Lévico Terme, *Italy* ... 29 C8
Levie, *France* ... 21 G13
Levier, *France* ... 19 F13
Levin, *N.Z.* ... 91 J5
Lévis, *Canada* ... 103 C5
Levis, L., *Canada* ... 104 A5
Levítha, *Greece* ... 39 D8
Levittown, *N.Y., U.S.A.* ... 111 F11
Levittown, *Pa., U.S.A.* ... 111 F10
Levka, *Bulgaria* ... 41 E10
Levkás, *Greece* ... 38 C2
Levkás □, *Greece* ... 38 C2
Levkímmi, *Greece* ... 36 B4
Levkímmi, Ákra, *Greece* ... 36 B4
Levkôsia = Nicosia, *Cyprus* ... 36 D12
Levoča, *Slovak Rep.* ... 27 B13
Levroux, *France* ... 19 F8
Levski, *Bulgaria* ... 41 C9
Levskigrad = Karlovo, *Bulgaria* ... 41 D8
Lewes, *U.K.* ... 13 G8
Lewes, *U.S.A.* ... 108 F8
Lewin Brzeski, *Poland* ... 45 H4
Lewis, *U.K.* ... 14 C2
Lewis →, *U.S.A.* ... 116 E4
Lewis, Butt of, *U.K.* ... 14 C2
Lewis Ra., *Australia* ... 92 C4
Lewis Range, *U.S.A.* ... 114 C7
Lewis Run, *U.S.A.* ... 110 E6
Lewisburg, *Pa., U.S.A.* ... 110 F8
Lewisburg, *Tenn., U.S.A.* ... 109 H2
Lewisburg, *W. Va., U.S.A.* ... 108 G5
Lewisporte, *Canada* ... 103 C8
Lewiston, *Idaho, U.S.A.* ... 114 C5
Lewiston, *Maine, U.S.A.* ... 109 C11
Lewiston, *N.Y., U.S.A.* ... 110 C5
Lewistown, *Mont., U.S.A.* ... 114 C9
Lewistown, *Pa., U.S.A.* ... 110 F7
Lexington, *Ill., U.S.A.* ... 112 E10
Lexington, *Ky., U.S.A.* ... 108 F3
Lexington, *Mich., U.S.A.* ... 110 C2
Lexington, *Mo., U.S.A.* ... 112 F8
Lexington, *N.C., U.S.A.* ... 109 H5
Lexington, *N.Y., U.S.A.* ... 111 D10
Lexington, *Nebr., U.S.A.* ... 112 E5
Lexington, *Ohio, U.S.A.* ... 110 F2
Lexington, *Tenn., U.S.A.* ... 109 H1
Lexington, *Va., U.S.A.* ... 108 G6
Lexington Park, *U.S.A.* ... 108 F7
Leyburn, *U.K.* ... 12 C6
Leye, *China* ... 58 E6
Leyland, *U.K.* ... 12 D5
Leyre →, *France* ... 20 D2
Leyte □, *Phil.* ... 61 F6
Leyte Gulf, *Phil.* ... 61 F6
Leżajsk, *Poland* ... 45 H9
Lezha, *Albania* ... 40 E3
Lezhi, *China* ... 58 B5
Lézignan-Corbières, *France* ... 20 E6
Lezoux, *France* ... 20 C7
Lgov, *Russia* ... 47 G8
Lhasa, *China* ... 60 D4
Lhazê, *China* ... 60 D3
Lhokkruet, *Indonesia* ... 62 D1

Lhokseumawe, Indonesia .. 62 C1
L'Hospitalet de Llobregat, Spain 32 D7
Lhuntsi Dzong, India 67 F17
Li, Thailand 64 D2
Li Shui →, China 59 C9
Li Xian, Gansu, China 56 G3
Li Xian, Hebei China 56 E8
Li Xian, Hunan, China 59 C8
Liádhoi, Greece 39 E8
Liancheng, China 59 E11
Lianga, Phil. 61 G7
Liangcheng, Nei Mongol Zizhiqu, China 56 D7
Liangcheng, Shandong, China 57 G10
Liangdang, China 56 H4
Lianghe, China 58 E2
Lianghekou, China 58 C7
Liangping, China 58 B6
Liangpran, Indonesia 62 D4
Lianhua, China 59 D9
Lianjiang, Fujian, China .. 59 D12
Lianjiang, Guangdong, China 59 G8
Lianping, China 59 E10
Lianshan, China 59 E9
Lianshanguan, China 57 D12
Lianshui, China 57 H10
Lianyuan, China 59 D8
Lianyungang, China 57 G10
Lianzhou, China 59 E9
Liao He →, China 57 D11
Liaocheng, China 56 F8
Liaodong Bandao, China ... 57 E12
Liaodong Wan, China 57 D11
Liaoning □, China 57 D12
Liaoyang, China 57 D12
Liaoyuan, China 57 C13
Liaozhong, China 57 D12
Liapádhes, Greece 38 B1
Liard →, Canada 104 A4
Liard River, Canada 104 B3
Liari, Pakistan 68 G2
Libau = Liepāja, Latvia .. 9 H19
Libby, U.S.A. 114 B6
Libenge, Dem. Rep. of the Congo . 84 D3
Liberal, U.S.A. 113 G4
Liberec, Czech Rep. 26 A8
Liberia, Costa Rica 120 D2
Liberia ■, W. Afr. 82 D3
Liberty, Mo., U.S.A. 112 F7
Liberty, N.Y., U.S.A. ... 111 E10
Liberty, Pa., U.S.A. 110 E7
Liberty, Tex., U.S.A. 113 K7
Libiąż, Poland 45 H6
Libîya, Sahrâ', Africa 79 C10
Libo, China 58 E6
Libobo, Tanjung, Indonesia 63 E7
Libode, S. Africa 89 E4
Libohava, Albania 40 F4
Libourne, France 20 D3
Libramont, Belgium 17 E5
Librazhdi, Albania 40 E4
Libreville, Gabon 84 D1
Libya ■, N. Afr. 79 C9
Libyan Desert = Libîya, Sahrâ', Africa 79 C10
Libyan Plateau = Ed-Déffa, Egypt 80 A2
Licantén, Chile 126 D1
Licata, Italy 30 E6
Lice, Turkey 73 C9
Licheng, China 56 F7
Lichfield, U.K. 13 E6
Lichinga, Mozam. 87 E4
Lichtenburg, S. Africa ... 88 D4
Lichtenfels, Germany 25 E7
Lichuan, Hubei, China ... 58 B7
Lichuan, Jiangxi, China .. 59 D11
Licking →, U.S.A. 108 F3
Licosa, Punta, Italy 31 B7
Lida, Belarus 9 K21
Liden, Sweden 10 B10
Lidhorikíon, Greece 38 C4
Lidhult, Sweden 11 H7
Lidköping, Sweden 11 F7
Lido, Italy 29 C9
Lido, Niger 83 C5
Lido di Roma = Ostia, Lido di, Italy 29 G9
Lidzbark, Poland 45 E6
Lidzbark Warmiński, Poland 44 D7
Liebenwalde, Germany ... 24 C9
Lieberose, Germany 24 D10
Liebig, Mt., Australia ... 92 D5
Liebling, Romania 42 E6
Liechtenstein ■, Europe ... 25 H5
Liège, Belgium 17 D5
Liège □, Belgium 17 D5
Liegnitz = Legnica, Poland 45 G3
Lienart, Dem. Rep. of the Congo . 86 B2
Lienyünchiangshih = Lianyungang, China 57 G10
Lienz, Austria 26 E5
Liepāja, Latvia 9 H19
Liepāja □, Latvia 44 B8
Liepājas ezers, Latvia 44 B8
Lier, Belgium 17 C4
Liernais, France 19 E11
Liești, Romania 43 E12
Liévin, France 19 B9
Lièvre →, Canada 102 C4
Liezen, Austria 26 D7
Liffey →, Ireland 15 C5
Lifford, Ireland 15 B4
Liffré, France 18 D5
Lifudzin, Russia 54 B7
Ligao, Phil. 61 E5

Lightning Ridge, Australia . 95 D4
Lignano Sabbiadoro, Italy .. 29 C10
Ligny-en-Barrois, France ... 19 D12
Ligonier, U.S.A. 110 F5
Ligoúrion, Greece 38 D5
Ligueil, France 18 E7
Liguria □, Italy 28 D5
Ligurian Sea, Medit. S. 6 G7
Lihou Reefs and Cays, Australia 94 B5
Lihue, U.S.A. 106 H15
Likasi, Dem. Rep. of the Congo . 87 E2
Likenäs, Sweden 10 D8
Likhoslavl, Russia 46 D8
Likhovskoy, Russia 47 H11
Likoma I., Malawi 87 E3
Likumburu, Tanzania 87 D4
L'Île-Bouchard, France ... 18 E7
L'Île-Rousse, France 21 F12
Liling, China 59 D9
Lilla Edet, Sweden 11 F6
Lille, France 19 B10
Lille Bælt, Denmark 11 J3
Lillebonne, France 18 C7
Lillehammer, Norway ... 9 F14
Lillesand, Norway 9 G13
Lillhärdal, Sweden 10 C8
Lillian Pt., Australia 93 E4
Lillo, Spain 34 F7
Lillooet, Canada 104 C4
Lillooet →, Canada 104 D4
Lilongwe, Malawi 87 E3
Liloy, Phil. 63 C6
Lim →, Bos.-H. 40 C3
Lima, Indonesia 63 E7
Lima, Peru 124 F3
Lima, Mont., U.S.A. 114 D7
Lima, Ohio, U.S.A. 108 E3
Lima →, Portugal 34 D2
Liman, Indonesia 63 G14
Liman, Russia 49 H8
Limanowa, Poland 45 J7
Limay →, Argentina ... 128 D3
Limay Mahuida, Argentina . 126 D2
Limbach-Oberfrohna, Germany 24 E8
Limbang, Brunei 62 D5
Limbara, Mte., Italy 30 B2
Limbaži, Latvia 9 H21
Limbdi, India 68 H4
Limbe, Cameroon 83 E6
Limburg, Germany 25 E4
Limburg □, Belgium ... 17 C5
Limburg □, Neths. 17 C5
Limedsforsen, Sweden ... 10 D7
Limeira, Brazil 127 A6
Limenária, Greece 41 F8
Limerick, Ireland 15 D3
Limerick, U.S.A. 111 C14
Limerick □, Ireland 15 D3
Limestone, U.S.A. 110 D6
Limestone →, Canada ... 105 B10
Limfjorden, Denmark ... 11 H3
Limia = Lima →, Portugal 34 D2
Limín Khersonísou, Greece . 39 F7
Limingen, Norway 8 D15
Limmared, Sweden 11 G7
Limmen Bight, Australia .. 94 A2
Limmen Bight →, Australia 94 B2
Límni, Greece 38 C5
Límnos, Greece 39 B7
Limoges, Canada 111 A9
Limoges, France 20 C5
Limón, Costa Rica 120 E3
Limon, U.S.A. 112 F3
Limone Piemonte, Italy .. 28 D4
Limousin, France 20 C5
Limousin, Plateaux du, France 20 C5
Limoux, France 20 E6
Limpopo →, Africa 89 D5
Limuru, Kenya 86 C4
Lin Xian, China 56 F6
Lin'an, China 59 B12
Linapacan I., Phil. 61 F3
Linapacan Str., Phil. ... 61 F3
Linares, Chile 126 D1
Linares, Mexico 119 C5
Linares, Spain 35 G7
Linaro, Capo, Italy 29 F8
Línas Mte., Italy 30 C1
Lincang, China 58 F3
Lincheng, China 56 F8
Linchuan, China 59 D11
Lincoln, Argentina 126 C3
Lincoln, N.Z. 91 K4
Lincoln, U.K. 12 D7
Lincoln, Calif., U.S.A. ... 116 G5
Lincoln, Ill., U.S.A. ... 112 E10
Lincoln, Kans., U.S.A. .. 112 F5
Lincoln, Maine, U.S.A. .. 109 C11
Lincoln, N.H., U.S.A. .. 111 B13
Lincoln, N. Mex., U.S.A. 115 K11
Lincoln, Nebr., U.S.A. .. 112 E6
Lincoln City, U.S.A. ... 114 D1
Lincoln Hav = Lincoln Sea, Arctic 4 A5
Lincoln Sea, Arctic 4 A5
Lincolnshire □, U.K. ... 12 D7
Lincolnshire Wolds, U.K. . 12 D7
Lincolnton, U.S.A. 109 H5
L'Incudine, France 21 G13
Lind, U.S.A. 114 C4
Linda, U.S.A. 116 F5
Lindau, Germany 25 H5
Linden, Guyana 124 B7
Linden, Ala., U.S.A. ... 109 J2

Linden, Calif., U.S.A. 116 G5
Linden, Tex., U.S.A. 113 J7
Lindenhurst, U.S.A. 111 F11
Lindesberg, Sweden 10 E9
Lindesnes, Norway 9 H12
Líndhos, Greece 36 C10
Líndhos, Ákra, Greece ... 36 C10
Lindi, Tanzania 87 D4
Lindi □, Tanzania 87 D4
Lindi →, Dem. Rep. of the Congo . 86 B2
Lindö, Sweden 11 F10
Lindome, Sweden 11 G6
Lindoso, Portugal 34 D2
Lindow, Germany 24 C9
Lindsay, Canada 102 D4
Lindsay, Calif., U.S.A. ... 116 J7
Lindsay, Okla., U.S.A. .. 113 H6
Lindsborg, U.S.A. 112 F6
Lindsdal, Sweden 11 H10
Linesville, U.S.A. 110 E4
Linfen, China 56 F6
Ling Xian, Hunan, China . 59 D9
Ling Xian, Shandong, China 56 F9
Lingao, China 64 C7
Lingayen, Phil. 63 A6
Lingayen G., Phil. 61 C4
Lingbi, China 57 H9
Lingbo, Sweden 10 C10
Lingchuan, Guangxi Zhuangzu, China 59 E8
Lingchuan, Shanxi, China . 56 G7
Lingen, Germany 24 C3
Lingga, Indonesia 62 E2
Lingga, Kepulauan, Indonesia 62 E2
Lingga Arch. = Lingga, Kepulauan, Indonesia 62 E2
Linghem, Sweden 11 F9
Lingle, U.S.A. 112 D2
Lingqiu, China 56 E8
Lingshan, China 58 F7
Lingshi, China 56 F6
Lingshou, China 56 E8
Lingshui, China 64 C8
Lingtai, China 56 G4
Linguère, Senegal 82 B1
Lingui, China 59 E8
Lingwu, China 56 E4
Lingyuan, China 57 D10
Lingyun, China 58 E6
Linhai, China 59 C13
Linhares, Brazil 125 G10
Linhe, China 56 D4
Linjiang, China 57 D14
Linköping, Sweden 11 F9
Linkou, China 57 B16
Linli, China 59 C8
Linqi, China 56 G7
Linqing, China 56 F8
Linqu, China 57 F10
Linru, China 56 G7
Lins, Brazil 127 A6
Linta →, Madag. 89 D7
Linth →, Switz. 25 H5
Linthal, Switz. 25 J5
Linton, Ind., U.S.A. ... 108 F2
Linton, N. Dak., U.S.A. . 112 B4
Lintong, China 56 G5
Linwood, Canada 110 C4
Linwu, China 59 E9
Linxi, China 57 C10
Linxia, China 60 C5
Linxiang, China 59 C9
Linyanti →, Africa 88 B4
Linyi, China 57 G10
Linz, Austria 26 C7
Linz, Germany 24 E3
Linzhenzhen, China 56 F5
Linzi, China 57 F10
Lion, G. du, France ... 20 E7
Lionárisso, Cyprus 36 D13
Lioni, Italy 31 B8
Lions, G. of = Lion, G. du, France 20 E7
Lion's Den, Zimbabwe .. 87 F3
Lion's Head, Canada ... 110 B3
Liozno = Lyozna, Belarus . 46 E6
Lipa, Phil. 61 E4
Lipali, Mozam. 87 F4
Lipany, Slovak Rep. ... 27 B13
Lípari, Italy 31 D7
Lípari →, Italy 31 D7
Lípari, Is. = Éolie, Ís., Italy 31 D7
Lipcani, Moldova 43 B11
Lipetsk, Russia 47 F10
Lipiany, Poland 45 E1
Lipkany = Lipcani, Moldova 43 B11
Lipljan, Kosovo, Yug. ... 40 D5
Lipník nad Bečvou, Czech Rep. 27 B10
Lipno, Poland 45 F6
Lipova, Romania 42 D6
Lipovcy Manzovka, Russia . 54 B6
Lipovets, Ukraine 47 H5
Lippe →, Germany ... 24 D2
Lippstadt, Germany ... 24 D4
Lipscomb, U.S.A. 113 G4
Lipsk, Poland 44 E10
Lipsko, Poland 45 G8
Lipsói, Greece 39 D8
Liptovský Hrádok, Slovak Rep. 27 B12
Liptovský Milkuláš, Slovak Rep. 27 B12
Liptrap C., Australia ... 95 F4
Lipu, China 59 E8
Lira, Uganda 86 B3

Liri →, Italy 30 A6
Liria = Lliria, Spain 33 F4
Lisala, Dem. Rep. of the Congo . 84 D4
Lisboa, Portugal 35 G1
Lisboa □, Portugal 35 F1
Lisbon = Lisboa, Portugal . 35 G1
Lisbon, N. Dak., U.S.A. .. 112 B6
Lisbon, N.H., U.S.A. ... 111 B13
Lisbon, Ohio, U.S.A. ... 110 F4
Lisbon Falls, U.S.A. ... 109 D10
Lisburn, U.K. 15 B5
Liscannor B., Ireland ... 15 D2
Liscia →, Italy 30 A2
Lishe Jiang →, China ... 58 E3
Lishi, China 56 F6
Lishu, China 57 C13
Lishui, Jiangsu, China ... 59 B12
Lishui, Zhejiang, China .. 59 C12
Lisianski I., Pac. Oc. 96 E10
Lisichansk = Lysychansk, Ukraine 47 H10
Lisieux, France 18 C7
Liski, Russia 47 G10
L'Isle-Jourdain, Gers, France 20 E5
L'Isle-Jourdain, Vienne, France 20 B4
L'Isle-sur-la-Sorgue, France . 21 E9
Lisle-sur-Tarn, France 20 E5
Lismore, Australia 95 D5
Lismore, Ireland 15 D4
Lista, Norway 9 G12
Lister, Mt., Antarctica ... 5 D11
Liston, Australia 95 D5
Listowel, Canada 102 D3
Listowel, Ireland 15 D2
Lit, Sweden 10 A8
Lit-et-Mixe, France 20 D2
Litang, Guangxi Zhuangzu, China 58 F7
Litang, Sichuan, China .. 58 B3
Litang Qu →, China ... 58 C3
Litani →, Lebanon 75 B4
Litchfield, Calif., U.S.A. .. 116 E6
Litchfield, Conn., U.S.A. . 111 E11
Litchfield, Ill., U.S.A. .. 112 F10
Litchfield, Minn., U.S.A. . 112 C7
Liteni, Romania 43 C11
Lithgow, Australia 95 E5
Líthinon, Ákra, Greece ... 36 E6
Lithuania ■, Europe ... 9 J20
Litija, Slovenia 29 B11
Lititz, U.S.A. 111 F8
Litókhoron, Greece 40 F6
Litoměřice, Czech Rep. .. 26 A7
Litomyšl, Czech Rep. ... 27 B9
Litschau, Austria 26 C8
Little Abaco I., Bahamas . 120 A4
Little Barrier I., N.Z. ... 91 G5
Little Belt Mts., U.S.A. .. 114 C8
Little Blue →, U.S.A. .. 112 F6
Little Buffalo →, Canada .. 104 A6
Little Cayman, I., Cayman Is. 120 C3
Little Churchill →, Canada 105 B9
Little Colorado →, U.S.A. 115 H8
Little Current, Canada ... 102 C3
Little Current →, Canada . 102 B3
Little Falls, Minn., U.S.A. . 112 C7
Little Falls, N.Y., U.S.A. .. 111 C10
Little Fork →, U.S.A. .. 112 A8
Little Grand Rapids, Canada 105 C9
Little Humboldt →, U.S.A. 114 F5
Little Inagua I., Bahamas . 121 B5
Little Karoo, S. Africa ... 88 E3
Little Lake, U.S.A. 117 K9
Little Laut Is. = Laut Kecil, Kepulauan, Indonesia ... 62 E5
Little-Mecatina = Petit-Mécatina →, Canada ... 103 B8
Little Minch, U.K. 14 D2
Little Missouri →, U.S.A. 112 B3
Little Ouse →, U.K. ... 13 E9
Little Rann, India 68 H4
Little Red →, U.S.A. .. 113 H9
Little River, N.Z. 91 K4
Little Rock, U.S.A. ... 113 H8
Little Ruaha →, Tanzania . 86 D4
Little Sable Pt., U.S.A. .. 108 D2
Little Scarcies →, S. Leone 82 D2
Little Sioux →, U.S.A. .. 112 E6
Little Smoky →, Canada . 104 C5
Little Snake →, U.S.A. .. 114 F9
Little Valley, U.S.A. ... 110 D6
Little Wabash →, U.S.A. 108 G1
Little White →, U.S.A. . 112 D4
Littlefield, U.S.A. 113 J3
Littlehampton, U.K. ... 13 G7
Littleton, U.S.A. 111 B13
Litvínov, Czech Rep. ... 26 A6
Liu He →, China 57 D11
Liu Jiang →, China ... 58 F7
Liuba, China 56 H4
Liucheng, China 58 E7
Liugou, China 57 D10
Liuhe, China 57 C13
Liuheng Dao, China ... 59 C14
Liujiang, China 58 E7
Liukang Tenggaja = Sabalana, Kepulauan, Indonesia 63 F5
Liuli, Tanzania 87 E3
Liuwa Plain, Zambia ... 85 G4
Liuyang, China 59 C9
Liuzhi, China 58 D5
Liuzhuang, China 57 H11
Livada, Romania 42 C8
Livadherón, Greece ... 40 F5
Livadhia, Cyprus 36 E12
Livádhion, Greece ... 38 A4
Livarot, France 18 D7

Live Oak, Calif., U.S.A. ... 116 F5
Live Oak, Fla., U.S.A. .. 109 K4
Liveras, Cyprus 36 D11
Livermore, U.S.A. 116 H5
Livermore, Mt., U.S.A. .. 113 K2
Livermore Falls, U.S.A. .. 109 C11
Liverpool, Canada 103 D7
Liverpool, U.K. 12 D4
Liverpool, U.S.A. 111 C8
Liverpool Bay, U.K. ... 12 D4
Liverpool Plains, Australia . 95 E5
Liverpool Ra., Australia .. 95 E5
Livigno, Italy 28 B7
Livingston, Guatemala ... 120 C2
Livingston, U.K. 14 F5
Livingston, Ala., U.S.A. .. 109 J1
Livingston, Calif., U.S.A. . 116 H6
Livingston, Mont., U.S.A. 114 D8
Livingston, S.C., U.S.A. .. 109 J5
Livingston, Tenn., U.S.A. . 109 G3
Livingston, Tex., U.S.A. .. 113 K7
Livingston, L., U.S.A. .. 113 K7
Livingston Manor, U.S.A. . 111 E10
Livingstone, Zambia ... 87 F2
Livingstone Mts., Tanzania . 87 D3
Livingstonia, Malawi ... 87 E3
Livno, Bos.-H. 42 G2
Livny, Russia 47 F9
Livonia, Mich., U.S.A. .. 108 D4
Livonia, N.Y., U.S.A. .. 110 D7
Livorno, Italy 28 E7
Livramento, Brazil 127 C4
Livron-sur-Drôme, France . 21 D8
Liwale, Tanzania 87 D4
Liwiec →, Poland 45 F8
Lixi, China 58 D3
Lixian, China 58 B4
Lixoúrion, Greece 38 C2
Liyang, China 59 B12
Lizard I., Australia ... 94 A4
Lizard Pt., U.K. 13 H2
Lizzano, Italy 31 B10
Ljig, Serbia, Yug. 40 B4
Ljubija, Bos.-H. 29 D13
Ljubinje, Bos.-H. 40 D2
Ljubljana, Slovenia ... 29 B11
Ljubno, Slovenia 29 B11
Ljubovija, Serbia, Yug. .. 40 B3
Ljugarn, Sweden 11 G12
Ljung, Sweden 11 G7
Ljungan →, Sweden .. 10 B11
Ljungaverk, Sweden ... 10 B10
Ljungby, Sweden 9 H15
Ljungbyholm, Sweden .. 11 H10
Ljungdalen, Sweden ... 10 B6
Ljungsbro, Sweden ... 11 F9
Ljungskile, Sweden ... 11 F5
Ljusdal, Sweden 10 C10
Ljusfallshammar, Sweden . 11 F9
Ljusnan →, Sweden ... 10 C11
Ljusne, Sweden 10 C11
Ljutomer, Slovenia ... 29 B13
Llagostera, Spain 32 D7
Llancanelo, Salina, Argentina 126 D2
Llandeilo, U.K. 13 F4
Llandovery, U.K. 13 F4
Llandrindod Wells, U.K. . 13 E4
Llandudno, U.K. 12 D4
Llanelli, U.K. 13 F3
Llanes, Spain 34 B6
Llangollen, U.K. 12 E4
Llanidloes, U.K. 13 E4
Llano, U.S.A. 113 K5
Llano →, U.S.A. 113 K5
Llano Estacado, U.S.A. . 113 J3
Llanos, S. Amer. 122 C3
Llanquihue, L., Chile ... 128 E1
Llanwrtyd Wells, U.K. .. 13 E4
Llebeig, C. des, Spain ... 37 B9
Lleida, Spain 32 D5
Lleida □, Spain 32 C6
Llentrisca, C., Spain ... 37 C7
Llera, Mexico 119 C5
Llerena, Spain 35 G5
Lleyn Peninsula, U.K. .. 12 E3
Llico, Chile 126 C1
Lliria, Spain 33 F4
Llobregat →, Spain ... 32 D7
Llodio, Spain 32 B2
Lloret de Mar, Spain ... 32 D7
Lloyd B., Australia ... 94 A3
Lloyd L., Canada 105 B7
Lloydminster, Canada .. 105 C7
Llucena del Cid, Spain .. 32 E4
Llucmajor, Spain 37 B9
Llullaillaco, Volcán, S. Amer. 126 A2
Lo →, Vietnam 64 B5
Loa, U.S.A. 115 G8
Loaita I., S. China Sea ... 62 B4
Loange →, Dem. Rep. of the Congo . 84 E4
Loano, Italy 28 D5
Lobatse, Botswana ... 88 D4
Löbau, Germany 24 D10
Lobenstein, Germany .. 24 E7
Lobería, Argentina ... 126 D4
Łobez, Poland 44 E2
Lobito, Angola 85 G2
Lobos, Argentina 126 D4
Lobos, I., Mexico 118 B2
Lobos, I. de, Canary Is. .. 37 F6
Łobżenica, Poland ... 45 E4
Loc Binh, Vietnam ... 64 B6
Loc Ninh, Vietnam ... 65 G6
Locarno, Switz. 25 J4
Loch Baghasdail = Lochboisdale, U.K. ... 14 D1

Loch Garman = Wexford,
Ireland 15 D5
Loch Nam Madadh =
Lochmaddy, U.K. 14 D1
Lochaber, U.K. 14 E3
Locharbriggs, U.K. 14 F5
Lochboisdale, U.K. 14 D1
Loche, L. La, Canada 105 B7
Lochem, Neths. 17 B6
Loches, France 18 E7
Lochgilphead, U.K. 14 E3
Lochinver, U.K. 14 C3
Lochmaddy, U.K. 14 D1
Lochnagar, Australia 94 C4
Lochnagar, U.K. 14 E5
Łochów, Poland 45 F8
Lochy, L., U.K. 14 E4
Lock, Australia 95 E2
Lock Haven, U.S.A. 110 E7
Lockeford, U.S.A. 116 G5
Lockeport, Canada 103 D6
Lockerbie, U.K. 14 F5
Lockhart, Australia 95 F4
Lockhart, U.S.A. 113 L6
Lockhart, L., Australia 93 F2
Lockhart River, Australia . 94 A3
Lockney, U.S.A. 113 H4
Lockport, U.S.A. 110 C6
Locminé, France 18 E4
Locri, Italy 31 D9
Locronan, France 18 D2
Lod, Israel 75 D3
Lodeinoye Pole, Russia ... 46 B7
Lodève, France 20 E6
Lodge Bay, Canada 103 B8
Lodge Grass, U.S.A. 114 D10
Lodgepole Cr. ➤, U.S.A. . 112 E2
Lodhran, Pakistan 68 E4
Lodi, Italy 28 C6
Lodi, Calif., U.S.A. 116 G5
Lodi, Ohio, U.S.A. 110 E3
Lodja,
  Dem. Rep. of the Congo . 86 C1
Lodosa, Spain 32 C2
Lödöse, Sweden 11 F6
Lodwar, Kenya 86 B4
Łódź, Poland 45 G6
Łódzkie □, Poland 45 G6
Loei, Thailand 64 D3
Loengo,
  Dem. Rep. of the Congo . 86 C2
Loeriesfontein, S. Africa ... 88 E2
Lofa ➤, Liberia 83 D2
Lofer, Austria 26 D5
Lofoten, Norway 8 B15
Lofsdalen, Sweden 10 B7
Lofsen ➤, Sweden 10 B7
Loftahammar, Sweden 11 G10
Loga, Niger 83 C5
Logan, Iowa, U.S.A. 112 E7
Logan, Ohio, U.S.A. 108 F4
Logan, Utah, U.S.A. 114 F8
Logan, W. Va., U.S.A. 108 G5
Logan, Mt., Canada 100 B5
Logandale, U.S.A. 117 J12
Logansport, Ind., U.S.A. . 108 E2
Logansport, La., U.S.A. .. 113 K8
Logirim, Sudan 81 G3
Logo, Sudan 81 F3
Logone ➤, Chad 79 F9
Logroño, Spain 32 C2
Logrosán, Spain 35 F5
Løgstør, Denmark 11 H3
Løgumkloster, Denmark .. 11 J2
Lohals, Denmark 11 J4
Lohardaga, India 69 H11
Loharia, India 68 H6
Loharu, India 68 E6
Lohja, Finland 9 F21
Löhne, Germany 24 C4
Lohr, Germany 25 F5
Lohri Wah ➤, Pakistan .. 68 F2
Loi-kaw, Burma 67 K20
Loimaa, Finland 9 F20
Loir ➤, France 18 E6
Loir-et-Cher □, France .. 18 E8
Loire □, France 21 C8
Loire ➤, France 18 E4
Loire-Atlantique □, France 18 E5
Loiret □, France 19 E9
Loitz, Germany 24 B9
Loja, Ecuador 124 D3
Loja, Spain 35 H6
Loji = Kawasi, Indonesia . 63 E7
Løjt Kirkeby, Denmark ... 11 J3
Lojung, China 58 E7
Loka, Sudan 81 G3
Lokandu,
  Dem. Rep. of the Congo . 86 C2
Lokeren, Belgium 17 C3
Lokgwabe, Botswana 88 C3
Lokhvitsa, Ukraine 47 G7
Lokichokio, Kenya 86 B3
Lokitaung, Kenya 86 B4
Lokkan tekojärvi, Finland . 8 C22
Løkken, Denmark 11 G3
Loknya, Russia 46 D6
Loko, Nigeria 83 D6
Lokoja, Nigeria 83 D6
Lokolama,
  Dem. Rep. of the Congo . 84 E3
Lol ➤, Sudan 81 F2
Lola, Guinea 82 D3
Lola, Mt., U.S.A. 116 F6
Lolibai, Gebel, Sudan 81 G3
Lolimi, Sudan 81 G3
Loliondo, Tanzania 86 C4
Lolland, Denmark 11 K5
Lollar, Germany 24 E4
Lolo, U.S.A. 114 C6
Lolodorf, Cameroon 83 E7
Lom, Bulgaria 40 C7

Lom ➤, Bulgaria 40 C7
Lom Kao, Thailand 64 D3
Lom Sak, Thailand 64 D3
Loma, U.S.A. 114 C8
Loma Linda, U.S.A. 117 L9
Lomami ➤,
  Dem. Rep. of the Congo . 86 B1
Lomas de Zamóra, Argentina 126 C4
Lombadina, Australia 92 C3
Lombárdia □, Italy 28 C6
Lombardy = Lombárdia □,
  Italy 28 C6
Lombez, France 20 E4
Lomblen, Indonesia 63 F6
Lombok, Indonesia 62 F5
Lomé, Togo 83 D5
Lomela,
  Dem. Rep. of the Congo . 84 E4
Lomela ➤,
  Dem. Rep. of the Congo . 84 E4
Lomianki, Poland 45 F7
Lomma, Sweden 11 J7
Lommel, Belgium 17 C5
Lomond, Canada 104 C6
Lomond, L., U.K. 14 E4
Lomphat, Cambodia 64 F6
Lompobatang, Indonesia . 63 F5
Lompoc, U.S.A. 117 L6
Łomża, Poland 45 E9
Loncoche, Chile 128 D2
Londa, India 66 M9
Londiani, Kenya 86 C4
Londinières, France 18 C8
London, Canada 102 D3
London, U.K. 13 F7
London, Ky., U.S.A. 108 G3
London, Ohio, U.S.A. 108 F4
London, Greater □, U.K. . 13 F7
Londonderry, U.K. 15 B4
Londonderry □, U.K. 15 B4
Londonderry, C., Australia . 92 B4
Londonderry, I., Chile 128 H2
Londres, Argentina 128 B3
Londrina, Brazil 127 A5
Lone Pine, U.S.A. 116 J8
Lonely Mine, Zimbabwe .. 89 B4
Long B., U.S.A. 109 J6
Long Beach, Calif., U.S.A. . 117 M8
Long Beach, N.Y., U.S.A. . 111 F11
Long Beach, Wash., U.S.A. 116 D2
Long Branch, U.S.A. 111 F11
Long Creek, U.S.A. 114 D4
Long Eaton, U.K. 12 E6
Long I., Australia 94 C4
Long I., Bahamas 121 B4
Long I., Canada 102 B4
Long I., Ireland 15 E2
Long I., U.S.A. 111 F11
Long Island Sd., U.S.A. .. 111 E12
Long L., Canada 102 C2
Long Lake, U.S.A. 111 C10
Long Point B., Canada ... 110 D4
Long Prairie ➤, U.S.A. .. 112 C7
Long Pt., Canada 110 D4
Long Range Mts., Canada . 103 C8
Long Reef, Australia 92 B4
Long Spruce, Canada 105 B10
Long Str. = Longa, Proliv,
  Russia 4 C16
Long Thanh, Vietnam 65 G6
Long Xian, China 56 G4
Long Xuyen, Vietnam 65 G5
Longá, Greece 38 E3
Longa, Proliv, Russia 4 C16
Long'an, China 58 F6
Longarone, Italy 29 B9
Longbenton, U.K. 12 B6
Longboat Key, U.S.A. 109 M4
Longchang, China 58 C5
Longchi, China 58 C4
Longchuan, Guangdong,
  China 59 E10
Longchuan, Yunnan, China 58 E1
Longde, China 56 G4
Longeau, France 19 E12
Longford, Australia 94 G4
Longford, Ireland 15 C4
Longford □, Ireland 15 C4
Longguan, China 56 D8
Longhai, China 59 E11
Longhua, China 57 D9
Longhui, China 59 D8
Longido, Tanzania 86 C4
Longiram, Indonesia 62 E5
Longkou, Jiangxi, China .. 59 D10
Longkou, Shandong, China 57 F11
Longlac, Canada 102 C2
Longli, China 58 D6
Longlin, China 58 E5
Longling, China 58 E2
Longmeadow, U.S.A. 111 D12
Longmen, China 59 F10
Longming, China 58 F6
Longmont, U.S.A. 112 E2
Longnan, China 59 E10
Longnawan, Indonesia ... 62 D4
Longobucco, Italy 31 C9
Longquan, China 59 C12
Longreach, Australia 94 C3
Longshan, China 58 C7
Longsheng, China 59 E8
Longué-Jumelles, France . 18 E6
Longueau, France 19 C9
Longueuil, Canada 111 A11
Longuyon, France 19 C12
Longvic, France 19 E12
Longview, Tex., U.S.A. ... 113 J7
Longview, Wash., U.S.A. . 116 D4
Longwy, France 19 C12
Longxi, China 56 G3
Longyan, China 59 E11

Longyou, China 59 C12
Longzhou, China 58 F6
Lonigo, Italy 29 C8
Löningen, Germany 24 C3
Lonja ➤, Croatia 29 C13
Lonoke, U.S.A. 113 H9
Lonquimay, Chile 128 D2
Lons-le-Saunier, France ... 19 F12
Lönsboda, Sweden 11 H8
Looe, U.K. 13 G3
Lookout, C., Canada 102 A3
Lookout, C., U.S.A. 109 H7
Loolmalasin, Tanzania ... 86 C4
Loon ➤, Alta., Canada .. 104 B5
Loon ➤, Man., Canada .. 105 B8
Loon Lake, Canada 105 C7
Loongana, Australia 93 F4
Loop Hd., Ireland 15 D2
Lop Buri, Thailand 64 E3
Lop Nor = Lop Nur, China 60 B4
Lop Nur, China 60 B4
Lopare, Bos.-H. 42 F3
Lopatin, Russia 49 J8
Lopatina, Gora, Russia ... 51 D15
Lopaye, Sudan 81 F3
Lopez, Phil. 61 E5
Lopez, U.S.A. 111 E8
Lopez, C., Gabon 84 E1
Lopphavet, Norway 8 A19
Lora ➤, Afghan. 66 D4
Lora, Hamun-i-, Pakistan . 66 E4
Lora Cr. ➤, Australia ... 95 D2
Lora del Río, Spain 35 H5
Lorain, U.S.A. 110 E2
Loralai, Pakistan 68 D3
Lorca, Spain 33 H3
Lord Howe I., Pac. Oc. .. 96 L7
Lord Howe Ridge, Pac. Oc. 96 L8
Lordsburg, U.S.A. 115 K9
Loreto, Brazil 125 E9
Loreto, Italy 29 E10
Loreto, Mexico 118 B2
Lorgues, France 21 E10
Lorhosso, Burkina Faso .. 82 C4
Lorient, France 18 E3
Lorin, India 69 H9
Lorn, Australia 95 E5
Lorn, Firth of, U.K. 14 E3
Lorne, Australia 95 F3
Loronyo, Sudan 81 G3
Lorovouno, Cyprus 36 D11
Lörrach, Germany 25 H3
Lorraine □, France 19 D13
Los, Sweden 10 C9
Los, Îles de, Guinea 82 D2
Los Alamos, Calif., U.S.A. 117 L6
Los Alamos, N. Mex.,
  U.S.A. 115 J10
Los Altos, U.S.A. 116 H4
Los Andes, Chile 126 C1
Los Angeles, Chile 126 D1
Los Angeles, U.S.A. 117 M8
Los Angeles, Bahia de,
  Mexico 118 B2
Los Angeles Aqueduct,
  U.S.A. 117 K9
Los Banos, U.S.A. 116 H6
Los Barrios, Spain 35 J5
Los Blancos, Argentina ... 126 A3
Los Chiles, Costa Rica ... 120 D3
Los Corrales de Buelna,
  Spain 34 B6
Los Cristianos, Canary Is. 37 F3
Los Gallardos, Spain 33 H3
Los Gatos, U.S.A. 116 H5
Los Hermanos Is., Venezuela 121 D7
Los Islotes, Canary Is. ... 37 E6
Los Llanos de Aridane,
  Canary Is. 37 F2
Los Loros, Chile 126 B1
Los Lunas, U.S.A. 115 J10
Los Mochis, Mexico 118 B3
Los Monegros, Spain 32 D4
Los Nietos, Spain 33 H4
Los Olivos, U.S.A. 117 L6
Los Palacios, Cuba 120 B3
Los Palacios y Villafranca,
  Spain 35 H5
Los Reyes, Mexico 118 D4
Los Roques Is., Venezuela 121 D6
Los Santos de Maimona,
  Spain 35 G4
Los Teques, Venezuela ... 124 A5
Los Testigos, Is., Venezuela 124 A6
Los Vilos, Chile 126 C1
Los Yébenes, Spain 35 F7
Łosice, Poland 45 F9
Loskop Dam, S. Africa ... 89 D4
Løsning, Denmark 11 J3
Lossiemouth, U.K. 14 D5
Lostwithiel, U.K. 13 G3
Lot □, France 20 D5
Lot ➤, France 20 D4
Lot-et-Garonne □, France . 20 D4
Lota, Chile 126 D1
Lotagipi Swamp, Sudan .. 81 G3
Loṭfābād, Iran 71 B8
Lothair, S. Africa 89 D5
Lotorp, Sweden 11 F9
Lötschbergtunnel, Switz. . 25 J3
Löttorp, Sweden 11 G11
Loubomo, Congo 84 E2
Loudéac, France 18 D4
Loudi, China 59 D8
Loudonville, U.S.A. 110 F2
Loudun, France 18 E7
Loue ➤, France 19 E12
Louga, Senegal 82 B1

Loughborough, U.K. 12 E6
Loughrea, Ireland 15 C3
Loughros More B., Ireland . 15 B3
Louhans, France 19 F12
Louis Trichardt, S. Africa . 89 C4
Louis XIV, Pte., Canada .. 102 B4
Louisa, U.S.A. 108 F4
Louisbourg, Canada 103 C8
Louise I., Canada 104 C2
Louiseville, Canada 102 C5
Louisiade Arch.,
  Papua N. G. 96 J7
Louisiana, U.S.A. 112 F9
Louisiana □, U.S.A. 113 K9
Louisville, Ky., U.S.A. ... 108 F3
Louisville, Miss., U.S.A. . 113 J10
Louisville, Ohio, U.S.A. .. 110 F3
Loulay, France 20 B3
Loulé, Portugal 35 H3
Louny, Czech Rep. 26 A6
Loup City, U.S.A. 112 E5
Loup, Lacs des,
  Canada 102 A5
Lourdes, France 20 E3
Lourenço-Marques =
  Maputo, Mozam. 89 D5
Lourinhã, Portugal 35 F1
Lousã, Portugal 34 E2
Louth, Australia 95 E4
Louth, Ireland 15 C5
Louth, U.K. 12 D7
Louth □, Ireland 15 C5
Loutrá Aidhipsoú, Greece . 38 C5
Loutráki, Greece 38 D4
Louvain = Leuven, Belgium 17 D4
Louviers, France 18 C8
Louwsburg, S. Africa 89 D5
Lovat ➤, Russia 46 C6
Lovćen, Montenegro, Yug. . 40 D2
Lovech, Bulgaria 41 C8
Lovech □, Bulgaria 41 C8
Loveland, U.S.A. 112 E2
Lovell, U.S.A. 114 D9
Lovelock, U.S.A. 114 F4
Lóvere, Italy 28 C7
Lovestad, Sweden 11 J7
Loviisa = Lovisa, Finland . 9 F22
Lovington, U.S.A. 113 J3
Lovisa, Finland 9 F22
Lovosice, Czech Rep. 26 A7
Lovran, Croatia 29 C11
Lovrin, Romania 42 E5
Lövstabruk, Sweden 10 D11
Lövstabuken, Sweden 10 D11
Low, L., Canada 102 B4
Low Pt., Australia 93 F4
Low Tatra = Nízké Tatry,
  Slovak Rep. 27 C12
Lowa,
  Dem. Rep. of the Congo . 86 C2
Lowa ➤,
  Dem. Rep. of the Congo . 86 C2
Lowell, U.S.A. 111 D13
Lowellville, U.S.A. 110 E4
Löwen ➤, Namibia 88 D2
Lower Alkali L., U.S.A. ... 114 F3
Lower Arrow L., Canada . 104 D5
Lower Austria =
  Niederösterreich □,
  Austria 26 C8
Lower California = Baja
  California, Mexico ... 118 A1
Lower Hutt, N.Z. 91 J5
Lower Lake, U.S.A. 116 G4
Lower Manitou L., Canada 105 D10
Lower Post, Canada 104 B3
Lower Red L., U.S.A. ... 112 B7
Lower Saxony =
  Niedersachsen □,
  Germany 24 C4
Lower Tunguska =
  Tunguska, Nizhnyaya ➤,
  Russia 51 C9
Lowestoft, U.K. 13 E9
Łowicz, Poland 45 F6
Lowville, U.S.A. 111 C9
Loxton, Australia 95 E3
Loxton, S. Africa 88 E3
Loyalton, U.S.A. 116 F6
Loyalty Is. = Loyauté, Is.,
  N. Cal. 96 K8
Loyang = Luoyang, China . 56 G7
Loyauté, Is., N. Cal. 96 K8
Loyev = Loyew, Belarus .. 47 G6
Loyew, Belarus 47 G6
Loyoro, Uganda 86 B3
Loż, Slovenia 29 C11
Lozère □, France 20 D7
Loznica, Serbia, Yug. 40 B3
Lozova, Ukraine 47 H9
Lü Shan, China 59 C11
Lü-Tao, Taiwan 59 F13
Luachimo, Angola 84 F4
Luajan ➤, India 69 G11
Lualaba ➤,
  Dem. Rep. of the Congo . 86 B2
Luampa, Zambia 87 F1
Lu'an, China 59 B11
Luan Chau, Vietnam 58 G4
Luan He ➤, China 57 E10
Luan Xian, China 57 E10
Luancheng,
  Guangxi Zhuangzu, China 58 F7
Luancheng, Hebei, China . 56 F8
Luanco, Spain 34 B5
Luanda, Angola 84 F2
Luang, Thale, Thailand ... 65 J3
Luang Prabang, Laos 58 H4
Luangwa, Zambia 87 F3

Luangwa ➤, Zambia 87 E3
Luangwa Valley, Zambia .. 87 E3
Luanne, China 57 D9
Luanping, China 57 D9
Luanshya, Zambia 87 E2
Luapula □, Zambia 87 E2
Luapula ➤, Africa 87 D2
Luarca, Spain 34 B4
Luashi,
  Dem. Rep. of the Congo . 87 E1
Luau, Angola 84 G4
Lubaczów, Poland 45 H10
Lubań, Poland 45 G2
Lubana, Ozero = Lubānas
  Ezers, Latvia 9 H22
Lubānas Ezers, Latvia ... 9 H22
Lubang, Phil. 61 E4
Lubang Is., Phil. 63 B6
Lubartów, Poland 45 G9
Lubawa, Poland 44 E6
Lübbecke, Germany 24 C4
Lübben, Germany 24 D9
Lübbenau, Germany 24 D9
Lubbock, U.S.A. 113 J4
Lübeck, Germany 24 B6
Lübecker Bucht, Germany . 24 A6
Lubefu,
  Dem. Rep. of the Congo . 86 C1
Lubefu ➤,
  Dem. Rep. of the Congo . 86 C1
Lubero = Luofu,
  Dem. Rep. of the Congo . 86 C2
Lubersac, France 20 C5
Lubicon L., Canada 104 B5
Lubień Kujawski, Poland . 45 F6
Lubilash ➤,
  Dem. Rep. of the Congo . 84 F4
Lubin, Poland 45 G3
Lublin, Poland 45 G9
Lubliniec, Poland 45 H5
Lubnān, Jabal, Lebanon .. 75 B4
Lubniewice, Poland 45 F2
Lubny, Ukraine 47 G7
Lubomierz, Poland 45 G2
Luboń, Poland 45 F3
Lubongola,
  Dem. Rep. of the Congo . 86 C2
L'ubotín, Slovak Rep. ... 27 B13
Lubraniec, Poland 45 F5
Lubsko, Poland 45 G1
Lübtheen, Germany 24 B7
Lubuagan, Phil. 61 C4
Lubudi,
  Dem. Rep. of the Congo . 84 F5
Lubudi ➤,
  Dem. Rep. of the Congo . 87 D2
Lubuklinggau, Indonesia . 62 E2
Lubuksikaping, Indonesia . 62 D2
Lubumbashi,
  Dem. Rep. of the Congo . 87 E2
Lubunda,
  Dem. Rep. of the Congo . 86 D2
Lubungu, Zambia 87 E2
Lubuskie □, Poland 45 F2
Lubutu,
  Dem. Rep. of the Congo . 86 C2
Luc An Chau, Vietnam .. 64 A5
Luc-en-Diois, France 21 D9
Lucan, Canada 110 C3
Lucania, Mt., Canada ... 100 B5
Lucas Channel, Canada .. 110 A3
Lucban, Phil. 61 D4
Lucca, Italy 28 E7
Luce ➤, France 18 E4
Luce Bay, U.K. 14 G4
Lucea, Jamaica 120 C4
Lucedale, U.S.A. 109 K1
Lucena, Phil. 61 D4
Lucena, Spain 35 H6
Lučenec, Slovak Rep. ... 27 C12
Lucera, Italy 31 A8
Lucerne = Luzern, Switz. . 25 H4
Lucerne, U.S.A. 116 F4
Lucerne Valley, U.S.A. ... 117 L10
Lucero, Mexico 118 A3
Luchena ➤, Spain 33 H3
Lucheng, China 56 F7
Lucheringo ➤, Mozam. .. 87 E4
Lüchow, Germany 24 C7
Luchuan, China 59 F8
Lucia, U.S.A. 116 J5
Lucinda, Australia 94 B4
Lucindale, Australia 95 F3
Luckau, Germany 24 D9
Luckenwalde, Germany .. 24 C9
Luckhoff, S. Africa 88 D3
Lucknow, Canada 110 C3
Lucknow, India 69 F9
Luçon, France 20 B2
Lüda = Dalian, China ... 57 E11
Luda Kamchiya ➤, Bulgaria 41 C11
Ludbreg, Croatia 29 B13
Lüdenscheid, Germany .. 24 D3
Lüderitz, Namibia 88 D2
Lüderitzbaai, Namibia ... 88 D2
Ludhiana, India 68 D6
Ludian, China 58 D4
Luding Qiao, China 58 C4
Lüdinghausen, Germany . 24 D3
Ludington, U.S.A. 108 D2
Ludlow, U.K. 13 E5
Ludlow, Calif., U.S.A. ... 117 L10
Ludlow, Vt., U.S.A. 111 C12
Ludus, Romania 43 D9
Ludvika, Sweden 10 D9
Ludwigsburg, Germany .. 25 G5
Ludwigsfelde, Germany .. 24 C9
Ludwigshafen, Germany . 25 F4
Ludwigslust, Germany ... 24 B7

Ludza, *Latvia* ... 46 D4
Lueki,
  Dem. Rep. of the Congo . 86 C2
Luena,
  Dem. Rep. of the Congo . 87 D2
Luena, *Zambia* ... 87 E3
Lüeyang, *China* ... 56 H4
Lufeng, *Guangdong, China* . 59 F10
Lufeng, *Yunnan, China* . 58 E4
Lufira →,
  Dem. Rep. of the Congo . 87 D2
Lufkin, *U.S.A.* ... 113 K7
Lufupa,
  Dem. Rep. of the Congo . 87 E1
Luga, *Russia* ... 46 C5
Luga →, *Russia* ... 46 C5
Lugano, *Switz.* ... 25 J4
Lugano, L. di, *Switz.* ... 28 C6
Lugansk = Luhansk, *Ukraine* 47 H10
Lugard's Falls, *Kenya* ... 86 C4
Lugela, *Mozam.* ... 87 F4
Lugenda →, *Mozam.* ... 87 E4
Lugh Ganana, *Somali Rep.* . 74 G3
Lugnaquilla, *Ireland* ... 15 D5
Lugo, *Italy* ... 29 D8
Lugo, *Spain* ... 34 B3
Lugo □, *Spain* ... 34 C3
Lugoj, *Romania* ... 42 E6
Lugovoy, *Kazakstan* ... 50 E8
Luhansk, *Ukraine* ... 47 H10
Luhe, *China* ... 59 A12
Luhe →, *Germany* ... 24 B6
Luhuo, *China* ... 58 B3
Luiana, *Angola* ... 88 B3
Luimneach = Limerick,
  Ireland ... 15 D3
Luing, *U.K.* ... 14 E3
Luino, *Italy* ... 28 C5
Luís Correia, *Brazil* ... 125 D10
Luitpold Coast, *Antarctica* . 5 D1
Luiza,
  Dem. Rep. of the Congo . 84 F4
Luizi,
  Dem. Rep. of the Congo . 86 D2
Luján, *Argentina* ... 126 C4
Lujiang, *China* ... 59 B11
Lukang, *Taiwan* ... 59 E13
Lukanga Swamp, *Zambia* . 87 E2
Lukavac, *Bos.-H.* ... 42 F3
Lukenie →,
  Dem. Rep. of the Congo . 84 E3
Lukhisaral, *India* ... 69 G12
Lüki, *Bulgaria* ... 41 E8
Lukolela,
  Dem. Rep. of the Congo . 86 D1
Lukosi, *Zimbabwe* ... 87 F2
Lukovë, *Albania* ... 40 G3
Lukovit, *Bulgaria* ... 41 C8
Łuków, *Poland* ... 45 G9
Lukoyanov, *Russia* ... 48 C7
Lule älv →, *Sweden* ... 8 D19
Luleå, *Sweden* ... 8 D20
Lüleburgaz, *Turkey* ... 41 E11
Luliang, *China* ... 58 E4
Luling, *U.S.A.* ... 113 L6
Lulong, *China* ... 57 E10
Lulonga →,
  Dem. Rep. of the Congo . 84 D3
Lulua →,
  Dem. Rep. of the Congo . 84 E4
Luluabourg = Kananga,
  Dem. Rep. of the Congo . 84 F4
Lumajang, *Indonesia* ... 63 H15
Lumbala N'guimbo, *Angola* . 85 G4
Lumberton, *U.S.A.* ... 109 H6
Lumbwa, *Kenya* ... 86 C4
Lumsden, *Canada* ... 105 C8
Lumsden, *N.Z.* ... 91 L2
Lumut, *Malaysia* ... 65 K3
Lumut, Tanjung, *Indonesia* . 62 E3
Luna, *India* ... 68 H3
Lunan, *China* ... 58 E4
Lunavada, *India* ... 68 H5
Lunca, *Romania* ... 43 C10
Lunca Corbului, *Romania* . 43 F9
Lund, *Sweden* ... 11 J7
Lundazi, *Zambia* ... 87 E3
Lunderskov, *Denmark* ... 11 J3
Lundi →, *Zimbabwe* ... 87 G3
Lundu, *Malaysia* ... 62 D3
Lundy, *U.K.* ... 13 F3
Lune →, *U.K.* ... 12 C5
Lüneburg, *Germany* ... 24 B6
Lüneburg Heath =
  Lüneburger Heide,
  Germany ... 24 B6
Lüneburger Heide, *Germany* 24 B6
Lunel, *France* ... 21 E8
Lünen, *Germany* ... 24 D3
Lunenburg, *Canada* ... 103 D7
Lunéville, *France* ... 19 D13
Lunga →, *Zambia* ... 87 E2
Lungi Airport, *S. Leone* ... 82 D2
Lunglei, *India* ... 67 H18
Luni, *India* ... 68 G5
Luni →, *India* ... 68 G4
Luninets = Luninyets,
  Belarus ... 47 F4
Luning, *U.S.A.* ... 114 G4
Lunino, *Russia* ... 48 D7
Luninyets, *Belarus* ... 47 F4
Lunkaransar, *India* ... 68 E5
Lunsemfwa →, *Zambia* ... 87 E3
Lunsemfwa Falls, *Zambia* . 87 E2
Luo He →, *China* ... 56 G6
Luocheng, *China* ... 58 E7
Luochuan, *China* ... 56 G5
Luoci, *China* ... 58 E4
Luodian, *China* ... 58 E6
Luoding, *China* ... 59 F8

Luofu,
  Dem. Rep. of the Congo . 86 C2
Luohe, *China* ... 56 H8
Luojiang, *China* ... 58 B5
Luonan, *China* ... 56 G6
Luoning, *China* ... 56 G6
Luoshan, *China* ... 59 A10
Luotian, *China* ... 59 B10
Luoxiao Shan, *China* ... 59 D10
Luoyang, *China* ... 56 G7
Luoyuan, *China* ... 59 D12
Luozigou, *China* ... 57 C16
Lupanshui, *China* ... 58 D5
Lupeni, *Romania* ... 43 E8
Lupilichi, *Mozam.* ... 87 E4
Łupków, *Poland* ... 45 J9
Luping, *China* ... 58 E5
Luquan, *China* ... 58 E4
Luque, *Paraguay* ... 126 B4
Lúras, *Italy* ... 30 B2
Luray, *U.S.A.* ... 108 F6
Lure, *France* ... 19 E13
Lurgan, *U.K.* ... 15 B5
Lusaka, *Zambia* ... 87 F2
Lusambo,
  Dem. Rep. of the Congo . 86 C1
Lusangaye,
  Dem. Rep. of the Congo . 86 C2
Luseland, *Canada* ... 105 C7
Lushan, *Henan, China* ... 56 H7
Lushan, *Sichuan, China* ... 58 B4
Lushi, *China* ... 56 G6
Lushnja, *Albania* ... 40 F3
Lushoto, *Tanzania* ... 86 C4
Lushui, *China* ... 58 E2
Lüshun, *China* ... 57 E11
Lusignan, *France* ... 20 B4
Lusigny-sur-Barse, *France* . 19 D11
Lusk, *U.S.A.* ... 112 D2
Lussac-les-Châteaux, *France* 20 B4
Lustenau, *Austria* ... 26 D2
Lüt, Dasht-e, *Iran* ... 71 D8
Luta = Dalian, *China* ... 57 E11
Lutherstadt Wittenberg,
  Germany ... 24 D8
Luton, *U.K.* ... 13 F7
Luton □, *U.K.* ... 13 F7
Lutselke, *Canada* ... 105 A6
Lutsk, *Ukraine* ... 47 G3
Lützow Holmbukta,
  Antarctica ... 5 C4
Lutzputs, *S. Africa* ... 88 D3
Luverne, *Ala., U.S.A.* ... 109 K2
Luverne, *Minn., U.S.A.* ... 112 D6
Luvua,
  Dem. Rep. of the Congo . 87 D2
Luvua →,
  Dem. Rep. of the Congo . 86 D2
Luvuvhu →, *S. Africa* ... 89 C5
Luwegu →, *Tanzania* ... 87 D4
Luwuk, *Indonesia* ... 63 E6
Luxembourg, *Lux.* ... 17 E6
Luxembourg □, *Belgium* ... 17 E5
Luxembourg ■, *Europe* ... 7 F7
Luxeuil-les-Bains, *France* . 19 E13
Luxi, *Hunan, China* ... 59 C8
Luxi, *Yunnan, China* ... 58 E4
Luxi, *Yunnan, China* ... 58 E2
Luxor = El Uqsur, *Egypt* ... 80 B3
Luy-de-Béarn →, *France* ... 20 E3
Luy-de-France →, *France* ... 20 E3
Luyi, *China* ... 56 H8
Luz-St-Sauveur, *France* ... 20 F4
Luzern, *Switz.* ... 25 H4
Luzern □, *Switz.* ... 25 H3
Luzhai, *China* ... 58 E7
Luzhi, *China* ... 58 D5
Luzhou, *China* ... 58 C5
Luziânia, *Brazil* ... 125 G9
Lužnice →, *Czech Rep.* ... 26 B7
Luzon, *Phil.* ... 61 D4
Luzy, *France* ... 19 F10
Luzzi, *Italy* ... 31 C9
Lviv, *Ukraine* ... 47 H3
Lvov = Lviv, *Ukraine* ... 47 H3
Lwówek, *Poland* ... 45 F3
Lwówek Śląski, *Poland* ... 45 G2
Lyakhavichy, *Belarus* ... 47 F4
Lyakhovskiye, Ostrova,
  Russia ... 51 B15
Lyaki = Läki, *Azerbaijan* ... 49 K8
Lyal I., *Canada* ... 110 B3
Lyallpur = Faisalabad,
  Pakistan ... 68 D5
Lyaskovets, *Bulgaria* ... 41 C9
Lybster, *U.K.* ... 14 C5
Lycaonia, *Turkey* ... 72 D5
Lychen, *Germany* ... 24 B9
Lychkova, *Russia* ... 46 D7
Lycia, *Turkey* ... 39 E11
Lyckebyån →, *Sweden* ... 11 H9
Lycksele, *Sweden* ... 8 D18
Lycosura, *Greece* ... 38 D3
Lydda = Lod, *Israel* ... 75 D3
Lydenburg, *S. Africa* ... 89 D5
Lydia, *Turkey* ... 39 C10
Łydynia →, *Poland* ... 45 F7
Lyell, *N.Z.* ... 91 J4
Lyell I., *Canada* ... 104 C2
Lyepyel, *Belarus* ... 46 E5
Lygnern, *Sweden* ... 11 G6
Lykens, *U.S.A.* ... 111 F8
Lyman, *U.S.A.* ... 114 F8
Lyme B., *U.K.* ... 13 G4
Lyme Regis, *U.K.* ... 13 G5
Lymington, *U.K.* ... 13 G6
Łyna →, *Poland* ... 9 J19
Lynchburg, *U.S.A.* ... 108 G6
Lynd →, *Australia* ... 94 B3
Lynd Ra., *Australia* ... 95 D4
Lynden, *Canada* ... 110 C4

Lynden, *U.S.A.* ... 116 B4
Lyndhurst, *Australia* ... 95 E2
Lyndon →, *Australia* ... 93 D1
Lyndonville, *N.Y., U.S.A.* ... 110 C6
Lyndonville, *Vt., U.S.A.* ... 111 B12
Lyngen, *Norway* ... 8 B19
Lynher Reef, *Australia* ... 92 C3
Lynn, *U.S.A.* ... 111 D14
Lynn Lake, *Canada* ... 105 B8
Lynnwood, *U.S.A.* ... 116 C4
Lynton, *U.K.* ... 13 F4
Lyntupy, *Belarus* ... 9 J22
Lynx L., *Canada* ... 105 A7
Lyon, *France* ... 21 C8
Lyonnais, *France* ... 21 C8
Lyons = Lyon, *France* ... 21 C8
Lyons, *Ga., U.S.A.* ... 109 J4
Lyons, *Kans., U.S.A.* ... 112 F5
Lyons, *N.Y., U.S.A.* ... 110 C8
Lyons →, *Australia* ... 93 E2
Lyons →, *U.S.A.* ... 111 C9
Lyozna, *Belarus* ... 46 E6
Lys = Leie →, *Belgium* ... 17 C3
Lysá nad Labem, *Czech Rep.* 26 A7
Lysekil, *Sweden* ... 11 F5
Lyskovo, *Russia* ... 48 B7
Lystrup, *Denmark* ... 11 H4
Lysva, *Russia* ... 10 D7
Lysvik, *Sweden* ... 10 D7
Lysychansk, *Ukraine* ... 47 H10
Lytham St. Anne's, *U.K.* ... 12 D4
Lytton, *Canada* ... 104 C4
Lyuban, *Russia* ... 46 C6
Lyubertsy, *Russia* ... 46 E9
Lyubim, *Russia* ... 46 C11
Lyuboml, *Ukraine* ... 47 G3
Lyubotyn, *Ukraine* ... 47 H8
Lyubytino, *Russia* ... 46 C7
Lyudinovo, *Russia* ... 46 F8

M

M.R. Gomez, Presa, *Mexico* 119 B5
Ma →, *Vietnam* ... 58 H5
Ma'adaba, *Jordan* ... 75 E4
Maamba, *Zambia* ... 88 B4
Ma'ān, *Jordan* ... 75 E4
Ma'ān □, *Jordan* ... 75 F5
Maanselkä, *Finland* ... 8 C23
Ma'anshan, *China* ... 59 B12
Maarianhamina, *Finland* ... 9 F18
Ma'arrat an Nu'mān, *Syria* . 70 C3
Maas →, *Neths.* ... 17 C4
Maaseik, *Belgium* ... 17 C5
Maasin, *Phil.* ... 63 B6
Maastricht, *Neths.* ... 17 D5
Maave, *Mozam.* ... 89 C5
Mababe Depression,
  Botswana ... 88 B3
Mabalane, *Mozam.* ... 89 C5
Mabel L., *Canada* ... 104 C5
Mabenge,
  Dem. Rep. of the Congo . 86 B1
Maberly, *Canada* ... 111 B8
Mabian, *China* ... 58 C4
Mabil, *Ethiopia* ... 81 E4
Mablethorpe, *U.K.* ... 12 D8
Mably, *France* ... 19 F11
Maboma,
  Dem. Rep. of the Congo . 86 B2
Mabonto, *S. Leone* ... 82 D2
Mabrouk, *Mali* ... 83 B4
Mac Bac, *Vietnam* ... 65 H6
Macachín, *Argentina* ... 126 D3
Macaé, *Brazil* ... 127 A7
Macael, *Spain* ... 33 H2
McAlester, *U.S.A.* ... 113 H7
McAllen, *U.S.A.* ... 113 M5
MacAlpine L., *Canada* ... 100 B9
Macamic, *Canada* ... 102 C4
Macao = Macau, *Asia* ... 59 F9
Macão, *Portugal* ... 35 F3
Macapá, *Brazil* ... 125 C8
McArthur →, *Australia* ... 94 B2
McArthur, Port, *Australia* . 94 B2
Macau, *Brazil* ... 125 E11
Macau, *Asia* ... 59 F9
McBride, *Canada* ... 104 C4
McCall, *U.S.A.* ... 114 D5
McCamey, *U.S.A.* ... 113 K3
McCammon, *U.S.A.* ... 114 E7
McCauley I., *Canada* ... 104 C2
McCleary, *U.S.A.* ... 116 C3
Macclenny, *U.S.A.* ... 109 K4
Macclesfield, *U.K.* ... 12 D5
M'Clintock Chan., *Canada* . 100 A9
McClintock Ra., *Australia* . 92 C4
McCloud, *U.S.A.* ... 114 F2
McClure, *U.S.A.* ... 110 F7
McClure, L., *U.S.A.* ... 116 H6
M'Clure Str., *Canada* ... 4 B2
McClusky, *U.S.A.* ... 112 B4
McComb, *U.S.A.* ... 113 K9
McConaughy, L., *U.S.A.* ... 112 E4
McCook, *U.S.A.* ... 112 E4
McCreary, *Canada* ... 105 C9
McCullough Mt., *U.S.A.* ... 117 K11
McCusker →, *Canada* ... 105 B7
McDame, *Canada* ... 104 B3
McDermitt, *U.S.A.* ... 114 F5
McDonald, *U.S.A.* ... 110 F4
Macdonald, L., *Australia* ... 92 D4
McDonald Is., *Ind. Oc.* ... 3 G13
MacDonnell Ranges,
  Australia ... 92 D5
MacDowell L., *Canada* ... 102 B1

Macduff, *U.K.* ... 14 D6
Maceda, *Spain* ... 34 C3
Macedonia, *U.S.A.* ... 110 E3
Macedonia ■, *Europe* ... 40 E5
Maceió, *Brazil* ... 125 E11
Maceira, *Portugal* ... 34 F2
Macenta, *Guinea* ... 82 D3
Macerata, *Italy* ... 29 E10
McFarland, *U.S.A.* ... 117 K7
McFarlane →, *Canada* ... 105 B7
Macfarlane, L., *Australia* ... 95 E2
McGehee, *U.S.A.* ... 113 J9
McGill, *U.S.A.* ... 114 G6
Macgillycuddy's Reeks,
  Ireland ... 15 E2
McGraw, *U.S.A.* ... 111 D8
McGregor, *U.S.A.* ... 112 D9
McGregor Ra., *Australia* ... 95 D3
Mach, *Pakistan* ... 66 E5
Māch Kowr, *Iran* ... 71 E9
Machado = Jiparaná →,
  Brazil ... 124 E6
Machagai, *Argentina* ... 126 B3
Machakos, *Kenya* ... 86 C4
Machala, *Ecuador* ... 124 D3
Machanga, *Mozam.* ... 89 C6
Machattie, L., *Australia* ... 94 C2
Machava, *Mozam.* ... 89 D5
Machece, *Mozam.* ... 87 F4
Machecoul, *France* ... 18 F5
Macheke, *Zimbabwe* ... 89 B5
Macheng, *China* ... 59 B10
Machero, *Spain* ... 35 F6
Machhu →, *India* ... 68 H4
Machias, *Maine, U.S.A.* ... 109 C12
Machias, *N.Y., U.S.A.* ... 110 D6
Machichi →, *Canada* ... 105 B10
Machico, *Madeira* ... 37 D3
Machilipatnam, *India* ... 67 L12
Machiques, *Venezuela* ... 124 A4
Machupicchu, *Peru* ... 124 F4
Machynlleth, *U.K.* ... 13 E4
Macia, *Mozam.* ... 89 D5
Maciejowice, *Poland* ... 45 G8
McIlwraith Ra., *Australia* ... 94 A3
Măcin, *Romania* ... 43 E13
Macina, *Mali* ... 82 C4
McInnes L., *Canada* ... 105 C10
McIntosh, *U.S.A.* ... 112 C4
McIntosh L., *Canada* ... 105 B8
Macintosh Ra., *Australia* ... 93 E4
Macintyre →, *Australia* ... 95 D5
Macizo Galaico, *Spain* ... 34 C3
Mackay, *Australia* ... 94 C4
Mackay, *U.S.A.* ... 114 E7
MacKay →, *Canada* ... 104 B6
Mackay, L., *Australia* ... 92 D4
McKay Ra., *Australia* ... 92 D3
McKeesport, *U.S.A.* ... 110 F5
McKellar, *Canada* ... 110 A5
McKenna, *U.S.A.* ... 116 D4
Mackenzie, *Canada* ... 104 B4
McKenzie, *U.S.A.* ... 109 G1
Mackenzie →, *Australia* ... 94 C4
Mackenzie →, *Canada* ... 100 B6
McKenzie →, *U.S.A.* ... 114 D2
Mackenzie Bay, *Canada* ... 4 B1
Mackenzie City = Linden,
  Guyana ... 124 B7
Mackenzie Mts., *Canada* ... 100 B6
Mackinaw City, *U.S.A.* ... 108 C3
McKinlay, *Australia* ... 94 C3
McKinlay →, *Australia* ... 94 C3
McKinley, Mt., *U.S.A.* ... 100 B4
McKinley Sea, *Arctic* ... 4 A7
McKinney, *U.S.A.* ... 113 J6
Mackinnon Road, *Kenya* ... 86 C4
McKittrick, *U.S.A.* ... 117 K7
Macklin, *Canada* ... 105 C7
Macksville, *Australia* ... 95 E5
McLaughlin, *U.S.A.* ... 112 C4
Maclean, *Australia* ... 95 D5
McLean, *U.S.A.* ... 113 H4
McLeansboro, *U.S.A.* ... 112 F10
Maclear, *S. Africa* ... 89 E4
Macleay →, *Australia* ... 95 E5
McLennan, *Canada* ... 104 B5
McLeod →, *Canada* ... 104 C5
MacLeod, B., *Canada* ... 105 A7
McLeod, L., *Australia* ... 93 D1
MacLeod Lake, *Canada* ... 104 C4
McLoughlin, Mt., *U.S.A.* ... 114 E2
McMechen, *U.S.A.* ... 110 G4
McMinnville, *Oreg., U.S.A.* 114 D2
McMinnville, *Tenn., U.S.A.* 109 H3
McMurdo Sd., *Antarctica* . 5 D11
McMurray = Fort
  McMurray, *Canada* ... 104 B6
McMurray, *U.S.A.* ... 116 B4
Macodoene, *Mozam.* ... 89 C6
Macomb, *U.S.A.* ... 112 E9
Macomer, *Italy* ... 30 B1
Mâcon, *France* ... 19 F11
Macon, *Ga., U.S.A.* ... 109 J4
Macon, *Miss., U.S.A.* ... 109 J1
Macon, *Mo., U.S.A.* ... 112 F8
Macossa, *Mozam.* ... 87 F3
Macoun, L., *Canada* ... 105 B8
Macovane, *Mozam.* ... 89 C6
McPherson, *U.S.A.* ... 112 F6
McPherson Pk., *U.S.A.* ... 117 L7
McPherson Ra., *Australia* .. 95 D5
Macquarie Harbour,
  Australia ... 94 G4
Macquarie Is., *Pac. Oc.* ... 96 N7
MacRobertson Land,
  Antarctica ... 5 D6
Macroom, *Ireland* ... 15 E3
MacTier, *Canada* ... 110 A5

Macubela, *Mozam.* ... 87 F4
Macugnaga, *Italy* ... 28 C4
Macuiza, *Mozam.* ... 87 F3
Macusani, *Peru* ... 124 F4
Macuse, *Mozam.* ... 87 F4
Macuspana, *Mexico* ... 119 D6
Macusse, *Angola* ... 88 B3
Mada →, *Nigeria* ... 83 D6
Madadeni, *S. Africa* ... 89 D5
Madagali, *Nigeria* ... 83 C7
Madagascar ■, *Africa* ... 89 C8
Madā'in Sālih, *Si. Arabia* ... 70 E3
Madama, *Niger* ... 79 D8
Madame I., *Canada* ... 103 C7
Madan, *Bulgaria* ... 41 E8
Madaoua, *Niger* ... 83 C6
Madara, *Nigeria* ... 83 C7
Madaripur, *Bangla.* ... 67 H17
Madauk, *Burma* ... 67 L20
Madawaska, *Canada* ... 110 A7
Madawaska →, *Canada* ... 102 C4
Madaya, *Burma* ... 67 H20
Madbar, *Sudan* ... 81 F3
Maddalena, *Italy* ... 30 A2
Maddaloni, *Italy* ... 31 A7
Madeira, *Atl. Oc.* ... 37 D3
Madeira →, *Brazil* ... 122 D5
Madeleine, Îs. de la, *Canada* 103 C7
Maden, *Turkey* ... 73 C8
Madera, *Mexico* ... 118 B3
Madera, *Calif., U.S.A.* ... 116 J6
Madera, *Pa., U.S.A.* ... 110 F6
Madha, *India* ... 66 L9
Madhavpur, *India* ... 68 J3
Madhepura, *India* ... 69 F12
Madhubani, *India* ... 69 F12
Madhupur, *India* ... 69 G12
Madhya Pradesh □, *India* .. 68 J8
Madian, *China* ... 59 A11
Madidi →, *Bolivia* ... 124 F5
Madikeri, *India* ... 66 N9
Madill, *U.S.A.* ... 113 H6
Madimba,
  Dem. Rep. of the Congo . 84 E3
Ma'din, *Syria* ... 70 C3
Madina, *Mali* ... 82 C3
Madinani, *Ivory C.* ... 82 D3
Madingou, *Congo* ... 84 E2
Madirovalo, *Madag.* ... 89 B8
Madison, *Calif., U.S.A.* ... 116 G5
Madison, *Fla., U.S.A.* ... 109 K4
Madison, *Ind., U.S.A.* ... 108 F3
Madison, *Nebr., U.S.A.* ... 112 E6
Madison, *Ohio, U.S.A.* ... 110 E3
Madison, *S. Dak., U.S.A.* ... 112 D6
Madison, *Wis., U.S.A.* ... 112 D10
Madison →, *U.S.A.* ... 114 D8
Madison Heights, *U.S.A.* ... 108 G6
Madisonville, *Ky., U.S.A.* .. 108 G2
Madisonville, *Tex., U.S.A.* . 113 K7
Madista, *Botswana* ... 88 C4
Madiun, *Indonesia* ... 63 G14
Madoc, *Canada* ... 110 B7
Madol, *Sudan* ... 81 F2
Madon →, *France* ... 19 D13
Madona, *Latvia* ... 9 H22
Madonie, *Italy* ... 30 E6
Madonna di Campiglio, *Italy* 28 B7
Madra Dağı, *Turkey* ... 39 B9
Madrakah, Ra's al, *Oman* .. 74 D6
Madras = Chennai, *India* .. 66 N12
Madras = Tamil Nadu □,
  India ... 66 P10
Madras, *U.S.A.* ... 114 D3
Madre, L., *Mexico* ... 119 C5
Madre, Laguna, *U.S.A.* ... 113 M6
Madre, Sierra, *Phil.* ... 61 C5
Madre de Dios →, *Bolivia* . 122 E4
Madre de Dios, I., *Chile* ... 122 J3
Madre del Sur, Sierra,
  Mexico ... 119 D5
Madre Occidental, Sierra,
  Mexico ... 118 B3
Madre Oriental, Sierra,
  Mexico ... 118 C5
Madri, *India* ... 68 G5
Madrid, *Spain* ... 34 E7
Madrid, *U.S.A.* ... 111 B9
Madrid □, *Spain* ... 34 E7
Madridejos, *Spain* ... 35 F7
Madrigal de las Altas Torres,
  Spain ... 34 D6
Madrona, Sierra, *Spain* ... 35 G6
Madroñera, *Spain* ... 35 F5
Madu, *Sudan* ... 81 E2
Madura, *Australia* ... 93 F4
Madura, *Indonesia* ... 63 G15
Madura, Selat, *Indonesia* .. 63 G15
Madurai, *India* ... 66 Q11
Madurantakam, *India* ... 66 N11
Madzhalis, *Russia* ... 49 J8
Mae Chan, *Thailand* ... 64 C2
Mae Hong Son, *Thailand* .. 64 C2
Mae Khlong →, *Thailand* .. 64 F3
Mae Phrik, *Thailand* ... 64 D2
Mae Ramat, *Thailand* ... 64 D2
Mae Sot, *Thailand* ... 64 D2
Mae Suai, *Thailand* ... 58 E4
Mae Tha, *Thailand* ... 64 C2
Maebashi, *Japan* ... 55 F9
Maella, *Spain* ... 32 D5
Maesteg, *U.K.* ... 13 F4
Maestra, Sierra, *Cuba* ... 120 B4
Maevatanana, *Madag.* ... 89 B8
Mafeking = Mafikeng,
  S. Africa ... 88 D4
Mafeteng, *Lesotho* ... 88 D4
Maféré, *Ivory C.* ... 82 D4
Mafeteng, *Lesotho* ... 88 D4
Maffra, *Australia* ... 95 F4

Mafia I., *Tanzania* 86 D4
Mafikeng, *S. Africa* 88 D4
Mafra, *Brazil* 127 B6
Mafra, *Portugal* 35 G1
Mafungabusi Plateau,
  Zimbabwe 87 F2
Magadan, *Russia* 51 D16
Magadi, *Kenya* 86 C4
Magadi, L., *Kenya* 86 C4
Magaliesburg, *S. Africa* 89 D4
Magallanes, Estrecho de,
  Chile 122 J3
Magaluf, *Spain* 33 F7
Magangué, *Colombia* 124 B4
Magaria, *Niger* 83 C6
Magburaka, *S. Leone* 82 D2
Magdalen Is. = Madeleine,
  Îs. de la, *Canada* 103 C7
Magdalena, *Argentina* 126 D4
Magdalena, *Bolivia* 124 F6
Magdalena, *Mexico* 118 A2
Magdalena, *U.S.A.* 115 J10
Magdalena →, *Colombia* . . . 122 B3
Magdalena →, *Mexico* 118 A2
Magdalena, B., *Mexico* 118 C2
Magdalena, Llano de la,
  Mexico 118 C2
Magdeburg, *Germany* 24 C7
Magdelaine Cays, *Australia* . 94 B5
Magdub, *Sudan* 81 E2
Magee, *U.S.A.* 113 K10
Magelang, *Indonesia* 63 G14
Magellan's Str. =
  Magallanes, Estrecho de,
  Chile 122 J3
Magenta, *Italy* 28 C5
Magenta, L., *Australia* 93 F2
Magerøya, *Norway* 8 A21
Maggia →, *Switz.* 25 J4
Maggiorasca, Mte., *Italy* . . . 28 D6
Maggiore, Lago, *Italy* 28 C5
Maghâgha, *Egypt* 80 B3
Maghama, *Mauritania* 82 B2
Magherafelt, *U.K.* 15 B5
Maghreb, *N. Afr.* 78 B5
Magione, *Italy* 29 E9
Magistralnyy, *Russia* 51 D11
Maglaj, *Bos.-H.* 42 F3
Magliano in Toscana, *Italy* . . 29 F8
Máglie, *Italy* 31 B11
Magnac-Laval, *France* 20 B5
Magnetic Pole (North) =
  North Magnetic Pole,
  Canada 4 B2
Magnetic Pole (South) =
  South Magnetic Pole,
  Antarctica 5 C9
Magnisía □, *Greece* 38 B5
Magnitogorsk, *Russia* 50 D6
Magnolia, *Ark., U.S.A.* 113 J8
Magnolia, *Miss., U.S.A.* . . . 113 K9
Magny-en-Vexin, *France* . . . 19 C8
Magog, *Canada* 103 C5
Magoro, *Uganda* 86 B3
Magosa = Famagusta,
  Cyprus 36 D12
Magouládhes, *Greece* 36 A3
Magoye, *Zambia* 87 F2
Magozal, *Mexico* 119 C5
Magpie, L., *Canada* 103 B7
Magrath, *Canada* 104 D6
Magre →, *Spain* 33 F4
Magrur, *Sudan* 81 E3
Magrur, Wadi →, *Sudan* . . . 81 D2
Magta Lahjar, *Mauritania* . . 82 B2
Maguan, *China* 58 F5
Maguarinho, C., *Brazil* 125 D9
Magude, *Mozam.* 89 D5
Maģsa = Famagusta,
  Cyprus 36 D12
Maguse L., *Canada* 105 A9
Maguse Pt., *Canada* 105 A10
Magvana, *India* 68 H3
Magwe, *Burma* 67 J19
Magwe, *Sudan* 81 G3
Maha Sarakham, *Thailand* . . 64 D7
Mahābād, *Iran* 70 B5
Mahabharat Lekh, *Nepal* . . . 69 E10
Mahabo, *Madag.* 89 C7
Mahadeo Hills, *India* 69 H8
Mahaffey, *U.S.A.* 110 F6
Mahagi,
  Dem. Rep. of the Congo . . 86 B3
Mahajamba →, *Madag.* . . . 89 B8
Mahajamba, Helodranon' i,
  Madag. 89 B8
Mahajan, *India* 68 E5
Mahajanga, *Madag.* 89 B8
Mahajanga □, *Madag.* 89 B8
Mahajilo →, *Madag.* 89 B8
Mahakam →, *Indonesia* 62 E5
Mahalapye, *Botswana* 88 C4
Maḥallāt, *Iran* 71 C6
Māhān, *Iran* 71 D8
Mahan →, *India* 69 H10
Mahanadi →, *India* 67 J15
Mahananda →, *India* 69 G12
Mahanoro, *Madag.* 89 B8
Mahanoy City, *U.S.A.* 111 F8
Maharashtra □, *India* 66 J9
Mahari Mts., *Tanzania* 86 D3
Mahasham, W. →, *Egypt* . . . 75 E3
Mahasoa, *Madag.* 89 C8
Mahasolo, *Madag.* 89 B8
Mahattat ash Shīdīyah,
  Jordan 75 F4
Mahattat 'Unayzah, *Jordan* . 75 E4
Mahavavy →, *Madag.* 89 B8
Mahaxay, *Laos* 64 D5
Mahbubnagar, *India* 66 L10
Maḥḍah, *Oman* 71 E7

Mahdia, *Tunisia* 79 A8
Mahe, *India* 69 C8
Mahendragarh, *India* 68 E7
Mahenge, *Tanzania* 87 D4
Maheno, *N.Z.* 91 L3
Mahesana, *India* 68 H5
Maheshwar, *India* 68 H6
Mahgawan, *India* 69 F8
Mahi →, *India* 68 H5
Mahia Pen., *N.Z.* 91 H6
Mahilyow, *Belarus* 46 F6
Mahmud Kot, *Pakistan* 68 D4
Mahmudia, *Romania* 43 E14
Mahmudiye, *Turkey* 39 B12
Mahmutbey, *Turkey* 41 E12
Mahnomen, *U.S.A.* 112 B7
Mahoba, *India* 69 G8
Mahón = Maó, *Spain* 37 B11
Mahone Bay, *Canada* 103 D7
Mahopac, *U.S.A.* 111 E11
Mahuta, *Nigeria* 83 C5
Mahuva, *India* 68 J4
Mahya Daği, *Turkey* 41 E11
Mai-Ndombe, L.,
  Dem. Rep. of the Congo . . 84 E3
Mai-Sai, *Thailand* 58 G2
Maia, *Portugal* 34 D2
Maia, *Spain* 32 B3
Maials, *Spain* 32 D5
Maïche, *France* 19 E13
Maicurú →, *Brazil* 125 D8
Máida, *Italy* 31 D9
Maidan Khula, *Afghan.* 68 C3
Maidenhead, *U.K.* 13 F7
Maidstone, *Canada* 105 C7
Maidstone, *U.K.* 13 F8
Maiduguri, *Nigeria* 83 C7
Măieruş, *Romania* 43 E10
Maigatari, *Nigeria* 83 C6
Maignelay Montigny, *France* . 19 C9
Maigo, *Phil.* 61 G5
Maigudo, *Ethiopia* 81 F4
Maihar, *India* 69 G9
Maijdi, *Bangla.* 67 H17
Maikala Ra., *India* 67 J12
Mailani, *India* 69 E9
Maillezais, *France* 20 B3
Mailsi, *Pakistan* 68 E5
Main →, *Germany* 25 F4
Main →, *U.K.* 15 B5
Mainburg, *Germany* 25 G7
Maine, *France* 18 D6
Maine □, *U.S.A.* 109 C11
Maine →, *Ireland* 15 D2
Maine-et-Loire □, *France* . . . 18 E6
Maïne-Soroa, *Niger* 83 C7
Maingkwan, *Burma* 67 F20
Mainit, L., *Phil.* 61 G6
Mainland, *Orkney, U.K.* 14 C5
Mainland, *Shet., U.K.* 14 A7
Mainoru, *Australia* 94 A1
Mainpuri, *India* 69 F8
Maintal, *Germany* 25 E4
Maintenon, *France* 19 D8
Maintirano, *Madag.* 89 B7
Mainz, *Germany* 25 E4
Maipú, *Argentina* 126 D4
Maiquetía, *Venezuela* 124 A5
Máira →, *Italy* 28 D4
Mairabari, *India* 67 F18
Maisí, *Cuba* 121 B5
Maisí, Pta. de, *Cuba* 121 B5
Maitland, *N.S.W., Australia* . 95 E5
Maitland, *S. Austral.,
  Australia* 95 E2
Maitland →, *Canada* 110 C3
Maiyema, *Nigeria* 83 C5
Maizuru, *Japan* 55 G7
Majalengka, *Indonesia* 63 G13
Majene, *Indonesia* 63 E5
Majevica, *Bos.-H.* 42 F3
Maji, *Ethiopia* 81 F4
Majiang, *China* 58 D6
Majorca = Mallorca, *Spain* . 37 B10
Maka, *Senegal* 82 C2
Makaha, *Zimbabwe* 89 B5
Makak, *Cameroon* 83 E7
Makalamabedi, *Botswana* . . 88 C3
Makale, *Indonesia* 63 E5
Makamba, *Burundi* 86 C2
Makari, *Cameroon* 83 C7
Makarikari = Makgadikgadi
  Salt Pans, *Botswana* 88 C4
Makarovo, *Russia* 51 D11
Makarska, *Croatia* 29 E14
Makaryev, *Russia* 48 B6
Makasar = Ujung Pandang,
  Indonesia 63 F5
Makasar, Selat, *Indonesia* . . 63 E5
Makasar, Str. of = Makasar,
  Selat, *Indonesia* 63 E5
Makat, *Kazakstan* 50 E6
Makedonija = Macedonia ■,
  Europe 40 E5
Makena, *U.S.A.* 106 H16
Makeni, *S. Leone* 82 D2
Makeyevka = Makiyivka,
  Ukraine 47 H9
Makgadikgadi Salt Pans,
  Botswana 88 C4
Makhachkala, *Russia* 49 J8
Makharadze = Ozurgeti,
  Georgia 49 K5
Makhmūr, *Iraq* 70 C4
Makian, *Indonesia* 63 D7
Makindu, *Kenya* 86 C4
Makinsk, *Kazakhstan* 50 D8
Makiyivka, *Ukraine* 47 H9

Makkah, *Si. Arabia* 74 C2
Makkovik, *Canada* 103 A8
Makó, *Hungary* 42 D5
Mako, *Senegal* 82 C2
Makokou, *Gabon* 84 D2
Makongo,
  Dem. Rep. of the Congo . 86 B2
Makoro,
  Dem. Rep. of the Congo . 86 B2
Maków Mazowiecki, *Poland* 45 F8
Maków Podhalański, *Poland* 45 J6
Makrá, *Greece* 39 E7
Makrai, *India* 66 H10
Makran Coast Range,
  Pakistan 66 G4
Makrana, *India* 68 F6
Mákri, *Greece* 41 F9
Makriyialos, *Greece* 36 D7
Mākū, *Iran* 70 B5
Makunda, *Botswana* 88 C3
Makung, *Taiwan* 59 F12
Makurazaki, *Japan* 55 J5
Makurdi, *Nigeria* 83 D6
Makūyeh, *Iran* 71 D7
Makwassie, *S. Africa* 88 D4
Makwiro, *Zimbabwe* 89 B5
Mâl, *Mauritania* 82 B2
Mal B., *Ireland* 15 D2
Mala, Pta., *Panama* 120 E3
Mala Belozërka, *Ukraine* . . . 47 J8
Mala Kapela, *Croatia* 29 D12
Mała Panew →, *Poland* 45 H4
Mala Vyska, *Ukraine* 47 H6
Malabang, *Phil.* 61 H6
Malabar Coast, *India* 66 P9
Malabo = Rey Malabo,
  Eq. Guin. 83 E6
Malabon, *Phil.* 61 D4
Malabu, *Nigeria* 83 D7
Malacca, Str. of, *Indonesia* . 65 L3
Malacky, *Slovak Rep.* 27 C10
Malad City, *U.S.A.* 114 E7
Maladeta, *Spain* 32 C5
Maladzyechna, *Belarus* 46 E4
Málaga, *Spain* 35 J6
Málaga □, *Spain* 35 J6
Malagarasi, *Tanzania* 86 D3
Malagarasi →, *Tanzania* . . . 86 D2
Malagasy Rep. =
  Madagascar ■, *Africa* . . . 89 C8
Malagón, *Spain* 35 F7
Malagón →, *Spain* 35 H3
Malahide, *Ireland* 15 C5
Malaimbandy, *Madag.* 89 C8
Malakâl, *Sudan* 81 F3
Malakand, *Pakistan* 68 B4
Malakwal, *Pakistan* 68 C5
Malamala, *Indonesia* 63 E6
Malanda, *Australia* 94 B4
Malang, *Indonesia* 63 G15
Malangen, *Norway* 8 B18
Malanje, *Angola* 84 F3
Mälaren, *Sweden* 10 E11
Malargüe, *Argentina* 126 D2
Malartic, *Canada* 102 C4
Malaryta, *Belarus* 47 G3
Malatya, *Turkey* 70 B3
Malawi ■, *Africa* 87 E3
Malawi, L. = Nyasa, L.,
  Africa 87 E3
Malay Pen., *Asia* 65 J3
Malaya Belozërka = Mala
  Belozërka, *Ukraine* 47 J8
Malaya Vishera, *Russia* 46 C7
Malaya Viska = Mala Vyska,
  Ukraine 47 H6
Malaybalay, *Phil.* 61 G6
Malāyer, *Iran* 71 C6
Malaysia ■, *Asia* 65 K4
Malazgirt, *Turkey* 70 B4
Malbaza, *Niger* 83 C6
Malbon, *Australia* 94 C3
Malbooma, *Australia* 95 E1
Malbork, *Poland* 44 D6
Malcésine, *Italy* 28 C7
Malchin, *Germany* 24 B8
Malchow, *Germany* 24 B8
Malcolm, *Australia* 93 E3
Malcolm, Pt., *Australia* 93 F3
Maldah, *India* 69 G13
Maldegem, *Belgium* 17 C3
Malden, *Mass., U.S.A.* 111 D13
Malden, *Mo., U.S.A.* 113 G10
Malden I., *Kiribati* 97 H12
Maldives ■, *Ind. Oc.* 52 J11
Maldonado, *Uruguay* 127 C5
Maldonado, Punta, *Mexico* . 119 D5
Malè, *Italy* 28 B7
Malé, *Maldives* 53 J11
Maléa, Ákra, *Greece* 38 E5
Malegaon, *India* 66 J9
Malei, *Mozam.* 87 F4
Malek, *Sudan* 81 F3
Malek Kandī, *Iran* 70 B5
Malela,
  Dem. Rep. of the Congo . 86 C2
Malema, *Mozam.* 87 E4
Máleme, *Greece* 36 D5
Maleny, *Australia* 95 D5
Mälerås, *Sweden* 11 H9
Malerkotla, *India* 68 D6
Máles, *Greece* 36 D7
Malesherbes, *France* 19 D9
Maleshevska Planina, *Europe* 40 E5
Malesína, *Greece* 38 C5
Malestroit, *France* 18 E4
Malfa, *Italy* 31 D7
Malgobek, *Russia* 49 J7
Malgomaj, *Sweden* 8 D17

Malgrat = Malgrat de Mar,
  Spain 32 D7
Malgrat de Mar, *Spain* 32 D7
Malha, *Sudan* 81 D2
Malhargarh, *India* 68 G6
Malheur →, *U.S.A.* 114 D5
Malheur L., *U.S.A.* 114 E4
Mali, *Guinea* 82 C2
Mali ■, *Africa* 82 C2
Mali →, *Burma* 67 G20
Mali Kanal, *Serbia, Yug.* . . . 42 E4
Mali Kyun, *Burma* 64 F2
Malibu, *U.S.A.* 117 L8
Maliku, *Indonesia* 63 E6
Malili, *Indonesia* 63 E6
Målilla, *Sweden* 11 G9
Malimba, Mts.,
  Dem. Rep. of the Congo . 86 D2
Malin Hd., *Ireland* 15 A4
Malin Pen., *Ireland* 15 A4
Malindi, *Kenya* 86 C5
Malines = Mechelen,
  Belgium 17 C4
Malino, *Indonesia* 63 D6
Malinyi, *Tanzania* 87 D4
Malipo, *China* 58 F5
Maliqi, *Albania* 40 F4
Malita, *Phil.* 63 C7
Maliwun, *Burma* 62 B1
Maliya, *India* 68 H4
Maljenik, *Serbia, Yug.* 40 C5
Malkara, *Turkey* 41 F10
Malkinia Górna, *Poland* . . . 45 F9
Malko Tŭrnovo, *Bulgaria* . . 41 E11
Mallacoota Inlet, *Australia* . 95 F4
Mallaig, *U.K.* 14 D3
Mallaoua, *Niger* 83 C6
Mallawan, *India* 69 F9
Mallawi, *Egypt* 80 B3
Mallemort, *France* 21 E9
Málles Venosta, *Italy* 28 B7
Mállia, *Greece* 36 D7
Mallión, Kólpos, *Greece* . . . 36 D7
Mallorca, *Spain* 37 B10
Mallorytown, *Canada* 111 B9
Mallow, *Ireland* 15 D3
Malmbäck, *Sweden* 11 G8
Malmberget, *Sweden* 8 C19
Malmédy, *Belgium* 17 D6
Malmesbury, *S. Africa* 88 E2
Malmköping, *Sweden* 10 E10
Malmö, *Sweden* 11 J6
Malmslätt, *Sweden* 11 F9
Malmyzh, *Russia* 48 B10
Malnaş, *Romania* 43 D10
Malo Konare, *Bulgaria* 41 D8
Maloarkhangelsk, *Russia* . . . 47 F9
Malolos, *Phil.* 63 B6
Malombe L., *Malawi* 87 E4
Małomice, *Poland* 45 G2
Malomir, *Bulgaria* 41 D10
Malone, *U.S.A.* 111 B10
Malong, *China* 58 E4
Małopolskie □, *Poland* 45 J7
Malorad, *Bulgaria* 40 C7
Måløy, *Norway* 9 F11
Maloyaroslovets, *Russia* . . . 46 E9
Malpartida, *Spain* 35 F4
Malpaso, *Canary Is.* 37 G1
Malpelo, I. de, *Colombia* . . . 124 C2
Malpica de Bergantiños,
  Spain 34 B2
Malpur, *India* 68 H5
Malpura, *India* 68 F6
Mals = Málles Venosta, *Italy* 28 B7
Malta, *Idaho, U.S.A.* 114 E7
Malta, *Mont., U.S.A.* 114 B10
Malta ■, *Europe* 36 D2
Maltahöhe, *Namibia* 88 C2
Malton, *Canada* 110 C5
Malton, *U.K.* 12 C7
Maluku, *Indonesia* 63 E7
Maluku □, *Indonesia* 63 E7
Maluku Sea = Molucca Sea,
  Indonesia 63 E6
Malumfashi, *Nigeria* 83 C6
Malung, *Sweden* 10 D7
Malungsfors, *Sweden* 10 D7
Maluwe, *Ghana* 82 D4
Malvan, *India* 66 L8
Malvern, *U.S.A.* 113 H8
Malvern Hills, *U.K.* 13 E5
Malvinas, Is. = Falkland
  Is. □, *Atl. Oc.* 128 G5
Malya, *Tanzania* 86 C3
Malyn, *Ukraine* 47 G5
Malyy Lyakhovskiy, Ostrov,
  Russia 51 B15
Mama, *Russia* 51 D12
Mamadysh, *Russia* 48 C10
Mamanguape, *Brazil* 125 E11
Mamarr Mitlā, *Egypt* 75 E1
Mamasa, *Indonesia* 63 E5
Mambasa,
  Dem. Rep. of the Congo . 86 B2
Mamberamo →, *Indonesia* . . 63 E9
Mambilima Falls, *Zambia* . . 87 E2
Mambirima,
  Dem. Rep. of the Congo . 87 E2
Mambo, *Tanzania* 86 C4
Mambrui, *Kenya* 86 C5
Mamburao, *Phil.* 61 E4
Mameigwess L., *Canada* . . . 102 B2
Mamers, *France* 18 D7
Mamfé, *Cameroon* 83 D6
Mammoth, *U.S.A.* 115 K8
Mammoth Cave National
  Park, *U.S.A.* 108 G3
Mamoré →, *Bolivia* 122 E4

Mamou, *Guinea* 82 C2
Mampatá, *Guinea-Biss.* 82 C2
Mampikony, *Madag.* 89 B8
Mampong, *Ghana* 83 D4
Mamry, Jezioro, *Poland* 44 D8
Mamuju, *Indonesia* 63 E5
Mamuno, *Botswana* 88 C3
Mamuras, *Albania* 40 E3
Man, *Ivory C.* 82 D3
Man, I. of, *U.K.* 12 C3
Man-Bazar, *India* 69 H12
Man Na, *Burma* 67 H20
Mana →, *Fr. Guiana* 125 B8
Manaar, G. of = Mannar,
  G. of, *Asia* 66 Q11
Manacapuru, *Brazil* 124 D6
Manacor, *Spain* 37 B10
Manado, *Indonesia* 63 D6
Managua, *Nic.* 120 D2
Managua, L. de, *Nic.* 120 D2
Manakara, *Madag.* 89 C8
Manali, *India* 68 C7
Manama = Al Manāmah,
  Bahrain 71 E6
Manambao →, *Madag.* 89 B7
Manambato, *Madag.* 89 A8
Manambolo →, *Madag.* 89 B7
Manambolosy, *Madag.* 89 B8
Mananara, *Madag.* 89 B8
Mananara →, *Madag.* 89 C8
Mananjary, *Madag.* 89 C8
Manankoro, *Mali* 82 C3
Manantenina, *Madag.* 89 C8
Manaos = Manaus, *Brazil* . . 124 D7
Manápire →, *Venezuela* . . . 124 B5
Manapouri, *N.Z.* 91 L1
Manapouri, L., *N.Z.* 91 L1
Manaqil, *Sudan* 81 E3
Manār, Jabal, *Yemen* 74 E3
Manaravolo, *Madag.* 89 C8
Manas, *China* 60 B3
Manas →, *India* 69 E11
Manaslu, *Nepal* 69 E11
Manasquan, *U.S.A.* 111 F10
Manassa, *U.S.A.* 115 H11
Manaung, *Burma* 67 K18
Manaus, *Brazil* 124 D7
Manavgat, *Turkey* 72 D4
Manawan L., *Canada* 105 B8
Manay, *Phil.* 61 H7
Manbij, *Syria* 70 B3
Mancha Real, *Spain* 35 H7
Manche □, *France* 18 C5
Manchegorsk, *Russia* 50 C4
Manchester, *U.K.* 12 D5
Manchester, *Calif., U.S.A.* . . 116 G3
Manchester, *Conn., U.S.A.* . . 111 E12
Manchester, *Ga., U.S.A.* . . . 109 J3
Manchester, *Iowa, U.S.A.* . . 112 D9
Manchester, *Ky., U.S.A.* . . . 108 G4
Manchester, *N.H., U.S.A.* . . 111 D13
Manchester, *N.Y., U.S.A.* . . 110 D7
Manchester, *Pa., U.S.A.* . . . 111 F8
Manchester, *Tenn., U.S.A.* . . 109 H2
Manchester, *Vt., U.S.A.* . . . 111 C11
Manchester L., *Canada* 105 A7
Manchhar L., *Pakistan* 68 F2
Manchuria = Dongbei,
  China 57 D13
Manchurian Plain, *China* . . . 52 D14
Manciano, *Italy* 29 F8
Mancifa, *Ethiopia* 81 F5
Mand →, *India* 69 J10
Mand →, *Iran* 71 D7
Manda, *Chunya, Tanzania* . . 86 D3
Manda, *Ludewe, Tanzania* . . 87 E3
Mandabé, *Madag.* 89 C7
Mandaguari, *Brazil* 127 A5
Mandah = Töhöm, *Mongolia* 56 B5
Mandal, *Norway* 9 G12
Mandala, Puncak, *Indonesia* 63 E10
Mandalay, *Burma* 67 J20
Mandale = Mandalay,
  Burma 67 J20
Mandalgarh, *India* 68 G6
Mandalgovi, *Mongolia* 56 B4
Mandalī, *Iraq* 70 C5
Mandan, *U.S.A.* 112 B4
Mandaon, *Phil.* 61 E5
Mandar, Teluk, *Indonesia* . . 63 E5
Mándas, *Italy* 30 C2
Mandaue, *Phil.* 61 F5
Mandelieu-la-Napoule,
  France 21 E10
Mandera, *Kenya* 86 B5
Mandi, *India* 68 D7
Mandi Dabwali, *India* 68 E6
Mandimba, *Mozam.* 87 E4
Mandioli, *Indonesia* 63 E7
Mandla, *India* 69 H9
Mandø, *Denmark* 11 J2
Mandorah, *Australia* 92 B5
Mandoto, *Madag.* 89 B8
Mandoúdhion, *Greece* 38 C5
Mandra, *Pakistan* 68 C5
Mándra, *Greece* 38 C5
Mandráki, *Greece* 39 E9
Mandrare →, *Madag.* 89 D8
Mandritsara, *Madag.* 89 B8
Mandronarivo, *Madag.* 89 C8
Mandsaur, *India* 68 G6
Mandurah, *Australia* 93 F2
Mandúria, *Italy* 31 B10
Mandvi, *India* 68 H3
Mandya, *India* 66 N10
Mandzai, *Pakistan* 68 D2
Mané, *Burkina Faso* 83 C4
Maneh, *Iran* 71 B8
Manengouba, Mts.,
  Cameroon 83 E6

Manera, *Madag.* 89 C7
Manérbio, *Italy* 28 C7
Maneroo Cr. →, *Australia* . 94 C3
Manfalût, *Egypt* 80 B3
Manfredónia, *Italy* 29 G12
Manfredónia, G. di, *Italy* . 29 G13
Manga, *Burkina Faso* 83 C4
Manga, *Niger* 83 C7
Mangabeiras, Chapada das,
    Brazil 125 F9
Mangalia, *Romania* 43 G13
Mangalore, *India* 66 N9
Mangan, *India* 69 F13
Mangaung, *S. Africa* 85 K5
Mangawan, *India* 69 G9
Mangawitu, *Indonesia* 91 H5
Manggar, *Indonesia* 62 E3
Manggawitu, *Indonesia* 63 E8
Mangindrano, *Madag.* 89 A8
Mangkalihat, Tanjung,
    Indonesia 63 D5
Mangla, *Pakistan* 68 C5
Mangla Dam, *Pakistan* 69 C5
Manglaur, *India* 68 E7
Mangnai, *China* 60 C4
Mango, *Togo* 83 C5
Mangoche, *Malawi* 87 E4
Mangoky →, *Madag.* 89 C7
Mangole, *Indonesia* 63 E6
Mangombe,
    Dem. Rep. of the Congo . 86 C2
Mangonui, *N.Z.* 91 F4
Mangoro →, *Madag.* 89 B8
Mangrol, *Mad. P., India* . . . 68 J4
Mangrol, *Raj., India* 68 G6
Mangualde, *Portugal* 34 E3
Mangueira, L. da, *Brazil* . . 127 C5
Mangum, *U.S.A.* 113 H5
Mangyshlak Poluostrov,
    Kazakstan 50 E6
Manhattan, *U.S.A.* 112 F6
Manhiça, *Mozam.* 89 D5
Mania →, *Madag.* 89 B8
Maniago, *Italy* 29 B9
Manica, *Mozam.* 89 B5
Manica □, *Mozam.* 89 B5
Manicaland □, *Zimbabwe* . . 87 F3
Manicoré, *Brazil* 124 E6
Manicouagan →, *Canada* . . 103 C6
Manicouagan, Rés., *Canada* 103 B6
Maniema □,
    Dem. Rep. of the Congo . 86 C2
Manîfah, *Si. Arabia* 71 E6
Manifold, C., *Australia* 94 C5
Maniganggo, *China* 58 B2
Manigotagan, *Canada* 105 C9
Manigotagan →, *Canada* . . 105 C9
Manihari, *India* 69 G12
Manihiki, *Cook Is.* 97 J11
Manika, Plateau de la,
    Dem. Rep. of the Congo . 87 E2
Manikpur, *India* 69 G9
Manila, *Phil.* 61 D4
Manila, *U.S.A.* 114 F9
Manila B., *Phil.* 61 D4
Manilla, *Australia* 95 E5
Manimpé, *Mali* 82 C3
Maningrida, *Australia* 94 A1
Maninian, *Ivory C.* 82 C3
Manipur □, *India* 67 G19
Manipur →, *Burma* 67 H19
Manisa, *Turkey* 39 C9
Manisa □, *Turkey* 39 C9
Manistee, *U.S.A.* 108 C2
Manistee →, *U.S.A.* 108 C2
Manistique, *U.S.A.* 108 C2
Manito L., *Canada* 105 C7
Manitoba □, *Canada* 105 B9
Manitoba, L., *Canada* 105 C9
Manitou, *Canada* 105 D9
Manitou, L., *Canada* 103 B6
Manitou Is., *U.S.A.* 108 C3
Manitou Springs, *U.S.A.* . . . 112 F2
Manitoulin I., *Canada* 102 C3
Manitouwadge, *Canada* 102 C3
Manitowoc, *U.S.A.* 108 C2
Manizales, *Colombia* 124 B3
Manja, *Madag.* 89 C7
Manjacaze, *Mozam.* 89 C5
Manjakandriana, *Madag.* . . . 89 B8
Manjhand, *Pakistan* 68 G3
Manjil, *Iran* 71 B6
Manjimup, *Australia* 93 F2
Manjra →, *India* 66 K10
Mankato, *Kans., U.S.A.* . . . 112 F5
Mankato, *Minn., U.S.A.* . . . 112 C8
Mankayane, *Swaziland* 89 D5
Mankera, *Pakistan* 68 D4
Mankim, *Cameroon* 83 D7
Mankono, *Ivory C.* 82 D3
Mankota, *Canada* 105 D7
Manlay = Üydzin, *Mongolia* 56 B4
Manlleu, *Spain* 32 C7
Manmad, *India* 66 J9
Mann Ranges, *Australia* . . . 93 E5
Manna, *Indonesia* 62 E2
Mannahill, *Australia* 95 E3
Mannar, *Sri Lanka* 66 Q11
Mannar, G. of, *Asia* 66 Q11
Mannar □, *Sri Lanka* 66 Q11
Mannheim, *Germany* 25 F4
Manning, *Canada* 104 B5
Manning, *Oreg., U.S.A.* . . . 116 E3
Manning, *S.C., U.S.A.* 109 J5
Manning Prov. Park, *Canada* 104 D4
Mannu →, *Italy* 30 C2
Mannu, C., *Italy* 30 B1
Mannum, *Australia* 95 E2
Mano, *S. Leone* 82 D2
Mano, *Liberia* 82 D2
Mano River, *Liberia* 82 D2

Manoharpur, *India* 69 H11
Manokwari, *Indonesia* 63 E8
Manolás, *Greece* 38 C3
Manombo, *Madag.* 89 C7
Manono,
    Dem. Rep. of the Congo . 86 D2
Manoppello, *Italy* 29 F11
Manosque, *France* 21 E9
Manotick, *Canada* 111 A9
Manouane →, *Canada* 103 C5
Manouane, L., *Canada* 103 B5
Manp'o, *N. Korea* 57 D14
Manpojin = Manp'o,
    N. Korea 57 D14
Manpur, *Mad. P., India* . . . 68 H6
Manpur, *Mad. P., India* . . . 69 H10
Manresa, *Spain* 32 D6
Mansa, *Gujarat, India* 68 H5
Mansa, *Punjab, India* 68 E6
Mansa, *Zambia* 87 E2
Månsåsen, *Sweden* 10 A8
Mansehra, *Pakistan* 68 B5
Mansel I., *Canada* 101 B11
Mansfield, *Australia* 95 F4
Mansfield, *U.K.* 12 D6
Mansfield, *La., U.S.A.* 113 J8
Mansfield, *Mass., U.S.A.* . . 111 D13
Mansfield, *Ohio, U.S.A.* . . . 110 F2
Mansfield, *Pa., U.S.A.* 110 E7
Mansfield, Mt., *U.S.A.* . . . 111 B12
Mansilla de las Mulas, *Spain* 34 C5
Mansle, *France* 20 C4
Mansoa, *Guinea-Biss.* 82 C1
Manson Creek, *Canada* 104 B4
Manta, *Ecuador* 124 D2
Mantalingajan, Mt., *Phil.* . . 61 G2
Mantare, *Tanzania* 86 C3
Manteca, *U.S.A.* 116 H5
Manteo, *U.S.A.* 109 H8
Mantes-la-Jolie, *France* 19 D8
Mántova, *Italy* 28 C7
Manton, *U.S.A.* 108 C3
Mantorp, *Sweden* 11 F9
Mäntta, *Finland* 9 E21
Mantua = Mántova, *Italy* . . 28 C7
Manturovo, *Russia* 48 A7
Manu, *Peru* 124 F4
Manu →, *Peru* 124 F4
Manua Is., *Amer. Samoa* . . . 91 B14
Manuel Alves →, *Brazil* . . . 125 F9
Manui, *Indonesia* 63 E6
Manuripi →, *Bolivia* 124 F5
Many, *U.S.A.* 113 K8
Manyara, L., *Tanzania* 86 C4
Manyas, *Turkey* 41 F11
Manych →, *Russia* 49 G5
Manych-Gudilo, Ozero,
    Russia 49 G6
Manyonga →, *Tanzania* . . . 86 C3
Manyoni, *Tanzania* 86 D3
Manzai, *Pakistan* 68 C4
Manzala, Bahra el, *Egypt* . . 80 H7
Manzanares, *Spain* 35 F7
Manzaneda, *Spain* 34 C3
Manzanillo, *Cuba* 120 B4
Manzanillo, *Mexico* 118 D4
Manzanillo, Pta., *Panama* . . 120 E4
Manzano Mts., *U.S.A.* 115 J10
Manẓarīyeh, *Iran* 71 C6
Manzhouli, *China* 60 B6
Manzini, *Swaziland* 89 D5
Mao, *Chad* 79 F9
Maó, *Spain* 37 B11
Maoke, Pegunungan,
    Indonesia 63 E9
Maolin, *China* 57 C12
Maoming, *China* 59 G8
Maopi T'ou, *China* 59 G13
Maouri, Dallol →, *Niger* . . . 83 C5
Maoxian, *China* 58 B4
Maoxing, *China* 57 B13
Mapam Yumco, *China* 60 C3
Mapastepec, *Mexico* 119 D6
Mapia, Kepulauan, *Indonesia* 63 D8
Mapimí, *Mexico* 118 B4
Mapimí, Bolsón de, *Mexico* 118 B4
Maping, *China* 59 B9
Mapinga, *Tanzania* 86 D4
Mapinhane, *Mozam.* 89 C6
Maple Creek, *Canada* 105 D7
Maple Valley, *U.S.A.* 116 C4
Mapleton, *U.S.A.* 114 D2
Mapuera →, *Brazil* 124 D7
Mapulanguene, *Mozam.* . . . 89 C5
Maputo, *Mozam.* 89 D5
Maputo □, *Mozam.* 89 D5
Maputo, B. de, *Mozam.* 89 D5
Maqiaohe, *China* 57 B16
Maqnā, *Si. Arabia* 70 D2
Maqueda, *Spain* 34 E6
Maquela do Zombo, *Angola* 84 F3
Maquinchao, *Argentina* . . . 128 E3
Maquoketa, *U.S.A.* 112 D9
Mar, Serra do, *Brazil* 127 B6
Mar Chiquita, L., *Argentina* 126 C3
Mar del Plata, *Argentina* . . 126 D4
Mar Menor, *Spain* 33 H4
Mara, *Tanzania* 86 C3
Mara □, *Tanzania* 86 C3
Maraã, *Brazil* 124 D5
Marabá, *Brazil* 125 E9
Maracá, I. de, *Brazil* 125 C8
Maracaibo, *Venezuela* 124 A4
Maracaibo, L. de, *Venezuela* 124 B4
Maracaju, *Brazil* 127 A4
Maracay, *Venezuela* 124 A5
Maracena, *Spain* 35 H7
Maradi, *Niger* 83 C6

Marágheh, *Iran* 70 B5
Marāh, *Si. Arabia* 70 E5
Marajó, I. de, *Brazil* 122 D6
Marākand, *Iran* 70 B5
Maralal, *Kenya* 86 B4
Maralinga, *Australia* 93 F5
Maramaraereğlisi, *Turkey* . . 41 F11
Marampa, *S. Leone* 82 D2
Maran, *Malaysia* 65 L4
Marana, *U.S.A.* 115 K8
Maranboy, *Australia* 92 B5
Maranchón, *Spain* 32 D2
Marand, *Iran* 70 B5
Marang, *Malaysia* 65 K4
Maranguape, *Brazil* 125 D11
Maranhão = São Luís, *Brazil* 125 D10
Maranhão □, *Brazil* 125 E9
Marano, L. di, *Italy* 29 C10
Maranoa →, *Australia* 95 D4
Marañón →, *Peru* 122 D3
Marão, *Mozam.* 89 C5
Maraş = Kahramanmaraş,
    Turkey 70 B3
Mărăşeşti, *Romania* 43 E12
Maratea, *Italy* 31 C8
Marateca, *Portugal* 35 G2
Marathasa □, *Cyprus* 36 E11
Marathókambos, *Greece* . . . 39 D8
Marathon, *Australia* 94 C3
Marathon, *Canada* 102 C2
Marathón, *Greece* 38 C5
Marathon, *N.Y., U.S.A.* . . . 111 D8
Marathon, *N.Y., U.S.A.* . . . 111 D8
Marathon, *Tex., U.S.A.* . . . 113 K3
Marathóvouno, *Cyprus* 36 D12
Maratua, *Indonesia* 63 D5
Maravatío, *Mexico* 118 D4
Marawi City, *Phil.* 61 G6
Marāwih, *U.A.E.* 71 E7
Marbella, *Spain* 35 J6
Marble Bar, *Australia* 92 D2
Marble Falls, *U.S.A.* 113 K5
Marblehead, *U.S.A.* 111 D14
Marburg, *Germany* 24 E4
Marcal →, *Hungary* 42 C2
Marcali, *Hungary* 42 D2
Marcaria, *Italy* 28 C7
Mărcăuţi, *Moldova* 43 B12
March, *U.K.* 13 E8
Marche, *France* 20 B5
Marche □, *Italy* 29 E10
Marche-en-Famenne,
    Belgium 17 D5
Marchena, *Spain* 35 H5
Marches = Marche □, *Italy* . 29 E10
Marciana Marina, *Italy* 28 F7
Marcianise, *Italy* 31 A7
Marcigny, *France* 19 F11
Marcillat-en-Combraille,
    France 19 F9
Marck, *France* 19 B8
Marckolsheim, *France* 19 D14
Marco, *U.S.A.* 109 N5
Marcos Juárez, *Argentina* . . 126 C3
Mărculeşti, *Moldova* 43 C13
Marcus I. = Minami-Tori-
    Shima, *Pac. Oc.* 96 E7
Marcus Necker Ridge,
    Pac. Oc. 96 F9
Marcy, Mt., *U.S.A.* 111 B11
Mardan, *Pakistan* 68 B5
Mardin, *Turkey* 70 B5
Mårdsjön, *Sweden* 10 A9
Marecchia →, *Italy* 29 D9
Maree, L., *U.K.* 14 D3
Mareeba, *Australia* 94 B4
Mareetsane, *S. Africa* 88 D4
Maremma, *Italy* 29 F8
Maréna, *Mali* 82 C2
Maréna, *Mali* 82 C3
Marengo, *U.S.A.* 112 E8
Marennes, *France* 20 C2
Marenyi, *Kenya* 86 C4
Marérano, *Madag.* 89 C7
Maréttimo, *Italy* 30 E5
Mareuil, *France* 20 C4
Marfa, *U.S.A.* 113 K2
Marfa Pt., *Malta* 36 D1
Marganets = Marhanets,
    Ukraine 47 J8
Margaret →, *Australia* 92 C4
Margaret Bay, *Canada* 104 C3
Margaret L., *Canada* 104 B5
Margaret River, *Australia* . . 93 F2
Margarita, I. de, *Venezuela* 122 B4
Margarítion, *Greece* 38 B2
Margaritovo, *Russia* 54 C7
Margate, *S. Africa* 89 E5
Margate, *U.K.* 13 F9
Margeride, Mts. de la,
    France 20 D7
Margherita di Savóia, *Italy* . 31 A9
Marghita, *Romania* 42 C7
Margonin, *Poland* 45 F4
Margosatubig, *Phil.* 61 H5
Mărgow, Dasht-e, *Afghan.* . . 66 D3
Marguerite, *Canada* 104 C4
Marhanets, *Ukraine* 47 J8
Mari El □, *Russia* 48 B8
Mari Indus, *Pakistan* 68 C4
Mari Republic = Mari El □,
    Russia 48 B8
María, Is. de, *Spain* 33 H2
María Elena, *Chile* 126 A2
María Grande, *Argentina* . . 126 C4
Maria I., *N. Terr., Australia* 94 A2
Maria I., *Tas., Australia* . . . 94 G4
Maria van Diemen, C., *N.Z.* 91 F4
Mariager, *Denmark* 11 H3
Mariager Fjord, *Denmark* . . 11 H4

Mariakani, *Kenya* 86 C4
Marian, *Australia* 94 C4
Marian L., *Canada* 104 A5
Mariana Trench, *Pac. Oc.* . . 52 H18
Marianao, *Cuba* 120 B3
Marianna, *Ark., U.S.A.* 113 H9
Marianna, *Fla., U.S.A.* 109 K3
Mariannelund, *Sweden* 11 G9
Mariánské Lázně,
    Czech Rep. 26 B5
Marias →, *U.S.A.* 114 C8
Mariato, Punta, *Panama* . . . 120 E3
Mariazell, *Austria* 26 D8
Maribo, *Denmark* 11 K5
Maribor, *Slovenia* 29 B12
Marico →, *Africa* 88 C4
Maricopa, *Ariz., U.S.A.* . . . 115 K7
Maricopa, *Calif., U.S.A.* . . . 117 K7
Marīdī, *Sudan* 81 G2
Maridi, Wadi →, *Sudan* 81 F2
Marié →, *Brazil* 124 D5
Marie Byrd Land, *Antarctica* . 5 D14
Marie-Galante, *Guadeloupe* 121 C7
Mariecourt = Kangiqsujuaq,
    Canada 101 B12
Mariefred, *Sweden* 10 E11
Mariehamn, *Sweden* 11 J7
Mariembourg, *Belgium* 17 D4
Marienbad = Mariánské
    Lázně, *Czech Rep.* 26 B5
Marienberg, *Germany* 24 E9
Mariental, *Namibia* 88 C2
Marienville, *U.S.A.* 110 E5
Mariestad, *Sweden* 11 F7
Marietta, *Ga., U.S.A.* 109 J3
Marietta, *Ohio, U.S.A.* 108 F5
Marieville, *Canada* 111 A11
Mariga →, *Nigeria* 83 C6
Marignane, *France* 21 E9
Marihatag, *Phil.* 61 G7
Mariinsk, *Russia* 50 D9
Mariinskiy Posad, *Russia* . . 48 B8
Marijampolė, *Lithuania* 9 J20
Marijampolė □, *Lithuania* . . 44 D10
Marília, *Brazil* 127 A6
Marín, *Spain* 34 C2
Marina, *U.S.A.* 116 J5
Marinduque, *Phil.* 63 B6
Marine City, *U.S.A.* 110 D2
Marineo, *Italy* 30 E6
Marinette, *U.S.A.* 108 C2
Maringá, *Brazil* 127 A5
Marinha Grande, *Portugal* . 34 F2
Marino, *Italy* 29 G9
Marion, *Ala., U.S.A.* 109 J2
Marion, *Ill., U.S.A.* 113 G10
Marion, *Ind., U.S.A.* 108 E3
Marion, *Iowa, U.S.A.* 112 D9
Marion, *Kans., U.S.A.* 112 F6
Marion, *N.C., U.S.A.* 109 H5
Marion, *Ohio, U.S.A.* 108 E4
Marion, *S.C., U.S.A.* 109 H6
Marion, *Va., U.S.A.* 109 G5
Marion, L., *U.S.A.* 109 J5
Mariposa, *U.S.A.* 116 H7
Mariscal Estigarribia,
    Paraguay 126 A3
Maritime Alps = Maritimes,
    Alpes, *Europe* 21 D11
Maritimes, Alpes, *Europe* . . 21 D11
Maritsa = Évros →,
    Bulgaria 72 B2
Maritsá, *Greece* 36 C10
Mariupol, *Ukraine* 47 J9
Marīvān, *Iran* 70 C5
Marj 'Uyūn, *Lebanon* 75 B4
Marka, *Si. Arabia* 80 D5
Markam, *China* 58 C2
Markaryd, *Sweden* 11 H7
Markazi □, *Iran* 71 C6
Markdale, *Canada* 110 B4
Marked Tree, *U.S.A.* 113 H9
Markelsdorfer Huk,
    Germany 24 A7
Market Drayton, *U.K.* 12 E5
Market Harborough, *U.K.* . . 13 E7
Market Rasen, *U.K.* 12 D7
Markham, *Canada* 110 C5
Markham, Mt., *Antarctica* . . . 5 E11
Marki, *Poland* 45 F8
Markkleeberg, *Germany* . . . 24 D8
Markleeville, *U.S.A.* 116 G7
Markoupoulon, *Greece* 38 D5
Markovac, *Serbia, Yug.* 40 B5
Markovo, *Russia* 51 C17
Markoye, *Burkina Faso* 83 C5
Marks, *Russia* 48 E8
Marksville, *U.S.A.* 113 K8
Markt Schwaben, *Germany* . 25 G7
Marktoberdorf, *Germany* . . 25 H6
Marktredwitz, *Germany* . . . 25 E8
Marl, *Germany* 24 D3
Marla, *Australia* 95 D1
Marlbank, *Canada* 110 B7
Marlboro, *Mass., U.S.A.* . . 111 D13
Marlboro, *N.Y., U.S.A.* . . . 111 E11
Marlborough, *Australia* 94 C4
Marlborough, *U.K.* 13 F6
Marlborough Downs, *U.K.* . . 13 F6
Marle, *France* 19 C10
Marlin, *U.S.A.* 113 K6
Marlow, *Germany* 24 A8
Marlow, *U.S.A.* 113 H6
Marmagao, *India* 66 M8
Marmande, *France* 20 D4
Marmara, *Turkey* 41 F11
Marmara, Sea of = Marmara
    Denizi, *Turkey* 41 F12
Marmara Denizi, *Turkey* . . . 41 F12
Marmara Gölü, *Turkey* 39 C10
Marmaris, *Turkey* 39 E10

Marmaris Limanı, *Turkey* . . 39 E10
Marmion, Mt., *Australia* . . . 93 E2
Marmion L., *Canada* 102 C1
Marmolada, Mte., *Italy* 29 B8
Marmolejo, *Spain* 35 G6
Marmora, *Canada* 102 D4
Mármora, La, *Italy* 30 C2
Marnay, *France* 19 E12
Marne □, *France* 19 D11
Marne →, *France* 19 D9
Marneuli, *Georgia* 49 K7
Maroala, *Madag.* 89 B8
Maroantsetra, *Madag.* 89 B8
Maroelaboom, *Namibia* 88 B2
Marofandilia, *Madag.* 89 C7
Marolambo, *Madag.* 89 C8
Maromandia, *Madag.* 89 A8
Maromokotro, *Madag.* 89 A8
Marondera, *Zimbabwe* 87 F3
Maroni →, *Fr. Guiana* 125 B8
Marónia, *Greece* 41 F9
Maronne →, *France* 20 C5
Maroochydore, *Australia* . . . 95 D5
Maroona, *Australia* 95 F3
Maros →, *Hungary* 42 D5
Marosakoa, *Madag.* 89 B8
Maroseranana, *Madag.* 89 B8
Maróstica, *Italy* 29 C8
Marotandrano, *Madag.* 89 B8
Marotaolano, *Madag.* 89 A8
Maroua, *Cameroon* 83 C7
Marovato, *Madag.* 89 B8
Marovoay, *Madag.* 89 B8
Marquard, *S. Africa* 88 D4
Marquesas Is. = Marquises,
    Is., *Pac. Oc.* 97 H14
Marquette, *U.S.A.* 108 B2
Marquise, *France* 19 B8
Marquises, Is., *Pac. Oc.* . . . 97 H14
Marra, Djebel, *Sudan* 79 F10
Marra, Gebel, *Sudan* 81 F2
Marracuene, *Mozam.* 89 D5
Marradi, *Italy* 29 D8
Marrakech, *Morocco* 78 B4
Marratxi, *Spain* 32 F7
Marrawah, *Australia* 94 G3
Marree, *Australia* 95 D2
Marrero, *U.S.A.* 113 L9
Marrimane, *Mozam.* 89 C5
Marromeu, *Mozam.* 89 B6
Marroquí, Punta, *Spain* 35 K5
Marrowie Cr. →, *Australia* . 95 E4
Marrubane, *Mozam.* 87 F4
Marrúbiu, *Italy* 30 C1
Marrupa, *Mozam.* 87 E4
Mars Hill, *U.S.A.* 109 B12
Marsá Alam, *Egypt* 80 B3
Marsá Matrûh, *Egypt* 80 A2
Marsa Sha'b, *Sudan* 80 C4
Marsabit, *Kenya* 86 B4
Marsala, *Italy* 30 E5
Marsalforn, *Malta* 36 C1
Mârşani, *Romania* 43 F9
Marsberg, *Germany* 24 D4
Marsciano, *Italy* 29 F9
Marsden, *Australia* 95 E4
Marseillan, *France* 20 E7
Marseille, *France* 21 E9
Marseilles = Marseille,
    France 21 E9
Marsh I., *U.S.A.* 113 L9
Marshall, *Liberia* 82 D2
Marshall, *Ark., U.S.A.* 113 H8
Marshall, *Mich., U.S.A.* . . . 108 D3
Marshall, *Minn., U.S.A.* . . . 112 C7
Marshall, *Mo., U.S.A.* 112 F8
Marshall, *Tex., U.S.A.* 113 J7
Marshall →, *Australia* 94 C2
Marshall Is. ■, *Pac. Oc.* . . . 96 G9
Marshalltown, *U.S.A.* 112 D8
Marshbrook, *Zimbabwe* 89 B5
Marshfield, *Mo., U.S.A.* . . . 113 G8
Marshfield, *Vt., U.S.A.* 111 B12
Marshfield, *Wis., U.S.A.* . . . 112 C9
Marshūn, *Iran* 71 B6
Mársico Nuovo, *Italy* 31 B8
Märsta, *Sweden* 10 E11
Marstal, *Denmark* 11 K4
Marstrand, *Sweden* 11 G5
Mart, *U.S.A.* 113 K6
Marta →, *Italy* 29 F8
Martaban, *Burma* 67 L20
Martaban, G. of, *Burma* . . . 67 L20
Martano, *Italy* 31 B11
Martapura, *Kalimantan,
    Indonesia* 62 E4
Martapura, *Sumatera,
    Indonesia* 62 E2
Marte, *Nigeria* 83 C7
Martel, *France* 20 D5
Martelange, *Belgium* 17 E5
Martellago, *Italy* 29 C9
Martés, Sierra, *Spain* 33 F4
Martfű, *Hungary* 42 C5
Martha's Vineyard, *U.S.A.* . 111 E14
Martigné-Ferchaud, *France* . 18 E5
Martigny, *Switz.* 25 J3
Martigues, *France* 21 E9
Martin, *Slovak Rep.* 27 B11
Martin, *S. Dak., U.S.A.* . . . 112 D4
Martin, *Tenn., U.S.A.* 113 G10
Martín →, *Spain* 32 D4
Martin L., *U.S.A.* 109 J3
Martina Franca, *Italy* 31 B10
Martinborough, *N.Z.* 91 J5
Martínez, *Calif., U.S.A.* . . . 116 G4
Martinez, *Ga., U.S.A.* 109 J4
Martinique ■, *W. Indies* . . . 121 D7
Martinique Passage,
    W. Indies 121 C7
Martínon, *Greece* 38 C5

Martinópolis, *Brazil* 127 A5
Martins Ferry, *U.S.A.* 110 F4
Martinsberg, *Austria* 26 C8
Martinshunga, *Pa., U.S.A.* ... 110 F6
Martinsburg, *W. Va., U.S.A.* 108 F7
Martinsicuro, *Italy* 29 F10
Martinsville, *Ind., U.S.A.* ... 108 F2
Martinsville, *Va., U.S.A.* ... 109 G6
Marton, *N.Z.* 91 J5
Martorell, *Spain* 32 D6
Martos, *Spain* 35 H7
Martuni, *Armenia* 49 K7
Maru, *Nigeria* 83 C6
Marudi, *Malaysia* 62 D4
Ma'ruf, *Afghan.* 66 D5
Marugame, *Japan* 55 G6
Marunga, *Angola* 88 B3
Marungu, Mts.,
  Dem. Rep. of the Congo . 86 D3
Marv Dasht, *Iran* 71 D7
Marvast, *Iran* 71 D7
Marvejols, *France* 20 D7
Marvel Loch, *Australia* 93 F2
Marwar, *India* 68 G5
Mary, *Turkmenistan* 50 F7
Maryborough = Port Laoise,
  Ireland 15 C4
Maryborough, *Queens.,*
  Australia 95 D5
Maryborough, *Vic., Australia* 95 F3
Maryfield, *Canada* 105 D8
Maryland □, *U.S.A.* 108 F7
Maryland Junction,
  Zimbabwe 87 F3
Maryport, *U.K.* 12 C4
Mary's Harbour, *Canada* ... 103 B8
Marystown, *Canada* 103 C8
Marysville, *Canada* 104 D5
Marysville, *Calif., U.S.A.* .. 116 F5
Marysville, *Kans., U.S.A.* .. 112 F6
Marysville, *Mich., U.S.A.* .. 110 D2
Marysville, *Ohio, U.S.A.* ... 108 E4
Marysville, *Wash., U.S.A.* .. 116 B4
Maryville, *Mo., U.S.A.* 112 E7
Maryville, *Tenn., U.S.A.* ... 109 H4
Marzūq, *Libya* 79 C8
Masahunga, *Tanzania* 86 C3
Masai Steppe, *Tanzania* 86 C4
Masaka, *Uganda* 86 C3
Masalembo, Kepulauan,
  Indonesia 62 F4
Masalima, Kepulauan,
  Indonesia 62 F5
Masallı, *Azerbaijan* 73 C13
Masamba, *Indonesia* 63 E6
Masan, *S. Korea* 57 G15
Masandam, Ra's, *Oman* ... 71 E8
Masasi, *Tanzania* 87 E4
Masaya, *Nic.* 120 D2
Masba, *Nigeria* 83 C7
Masbate, *Phil.* 61 E5
Máscali, *Italy* 31 E8
Mascara, *Algeria* 78 A6
Mascota, *Mexico* 118 C4
Masela, *Indonesia* 63 F7
Maseru, *Lesotho* 88 D4
Mashaba, *Zimbabwe* 87 G3
Mashābih, *Si. Arabia* 70 E3
Mashan, *China* 58 F7
Mashar, *Sudan* 81 F2
Mashegu, *Nigeria* 83 D6
Masherbrum, *Pakistan* 69 B7
Mashhad, *Iran* 71 B8
Mashi, *Nigeria* 83 C6
Mashīz, *Iran* 71 D8
Mashkel, Hamun-i, *Pakistan* 66 E3
Mashki Chāh, *Pakistan* 66 E3
Mashonaland, *Zimbabwe* ... 85 H6
Mashonaland Central □,
  Zimbabwe 89 B5
Mashonaland East □,
  Zimbabwe 89 B5
Mashonaland West □,
  Zimbabwe 89 B4
Mashrakh, *India* 69 F11
Mashtaga = Maştağa,
  Azerbaijan 49 K10
Masindi, *Uganda* 86 B3
Masindi Port, *Uganda* 86 B3
Maşīrah, *Oman* 74 C6
Maşīrah, Khalīj, *Oman* 74 C6
Masisi,
  Dem. Rep. of the Congo . 86 C2
Masjed Soleyman, *Iran* 71 D6
Mask, L., *Ireland* 15 C2
Maskin, *Oman* 71 F8
Maslen Nos, *Bulgaria* 41 D11
Maslinica, *Croatia* 29 E13
Masnou = El Masnou, *Spain* 32 D7
Masoala, Tanjon' i, *Madag.* 89 B9
Masoarivo, *Madag.* 89 B7
Masohi = Amahai, *Indonesia* 63 E7
Masomeloka, *Madag.* 89 C8
Mason, *Nev., U.S.A.* 116 G7
Mason, *Tex., U.S.A.* 113 K5
Mason City, *U.S.A.* 112 D8
Maspalomas, *Canary Is.* 37 G4
Maspalomas, Pta., *Canary Is.* 37 G4
Masqat, *Oman* 74 C6
Massa, *Italy* 28 D7
Massa Maríttima, *Italy* 28 E7
Massachusetts □, *U.S.A.* ... 111 D13
Massachusetts B., *U.S.A.* ... 111 D14
Massafra, *Italy* 31 B10
Massakory, *Chad* 79 F9
Massangena, *Mozam.* 89 C5
Massango, *Angola* 84 F3
Massat, *France* 20 F5
Massawa = Mitsiwa, *Eritrea* 81 D4
Massena, *U.S.A.* 111 B10

Massénya, *Chad* 79 F9
Masset, *Canada* 104 C2
Masseube, *France* 20 E4
Massiac, *France* 20 C7
Massif Central, *France* 20 D7
Massigui, *Mali* 82 C3
Massillon, *U.S.A.* 110 F3
Massinga, *Mozam.* 89 C6
Massingir, *Mozam.* 89 C5
Mässlingen, *Sweden* 10 B6
Masson, *Canada* 111 A9
Masson I., *Antarctica* 5 C7
Maştağa, *Azerbaijan* 49 K10
Mastanli = Momchilgrad,
  Bulgaria 41 E9
Masterton, *N.Z.* 91 J5
Mastic, *U.S.A.* 111 F12
Mástikho, Ákra, *Greece* 39 C8
Mastuj, *Pakistan* 69 A5
Mastung, *Pakistan* 66 E5
Mastūrah, *Si. Arabia* 80 C4
Masty, *Belarus* 46 F3
Masuda, *Japan* 55 G5
Masvingo, *Zimbabwe* 87 G3
Masvingo □, *Zimbabwe* 87 G3
Maşyāf, *Syria* 70 C3
Maszewo, *Poland* 44 E2
Matabeleland, *Zimbabwe* .. 85 H5
Matabeleland North □,
  Zimbabwe 87 F2
Matabeleland South □,
  Zimbabwe 87 G2
Matachel →, *Spain* 35 G4
Matachewan, *Canada* 102 C3
Matadi,
  Dem. Rep. of the Congo . 84 F2
Matagalpa, *Nic.* 120 D2
Matagami, *Canada* 102 C4
Matagami, L., *Canada* 102 C4
Matagorda B., *U.S.A.* 113 L6
Matagorda I., *U.S.A.* 113 L6
Matak, *Indonesia* 65 L6
Mátala, *Greece* 36 E6
Matam, *Senegal* 82 B2
Matameye, *Niger* 83 C6
Matamoros, *Campeche,*
  Mexico 119 D6
Matamoros, *Coahuila,*
  Mexico 118 B4
Matamoros, *Tamaulipas,*
  Mexico 119 B5
Ma'ţan as Sarra, *Libya* 79 D10
Matandu →, *Tanzania* 87 D3
Matane, *Canada* 103 C6
Matang, *China* 58 F5
Matankari, *Niger* 83 C5
Matanomadh, *India* 68 H3
Matanzas, *Cuba* 120 B3
Matapa, *Botswana* 88 C3
Matapan, C. = Taínaron,
  Ákra, *Greece* 38 E4
Matapédia, *Canada* 103 C6
Matara, *Sri Lanka* 66 S12
Mataram, *Indonesia* 62 F5
Matarani, *Peru* 124 G4
Mataranka, *Australia* 92 B5
Matarma, Râs, *Egypt* 75 E1
Mataró, *Spain* 32 D7
Matarraña →, *Spain* 32 D5
Mataruška Banja,
  Serbia, Yug. 40 C4
Matatiele, *S. Africa* 89 E4
Mataura, *N.Z.* 91 M2
Matehuala, *Mexico* 118 C4
Mateke Hills, *Zimbabwe* ... 87 G3
Matera, *Italy* 31 B9
Matese, Monti del, *Italy* ... 31 A7
Mátészalka, *Hungary* 42 C7
Matetsi, *Zimbabwe* 87 F2
Matha, *France* 20 C3
Mathis, *U.S.A.* 113 L6
Mathráki, *Greece* 36 A3
Mathura, *India* 68 F7
Mati, *Phil.* 61 H7
Mati →, *Albania* 40 E3
Matiakoali, *Burkina Faso* ... 83 C5
Matiali, *India* 69 F13
Matías Romero, *Mexico* 119 D5
Matibane, *Mozam.* 87 E5
Matima, *Botswana* 88 C3
Matiri Ra., *N.Z.* 91 J4
Matjiesfontein, *S. Africa* ... 88 E3
Matla →, *India* 69 J13
Matlamanyane, *Botswana* .. 88 B4
Matli, *Pakistan* 68 G3
Matlock, *U.K.* 12 D6
Matna, *Sudan* 81 E4
Matopo Hills, *Zimbabwe* ... 87 G2
Matopos, *Zimbabwe* 87 G2
Matosinhos, *Portugal* 34 D2
Matour, *France* 19 F11
Maţraḩ, *Oman* 74 C6
Matroosberg, *S. Africa* 88 E2
Matsena, *Nigeria* 83 C7
Matsesta, *Russia* 49 J4
Matsu Tao, *Taiwan* 59 E13
Matsumae, *Japan* 54 D10
Matsumoto, *Japan* 55 F9
Matsusaka, *Japan* 55 G8
Matsuō, *Japan* 55 F8
Matsuura, *Japan* 55 H4
Matsuyama, *Japan* 55 H6
Mattagami →, *Canada* 102 B3

Mattancheri, *India* 66 Q10
Mattawa, *Canada* 102 C4
Matterhorn, *Switz.* 25 K3
Mattersburg, *Austria* 27 D9
Matthew Town, *Bahamas* .. 121 B5
Matthew's Ridge, *Guyana* . 124 B6
Mattice, *Canada* 102 C3
Mattituck, *U.S.A.* 111 F12
Mattoon, *U.S.A.* 108 F1
Matuba, *Mozam.* 89 C5
Matucana, *Peru* 124 F3
Matūn = Khowst, *Afghan.* . 68 C3
Maturín, *Venezuela* 124 B6
Matxitxako, C., *Spain* 32 B2
Mau, *Mad. P., India* 69 F8
Mau, *Ut. P., India* 69 G10
Mau, *Ut. P., India* 69 G9
Mau Escarpment, *Kenya* ... 86 C4
Mau Ranipur, *India* 69 G8
Maubeuge, *France* 19 B10
Maubourguet, *France* 20 E4
Maud, Pt., *Australia* 92 D1
Maude, *Australia* 95 E3
Maudin Sun, *Burma* 67 M19
Maués, *Brazil* 124 D7
Mauganj, *India* 67 G12
Maughold Hd., *U.K.* 12 C3
Mauguio, *France* 20 E7
Maui, *U.S.A.* 106 H16
Maulamyaing = Moulmein,
  Burma 67 L20
Maule □, *Chile* 126 D1
Mauléon-Licharre, *France* .. 20 E3
Maumee, *U.S.A.* 108 E4
Maumee →, *U.S.A.* 108 E4
Maumere, *Indonesia* 63 F6
Maumusson, Pertuis de,
  France 20 C2
Maun, *Botswana* 88 C3
Mauna Kea, *U.S.A.* 106 J17
Mauna Loa, *U.S.A.* 106 J17
Maungmagan Is., *Burma* ... 64 E1
Maungmagan Kyunzu,
  Burma 67 N20
Maupin, *U.S.A.* 114 D3
Maure-de-Bretagne, *France* 18 E5
Maurepas, L., *U.S.A.* 113 K9
Maures, *France* 21 E10
Mauriac, *France* 20 C6
Maurice, L., *Australia* 93 E5
Mauricie, Parc Nat. de la,
  Canada 102 C5
Maurienne, *France* 21 C10
Mauritania ■, *Africa* 78 E3
Mauritius ■, *Ind. Oc.* 77 J9
Mauron, *France* 18 D4
Maurs, *France* 20 D6
Mauston, *U.S.A.* 112 D9
Mauterndorf, *Austria* 26 D6
Mauthen, *Austria* 26 E6
Mauvezin, *France* 20 E4
Mauzé-sur-le-Mignon, *France* 20 B3
Mavli, *India* 68 G5
Mavrova, *Albania* 40 F3
Mavuradonha Mts.,
  Zimbabwe 87 F3
Mawa,
  Dem. Rep. of the Congo . 86 B2
Mawai, *India* 69 H9
Mawana, *India* 68 E7
Mawand, *Pakistan* 68 E3
Mawk Mai, *Burma* 67 J20
Mawlaik, *Burma* 67 H19
Mawlamyine = Moulmein,
  Burma 67 L20
Mawqaq, *Si. Arabia* 70 E4
Mawson Coast, *Antarctica* . 5 C6
Max, *U.S.A.* 112 B4
Maxcanú, *Mexico* 119 C6
Maxesibeni, *S. Africa* 89 E4
Maxhamish L., *Canada* 104 B4
Maxixe, *Mozam.* 89 C6
Maxville, *Canada* 111 A10
Maxwell, *U.S.A.* 116 F4
Maxwelton, *Australia* 94 C3
May, C., *U.S.A.* 108 F8
May Pen, *Jamaica* 120 C4
Maya →, *Russia* 51 D14
Maya Mts., *Belize* 119 D7
Mayaguana, *Bahamas* 121 B5
Mayagüez, *Puerto Rico* 121 C6
Mayahi, *Niger* 83 C6
Mayals = Maials, *Spain* 32 D5
Mayāmey, *Iran* 71 B7
Mayang, *China* 58 D7
Mayanup, *Australia* 93 F2
Mayapan, *Mexico* 119 C7
Mayarí, *Cuba* 121 B4
Maybell, *U.S.A.* 114 F9
Maybole, *U.K.* 14 F4
Maychew, *Ethiopia* 81 E4
Maydān, *Iraq* 70 C5
Maydena, *Australia* 94 G4
Mayen, *Germany* 25 E3
Mayenne, *France* 18 D6
Mayenne □, *France* 18 D6
Mayenne →, *France* 18 E6
Mayer, *U.S.A.* 115 J7
Mayerthorpe, *Canada* 104 C5
Mayfield, *Ky., U.S.A.* 109 G1
Mayfield, *N.Y., U.S.A.* 111 D10
Mayhill, *U.S.A.* 115 K11
Maykop, *Russia* 49 H5
Maymyo, *Burma* 67 H20
Maynard, *Mass., U.S.A.* ... 111 D13
Maynard, *Wash., U.S.A.* .. 116 C4
Maynard Hills, *Australia* ... 93 E2
Mayne →, *Australia* 94 C3
Maynooth, *Ireland* 15 C5
Mayo, *Canada* 100 B6

Mayo □, *Ireland* 15 C2
Mayo Daga, *Nigeria* 83 D7
Mayo Faran, *Nigeria* 83 D7
Mayon Volcano, *Phil.* 61 E5
Mayor I., *N.Z.* 91 G6
Mayorga, *Spain* 34 C5
Mayotte, *Ind. Oc.* 85 G9
Mayraira Pt., *Phil.* 61 B4
Mayskiy, *Russia* 49 J7
Maysville, *U.S.A.* 108 F4
Mayu, *Indonesia* 63 D7
Mayville, *N. Dak., U.S.A.* . 112 B6
Mayville, *N.Y., U.S.A.* 110 D5
Mayya, *Russia* 51 C14
Mazabuka, *Zambia* 87 F2
Mazagán = El Jadida,
  Morocco 78 B4
Mazagão, *Brazil* 125 D8
Mazamet, *France* 20 E6
Mazán, *Peru* 124 D4
Māzandarān □, *Iran* 71 B7
Mazapil, *Mexico* 118 C4
Mazara del Vallo, *Italy* 30 E5
Mazarrón, *Spain* 33 H3
Mazarrón, G. de, *Spain* ... 33 H3
Mazaruni →, *Guyana* 124 B7
Mazatán, *Mexico* 118 B2
Mazatenango, *Guatemala* .. 120 D1
Mazatlán, *Mexico* 118 C3
Mažeikiai, *Lithuania* 9 H20
Māzhān, *Iran* 71 C8
Mazīnān, *Iran* 71 B8
Mazoe, *Mozam.* 87 F3
Mazoe →, *Mozam.* 87 F3
Mazowe, *Zimbabwe* 87 F3
Mazowieckie □, *Poland* 45 F8
Mazrūb, *Sudan* 81 E2
Mazu Dao, *China* 59 D12
Mazurian Lakes = Mazurski,
  Pojezierze, *Poland* ......
Mazurski, Pojezierze, *Poland* 44 E7
Mazyr, *Belarus* 47 F5
Mazzarino, *Italy* 31 E7
Mbaba, *Senegal* 82 C1
Mbabane, *Swaziland* 89 D5
Mbagne, *Mauritania* 82 B2
Mbaiki, *C.A.R.* 84 D3
Mbala, *Zambia* 87 D3
Mbalabala, *Zimbabwe* 89 C4
Mbale, *Uganda* 86 B3
Mbalmayo, *Cameroon* 83 E7
Mbam →, *Cameroon* 83 D7
Mbamba Bay, *Tanzania* 87 E3
Mbandaka,
  Dem. Rep. of the Congo . 84 D3
Mbanga, *Cameroon* 83 E6
Mbanza Congo, *Angola* 84 F2
Mbanza Ngungu,
  Dem. Rep. of the Congo . 84 F2
Mbarara, *Uganda* 86 C3
Mbashe →, *S. Africa* 89 E4
Mbatto, *Ivory C.* 82 D4
Mbenkuru →, *Tanzania* 87 D4
Mberengwa, *Zimbabwe* 87 G2
Mberengwa, Mt., *Zimbabwe* 87 G2
Mberubu, *Nigeria* 83 D6
Mbesuma, *Zambia* 87 E3
Mbeya, *Tanzania* 87 D3
Mbeya □, *Tanzania* 86 D3
Mbinga, *Tanzania* 87 E4
Mbini □, *Eq. Guin.* 84 D2
Mboki, *C.A.R.* 81 F2
M'bonge, *Cameroon* 83 E6
Mboro, *Senegal* 82 B1
Mboune, *Senegal* 82 C2
Mbour, *Senegal* 82 C1
Mbout, *Mauritania* 82 B2
Mbuji-Mayi,
  Dem. Rep. of the Congo . 86 D1
Mbulu, *Tanzania* 86 C4
Mburucuyá, *Argentina* 126 B4
Mchinja, *Tanzania* 87 D4
Mchinji, *Malawi* 87 E3
Mdantsane, *S. Africa* 85 L5
Mead, L., *U.S.A.* 117 J12
Meade, *U.S.A.* 113 G4
Meadow Lake, *Canada* 105 C7
Meadow Lake Prov. Park,
  Canada 105 C7
Meadow Valley Wash →,
  U.S.A. 117 J12
Meadville, *U.S.A.* 110 E4
Meaford, *Canada* 102 D3
Mealhada, *Portugal* 34 E2
Mealy Mts., *Canada* 103 B8
Meander River, *Canada* ... 104 B5
Mearim →, *Brazil* 125 D10
Meares, C., *U.S.A.* 114 D2
Mearns, Serra de, *Spain* ... 34 B3
Meath □, *Ireland* 15 C5
Meath Park, *Canada* 105 C7
Meaulne, *France* 19 F9
Meaux, *France* 19 D9
Mebechi-Gawa →, *Japan* .. 54 D10
Mecanhelas, *Mozam.* 87 F4
Mecca = Makkah, *Si. Arabia* 80 C2
Mecca, *U.S.A.* 117 M10
Mechanicsburg, *U.S.A.* 110 F8
Mechanicville, *U.S.A.* 111 D11
Mechara, *Ethiopia* 81 F5
Mechelen, *Belgium* 17 C4
Mecheria, *Algeria* 78 B5
Mechernich, *Germany* 24 E2
Mechetinskaya, *Russia* 49 G5
Mecitözü, *Turkey* 72 B6
Mecklenburg-
  Vorpommern □, *Germany* 24 B8
Mecklenburger Bucht,
  Germany 24 A7

Meconta, *Mozam.* 87 E4
Mecsek, *Hungary* 42 D3
Meda, *Portugal* 34 E3
Medan, *Indonesia* 62 D1
Medanosa, Pta., *Argentina* . 128 F3
Mede, *Italy* 28 C5
Medéa, *Algeria* 78 A6
Mededa, *Bos.-H.* 42 G4
Medellín, *Colombia* 124 B3
Medelpad, *Sweden* 10 B10
Medemblik, *Neths.* 17 B5
Mederdra, *Mauritania* 82 B1
Medford, *Mass., U.S.A.* ... 111 D13
Medford, *Oreg., U.S.A.* ... 114 E2
Medford, *Wis., U.S.A.* 112 C9
Medgidia, *Romania* 43 F13
Medi, *Sudan* 81 F3
Media Agua, *Argentina* 126 C2
Media Luna, *Argentina* 126 C2
Medianeira, *Brazil* 127 B5
Mediaş, *Romania* 43 D9
Medicina, *Italy* 29 D8
Medicine Bow, *U.S.A.* 114 F10
Medicine Bow Pk., *U.S.A.* . 114 F10
Medicine Bow Ra., *U.S.A.* . 114 F10
Medicine Hat, *Canada* 105 D6
Medicine Lake, *U.S.A.* 112 A2
Medicine Lodge, *U.S.A.* ... 113 G5
Medina = Al Madīnah,
  Si. Arabia 70 E3
Medina, *N. Dak., U.S.A.* .. 112 B5
Medina, *N.Y., U.S.A.* 110 C6
Medina, *Ohio, U.S.A.* 110 E3
Medina →, *U.S.A.* 113 L5
Medina de Pomar, *Spain* ... 34 C7
Medina de Ríoseco, *Spain* . 34 D5
Medina del Campo, *Spain* . 34 D6
Medina L., *U.S.A.* 113 L5
Medina Sidonia, *Spain* 35 J5
Medinaceli, *Spain* 32 D2
Medinipur, *India* 69 H12
Mediterranean Sea, *Europe* 6 H7
Médoc, *France* 20 C3
Medulin, *Croatia* 29 D10
Medveđa, *Serbia, Yug.* 40 D5
Medvedevo, *Russia* 48 B8
Medveditsa →, *Tver, Russia* 48 B9
Medveditsa →, *Volgograd,*
  Russia 48 F6
Medvedok, *Russia* 48 B10
Medvezhi, Ostrava, *Russia* . 51 B17
Medvezhyegorsk, *Russia* ... 50 C4
Medway →, *U.K.* 13 F8
Medway Towns □, *U.K.* ... 13 F8
Medzev, *Slovak Rep.* 27 C13
Medzilaborce, *Slovak Rep.* . 27 B14
Medžitlija, *Macedonia* 40 F5
Meekatharra, *Australia* 93 E2
Meeker, *U.S.A.* 114 F10
Meelpaeg Res., *Canada* 103 C8
Meerut, *Germany* 25 H5
Meerut, *India* 68 E7
Meeteetse, *U.S.A.* 114 D9
Mega, *Ethiopia* 81 G4
Megálo Khorío, *Greece* 39 E9
Megálo Petalí, *Greece* 38 D6
Megalópolis, *Greece* 38 D4
Meganísi, *Greece* 38 C2
Mégara, *Greece* 38 D5
Megasini, *India* 69 J12
Megdhova →, *Greece* 38 C3
Megève, *France* 21 C10
Meghalaya □, *India* 67 G17
Meghezez, *Ethiopia* 81 F4
Mégiscane, L., *Canada* 102 C4
Megiste, *Greece* 39 E11
Megra, *Russia* 46 B9
Mehadia, *Romania* 42 F7
Meharry, Mt., *Australia* ... 92 D2
Mehedeby, *Sweden* 10 D11
Mehedinți □, *Romania* 42 F7
Meheisa, *Sudan* 80 D3
Mehlville, *U.S.A.* 112 F9
Mehndawal, *India* 69 F10
Mehr Jān, *Iran* 71 C7
Mehrābād, *Iran* 70 B5
Mehrān, *Iran* 70 C5
Mehrīz, *Iran* 71 D7
Mehun-sur-Yèvre, *France* .. 19 E9
Mei Jiang →, *China* 59 E11
Mei Xian, *China* 56 G4
Meichengzhen, *China* 59 C9
Meichuan, *China* 59 B10
Meigu, *China* 58 C4
Meiktila, *Burma* 67 J19
Meinerzhagen, *Germany* ... 24 D3
Meiningen, *Germany* 24 E6
Meira, Serra de, *Spain* 34 B3
Meishan, *China* 58 B4
Meissen, *Germany* 24 D9
Meissner, *Germany* 24 D5
Meitan, *China* 58 D6
Meizhou, *China* 59 E11
Meja, *India* 69 G10
Mejillones, *Chile* 126 A1
Mekdela, *Ethiopia* 81 E4
Mekele, *Ethiopia* 81 E4
Mekhtar, *Pakistan* 66 D6
Meknès, *Morocco* 78 B4
Meko, *Nigeria* 83 D5
Mekong →, *Asia* 65 H6
Mekongga, *Indonesia* 63 E6
Mekrou →, *Benin* 83 C5
Mekvari = Kür →,
  Azerbaijan 73 C13
Mel, *Italy* 29 B9
Melagiri Hills, *India* 66 N10
Melaka, *Malaysia* 65 L4
Melalap, *Malaysia* 62 C5

Mélambes, Greece 36 D6
Melanesia, Pac. Oc. 96 H7
Melbourne, Australia .. 95 F4
Melbourne, U.S.A. .. 109 L5
Melchor Múzquiz, Mexico .. 118 B4
Melchor Ocampo, Mexico .. 118 C4
Méldola, Italy 29 D9
Meldorf, Germany 24 A5
Melegnano, Italy 28 C6
Melenci, Serbia, Yug. 42 E5
Melenki, Russia 48 C5
Mélèzes →, Qué., Canada . 101 C12
Mélèzes →, Qué., Canada . 102 A5
Melfi, Italy 31 B8
Melfort, Canada 105 C8
Melfort, Zimbabwe 87 F3
Melgaço, Portugal 34 C2
Melgar de Fernamental, Spain 34 C6
Melhus, Norway 8 E14
Melide, Spain 34 C2
Meligalá, Greece 38 D3
Melilla, N. Afr. 78 A5
Melilli, Italy 31 E8
Melipilla, Chile 126 C1
Mélissa, Ákra, Greece 36 D6
Mélissa Óros, Greece 39 D8
Melita, Canada 105 D8
Mélito di Porto Salvo, Italy . 31 E8
Melitopol, Ukraine 47 J8
Melk, Austria 26 C8
Mellan Fryken, Sweden ... 10 E7
Mellansel, Sweden 8 E18
Mellbystrand, Sweden 11 H6
Melle, France 20 B3
Melle, Germany 24 C4
Mellen, U.S.A. 112 B9
Mellerud, Sweden 11 F6
Mellette, U.S.A. 112 C5
Mellid = Melide, Spain ... 34 C2
Mellieha, Malta 36 D1
Mellit, Sudan 81 E2
Mellrichstadt, Germany ... 24 E6
Melnik, Bulgaria 40 E7
Mělník, Czech Rep. 26 A7
Melo, Uruguay 127 C5
Melolo, Indonesia 63 F6
Melouprey, Cambodia 64 F5
Melrose, Australia 95 E4
Melrose, U.K. 14 F6
Melrose, Minn., U.S.A. ... 112 C7
Melrose, N. Mex., U.S.A. . 113 H3
Melstone, U.S.A. 114 C10
Melsungen, Germany 24 D5
Melton Mowbray, U.K. 12 E7
Melun, France 19 D9
Melut, Sudan 81 E3
Melville, Canada 105 C8
Melville, C., Australia 94 A3
Melville, L., Canada 103 B8
Melville B., Australia 94 A2
Melville I., Australia 92 B5
Melville I., Canada 4 B2
Melville Pen., Canada 101 B11
Mélykút, Hungary 42 D4
Memaliaj, Albania 40 F3
Memba, Mozam. 87 E5
Memboro, Indonesia 63 F5
Membrilla, Spain 35 G7
Memel = Klaìpėda, Lithuania 9 J19
Memel, S. Africa 89 D4
Memmingen, Germany 25 H6
Mempawah, Indonesia 62 D3
Memphis, Egypt 80 J7
Memphis, Mich., U.S.A. .. 110 D2
Memphis, Tenn., U.S.A. .. 113 H10
Memphis, Tex., U.S.A. ... 113 H4
Memphremagog, L., U.S.A. 111 B12
Mena, Ukraine 47 G7
Mena, U.S.A. 113 H7
Mena →, Ethiopia 81 F5
Menai Strait, U.K. 12 D3
Ménaka, Mali 83 B5
Menan = Chao Phraya →, Thailand 64 F3
Menarandra →, Madag. .. 89 D7
Menard, U.S.A. 113 K5
Menawashei, Sudan 81 E1
Mendawai →, Indonesia ... 62 E4
Mende, France 20 D7
Mendebo, Ethiopia 81 F4
Menden, Germany 24 D3
Menderes, Turkey 39 C9
Mendez, Mexico 119 B5
Mendhar, India 69 C6
Mendi, Ethiopia 81 F4
Mendip Hills, U.K. 13 F5
Mendocino, U.S.A. 114 G2
Mendocino, C., U.S.A. ... 114 F1
Mendooran, Australia 95 E4
Mendota, Calif., U.S.A. .. 116 J6
Mendota, Ill., U.S.A. 112 E10
Mendoza, Argentina 126 C2
Mendoza □, Argentina ... 126 C2
Mene Grande, Venezuela .. 124 B4
Menemen, Turkey 39 C9
Menen, Belgium 17 D3
Menfi, Italy 30 E5
Mengdingjie, China 58 F2
Mengeš, Slovenia 29 B11
Menggala, Indonesia 62 E3
Menghai, China 58 G3
Mengíbar, Spain 35 H7
Mengjin, China 56 G7
Mengla, China 58 G3
Menglian, China 58 F2
Mengshan, China 59 E8
Mengyin, China 57 G9
Mengzhe, China 58 F3
Mengzi, China 58 F4

Menihek, Canada 103 B6
Menihek L., Canada 103 B6
Menin = Menen, Belgium . 17 D3
Menindee, Australia 95 E3
Menindee L., Australia ... 95 E3
Meningie, Australia 95 F2
Menlo Park, U.S.A. 116 H4
Menominee, U.S.A. 108 C2
Menominee →, U.S.A. ... 108 C2
Menomonie, U.S.A. 112 C9
Menongue, Angola 85 G3
Menorca, Spain 37 B11
Mentakab, Malaysia 65 L4
Mentawai, Kepulauan, Indonesia 62 E1
Menton, France 21 E11
Mentor, U.S.A. 110 E3
Menzies, Australia 93 E3
Meob B., Namibia 88 B2
Me'ona, Israel 75 B4
Meoqui, Mexico 118 B3
Mepaco, Mozam. 87 F3
Meppel, Neths. 17 B6
Meppen, Germany 24 C3
Mequinenza, Spain 32 D5
Mequinenza, Embalse de, Spain 32 D5
Mer, France 18 E8
Merabéllou, Kólpos, Greece 36 D7
Merak, Indonesia 63 F12
Meramangye, L., Australia . 93 E5
Meran = Merano, Italy ... 29 B8
Merano, Italy 29 B8
Merate, Italy 28 C6
Merauke, Indonesia 63 F10
Merbein, Australia 95 E3
Merca, Somali Rep. 74 G3
Mercato Saraceno, Italy .. 29 E9
Merced, U.S.A. 116 H6
Merced →, U.S.A. 116 H6
Merced Pk., U.S.A. 116 H7
Mercedes, Buenos Aires, Argentina 126 C4
Mercedes, Corrientes, Argentina 126 B4
Mercedes, San Luis, Argentina 126 C2
Mercedes, Uruguay 126 C4
Mercedes, U.S.A. 113 M6
Merceditas, Chile 126 B1
Mercer, N.Z. 91 G5
Mercer, U.S.A. 110 E4
Mercer Island, U.S.A. ... 116 C4
Mercury, U.S.A. 117 J11
Mercy C., Canada 101 B13
Merdrignac, France 18 D4
Mere, U.K. 13 F5
Meredith, C., Falk. Is. ... 128 G4
Meredith, L., U.S.A. 113 H4
Merefa, Ukraine 47 H9
Merei, Romania 43 E11
Merga = Nukheila, Sudan . 80 D2
Mergui, Burma 64 F2
Mergui Arch. = Myeik Kyunzu, Burma 65 G1
Meriç, Turkey 41 E10
Meriç →, Turkey 41 F10
Mérida, Mexico 119 C7
Mérida, Spain 35 G4
Mérida, Venezuela 124 B4
Mérida, Cord. de, Venezuela 122 C3
Meriden, U.K. 13 E6
Meriden, U.S.A. 111 E12
Meridian, Calif., U.S.A. .. 116 F5
Meridian, Idaho, U.S.A. .. 114 E5
Meridian, Miss., U.S.A. .. 109 J1
Mérignac, France 20 D3
Merimbula, Australia 95 F4
Mérinaghène, Senegal ... 82 B1
Merinda, Australia 94 C4
Mering, Germany 25 G6
Meringa, Nigeria 83 C7
Meringur, Australia 95 E3
Merir, Pac. Oc. 63 D8
Merirumã, Brazil 125 C8
Merkel, U.S.A. 113 J5
Mermaid Reef, Australia . 92 C2
Merowe, Sudan 80 D3
Merredin, Australia 93 F2
Merrick, U.K. 14 F4
Merrickville, Canada 111 B9
Merrill, Oreg., U.S.A. 114 E3
Merrill, Wis., U.S.A. 112 C10
Merrimack →, U.S.A. ... 111 D14
Merriman, U.S.A. 112 D4
Merritt, Canada 104 C4
Merritt Island, U.S.A. ... 109 L5
Merriwa, Australia 95 E5
Merry I., Canada 102 A4
Merryville, U.S.A. 113 K8
Mersa Fatma, Eritrea 81 E5
Mersch, Lux. 17 E6
Merse →, Italy 29 E8
Mersea I., U.K. 13 F8
Merseburg, Germany 24 D7
Mersey →, U.K. 12 D4
Merseyside □, U.K. 12 D4
Mersin, Turkey 70 B2
Mersing, Malaysia 65 L4
Merta, India 68 F6
Merta Road, India 68 F5
Merthyr Tydfil, U.K. 13 F4
Merthyr Tydfil □, U.K. .. 13 F4
Mértola, Portugal 35 H3
Mertzon, U.S.A. 113 K4
Méru, France 19 C9
Meru, Kenya 86 B4
Meru, Tanzania 86 C4
Merville, France 19 B9
Méry-sur-Seine, France .. 19 D10
Merzifon, Turkey 72 B6

Merzig, Germany 25 F2
Mesa, U.S.A. 115 K8
Mesa Verde National Park, U.S.A. 115 H9
Mesagne, Italy 31 B10
Mesanagrós, Greece 36 C9
Mesaoría □, Cyprus 36 D12
Mesarás, Kólpos, Greece .. 36 D6
Meschede, Germany 24 D4
Mescit, Turkey 73 B9
Mesfinto, Ethiopia 81 E4
Mesgouez, L., Canada 102 B5
Meshchovsk, Russia 46 E8
Meshed = Mashhad, Iran . 71 B8
Meshoppen, U.S.A. 111 E8
Meshra er Req, Sudan ... 81 F2
Mesilinka →, Canada ... 104 B4
Mesilla, U.S.A. 115 K10
Meslay-du-Maine, France . 18 E6
Mesocco, Switz. 25 J5
Mesolóngion, Greece 38 C3
Mesopotamia = Al Jazirah, Iraq 70 C5
Mesopotamia, U.S.A. 110 E4
Mesopótamon, Greece ... 38 B2
Mesoraca, Italy 31 C9
Mésou Volímais = Volímai, Greece 38 D2
Mesquite, U.S.A. 115 H6
Messac, France 18 E5
Messad, Algeria 78 B6
Messalo →, Mozam. 87 E4
Méssaména, Cameroon ... 83 E7
Messeue, Greece 38 D3
Messina, Italy 31 D8
Messina, S. Africa 89 C5
Messina, Str. di, Italy ... 31 D8
Messíni, Greece 38 D4
Messíni, Greece 38 D3
Messiniakós Kólpos, Greece 38 E4
Messkirch, Germany 25 H5
Messologi →, Bulgaria .. 40 E7
Messonghi, Greece 36 B3
Mesta →, Bulgaria 40 E7
Mestá, Ákra, Greece 39 C7
Mestanza, Spain 35 G6
Mestre, Italy 29 C9
Mesudiye, Turkey 72 B7
Meta →, S. Amer. 122 C4
Meta Incógnita Peninsula, Canada 101 B13
Metabetchouan, Canada .. 103 C5
Metairie, U.S.A. 113 L9
Metalici, Munții, Romania . 42 D7
Metaline Falls, U.S.A. ... 114 B5
Metallifere, Colline, Italy . 28 E8
Metán, Argentina 126 B3
Metangula, Mozam. 87 E3
Metauro →, Italy 29 E10
Metema, Ethiopia 81 E4
Metengobalame, Mozam. . 87 E3
Méthana, Greece 38 D5
Methóni, Greece 38 E3
Methven, N.Z. 91 K3
Metil, Mozam. 87 F4
Metkovets, Bulgaria 40 C7
Metković, Croatia 29 E14
Metlakatla, U.S.A. 100 C6
Metlika, Slovenia 29 C12
Metropolis, U.S.A. 113 G10
Métsovon, Greece 38 B3
Mettur Dam, India 66 P10
Metu, Ethiopia 81 F4
Metz, France 19 C13
Metzingen, Germany 25 G5
Meulaboh, Indonesia 62 D1
Meung-sur-Loire, France . 19 E8
Meureudu, Indonesia 62 C1
Meurthe →, France 19 D13
Meurthe-et-Moselle □, France 19 D13
Meuse □, France 19 C12
Meuse →, Europe 17 D5
Meuselwitz, Germany ... 24 D8
Mexia, U.S.A. 113 K6
Mexiana, I., Brazil 125 D9
Mexicali, Mexico 117 N11
Mexican Plateau, Mexico . 98 G9
Mexican Water, U.S.A. .. 115 H9
México, Mexico 119 D5
Mexico, Maine, U.S.A. ... 111 B14
Mexico, Mo., U.S.A. 112 F9
Mexico, N.Y., U.S.A. 111 C8
México □, Mexico 119 D5
Mexico ■, Cent. Amer. .. 118 C4
Mexico, G. of, Cent. Amer. 119 C7
Mexico B., U.S.A. 111 C8
Meydān-e Naftūn, Iran ... 71 D6
Meydani, Ra's-e, Iran ... 71 E8
Meyenburg, Germany ... 24 B8
Meymac, France 20 C6
Meymaneh, Afghan. 66 B4
Meyrueis, France 20 D7
Meyssac, France 20 C5
Meyzieu, France 21 C8
Mezdra, Bulgaria 40 C7
Mèze, France 20 E7
Mezen, Russia 50 C5
Mezen →, Russia 50 C5
Mézenc, Mt., France 21 D8
Mezhdurechensk, Russia . 50 D9
Mezhdurechenskiy, Russia . 50 C7
Mezha →, Russia 46 E6
Mézidon-Canon, France . 18 C6
Mézières-en-Brenne, France 21 B5
Mézilhac, France 21 D8
Mézin, France 20 D4
Mezőberény, Hungary ... 42 D6
Mezőfalva, Hungary 42 D3
Mezőhegyes, Hungary ... 42 D5
Mezőkövácsháza, Hungary 42 D5
Mezőkövesd, Hungary ... 42 C5

Mézos, France 20 D2
Mezőtúr, Hungary 42 C5
Mezzolombardo, Italy ... 28 B8
Mfolozi →, S. Africa 89 D5
Mgeta, Tanzania 87 D4
Mglin, Russia 47 F7
Mhlaba Hills, Zimbabwe . 87 F3
Mhow, India 68 H6
Miahuatlán, Mexico 119 D5
Miajadas, Spain 35 F5
Miami, Fla., U.S.A. 109 N5
Miami, Okla., U.S.A. 113 G7
Miami, Tex., U.S.A. 113 H4
Miami Beach, U.S.A. 109 N5
Mian Xian, China 56 H4
Mianchi, China 56 G6
Miāndarreh, Iran 71 C7
Miāndowāb, Iran 70 B5
Miandrivazo, Madag. 89 B8
Miāneh, Iran 70 B5
Mianning, China 58 C4
Mianwali, Pakistan 68 C4
Mianyang, China 58 B5
Mianzhu, China 58 B5
Miaoli, Taiwan 59 E13
Miarinarivo, Antananarivo, Madag. 89 B8
Miarinarivo, Toamasina, Madag. 89 B8
Miariravaratra, Madag. .. 89 C8
Miass, Russia 50 D7
Miastko, Poland 44 E3
Mica, S. Africa 89 C5
Micăsasa, Romania 43 D9
Michalovce, Slovak Rep. . 27 C14
Michigan □, U.S.A. 108 C3
Michigan, L., U.S.A. 108 D2
Michigan City, U.S.A. ... 108 E2
Michika, Nigeria 83 C7
Michipicoten I., Canada .. 102 C2
Michoacan □, Mexico ... 118 D4
Michurin, Bulgaria 41 D11
Michurinsk, Russia 48 D5
Mico, Pta., Nic. 120 D3
Micronesia, Pac. Oc. 96 G7
Micronesia, Federated States of ■, Pac. Oc. 96 G7
Midai, Indonesia 65 L6
Midale, Canada 105 D8
Middelburg, Neths. 17 C3
Middelburg, Eastern Cape, S. Africa 88 E4
Middelburg, Mpumalanga, S. Africa 89 D4
Middelfart, Denmark 11 J3
Middelpos, S. Africa 88 E3
Middelwit, S. Africa 88 C4
Middle Alkali L., U.S.A. . 114 F3
Middle Bass I., U.S.A. ... 110 E2
Middle East, Asia 52 F7
Middle Fork Feather →, U.S.A. 116 F5
Middle I., Australia 93 F3
Middle Loup →, U.S.A. . 112 E5
Middle Sackville, Canada . 103 D7
Middleboro, U.S.A. 111 E14
Middleburg, Fla., U.S.A. . 109 K5
Middleburg, N.Y., U.S.A. . 111 D10
Middleburg, Pa., U.S.A. . 110 F7
Middlebury, U.S.A. 111 B11
Middlemount, Australia .. 94 C4
Middleport, N.Y., U.S.A. . 110 C6
Middleport, Ohio, U.S.A. . 108 F4
Middlesboro, U.S.A. 109 G4
Middlesbrough, U.K. 12 C6
Middlesbrough □, U.K. .. 12 C6
Middlesex, Belize 120 C2
Middlesex, N.J., U.S.A. .. 111 F10
Middlesex, N.Y., U.S.A. . 110 D7
Middleton, Australia 94 C3
Middleton, Canada 103 D6
Middleton Cr. →, Australia 94 C3
Middletown, U.K. 15 B5
Middletown, Calif., U.S.A. 116 G4
Middletown, Conn., U.S.A. 111 E12
Middletown, N.Y., U.S.A. 111 E10
Middletown, Ohio, U.S.A. 108 F3
Middletown, Pa., U.S.A. . 111 F8
Midhurst, U.K. 13 G7
Midi, Canal du →, France 20 E5
Midi d'Ossau, Pic du, France 20 F3
Midi-Pyrénées □, France . 20 E5
Midland, Canada 102 D4
Midland, Calif., U.S.A. .. 117 M12
Midland, Mich., U.S.A. .. 108 D3
Midland, Pa., U.S.A. 110 F4
Midland, Tex., U.S.A. ... 113 K3
Midlands □, Zimbabwe .. 87 F2
Midleton, Ireland 15 E3
Midlothian, U.S.A. 113 J6
Midlothian □, U.K. 14 F5
Midongy, Tangorombohitr' i, Madag. 89 C8
Midongy Atsimo, Madag. . 89 C8
Midou →, France 20 E3
Midouze →, France 20 E3
Midsayap, Phil. 61 H6
Midu, China 58 E3
Midway Is., Pac. Oc. 96 E10
Midway Wells, U.S.A. ... 117 N11
Midwest, U.S.A. 107 B9
Midwest, Wyo., U.S.A. .. 114 E10
Midyat, Turkey 70 B4
Midzŏr, Bulgaria 40 C6
Mie □, Japan 55 G8
Miechów, Poland 45 H7

Miedwie, Jezioro, Poland .. 45 E1
Międzybórz, Poland 45 G4
Międzychód, Poland 45 F2
Międzylesie, Poland 45 H3
Międzyrzec Podlaski, Poland 45 G9
Międzyrzecz, Poland 45 F2
Międzyzdroje, Poland 44 E1
Miejska Górka, Poland ... 45 G3
Miélan, France 20 E4
Mielec, Poland 45 H8
Mienga, Angola 88 B2
Miercurea-Ciuc, Romania . 43 D10
Miercurea Sibiului, Romania 43 E8
Mieres, Spain 34 B5
Mieroszów, Poland 45 H3
Mieso, Ethiopia 81 F5
Mieszkowice, Poland 45 F1
Mifflintown, U.S.A. 110 F7
Mifraz Ḥefa, Israel 75 C4
Migennes, France 19 E10
Migliarino, Italy 29 D8
Miguel Alemán, Presa, Mexico 119 D5
Miguelturra, Spain 35 G7
Mihăileni, Romania 43 C11
Mihăilești, Romania 43 F10
Mihailovca, Moldova 43 D13
Mihara, Japan 55 G6
Miheșu de Cîmpie, Romania 43 D9
Mijas, Spain 35 J6
Mikese, Tanzania 86 D4
Mikha-Tskhakaya = Senaki, Georgia 49 J6
Mikhailovka = Mykhaylivka, Ukraine 47 J8
Mikhaylov, Russia 46 E10
Mikhaylovgrad = Montana, Bulgaria 40 C7
Mikhaylovka, Russia 48 E6
Mikhnevo, Russia 46 E9
Mikínai, Greece 38 D4
Mikkeli, Finland 9 F22
Mikkwa →, Canada 104 B6
Mikniya, Sudan 81 D3
Mikołajki, Poland 44 E8
Míkonos, Greece 39 D7
Mikrí Préspa, Límni, Greece 40 F5
Mikrón Dhérion, Greece .. 41 E10
Mikstat, Poland 45 G4
Mikulov, Czech Rep. 27 C9
Mikumi, Tanzania 86 D4
Milaca, U.S.A. 112 C8
Milagro, Ecuador 124 D3
Milagros, Phil. 61 E5
Milan = Milano, Italy ... 28 C6
Milan, Mo., U.S.A. 112 E8
Milan, Tenn., U.S.A. 109 H1
Milang, Australia 95 F2
Milange, Mozam. 87 F4
Milano, Italy 28 C6
Milanoa, Madag. 89 A8
Milâs, Turkey 39 D9
Milatos, Greece 36 D7
Milazzo, Italy 31 D8
Milbank, U.S.A. 112 C6
Milbanke Sd., Canada ... 104 C3
Milden, Canada 105 C7
Mildenhall, U.K. 13 E8
Mildmay, Canada 110 B3
Mildura, Australia 95 E3
Mile, China 58 E4
Miléai, Greece 38 B5
Miles, Australia 95 D5
Miles City, U.S.A. 112 B2
Milești, Moldova 43 C13
Milestone, Canada 105 D8
Mileto, Italy 31 D9
Miletto, Mte., Italy 31 A7
Miletus, Turkey 39 D9
Milevsko, Czech Rep. ... 26 B7
Milford, Calif., U.S.A. ... 116 E6
Milford, Conn., U.S.A. ... 111 E11
Milford, Del., U.S.A. 108 F8
Milford, Mass., U.S.A. .. 111 D13
Milford, N.H., U.S.A. ... 111 D13
Milford, Pa., U.S.A. 111 E10
Milford, Utah, U.S.A. ... 115 G7
Milford Haven, U.K. 13 F2
Milford Sd., N.Z. 91 L1
Milḥ, Baḥr al, Iraq 70 C4
Milicz, Poland 45 G4
Milikapiti, Australia 92 B5
Miling, Australia 93 F2
Militello in Val di Catánia, Italy 31 E7
Milk →, U.S.A. 114 B10
Milk, Wadi el →, Sudan . 80 D3
Milk River, Canada 104 D6
Mill I., Antarctica 5 C8
Mill Valley, U.S.A. 116 H4
Millárs →, Spain 32 E4
Millau, France 20 D7
Millbridge, Canada 110 B7
Millbrook, Canada 110 B6
Millbrook, U.S.A. 111 E11
Mille Lacs, L. des, Canada 102 C1
Mille Lacs L., U.S.A. 112 B8
Milledgeville, U.S.A. 109 J4
Millen, U.S.A. 109 J5
Miller, U.S.A. 112 C5
Millerovo, Russia 49 F5
Millersburg, Ohio, U.S.A. 110 F3
Millersburg, Pa., U.S.A. . 110 F8
Millerton, U.S.A. 111 E11
Millerton L., U.S.A. 116 J7
Millevaches, Plateau de, France 20 C6
Millheim, U.S.A. 110 F7
Millicent, Australia 95 F3

Millington, U.S.A.	113	H10
Millinocket, U.S.A.	109	C11
Millmerran, Australia	95	D5
Millom, U.K.	12	C4
Mills L., Canada	104	A5
Millsboro, U.S.A.	110	G5
Milltown Malbay, Ireland	15	D2
Millville, N.J., U.S.A.	108	F8
Millville, Pa., U.S.A.	111	E8
Millwood L., U.S.A.	113	J8
Milna, Croatia	29	E13
Milne →, Australia	94	C2
Milo, U.S.A.	109	C11
Mílos, Greece	38	E6
Miłosław, Poland	45	F4
Milot, Albania	40	E3
Milparinka, Australia	95	D3
Miltenberg, Germany	25	F5
Milton, N.S., Canada	103	D7
Milton, Ont., Canada	110	C5
Milton, N.Z.	91	M2
Milton, Calif., U.S.A.	116	G6
Milton, Fla., U.S.A.	109	K2
Milton, Pa., U.S.A.	110	F8
Milton, Vt., U.S.A.	111	B11
Milton-Freewater, U.S.A.	114	D4
Milton Keynes, U.K.	13	E7
Milton Keynes □, U.K.	13	E7
Miluo, China	59	C9
Milverton, U.S.A.	110	C4
Milwaukee, U.S.A.	108	D2
Milwaukee Deep, Atl. Oc.	121	C6
Milwaukie, U.S.A.	116	E4
Mim, Ghana	82	D4
Mimizan, France	20	D2
Mimoň, Czech Rep.	26	A7
Min Jiang →, Fujian, China	59	E12
Min Jiang →, Sichuan, China	58	C5
Min Xian, China	56	G3
Mina Pirquitas, Argentina	126	A2
Mīnā Su'ud, Kuwait	71	D6
Mīnā'al Aḥmadī, Kuwait	71	D6
Minago →, Canada	105	C9
Minaki, Canada	105	D10
Minamata, Japan	55	H5
Minami-Tori-Shima, Pac. Oc.	96	E7
Minas, Uruguay	127	C4
Minas, Sierra de las, Guatemala	120	C2
Minas Basin, Canada	103	C7
Minas de Rio Tinto = Minas de Riotinto, Spain	35	H4
Minas de Riotinto, Spain	35	H4
Minas Gerais □, Brazil	125	G9
Minatitlán, Mexico	119	D6
Minbu, Burma	67	J19
Minchinabad, Pakistan	68	D5
Mincio →, Italy	28	C7
Minčol, Slovak Rep.	27	B13
Mindanao, Phil.	61	H6
Mindanao Sea = Bohol Sea, Phil.	63	C6
Mindanao Trench, Pac. Oc.	61	F7
Mindel →, Germany	25	G6
Mindelheim, Germany	25	G6
Minden, Canada	110	B6
Minden, Germany	24	C4
Minden, La., U.S.A.	113	J8
Minden, Nev., U.S.A.	116	G7
Mindiptana, Indonesia	63	F10
Mindoro, Phil.	61	E4
Mindoro Str., Phil.	61	E4
Mine, Japan	55	G5
Minehead, U.K.	13	F4
Mineola, N.Y., U.S.A.	111	F11
Mineola, Tex., U.S.A.	113	J7
Mineral King, U.S.A.	116	J8
Mineral Wells, U.S.A.	113	J5
Mineralnyye Vody, Russia	49	H6
Minersville, U.S.A.	111	F8
Minerva, U.S.A.	110	F3
Minervino Murge, Italy	31	A9
Minetto, U.S.A.	111	C8
Mingäçevir, Azerbaijan	49	K8
Mingäçevir Su Anbarı, Azerbaijan	49	K8
Mingan, Canada	103	B7
Mingechaur = Mingäçevir, Azerbaijan	49	K8
Mingechaurskoye Vdkhr. = Mingäçevir Su Anbarı, Azerbaijan	49	K8
Mingela, Australia	94	B4
Mingenew, Australia	93	E2
Mingera Cr. →, Australia	94	C2
Minggang, China	59	A10
Mingguang, China	59	A11
Mingin, Burma	67	H19
Mingir, Moldova	43	D13
Minglanilla, Spain	33	F3
Minglun, China	58	E7
Mingo Junction, U.S.A.	110	F4
Mingorria, Spain	34	E6
Mingshan, China	58	B4
Mingxi, China	59	D11
Mingyuegue, China	57	C15
Minho = Miño →, Spain	34	D2
Minho □, Portugal	34	D2
Minhou, China	59	E12
Minićevo, Serbia, Yug.	42	G7
Minidoka, U.S.A.	114	E7
Minigwal, L., Australia	93	E3
Minilya →, Australia	93	D1
Minilya Roadhouse, Australia	93	D1
Minipi L., Canada	103	B7
Mink L., Canada	104	A5
Minkammen, Sudan	81	F3
Minna, Nigeria	83	D6
Minneapolis, Kans., U.S.A.	112	F6
Minneapolis, Minn., U.S.A.	112	C8
Minnedosa, Canada	105	C9
Minnesota □, U.S.A.	112	B8
Minnesota →, U.S.A.	112	C8
Minnewaukan, U.S.A.	112	A5
Minnipa, Australia	95	E2
Minnitaki L., Canada	102	C1
Mino, Japan	55	G8
Miño, Spain	34	B2
Miño →, Spain	34	D2
Minoa, Greece	39	F7
Minorca = Menorca, Spain	37	B11
Minot, U.S.A.	112	A4
Minqin, China	56	E2
Minqing, China	59	D12
Minsen, Germany	24	B3
Minsk, Belarus	46	F4
Mińsk Mazowiecki, Poland	45	F8
Mintabie, Australia	95	D1
Mintaka Pass, Pakistan	69	A6
Minteke Daban = Mintaka Pass, Pakistan	69	A6
Minto, Canada	103	C6
Minto, L., Canada	102	A5
Minton, Canada	105	D8
Minturn, U.S.A.	114	G10
Minturno, Italy	30	A6
Minûf, Egypt	80	H7
Minusinsk, Russia	51	D10
Minutang, India	67	E20
Minya el Qamh, Egypt	80	H7
Mionica, Bos.-H.	42	F3
Mionica, Serbia, Yug.	40	B4
Miquelon, Canada	102	C4
Miquelon, St- P. & M.	103	C8
Mir, Niger	83	C7
Mīr Kūh, Iran	71	E8
Mīr Shahdād, Iran	71	E8
Mira, Italy	29	C9
Mira, Portugal	34	E2
Mira →, Portugal	35	H2
Mira por vos Cay, Bahamas	121	B5
Mirabella Eclano, Italy	31	A7
Miraj, India	66	L9
Miram Shah, Pakistan	68	C4
Miramar, Argentina	126	D4
Miramar, Mozam.	89	C6
Miramas, France	21	E8
Mirambeau, France	20	C3
Miramichi, Canada	103	C6
Miramichi B., Canada	103	C7
Miramont-de-Guyenne, France	20	D4
Miranda, Brazil	125	H7
Miranda →, Brazil	124	G7
Miranda de Ebro, Spain	32	C2
Miranda do Corvo, Portugal	34	E2
Miranda do Douro, Portugal	34	D4
Mirande, France	20	E4
Mirandela, Portugal	34	D3
Mirándola, Italy	28	D8
Mirandópolis, Brazil	127	A5
Mirango, Malawi	87	E3
Mirano, Italy	29	C9
Miras, Albania	40	F4
Mirassol, Brazil	127	A6
Mirbāṭ, Oman	74	D5
Mirear, Egypt	80	C4
Mirebeau, Côte-d'Or, France	19	E12
Mirebeau, Vienne, France	18	F7
Mirecourt, France	19	D13
Mirgorod = Myrhorod, Ukraine	47	H7
Miri, Malaysia	62	D4
Miriam Vale, Australia	94	C5
Miribel, France	19	G11
Mirim, L., S. Amer.	127	C5
Mirnyy, Russia	51	C12
Miroč, Serbia, Yug.	40	B6
Mirokhan, Pakistan	68	F3
Mirond L., Canada	105	B8
Mirosławiec, Poland	44	E3
Mirpur, Pakistan	69	C5
Mirpur Batoro, Pakistan	68	G3
Mirpur Bibiwari, Pakistan	68	E2
Mirpur Khas, Pakistan	68	G3
Mirpur Sakro, Pakistan	68	G2
Mirria, Niger	83	C6
Mirsk, Poland	45	H2
Mirtağ, Turkey	70	B4
Miryang, S. Korea	57	G15
Mirzaani, Georgia	49	K8
Mirzapur, India	69	G10
Mirzapur-cum-Vindhyachal = Mirzapur, India	69	G10
Misantla, Mexico	119	D5
Misawa, Japan	54	D10
Miscou I., Canada	103	C7
Mish'āb, Ra's al, Si. Arabia	71	D6
Mishan, China	60	B8
Mishawaka, U.S.A.	108	E2
Mishbih, Gebel, Egypt	80	C3
Mishima, Japan	55	G9
Misión, Mexico	117	N10
Misiones □, Argentina	127	B5
Misiones □, Paraguay	126	B4
Miskah, Si. Arabia	70	E4
Miskitos, Cayos, Nic.	120	D3
Miskolc, Hungary	42	B5
Misoke, Dem. Rep. of the Congo	86	C2
Misool, Indonesia	63	E8
Mişrātah, Libya	79	B9
Missanabie, Canada	102	C3
Missinaibi →, Canada	102	B3
Missinaibi L., Canada	102	C3
Mission, Canada	104	D4
Mission, S. Dak., U.S.A.	112	D4
Mission, Tex., U.S.A.	113	M5
Mission Beach, Australia	94	B4
Mission Viejo, U.S.A.	117	M9
Missira, Senegal	82	C1
Missisa L., Canada	102	B2
Missiscabi →, Canada	102	B4
Mississagi →, Canada	102	C3
Mississauga, Canada	110	C5
Mississippi □, U.S.A.	113	J10
Mississippi →, U.S.A.	113	L10
Mississippi L., Canada	111	A8
Mississippi River Delta, U.S.A.	113	L9
Mississippi Sd., U.S.A.	113	K10
Missoula, U.S.A.	114	C7
Missouri □, U.S.A.	112	F8
Missouri →, U.S.A.	112	F9
Missouri City, U.S.A.	113	L7
Missouri Valley, U.S.A.	112	E7
Mist, U.S.A.	116	E3
Mistassibi →, Canada	103	B5
Mistassini, Canada	103	C5
Mistassini →, Canada	103	C5
Mistassini, L., Canada	102	B5
Mistastin L., Canada	103	A7
Mistelbach, Austria	27	C9
Misterbianco, Italy	31	E8
Mistinibi, L., Canada	103	A7
Mistretta, Italy	31	E7
Misty L., Canada	105	B8
Misurata = Mişrātah, Libya	79	B9
Mît Ghamr, Egypt	80	H7
Mitatib, Sudan	81	D4
Mitchell, Australia	95	D4
Mitchell, Canada	110	C3
Mitchell, Nebr., U.S.A.	112	E3
Mitchell, Oreg., U.S.A.	114	D3
Mitchell, S. Dak., U.S.A.	112	D6
Mitchell →, Australia	94	B3
Mitchell, Mt., U.S.A.	109	H4
Mitchell Ranges, Australia	94	A2
Mitchelstown, Ireland	15	D3
Mitha Tiwana, Pakistan	68	C5
Mithi, Pakistan	68	G3
Mithrao, Pakistan	68	F3
Míthymna, Greece	39	B8
Mitilíni, Greece	39	B8
Mitilinoí, Greece	39	D8
Mito, Japan	55	F10
Mitrofanovka, Russia	47	H10
Mitrovica = Kosovska Mitrovica, Kosovo, Yug.	40	D4
Mitsinjo, Madag.	89	B8
Mitsiwa, Eritrea	81	D4
Mitsiwa Channel, Eritrea	81	D5
Mitsukaidō, Japan	55	F9
Mittagong, Australia	95	E5
Mittelberg, Austria	26	D3
Mittelfranken □, Germany	25	F6
Mittellandkanal →, Germany	24	C4
Mittenwalde, Germany	24	C9
Mittersill, Austria	26	D5
Mitterteich, Germany	25	F8
Mittweida, Germany	24	E8
Mitú, Colombia	124	C4
Mitumba, Tanzania	86	D3
Mitumba, Mts., Dem. Rep. of the Congo	86	D2
Mitwaba, Dem. Rep. of the Congo	87	D2
Mityana, Uganda	86	B3
Mixteco →, Mexico	119	D5
Miyagi □, Japan	54	E10
Miyāh, W. el →, Egypt	80	C3
Miyah, W. el →, Syria	70	C3
Miyake-Jima, Japan	55	G9
Miyako, Japan	54	E10
Miyako-Jima, Japan	55	M2
Miyako-Rettō, Japan	55	M2
Miyakonojō, Japan	55	J5
Miyani, India	68	J3
Miyanoura-Dake, Japan	55	J5
Miyazaki, Japan	55	J5
Miyazaki □, Japan	55	H5
Miyazu, Japan	55	G7
Miyet, Bahr el = Dead Sea, Asia	75	D4
Miyi, China	58	D4
Miyoshi, Japan	55	G6
Miyun, China	56	D9
Miyun Shuiku, China	57	D9
Mizan Teferi, Ethiopia	81	F4
Mizdah, Libya	79	B8
Mizen Hd., Cork, Ireland	15	E2
Mizen Hd., Wick., Ireland	15	D5
Mizhi, China	56	F6
Mizil, Romania	43	F11
Mizoram □, India	67	H18
Mizpe Ramon, Israel	75	E3
Mizusawa, Japan	54	E10
Mjällby, Sweden	11	H8
Mjölby, Sweden	11	F9
Mjörn, Sweden	11	G6
Mjøsa, Norway	9	F14
Mkata, Tanzania	86	D4
Mkokotoni, Tanzania	86	D4
Mkomazi, Tanzania	86	C4
Mkomazi →, S. Africa	89	E5
Mkulwe, Tanzania	87	D3
Mkumbi, Ras, Tanzania	86	D4
Mkushi, Zambia	87	E2
Mkushi River, Zambia	87	E2
Mkuze, S. Africa	89	D5
Mladá Boleslav, Czech Rep.	26	A7
Mladenovac, Serbia, Yug.	40	B4
Mlala Hills, Tanzania	86	D3
Mlange = Mulanje, Malawi	87	F4
Mlanje, Pic, Malawi	85	H7
Mlava →, Serbia, Yug.	40	B5
Mława, Poland	45	E7
Mlinište, Bos.-H.	29	D13
Mljet, Croatia	29	F14
Mljetski Kanal, Croatia	29	F14
Młynary, Poland	44	D6
Mmabatho, S. Africa	88	D4
Mme, Cameroon	83	D7
Mnichovo Hradiště, Czech Rep.	26	A7
Mo i Rana, Norway	8	C16
Moa, Cuba	121	B4
Moa, Indonesia	63	F7
Moa →, S. Leone	82	D2
Moab, U.S.A.	115	G9
Moala, Fiji	91	D8
Moama, Australia	95	F3
Moamba, Mozam.	89	D5
Moapa, U.S.A.	117	J12
Moate, Ireland	15	C4
Moba, Dem. Rep. of the Congo	86	D2
Mobārakābād, Iran	71	D7
Mobaye, C.A.R.	84	D4
Mobayi, Dem. Rep. of the Congo	84	D4
Moberley Lake, Canada	104	B4
Moberly, U.S.A.	112	F8
Mobile, U.S.A.	109	K1
Mobile B., U.S.A.	109	K2
Mobridge, U.S.A.	112	C4
Mobutu Sese Seko, L. = Albert L., Africa	86	B3
Moc Chau, Vietnam	64	B5
Moc Hoa, Vietnam	65	G5
Mocabe Kasari, Dem. Rep. of the Congo	87	D2
Moçambique, Mozam.	87	F5
Moçâmedes = Namibe, Angola	85	H2
Mocanaqua, U.S.A.	111	E8
Mochudi, Botswana	88	C4
Mocimboa da Praia, Mozam.	87	E5
Mociu, Romania	43	D9
Mocoa, Colombia	124	C3
Mococa, Brazil	127	A6
Mocorito, Mexico	118	B3
Moctezuma, Mexico	118	B3
Moctezuma →, Mexico	119	C5
Mocuba, Mozam.	87	F4
Mocúzari, Presa, Mexico	118	B3
Modane, France	21	C10
Modasa, India	68	H5
Modder →, S. Africa	88	D3
Modderrivier, S. Africa	88	D3
Módena, Italy	28	D7
Modena, U.S.A.	115	H7
Modesto, U.S.A.	116	H6
Módica, Italy	31	F7
Mödling, Austria	27	C9
Modo, Sudan	81	F3
Modra, Slovak Rep.	27	C10
Modriča, Bos.-H.	42	F3
Moe, Australia	95	F4
Moebase, Mozam.	87	F4
Moëlan-sur-Mer, France	18	E3
Moengo, Surinam	125	B8
Moffat, U.K.	14	F5
Moga, India	68	D6
Mogadishu = Muqdisho, Somali Rep.	74	G4
Mogador = Essaouira, Morocco	78	B4
Mogadouro, Portugal	34	D4
Mogalakwena →, S. Africa	89	C4
Mogami-Gawa →, Japan	54	E10
Mogán, Canary Is.	37	G4
Mogaung, Burma	67	G20
Mogente = Moixent, Spain	33	G4
Mogho, Ethiopia	81	G5
Mogi das Cruzes, Brazil	127	A6
Mogi-Guaçu →, Brazil	127	A6
Mogi-Mirim, Brazil	127	A6
Mogielnica, Poland	45	G7
Mogige, Ethiopia	81	F4
Mogilev = Mahilyow, Belarus	46	F6
Mogilno, Poland	45	F4
Mogincual, Mozam.	87	F5
Mogliano Véneto, Italy	29	C9
Mogocha, Russia	51	D12
Mogok, Burma	67	H20
Mogollon Rim, U.S.A.	115	J8
Mógoro, Italy	30	C1
Mograt, Sudan	80	D3
Moguer, Spain	35	H4
Mogumber, Australia	93	F2
Mohács, Hungary	42	F3
Mohales Hoek, Lesotho	88	E4
Mohall, U.S.A.	112	A4
Mohammadābād, Iran	71	B8
Mohammedia, Morocco	78	B4
Mohana →, India	69	G11
Mohanlalganj, India	69	F9
Mohave, L., U.S.A.	117	K12
Mohawk →, U.S.A.	111	D11
Moheda, Sweden	11	G8
Mohenjodaro, Pakistan	68	F3
Mohicanville Reservoir, U.S.A.	110	F3
Möhne →, Germany	24	D4
Mohoro, Tanzania	86	D4
Mohyliv-Podilskyy, Ukraine	47	H4
Moia, Sudan	81	F2
Moidart, L., U.K.	14	E3
Moineşti, Romania	43	D11
Moira →, Canada	110	B7
Moirans, France	21	C9
Moirans-en-Montagne, France	19	F12
Moíres, Greece	36	D6
Moisaküla, Estonia	9	G21
Moisie, Canada	103	B6
Moisie →, Canada	103	B6
Moissac, France	20	D5
Moita, Portugal	35	G2
Moixent, Spain	33	G4
Möja, Sweden	10	E12
Mojácar, Spain	33	H3
Mojados, Spain	34	D6
Mojave, U.S.A.	117	K8
Mojave Desert, U.S.A.	117	L10
Mojiang, China	58	F3
Mojo, Bolivia	126	A2
Mojo, Ethiopia	81	F4
Mojokerto, Indonesia	63	G15
Mokai, N.Z.	91	H5
Mokambo, Dem. Rep. of the Congo	87	E2
Mokameh, India	69	G11
Mokelumne →, U.S.A.	116	G5
Mokelumne Hill, U.S.A.	116	G6
Mokhós, Greece	36	D7
Mokhotlong, Lesotho	89	D4
Möklinta, Sweden	10	D10
Mokokchung, India	67	F19
Mokolo, Cameroon	83	C7
Mokolo →, S. Africa	89	C4
Mokp'o, S. Korea	57	G14
Mokra Gora, Yugoslavia	40	D4
Mokronog, Slovenia	29	C12
Moksha →, Russia	48	C6
Mokshan, Russia	48	D7
Mokwa, Nigeria	83	D6
Mol, Belgium	17	C5
Mola di Bari, Italy	31	A10
Molale, Ethiopia	81	E4
Moláoi, Greece	38	E4
Molara, Italy	30	B2
Molat, Croatia	29	D11
Molchanovo, Russia	50	D9
Mold, U.K.	12	D4
Moldava nad Bodvou, Slovak Rep.	27	C14
Moldavia = Moldova ■, Europe	43	C13
Moldavia, Romania	43	D12
Molde, Norway	8	E12
Moldova ■, Europe	43	C13
Moldova →, Romania	43	C11
Moldova Nouă, Romania	42	F6
Moldoveana, Vf., Romania	43	E9
Moldoviţa, Romania	43	C10
Mole →, U.K.	13	F7
Mole Creek, Australia	94	G4
Molepolole, Botswana	88	C4
Molfetta, Italy	31	A9
Molina de Aragón, Spain	32	E3
Molina de Segura, Spain	33	G3
Moline, U.S.A.	112	E9
Molinella, Italy	29	D8
Molinos, Argentina	126	B2
Moliro, Dem. Rep. of the Congo	86	D3
Moliterno, Italy	31	B8
Molkom, Sweden	10	E7
Mölle, Sweden	11	H6
Molledo, Spain	34	B6
Mollendo, Peru	124	G4
Mollerin, L., Australia	93	F2
Mollerussa, Spain	32	D5
Mollina, Spain	35	H6
Mölln, Germany	24	B6
Mölltorp, Sweden	11	F8
Mölndal, Sweden	11	G6
Mölnlycke, Sweden	11	G6
Molochansk, Ukraine	47	J8
Molochnoye, Ozero, Ukraine	47	J8
Molodechno = Maladzyechna, Belarus	46	E4
Molokai, U.S.A.	106	H16
Molong, Australia	95	E4
Molopo →, Africa	88	D3
Mólos, Greece	38	C4
Molotov = Perm, Russia	50	D6
Molsheim, France	19	D14
Molson L., Canada	105	C9
Molteno, S. Africa	88	E4
Molu, Indonesia	63	F8
Molucca Sea, Indonesia	63	E7
Moluccas = Maluku, Indonesia	63	E7
Moma, Dem. Rep. of the Congo	86	C1
Moma, Mozam.	87	F4
Mombasa, Kenya	86	C4
Mombetsu, Japan	54	B11
Mombuey, Spain	34	C4
Momchilgrad, Bulgaria	41	E9
Momi, Dem. Rep. of the Congo	86	C2
Mompós, Colombia	124	B4
Møn, Denmark	11	K6
Mon →, Burma	67	J19
Mona, Canal de la, W. Indies	121	C6
Mona, Isla, Puerto Rico	121	C6
Mona, Pta., Costa Rica	120	E3
Monaca, U.S.A.	110	F4
Monaco ■, Europe	21	E11
Monadhliath Mts., U.K.	14	D4
Monadnock, Mt., U.S.A.	111	D12
Monaghan, Ireland	15	B5
Monaghan □, Ireland	15	B5
Monahans, U.S.A.	113	K3
Monapo, Mozam.	87	E5
Monar, L., U.K.	14	D3
Monarch Mts., Canada	104	C3
Monashee Mts., Canada	104	C5
Monasterevin, Ireland	15	C4

Monastir = Bitola, Macedonia ... 40 E5
Moncada, Phil. ... 61 D4
Moncalieri, Italy ... 28 C4
Moncalvo, Italy ... 28 C5
Moncão, Portugal ... 34 C2
Moncarapacho, Portugal ... 35 H3
Moncayo, Sierra del, Spain . 32 D3
Mönchengladbach, Germany ... 24 D2
Monchique, Portugal ... 35 H2
Moncks Corner, U.S.A. ... 109 J5
Monclova, Mexico ... 118 B4
Moncontour, France ... 18 D4
Moncton, Canada ... 103 C7
Mondariz, Spain ... 34 C2
Mondego →, Portugal ... 34 E2
Mondego, C., Portugal ... 34 E2
Mondeodo, Indonesia ... 63 E6
Mondeville, France ... 18 C6
Mondolfo, Italy ... 29 E10
Mondoñedo, Spain ... 34 B3
Mondovì, Italy ... 28 D4
Mondragon, Phil. ... 61 E6
Mondragone, Italy ... 30 A6
Mondrain I., Australia ... 93 F3
Monemvasía, Greece ... 38 E5
Monessen, U.S.A. ... 110 F5
Monesterio, Spain ... 35 G4
Monestier-de-Clermont, France ... 21 D9
Monett, U.S.A. ... 113 G8
Moneymore, U.K. ... 15 B5
Monfalcone, Italy ... 29 C10
Monflanquin, France ... 20 D4
Monforte, Portugal ... 35 F3
Monforte de Lemos, Spain ... 34 C3
Mong Hsu, Burma ... 58 G2
Mong Kung, Burma ... 67 J20
Mong Nai, Burma ... 67 J20
Mong Pawk, Burma ... 67 H21
Mong Ping, Burma ... 58 G2
Mong Ton, Burma ... 67 J21
Mong Wa, Burma ... 67 J22
Mong Yai, Burma ... 67 H21
Mongalla, Sudan ... 81 F3
Mongers, L., Australia ... 93 E2
Monghyr = Munger, India . 69 G12
Mongibello = Etna, Italy . 31 E7
Mongo, Chad ... 79 F9
Mongo →, S. Leone ... 82 D2
Mongolia ■, Asia ... 51 E10
Mongonu, Nigeria ... 83 C7
Mongu, Zambia ... 85 H4
Môngua, Angola ... 88 B2
Monifieth, U.K. ... 14 E6
Monistrol-sur-Loire, France ... 21 C8
Monkey Bay, Malawi ... 87 E4
Monkey Mia, Australia ... 93 E1
Monkey River, Belize ... 119 D7
Mońki, Poland ... 44 E9
Monkoto, Dem. Rep. of the Congo . 84 E4
Monkton, Canada ... 110 C3
Monmouth, U.K. ... 13 F5
Monmouth, Ill., U.S.A. ... 112 E9
Monmouth, Oreg., U.S.A. ... 114 D2
Monmouthshire □, U.K. ... 13 F5
Mono L., U.S.A. ... 116 H7
Monolith, U.S.A. ... 117 K8
Monólithos, Greece ... 36 C9
Monongahela, U.S.A. ... 110 F5
Monópoli, Italy ... 31 B10
Monor, Hungary ... 42 C4
Monóvar, Spain ... 33 G4
Monreal del Campo, Spain . 32 E3
Monreale, Italy ... 30 D6
Monroe, Ga., U.S.A. ... 109 J4
Monroe, La., U.S.A. ... 113 J8
Monroe, Mich., U.S.A. ... 108 E4
Monroe, N.C., U.S.A. ... 109 H5
Monroe, N.Y., U.S.A. ... 111 E10
Monroe, Utah, U.S.A. ... 115 G7
Monroe, Wash., U.S.A. ... 116 C5
Monroe, Wis., U.S.A. ... 112 D10
Monroe City, U.S.A. ... 112 F9
Monroeton, U.S.A. ... 111 E8
Monroeville, Ala., U.S.A. ... 109 K2
Monroeville, Pa., U.S.A. ... 110 F5
Monrovia, Liberia ... 82 D2
Mons, Belgium ... 17 D3
Møns Klint, Denmark ... 11 K6
Monsaraz, Portugal ... 35 G3
Monse, Indonesia ... 63 E6
Monségur, France ... 20 D4
Monsélice, Italy ... 29 C8
Mönsterås, Sweden ... 11 G10
Mont Cenis, Col du, France . 21 C10
Mont-de-Marsan, France ... 20 E3
Mont-Joli, Canada ... 103 C6
Mont-Laurier, Canada ... 102 C4
Mont-Louis, Canada ... 103 C6
Mont-roig del Camp, Spain . 32 D5
Mont-St-Michel, Le = Le Mont-St-Michel, France .. 18 D5
Mont Tremblant, Parc Recr. du, Canada ... 102 C5
Montabaur, Germany ... 24 E3
Montagnac, France ... 20 E7
Montagnana, Italy ... 29 C8
Montagu, S. Africa ... 88 E3
Montagu I., Antarctica ... 5 B1
Montague, Canada ... 103 C7
Montague, I., Mexico ... 118 A2
Montague Ra., Australia ... 93 E2
Montague Sd., Australia ... 92 B4
Montaigu, France ... 18 F5
Montalbán, Spain ... 32 E4
Montalbano Iónico, Italy . 31 B9
Montalbo, Spain ... 32 F2
Montalcino, Italy ... 29 E8
Montalegre, Portugal ... 34 D3

Montalto, Italy ... 31 D8
Montalto di Castro, Italy ... 29 F8
Montalto Uffugo, Italy ... 31 C9
Montalvo, U.S.A. ... 117 L7
Montamarta, Spain ... 34 D5
Montana, Bulgaria ... 40 C7
Montaña, Peru ... 124 E4
Montana □, Bulgaria ... 40 C7
Montana □, U.S.A. ... 114 C9
Montaña Clara, I., Canary Is. ... 37 E6
Montánchez, Spain ... 35 F4
Montargil, Portugal ... 35 F2
Montargis, France ... 19 E9
Montauban, France ... 20 D5
Montauk, U.S.A. ... 111 E13
Montauk Pt., U.S.A. ... 111 E13
Montbard, France ... 19 E11
Montbarrey, France ... 19 E12
Montbéliard, France ... 19 E13
Montblanc, Spain ... 32 D6
Montbrison, France ... 21 C8
Montceau-les-Mines, France . 19 F11
Montcenis, France ... 21 B8
Montclair, U.S.A. ... 111 F10
Montcornet, France ... 19 C11
Montcuq, France ... 20 D5
Montdidier, France ... 19 C9
Monte Albán, Mexico ... 119 D5
Monte Alegre, Brazil ... 125 D8
Monte Azul, Brazil ... 125 G10
Monte Bello Is., Australia . 92 D2
Monte-Carlo, Monaco ... 21 E11
Monte Caseros, Argentina . 126 C4
Monte Comán, Argentina ... 126 C2
Monte Cristi, Dom. Rep. ... 121 C5
Monte Lindo →, Paraguay . 126 A4
Monte Patria, Chile ... 126 C1
Monte Quemado, Argentina 126 B3
Monte Redondo, Portugal .. 34 F2
Monte Rio, U.S.A. ... 116 G4
Monte San Giovanni Campano, Italy ... 30 A6
Monte San Savino, Italy ... 29 E8
Monte Sant' Ángelo, Italy ... 29 G12
Monte Santu, C. di, Italy ... 30 B2
Monte Vista, U.S.A. ... 115 H10
Monteagudo, Argentina ... 127 B5
Montealegre del Castillo, Spain ... 33 G3
Montebello, Canada ... 102 C5
Montebello Iónico, Italy ... 31 E8
Montebelluna, Italy ... 29 C9
Montebourg, France ... 18 C5
Montecastrilli, Italy ... 29 F9
Montecatini Terme, Italy ... 28 E7
Montecito, U.S.A. ... 117 L7
Montecristo, Italy ... 28 F7
Montefalco, Italy ... 29 F9
Montefiascone, Italy ... 29 F9
Montefrío, Spain ... 35 H7
Montegiórgio, Italy ... 29 E10
Montego Bay, Jamaica ... 120 C4
Montehermoso, Spain ... 34 E4
Montejicar, Spain ... 35 H7
Montélimar, France ... 21 D8
Montella, Italy ... 31 B8
Montellano, Spain ... 35 J5
Montello, U.S.A. ... 112 D10
Montemor-o-Novo, Portugal 35 G2
Montemor-o-Velho, Portugal 34 E2
Montemorelos, Mexico ... 119 B5
Montendre, France ... 20 C3
Montenegro, Brazil ... 127 B5
Montenegro □, Yugoslavia . 40 D3
Montenero di Bisáccia, Italy 29 G11
Montepuez, Mozam. ... 87 E4
Montepuez →, Mozam. ... 87 E5
Montepulciano, Italy ... 29 E8
Montereale, Italy ... 29 F10
Montereau-Faut-Yonne, France ... 19 D9
Monterey, U.S.A. ... 116 J5
Monterey B., U.S.A. ... 116 J5
Montería, Colombia ... 124 B3
Monteros, Argentina ... 126 B2
Monterotondo, Italy ... 29 F9
Monterrey, Mexico ... 118 B4
Montes Claros, Brazil ... 125 G10
Montesano, U.S.A. ... 116 D3
Montesano sulla Marcellana, Italy ... 31 B8
Montesárchio, Italy ... 31 A7
Montescaglioso, Italy ... 31 B9
Montesilvano, Italy ... 29 F11
Montevarchi, Italy ... 29 E8
Montevideo, Uruguay ... 127 C4
Montevideo, U.S.A. ... 112 C7
Montezuma, U.S.A. ... 112 E8
Montfaucon, France ... 18 E5
Montfaucon-d'Argonne, France ... 19 C12
Montfaucon-en-Velay, France ... 21 C8
Montfort, France ... 18 D5
Montfort-le-Gesnois, France . 18 D7
Montgenèvre, France ... 21 D10
Montgomery = Sahiwal, Pakistan ... 68 D5
Montgomery, U.K. ... 13 E4
Montgomery, Ala., U.S.A. . 109 J2
Montgomery, Pa., U.S.A. .. 110 E8
Montgomery, W. Va., U.S.A. ... 108 F5
Montgomery City, U.S.A. ... 112 F9
Montguyon, France ... 20 C3
Monthermé, France ... 19 C11
Monthey, Switz. ... 25 J2
Monthois, France ... 19 C11
Monti, Italy ... 30 B2

Monticelli d'Ongina, Italy .. 28 C6
Monticello, Ark., U.S.A. ... 113 J9
Monticello, Fla., U.S.A. ... 109 K4
Monticello, Ind., U.S.A. ... 108 E2
Monticello, Iowa, U.S.A. ... 112 D9
Monticello, Ky., U.S.A. ... 109 G3
Monticello, Minn., U.S.A. .. 112 C8
Monticello, Miss., U.S.A. .. 113 K9
Monticello, N.Y., U.S.A. ... 111 E10
Monticello, Utah, U.S.A. ... 115 H9
Montichiari, Italy ... 28 C7
Montier-en-Der, France ... 19 D11
Montignac, France ... 20 C5
Montigny-les-Metz, France . 19 C13
Montigny-sur-Aube, France . 19 E11
Montijo, Portugal ... 35 G2
Montijo, Spain ... 35 G4
Montilla, Spain ... 35 H6
Montivilliers, France ... 18 C7
Montluçon, France ... 19 F9
Montmagny, Canada ... 103 C5
Montmarault, France ... 19 F9
Montmartre, Canada ... 105 C8
Montmédy, France ... 19 C12
Montmélian, France ... 21 C10
Montmirail, France ... 19 D10
Montmoreau-St-Cybard, France ... 20 C4
Montmorillon, France ... 20 B4
Montmort-Lucy, France ... 19 D10
Monto, Australia ... 94 C5
Montoire-sur-le-Loir, France 18 E7
Montório al Vomano, Italy . 29 F10
Montoro, Spain ... 35 G6
Montour Falls, U.S.A. ... 110 D8
Montoursville, U.S.A. ... 110 E8
Montpelier, Idaho, U.S.A. .. 114 E8
Montpelier, Vt., U.S.A. ... 111 B12
Montpellier, France ... 20 E7
Montpezat-de-Quercy, France ... 20 D5
Montpon-Ménestérol, France 20 D4
Montréal, Canada ... 102 C5
Montréal, Aude, France ... 20 E6
Montréal, Gers, France ... 20 E4
Montreal →, Canada ... 102 C3
Montreal L., Canada ... 105 C7
Montreal Lake, Canada ... 105 C7
Montredon-Labessonnié, France ... 20 E6
Montrésor, France ... 18 E8
Montret, France ... 19 F12
Montreuil, Pas-de-Calais, France ... 19 B8
Montreuil, Seine-St-Denis, France ... 19 D9
Montreuil-Bellay, France ... 18 E6
Montreux, Switz. ... 25 J2
Montrevel-en-Bresse, France 19 F12
Montrichard, France ... 18 E8
Montrose, U.K. ... 14 E6
Montrose, Colo., U.S.A. ... 115 G10
Montrose, Pa., U.S.A. ... 111 E9
Monts, Pte. des, Canada ... 103 C6
Montsalvy, France ... 20 D6
Montsant, Serra de, Spain .. 32 D6
Montsauche-les-Settons, France ... 19 E11
Montsec, Serra del, Spain ... 32 C5
Montserrat, Spain ... 32 D6
Montserrat ■, W. Indies ... 121 C7
Montuenga, Spain ... 34 D6
Montuiri, Spain ... 37 B9
Monywa, Burma ... 67 H19
Monza, Italy ... 28 C6
Monze, Zambia ... 87 F2
Monze, C., Pakistan ... 68 G2
Monzón, Spain ... 32 D5
Mooers, U.S.A. ... 111 B11
Mooi →, S. Africa ... 89 D5
Mooi River, S. Africa ... 89 D4
Moonah →, Australia ... 94 C2
Moonda, L., Australia ... 94 D3
Moonie, Australia ... 95 D5
Moonie →, Australia ... 95 D4
Moonta, Australia ... 95 E2
Moora, Australia ... 93 F2
Moorcroft, U.S.A. ... 112 C2
Moore →, Australia ... 93 F2
Moore, L., Australia ... 93 E2
Moore Park, Australia ... 94 C5
Moore Reefs, Australia ... 94 B4
Moorefield, U.S.A. ... 108 F6
Moores Res., U.S.A. ... 111 B13
Moorfoot Hills, U.K. ... 14 F5
Moorhead, U.S.A. ... 112 B6
Moormerland, Germany ... 24 B3
Moorpark, U.S.A. ... 117 L8
Moorreesburg, S. Africa ... 88 E2
Moosburg, Germany ... 25 G7
Moose →, Canada ... 102 B3
Moose →, U.S.A. ... 111 C9
Moose Creek, Canada ... 111 A10
Moose Factory, Canada ... 102 B3
Moose Jaw, Canada ... 105 C7
Moose Jaw →, Canada ... 105 C7
Moose Lake, Canada ... 105 C8
Moose Lake, U.S.A. ... 112 B8
Moose Mountain Prov. Park, Canada ... 105 D8
Moosehead L., U.S.A. ... 109 C11
Mooselookmeguntic L., U.S.A. ... 109 C10
Moosilauke, Mt., U.S.A. ... 111 B13
Moosomin, Canada ... 105 C8
Moosonee, Canada ... 102 B3
Moosup, U.S.A. ... 111 E13
Mopane, S. Africa ... 89 C4
Mopeia Velha, Mozam. ... 87 F4
Mopipi, Botswana ... 88 C3

Mopoi, C.A.R. ... 86 A2
Mopti, Mali ... 82 C4
Moqatta, Sudan ... 81 E4
Moqor, Afghan. ... 68 C2
Moquegua, Peru ... 124 G4
Mór, Hungary ... 42 C3
Móra, Portugal ... 35 G2
Mora, Spain ... 35 F7
Mora, Sweden ... 10 C8
Mora, Minn., U.S.A. ... 112 C8
Mora, N. Mex., U.S.A. ... 115 J11
Mora →, U.S.A. ... 113 H2
Mora de Ebro = Mòra d'Ebre, Spain ... 32 D5
Mora de Rubielos, Spain ... 32 E4
Mòra d'Ebre, Spain ... 32 D5
Mora la Nova, Spain ... 32 D5
Morača →, Montenegro, Yug. ... 40 D3
Moradabad, India ... 69 E8
Morafenobe, Madag. ... 89 B7
Morag, Poland ... 44 E6
Moral de Calatrava, Spain . 35 G7
Moraleja, Spain ... 34 E4
Moramanga, Madag. ... 89 B8
Moran, Kans., U.S.A. ... 113 G7
Moran, Wyo., U.S.A. ... 114 E8
Moranbah, Australia ... 94 C4
Morano Cálabro, Italy ... 31 C9
Morant Cays, Jamaica ... 120 C4
Morant Pt., Jamaica ... 120 C4
Morar, India ... 68 F8
Morar, L., U.K. ... 14 E3
Moratalla, Spain ... 33 G3
Moratuwa, Sri Lanka ... 66 R11
Morava →, Slovak Rep. ... 27 C9
Morava →, Serbia, Yug. ... 40 C3
Moravia, U.S.A. ... 111 D8
Moravian Hts. = Českomoravská Vrchovina, Czech Rep. ... 26 B8
Moravica →, Serbia, Yug. . 40 C4
Moravița, Romania ... 42 E6
Moravská Třebová, Czech Rep. ... 27 B9
Moravské Budějovice, Czech Rep. ... 26 B8
Morawa, Australia ... 93 E2
Morawhanna, Guyana ... 124 B7
Moray □, U.K. ... 14 D5
Moray Firth, U.K. ... 14 D5
Morbach, Germany ... 25 F3
Morbegno, Italy ... 28 B6
Morbi, India ... 68 H4
Morbihan □, France ... 18 E4
Mörbylånga, Sweden ... 11 H10
Morcenx, France ... 20 D3
Morcone, Italy ... 31 A7
Mordelles, France ... 18 E5
Morden, Canada ... 105 D9
Mordovian Republic = Mordvinia □, Russia ... 48 C7
Mordovo, Russia ... 48 D5
Mordvinia □, Russia ... 48 C7
Mordy, Poland ... 45 F9
Morea, Greece ... 6 H10
Moreau →, U.S.A. ... 112 C4
Morecambe, U.K. ... 12 C5
Morecambe B., U.K. ... 12 C5
Moree, Australia ... 95 D4
Morehead, U.S.A. ... 108 F4
Morehead City, U.S.A. ... 109 H7
Morel →, India ... 68 F7
Morelia, Mexico ... 118 D4
Morella, Australia ... 94 C3
Morella, Spain ... 32 E4
Morelos, Mexico ... 118 B3
Morelos □, Mexico ... 119 D5
Morena, India ... 68 F8
Morena, Sierra, Spain ... 35 G7
Moreni, Romania ... 43 F10
Moreno Valley, U.S.A. ... 117 M10
Moresby I., Canada ... 104 C2
Morestel, France ... 21 C9
Moreton I., Australia ... 95 D5
Moreuil, France ... 19 C9
Morey, Spain ... 37 B10
Morez, France ... 19 F13
Morgan, U.S.A. ... 114 F8
Morgan City, U.S.A. ... 113 L9
Morgan Hill, U.S.A. ... 116 H5
Morganfield, U.S.A. ... 108 G2
Morganton, U.S.A. ... 109 H5
Morgantown, U.S.A. ... 108 F6
Morgenzon, S. Africa ... 89 D4
Morges, Switz. ... 25 J2
Morghak, Iran ... 71 D8
Morgongåva, Sweden ... 10 E10
Morhange, France ... 19 D13
Mori, Italy ... 28 C7
Moriarty, U.S.A. ... 115 J10
Moribaya, Guinea ... 82 D3
Morice L., Canada ... 104 C3
Moriki, Nigeria ... 83 C6
Morinville, Canada ... 104 C6
Morioka, Japan ... 54 E10
Moris, Mexico ... 118 B3
Morlaàs, France ... 20 E3
Morlaix, France ... 18 D3
Mörlunda, Sweden ... 11 G9
Mormanno, Italy ... 31 C8
Mormant, France ... 19 D9
Mornington, Australia ... 95 F4
Mornington, I., Chile ... 128 F1
Mornington I., Australia ... 94 B2
Mórnos →, Greece ... 38 C3
Moro, Pakistan ... 68 F2
Moro, Sudan ... 81 E3

Moro →, Pakistan ... 68 E2
Moro G., Phil. ... 61 H5
Morocco ■, N. Afr. ... 78 B4
Morogoro, Tanzania ... 86 D4
Morogoro □, Tanzania ... 86 D4
Moroleón, Mexico ... 118 C4
Morombe, Madag. ... 89 C7
Moron, Argentina ... 126 C4
Morón, Cuba ... 120 B4
Morón de Almazán, Spain . 32 D2
Morón de la Frontera, Spain 35 H5
Morona →, Peru ... 124 D3
Morondava, Madag. ... 89 C7
Morongo Valley, U.S.A. ... 117 L10
Moroni, Comoros Is. ... 77 H8
Moroni, U.S.A. ... 114 G8
Moronou, Ivory C. ... 82 D4
Morotai, Indonesia ... 63 D7
Moroto, Uganda ... 86 B3
Moroto Summit, Kenya ... 86 B3
Morozov, Bulgaria ... 41 D9
Morozovsk, Russia ... 49 F5
Morpeth, U.K. ... 12 B6
Morphou, Cyprus ... 36 D11
Morphou Bay, Cyprus ... 36 D11
Morrilton, U.S.A. ... 113 H8
Morrinhos, Brazil ... 125 G9
Morrinsville, N.Z. ... 91 G5
Morris, Canada ... 105 D9
Morris, Ill., U.S.A. ... 112 E10
Morris, Minn., U.S.A. ... 112 C7
Morris, N.Y., U.S.A. ... 111 D9
Morris, Pa., U.S.A. ... 110 E7
Morris, Mt., Australia ... 93 E5
Morrisburg, Canada ... 111 B9
Morrison, Ariz., U.S.A. ... 115 K7
Morristown, N.J., U.S.A. ... 111 F10
Morristown, N.Y., U.S.A. .. 111 B9
Morristown, Tenn., U.S.A. . 109 G4
Morrisville, N.Y., U.S.A. ... 111 D9
Morrisville, Pa., U.S.A. ... 111 F10
Morrisville, Vt., U.S.A. ... 111 B12
Morro, Pta., Chile ... 126 B1
Morro Bay, U.S.A. ... 116 K6
Morro del Jable, Canary Is. 37 F5
Morro Jable, Pta. de, Canary Is. ... 37 F5
Morrosquillo, G. de, Colombia ... 120 E4
Mörrum, Sweden ... 11 H8
Morrumbene, Mozam. ... 89 C6
Mörrumsån →, Sweden ... 11 H8
Mors, Denmark ... 11 H2
Morshansk, Russia ... 48 D5
Mörsil, Sweden ... 10 A7
Mortagne →, France ... 19 D13
Mortagne-au-Perche, France 18 D7
Mortagne-sur-Gironde, France ... 20 C3
Mortagne-sur-Sèvre, France 18 F6
Mortain, France ... 18 D6
Mortara, Italy ... 28 C5
Morteau, France ... 19 E13
Morteros, Argentina ... 126 C3
Mortlach, Canada ... 105 C7
Mortlake, Australia ... 95 F3
Morton, Tex., U.S.A. ... 113 J3
Morton, Wash., U.S.A. ... 116 D4
Morundah, Australia ... 95 E4
Moruya, Australia ... 95 F5
Morvan, France ... 19 E11
Morven, Australia ... 95 D4
Morvern, U.K. ... 14 E3
Morwell, Australia ... 95 F4
Moryń, Poland ... 45 F1
Morzine, France ... 19 F13
Mosalsk, Russia ... 46 E8
Mosbach, Germany ... 25 F5
Mošćenice, Croatia ... 29 C11
Mosciano Sant' Ángelo, Italy 29 F10
Moscos Is., Burma = Maungmagan Is., Burma ... 64 E1
Moscow = Moskva, Russia . 46 E9
Moscow, Idaho, U.S.A. ... 114 C5
Moscow, Pa., U.S.A. ... 111 E9
Mosel →, Europe ... 19 B14
Moselle = Mosel →, Europe 19 B14
Moselle □, France ... 19 D13
Moses Lake, U.S.A. ... 114 C4
Mosgiel, N.Z. ... 91 L3
Moshaweng →, S. Africa .. 88 D3
Moshi, Tanzania ... 86 C4
Moshupa, Botswana ... 88 C4
Mosina, Poland ... 45 F3
Mosjøen, Norway ... 8 D15
Moskenesøya, Norway ... 8 C15
Moskenstraumen, Norway .. 8 C15
Moskva, Russia ... 46 E9
Moskva →, Russia ... 46 E10
Moslavačka Gora, Croatia .. 29 C13
Mosomane, Botswana ... 88 C4
Moson-magyaróvár, Hungary 42 C2
Mošorin, Serbia, Yug. ... 42 E5
Mospino, Ukraine ... 47 J9
Mosquera, Colombia ... 124 C3
Mosquero, U.S.A. ... 113 H3
Mosqueruela, Spain ... 32 E4
Mosquitia, Honduras ... 120 C3
Mosquito Coast = Mosquitia, Honduras ... 120 C3
Mosquito Creek L., U.S.A. . 110 E4
Mosquito L., Canada ... 105 A8
Mosquitos, G. de los, Panama ... 120 E3
Moss, Norway ... 9 G14
Moss Vale, Australia ... 95 E5
Mossbank, Canada ... 105 D7
Mossburn, N.Z. ... 91 L2
Mosselbaai, S. Africa ... 88 E3

Mossendjo, *Congo*	84	E2
Mossgiel, *Australia*	95	E3
Mossingen, *Germany*	25	G5
Mossman, *Australia*	94	B4
Mossoró, *Brazil*	125	E11
Mossuril, *Mozam.*	87	E5
Most, *Czech Rep.*	26	A6
Mosta, *Malta*	36	D1
Moşţafáábád, *Iran*	71	C7
Mostaganem, *Algeria*	78	A6
Mostar, *Bos.-H.*	42	G2
Mostardas, *Brazil*	127	C5
Mostiska = Mostyska, *Ukraine*	47	H2
Móstoles, *Spain*	34	E7
Mosty = Masty, *Belarus*	46	F3
Mostyska, *Ukraine*	47	H2
Mosul = Al Mawşil, *Iraq*	70	B4
Mosûlpo, *S. Korea*	57	H14
Mota, *Ethiopia*	81	E4
Mota del Cuervo, *Spain*	33	F2
Mota del Marqués, *Spain*	34	D5
Motagua →, *Guatemala*	120	C2
Motala, *Sweden*	11	F9
Motaze, *Mozam.*	89	C5
Moţca, *Romania*	43	C11
Moth, *India*	69	G8
Motherwell, *U.K.*	14	F5
Motihari, *India*	69	F11
Motilla del Palancar, *Spain*	33	F3
Motnik, *Slovenia*	29	B11
Motovun, *Croatia*	29	C10
Motozintla de Mendoza, *Mexico*	119	D6
Motril, *Spain*	35	J7
Motru, *Romania*	42	F7
Motru →, *Romania*	43	F8
Mott, *U.S.A.*	112	B3
Móttola, *Italy*	31	B10
Motueka, *N.Z.*	91	J4
Motueka →, *N.Z.*	91	J4
Motul, *Mexico*	119	C7
Mouchalagane →, *Canada*	103	B6
Moúdhros, *Greece*	39	B7
Mouding, *China*	58	E3
Moudjeria, *Mauritania*	82	B2
Moudon, *Switz.*	25	J2
Mouila, *Gabon*	84	E2
Moulamein, *Australia*	95	F3
Mouliana, *Greece*	36	D7
Moulins, *France*	19	F10
Moulmein, *Burma*	67	L20
Moulouya, O. →, *Morocco*	78	B5
Moultrie, *U.S.A.*	109	K4
Moultrie, L., *U.S.A.*	109	J5
Mound City, *Mo., U.S.A.*	112	E7
Mound City, *S. Dak., U.S.A.*	112	C4
Moúnda, Ákra, *Greece*	38	C2
Moundou, *Chad*	79	G9
Moundsville, *U.S.A.*	110	G4
Moung, *Cambodia*	64	F4
Mount Airy, *U.S.A.*	109	G5
Mount Albert, *Canada*	110	B5
Mount Barker, *S. Austral., Australia*	95	F2
Mount Barker, *W. Austral., Australia*	93	F2
Mount Beauty, *Australia*	95	F4
Mount Brydges, *Canada*	110	D3
Mount Burr, *Australia*	95	F3
Mount Carmel, *Ill., U.S.A.*	108	F2
Mount Carmel, *Pa., U.S.A.*	111	F8
Mount Charleston, *U.S.A.*	117	J11
Mount Clemens, *U.S.A.*	110	D2
Mount Coolon, *Australia*	94	C4
Mount Darwin, *Zimbabwe*	87	F3
Mount Desert I., *U.S.A.*	109	C11
Mount Dora, *U.S.A.*	109	L5
Mount Edziza Prov. Park, *Canada*	104	B2
Mount Fletcher, *S. Africa*	89	E4
Mount Forest, *Canada*	102	D3
Mount Gambier, *Australia*	95	F3
Mount Garnet, *Australia*	94	B4
Mount Holly, *U.S.A.*	111	G10
Mount Holly Springs, *U.S.A.*	110	F7
Mount Hope, *N.S.W., Australia*	95	E4
Mount Hope, *S. Austral., Australia*	95	E2
Mount Isa, *Australia*	94	C2
Mount Jewett, *U.S.A.*	110	E6
Mount Kisco, *U.S.A.*	111	E11
Mount Laguna, *U.S.A.*	117	N10
Mount Larcom, *Australia*	94	C5
Mount Lofty Ra., *Australia*	95	E2
Mount Magnet, *Australia*	93	E2
Mount Maunganui, *N.Z.*	91	G6
Mount Molloy, *Australia*	94	B4
Mount Morgan, *Australia*	94	C5
Mount Morris, *U.S.A.*	110	D7
Mount Pearl, *Canada*	103	C9
Mount Penn, *U.S.A.*	111	F9
Mount Perry, *Australia*	95	D5
Mount Pleasant, *Iowa, U.S.A.*	112	E9
Mount Pleasant, *Mich., U.S.A.*	108	D3
Mount Pleasant, *Pa., U.S.A.*	110	F5
Mount Pleasant, *S.C., U.S.A.*	109	J6
Mount Pleasant, *Tenn., U.S.A.*	109	H2
Mount Pleasant, *Tex., U.S.A.*	113	J7
Mount Pleasant, *Utah, U.S.A.*	114	G8
Mount Pocono, *U.S.A.*	111	E9
Mount Rainier Nat. Park, *U.S.A.*	116	D5
Mount Revelstoke Nat. Park, *Canada*	104	C5
Mount Robson Prov. Park, *Canada*	104	C5
Mount Selinda, *Zimbabwe*	89	C5
Mount Shasta, *U.S.A.*	114	F2
Mount Signal, *U.S.A.*	117	N11
Mount Sterling, *Ill., U.S.A.*	112	F9
Mount Sterling, *Ky., U.S.A.*	108	F4
Mount Surprise, *Australia*	94	B3
Mount Union, *U.S.A.*	110	F7
Mount Upton, *U.S.A.*	111	D9
Mount Vernon, *Ill., U.S.A.*	108	F1
Mount Vernon, *Ind., U.S.A.*	112	F10
Mount Vernon, *N.Y., U.S.A.*	111	F11
Mount Vernon, *Ohio, U.S.A.*	110	F2
Mount Vernon, *Wash., U.S.A.*	116	B4
Mountain Ash, *U.K.*	13	F4
Mountain Center, *U.S.A.*	117	M10
Mountain City, *Nev., U.S.A.*	114	F6
Mountain City, *Tenn., U.S.A.*	109	G5
Mountain Dale, *U.S.A.*	111	E10
Mountain Grove, *U.S.A.*	113	G8
Mountain Home, *Ark., U.S.A.*	113	G8
Mountain Home, *Idaho, U.S.A.*	114	E6
Mountain Iron, *U.S.A.*	112	B8
Mountain Pass, *U.S.A.*	117	K11
Mountain View, *Ark., U.S.A.*	113	H8
Mountain View, *Calif., U.S.A.*	116	H4
Mountain View, *Hawaii, U.S.A.*	106	J17
Mountainair, *U.S.A.*	115	J10
Mountlake Terrace, *U.S.A.*	116	C4
Mountmellick, *Ireland*	15	C4
Mountrath, *Ireland*	15	D4
Moura, *Australia*	94	C4
Moura, *Brazil*	124	D6
Moura, *Portugal*	35	G3
Mourão, *Portugal*	35	G3
Mourdi, Dépression du, *Chad*	79	E10
Mourdiah, *Mali*	82	C3
Mourenx-Ville-Nouvelle, *France*	20	E3
Mouri, *Ghana*	83	D4
Mourilyan, *Australia*	94	B4
Mourmelon-le-Grand, *France*	19	C11
Mourne →, *U.K.*	15	B4
Mourne Mts., *U.K.*	15	B5
Mourniaí, *Greece*	36	D6
Mournies = Mourniaí, *Greece*	36	D6
Mouscron, *Belgium*	17	D3
Moussoro, *Chad*	79	F9
Mouthe, *France*	19	F13
Moutier, *Switz.*	25	H3
Moûtiers, *France*	21	C10
Moutohara, *N.Z.*	91	H6
Moutong, *Indonesia*	63	D6
Mouy, *France*	19	C9
Mouzáki, *Greece*	38	B3
Mouzon, *France*	19	C12
Movas, *Mexico*	118	B3
Moville, *Ireland*	15	A4
Mowandjum, *Australia*	92	C3
Moy →, *Ireland*	15	B2
Moyale, *Kenya*	81	G4
Moyamba, *S. Leone*	82	D2
Moyen Atlas, *Morocco*	78	B4
Moyne, L. le, *Canada*	103	A6
Moyo, *Indonesia*	62	F5
Moyobamba, *Peru*	124	E3
Moyyero →, *Russia*	51	C11
Moyynty, *Kazakhstan*	50	E8
Mozambique = Moçambique, *Mozam.*	87	F5
Mozambique ■, *Africa*	87	F4
Mozambique Chan., *Africa*	89	B7
Mozdok, *Russia*	49	J7
Mozdūrān, *Iran*	71	B9
Mozhaysk, *Russia*	46	E9
Mozhga, *Russia*	48	B11
Mozhnābād, *Iran*	71	C9
Mozirje, *Slovenia*	29	B11
Mozyr = Mazyr, *Belarus*	47	F5
Mpanda, *Tanzania*	86	D3
Mpésoba, *Mali*	82	C3
Mphoengs, *Zimbabwe*	89	C4
Mpika, *Zambia*	87	E3
Mpulungu, *Zambia*	87	D3
Mpumalanga, *S. Africa*	89	D5
Mpumalanga □, *S. Africa*	89	B5
Mpwapwa, *Tanzania*	86	D4
Mqanduli, *S. Africa*	89	E4
Mqinvartsveri = Kazbek, *Russia*	49	J7
Mragowo, *Poland*	44	E8
Mramor, *Serbia, Yug.*	40	C5
Mrkonjić Grad, *Bos.-H.*	42	F2
Mrkopalj, *Croatia*	29	C11
Mrocza, *Poland*	45	E4
Msambansovu, *Zimbabwe*	87	F3
M'sila →, *Algeria*	78	A6
Msoro, *Zambia*	87	E3
Msta →, *Russia*	46	C6
Mstislavl = Mstsislaw, *Belarus*	46	E6
Mstsislaw, *Belarus*	46	E6
Mszana Dolna, *Poland*	45	J7
Mszczonów, *Poland*	45	G7
Mtama, *Tanzania*	87	E4
Mtamvuna →, *S. Africa*	89	E5
Mtilikwe →, *Zimbabwe*	87	G3
Mtsensk, *Russia*	46	F9
Mtskheta, *Georgia*	49	K7
Mtubatuba, *S. Africa*	89	D5
Mtwalume, *S. Africa*	89	E5
Mtwara-Mikindani, *Tanzania*	87	E5
Mu Gia, Deo, *Vietnam*	64	D5
Mu Us Shamo, *China*	56	E5
Muang Chiang Rai = Chiang Rai, *Thailand*	58	H2
Muang Khong, *Laos*	64	E5
Muang Lamphun, *Thailand*	64	C2
Muang Pak Beng, *Laos*	58	H3
Muar, *Malaysia*	65	L4
Muarabungo, *Indonesia*	62	E2
Muaraenim, *Indonesia*	62	E2
Muarajuloi, *Indonesia*	62	E4
Muarakaman, *Indonesia*	62	E5
Muaratebo, *Indonesia*	62	E2
Muaratembesi, *Indonesia*	62	E2
Muaratewe, *Indonesia*	62	E4
Mubarakpur, *India*	69	F10
Mubarraz = Al Mubarraz, *Si. Arabia*	71	E6
Mubende, *Uganda*	86	B3
Mubi, *Nigeria*	83	C7
Mubur, Pulau, *Indonesia*	65	L6
Mucajaí →, *Brazil*	124	C6
Muchachos, Roque de los, *Canary Is.*	37	F2
Mücheln, *Germany*	24	D7
Muchinga Mts., *Zambia*	87	E3
Muchkapskiy, *Russia*	48	E6
Muchuan, *China*	58	C5
Muck, *U.K.*	14	E2
Muckadilla, *Australia*	95	D4
Mucur, *Turkey*	72	C6
Mucuri, *Brazil*	125	G11
Mucusso, *Angola*	88	B3
Muda, *Canary Is.*	37	F6
Mudanjiang, *China*	57	B15
Mudanya, *Turkey*	41	F12
Muddy Cr. →, *U.S.A.*	115	H8
Mudgee, *Australia*	95	E4
Mudjatik →, *Canada*	105	B7
Mudurnu, *Turkey*	72	B4
Mueda, *Mozam.*	87	E4
Mueller Ra., *Australia*	92	C4
Muende, *Mozam.*	87	E3
Muerto, Mar, *Mexico*	119	D6
Mufu Shan, *China*	59	C10
Mufulira, *Zambia*	87	E2
Mufumbiro Range, *Africa*	86	C2
Mugardos, *Spain*	34	B2
Muge, *Portugal*	35	F2
Múggia, *Italy*	29	C10
Mughal Sarai, *India*	69	G10
Mughayrā', *Si. Arabia*	70	D3
Mugi, *Japan*	55	H7
Mugia = Muxía, *Spain*	34	B1
Mugila, Mts., *Dem. Rep. of the Congo*	86	D2
Muğla, *Turkey*	39	D10
Muğla □, *Turkey*	39	D10
Muglad, *Sudan*	81	E2
Muğlizh, *Bulgaria*	41	D9
Mugu, *Nepal*	69	E10
Muhammad, Ras, *Egypt*	70	E2
Muhammad Qol, *Sudan*	80	C4
Muhammadabad, *India*	69	F10
Muhesi →, *Tanzania*	86	D4
Mühlacker, *Germany*	25	G4
Mühldorf, *Germany*	25	G8
Mühlhausen, *Germany*	24	D6
Mühlig Hofmann fjell, *Antarctica*	5	D3
Mühlviertel, *Austria*	26	C7
Mühos, *Finland*	8	D22
Muhu, *Estonia*	9	G20
Muhutwe, *Tanzania*	86	C3
Muine Bheag, *Ireland*	15	D5
Muir, L., *Australia*	93	F2
Mukacheve, *Ukraine*	47	H2
Mukachevo = Mukacheve, *Ukraine*	47	H2
Mukah, *Malaysia*	62	D4
Mukandwara, *India*	68	G6
Mukawwa, Geziret, *Egypt*	80	C4
Mukawwar, *Sudan*	80	C4
Mukdahan, *Thailand*	64	D5
Mukden = Shenyang, *China*	57	D12
Mukerian, *India*	68	D6
Mukhtolovo, *Russia*	48	C6
Mukhtuya = Lensk, *Russia*	51	C12
Mukinbudin, *Australia*	93	F2
Mukishi, *Dem. Rep. of the Congo*	87	D1
Mukomuko, *Indonesia*	62	E2
Mukomwenze, *Dem. Rep. of the Congo*	86	D2
Muktsar, *India*	68	D6
Mukur = Moqor, *Afghan.*	68	C2
Mukutawa →, *Canada*	105	C9
Mukwela, *Zambia*	87	F2
Mula, *Spain*	33	G3
Mula →, *Pakistan*	68	F2
Mulange, *Dem. Rep. of the Congo*	86	C2
Mulanje, *Malawi*	87	F4
Mulchén, *Chile*	126	D1
Mulde →, *Germany*	24	D8
Mule Creek Junction, *U.S.A.*	112	D2
Muleba, *Tanzania*	86	C3
Mulejé, *Mexico*	118	B2
Muleshoe, *U.S.A.*	113	H3
Muletta, Gara, *Ethiopia*	81	F5
Mulgrave, *Canada*	103	C7
Mulhacén, *Spain*	35	H7
Mülheim, *Germany*	24	D2
Mulhouse, *France*	19	E14
Muli, *China*	58	D3
Muling, *China*	57	B16
Mull, *U.K.*	14	E3
Mull, Sound of, *U.K.*	14	E3
Mullaittivu, *Sri Lanka*	66	Q12
Mullen, *U.S.A.*	112	D4
Mullens, *U.S.A.*	108	G5
Muller, Pegunungan, *Indonesia*	62	D4
Mullet Pen., *Ireland*	15	B1
Mullewa, *Australia*	93	E2
Mülheim, *Germany*	25	H3
Mulligan →, *Australia*	94	D2
Mullingar, *Ireland*	15	C4
Mullins, *U.S.A.*	109	H6
Mullsjö, *Sweden*	11	G7
Mullumbimby, *Australia*	95	D5
Mulobezi, *Zambia*	87	F2
Mulroy B., *Ireland*	15	A4
Multan, *Pakistan*	68	D4
Mulumbe, Mts., *Dem. Rep. of the Congo*	87	D2
Mulungushi Dam, *Zambia*	87	E2
Mulvane, *U.S.A.*	113	G6
Mulwad, *Sudan*	80	D3
Mulwala, *Australia*	95	F4
Mumbai, *India*	66	K8
Mumbwa, *Zambia*	87	F2
Mumra, *Russia*	49	H8
Mun →, *Thailand*	64	E5
Muna, *Indonesia*	63	F6
Munabao, *India*	68	G4
Munamagi, *Estonia*	9	H22
Münchberg, *Germany*	25	E7
Müncheberg, *Germany*	24	C10
München, *Germany*	25	G7
Munchen-Gladbach = Mönchengladbach, *Germany*	24	D2
Muncho Lake, *Canada*	104	B3
Munch'ŏn, *N. Korea*	57	E14
Muncie, *U.S.A.*	108	E3
Muncoonie, L., *Australia*	94	D2
Mundabbera, *Australia*	95	D5
Munday, *U.S.A.*	113	J5
Münden, *Germany*	24	D5
Mundiwindi, *Australia*	92	D3
Mundo →, *Spain*	33	G2
Mundo Novo, *Brazil*	125	F10
Mundra, *India*	68	H3
Mundrabilla, *Australia*	93	F4
Munera, *Spain*	33	F2
Mungallala, *Australia*	95	D4
Mungallala Cr. →, *Australia*	95	D4
Mungana, *Australia*	94	B3
Mungaoli, *India*	68	G8
Mungari, *Mozam.*	87	F3
Mungbere, *Dem. Rep. of the Congo*	86	B2
Mungeli, *India*	69	H9
Munger, *India*	69	G12
Munich = München, *Germany*	25	G7
Munising, *U.S.A.*	108	B2
Munka-Ljungby, *Sweden*	11	H6
Munkebo, *Denmark*	11	J4
Munkedal, *Sweden*	11	F5
Munkfors, *Sweden*	10	E7
Munku-Sardyk, *Russia*	51	D11
Münnerstadt, *Germany*	25	E6
Muñoz Gamero, Pen., *Chile*	128	G2
Munroe L., *Canada*	105	B9
Munsan, *S. Korea*	57	F14
Munster, *France*	19	D14
Munster, *Niedersachsen, Germany*	24	C6
Münster, *Nordrhein-Westfalen, Germany*	24	D3
Munster □, *Ireland*	15	D3
Muntadgin, *Australia*	93	F2
Muntele Mare, Vf., *Romania*	43	D8
Muntok, *Indonesia*	62	E3
Munyama, *Zambia*	87	F2
Munzur Dağları, *Turkey*	73	C8
Muong Beng, *Laos*	58	G3
Muong Boum, *Vietnam*	58	F4
Muong Et, *Laos*	64	B5
Muong Hai, *Laos*	58	G3
Muong Hiem, *Laos*	58	B4
Muong Houn, *Laos*	58	G3
Muong Hung, *Vietnam*	58	G4
Muong Kau, *Laos*	64	E5
Muong Khao, *Laos*	64	C4
Muong Khoua, *Laos*	58	B4
Muong Liep, *Laos*	64	C3
Muong May, *Laos*	64	E6
Muong Ngeun, *Laos*	58	G3
Muong Ngoi, *Laos*	58	B4
Muong Nhie, *Vietnam*	58	F4
Muong Nong, *Laos*	64	D6
Muong Ou Tay, *Laos*	58	F3
Muong Oua, *Laos*	64	C3
Muong Peun, *Laos*	58	B4
Muong Phalane, *Laos*	64	D5
Muong Phieng, *Laos*	64	C3
Muong Phine, *Laos*	64	D6
Muong Sai, *Laos*	58	G3
Muong Saiapoun, *Laos*	64	C3
Muong Sen, *Vietnam*	64	C5
Muong Sing, *Laos*	58	G3
Muong Son, *Laos*	58	B4
Muong Soui, *Laos*	64	C4
Muong Va, *Laos*	58	G4
Muong Xia, *Vietnam*	64	B5
Muqdisho, *Somali Rep.*	74	G4
Mur →, *Austria*	27	E9
Mur-de-Bretagne, *France*	18	D4
Muradiye, *Manisa, Turkey*	39	C9
Muradiye, *Van, Turkey*	73	C10
Murakami, *Japan*	54	E9
Murallón, Cerro, *Chile*	128	F2
Muranda, *Rwanda*	86	C2
Murang'a, *Kenya*	86	C4
Murashi, *Russia*	50	D5
Murat, *France*	20	C6
Murat →, *Turkey*	73	C9
Murat Dağı, *Turkey*	39	C11
Muratlı, *Turkey*	41	E11
Murato, *France*	21	F13
Murau, *Austria*	26	D7
Muravera, *Italy*	30	C2
Murayama, *Japan*	54	E10
Murban, *U.A.E.*	71	F7
Murça, *Portugal*	34	D3
Murchison →, *Australia*	93	E1
Murchison, Mt., *Antarctica*	5	D11
Murchison Falls, *Uganda*	86	B3
Murchison Ra., *Australia*	94	C1
Murchison Rapids, *Malawi*	87	F3
Murcia, *Spain*	33	G3
Murcia □, *Spain*	33	H3
Murdo, *U.S.A.*	112	D4
Murdoch Pt., *Australia*	94	A3
Mûrefte, *Turkey*	41	F11
Mureş □, *Romania*	43	D9
Mureş →, *Romania*	42	D5
Mureşul = Mureş →, *Romania*	42	D5
Muret, *France*	20	E5
Murewa, *Zimbabwe*	89	B5
Murfreesboro, *N.C., U.S.A.*	109	G7
Murfreesboro, *Tenn., U.S.A.*	109	H2
Murgab = Murghob, *Tajikistan*	50	F8
Murgab →, *Turkmenistan*	71	B9
Murgenella, *Australia*	92	B5
Murgeni, *Romania*	43	D13
Murgha Kibzai, *Pakistan*	68	D3
Murghob, *Tajikistan*	50	F8
Murgon, *Australia*	95	D5
Muri, *India*	69	H11
Muria, *Indonesia*	63	G14
Muriaé, *Brazil*	127	A7
Murias de Paredes, *Spain*	34	C4
Muriel Mine, *Zimbabwe*	87	F3
Müritz, *Germany*	24	B8
Murka, *Kenya*	86	C4
Murliganj, *India*	69	G12
Murmansk, *Russia*	50	C5
Murnau, *Germany*	25	H7
Muro, *France*	21	F12
Muro, *Spain*	37	B10
Muro, C. de, *France*	21	G12
Muro de Alcoy, *Spain*	33	G4
Muro Lucano, *Italy*	31	B8
Murom, *Russia*	48	C6
Muroran, *Japan*	54	C10
Muros, *Spain*	34	C1
Muros y de Noya, Ría de, *Spain*	34	C1
Muroto, *Japan*	55	H7
Muroto-Misaki, *Japan*	55	H7
Murowana Goślina, *Poland*	45	F3
Murphy, *U.S.A.*	114	E5
Murphys, *U.S.A.*	116	G6
Murrat, *Sudan*	80	D2
Murray, *Ky., U.S.A.*	109	G1
Murray, *Utah, U.S.A.*	114	F8
Murray →, *Australia*	95	F2
Murray, L., *U.S.A.*	109	H5
Murray Bridge, *Australia*	95	F2
Murray Harbour, *Canada*	103	C7
Murraysburg, *S. Africa*	88	E3
Murree, *Pakistan*	68	C5
Murrieta, *U.S.A.*	117	M9
Murro di Porco, Capo, *Italy*	31	F8
Murrumbidgee →, *Australia*	95	E3
Murrumburrah, *Australia*	95	E4
Murrurundi, *Australia*	95	E5
Murshid, *Sudan*	80	C3
Murshidabad, *India*	69	G13
Murska Sobota, *Slovenia*	29	B13
Murtle L., *Canada*	104	C5
Murtoa, *Australia*	95	F3
Murtosa, *Portugal*	34	E2
Murungu, *Tanzania*	86	C3
Mururoa, *Pac. Oc.*	97	K14
Murwara, *India*	69	H9
Murwillumbah, *Australia*	95	D5
Mürz →, *Austria*	26	D8
Mürzzuschlag, *Austria*	26	D8
Muş, *Turkey*	70	B4
Mûsa, Gebel, *Egypt*	70	D2
Musa Khel, *Pakistan*	68	D3
Mûsá Qal'eh, *Afghan.*	66	C4
Musaffargarh, *Pakistan*	68	D4
Musafirkhana, *India*	69	F9
Musala, *Bulgaria*	40	D7
Musala, *Indonesia*	62	D1
Musan, *N. Korea*	57	C15
Musangu, *Dem. Rep. of the Congo*	87	E1
Musasa, *Tanzania*	86	C3
Musay'īd, *Qatar*	71	E6
Muscat = Masqat, *Oman*	74	C6
Muscat & Oman = Oman ■, *Asia*	74	C6
Muscatine, *U.S.A.*	112	E9
Musgrave Harbour, *Canada*	103	C9
Musgrave Ranges, *Australia*	93	E5
Mushie, *Dem. Rep. of the Congo*	84	E3
Mushin, *Nigeria*	83	D5

Natalinci

Musi →, *Indonesia* 62 E2
Muskeg →, *Canada* 104 A4
Muskegon, *U.S.A.* 108 D2
Muskegon →, *U.S.A.* 108 D2
Muskegon Heights, *U.S.A.* 108 D2
Muskogee, *U.S.A.* 113 H7
Muskoka, L., *Canada* 110 B5
Muskwa →, *Canada* 104 B4
Muslīmiyah, *Syria* 70 B3
Musmar, *Sudan* 80 D4
Musofu, *Zambia* 87 E2
Musoma, *Tanzania* 86 C3
Musquaro, L., *Canada* 103 B7
Musquodoboit Harbour, *Canada* 103 D7
Musselburgh, *U.K.* 14 F5
Musselshell →, *U.S.A.* 114 C10
Mussidan, *France* 20 C4
Mussomeli, *Italy* 30 E6
Mussoorie, *India* 68 D8
Mussuco, *Angola* 88 B2
Mustafakemalpaşa, *Turkey* 41 F12
Mustang, *Nepal* 69 E10
Musters, L., *Argentina* 128 F3
Musudan, *N. Korea* 57 D15
Muswellbrook, *Australia* 95 E5
Muszyna, *Poland* 45 J7
Mût, *Egypt* 80 B2
Mut, *Turkey* 70 B2
Mutanda, *Mozam.* 89 C5
Mutanda, *Zambia* 87 E2
Mutare, *Zimbabwe* 87 F3
Muting, *Indonesia* 63 F10
Mutoko, *Zimbabwe* 89 B5
Mutoray, *Russia* 51 C11
Mutshatsha, *Dem. Rep. of the Congo* 87 E1
Mutsu, *Japan* 54 D10
Mutsu-Wan, *Japan* 54 D10
Muttaburra, *Australia* 94 C3
Muttalip, *Turkey* 39 B12
Mutton I., *Ireland* 15 D2
Mutuáli, *Mozam.* 87 E4
Mutum Biyu, *Nigeria* 83 D7
Muweilih, *Egypt* 75 E3
Muxía, *Spain* 34 B1
Muy Muy, *Nic.* 120 D2
Muyinga, *Burundi* 86 C3
Muynak, *Uzbekistan* 50 E6
Muzaffarabad, *Pakistan* 69 B5
Muzaffargarh, *Pakistan* 68 D4
Muzaffarnagar, *India* 68 E7
Muzaffarpur, *India* 69 F11
Muzafirpur, *Pakistan* 68 D3
Muzhi, *Russia* 50 C7
Muzillac, *France* 18 E4
Muzūra, *Egypt* 80 J7
Mvôlô, *Sudan* 81 F2
Mvuma, *Zimbabwe* 87 F3
Mvurwi, *Zimbabwe* 87 F3
Mwadui, *Tanzania* 86 C3
Mwambo, *Tanzania* 87 E5
Mwandi, *Zambia* 87 F1
Mwanza, *Dem. Rep. of the Congo* 86 D2
Mwanza, *Tanzania* 86 C3
Mwanza, *Zambia* 87 F1
Mwanza □, *Tanzania* 86 C3
Mwaya, *Tanzania* 87 D3
Mweelrea, *Ireland* 15 C2
Mweka, *Dem. Rep. of the Congo* 84 E4
Mwenezi, *Zimbabwe* 87 G3
Mwenezi →, *Mozam.* 87 G3
Mwenga, *Dem. Rep. of the Congo* 86 C2
Mweru, L., *Zambia* 87 D2
Mweza Range, *Zimbabwe* 87 G3
Mwilambwe, *Dem. Rep. of the Congo* 86 D2
Mwimbi, *Tanzania* 87 D3
Mwinilunga, *Zambia* 87 E1
My Tho, *Vietnam* 65 G6
Myajlar, *India* 68 F4
Myanaung, *Burma* 67 K19
Myanmar = Burma ■, *Asia* 67 J20
Myaungmya, *Burma* 67 L19
Myeik Kyunzu, *Burma* 65 G1
Myers Chuck, *U.S.A.* 104 B2
Myerstown, *U.S.A.* 111 F8
Myingyan, *Burma* 67 J19
Myitkyina, *Burma* 67 G20
Myjava, *Slovak Rep.* 27 C10
Mykhaylivka, *Ukraine* 47 J8
Mykines, *Færoe Is.* 8 E9
Mykolayiv, *Ukraine* 47 J7
Mymensingh, *Bangla.* 67 G17
Mynydd Du, *U.K.* 13 F4
Mýrdalsjökull, *Iceland* 8 E4
Myrhorod, *Ukraine* 47 H7
Myrtle Beach, *U.S.A.* 109 J6
Myrtle Creek, *U.S.A.* 114 E2
Myrtle Point, *U.S.A.* 114 E1
Myrtou, *Cyprus* 36 D12
Mysia, *Turkey* 41 G11
Myślenice, *Poland* 45 J6
Myślibórz, *Poland* 45 F1
Mysłowice, *Poland* 45 H6
Mysore = Karnataka □, *India* 66 N10
Mysore, *India* 66 N10
Mystic, *U.S.A.* 111 E13
Myszków, *Poland* 45 H6
Myszyniec, *Poland* 44 E8
Mytishchi, *Russia* 46 E9
Mývatn, *Iceland* 8 D5
Mže →, *Czech Rep.* 26 B6
Mzimba, *Malawi* 87 E3
Mzimkulu →, *S. Africa* 89 E5
Mzimvubu →, *S. Africa* 89 E4
Mzuzu, *Malawi* 87 E3

N

Na Hearadh = Harris, *U.K.* 14 D2
Na Noi, *Thailand* 64 C3
Na Phao, *Laos* 64 D5
Na Sam, *Vietnam* 58 F6
Na San, *Vietnam* 64 B5
Naab →, *Germany* 25 F8
Na'am, *Sudan* 81 F2
Na'am →, *Sudan* 81 F2
Naantali, *Finland* 9 F19
Naas, *Ireland* 15 C5
Nababeep, *S. Africa* 88 D2
Nabadwip = Navadwip, *India* 69 H13
Nabari, *Japan* 55 G8
Nabawa, *Australia* 93 E1
Nabberu, L., *Australia* 93 E3
Nabburg, *Germany* 25 F8
Naberezhnyye Chelny, *Russia* 48 C11
Nabeul, *Tunisia* 79 A8
Nabha, *India* 68 D7
Nabīd, *Iran* 71 D8
Nabire, *Indonesia* 63 E9
Nabisar, *Pakistan* 68 G3
Nabisipi →, *Canada* 103 B7
Nabiswera, *Uganda* 86 B3
Nablus = Nābulus, *West Bank* 75 C4
Naboomspruit, *S. Africa* 89 C4
Nabou, *Burkina Faso* 82 C4
Nabua, *Phil.* 61 E5
Nābulus, *West Bank* 75 C4
Nacala, *Mozam.* 87 E5
Nacala-Velha, *Mozam.* 87 E5
Nacaome, *Honduras* 120 D2
Nacaroa, *Mozam.* 87 E4
Naches, *U.S.A.* 114 C3
Naches →, *U.S.A.* 116 D6
Nachicapau, L., *Canada* 103 A6
Nachingwea, *Tanzania* 87 E4
Nachna, *India* 68 F4
Náchod, *Czech Rep.* 26 A9
Nacimiento L., *U.S.A.* 116 K6
Naco, *Mexico* 118 A3
Nacogdoches, *U.S.A.* 113 K7
Nácori Chico, *Mexico* 118 B3
Nacozari, *Mexico* 118 A3
Nadi, *Sudan* 80 D3
Nadiad, *India* 68 H5
Nădlac, *Romania* 42 D5
Nador, *Morocco* 78 B5
Nadur, *Malta* 36 C1
Nadūshan, *Iran* 71 C7
Nadvirna, *Ukraine* 47 H3
Nadvornaya = Nadvirna, *Ukraine* 47 H3
Nadym, *Russia* 50 C8
Nadym →, *Russia* 50 C8
Nærbø, *Norway* 9 G11
Næstved, *Denmark* 11 J5
Nafada, *Nigeria* 83 C7
Naft-e Safīd, *Iran* 71 D6
Naftshahr, *Iran* 70 C5
Nafud Desert = An Nafūd, *Si. Arabia* 70 D4
Nag Hammâdi, *Egypt* 80 B3
Naga, *Phil.* 61 E5
Nagahama, *Japan* 55 G8
Nagai, *Japan* 54 E10
Nagaland □, *India* 67 G19
Nagano, *Japan* 55 F9
Nagano □, *Japan* 55 F9
Nagaoka, *Japan* 55 F9
Nagappattinam, *India* 66 P11
Nagar →, *Bangla.* 69 G13
Nagar Parkar, *Pakistan* 68 G4
Nagasaki, *Japan* 55 H4
Nagasaki □, *Japan* 55 H4
Nagato, *Japan* 55 G5
Nagaur, *India* 68 F5
Nagda, *India* 68 H6
Nagercoil, *India* 66 Q10
Nagina, *India* 69 E8
Nagīneh, *Iran* 71 C8
Nagir, *Pakistan* 69 A6
Naglarby, *Sweden* 10 D9
Nagod, *India* 69 G9
Nagold, *Germany* 25 G4
Nagold →, *Germany* 25 G4
Nagoorin, *Australia* 94 C5
Nagorno-Karabakh, *Azerbaijan* 70 B5
Nagornyy, *Russia* 51 D13
Nagoya, *Japan* 55 G8
Nagpur, *India* 66 J11
Nagua, *Dom. Rep.* 121 C6
Nagyatád, *Hungary* 42 D2
Nagyecsed, *Hungary* 42 C7
Nagykálló, *Hungary* 42 C6
Nagykanizsa, *Hungary* 42 D2
Nagykáta, *Hungary* 42 C4
Nagykőrös, *Hungary* 42 C4
Naha, *Japan* 55 L3
Nahan, *India* 68 D7
Nahanni Butte, *Canada* 104 A4
Nahanni Nat. Park, *Canada* 104 A4
Nahargarh, *Mad. P., India* 68 G6
Nahargarh, *Raj., India* 68 G7
Nahariyya, *Israel* 70 C2
Nahāvand, *Iran* 71 C6
Nahe →, *Germany* 25 F3
Nahîya, W. →, *Egypt* 80 B3
Naicá, *Mexico* 118 B3
Naicam, *Canada* 105 C8
Naikoon Prov. Park, *Canada* 104 C2
Naila, *Germany* 25 E7
Naimisharanya, *India* 69 F9
Nain, *Canada* 103 A7
Nā'īn, *Iran* 71 C7
Naini Tal, *India* 69 E8
Nainpur, *India* 66 H12
Naintré, *France* 18 F7
Nainwa, *India* 68 G6
Naipu, *Romania* 43 F10
Nairn, *U.K.* 14 D5
Nairobi, *Kenya* 86 C4
Naissaar, *Estonia* 9 G21
Naita, Mt., *Ethiopia* 81 F4
Naivasha, *Kenya* 86 C4
Naivasha, L., *Kenya* 86 C4
Najac, *France* 20 D5
Najafābād, *Iran* 71 C6
Najd, *Si. Arabia* 74 B3
Nájera, *Spain* 32 C2
Najerilla →, *Spain* 32 C2
Najibabad, *India* 68 E8
Najin, *N. Korea* 57 C16
Najmah, *Si. Arabia* 71 E6
Naju, *S. Korea* 57 G14
Nakadōri-Shima, *Japan* 55 H4
Nakalagba, *Dem. Rep. of the Congo* 86 B2
Nakaminato, *Japan* 55 F10
Nakamura, *Japan* 55 H6
Nakano, *Japan* 55 F9
Nakano-Shima, *Japan* 55 K4
Nakashibetsu, *Japan* 54 C12
Nakfa, *Eritrea* 81 D4
Nakhfar al Buşayyah, *Iraq* 70 D5
Nakhichevan = Naxçıvan, *Azerbaijan* 70 B5
Nakhichevan Republic = Naxçıvan □, *Azerbaijan* 50 F5
Nakhl, *Egypt* 75 F2
Nakhl-e Taqī, *Iran* 71 E7
Nakhodka, *Russia* 51 E14
Nakhon Nayok, *Thailand* 64 E3
Nakhon Pathom, *Thailand* 64 F3
Nakhon Phanom, *Thailand* 64 D5
Nakhon Ratchasima, *Thailand* 64 E4
Nakhon Sawan, *Thailand* 64 E3
Nakhon Si Thammarat, *Thailand* 65 H3
Nakhon Thai, *Thailand* 64 D3
Nakhtarana, *India* 68 H3
Nakina, *Canada* 102 B2
Nakło nad Notecią, *Poland* 45 E4
Nako, *Burkina Faso* 82 C4
Nakodar, *India* 68 D6
Nakskov, *Denmark* 11 K5
Naktong →, *S. Korea* 57 G15
Nakuru, *Kenya* 86 C4
Nakuru, L., *Kenya* 86 C4
Nakusp, *Canada* 104 C5
Nal, *Pakistan* 68 F2
Nal →, *Pakistan* 68 G1
Nalázi, *Mozam.* 89 C5
Nalchik, *Russia* 49 J6
Nałęczów, *Poland* 45 G9
Nalerigu, *Ghana* 83 C4
Nalgonda, *India* 66 L11
Nalhati, *India* 69 G12
Naliya, *India* 68 H3
Nallamalai Hills, *India* 66 M11
Nallıhan, *Turkey* 72 B4
Nalón →, *Spain* 34 B4
Nam Can, *Vietnam* 65 H5
Nam-ch'on, *N. Korea* 57 E14
Nam Co, *China* 60 C4
Nam Dinh, *Vietnam* 58 G6
Nam Du, Hon, *Vietnam* 65 H5
Nam Ngum Dam, *Laos* 64 C4
Nam-Phan = Cochin China, *Vietnam* 65 G6
Nam Phong, *Thailand* 64 D4
Nam Tha, *Laos* 58 G3
Nam Tok, *Thailand* 64 E2
Namacunde, *Angola* 88 B2
Namacurra, *Mozam.* 89 B6
Namak, Daryācheh-ye, *Iran* 71 C7
Namak, Kavir-e, *Iran* 71 C8
Namakzār, Daryācheh-ye, *Iran* 71 C9
Namaland, *Namibia* 88 C2
Namangan, *Uzbekistan* 50 E8
Namapa, *Mozam.* 87 E4
Namaqualand, *S. Africa* 88 E2
Namasagali, *Uganda* 86 B3
Namber, *Indonesia* 63 E8
Nambour, *Australia* 95 D5
Nambucca Heads, *Australia* 95 E5
Namche Bazar, *Nepal* 69 F12
Namchonjŏm = Nam-ch'on, *N. Korea* 57 E14
Namecunda, *Mozam.* 87 E4
Nameponda, *Mozam.* 87 F4
Náměšť nad Oslavou, *Czech Rep.* 27 B9
Námestovo, *Slovak Rep.* 27 B12
Nametil, *Mozam.* 87 F4
Namew L., *Canada* 105 C8
Namgia, *India* 69 D8
Namhkam, *Burma* 58 E1
Namib Desert = Namibwoestyn, *Namibia* 88 C2
Namibe, *Angola* 85 H2
Namibe □, *Angola* 88 B1
Namibia ■, *Africa* 88 C2
Namibwoestyn, *Namibia* 88 C2
Namīn, *Iran* 73 C13
Namlea, *Indonesia* 63 E7
Namoi →, *Australia* 95 E4
Nampa, *U.S.A.* 114 E5
Nampala, *Mali* 82 B3
Namp'o, *N. Korea* 57 E13
Nampō-Shotō, *Japan* 55 J10
Nampula, *Mozam.* 87 F4
Namrole, *Indonesia* 63 E7
Namse Shankou, *China* 67 E13
Namsen →, *Norway* 8 D14
Namsos, *Norway* 8 D14
Namtsy, *Russia* 51 C13
Namtu, *Burma* 67 H20
Namtumbo, *Tanzania* 87 E4
Namu, *Canada* 104 C3
Namur, *Belgium* 17 D4
Namur □, *Belgium* 17 D4
Namutoni, *Namibia* 88 B2
Namwala, *Zambia* 87 F2
Namwŏn, *S. Korea* 57 G14
Namysłów, *Poland* 45 G4
Nan, *Thailand* 64 C3
Nan →, *Thailand* 64 E3
Nan-ch'ang = Nanchang, *China* 59 C10
Nan Ling, *China* 59 E8
Nan Xian, *China* 59 C9
Nana, *Romania* 43 F11
Nana Kru, *Liberia* 82 E3
Nanaimo, *Canada* 104 D4
Nanam, *N. Korea* 57 D15
Nanan, *China* 59 E12
Nanango, *Australia* 95 D5
Nan'ao, *China* 59 F11
Nanao, *Japan* 55 F8
Nanbu, *China* 58 B6
Nanchang, *Jiangxi, China* 59 C10
Nanchang, *Kiangsi, China* 59 C10
Nancheng, *China* 59 D11
Nanching = Nanjing, *China* 59 A12
Nanchong, *China* 58 B6
Nanchuan, *China* 58 C6
Nancy, *France* 19 D13
Nanda Devi, *India* 69 D8
Nanda Kot, *India* 69 D9
Nandan, *China* 58 E6
Nandan, *Japan* 55 G7
Nanded, *India* 66 K10
Nandewar Ra., *Australia* 95 E5
Nandi, *Fiji* 91 C7
Nandigram, *India* 69 H12
Nandurbar, *India* 66 J9
Nandyal, *India* 66 M11
Nanfeng, *Guangdong, China* 59 F8
Nanfeng, *Jiangxi, China* 59 D11
Nanga-Eboko, *Cameroon* 83 E7
Nanga Parbat, *Pakistan* 69 B6
Nangade, *Mozam.* 87 E4
Nangapinoh, *Indonesia* 62 E4
Nangarhār □, *Afghan.* 66 B7
Nangatayap, *Indonesia* 62 E4
Nangeya Mts., *Uganda* 86 B3
Nangis, *France* 19 D10
Nangong, *China* 56 F8
Nanhua, *China* 58 E3
Nanhuang, *China* 57 F11
Nanhui, *China* 59 B13
Nanjeko, *Zambia* 87 F1
Nanji Shan, *China* 59 D13
Nanjian, *China* 58 E3
Nanjiang, *China* 58 A6
Nanjing, *Fujian, China* 59 E11
Nanjing, *Jiangsu, China* 59 A12
Nanjirinji, *Tanzania* 87 D4
Nankana Sahib, *Pakistan* 68 D5
Nankang, *China* 59 E10
Nanking = Nanjing, *China* 59 A12
Nankoku, *Japan* 55 H6
Nanling, *China* 59 B12
Nanning, *China* 58 F7
Nannup, *Australia* 93 F2
Nanpan Jiang →, *China* 58 E6
Nanpara, *India* 69 F9
Nanpi, *China* 56 E9
Nanping, *Fujian, China* 59 D12
Nanping, *Henan, China* 59 C9
Nanri Dao, *China* 59 E12
Nanripe, *Mozam.* 87 E4
Nansei-Shotō = Ryūkyū-rettō, *Japan* 55 M3
Nansen Sd., *Canada* 4 A3
Nanshan I., *S. China Sea* 62 B5
Nansio, *Tanzania* 86 C3
Nant, *France* 20 D7
Nanterre, *France* 19 D9
Nantes, *France* 18 E5
Nantiat, *France* 20 B5
Nanticoke, *U.S.A.* 111 E8
Nanton, *Canada* 104 C6
Nantong, *China* 59 A13
Nantou, *Taiwan* 59 F13
Nantua, *France* 19 F12
Nantucket I., *U.S.A.* 108 E10
Nantwich, *U.K.* 12 D5
Nanty Glo, *U.S.A.* 110 F6
Nanuque, *Brazil* 125 G10
Nanusa, Kepulauan, *Indonesia* 63 D7
Nanutarra Roadhouse, *Australia* 92 D2
Nanxi, *China* 58 C5
Nanxiong, *China* 59 E10
Nanyang, *China* 56 H7
Nanyi Hu, *China* 59 B12
Nanyuan, *China* 56 E9
Nanyuki, *Kenya* 86 B4
Nanzhang, *China* 59 B8
Nao, C. de la, *Spain* 33 G5
Naococane, L., *Canada* 103 B5
Náousa, *Imathía, Greece* 40 F6
Náousa, *Kikládhes, Greece* 39 D7
Naozhou Dao, *China* 59 G8
Napa, *U.S.A.* 116 G4
Napa →, *U.S.A.* 116 G4
Napanee, *Canada* 102 D4
Napanoch, *U.S.A.* 111 E10
Nape, *Laos* 64 C5
Nape Pass = Keo Neua, Deo, *Vietnam* 64 C5
Napier, *N.Z.* 91 H6
Napier Broome B., *Australia* 92 B4
Napier Pen., *Australia* 94 A2
Napierville, *Canada* 111 A11
Naples = Nápoli, *Italy* 31 B7
Naples, *U.S.A.* 109 M5
Napo, *China* 58 F5
Napo →, *Peru* 122 D3
Napoleon, *N. Dak., U.S.A.* 112 B5
Napoleon, *Ohio, U.S.A.* 108 E3
Nápoli, *Italy* 31 B7
Nápoli, G. di, *Italy* 31 B7
Napopo, *Dem. Rep. of the Congo* 86 B2
Naqâda, *Egypt* 80 B3
Naqadeh, *Iran* 73 D11
Naqb, Ra's an, *Jordan* 75 F4
Naqqāsh, *Iran* 71 C6
Nara, *Japan* 55 G7
Nara, *Mali* 82 B3
Nara □, *Japan* 55 G8
Nara Canal, *Pakistan* 68 G3
Nara Visa, *U.S.A.* 113 H3
Naracoorte, *Australia* 95 F3
Naradhan, *Australia* 95 E4
Naraini, *India* 69 G9
Narasapur, *India* 67 L12
Narathiwat, *Thailand* 65 J3
Narayanganj, *Bangla.* 67 H17
Narayanpet, *India* 66 L10
Narbonne, *France* 20 E7
Narcea →, *Spain* 34 B4
Nardīn, *Iran* 71 B7
Nardò, *Italy* 31 B11
Narembeen, *Australia* 93 F2
Narendranagar, *India* 68 D8
Nares Str., *Arctic* 98 A13
Naretha, *Australia* 93 F3
Narew →, *Poland* 45 F7
Nari →, *Pakistan* 68 F2
Narin, *Afghan.* 66 A6
Narindra, Helodranon' i, *Madag.* 89 A8
Narita, *Japan* 55 G10
Närke, *Sweden* 10 E8
Narmada →, *India* 68 J5
Narman, *Turkey* 73 B9
Narmland, *Sweden* 9 F15
Narnaul, *India* 68 E7
Narni, *Italy* 29 F9
Naro, *Ghana* 82 C4
Naro Fominsk, *Russia* 46 E9
Narodnaya, *Russia* 6 B17
Narok, *Kenya* 86 C4
Narón, *Spain* 34 B2
Narooma, *Australia* 95 F5
Narowal, *Pakistan* 68 C6
Narrabri, *Australia* 95 E4
Narran →, *Australia* 95 D4
Narrandera, *Australia* 95 E4
Narrogin, *Australia* 93 F2
Narromine, *Australia* 95 E4
Narrow Hills Prov. Park, *Canada* 105 C8
Narsimhapur, *India* 69 H8
Narsinghgarh, *India* 68 H7
Nartes, L. e, *Albania* 40 F3
Nartkala, *Russia* 49 J6
Naruto, *Japan* 55 G7
Narva, *Estonia* 46 C5
Narva →, *Russia* 9 G22
Narvik, *Norway* 8 B17
Narvskoye Vdkhr., *Russia* 46 C5
Narwana, *India* 68 E7
Naryan-Mar, *Russia* 50 C6
Narym, *Russia* 50 D9
Naryn, *Kyrgyzstan* 50 E8
Nasa, *Norway* 8 C16
Nasarawa, *Nigeria* 83 D6
Năsăud, *Romania* 43 C9
Naseby, *N.Z.* 91 L3
Naselle, *U.S.A.* 116 D3
Naser, Buheirat en, *Egypt* 80 C3
Nashua, *Mont., U.S.A.* 114 B10
Nashua, *N.H., U.S.A.* 111 D13
Nashville, *Ark., U.S.A.* 113 J8
Nashville, *Ga., U.S.A.* 109 K4
Nashville, *Tenn., U.S.A.* 109 G2
Našice, *Croatia* 42 E3
Nasielsk, *Poland* 45 F7
Nasik, *India* 66 K8
Nasipit, *Phil.* 61 G6
Nasir, *Sudan* 81 F3
Nasirabad, *India* 68 F6
Nasirabad, *Pakistan* 68 E3
Naskaupi →, *Canada* 103 B7
Naso, *Italy* 31 D7
Naşrābād, *Iran* 71 C6
Naşriān-e Pā'īn, *Iran* 70 C5
Nass →, *Canada* 104 C3
Nassarawa □, *Nigeria* 83 D6
Nassau, *Bahamas* 120 A4
Nassau, *U.S.A.* 111 D11
Nassau, B., *Chile* 128 H3
Nasser, L. = Naser, Buheirat en, *Egypt* 80 C3
Nasser City = Kôm Ombo, *Egypt* 80 C3
Nassian, *Ivory C.* 82 D4
Nässjö, *Sweden* 11 G8
Nastapoka →, *Canada* 102 A4
Nastapoka, Is., *Canada* 102 A4
Nasugbu, *Phil.* 61 D4
Näsum, *Sweden* 11 H8
Näsviken, *Sweden* 10 C10
Nata, *Botswana* 88 C4
Nata →, *Botswana* 88 C4
Natal, *Brazil* 125 E11
Natal, *Indonesia* 62 D1
Natal, *S. Africa* 85 K6
Natalinci, *Serbia, Yug.* 42 F5

Naţanz, *Iran*	71	C6
Natashquan, *Canada*	103	B7
Natashquan →, *Canada*	103	B7
Natchez, *U.S.A.*	113	K9
Natchitoches, *U.S.A.*	113	K8
Nathalia, *Australia*	95	F4
Nathdwara, *India*	68	G5
Nati, Pta., *Spain*	37	A10
Natimuk, *Australia*	95	F3
Nation →, *Canada*	104	B4
National City, *U.S.A.*	117	N9
Natitingou, *Benin*	83	C5
Natividad, I., *Mexico*	118	B1
Natkyizin, *Burma*	64	E1
Natron, L., *Tanzania*	86	C4
Natrona Heights, *U.S.A.*	110	F5
Natrûn, W. el →, *Egypt*	80	H7
Nättraby, *Sweden*	11	H9
Natukanaoka Pan, *Namibia*	88	B2
Natuna Besar, Kepulauan, *Indonesia*	65	L7
Natuna Is. = Natuna Besar, Kepulauan, *Indonesia*	65	L7
Natuna Selatan, Kepulauan, *Indonesia*	65	L7
Natural Bridge, *U.S.A.*	111	B9
Naturaliste, C., *Australia*	94	G4
Nau Qala, *Afghan.*	68	B3
Naucelle, *France*	20	D6
Nauders, *Austria*	26	E3
Nauen, *Germany*	24	C8
Naugatuck, *U.S.A.*	111	E11
Naujoji Akmenė, *Lithuania*	44	B9
Naumburg, *Germany*	24	D7
Nā'ūr at Tunayb, *Jordan*	75	D4
Nauru ■, *Fac. Oc.*	96	H8
Naushahra = Nowshera, *Pakistan*	66	C8
Naushahro, *Pakistan*	68	F3
Naushon I., *U.S.A.*	111	E14
Nauta, *Peru*	124	D4
Nautanwa, *India*	67	F13
Nautla, *Mexico*	119	C5
Nava, *Mexico*	118	B4
Nava, *Spain*	34	B5
Nava del Rey, *Spain*	34	D5
Navadwip, *India*	69	H13
Navahermosa, *Spain*	35	F6
Navahrudak, *Belarus*	46	F3
Navajo Reservoir, *U.S.A.*	115	H10
Navalcarnero, *Spain*	34	E6
Navalmoral de la Mata, *Spain*	34	F5
Navalvillar de Pela, *Spain*	35	F5
Navan = An Uaimh, *Ireland*	15	C5
Navapolatsk, *Belarus*	46	E5
Navarino, I., *Chile*	128	H3
Navarra □, *Spain*	32	C3
Navarre, *U.S.A.*	110	F3
Navarro →, *U.S.A.*	116	F3
Navas de San Juan, *Spain*	35	G7
Navasota, *U.S.A.*	113	K6
Navassa I., *W. Indies*	121	C5
Nävekvarn, *Sweden*	11	F10
Naver →, *U.K.*	14	C4
Navia, *Spain*	34	B4
Navia →, *Spain*	34	B4
Navia de Suarna, *Spain*	34	C3
Navibandar, *India*	68	J3
Navidad, *Chile*	126	C1
Naviraí, *Brazil*	127	A5
Navlakhi, *India*	68	H4
Navlya, *Russia*	47	F8
Năvodari, *Romania*	43	F13
Navoi = Nawoiy, *Uzbekistan*	50	E7
Navojoa, *Mexico*	118	B3
Navolato, *Mexico*	118	C3
Návpaktos, *Greece*	38	C3
Návplion, *Greece*	38	D4
Navrongo, *Ghana*	83	C4
Navsari, *India*	66	J8
Nawa Kot, *Pakistan*	68	E4
Nawab Khan, *Pakistan*	68	D3
Nawabganj, *Ut. P., India*	69	F9
Nawabganj, *Ut. P., India*	69	E8
Nawabshah, *Pakistan*	68	F3
Nawada, *India*	69	G11
Nawakot, *Nepal*	69	F11
Nawalgarh, *India*	68	F6
Nawanshahr, *India*	69	C6
Nawar, Dasht-i-, *Afghan.*	68	C3
Nawi, *Sudan*	80	D3
Nawoiy, *Uzbekistan*	50	E7
Naxçıvan, *Azerbaijan*	70	B5
Naxçıvan □, *Azerbaijan*	50	F5
Náxos, *Greece*	39	D7
Nay, *France*	20	E3
Nay, Mui, *Vietnam*	62	B3
Nāy Band, *Būshehr, Iran*	71	E7
Nāy Band, *Khorāsān, Iran*	71	C8
Nayakhan, *Russia*	51	C16
Nayarit □, *Mexico*	118	C4
Nayé, *Senegal*	82	C2
Nayong, *China*	58	D5
Nayoro, *Japan*	54	B11
Nayyāl, W. →, *Si. Arabia*	70	D3
Nazaré, *Brazil*	125	F11
Nazaré, *Portugal*	35	F1
Nazareth = Nazerat, *Israel*	75	C4
Nazareth, *U.S.A.*	111	F9
Nazas, *Mexico*	118	B4
Nazas →, *Mexico*	118	B4
Nazca, *Peru*	124	F4
Naze, The, *U.K.*	13	F9
Nazerat, *Israel*	75	C4
Nāzık, *Iran*	70	B5
Nazilli, *Turkey*	39	D10
Nazir Hat, *Bangla.*	67	H17
Nazko, *Canada*	104	C4
Nazko →, *Canada*	104	C4
Nazret, *Ethiopia*	81	F4
Nazwá, *Oman*	74	C6
Nchanga, *Zambia*	87	E2
Ncheu, *Malawi*	87	E3
Ndala, *Tanzania*	86	C3
Ndalatando, *Angola*	84	F2
Ndali, *Benin*	83	D5
Ndareda, *Tanzania*	86	C4
Ndélé, *C.A.R.*	84	C4
Ndikiniméki, *Cameroon*	83	E7
N'Dioum, *Senegal*	82	B2
Ndjamena, *Chad*	79	F8
Ndola, *Zambia*	87	E2
Ndoto Mts., *Kenya*	86	B4
Nduguti, *Tanzania*	86	C3
Néa Alikarnassós, *Greece*	39	F7
Néa Ankhíalos, *Greece*	38	B4
Néa Epídhavros, *Greece*	38	D5
Néa Flippiás, *Greece*	38	B2
Néa Ionía, *Greece*	38	B4
Néa Kallikrátia, *Greece*	40	F7
Néa Mákri, *Greece*	38	C5
Néa Moudhaniá, *Greece*	40	F7
Néa Péramos, *Attikí, Greece*	38	C5
Néa Péramos, *Kaválla, Greece*	41	F8
Néa Víssi, *Greece*	41	E10
Néa Zíkhna, *Greece*	40	E7
Neagh, Lough, *U.K.*	15	B5
Neah Bay, *U.S.A.*	116	B2
Neale, L., *Australia*	92	D5
Neamţ □, *Romania*	43	C11
Neápolis, *Kozáni, Greece*	40	F5
Neápolis, *Kríti, Greece*	36	D7
Neápolis, *Lakonía, Greece*	38	E5
Near Is., *U.S.A.*	100	C1
Neath, *U.K.*	13	F4
Neath Port Talbot □, *U.K.*	13	F4
Nebbou, *Burkina Faso*	83	C4
Nebine Cr. →, *Australia*	95	D4
Nebitdag, *Turkmenistan*	50	F6
Nebo, *Australia*	94	C4
Nebolchy, *Russia*	46	C7
Nebraska □, *U.S.A.*	112	E5
Nebraska City, *U.S.A.*	112	E7
Nébrodi, Monti, *Italy*	31	E7
Necedah, *U.S.A.*	112	C9
Nechako →, *Canada*	104	C4
Neches →, *U.S.A.*	113	L8
Neckar →, *Germany*	25	F4
Necochea, *Argentina*	126	D4
Neda, *Spain*	34	B2
Nedelino, *Bulgaria*	41	E9
Nedelišće, *Croatia*	29	B13
Nédha →, *Greece*	38	D3
Needles, *Canada*	104	D5
Needles, *U.S.A.*	117	L12
Needles, The, *U.K.*	13	G6
Ñeembucú □, *Paraguay*	126	B4
Neemuch = Nimach, *India*	68	G6
Neenah, *U.S.A.*	108	C1
Neepawa, *Canada*	105	C9
Neftçala, *Azerbaijan*	71	B6
Neftegorsk, *Russia*	49	H4
Neftekumsk, *Russia*	49	H7
Nefyn, *U.K.*	12	E3
Négala, *Mali*	82	C3
Negapatam = Nagappattinam, *India*	66	P11
Negaunee, *U.S.A.*	108	B2
Negele, *Ethiopia*	81	F4
Negev Desert = Hanegev, *Israel*	75	E4
Negoiul, Vf., *Romania*	43	E9
Negombo, *Sri Lanka*	66	R11
Negotin, *Serbia, Yug.*	40	B6
Negotino, *Macedonia*	40	E6
Negra, Peña, *Spain*	34	C4
Negra, Pta., *Peru*	122	D2
Negrais, C. = Maudin Sun, *Burma*	67	M19
Negreşti, *Romania*	43	D12
Negreşti-Oaş, *Romania*	43	C8
Negril, *Jamaica*	120	C4
Negro →, *Argentina*	122	H4
Negro →, *Brazil*	122	D4
Negro →, *Uruguay*	127	C4
Negros, *Phil.*	61	G5
Negru Vodă, *Romania*	43	G13
Neguac, *Canada*	103	C6
Nehalem →, *U.S.A.*	116	E3
Nehāvand, *Iran*	71	C6
Nehbandān, *Iran*	71	D9
Nehoiu, *Romania*	43	E11
Nei Mongol Zizhiqu □, *China*	56	D7
Neijiang, *China*	58	C5
Neillsville, *U.S.A.*	112	C9
Neilton, *U.S.A.*	114	C2
Neiqiu, *China*	56	F8
Neiva, *Colombia*	124	C3
Neixiang, *China*	56	H6
Nejanilini L., *Canada*	105	B9
Nejd = Najd, *Si. Arabia*	74	B3
Nejo, *Ethiopia*	81	F4
Nekā, *Iran*	71	B7
Nekemte, *Ethiopia*	81	F4
Nêkheb, *Egypt*	80	B3
Neksø, *Denmark*	11	J9
Nelas, *Portugal*	34	E3
Nelia, *Australia*	94	C3
Nelidovo, *Russia*	46	D7
Neligh, *U.S.A.*	112	D5
Nelkan, *Russia*	51	D14
Nellore, *India*	66	M11
Nelson, *Canada*	104	D5
Nelson, *N.Z.*	91	J4
Nelson, *U.K.*	12	D5
Nelson, *Ariz., U.S.A.*	115	J7
Nelson, *Nev., U.S.A.*	117	K12
Nelson →, *Canada*	105	C9
Nelson, C., *Australia*	95	F3
Nelson, Estrecho, *Chile*	128	G2
Nelson Bay, *Australia*	95	E5
Nelson Forks, *Canada*	104	B4
Nelson House, *Canada*	105	B9
Nelson L., *Canada*	105	B8
Nelspoort, *S. Africa*	88	E3
Nelspruit, *S. Africa*	89	D5
Néma, *Mauritania*	82	B3
Neman, *Russia*	9	J20
Neman →, *Lithuania*	9	J20
Neméa, *Greece*	38	D4
Nemeiben L., *Canada*	105	B7
Nemërçkës, Mal, *Albania*	40	F4
Nemira, Vf., *Romania*	43	D11
Némiscau, *Canada*	102	B4
Némiscau, L., *Canada*	102	B4
Nemours, *France*	19	D9
Nemšová, *Slovak Rep.*	27	C11
Nemunas = Neman →, *Lithuania*	9	J20
Nemuro, *Japan*	54	C12
Nemuro-Kaikyō, *Japan*	54	C12
Nen Jiang →, *China*	57	B13
Nenagh, *Ireland*	15	D3
Nenasi, *Malaysia*	65	L4
Nene →, *U.K.*	13	E8
Nénita, *Greece*	39	C8
Nenjiang, *China*	60	B7
Neno, *Malawi*	87	F3
Neodesha, *U.S.A.*	113	G7
Neokhórion, *Aitolía kai Akarnanía, Greece*	38	C3
Neokhórion, *Árta, Greece*	38	B2
Néon Karlovásion, *Greece*	39	D8
Néon Petrítsi, *Greece*	40	E7
Neosho, *U.S.A.*	113	G7
Neosho →, *U.S.A.*	113	H7
Nepal ■, *Asia*	69	F11
Nepalganj, *Nepal*	69	E9
Nepalganj Road, *India*	69	E9
Nephi, *U.S.A.*	114	G8
Nephin, *Ireland*	15	B2
Nepi, *Italy*	29	F9
Nepomuk, *Czech Rep.*	26	B6
Neptune, *U.S.A.*	111	F10
Nera →, *Italy*	29	F9
Nera →, *Romania*	42	F6
Nérac, *France*	20	D4
Nerang, *Australia*	95	D5
Neratovice, *Czech Rep.*	26	A7
Nerchinsk, *Russia*	51	D12
Nereju, *Romania*	43	E11
Nerekhta, *Russia*	46	D11
Néret, L., *Canada*	103	B5
Neretvanski Kanal, *Croatia*	29	E14
Neringa, *Lithuania*	9	J19
Nerja, *Spain*	35	J7
Nerl →, *Russia*	46	D11
Nerpio, *Spain*	33	G2
Nerva, *Spain*	35	H4
Nervi, *Italy*	28	D6
Neryungri, *Russia*	51	D13
Nescopeck, *U.S.A.*	111	E8
Nesebŭr, *Bulgaria*	41	D11
Ness, L., *U.K.*	14	D4
Ness City, *U.S.A.*	112	F5
Nesterov, *Poland*	47	G2
Nestórion, *Greece*	40	F5
Néstos →, *Greece*	41	E8
Nesvady, *Slovak Rep.*	27	D11
Nesvizh = Nyasvizh, *Belarus*	47	F4
Netanya, *Israel*	75	C3
Netarhat, *India*	69	H11
Nete →, *Belgium*	17	C4
Netherdale, *Australia*	94	C4
Netherlands ■, *Europe*	17	C5
Netherlands Antilles ■, *W. Indies*	124	A5
Neto →, *Italy*	31	C10
Nettancourt, *France*	19	D11
Nettetal, *Germany*	24	D2
Nettilling L., *Canada*	101	B12
Nettuno, *Italy*	30	A5
Netzahualcoyotl, Presa, *Mexico*	119	D6
Neu-Isenburg, *Germany*	25	E4
Neu-Ulm, *Germany*	25	G6
Neubrandenburg, *Germany*	24	B9
Neubukow, *Germany*	24	A7
Neuburg, *Germany*	25	G7
Neuchâtel, *Switz.*	25	J2
Neuchâtel □, *Switz.*	25	J2
Neuchâtel, Lac de, *Switz.*	25	J2
Neudau, *Austria*	26	D9
Neuenhagen, *Germany*	24	C9
Neuenhaus, *Germany*	24	C2
Neuf-Brisach, *France*	19	D14
Neufahrn, *Bayern, Germany*	25	G8
Neufahrn, *Bayern, Germany*	25	G7
Neufchâteau, *Belgium*	17	E5
Neufchâteau, *France*	19	D12
Neufchâtel-en-Bray, *France*	18	C8
Neufchâtel-sur-Aisne, *France*	19	C11
Neuhaus, *Germany*	24	B6
Neuillé-Pont-Pierre, *France*	18	E7
Neuilly-St-Front, *France*	19	C10
Neukalen, *Germany*	24	B8
Neumarkt, *Germany*	25	F7
Neumünster, *Germany*	24	A5
Neung-sur-Beuvron, *France*	19	E8
Neunkirchen, *Austria*	26	D9
Neunkirchen, *Germany*	25	F3
Neuquén, *Argentina*	128	D3
Neuquén □, *Argentina*	126	D2
Neuruppin, *Germany*	24	C8
Neusäss, *Germany*	25	G6
Neuse →, *U.S.A.*	109	H7
Neusiedl, *Austria*	27	D9
Neusiedler See, *Austria*	27	D9
Neuss, *Germany*	24	D2
Neussargues-Moissac, *France*	20	C7
Neustadt, *Bayern, Germany*	25	F8
Neustadt, *Bayern, Germany*	25	G7
Neustadt, *Bayern, Germany*	25	F6
Neustadt, *Bayern, Germany*	25	E7
Neustadt, *Brandenburg, Germany*	24	C8
Neustadt, *Hessen, Germany*	24	E5
Neustadt, *Niedersachsen, Germany*	24	C5
Neustadt, *Rhld.-Pfz., Germany*	25	F4
Neustadt, *Sachsen, Germany*	24	D10
Neustadt, *Schleswig-Holstein, Germany*	24	A6
Neustadt, *Thüringen, Germany*	24	E7
Neustrelitz, *Germany*	24	B9
Neuvic, *France*	20	C6
Neuville-sur-Saône, *France*	21	C8
Neuvy-le-Roi, *France*	18	E7
Neuvy-St-Sépulchre, *France*	19	F8
Neuvy-sur-Barangeon, *France*	19	E9
Neuwerk, *Germany*	24	B4
Neuwied, *Germany*	24	E3
Neva →, *Russia*	46	C6
Nevada, *Iowa, U.S.A.*	112	D8
Nevada, *Mo., U.S.A.*	113	G7
Nevada □, *U.S.A.*	114	G5
Nevada, Sierra, *Spain*	35	H7
Nevada, Sierra, *U.S.A.*	114	G3
Nevada City, *U.S.A.*	116	F6
Nevado, Cerro, *Argentina*	126	D2
Nevel, *Russia*	46	D5
Nevers, *France*	19	F10
Nevertire, *Australia*	95	E4
Nevesinje, *Bos.-H.*	40	C2
Nevinnomyssk, *Russia*	49	H6
Nevis, *W. Indies*	121	C7
Nevrokop = Gotse Delchev, *Bulgaria*	40	E7
Nevşehir, *Turkey*	70	B2
New →, *U.S.A.*	108	F5
New Aiyansh, *Canada*	104	B3
New Albany, *Ind., U.S.A.*	108	F3
New Albany, *Miss., U.S.A.*	113	H10
New Albany, *Pa., U.S.A.*	111	E8
New Amsterdam, *Guyana*	124	B7
New Angledool, *Australia*	95	D4
New Baltimore, *U.S.A.*	110	D2
New Bedford, *U.S.A.*	111	E14
New Berlin, *N.Y., U.S.A.*	111	D9
New Berlin, *Pa., U.S.A.*	110	F8
New Bern, *U.S.A.*	109	H7
New Bethlehem, *U.S.A.*	110	F5
New Bloomfield, *U.S.A.*	110	F7
New Boston, *U.S.A.*	113	J7
New Braunfels, *U.S.A.*	113	L5
New Brighton, *N.Z.*	91	K4
New Brighton, *U.S.A.*	110	F4
New Britain, *Papua N. G.*	96	H7
New Britain, *U.S.A.*	111	E12
New Brunswick, *U.S.A.*	111	F10
New Brunswick □, *Canada*	103	C6
New Bussa, *Nigeria*	83	D5
New Caledonia ■, *Pac. Oc.*	96	K8
New Castile = Castilla-La Mancha □, *Spain*	6	H5
New Castle, *Ind., U.S.A.*	108	F3
New Castle, *Pa., U.S.A.*	110	F4
New City, *U.S.A.*	111	E11
New Concord, *U.S.A.*	110	G3
New Cumberland, *U.S.A.*	110	F4
New Cuyama, *U.S.A.*	117	L7
New Delhi, *India*	68	E7
New Denver, *Canada*	104	D5
New Don Pedro Reservoir, *U.S.A.*	116	H6
New England, *U.S.A.*	112	B3
New England Ra., *Australia*	95	E5
New Forest, *U.K.*	13	G6
New Galloway, *U.K.*	14	F4
New Glasgow, *Canada*	103	C7
New Guinea, *Oceania*	52	K17
New Hamburg, *Canada*	110	C4
New Hampshire □, *U.S.A.*	111	C13
New Hampton, *U.S.A.*	112	D8
New Hanover, *S. Africa*	89	D5
New Hartford, *U.S.A.*	111	C9
New Haven, *Conn., U.S.A.*	111	E12
New Haven, *Mich., U.S.A.*	110	D2
New Hazelton, *Canada*	104	B3
New Hebrides = Vanuatu ■, *Pac. Oc.*	96	J8
New Holland, *U.S.A.*	111	F8
New Iberia, *U.S.A.*	113	K9
New Ireland, *Papua N. G.*	96	H7
New Jersey □, *U.S.A.*	108	E8
New Kensington, *U.S.A.*	110	F5
New Lexington, *U.S.A.*	108	F4
New Liskeard, *Canada*	102	C4
New London, *Conn., U.S.A.*	111	E12
New London, *Ohio, U.S.A.*	110	E2
New London, *Wis., U.S.A.*	112	C10
New Madrid, *U.S.A.*	113	G10
New Martinsville, *U.S.A.*	108	F5
New Meadows, *U.S.A.*	114	D5
New Melones L., *U.S.A.*	116	H6
New Mexico □, *U.S.A.*	115	J10
New Milford, *Conn., U.S.A.*	111	E11
New Milford, *Pa., U.S.A.*	111	E9
New Norcia, *Australia*	93	F2
New Norfolk, *Australia*	94	G4
New Orleans, *U.S.A.*	113	L9
New Philadelphia, *U.S.A.*	110	F3
New Plymouth, *N.Z.*	91	H5
New Plymouth, *U.S.A.*	114	E5
New Port Richey, *U.S.A.*	109	L4
New Providence, *Bahamas*	120	A4
New Quay, *U.K.*	13	E3
New Radnor, *U.K.*	13	E4
New Richmond, *Canada*	103	C6
New Richmond, *U.S.A.*	112	C8
New Roads, *U.S.A.*	113	K9
New Rochelle, *U.S.A.*	111	F11
New Rockford, *U.S.A.*	112	B5
New Romney, *U.K.*	13	G8
New Ross, *Ireland*	15	D5
New Salem, *U.S.A.*	112	B4
New Scone, *U.K.*	14	E5
New Siberian I. = Novaya Sibir, Ostrov, *Russia*	51	B16
New Siberian Is. = Novosibirskiye Ostrova, *Russia*	51	B15
New Smyrna Beach, *U.S.A.*	109	L5
New South Wales □, *Australia*	95	E4
New Town, *U.S.A.*	112	B3
New Tredegar, *U.K.*	13	F4
New Ulm, *U.S.A.*	112	C7
New Waterford, *Canada*	103	C7
New Westminster, *Canada*	116	A4
New York, *U.S.A.*	111	F11
New York □, *U.S.A.*	111	D9
New York Mts., *U.S.A.*	115	J6
New Zealand ■, *Oceania*	91	J6
Newala, *Tanzania*	87	E4
Newark, *Del., U.S.A.*	108	F8
Newark, *N.J., U.S.A.*	111	F10
Newark, *N.Y., U.S.A.*	110	C7
Newark, *Ohio, U.S.A.*	110	F2
Newark-on-Trent, *U.K.*	12	D7
Newark Valley, *U.S.A.*	111	D8
Newberg, *U.S.A.*	114	D2
Newberry, *Mich., U.S.A.*	108	B3
Newberry, *S.C., U.S.A.*	109	H5
Newberry Springs, *U.S.A.*	117	L10
Newboro L., *Canada*	111	B8
Newbridge = Droichead Nua, *Ireland*	15	C5
Newburgh, *Canada*	111	B8
Newburgh, *U.S.A.*	111	E10
Newbury, *U.K.*	13	F6
Newbury, *Vt., U.S.A.*	111	B12
Newburyport, *U.S.A.*	109	D10
Newcastle, *Australia*	95	E5
Newcastle, *N.B., Canada*	103	C6
Newcastle, *Ont., Canada*	102	D4
Newcastle, *S. Africa*	89	D4
Newcastle, *U.K.*	15	B6
Newcastle, *Calif., U.S.A.*	116	G5
Newcastle, *Wyo., U.S.A.*	112	D2
Newcastle Emlyn, *U.K.*	13	E3
Newcastle Ra., *Australia*	92	C5
Newcastle-under-Lyme, *U.K.*	12	D5
Newcastle-upon-Tyne, *U.K.*	12	C6
Newcastle Waters, *Australia*	94	B1
Newcastle West, *Ireland*	15	D2
Newcomb, *U.S.A.*	111	C10
Newcomerstown, *U.S.A.*	110	F3
Newdegate, *Australia*	93	F2
Newell, *Australia*	94	B4
Newell, *U.S.A.*	112	C3
Newfane, *U.S.A.*	110	C6
Newfield, *U.S.A.*	111	D8
Newfound L., *U.S.A.*	111	C13
Newfoundland, *N. Amer.*	98	C14
Newfoundland, *U.S.A.*	111	E9
Newfoundland □, *Canada*	103	B8
Newhall, *U.S.A.*	117	L8
Newhaven, *U.K.*	13	G8
Newkirk, *U.S.A.*	113	G6
Newlyn, *U.K.*	13	G2
Newman, *Australia*	92	D2
Newman, *U.S.A.*	116	H5
Newmarket, *Canada*	110	B5
Newmarket, *Ireland*	15	D2
Newmarket, *U.K.*	13	E8
Newmarket, *N.H., U.S.A.*	111	C14
Newmarket, *N.H., U.S.A.*	111	C14
Newnan, *U.S.A.*	109	J3
Newport, *I. of W., U.K.*	13	G6
Newport, *Newp., U.K.*	13	F5
Newport, *Ark., U.S.A.*	113	H9
Newport, *Ky., U.S.A.*	108	F3
Newport, *N.H., U.S.A.*	111	C12
Newport, *N.Y., U.S.A.*	111	C9
Newport, *Oreg., U.S.A.*	114	D1
Newport, *Pa., U.S.A.*	110	F7
Newport, *R.I., U.S.A.*	111	E13
Newport, *Tenn., U.S.A.*	109	H4
Newport, *Vt., U.S.A.*	111	B12
Newport, *Wash., U.S.A.*	114	B5
Newport □, *U.K.*	13	F5
Newport Beach, *U.S.A.*	117	M9
Newport News, *U.S.A.*	108	G7
Newport Pagnell, *U.K.*	13	E7
Newquay, *U.K.*	13	G2
Newry, *U.K.*	15	B5
Newton, *Ill., U.S.A.*	112	F10
Newton, *Iowa, U.S.A.*	112	E8
Newton, *Kans., U.S.A.*	113	F6
Newton, *Mass., U.S.A.*	111	D13
Newton, *Miss., U.S.A.*	113	J10
Newton, *N.C., U.S.A.*	109	H5
Newton, *N.J., U.S.A.*	111	E10
Newton, *Texas, U.S.A.*	113	K8
Newton Abbot, *U.K.*	13	G4
Newton Aycliffe, *U.K.*	12	C6
Newton Falls, *U.S.A.*	110	E4
Newton Stewart, *U.K.*	14	G4
Newtonmore, *U.K.*	14	D4
Newtown, *U.K.*	13	E4
Newtownabbey, *U.K.*	15	B6

Newtownards, *U.K.* 15 B6
Newtownbarry = Bunclody,
  Ireland 15 D5
Newtownstewart, *U.K.* 15 B4
Newville, *U.S.A.* 110 F7
Nexon, *France* 20 C5
Neya, *Russia* 48 A6
Neyrīz, *Iran* 71 D7
Neyshābūr, *Iran* 71 B8
Nezhin = Nizhyn, *Ukraine* . 47 G6
Nezperce, *U.S.A.* 114 C4
Ngabang, *Indonesia* 62 D3
Ngabordamlu, Tanjung,
  Indonesia 63 F8
N'Gage, *Angola* 84 F3
Ngala, *Nigeria* 83 C7
Ngambé, *Cameroon* 83 D7
Ngambé, *Cameroon* 83 D7
Ngami Depression, *Botswana* 88 C3
Ngamo, *Zimbabwe* 87 F2
Ngangala, *Sudan* 81 G3
Nganglong Kangri, *China* . 67 C12
Ngao, *Thailand* 64 C2
Ngaoundéré, *Cameroon* ... 84 C2
Ngapara, *N.Z.* 91 L3
Ngara, *Tanzania* 86 C3
Ngawi, *Indonesia* 63 G14
Nghia Lo, *Vietnam* 58 G5
Ngoboli, *Sudan* 81 G3
Ngoma, *Malawi* 87 E3
Ngomahura, *Zimbabwe* ... 87 G3
Ngomba, *Tanzania* 87 D3
Ngop, *Sudan* 81 F3
Ngoring Hu, *China* 60 C4
Ngorkou, *Mali* 82 B4
Ngorongoro, *Tanzania* 86 C4
Ngozi, *Burundi* 86 C2
Ngudu, *Tanzania* 86 C3
Nguigmi, *Niger* 79 F8
Nguila, *Cameroon* 83 E7
Nguiu, *Australia* 92 B5
Ngukurr, *Australia* 94 A1
Ngulu Atoll, *Pac. Oc.* 63 C9
Ngunga, *Tanzania* 86 C3
Nguru, *Nigeria* 83 C7
Nguru Mts., *Tanzania* 86 D4
Nguyen Binh, *Vietnam* 58 F5
Nha Trang, *Vietnam* 65 F7
Nhacoongo, *Mozam.* 89 C6
Nhamaabué, *Mozam.* 87 F4
Nhamundá →, *Brazil* 125 D7
Nhangulaze, L., *Mozam.* ... 89 C5
Nhill, *Australia* 95 F3
Nho Quan, *Vietnam* 58 G5
Nhulunbuy, *Australia* 94 A2
Nia-nia,
  Dem. Rep. of the Congo . 86 B2
Niafounké, *Mali* 82 B4
Niagara Falls, *Canada* ... 102 D4
Niagara Falls, *U.S.A.* 110 C6
Niagara-on-the-Lake, *Canada* 110 C5
Niah, *Malaysia* 62 D4
Niamey, *Niger* 83 C5
Niandan-Koro, *Guinea* ... 82 C3
Nianforando, *Guinea* 82 D2
Niangara,
  Dem. Rep. of the Congo . 86 B2
Niangbo, *Ivory C.* 82 D3
Niangoloko, *Burkina Faso* . 82 C4
Niantic, *U.S.A.* 111 E12
Niaro, *Sudan* 81 E3
Nias, *Indonesia* 62 D1
Niassa □, *Mozam.* 87 E4
Nibāk, *Si. Arabia* 71 E7
Nibe, *Denmark* 11 H3
Nicaragua ■, *Cent. Amer.* . 120 D2
Nicaragua, L. de, *Nic.* 120 D2
Nicastro, *Italy* 31 D9
Nice, *France* 21 E11
Niceville, *U.S.A.* 109 K2
Nichicun, L., *Canada* 103 B5
Nichinan, *Japan* 55 J5
Nicholás, Canal, *W. Indies* . 120 B3
Nicholasville, *U.S.A.* 108 G3
Nichols, *U.S.A.* 111 D8
Nicholson, *Australia* 92 C4
Nicholson, *U.S.A.* 111 E9
Nicholson →, *Australia* ... 94 B2
Nicholson L., *Canada* 105 A8
Nicholson Ra., *Australia* .. 93 E2
Nicholville, *U.S.A.* 111 B10
Nicobar Is., *Ind. Oc.* 52 J13
Nicola, *Canada* 104 C4
Nicolls Town, *Bahamas* .. 120 A4
Nicopolis, *Greece* 38 B2
Nicosia, *Cyprus* 36 D12
Nicosia, *Italy* 31 E7
Nicótera, *Italy* 31 D8
Nicoya, *Costa Rica* 120 D2
Nicoya, G. de, *Costa Rica* . 120 E3
Nicoya, Pen. de, *Costa Rica* 120 E2
Nidd →, *U.K.* 12 D6
Nidda, *Germany* 25 E5
Nidda →, *Germany* 25 E4
Nidwalden □, *Switz.* 25 J4
Nidzica, *Poland* 45 E7
Niebüll, *Germany* 24 A4
Nied →, *Germany* 19 C13
Niederaula, *Germany* 24 E5
Niederbayern □, *Germany* . 25 G8
Niederbronn-les-Bains,
  France 19 D14
Niedere Tauern, *Austria* .. 26 D7
Niederlausitz, *Germany* .. 24 D9
Niederösterreich □, *Austria* 26 C8
Niedersachsen □, *Germany* 24 C4
Niekerkshoop, *S. Africa* .. 88 D3
Niellé, *Ivory C.* 82 C3
Niemba,
  Dem. Rep. of the Congo . 86 D2

Niemen = Neman →,
  Lithuania 9 J20
Niemodlin, *Poland* 45 H4
Nienburg, *Germany* 24 C5
Niepołomice, *Poland* 45 H7
Niers →, *Germany* 24 D1
Niesky, *Germany* 24 D10
Nieszawa, *Poland* 45 F5
Nieu Bethesda, *S. Africa* .. 88 E3
Nieuw Amsterdam, *Surinam* 125 B7
Nieuw Nickerie, *Surinam* .. 125 B7
Nieuwoudtville, *S. Africa* .. 88 E2
Nieuwpoort, *Belgium* 17 C2
Nieves, Pico de las,
  Canary Is. 37 G4
Nièvre □, *France* 19 E10
Niga, *Mali* 82 C3
Niğde, *Turkey* 70 B2
Nigel, *S. Africa* 89 D4
Niger □, *Nigeria* 83 D6
Niger ■, *W. Afr.* 83 B7
Niger →, *W. Afr.* 83 D6
Niger Delta, *Africa* 83 E6
Nigeria ■, *W. Afr.* 83 D6
Nighasin, *India* 69 E9
Nightcaps, *N.Z.* 91 L2
Nigríta, *Greece* 40 F7
Nii-Jima, *Japan* 55 G9
Niigata, *Japan* 54 F9
Niigata □, *Japan* 55 F9
Niihama, *Japan* 55 H6
Niihau, *U.S.A.* 106 H14
Niimi, *Japan* 55 G6
Niitsu, *Japan* 54 F9
Níjar, *Spain* 33 J2
Nijil, *Jordan* 75 E4
Nijkerk, *Neths.* 17 B5
Nijmegen, *Neths.* 17 C5
Nijverdal, *Neths.* 17 B6
Nīk Pey, *Iran* 71 B6
Nike, *Nigeria* 83 D6
Nikiniki, *Indonesia* 63 F6
Nikísiani, *Greece* 41 F8
Nikítas, *Greece* 40 F7
Nikki, *Benin* 83 D5
Nikkō, *Japan* 55 F9
Nikolayev = Mykolayiv,
  Ukraine 47 J7
Nikolayevsk, *Russia* 48 E7
Nikolayevsk-na-Amur,
  Russia 51 D15
Nikolsk, *Russia* 48 D8
Nikolskoye, *Russia* 51 D17
Nikopol, *Bulgaria* 41 C8
Nikopol, *Ukraine* 47 J8
Niksar, *Turkey* 72 B7
Nīkshahr, *Iran* 71 E9
Nikšić, *Montenegro, Yug.* .. 40 D2
Nîl, Nahr en →, *Africa* ... 80 H7
Nîl el Abyad →, *Sudan* ... 81 D3
Nîl el Azraq →, *Sudan* ... 81 D3
Nila, *Indonesia* 63 F7
Niland, *U.S.A.* 117 M11
Nile = Nîl, Nahr en →,
  Africa 80 H7
Niles, *Mich., U.S.A.* 108 D2
Niles, *Ohio, U.S.A.* 110 E4
Nilüfer →, *Turkey* 41 F12
Nim Ka Thana, *India* 68 F6
Nimach, *India* 68 G6
Nimbahera, *India* 68 G6
Nîmes, *France* 21 E8
Nimfaíon, Ákra = Pínnes,
  Ákra, *Greece* 41 F8
Nimmitabel, *Australia* ... 95 F4
Nimule, *Sudan* 81 G3
Nin, *Croatia* 29 D12
Nindigully, *Australia* 95 D4
Nineveh = Nīnawā, *Iraq* .. 70 B4
Ning Xian, *China* 56 G4
Ning'an, *China* 57 B15
Ningbo, *China* 59 C13
Ningcheng, *China* 57 D10
Ningde, *China* 59 D12
Ningdu, *China* 59 D10
Ninggang, *China* 59 D9
Ningguo, *China* 59 B12
Ninghai, *China* 59 C13
Ninghua, *China* 59 D11
Ningi, *Nigeria* 83 C6
Ningjin, *China* 56 F8
Ningjing Shan, *China* 58 C2
Ninglang, *China* 58 D3
Ningling, *China* 56 G8
Ningming, *China* 58 F6
Ningnan, *China* 58 D4
Ningpo = Ningbo, *China* . 59 C13
Ningqiang, *China* 56 H4
Ningshan, *China* 56 H5
Ningsia Hui A.R. = Ningxia
  Huizu Zizhiqu □, *China* . 56 F4
Ningwu, *China* 56 E7
Ningxia Huizu Zizhiqu □,
  China 56 F4
Ningxiang, *China* 59 C9
Ningyang, *China* 56 G9
Ningyuan, *China* 59 E8
Ninh Binh, *Vietnam* 58 G5
Ninh Giang, *Vietnam* 64 B6
Ninh Hoa, *Vietnam* 64 F7
Ninh Ma, *Vietnam* 64 F7
Ninove, *Belgium* 17 D4
Nioaque, *Brazil* 127 A4
Niobrara, *U.S.A.* 112 D6
Niobrara →, *U.S.A.* 112 D6
Niono, *Mali* 82 C3
Nionsamoridougou, *Guinea* 82 D3
Nioro du Rip, *Senegal* ... 82 C1
Nioro du Sahel, *Mali* 82 B3
Niort, *France* 20 B3

Nipawin, *Canada* 105 C8
Nipfjället, *Sweden* 10 C6
Nipigon, *Canada* 102 C2
Nipigon, L., *Canada* 102 C2
Nipishish L., *Canada* 103 B7
Nipissing, L., *Canada* 102 C4
Nipomo, *U.S.A.* 117 K6
Nipton, *U.S.A.* 117 K11
Niquelândia, *Brazil* 125 F9
Nīr, *Iran* 70 B5
Nirasaki, *Japan* 55 G9
Nirmal, *India* 66 K11
Nirmali, *India* 69 F12
Nisa, *Portugal* 35 F3
Nişāb, *Si. Arabia* 70 D5
Nişāb, *Yemen* 74 E4
Nišava →, *Serbia, Yug.* .. 40 C5
Niscemi, *Italy* 31 E7
Nishinomiya, *Japan* 55 G7
Nishino'omote, *Japan* ... 55 J5
Nishiwaki, *Japan* 55 G7
Nísíros, *Greece* 39 E9
Niška Banja, *Serbia, Yug.* . 40 C6
Niskibi →, *Canada* 102 A2
Nisko, *Poland* 45 H9
Nisporeni, *Moldova* 43 C13
Nisqually →, *U.S.A.* 116 C4
Nissáki, *Greece* 36 A3
Nissan →, *Sweden* 11 H6
Nissum Bredning, *Denmark* 11 H2
Nissum Fjord, *Denmark* .. 11 H2
Nistru = Dnister →, *Europe* 47 J6
Nisutlin →, *Canada* 104 A2
Nitchequon, *Canada* 103 B5
Niterói, *Brazil* 127 A7
Nith →, *Canada* 110 C4
Nith →, *U.K.* 14 F5
Nitra, *Slovak Rep.* 27 C11
Nitra →, *Slovak Rep.* ... 27 D11
Nitriansky □, *Slovak Rep.* . 27 C11
Nittenau, *Germany* 25 F8
Niuafo'ou, *Tonga* 91 B11
Niue, *Cook Is.* 97 J11
Niulan Jiang →, *China* .. 58 D4
Niut, *Indonesia* 62 D4
Niutou Shan, *China* 59 C13
Niuzhuang, *China* 57 D12
Nivala, *Finland* 8 E21
Nivelles, *Belgium* 17 D4
Nivernais, *France* 19 E10
Niwas, *India* 69 H9
Nixon, *U.S.A.* 113 L6
Nizamabad, *India* 66 K11
Nizamghat, *India* 67 E19
Nizhne Kolymsk, *Russia* .. 51 C17
Nizhnegorskiy =
  Nyzhnohirskyy, *Ukraine* . 47 K8
Nizhnekamsk, *Russia* ... 48 C10
Nizhneudinsk, *Russia* ... 51 D10
Nizhnevartovsk, *Russia* .. 50 C8
Nizhniy Chir, *Russia* 49 F6
Nizhniy Lomov, *Russia* .. 48 D6
Nizhniy Novgorod, *Russia* 48 B7
Nizhniy Tagil, *Russia* ... 50 D6
Nizhyn, *Ukraine* 47 G6
Nizina Mazowiecka, *Poland* 45 F8
Nizip, *Turkey* 70 B3
Nízké Tatry, *Slovak Rep.* .. 27 C12
Nízký Jeseník, *Czech Rep.* . 27 B10
Nizza Monferrato, *Italy* .. 28 D5
Njakwal, *Malawi* 87 E3
Njanji, *Zambia* 87 E3
Njegoš, *Montenegro, Yug.* .. 40 D2
Njinjo, *Tanzania* 87 D4
Njombe, *Tanzania* 86 D4
Njombe →, *Tanzania* ... 87 D3
Njurundabommen, *Sweden* 10 B11
Nkambe, *Cameroon* 83 D7
Nkana, *Zambia* 87 E2
Nkandla, *S. Africa* 89 D5
Nkawkaw, *Ghana* 83 D4
Nkayi, *Zimbabwe* 87 F2
Nkhotakota, *Malawi* 87 E3
Nkongsamba, *Cameroon* . 83 E6
Nkurenkuru, *Namibia* ... 88 B2
Nkwanta, *Ghana* 82 D4
Nmai →, *Burma* 58 F2
Noakhali = Maijdi, *Bangla* . 67 H17
Nobel, *Canada* 110 A4
Nobeoka, *Japan* 55 H5
Noblejas, *Spain* 34 F7
Noblesville, *U.S.A.* 108 E3
Noce →, *Italy* 28 B8
Nocera Inferiore, *Italy* .. 31 B7
Nocera Umbra, *Italy* ... 29 E9
Noci, *Italy* 31 B10
Nocona, *U.S.A.* 113 J6
Nocrich, *Romania* 43 E9
Noda, *Japan* 55 G9
Nogales, *Mexico* 118 A2
Nogales, *U.S.A.* 115 L8
Nogaro, *France* 20 E3
Nogat →, *Poland* 44 D6
Nōgata, *Japan* 55 H5
Nogent, *France* 19 D12
Nogent-le-Rotrou, *France* . 18 D7
Nogent-sur-Seine, *France* . 19 D10
Noggerup, *Australia* ... 93 F2
Noginsk, *Moskva, Russia* . 46 E10
Noginsk, *Tunguska, Russia* 51 C10
Nogoa →, *Australia* 94 C4
Nogoyá, *Argentina* 126 C4
Nógrád □, *Hungary* 27 C10
Noguera Pallaresa →, *Spain* 32 D5
Noguera Ribagorzana →,
  Spain 32 D5
Nohar, *India* 68 E6
Nohfelden, *Germany* ... 25 F3
Nohta, *India* 69 H8
Noia, *Spain* 34 C2

Noire, Montagne, *France* .. 20 E6
Noire, Mt., *France* 18 D3
Noirétable, *France* 20 C7
Noirmoutier, Î. de, *France* . 18 F4
Noirmoutier-en-l'Île, *France* 18 F4
Nojane, *Botswana* 88 C3
Nojima-Zaki, *Japan* 55 G9
Nok Kundi, *Pakistan* 66 E3
Nokaneng, *Botswana* ... 88 B3
Nokia, *Finland* 9 F20
Nokomis, *Canada* 105 C8
Nokomis L., *Canada* 105 B8
Nol, *Sweden* 11 G6
Nola, *C.A.R.* 84 D3
Nola, *Italy* 31 B7
Nolay, *France* 19 F11
Noli, C. di, *Italy* 28 D5
Nolinsk, *Russia* 48 B9
Noma Omuramba →,
  Namibia 88 B3
Nombre de Dios, *Panama* . 120 E4
Nome, *U.S.A.* 100 B3
Nomo-Zaki, *Japan* 55 H4
Nonacho L., *Canada* 105 A7
Nonancourt, *France* 18 D8
Nonda, *Australia* 94 C3
None, *Italy* 28 D4
Nong Chang, *Thailand* .. 64 E2
Nong Het, *Laos* 64 C4
Nong Khai, *Thailand* ... 64 D4
Nong'an, *China* 57 B13
Nongoma, *S. Africa* 89 D5
Nonoava, *Mexico* 118 B3
Nonoava →, *Mexico* ... 118 B3
Nonthaburi, *Thailand* ... 64 F3
Nontron, *France* 20 C4
Nonza, *France* 21 F13
Noonamah, *Australia* ... 92 B5
Noonan, *U.S.A.* 112 A3
Noonkanbah, *Australia* . 92 C3
Noord Brabant □, *Neths.* . 17 C5
Noord Holland □, *Neths.* . 17 B4
Noordbeveland, *Neths.* .. 17 C3
Noordoostpolder, *Neths.* .. 17 B5
Noordwijk, *Neths.* 17 B4
Nootka I., *Canada* 104 D3
Nopiming Prov. Park,
  Canada 105 C9
Nora, *Eritrea* 81 D5
Nora, *Sweden* 10 E9
Noralee, *Canada* 104 C3
Noranda = Rouyn-Noranda,
  Canada 102 C4
Norberg, *Sweden* 10 D9
Nórcia, *Italy* 29 F10
Norco, *U.S.A.* 117 M9
Nord □, *France* 19 B10
Nord-Kivu □,
  Dem. Rep. of the Congo . 86 C2
Nord-Ostsee-Kanal,
  Germany 24 A5
Nord-Pas-de-Calais □,
  France 19 B9
Nordaustlandet, *Svalbard* .. 4 B9
Nordborg, *Denmark* 11 J3
Nordby, *Denmark* 11 J2
Norddeich, *Germany* ... 24 B3
Nordegg, *Canada* 104 C5
Norden, *Germany* 24 B3
Nordenham, *Germany* .. 24 B4
Norderney, *Germany* ... 24 B3
Norderstedt, *Germany* .. 24 B6
Nordfjord, *Norway* 9 F11
Nordfriesische Inseln,
  Germany 24 A4
Nordhausen, *Germany* .. 24 D6
Nordhorn, *Germany* 24 C3
Nordøyar, *Færoe Is.* 8 E9
Nordingrå, *Sweden* 10 B12
Nordjyllands
  Amtskommune □,
  Denmark 11 G4
Nordkapp, *Norway* 8 A21
Nordkapp, *Svalbard* 4 A9
Nordkinn = Kinnarodden,
  Norway 6 A11
Nordkinn-halvøya, *Norway* . 8 A22
Nördlingen, *Germany* ... 25 G6
Nordrhein-Westfalen □,
  Germany 24 D3
Nordstrand, *Germany* ... 24 A4
Nordvik, *Russia* 51 B12
Nore, *Ireland* 15 D4
Nore →, *Ireland* 15 D4
Norfolk, *Nebr., U.S.A.* .. 112 D6
Norfolk, *Va., U.S.A.* 108 G7
Norfolk □, *U.K.* 13 E8
Norfolk I., *Pac. Oc.* 96 K8
Nork L., *U.S.A.* 113 G8
Norilsk, *Russia* 51 C9
Norma, Mt., *Australia* .. 94 C3
Normal, *U.S.A.* 112 E10
Norman, *U.S.A.* 113 H6
Norman →, *Australia* .. 94 B3
Norman Wells, *Canada* . 100 B7
Normanby →, *Australia* . 94 A3
Normandin, *Canada* ... 102 C5
Normanhurst, Mt., *Australia* 93 E3
Normanton, *Australia* .. 94 B3
Normétal, *Canada* 102 C4
Norquay, *Canada* 105 C8
Norquinco, *Argentina* .. 128 E2
Norra Dellen, *Sweden* .. 10 C10
Norra Ulvön, *Sweden* .. 10 A12
Norrahammar, *Sweden* . 11 G8
Nørre Åby, *Denmark* .. 11 J3
Nørre Alslev, *Denmark* . 11 K5
Nørresundby, *Denmark* . 11 G3
Norrhult, *Sweden* 11 H9
Norris Point, *Canada* .. 103 C8
Norristown, *U.S.A.* 111 F9
Norrköping, *Sweden* ... 11 F10
Norrland, *Sweden* 9 E16

Norrsundet, *Sweden* 10 D11
Norrtälje, *Sweden* 10 E12
Norseman, *Australia* 93 F3
Norsk, *Russia* 51 D14
Norte, Pta. del, *Canary Is.* . 37 G2
Norte, Serra do, *Brazil* 124
North, C., *Canada* 103 C7
North Adams, *U.S.A.* 111 D11
North Arm, *Canada* 104 A5
North Augusta, *U.S.A.* ... 109 J5
North Ayrshire □, *U.K.* .. 14 F4
North Bass I., *U.S.A.* 110 E2
North Battleford, *Canada* . 105 C7
North Bay, *Canada* 102 C4
North Belcher Is., *Canada* . 102 A4
North Bend, *Oreg., U.S.A.* . 114 E1
North Bend, *Pa., U.S.A.* .. 110 E7
North Bend, *Wash., U.S.A.* 116 C5
North Bennington, *U.S.A.* . 111 D11
North Berwick, *U.K.* 14 E6
North Berwick, *U.S.A.* ... 111 C14
North C., *Canada* 103 C7
North C., *N.Z.* 91 F4
North Canadian →, *U.S.A.* 113 H7
North Canton, *U.S.A.* ... 110 F3
North Cape = Nordkapp,
  Norway 8 A21
North Cape = Nordkapp,
  Svalbard 4 A9
North Caribou L., *Canada* . 102 B1
North Carolina □, *U.S.A.* .. 109 H6
North Cascades National
  Park, *U.S.A.* 114 B3
North Channel, *Canada* .. 102 C3
North Channel, *U.K.* 14 F3
North Charleston, *U.S.A.* . 109 J6
North Chicago, *U.S.A.* ... 108 D2
North Creek, *U.S.A.* 111 C11
North Dakota □, *U.S.A.* .. 112 B5
North Downs, *U.K.* 13 F8
North East, *U.S.A.* 110 D5
North East Frontier
  Agency = Arunachal
  Pradesh □, *India* 67 F19
North East Lincolnshire □,
  U.K. 12 D7
North Eastern □, *Kenya* .. 86 B5
North Esk →, *U.K.* 14 E6
North European Plain,
  Europe 6 E10
North Foreland, *U.K.* ... 13 F9
North Fork, *U.S.A.* 116 H7
North Fork American →,
  U.S.A. 116 G5
North Fork Feather →,
  U.S.A. 116 F5
North Fork Grand →,
  U.S.A. 112 C3
North Fork Red →, *U.S.A.* 113 H5
North Frisian Is. =
  Nordfriesische Inseln,
  Germany 24 A4
North Gower, *Canada* ... 111 A9
North Hd., *Australia* 93 F1
North Henik L., *Canada* . 105 A9
North Highlands, *U.S.A.* . 116 G5
North Horr, *Kenya* 86 B4
North I., *Kenya* 86 B4
North I., *N.Z.* 91 H5
North Kingsville, *U.S.A.* . 110 E4
North Knife →, *Canada* . 105 B10
North Koel →, *India* ... 69 G10
North Korea ■, *Asia* 57 E14
North Lakhimpur, *India* . 67 F19
North Lanarkshire □, *U.K.* 14 F5
North Las Vegas, *U.S.A.* . 117 J11
North Lincolnshire □, *U.K.* 12 D7
North Little Rock, *U.S.A.* . 113 H8
North Loup →, *U.S.A.* .. 112 E5
North Magnetic Pole,
  Canada 4 B2
North Minch, *U.K.* 14 C3
North Moose L., *Canada* . 105 C8
North Myrtle Beach, *U.S.A.* 109 J6
North Nahanni →, *Canada* 104 A4
North Olmsted, *U.S.A.* .. 110 E3
North Ossetia □, *Russia* .. 49 J7
North Pagai, I. = Pagai
  Utara, Pulau, *Indonesia* . 62 E2
North Palisade, *U.S.A.* .. 116 H8
North Platte, *U.S.A.* 112 E4
North Platte →, *U.S.A.* .. 112 E4
North Pole, *Arctic* ...... 4 A
North Portal, *Canada* ... 105 D8
North Powder, *U.S.A.* ... 114 D5
North Pt., *U.S.A.* 110 A1
North Rhine Westphalia =
  Nordrhein-Westfalen □,
  Germany 24 D3
North River, *Canada* ... 103 B8
North Ronaldsay, *U.K.* .. 14 B6
North Saskatchewan →,
  Canada 105 C7
North Sea, *Europe* 6 D6
North Seal →, *Canada* .. 105 B9
North Somerset □, *U.K.* . 13 F5
North Sporades = Vóriai
  Sporádhes, *Greece* 38 B5
North Sydney, *Canada* .. 103 C7
North Taranaki Bight, *N.Z.* 91 H5
North Thompson →,
  Canada 104 C4
North Tonawanda, *U.S.A.* 110 C6
North Troy, *U.S.A.* 111 B12
North Truchas Pk., *U.S.A.* 115 J11
North Twin I., *Canada* .. 102 B4
North Tyne →, *U.K.* 12 B5
North Uist, *U.K.* 14 D1
North Vancouver, *Canada* 104 D4
North Vernon, *U.S.A.* ... 108 F3

North Wabasca L., *Canada*	.	104	B6
North Walsham, *U.K.*		12	E9
North-West □, *S. Africa*		88	D4
North West C., *Australia*		92	D1
North West Christmas I. Ridge, *Pac. Oc.*		97	G11
North West Frontier □, *Pakistan*		68	C4
North West Highlands, *U.K.*		14	D4
North West River, *Canada*		103	B7
North Western □, *Zambia*		87	E2
North Wildwood, *U.S.A.*		108	F8
North York Moors, *U.K.*		12	C7
North Yorkshire □, *U.K.*		12	C6
Northallerton, *U.K.*		12	C6
Northam, *Australia*		93	F2
Northam, *S. Africa*		88	C4
Northampton, *Australia*		93	E1
Northampton, *U.K.*		13	E7
Northampton, *Mass., U.S.A.*		111	D12
Northampton, *Pa., U.S.A.*		111	F9
Northamptonshire □, *U.K.*		13	E7
Northbridge, *U.S.A.*		111	D13
Northcliffe, *Australia*		93	F2
Northeast Providence Chan., *W. Indies*		120	A4
Northeim, *Germany*		24	D6
Northern □, *Ghana*		83	D4
Northern □, *Malawi*		87	E3
Northern □, *Uganda*		86	B3
Northern □, *Zambia*		87	E3
Northern Cape □, *S. Africa*		88	D3
Northern Circars, *India*		67	L13
Northern Indian L., *Canada*		105	B9
Northern Ireland □, *U.K.*		15	B5
Northern Light L., *Canada*		102	C1
Northern Marianas ■, *Pac. Oc.*		96	F6
Northern Province □, *S. Leone*		82	D2
Northern Province □, *S. Africa*		89	C4
Northern Territory □, *Australia*		92	D5
Northfield, *Minn., U.S.A.*		112	C8
Northfield, *Vt., U.S.A.*		111	B12
Northland □, *N.Z.*		91	F4
Northome, *U.S.A.*		112	B7
Northport, *Ala., U.S.A.*		109	J2
Northport, *Wash., U.S.A.*		114	B5
Northumberland □, *U.K.*		12	B6
Northumberland, C., *Australia*		95	F3
Northumberland Is., *Australia*		94	C4
Northumberland Str., *Canada*		103	C7
Northville, *U.S.A.*		111	C10
Northwest Providence Channel, *W. Indies*		120	A4
Northwest Territories □, *Canada*		100	B9
Northwood, *Iowa, U.S.A.*		112	D8
Northwood, *N. Dak., U.S.A.*		112	B6
Norton, *U.S.A.*		112	F5
Norton, *Zimbabwe*		87	F3
Norton Sd., *U.S.A.*		100	B3
Nortorf, *Germany*		24	A5
Norwalk, *Calif., U.S.A.*		117	M8
Norwalk, *Conn., U.S.A.*		111	E11
Norwalk, *Iowa, U.S.A.*		112	E8
Norwalk, *Ohio, U.S.A.*		110	E2
Norway, *Maine, U.S.A.*		109	C10
Norway, *Mich., U.S.A.*		108	C2
Norway ■, *Europe*		8	E14
Norway House, *Canada*		105	C9
Norwegian Sea, *Atl. Oc.*		4	C8
Norwich, *Canada*		110	D4
Norwich, *U.K.*		13	E9
Norwich, *Conn., U.S.A.*		111	E12
Norwich, *N.Y., U.S.A.*		111	D9
Norwood, *Canada*		110	B7
Norwood, *U.S.A.*		111	B10
Noshiro, *Japan*		54	D10
Nosivka, *Ukraine*		47	G6
Nosovka = Nosivka, *Ukraine*		47	G6
Noṣratābād, *Iran*		71	D8
Noss Hd., *U.K.*		14	C5
Nossebro, *Sweden*		11	F6
Nossob →, *S. Africa*		88	D3
Nossombougou, *Mali*		82	C3
Nosy Barren, *Madag.*		85	H8
Nosy Be, *Madag.*		85	G9
Nosy Boraha, *Madag.*		89	B8
Nosy Lava, *Madag.*		89	A8
Nosy Varika, *Madag.*		89	C8
Noteć →, *Poland*		45	F2
Notikewin →, *Canada*		104	B5
Notios Evvoïkos Kólpos, *Greece*		38	C5
Noto, *Italy*		31	F8
Noto, G. di, *Italy*		31	F8
Notodden, *Norway*		9	G13
Notre Dame B., *Canada*		103	C8
Notre Dame de Koartac = Quaqtaq, *Canada*		101	B13
Notre-Dame-des-Bois, *Canada*		111	A13
Notre Dame d'Ivugivic = Ivujivik, *Canada*		101	B12
Notre-Dame-du-Nord, *Canada*		102	C4
Notsé, *Togo*		83	D5
Nottawasaga B., *Canada*		110	B4
Nottaway →, *Canada*		102	B4
Nottingham, *U.K.*		12	E6
Nottingham, City of □, *U.K.*		12	E6
Nottingham I., *Canada*		101	B12
Nottinghamshire □, *U.K.*		12	D6
Nottoway →, *U.S.A.*		108	G7
Notwane →, *Botswana*		88	C4

Nouâdhibou, *Mauritania*		78	D2
Nouâdhibou, Ras, *Mauritania*		78	D2
Nouakchott, *Mauritania*		82	B1
Nouâmghâr, *Mauritania*		82	B1
Nouméa, *N. Cal.*		96	K8
Nouna, *Burkina Faso*		82	C4
Noupoort, *S. Africa*		88	E3
Nouveau Comptoir = Wemindji, *Canada*		102	B4
Nouvelle-Amsterdam, I., *Ind. Oc.*		3	F13
Nouvelle-Calédonie = New Caledonia ■, *Pac. Oc.*		96	K8
Nouzonville, *France*		19	C11
Nová Baňa, *Slovak Rep.*		27	C11
Nová Bystřice, *Czech Rep.*		26	B8
Nova Casa Nova, *Brazil*		125	E10
Nova Esperança, *Brazil*		127	A5
Nova Friburgo, *Brazil*		127	A7
Nova Gaia = Cambundi-Catembo, *Angola*		84	G3
Nova Gorica, *Slovenia*		29	C10
Nova Gradiška, *Croatia*		42	E2
Nova Iguaçu, *Brazil*		127	A7
Nova Iorque, *Brazil*		125	E10
Nova Kakhovka, *Ukraine*		47	J7
Nova Lamego, *Guinea-Biss.*		82	C2
Nova Lima, *Brazil*		127	A7
Nova Lisboa = Huambo, *Angola*		85	G3
Nova Lusitânia, *Mozam.*		87	F3
Nova Mambone, *Mozam.*		89	C6
Nova Odesa, *Ukraine*		47	J6
Nová Paka, *Czech Rep.*		26	A8
Nova Pavova, *Serbia, Yug.*		42	F5
Nova Scotia □, *Canada*		103	C7
Nova Siri, *Italy*		31	B9
Nova Sofala, *Mozam.*		89	C5
Nova Varoš, *Serbia, Yug.*		40	C3
Nova Venécia, *Brazil*		125	G10
Nova Zagora, *Bulgaria*		41	D10
Novaci, *Macedonia*		40	E5
Novaci, *Romania*		43	E8
Novaféltria, *Italy*		29	E9
Novaleksandrovskaya = Novoaleksandrovsk, *Russia*		49	H5
Novannenskiy = Novoannenskiy, *Russia*		48	E6
Novar, *Canada*		110	A5
Novara, *Italy*		28	C5
Novato, *U.S.A.*		116	G4
Novaya Kakhovka = Nova Kakhovka, *Ukraine*		47	J7
Novaya Kazanka, *Kazakstan*		49	F9
Novaya Ladoga, *Russia*		46	B7
Novaya Lyalya, *Russia*		50	D7
Novaya Sibir, Ostrov, *Russia*		51	B16
Novaya Zemlya, *Russia*		50	B6
Nové Město, *Slovak Rep.*		27	C10
Nové Město na Moravě, *Czech Rep.*		26	B9
Nové Město nad Metují, *Czech Rep.*		27	A9
Nové Zámky, *Slovak Rep.*		27	C11
Novelda, *Spain*		33	G4
Novellara, *Italy*		28	D7
Noventa Vicentina, *Italy*		29	C8
Novgorod, *Russia*		46	C6
Novgorod-Severskiy = Novhorod-Siverskyy, *Ukraine*		47	G7
Novhorod-Siverskyy, *Ukraine*		47	G7
Novi Bečej, *Serbia, Yug.*		42	E5
Novi Iskar, *Bulgaria*		40	D7
Novi Kneževac, *Serbia, Yug.*		42	D5
Novi Lígure, *Italy*		28	D5
Novi Pazar, *Bulgaria*		41	C11
Novi Pazar, *Serbia, Yug.*		40	C4
Novi Sad, *Serbia, Yug.*		42	E4
Novi Slankamen, *Serbia, Yug.*		42	E5
Novi Travnik, *Bos.-H.*		42	F2
Novi Vinodolski, *Croatia*		29	C11
Novigrad, *Istra, Croatia*		29	C10
Novigrad, *Zadar, Croatia*		29	D12
Novigradsko More, *Croatia*		29	D12
Nôvo Hamburgo, *Brazil*		127	B5
Novo Mesto, *Slovenia*		29	C12
Novo Miloševo, *Serbia, Yug.*		42	E5
Novo Remanso, *Brazil*		125	E10
Novoaleksandrovsk, *Russia*		49	H5
Novoannenskiy, *Russia*		48	E6
Novoataysk, *Russia*		50	D9
Novoazovsk, *Ukraine*		47	J10
Novocheboksarsk, *Russia*		48	B8
Novocherkassk, *Russia*		49	G5
Novodevichye, *Russia*		48	D9
Novogrudok = Navahrudak, *Belarus*		46	F3
Novohrad-Volynskyy, *Ukraine*		47	G4
Novokachalinsk, *Russia*		54	B6
Novokazalinsk = Zhangaqazaly, *Kazakstan*		50	E7
Novokhopersk, *Russia*		48	E5
Novokuybyshevsk, *Russia*		48	D9
Novokuznetsk, *Russia*		50	D9
Novomirgorod, *Ukraine*		47	H6
Novomoskovsk, *Russia*		46	E10
Novomoskovsk, *Ukraine*		47	H8
Novopolotsk = Navapolatsk, *Belarus*		46	E5
Novorossiysk, *Russia*		47	K9
Novorybnoye, *Russia*		51	B11
Novorzhev, *Russia*		46	D5
Novosej, *Albania*		40	E4
Novoselytsya, *Ukraine*		47	H4
Novoshakhtinsk, *Russia*		47	J10
Novosibirsk, *Russia*		50	D9

Novosibirskiye Ostrova, *Russia*		51	B15
Novosil, *Russia*		47	F9
Novosokolniki, *Russia*		46	D6
Novotitarovskaya, *Russia*		49	H4
Novotroitsk, *Russia*		50	D6
Novoukrayinka, *Ukraine*		47	H6
Novouzensk, *Russia*		48	E9
Novovolynsk, *Ukraine*		47	G3
Novovoronezhskiy, *Russia*		47	G10
Novozybkov, *Russia*		47	F6
Novska, *Croatia*		29	C14
Novvy Urengoy, *Russia*		50	C8
Nové Bor, *Czech Rep.*		26	A7
Novy Bug = Novyy Buh, *Ukraine*		47	J7
Nový Bydžov, *Czech Rep.*		26	A8
Nový Dwór Mazowiecki, *Poland*		45	F7
Nový Jičín, *Czech Rep.*		27	B11
Novyy Afon, *Georgia*		49	J5
Novyy Buh, *Ukraine*		47	J7
Novyy Oskol, *Russia*		47	G9
Novyy Port, *Russia*		50	C8
Now Shahr, *Iran*		71	B6
Nowa Deba, *Poland*		45	H8
Nowa Ruda, *Poland*		45	H3
Nowa Sarzyna, *Poland*		45	H9
Nowa Sól, *Poland*		45	G2
Nowata, *U.S.A.*		113	G7
Nowbarān, *Iran*		71	C6
Nowe, *Poland*		44	E5
Nowe Miasteczko, *Poland*		45	G2
Nowe Miasto, *Poland*		45	G7
Nowe Miasto Lubawskie, *Poland*		44	E6
Nowe Skalmierzyce, *Poland*		45	G4
Nowe Warpno, *Poland*		44	E1
Nowghāb, *Iran*		71	C8
Nowgong, *Assam, India*		67	F18
Nowgong, *Mad. P., India*		69	G8
Nowogard, *Poland*		44	E2
Nowogród, *Poland*		45	E8
Nowogród Bobrzanski, *Poland*		45	G2
Nowogrodziec, *Poland*		45	G2
Nowra-Bomaderry, *Australia*		95	E5
Nowshera, *Pakistan*		66	C8
Nowy Dwór Gdański, *Poland*		44	D6
Nowy Sącz, *Poland*		45	J7
Nowy Staw, *Poland*		44	D6
Nowy Targ, *Poland*		45	J7
Nowy Tomyśl, *Poland*		45	F3
Nowy Wiśnicz, *Poland*		45	J7
Noxen, *U.S.A.*		111	E8
Noxon, *U.S.A.*		114	C6
Noyabr'sk, *Russia*		50	C8
Noyant, *France*		18	E7
Noyers, *France*		19	E10
Noyon, *France*		19	C9
Noyon, *Mongolia*		56	C2
Nozay, *France*		18	E5
Nqutu, *S. Africa*		89	D5
Nsanje, *Malawi*		87	F4
Nsawam, *Ghana*		83	D4
Nsomba, *Zambia*		87	E2
Nsukka, *Nigeria*		83	D6
Ntui, *Cameroon*		83	E7
Nu Jiang →, *China*		58	E2
Nu Shan, *China*		58	E2
Nuba Mts. = Nubah, Jibalal, *Sudan*		81	E3
Nubah, Jibalal, *Sudan*		81	E3
Nubia, *Africa*		76	D7
Nubian Desert = Nûbîya, Es Sahrâ en, *Sudan*		80	C3
Nûbîya, Es Sahrâ en, *Sudan*		80	C3
Nubledo, *Spain*		34	B5
Nuboai, *Indonesia*		63	E9
Nubra →, *India*		69	B7
Nucet, *Romania*		42	D7
Nueces →, *U.S.A.*		113	M6
Nueltin L., *Canada*		105	A9
Nueva Asunción □, *Paraguay*		126	A3
Nueva Carteya, *Spain*		35	H6
Nueva Gerona, *Cuba*		120	B3
Nueva Palmira, *Uruguay*		126	C4
Nueva Rosita, *Mexico*		118	B4
Nueva San Salvador, *El Salv.*		120	D2
Nueva Tabarca, *Spain*		33	G4
Nuéve de Julio, *Argentina*		126	D3
Nuevitas, *Cuba*		120	B4
Nuevo, G., *Argentina*		128	E4
Nuevo Casas Grandes, *Mexico*		118	A3
Nuevo Guerrero, *Mexico*		119	B5
Nuevo Laredo, *Mexico*		119	B5
Nuevo León □, *Mexico*		118	C5
Nuevo Rocafuerte, *Ecuador*		124	D3
Nugget Pt., *N.Z.*		91	M2
Nugrus, Gebel, *Egypt*		80	C3
Nuhaka, *N.Z.*		91	H6
Nukey Bluff, *Australia*		95	E2
Nukheila, *Sudan*		80	D2
Nukhuyb, *Iraq*		70	C4
Nuku'alofa, *Tonga*		91	E12
Nukus, *Uzbekistan*		50	E6
Nules, *Spain*		32	F4
Nullagine, *Australia*		92	D3
Nullagine →, *Australia*		92	D3
Nullarbor, *Australia*		93	F5
Nullarbor Plain, *Australia*		93	F4
Numalla, L., *Australia*		95	D3
Numan, *Nigeria*		83	D7
Numata, *Japan*		55	F9
Numatinna →, *Sudan*		81	F2
Numazu, *Japan*		55	G9
Numbulwar, *Australia*		94	A2

Numfoor, *Indonesia*		63	E8
Numurkah, *Australia*		95	F4
Nunaksaluk I., *Canada*		103	A7
Nunap Isua, *Greenland*		101	D15
Nunavut □, *Canada*		101	B11
Nunda, *U.S.A.*		110	D7
Nungarin, *Australia*		93	F2
Nungo, *Mozam.*		87	E4
Nungwe, *Tanzania*		86	C3
Nunivak I., *U.S.A.*		100	B3
Nunkun, *India*		69	C7
Núoro, *Italy*		30	B2
Nūrābād, *Iran*		71	E8
Nure →, *Italy*		28	C7
Nuremberg = Nürnberg, *Germany*		25	F7
Nuri, *Mexico*		118	B3
Nuriootpa, *Australia*		95	E2
Nurlat, *Russia*		48	C10
Nurmes, *Finland*		8	E23
Nürnberg, *Germany*		25	F7
Nurpur, *Pakistan*		68	D4
Nurra, La, *Italy*		30	B1
Nurran, L. = Terewah, L., *Australia*		95	D4
Nurrari Lakes, *Australia*		93	E5
Nurri, *Italy*		30	C2
Nürtingen, *Germany*		25	G5
Nurzec →, *Poland*		45	F9
Nus, *Italy*		28	C4
Nusa Barung, *Indonesia*		63	H15
Nusa Kambangan, *Indonesia*		63	G13
Nusa Tenggara Barat □, *Indonesia*		62	F5
Nusa Tenggara Timur □, *Indonesia*		63	F6
Nusaybin, *Turkey*		73	D9
Nushki, *Pakistan*		68	E2
Nuuk, *Greenland*		101	B14
Nuwakot, *Nepal*		69	E10
Nuweiba', *Egypt*		70	D2
Nuwerus, *S. Africa*		88	E2
Nuweveldberge, *S. Africa*		88	E3
Nuyts, C., *Australia*		93	F5
Nuyts, Pt., *Australia*		93	G2
Nuyts Arch., *Australia*		95	E1
Nxau-Nxau, *Botswana*		88	B3
Nyaake, *Liberia*		82	E3
Nyabing, *Australia*		93	F2
Nyack, *U.S.A.*		111	E11
Nyagan, *Russia*		50	C7
Nyahanga, *Tanzania*		86	C3
Nyahua, *Tanzania*		86	D3
Nyahururu, *Kenya*		86	B4
Nyainqentanglha Shan, *China*		60	C4
Nyakanazi, *Tanzania*		86	C3
Nyakrom, *Ghana*		83	D4
Nyâlâ, *Sudan*		81	E1
Nyamandhlovu, *Zimbabwe*		87	F2
Nyambiti, *Tanzania*		86	C3
Nyamlell, *Sudan*		81	F2
Nyamwaga, *Tanzania*		86	C3
Nyandekwa, *Tanzania*		86	C3
Nyanding →, *Sudan*		81	F3
Nyandoma, *Russia*		46	B11
Nyangana, *Namibia*		88	B3
Nyanguge, *Tanzania*		86	C3
Nyankpala, *Ghana*		83	D4
Nyanza, *Rwanda*		86	C2
Nyanza □, *Kenya*		86	C3
Nyanza-Lac, *Burundi*		86	C2
Nyapongeta, *Sudan*		81	F3
Nyasa, L., *Africa*		87	E3
Nyasvizh, *Belarus*		47	F4
Nyazura, *Zimbabwe*		87	F3
Nyazwidzi →, *Zimbabwe*		87	G3
Nyborg, *Denmark*		11	J4
Nybro, *Sweden*		11	H9
Nyda, *Russia*		50	C8
Nyeri, *Kenya*		86	C4
Nyerol, *Sudan*		81	F3
Nyhammar, *Sweden*		10	D8
Nyinahin, *Ghana*		82	D4
Nyíradony, *Hungary*		42	C6
Nyírbátor, *Hungary*		42	C7
Nyíregyháza, *Hungary*		42	C6
Nykøbing, Storstrøm, *Denmark*		11	K5
Nykøbing, Vestsjælland, *Denmark*		11	J5
Nykøbing, Viborg, *Denmark*		11	H2
Nyköping, *Sweden*		11	F11
Nykroppa, *Sweden*		10	E8
Nykvarn, *Sweden*		10	E11
Nyland, *Sweden*		10	A11
Nylstroom, *S. Africa*		89	C4
Nymagee, *Australia*		95	E4
Nymburk, *Czech Rep.*		26	A8
Nynäshamn, *Sweden*		11	F11
Nyngan, *Australia*		95	E4
Nyoma Rap, *India*		69	C8
Nyoman = Neman →, *Lithuania*		9	J20
Nyon, *Switz.*		25	J2
Nyong →, *Cameroon*		83	E6
Nyons, *France*		21	D9
Nyou, *Burkina Faso*		83	C4
Ný̌rsko, *Czech Rep.*		26	B6
Nysa, *Poland*		45	H4
Nysa →, *Europe*		24	C10
Nysa Kłodzka →, *Poland*		45	H4
Nysäter, *Sweden*		10	E6
Nyssa, *U.S.A.*		114	E5
Nysted, *Denmark*		11	K5
Nyunzu, *Dem. Rep. of the Congo*		86	D2
Nyurba, *Russia*		51	C12
Nyzhnohirskyy, *Ukraine*		47	K8
Nzébéla, *Guinea*		82	D3

Nzega, *Tanzania*		86	C3
Nzérékoré, *Guinea*		82	D3
Nzeto, *Angola*		84	F2
Nzilo, Chutes de, *Dem. Rep. of the Congo*		87	E2
Nzo →, *Ivory C.*		82	D3
Nzubuka, *Tanzania*		86	C3

O

O Barco, *Spain*		34	C4
O Carballiño, *Spain*		34	C2
O Corgo, *Spain*		34	C3
O Pino, *Spain*		34	C2
O Porriño, *Spain*		34	C2
Ō-Shima, *Japan*		55	G9
Oa, Mull of, *U.K.*		14	F2
Oacoma, *U.S.A.*		112	D5
Oahe, L., *U.S.A.*		112	C4
Oahe Dam, *U.S.A.*		112	C4
Oahu, *U.S.A.*		106	H16
Oak Harbor, *U.S.A.*		116	B4
Oak Hill, *U.S.A.*		108	G5
Oak Ridge, *U.S.A.*		109	G3
Oak View, *U.S.A.*		117	L7
Oakan-Dake, *Japan*		54	C12
Oakdale, *Calif., U.S.A.*		116	H6
Oakdale, *La., U.S.A.*		113	K8
Oakes, *U.S.A.*		112	B5
Oakesdale, *U.S.A.*		114	C5
Oakey, *Australia*		95	D5
Oakfield, *U.S.A.*		110	C6
Oakham, *U.K.*		13	E7
Oakhurst, *U.S.A.*		116	H7
Oakland, *U.S.A.*		116	H4
Oakley, *Idaho, U.S.A.*		114	E7
Oakley, *Kans., U.S.A.*		112	F4
Oakover →, *Australia*		92	D3
Oakridge, *U.S.A.*		114	E2
Oakville, *Canada*		110	C5
Oakville, *U.S.A.*		116	D3
Oamaru, *N.Z.*		91	L3
Oancea, *Romania*		43	E12
Oasis, *Calif., U.S.A.*		117	M10
Oasis, *Nev., U.S.A.*		116	H9
Oates Land, *Antarctica*		5	C11
Oatlands, *Australia*		95	G4
Oatman, *U.S.A.*		117	K12
Oaxaca, *Mexico*		119	D5
Oaxaca □, *Mexico*		119	D5
Ob →, *Russia*		50	C7
Oba, *Canada*		102	C3
Obala, *Cameroon*		83	E7
Obama, *Japan*		55	G7
Oban, *Nigeria*		83	D6
Oban, *U.K.*		14	E3
Obbia = Hobyo, *Somali Rep.*		74	F4
Obera, *Argentina*		127	B4
Oberammergau, *Germany*		25	H7
Oberasbach, *Germany*		25	F6
Oberbayern □, *Germany*		25	G7
Oberdrauburg, *Austria*		26	E5
Oberfranken □, *Germany*		25	E7
Oberhausen, *Germany*		24	D2
Oberkirch, *Germany*		25	G4
Oberlausitz, *Germany*		24	D10
Oberlin, *Kans., U.S.A.*		112	F4
Oberlin, *La., U.S.A.*		113	K8
Oberlin, *Ohio, U.S.A.*		110	E2
Obernai, *France*		19	D14
Oberndorf, *Germany*		25	G4
Oberon, *Australia*		95	E4
Oberösterreich □, *Austria*		26	C7
Oberpfalz □, *Germany*		25	F8
Oberpfälzer Wald, *Germany*		25	F8
Oberstdorf, *Germany*		25	H6
Obersdorf, *Germany*		25	H6
Oberursel, *Germany*		25	E4
Oberwart, *Austria*		27	D9
Obi, Kepulauan, *Indonesia*		63	E7
Obi Is. = Obi, Kepulauan, *Indonesia*		63	E7
Obiaruku, *Nigeria*		83	D6
Óbidos, *Brazil*		125	D7
Óbidos, *Portugal*		35	F1
Obihiro, *Japan*		54	C11
Obilatu, *Indonesia*		63	E7
Obilnoye, *Russia*		49	G7
Obing, *Germany*		25	G8
Objat, *France*		20	C5
Obluchye, *Russia*		51	E14
Obninsk, *Russia*		46	E9
Obo, *C.A.R.*		86	A2
Oboa, Mt., *Uganda*		86	B3
Obock, *Djibouti*		81	E5
Oborniki, *Poland*		45	F3
Oborniki Śląskie, *Poland*		45	G3
Oboyan, *Russia*		47	G9
Obozerskaya = Obozerskiy, *Russia*		50	C5
Obozerskiy, *Russia*		50	C5
Obrenovac, *Serbia, Yug.*		40	B4
Obrovac, *Croatia*		29	D12
Obruk, *Turkey*		72	C5
Observatory Inlet, *Canada*		104	B3
Obshchi Syrt, *Russia*		6	E16
Obskaya Guba, *Russia*		50	C8
Obuasi, *Ghana*		83	D4
Obubra, *Nigeria*		83	D6
Obudu, *Nigeria*		83	D6
Obwalden □, *Switz.*		25	J4
Obzor, *Bulgaria*		41	D11
Ocala, *U.S.A.*		109	L4
Ocampo, *Chihuahua, Mexico*		118	B3
Ocampo, *Tamaulipas, Mexico*		119	C5
Ocaña, *Spain*		34	F7
Ocanomowoc, *U.S.A.*		112	D10

Occidental, Cordillera,
  Colombia 122 C3
Ocean City, Md., U.S.A. .. 108 F8
Ocean City, N.J., U.S.A. .. 108 F8
Ocean City, Wash., U.S.A. 116 C2
Ocean Falls, Canada 104 C3
Ocean I. = Banaba, Kiribati 96 H8
Ocean Park, U.S.A. 116 C2
Oceano, U.S.A. 117 K6
Oceanport, U.S.A. 111 F10
Oceanside, U.S.A. 117 M9
Ochagavía, Spain 32 C3
Ochakiv, Ukraine 47 J6
Ochamchira, Georgia 49 J5
Ochil Hills, U.K. 14 E5
Ochsenfurt, Germany 25 F6
Ochsenhausen, Germany ... 25 G5
Ocilla, U.S.A. 109 K4
Ockelbo, Sweden 10 D10
Ocmulgee →, U.S.A. 109 K4
Ocna Mureş, Romania 43 D8
Ocna Sibiului, Romania .. 43 E9
Ocnele Mari, Romania ... 43 E9
Ocniţa, Moldova 43 B12
Oconee →, U.S.A. 109 K4
Oconto, U.S.A. 108 C2
Oconto Falls, U.S.A. 108 C1
Ocosingo, Mexico 119 D6
Ocotal, Nic. 120 D2
Ocotlán, Mexico 118 C4
Ocotlán de Morelos, Mexico 119 D5
Ocreza →, Portugal 35 F3
Ócsa, Hungary 42 C4
Octeville, France 18 C5
Oda, Ghana 83 D4
Ōda, Japan 55 G6
Oda, J., Sudan 80 C4
Ódáðahraun, Iceland 8 D5
Ódákra, Sweden 11 H6
Odate, Japan 54 D10
Odawara, Japan 55 G9
Odda, Norway 9 F12
Odder, Denmark 11 J4
Odei →, Canada 105 B9
Odemira, Portugal 35 H2
Ödemiş, Turkey 39 C9
Odendaalsrus, S. Africa ... 88 D4
Odensbacken, Sweden 10 E9
Odense, Denmark 11 J4
Odenwald, Germany 25 F5
Oder →, Europe 24 B10
Oder-Havel Kanal, Germany 24 C10
Oderzo, Italy 29 C9
Odesa, Ukraine 47 J6
Ödeshög, Sweden 11 F8
Odessa = Odesa, Ukraine . 47 J6
Odessa, Canada 111 B8
Odessa, Tex., U.S.A. 113 K3
Odessa, Wash., U.S.A. ... 114 C4
Odiakwe, Botswana 88 C4
Odiel →, Spain 35 H4
Odienné, Ivory C. 82 D3
Odintsovo, Russia 46 E9
Odiongan, Phil. 61 E4
Odobeşti, Romania 43 E12
Odolanów, Poland 45 G4
O'Donnell, U.S.A. 113 J4
Odorheiu Secuiesc, Romania 43 D10
Odoyevo, Russia 46 F9
Odra = Oder →, Europe .. 24 B10
Odra →, Spain 34 C6
Odžaci, Serbia, Yug. 42 E4
Odžak, Bos.-H. 42 E4
Odzi, Zimbabwe 89 B5
Odzi →, Zimbabwe 89 B5
Oebisfelde, Germany 24 C6
Oeiras, Brazil 125 E10
Oeiras, Portugal 35 G1
Oelrichs, U.S.A. 112 D3
Oelsnitz, Germany 25 E8
Oelwein, U.S.A. 112 D9
Oenpelli, Australia 92 B5
Oetz, Austria 26 D3
Of, Turkey 73 B9
Ofanto →, Italy 31 A9
Offa, Nigeria 83 D5
Offaly □, Ireland 15 C4
Offenbach, Germany 25 E4
Offenburg, Germany 25 G3
Offida, Italy 29 F10
Ofidhousa, Greece 39 E8
Ofotfjorden, Norway 8 B17
Ōfunato, Japan 54 E10
Oga, Japan 54 E9
Oga-Hantō, Japan 54 E9
Ōgaki, Japan 55 G8
Ogallala, U.S.A. 112 E4
Ogasawara Gunto, Pac. Oc. 52 G18
Ogbomosho, Nigeria 83 D5
Ogden, U.S.A. 114 F7
Ogdensburg, U.S.A. 111 B9
Ogeechee →, U.S.A. 109 K5
Ogilby, U.S.A. 117 N12
Oglio →, Italy 28 C7
Ogmore, Australia 94 C4
Ognon →, France 19 E12
Ogoja, Nigeria 83 D6
Ogoki, Canada 102 B2
Ogoki →, Canada 102 B2
Ogoki L., Canada 102 B2
Ogoki Res., Canada 102 B2
Ogooué →, Gabon 84 E1
Ogosta →, Bulgaria 40 C7
Ogowe = Ogooué →,
  Gabon 84 E1
Ogr = Sharafa, Sudan ... 81 E2
Ograźden, Macedonia ... 40 E6
Ogre, Latvia 9 H21
Ogrein, Sudan 80 D3
Ogulin, Croatia 29 C12

Ogun □, Nigeria 83 D5
Ogurchinskiy, Ostrov,
  Turkmenistan 71 B7
Oguta, Nigeria 83 D6
Ogwashi-Uku, Nigeria .. 83 D6
Ogwe, Nigeria 83 E6
Ohai, N.Z. 91 L2
Ohakune, N.Z. 91 H5
Ohata, Japan 54 D10
Ohau, L., N.Z. 91 L2
Ohio □, U.S.A. 110 F2
Ohio →, U.S.A. 108 G1
Ohře →, Czech Rep. 26 A7
Ohre →, Germany 24 C7
Ohrid, Macedonia 40 E4
Ohridsko Jezero, Macedonia 40 E4
Ohrigstad, S. Africa 89 C5
Öhringen, Germany 25 F5
Oi Qu, China 58 C2
Oiapoque, Brazil 125
Oikou, China 57 E9
Oil City, U.S.A. 110 E5
Oil Springs, Canada ... 110 D2
Oildale, U.S.A. 117 K7
Oinousa, Greece 39 C8
Oise □, France 19 C9
Oise →, France 19 C9
Ōita, Japan 55 H5
Ōita □, Japan 55 H5
Oiticica, Brazil 125 E10
Ojacaliente, Mexico ... 118 C4
Ojai, U.S.A. 117 L7
Ojinaga, Mexico 118 B4
Ojiya, Japan 55 F9
Ojos del Salado, Cerro,
  Argentina 126 B2
Okaba, Indonesia 63 F9
Okahandja, Namibia ... 88 C2
Okahukura, N.Z. 91 H5
Okanagan L., Canada .. 104 D5
Okanogan, U.S.A. 114 B4
Okanogan →, U.S.A. .. 114 B4
Okány, Hungary 42 D6
Okaputa, Namibia 88 C2
Okara, Pakistan 68 D5
Okarito, N.Z. 91 K3
Okaukuejo, Namibia .. 88 B2
Okavango Swamps,
  Botswana 88 B3
Okaya, Japan 55 F9
Okayama, Japan 55 G6
Okayama □, Japan 55 G6
Okazaki, Japan 55 G8
Oke-Iho, Nigeria 83 D5
Okeechobee, U.S.A. .. 109 M5
Okeechobee, L., U.S.A. 109 M5
Okefenokee Swamp, U.S.A. 109 K4
Okehampton, U.K. ... 13 G4
Okene, Nigeria 83 D6
Oker →, Germany 24 C6
Okha, India 68 H3
Okha, Russia 51 D15
Ókhi Óros, Greece 38 C6
Okhotsk, Russia 51 D15
Okhotsk, Sea of, Asia . 51 D15
Okhotskiy Perevoz, Russia 51 C14
Okhtyrka, Ukraine ... 47 G8
Oki-Shotō, Japan 55 F6
Okiep, S. Africa 88 D2
Okigwi, Nigeria 83 D6
Okija, Nigeria 83 D6
Okinawa □, Japan ... 55 L4
Okinawa-Guntō, Japan 55 L4
Okinawa-Jima, Japan . 55 L4
Okino-erabu-Shima, Japan . 55 L4
Okitipupa, Nigeria ... 83 D5
Oklahoma □, U.S.A. . 113 H6
Oklahoma City, U.S.A. 113 H6
Okmulgee, U.S.A. ... 113 H7
Oknitsa = Ocniţa, Moldova 43 B12
Oko, W. →, Sudan ... 80 C4
Okolo, Uganda 86 B3
Okolona, U.S.A. 113 J10
Okombahe, Namibia .. 88 C2
Okonek, Poland 44 E3
Okotoks, Canada 104 C6
Okrika, Nigeria 83 E6
Oksibil, Indonesia ... 63 E10
Oktabrsk = Oktyabrsk,
  Kazakstan 50 E6
Oktyabrsk, Kazakstan . 50 E6
Oktyabrsk, Russia ... 48 D9
Oktyabrskiy = Aktsyabrski,
  Belarus 47 F5
Oktyabrskiy, Russia .. 49 G5
Oktyabrskoy Revolyutsii,
  Ostrov, Russia 51 B10
Oktyabrskoye = Zhovtneve,
  Ukraine 47 J7
Okulovka, Russia 46 C7
Okuru, N.Z. 91 K2
Okushiri-Tō, Japan .. 54 C9
Okuta, Nigeria 83 D5
Okwa →, Botswana .. 88 C3
Ola, U.S.A. 113 H8
Ólafsfjörður, Iceland . 8 C4
Ólafsvík, Iceland 8 D2
Olaine, Latvia 44 B10
Olancha, U.S.A. 117 J8
Olancha Pk., U.S.A. . 117 J8
Olanchito, Honduras . 120 C2
Öland, Sweden 11 H10
Ölands norra udde, Sweden 11 G11
Ölands södra udde, Sweden 11 H10
Olargues, France 20 E6
Olary, Australia 95 E3
Olascoaga, Argentina . 126 D3
Olathe, U.S.A. 112 F7
Olavarría, Argentina . 126 D3
Oława, Poland 45 H4

Olbernhau, Germany 24 E9
Ólbia, Italy 30 B2
Ólbia, G. di, Italy 30 B2
Olching, Germany 25 G7
Olcott, U.S.A. 110 C6
Old Bahama Chan. =
  Bahama, Canal Viejo de,
  W. Indies 120 B4
Old Baldy Pk. = San
  Antonio, Mt., U.S.A. ... 117 L9
Old Castile = Castilla y
  Leon □, Spain 34 D6
Old Crow, Canada 100 B6
Old Dale, U.S.A. 117 L11
Old Dongola, Sudan 80 D3
Old Forge, N.Y., U.S.A. .. 111 C10
Old Forge, Pa., U.S.A. .. 111 E9
Old Perlican, Canada ... 103 C9
Old Shinyanga, Tanzania . 86 C3
Old Speck Mt., U.S.A. .. 111 B14
Old Town, U.S.A. 109 C11
Old Washington, U.S.A. . 110 F3
Old Wives L., Canada ... 105 C7
Oldbury, U.K. 13 F5
Oldcastle, Ireland 15 C4
Oldeani, Tanzania 86 C4
Oldenburg, Niedersachsen,
  Germany 24 B4
Oldenburg,
  Schleswig-Holstein,
  Germany 24 A6
Oldenzaal, Neths. 17 B6
Oldham, U.K. 12 D5
Oldman →, Canada 104 D6
Oldmeldrum, U.K. 14 D6
Olds, Canada 104 C6
Oldziyt, Mongolia 56 B5
Olean, U.S.A. 110 D6
Olecko, Poland 44 D9
Oléggio, Italy 28 C5
Oleiros, Portugal 34 F3
Oleiros, Spain 34 B2
Olekma →, Russia 51 C13
Olekminsk, Russia 51 C13
Oleksandriya, Kirovohrad,
  Ukraine 47 H7
Oleksandriya, Rivne, Ukraine 47 G4
Oleksandrovka, Ukraine . 47 H7
Olema, U.S.A. 116 G4
Olenek, Russia 51 C12
Olenek →, Russia 51 B13
Olenino, Russia 46 D7
Oléron, Î. d', France ... 20 C2
Oleśnica, Poland 45 G4
Olesno, Poland 45 H5
Olevsk, Ukraine 47 G4
Olga, Russia 51 E14
Olga, L., Canada 102 C4
Olga, Mt., Australia ... 93 E5
Ølgod, Denmark 11 J2
Olhão, Portugal 35 H3
Olib, Croatia 29 D11
Oliena, Italy 30 B2
Oliete, Spain 32 D4
Olifants →, Africa 89 C5
Olifants →, Namibia .. 88 C2
Olifantshoek, S. Africa . 88 D3
Ólimbos, Greece 39 F9
Ólimbos, Óros, Greece . 40 F6
Olímpia, Brazil 127 A6
Olinda, Brazil 125 E12
Olite, Spain 32 C3
Oliva, Argentina 126 C3
Oliva, Spain 33 G4
Oliva, Punta del, Spain . 34 B5
Oliva de la Frontera, Spain . 35 G4
Olivares, Spain 32 F2
Olivehurst, U.S.A. ... 116 F5
Oliveira de Azeméis,
  Portugal 34 E2
Oliveira do Douro, Portugal 34 D2
Olivenza, Spain 35 G3
Oliver, Canada 104 D5
Oliver L., Canada 105 B8
Olivet, France 19 E8
Olkhovka, Russia ... 48 F7
Olkusz, Poland 45 H6
Ollagüe, Chile 126 A2
Olmedo, Spain 34 D6
Olmeto, France 21 G12
Olney, Ill., U.S.A. .. 108 F1
Olney, Tex., U.S.A. . 113 J5
Olofström, Sweden .. 11 H8
Oloma, Cameroon ... 83 E7
Olomane →, Canada . 103 B7
Olomouc, Czech Rep. . 27 B10
Olonets, Russia 46 B7
Olongapo, Phil. 61 D4
Olonne-sur-Mer, France 20 B2
Oloron, Gave d' →, France 20 E2
Oloron-Ste-Marie, France .. 20 E3
Olot, Spain 32 C7
Olovo, Bos.-H. 42 F3
Olovyannaya, Russia . 51 D12
Oloy →, Russia 51 C16
Olsberg, Germany ... 24 D4
Olshanka, Ukraine .. 47 H6
Olshany, Ukraine ... 47 G8
Olsztyn, Poland 44 E7
Olsztynek, Poland .. 44 E7
Olt □, Romania 43 F9
Olt →, Romania 43 G9
Oltenița, Romania .. 43 F11
Oltet →, Romania .. 43 F9
Oltu, Turkey 73 B9
Oluanpi, Taiwan ... 59 G13
Olula del Rio, Spain . 33 H2
Olur, Turkey 73 B10
Olutanga, Phil. 61 H5

Olvega, Spain 32 D2
Olvera, Spain 35 J5
Olymbos, Cyprus 36 D12
Olympia, Greece 38 D3
Olympia, U.S.A. 116 D4
Olympic Dam, Australia . 95 E2
Olympic Mts., U.S.A. .. 116 C3
Olympic Nat. Park, U.S.A. 116 C3
Olympus, Cyprus 36 E11
Olympus, Mt. = Ólimbos,
  Óros, Greece 40 F6
Olympus, Mt., U.S.A. .. 116 C3
Olympus, Mt. = Uludağ,
  Turkey 41 F13
Om →, Russia 50 D8
Om Hajer, Eritrea 81 E4
Om Koi, Thailand 64 D2
Ōma, Japan 54 D10
Ōmachi, Japan 55 F8
Omae-Zaki, Japan 55 G9
Ōmagari, Japan 54 E10
Omagh, U.K. 15 B4
Omagh □, U.K. 15 B4
Omaha, U.S.A. 112 E7
Omak, U.S.A. 114 B4
Omalos, Greece 36 D5
Oman ■, Asia 74 C6
Oman, G. of, Asia 71 E8
Omaruru, Namibia ... 88 C2
Omaruru →, Namibia . 88 C1
Omate, Peru 124 G4
Ombai, Selat, Indonesia . 63 F6
Omboué, Gabon 84 E1
Ombrone →, Italy ... 28 F8
Omdurmân, Sudan ... 81 D3
Omega, Italy 28 C5
Omemee, Canada ... 110 B6
Omeo, Australia 95 F4
Omeonga,
  Dem. Rep. of the Congo . 86 C1
Ometepe, I. de, Nic. .. 120 D2
Ometepec, Mexico ... 119 D5
Ominato, Japan 54 D10
Omineca →, Canada . 104 B4
Omiš, Croatia 29 E13
Omišalj, Croatia 29 C11
Omitara, Namibia ... 88 C2
Ōmiya, Japan 55 G9
Omme Å →, Denmark 11 J2
Ommen, Neths. 17 B6
Ömnögovi □, Mongolia 56 C3
Omo →, Ethiopia ... 81 F4
Omodeo, L., Italy ... 30 B1
Omodhos, Cyprus ... 36 E11
Omoko, Nigeria 83 D6
Omolon →, Russia .. 51 C16
Omono-Gawa →, Japan 54 E10
Omsk, Russia 50 D8
Omsukchan, Russia . 51 C16
Ōmu, Japan 54 B11
Omul, Vf., Romania . 43 E10
Omulew →, Poland . 45 E8
Ōmura, Japan 55 H4
Omuramba Omatako →,
  Namibia 88 B2
Omuramba Ovambo →,
  Namibia 88 B2
Omurtag, Bulgaria .. 41 C10
Ōmuta, Japan 55 H5
Oña, Spain 34 C7
Onaga, U.S.A. 112 F6
Onalaska, U.S.A. ... 112 D9
Onancock, U.S.A. .. 108 G8
Onang, Indonesia .. 63 E5
Onaping L., Canada . 102 C3
Oñati, Spain 32 B2
Onavas, Mexico 118 B3
Onawa, U.S.A. 112 D6
Oncócua, Angola .. 88 B1
Onda, Spain 32 F4
Ondaejin, N. Korea . 57 D15
Ondangua, Namibia . 88 B2
Ondarroa, Spain ... 32 B2
Ondava →, Slovak Rep. 27 C14
Ondjiva, Angola ... 88 B2
Ondo, Nigeria 83 D5
Ondo □, Nigeria ... 83 D5
Öndörhaan, Mongolia 56 B6
Öndörshil, Mongolia . 56 B5
Öndverðarnes, Iceland . 8 D1
One Tree, Australia .. 95 E3
Onega, Russia 50 C4
Onega →, Russia ... 6 C13
Onega, L. = Onezhskoye
  Ozero, Russia 46 B8
Onehunga, N.Z. ... 91 G5
Oneida, U.S.A. 111 C9
Oneida L., U.S.A. .. 111 C9
O'Neill, U.S.A. 112 D5
Onekotan, Ostrov, Russia 51 E16
Onema,
  Dem. Rep. of the Congo . 86 C1
Oneonta, U.S.A. ... 111 D9
Oneşti, Romania ... 43 D11
Onezhskoye Ozero, Russia 46 B8
Ongarue, N.Z. 91 H5
Ongers →, S. Africa . 88 E3
Ongerup, Australia . 93 F2
Ongjin, N. Korea .. 57 F13
Ongkharak, Thailand 64 E3
Ongniud Qi, China . 57 C10
Ongoka,
  Dem. Rep. of the Congo . 86 C2
Ongole, India 66 M12
Ongon = Havirga, Mongolia 56 B7
Oni, Georgia 49 J6
Onida, U.S.A. 112 C4
Onilahy →, Madag. . 89 C7
Onitsha, Nigeria ... 83 D6
Onoda, Japan 55 G5
Onpyŏng-ni, S. Korea . 57 H14

Ons, I. de, Spain 34 C2
Onslow, Australia 92 D2
Onslow B., U.S.A. 109 H7
Ontake-San, Japan 55 G8
Ontario, Calif., U.S.A. .. 117 L9
Ontario, Oreg., U.S.A. .. 114 D5
Ontario □, Canada 102 B2
Ontario, L., N. Amer. ... 102 D4
Ontinyent, Spain 33 G4
Ontonagon, U.S.A. 112 B10
Ontur, Spain 33 G3
Onyx, U.S.A. 117 K8
Oodnadatta, Australia .. 95 D2
Ooldea, Australia 93 F5
Oombulgurri, Australia . 92 C4
Oorindi, Australia 94 C3
Oost-Vlaanderen □, Belgium 17 C3
Oostende, Belgium 17 C2
Oosterhout, Neths. 17 C4
Oosterschelde →, Neths. . 17 C4
Oosterwolde, Neths. ... 17 B6
Ootacamund =
  Udagamandalam, India . 66 P10
Ootsa L., Canada 104 C3
Opaka, Bulgaria 41 C10
Opala,
  Dem. Rep. of the Congo . 86 C1
Opalenica, Poland 45 F3
Opan, Bulgaria 41 D9
Opanake, Sri Lanka ... 66 R12
Opasatika, Canada ... 102 C3
Opasquia Prov. Park,
  Canada 102 B1
Opatija, Croatia 29 C11
Opatów, Poland 45 H8
Opava, Czech Rep. ... 27 B10
Opelika, U.S.A. 109 J3
Opelousas, U.S.A. ... 113 K8
Opémisca, L., Canada . 102 C5
Opheim, U.S.A. 114 B10
Ophthalmia Ra., Australia . 92 D2
Opi, Nigeria 83 D6
Opinaca →, Canada .. 102 B4
Opinaca, Rés., Canada . 102 B4
Opinnagau →, Canada . 102 B3
Opiscoteo, L., Canada . 103 B6
Opobo, Nigeria 83 E6
Opochka, Russia 46 D5
Opoczno, Poland 45 G7
Opol, Phil. 61 G6
Opole, Poland 45 H4
Opole Lubelskie, Poland . 45 G8
Opolskie □, Poland ... 45 H5
Oponono L., Namibia . 88 B2
Oporto = Porto, Portugal . 34 D2
Opotiki, N.Z. 91 H6
Opp, U.S.A. 109 K2
Oppdal, Norway 9 E13
Óppido Mamertina, Italy . 31 D8
Opportunity, U.S.A. .. 114 C5
Oprişor, Romania ... 42 F8
Oprtalj, Croatia 29 C10
Opua, N.Z. 91 F5
Opunake, N.Z. 91 H4
Opuwo, Namibia ... 88 B1
Opuzen, Croatia ... 29 E14
Ora, Cyprus 36 E12
Oracle, U.S.A. 115 K8
Oradea, Romania ... 42 C6
Öræfajökull, Iceland . 8 D5
Orahovac, Kosovo, Yug. . 40 D4
Orahovica, Croatia .. 42 E2
Orai, India 69 G8
Oraison, France 21 E9
Oral = Zhayyq →,
  Kazakstan 50 E6
Oral, Kazakstan 48 E10
Oran, Algeria 78 A5
Orange, Australia ... 95 E4
Orange, France 21 D8
Orange, Calif., U.S.A. . 117 M9
Orange, Mass., U.S.A. . 111 D12
Orange, Tex., U.S.A. . 113 K8
Orange, Va., U.S.A. .. 108 F6
Orange →, S. Africa .. 88 D2
Orange, C., Brazil ... 122 C5
Orange Cove, U.S.A. . 116 J7
Orange Free State = Free
  State □, S. Africa ... 88 D4
Orange Grove, U.S.A. . 113 M6
Orange Walk, Belize .. 119 D7
Orangeburg, U.S.A. .. 109 J5
Orangeville, Canada .. 102 D3
Orango, Guinea-Biss. .. 82 C1
Orani, Phil. 61 D4
Oranienburg, Germany . 24 C9
Oranje = Orange →,
  S. Africa 88 D2
Oranje Vrystaat = Free
  State □, S. Africa ... 88 D4
Oranjemund, Namibia . 88 D2
Oranjerivier, S. Africa . 88 D3
Orapa, Botswana 85 J5
Orarak, Sudan 81 F3
Oras, Phil. 61 E6
Orašje, Bos.-H. 42 E3
Orăştie, Romania ... 43 E8
Oraşul Stalin = Braşov,
  Romania 43 E10
Orava →, Slovak Rep. . 27 B12
Orava, Vodna nádrž,
  Slovak Rep. 27 B12
Oravița, Romania ... 42 E6
Orb →, France 20 E7
Orbe, Switz. 25 J2
Orbec, France 18 C7
Orbetello, Italy 29 F8
Órbigo →, Spain 34 C5
Orbisonia, U.S.A. ... 110 F7

Orbost, *Australia* 95 F4
Örbyhus, *Sweden* 10 D11
Orcas I., *U.S.A.* 116 B4
Orce, *Spain* 33 H2
Orce →, *Spain* 33 H2
Orchard City, *U.S.A.* 115 G10
Orchies, *France* 19 B10
Orchila, I., *Venezuela* 121 D6
Órcia →, *Italy* 29 F8
Orco →, *Italy* 28 C4
Orcutt, *U.S.A.* 117 L6
Ord, *U.S.A.* 112 E5
Ord →, *Australia* 92 C4
Ord, Mt., *Australia* 92 C4
Ordenes = Ordes, *Spain* .. 34 B2
Orderville, *U.S.A.* 115 H7
Ordes, *Spain* 34 B2
Ording = St-Peter-Ording,
  Germany 24 A4
Ordos = Mu Us Shamo,
  China 56 E5
Ordu, *Turkey* 72 B7
Ordubad, *Azerbaijan* 73 C12
Orduña, *Álava, Spain* 32 C2
Orduña, *Granada, Spain* .. 35 H7
Ordway, *U.S.A.* 112 F3
Ordzhonikidze =
  Vladikavkaz, *Russia* ... 49 J7
Ordzhonikidze, *Ukraine* ... 47 J8
Ore,
  Dem. Rep. of the Congo . 86 B2
Ore Mts. = Erzgebirge,
  Germany 24 E8
Orebić, *Croatia* 29 F14
Örebro, *Sweden* 10 E9
Örebro län □, *Sweden* 10 E8
Oregon, *U.S.A.* 112 D10
Oregon □, *U.S.A.* 114 E3
Oregon City, *U.S.A.* 116 E4
Öregrund, *Sweden* 10 D12
Öregrundsgrepen, *Sweden* . 10 D12
Orekhov = Orikhiv, *Ukraine* 47 J8
Orekhovo-Zuyevo, *Russia* . 46 E10
Orel, *Russia* 47 F9
Orel →, *Ukraine* 47 H8
Orellana, *Spain* 35 F5
Orellana, Canal de, *Spain* . 35 F5
Orellana, Embalse de, *Spain* 35 F5
Orem, *U.S.A.* 114 F8
Ören, *Turkey* 39 D9
Orenburg, *Russia* 50 D6
Örencik, *Turkey* 39 B11
Orense = Ourense, *Spain* .. 34 C3
Orense □, *Spain* 34 C3
Orepuki, *N.Z.* 91 M1
Orestiás, *Greece* 41 E10
Orestos Pereyra, *Mexico* .. 118 B3
Øresund, *Europe* 11 J6
Orford Ness, *U.K.* 13 E9
Organã = Organyà, *Spain* . 32 C6
Organos, Pta. de los,
  Canary Is. 37 F2
Organyà, *Spain* 32 C6
Orgaz, *Spain* 35 F7
Orgeyev = Orhei, *Moldova* . 43 C13
Orhaneli, *Turkey* 41 G12
Orhaneli →, *Turkey* 41 G12
Orhangazi, *Turkey* 41 F13
Orhei, *Moldova* 43 C13
Orhon Gol →, *Mongolia* .. 60 A5
Óría, *Italy* 31 B10
Oriental, Cordillera,
  Colombia 122 C3
Orientale □,
  Dem. Rep. of the Congo . 86 B2
Oriente, *Argentina* 126 D3
Orihuela, *Spain* 33 G4
Orihuela del Tremedal,
  Spain 32 E3
Orikhiv, *Ukraine* 47 J8
Oriku, *Albania* 40 F3
Orillia, *Canada* 102 D4
Orinoco →, *Venezuela* 122 C4
Orion, *Canada* 105 D6
Oriskany, *U.S.A.* 111 C9
Orissa □, *India* 67 K14
Orissaare, *Estonia* 9 G20
Oristano, *Italy* 30 C1
Oristano, G. di, *Italy* 30 C1
Orizaba, *Mexico* 119 D5
Orizare, *Bulgaria* 41 D11
Orjen, *Bos.-H.* 40 D2
Orjiva, *Spain* 35 J7
Orkanger, *Norway* 8 E13
Örkelljunga, *Sweden* 11 H7
Örken, *Sweden* 11 G9
Örkény, *Hungary* 42 C4
Orkla →, *Norway* 8 E13
Orkney, *S. Africa* 88 D4
Orkney □, *U.K.* 14 B5
Orkney Is., *U.K.* 14 B6
Orland, *U.S.A.* 116 F4
Orlando, *U.S.A.* 109 L5
Orlando, C. d', *Italy* 31 D7
Orléanais, *France* 19 E9
Orléans, *France* 19 E8
Orleans, *U.S.A.* 111 B12
Orléans, I. d', *Canada* 103 C5
Orlice →, *Czech Rep.* 26 A8
Orlov, *Slovak Rep.* 27 B13
Orlov Gay, *Russia* 48 E9
Orlová, *Czech Rep.* 27 B11
Orlovat, *Serbia, Yug.* 42 E5
Ormara, *Pakistan* 66 G4
Ormea, *Italy* 28 D4
Ormília, *Greece* 40 F7
Ormoc, *Phil.* 61 F6
Ormond, *N.Z.* 91 H6
Ormond Beach, *U.S.A.* ... 109 L5
Ormož, *Slovenia* 29 B13
Ormskirk, *U.K.* 12 D5

Ormstown, *Canada* 111 A11
Ornans, *France* 19 E13
Orne □, *France* 18 D7
Orne →, *France* 18 C6
Orneta, *Poland* 44 D7
Örnö, *Sweden* 10 E12
Örnsköldsvik, *Sweden* 10 A12
Oro, *N. Korea* 57 D14
Oro →, *Mexico* 118 B3
Oro Grande, *U.S.A.* 117 L9
Oro Valley, *U.S.A.* 115 K8
Orobie, Alpi, *Italy* 28 B6
Orocué, *Colombia* 124 C4
Orodara, *Burkina Faso* ... 82 C4
Orodo, *Nigeria* 83 D6
Orofino, *U.S.A.* 114 C5
Orol Dengizi = Aral Sea,
  Asia 50 E7
Oromocto, *Canada* 103 C6
Oron, *Nigeria* 83 E6
Orono, *Canada* 110 C6
Orono, *U.S.A.* 109 C11
Oronsay, *U.K.* 14 E2
Oropesa, *Spain* 34 F5
Oroquieta, *Phil.* 61 G5
Orosei, *Italy* 30 B2
Orosei, G. di, *Italy* 30 B2
Orosháza, *Hungary* 42 D5
Oroszlány, *Hungary* 42 C3
Orotukan, *Russia* 51 C16
Oroville, *Calif., U.S.A.* ... 116 F5
Oroville, *Wash., U.S.A.* .. 114 B4
Oroville, L., *U.S.A.* 116 F5
Orrefors, *Sweden* 11 H9
Orroroo, *Australia* 95 E2
Orrville, *U.S.A.* 110 F3
Orsa, *Sweden* 10 C8
Orsara di Púglia, *Italy* ... 31 A8
Orsasjön, *Sweden* 10 C8
Orsha, *Belarus* 46 E6
Örsjö, *Sweden* 11 H9
Orsk, *Russia* 50 D6
Orşova, *Romania* 42 F7
Ørsted, *Denmark* 11 H4
Ørsundsbro, *Sweden* 10 E11
Orta, L. d', *Italy* 28 C5
Orta Nova, *Italy* 31 A8
Ortaca, *Turkey* 39 E10
Ortakent, *Turkey* 39 D9
Ortaklar, *Turkey* 39 D9
Ortaköy, *Çorum, Turkey* . 72 B6
Ortaköy, *Niğde, Turkey* .. 72 C6
Orte, *Italy* 29 F9
Ortegal, C., *Spain* 34 B3
Orthez, *France* 20 E3
Ortigueira, *Spain* 34 B3
Orting, *U.S.A.* 116 C4
Ortisei, *Italy* 29 B8
Ortles, *Italy* 28 B7
Ortón →, *Bolivia* 124 F5
Ortona, *Italy* 29 F11
Ortonville, *U.S.A.* 112 C6
Orūmīyeh, *Iran* 70 B5
Orūmīyeh, Daryācheh-ye,
  Iran 70 B5
Orune, *Italy* 30 B2
Oruro, *Bolivia* 124 G5
Orust, *Sweden* 11 F5
Oruzgān □, *Afghan.* 66 C5
Orvault, *France* 18 E5
Orvieto, *Italy* 29 F9
Orwell, *N.Y., U.S.A.* 111 C9
Orwell, *Ohio, U.S.A.* 110 E4
Orwell →, *U.K.* 13 F9
Orwigsburg, *U.S.A.* 111 F8
Oryakhovo, *Bulgaria* 40 C7
Orzinuovi, *Italy* 28 C6
Orzyc →, *Poland* 45 F8
Orzysz, *Poland* 44 E8
Osa, *Poland* 44 E5
Osa, Pen. de, *Costa Rica* . 120 E3
Osage, *U.S.A.* 112 D8
Osage →, *U.S.A.* 112 F9
Osage City, *U.S.A.* 112 F7
Ōsaka, *Japan* 55 G7
Osan, *S. Korea* 57 F14
Osawatomie, *U.S.A.* 112 F7
Osborne, *U.S.A.* 112 F5
Osby, *Sweden* 11 H7
Osceola, *Ark., U.S.A.* ... 113 H10
Osceola, *Iowa, U.S.A.* ... 112 E8
Oschatz, *Germany* 24 D9
Oschersleben, *Germany* ... 24 C7
Óschiri, *Italy* 30 B2
Oscoda, *U.S.A.* 110 B1
Osečina, *Serbia, Yug.* 40 B3
Ösel = Saaremaa, *Estonia* . 9 G20
Osery, *Russia* 46 E10
Osgoode, *Canada* 111 A9
Osh, *Kyrgyzstan* 50 E8
Oshakati, *Namibia* 85 H3
Oshawa, *Canada* 102 D4
Oshigambo, *Namibia* 88 B2
Oshkosh, *Nebr., U.S.A.* .. 112 E3
Oshkosh, *Wis., U.S.A.* ... 112 C10
Oshmyany = Ashmyany,
  Belarus 9 J21
Oshnovīyeh, *Iran* 70 B5
Oshogbo, *Nigeria* 83 D5
Oshtorīnān, *Iran* 71 C6
Oshwe,
  Dem. Rep. of the Congo . 84 E3
Osi, *Nigeria* 83 D6
Osieczna, *Poland* 45 G3
Osijek, *Croatia* 42 E3
Ósilo, *Italy* 30 B1
Ósimo, *Italy* 29 E10
Osintorf, *Belarus* 46 E6
Osipenko = Berdyansk,
  Ukraine 47 J9

Osipovichi = Asipovichy,
  Belarus 46 F5
Osiyan, *India* 68 F5
Osizweni, *S. Africa* 89 D5
Oskaloosa, *U.S.A.* 112 E8
Oskarshamn, *Sweden* 11 G10
Oskarström, *Sweden* 11 H6
Oskélanéo, *Canada* 102 C4
Öskemen, *Kazakstan* 50 E9
Oskol →, *Ukraine* 47 H9
Oslo, *Norway* 9 G14
Oslob, *Phil.* 61 G5
Oslofjorden, *Norway* 9 G14
Osmanabad, *India* 66 K10
Osmancık, *Turkey* 72 B6
Osmaniye, *Turkey* 70 B3
Osmanlı, *Turkey* 41 E10
Ösmo, *Sweden* 10 F11
Osnabrück, *Germany* 24 C4
Ośno Lubuskie, *Poland* ... 45 F1
Osoblaha, *Czech Rep.* ... 27 A10
Osogovska Planina,
  Macedonia 40 D6
Osor, *Italy* 29 D11
Osorio, *Brazil* 127 B5
Osorno, *Chile* 128 E2
Osorno, *Spain* 34 C6
Osoyoos, *Canada* 104 D5
Osøyro, *Norway* 9 F11
Ospika →, *Canada* 104 B4
Osprey Reef, *Australia* ... 94 A4
Oss, *Neths.* 17 C5
Ossa, Mt., *Australia* 94 G4
Óssa, Óros, *Greece* 38 B4
Ossa de Montiel, *Spain* ... 33 G2
Ossabaw I., *U.S.A.* 109 K5
Osse →, *France* 20 D4
Osse →, *Nigeria* 83 D6
Ossi, *Italy* 30 B1
Ossining, *U.S.A.* 111 E11
Ossipee, *U.S.A.* 111 C13
Ossokmanuan L., *Canada* . 103 B7
Ossora, *Russia* 51 D17
Ostashkov, *Russia* 46 D7
Östavall, *Sweden* 10 B9
Oste →, *Germany* 24 B5
Ostend = Oostende, *Belgium* 17 C2
Oster, *Ukraine* 47 G6
Osterburg, *Germany* 24 C7
Osterburg, *U.S.A.* 110 F6
Osterburken, *Germany* ... 25 F5
Österbybruk, *Sweden* 10 D11
Österbymo, *Sweden* 11 G9
Österdalälven, *Sweden* ... 10 C7
Østerdalen, *Norway* 9 F14
Österfärnebo, *Sweden* 10 D10
Österforse, *Sweden* 10 A11
Östergötlands län □, *Sweden* 11 F9
Osterholz-Scharmbeck,
  Germany 24 B4
Østerild, *Denmark* 11 G2
Osterode, *Germany* 24 D6
Östersund, *Sweden* 10 A8
Östervåla, *Sweden* 10 D11
Ostfriesische Inseln,
  Germany 24 B3
Ostfriesland, *Germany* ... 24 B3
Östhammar, *Sweden* 10 D12
Óstia, Lido di, *Italy* 29 G9
Ostíglia, *Italy* 29 C8
Östmark, *Sweden* 10 D6
Östra Husby, *Sweden* 11 F10
Ostrava, *Czech Rep.* 27 B11
Ostróda, *Poland* 44 E6
Ostrogozhsk, *Russia* 47 G10
Ostroh, *Ukraine* 47 G4
Ostrołęka, *Poland* 45 E8
Ostrov, *Bulgaria* 41 C8
Ostrov, *Czech Rep.* 26 A5
Ostrov, *Romania* 43 F12
Ostrov, *Russia* 46 D5
Ostrów Lubelski, *Poland* .. 45 G9
Ostrów Mazowiecka, *Poland* 45 F8
Ostrów Wielkopolski, *Poland* 45 G4
Ostrowiec-Świętokrzyski,
  Poland 45 H8
Ostrożac, *Bos.-H.* 42 G2
Ostrzeszów, *Poland* 45 G4
Ostseebad Kühlungsborn,
  Germany 24 A7
Ostuni, *Italy* 31 B10
Osüm →, *Bulgaria* 41 C8
Osum →, *Albania* 40 F4
Ōsumi-Kaikyō, *Japan* 55 J5
Ōsumi-Shotō, *Japan* 55 J5
Osun □, *Nigeria* 83 D5
Osuna, *Spain* 35 H5
Oswegatchie →, *U.S.A.* .. 111 B9
Oswego, *U.S.A.* 111 C8
Oswego →, *U.S.A.* 111 C8
Oswestry, *U.K.* 12 E4
Oświęcim, *Poland* 45 H6
Otaci, *Moldova* 43 B12
Otago □, *N.Z.* 91 L2
Otago Harbour, *N.Z.* 91 L3
Otaki, *N.Z.* 91 J5
Otake, *Japan* 55 G6
Otaru, *Japan* 54 C10
Otaru-Wan = Ishikari-Wan,
  Japan 54 C10
Otava →, *Czech Rep.* 26 B7
Otavalo, *Ecuador* 124 C3
Otavi, *Namibia* 88 B2
Otchinjau, *Angola* 88 B1
Otelec, *Romania* 42 E5
Otelnuk L., *Canada* 103 A6
Oţelu Roşu, *Romania* 42 E7
Otero de Rey = Outeiro de
  Rei, *Spain* 34 B3
Othello, *U.S.A.* 114 C4

Othonoí, *Greece* 38 B1
Óthris, Óros, *Greece* 38 B4
Otira Gorge, *N.Z.* 91 K3
Otjiwarongo, *Namibia* 88 C2
Otočac, *Croatia* 29 D12
Otoineppu, *Japan* 54 B11
Otok, *Croatia* 29 E13
Otorohanga, *N.Z.* 91 H5
Otoskwin →, *Canada* 102 B2
Otra →, *Norway* 9 G13
Otradnyy, *Russia* 48 D10
Otranto, *Italy* 31 B11
Otranto, C. d', *Italy* 31 B11
Otranto, Str. of, *Italy* 31 B11
Otrokovice, *Czech Rep.* .. 27 B10
Otse, *S. Africa* 88 D4
Ōtsu, *Japan* 55 G7
Ōtsuki, *Japan* 55 G9
Ottawa = Outaouais →,
  Canada 102 C5
Ottawa, *Canada* 102 C4
Ottawa, *Ill., U.S.A.* 112 E10
Ottawa, *Kans., U.S.A.* ... 112 F7
Ottawa Is., *Canada* 101 C11
Ottélé, *Cameroon* 83 E7
Ottensheim, *Austria* 26 C7
Otter Cr. →, *U.S.A.* 111 B11
Otter L., *Canada* 105 B8
Otterndorf, *Germany* 24 B4
Otterup, *Denmark* 11 J4
Otterville, *Canada* 110 D4
Ottery St. Mary, *U.K.* ... 13 G4
Otto Beit Bridge, *Zimbabwe* 87 F2
Ottosdal, *S. Africa* 88 D4
Ottumwa, *U.S.A.* 112 E8
Otu, *Nigeria* 83 D5
Otukpa, *Nigeria* 83 D6
Oturkpo, *Nigeria* 83 D6
Otway, B., *Chile* 128 G2
Otway, C., *Australia* 95 F3
Otwock, *Poland* 45 F8
Ötztaler Ache →, *Austria* . 26 D3
Ötztaler Alpen, *Austria* ... 26 E3
Ou →, *Laos* 64 B4
Ou Neua, *Laos* 58 F3
Ou-Sammyaku, *Japan* 54 E10
Ouachita →, *U.S.A.* 113 K9
Ouachita, L., *U.S.A.* 113 H8
Ouachita Mts., *U.S.A.* ... 113 H7
Ouagadougou, *Burkina Faso* 83 C4
Ouahigouya, *Burkina Faso* . 82 C4
Ouahran = Oran, *Algeria* . 78 A5
Oualâta, *Mauritania* 82 B3
Ouallam, *Niger* 83 C5
Ouallene, *Algeria* 78 D6
Ouargaye, *Burkina Faso* .. 83 C5
Ouargla, *Algeria* 78 B7
Ouarkoye, *Burkina Faso* .. 82 C4
Ouarzazate, *Morocco* 78 B4
Ouassouas, *Mali* 83 B5
Ouatagouna, *Mali* 83 B5
Oubangi →,
  Dem. Rep. of the Congo . 84 E3
Ouche →, *France* 19 E12
Ouddorp, *Neths.* 17 C3
Oude Rijn →, *Neths.* 17 B4
Oudenaarde, *Belgium* 17 D3
Oudon →, *France* 18 E6
Oudtshoorn, *S. Africa* 88 E3
Ouellé, *Ivory C.* 82 D4
Ouéme →, *Benin* 83 D5
Ouessa, *Burkina Faso* 82 C4
Ouessant, Î. d', *France* ... 18 D1
Ouesso, *Congo* 84 D3
Ouest, Pte. de l', *Canada* . 103 C7
Ouezzane, *Morocco* 78 B4
Ougarou, *Burkina Faso* ... 83 C5
Oughterard, *Ireland* 15 C2
Ouidah, *Benin* 83 D5
Ouidi, *Niger* 83 C7
Ouistreham, *France* 18 C6
Oujda, *Morocco* 78 B5
Oujeft, *Mauritania* 82 D2
Oulainen, *Finland* 8 D21
Ould Yenjé, *Mauritania* ... 82 B2
Oullins, *France* 21 C8
Oulu, *Finland* 8 D21
Oulujärvi, *Finland* 8 D22
Oulujoki →, *Finland* 8 D21
Oulx, *Italy* 28 C3
Oum Chalouba, *Chad* 79 E10
Oum Hadjer, *Chad* 79 F9
Oumé, *Ivory C.* 82 D3
Ounasjoki →, *Finland* 8 C21
Oungati, *Namibia* 88 C2
Ounianga Sérir, *Chad* 79 E10
Our →, *Lux.* 17 E6
Ouranópolis, *Greece* 40 F7
Ourârene, *Niger* 83 B6
Ouray, *U.S.A.* 115 G10
Ourcq →, *France* 19 C10
Ourense, *Spain* 34 C3
Ouricuri, *Brazil* 125 E10
Ourinhos, *Brazil* 127 A6
Ouro Fino, *Brazil* 127 A6
Ouro-Ndia, *Mali* 82 B4
Ouro Prêto, *Brazil* 127 A7
Ouro Sogui, *Senegal* 82 B2
Oursi, *Burkina Faso* 83 C4
Ourthe →, *Belgium* 17 D5
Ouse →, *E. Susx., U.K.* .. 13 G8
Ouse →, *N. Yorks., U.K.* . 12 D7
Oust, *France* 20 F5
Oust →, *France* 18 E4
Outaouais →, *Canada* 102 C5
Outardes →, *Canada* 103 C6
Outeiro de Rei, *Spain* 34 B3
Outer Hebrides, *U.K.* 14 D1

Outes = Serra de Outes,
  Spain 34 C2
Outjo, *Namibia* 88 C2
Outlook, *Canada* 105 C7
Outokumpu, *Finland* 8 E23
Outreau, *France* 19 B8
Ouvèze →, *France* 21 E8
Ouyen, *Australia* 95 F3
Ouzouer-le-Marché, *France* 19 E8
Ovada, *Italy* 28 D5
Ovalau, *Fiji* 91 C8
Ovalle, *Chile* 126 C1
Ovamboland, *Namibia* ... 88 B2
Ovar, *Portugal* 34 E2
Overath, *Germany* 24 E3
Overflakkee, *Neths.* 17 C4
Overijssel □, *Neths.* 17 B6
Overland Park, *U.S.A.* ... 112 F7
Overton, *U.S.A.* 117 J12
Övertorneå, *Sweden* 8 C20
Överum, *Sweden* 11 F10
Ovid, *U.S.A.* 111 D8
Ovidiopol, *Ukraine* 47 J6
Ovidiu, *Romania* 43 F13
Oviedo, *Spain* 34 B5
Oviksfjällen, *Sweden* 10 A7
Oviši, *Latvia* 9 H19
Ovoot, *Mongolia* 56 B7
Övör Hangay □, *Mongolia* . 56 B2
Ovoro, *Nigeria* 83 D6
Øvre Årdal, *Norway* 9 F12
Øvre Fryken, *Sweden* 10 E7
Ovruch, *Ukraine* 47 G5
Owaka, *N.Z.* 91 M2
Owambo = Ovamboland,
  Namibia 88 B2
Owasco L., *U.S.A.* 111 D8
Owase, *Japan* 55 G8
Owatonna, *U.S.A.* 112 C8
Owbeh, *Afghan.* 66 B3
Owego, *U.S.A.* 111 D8
Owen Falls Dam, *Uganda* . 86 B3
Owen Sound, *Canada* 102 D3
Owens →, *U.S.A.* 116 J9
Owens L., *U.S.A.* 117 J9
Owensboro, *U.S.A.* 108 G2
Owensville, *U.S.A.* 112 F9
Owerri, *Nigeria* 83 D6
Owl →, *Canada* 105 B10
Owo, *Nigeria* 83 D6
Owosso, *U.S.A.* 108 D3
Owyhee, *U.S.A.* 114 F5
Owyhee →, *U.S.A.* 114 E5
Owyhee, L., *U.S.A.* 114 E5
Ox Mts. = Slieve Gamph,
  Ireland 15 B3
Oxbow, *Canada* 105 D8
Oxelösund, *Sweden* 11 F11
Oxford, *N.Z.* 91 K4
Oxford, *U.K.* 13 F6
Oxford, *Mass., U.S.A.* ... 111 D13
Oxford, *Miss., U.S.A.* ... 113 H10
Oxford, *N.C., U.S.A.* 109 G6
Oxford, *N.Y., U.S.A.* 111 D9
Oxford, *Ohio, U.S.A.* 108 F3
Oxford L., *Canada* 105 C9
Oxfordshire □, *U.K.* 13 F6
Oxía, *Greece* 38 C3
Oxie, *Sweden* 11 J7
Oxilithos, *Greece* 38 C6
Oxnard, *U.S.A.* 117 L7
Oxsjövalen, *Sweden* 10 B7
Oxus = Amudarya →,
  Uzbekistan 50 E6
Oya, *Malaysia* 62 D4
Oyama, *Japan* 55 F9
Oyem, *Gabon* 84 D2
Oyen, *Canada* 105 C6
Oykel →, *U.K.* 14 D4
Oymyakon, *Russia* 51 C15
Oyo, *Nigeria* 83 D5
Oyo □, *Nigeria* 83 D5
Oyonnax, *France* 19 F12
Oyster Bay, *U.S.A.* 111 F11
Ōyūbari, *Japan* 54 C11
Özalp, *Turkey* 70 B5
Ozamiz, *Phil.* 61 G5
Ozark, *Ala., U.S.A.* 109 K3
Ozark, *Ark., U.S.A.* 113 H8
Ozark, *Mo., U.S.A.* 113 G8
Ozark Plateau, *U.S.A.* ... 113 G9
Ozarks, L. of the, *U.S.A.* . 112 F8
Ożarów, *Poland* 45 H8
Ózd, *Hungary* 42 B5
Ozernoye, *Russia* 48 E10
Ozette L., *U.S.A.* 116 B2
Ozieri, *Italy* 30 B2
Ozimek, *Poland* 45 H5
Ozinki, *Russia* 48 E9
Ozona, *U.S.A.* 113 K4
Ozorków, *Poland* 45 G6
Ozren, *Bos.-H.* 42 G3
Ozuluama, *Mexico* 119 C5
Ozun, *Romania* 43 E10
Ozurgeti, *Georgia* 49 K5

P

Pa, *Burkina Faso* 82 C4
Pa-an, *Burma* 67 L20
Pa Mong Dam, *Thailand* . 64 D4
Pa Sak →, *Thailand* 62 B2
Paamiut, *Greenland* 4 C5
Paar →, *Germany* 25 G7
Paarl, *S. Africa* 88 E2
Paauilo, *U.S.A.* 106 H17
Pab Hills, *Pakistan* 68 F2
Pabbay, *U.K.* 14 D1

Pabianice, Poland 45 G6
Pabna, Bangla. 67 G16
Pabo, Uganda 86 B3
Pacaja →, Brazil 125 D8
Pacaraima, Sa., S. Amer. .. 122 C4
Pacasmayo, Peru 124 E3
Paceco, Italy 30 E5
Pachhar, India 68 G7
Pachino, Italy 31 F8
Pachitea →, Peru 124 E4
Pachmarhi, India 69 H8
Pachpadra, India 66 G8
Pachuca, Mexico 119 C5
Pacific, Canada 104 C3
Pacific-Antarctic Ridge,
  Pac. Oc. 97 M16
Pacific Grove, U.S.A. 116 J5
Pacific Ocean, Pac. Oc. ... 97 G14
Pacific Rim Nat. Park,
  Canada 116 B2
Pacifica, U.S.A. 116 H4
Pacitan, Indonesia 63 H14
Packwood, U.S.A. 116 D5
Pacov, Czech Rep. 26 B8
Pacy-sur-Eure, France ... 18 C8
Padaido, Kepulauan,
  Indonesia 63 E9
Padang, Indonesia 62 E2
Padang Endau, Malaysia .. 65 L4
Padangpanjang, Indonesia . 62 E2
Padangsidempuan, Indonesia 62 D1
Padborg, Denmark 11 K3
Paddle Prairie, Canada ... 104 B5
Paddockwood, Canada ... 105 C7
Paderborn, Germany 24 D4
Padeş, Vf., Romania 42 E7
Padina, Romania 43 F12
Padma, India 69 G11
Pádova, Italy 29 C8
Padra, India 68 H5
Padrauna, India 69 F10
Padre I., U.S.A. 113 M6
Padrón, Spain 34 C2
Padstow, U.K. 13 G3
Padua = Pádova, Italy ... 29 C8
Paducah, Ky., U.S.A. 108 G1
Paducah, Tex., U.S.A. ... 113 H4
Padul, Spain 35 H7
Paengnyŏng-do, S. Korea . 57 F13
Paeroa, N.Z. 91 G5
Paesana, Italy 28 D4
Pafúri, Mozam. 89 C5
Pag, Croatia 29 D12
Paga, Ghana 83 C4
Pagadian, Phil. 61 H5
Pagai Selatan, Pulau,
  Indonesia 62 E2
Pagai Utara, Pulau,
  Indonesia 62 E2
Pagalu = Annobón, Atl. Oc. 77 G4
Pagara, India 69 G9
Pagastikós Kólpos, Greece . 38 B5
Pagatan, Indonesia 62 E5
Page, U.S.A. 115 H8
Pagégiai, Lithuania 44 C8
Pago Pago, Amer. Samoa . 91 B13
Pagosa Springs, U.S.A. .. 115 H10
Pagwa River, Canada 102 B2
Pahala, U.S.A. 106 J17
Pahang →, Malaysia 65 L4
Pahiatua, N.Z. 91 J5
Pahokee, U.S.A. 109 M5
Pahrump, U.S.A. 117 J11
Pahute Mesa, U.S.A. 116 H10
Pai, Thailand 64 C2
Paia, U.S.A. 106 H16
Paicines, U.S.A. 116 J5
Paide, Estonia 9 G21
Paignton, U.K. 13 G4
Paihia, Taiwan 59 F13
Päijänne, Finland 9 F21
Pailani, India 69 G9
Pailin, Cambodia 64 F4
Paimpol, France 18 D3
Painan, Indonesia 62 E2
Painesville, U.S.A. 110 E3
Paint Hills = Wemindji,
  Canada 102 B4
Paint L., Canada 105 B9
Painted Desert, U.S.A. .. 115 J8
Paintsville, U.S.A. 108 G4
País Vasco □, Spain 32 C2
Paisley, Canada 110 B3
Paisley, U.K. 14 F4
Paisley, U.S.A. 114 E3
Paita, Peru 124 E2
Paiva →, Portugal 34 D2
Paizhou, China 59 B9
Pajares, Spain 34 B5
Pajares, Puerto de, Spain . 34 C5
Pajęczno, Poland 45 G5
Pak Lay, Laos 64 C3
Pak Phanang, Thailand .. 65 H3
Pak Sane, Laos 64 C4
Pak Song, Laos 64 E6
Pak Suong, Laos 58 H4
Pakaur, India 69 G12
Pakenham, Canada 111 A8
Pákhnes, Greece 36 D6
Pakhuis, S. Africa 88 E2
Pakistan ■, Asia 68 E4
Pakkading, Laos 64 C4
Pakokku, Burma 67 J19
Pakość, Poland 45 F5
Pakowki L., Canada 105 D6
Pakpattan, Pakistan 68 D5
Pakrac, Croatia 42 E2
Pakruojis, Lithuania 44 C10
Paks, Hungary 42 D3
Paktīā □, Afghan. 66 C6
Pakwach, Uganda 86 B3

Pakxe, Laos 64 E5
Pal Lahara, India 69 J11
Pala, Chad 79 G9
Pala,
  Dem. Rep. of the Congo . 86 D2
Pala, U.S.A. 117 M9
Palabek, Uganda 86 B3
Palacios, U.S.A. 113 L6
Palafrugell, Spain 32 D8
Palagiano, Italy 31 B10
Palagonía, Italy 31 E7
Palagruža, Croatia 29 F13
Palaiókastron, Greece ... 36 D8
Palaiokhóra, Greece 36 D5
Pálairos, Greece 38 C2
Palaiseau, France 19 D9
Palam, India 66 K10
Palamás, Greece 38 B4
Palamòs, Spain 32 D8
Palampur, India 68 C7
Palamut, Turkey 39 C9
Palana, Australia 94 F4
Palana, Russia 51 D16
Palanan, Phil. 61 C5
Palanan Pt., Phil. 61 C5
Palandri, Pakistan 69 C5
Palanga, Lithuania 9 J19
Palangkaraya, Indonesia . 62 E4
Palani Hills, India 66 P10
Palanpur, India 68 G5
Palapye, Botswana 88 C4
Palas, Pakistan 69 B5
Palas de Rei, Spain 34 C3
Palashi, India 69 H13
Palasponga, India 69 J11
Palatka, Russia 51 C16
Palatka, U.S.A. 109 L5
Palau ■, Pac. Oc. 63 C8
Palau, Italy 30 A2
Palauk, Burma 64 F2
Palawan, Phil. 61 G3
Palayankottai, India ... 66 Q10
Palazzo, Pte., France ... 21 F12
Palazzo San Gervásio, Italy . 31 B8
Palazzolo Acréide, Italy .. 31 E7
Paldiski, Estonia 9 G21
Pale, Bos.-H. 42 G3
Paleleh, Indonesia 63 D6
Palembang, Indonesia ... 62 E2
Palencia, Spain 34 C6
Palencia □, Spain 34 C6
Palenque, Mexico 119 D6
Paleokastrítsa, Greece ... 36 A3
Paleometokho, Cyprus ... 36 D12
Palermo, Italy 30 D6
Palermo, U.S.A. 114 G3
Palestina, Chile 128 A3
Palestine, Asia 75 D4
Palestine, U.S.A. 113 K7
Palestrina, Italy 29 G9
Paletwa, Burma 67 J18
Palghat, India 66 P10
Palgrave, Mt., Australia . 92 D2
Pali, India 68 G5
Palikir, Micronesia 96 G7
Palinuro, Italy 31 B8
Palinuro, C., Italy 31 B8
Palioúrion, Ákra, Greece . 40 G7
Palisades Reservoir, U.S.A. 114 E8
Paliseul, Belgium 17 E5
Palitana, India 68 J4
Palizada, Mexico 119 D6
Palk Bay, Asia 66 Q11
Palk Strait, Asia 66 Q11
Palkānah, Iraq 70 C5
Palkot, India 69 H11
Palla Road = Dinokwe,
  Botswana 88 C4
Pallanza = Verbánia, Italy . 28 C5
Pallarenda, Australia ... 94 B4
Pallasovka, Russia 48 E8
Pallès, Bishti i, Albania .. 40 E3
Pallinup →, Australia ... 93 F2
Pallisa, Uganda 86 B3
Pallu, India 68 E6
Palm Bay, U.S.A. 109 L5
Palm Beach, U.S.A. 109 M6
Palm Coast, U.S.A. 109 L5
Palm Desert, U.S.A. 117 M10
Palm Is., Australia 94 B4
Palm Springs, U.S.A. ... 117 M10
Palma, Mozam. 87 E5
Palma, B. de, Spain 37 B9
Palma, La, Spain 37 B9
Palma del Río, Spain 35 H5
Palma di Montechiaro, Italy . 30 E6
Palma Soriano, Cuba 120 B4
Palmares, Brazil 125 E11
Palmarola, Italy 30 B5
Palmas, Brazil 127 B5
Palmas, C., Liberia 82 E3
Pálmas, G. di, Italy 30 D1
Palmdale, U.S.A. 117 L8
Palmeira das Missões, Brazil 127 B5
Palmeira dos Índios, Brazil . 125 E11
Palmela, Portugal 35 G2
Palmer, U.S.A. 100 B5
Palmer →, Australia 94 B3
Palmer Arch., Antarctica . 5 C17
Palmer Lake, U.S.A. 112 F2
Palmer Land, Antarctica . 5 D18
Palmerston, Canada 110 C4
Palmerston, N.Z. 91 L3
Palmerston North, N.Z. .. 91 J5
Palmerton, U.S.A. 111 F9
Palmetto, U.S.A. 109 M4
Palmi, Italy 31 D8
Palmira, Argentina 126 C2
Palmira, Colombia 124 C3
Palmyra = Tudmur, Syria . 70 C3
Palmyra, Mo., U.S.A. ... 112 F9

Palmyra, N.J., U.S.A. ... 111 F9
Palmyra, N.Y., U.S.A. .. 110 C7
Palmyra, Pa., U.S.A. 111 F8
Palmyra Is., Pac. Oc. 97 G11
Palo Alto, U.S.A. 116 H4
Palo Verde, U.S.A. 117 M12
Paloich, Sudan 81 E3
Palompon, Phil. 61 F6
Palopo, Indonesia 63 E6
Palos, C. de, Spain 33 H4
Palos de la Frontera, Spain . 35 H4
Palos Verdes, U.S.A. 117 M8
Palos Verdes, Pt., U.S.A. . 117 M8
Pålsboda, Sweden 10 E9
Palu, Indonesia 63 E5
Palu, Turkey 70 B3
Paluke, Liberia 82 D3
Paluzza, Italy 29 B10
Palwal, India 68 E7
Pama, Burkina Faso 83 C5
Pamanukan, Indonesia .. 63 G12
Pamiers, France 20 E5
Pamir, Tajikistan 50 F8
Pamlico →, U.S.A. 109 H7
Pamlico Sd., U.S.A. 109 H8
Pampa, U.S.A. 113 H4
Pampa de las Salinas,
  Argentina 126 C2
Pampanua, Indonesia ... 63 E6
Pampas, Argentina 126 D3
Pampas, Peru 124 F4
Pamphylia, Turkey 72 D4
Pamplona, Colombia 124 B4
Pamplona, Spain 32 C3
Pampoenpoort, S. Africa . 88 E3
Pamukçu, Turkey 39 B9
Pamukkale, Turkey 39 D11
Pan Xian, China 58 E5
Pana, U.S.A. 112 F10
Panabo, Phil. 61 H6
Panaca, U.S.A. 115 H6
Panagyurishte, Bulgaria . 41 D8
Panaitan, Indonesia 63 G11
Panaji, India 66 M8
Panamá, Panama 120 E4
Panama ■, Cent. Amer. . 120 E4
Panamá, G. de, Panama . 120 E4
Panama Canal, Panama .. 120 E4
Panama City, U.S.A. 109 K3
Panamint Range, U.S.A. . 117 J9
Panamint Springs, U.S.A. . 117 J9
Panão, Peru 124 E3
Panaon I., Phil. 61 F6
Panare, Thailand 65 J3
Panarea, Italy 31 D8
Panaro →, Italy 29 D8
Panay, Phil. 61 F5
Panay, G., Phil. 63 B6
Pančevo, Serbia, Yug. ... 42 F5
Panch'iao, Taiwan 59 E13
Panciu, Romania 43 E12
Pancorbo, Desfiladero, Spain 34 C7
Pâncota, Romania 42 D6
Panda, Mozam. 89 C5
Pandan, Antique, Phil. .. 61 F5
Pandan, Catanduanes, Phil. . 61 D6
Pandegelang, Indonesia .. 63 G12
Pandhana, India 68 J7
Pandharpur, India 66 L9
Pando, Uruguay 127 C4
Pando, L. = Hope, L.,
  Australia 95 D2
Pandokrátor, Greece 36 A3
Pandora, Costa Rica 120 E3
Pandrup, Denmark 11 G3
Panevėžys, Lithuania ... 9 J21
Panfilov, Kazakstan 50 E8
Panfilovo, Russia 48 E6
Pang-Long, Burma 67 H21
Pang-Yang, Burma 67 H21
Panga,
  Dem. Rep. of the Congo . 86 B2
Pangaíon Óros, Greece .. 41 F8
Pangalanes, Canal des =
  Ampangalana,
  Lakandranon', Madag. .. 89 C8
Pangani, Tanzania 86 D4
Pangani →, Tanzania ... 86 D4
Pangfou = Bengbu, China . 57 H9
Pangil,
  Dem. Rep. of the Congo . 86 C2
Pangkah, Tanjung, Indonesia 63 G15
Pangkajene, Indonesia ... 63 E5
Pangkalanbrandan, Indonesia 62 D1
Pangkalanbuun, Indonesia . 62 E4
Pangkalpinang, Indonesia . 62 E3
Pangnirtung, Canada 101 B13
Pangong Tso, India 68 B8
Panguitch, U.S.A. 115 H7
Pangutaran Group, Phil. . 61 H4
Panhandle, U.S.A. 113 H4
Pani Mines, India 68 H5
Pania-Mutombo,
  Dem. Rep. of the Congo . 86 D1
Panikota I., India 68 J4
Panipat, India 68 E7
Panjal Range, India 68 C7
Panjang, Hon, Vietnam .. 65 H4
Panjgur, Pakistan 66 F4
Panjim = Panaji, India .. 66 M8
Panjin, China 57 D12
Panjnad Barrage, Pakistan . 68 E4
Panjnad →, Pakistan ... 68 E4
Panjwai, Afghan. 68 D1
Panmunjom, N. Korea ... 57 F14
Panna, India 69 G9
Panna Hills, India 69 G9
Pannawonica, Australia .. 92 D2
Pano Akil, Pakistan 68 F3
Pano Lefkara, Cyprus ... 36 E12

Pano Panayia, Cyprus ... 36 E11
Panorama, Brazil 127 A5
Pánormon, Greece 36 D6
Pansemal, India 68 J6
Panshan = Panjin, China . 57 D12
Panshi, China 57 C14
Pantanal, Brazil 124 H7
Pantar, Indonesia 63 F6
Pante Macassar, Indonesia . 63 F6
Pantelleria, Italy 30 F4
Pantón, Spain 34 C3
Pánuco, Mexico 119 C5
Panyam, Nigeria 83 D6
Panyu, China 59 F9
Páola, Italy 31 C9
Paola, Malta 36 D2
Paola, U.S.A. 112 F7
Paonia, U.S.A. 115 G10
Paoting = Baoding, China . 56 E8
Paot'ou = Baotou, China . 56 D6
Paoua, C.A.R. 84 C3
Pápa, Hungary 42 C2
Papa Stour, U.K. 14 A7
Papa Westray, U.K. 14 B6
Papagayo →, Mexico ... 119 D5
Papagayo, G. de, Costa Rica 120 D2
Papakura, N.Z. 91 G5
Papantla, Mexico 119 C5
Papar, Malaysia 62 C5
Pápas, Ákra, Greece 38 C3
Papeete, Tahiti 97 J13
Papenburg, Germany 24 B3
Paphlagonia, Turkey 72 B5
Paphos, Cyprus 36 E11
Papien Chiang = Da →,
  Vietnam 58 G5
Papigochic →, Mexico .. 118 B3
Paposo, Chile 126 B1
Papoutsa, Cyprus 36 E12
Papua New Guinea ■,
  Oceania 96 H6
Papudo, Chile 126 C1
Papuk, Croatia 42 E2
Papun, Burma 67 K20
Papunya, Australia 92 D5
Pará = Belém, Brazil 125 D9
Pará □, Brazil 125 D8
Parábita, Italy 31 B11
Paraburdoo, Australia .. 92 D2
Paracale, Phil. 61 D5
Paracatu, Brazil 125 G9
Paracel Is., S. China Sea . 62 A4
Parachilna, Australia ... 95 E2
Parachinar, Pakistan ... 68 C4
Paraćin, Serbia, Yug. ... 40 C5
Paradas, Spain 35 H5
Paradela, Spain 34 C3
Paradhísi, Greece 36 C10
Paradip, India 67 J15
Paradise, Calif., U.S.A. . 116 F5
Paradise, Nev., U.S.A. .. 117 J11
Paradise →, Canada 103 B8
Paradise Hill, Canada ... 105 C7
Paradise River, Canada .. 103 B8
Paradise Valley, U.S.A. .. 114 F5
Parado, Indonesia 63 F5
Paragould, U.S.A. 113 G9
Paragua →, Venezuela .. 124 B6
Paraguaçu →, Brazil ... 125 F11
Paraguaçu Paulista, Brazil . 127 A5
Paraguaná, Pen. de,
  Venezuela 124 A5
Paraguarí, Paraguay 126 B4
Paraguarí □, Paraguay .. 126 B4
Paraguay ■, S. Amer. ... 126 A4
Paraguay →, Paraguay .. 126 B4
Paraíba = João Pessoa,
  Brazil 125 E12
Paraíba □, Brazil 125 E11
Paraíba do Sul →, Brazil . 127 A7
Parainen, Finland 9 F20
Paraiso, Mexico 119 D6
Parak, Iran 71 E7
Parakhino Paddube, Russia 46 C7
Parakou, Benin 83 D5
Paralimni, Cyprus 36 D12
Parálion-Astros, Greece .. 38 D4
Paramaribo, Surinam ... 125 B7
Paramithiá, Greece 38 B2
Paramushir, Ostrov, Russia . 51 D16
Paran →, Israel 75 E4
Paraná, Argentina 126 C3
Paraná, Brazil 125 F9
Paraná □, Brazil 127 A5
Paraná →, Argentina ... 126 C4
Paranã →, Brazil 125 F9
Paranaguá, Brazil 127 B6
Paranaíba, Brazil 125 G8
Paranaíba →, Brazil ... 125 H8
Paranapanema →, Brazil . 127 A5
Paranapiacaba, Serra do,
  Brazil 127 A6
Paranavaí, Brazil 127 A5
Parang, Maguindanao, Phil. . 63 C6
Parang, Sulu, Phil. 61 J4
Parângul Mare, Vf.,
  Romania 43 E8
Parapóla, Greece 38 E5
Paraspóri, Ákra, Greece . 39 F9
Parbati →, Mad. P., India . 68 G7
Parbati →, Raj., India .. 68 G7
Parbhani, India 66 K10
Parchim, Germany 24 B7
Parczew, Poland 45 G9
Pardes Hanna-Karkur, Israel 75 C3
Pardilla, Spain 34 D7
Pardo →, Bahia, Brazil .. 125 G11
Pardo →, Mato Grosso,
  Brazil 127 A5
Pardubice, Czech Rep. ... 26 A8

Pare, Indonesia 63 G15
Pare Mts., Tanzania 86 C4
Parecis, Serra dos, Brazil . 124 F7
Paredes de Nava, Spain .. 34 C6
Paren, Russia 51 C17
Parent, Canada 102 C5
Parent, L., Canada 102 C4
Parentis-en-Born, France . 20 D2
Parepare, Indonesia 63 E5
Párga, Greece 38 B2
Pargo, Pta. do, Madeira .. 37 D2
Pariaguán, Venezuela ... 124 B6
Pariaman, Indonesia 62 E2
Paricutín, Cerro, Mexico . 118 D4
Parigi, Indonesia 63 E6
Parika, Guyana 124 B7
Parikkala, Finland 46 B5
Parima, Serra, Brazil 124 C6
Parinari, Peru 124 D4
Pariñas, Pta., S. Amer. .. 122 D2
Parincea, Romania 43 D12
Parintins, Brazil 125 D7
Pariparit Kyun, Burma .. 67 M18
Paris, Canada 110 C4
Paris, France 19 D9
Paris, Idaho, U.S.A. 114 E8
Paris, Ky., U.S.A. 108 F3
Paris, Tenn., U.S.A. 109 G1
Paris, Tex., U.S.A. 113 J7
Paris, Ville de □, France .. 19 D9
Parish, U.S.A. 111 C8
Parishville, U.S.A. 111 B10
Park, U.S.A. 116 B4
Park City, U.S.A. 113 G6
Park Falls, U.S.A. 112 C9
Park Head, Canada 110 B3
Park Hills, U.S.A. 113 G9
Park Range, U.S.A. 114 G10
Park Rapids, U.S.A. 112 B7
Park River, U.S.A. 112 A6
Park Rynie, S. Africa ... 89 E5
Parkā Bandar, Iran 71 E8
Parkano, Finland 9 E20
Parker, Ariz., U.S.A. ... 117 L12
Parker, Pa., U.S.A. 110 E5
Parker Dam, U.S.A. 117 L12
Parkersburg, U.S.A. 108 F5
Parkes, Australia 95 E4
Parkfield, U.S.A. 116 K6
Parkhill, Canada 110 C3
Parkland, U.S.A. 116 C4
Parkston, U.S.A. 112 D6
Parksville, Canada 104 D4
Parla, Spain 34 E7
Pârlița, Moldova 43 C12
Parma, Idaho, U.S.A. ... 114 E5
Parma, Ohio, U.S.A. ... 110 E3
Parma, Italy 28 D7
Parnaguá, Brazil 125 F10
Parnaíba, Brazil 125 D10
Parnaíba →, Brazil 122 D6
Parnassós, Greece 38 C4
Párnis, Greece 38 C5
Párnon Óros, Greece 38 D4
Pärnu, Estonia 9 G21
Paroo →, Australia 95 E3
Páros, Greece 39 D7
Parowan, U.S.A. 115 H7
Parpaillon, France 21 D10
Parral, Chile 126 D1
Parras, Mexico 118 B4
Parrett →, U.K. 13 F4
Parris I., U.S.A. 109 J5
Parrsboro, Canada 103 C7
Parry I., Canada 110 A4
Parry Is., Canada 4 B2
Parry Sound, Canada ... 102 C4
Parsberg, Germany 25 F7
Parshall, U.S.A. 112 B3
Parsnip →, Canada 104 B4
Parsons, U.S.A. 113 G7
Parsons Ra., Australia .. 94 A2
Partanna, Italy 30 E5
Parthenay, France 18 F6
Partinico, Italy 30 D6
Partizánske, Slovak Rep. . 27 C11
Partridge I., Canada 102 A2
Paru →, Brazil 125 D8
Parvān □, Afghan. 66 B6
Parvatipuram, India 67 K13
Parvatsar, India 68 F6
Påryd, Sweden 11 H9
Pas, Pta. des, Spain 37 C7
Pas-de-Calais □, France . 19 B9
Pasada, Spain 34 B5
Pasadena, Canada 103 C8
Pasadena, Calif., U.S.A. . 117 L8
Pasadena, Tex., U.S.A. .. 113 L7
Pasaje →, Argentina ... 126 B3
Paşalimanı, Turkey 41 F11
Pasay, Phil. 61 D4
Pascagoula, U.S.A. 113 K10
Pascagoula →, U.S.A. .. 113 K10
Paşcani, Romania 43 C11
Pasco, U.S.A. 114 C4
Pasco, Cerro de, Peru ... 124 F3
Pasco I., Australia 92 D2
Pascoag, U.S.A. 111 E13
Pascua, I. de, Pac. Oc. .. 97 K17
Pasewalk, Germany 24 B9
Pasfield L., Canada 105 B7
Pasha →, Russia 46 B7
Pashiwari, Pakistan 69 B6
Pashmakli = Smolyan,
  Bulgaria 41 E8
Pasinler, Turkey 73 C9
Pasir Mas, Malaysia 65 J4
Pasir Putih, Malaysia ... 65 K4
Pasirian, Indonesia 63 H15

Pasirkuning, Indonesia 62 E2
Påskallavik, Sweden 11 G10
Paskūh, Iran 71 E9
Pasłęk, Poland 44 D6
Pasłęka →, Poland 44 D6
Pasley, C., Australia 93 F3
Pašman, Croatia 29 E12
Pasni, Pakistan 66 G3
Paso Cantinela, Mexico 117 N11
Paso de Indios, Argentina . 128 E3
Paso de los Libres, Argentina 126 B4
Paso de los Toros, Uruguay . 126 C4
Paso Robles, U.S.A. 115 J3
Paspébiac, Canada 103 C6
Pasrur, Pakistan 68 C6
Passage West, Ireland 15 E3
Passaic, U.S.A. 111 F10
Passau, Germany 25 G9
Passero, C., Italy 31 F8
Passo Fundo, Brazil 127 B5
Passos, Brazil 125 H9
Passow, Germany 24 B10
Passy, France 21 C10
Pastavy, Belarus 9 J22
Pastaza →, Peru 124 D3
Pasto, Colombia 124 C3
Pastrana, Spain 32 E2
Pasuruan, Indonesia 63 G15
Pasym, Poland 44 E7
Pásztó, Hungary 42 C4
Patagonia, Argentina 122 H4
Patagonia, U.S.A. 115 L8
Patambar, Iran 71 D9
Patan, Gujarat, India 66 H8
Patan, Maharashtra, India .. 68 H5
Patan, Nepal 67 F14
Patani, Indonesia 63 D7
Pătârlagele, Romania 43 E11
Pataudi, India 68 E7
Patchewollock, Australia .. 95 F3
Patchogue, U.S.A. 111 F11
Patea, N.Z. 91 H5
Pategi, Nigeria 83 D6
Patensie, S. Africa 88 E3
Paterna, Spain 33 F4
Paternion, Austria 26 E6
Paternò, Italy 31 E7
Pateros, U.S.A. 114 B4
Paterson, U.S.A. 111 F10
Paterson Ra., Australia .. 92 D3
Pathankot, India 68 C6
Pathfinder Reservoir, U.S.A. 114 E10
Pathiu, Thailand 65 G2
Pathum Thani, Thailand .. 64 E3
Pati, Indonesia 63 G14
Patía →, Colombia 124 C3
Patiala, Punjab, India 68 D7
Patiala, Ut. P., India 69 F8
Patine Kouka, Senegal .. 82 C2
Patitírion, Greece 38 B5
Patkai Bum, India 67 F19
Pátmos, Greece 39 D8
Patna, India 69 G11
Patnos, Turkey 73 C10
Pato Branco, Brazil 127 B5
Patonga, Uganda 86 B3
Patos, Brazil 125 E11
Patos, L. dos, Brazil 127 C5
Patos, Río de los →, Argentina 126 C2
Patos de Minas, Brazil ... 125 G9
Patosi, Albania 40 F3
Patquía, Argentina 126 C2
Pátrai, Greece 38 C3
Pátraikós Kólpos, Greece .. 38 C3
Patras = Pátrai, Greece .. 38 C3
Patrocínio, Brazil 125 G9
Patta, Kenya 86 C5
Pattada, Italy 30 B2
Pattani, Thailand 65 J3
Pattaya, Thailand 62 B2
Patten, U.S.A. 109 C11
Patterson, Calif., U.S.A. .. 116 H5
Patterson, La., U.S.A. 113 L9
Patterson, Mt., U.S.A. 116 G7
Patti, Punjab, India 68 D6
Patti, Ut. P., India 69 G10
Patti, Italy 31 D7
Pattoki, Pakistan 68 D5
Patton, U.S.A. 110 F6
Patuakhali, Bangla. 67 H17
Patuanak, Canada 105 B7
Patuca →, Honduras 120 C3
Patuca, Punta, Honduras .. 120 C3
Pătulele, Romania 42 F7
Pátzcuaro, Mexico 118 D4
Pau, France 20 E3
Pau, Gave de →, France .. 20 E2
Pauillac, France 20 D3
Pauk, Burma 67 J19
Paul I., Canada 103 A7
Paul Smiths, U.S.A. 111 B10
Paulatuk, Canada 100 B7
Paulhan, France 20 E7
Paulis = Isiro,
  Dem. Rep. of the Congo . 86 B2
Paulistana, Brazil 125 E10
Paulo Afonso, Brazil 125 E11
Paulpietersburg, S. Africa . 89 D5
Pauls Valley, U.S.A. 113 H6
Pauma Valley, U.S.A. 117 M10
Pauri, India 69 D8
Pāveh, Iran 70 C5
Pavelets, Russia 46 F10
Pavia, Italy 28 C6
Pavilion, U.S.A. 110 D6
Pavilly, France 18 C7
Pāvilosta, Latvia 9 H19
Pavlikeni, Bulgaria 41 C9
Pavlodar, Kazakhstan 50 D8

Pavlograd = Pavlohrad,
  Ukraine 47 H8
Pavlohrad, Ukraine 47 H8
Pavlovo, Russia 48 C5
Pavlovsk, Russia 48 E5
Pavlovskaya, Russia 49 G4
Pavlovskiy-Posad, Russia .. 46 E10
Pawayan, India 69 E9
Pawhuska, U.S.A. 113 G6
Pawling, U.S.A. 111 E11
Pawnee, U.S.A. 113 G6
Pawnee City, U.S.A. 112 E6
Pawtucket, U.S.A. 111 E13
Paximádhia, Greece 36 E6
Paxoí, Greece 38 B2
Paxton, Ill., U.S.A. 108 E1
Paxton, Nebr., U.S.A. 112 E4
Payakumbuh, Indonesia ... 62 E2
Payette, U.S.A. 114 D5
Paymogo, Spain 35 H3
Payne Bay = Kangirsuk,
  Canada 101 B13
Payne L., Canada 101 C12
Paynes Find, Australia ... 93 E2
Paynesville, Liberia 82 D2
Paynesville, U.S.A. 112 C7
Pays de la Loire □, France . 18 E6
Paysandú, Uruguay 126 C4
Payson, U.S.A. 115 J8
Paz →, Guatemala 120 D1
Paz, B. la, Mexico 118 C2
Pāzanān, Iran 71 D6
Pazar, Turkey 73 B9
Pazarcık, Turkey 72 D7
Pazardzhik, Bulgaria 41 D8
Pazarköy, Turkey 39 B9
Pazarlar, Turkey 39 C11
Pazaryeri, Turkey 39 B11
Pazaryolu, Turkey 73 B9
Pazin, Croatia 29 C10
Pčinja →, Macedonia 40 E5
Pe Ell, U.S.A. 116 D3
Peabody, U.S.A. 111 D14
Peace →, Canada 104 B6
Peace Point, Canada 104 B6
Peace River, Canada 104 B5
Peach Springs, U.S.A. 115 J7
Peachland, Canada 104 D5
Peachtree City, U.S.A. 109 J3
Peak, The = Kinder Scout,
  U.K. 12 D6
Peak District, U.K. 12 D6
Peak Hill, N.S.W., Australia 95 E4
Peak Hill, W. Austral.,
  Australia 93 E2
Peak Ra., Australia 94 C4
Peake Cr. →, Australia ... 95 D2
Peal de Becerro, Spain ... 35 H7
Peale, Mt., U.S.A. 115 G9
Pearblossom, U.S.A. 117 L9
Pearl →, U.S.A. 113 K10
Pearl City, U.S.A. 106 H16
Pearl Harbor, U.S.A. 106 H16
Pearl River, U.S.A. 111 E10
Pearsall, U.S.A. 113 L5
Pearse I., Canada 104 B2
Peary Land, Greenland ... 4 A6
Pease →, U.S.A. 113 H5
Peawanuck, Canada 101 C11
Pebane, Mozam. 87 F4
Pebas, Peru 124 D4
Pebble Beach, U.S.A. 116 J5
Peč, Kosovo, Yug. 40 D4
Péccioli, Italy 28 E7
Pechea, Romania 43 E12
Pechenga, Russia 50 C4
Pechenizhyn, Ukraine 47 H3
Pechiguera, Pta., Canary Is. 37 F6
Pechnezhskoye Vdkhr.,
  Ukraine 47 G9
Pechora, Russia 50 C6
Pechora →, Russia 50 C6
Pechorskaya Guba, Russia . 50 C6
Pecica, Romania 42 D6
Pecka, Serbia, Yug. 40 B3
Pécora, C., Italy 30 C1
Pečory, Russia 9 H22
Pecos, U.S.A. 113 K3
Pecos →, U.S.A. 113 L3
Pécs, Hungary 42 D3
Pedder, L., Australia 94 G4
Peddie, S. Africa 89 E4
Pédernales, Dom. Rep. 121 C5
Pedirka, Australia 95 D2
Pedra Azul, Brazil 125 G10
Pedreguer, Spain 33 G5
Pedreiras, Brazil 125 D10
Pedro Afonso, Brazil 125 E9
Pedro Cays, Jamaica 120 C4
Pedro de Valdivia, Chile .. 126 A2
Pedro Juan Caballero,
  Paraguay 127 A4
Pedro Muñoz, Spain 35 F8
Pedrógão Grande, Portugal 34 F2
Pee Dee →, U.S.A. 109 J6
Peebinga, Australia 95 E3
Peebles, U.K. 14 F5
Peekskill, U.S.A. 111 E11
Peel, U.K. 12 C3
Peel →, Australia 95 E5
Peel →, Canada 100 B6
Peel Sound, Canada 100 A10
Peene →, Germany 24 A9
Peera Peera Poolanna L.,
  Australia 95 D2
Peerless Lake, Canada 104 B6
Peers, Canada 104 C5
Pegasus Bay, N.Z. 91 K4
Peggau, Austria 26 D8

Pegnitz, Germany 25 F7
Pegnitz →, Germany 25 F6
Pego, Spain 33 G4
Pegu, Burma 67 L20
Pegu Yoma, Burma 67 K20
Pehčevo, Macedonia 40 E6
Pehlivanköy, Turkey 41 E10
Pehuajó, Argentina 126 D3
Pei Xian = Pizhou, China . 56 G9
Peine, Chile 126 A2
Peine, Germany 24 C6
Peip'ing = Beijing, China .. 56 E9
Peipus, L. = Chudskoye,
  Ozero, Russia 9 G22
Peissenberg, Germany 25 H7
Peitz, Germany 24 D10
Peixe, Brazil 125 F9
Peixe →, Brazil 125 H8
Pek →, Serbia, Yug. 40 B5
Pekalongan, Indonesia 63 G13
Pekan, Malaysia 65 L4
Pekanbaru, Indonesia 62 D2
Pekang, Taiwan 59 F13
Pekin, U.S.A. 112 E10
Peking = Beijing, China ... 56 E9
Péla, Guinea 82 D3
Pelabuhan Kelang, Malaysia 65 L3
Pelabuhan Ratu, Teluk,
  Indonesia 63 G12
Pelabuhanratu, Indonesia .. 63 G12
Pélagos, Greece 38 B6
Pelaihari, Indonesia 62 E4
Pelat, Mt., France 21 D10
Pełczyce, Poland 45 E2
Peleaga, Vf., Romania 42 E7
Pelée, Mt., Martinique ... 121 D7
Pelee, Pt., Canada 102 D3
Pelee I., Canada 102 D3
Pelekech, Kenya 86 B4
Peleng, Indonesia 63 E6
Pélézi, Ivory C. 82 D3
Pelhřimov, Czech Rep. 26 B8
Pelican, U.S.A. 104 B1
Pelican, Canada 105 C8
Pelican Narrows, Canada .. 105 B8
Pelješac, Croatia 29 F14
Pelkosenniemi, Finland ... 8 C22
Pella, Greece 40 F6
Pella, S. Africa 88 D2
Pella, U.S.A. 112 E8
Péla □, Greece 40 F6
Pello, Finland 8 C21
Pellworm, Germany 24 A4
Pelly →, Canada 100 B6
Pelly Bay, Canada 101 B11
Peloponnese =
  Pelopónnisos □, Greece . 38 D4
Pelopónnisos □, Greece ... 38 D4
Peloritani, Monti, Italy ... 31 D8
Pelorus Sd., N.Z. 91 J4
Pelotas, Brazil 127 C5
Pelotas →, Brazil 127 B5
Pelovo, Bulgaria 41 C8
Pelplin, Poland 44 E5
Pelvoux, Massif du, France . 21 D10
Pemalang, Indonesia 63 G13
Pemanggil, Pulau, Malaysia 65 L5
Pematangsiantar, Indonesia . 62 D1
Pemba, Mozam. 87 E5
Pemba, Zambia 87 F2
Pemba I., Tanzania 86 D4
Pemba Channel, Tanzania . 86 D4
Pemberton, Australia 93 F2
Pemberton, Canada 104 C4
Pembina, U.S.A. 112 A6
Pembroke, Canada 102 C4
Pembroke, U.K. 13 F3
Pembrokeshire □, U.K. ... 13 F3
Pen-y-Ghent, U.K. 12 C5
Peña, Sierra de la, Spain .. 32 C4
Peña de Francia, Sierra de
  la, Spain 34 E4
Penafiel, Portugal 34 D2
Peñafiel, Spain 34 D6
Peñaflor, Spain 35 H5
Peñalara, Spain 34 E7
Penamacôr, Portugal 34 E3
Penang = Pinang, Malaysia 65 K3
Penápolis, Brazil 127 A6
Peñaranda de Bracamonte,
  Spain 34 E4
Peñarroya, Spain 32 E4
Peñarroya-Pueblonuevo,
  Spain 35 G5
Penarth, U.K. 13 F4
Peñas, C. de, Spain 34 B5
Peñas de San Pedro, Spain . 33 G3
Peñas del Chache, Canary Is. 37 E6
Peñausende, Spain 34 D5
Pench'i = Benxi, China ... 57 D12
Pend Oreille →, U.S.A. ... 114 B5
Pend Oreille, L., U.S.A. ... 114 C5
Pendálofon, Greece 40 F5
Pendembu, Eastern,
  S. Leone 82 D2
Pendembu, Northern,
  S. Leone 82 D2
Pender B., Australia 92 C3
Pendik, Turkey 41 F13
Pendjari →, Benin 83 C5
Pendleton, U.S.A. 114 D4
Pendra, India 69 H9
Penedo, Brazil 125 F11
Penetanguishene, Canada .. 102 D4
Penfield, U.S.A. 110 E6
Pengalengan, Indonesia ... 63 G12
Penge, Kasai-Or.,
  Dem. Rep. of the Congo . 86 D1
Penge, Sud-Kivu,
  Dem. Rep. of the Congo . 86 C2

Penghu, Taiwan 59 F12
Penglai, China 57 F11
Pengshan, China 58 B4
Pengshui, China 58 C7
Penguin, Australia 94 G4
Pengxi, China 58 B5
Pengze, China 59 C11
Penhalonga, Zimbabwe ... 87 F3
Peniche, Portugal 35 F1
Penicuik, U.K. 14 F5
Penida, Indonesia 62 F5
Peninnes, Alpes = Pennine,
  Alpi, Alps 25 J3
Peninsular Malaysia □,
  Malaysia 65 L4
Peñíscola, Spain 32 E5
Penitente, Serra do, Brazil . 125 E9
Penkridge, U.K. 12 E5
Penmarch, France 18 E2
Penmarch, Pte. de, France . 18 E2
Penn Hills, U.S.A. 110 F5
Penn Yan, U.S.A. 110 D7
Penna, Punta della, Italy .. 29 F11
Pennant, Canada 105 C7
Penne, Italy 29 F10
Penner →, India 66 M12
Pennine, Alpi, Alps 25 J3
Pennines, U.K. 12 C5
Pennington, U.S.A. 116 F5
Pennington →, Nigeria ... 83 E6
Pennsburg, U.S.A. 111 F9
Pennsylvania □, U.S.A. ... 108 E7
Penny, Canada 104 C4
Penobscot →, U.S.A. 109 C11
Penobscot B., U.S.A. 109 C11
Penola, Australia 95 F3
Penong, Australia 93 F5
Penonomé, Panama 120 E3
Penrith, Australia 95 E5
Penrith, U.K. 12 C5
Penryn, U.K. 13 G2
Pensacola, U.S.A. 109 K2
Pensacola Mts., Antarctica . 5 E1
Pense, Canada 105 C8
Penshurst, Australia 95 F3
Penticton, Canada 104 D5
Pentland, Australia 94 C4
Pentland Firth, U.K. 14 C5
Pentland Hills, U.K. 14 F5
Penza, Russia 48 D7
Penzance, U.K. 13 G2
Penzberg, Germany 25 H7
Penzhino, Russia 51 C17
Penzhinskaya Guba, Russia 51 C17
Penzhou, China 58 B4
Penzlin, Germany 24 B9
Peoria, Ariz., U.S.A. 115 K7
Peoria, Ill., U.S.A. 112 E10
Pepacton Reservoir, U.S.A. 111 D10
Pepani →, S. Africa 88 D3
Pepel, S. Leone 82 D2
Peqini, Albania 40 E3
Pera Hd., Australia 94 A3
Perabumulih, Indonesia ... 62 E2
Perak →, Malaysia 65 K3
Perakhóra, Greece 38 C4
Perales de Alfambra, Spain 32 E4
Perales del Puerto, Spain .. 34 E4
Pérama, Kérkira, Greece .. 36 A3
Pérama, Kríti, Greece 36 D6
Peräpohjola, Finland 8 C22
Perast, Montenegro, Yug. . 40 D2
Percé, Canada 103 C7
Perche, France 18 D8
Perchtoldsdorf, Austria ... 27 C9
Percival Lakes, Australia .. 92 D4
Percy, France 18 D5
Percy Is., Australia 94 C5
Perdido, Mte., Spain 32 C5
Perdu, Mt. = Perdido, Mte.,
  Spain 32 C5
Pereira, Colombia 124 C3
Perelazovskiy, Russia 49 F6
Perenjori, Australia 93 E2
Peresecina, Moldova 43 C13
Pereslavl-Zalesskiy, Russia . 46 D10
Peretu, Romania 43 F10
Pereyaslav-Khmelnytskyy,
  Ukraine 47 G6
Pérez, I., Mexico 119 C7
Perg, Austria 26 C7
Pergamino, Argentina 126 C3
Pergau →, Malaysia 65 K3
Pérgine Valsugana, Italy .. 29 B8
Pérgola, Italy 29 E9
Perham, U.S.A. 112 B7
Perhentian, Kepulauan,
  Malaysia 62 C2
Periam, Romania 42 D5
Péribonca →, Canada 103 C5
Péribonca, L., Canada 103 B5
Perico, Argentina 126 A2
Pericos, Mexico 118 B3
Périers, France 18 C5
Périgord, France 20 D4
Périgueux, France 20 C4
Perijá, Sierra de, Colombia . 124 B4
Peristéra, Greece 38 B5
Peristerona →, Cyprus 36 D12
Perito Moreno, Argentina . 128 F2
Perivol = Dragovishtitsa,
  Bulgaria 40 D6
Perkasie, U.S.A. 111 F9
Perković, Croatia 29 E13
Perlas, Arch. de las, Panama 120 E4
Perlas, Punta de, Nic. 120 D3
Perleberg, Germany 24 B7
Perlez, Serbia, Yug. 42 E5
Perm, Russia 50 D6

Përmeti, Albania 40 F4
Pernambuco = Recife, Brazil 125 E12
Pernambuco □, Brazil 125 E11
Pernatty Lagoon, Australia . 95 E2
Pernik, Bulgaria 40 D7
Peron Is., Australia 92 B5
Peron Pen., Australia 93 E1
Péronne, France 19 C9
Perosa Argentina, Italy ... 28 D4
Perow, Canada 104 C3
Perpendicular Pt., Australia 95 E5
Perpignan, France 20 F6
Perris, U.S.A. 117 M9
Perros-Guirec, France 18 D3
Perry, Fla., U.S.A. 109 K4
Perry, Ga., U.S.A. 109 J4
Perry, Iowa, U.S.A. 112 E7
Perry, Okla., U.S.A. 113 G6
Perryton, U.S.A. 113 G4
Perryville, U.S.A. 113 G10
Persan, France 19 C9
Persberg, Sweden 10 E8
Perşembe, Turkey 72 B7
Persepolis, Iran 71 D7
Pershotravensk, Ukraine .. 47 G4
Persia = Iran ■, Asia 71 C7
Persian Gulf = Gulf, The,
  Asia 71 E6
Perstorp, Sweden 11 H7
Pertek, Turkey 73 C8
Perth, Australia 93 F2
Perth, Canada 102 D4
Perth, U.K. 14 E5
Perth & Kinross □, U.K. .. 14 E5
Perth Amboy, U.S.A. 111 F10
Perth-Andover, Canada ... 103 C6
Pertuis, France 21 E9
Pertusato, C., France 21 G13
Peru, Ind., U.S.A. 108 E2
Peru, N.Y., U.S.A. 111 B11
Peru ■, S. Amer. 124 D4
Peru-Chile Trench, Pac. Oc. 124 G3
Perúgia, Italy 29 E9
Perušić, Croatia 29 D12
Pervomaysk, Russia 48 C6
Pervomaysk, Ukraine 47 H6
Pervouralsk, Russia 50 D6
Pésaro, Italy 29 E9
Pescadores = Penghu,
  Taiwan 59 F12
Pescara, Italy 29 F11
Pescara →, Italy 29 F11
Peschanokopskoye, Russia . 49 G5
Péscia, Italy 28 E7
Pescina, Italy 29 F10
Peshawar, Pakistan 68 B4
Peshkopi, Albania 40 E4
Peshtera, Bulgaria 41 D8
Peshtigo, U.S.A. 108 C2
Peski, Russia 48 E6
Pêso da Régua, Portugal .. 34 D3
Pesqueira, Brazil 125 E11
Pessac, France 20 D3
Pest □, Hungary 42 C4
Pestovo, Russia 46 C8
Pestravka, Russia 48 D9
Péta, Greece 38 B3
Petah Tiqwa, Israel 75 C3
Petalídhion, Greece 38 E3
Petaling Jaya, Malaysia ... 65 L3
Petaloudhes, Greece 36 C10
Petaluma, U.S.A. 116 G4
Pétange, Lux. 17 E5
Petaro, Pakistan 68 G3
Petatlán, Mexico 118 D4
Petauke, Zambia 87 E3
Petawawa, Canada 102 C4
Petén Itzá, L., Guatemala . 120 C2
Peter I.s Øy, Antarctica ... 5 C16
Peter Pond L., Canada 105 B7
Peterbell, Canada 102 C3
Peterborough, Australia ... 95 E2
Peterborough, Canada 102 D4
Peterborough, U.K. 13 E7
Peterborough, U.S.A. 111 D13
Peterborough □, U.K. 13 E7
Peterculter, U.K. 14 D6
Peterhead, U.K. 14 D7
Peterlee, U.K. 12 C6
Petermann Bjerg, Greenland 98 B17
Petermann Ranges, Australia 92 E5
Petersburg, Alaska, U.S.A. . 100 C6
Petersburg, Pa., U.S.A. ... 110 F6
Petersburg, Va., U.S.A. ... 108 G7
Petersburg, W. Va., U.S.A. 108 F6
Petersfield, U.K. 13 F7
Petershagen, Germany 24 C4
Petília Policastro, Italy ... 31 C9
Petit Goâve, Haiti 121 C5
Petit Jardin, Canada 103 C8
Petit Lac Manicouagan,
  Canada 103 B6
Petit-Mécatina →, Canada . 103 B8
Petit-Mécatina, I. du,
  Canada 103 B8
Petit Saint Bernard, Col du,
  Italy 21 C10
Petitcodiac, Canada 103 C6
Petite Baleine →, Canada . 102 A4
Petite Saguenay, Canada .. 103 C5
Petitot →, Canada 104 A4
Petitsikapau L., Canada ... 103 B6
Petlad, India 68 H5
Peto, Mexico 119 C7
Petone, N.Z. 91 J5
Petorca, Chile 126 C1
Petoskey, U.S.A. 108 C3
Petra, Jordan 75 E4
Petra, Spain 37 B10
Petra, Ostrova, Russia 4 B13
Petra Velikogo, Zaliv, Russia 54 C6

Petrel = Petrer, *Spain* 33 G4
Petrella, Monte, *Italy* 30 A6
Petrer, *Spain* 33 G4
Petreto-Bicchisano, *France* .. 21 G12
Petrich, *Bulgaria* 40 E7
Petrified Forest National
  Park, *U.S.A.* 115 J9
Petrijanec, *Croatia* 29 B13
Petrikov = Pyetrikaw,
  Belarus 47 F5
Petrila, *Romania* 43 E8
Petrinja, *Croatia* 29 C13
Petrodvorets, *Russia* 46 C5
Petrograd = Sankt-
  Peterburg, *Russia* 46 C6
Petrolândia, *Brazil* 125 E11
Petrolia, *Canada* 102 D3
Petrolina, *Brazil* 125 E10
Petropavl, *Kazakstan* 50 D7
Petropavlovsk = Petropavl,
  Kazakstan 50 D7
Petropavlovsk-Kamchatskiy,
  Russia 51 D16
Petropavlovskiy =
  Akhtubinsk, *Russia* 49 F8
Petrópolis, *Brazil* 127 A7
Petroşani, *Romania* 43 E8
Petrova Gora, *Croatia* 29 C12
Petrovac, *Montenegro, Yug.* .. 40 D2
Petrovac, *Serbia, Yug.* 40 B5
Petrovaradin, *Serbia, Yug.* .. 42 E4
Petrovsk, *Russia* 48 D7
Petrovsk-Zabaykalskiy,
  Russia 51 D11
Petrovskaya, *Russia* 47 K9
Petrovskoye = Svetlograd,
  Russia 49 H6
Petrozavodsk, *Russia* 46 B8
Petrus Steyn, *S. Africa* 89 D4
Petrusburg, *S. Africa* 88 D4
Petzeck, *Austria* 26 E5
Peumo, *Chile* 126 C1
Peureulak, *Indonesia* 62 D1
Pevek, *Russia* 51 C18
Peveragno, *Italy* 28 D4
Peyrehorade, *France* 20 E2
Peyruis, *France* 21 D9
Pézenas, *France* 20 E7
Pezinok, *Slovak Rep.* 27 C10
Pfaffenhofen, *Germany* 25 G7
Pfarrkirchen, *Germany* 25 G8
Pfeffenhausen, *Germany* 25 G7
Pforzheim, *Germany* 25 G4
Pfullendorf, *Germany* 25 H5
Pfungstadt, *Germany* 25 F4
Phagwara, *India* 66 D9
Phaistós, *Greece* 36 D6
Phala, *Botswana* 88 C4
Phalera = Phulera, *India* .. 68 F6
Phalodi, *India* 68 F5
Phalsbourg, *France* 19 D14
Phan, *Thailand* 64 C2
Phan Rang, *Vietnam* 65 G7
Phan Ri = Hoa Da, *Vietnam* .. 65 G7
Phan Thiet, *Vietnam* 65 G7
Phanae, *Greece* 39 C7
Phanat Nikhom, *Thailand* .. 64 F3
Phangan, Ko, *Thailand* 65 H3
Phangnga, *Thailand* 65 H2
Phanh Bho Ho Chi Minh,
  Vietnam 65 G6
Phanom Sarakham, *Thailand* 64 F3
Phaphund, *India* 69 F8
Pharenda, *India* 69 F10
Pharr, *U.S.A.* 113 M5
Phatthalung, *Thailand* 65 J3
Phayao, *Thailand* 64 C2
Phelps, *U.S.A.* 110 D7
Phelps L., *Canada* 105 B8
Phenix City, *U.S.A.* 109 J3
Phet Buri, *Thailand* 64 F2
Phetchabun, *Thailand* 64 D3
Phetchabun, Thiu Khao,
  Thailand 64 E3
Phetchaburi = Phet Buri,
  Thailand 64 F2
Phi Phi, Ko, *Thailand* 65 J2
Phiafay, *Laos* 64 E6
Phibun Mangsahan, *Thailand* 64 E5
Phichai, *Thailand* 64 D3
Phichit, *Thailand* 64 D3
Philadelphia, *Miss., U.S.A.* 113 J10
Philadelphia, *N.Y., U.S.A.* .. 111 B9
Philadelphia, *Pa., U.S.A.* .. 111 G9
Philip, *U.S.A.* 112 C4
Philippeville, *Belgium* 17 D4
Philippi, *Greece* 41 E8
Philippi, *U.S.A.* 108 F5
Philippi L., *Australia* 94 C2
Philippines ■, *Asia* 61 F5
Philippolis, *S. Africa* 88 E4
Philippopolis = Plovdiv,
  Bulgaria 41 D8
Philipsburg, *Canada* 111 A11
Philipsburg, *Mont., U.S.A.* .. 114 C7
Philipsburg, *Pa., U.S.A.* ... 110 F6
Philipstown = Daingean,
  Ireland 15 C4
Philipstown, *S. Africa* 88 E3
Phillip I., *Australia* 95 F4
Phillips, *U.S.A.* 112 C9
Phillipsburg, *Kans., U.S.A.* 112 F5
Phillipsburg, *N.J., U.S.A.* .. 111 F9
Philomont, *U.S.A.* 111 D11
Philomath, *U.S.A.* 114 D2
Phimai, *Thailand* 64 E4
Phitsanulok, *Thailand* 64 D3
Phnom Dangrek, *Thailand* .. 62 B2
Phnom Penh, *Cambodia* 65 G5
Phnum Penh = Phnom Penh,
  Cambodia 65 G5

Phoenicia, *U.S.A.* 111 D10
Phoenix, *Ariz., U.S.A.* 115 K7
Phoenix, *N.Y., U.S.A.* 111 C8
Phoenix Is., *Kiribati* 96 H10
Phoenixville, *U.S.A.* 111 F9
Phon, *Thailand* 64 E4
Phon Tiou, *Laos* 64 D5
Phong →, *Thailand* 64 D4
Phong Saly, *Laos* 58 G4
Phong Tho, *Vietnam* 64 A4
Phonhong, *Laos* 64 C4
Phonum, *Thailand* 65 H2
Phra Nakhon Si Ayutthaya,
  Thailand 64 E3
Phra Thong, Ko, *Thailand* . 65 H2
Phrae, *Thailand* 64 C3
Phrom Phiram, *Thailand* .. 64 D3
Phrygia, *Turkey* 72 C4
Phu Dien, *Vietnam* 64 C5
Phu Loi, *Laos* 64 B4
Phu Ly, *Vietnam* 58 G5
Phu Quoc, Dao, *Vietnam* .. 65 G4
Phu Tho, *Vietnam* 58 G5
Phuc Yen, *Vietnam* 58 G5
Phuket, *Thailand* 65 J2
Phuket, Ko, *Thailand* 65 J2
Phul, *India* 68 D6
Phulad, *India* 68 G5
Phulchari, *Bangla.* 69 G13
Phulera, *India* 68 F6
Phulpur, *India* 69 G10
Phun Phin, *Thailand* 65 H2
Piacenza, *Italy* 28 C6
Pian Cr. →, *Australia* 95 E4
Piana, *France* 21 F12
Pianella, *Italy* 29 F11
Pianosa, *Puglia, Italy* 29 F12
Pianosa, *Toscana, Italy* .. 28 F7
Piapot, *Canada* 105 D7
Pias, *Portugal* 35 G3
Piaseczno, *Poland* 45 F8
Piaski, *Poland* 45 G9
Piastów, *Poland* 45 F7
Piatra, *Romania* 43 G10
Piatra Neamţ, *Romania* .. 43 D11
Piatra Olt, *Romania* 43 F9
Piauí □, *Brazil* 125 E10
Piauí →, *Brazil* 125 E10
Piave →, *Italy* 29 C9
Piazza Ármerina, *Italy* .. 31 E7
Pibor →, *Sudan* 81 F3
Pibor Post, *Sudan* 81 F3
Picardie, *France* 19 C10
Picardie, Plaine de, *France* . 19 C9
Picardy = Picardie, *France* . 19 C10
Picayune, *U.S.A.* 113 K10
Picerno, *Italy* 31 B8
Pichhor, *India* 69 G8
Pichilemu, *Chile* 126 C1
Pichor, *India* 68 G8
Pickerel L., *Canada* 102 C1
Pickering, *U.K.* 12 C7
Pickering, Vale of, *U.K.* .. 12 C7
Pickle Lake, *Canada* 102 B1
Pickwick L., *U.S.A.* 109 H1
Pico Truncado, *Argentina* . 128 F3
Picos, *Brazil* 125 E10
Picton, *Australia* 95 E5
Picton, *Canada* 102 D4
Picton, *N.Z.* 91 J5
Pictou, *Canada* 103 C7
Picture Butte, *Canada* 104 D6
Picún Leufú, *Argentina* .. 128 D3
Pidurutalagala, *Sri Lanka* .. 66 R12
Piechowice, *Poland* 45 H2
Piedmont = Piemonte □,
  Italy 28 D5
Piedmont, *Ala., U.S.A.* .. 109 J3
Piedmont, *S.C., U.S.A.* .. 107 D10
Piedmonte Matese, *Italy* .. 31 A7
Piedra →, *Spain* 32 D3
Piedrabuena, *Spain* 35 G6
Piedrahita, *Spain* 34 E5
Piedralaves, *Spain* 34 E6
Piedras Blancas, *Spain* .. 34 B5
Piedras Negras, *Mexico* .. 118 B4
Piekary Śląskie, *Poland* .. 45 H5
Pieksämäki, *Finland* 9 E22
Piemonte □, *Italy* 28 D5
Pienaarsrivier, *S. Africa* .. 89 D4
Pieniężno, *Poland* 44 D7
Pieńsk, *Poland* 45 G2
Piercefield, *U.S.A.* 111 B10
Pierceland, *Canada* 105 C7
Pieria □, *Greece* 40 F6
Pierpont, *U.S.A.* 110 E4
Pierre, *U.S.A.* 112 C4
Pierre-Buffière, *France* .. 20 C5
Pierre-de-Bresse, *France* .. 19 F12
Pierrefontaine-les-Varans,
  France 19 E13
Pierrefort, *France* 20 D6
Pierrelatte, *France* 21 D8
Piešťany, *Slovak Rep.* 27 C10
Piesting →, *Austria* 27 C9
Pieszyce, *Poland* 45 H3
Piet Retief, *S. Africa* 89 D5
Pietarsaari, *Finland* 8 E20
Pietermaritzburg, *S. Africa* .. 89 D5
Pietersburg, *S. Africa* 89 C4
Pietragalla, *Italy* 31 B8
Pietrasanta, *Italy* 28 E7
Pietroşiţa, *Romania* 43 E10
Pietrosul, Vf., *Maramureş,
  Romania* 43 C9
Pietrosul, Vf., *Suceava,
  Romania* 43 C10
Pieve di Cadore, *Italy* .. 29 B9
Pieve di Teco, *Italy* 28 D4

Pievepélago, *Italy* 28 D7
Pigadhítsa, *Greece* 40 G5
Pigeon L., *Canada* 110 B6
Piggott, *U.S.A.* 113 G9
Pigna, *Italy* 28 E4
Pigüe, *Argentina* 126 D3
Pihani, *India* 69 F9
Pihlajavesi, *Finland* 9 F23
Pijijiapan, *Mexico* 119 D6
Pikalevo, *Russia* 46 C8
Pikangikum Berens, *Canada* 105 C10
Pikes Peak, *U.S.A.* 112 F2
Piketberg, *S. Africa* 88 E2
Pikeville, *U.S.A.* 108 G4
Pikou, *China* 57 E12
Pikwitonei, *Canada* 105 B9
Piła, *Poland* 45 E3
Pila, *Spain* 33 G3
Pilaía, *Greece* 40 F6
Pilani, *India* 68 E6
Pilar, *Brazil* 126 B4
Pilar de la Horadada, *Spain* 33 H4
Pilawa, *Poland* 45 G8
Pilaya →, *Bolivia* 124 H6
Pilbara, *Australia* 92 D2
Pilcomayo →, *Paraguay* .. 126 B4
Pilgrim's Rest, *S. Africa* .. 89 C5
Pilgrimstad, *Sweden* 10 B9
Píli, *Greece* 39 E9
Pilibhit, *India* 69 E8
Pilica →, *Poland* 45 G8
Pilion, *Greece* 38 B5
Pilis, *Hungary* 42 C4
Pilisvörösvár, *Hungary* .. 42 C3
Pilkhawa, *India* 68 E7
Pilliga, *Australia* 95 E4
Pílos, *Greece* 38 E3
Pilot Mound, *Canada* 105 D9
Pilot Point, *U.S.A.* 113 J6
Pilot Rock, *U.S.A.* 114 D4
Pilsen = Plzeň, *Czech Rep.* .. 26 B6
Pilštanj, *Slovenia* 29 B12
Piltene, *Latvia* 44 A8
Pilzno, *Poland* 45 J8
Pima, *U.S.A.* 115 K9
Pimba, *Australia* 95 E2
Pimenta Bueno, *Brazil* .. 124 F6
Pimentel, *Peru* 124 E3
Pina de Ebro, *Spain* 32 D4
Pinamalayan, *Phil.* 61 E4
Pinang, *Malaysia* 65 K3
Pinar, C. des, *Spain* 37 B10
Pinar del Río, *Cuba* 120 B3
Pınarbaşı, *Çanakkale, Turkey* 39 B8
Pınarbaşı, *Kayseri, Turkey* . 72 C7
Pınarhisar, *Turkey* 41 E11
Pinatubo, Mt., *Phil.* 61 D3
Pincehely, *Hungary* 42 D3
Pinchang, *China* 58 B6
Pincher Creek, *Canada* .. 104 D6
Pinchi L., *Canada* 104 C4
Pinckneyville, *U.S.A.* .. 112 F10
Pińczów, *Poland* 45 H7
Pindar, *Australia* 93 E2
Pindi Gheb, *Pakistan* 68 C5
Pindiga, *Nigeria* 83 D7
Pindos Óros, *Greece* 38 B3
Pindus Mts. = Pindos Óros,
  Greece 38 B3
Pine →, *B.C., Canada* .. 104 B4
Pine →, *Sask., Canada* .. 105 B7
Pine, C., *Canada* 103 C9
Pine Bluff, *U.S.A.* 113 H9
Pine Bluffs, *U.S.A.* 112 E2
Pine City, *U.S.A.* 112 C8
Pine Cr. →, *U.S.A.* 110 E7
Pine Creek, *Australia* .. 92 B5
Pine Falls, *Canada* 105 C9
Pine Flat Res., *U.S.A.* .. 116 J7
Pine Grove, *U.S.A.* 111 F8
Pine Pass, *Canada* 104 B4
Pine Point, *Canada* 104 A6
Pine Ridge, *U.S.A.* 112 D3
Pine River, *Canada* 105 C8
Pine River, *U.S.A.* 112 B7
Pine Valley, *U.S.A.* 117 N10
Pinecrest, *U.S.A.* 116 G6
Pineda de Mar, *Spain* .. 32 D7
Pinedale, *Calif., U.S.A.* .. 116 J7
Pinedale, *Wyo., U.S.A.* .. 114 E9
Pinega →, *Russia* 50 C5
Pinehill, *Australia* 94 C4
Pinehouse L., *Canada* .. 105 B7
Pineimuta →, *Canada* .. 102 B1
Pinerolo, *Italy* 28 D4
Pineto, *Italy* 29 F11
Pinetop, *U.S.A.* 115 J9
Pinetown, *S. Africa* 89 D5
Pineville, *U.S.A.* 113 K8
Piney, *France* 19 D11
Ping →, *Thailand* 64 E3
Pingaring, *Australia* 93 F2
Pingba, *China* 58 D6
Pingbian, *China* 58 F4
Pingchuan, *China* 58 D3
Pingding, *China* 56 F7
Pingdingshan, *China* 56 H7
Pingdong, *Taiwan* 59 F13
Pingdu, *China* 57 F10
Pingelly, *Australia* 93 F2
Pingguo, *China* 58 F6
Pinghe, *China* 59 E11
Pingjiang, *China* 59 B13
Pingle, *China* 59 E8
Pingli, *China* 58 A7
Pingliang, *China* 56 G4
Pinglu, *China* 56 E7
Pingluo, *China* 56 E4
Pingnan, *Fujian, China* .. 59 D12

Pingnan, *Guangxi Zhuangzu,
  China* 59 F8
Pingquan, *China* 57 D10
Pingrup, *Australia* 93 F2
Pingshan, *China* 58 C5
Pingtan, *China* 59 E12
Pingtang, *China* 58 E6
P'ingtung, *Taiwan* 59 F13
Pingwu, *China* 56 H3
Pingxiang,
  Guangxi Zhuangzu, China 58 F6
Pingxiang, *Jiangxi, China* .. 59 D9
Pingyao, *China* 56 F7
Pingyi, *China* 57 G9
Pingyin, *China* 56 F9
Pingyuan, *Guangdong, China* 59 E10
Pingyuan, *Shandong, China* 56 F9
Pingyuanjie, *China* 58 F4
Pinhal, *Brazil* 127 A6
Pinhal Novo, *Portugal* .. 35 G2
Pinheiro, *Brazil* 125 D9
Pinheiro Machado, *Brazil* . 127 C5
Pinhel, *Portugal* 34 E3
Pini, *Indonesia* 62 D1
Piniós →, *Ilía, Greece* .. 38 D3
Piniós →, *Tríkkala, Greece* 38 B4
Pinjarra, *Australia* 93 F2
Pink Mountain, *Canada* .. 104 B4
Pinkafeld, *Austria* 27 D9
Pinnacles, *U.S.A.* 116 J5
Pinnaroo, *Australia* 95 F3
Pinneberg, *Germany* 24 B5
Pínnes, Ákra, *Greece* 41 F8
Pinon Hills, *U.S.A.* 117 L9
Pinos, *Mexico* 118 C4
Pinos, Mt., *U.S.A.* 117 L7
Pinos Pt., *U.S.A.* 115 H3
Pinos Puente, *Spain* 35 H7
Pinotepa Nacional, *Mexico* . 119 D5
Pinrang, *Indonesia* 63 E5
Pins, Pte. aux, *Canada* .. 110 D3
Pinsk, *Belarus* 47 F4
Pintados, *Chile* 124 H5
Pinyang, *China* 59 D13
Pinyug, *Russia* 50 C5
Pioche, *U.S.A.* 115 H6
Piombino, *Italy* 28 F7
Piombino, Canale di, *Italy* . 28 F7
Pioner, Ostrov, *Russia* .. 51 B10
Pionki, *Poland* 45 G8
Piorini →, *Brazil* 124 D6
Piotrków Trybunalski,
  Poland 45 G6
Piove di Sacco, *Italy* 29 C9
Pip, *Iran* 71 E9
Pipar, *India* 68 F5
Pipar Road, *India* 68 F5
Piparia, *Mad. P., India* .. 68 H8
Piparia, *Mad. P., India* .. 68 J7
Pipéri, *Greece* 38 B6
Pipestone, *U.S.A.* 112 D6
Pipestone →, *Canada* .. 102 B2
Pipestone Cr. →, *Canada* . 105 D8
Piplan, *Pakistan* 68 C4
Piploda, *India* 68 H6
Pipmuacan, Rés., *Canada* . 103 C5
Pippingarra, *Australia* .. 92 D2
Pipriac, *France* 18 E5
Piqua, *U.S.A.* 108 E3
Piquiri →, *Brazil* 127 A5
Pīr Sohrāb, *Iran* 71 E9
Pira, *Benin* 83 D5
Piracicaba, *Brazil* 127 A6
Piracuruca, *Brazil* 125 D10
Piræus = Piraiévs, *Greece* .. 38 D5
Piraiévs, *Greece* 38 D5
Pirajuí, *Brazil* 127 A6
Piram I., *India* 68 J5
Piran, *Slovenia* 29 C10
Pirané, *Argentina* 126 B4
Pirano = Piran, *Slovenia* .. 29 C10
Pirapora, *Brazil* 125 G10
Pirawa, *India* 68 G7
Pirdop, *Bulgaria* 41 D8
Pirin Planina, *Bulgaria* .. 40 E7
Piripiri, *Brazil* 125 D10
Pirmasens, *Germany* 25 F3
Pirna, *Germany* 24 E9
Pirot, *Serbia, Yug.* 40 C6
Piru, *Indonesia* 63 E7
Piru, *U.S.A.* 117 L8
Piryatin = Pyryatyn, *Ukraine* 47 G7
Piryí, *Greece* 39 C7
Pisa, *Italy* 28 E7
Pisa →, *Poland* 45 E8
Pisagne, *Italy* 28 C7
Pisagua, *Chile* 124 G4
Pisarovina, *Croatia* 29 C12
Pisco, *Peru* 124 F3
Piscu, *Romania* 43 E12
Písek, *Czech Rep.* 26 B7
Pishan, *China* 60 C2
Pīshīn, *Iran* 71 E9
Pishin, *Pakistan* 68 D2
Pishin Lora →, *Pakistan* .. 68 E1
Pisidia, *Turkey* 72 D4
Pising, *Indonesia* 63 F6
Pismo Beach, *U.S.A.* 117 K6
Piso, L., *Liberia* 82 D2
Pissila, *Burkina Faso* .. 83 C4
Pissis, Cerro, *Argentina* .. 126 B2
Pissos, *France* 20 D3
Pissouri, *Cyprus* 36 E11
Pisticci, *Italy* 31 B9
Pistóia, *Italy* 28 E7

Pistol B., *Canada* 105 A10
Pisuerga →, *Spain* 34 D6
Pisz, *Poland* 44 E8
Pit →, *U.S.A.* 114 F2
Pita, *Guinea* 82 C2
Pitarpunga, L., *Australia* .. 95 E3
Pitcairn I., *Pac. Oc.* 97 K14
Pite älv →, *Sweden* 8 D19
Piteå, *Sweden* 8 D19
Piterka, *Russia* 48 E8
Piteşti, *Romania* 43 F9
Pithapuram, *India* 67 L13
Pithara, *Australia* 93 F2
Píthion, *Greece* 41 E10
Pithiviers, *France* 19 D9
Pithoragarh, *India* 69 E9
Pithoro, *Pakistan* 68 G3
Pitigliano, *Italy* 29 F8
Pitkyaranta, *Russia* 46 B6
Pitlochry, *U.K.* 14 E5
Pitsilía □, *Cyprus* 36 E12
Pitt I., *Canada* 104 C3
Pittsburg, *Calif., U.S.A.* .. 116 G5
Pittsburg, *Kans., U.S.A.* .. 113 G7
Pittsburg, *Tex., U.S.A.* .. 113 J7
Pittsburgh, *U.S.A.* 110 F5
Pittsfield, *Ill., U.S.A.* .. 112 F9
Pittsfield, *Maine, U.S.A.* .. 109 C11
Pittsfield, *Mass., U.S.A.* .. 111 D11
Pittsfield, *N.H., U.S.A.* .. 111 C13
Pittston, *U.S.A.* 111 E9
Pittsworth, *Australia* .. 95 D5
Pituri →, *Australia* 94 C2
Piura, *Peru* 124 E2
Piva →, *Montenegro, Yug.* 40 C2
Piwniczna, *Poland* 45 J7
Pixley, *U.S.A.* 116 K7
Piyai, *Greece* 38 B3
Pizarra, *Spain* 35 J6
Pizhou, *China* 56 G9
Pizzo, *Italy* 31 D9
Placentia, *Canada* 103 C9
Placentia B., *Canada* .. 103 C9
Placer, *Masbate, Phil.* .. 61 F5
Placer, *Surigao N., Phil.* .. 61 G6
Placerville, *U.S.A.* 116 G6
Placetas, *Cuba* 120 B4
Plačkovica, *Macedonia* .. 40 E6
Plainfield, *N.J., U.S.A.* .. 111 F10
Plainfield, *Ohio, U.S.A.* .. 110 F3
Plainfield, *Vt., U.S.A.* .. 111 B12
Plains, *Mont., U.S.A.* .. 114 C6
Plains, *Tex., U.S.A.* 113 J3
Plainview, *Nebr., U.S.A.* .. 112 D6
Plainview, *Tex., U.S.A.* .. 113 H4
Plainwell, *U.S.A.* 108 D3
Plaisance, *France* 20 E4
Plaistow, *U.S.A.* 111 D13
Pláka, *Greece* 39 B7
Pláka, Ákra, *Greece* 36 D8
Plakenska Planina,
  Macedonia 40 E5
Planá, *Czech Rep.* 26 B5
Plana Cays, *Bahamas* 121 B5
Planada, *U.S.A.* 116 H6
Plancoët, *France* 18 D4
Plandište, *Serbia, Yug.* .. 42 E6
Plano, *U.S.A.* 113 J6
Plant City, *U.S.A.* 109 M4
Plaquemine, *U.S.A.* 113 K9
Plasencia, *Spain* 34 E4
Plaški, *Croatia* 29 C12
Plaster City, *U.S.A.* 117 N11
Plaster Rock, *Canada* .. 103 C6
Plastun, *Russia* 54 B8
Plasy, *Czech Rep.* 26 B6
Plata, Río de la, *S. Amer.* .. 126 C4
Plátani →, *Italy* 30 E6
Plátanos, *Greece* 36 D5
Plateau □, *Nigeria* 83 D6
Plati, Ákra, *Greece* 41 F8
Platte, *U.S.A.* 112 D5
Platte →, *Mo., U.S.A.* .. 112 F7
Platte →, *Nebr., U.S.A.* .. 112 E7
Platteville, *U.S.A.* 112 D9
Plattling, *Germany* 25 G8
Plattsburgh, *U.S.A.* 111 B11
Plattsmouth, *U.S.A.* 112 E7
Plau, *Germany* 24 B8
Plauen, *Germany* 24 E8
Plauer See, *Germany* 24 B8
Plav, *Montenegro, Yug.* .. 40 D3
Plavinas, *Latvia* 9 H21
Plavnica, *Montenegro, Yug.* 40 D3
Plavno, *Croatia* 29 D13
Plavsk, *Russia* 46 F9
Playa Blanca, *Canary Is.* .. 37 F6
Playa Blanca Sur, *Canary Is.* 37 F6
Playa de las Americas,
  Canary Is. 37 F3
Playa de Mogán, *Canary Is.* 37 G4
Playa del Inglés, *Canary Is.* 37 G4
Playa Esmeralda, *Canary Is.* 37 F5
Playgreen L., *Canada* 105 C9
Pleasant Bay, *Canada* .. 103 C7
Pleasant Hill, *U.S.A.* .. 116 H4
Pleasant Mount, *U.S.A.* .. 111 E9
Pleasanton, *Calif., U.S.A.* .. 116 H5
Pleasanton, *Tex., U.S.A.* .. 113 L5
Pleasantville, *N.J., U.S.A.* 108 F8
Pleasantville, *Pa., U.S.A.* .. 110 E5
Pléaux, *France* 20 C6
Plei Ku, *Vietnam* 64 F7
Plélan-le-Grand, *France* .. 18 D4
Pléneuf-Val-André, *France* . 18 D4
Plenita, *Romania* 43 F8
Plenty →, *Australia* 94 C2
Plenty, B. of, *N.Z.* 91 G6
Plentywood, *U.S.A.* 112 A2
Plérin, *France* 18 D4
Plessisville, *Canada* 103 C5

Plestin-les-Grèves, *France* 18 D3
Pleszew, *Poland* 45 G4
Pleternica, *Croatia* 42 E2
Plétipi, L., *Canada* 103 B5
Pleven, *Bulgaria* 41 C8
Plevlja, *Montenegro, Yug.* .. 40 C3
Plevna, *Canada* 110 B8
Pljesevica, *Croatia* 29 D12
Ploaghe, *Italy* 30 B1
Plo'ana, *Slovak Rep.* 27 C12
Ploce, *Croatia* 29 E14
Plock, *Poland* 45 F6
Plöckenpass, *Italy* 29 B9
Plöckenstein, *Germany* 25 G9
Ploemeur, *France* 18 E3
Ploërmel, *France* 18 E4
Ploiesti, *Romania* 43 F11
Plomárion, *Greece* 39 C8
Plombières-les-Bains, *France* 19 E13
Plomin, *Croatia* 29 C11
Plön, *Germany* 24 A6
Plonge, Lac la, *Canada* ... 105 B7
Plonsk, *Poland* 45 F7
Plopeni, *Romania* 43 E10
Plopisului, Muntii, *Romania* 42 C7
Ploty, *Poland* 44 E2
Plouaret, *France* 18 D3
Plouay, *France* 18 E3
Ploucnice →, *Czech Rep.* .. 26 A7
Ploudalmézeau, *France* 18 D2
Plouescat, *France* 18 D2
Plougasnou, *France* 18 D3
Plougastel-Daoulas, *France* . 18 D2
Plouguerneau, *France* 18 D2
Plouha, *France* 18 D4
Plouhinec, *France* 18 E2
Plovdiv, *Bulgaria* 41 D8
Plovdiv □, *Bulgaria* 41 D8
Plum, *U.S.A.* 110 F5
Plum I., *U.S.A.* 111 E12
Plumas, *U.S.A.* 116 F7
Plummer, *U.S.A.* 114 C5
Plumtree, *Zimbabwe* 87 G2
Plunge, *Lithuania* 9 J19
Pluvigner, *France* 18 E3
Plymouth, *U.K.* 13 G3
Plymouth, *Calif., U.S.A.* ... 116 G6
Plymouth, *Ind., U.S.A.* ... 108 E2
Plymouth, *Mass., U.S.A.* .. 111 E14
Plymouth, *N.C., U.S.A.* ... 109 H7
Plymouth, *N.H., U.S.A.* ... 111 C13
Plymouth, *Pa., U.S.A.* 111 E9
Plymouth, *Wis., U.S.A.* ... 108 D2
Plynlimon = Pumlumon
  Fawr, *U.K.* 13 E4
Plyusa, *Russia* 46 C5
Plyusa →, *Russia* 46 C5
Plyussa = Plyusa, *Russia* .. 46 C5
Plyussa → = Plyusa →,
  Russia 46 C5
Plzen, *Czech Rep.* 26 B6
Pniewy, *Poland* 45 F3
Pô, *Burkina Faso* 83 C4
Po →, *Italy* 29 D9
Po, Foci del, *Italy* 29 D9
Po Hai = Bo Hai, *China* .. 57 E10
Pobé, *Benin* 83 D5
Pobé, *Burkina Faso* 83 C4
Pobeda, *Russia* 51 C15
Pobedy, Pik, *Kyrgyzstan* .. 50 E8
Pobiedziska, *Poland* 45 F4
Pobla de Segur, *Spain* 32 C5
Pobladura del Valle, *Spain* . 34 C5
Pobra de Trives, *Spain* ... 34 C3
Pocahontas, *Ark., U.S.A.* . 113 G9
Pocahontas, *Iowa, U.S.A.* . 112 D7
Pocatello, *U.S.A.* 114 E7
Pocatky, *Czech Rep.* 26 B8
Pochep, *Russia* 47 F7
Pochinki, *Russia* 48 C7
Pochinok, *Russia* 46 E7
Pöchlarn, *Austria* 26 C8
Pochutla, *Mexico* 119 D5
Pocito Casas, *Mexico* 118 B2
Pocking, *Germany* 25 G9
Pocomoke City, *U.S.A.* 108 F8
Poços de Caldas, *Brazil* ... 127 A6
Podbofany, *Czech Rep.* ... 26 A6
Poddebice, *Poland* 45 G5
Podebrady, *Czech Rep.* 26 A8
Podensac, *France* 20 D3
Podenzano, *Italy* 28 D6
Podgorac, *Croatia* 42 E3
Podgorica, *Montenegro, Yug.* 40 D3
Podgorie, *Albania* 40 F4
Podilska Vysochyna, *Ukraine* 47 H4
Podkarpackie □, *Poland* ... 45 H9
Podkova, *Bulgaria* 41 E9
Podlapaca, *Croatia* 29 D12
Podlaskie □, *Poland* 45 E10
Podoleni, *Romania* 43 D11
Podolínec, *Slovak Rep.* 27 B13
Podolsk, *Russia* 46 E9
Podor, *Senegal* 82 B1
Podporozhye, *Russia* 46 B8
Podu Iloaiei, *Romania* 43 C12
Podu Turcului, *Romania* ... 43 D12
Podujevo, *Kosovo, Yug.* ... 40 D5
Poel, *Germany* 24 B6
Pofadder, *S. Africa* 88 D2
Poggiardo, *Italy* 31 B11
Poggibonsi, *Italy* 28 E8
Póggio Mirteto, *Italy* 29 F9
Pogoanele, *Romania* 43 F12
Pogorzela, *Poland* 45 G4
Pogradeci, *Albania* 40 F4
Pogranitsnyi, *Russia* 54 B5
Poh, *Indonesia* 63 E6
P'ohang, *S. Korea* 57 F15
Pohjanmaa, *Finland* 8 E20
Pohnpei, *Micronesia* 96 G7

Pohorelá, *Slovak Rep.* 27 C13
Pohorelice, *Czech Rep.* 27 C9
Pohorje, *Slovenia* 29 B12
Pohri, *India* 68 G6
Poiana Mare, *Romania* 42 G8
Poiana Ruscai, Muntii,
  Romania 42 E7
Poiana Stampei, *Romania* .. 43 C10
Poinsett, C., *Antarctica* 5 C8
Point Arena, *U.S.A.* 116 G3
Point Baker, *U.S.A.* 104 B2
Point Edward, *Canada* 102 D3
Point Hope, *U.S.A.* 100 B3
Point L., *Canada* 100 B8
Point Pedro, *Sri Lanka* 66 Q12
Point Pleasant, *N.J., U.S.A.* 111 F10
Point Pleasant, *W. Va.,*
  U.S.A. 108 F4
Pointe-à-Pitre, *Guadeloupe* . 121 C7
Pointe-Claire, *Canada* 111 A11
Pointe-Gatineau, *Canada* .. 111 A9
Pointe-Noire, *Congo* 84 E2
Poio, *Spain* 34 C2
Poirino, *Italy* 28 D4
Poisonbush Ra., *Australia* .. 92 D3
Poissonnier Pt., *Australia* .. 92 C2
Poitiers, *France* 18 F7
Poitou, *France* 20 B3
Poitou-Charentes □, *France* 20 B4
Poix-de-Picardie, *France* .. 19 C8
Poix-Terron, *France* 19 C11
Pojoaque, *U.S.A.* 115 J11
Pokaran, *India* 66 F7
Pokataroo, *Australia* 95 D4
Pokhara, *Nepal* 69 E10
Pokhvistnevo, *Russia* 48 D11
Poko,
  Dem. Rep. of the Congo . 86 B2
Poko, *Sudan* 81 F3
Pokrov, *Russia* 46 E10
Pokrovsk = Engels, *Russia* . 48 E8
Pokrovsk, *Russia* 51 C13
Pokrovskoye, *Russia* 47 J10
Pola = Pula, *Croatia* 29 D10
Pola, *Russia* 46 D7
Pola de Allande, *Spain* 34 B4
Pola de Lena, *Spain* 34 B5
Pola de Siero, *Spain* 34 B5
Pola de Somiedo, *Spain* ... 34 B4
Polacca, *U.S.A.* 115 J8
Polan, *Iran* 71 E9
Poland ■, *Europe* 45 G3
Polanica-Zdrój, *Poland* 45 H3
Polaniec, *Poland* 45 H8
Polanów, *Poland* 44 D3
Polar Bear Prov. Park,
  Canada 102 A2
Polatlı, *Turkey* 72 C5
Polatsk, *Belarus* 46 E5
Polcura, *Chile* 126 D1
Polczyn-Zdrój, *Poland* 44 E3
Polessk, *Russia* 9 J19
Polesye = Pripet Marshes,
  Europe 47 F5
Polgar, *Hungary* 42 C6
Polgyo-ri, *S. Korea* 57 G14
Poli, *Cameroon* 83 C7
Poliaigos, *Greece* 38 E6
Police, *Poland* 44 E1
Policka, *Czech Rep.* 27 B9
Policoro, *Italy* 31 B9
Polignano a Mare, *Italy* ... 31 A9
Poligny, *France* 19 F12
Políkhnitos, *Greece* 39 B8
Polillo Is., *Phil.* 61 D4
Polillo Strait, *Phil.* 61 D4
Polis, *Cyprus* 36 D11
Polístena, *Italy* 31 D9
Políyiros, *Greece* 40 F7
Polk, *U.S.A.* 110 E5
Polkowice, *Poland* 45 G3
Polla, *Italy* 31 B8
Pollachi, *India* 66 P10
Pollença, *Spain* 37 B10
Pollença, B. de, *Spain* 37 B10
Póllica, *Italy* 31 B8
Pollino, Mte., *Italy* 31 C9
Polna, *Russia* 46 C5
Polnovat, *Russia* 50 C7
Pology, *Ukraine* 47 J9
Polonne, *Ukraine* 47 G4
Polonnoye = Polonne,
  Ukraine 47 G4
Polski Trumbesh, *Bulgaria* . 41 C9
Polsko Kosovo, *Bulgaria* ... 41 C9
Polson, *U.S.A.* 114 C6
Poltár, *Slovak Rep.* 27 C12
Poltava, *Ukraine* 47 H8
Põltsamaa, *Estonia* 9 G21
Polunochnoye, *Russia* 50 C7
Põlva, *Estonia* 9 G22
Polynesia, *Pac. Oc.* 97 J11
Polynésie française = French
  Polynesia ■, *Pac. Oc.* .. 97 K13
Pomarance, *Italy* 28 E7
Pomaro, *Mexico* 118 D4
Pombal, *Portugal* 34 F2
Pómbia, *Greece* 36 E6
Pomene, *Mozam.* 89 C6
Pomeroy, *Ohio, U.S.A.* ... 108 F4
Pomeroy, *Wash., U.S.A.* .. 114 C5
Pomézia, *Italy* 30 A5
Pomichna, *Ukraine* 47 H6
Pomona, *Australia* 95 D5
Pomona, *U.S.A.* 117 L9
Pomorie, *Bulgaria* 41 D11
Pomorskie □, *Poland* 44 D5
Pomorskie, Pojezierze,
  Poland 44 E3
Pomos, *Cyprus* 36 D11

Pomos, C., *Cyprus* 36 D11
Pompano Beach, *U.S.A.* ... 109 M5
Pompei, *Italy* 31 B7
Pompey, *France* 19 D13
Pompeys Pillar, *U.S.A.* 114 D10
Pompton Lakes, *U.S.A.* ... 111 F10
Ponape = Pohnpei,
  Micronesia 96 G7
Ponask L., *Canada* 102 B1
Ponca, *U.S.A.* 112 D6
Ponca City, *U.S.A.* 113 G6
Ponce, *Puerto Rico* 121 C6
Ponchatoula, *U.S.A.* 113 K9
Poncheville, L., *Canada* ... 102 B4
Pond, *U.S.A.* 117 K7
Pond Inlet, *Canada* 101 A12
Ponds, I. of, *Canada* 103 B8
Ponferrada, *Spain* 34 C4
Pongo, Wadi →, *Sudan* ... 81 F2
Pongo, Wadi →, *Sudan* ... 81 F2
Poniatowa, *Poland* 45 G9
Poniec, *Poland* 45 G3
Ponikva, *Slovenia* 29 B12
Ponnani, *India* 66 P9
Ponnyadaung, *Burma* 67 J19
Ponoka, *Canada* 104 C6
Ponorogo, *Indonesia* 63 G14
Pons = Ponts, *Spain* 32 D6
Pons, *France* 20 C3
Ponsul →, *Portugal* 34 F3
Pont-à-Mousson, *France* .. 19 D13
Pont-Audemer, *France* 18 C7
Pont-Aven, *France* 18 E3
Pont Canavese, *Italy* 28 C4
Pont-d'Ain, *France* 19 F12
Pont-de-Roide, *France* 19 E13
Pont-de-Salars, *France* 20 D6
Pont-de-Vaux, *France* 19 F11
Pont-de-Veyle, *France* 19 F11
Pont-du-Château, *France* .. 19 G10
Pont-l'Abbé, *France* 18 E2
Pont-l'Évêque, *France* 18 C7
Pont-St-Esprit, *France* 21 D8
Pont-St-Martin, *Italy* 28 C4
Pont-Ste-Maxence, *France* . 19 C9
Pont-sur-Yonne, *France* ... 19 D10
Ponta do Sol, *Madeira* 37 D2
Ponta Grossa, *Brazil* 127 B5
Ponta Pora, *Brazil* 127 A4
Pontacq, *France* 20 E3
Pontailler-sur-Saône, *France* 19 E12
Pontarlier, *France* 19 F13
Pontassieve, *Italy* 29 E8
Pontaumur, *France* 20 C6
Pontcharra, *France* 21 C10
Pontchartrain L., *U.S.A.* ... 113 K10
Pontchâteau, *France* 18 E4
Ponte da Barca, *Portugal* .. 34 D2
Ponte de Sor, *Portugal* 35 F2
Ponte dell'Ólio, *Italy* 28 D6
Ponte di Legno, *Italy* 28 B7
Ponte de Lima, *Portugal* ... 34 D2
Ponte do Pungué, *Mozam.* . 87 F3
Ponte-Leccia, *France* 21 F13
Ponte nelle Alpi, *Italy* 29 B9
Ponte Nova, *Brazil* 127 A7
Ponteareas, *Spain* 34 C2
Pontebba, *Italy* 29 B10
Ponteceso, *Spain* 34 B2
Pontecorvo, *Italy* 30 A6
Pontedeume, *Spain* 34 B2
Ponteix, *Canada* 105 D7
Pontevedra, *Spain* 34 C2
Pontevedra □, *Spain* 34 C2
Pontevedra, R. de →, *Spain* 34 C2
Pontevico, *Italy* 28 C7
Pontiac, *Ill., U.S.A.* 112 E10
Pontiac, *Mich., U.S.A.* 108 D4
Pontian Kecil, *Malaysia* ... 65 M4
Pontianak, *Indonesia* 62 E3
Pontine Is. = Ponziane,
  Ísole, *Italy* 30 B5
Pontine Mts. = Kuzey
  Anadolu Dagları, *Turkey* 72 B7
Pontinía, *Italy* 30 A6
Pontivy, *France* 18 D4
Pontoise, *France* 19 C9
Ponton →, *Canada* 104 B5
Pontorson, *France* 18 D5
Pontrémoli, *Italy* 28 D6
Pontrieux, *France* 18 D3
Ponts, *Spain* 32 D6
Pontypool, *Canada* 110 B6
Pontypool, *U.K.* 13 F4
Pontypridd, *U.K.* 13 F4
Ponza, *Italy* 30 B5
Ponziane, Ísole, *Italy* 30 B5
Poochera, *Australia* 95 E1
Poole, *U.K.* 13 G6
Poole □, *U.K.* 13 G6
Poona = Pune, *India* 66 K8
Pooncarie, *Australia* 95 E3
Poopelloe L., *Australia* 95 E3
Poopó, L. de, *Bolivia* 122 G5
Popayán, *Colombia* 124 C3
Popilta L., *Australia* 95 E3
Popina, *Bulgaria* 41 B10
Popio L., *Australia* 95 E3
Poplar, *U.S.A.* 112 A2
Poplar →, *Canada* 105 C9
Poplar Bluff, *U.S.A.* 113 G9
Poplarville, *U.S.A.* 113 K10
Popocatépetl, Volcán,
  Mexico 119 D5
Popokabaka,
  Dem. Rep. of the Congo . 84 F3
Pópoli, *Italy* 29 F10
Popovača, *Croatia* 29 C13
Popovo, *Bulgaria* 41 C10
Poppberg, *Germany* 25 F7
Poppi, *Italy* 29 E8

Poprad, *Slovak Rep.* 27 B13
Poprad →, *Slovak Rep.* ... 27 B13
Porali →, *Pakistan* 68 G2
Porbandar, *India* 66 J6
Porcher I., *Canada* 104 C2
Porcuna, *Spain* 35 H6
Porcupine →, *Canada* 105 B8
Porcupine →, *U.S.A.* 100 B5
Pordenone, *Italy* 29 C9
Pordim, *Bulgaria* 41 C8
Poretskoye, *Russia* 48 C8
Pori, *Finland* 9 F19
Porí, *Greece* 38 F5
Porkhov, *Russia* 46 D5
Porlamar, *Venezuela* 124 A6
Porlezza, *Italy* 28 B6
Porma →, *Spain* 34 C5
Pornic, *France* 18 E4
Poronaysk, *Russia* 51 E15
Póros, *Greece* 38 D5
Poroshiri-Dake, *Japan* 54 C11
Poroszló, *Hungary* 42 C5
Poroto Mts., *Tanzania* 87 D3
Porpoise B., *Antarctica* 5 C9
Porquera, *Spain* 34 C4
Porquerolles, Î. de, *France* . 21 F10
Porrentruy, *Switz.* 25 H3
Porreres, *Spain* 37 B10
Porlezza, *Italy* 28 B6
Porsangen, *Norway* 8 A21
Porsgrunn, *Norway* 9 G13
Port Alberni, *Canada* 104 D4
Port Alfred, *S. Africa* 88 E4
Port Alice, *Canada* 104 C3
Port Allegany, *U.S.A.* 110 E6
Port Allen, *U.S.A.* 113 K9
Port Alma, *Australia* 94 C5
Port Angeles, *U.S.A.* 116 B3
Port Antonio, *Jamaica* 120 C4
Port Aransas, *U.S.A.* 113 M6
Port Arthur = Lüshun,
  China 57 E11
Port Arthur, *Australia* 94 G4
Port Arthur, *U.S.A.* 113 L8
Port au Choix, *Canada* 103 B8
Port au Port B., *Canada* ... 103 C8
Port-au-Prince, *Haiti* 121 C5
Port Augusta, *Australia* ... 95 E2
Port Austin, *U.S.A.* 110 B2
Port Bell, *Uganda* 86 B3
Port Bergé Vaovao, *Madag.* 89 B8
Port Blandford, *Canada* ... 103 C9
Port-Bouët, *Ivory C.* 82 D4
Port Bradshaw, *Australia* .. 94 A2
Port Broughton, *Australia* . 95 E2
Port Burwell, *Canada* 110 D4
Port Campbell, *Australia* .. 95 F3
Port Canning, *India* 69 H13
Port-Cartier, *Canada* 103 B6
Port Chalmers, *N.Z.* 91 L3
Port Charlotte, *U.S.A.* 109 M4
Port Chester, *U.S.A.* 111 F11
Port Clements, *Canada* ... 104 C2
Port Clinton, *U.S.A.* 108 E4
Port Colborne, *Canada* 102 D4
Port Coquitlam, *Canada* ... 104 D4
Port Credit, *Canada* 110 C5
Port Curtis, *Australia* 94 C5
Port d'Alcúdia, *Spain* 37 B10
Port Dalhousie, *Canada* ... 110 C5
Port Darwin, *Australia* 92 B5
Port Darwin, *Falk. Is.* 128 G5
Port Davey, *Australia* 94 G4
Port-de-Bouc, *France* 21 E8
Port-de-Paix, *Haiti* 121 C5
Port de Pollença, *Spain* ... 37 B10
Port de Sóller, *Spain* 37 B9
Port Dickson, *Malaysia* ... 65 L3
Port Douglas, *Australia* ... 94 B4
Port Dover, *Canada* 110 D4
Port Edward, *Canada* 104 C2
Port Elgin, *Canada* 102 D3
Port Elizabeth, *S. Africa* ... 88 E4
Port Ellen, *U.K.* 14 F2
Port-en-Bessin, *France* 18 C6
Port Erin, *U.K.* 12 C3
Port Essington, *Australia* .. 92 B5
Port Etienne = Nouâdhibou,
  Mauritania 78 D2
Port Ewen, *U.S.A.* 111 E11
Port Fairy, *Australia* 95 F3
Port Fouâd = Bûr Fuad,
  Egypt 80 H8
Port-Gentil, *Gabon* 84 E1
Port Germein, *Australia* ... 95 E2
Port Gibson, *U.S.A.* 113 K9
Port Glasgow, *U.K.* 14 F4
Port Harcourt, *Nigeria* 83 E6
Port Hardy, *Canada* 104 C3
Port Harrison = Inukjuak,
  Canada 101 C12
Port Hawkesbury, *Canada* . 103 C7
Port Hedland, *Australia* ... 92 D2
Port Henry, *U.S.A.* 111 B11
Port Hood, *Canada* 103 C7
Port Hope, *Canada* 102 D4
Port Hope, *U.S.A.* 110 C2
Port Hope Simpson, *Canada* 103 B8
Port Hueneme, *U.S.A.* 117 L7
Port Huron, *U.S.A.* 110 D2
Port Ilîç, *Azerbaijan* 73 C13
Port Jefferson, *U.S.A.* 111 F11
Port Jervis, *U.S.A.* 111 E10
Port-Joinville, *France* 18 F4
Port Katon, *Russia* 47 J10
Port Kelang = Pelabuhan
  Kelang, *Malaysia* 65 L3
Port Kembla, *Australia* 95 E5
Port Kenny, *Australia* 95 E1
Port-la-Nouvelle, *France* ... 20 E7
Port Laoise, *Ireland* 15 C4

Port Laoise, *Ireland* 15 C4
Port Lavaca, *U.S.A.* 113 L6
Port Leyden, *U.S.A.* 111 C9
Port Lincoln, *Australia* 95 E2
Port Loko, *S. Leone* 82 D2
Port Louis, *France* 18 E3
Port Louis, *Mauritius* 77 H9
Port Lyautey = Kenitra,
  Morocco 78 B4
Port MacDonnell, *Australia* 95 F3
Port McNeill, *Canada* 104 C3
Port Macquarie, *Australia* . 95 E5
Port Maria, *Jamaica* 120 C4
Port Matilda, *U.S.A.* 110 F6
Port Mellon, *Canada* 104 D4
Port-Menier, *Canada* 103 C7
Port Moody, *Canada* 116 A4
Port Morant, *Jamaica* 120 C4
Port Moresby, *Papua N. G.* 96 H6
Port Musgrave, *Australia* .. 94 A3
Port-Navalo, *France* 18 E4
Port Neches, *U.S.A.* 113 L8
Port Nolloth, *S. Africa* 88 D2
Port Nouveau-Québec =
  Kangiqsualujjuaq, *Canada* 101 C13
Port of Spain, *Trin. & Tob.* 121 D7
Port Orange, *U.S.A.* 109 L5
Port Orchard, *U.S.A.* 116 C4
Port Orford, *U.S.A.* 114 E1
Port Pegasus, *N.Z.* 91 M1
Port Perry, *Canada* 102 D4
Port Phillip B., *Australia* .. 95 F3
Port Pirie, *Australia* 95 E2
Port Radium = Echo Bay,
  Canada 100 B8
Port Renfrew, *Canada* 104 D4
Port Roper, *Australia* 94 A2
Port Rowan, *Canada* 110 D4
Port Safaga = Bûr Safâga,
  Egypt 70 E2
Port Said = Bûr Sa'îd, *Egypt* 80 H8
Port St. Joe, *U.S.A.* 109 L3
Port St. Johns =
  Umzimvubu, *S. Africa* .. 89 E4
Port-St-Louis-du-Rhône,
  France 21 E8
Port St. Lucie, *U.S.A.* 109 M5
Port-Ste-Marie, *France* 20 D4
Port Sanilac, *U.S.A.* 110 C2
Port Severn, *Canada* 110 B5
Port Shepstone, *S. Africa* .. 89 E5
Port Simpson, *Canada* 104 C2
Port Stanley = Stanley,
  Falk. Is. 128 G5
Port Stanley, *Canada* 102 D3
Port Sudan = Bûr Sûdân,
  Sudan 80 D4
Port Sulphur, *U.S.A.* 113 L10
Port-sur-Saône, *France* 19 E13
Port Talbot, *U.K.* 13 F4
Port Taufiq = Bûr Taufiq,
  Egypt 80 J8
Port Townsend, *U.S.A.* 116 B4
Port-Vendres, *France* 20 F7
Port Vila, *Vanuatu* 96 J8
Port Wakefield, *Australia* .. 95 E2
Port Washington, *U.S.A.* .. 108 D2
Port Weld = Kuala
  Sepetang, *Malaysia* 65 K3
Portadown, *U.K.* 15 B5
Portaferry, *U.K.* 15 B6
Portage, *Pa., U.S.A.* 110 F6
Portage, *Wis., U.S.A.* 112 D10
Portage La Prairie, *Canada* . 105 D9
Portageville, *U.S.A.* 113 G10
Portalegre, *Portugal* 35 F3
Portalegre □, *Portugal* 35 F3
Portales, *U.S.A.* 113 H3
Portarlington, *Ireland* 15 C4
Portbou, *Spain* 32 C8
Portel, *Portugal* 35 G3
Porter L., *N.W.T., Canada* . 105 A7
Porter L., *Sask., Canada* ... 105 B7
Porterville, *S. Africa* 88 E2
Porterville, *U.S.A.* 116 J8
Portes-lès-Valence, *France* . 21 D8
Porthcawl, *U.K.* 13 F4
Porthill, *U.S.A.* 114 B5
Porthmadog, *U.K.* 12 E3
Portile de Fier, *Europe* 42 F7
Portimão, *Portugal* 35 H2
Portishead, *U.K.* 13 F5
Portitei, Gura, *Romania* ... 43 F14
Portknockie, *U.K.* 14 D6
Portland, *N.S.W., Australia* 95 E5
Portland, *Vic., Australia* ... 95 F3
Portland, *Canada* 111 B8
Portland, *Conn., U.S.A.* ... 111 E12
Portland, *Maine, U.S.A.* ... 101 D12
Portland, *Mich., U.S.A.* ... 108 D3
Portland, *Oreg., U.S.A.* ... 116 E4
Portland, *Pa., U.S.A.* 111 F9
Portland, *Tex., U.S.A.* 113 M6
Portland, B., *Australia* 95 F3
Portland Bill, *U.K.* 13 G5
Portland Canal, *U.S.A.* 104 B2
Portmadoc = Porthmadog,
  U.K. 12 E3
Porto, *France* 21 F12
Porto, *Portugal* 34 D2
Porto □, *Portugal* 34 D2
Porto, G. de, *France* 21 F12
Porto Alegre, *Brazil* 127 C5
Porto Amboim = Gunza,
  Angola 84 G2
Porto Azzurro, *Italy* 28 F7
Porto Cristo, *Spain* 37 B10
Pôrto de Móz, *Brazil* 125 D8
Porto Empédocle, *Italy* 30 E6
Pôrto Esperança, *Brazil* ... 124 G7

Pôrto Franco, Brazil ... 125 E9
Pôrto Lágos, Greece ... 41 E9
Porto Mendes, Brazil ... 127 A5
Porto Moniz, Madeira ... 37 D2
Pôrto Murtinho, Brazil ... 124 H7
Pôrto Nacional, Brazil ... 125 E9
Porto-Novo, Benin ... 83 D5
Porto Petro, Spain ... 37 B10
Porto San Giórgio, Italy ... 29 E10
Porto Sant' Elpídio, Italy ... 29 E10
Porto Santo, Madeira ... 78 B2
Porto Santo Stéfano, Italy ... 28 F8
Pôrto São José, Brazil ... 127 A5
Pôrto Seguro, Brazil ... 125 G11
Porto Tolle, Italy ... 29 D9
Porto Tórres, Italy ... 30 B1
Pôrto União, Brazil ... 127 B5
Pôrto Válter, Brazil ... 124 E4
Porto-Vecchio, France ... 21 G13
Pôrto Velho, Brazil ... 124 E6
Portobelo, Panama ... 120 E4
Portoferráio, Italy ... 28 F7
Portomaggiore, Italy ... 29 C9
Portoscuso, Italy ... 30 C1
Portovénere, Italy ... 28 D6
Portoviejo, Ecuador ... 124 D2
Portpatrick, U.K. ... 14 G3
Portree, U.K. ... 14 D2
Portrush, U.K. ... 15 A5
Portsmouth, Domin. ... 121 C7
Portsmouth, U.K. ... 13 G6
Portsmouth, N.H., U.S.A. ... 109 D10
Portsmouth, Ohio, U.S.A. ... 108 F4
Portsmouth, R.I., U.S.A. ... 111 E13
Portsmouth, Va., U.S.A. ... 108 G7
Portsmouth □, U.K. ... 13 G6
Portsoy, U.K. ... 14 D6
Portstewart, U.K. ... 15 A5
Porttipahtan tekojärvi, Finland ... 8 B22
Portugal ■, Europe ... 34 F3
Portugalete, Spain ... 32 B1
Portumna, Ireland ... 15 C3
Portville, U.S.A. ... 110 D6
Porvenir, Chile ... 128 G2
Porvoo, Finland ... 9 F21
Porzuna, Spain ... 35 F6
Posada, Italy ... 30 B2
Posada →, Italy ... 30 B2
Posadas, Argentina ... 127 B4
Posadas, Spain ... 35 H5
Poschiavo, Switz. ... 25 J6
Posets, Spain ... 32 C5
Poshan = Boshan, China ... 57 F9
Posht-e-Badam, Iran ... 71 C7
Posídhion, Ákra, Greece ... 40 G7
Posidium, Greece ... 39 F7
Poso, Indonesia ... 63 E6
Posong, S. Korea ... 57 G14
Posse, Brazil ... 125 F9
Possession I., Antarctica ... 5 D11
Pössneck, Germany ... 24 E7
Possum Kingdom L., U.S.A. ... 113 J5
Post, U.S.A. ... 113 J4
Post Falls, U.S.A. ... 114 C5
Postavy = Pastavy, Belarus ... 9 J22
Poste-de-la-Baleine = Kuujjuarapik, Canada ... 102 A4
Postmasburg, S. Africa ... 88 D3
Postojna, Slovenia ... 29 C11
Poston, U.S.A. ... 117 M12
Postville, Canada ... 103 B8
Potamós, Andíkithira, Greece ... 38 F4
Potamós, Kíthira, Greece ... 38 E4
Potchefstroom, S. Africa ... 88 D4
Potcoava, Romania ... 43 F9
Poteau, U.S.A. ... 113 H7
Poteet, U.S.A. ... 113 L5
Potenza, Italy ... 31 B8
Potenza →, Italy ... 29 E10
Potenza Picena, Italy ... 29 E10
Poteriteri, L., N.Z. ... 91 M1
Potgietersrus, S. Africa ... 89 C4
Poti, Georgia ... 49 J5
Potiskum, Nigeria ... 83 C7
Potlogi, Romania ... 43 F10
Potomac →, U.S.A. ... 108 G7
Potosí, Bolivia ... 124 G5
Potosi Mt., U.S.A. ... 117 K11
Pototan, Phil. ... 61 F5
Potrerillos, Chile ... 126 B2
Potsdam, Germany ... 24 C9
Potsdam, U.S.A. ... 111 B10
Pottenstein, Germany ... 25 F7
Pottsville, U.S.A. ... 111 C11
Pottery Hill = Abu Ballas, Egypt ... 80 C2
Pottstown, U.S.A. ... 111 F9
Pottsville, U.S.A. ... 111 F8
Pottuvil, Sri Lanka ... 66 R12
P'otzu, Taiwan ... 59 F13
Pouancé, France ... 18 E5
Pouce Coupé, Canada ... 104 B4
Poughkeepsie, U.S.A. ... 111 E11
Pouilly-sur-Loire, France ... 19 E9
Poulaphouca Res., Ireland ... 15 C5
Poulsbo, U.S.A. ... 116 C4
Poulton-le-Fylde, U.K. ... 12 D5
Pouso Alegre, Brazil ... 127 A6
Pout, Senegal ... 82 C1
Pouthisat, Cambodia ... 64 F4
Pouzauges, France ... 18 F6
Pova de Sta. Iria, Portugal ... 35 G1
Poverty B., N.Z. ... 91 H7
Povlen, Serbia, Yug. ... 40 B3
Póvoa de Lanhosa, Portugal ... 34 D2

Póvoa de Varzim, Portugal ... 34 D2
Povorino, Russia ... 48 E6
Povungnituk = Puvirnituq, Canada ... 101 B12
Powassan, Canada ... 102 C4
Poway, U.S.A. ... 117 N9
Powder →, U.S.A. ... 112 B2
Powder River, U.S.A. ... 114 E10
Powell, U.S.A. ... 114 D9
Powell, L., U.S.A. ... 115 H8
Powell River, Canada ... 104 D4
Powers, U.S.A. ... 108 C2
Powys □, U.K. ... 13 E4
Poyang Hu, China ... 59 C11
Poyarkovo, Russia ... 51 E13
Poysdorf, Austria ... 27 C9
Poza de la Sal, Spain ... 34 C7
Poza Rica, Mexico ... 119 C5
Pozanti, Turkey ... 72 D6
Požarevac, Serbia, Yug. ... 40 B5
Pozazal, Puerto, Spain ... 34 C6
Požega, Croatia ... 42 E2
Požega, Serbia, Yug. ... 40 C4
Poznań, Poland ... 45 F3
Pozo, U.S.A. ... 117 K6
Pozo Alcón, Spain ... 35 H8
Pozo Almonte, Chile ... 124 H5
Pozo Colorado, Paraguay ... 126 A4
Pozoblanco, Spain ... 35 G6
Pozzallo, Italy ... 31 F7
Pozzomaggiore, Italy ... 30 B1
Pozzuoli, Italy ... 31 B7
Pra →, Ghana ... 83 D4
Prabuty, Poland ... 44 E6
Prača, Bos.-H. ... 42 G3
Prachatice, Czech Rep. ... 26 B6
Prachin Buri, Thailand ... 64 E3
Prachuap Khiri Khan, Thailand ... 65 G2
Pradelles, France ... 20 D7
Prades, France ... 20 F6
Prado, Brazil ... 125 G11
Prado del Rey, Spain ... 35 J5
Præstø, Denmark ... 11 J6
Pragersko, Slovenia ... 29 B12
Prague = Praha, Czech Rep. ... 26 A7
Praha, Czech Rep. ... 26 A7
Prahecq, France ... 20 B3
Prahova □, Romania ... 43 E10
Prahova →, Romania ... 43 F10
Praia, C. Verde Is. ... 77 E1
Práia a Mare, Italy ... 31 C8
Praid, Romania ... 43 D10
Prainha, Amazonas, Brazil ... 124 E6
Prainha, Pará, Brazil ... 125 D8
Prairie, Australia ... 94 C3
Prairie City, U.S.A. ... 114 D4
Prairie Dog Town Fork →, U.S.A. ... 113 H5
Prairie du Chien, U.S.A. ... 112 D9
Prairies, L. of the, Canada ... 105 C8
Pramánda, Greece ... 38 B3
Prampram, Ghana ... 83 D5
Pran Buri, Thailand ... 64 F2
Prang, Ghana ... 83 D4
Prapat, Indonesia ... 62 D1
Prasonísi, Ákra, Greece ... 36 D9
Prästmon, Sweden ... 10 A11
Praszka, Poland ... 45 G5
Prata, Brazil ... 125 G9
Pratabpur, India ... 69 H10
Pratapgarh, Raj., India ... 68 G6
Pratapgarh, Ut. P., India ... 69 G9
Prato, Italy ... 28 E8
Prátola Peligna, Italy ... 29 F10
Prats-de-Mollo-la-Preste, France ... 20 F6
Pratt, U.S.A. ... 113 G5
Prattville, U.S.A. ... 109 J2
Pravdinsk, Russia ... 48 B6
Pravets, Bulgaria ... 40 D7
Pravia, Spain ... 34 B4
Praya, Indonesia ... 62 F5
Pré-en-Pail, France ... 18 D6
Precordillera, Argentina ... 126 C2
Predáppio, Italy ... 29 D8
Predazzo, Italy ... 29 B8
Predejane, Serbia, Yug. ... 40 D6
Preeceville, Canada ... 105 C8
Preetz, Germany ... 24 A6
Pregrada, Croatia ... 29 B12
Preiļi, Latvia ... 9 H22
Preko, Croatia ... 29 D12
Prelog, Croatia ... 29 B13
Prémery, France ... 19 E10
Premià de Mar, Spain ... 32 D7
Premont, U.S.A. ... 113 M5
Premuda, Croatia ... 29 D11
Prenjasi, Albania ... 40 E4
Prentice, U.S.A. ... 112 C9
Prenzlau, Germany ... 24 B9
Preobrazheniye, Russia ... 54 C6
Preparis North Channel, Ind. Oc. ... 67 M18
Preparis South Channel, Ind. Oc. ... 67 M18
Přerov, Czech Rep. ... 27 B10
Prescot, Canada ... 102 D4
Prescott, U.S.A. ... 115 J7
Prescott, Ark., U.S.A. ... 113 J8
Prescott Valley, U.S.A. ... 115 J7
Preservation Inlet, N.Z. ... 91 M1
Preševo, Serbia, Yug. ... 40 D5
Presho, U.S.A. ... 112 D4
Presicce, Italy ... 31 C11
Presidencia de la Plaza, Argentina ... 126 B4
Presidencia Roque Saenz Peña, Argentina ... 126 B3

Presidente Epitácio, Brazil ... 125 H8
Presidente Hayes □, Paraguay ... 126 A4
Presidente Prudente, Brazil ... 127 A5
Presidio, Mexico ... 118 B4
Presidio, U.S.A. ... 113 L2
Preslav, Bulgaria ... 41 C10
Preslavska Planina, Bulgaria ... 41 C10
Prešov, Slovak Rep. ... 27 B14
Prešovský □, Slovak Rep. ... 27 B13
Prespa, Bulgaria ... 41 E8
Prespa, L. = Prespansko Jezero, Macedonia ... 40 F5
Prespansko Jezero, Macedonia ... 40 F5
Presque I., U.S.A. ... 110 D4
Presque Isle, U.S.A. ... 109 B12
Prestatyn, U.K. ... 12 D4
Prestea, Ghana ... 82 D4
Presteigne, U.K. ... 13 E5
Prestice, Czech Rep. ... 26 B6
Preston, Canada ... 110 C4
Preston, U.K. ... 12 D5
Preston, Idaho, U.S.A. ... 114 E8
Preston, Minn., U.S.A. ... 112 D8
Preston, C., Australia ... 92 D2
Prestonburg, U.S.A. ... 108 G4
Prestwick, U.K. ... 14 F4
Pretoria, S. Africa ... 89 D4
Preuilly-sur-Claise, France ... 18 F7
Préveza, Greece ... 38 C2
Préveza □, Greece ... 38 B2
Prey Veng, Cambodia ... 65 G5
Priazovskoye, Ukraine ... 47 J8
Pribilof Is., U.S.A. ... 100 C2
Priboj, Serbia, Yug. ... 40 C3
Příbram, Czech Rep. ... 26 B7
Price, U.S.A. ... 114 G8
Price I., Canada ... 104 C3
Prichard, U.S.A. ... 109 K1
Priego, Spain ... 32 E2
Priego de Córdoba, Spain ... 35 H6
Priekule, Latvia ... 9 H19
Prien, Germany ... 25 H8
Prienai, Lithuania ... 9 J20
Prieska, S. Africa ... 88 D3
Priest L., U.S.A. ... 114 B5
Priest River, U.S.A. ... 114 B5
Priest Valley, U.S.A. ... 116 J6
Prievidza, Slovak Rep. ... 27 C11
Prignitz, Germany ... 24 B7
Prijedor, Bos.-H. ... 29 D13
Prijepolje, Serbia, Yug. ... 40 C3
Prikaspiyskaya Nizmennost = Caspian Depression, Eurasia ... 49 G9
Prikro, Ivory C. ... 82 D4
Prikubanskaya Nizmennost, Russia ... 49 H4
Prilep, Macedonia ... 40 E5
Priluki = Pryluky, Ukraine ... 47 G7
Prime Seal I., Australia ... 94 G4
Primorsk, Russia ... 46 B5
Primorsko, Bulgaria ... 41 D11
Primorsko-Akhtarsk, Russia ... 47 J10
Primorskoye, Ukraine ... 47 J9
Primrose L., Canada ... 105 C7
Prince Albert, Canada ... 105 C7
Prince Albert, S. Africa ... 88 E3
Prince Albert Mts., Antarctica ... 5 D11
Prince Albert Nat. Park, Canada ... 105 C7
Prince Albert Pen., Canada ... 100 A8
Prince Albert Sd., Canada ... 100 A8
Prince Alfred, C., Canada ... 4 B1
Prince Charles I., Canada ... 101 B12
Prince Charles Mts., Antarctica ... 5 D6
Prince Edward I. □, Canada ... 103 C7
Prince Edward Is., Ind. Oc. ... 3 G11
Prince Edward Pt., Canada ... 110 C8
Prince George, Canada ... 104 C4
Prince of Wales, C., U.S.A. ... 98 C3
Prince of Wales I., Australia ... 94 A3
Prince of Wales I., Canada ... 100 A10
Prince of Wales I., U.S.A. ... 100 C6
Prince Patrick I., Canada ... 4 B2
Prince Regent Inlet, Canada ... 4 B3
Prince Rupert, Canada ... 104 C2
Princess Charlotte B., Australia ... 94 A3
Princess May Ranges, Australia ... 92 C4
Princess Royal I., Canada ... 104 C3
Princeton, Canada ... 104 D4
Princeton, Calif., U.S.A. ... 116 F4
Princeton, Ill., U.S.A. ... 112 E10
Princeton, Ind., U.S.A. ... 108 F2
Princeton, Ky., U.S.A. ... 108 G2
Princeton, Mo., U.S.A. ... 112 E8
Princeton, N.J., U.S.A. ... 111 F10
Princeton, W. Va., U.S.A. ... 108 G5
Principe, I. de, Atl. Oc. ... 76 F4
Principe da Beira, Brazil ... 124 F6
Prineville, U.S.A. ... 114 D3
Prins Harald Kyst, Antarctica ... 5 D4
Prinsesse Astrid Kyst, Antarctica ... 5 D3
Prinsesse Ragnhild Kyst, Antarctica ... 5 D4
Prinzapolca, Nic. ... 120 D3
Prior, C., Spain ... 34 B2
Priozersk, Russia ... 46 B6
Pripet = Prypyat →, Europe ... 47 G9
Pripet Marshes = Pripyat Marshes, Europe ... 47 F5
Pripyat Marshes = Pripet Marshes, Europe ... 47 F5
Pripyats = Prypyat →, Europe ... 47 G6
Prislop, Pasul, Romania ... 43 C9

Pristen, Russia ... 47 G9
Priština, Kosovo, Yug. ... 40 D5
Pritzwalk, Germany ... 24 B8
Privas, France ... 21 D8
Priverno, Italy ... 30 A6
Privolzhsk, Russia ... 48 B5
Privolzhskaya Vozvyshennost, Russia ... 48 E7
Privolzhskiy, Russia ... 48 E8
Privolzhye, Russia ... 48 D9
Priyutnoye, Russia ... 49 G6
Prizren, Kosovo, Yug. ... 40 D4
Prizzi, Italy ... 30 E6
Prnjavor, Bos.-H. ... 42 F2
Probolinggo, Indonesia ... 63 G15
Prochowice, Poland ... 45 G3
Proctor, U.S.A. ... 111 C11
Proddatur, India ... 66 M11
Prodhromos, Cyprus ... 36 E11
Proença-a-Nova, Portugal ... 34 F3
Profitis Ilías, Greece ... 36 C9
Profondeville, Belgium ... 17 D4
Progreso, Coahuila, Mexico ... 118 B4
Progreso, Yucatán, Mexico ... 119 C7
Prokhladnyy, Russia ... 49 J7
Prokletije, Albania ... 40 D3
Prokopyevsk, Russia ... 50 D9
Prokuplje, Serbia, Yug. ... 40 C5
Proletarsk, Russia ... 49 G5
Proletarskaya = Proletarsk, Russia ... 49 G5
Prome = Pyè, Burma ... 67 K19
Prophet →, Canada ... 104 B4
Prophet River, Canada ... 104 B4
Propriá, Brazil ... 125 F11
Propriano, France ... 21 G12
Prosper, Australia ... 94 C4
Proserpine, Australia ... 94 C4
Prosna →, Poland ... 45 F4
Prospect, U.S.A. ... 111 C9
Prosser, U.S.A. ... 114 C4
Prostějov, Czech Rep. ... 27 B10
Prostki, Poland ... 44 E9
Proston, Australia ... 95 D5
Proszowice, Poland ... 45 H7
Próti, Greece ... 38 D3
Provadiya, Bulgaria ... 41 C11
Provence, France ... 21 E9
Provence-Alpes-Côte d'Azur □, France ... 21 D10
Providence, Ky., U.S.A. ... 108 G2
Providence, R.I., U.S.A. ... 111 E13
Providence Bay, Canada ... 102 C3
Providence Mts., U.S.A. ... 117 K11
Providencia, I. de, Colombia ... 120 D3
Provideniya, Russia ... 51 C19
Provins, France ... 19 D10
Provo, U.S.A. ... 114 F8
Provost, Canada ... 105 C6
Prozor, Bos.-H. ... 42 G2
Prudhoe Bay, U.S.A. ... 100 A5
Prudhoe I., Australia ... 94 C4
Prud'homme, Canada ... 105 C7
Prudnik, Poland ... 45 H4
Prüm, Germany ... 25 E2
Pruszcz Gdański, Poland ... 44 D5
Pruszków, Poland ... 45 F7
Prut →, Romania ... 43 E13
Pruzhany, Belarus ... 47 F3
Prvić, Croatia ... 29 D11
Prydz B., Antarctica ... 5 C6
Pryluky, Ukraine ... 47 G7
Pryor, U.S.A. ... 113 G7
Prypyat →, Europe ... 47 G9
Przasnysz, Poland ... 45 E7
Przedbórz, Poland ... 45 G6
Przedecz, Poland ... 45 F5
Przemków, Poland ... 45 G2
Przemyśl, Poland ... 45 J9
Przeworsk, Poland ... 45 H9
Przewalsk, Kyrgyzstan ... 50 E8
Przhevalsk, Kyrgyzstan ... 50 E8
Psakhná, Greece ... 38 C5
Psará, Greece ... 39 C7
Psathoúra, Greece ... 38 B6
Psel →, Ukraine ... 47 H7
Pserimos, Greece ... 39 E9
Psíra, Greece ... 36 D7
Pskov, Russia ... 46 D5
Pskovskoye, Ozero, Russia ... 9 H22
Ptich = Ptsich →, Belarus ... 47 F5
Ptolemaís, Greece ... 40 F5
Ptsich →, Belarus ... 47 F5
Ptuj, Slovenia ... 29 B12
Ptujska Gora, Slovenia ... 29 B12
Pu Xian, China ... 56 F6
Pua, Thailand ... 64 C3
Puán, Argentina ... 126 D3
Pu'an, China ... 58 E5
Pubei, China ... 58 F7
Pucallpa, Peru ... 124 E4
Pucheng, China ... 59 D12
Pucheni, Romania ... 43 E10
Puchheim, Germany ... 25 G7
Puchov, Slovak Rep. ... 27 B11
Pucioasa, Romania ... 43 E10
Pučišća, Croatia ... 29 E13
Puck, Poland ... 44 D5
Pucka, Zatoka, Poland ... 44 D5
Puçol, Spain ... 33 F4
Pudasjärvi, Finland ... 8 D22
Pudong, China ... 59 B13
Pudozh, Russia ... 46 B9
Pudukkottai, India ... 66 P11
Puebla, Mexico ... 119 D5
Puebla □, Mexico ... 119 D5
Puebla de Alcocer, Spain ... 35 G5

Puebla de Don Fadrique, Spain ... 33 H2
Puebla de Don Rodrigo, Spain ... 35 F6
Puebla de Guzmán, Spain ... 35 H3
Puebla de la Calzada, Spain ... 35 G4
Puebla de Sanabria, Spain ... 34 C4
Puebla de Trives = Pobra de Trives, Spain ... 34 C3
Pueblo, U.S.A. ... 112 F2
Pueblo Hundido, Chile ... 126 B1
Puelches, Argentina ... 126 D2
Puelén, Argentina ... 126 D2
Puente Alto, Chile ... 126 C1
Puente-Genil, Spain ... 35 H6
Puente la Reina, Spain ... 32 C3
Puenteareas = Ponteareas, Spain ... 34 C2
Puentedeume = Pontedeume, Spain ... 34 B2
Puentes de Garcia Rodriguez = As Pontes de García Rodríguez, Spain ... 34 B3
Pu'er, China ... 58 F3
Puerco →, U.S.A. ... 115 J10
Puerto, Canary Is. ... 37 F2
Puerto Aisén, Chile ... 128 F2
Puerto Ángel, Mexico ... 119 D5
Puerto Arista, Mexico ... 119 D6
Puerto Armuelles, Panama ... 120 E3
Puerto Ayacucho, Venezuela ... 124 B5
Puerto Barrios, Guatemala ... 120 C2
Puerto Bermejo, Argentina ... 126 B4
Puerto Bermúdez, Peru ... 124 F4
Puerto Bolívar, Ecuador ... 124 D3
Puerto Cabello, Venezuela ... 124 A5
Puerto Cabezas, Nic. ... 120 D3
Puerto Cabo Gracias á Dios, Nic. ... 120 D3
Puerto Carreño, Colombia ... 124 B5
Puerto Castilla, Honduras ... 120 C2
Puerto Chicama, Peru ... 124 E3
Puerto Coig, Argentina ... 128 G3
Puerto Cortés, Costa Rica ... 120 E3
Puerto Cortés, Honduras ... 120 C2
Puerto Cumarebo, Venezuela ... 124 A5
Puerto de Alcudia = Port d'Alcúdia, Spain ... 37 B10
Puerto de Andraitx, Spain ... 37 B9
Puerto de Cabrera, Spain ... 37 B9
Puerto de Gran Tarajal, Canary Is. ... 37 F5
Puerto de la Cruz, Canary Is. ... 37 F3
Puerto de Mazarrón, Spain ... 33 H3
Puerto de Pozo Negro, Canary Is. ... 37 F6
Puerto de Sóller = Port de Sóller, Spain ... 37 B9
Puerto de Somosierra, Spain ... 34 D7
Puerto del Carmen, Canary Is. ... 37 F6
Puerto del Rosario, Canary Is. ... 37 F6
Puerto Deseado, Argentina ... 128 F3
Puerto Escondido, Mexico ... 119 D5
Puerto Heath, Bolivia ... 124 F5
Puerto Inírida, Colombia ... 124 C5
Puerto Juárez, Mexico ... 119 C7
Puerto La Cruz, Venezuela ... 124 A6
Puerto Leguízamo, Colombia ... 124 D4
Puerto Limón, Colombia ... 124 C4
Puerto Lobos, Argentina ... 128 E3
Puerto Lumbreras, Spain ... 33 H3
Puerto Madryn, Argentina ... 128 E3
Puerto Maldonado, Peru ... 124 F5
Puerto Manotí, Cuba ... 120 B4
Puerto Mazarrón = Puerto de Mazarrón, Spain ... 33 H3
Puerto Montt, Chile ... 128 E2
Puerto Morazán, Nic. ... 120 D2
Puerto Morelos, Mexico ... 119 C7
Puerto Natales, Chile ... 128 G2
Puerto Padre, Cuba ... 120 B4
Puerto Páez, Venezuela ... 124 B5
Puerto Peñasco, Mexico ... 118 A2
Puerto Pinasco, Paraguay ... 126 A4
Puerto Plata, Dom. Rep. ... 121 C5
Puerto Pollensa = Port de Pollença, Spain ... 37 B10
Puerto Quepos, Costa Rica ... 120 E3
Puerto Real, Spain ... 35 J4
Puerto Rico, Canary Is. ... 37 G4
Puerto Rico ■, W. Indies ... 121 C6
Puerto Rico Trench, Atl. Oc. ... 121 C6
Puerto San Julián, Argentina ... 128 F3
Puerto Sastre, Paraguay ... 126 A4
Puerto Serrano, Spain ... 35 J5
Puerto Suárez, Bolivia ... 124 G7
Puerto Vallarta, Mexico ... 118 C3
Puerto Wilches, Colombia ... 124 B4
Puertollano, Spain ... 35 G6
Pueyrredón, L., Argentina ... 128 F2
Puffin I., Ireland ... 15 E1
Pugachev, Russia ... 48 D9
Pugal, India ... 68 E5
Puge, China ... 58 D4
Puge, Tanzania ... 86 C3
Puget Sound, U.S.A. ... 114 C2
Puget-Théniers, France ... 21 E10
Púglia □, Italy ... 31 A9
Pugödong, N. Korea ... 57 C16
Pugu, Tanzania ... 86 D4
Pūgünzī, Iran ... 71 E8
Pui, Romania ... 42 E8
Puiești, Romania ... 43 D12
Puig Major, Spain ... 37 B9
Puigcerdà, Spain ... 32 C6
Puigmal, Spain ... 32 C7
Puigpunyent, Spain ... 37 B9
Puijiang, China ... 58 B4

Puisaye, Collines de la,
  France 19 E10
Puiseaux, *France* 19 D9
Pujehun, *S. Leone* 82 D2
Pujiang, *China* 59 C12
Pujols, *France* 20 D3
Pujon-chŏsuji, *N. Korea* ... 57 D14
Pukaki L., *N.Z.* 91 L3
Pukapuka, *Cook Is.* 97 J11
Pukaskwa Nat. Park, *Canada* 102 C2
Pukatawagan, *Canada* 105 B8
Pukchin, *N. Korea* 57 D13
Pukch'ŏng, *N. Korea* 57 D15
Pukekohe, *N.Z.* 91 G5
Pukhrayan, *India* 69 F8
Pukou, *China* 59 A12
Pula, *Croatia* 29 D10
Pula, *Italy* 30 C1
Pulacayo, *Bolivia* 124 H5
Pulandian, *China* 57 E11
Pularumpi, *Australia* 92 B5
Pulaski, *N.Y., U.S.A.* ... 111 C8
Pulaski, *Tenn., U.S.A.* .. 109 H2
Pulaski, *Va., U.S.A.* ... 108 G5
Pulau →, *Indonesia* 63 F9
Puławy, *Poland* 45 G8
Pulga, *U.S.A.* 116 F5
Pulicat L., *India* 66 N12
Pullman, *U.S.A.* 114 C5
Pulo-Anna, *Pac. Oc.* 63 D8
Pulog, Mt., *Phil.* 61 C4
Pułtusk, *Poland* 45 F8
Pülümür, *Turkey* 73 C8
Pumlumon Fawr, *U.K.* .. 13 E4
Puná, I., *Ecuador* 124 D2
Punakha, *Bhutan* 67 F16
Punasar, *India* 68 F5
Punata, *Bolivia* 124 G5
Punch, *India* 69 C6
Punch →, *Pakistan* 68 C5
Punda Maria, *S. Africa* . 89 C5
Pune, *India* 66 K8
P'ungsan, *N. Korea* 57 D15
Pungue, Ponte de, *Mozam.* 87 F3
Puning, *China* 59 F11
Punjab □, *India* 68 D7
Punjab □, *Pakistan* 68 E6
Puno, *Peru* 124 G4
Punpun →, *India* 69 G11
Punta Alta, *Argentina* .. 128 D4
Punta Arenas, *Chile* 128 G2
Punta de Díaz, *Chile* ... 126 B1
Punta Gorda, *Belize* 119 D7
Punta Gorda, *U.S.A.* ... 109 M5
Punta Prieta, *Mexico* ... 118 B2
Punta Prima, *Spain* 37 B11
Punta Umbría, *Spain* ... 35 H4
Puntarenas, *Costa Rica* . 120 E3
Punto Fijo, *Venezuela* .. 124 A4
Punxsatawney, *U.S.A.* .. 110 F6
Puqi, *China* 59 C9
Puquio, *Peru* 124 F4
Pur →, *Russia* 50 C8
Purace, Vol., *Colombia* . 124 C3
Puračić, *Bos.-H.* 42 F3
Puralia = Puruliya, *India* 69 H12
Puranpur, *India* 69 E9
Purbeck, Isle of, *U.K.* .. 13 G6
Purcell, *U.S.A.* 113 H6
Purcell Mts., *Canada* ... 104 D5
Puri, *India* 67 K14
Purmerend, *Neths.* 17 B4
Purnia, *India* 69 G12
Pursat = Pouthisat,
  Cambodia 64 F4
Purukcahu, *Indonesia* .. 62 E4
Puruliya, *India* 69 H12
Purus →, *Brazil* 122 D4
Puruvesi, *Finland* 46 B5
Purvis, *U.S.A.* 113 K10
Pŭrvomay, *Bulgaria* ... 41 D9
Purwa, *India* 69 F9
Purwakarta, *Indonesia* . 63 G12
Purwodadi, *Indonesia* .. 63 G14
Purwokerto, *Indonesia* . 63 G13
Puryŏng, *N. Korea* 57 C15
Pusa, *India* 69 G11
Pusan, *S. Korea* 57 G15
Pushkin, *Russia* 46 C6
Pushkino, *Moskva, Russia* 46 D9
Pushkino, *Saratov, Russia* 48 E8
Püspökladány, *Hungary* . 42 C6
Pustoshka, *Russia* 46 D5
Puszczykowo, *Poland* .. 45 F3
Putahow L., *Canada* ... 105 B8
Putao, *Burma* 67 F20
Putaruru, *N.Z.* 91 H5
Putbus, *Germany* 24 A9
Puthein Myit →, *Burma* 67 M19
Putian, *China* 59 E12
Putignano, *Italy* 31 B10
Putina, *Romania* 43 C10
Putna →, *Romania* 43 E12
Putnam, *U.S.A.* 111 E13
Putnok, *Hungary* 42 B5
Putorana, Gory, *Russia* . 51 C10
Puttalam, *Sri Lanka* ... 66 Q11
Puttgarden, *Germany* .. 24 A7
Püttlingen, *Germany* ... 25 F7
Putumayo →, *S. Amer.* 122 D4
Putuo, *China* 59 C14
Putussibau, *Indonesia* . 62 D4
Puvirnituq, *Canada* 101 B12
Puy-de-Dôme, *France* .. 20 C6
Puy-de-Dôme □, *France* 20 C7
Puy-l'Évêque, *France* .. 20 D5
Puyallup, *U.S.A.* 116 C4
Puyang, *China* 56 G8

Puylaurens, *France* 20 E6
Pūzeh Rīg, *Iran* 71 E8
Pwani □, *Tanzania* 86 D4
Pweto,
  Dem. Rep. of the Congo . 87 D2
Pwllheli, *U.K.* 12 E3
Pyana →, *Russia* 48 C8
Pyapon, *Burma* 67 L19
Pyasina →, *Russia* 51 B9
Pyatigorsk, *Russia* 49 H6
Pyatykhatky, *Ukraine* .. 47 H7
Pydna, *Greece* 40 F6
Pyè, *Burma* 67 K19
Pyetrikaw, *Belarus* 47 F5
Pyhäjoki, *Finland* 8 D21
Pyinmana, *Burma* 67 K20
Pyla, C., *Cyprus* 36 E12
Pymatuning Reservoir,
  U.S.A. 110 E4
Pyŏktong, *N. Korea* ... 57 D13
Pyŏnggang, *N. Korea* .. 57 E14
P'yŏngt'aek, *S. Korea* .. 57 F14
P'yŏngyang, *N. Korea* . 57 E13
Pyote, *U.S.A.* 113 K3
Pyramid L., *U.S.A.* 114 G4
Pyramid Pk., *U.S.A.* ... 117 J10
Pyramids, *Egypt* 80 J7
Pyrénées, *Europe* 20 F4
Pyrénées-Atlantiques □,
  France 20 E3
Pyrénées-Orientales □,
  France 20 F6
Pyryatyn, *Ukraine* 47 G7
Pyrzyce, *Poland* 45 E1
Pyskowice, *Poland* 45 H5
Pytalovo, *Russia* 46 D4
Pyu, *Burma* 67 K20
Pyzdry, *Poland* 45 F4

Q

Qaanaaq, *Greenland* 4 B4
Qabirri →, *Azerbaijan* .. 49 K8
Qachasnek, *S. Africa* .. 89 E4
Qa'el Jafr, *Jordan* 75 E5
Qa'emābād, *Iran* 71 D9
Qā'emshahr, *Iran* 71 B7
Qagan Nur, *China* 56 C8
Qahar Youyi Zhongqi, *China* 56 D7
Qahremānshahr =
  Bākhtarān, *Iran* 70 C5
Qaidam Pendi, *China* .. 60 C4
Qajarīyeh, *Iran* 71 D6
Qala, Ras il, *Malta* 36 C1
Qala-i-Jadid = Spīn Búldak,
  Afghan. 68 D2
Qala Viala, *Pakistan* ... 68 D2
Qala Yangi, *Afghan.* ... 68 B2
Qal'at al Akhḍar, *Si. Arabia* 70 E3
Qal'at Dīzah, *Iraq* 70 B5
Qal'at Şāliḥ, *Iraq* 70 D5
Qal'at Sukkar, *Iraq* 70 D5
Qal'eh Shaharak, *Afghan.* 66 B4
Qalyûb, *Egypt* 80 H7
Qamdo, *China* 58 B1
Qamruddin Karez, *Pakistan* 68 D3
Qandahār, *Afghan.* 66 D4
Qandahār □, *Afghan.* .. 66 D4
Qapān, *Iran* 71 B7
Qapshaghay, *Kazakhstan* 50 E8
Qaqortoq, *Greenland* ... 4 C5
Qâra, *Egypt* 80 B2
Qara Qash →, *India* ... 69 B8
Qarabutaq, *Kazakhstan* . 50 E7
Qaraçala, *Azerbaijan* ... 49 L9
Qaraghandy, *Kazakhstan* 50 E8
Qārah, *Si. Arabia* 70 D4
Qarataū, *Kazakhstan* ... 50 E8
Qardud, *Sudan* 81 E2
Qareh →, *Iran* 70 B5
Qareh Tekān, *Iran* 71 B6
Qarqan He →, *China* .. 60 C3
Qarqaraly, *Kazakhstan* . 50 E8
Qarrasa, *Sudan* 81 E3
Qarshi, *Uzbekistan* 50 F7
Qartabā, *Lebanon* 75 A4
Qaryat al Gharab, *Iraq* . 70 D5
Qaryat al 'Ulyā, *Si. Arabia* 70 E5
Qasr 'Amra, *Jordan* ... 70 D3
Qaşr-e Qand, *Iran* 71 E9
Qasr Farâfra, *Egypt* ... 80 B2
Qatanā, *Syria* 75 B5
Qatar ■, *Asia* 71 E6
Qatlīsh, *Iran* 71 B8
Qattâra, *Egypt* 80 A2
Qattâra, Munkhafed el,
  Egypt 80 B2
Qattâra Depression =
  Qattâra, Munkhafed el,
  Egypt 80 B2
Qawâm al Ḥamzah, *Iraq* 70 D5
Qāyen, *Iran* 71 C8
Qazaqstan = Kazakhstan ■,
  Asia 50 E7
Qazimämmäd, *Azerbaijan* 49 K9
Qazvin, *Iran* 71 B6
Qeissan, *Sudan* 81 E3
Qena, *Egypt* 80 B3
Qena, W. →, *Egypt* ... 80 B3
Qeqertarsuaq, *Greenland* 4 C5
Qeqertarsuaq, *Greenland* 4 C5
Qeshlāq, *Iran* 70 C5
Qeshm, *Iran* 71 E8
Qeys, *Iran* 71 E7
Qezel Owzen →, *Iran* .. 71 B6
Qezi'ot, *Israel* 75 E3
Qi Xian, *China* 56 G8
Qian Gorlos, *China* 57 B13

Qian Xian, *China* 56 G5
Qiancheng, *China* 58 D7
Qianjiang,
  Guangxi Zhuangzu, China 58 F7
Qianjiang, *Hubei, China* 59 B9
Qianjiang, *Sichuan, China* 58 C7
Qianshan, *China* 59 B11
Qianwei, *China* 58 C4
Qianxi, *China* 58 D6
Qianyang, *Hunan, China* 59 D8
Qianyang, *Shaanxi, China* 56 G4
Qianyang, *Zhejiang, China* 59 B12
Qiaojia, *China* 58 D4
Qiaojia, *China* 58 D4
Qibā', *Si. Arabia* 70 E5
Qichun, *China* 59 B10
Qidong, *Hunan, China* . 59 D9
Qidong, *Jiangsu, China* . 59 B13
Qijiang, *China* 58 C6
Qikiqtarjuaq, *Canada* .. 101 B13
Qila Safed, *Pakistan* ... 66 E2
Qila Saifullāh, *Pakistan* 68 D3
Qilian Shan, *China* 60 C4
Qimen, *China* 59 C11
Qin He →, *China* 56 G7
Qin Jiang →,
  Guangxi Zhuangzu, China 58 F7
Qin Jiang →, *Jiangxi, China* 59 D10
Qin Ling = Qinling Shandi,
  China 56 H5
Qin'an, *China* 56 G3
Qing Xian, *China* 56 E9
Qingcheng, *China* 57 F9
Qingdao, *China* 57 F11
Qingfeng, *China* 56 G8
Qinghai □, *China* 60 C4
Qinghai Hu, *China* 60 C5
Qinghecheng, *China* ... 57 D13
Qinghemen, *China* 57 D11
Qingjian, *China* 56 F6
Qingjiang = Huaiyin, *China* 57 H10
Qingliu, *China* 59 D11
Qinglong, *China* 58 E5
Qingping, *China* 58 D6
Qingpu, *China* 59 B13
Qingshui, *China* 56 G4
Qingshuihe, *China* 56 E6
Qingtian, *China* 59 C13
Qingtongxia Shuiku, *China* 56 F3
Qingxi, *China* 58 D7
Qingxu, *China* 56 F7
Qingyang, *Anhui, China* 59 B11
Qingyang, *Gansu, China* 56 F4
Qingyi Jiang →, *China* . 58 C4
Qingyuan, *Guangdong,*
  China 59 F9
Qingyuan, *Liaoning, China* 57 C13
Qingyuan, *Zhejiang, China* 59 D12
Qingyun, *China* 57 F9
Qingzhen, *China* 58 D6
Qinhuangdao, *China* ... 57 E10
Qinling Shandi, *China* . 56 H5
Qinshui, *China* 56 G7
Qinyang = Jiyuan, *China* 56 G7
Qinyuan, *China* 56 F7
Qinzhou, *China* 58 G7
Qionghai, *China* 64 C8
Qionglai, *China* 58 B4
Qionglai Shan, *China* .. 58 B4
Qiongzhou Haixia, *China* 58 B8
Qiqihar, *China* 51 E13
Qiraîya, W. →, *Egypt* . 75 E3
Qiryat Ata, *Israel* 75 C4
Qiryat Gat, *Israel* 75 D3
Qiryat Mal'akhi, *Israel* . 75 D3
Qiryat Shemona, *Israel* . 75 B4
Qiryat Yam, *Israel* 75 C4
Qishan, *China* 56 G4
Qitai, *China* 60 B3
Qiubei, *China* 58 E5
Qixia, *China* 57 F11
Qiyang, *China* 59 D8
Qızlağac Körfäzi, *Azerbaijan* 71 B6
Qojūr, *Iran* 70 B5
Qom, *Iran* 71 C6
Qomolangma Feng =
  Everest, Mt., *Nepal* .. 69 E12
Qomsheh, *Iran* 71 D6
Qorveh, *Iran* 73 C12
Qostanay, *Kazakhstan* .. 50 D7
Qoţūr, *Iran* 73 C11
Qu Jiang →, *China* 58 B6
Qu Xian, *China* 58 B6
Quabbin Reservoir, *U.S.A.* 111 D12
Quairading, *Australia* .. 93 F2
Quakenbrück, *Germany* . 24 C3
Quakertown, *U.S.A.* ... 111 F9
Qualicum Beach, *Canada* 104 D4
Quambatook, *Australia* . 95 F3
Quambone, *Australia* .. 95 E4
Quamby, *Australia* 94 C3
Quan Long = Ca Mau,
  Vietnam 65 H5
Quanah, *U.S.A.* 113 H5
Quang Ngai, *Vietnam* .. 64 E7
Quang Tri, *Vietnam* ... 64 D6
Quang Yen, *Vietnam* .. 58 G6
Quannan, *China* 59 E10
Quanzhou,
  Guangxi Zhuangzu, China 59 E8
Qu'Appelle, *Canada* ... 105 C8
Quaqtaq, *Canada* 101 B13
Quaraí, *Brazil* 126 C4
Quaraí →, *Brazil* 126 C4
Quarré-les-Tombes, *France* 19 E11
Quarteira, *Portugal* 35 H2
Quartu Sant'Élena, *Italy* 30 C2
Quartzsite, *U.S.A.* 117 M12
Quatsino Sd., *Canada* .. 104 C2
Quba, *Azerbaijan* 49 K9

Queanbeyan, *Australia* .. 95 F4
Québec, *Canada* 103 C5
Québec □, *Canada* 103 C6
Quedlinburg, *Germany* . 24 D7
Queen Alexandra Ra.,
  Antarctica 5 E11
Queen Charlotte City,
  Canada 104 C2
Queen Charlotte Is., *Canada* 104 C2
Queen Charlotte Sd.,
  Canada 104 C3
Queen Charlotte Strait,
  Canada 104 C3
Queen Elizabeth Is., *Canada* 98 B10
Queen Elizabeth Nat. Park,
  Uganda 86 C3
Queen Mary Land,
  Antarctica 5 D7
Queen Maud G., *Canada* . 100 B9
Queen Maud Land,
  Antarctica 5 D3
Queen Maud Mts.,
  Antarctica 5 E13
Queens Chan., *Australia* . 92 C4
Queenscliff, *Australia* .. 95 F3
Queensland □, *Australia* 94 C3
Queenstown, *Australia* . 94 G4
Queenstown, *N.Z.* 91 L2
Queenstown, *S. Africa* . 88 E4
Queets, *U.S.A.* 116 C2
Queguay Grande →,
  Uruguay 126 C4
Queimadas, *Brazil* 125 F11
Quelimane, *Mozam.* ... 87 F4
Quellón, *Chile* 128 E2
Quelpart = Cheju do,
  S. Korea 57 H14
Queluz, *Portugal* 35 G1
Quemado, *N. Mex., U.S.A.* 115 J9
Quemado, *Tex., U.S.A.* . 113 L4
Quemoy = Chinmen, *Taiwan* 59 E13
Quemú-Quemú, *Argentina* 126 D3
Quequén, *Argentina* ... 126 D4
Querétaro, *Mexico* 118 C4
Querétaro □, *Mexico* .. 118 C5
Querfurt, *Germany* 24 D7
Quérigut, *France* 20 F6
Querqueville, *France* ... 18 C5
Quesada, *Spain* 35 H7
Queshan, *China* 56 H8
Quesnel, *Canada* 104 C4
Quesnel →, *Canada* ... 104 C4
Quesnel L., *Canada* ... 104 C4
Questa, *U.S.A.* 115 H11
Questembert, *France* ... 18 E4
Quetico Prov. Park, *Canada* 102 C1
Quetta, *Pakistan* 68 D2
Quezaltenango, *Guatemala* 120 D1
Quezon City, *Phil.* 61 D4
Qufār, *Si. Arabia* 70 E4
Qui Nhon, *Vietnam* ... 64 F7
Quiaca, *Angola* 84 F2
Quibaxe, *Angola* 84 F2
Quibdo, *Colombia* 124 B3
Quiberon, *France* 18 E3
Quiberon, Presqu'île de,
  France 18 E3
Quickborn, *Germany* .. 24 B5
Quiet L., *Canada* 104 A2
Quiindy, *Paraguay* 126 B4
Quila, *Mexico* 118 C3
Quilán, C., *Chile* 128 E2
Quilcene, *U.S.A.* 116 C4
Quilimarí, *Chile* 126 C1
Quilino, *Argentina* 126 C3
Quill Lakes, *Canada* ... 105 C8
Quillabamba, *Peru* 124 F4
Quillagua, *Chile* 126 A2
Quillaicillo, *Chile* 126 C1
Quillan, *France* 20 F6
Quillota, *Chile* 126 C1
Quilmes, *Argentina* 126 C4
Quilon, *India* 66 Q10
Quilpie, *Australia* 95 D3
Quilpué, *Chile* 126 C1
Quilua, *Mozam.* 87 F4
Quimilí, *Argentina* 126 B3
Quimper, *France* 18 D2
Quimperlé, *France* 18 E3
Quinault →, *U.S.A.* ... 116 C2
Quincy, *Calif., U.S.A.* . 116 F6
Quincy, *Fla., U.S.A.* .. 109 K3
Quincy, *Ill., U.S.A.* ... 112 F9
Quincy, *Mass., U.S.A.* . 111 D14
Quincy, *Wash., U.S.A.* . 114 C4
Quines, *Argentina* 126 C2
Quinga, *Mozam.* 87 F5
Quingey, *France* 19 E12
Quinns Rocks, *Australia* 93 F2
Quintana de la Serena, *Spain* 35 G5
Quintana Roo □, *Mexico* 119 D7
Quintanar de la Orden,
  Spain 35 F7
Quintanar de la Sierra, *Spain* 32 C2
Quintanar del Rey, *Spain* 33 F3
Quintero, *Chile* 126 C1
Quintin, *France* 18 D4
Quinto, *Spain* 32 D4
Quípar →, *Spain* 33 G3
Quirihue, *Chile* 126 D1
Quirindi, *Australia* 95 E5
Quirinópolis, *Brazil* ... 125 G8
Quiroga, *Spain* 34 C3
Quissac, *France* 21 E8
Quissanga, *Mozam.* ... 87 E5
Quissico, *Mozam.* 89 C5
Quitilipi, *Argentina* ... 126 B3
Quitman, *U.S.A.* 109 K4
Quito, *Ecuador* 124 D3
Quixadá, *Brazil* 125 D11
Quixaxe, *Mozam.* 87 F5
Qujing, *China* 58 E4

Qul'ân, Jazâ'ir, *Egypt* .. 70 E2
Qumbu, *S. Africa* 89 E4
Quneitra, *Syria* 75 B4
Qûnghirot, *Uzbekistan* . 50 E6
Qu'nyido, *China* 58 B2
Quoin I., *Australia* 92 B4
Quoin Pt., *S. Africa* ... 88 E2
Quorn, *Australia* 95 E2
Qŭqon, *Uzbekistan* 50 E8
Qurein, *Sudan* 81 E3
Qurnat as Sawdâ', *Lebanon* 75 A5
Qûs, *Egypt* 80 B3
Qusar, *Azerbaijan* 49 K9
Quşaybā', *Si. Arabia* .. 70 E4
Quşaybah, *Iraq* 70 C4
Quseir, *Egypt* 70 E2
Qūshchī, *Iran* 70 B5
Quthing, *Lesotho* 89 E4
Qūtīābād, *Iran* 71 C6
Quwo, *China* 56 G6
Quyang, *China* 56 E8
Quynh Nhai, *Vietnam* .. 64 B4
Quyon, *Canada* 111 A8
Quzhou, *China* 59 C12
Quzi, *China* 56 F4
Qvareli, *Georgia* 49 K7
Qytet Stalin = Kuçovë,
  Albania 40 F3
Qyzylorda, *Kazakhstan* . 50 E7

R

Ra, Ko, *Thailand* 65 H2
Raab, *Austria* 26 C6
Raahe, *Finland* 8 D21
Raalte, *Neths.* 17 B6
Raasay, *U.K.* 14 D2
Raasay, Sd. of, *U.K.* ... 14 D2
Rab, *Croatia* 29 D11
Raba, *Indonesia* 63 F5
Rába →, *Hungary* 42 C2
Raba →, *Poland* 45 H7
Rabaçal →, *Portugal* .. 34 D3
Rabah, *Nigeria* 83 C6
Rabai, *Kenya* 86 C4
Rabak, *Sudan* 81 E3
Rabastens, *France* 20 E5
Rabastens-de-Bigorre, *France* 20 E4
Rabat, *Malta* 36 D1
Rabat, *Morocco* 78 B4
Rabaul, *Papua N. G.* .. 96 H7
Rābigh, *Si. Arabia* 74 C2
Rabka, *Poland* 45 J6
Râbniţa, *Moldova* 43 C14
Râbor, *Iran* 71 D8
Rača, *Serbia, Yug.* 40 B4
Răcăciuni, *Romania* ... 43 D11
Răcăşdia, *Romania* ... 42 F6
Racconigi, *Italy* 28 D4
Race, C., *Canada* 103 C9
Rach Gia, *Vietnam* 65 G5
Rachid, *Mauritania* ... 82 B2
Raciąż, *Poland* 45 F7
Racibórz, *Poland* 45 H5
Racine, *U.S.A.* 108 D2
Rackerby, *U.S.A.* 116 F5
Radama, Nosy, *Madag.* . 89 A8
Radama, Saikanosy, *Madag.* 89 A8
Radan, *Serbia, Yug.* ... 40 D5
Rădăuţi, *Romania* 43 C10
Rădăuţi-Prut, *Romania* . 43 B11
Radbuza →, *Czech Rep.* 26 D3
Radcliff, *U.S.A.* 108 G3
Radebeul, *Germany* 24 D9
Radeburg, *Germany* ... 24 D9
Radeče, *Slovenia* 29 B12
Radekhiv, *Ukraine* 47 G3
Radekhov = Radekhiv,
  Ukraine 47 G3
Radenthein, *Austria* ... 26 E6
Radew →, *Poland* 44 E2
Radford, *U.S.A.* 108 G5
Radhanpur, *India* 68 H4
Radhwa, Jabal, *Si. Arabia* 70 E3
Radika →, *Macedonia* . 40 E4
Radisson, *Qué., Canada* 102 B5
Radisson, *Sask., Canada* 105 C7
Radium Hot Springs, *Canada* 104 C5
Radlje ob Dravi, *Slovenia* 29 B12
Radnevo, *Bulgaria* 41 D9
Radnor Forest, *U.K.* ... 13 E4
Radolfzell, *Germany* ... 25 H4
Radom, *Poland* 45 G8
Radom →, *Poland* 45 G8
Radomka →, *Poland* .. 45 G8
Radomsko, *Poland* 45 G6
Radomyshl, *Ukraine* ... 47 G5
Radomyśl Wielki, *Poland* 45 H8
Radoszyce, *Poland* 45 G7
Radoviš, *Macedonia* ... 40 E5
Radovljica, *Slovenia* ... 29 B11
Radstadt, *Austria* 26 D6
Radstock, *U.K.* 13 F5
Răducăneni, *Romania* . 43 D12
Raduša, *Macedonia* ... 40 E4
Radviliškis, *Lithuania* . 9 J20
Radville, *Canada* 105 D8
Radymno, *Poland* 45 J9
Radzanów, *Poland* 45 F7
Radziejów, *Poland* 45 F5
Radzyń Chełmiński, *Poland* 45 E5
Radzyń Podlaski, *Poland* 45 G9
Rae, *Canada* 104 A5
Rae Bareli, *India* 69 F9
Rae Isthmus, *Canada* .. 101 B11
Raeren, *Belgium* 17 D6

Raeside, L., *Australia* 93 E3
Raetihi, *N.Z.* 91 H5
Rafaela, *Argentina* 126 C3
Rafah, *Gaza Strip* 75 D3
Rafai, *C.A.R.* 86 B1
Raffadali, *Italy* 30 E6
Raffili, *Sudan* 81 F2
Rafhā, *Si. Arabia* 70 D4
Rafsanjān, *Iran* 71 D8
Raft Pt., *Australia* 92 C3
Râgâ, *Sudan* 81 F2
Raga →, *Sudan* 81 F2
Ragachow, *Belarus* 47 F6
Ragag, *Sudan* 81 E1
Ragama, *Sri Lanka* 66 R11
Ragged, Mt., *Australia* 93 F3
Raghunathpalli, *India* 69 H11
Raghunathpur, *India* 69 H12
Raglan, *N.Z.* 91 G5
Ragusa, *Italy* 31 F7
Raha, *Indonesia* 63 E6
Rahad, Nahr ar →, *Sudan* 81 E3
Rahaeng = Tak, *Thailand* .. 64 D2
Rahatgarh, *India* 69 H8
Rahden, *Germany* 24 C4
Raheita, *Eritrea* 81 E5
Raḥīmah, *Si. Arabia* 71 E6
Rahimyar Khan, *Pakistan* .. 68 E4
Rāhjerd, *Iran* 71 C6
Rahon, *India* 68 D7
Raichur, *India* 66 L10
Raiganj, *India* 69 G13
Raigarh, *India* 67 J13
Raijua, *Indonesia* 63 F6
Raikot, *India* 68 D6
Railton, *Australia* 94 G4
Rainbow Lake, *Canada* 104 B5
Rainier, *U.S.A.* 116 D4
Rainier, Mt., *U.S.A.* 116 D5
Rainy L., *Canada* 105 D10
Rainy River, *Canada* 105 D10
Raippaluoto, *Finland* 8 E19
Raipur, *India* 67 J12
Ra'is, *Si. Arabia* 80 C4
Raisen, *India* 68 H8
Raisio, *Finland* 9 F20
Raj Nandgaon, *India* 67 J12
Raj Nilgiri, *India* 69 J12
Raja, Ujung, *Indonesia* 62 D1
Raja Ampat, Kepulauan,
  Indonesia 63 E7
Rajahmundry, *India* 67 L12
Rajang →, *Malaysia* 62 D4
Rajanpur, *Pakistan* 68 E4
Rajapalaiyam, *India* 66 Q10
Rajasthan □, *India* 68 F5
Rajasthan Canal, *India* 68 F5
Rajauri, *India* 69 C6
Rajgarh, *Mad. P., India* ... 68 G7
Rajgarh, *Raj., India* 68 F7
Rajgarh, *Raj., India* 68 E6
Rajgir, *India* 69 G11
Rajgród, *Poland* 44 E9
Rajkot, *India* 68 H4
Rajmahal Hills, *India* 69 G12
Rajpipla, *India* 66 J8
Rajpur, *India* 68 H6
Rajpura, *India* 68 D7
Rajshahi, *Bangla.* 67 G16
Rajshahi □, *Bangla.* 69 G13
Rajula, *India* 68 J4
Rakaia, *N.Z.* 91 K4
Rakaia →, *N.Z.* 91 K4
Rakan, Ra's, *Qatar* 71 E6
Rakaposhi, *Pakistan* 69 A6
Rakata, Pulau, *Indonesia* .. 62 F3
Rakhiv, *Ukraine* 47 H3
Rakhni, *Pakistan* 68 D3
Rakhni →, *Pakistan* 68 E3
Rakitnoye, *Russia* 54 B7
Rakitovo, *Bulgaria* 41 E8
Rakoniewice, *Poland* 45 F3
Rakops, *Botswana* 88 C3
Rakovica, *Croatia* 29 D12
Rakovník, *Czech Rep.* 26 A6
Rakovski, *Bulgaria* 41 D8
Rakvere, *Estonia* 9 G22
Raleigh, *U.S.A.* 109 H6
Raleigh B., *U.S.A.* 107 D11
Ralja, *Serbia, Yug.* 40 B4
Ralls, *U.S.A.* 113 J4
Ralston, *U.S.A.* 110 E8
Ram →, *Canada* 104 A4
Rām Allāh, *West Bank* 75 D4
Ram Hd., *Australia* 95 F4
Rama, *Nic.* 120 D3
Ramacca, *Italy* 31 E7
Ramakona, *India* 69 J8
Ramales de la Victoria,
  Spain 34 B7
Raman, *Thailand* 65 J3
Ramanathapuram, *India* ... 66 Q11
Ramanetaka, B. de, *Madag.* 89 A8
Ramanujganj, *India* 69 H10
Ramat Gan, *Israel* 75 C3
Ramatlhabama, *S. Africa* .. 88 D4
Ramban, *India* 69 C6
Rambervillers, *France* 19 D13
Rambipuji, *Indonesia* 63 H15
Rambouillet, *France* 19 D8
Ramechhap, *Nepal* 69 F12
Ramenskoye, *Russia* 46 E10
Ramganga →, *India* 69 F8
Ramgarh, *Bihar, India* 69 H11
Ramgarh, *Raj., India* 68 F6
Ramgarh, *Raj., India* 68 F4
Rāmhormoz, *Iran* 71 D6
Ramīān, *Iran* 71 B7
Ramingining, *Australia* 94 A2
Ramla, *Israel* 75 D3
Ramlu, *Eritrea* 81 E5

Râmna →, *Romania* 43 E12
Ramnad =
  Ramanathapuram, *India* . 66 Q11
Ramnagar,
  Jammu & Kashmir, India 69 C6
Ramnagar, *Ut. P., India* ... 69 E8
Ramnäs, *Sweden* 10 E10
Râmnicu Sărat, *Romania* ... 43 E12
Râmnicu Vâlcea, *Romania* .. 43 E9
Ramon, *Russia* 47 G10
Ramona, *U.S.A.* 117 M10
Ramonville-St-Agne, *France* 20 E5
Ramore, *Canada* 102 C3
Ramos →, *Nigeria* 83 D6
Ramotswa, *Botswana* 88 C4
Rampur, *H.P., India* 68 D7
Rampur, *Mad. P., India* ... 68 H5
Rampur, *Ut. P., India* 69 E8
Rampur Hat, *India* 69 G12
Rampura, *India* 68 G6
Ramrama Tola, *India* 69 J8
Ramree I. = Ramree Kyun,
  Burma 67 K19
Ramree Kyun, *Burma* 67 K19
Rāmsar, *Iran* 71 B6
Ramsey, *U.K.* 12 C3
Ramsey, *U.S.A.* 111 E10
Ramsey L., *Canada* 102 C3
Ramsgate, *U.K.* 13 F9
Ramsjö, *Sweden* 10 B9
Ramstein, *Germany* 25 F3
Ramtek, *India* 66 J11
Ramvik, *Sweden* 10 B11
Rana Pratap Sagar Dam,
  India 68 G6
Ranaghat, *India* 69 H13
Ranahu, *Pakistan* 68 G3
Ranau, *Malaysia* 62 C5
Rancagua, *Chile* 126 C1
Rance →, *France* 18 D5
Rancheria →, *Canada* 104 A3
Ranchester, *U.S.A.* 114 D10
Ranchi, *India* 69 H11
Rancho Cucamonga, *U.S.A.* 117 L9
Randalstown, *U.K.* 15 B5
Randan, *France* 19 F10
Randazzo, *Italy* 31 E7
Randers, *Denmark* 11 H4
Randers Fjord, *Denmark* ... 11 H4
Randfontein, *S. Africa* 89 D4
Randle, *U.S.A.* 116 D5
Randolph, *Mass., U.S.A.* .. 111 D13
Randolph, *N.Y., U.S.A.* ... 110 D6
Randolph, *Utah, U.S.A.* ... 114 F8
Randolph, *Vt., U.S.A.* 111 C12
Randsburg, *U.S.A.* 117 K9
Råne älv →, *Sweden* 8 D20
Rangae, *Thailand* 65 J3
Rangaunu B., *N.Z.* 91 F4
Rangeley, *U.S.A.* 111 B14
Rangeley L., *U.S.A.* 111 B14
Rangely, *U.S.A.* 114 F9
Ranger, *U.S.A.* 113 J5
Rangia, *India* 67 F17
Rangiora, *N.Z.* 91 K4
Rangitaiki →, *N.Z.* 91 G6
Rangitata →, *N.Z.* 91 K3
Rangkasbitung, *Indonesia* .. 63 G12
Rangon →, *Burma* 67 L20
Rangoon, *Burma* 67 L20
Rangpur, *Bangla.* 67 G16
Rangsit, *Thailand* 64 F3
Ranibennur, *India* 66 M9
Raniganj, *Ut. P., India* 69 F9
Raniganj, *W. Bengal, India* . 67 H15
Ranikhet, *India* 69 E8
Raniwara, *India* 66 G8
Rāniyah, *Iraq* 70 B5
Ranka, *India* 69 H10
Ranken →, *Australia* 94 C2
Rankin, *U.S.A.* 113 K4
Rankin Inlet, *Canada* 100 B10
Rankins Springs, *Australia* . 95 E4
Rankweil, *Austria* 26 D2
Rannoch, L., *U.K.* 14 E4
Rannoch Moor, *U.K.* 14 E4
Ranobe, Helodran an' i,
  Madag. 89 C7
Ranohira, *Madag.* 89 C8
Ranomafana, Toamasina,
  Madag. 89 B8
Ranomafana, Toliara,
  Madag. 89 C8
Ranomena, *Madag.* 89 C8
Ranong, *Thailand* 65 H2
Ranotsara Nord, *Madag.* ... 89 C8
Ransiki, *Indonesia* 63 E8
Rantabe, *Madag.* 89 B8
Rantauprapat, *Indonesia* ... 62 D1
Rantemario, *Indonesia* 63 E5
Rantoul, *U.S.A.* 108 E1
Ranum, *Denmark* 11 H3
Ranyah, W. →, *Si. Arabia* . 80 C5
Raon l'Étape, *France* 19 D13
Raoping, *China* 59 F11
Raoyang, *China* 56 E8
Rapa, *Pac. Oc.* 97 K13
Rapallo, *Italy* 28 D6
Rapar, *India* 68 H4
Rāpch, *Iran* 71 E8
Raper, C., *Canada* 101 B13
Rapid City, *U.S.A.* 112 D3
Rapid River, *U.S.A.* 108 C2
Rapla, *Estonia* 9 G21
Rapti →, *India* 69 F10
Rapu Rapu I., *Phil.* 61 E6
Raqaba ez Zarqa →, *Sudan* 81 F2
Raquette →, *U.S.A.* 111 B10
Raquette Lake, *U.S.A.* 111 C10
Rarotonga, *Cook Is.* 97 K12

Ra's al 'Ayn, *Syria* 70 B4
Ra's al Khaymah, *U.A.E.* .. 71 E7
Râs el Mâ, *Mali* 82 B4
Ras Ghārib, *Egypt* 80 B3
Ras Mallap, *Egypt* 80 B3
Râs Timirist, *Mauritania* .. 82 B1
Rasca, Pta. de la, *Canary Is.* 37 G3
Râscani, *Moldova* 43 C12
Raseiniai, *Lithuania* 9 J20
Rashad, *Sudan* 81 E3
Rashīd, *Egypt* 80 H7
Rashīd, Masabb, *Egypt* 80 H7
Rashmi, *India* 68 G6
Rasht, *Iran* 71 B6
Rasi Salai, *Thailand* 64 E5
Raška, *Serbia, Yug.* 40 C4
Rason L., *Australia* 93 E3
Raşova, *Romania* 43 F12
Rasovo, *Bulgaria* 40 C7
Rasra, *India* 69 G10
Rasskazovo, *Russia* 48 D5
Rast, *Romania* 43 G8
Rastatt, *Germany* 25 G4
Rastede, *Germany* 24 B4
Răstoliţa, *Romania* 43 D9
Rasul, *Pakistan* 68 C5
Raszków, *Poland* 45 G4
Rat Buri, *Thailand* 64 F2
Rat Islands, *U.S.A.* 100 C1
Rat L., *Canada* 105 B9
Ratangarh, *India* 68 E6
Rätansbyn, *Sweden* 10 B8
Ratcatchers L., *Australia* .. 95 E3
Rath, *India* 69 G8
Rath Luirc, *Ireland* 15 D3
Rathdrum, *Ireland* 15 D5
Rathenow, *Germany* 24 C8
Rathkeale, *Ireland* 15 D3
Rathlin I., *U.K.* 15 A5
Rathmelton, *Ireland* 15 A4
Ratibor = Racibórz, *Poland* 45 H5
Rätikon, *Austria* 26 D2
Ratingen, *Germany* 24 D2
Ratlam, *India* 68 H6
Ratnagiri, *India* 66 L8
Ratodero, *Pakistan* 68 F3
Raton, *U.S.A.* 113 G2
Rattaphum, *Thailand* 65 J3
Ratten, *Austria* 26 D8
Rattray Hd., *U.K.* 14 D7
Rättvik, *Sweden* 10 D9
Ratz, Mt., *Canada* 104 B2
Ratzeburg, *Germany* 24 B6
Raub, *Malaysia* 65 L3
Rauch, *Argentina* 126 D4
Raudales de Malpaso,
  Mexico 119 D6
Raufarhöfn, *Iceland* 8 C6
Raufoss, *Norway* 9 F14
Raukumara Ra., *N.Z.* 91 H6
Rauma, *Finland* 9 F19
Raurkela, *India* 69 H11
Rausu-Dake, *Japan* 54 B12
Răut →, *Moldova* 43 C14
Rava Russkaya = Rava-
  Ruska, *Poland* 47 G2
Rava Russkaya = Rava-
  Ruska, *Poland* 47 G2
Ravalli, *U.S.A.* 114 C6
Ravānsar, *Iran* 70 C5
Ravanusa, *Italy* 30 E6
Rāvar, *Iran* 71 D8
Ravena, *U.S.A.* 111 D11
Ravenna, *Italy* 29 D9
Ravenna, *Nebr., U.S.A.* ... 112 E5
Ravenna, *Ohio, U.S.A.* ... 110 E3
Ravensburg, *Germany* 25 H5
Ravenshoe, *Australia* 94 B4
Ravensthorpe, *Australia* ... 93 F3
Ravenswood, *Australia* 94 C4
Ravenswood, *U.S.A.* 108 F5
Ravi →, *Pakistan* 68 D4
Ravna Gora, *Croatia* 29 C11
Ravna Reka, *Serbia, Yug.* . 40 B5
Ravne na Koroškem,
  Slovenia 29 B11
Rawa Mazowiecka, *Poland* . 45 G7
Rawalpindi, *Pakistan* 68 C5
Rawāndūz, *Iraq* 70 B5
Rawang, *Malaysia* 65 L3
Rawene, *N.Z.* 91 F4
Rawicz, *Poland* 45 G3
Rawka →, *Poland* 45 F7
Rawlinna, *Australia* 93 F4
Rawlins, *U.S.A.* 114 F10
Rawlinson Ra., *Australia* ... 93 D4
Rawson, *Argentina* 128 E3
Raxaul, *India* 69 F11
Ray, *U.S.A.* 112 A3
Ray, C., *Canada* 103 C8
Rayadurg, *India* 66 M10
Rayagada, *India* 67 K13
Raychikhinsk, *Russia* 51 E13
Rāyen, *Iran* 71 D8
Rayleigh, *U.K.* 13 F8
Raymond, *Canada* 104 D6
Raymond, *Calif., U.S.A.* ... 116 H7
Raymond, *N.H., U.S.A.* ... 111 C13
Raymond, *Wash., U.S.A.* .. 116 D3
Raymond Terrace, *Australia* 95 E5
Raymondville, *U.S.A.* 113 M6
Raymore, *Canada* 105 C8
Rayón, *Mexico* 118 B2
Rayong, *Thailand* 64 F3
Rayville, *U.S.A.* 113 J9
Raz, Pte. du, *France* 18 D2
Razan, *Iran* 71 C6
Ražana, *Serbia, Yug.* 40 B3
Ražanj, *Serbia, Yug.* 40 C5
Razdelna, *Bulgaria* 41 C11

Razdolnaya = Rozdilna,
  Ukraine 47 J6
Razdolnoye, *Russia* 54 C5
Razdolnoye, *Ukraine* 47 K7
Razeh, *Iran* 71 C6
Razgrad, *Bulgaria* 41 C10
Razim, Lacul, *Romania* ... 43 F13
Razlog, *Bulgaria* 40 E7
Razmak, *Pakistan* 68 C3
Ré, Î. de, *France* 20 B2
Reading, *U.K.* 13 F7
Reading, *U.S.A.* 111 F9
Reading □, *U.K.* 13 F7
Realicó, *Argentina* 126 D3
Réalmont, *France* 20 E6
Ream, *Cambodia* 65 G4
Reata, *Mexico* 118 B4
Rebais, *France* 19 D10
Rebi, *Indonesia* 63 F8
Rebiana, *Libya* 79 D10
Rebun-Tō, *Japan* 54 B10
Recanati, *Italy* 29 E10
Recaș, *Romania* 42 E6
Recco, *Italy* 28 D6
Recherche, Arch. of the,
  Australia 93 F3
Rechna Doab, *Pakistan* ... 68 D5
Rechytsa, *Belarus* 47 F6
Recife, *Brazil* 125 E12
Recklinghausen, *Germany* .. 17 C7
Reconquista, *Argentina* ... 126 B4
Recreo, *Argentina* 126 B2
Recz, *Poland* 45 E2
Red →, *La., U.S.A.* 113 K9
Red →, *N. Dak., U.S.A.* .. 100 C10
Red Bank, *U.S.A.* 111 F10
Red Bay, *Canada* 103 B8
Red Bluff, *U.S.A.* 114 F2
Red Bluff L., *U.S.A.* 113 K3
Red Cliffs, *Australia* 95 E3
Red Cloud, *U.S.A.* 112 E5
Red Creek, *U.S.A.* 111 C8
Red Deer, *Canada* 104 C6
Red Deer →, *Alta., Canada* 105 C7
Red Deer →, *Man., Canada* 105 C8
Red Deer L., *Canada* 105 C8
Red Hook, *U.S.A.* 111 E11
Red Indian L., *Canada* 103 C8
Red L., *Canada* 105 C10
Red Lake, *Canada* 105 C10
Red Lake Falls, *U.S.A.* ... 112 B6
Red Lake Road, *Canada* ... 105 C10
Red Lodge, *U.S.A.* 114 D9
Red Mountain, *U.S.A.* 117 K9
Red Oak, *U.S.A.* 112 E7
Red Rock, *Canada* 102 C2
Red Rock, L., *U.S.A.* 112 E8
Red Rocks Pt., *Australia* .. 93 F4
Red Sea, *Asia* 74 C2
Red Slate Mt., *U.S.A.* 116 H8
Red Sucker L., *Canada* 102 B1
Red Tower Pass = Turnu
  Roşu, P., *Romania* 43 E9
Red Wing, *U.S.A.* 112 C8
Reda, *Poland* 44 D5
Redang, *Malaysia* 62 C2
Redange, *Lux.* 17 E5
Redcar, *U.K.* 12 C6
Redcar & Cleveland □, *U.K.* 12 C7
Redcliff, *Canada* 105 C6
Redcliffe, *Australia* 95 D5
Redcliffe, Mt., *Australia* ... 93 E3
Reddersburg, *S. Africa* 88 D4
Redding, *U.S.A.* 114 F2
Redditch, *U.K.* 13 E6
Redfield, *U.S.A.* 112 C5
Redford, *U.S.A.* 111 B11
Redkino, *Russia* 46 D9
Redlands, *U.S.A.* 117 M9
Redmond, *Oreg., U.S.A.* .. 114 D3
Redmond, *Wash., U.S.A.* .. 116 C4
Redon, *France* 18 E4
Redonda, *Antigua* 121 C7
Redondela, *Spain* 34 C2
Redondo, *Portugal* 35 G3
Redondo Beach, *U.S.A.* ... 117 M8
Redruth, *U.K.* 13 G2
Redvers, *Canada* 105 D8
Redwater, *Canada* 104 C6
Redwood, *U.S.A.* 111 B9
Redwood City, *U.S.A.* 116 H4
Redwood Falls, *U.S.A.* 112 C7
Redwood National Park,
  U.S.A. 114 F1
Ree, L., *Ireland* 15 C3
Reed, L., *Canada* 105 C8
Reed City, *U.S.A.* 108 D3
Reedley, *U.S.A.* 116 J7
Reedsburg, *U.S.A.* 112 D9
Reedsport, *U.S.A.* 114 E1
Reedsville, *U.S.A.* 110 F7
Reefton, *N.Z.* 91 K3
Rees, *Germany* 24 D2
Reese →, *U.S.A.* 114 F5
Refahiye, *Turkey* 73 C8
Reftele, *Sweden* 11 G7
Refugio, *U.S.A.* 113 L6
Rega →, *Poland* 44 D2
Regalbuto, *Italy* 31 E7
Regen, *Germany* 25 G9
Regen →, *Germany* 25 F8
Regensburg, *Germany* 25 F8
Regenstauf, *Germany* 25 F8
Reggello, *Italy* 29 E8
Réggio di Calábria, *Italy* ... 31 D8
Réggio nell'Emília, *Italy* ... 28 D7
Reghin, *Romania* 43 D9
Regina, *Canada* 105 C8
Regina Beach, *Canada* 105 C8
Registro, *Brazil* 127 A6

Reguengos de Monsaraz,
  Portugal 35 G3
Rehar →, *India* 69 H10
Rehli, *India* 69 H8
Rehoboth, *Namibia* 88 C2
Rehovot, *Israel* 75 D3
Reichenbach, *Germany* 24 E8
Reid, *Australia* 93 F4
Reidsville, *U.S.A.* 109 G6
Reigate, *U.K.* 13 F7
Reillo, *Spain* 32 F3
Reims, *France* 19 C11
Reina Adelaida, Arch., *Chile* 128 G2
Reinbek, *Germany* 24 B6
Reindeer →, *Canada* 105 B8
Reindeer I., *Canada* 105 C9
Reindeer L., *Canada* 105 B8
Reinga, C., *N.Z.* 91 F4
Reinosa, *Spain* 34 B6
Reitz, *S. Africa* 89 D4
Reivilo, *S. Africa* 88 D3
Rejaf, *Sudan* 81 G3
Rejmyre, *Sweden* 11 F9
Rejowiec Fabryczny, *Poland* 45 G10
Reka →, *Slovenia* 29 C11
Rekovac, *Serbia, Yug.* 40 C5
Reliance, *Canada* 105 A7
Rémalard, *France* 18 D7
Remarkable, Mt., *Australia* 95 E2
Rembang, *Indonesia* 63 G14
Remedios, *Panama* 120 E3
Remeshk, *Iran* 71 E8
Remetea, *Romania* 43 D10
Remich, *Lux.* 17 E6
Remiremont, *France* 19 D13
Remo, *Ethiopia* 81 F5
Remontnoye, *Russia* 49 G6
Remoulins, *France* 21 E8
Remscheid, *Germany* 17 C7
Ren Xian, *China* 56 F8
Rende, *Italy* 31 C9
Rendína, *Greece* 38 B3
Rendsburg, *Germany* 24 A5
Renfrew, *Canada* 102 C4
Renfrewshire □, *U.K.* 14 F4
Rengat, *Indonesia* 62 E2
Rengo, *Chile* 126 C1
Renhua, *China* 59 E9
Renhuai, *China* 58 D6
Reni, *Ukraine* 47 K5
Renk, *Sudan* 81 E3
Renmark, *Australia* 95 E3
Rennell Sd., *Canada* 104 C2
Renner Springs, *Australia* . 94 B1
Rennes, *France* 18 D5
Rennie L., *Canada* 105 A7
Reno, *U.S.A.* 116 F7
Reno →, *Italy* 29 D9
Renovo, *U.S.A.* 110 E7
Renqiu, *China* 56 E9
Rens, *Denmark* 11 K3
Renshou, *China* 58 C5
Rensselaer, Ind., *U.S.A.* ... 108 E2
Rensselaer, N.Y., *U.S.A.* .. 111 D11
Rentería, *Spain* 32 B3
Renton, *U.S.A.* 116 C4
Réo, *Burkina Faso* 82 C4
Reocín, *Spain* 34 B6
Reotipur, *India* 69 G10
Répcelak, *Hungary* 42 C2
Republic, *Mo., U.S.A.* 113 G8
Republic, *Wash., U.S.A.* .. 114 B4
Republican →, *U.S.A.* 112 F6
Repulse Bay, *Canada* 101 B11
Requena, *Peru* 124 E4
Requena, *Spain* 33 F3
Réquista, *France* 20 D6
Reşadiye = Datça, *Turkey* . 39 E9
Reşadiye, *Turkey* 73 B8
Reşadiye Yarımadası, *Turkey* 39 E9
Resavica, *Serbia, Yug.* 40 B5
Resen, *Macedonia* 40 E5
Reserve, *U.S.A.* 115 K9
Resht = Rasht, *Iran* 71 B6
Resistencia, *Argentina* 126 B4
Reşiţa, *Romania* 42 E6
Resko, *Poland* 44 E2
Resolution I., *Canada* 101 B13
Resolution I., *N.Z.* 91 L1
Ressano Garcia, *Mozam.* .. 89 D5
Reston, *Canada* 105 D8
Reszel, *Poland* 44 D8
Retalhuleu, *Guatemala* 120 D1
Retenue, L. de,
  Dem. Rep. of the Congo 87 E2
Retezat, Munţii, *Romania* . 42 E8
Retford, *U.K.* 12 D7
Rethel, *France* 19 C11
Rethem, *Germany* 24 C5
Réthímno, *Greece* 36 D6
Réthímnon □, *Greece* 36 D6
Reti, *Pakistan* 68 E3
Retiche, Alpi, *Switz.* 25 J6
Retiers, *France* 18 E5
Retortillo, *Spain* 34 E4
Retournac, *France* 21 C8
Rétság, *Hungary* 42 C4
Réunion ■, *Ind. Oc.* 77 J9
Reus, *Spain* 32 D6
Reuterstadt Stavenhagen,
  Germany 24 B8
Reutlingen, *Germany* 25 G5
Reutte, *Austria* 26 D3
Reval = Tallinn, *Estonia* ... 9 G21
Revel, *France* 20 E6
Revelganj, *India* 69 G11
Reventazón, *Peru* 124 E2
Revelstoke, *Canada* 104 C5
Revigny-sur-Ornain, *France* 19 D11
Revillagigedo, Is. de,
  Pac. Oc. 118 D2

199

Revin, France	19	C11
Revúca, Slovak Rep.	27	C13
Revuè ➤, Mozam.	87	F3
Rewa, India	69	G9
Rewari, India	68	E7
Rexburg, U.S.A.	114	E8
Rey, Iran	71	C6
Rey, I. del, Panama	120	E4
Rey, Rio del ➤, Nigeria	83	E6
Rey Malabo, Eq. Guin.	83	E6
Reyðarfjörður, Iceland	8	D6
Reyes, Pt., U.S.A.	116	H3
Reyhanlı, Turkey	72	D7
Reykjahlíð, Iceland	8	D5
Reykjanes, Iceland	8	E2
Reykjavík, Iceland	8	D3
Reynolds Ra., Australia	92	D5
Reynoldsville, U.S.A.	110	E6
Reynosa, Mexico	119	B5
Rēzekne, Latvia	9	H22
Rezina, Moldova	43	C13
Rezovo, Bulgaria	41	D12
Rezvān, Iran	71	E8
Rgotina, Serbia, Yug.	40	B6
Rhamnus, Greece	38	C6
Rhayader, U.K.	13	E4
Rheda-Wiedenbrück, Germany	24	D4
Rhede, Germany	24	D2
Rhein ➤, Europe	17	C6
Rhein-Main-Donau-Kanal, Germany	25	F7
Rheinbach, Germany	24	E2
Rheine, Germany	24	C3
Rheinfelden, Germany	25	H3
Rheinhessen-Pfalz □, Germany	25	F3
Rheinland-Pfalz □, Germany	24	B8
Rhin = Rhein ➤, Europe	17	C6
Rhine = Rhein ➤, Europe	17	C6
Rhinebeck, U.S.A.	111	E11
Rhineland-Palatinate = Rheinland-Pfalz □, Germany	25	E2
Rhinelander, U.S.A.	112	C10
Rhinns Pt., U.K.	14	F2
Rhino Camp, Uganda	86	B3
Rhir, Cap, Morocco	78	B4
Rho, Italy	28	C6
Rhode Island □, U.S.A.	111	E13
Rhodes = Ródhos, Greece	36	C10
Rhodesia = Zimbabwe ■, Africa	87	F3
Rhodope Mts. = Rhodopi Planina, Bulgaria	41	E8
Rhodopi Planina, Bulgaria	41	E8
Rhön, Germany	24	E5
Rhondda, U.K.	13	F4
Rhondda Cynon Taff □, U.K.	13	F4
Rhône □, France	21	C8
Rhône ➤, France	21	E8
Rhône-Alpes □, France	21	C9
Rhum, U.K.	14	E2
Rhyl, U.K.	12	D4
Ri-Aba, Eq. Guin.	83	E6
Riachão, Brazil	125	E9
Riangnom, Sudan	81	F3
Riaño, Spain	34	C6
Rians, France	21	E9
Riansáres ➤, Spain	35	F7
Riasi, India	69	C6
Riau □, Indonesia	62	D2
Riau, Kepulauan, Indonesia	62	D2
Riau Arch. = Riau, Kepulauan, Indonesia	62	D2
Riaza, Spain	34	D7
Riaza ➤, Spain	34	D7
Riba de Saelices, Spain	32	E2
Riba-Roja de Turia, Spain	33	F4
Ribadavia, Spain	34	C2
Ribadeo, Spain	34	B3
Ribadesella, Spain	34	B5
Ribado, Nigeria	83	D7
Ribao, Cameroon	83	D7
Ribas = Ribes de Freser, Spain	32	C7
Ribas do Rio Pardo, Brazil	125	H8
Ribble ➤, U.K.	12	D5
Ribe, Denmark	11	J2
Ribe Amtskommune □, Denmark	11	J2
Ribeauvillé, France	19	D14
Ribécourt-Dreslincourt, France	19	C9
Ribeira = Santa Uxía, Spain	34	C2
Ribeira Brava, Madeira	37	D2
Ribeirão Prêto, Brazil	127	A6
Ribemont, France	19	C10
Ribera, Italy	30	E6
Ribérac, France	20	C4
Riberalta, Bolivia	124	F5
Ribes de Freser, Spain	32	C7
Ribnica, Slovenia	29	C11
Ribnitz-Damgarten, Germany	24	A8
Ričany, Czech Rep.	26	B7
Riccarton, N.Z.	91	K4
Ríccia, Italy	31	A7
Riccione, Italy	29	E9
Rice, U.S.A.	117	L12
Rice L., U.S.A.	110	B6
Rice Lake, U.S.A.	112	C9
Rich, C., U.S.A.	110	B4
Richard Toll, Senegal	82	B1
Richards Bay, S. Africa	89	D5
Richardson ➤, Canada	105	B6
Richardson Lakes, U.S.A.	108	C10
Richardson Springs, U.S.A.	116	F5
Riche, C., Australia	93	F2

Richelieu, France	18	E7
Richey, U.S.A.	112	B2
Richfield, U.S.A.	115	G8
Richfield Springs, U.S.A.	111	D10
Richford, U.S.A.	111	B12
Richibucto, Canada	103	C7
Richland, Ga., U.S.A.	109	J3
Richland, Wash., U.S.A.	114	C4
Richland Center, U.S.A.	112	D9
Richlands, U.S.A.	108	G5
Richmond, Australia	94	C3
Richmond, N.Z.	91	J4
Richmond, U.K.	12	C6
Richmond, Calif., U.S.A.	116	H4
Richmond, Ind., U.S.A.	108	F3
Richmond, Ky., U.S.A.	108	G3
Richmond, Mich., U.S.A.	110	D2
Richmond, Mo., U.S.A.	112	F8
Richmond, Tex., U.S.A.	113	L7
Richmond, Utah, U.S.A.	114	F8
Richmond, Va., U.S.A.	108	G7
Richmond, Vt., U.S.A.	111	B12
Richmond Hill, Canada	110	C5
Richmond Ra., Australia	95	D5
Richwood, U.S.A.	108	F5
Ricla, Spain	32	D3
Ridder = Leninogorsk, Kazakstan	50	D9
Riddlesburg, U.S.A.	110	F6
Ridgecrest, U.S.A.	117	K9
Ridgefield, Conn., U.S.A.	111	E11
Ridgefield, Wash., U.S.A.	116	E4
Ridgeland, U.S.A.	109	J5
Ridgetown, Canada	102	D3
Ridgewood, U.S.A.	111	F10
Ridgway, U.S.A.	110	E6
Riding Mountain Nat. Park, Canada	105	C9
Ridley, Mt., Australia	93	F3
Riebeek-Oos, S. Africa	88	E4
Ried, Austria	26	C6
Riedlingen, Germany	25	G5
Riedstadt, Germany	25	F4
Rienza ➤, Italy	29	B8
Riesa, Germany	24	D9
Riesi, Italy	31	E7
Riet ➤, S. Africa	88	D3
Rietavas, Lithuania	44	C8
Rietbron, S. Africa	88	E3
Rietfontein, Namibia	88	C3
Rieti, Italy	29	F9
Rieupeyroux, France	20	D6
Riez, France	21	E10
Riffe L., U.S.A.	116	D4
Rifle, U.S.A.	114	G10
Rift Valley □, Kenya	86	B4
Rīga, Latvia	9	H21
Riga, G. of, Latvia	9	H20
Rigacikun, Nigeria	83	C6
Rīgān, Iran	71	D8
Rīgas Jūras Līcis = Riga, G. of, Latvia	9	H20
Rigaud, Canada	111	A10
Rigby, U.S.A.	114	E8
Rīgestān □, Afghan.	66	D4
Riggins, U.S.A.	114	D5
Rignac, France	20	D6
Rigolet, Canada	103	B8
Rihand Dam, India	69	G10
Riihimäki, Finland	9	F21
Riiser-Larsen-halvøya, Antarctica	5	C4
Rijau, Nigeria	83	C6
Rijeka, Croatia	29	C11
Rijeka Crnojevića, Montenegro, Yug.	40	D3
Rijssen, Neths.	17	B6
Rike, Ethiopia	81	E4
Rikuzentakada, Japan	54	E10
Rila, Bulgaria	40	D7
Rila Planina, Bulgaria	40	D7
Riley, U.S.A.	114	E4
Rima ➤, Nigeria	83	C6
Rimah, Wadi ar ➤, Si. Arabia	70	E4
Rimavská Sobota, Slovak Rep.	27	C13
Rimbey, Canada	104	C6
Rimbo, Sweden	10	E12
Rimersburg, U.S.A.	110	E5
Rimforsa, Sweden	11	F9
Rimi, Nigeria	83	C6
Rímini, Italy	29	D9
Rimouski, Canada	103	C6
Rimrock, U.S.A.	116	D5
Rinca, Indonesia	63	F5
Rincón de la Victoria, Spain	35	J6
Rincón de Romos, Mexico	118	C4
Rinconada, Argentina	126	A2
Rind ➤, India	69	G9
Ringarum, Sweden	11	F10
Ringas, India	68	F6
Ringe, Denmark	11	J4
Ringim, Nigeria	83	C6
Ringkøbing, Denmark	11	H2
Ringkøbing Amtskommune □, Denmark	11	H2
Ringkøbing Fjord, Denmark	11	H2
Ringsjön, Sweden	11	J7
Ringsted, Denmark	11	J5
Ringvassøy, Norway	8	B18
Ringwood, U.S.A.	111	E10
Rinía, Greece	39	D7
Rinjani, Indonesia	62	F5
Rinteln, Germany	24	C5
Río, Punta del, Spain	33	J2
Rio Branco, Brazil	124	E5
Río Branco, Uruguay	127	C5
Río Bravo del Norte ➤, Mexico	119	B5

Rio Brilhante, Brazil	127	A5
Rio Claro, Brazil	127	A6
Rio Claro, Trin. & Tob.	121	D7
Río Colorado, Argentina	128	D4
Río Cuarto, Argentina	126	C3
Rio das Pedras, Mozam.	89	C6
Rio de Janeiro, Brazil	127	A7
Rio de Janeiro □, Brazil	127	A7
Rio do Sul, Brazil	127	B6
Rio Grande = Grande, Rio ➤, U.S.A.	113	N6
Rio Grande, Argentina	128	G3
Rio Grande, Brazil	127	C5
Río Grande, Mexico	118	C4
Río Grande, Nic.	120	D3
Rio Grande City, U.S.A.	113	M5
Rio Grande de Santiago ➤, Mexico	118	C3
Rio Grande do Norte □, Brazil	125	E11
Rio Grande do Sul □, Brazil	127	C5
Río Hato, Panama	120	E3
Rio Lagartos, Mexico	119	C7
Rio Largo, Brazil	125	E11
Rio Maior, Portugal	35	F2
Rio Marina, Italy	28	F7
Río Mulatos, Bolivia	124	G5
Río Muni = Mbini □, Eq. Guin.	84	D2
Rio Negro, Brazil	127	B6
Rio Pardo, Brazil	127	C5
Rio Rancho, U.S.A.	115	J10
Río Segundo, Argentina	126	C3
Río Tercero, Argentina	126	C3
Rio Tinto, Portugal	34	D2
Rio Verde, Brazil	125	G8
Río Verde, Mexico	119	C5
Rio Vista, U.S.A.	116	G5
Ríobamba, Ecuador	124	D3
Ríohacha, Colombia	124	A4
Riom, France	20	C7
Riom-ès-Montagnes, France	20	C6
Rion-des-Landes, France	20	E3
Rionero in Vúlture, Italy	31	B8
Rioni ➤, Georgia	49	J5
Ríos, Spain	34	D3
Ríosucio, Colombia	124	B3
Riou L., Canada	105	B7
Rioz, France	19	E13
Ripatransone, Italy	29	F10
Ripley, Canada	110	B3
Ripley, Calif., U.S.A.	117	M12
Ripley, N.Y., U.S.A.	110	D5
Ripley, Tenn., U.S.A.	113	H10
Ripley, W. Va., U.S.A.	108	F5
Ripoll, Spain	32	C7
Ripon, U.K.	12	C6
Ripon, Calif., U.S.A.	116	H5
Ripon, Wis., U.S.A.	108	D1
Riposto, Italy	31	E8
Risan, Montenegro, Yug.	40	D2
Riscle, France	20	E3
Rishā', W. ar ➤, Si. Arabia	70	E5
Rishiri-Tō, Japan	54	B10
Rishon le Ziyyon, Israel	75	D3
Risle ➤, France	18	C7
Rison, U.S.A.	113	J8
Risør, Norway	9	G13
Rita Blanca Cr. ➤, U.S.A.	113	H3
Riti, Nigeria	83	D6
Ritter, Mt., U.S.A.	116	H7
Rittman, U.S.A.	110	F3
Ritzville, U.S.A.	114	C4
Riva del Garda, Italy	28	C7
Riva Lígure, Italy	28	E4
Rivadavia, Buenos Aires, Argentina	126	D3
Rivadavia, Mendoza, Argentina	126	C2
Rivadavia, Salta, Argentina	126	A3
Rivadavia, Chile	126	B1
Rivarolo Canavese, Italy	28	C4
Rivas, Nic.	120	D2
Rive-de-Gier, France	21	C8
River Cess, Liberia	82	D3
River Jordan, Canada	116	B2
Rivera, Argentina	126	D3
Rivera, Uruguay	127	C4
Riverbank, U.S.A.	116	H6
Riverdale, U.S.A.	116	J7
Riverhead, U.S.A.	111	F12
Riverhurst, Canada	105	C7
Rivers, Canada	105	C8
Rivers □, Nigeria	83	E6
Rivers Inlet, Canada	104	C3
Riversdale, S. Africa	88	E3
Riverside, U.S.A.	117	M9
Riverton, Australia	95	E2
Riverton, Canada	105	C9
Riverton, N.Z.	91	M2
Riverton Heights, U.S.A.	116	C4
Rives, France	21	C9
Rivesaltes, France	20	F6
Riviera di Levante, Italy	28	D6
Riviera di Ponente, Italy	28	D5
Rivière-au-Renard, Canada	103	C7
Rivière-du-Loup, Canada	103	C6
Rivière-Pentecôte, Canada	103	C6
Rivière-Pilote, Martinique	121	D7
Rivière St. Paul, Canada	103	B8
Rivne, Ukraine	47	G4
Rívoli, Italy	28	C4
Rívoli B., Australia	95	F3
Rixheim, France	19	E14
Riyadh = Ar Riyāḍ, Si. Arabia	70	E5
Rize, Turkey	73	B9
Rizhao, China	57	G10

Rizokarpaso, Cyprus	36	D13
Rizzuto, C., Italy	31	D10
Rjukan, Norway	9	G13
Ro, Greece	39	E11
Roa, Spain	34	D7
Road Town, Virgin Is.	121	C7
Roan Plateau, U.S.A.	114	G9
Roanne, France	19	F11
Roanoke, Ala., U.S.A.	109	J3
Roanoke, Va., U.S.A.	108	G6
Roanoke ➤, U.S.A.	109	H7
Roanoke I., U.S.A.	109	H8
Roanoke Rapids, U.S.A.	109	G7
Roatán, Honduras	120	C2
Robāt Sang, Iran	71	C8
Robbins I., Australia	94	G4
Róbbio, Italy	28	C5
Robe, Australia	95	F2
Robe ➤, Australia	92	D2
Röbel, Germany	24	B8
Robert Lee, U.S.A.	113	K4
Robertsdale, U.S.A.	110	F6
Robertsganj, India	69	G10
Robertson, S. Africa	88	E2
Robertson I., Antarctica	5	C18
Robertson Ra., Australia	92	D3
Robertsport, Liberia	82	D2
Robertstown, Australia	95	E2
Roberval, Canada	103	C5
Robeson Chan., Greenland	4	A4
Robesonia, U.S.A.	111	F8
Robi, Ethiopia	81	F4
Robinson, U.S.A.	108	F2
Robinson ➤, Australia	94	B2
Robinson Ra., Australia	93	E2
Robinvale, Australia	95	E3
Robledo, Spain	33	G2
Roblin, Canada	105	C8
Roboré, Bolivia	124	G7
Robson, Canada	104	D5
Robson, Mt., Canada	104	C5
Robstown, U.S.A.	113	M6
Roca, C. da, Portugal	35	G1
Rocas, I., Brazil	125	D12
Rocca San Casciano, Italy	29	D8
Roccadáspide, Italy	31	B8
Roccastrada, Italy	29	F8
Roccella Iónica, Italy	31	D9
Rocha, Uruguay	127	C5
Rochdale, U.K.	12	D5
Rochechouart, France	20	C4
Rochefort, Belgium	17	D5
Rochefort, France	20	C3
Rochefort-en-Terre, France	18	E4
Rochelle, U.S.A.	112	E10
Rocher River, Canada	104	A6
Rocheservière, France	18	F5
Rochester, U.K.	13	F8
Rochester, Ind., U.S.A.	108	E2
Rochester, Minn., U.S.A.	112	C8
Rochester, N.H., U.S.A.	111	C14
Rochester, N.Y., U.S.A.	110	C7
Rociu, Romania	43	F10
Rock ➤, Canada	104	A3
Rock Creek, U.S.A.	110	E4
Rock Falls, U.S.A.	112	E10
Rock Hill, U.S.A.	109	H5
Rock Island, U.S.A.	112	E9
Rock Rapids, U.S.A.	112	D6
Rock Sound, Bahamas	120	B4
Rock Springs, Mont., U.S.A.	114	C10
Rock Springs, Wyo., U.S.A.	114	F9
Rock Valley, U.S.A.	112	D6
Rockall, Atl. Oc.	6	D3
Rockdale, Tex., U.S.A.	113	K6
Rockdale, Wash., U.S.A.	116	C5
Rockefeller Plateau, Antarctica	5	E14
Rockford, U.S.A.	112	D10
Rockglen, Canada	105	D7
Rockhampton, Australia	94	C5
Rockingham, Australia	93	F2
Rockingham B., Australia	94	B4
Rocklake, U.S.A.	112	A5
Rockland, Canada	111	A9
Rockland, Idaho, U.S.A.	114	E7
Rockland, Maine, U.S.A.	109	C11
Rockland, Mich., U.S.A.	112	B10
Rocklin, U.S.A.	116	G5
Rockport, Mass., U.S.A.	111	D14
Rockport, Mo., U.S.A.	112	E7
Rockport, Tex., U.S.A.	113	L6
Rockville, Conn., U.S.A.	111	E12
Rockville, Md., U.S.A.	108	F7
Rockwall, U.S.A.	113	J6
Rockwell City, U.S.A.	112	D7
Rockwood, Canada	110	C4
Rockwood, Maine, U.S.A.	109	C11
Rockwood, Tenn., U.S.A.	109	H3
Rocky Ford, U.S.A.	112	F3
Rocky Gully, Australia	93	F2
Rocky Harbour, Canada	103	C8
Rocky Island L., Canada	102	C3
Rocky Lane, Canada	104	B5
Rocky Mount, U.S.A.	109	H7
Rocky Mountain House, Canada	104	C6
Rocky Mountain National Park, U.S.A.	114	F11
Rocky Mts., N. Amer.	114	G10
Rocky Point, Namibia	88	B2
Rod, Pakistan	66	E3
Rødby, Denmark	11	K5
Rødbyhavn, Denmark	11	K5
Rødding, Denmark	11	J3

Rödeby, Sweden	11	H9
Rødekro, Denmark	11	J3
Rodenkirchen, Germany	24	B4
Rodez, France	20	D6
Rodholívas, Greece	40	F7
Rodhópi, Greece	41	E9
Rodhopoú, Greece	36	D5
Ródhos, Greece	36	C10
Rodi Gargánico, Italy	29	G12
Rodna, Romania	43	C9
Rodnei, Munţii, Romania	43	C9
Rodney, Canada	110	D3
Rodney, C., N.Z.	91	G5
Rodniki, Russia	48	B5
Rodonit, Kepi i, Albania	40	E3
Rodriguez, Ind. Oc.	3	E13
Roe ➤, U.K.	15	A5
Roebling, U.S.A.	111	F10
Roebourne, Australia	92	D2
Roebuck B., Australia	92	C3
Roermond, Neths.	17	C6
Roes Welcome Sd., Canada	101	B11
Roeselare, Belgium	17	D3
Rogachev = Ragachow, Belarus	47	F6
Rogačica, Serbia, Yug.	40	B3
Rogagua, L., Bolivia	124	F5
Rogaška Slatina, Slovenia	29	B12
Rogatec, Slovenia	29	B12
Rogatica, Bos.-H.	42	G4
Rogatyn, Ukraine	47	H3
Rogdhia, Greece	36	D7
Rogers, U.S.A.	113	G7
Rogers City, U.S.A.	108	C4
Rogersville, Canada	103	C6
Roggan ➤, Canada	102	B4
Roggan L., Canada	102	B4
Roggeveldberge, S. Africa	88	E3
Roggiano Gravina, Italy	31	C9
Rogliano, France	21	F13
Rogliano, Italy	31	C9
Rogoaguado, L., Bolivia	124	F5
Rogoźno, Poland	45	F3
Rogue ➤, U.S.A.	114	E1
Rohan, France	18	D4
Róhda, Greece	36	A3
Rohnert Park, U.S.A.	116	G4
Rohri, Pakistan	68	F3
Rohri Canal, Pakistan	68	F3
Rohtak, India	68	E7
Roi Et, Thailand	64	D4
Roja, Latvia	9	H20
Rojas, Argentina	126	C3
Rojiște, Romania	43	F9
Rojo, C., Mexico	119	C5
Rokan ➤, Indonesia	62	D2
Rokel ➤, S. Leone	82	D2
Rokiškis, Lithuania	9	J21
Rokitno, Russia	47	G8
Rokycany, Czech Rep.	26	B6
Rolândia, Brazil	127	A5
Rolla, U.S.A.	113	G9
Rolleston, Australia	94	C4
Rollingstone, Australia	94	B4
Rom, Sudan	81	F3
Roma, Australia	95	D4
Roma, Italy	29	G9
Roma, Sweden	11	G12
Roma, U.S.A.	113	M5
Romain C., U.S.A.	109	J6
Romaine, Canada	103	B7
Romaine ➤, Canada	103	B7
Roman, Bulgaria	40	C7
Roman, Romania	43	D11
Roman-Kosh, Gora, Ukraine	47	K8
Romanche ➤, France	21	C9
Romang, Indonesia	63	F7
Români, Bos.-H.	42	G3
Romania ■, Europe	43	D10
Romano, Cayo, Cuba	120	B4
Romanovka = Basarabeasca, Moldova	43	D13
Romans-sur-Isère, France	21	C9
Romanshorn, Switz.	25	H5
Rombari, Sudan	81	G4
Romblon, Phil.	61	E5
Rome = Roma, Italy	29	G9
Rome, Ga., U.S.A.	109	H3
Rome, N.Y., U.S.A.	111	C9
Rome, Pa., U.S.A.	111	E8
Rometta, Italy	31	D8
Romilly-sur-Seine, France	19	D10
Romney, U.S.A.	108	F6
Romney Marsh, U.K.	13	F8
Romny, Ukraine	47	G7
Rømø, Denmark	11	J2
Romodan, Ukraine	47	G7
Romodanovo, Russia	48	C7
Romont, Switz.	25	J2
Romorantin-Lanthenay, France	19	E8
Romsdalen, Norway	9	E12
Romsey, U.K.	13	G6
Ron, Vietnam	64	D6
Ronan, U.S.A.	114	C6
Roncador, Cayos, Caribbean	120	D3
Roncador, Serra do, Brazil	125	F8
Ronciglione, Italy	29	F9
Ronco ➤, Italy	29	D9
Ronda, Spain	35	J5
Ronda, Serranía de, Spain	35	J5
Rondane, Norway	9	F13
Rondônia □, Brazil	124	F6
Rondonópolis, Brazil	125	G8
Rong, Koh, Cambodia	65	G4
Rong Jiang ➤, China	58	E7
Rong Xian, Guangxi Zhuangzu, China	59	F8
Rong Xian, Sichuan, China	58	C5

Rong'an, China 58 E7
Rongchang, China 58 C5
Ronge, L. la, Canada 105 B7
Rongjiang, China 58 E7
Rongshui, China 58 E7
Rønne, Denmark 11 J8
Ronne Ice Shelf, Antarctica 5 D18
Ronneby, Sweden 11 H9
Ronnebyån →, Sweden 11 H9
Rönneshytta, Sweden 11 F9
Ronsard, C., Australia 93 D1
Ronse, Belgium 17 D3
Roodepoort, S. Africa 89 D4
Roof Butte, U.S.A. 115 H9
Rooiboklaagte →, Namibia 88 C3
Roorkee, India 68 E7
Roosendaal, Neths. 17 C4
Roosevelt, U.S.A. 114 F8
Roosevelt →, Brazil 122 D4
Roosevelt, Mt., Canada 104 B3
Roosevelt I., Antarctica 5 D12
Ropczyce, Poland 45 H8
Roper →, Australia 94 A2
Roper Bar, Australia 94 A1
Roque Pérez, Argentina 126 D4
Roquefort, France 20 D3
Roquemaure, France 21 D8
Roquetas de Mar, Spain 33 J2
Roquetes, Spain 32 E5
Roquevaire, France 21 E9
Roraima □, Brazil 124 C6
Roraima, Mt., Venezuela 122 C4
Røros, Norway 9 E14
Rorschach, Switz. 25 H5
Rosa, Zambia 87 D3
Rosa, L., Bahamas 121 B5
Rosa, Monte, Italy 28 C4
Rosal de la Frontera, Spain 35 H3
Rosalia, U.S.A. 114 C5
Rosamond, U.S.A. 117 L8
Rosans, France 21 D9
Rosário, Argentina 126 C3
Rosário, Brazil 125 D10
Rosario, Baja Calif., Mexico 118 B1
Rosario, Sinaloa, Mexico 118 C3
Rosario, Paraguay 126 A4
Rosario de la Frontera, Argentina 126 B3
Rosario de Lerma, Argentina 126 A2
Rosario del Tala, Argentina 126 C4
Rosário do Sul, Brazil 127 C5
Rosarito, Mexico 117 N9
Rosarno, Italy 31 D8
Rosas = Roses, Spain 32 C8
Roscoe, U.S.A. 111 E10
Roscoff, France 18 D3
Roscommon, Ireland 15 C3
Roscommon □, Ireland 15 C3
Roscrea, Ireland 15 D4
Rose →, Australia 94 A2
Rose Blanche, Canada 103 C8
Rose Pt., Canada 104 C2
Rose Valley, Canada 105 C8
Roseau, Domin. 121 C7
Roseau, U.S.A. 112 A7
Rosebery, Australia 94 G4
Rosebud, S. Dak., U.S.A. 112 D4
Rosebud, Tex., U.S.A. 113 K6
Roseburg, U.S.A. 114 E2
Rosedale, U.S.A. 113 J9
Roseland, U.S.A. 116 G4
Rosemary, Canada 104 C6
Rosenberg, U.S.A. 113 L7
Rosendaël, France 19 A9
Rosenheim, Germany 25 H8
Roses, Spain 32 C8
Roses, G. de, Spain 32 C8
Roseto degli Abruzzi, Italy 29 F11
Rosetown, Canada 105 C7
Rosetta = Rashîd, Egypt 80 H7
Roseville, Calif., U.S.A. 116 G5
Roseville, Mich., U.S.A. 110 D2
Rosewood, Australia 95 D5
Roshkhvār, Iran 71 C8
Rosières-en-Santerre, France 19 C9
Rosignano Maríttimo, Italy 28 E7
Rosignol, Guyana 124 B7
Roșiori de Vede, Romania 43 F10
Rositsa →, Bulgaria 41 C11
Rosita, Bulgaria 41 C9
Roskilde, Denmark 11 J6
Roskilde Amtskommune □, Denmark 11 J6
Roskovec, Albania 40 F3
Roslavl, Russia 46 F7
Rosmaninhal, Portugal 34 F3
Rosmead, S. Africa 88 E4
Røsnæs, Denmark 11 J4
Rosolini, Italy 31 F7
Rosporden, France 18 E3
Ross, N.Z. 91 K3
Ross Béthio, Mauritania 82 B1
Ross I., Antarctica 5 D11
Ross Ice Shelf, Antarctica 5 E12
Ross L., U.S.A. 114 B3
Ross-on-Wye, U.K. 13 F5
Ross River, Australia 94 C1
Ross River, Canada 104 A2
Ross Sea, Antarctica 5 D11
Rossall Pt., Ireland 15 D4
Rossan Pt., Ireland 15 B3
Rossano, Italy 31 C9
Rossburn, Canada 105 C8
Rosseau, Canada 110 A5
Rosseau, L., Canada 110 A5
Rosses, The, Ireland 15 A3
Rossignol, L., Canada 102 B5
Rossignol Res., Canada 103 D6
Rossland, Canada 104 D5
Rosslare, Ireland 15 D5

Rosslau, Germany 24 D8
Rosso, Mauritania 82 B1
Rosso, C., France 21 F12
Rossosh, Russia 47 G10
Røssvatnet, Norway 8 D16
Røst, Norway 8 C15
Rosthern, Canada 105 C7
Rostock, Germany 24 A8
Rostov, Don, Russia 47 J10
Rostov, Yaroslavl, Russia 46 D10
Rostrenen, France 18 D3
Roswell, Ga., U.S.A. 109 H3
Roswell, N. Mex., U.S.A. 113 J2
Rota, Spain 35 J4
Rotan, U.S.A. 113 J4
Rotenburg, Hessen, Germany 24 E5
Rotenburg, Niedersachsen, Germany 24 B5
Roth, Germany 25 F7
Rothaargebirge, Germany 24 D4
Rothenburg ob der Tauber, Germany 25 F6
Rother →, U.K. 13 G8
Rotherham, U.K. 12 D6
Rothes, U.K. 14 D5
Rothesay, Canada 103 C6
Rothesay, U.K. 14 F3
Roti, Indonesia 63 F6
Rotja, Pta., Spain 33 G6
Roto, Australia 95 E4
Rotoroa, L., N.Z. 91 J4
Rotorua, N.Z. 91 H6
Rotorua, L., N.Z. 91 H6
Rott →, Germany 25 G9
Rottenburg, Germany 25 G4
Rottenmann, Austria 26 D7
Rotterdam, Neths. 17 C4
Rotterdam, U.S.A. 111 D10
Rottne, Sweden 11 G8
Rottnest I., Australia 93 F2
Rottumeroog, Neths. 17 A6
Rottweil, Germany 25 G4
Rotuma, Fiji 96 J9
Roubaix, France 19 B10
Roudnice nad Labem, Czech Rep. 26 A7
Rouen, France 18 C8
Rouergue, France 20 D5
Rouillac, France 20 C3
Rouleau, Canada 105 C8
Round Mountain, U.S.A. 114 G5
Round Mt., Australia 95 E5
Round Rock, U.S.A. 113 K6
Roundup, U.S.A. 114 C9
Rousay, U.K. 14 B5
Rouses Point, U.S.A. 111 B11
Rouseville, U.S.A. 110 E5
Roussillon, Isère, France 21 C8
Roussillon, Pyrénées-Or., France 20 F6
Rouxville, S. Africa 88 E4
Rouyn-Noranda, Canada 102 C4
Rovaniemi, Finland 8 C21
Rovato, Italy 28 C7
Rovenki, Ukraine 47 H10
Rovereto, Italy 28 C8
Rovigo, Italy 29 C8
Rovinj, Croatia 29 C10
Rovno = Rivne, Ukraine 47 G4
Rovnoye, Russia 48 E8
Rovuma = Ruvuma →, Tanzania 87 E5
Row'ān, Iran 71 C6
Rowena, Australia 95 D4
Rowley Shoals, Australia 92 C2
Roxa, Guinea-Biss. 82 C1
Roxas, Capiz, Phil. 61 F5
Roxas, Isabela, Phil. 61 C4
Roxas, Mind. Or., Phil. 61 E4
Roxboro, U.S.A. 109 G6
Roxburgh, N.Z. 91 L2
Roxbury, U.S.A. 110 F7
Roxen, Sweden 11 F9
Roy, Mont., U.S.A. 114 C9
Roy, N. Mex., U.S.A. 113 H2
Roy, Utah, U.S.A. 114 F7
Royal Canal, Ireland 15 C4
Royal Leamington Spa, U.K. 13 E6
Royal Tunbridge Wells, U.K. 13 F8
Royan, France 20 C2
Roye, France 19 C9
Royston, U.K. 13 E7
Rožaj, Montenegro, Yug. 40 D4
Różan, Poland 45 F8
Rozay-en-Brie, France 19 D9
Rozdilna, Ukraine 47 J6
Rozhyshche, Ukraine 47 G3
Rožmitál pod Třemšínem, Czech Rep. 26 B6
Rožňava, Slovak Rep. 27 C13
Rozogi, Poland 44 E8
Rozoy-sur-Serre, France 19 C11
Rozzano, Italy 28 C6
Rrëshen, Albania 40 E3
Rrogozhinë, Albania 40 E3
Rtanj, Serbia, Yug. 40 C5
Rtishchevo, Russia 48 D6
Rúa = La Rúa, Spain 34 C3
Ruacaná, Angola 88 B1
Ruahine Ra., N.Z. 91 H6
Ruapehu, N.Z. 91 H5
Ruapuke I., N.Z. 91 M2
Ruâq, W. →, Egypt 75 F2
Rub' al Khālī, Si. Arabia 74 D4
Rubeho Mts., Tanzania 86 D4
Rubezhnoye = Rubizhne, Ukraine 47 H10
Rubh a' Mhail, U.K. 14 F2
Rubha Hunish, U.K. 14 D2
Rubha Robhanais = Lewis, Butt of, U.K. 14 C2

Rubi, Spain 32 D7
Rubicon →, U.S.A. 116 G5
Rubicone →, Italy 29 D9
Rubik, Albania 40 E3
Rubino, Ivory C. 82 D4
Rubio, Venezuela 124 B4
Rubizhne, Ukraine 47 H10
Rubtsovsk, Russia 50 D9
Ruby L., U.S.A. 114 F6
Ruby Mts., U.S.A. 114 F6
Rubyvale, Australia 94 C4
Rucheng, China 59 E9
Ruciane-Nida, Poland 44 E8
Rüd Sar, Iran 71 B6
Ruda, Sweden 11 G10
Ruda Śląska, Poland 45 H5
Rudall, Australia 95 E2
Rudall →, Australia 92 D3
Rudewa, Tanzania 87 E3
Rudna, Poland 45 G3
Rudnik, Bulgaria 41 D11
Rudnik, Poland 45 H9
Rudnik, Serbia, Yug. 40 B4
Rudnya, Russia 46 E6
Rudnyy, Kazakstan 50 D7
Rudo, Bos.-H. 42 G4
Rudolfa, Ostrov, Russia 50 A6
Rudolstadt, Germany 24 E7
Rudong, China 59 A13
Rudozem, Bulgaria 41 E8
Rudyard, U.S.A. 108 B3
Rue, France 19 B8
Rufa'a, Sudan 81 E3
Rufiji →, Tanzania 86 D4
Rufino, Argentina 126 C3
Rufisque, Senegal 82 C1
Rufunsa, Zambia 87 F2
Rugao, China 59 A13
Rugby, U.K. 13 E6
Rugby, U.S.A. 112 A5
Rügen, Germany 24 A9
Rugles, France 18 D7
Ruhengeri, Rwanda 86 C2
Ruhla, Germany 24 E6
Ruhland, Germany 24 D9
Ruhnu, Estonia 9 H20
Ruhr →, Germany 24 D2
Ruhuhu →, Tanzania 87 E3
Rui'an, China 59 D13
Ruichang, China 59 C10
Ruidoso, U.S.A. 115 K11
Ruijin, China 59 E10
Ruili, China 58 E1
Ruivo, Pico, Madeira 37 D3
Ruj, Bulgaria 40 D6
Rujen, Macedonia 40 D6
Rujm Tal'at al Jamā'ah, Jordan 75 E4
Ruk, Pakistan 68 F3
Rukhla, Pakistan 68 C4
Ruki →, Dem. Rep. of the Congo 84 E3
Rukwa □, Tanzania 86 D3
Rukwa, L., Tanzania 86 D3
Rulhieres, C., Australia 92 B4
Rum = Rhum, U.K. 14 E2
Rum Cay, Bahamas 121 B5
Rum Jungle, Australia 92 B5
Ruma, Serbia, Yug. 42 E4
Rumāḥ, Si. Arabia 70 E5
Rumania = Romania ■, Europe 43 D10
Rumaylah, Iraq 70 D5
Rumbêk, Sudan 81 F2
Rumburk, Czech Rep. 26 A7
Rumford, U.S.A. 109 C10
Rumia, Poland 44 D5
Rumilly, France 21 C9
Rumoi, Japan 54 C10
Rumonge, Burundi 86 C2
Rumson, U.S.A. 111 F11
Rumuruti, Kenya 86 B4
Runan, China 56 H8
Runanga, N.Z. 91 K3
Runaway, C., N.Z. 91 G6
Runcorn, U.K. 12 D5
Rundu, Namibia 88 B2
Rungwa, Tanzania 86 D3
Rungwa →, Tanzania 86 D3
Rungwe, Tanzania 87 D3
Rungwe, Mt., Tanzania 84 F6
Runka, Nigeria 83 C6
Runn, Sweden 10 D9
Ruokolahti, Finland 46 B5
Ruoqiang, China 60 C3
Rupa, India 67 F18
Rupar, India 68 D7
Rupat, Indonesia 62 D2
Rupea, Romania 43 D10
Rupen →, India 68 H4
Rupert, U.S.A. 114 E7
Rupert →, Canada 102 B4
Rupert B., Canada 102 B4
Rupert House = Waskaganish, Canada 102 B4
Rupsa, India 69 J12
Rurrenabaque, Bolivia 124 F5
Rur →, Germany 24 D1
Rus →, Spain 33 F2
Rusambo, Zimbabwe 87 F3
Rusape, Zimbabwe 87 F3
Ruschuk = Ruse, Bulgaria 41 C9
Ruse, Bulgaria 41 C9
Ruse □, Bulgaria 41 C10
Ruşeţu, Romania 43 F12
Rush, Ireland 15 C5
Rushan, China 57 F11
Rushden, U.K. 13 E7

Rushmore, Mt., U.S.A. 112 D3
Rushville, Ill., U.S.A. 112 E9
Rushville, Ind., U.S.A. 108 F3
Rushville, Nebr., U.S.A. 112 D3
Russas, Brazil 125 D11
Russell, Canada 105 C8
Russell, Kans., U.S.A. 112 F5
Russell, N.Y., U.S.A. 111 B9
Russell, Pa., U.S.A. 110 E5
Russell L., Man., Canada 105 B8
Russell L., N.W.T., Canada 104 A5
Russellkonda, India 67 K14
Russellville, Ala., U.S.A. 109 H2
Russellville, Ark., U.S.A. 113 H8
Russellville, Ky., U.S.A. 109 G2
Rüsselsheim, Germany 25 F4
Russi, Italy 29 D9
Russia ■, Eurasia 51 C11
Russian →, U.S.A. 116 G3
Russkoye Ustie, Russia 4 B15
Rust, Austria 27 D9
Rustam, Pakistan 68 B5
Rustam Shahr, Pakistan 68 F2
Rustavi, Georgia 49 K7
Rustenburg, S. Africa 88 D4
Ruston, U.S.A. 113 J8
Rutana, Burundi 86 C3
Rute, Spain 35 H6
Ruteng, Indonesia 63 F6
Ruth, U.S.A. 110 C2
Rutherford, U.S.A. 116 G4
Rutland, U.S.A. 111 C12
Rutland □, U.K. 13 E7
Rutland Water, U.K. 13 E7
Rutledge →, Canada 105 A6
Rutledge L., Canada 105 A6
Rutqa, W. →, Syria 73 E9
Rutshuru, Dem. Rep. of the Congo 86 C2
Ruvo di Púglia, Italy 31 A9
Ruvu, Tanzania 86 D4
Ruvu →, Tanzania 86 D4
Ruvuma □, Tanzania 87 E4
Ruvuma →, Tanzania 87 E5
Ruwais, U.A.E. 71 E7
Ruwenzori, Africa 86 B2
Ruya →, Zimbabwe 89 B5
Ruyigi, Burundi 86 C3
Ruyuan, China 59 E9
Ruzayevka, Russia 48 C7
Růžhevo Konare, Bulgaria 41 D8
Ružomberok, Slovak Rep. 27 B12
Rwanda ■, Africa 86 C3
Ryakhovo, Bulgaria 41 C10
Ryan, L., U.K. 14 G3
Ryazan, Russia 46 E10
Ryazhsk, Russia 46 F11
Rybache = Rybachye, Kazakhstan 50 E9
Rybachye, Kazakstan 50 E9
Rybinsk, Russia 46 C10
Rybinskoye Vdkhr., Russia 46 C10
Rybnik, Poland 45 H5
Rybnitsa = Râbniţa, Moldova 43 C14
Rybnoye, Russia 46 E10
Rychnov nad Kněžnou, Czech Rep. 27 A9
Rychwał, Poland 45 F5
Rycroft, Canada 104 B5
Ryd, Sweden 11 H8
Rydaholm, Sweden 11 H8
Ryde, U.K. 13 G6
Ryderwood, U.S.A. 116 D3
Rydzyna, Poland 45 G3
Rye →, U.K. 12 C7
Rye Bay, U.K. 13 G8
Rye Patch Reservoir, U.S.A. 114 F4
Ryegate, U.S.A. 114 C9
Ryki, Poland 45 G8
Ryley, Canada 104 C6
Rylsk, Russia 47 G8
Rylstone, Australia 95 E4
Rymanów, Poland 45 J8
Ryn, Poland 44 E8
Ryn Peski, Kazakstan 49 G9
Rypin, Poland 45 E6
Ryssby, Sweden 11 H8
Ryūgasaki, Japan 55 G10
Ryūkyū Is. = Ryūkyū-rettō, Japan 55 M3
Ryūkyū-rettō, Japan 55 M3
Rzepin, Poland 45 F1
Rzeszów, Poland 45 H8
Rzhev, Russia 46 D8

S

Sa, Thailand 64 C3
Sa Canal, Spain 37 C7
Sa Conillera, Spain 37 C7
Sa Dec, Vietnam 65 G5
Sa Dragonera, Spain 37 B9
Sa Mesquida, Spain 37 B11
Sa Pobla, Spain 32 F8
Sa Savina, Spain 37 C7
Sa'ādatābād, Fārs, Iran 71 D7
Sa'ādatābād, Hormozgān, Iran 71 D7
Sa'ādatābād, Kermān, Iran 71 D7
Saale →, Germany 24 D7
Saaler Bodden, Germany 24 A8
Saalfeld, Germany 24 E7
Saalfelden, Austria 26 D5
Saane →, Switz. 25 H3
Saar →, Europe 17 E6

Saarbrücken, Germany 25 F2
Saarburg, Germany 25 F2
Saaremaa, Estonia 9 G20
Saarijärvi, Finland 9 E21
Saariselkä, Finland 8 B23
Saarland □, Germany 25 F2
Saarlouis, Germany 25 F2
Sab 'Ābar, Syria 70 C3
Saba, W. Indies 121 C7
Šabac, Serbia, Yug. 40 B3
Sabadell, Spain 32 D7
Sabah □, Malaysia 62 C5
Sabak Bernam, Malaysia 65 L3
Sabalān, Kūhhā-ye, Iran 70 B5
Sabalana, Kepulauan, Indonesia 63 F5
Sábana de la Mar, Dom. Rep. 121 C6
Sábanalarga, Colombia 124 A4
Sabang, Indonesia 62 C1
Săbăoani, Romania 43 C11
Sabará, Brazil 125 G10
Sabarmati →, India 68 H5
Sabattis, U.S.A. 111 B10
Sabáudia, Italy 30 A6
Saberania, Indonesia 63 E9
Sabhā, Libya 79 C8
Sabi →, India 68 E7
Sabidana, J., Sudan 80 D4
Sabie, S. Africa 89 D5
Sabinal, Mexico 118 A3
Sabinal, U.S.A. 113 L5
Sabiñánigo, Spain 32 C4
Sabinar, Punta del, Spain 33 J2
Sabinas, Mexico 118 B4
Sabinas →, Mexico 118 B4
Sabinas Hidalgo, Mexico 118 B4
Sabine →, U.S.A. 113 L8
Sabine L., U.S.A. 113 L8
Sabine Pass, U.S.A. 113 L8
Sabinov, Slovak Rep. 27 B14
Sabinsville, U.S.A. 110 E7
Sabirabad, Azerbaijan 49 K9
Sabkhet el Bardawîl, Egypt 75 D2
Sablayan, Phil. 61 E4
Sable, C., Canada 103 A6
Sable, C., U.S.A. 107 F10
Sable I., Canada 103 D8
Sablé-sur-Sarthe, France 18 E6
Sabonkafi, Niger 83 C6
Sabor →, Portugal 34 D3
Sabou, Burkina Faso 82 C4
Sabres, France 20 D3
Sabrina Coast, Antarctica 5 C9
Sabugal, Portugal 34 E3
Sabulubbek, Indonesia 62 E1
Sabuncu, Turkey 39 B12
Sabzevār, Iran 71 B8
Sabzvārān, Iran 71 D8
Sac City, U.S.A. 112 D7
Sacedón, Spain 32 E2
Săcele, Romania 43 E10
Sachigo →, Canada 102 A2
Sachigo, L., Canada 102 B1
Sachkhere, Georgia 49 J6
Sachsen □, Germany 24 D9
Sachsen-Anhalt □, Germany 24 D7
Sacile, Italy 29 C9
Sackets Harbor, U.S.A. 111 C8
Sackville, Canada 103 C7
Saco, Maine, U.S.A. 109 D10
Saco, Mont., U.S.A. 114 B10
Sacramento, U.S.A. 116 G5
Sacramento →, U.S.A. 116 G5
Sacramento Mts., U.S.A. 115 K11
Sacramento Valley, U.S.A. 116 G5
Sacratif, C., Spain 35 J7
Săcueni, Romania 42 C7
Sada, Spain 34 B2
Sada-Misaki, Japan 55 H6
Sádaba, Spain 32 C3
Sadabad, India 68 F8
Sadani, Tanzania 86 D4
Sadao, Thailand 65 J3
Sadd el Aali, Egypt 80 C3
Saddle Mt., U.S.A. 116 E3
Sade, Nigeria 83 C7
Sadimi, Dem. Rep. of the Congo 87 D1
Sadiola, Mali 82 C2
Sa'dīyah, Hawr as, Iraq 73 F12
Sado, Japan 54 F9
Sado →, Portugal 35 G2
Sadon, Burma 67 G20
Sadon, Russia 49 J6
Sadra, India 68 H5
Sadri, India 68 G5
Sæby, Denmark 11 G4
Saegertown, U.S.A. 110 E4
Saelices, Spain 32 F2
Safaalan, Turkey 41 E12
Safaga, Egypt 80 B3
Šafárikovo = Tornal'a, Slovak Rep. 27 C13
Säffle, Sweden 10 E6
Safford, U.S.A. 115 K9
Saffron Walden, U.K. 13 E8
Safi, Morocco 78 B4
Safīd Dasht, Iran 71 C6
Şafījah, Si. Arabia 70 D5
Safid Kūh, Afghan. 66 B3
Safid Rūd →, Iran 71 B6
Safipur, India 69 F9
Safonovo, Russia 46 E7
Safranbolu, Turkey 72 B5
Saft Rashîn, Egypt 80 J7
Safwān, Iraq 70 D5
Sag Harbor, U.S.A. 111 F12
Saga, Japan 55 H5

Saga □, Japan ... 55 H5
Sagae, Japan ... 54 E10
Sagala, Mali ... 82 C3
Sagamore, U.S.A. ... 110 F5
Sagar, Karnataka, India ... 66 M9
Sagar, Mad. P., India ... 69 H8
Sagara, L., Tanzania ... 86 D3
Sagay, Phil. ... 61 F5
Saginaw, U.S.A. ... 108 D4
Saginaw →, U.S.A. ... 108 D4
Saginaw B., U.S.A. ... 108 D4
Sagleipie, Liberia ... 82 D3
Saglouc = Salluit, Canada ... 101 B12
Sagŏ-ri, S. Korea ... 57 G14
Sagone, France ... 21 F12
Sagone, G. de, France ... 21 F12
Sagres, Portugal ... 35 J2
Sagua la Grande, Cuba ... 120 B3
Saguache, U.S.A. ... 115 G10
Saguaro Nat. Park, U.S.A. ... 115 K8
Saguenay →, Canada ... 103 C5
Sagunt, Spain ... 32 F4
Sagunto = Sagunt, Spain ... 32 F4
Sagwara, India ... 68 H6
Sahaba, Sudan ... 80 D3
Sahagún, Spain ... 34 C5
Saham al Jawlān, Syria ... 75 C4
Sahamandrevo, Madag. ... 89 C8
Sahand, Kūh-e, Iran ... 70 B5
Sahara, Africa ... 78 D6
Saharan Atlas = Saharien, Atlas, Algeria ... 78 B6
Saharanpur, India ... 68 E7
Saharien, Atlas, Algeria ... 78 B6
Saharsa, India ... 69 G12
Sahasinaka, Madag. ... 89 C8
Sahaswan, India ... 69 E8
Sahel, Africa ... 78 E5
Sahel, Canal du, Mali ... 82 C3
Sahibganj, India ... 69 G12
Sahiwal, Pakistan ... 68 D5
Şahneh, Iran ... 70 C5
Sahuaripa, Mexico ... 118 B3
Sahuarita, U.S.A. ... 115 L8
Sahuayo, Mexico ... 118 C4
Šahy, Slovak Rep. ... 27 C11
Sai →, India ... 69 G10
Sai Buri, Thailand ... 65 J3
Sa'id Bundās, Sudan ... 81 F1
Sa'īdābād, Kermān, Iran ... 71 D7
Sa'īdābād, Semnān, Iran ... 71 B7
Sa'īdīyeh, Iran ... 71 B6
Saidpur, Bangla. ... 67 G16
Saidpur, India ... 69 G10
Saidu, Pakistan ... 69 B5
Saignes, France ... 20 C6
Saigon = Phanh Bho Ho Chi Minh, Vietnam ... 65 G6
Saijō, Japan ... 55 H6
Saikanosy Masoala, Madag. ... 89 B9
Saikhoa Ghat, India ... 67 F19
Saiki, Japan ... 55 H5
Sailana, India ... 68 H6
Saillans, France ... 21 D9
Sailolof, Indonesia ... 63 E8
Saimaa, Finland ... 9 F23
Saimbeyli, Turkey ... 72 D7
Şa'in Dezh, Iran ... 70 B5
St. Abb's Head, U.K. ... 14 F6
St-Affrique, France ... 20 E6
St-Agrève, France ... 21 C8
St-Aignan, France ... 18 E8
St. Alban's, Canada ... 103 C8
St. Albans, U.K. ... 13 F7
St. Albans, Vt., U.S.A. ... 111 B11
St. Albans, W. Va., U.S.A. ... 108 F5
St. Alban's Head, U.K. ... 13 G5
St. Albert, Canada ... 104 C6
St-Amand-en-Puisaye, France ... 19 E10
St-Amand-les-Eaux, France ... 19 B10
St-Amand-Montrond, France ... 19 F9
St-Amarin, France ... 19 E14
St-Amour, France ... 19 F12
St-André-de-Cubzac, France ... 20 D3
St-André-les-Alpes, France ... 21 E10
St. Andrew's, Canada ... 103 C8
St. Andrews, U.K. ... 14 E6
St-Anicet, Canada ... 111 A10
St. Ann B., Canada ... 103 C7
St. Ann's Bay, Jamaica ... 120 C4
St. Anthony, Canada ... 103 B8
St. Anthony, U.S.A. ... 114 E8
St-Antoine, Canada ... 103 C7
St-Antonin-Noble-Val, France ... 20 D5
St. Arnaud, Australia ... 95 F3
St-Astier, France ... 20 C4
St-Aubin-du-Cormier, France ... 18 D5
St-Augustin →, Canada ... 103 B8
St-Augustin-Saguenay, Canada ... 103 B8
St. Augustine, U.S.A. ... 109 L5
St-Aulaye, France ... 20 C4
St. Austell, U.K. ... 13 G3
St-Avold, France ... 19 C13
St. Barbe, Canada ... 103 B8
St-Barthélemy, W. Indies ... 121 C7
St-Béat, France ... 20 F4
St. Bees Hd., U.K. ... 12 C4
St-Benoît-du-Sault, France ... 20 B5
St-Bonnet, France ... 21 D10
St-Brévin-les-Pins, France ... 18 E4
St-Brice-en-Coglès, France ... 18 D5
St. Bride's, Canada ... 103 C9
St. Brides B., U.K. ... 13 F2
St-Brieuc, France ... 18 D4
St-Calais, France ... 18 E7
St-Cast-le-Guildo, France ... 18 D4
St. Catharines, Canada ... 102 D4
St. Catherines I., U.S.A. ... 109 K5

St. Catherine's Pt., U.K. ... 13 G6
St-Céré, France ... 20 D5
St-Cergue, Switz. ... 25 J2
St-Cernin, France ... 20 C6
St-Chamond, France ... 21 C8
St. Charles, Ill., U.S.A. ... 108 E1
St. Charles, Mo., U.S.A. ... 112 F9
St. Charles, Va., U.S.A. ... 108 F7
St-Chély-d'Apcher, France ... 20 D7
St-Chinian, France ... 20 E6
St. Christopher-Nevis = St. Kitts & Nevis ■, W. Indies ... 121 C7
St-Ciers-sur-Gironde, France ... 20 C3
St. Clair, Mich., U.S.A. ... 110 D2
St. Clair, Pa., U.S.A. ... 111 F8
St. Clair →, U.S.A. ... 110 D2
St. Clair, L., Canada ... 102 D3
St. Clair, L., U.S.A. ... 110 D2
St. Clairsville, U.S.A. ... 110 F4
St-Claud, France ... 20 C4
St. Claude, Canada ... 105 D9
St-Claude, France ... 19 F12
St-Clet, Canada ... 111 A10
St. Cloud, Fla., U.S.A. ... 109 L5
St. Cloud, Minn., U.S.A. ... 112 C7
St-Cricq, C., Australia ... 93 E1
St. Croix, Virgin Is. ... 121 C7
St. Croix →, U.S.A. ... 112 C8
St. Croix Falls, U.S.A. ... 112 C8
St-Cyprien, France ... 20 F7
St-Cyr-sur-Mer, France ... 21 E9
St. David's, Canada ... 103 C8
St. David's, U.K. ... 13 F2
St. David's Head, U.K. ... 13 F2
St-Denis, France ... 19 D9
St-Dié, France ... 19 D13
St-Dizier, France ... 19 D11
St-Égrève, France ... 21 C9
St. Elias, Mt., U.S.A. ... 100 B5
St. Elias Mts., Canada ... 104 A1
St. Elias Mts., U.S.A. ... 100 C6
St-Éloy-les-Mines, France ... 19 F9
St-Émilion, France ... 20 D3
St-Étienne, France ... 21 C8
St-Étienne-de-Tinée, France ... 21 D10
St-Étienne-du-Rouvray, France ... 18 C8
St. Eugène, Canada ... 111 A10
St. Eustatius, W. Indies ... 121 C7
St-Fargeau, France ... 19 E10
St-Félicien, Canada ... 102 C5
St-Florent, France ... 21 F13
St-Florent, G. de, France ... 21 F13
St-Florent-sur-Cher, France ... 19 F9
St-Florentin, France ... 19 E10
St-Flour, France ... 20 C7
St. Francis, U.S.A. ... 112 F4
St. Francis →, U.S.A. ... 113 H9
St. Francis, C., S. Africa ... 88 E3
St. Francisville, U.S.A. ... 113 K9
St-François, L., Canada ... 111 A10
St-Fulgent, France ... 18 F5
St-Gabriel, Canada ... 102 C5
St. Gallen = Sankt Gallen, Switz. ... 25 H5
St-Galmier, France ... 19 G11
St-Gaudens, France ... 20 E4
St-Gaultier, France ... 18 F8
St-Gengoux-le-National, France ... 19 F11
St-Geniez-d'Olt, France ... 20 D6
St. George, Australia ... 95 D4
St. George, Canada ... 103 C6
St. George, S.C., U.S.A. ... 109 J5
St. George, Utah, U.S.A. ... 115 H7
St. George, C., Canada ... 103 C8
St. George, C., U.S.A. ... 109 L3
St. George Ra., Australia ... 92 C4
St. George's, Canada ... 103 C8
St-Georges, Canada ... 103 C5
St. George's, Grenada ... 121 D7
St. George's B., Canada ... 103 C8
St. Georges Basin, N.S.W., Australia ... 95 F5
St. Georges Basin, W. Austral., Australia ... 92 C4
St. George's Channel, Europe ... 15 E6
St. Georges Hd., Australia ... 95 F5
St-Georges-lès-Baillargeaux, France ... 20 B4
St-Germain-de-Calberte, France ... 20 D7
St-Germain-en-Laye, France ... 19 D9
St-Germain-Lembron, France ... 20 C7
St-Gervais-d'Auvergne, France ... 19 F9
St-Gervais-les-Bains, France ... 21 C10
St-Gildas, Pte. de, France ... 18 E4
St-Gilles, France ... 21 E8
St-Girons, Ariège, France ... 20 F5
St-Girons, Landes, France ... 20 E2
St. Gotthard P. = San Gottardo, P. del, Switz. ... 25 J4
St. Helena, U.S.A. ... 114 G4
St. Helena ■, Atl. Oc. ... 76 H3
St. Helena, Mt., U.S.A. ... 116 G4
St. Helena B., S. Africa ... 88 E2
St. Helens, Australia ... 94 G4
St. Helens, U.K. ... 12 D5
St. Helens, U.S.A. ... 116 E4
St. Helens, Mt., U.S.A. ... 116 D4
St. Helier, U.K. ... 13 H5
St-Herblain, France ... 18 E5
St-Hilaire-du-Harcouët, France ... 18 D5
St-Hippolyte, France ... 19 E13
St-Hippolyte-du-Fort, France ... 20 E7
St-Honoré-les-Bains, France ... 19 F10
St-Hubert, Belgium ... 17 D5
St-Hyacinthe, Canada ... 102 C5

St. Ignace, U.S.A. ... 108 C3
St. Ignace I., Canada ... 102 C2
St. Ignatius, U.S.A. ... 114 C6
St-Imier, Switz. ... 25 H2
St. Ives, U.K. ... 13 G2
St-James, France ... 18 D5
St. James, U.S.A. ... 112 D7
St-Jean →, Canada ... 103 B7
St-Jean, L., Canada ... 103 C5
St-Jean-d'Angély, France ... 20 C3
St-Jean-de-Braye, France ... 19 E8
St-Jean-de-Luz, France ... 20 E2
St-Jean-de-Maurienne, France ... 21 C10
St-Jean-de-Monts, France ... 18 F4
St-Jean-du-Gard, France ... 20 D7
St-Jean-en-Royans, France ... 21 C9
St-Jean-Pied-de-Port, France ... 20 E2
St-Jean-Port-Joli, Canada ... 103 C5
St-Jean-sur-Richelieu, Canada ... 102 C5
St-Jérôme, Canada ... 102 C5
St. John, Canada ... 103 C6
St. John, U.S.A. ... 113 G5
St. John →, Liberia ... 82 D2
St. John →, U.S.A. ... 109 C12
St. John, C., Canada ... 103 B8
St. John's, Antigua ... 121 C7
St. John's, Canada ... 103 C9
St. Johns, Ariz., U.S.A. ... 115 J9
St. Johns, Mich., U.S.A. ... 108 D3
St. Johns →, U.S.A. ... 109 K5
St. John's Pt., Ireland ... 15 B3
St. Johnsbury, U.S.A. ... 111 B12
St. Johnsville, U.S.A. ... 111 D10
St. Joseph, La., U.S.A. ... 113 K9
St. Joseph, Mo., U.S.A. ... 112 F7
St. Joseph →, U.S.A. ... 108 D2
St. Joseph, I., Canada ... 102 C3
St. Joseph, L., Canada ... 102 B1
St-Jovite, Canada ... 102 C5
St-Juéry, France ... 20 E6
St-Julien-Chapteuil, France ... 21 C8
St-Julien-de-Vouvantes, France ... 18 E5
St-Julien-en-Genevois, France ... 19 F13
St-Junien, France ... 20 C4
St-Just-en-Chaussée, France ... 19 C9
St-Just-en-Chevalet, France ... 20 C7
St. Kilda, N.Z. ... 91 L3
St. Kitts & Nevis ■, W. Indies ... 121 C7
St. Laurent, Canada ... 105 C9
St-Laurent-de-la-Salanque, France ... 20 F6
St-Laurent-du-Pont, France ... 21 C9
St-Laurent-en-Grandvaux, France ... 19 F12
St-Laurent-et-Benon, France ... 20 C3
St. Lawrence, Australia ... 94 C4
St. Lawrence, Canada ... 103 C8
St. Lawrence →, Canada ... 103 C6
St. Lawrence, Gulf of, Canada ... 103 C7
St. Lawrence I., U.S.A. ... 100 B3
St. Leonard, Canada ... 103 C6
St-Léonard-de-Noblat, France ... 20 C5
St. Lewis →, Canada ... 103 B8
St-Lô, France ... 18 C5
St-Louis, France ... 19 E14
St. Louis, Senegal ... 82 B1
St. Louis, U.S.A. ... 112 F9
St. Louis →, U.S.A. ... 112 B8
St-Loup-sur-Semouse, France ... 19 E13
St. Lucia ■, W. Indies ... 121 D7
St. Lucia, L., S. Africa ... 89 D5
St. Lucia Channel, W. Indies ... 121 D7
St. Maarten, W. Indies ... 121 C7
St. Magnus B., U.K. ... 14 A7
St-Maixent-l'École, France ... 20 B3
St-Malo, France ... 18 D4
St-Malo, G. de, France ... 18 D4
St-Mandrier-sur-Mer, France ... 21 E9
St-Marc, Haiti ... 121 C5
St-Marcellin, France ... 21 C9
St-Marcouf, Îs., France ... 18 C5
St. Maries, U.S.A. ... 114 C5
St. Martin, W. Indies ... 121 C7
St. Martin, L., Canada ... 105 C9
St-Martin-de-Crau, France ... 21 E8
St-Martin-de-Ré, France ... 20 B2
St-Martin-d'Hères, France ... 21 C9
St-Martin-Vésubie, France ... 21 D11
St-Martory, France ... 20 E4
St. Mary Pk., Australia ... 95 E2
St. Marys, Australia ... 94 G4
St. Marys, Canada ... 110 C3
St. Marys, Corn., U.K. ... 13 H1
St. Mary's, Orkney, U.K. ... 14 C6
St. Marys, Ga., U.S.A. ... 109 K5
St. Marys, Pa., U.S.A. ... 110 E6
St. Mary's, C., Canada ... 103 C9
St. Mary's B., Canada ... 103 C9
St. Marys Bay, Canada ... 103 D6
St. Mathieu, Pte., France ... 18 D2
St. Matthews, I. = Zadetkyi Kyun, Burma ... 65 G1
St-Maurice →, Canada ... 102 C5
St-Maximin-la-Ste-Baume, France ... 21 E9
St-Médard-en-Jalles, France ... 20 D3
St-Menehould, France ... 19 C11
St-Mère-Église, France ... 18 C5
St-Mihiel, France ... 19 D12
St. Moritz, Switz. ... 25 J5
St-Nazaire, France ... 18 E4
St. Neots, U.K. ... 13 E7
St-Nicolas-de-Port, France ... 19 D13
St-Niklaas, Belgium ... 17 C4

St-Omer, France ... 19 B9
St-Palais-sur-Mer, France ... 20 C2
St-Pamphile, Canada ... 103 C6
St-Pardoux-la-Rivière, France ... 20 C4
St. Pascal, Canada ... 103 C6
St. Paul, Canada ... 104 C6
St. Paul, France ... 21 D10
St. Paul, Minn., U.S.A. ... 112 C8
St. Paul, Nebr., U.S.A. ... 112 E5
St. Paul →, Canada ... 103 B8
St. Paul →, Liberia ... 82 D2
St. Paul, I., Ind. Oc. ... 3 F13
St-Paul-de-Fenouillet, France ... 20 F6
St. Paul I., Canada ... 103 C7
St-Paul-lès-Dax, France ... 20 E2
St-Péray, France ... 21 D8
St. Peter, U.S.A. ... 112 C8
St. Peter-Ording, Germany ... 24 A4
St. Peter Port, U.K. ... 13 H5
St. Peters, N.S., Canada ... 103 C7
St. Peters, P.E.I., Canada ... 103 C7
St. Petersburg = Sankt-Peterburg, Russia ... 46 C6
St. Petersburg, U.S.A. ... 109 M4
St-Philbert-de-Grand-Lieu, France ... 18 E5
St-Pie, Canada ... 111 A12
St-Pierre, St- P. & M. ... 103 C8
St-Pierre, L., Canada ... 102 C5
St-Pierre-d'Oléron, France ... 20 C2
St-Pierre-en-Port, France ... 18 C7
St-Pierre et Miquelon □, St- P. & M. ... 103 C8
St-Pierre-le-Moûtier, France ... 19 F10
St-Pierre-sur-Dives, France ... 18 C6
St-Pol-de-Léon, France ... 18 D3
St-Pol-sur-Mer, France ... 19 A9
St-Pol-sur-Ternoise, France ... 19 B9
St-Pons, France ... 20 E6
St-Pourçain-sur-Sioule, France ... 19 F10
St-Priest, France ... 21 C8
St-Quay-Portrieux, France ... 18 D4
St. Quentin, Canada ... 103 C6
St-Quentin, France ... 19 C10
St-Rambert-d'Albon, France ... 21 C8
St-Raphaël, France ... 21 E10
St-Régis, U.S.A. ... 114 C6
St-Renan, France ... 18 D2
St-Saëns, France ... 18 C8
St-Savin, France ... 20 B4
St-Savinien, France ... 20 C3
St. Sebastien, Tanjon' i, Madag. ... 89 A8
St-Seine-l'Abbaye, France ... 19 E11
St-Sernin-sur-Rance, France ... 20 E6
St-Sever, France ... 20 E3
St-Siméon, Canada ... 103 C6
St. Simons I., U.S.A. ... 109 K5
St. Simons Island, U.S.A. ... 109 K5
St. Stephen, Canada ... 103 C6
St-Sulpice, France ... 20 E5
St-Sulpice-Laurière, France ... 20 B5
St-Sulpice-les-Feuilles, France ... 20 B5
St-Syprien = St-Cyprien, France ... 20 F7
St-Thégonnec, France ... 18 D3
St. Thomas, Canada ... 102 D3
St. Thomas I., Virgin Is. ... 121 C7
St-Tite, Canada ... 102 C5
St-Tropez, France ... 21 E10
St. Trond = St. Truiden, Belgium ... 17 D5
St. Truiden, Belgium ... 17 D5
St-Vaast-la-Hougue, France ... 18 C5
St-Valery-en-Caux, France ... 18 C7
St-Valéry-sur-Somme, France ... 19 B8
St-Vallier, France ... 19 F11
St-Vallier-de-Thiey, France ... 21 E10
St-Varent, France ... 18 F6
St-Vaury, France ... 20 B5
St. Vincent, Italy ... 28 C4
St. Vincent, G., Australia ... 95 F2
St. Vincent & the Grenadines ■, W. Indies ... 121 D7
St-Vincent-de-Tyrosse, France ... 20 E2
St. Vincent Passage, W. Indies ... 121 D7
St-Vith, Belgium ... 17 D6
St-Vivien-de-Médoc, France ... 20 C2
St. Walburg, Canada ... 105 C7
St-Yrieix-la-Perche, France ... 20 C5
St-Adresse, France ... 18 C7
Ste-Agathe-des-Monts, Canada ... 102 C5
Ste-Anne, L., Canada ... 103 B6
Ste-Anne-des-Monts, Canada ... 103 C6
Ste-Croix, Switz. ... 25 J2
Ste-Énimie, France ... 20 D7
Ste-Foy-la-Grande, France ... 20 D4
Ste. Genevieve, U.S.A. ... 112 G9
Ste-Hermine, France ... 18 B2
Ste-Livrade-sur-Lot, France ... 20 D4
Ste-Marguerite →, Canada ... 103 B6
Ste-Marie, Martinique ... 121 D7
Ste-Marie-aux-Mines, France ... 19 D14
Ste-Marie de la Madeleine, Canada ... 103 C5
Ste-Maure-de-Touraine, France ... 18 E7
Ste-Maxime, France ... 21 E10
Ste-Menehould, France ... 19 C11
Ste-Mère-Église, France ... 18 C5
Ste-Rose, Guadeloupe ... 121 C7
Ste. Rose du Lac, Canada ... 105 C9
Ste-Savine, France ... 19 D11
Ste-Sigolène, France ... 21 C8
Saintes, France ... 20 C3
Saintes, I. des, Guadeloupe ... 121 C7

Stes-Maries-de-la-Mer, France ... 21 E8
Saintfield, U.K. ... 15 B6
Saintonge, France ... 20 C3
Saipan, Pac. Oc. ... 96 F6
Sairang, India ... 67 H18
Sairecábur, Cerro, Bolivia ... 126 A2
Saitama □, Japan ... 55 F9
Saiteli = Kadınhanı, Turkey ... 72 C5
Saiti, Moldova ... 43 D14
Saiyid, Pakistan ... 68 C5
Sajama, Bolivia ... 124 G5
Sajan, Serbia, Yug. ... 42 E5
Sajó →, Hungary ... 42 E5
Sajószentpéter, Hungary ... 42 B5
Sajum, India ... 69 C8
Sak →, S. Africa ... 88 E3
Sakaba, Nigeria ... 83 C6
Sakai, Japan ... 55 G7
Sakaide, Japan ... 55 G6
Sakaiminato, Japan ... 55 G6
Sakākah, Si. Arabia ... 70 D4
Sakakawea, L., U.S.A. ... 112 B4
Sakami →, Canada ... 102 B4
Sakami, L., Canada ... 102 B4
Sâkâne, 'Erg i-n, Mali ... 83 A4
Sakania, Dem. Rep. of the Congo ... 87 E2
Sakaraha, Madag. ... 89 C7
Sakarya, Turkey ... 72 B4
Sakarya →, Turkey ... 72 B4
Sakashima-Guntō, Japan ... 55 M2
Sakassou, Ivory C. ... 82 D3
Sakata, Japan ... 54 E9
Sakchu, N. Korea ... 57 D13
Sakeny →, Madag. ... 89 C8
Sakété, Benin ... 83 D5
Sakha □, Russia ... 51 C13
Sakhalin, Russia ... 51 D15
Sakhalinskiy Zaliv, Russia ... 51 D15
Şaki, Azerbaijan ... 49 K8
Sakiai, Lithuania ... 9 J20
Sakon Nakhon, Thailand ... 64 D5
Sakrand, Pakistan ... 68 F3
Sakri, India ... 69 F12
Sakrivier, S. Africa ... 88 E3
Sakskøbing, Denmark ... 11 K5
Sakti, India ... 69 H10
Sakuma, Japan ... 55 G8
Sakurai, Japan ... 55 G7
Saky, Ukraine ... 47 K7
Sal →, Russia ... 49 G5
Sal, Eritrea ... 81 D4
Šal'a, Slovak Rep. ... 27 C10
Sala, Sweden ... 10 E10
Sala →, Eritrea ... 81 D4
Sala Consilina, Italy ... 31 B8
Sala-y-Gómez, Pac. Oc. ... 97 K17
Salaberry-de-Valleyfield, Canada ... 102 C5
Saladas, Argentina ... 126 B4
Saladillo, Argentina ... 126 D4
Salado →, Buenos Aires, Argentina ... 126 D4
Salado →, La Pampa, Argentina ... 128 D3
Salado →, Santa Fe, Argentina ... 126 C3
Salado →, Mexico ... 113 M5
Salaga, Ghana ... 83 D4
Šalāh, Syria ... 75 C5
Sălaj □, Romania ... 42 C8
Sálakhos, Greece ... 36 C9
Salala, Liberia ... 82 D2
Salala, Sudan ... 80 C4
Salālah, Oman ... 74 C5
Salamanca, Chile ... 126 C1
Salamanca, Spain ... 34 B5
Salamanca, U.S.A. ... 110 D6
Salamanca □, Spain ... 34 E5
Salamātābād, Iran ... 70 C5
Salamis, Cyprus ... 36 D12
Salamís, Greece ... 38 D5
Salar de Atacama, Chile ... 126 A2
Salar de Uyuni, Bolivia ... 124 H5
Sălard, Romania ... 42 C7
Salas, Spain ... 34 B4
Salas de los Infantes, Spain ... 34 C7
Salatiga, Indonesia ... 63 G14
Salaverry, Peru ... 124 E3
Salawati, Indonesia ... 63 E8
Salaya, India ... 68 H3
Salayar, Indonesia ... 63 F6
Salazar →, Spain ... 32 C3
Salbris, France ... 19 E9
Salcia, Romania ... 43 G9
Sălciua, Romania ... 43 D8
Salcombe, U.K. ... 13 G4
Saldaña, Spain ... 34 C6
Saldanha, S. Africa ... 88 E2
Saldanha B., S. Africa ... 88 E2
Saldus, Latvia ... 9 H20
Saldus □, Latvia ... 44 B9
Sale, Australia ... 95 F4
Sale, Italy ... 28 D5
Salé, Morocco ... 78 B4
Sale, U.K. ... 12 D5
Salekhard, Russia ... 50 C7
Salem, India ... 66 P11
Salem, Ill., U.S.A. ... 108 F1
Salem, Ind., U.S.A. ... 108 F2
Salem, Mass., U.S.A. ... 111 D14
Salem, Mo., U.S.A. ... 113 G9
Salem, N.H., U.S.A. ... 111 D13
Salem, N.J., U.S.A. ... 108 F8
Salem, N.Y., U.S.A. ... 111 C11
Salem, Ohio, U.S.A. ... 110 F4
Salem, Oreg., U.S.A. ... 114 D2
Salem, S. Dak., U.S.A. ... 112 D6
Salem, Va., U.S.A. ... 108 G5
Salemi, Italy ... 30 E5

Sälen, Sweden 10 C7
Salernes, France 21 E10
Salerno, Italy 31 B7
Salerno, G. di, Italy 31 B7
Salford, U.K. 12 D5
Salgir →, Ukraine 47 K8
Salgótarján, Hungary 42 B4
Salgueiro, Brazil 125 E11
Salibabu, Indonesia 63 D7
Salida, U.S.A. 106 C5
Salies-de-Béarn, France 20 E3
Salihli, Turkey 72 C3
Salihorsk, Belarus 47 F4
Salima, Malawi 85 G6
Salina, Italy 31 D7
Salina, Kans., U.S.A. 112 F6
Salina, Utah, U.S.A. 115 G8
Salina Cruz, Mexico 119 D5
Salinas, Brazil 125 G10
Salinas, Chile 126 A2
Salinas, Ecuador 124 D2
Salinas, U.S.A. 116 J5
Salinas →, Guatemala 119 D6
Salinas →, U.S.A. 116 J5
Salinas, B. de, Nic. 120 D2
Salinas, Pampa de las,
  Argentina 126 C2
Salinas Ambargasta,
  Argentina 126 B3
Salinas de Hidalgo, Mexico . 118 C4
Salinas Grandes, Argentina . 126 C3
Saline →, Ark., U.S.A. 113 J8
Saline →, Kans., U.S.A. ... 112 F6
Salines, Spain 37 B10
Salines, C. de ses, Spain ... 37 B10
Salinópolis, Brazil 125 D9
Salins-les-Bains, France ... 19 F12
Salir, Portugal 35 H2
Salisbury = Harare,
  Zimbabwe 87 F3
Salisbury, U.K. 13 F6
Salisbury, Md., U.S.A. 108 F8
Salisbury, N.C., U.S.A. ... 109 H5
Salisbury I., Canada 101 B12
Salisbury Plain, U.K. 13 F6
Sălişte, Romania 43 E8
Salka, Nigeria 83 C5
Şalkhad, Syria 75 C5
Salla, Finland 8 C23
Sallanches, France 21 C10
Sallent, Spain 32 D6
Salles, France 20 D3
Salles-Curan, France 20 D6
Salling, Denmark 11 H2
Salliq, Canada 101 B11
Sallisaw, U.S.A. 113 H7
Sallom Junction, Sudan 80 D4
Salluit, Canada 101 B12
Salmās, Iran 70 B5
Salmerón, Spain 32 E2
Salmo, Canada 104 D5
Salmon, U.S.A. 114 D7
Salmon →, Canada 104 C4
Salmon →, U.S.A. 114 D5
Salmon Arm, Canada 104 C5
Salmon Gums, Australia ... 93 F3
Salmon River Mts., U.S.A. . 114 D6
Salo, Finland 9 F20
Salò, Italy 28 C7
Salobreña, Spain 35 J7
Salome, U.S.A. 117 M13
Salon, India 69 F9
Salon-de-Provence, France . 21 E9
Salonica = Thessaloníki,
  Greece 40 F6
Salonta, Romania 42 D6
Salor →, Spain 35 F3
Salou, Spain 32 D6
Salou, C. de, Spain 32 D6
Saloum →, Senegal 82 C1
Salpausselkä, Finland 9 F22
Salsacate, Argentina 126 C2
Salses, France 20 F6
Salsk, Russia 49 G5
Salso →, Italy 30 E6
Salsomaggiore Terme, Italy . 28 D7
Salt, Spain 32 D7
Salt →, Canada 104 B6
Salt →, U.S.A. 115 K7
Salt Lake City, U.S.A. 114 F8
Salt Range, Pakistan 68 C5
Salta, Argentina 126 A2
Salta □, Argentina 126 A2
Saltara, Italy 29 E9
Saltash, U.K. 13 G3
Saltburn by the Sea, U.K. .. 12 C7
Saltcoats, U.K. 14 F4
Saltee Is., Ireland 15 D5
Saltfjellet, Norway 8 C16
Saltfjorden, Norway 8 C16
Saltholm, Denmark 11 J6
Saltillo, Mexico 118 B4
Salto, Argentina 126 C3
Salto, Uruguay 126 C4
Salto del Guaíra, Paraguay . 127 A5
Salton City, U.S.A. 117 M11
Salton Sea, U.S.A. 117 M11
Saltpond, Ghana 83 D4
Saltsburg, U.S.A. 110 F5
Saltsjöbaden, Sweden 10 E12
Saluda →, U.S.A. 109 J5
Salûm, Egypt 80 A2
Salûm, Khâlig el, Egypt ... 80 A2
Salur, India 67 K13
Saluzzo, Italy 28 D4
Salvador, Brazil 125 F11
Salvador, Canada 105 C7
Salvador, L., U.S.A. 113 L9
Salvaterra de Magos,
  Portugal 35 F2
Sálvora, I. de, Spain 34 C2

Salween →, Burma 67 L20
Salyan, Azerbaijan 50 F5
Salza →, Austria 26 D7
Salzach →, Austria 26 C5
Salzburg, Austria 26 D6
Salzburg □, Austria 26 D6
Salzgitter, Germany 24 C6
Salzkotten, Germany 24 D4
Salzwedel, Germany 24 C7
Sam, India 68 F4
Sam Neua, Laos 58 G5
Sam Ngao, Thailand 64 D2
Sam Rayburn Reservoir,
  U.S.A. 113 K7
Sam Son, Vietnam 64 C5
Sam Teu, Laos 64 C5
Sama de Langreo =
  Langreo, Spain 34 B5
Samagaltay, Russia 51 D10
Samales Group, Phil. 61 J4
Samâlût, Egypt 80 B3
Samana, India 68 D7
Samaná □, Dom. Rep. ... 121 C6
Samana Cay, Bahamas 121 B5
Samandağı, Turkey 72 D6
Samandıra, Turkey 41 F13
Samanga, Tanzania 87 D4
Samangwa,
  Dem. Rep. of the Congo . 86 C1
Samani, Japan 54 C11
Samanli Dağları, Turkey .. 41 F13
Samar, Phil. 61 F6
Samara, Russia 48 D10
Samara →, Russia 48 D10
Samara →, Ukraine 47 H8
Samaria = Shōmrōn,
  West Bank 75 C4
Samariá, Greece 36 D5
Samarinda, Indonesia 62 E5
Samarkand = Samarqand,
  Uzbekistan 50 F7
Samarqand, Uzbekistan ... 50 F7
Sāmarrā, Iraq 70 C4
Samastipur, India 69 G11
Şamaxı, Azerbaijan 49 K9
Samba,
  Dem. Rep. of the Congo . 86 C2
Samba, India 69 C6
Sambalpur, India 67 J14
Sambar, Tanjung, Indonesia 62 E4
Sambas, Indonesia 62 D3
Sambava, Madag. 89 A9
Sambawizi, Zimbabwe 87 F2
Sambhal, India 69 E8
Sambhar, India 68 F6
Sambhar L., India 68 F6
Sambiase, Italy 31 D9
Sambir, Ukraine 47 H2
Sambor, Cambodia 64 F6
Samborombón, B., Argentina 126 D4
Sambuca di Sicília, Italy .. 30 E6
Samch'ŏk, S. Korea 57 F15
Samch'onp'o, S. Korea ... 57 G15
Same, Tanzania 86 C4
Samer, France 19 B8
Samfya, Zambia 87 E2
Sámi, Greece 38 C2
Şämkir, Azerbaijan 49 K8
Şamlı, Turkey 39 B9
Samnah, Si. Arabia 70 E3
Samo Alto, Chile 126 C1
Samoa = Western Samoa ■,
  Pac. Oc. 91 B13
Samobor, Croatia 29 C12
Samoëns, France 19 F13
Samokov, Bulgaria 40 D7
Šamorín, Slovak Rep. 27 C10
Samorogouan, Burkina Faso 82 C4
Sámos, Greece 39 D8
Samoš, Serbia, Yug. 42 E5
Samos, Spain 34 C3
Sámos □, Greece 39 D8
Samothráki = Mathráki,
  Greece 36 A3
Samothráki, Greece 41 F9
Samothráki, Évros, Greece . 41 F9
Samoylovka, Russia 48 E6
Sampa, Ghana 82 D4
Sampacho, Argentina 126 C3
Sampang, Indonesia 63 G15
Samper de Calanda, Spain . 32 D4
Sampéyre, Italy 28 D4
Sampit, Indonesia 62 E4
Sampit, Teluk, Indonesia .. 62 E4
Samrong, Cambodia 64 E4
Samrong, Thailand 64 E3
Samsø, Denmark 11 J4
Samsø Bælt, Denmark ... 11 J4
Samsun, Turkey 72 B7
Samtredia, Georgia 49 J6
Samui, Ko, Thailand 65 H3
Samur →, Russia 49 K9
Samurskiy Khrebet, Russia . 49 K8
Samusole,
  Dem. Rep. of the Congo . 87 E1
Samut Prakan, Thailand .. 64 F3
Samut Songkhram →,
  Thailand 62 B1
Samwari, Pakistan 68 E2
San, Mali 82 C4
San →, Cambodia 64 F5
San →, Poland 45 H8
San Adrián, Spain 32 C3
San Adrián, C. de, Spain .. 34 B2
San Agustin, C., Phil. 61 H7
San Agustín de Valle Fértil,
  Argentina 126 C2
San Ambrosio, Pac. Oc. .. 122 F3
San Andreas, U.S.A. 116 G6
San Andres, Phil. 61 E6
San Andrés, I. de, Caribbean 120 D3

San Andrês del Rabanedo,
  Spain 34 C5
San Andres Mts., U.S.A. .. 115 K10
San Andrés Tuxtla, Mexico . 119 D5
San Angelo, U.S.A. 113 K4
San Anselmo, U.S.A. 116 H4
San Antonio, Belize 119 D7
San Antonio, Chile 126 C1
San Antonio, Phil. 61 D4
San Antonio, N. Mex.,
  U.S.A. 115 K10
San Antonio, Tex., U.S.A. . 113 L5
San Antonio →, U.S.A. .. 113 L6
San Antonio, C., Argentina 126 D4
San Antonio, C., Cuba ... 120 B3
San Antonio, C. de, Spain . 33 G5
San Antonio, Mt., U.S.A. .. 117 L9
San Antonio de los Baños,
  Cuba 120 B3
San Antonio de los Cobres,
  Argentina 126 A2
San Antonio Oeste,
  Argentina 128 E4
San Arcángelo, Italy 31 B9
San Ardo, U.S.A. 116 J6
San Augustín, Canary Is. .. 37 G4
San Augustine, U.S.A. 113 K7
San Bartolomé, Canary Is. . 37 F6
San Bartolomé de Tirajana,
  Canary Is. 37 G4
San Bartolomeo in Galdo,
  Italy 31 A8
San Benedetto del Tronto,
  Italy 29 F10
San Benedetto Po, Italy ... 28 C7
San Benedicto, I., Mexico . 118 D2
San Benito, U.S.A. 113 M6
San Benito →, U.S.A. ... 116 J5
San Benito Mt., U.S.A. ... 116 J6
San Bernardino, U.S.A. ... 117 L9
San Bernardino Mts., U.S.A. 117 L10
San Bernardino Str., Phil. .. 61 E6
San Bernardo, Chile 126 C1
San Bernardo, I. de,
  Colombia 124 B3
San Blas, Mexico 118 C3
San Blas, Arch. de, Panama 120 E4
San Blas, C., U.S.A. 109 L3
San Bonifacio, Italy 29 C8
San Borja, Bolivia 124 F5
San Buenaventura, Mexico . 118 B4
San Carlos = Butuku-Luba,
  Eq. Guin. 83 E6
San Carlos = Sant Carles,
  Spain 37 B8
San Carlos, Argentina 126 C2
San Carlos, Chile 126 D1
San Carlos, Baja Calif. S.,
  Mexico 118 C2
San Carlos, Coahuila,
  Mexico 118 B4
San Carlos, Nic. 120 D3
San Carlos, Neg. Occ., Phil. 61 F5
San Carlos, Pangasinan,
  Phil. 61 D4
San Carlos, Uruguay 127 C5
San Carlos, U.S.A. 115 K8
San Carlos, Venezuela 124 B5
San Carlos de Bariloche,
  Argentina 128 E2
San Carlos de Bolívar,
  Argentina 128 D4
San Carlos de la Rápita =
  Sant Carles de la Ràpita,
  Spain 32 E5
San Carlos del Zulia,
  Venezuela 124 B4
San Carlos L., U.S.A. 115 K8
San Cataldo, Italy 30 E6
San Celoni = Sant Celoni,
  Spain 32 D7
San Clemente, Chile 126 D1
San Clemente, Spain 33 F2
San Clemente, U.S.A. 117 M9
San Clemente I., U.S.A. .. 117 N8
San Cristóbal = Es Migjorn
  Gran, Spain 37 B11
San Cristóbal, Argentina .. 126 C3
San Cristóbal, Dom. Rep. . 121 C5
San Cristóbal, Venezuela .. 124 B4
San Cristóbal de la Casas,
  Mexico 119 D6
San Damiano d'Asti, Italy . 28 D5
San Daniele del Friuli, Italy 29 B10
San Diego, Calif., U.S.A. .. 117 N9
San Diego, Tex., U.S.A. ... 113 M5
San Diego, C., Argentina .. 128 G3
San Diego de la Unión,
  Mexico 118 C4
San Dimitri, Ras, Malta ... 36 C1
San Donà di Piave, Italy ... 29 C9
San Estanislao, Paraguay .. 126 A4
San Esteban de Gormaz,
  Spain 32 D1
San Felice Circeo, Italy ... 30 A6
San Felice sul Panaro, Italy . 29 D8
San Felipe, Chile 126 C1
San Felipe, Mexico 118 A2
San Felipe, Venezuela 124 A5
San Felipe →, U.S.A. ... 117 M11
San Felix, Chile 126 B1
San Félix, Pac. Oc. 122 F2
San Fernando = Sant
  Ferran, Spain 37 C7
San Fernando, Chile 126 C1
San Fernando, Baja Calif.,
  Mexico 118 B1
San Fernando, Tamaulipas,
  Mexico 119 C5
San Fernando, La Union,
  Phil. 61 C4

San Fernando, Pampanga,
  Phil. 61 D4
San Fernando, Spain 35 J4
San Fernando, Trin. & Tob. . 121 D7
San Fernando, U.S.A. 117 L8
San Fernando de Apure,
  Venezuela 124 B5
San Fernando de Atabapo,
  Venezuela 124 C5
San Fernando di Púglia, Italy 31 A9
San Francisco, Argentina .. 126 C3
San Francisco, U.S.A. 116 H4
San Francisco →, U.S.A. . 115 K9
San Francisco, Paso de,
  S. Amer. 126 B2
San Francisco de Macorís,
  Dom. Rep. 121 C5
San Francisco del Monte de
  Oro, Argentina 126 C2
San Francisco del Oro,
  Mexico 118 B3
San Francisco Javier = Sant
  Francesc de Formentera,
  Spain 37 C7
San Francisco Solano, Pta.,
  Colombia 122 C3
San Fratello, Italy 31 D7
San Gabriel, Chile 126 C1
San Gabriel Mts., U.S.A. .. 117 L9
San Gavino Monreale, Italy 30 C1
San Gimignano, Italy 28 E8
San Giórgio di Nogaro, Italy 29 C10
San Giórgio Iónico, Italy .. 31 B10
San Giovanni Bianco, Italy . 28 C6
San Giovanni in Fiore, Italy 31 C9
San Giovanni in Persiceto,
  Italy 29 D8
San Giovanni Rotondo, Italy 29 G12
San Giovanni Valdarno, Italy 29 E8
San Giuliano Terme, Italy .. 28 E7
San Gorgonio Mt., U.S.A. . 117 L10
San Gottardo, P. del, Switz. 25 J4
San Gregorio, Uruguay 127 C4
San Gregorio, U.S.A. 116 H4
San Guiseppe Jato, Italy ... 30 E6
San Ignacio, Belize 119 D7
San Ignacio, Bolivia 124 G6
San Ignacio, Mexico 118 B2
San Ignacio, Paraguay 120 C2
San Ignacio, L., Mexico ... 118 B2
San Ildefonso, C., Phil. ... 61 C5
San Isidro, Argentina 126 C4
San Isidro, Phil. 61 H7
San Jacinto, U.S.A. 117 M10
San Jaime = Sant Jaume,
  Spain 37 B11
San Javier, Misiones,
  Argentina 127 B4
San Javier, Santa Fe,
  Argentina 126 C4
San Javier, Bolivia 124 G6
San Javier, Chile 126 D1
San Javier, Spain 33 H4
San Jeronimo Taviche,
  Mexico 119 D5
San Joaquin, U.S.A. 116 J6
San Joaquin →, U.S.A. .. 116 G5
San Joaquin Valley, U.S.A. . 116 J6
San Jon, U.S.A. 113 H3
San Jordi = Sant Jordi,
  Spain 37 B9
San Jorge, Argentina 126 C3
San Jorge, Spain 37 C7
San Jorge, B. de, Mexico .. 118 A2
San Jorge, G., Argentina .. 128 F3
San Jorge, G. of, Argentina 122 H4
San José = San Josep, Spain 37 C7
San José, Costa Rica 120 D3
San José, Guatemala 120 D1
San Jose, Mind. Occ., Phil. . 61 E4
San Jose, Nueva Ecija, Phil. 61 D4
San Jose, U.S.A. 116 H5
San Jose →, U.S.A. 115 J10
San Jose de Buenavista, Phil. 63 B6
San José de Chiquitos,
  Bolivia 124 G6
San José de Feliciano,
  Argentina 126 C4
San José de Jáchal,
  Argentina 126 C2
San José de Mayo, Uruguay 126 C4
San José del Cabo, Mexico . 118 C3
San José del Guaviare,
  Colombia 124 C4
San Josep, Spain 37 C7
San Juan, Argentina 126 C2
San Juan, Mexico 118 C4
San Juan, Phil. 61 F6
San Juan, Puerto Rico 121 C6
San Juan □, Argentina ... 126 C2
San Juan □, Dom. Rep. .. 121 C5
San Juan →, Argentina ... 126 C2
San Juan →, Nic. 120 D3
San Juan →, U.S.A. 115 H8
San Juan Bautista = Sant
  Joan Baptista, Spain 37 B8
San Juan Bautista, Paraguay 126 B4
San Juan Bautista, U.S.A. . 116 J5
San Juan Bautista Valle
  Nacional, Mexico 119 D5
San Juan Capistrano, U.S.A. 117 M9
San Juan Cr. →, U.S.A. . 116 J5
San Juan de Alicante, Spain 33 G4
San Juan de Guadalupe,
  Mexico 118 C4
San Juan de la Costa, Mexico 118 C2
San Juan de los Morros,
  Venezuela 124 B5
San Juan del Norte, Nic. ... 120 D3

San Juan del Norte, B. de,
  Nic. 120 D3
San Juan del Río, Mexico .. 119 C5
San Juan del Sur, Nic. 120 D2
San Juan I., U.S.A. 116 B3
San Juan Mts., U.S.A. 115 H10
San Just, Sierra de, Spain . 32 E4
San Justo, Argentina 126 C3
San Kamphaeng, Thailand . 64 C2
San Lázaro, C., Mexico ... 118 C2
San Lázaro, Sa., Mexico ... 118 C3
San Leandro, U.S.A. 116 H4
San Leonardo de Yagüe,
  Spain 32 D1
San Lorenzo = Sant Llorenç
  des Cardassar, Spain 37 B10
San Lorenzo, Argentina ... 126 C3
San Lorenzo, Ecuador 124 C3
San Lorenzo, Paraguay ... 126 B4
San Lorenzo →, Mexico .. 118 C3
San Lorenzo, I., Mexico ... 118 B2
San Lorenzo, Mte.,
  Argentina 128 F2
San Lorenzo de la Parrilla,
  Spain 32 F2
San Lorenzo de Morunys =
  Sant Llorenç de Morunys,
  Spain 32 C6
San Lucas, Bolivia 124 H5
San Lucas, Baja Calif. S.,
  Mexico 118 C3
San Lucas, Baja Calif. S.,
  Mexico 118 B2
San Lucas, U.S.A. 116 J5
San Lucas, C., Mexico 118 C3
San Lúcido, Italy 31 C9
San Luis, Argentina 126 C2
San Luis, Cuba 120 B3
San Luis, Guatemala 120 C2
San Luis, Ariz., U.S.A. ... 115 K6
San Luis, Colo., U.S.A. ... 115 H11
San Luis □, Argentina 126 C2
San Luis, I., Mexico 118 B2
San Luis, Sierra de,
  Argentina 126 C2
San Luis de la Paz, Mexico . 118 C4
San Luis Obispo, U.S.A. .. 117 K6
San Luis Potosí, Mexico ... 118 C4
San Luis Potosí □, Mexico . 118 C4
San Luis Reservoir, U.S.A. . 116 H5
San Luis Río Colorado,
  Mexico 118 A2
San Manuel, U.S.A. 115 K8
San Marco, C., Italy 30 C1
San Marco Argentano, Italy 31 C9
San Marco in Lámis, Italy . 29 G12
San Marcos, Guatemala ... 120 D1
San Marcos, Mexico 118 B2
San Marcos, Calif., U.S.A. . 117 M9
San Marcos, Tex., U.S.A. .. 113 L6
San Marino, San Marino .. 29 E9
San Marino ■, Europe 29 E9
San Martín, Argentina 126 C2
San Martín →, Bolivia ... 124 F6
San Martín, L., Argentina . 128 F2
San Martín de la Vega, Spain 34 E7
San Martín de los Andes,
  Argentina 128 E2
San Martín de Valdeiglesias,
  Spain 34 E6
San Mateo = Sant Mateu,
  Baleares, Spain 37 B7
San Mateo = Sant Mateu,
  Valencia, Spain 32 E5
San Mateo, Phil. 61 C4
San Mateo, U.S.A. 116 H4
San Matías, Bolivia 124 G7
San Matías, G., Argentina . 122 H4
San Miguel = Sant Miquel,
  Spain 37 B7
San Miguel, El Salv. 120 D2
San Miguel, Panama 120 E4
San Miguel, U.S.A. 116 K6
San Miguel →, Bolivia ... 124 F6
San Miguel de Tucumán,
  Argentina 126 B2
San Miguel del Monte,
  Argentina 126 D4
San Miguel I., U.S.A. 117 L6
San Miniato, Italy 28 E7
San Nicolás, Canary Is. ... 37 G4
San Nicolás, Phil. 61 B4
San Nicolás de los Arroyas,
  Argentina 126 C3
San Nicolas I., U.S.A. 117 M7
San Onofre, U.S.A. 117 M9
San Pablo, Bolivia 126 A2
San Pablo, Phil. 61 D4
San Pablo, U.S.A. 116 H4
San Páolo di Civitate, Italy . 29 G12
San Pedro, Buenos Aires,
  Argentina 126 C4
San Pedro, Misiones,
  Argentina 127 B5
San Pedro, Chile 126 C1
San Pédro, Ivory C. 82 E3
San Pedro, Mexico 118 C2
San Pedro □, Paraguay ... 126 A4
San Pedro →, Chihuahua,
  Mexico 118 B3
San Pedro →, Nayarit,
  Mexico 118 C3
San Pedro →, U.S.A. ... 115 K8
San Pedro, Pta., Chile 126 B1
San Pedro, Sierra de, Spain 35 F4
San Pedro Channel, U.S.A. . 117 M8
San Pedro de Atacama, Chile 126 A2
San Pedro de Jujuy,
  Argentina 126 A3
San Pedro de las Colonias,
  Mexico 118 B4

203

San Pedro de Macorís,
  Dom. Rep. 121 C6
San Pedro del Norte, *Nic.* .. 120 D3
San Pedro del Paraná,
  Paraguay 126 B4
San Pedro del Pinatar, *Spain* 33 H4
San Pedro Mártir, Sierra,
  Mexico 118 A1
San Pedro Mixtepec, *Mexico* 119 D5
San Pedro Ocampo =
  Melchor Ocampo, *Mexico* 118 C4
San Pedro Sula, *Honduras* . 120 C2
San Pietro, *Italy* 30 C1
San Pietro Vernótico, *Italy* . 31 B11
San Quintín, *Mexico* 118 A1
San Rafael, *Argentina* 126 C2
San Rafael, *Calif., U.S.A.* . 116 H4
San Rafael, *N. Mex., U.S.A.* 115 J10
San Rafael Mt., *U.S.A.* 117 L7
San Rafael Mts., *U.S.A.* ... 117 L7
San Ramón de la Nueva
  Orán, *Argentina* 126 A3
San Remo, *Italy* 28 E4
San Roque, *Argentina* 126 B4
San Roque, *Spain* 35 J5
San Rosendo, *Chile* 126 D1
San Saba, *U.S.A.* 113 K5
San Salvador, *El Salv.* 120 D2
San Salvador, *Spain* 37 B10
San Salvador de Jujuy,
  Argentina 126 A3
San Salvador I., *Bahamas* . 121 C6
San Salvo, *Italy* 29 F11
San Sebastián = Donostia-
  San Sebastián, *Spain* ... 32 B3
San Sebastián, *Argentina* ... 128 G3
San Sebastian de la Gomera,
  Canary Is. 37 F2
San Serra = Son Serra,
  Spain 37 B10
San Serverino Marche, *Italy* 29 E10
San Severo, *Italy* 29 G12
San Simeon, *U.S.A.* 116 K5
San Simon, *U.S.A.* 115 K9
San Stéfano di Cadore, *Italy* 29 B9
San Stino di Livenza, *Italy* . 29 C9
San Telmo = Sant Telm,
  Spain 37 B9
San Telmo, *Mexico* 118 A1
San Tiburcio, *Mexico* 118 C4
San Valentin, Mte., *Chile* . 122 H3
San Vicente de Alcántara,
  Spain 35 F3
San Vicente de la Barquera,
  Spain 34 B6
San Vincente del Raspeig,
  Spain 33 G4
San Vincenzo, *Italy* 28 E7
San Vito, *Costa Rica* 120 E3
San Vito, *Italy* 30 C2
San Vito, C., *Italy* 30 D5
San Vito al Tagliamento,
  Italy 29 C9
San Vito Chietino, *Italy* 29 F11
San Vito dei Normanni, *Italy* 31 B10
Sana', *Yemen* 74 D3
Sana →, *Bos.-H.* 29 C13
Sanaba, *Burkina Faso* 82 C4
Şanâfir, *Si. Arabia* 80 B3
Sanaga →, *Cameroon* 83 E6
Sanaloa, Presa, *Mexico* 118 C3
Sanana, *Indonesia* 63 E7
Sanand, *India* 68 H5
Sanandaj, *Iran* 70 C5
Sanandita, *Bolivia* 126 A3
Sanary-sur-Mer, *France* ... 21 E9
Sanawad, *India* 68 H7
Sancellas = Sencelles, *Spain* 37 B9
Sancergues, *France* 19 E9
Sancerre, *France* 19 E9
Sancerrois, Collines du,
  France 19 E9
Sancha He →, *China* 58 D6
Sanchahe, *China* 57 B14
Sánchez, *Dom. Rep.* 121 C6
Sanchor, *India* 68 G4
Sancoins, *France* 19 F9
Sancti Spíritus, *Cuba* 120 B4
Sancy, Puy de, *France* 20 C6
Sand →, *S. Africa* 89 C5
Sand Hills, *U.S.A.* 112 D4
Sand Springs, *U.S.A.* 113 G6
Sanda, *Japan* 55 G7
Sandakan, *Malaysia* 62 C5
Sandan = Sambor,
  Cambodia 64 F6
Sandanski, *Bulgaria* 40 E7
Sandaré, *Mali* 82 C2
Sandared, *Sweden* 11 G6
Sandarne, *Sweden* 10 C11
Sanday, *U.K.* 14 B6
Sandefjord, *Norway* 9 G14
Sanders, *U.S.A.* 115 J9
Sanderson, *U.S.A.* 113 K3
Sandersville, *U.S.A.* 109 J4
Sandfire Roadhouse,
  Australia 92 C3
Sandfly L., *Canada* 105 B7
Sandfontein, *Namibia* 88 C2
Sandhammaren, C., *Sweden* 11 J8
Sandía, *Peru* 124 F5
Sandıklı, *Turkey* 39 C12
Sandila, *India* 69 F9
Sandnes, *Norway* 9 G11
Sandnessjøen, *Norway* 8 C15
Sandoa,
  Dem. Rep. of the Congo . 84 F4
Sandomierz, *Poland* 45 H8
Sândominic, *Romania* 43 D10
Sandover →, *Australia* 94 C2
Sandoway, *Burma* 67 K19

Sandoy, *Færoe Is.* 8 F9
Sandpoint, *U.S.A.* 114 B5
Sandray, *U.K.* 14 E1
Sandringham, *U.K.* 12 E8
Sandstone, *Australia* 93 E2
Sandu, *China* 58 E6
Sandusky, *Mich., U.S.A.* .. 110 C2
Sandusky, *Ohio, U.S.A.* ... 110 E2
Sandvig, *Sweden* 11 J8
Sandviken, *Sweden* 10 D10
Sandwich, C., *Australia* ... 94 B4
Sandwich B., *Canada* 103 B8
Sandwich B., *Namibia* 88 C1
Sandwip Chan., *Bangla.* ... 67 H17
Sandy, *Oreg., U.S.A.* 116 E4
Sandy, *Pa., U.S.A.* 110 E6
Sandy, *Utah, U.S.A.* 114 F8
Sandy Bay, *Canada* 105 B8
Sandy Bight, *Australia* 93 F3
Sandy C., *Queens., Australia* 94 C5
Sandy C., *Tas., Australia* .. 94 G3
Sandy Cay, *Bahamas* 121 B4
Sandy Cr. →, *U.S.A.* 114 F9
Sandy L., *Canada* 102 B1
Sandy Lake, *Canada* 102 B1
Sandy Valley, *U.S.A.* 117 K11
Sanford, *Fla., U.S.A.* 109 L5
Sanford, *Maine, U.S.A.* ... 109 D10
Sanford, *N.C., U.S.A.* 109 H6
Sanford →, *Australia* 93 E2
Sanford, Mt., *U.S.A.* 100 B5
Sang-i-Masha, *Afghan.* 68 C2
Sanga, *Mozam.* 87 E4
Sanga →, *Congo* 84 E3
Sanga, *India* 68 C1
Sangamner, *India* 66 K9
Sangar, *Afghan.* 68 C1
Sangar, *Russia* 51 C13
Sangar Sarai, *Afghan.* 68 B4
Sangaredi, *Guinea* 82 C2
Sangarh →, *Pakistan* 68 D4
Sangasso, *Mali* 82 C3
Sangatte, *France* 19 B8
Sangay, *Ecuador* 124 D3
Sange,
  Dem. Rep. of the Congo . 86 D2
Sangeang, *Indonesia* 63 F5
Sângeorz-Băi, *Romania* ... 43 C9
Sanger, *U.S.A.* 116 J7
Sângera, *Moldova* 43 D13
Sangerhausen, *Germany* .. 24 D7
Sanggan He →, *China* 56 E9
Sanggau, *Indonesia* 62 D4
Sanghar, *Pakistan* 68 F3
Sangihe, Kepulauan,
  Indonesia 63 D7
Sangihe, Pulau, *Indonesia* . 63 D7
Sangju, *S. Korea* 57 F15
Sangkapura, *Indonesia* 62 F4
Sangkhla, *Thailand* 64 E2
Sangkulirang, *Indonesia* ... 62 D5
Sangla, *Pakistan* 68 D5
Sangli, *India* 66 L9
Sangmélima, *Cameroon* ... 83 E7
Sangod, *India* 68 G7
Sangre de Cristo Mts.,
  U.S.A. 113 G2
Sangro →, *Italy* 29 F11
Sangrur, *India* 68 D6
Sangudo, *Canada* 104 C6
Sangue →, *Brazil* 124 F7
Sangüesa, *Spain* 32 C3
Sanguinaires, Îs., *France* .. 21 G12
Sangzhi, *China* 59 C8
Sanhala, *Ivory C.* 82 C3
Sanibel, *U.S.A.* 109 M4
Sanirajak, *Canada* 101 B11
Sanjawi, *Pakistan* 68 D3
Sanje, *Uganda* 86 C3
Sanjiang, *China* 58 E7
Sanjo, *Japan* 54 F9
Sankh →, *India* 69 H11
Sankt Andrä, *Austria* 26 E7
Sankt Augustin, *Germany* . 24 E3
Sankt Blasien, *Germany* .. 25 H4
Sankt Gallen, *Switz.* 25 H5
Sankt Gallen □, *Switz.* ... 25 H5
Sankt Goar, *Germany* 25 E3
Sankt Ingbert, *Germany* .. 25 F3
Sankt Johann im Pongau,
  Austria 26 D6
Sankt Johann in Tirol,
  Austria 26 D5
Sankt-Peterburg, *Russia* .. 46 C6
Sankt Pölten, *Austria* 26 C8
Sankt Ulrich = Ortisei, *Italy* 29 B8
Sankt Valentin, *Austria* ... 26 C7
Sankt Veit an der Glan,
  Austria 26 E7
Sankt Wendel, *Germany* .. 25 F3
Sankt Wolfgang, *Austria* .. 26 D6
Sankuru →,
  Dem. Rep. of the Congo . 84 E4
Sanliurfa, *Turkey* 70 B3
Sanlúcar de Barrameda,
  Spain 35 J4
Sanluri, *Italy* 30 C1
Sânmartin, *Romania* 43 D10
Sanmen, *China* 59 C13
Sanmenxia, *China* 56 G6
Sanming, *China* 59 D11
Sannaspos, *S. Africa* 88 D4
Sannicandro Gargánico, *Italy* 29 G12
Sânnicolau Mare, *Romania* 42 D5
Sannieshof, *S. Africa* 88 D4
Sannīn, J., *Lebanon* 75 B4
Sanniquellie, *Liberia* 82 D3
Sannûr, W. →, *Egypt* 80 B3
Sanok, *Poland* 45 J9
Sanquhar, *U.K.* 14 F5
Sansanding, *Mali* 82 C3
Sansepolcro, *Italy* 29 E9

Sansha, *China* 59 D13
Sanshui, *China* 59 F9
Sanski Most, *Bos.-H.* 29 D13
Sansui, *China* 58 D7
Sant Antoni Abat, *Spain* .. 37 C7
Sant Boi de Llobregat, *Spain* 32 D7
Sant Carles, *Spain* 37 B8
Sant Carles de la Ràpita,
  Spain 32 E5
Sant Celoni, *Spain* 32 D7
Sant Feliu de Guíxols, *Spain* 32 D8
Sant Feliu de Llobregat,
  Spain 32 D7
Sant Ferran, *Spain* 37 C7
Sant Francesc de
  Formentera, *Spain* 37 C7
Sant Jaume, *Spain* 37 B11
Sant Joan Baptista, *Spain* . 37 B8
Sant Jordi, *Spain* 37 B9
Sant Jordi, G. de, *Spain* .. 32 E6
Sant Llorenç de Morunys,
  Spain 32 C6
Sant Llorenç des Cardassar,
  Spain 37 B10
Sant Mateu, *Baleares, Spain* 37 B7
Sant Mateu, *Valencia, Spain* 32 E5
Sant Miquel, *Spain* 37 B7
Sant Telm, *Spain* 37 B9
Sant' Ágata Militello, *Italy* . 31 D7
Santa Agnés, *Spain* 37 B7
Santa Ana, *Bolivia* 124 F5
Santa Ana, *El Salv.* 120 D2
Santa Ana, *Mexico* 118 A2
Santa Ana, *U.S.A.* 117 M9
Sant' Ángelo Lodigiano, *Italy* 28 C6
Sant' Antíoco, *Italy* 30 C1
Santa Bárbara, *Colombia* .. 124 A4
Santa Bárbara, *Honduras* . 120 D2
Santa Bárbara, *Mexico* ... 118 B3
Santa Bárbara, *Spain* 32 E5
Santa Barbara, *U.S.A.* ... 117 L7
Santa Bárbara, Mt., *Spain* . 33 H2
Santa Barbara Channel,
  U.S.A. 117 L7
Santa Barbara I., *U.S.A.* .. 117 M7
Santa Catalina, Gulf of,
  U.S.A. 117 N9
Santa Catalina I., *Mexico* . 118 B2
Santa Catalina I., *U.S.A.* .. 117 M8
Santa Catarina □, *Brazil* .. 127 B6
Santa Catarina, I. de, *Brazil* 127 B6
Santa Caterina di Pittinuri,
  Italy 30 B1
Santa Caterina Villarmosa,
  Italy 31 E7
Santa Cecília, *Brazil* 127 B5
Santa Clara, *Cuba* 120 B4
Santa Clara, *Calif., U.S.A.* . 116 H5
Santa Clara, *Utah, U.S.A.* . 115 H7
Santa Clara, El Golfo de,
  Mexico 118 A2
Santa Clara de Olimar,
  Uruguay 127 C5
Santa Clarita, *U.S.A.* 117 L8
Santa Clotilde, *Peru* 124 D4
Santa Coloma de Farners,
  Spain 32 D7
Santa Coloma de Gramenet,
  Spain 32 D7
Santa Comba, *Spain* 34 B2
Santa Croce Camerina, *Italy* 31 F7
Santa Croce di Magliano,
  Italy 29 G11
Santa Cruz, *Argentina* ... 128 G3
Santa Cruz, *Bolivia* 124 G6
Santa Cruz, *Chile* 126 C1
Santa Cruz, *Costa Rica* ... 120 D2
Santa Cruz, *Madeira* 37 D3
Santa Cruz, *Phil.* 61 D4
Santa Cruz, *U.S.A.* 116 J4
Santa Cruz →, *Argentina* . 128 G3
Santa Cruz de la Palma,
  Canary Is. 37 F2
Santa Cruz de Mudela, *Spain* 35 G7
Santa Cruz de Tenerife,
  Canary Is. 37 F3
Santa Cruz del Norte, *Cuba* 120 B3
Santa Cruz del Retamar,
  Spain 34 E6
Santa Cruz del Sur, *Cuba* . 120 B4
Santa Cruz do Rio Pardo,
  Brazil 127 A6
Santa Cruz do Sul, *Brazil* . 127 B5
Santa Cruz I., *U.S.A.* 117 M7
Santa Cruz Is., *Solomon Is.* 96 J8
Santa Domingo, Cay,
  Bahamas 120 B4
Sant' Egídio alla Vibrata,
  Italy 29 F10
Santa Elena, *Argentina* ... 126 C4
Santa Elena, C., *Costa Rica* 120 D2
Sant' Eufémia, G. di, *Italy* . 31 D9
Santa Eulàlia des Riu, *Spain* 37 C8
Santa Fe, *Argentina* 126 C3
Santa Fe, *Spain* 35 H7
Santa Fe, *U.S.A.* 115 J11
Santa Fé →, *Argentina* ... 126 C3
Santa Fé do Sul, *Brazil* ... 125 H8
Santa Filomena, *Brazil* ... 125 E9
Santa Fiora, *Italy* 29 F8
Santa Gertrudis, *Spain* ... 37 C7
Santa Giusta, *Italy* 30 C1
Santa Inês, *Brazil* 125 F11
Santa Inés, *Spain* 35 G5
Santa Inés, I., *Chile* 122 J3
Santa Isabel = Rey Malabo,
  Eq. Guin. 83 E6
Santa Isabel, *Argentina* ... 126 D2
Santa Isabel, Pico de, *Eq. Guin.* 83 E6
Santa Isabel do Morro,
  Brazil 125 F8

Santa Lucía, *Corrientes,
  Argentina* 126 B4
Santa Lucía, *San Juan,
  Argentina* 126 C2
Santa Lucía, *Spain* 33 H4
Santa Lucia, *Uruguay* 126 C4
Santa Lucia Range, *U.S.A.* 116 K5
Santa Magdalena, I., *Mexico* 118 C2
Santa Margarita, *Argentina* 126 D3
Santa Margarita, *Spain* ... 37 B10
Santa Margarita →, *U.S.A.* 117 M9
Santa Margarita, I., *Mexico* 118 C2
Santa Margherita, *Italy* ... 30 D1
Santa Margherita Ligure,
  Italy 28 D6
Santa María, *Argentina* ... 126 B2
Santa Maria, *Brazil* 127 B5
Santa María, *Phil.* 61 C4
Santa Maria, *U.S.A.* 117 L6
Santa María →, *Mexico* .. 118 A3
Santa María, B. de, *Mexico* 118 B3
Santa María, C. de, *Portugal* 35 J3
Santa Maria Cápua Vétere,
  Italy 31 A7
Santa Maria da Feira,
  Portugal 34 E2
Santa Maria da Vitória,
  Brazil 125 F10
Santa Maria del Camí, *Spain* 37 B9
Santa Maria di Léuca, C.,
  Italy 31 C11
Santa Marinella, *Italy* 29 F8
Santa Marta, *Colombia* ... 124 A4
Santa Marta, Sierra Nevada
  de, *Colombia* 122 B3
Santa Marta de Tormes,
  Spain 34 E5
Santa Marta Grande, C.,
  Brazil 127 B6
Santa Marta Ortigueira, Ría
  de, *Spain* 34 B3
Santa Maura = Levkás,
  Greece 38 C2
Santa Monica, *U.S.A.* 117 M8
Santa Olalla, *Huelva, Spain* 35 H4
Santa Olalla, *Toledo, Spain* 34 E6
Santa Paula, *U.S.A.* 117 L7
Santa Pola, *Spain* 33 G4
Santa Ponsa, *Spain* 37 B9
Santa Rita, *U.S.A.* 115 K10
Santa Rosa, *La Pampa,
  Argentina* 126 D3
Santa Rosa, *San Luis,
  Argentina* 126 C2
Santa Rosa, *Brazil* 127 B5
Santa Rosa, *Calif., U.S.A.* . 116 G4
Santa Rosa, *N. Mex., U.S.A.* 113 H2
Santa Rosa de Copán,
  Honduras 120 D2
Santa Rosa de Río Primero,
  Argentina 126 C3
Santa Rosa del Sara, *Bolivia* 124 G6
Santa Rosa I., *U.S.A.* 117 M6
Santa Rosa Range, *U.S.A.* . 114 F5
Santa Rosalía, *Mexico* 118 B2
Santa Sylvina, *Argentina* .. 126 B3
Santa Tecla = Nueva San
  Salvador, *El Salv.* 120 D2
Santa Teresa, *Argentina* .. 126 C3
Santa Teresa, *Australia* ... 94 C1
Santa Teresa, *Mexico* 119 B5
Santa Teresa di Riva, *Italy* . 31 E8
Santa Teresa Gallura, *Italy* . 30 A2
Santa Uxía, *Spain* 34 C2
Santa Vitória do Palmar,
  Brazil 127 C5
Santa Ynez →, *U.S.A.* ... 117 L6
Santa Ynez Mts., *U.S.A.* .. 117 L6
Santa Ysabel, *U.S.A.* 117 M10
Santadi, *Italy* 30 C1
Santaella, *Spain* 35 H6
Santai, *China* 58 B5
Santana, *Madeira* 37 D3
Sântana, *Romania* 42 D6
Santana, Coxilha de, *Brazil* 127 C4
Santana do Livramento,
  Brazil 127 C4
Santander, *Spain* 34 B7
Santander Jiménez, *Mexico* 119 C5
Santanyí, *Spain* 37 B10
Santaquin, *U.S.A.* 114 G8
Santarcángelo di Romagna,
  Italy 29 D9
Santarém, *Brazil* 125 D8
Santarém, *Portugal* 35 F2
Santarém □, *Portugal* 35 F2
Santaren Channel, *W. Indies* 120 B4
Santee, *U.S.A.* 109 J6
Santee →, *U.S.A.* 109 J6
Santéramo in Colle, *Italy* .. 31 A9
Santerno →, *Italy* 29 D8
Santhià, *Italy* 28 C5
Santiago, *Brazil* 127 B5
Santiago, *Chile* 126 C1
Santiago, *Panama* 120 E3
Santiago, *Phil.* 61 C4
Santiago □, *Chile* 126 C1
Santiago →, *Mexico* 98 G9
Santiago →, *Peru* 124 D3
Santiago, Punta de,
  Eq. Guin. 83 E6
Santiago de Compostela,
  Spain 34 C2
Santiago de Cuba, *Cuba* .. 120 C4
Santiago de los Cabelleros,
  Dom. Rep. 121 C5
Santiago del Estero,
  Argentina 126 B3

Santiago del Estero □,
  Argentina 126 B3
Santiago del Teide,
  Canary Is. 37 F3
Santiago do Cacém, *Portugal* 35 G2
Santiago Ixcuintla, *Mexico* . 118 C3
Santiago Papasquiaro,
  Mexico 118 C3
Santiaguillo, L. de, *Mexico* 118 C4
Santiguila, *Mali* 82 C3
Santillana, *Spain* 34 B6
Santisteban del Puerto, *Spain* 35 G7
Santo Amaro, *Brazil* 125 F11
Santo Anastácio, *Brazil* ... 127 A5
Santo André, *Brazil* 127 A6
Santo Ângelo, *Brazil* 127 B5
Santo Antônio do Içá, *Brazil* 124 D5
Santo Antônio do Leverger,
  Brazil 125 G7
Santo Domingo, *Baja Calif.,
  Mexico* 118 A1
Santo Domingo,
  Baja Calif. S., Mexico ... 118 B2
Santo Domingo, *Nic.* 120 D3
Santo Domingo de la
  Calzada, *Spain* 32 C2
Santo Domingo de los
  Colorados, *Ecuador* ... 124 D3
Santo Domingo Pueblo,
  U.S.A. 115 J10
Santo Stéfano di Camastro,
  Italy 31 D7
Santo Tirso, *Portugal* 34 D2
Santo Tomás, *Mexico* 118 A1
Santo Tomás, *Peru* 124 F4
Santo Tomé, *Argentina* ... 127 B4
Santo Tomé de Guayana =
  Ciudad Guayana,
  Venezuela 124 B6
Santomera, *Spain* 33 G3
Santoña, *Spain* 34 B7
Santoríni = Thíra, *Greece* . 39 E7
Santos, *Brazil* 127 A6
Santos, Sierra de los, *Spain* 35 G5
Santos Dumont, *Brazil* ... 127 A7
Sanwer, *India* 68 H6
Sanxenxo, *Spain* 34 C2
Sanyuan, *China* 56 G5
São Bartolomeu de Messines,
  Portugal 35 H2
São Bernardo do Campo,
  Brazil 127 A6
São Borja, *Brazil* 127 B4
São Brás de Alportel,
  Portugal 35 H3
São Carlos, *Brazil* 127 A6
São Cristóvão, *Brazil* 125 F11
São Domingos, *Brazil* 125 F9
São Domingos, *Guinea-Biss.* 82 C1
São Francisco, *Brazil* 125 G10
São Francisco →, *Brazil* .. 122 E7
São Francisco do Sul, *Brazil* 127 B6
São Gabriel, *Brazil* 127 C5
São Gonçalo, *Brazil* 127 A7
Sao Hill, *Tanzania* 87 D4
São João, *Guinea-Biss.* ... 82 C1
São João da Boa Vista,
  Brazil 127 A6
São João da Madeira,
  Portugal 34 E2
São João da Pesqueira,
  Portugal 34 D3
São João del Rei, *Brazil* ... 127 A7
São João do Araguaia, *Brazil* 125 E9
São João do Piauí, *Brazil* .. 125 E10
São Joaquim, *Brazil* 127 B6
São Jorge, Pta. de, *Madeira* 37 D3
São José, *Brazil* 127 B5
São José do Norte, *Brazil* .. 127 C5
São José do Rio Prêto,
  Brazil 127 A6
São José dos Campos, *Brazil* 127 A6
São Leopoldo, *Brazil* 127 B5
São Lourenço, *Brazil* 127 A6
São Lourenço →, *Brazil* .. 125 G7
São Lourenço, Pta. de,
  Madeira 37 D3
São Lourenço do Sul, *Brazil* 127 C5
São Luís, *Brazil* 125 D10
São Luís Gonzaga, *Brazil* .. 127 B5
São Marcos →, *Brazil* ... 125 G9
São Marcos, B. de, *Brazil* . 125 D10
São Martinho da Cortiça,
  Portugal 34 E2
São Mateus, *Brazil* 125 G11
São Mateus do Sul, *Brazil* . 127 B5
São Miguel do Oeste, *Brazil* 127 B5
São Paulo, *Brazil* 127 A6
São Paulo □, *Brazil* 127 A6
São Paulo, I., *Atl. Oc.* 2 D8
São Paulo de Olivença,
  Brazil 124 D5
São Pedro do Sul, *Portugal* 34 E2
São Roque, *Madeira* 37 D3
São Roque, C. de, *Brazil* .. 122 D7
São Sebastião do Paraíso,
  Brazil 127 A6
São Teotónio, *Portugal* ... 35 H2
São Tomé, *Atl. Oc.* 76 F4
São Tomé, C. de, *Brazil* ... 127 A7
São Tomé & Principe ■,
  Africa 77 F4
São Vicente, *Brazil* 127 A6
São Vicente, *Madeira* 37 D3
São Vicente, C. de, *Portugal* 35 H1
Saona, I., *Dom. Rep.* 121 C6
Saône →, *France* 19 G11
Saône-et-Loire □, *France* .. 19 F11
Saonek, *Indonesia* 63 E8

Sápai, Greece ... 41 E9
Sapanca, Turkey ... 72 B4
Saparua, Indonesia ... 63 E7
Sapele, Nigeria ... 83 D6
Sapelo I., U.S.A. ... 109 K5
Şaphane, Turkey ... 39 B11
Sapiéntza, Greece ... 38 E3
Sapone, Burkina Faso ... 83 C4
Saposoa, Peru ... 124 E3
Sapouy, Burkina Faso ... 83 C4
Sapozhok, Russia ... 48 D5
Sapphire, Australia ... 94 C4
Sappho, U.S.A. ... 116 B2
Sapporo, Japan ... 54 C10
Sapri, Italy ... 31 B8
Sapulpa, U.S.A ... 113 H6
Saqqez, Iran ... 70 B5
Sar Dasht, Iran ... 71 C6
Sar Gachineh, Iran ... 71 D6
Sar Planina, Macedonia ... 40 E4
Sara, Burkina Faso ... 82 C4
Sara, Phil. ... 61 F5
Sara Buri = Saraburi,
  Thailand ... 64 E3
Sarāb, Iran ... 70 B5
Sarabadi, Iraq ... 70 C5
Saraburi, Thailand ... 64 E3
Sarada →, India ... 67 F12
Saradiya, India ... 68 J4
Saraféré, Mali ... 82 C4
Saragossa = Zaragoza, Spain 32 D4
Saraguro, Ecuador ... 124 D3
Sarai Naurang, Pakistan ... 68 C4
Saraikela, India ... 69 H11
Saraiu, Romania ... 43 F13
Sarajevo, Bos.-H. ... 42 G3
Sarakhs, Turkmenistan ... 71 B9
Saran, Gunung, Indonesia ... 62 E4
Saranac L., U.S.A. ... 111 B10
Saranac Lake, U.S.A. ... 111 B10
Saranda, Tanzania ... 86 D3
Sarandë, Albania ... 40 G3
Sarandí del Yi, Uruguay ... 127 C4
Sarandí Grande, Uruguay ... 126 C4
Sarangani B., Phil. ... 61 J6
Sarangani Is., Phil. ... 61 J6
Sarangarh, India ... 67 J13
Saransk, Russia ... 48 C7
Sarapul, Russia ... 50 D6
Sarasota, U.S.A. ... 109 M4
Saratoga, Calif., U.S.A. ... 116 H4
Saratoga, Wyo., U.S.A. ... 114 F10
Saratoga Springs, U.S.A. ... 111 C11
Saratok, Malaysia ... 62 D4
Saratov, Russia ... 48 E7
Saravane, Laos ... 64 E6
Sarawak □, Malaysia ... 62 D4
Saray, Tekirdağ, Turkey ... 41 E11
Saray, Van, Turkey ... 73 C11
Saraya, Guinea ... 82 C2
Saraya, Senegal ... 82 C2
Sarayçık, Turkey ... 39 B11
Sarayköy, Turkey ... 39 D10
Saraylar, Turkey ... 41 F11
Sarayönü, Turkey ... 72 C5
Sarbāz, Iran ... 71 E9
Sarbisheh, Iran ... 71 C8
Sárbogárd, Hungary ... 42 D3
Sarca →, Italy ... 28 C7
Sarcelles, France ... 19 D9
Sarda = Sarada →, India ... 67 F12
Sardarshahr, India ... 68 E6
Sardegna □, Italy ... 30 B1
Sardhana, India ... 68 E7
Sardina, Pta., Canary Is. ... 37 F4
Sardinia = Sardegna □, Italy 30 B1
Sardis, Turkey ... 39 C10
Sārdūīyeh = Dar Mazār,
  Iran ... 71 D8
S'Arenal, Spain ... 37 B9
Sarentino, Italy ... 29 B8
Saréyamou, Mali ... 82 B4
Sargasso Sea, Atl. Oc. ... 97 D20
Sargodha, Pakistan ... 68 C5
Sarh, Chad ... 79 G9
Sarhala, Ivory C. ... 82 D3
Sārī, Iran ... 71 B7
Sari d'Orcino, France ... 21 F12
Sária, Greece ... 39 F9
Saria, India ... 69 J10
Sariab, Pakistan ... 68 D2
Sarıbeyler, Turkey ... 39 B9
Sarıgöl, Turkey ... 72 C3
Sarıkamış, Turkey ... 73 B10
Sarıkaya, Turkey ... 72 C6
Sarikei, Malaysia ... 62 D4
Sarıköy, Turkey ... 41 F11
Sarila, India ... 69 G8
Sarina, Australia ... 94 C4
Sariñena, Spain ... 32 D4
Sarita, U.S.A. ... 113 M6
Sariwŏn, N. Korea ... 57 E13
Sariyar Baraji, Turkey ... 72 B4
Sarıyer, Turkey ... 41 E13
Sarju →, India ... 69 F9
Sark, U.K. ... 13 H5
Sarkad, Hungary ... 42 D6
Sarkari Tala, India ... 68 F4
Şarkışla, Turkey ... 72 C7
Şarköy, Turkey ... 41 F11
Sarlat-la-Canéda, France ... 20 D5
Sărmaşu, Romania ... 43 C7
Sărmaşu, Romania ... 43 D9
Sarmi, Indonesia ... 63 E9
Sarmiento, Argentina ... 128 F3
Sarmizegetusa, Romania ... 42 E7
Särna, Sweden ... 10 C7
Sarnano, Italy ... 29 E10
Sarnen, Switz. ... 25 J4
Sarnia, Canada ... 102 D3
Sarno, Italy ... 31 B7

Sarnthein = Sarentino, Italy 29 B8
Särö, Sweden ... 11 G5
Sarolangun, Indonesia ... 62 E2
Saronikós Kólpos, Greece ... 38 D5
Saronno, Italy ... 28 C6
Saros Körfezi, Turkey ... 41 F10
Sárospatak, Hungary ... 42 B6
Sarpsborg, Norway ... 9 G14
Sarracín, Spain ... 34 C7
Sarralbe, France ... 19 D14
Sarre = Saar →, Europe ... 17 E6
Sarre, Italy ... 28 C4
Sarre-Union, France ... 19 D14
Sarrebourg, France ... 19 D14
Sarreguemines, France ... 19 C14
Sarria, Spain ... 34 C3
Sarrión, Spain ... 32 E4
Sarro, Mali ... 82 C3
Sarstedt, Germany ... 24 C5
Sartène, France ... 21 G12
Sarthe □, France ... 18 D7
Sarthe →, France ... 18 E6
Sartilly, France ... 18 D5
Saruhanlı, Turkey ... 39 C9
Sărulești, Romania ... 43 F11
Saruna →, Pakistan ... 68 F2
Sárvár, Hungary ... 42 C1
Sarvar, India ... 68 F6
Sarvestān, Iran ... 71 D7
Särvfjället, Sweden ... 10 B7
Sárviz →, Hungary ... 42 D3
Sary-Tash, Kyrgyzstan ... 50 F8
Sarych, Mys, Ukraine ... 47 K7
Saryshagan, Kazakhstan ... 50 E8
Sarzana, Italy ... 28 D6
Sarzeau, France ... 18 E4
Sasan Gir, India ... 68 J4
Sasaram, India ... 69 G11
Sasebo, Japan ... 55 H4
Saser, India ... 69 B7
Saskatchewan □, Canada ... 105 C7
Saskatchewan →, Canada ... 105 C8
Saskatoon, Canada ... 105 C7
Saskylakh, Russia ... 51 B12
Sasolburg, S. Africa ... 89 D4
Sasovo, Russia ... 48 C5
Sassandra, Ivory C. ... 82 E3
Sassandra →, Ivory C. ... 82 E3
Sássari, Italy ... 30 B1
Sassnitz, Germany ... 24 A9
Sasso Marconi, Italy ... 29 D8
Sassocorvaro, Italy ... 29 E9
Sassoferrato, Italy ... 29 E9
Sasstown, Liberia ... 82 E3
Sassuolo, Italy ... 28 D7
Sástago, Spain ... 32 D4
Sasumua Dam, Kenya ... 86 C4
Sasyk, Ozero, Ukraine ... 47 K5
Sata-Misaki, Japan ... 55 J5
Satadougou, Mali ... 82 C2
Satakunta, Finland ... 9 F20
Satama-Soukoura, Ivory C. ... 82 D4
Satara, India ... 66 L8
Satara, S. Africa ... 89 C5
Satbarwa, India ... 69 H11
Sätenäs, Sweden ... 11 F6
Säter, Sweden ... 10 D9
Satevó, Mexico ... 118 B3
Satilla →, U.S.A. ... 109 K5
Satmala Hills, India ... 66 J9
Satna, India ... 69 G9
Šator, Bos.-H. ... 29 D13
Satpura Ra., India ... 66 J10
Satrup, Germany ... 24 A5
Satsuna-Shotō, Japan ... 55 K5
Sattahip, Thailand ... 64 F3
Satu Mare, Romania ... 42 C7
Satu Mare □, Romania ... 42 C8
Satui, Indonesia ... 62 E5
Satun, Thailand ... 65 J3
Saturnina →, Brazil ... 124 F7
Sauce, Argentina ... 126 C4
Sauceda, Mexico ... 118 B4
Saucillo, Mexico ... 118 B3
Sauda, Norway ... 9 G12
Sauðarkrókur, Iceland ... 8 D4
Saudi Arabia ■, Asia ... 74 B3
Saugeen →, Canada ... 110 B3
Saugerties, U.S.A. ... 111 D11
Saugues, France ... 20 D7
Saugus, U.S.A. ... 117 L8
Saujon, France ... 20 C3
Sauk Centre, U.S.A. ... 112 C7
Sauk Rapids, U.S.A. ... 112 C7
Saulgau, Germany ... 25 G5
Saulieu, France ... 19 E11
Sault, France ... 21 D9
Sault Ste. Marie, Canada ... 102 C3
Sault Ste. Marie, U.S.A. ... 101 D11
Saumlaki, Indonesia ... 63 F8
Saumur, France ... 18 E6
Saunders C., N.Z. ... 91 L3
Saunders I., Antarctica ... 5 B1
Saunders Point, Australia ... 93 E4
Sauri, Nigeria ... 83 C6
Saurimo, Angola ... 84 F4
Sausalito, U.S.A. ... 116 H4
Sauveterre-de-Béarn, France 20 E3
Sauze-Vaussais, France ... 20 B4
Savá, Honduras ... 120 C2
Sava, Italy ... 31 B10
Sava →, Serbia, Yug. ... 42 F5
Savage, U.S.A. ... 112 B2
Savage I. = Niue, Cook Is. ... 97 J11
Savage River, Australia ... 94 G4
Savai'i, W. Samoa ... 91 A12
Savalou, Benin ... 83 D5
Savane, Mozam. ... 87 F4
Savanna, U.S.A. ... 112 D9
Savanna-la-Mar, Jamaica ... 120 C4

Savannah, Ga., U.S.A. ... 109 J5
Savannah, Mo., U.S.A. ... 112 F7
Savannah, Tenn., U.S.A. ... 109 H1
Savannah →, U.S.A. ... 109 J5
Savannakhet, Laos ... 64 D5
Savant L., Canada ... 102 B1
Savant Lake, Canada ... 102 B1
Savanur, India ... 66 M9
Săvârşin, Romania ... 42 D7
Savaştepe, Turkey ... 39 B9
Savé, Benin ... 83 D5
Save →, France ... 20 E5
Save →, Mozam. ... 89 C5
Săveh, Iran ... 71 C6
Savelugu, Ghana ... 83 D4
Savenay, France ... 18 E5
Săveni, Romania ... 43 C11
Saverdun, France ... 20 E5
Saverne, France ... 19 D14
Savigliano, Italy ... 28 D4
Savigny-sur-Braye, France ... 18 E7
Sávio →, Italy ... 29 D9
Šavnik, Montenegro, Yug. ... 40 D3
Savo, Finland ... 8 E22
Savoie □, France ... 21 C10
Savona, Italy ... 28 D5
Savona, U.S.A. ... 110 D7
Savonlinna, Finland ... 46 B5
Savoy = Savoie □, France ... 21 C10
Şavşat, Turkey ... 73 B10
Sävsjö, Sweden ... 11 G8
Savur, Turkey ... 70 B4
Sawahlunto, Indonesia ... 62 E2
Sawai, Indonesia ... 63 E7
Sawai Madhopur, India ... 68 G7
Sawang Daen Din, Thailand 64 D4
Sawankhalok, Thailand ... 64 D2
Sawara, Japan ... 55 G10
Sawatch Range, U.S.A. ... 115 G10
Sawel Mt., U.K. ... 15 B4
Sawi, Thailand ... 65 G2
Sawla, Ghana ... 82 D4
Sawmills, Zimbabwe ... 87 F2
Sawtooth Range, U.S.A. ... 114 K6
Sawu, Indonesia ... 63 F6
Sawu Sea, Indonesia ... 63 F6
Saxby →, Australia ... 94 B3
Saxmundham, U.K. ... 13 E9
Saxony = Sachsen □,
  Germany ... 24 E9
Saxony, Lower =
  Niedersachsen □,
  Germany ... 24 C4
Saxton, U.S.A. ... 110 F6
Say, Mali ... 82 C4
Say, Niger ... 83 C5
Saya, Nigeria ... 83 D5
Sayabec, Canada ... 103 C6
Sayaboury, Laos ... 64 C3
Sayán, Peru ... 124 F3
Sayan, Vostochnyy, Russia 51 D10
Sayan, Zapadnyy, Russia ... 51 D10
Saydā, Lebanon ... 75 B4
Sayhandulaan = Oldziyt,
  Mongolia ... 56 B5
Sayhūt, Yemen ... 74 D5
Saykhin, Kazakhstan ... 49 F8
Saynshand, Mongolia ... 56 B6
Sayre, Okla., U.S.A. ... 113 H5
Sayre, Pa., U.S.A. ... 111 E8
Sayreville, U.S.A. ... 111 F10
Sayula, Mexico ... 118 D4
Sayward, Canada ... 104 C3
Sazanit, Albania ... 40 F3
Sázava →, Czech Rep. ... 26 B7
Sazin, Pakistan ... 69 B5
Sazlika →, Bulgaria ... 41 E9
Scaër, France ... 18 D3
Scafell Pike, U.K. ... 12 C4
Scalea, Italy ... 31 C8
Scalloway, U.K. ... 14 A7
Scalpay, U.K. ... 14 D3
Scandia, Canada ... 104 C6
Scandiano, Italy ... 28 D7
Scandicci, Italy ... 29 E8
Scandinavia, Europe ... 6 C8
Scansano, Italy ... 29 F8
Scapa Flow, U.K. ... 14 C5
Scappoose, U.S.A. ... 116 E4
Scarámia, Capo, Italy ... 31 F7
Scarba, U.K. ... 14 E3
Scarborough, Trin. & Tob. ... 121 D7
Scarborough, U.K. ... 12 C7
Scariff I., Ireland ... 15 E1
Scarp, U.K. ... 14 C1
Scebeli, Wabi →,
  Somali Rep. ... 74 G3
Ščedro, Croatia ... 29 E13
Schaal See, Germany ... 24 B6
Schaffhausen, Switz. ... 25 H4
Schagen, Neths. ... 17 B4
Schaghticoke, U.S.A. ... 111 D11
Schärding, Austria ... 26 C6
Scharhörn, Germany ... 24 B4
Scheessel, Germany ... 24 B5
Schefferville, Canada ... 103 B6
Scheibbs, Austria ... 26 C8
Schelde →, Belgium ... 17 C4
Schell Creek Ra., U.S.A. ... 114 G6
Schellsburg, U.S.A. ... 110 F6
Schenectady, U.S.A. ... 111 D11
Schenevus, U.S.A. ... 111 D10
Scherfede, Germany ... 24 D5
Schesslitz, Germany ... 25 F7
Schiedam, Neths. ... 17 C4
Schiermonnikoog, Neths. ... 17 A6
Schiltigheim, France ... 19 D14
Schio, Italy ... 29 C8
Schladming, Austria ... 26 D6
Schlanders = Silandro, Italy 28 B7
Schlei →, Germany ... 24 A5

Schleiden, Germany ... 24 E2
Schleiz, Germany ... 24 E7
Schleswig, Germany ... 24 A5
Schleswig-Holstein □,
  Germany ... 24 A5
Schlüchtern, Germany ... 25 E5
Schmalkalden, Germany ... 24 E6
Schmölln, Germany ... 24 E8
Schneeberg, Austria ... 26 D8
Schneeberg, Germany ... 24 E8
Schneverdingen, Germany ... 24 B5
Schoharie, U.S.A. ... 111 D10
Schoharie →, U.S.A. ... 111 D10
Scholls, U.S.A. ... 116 E4
Schönberg,
  Mecklenburg-Vorpommern,
  Germany ... 24 B6
Schönberg,
  Schleswig-Holstein,
  Germany ... 24 A6
Schönebeck, Germany ... 24 C7
Schongau, Germany ... 25 H6
Schöningen, Germany ... 24 C6
Schopfheim, Germany ... 25 H3
Schorndorf, Germany ... 25 G5
Schortens, Germany ... 24 B3
Schouten I., Australia ... 94 G4
Schouten Is. = Supiori,
  Indonesia ... 63 E9
Schouwen, Neths. ... 17 C3
Schramberg, Germany ... 25 G4
Schrankogel, Austria ... 26 D4
Schreiber, Canada ... 102 C2
Schrems, Austria ... 26 C8
Schrobenhausen, Germany ... 25 G7
Schroffenstein, Namibia ... 88 D2
Schroon Lake, U.S.A. ... 111 C11
Schruns, Austria ... 26 D2
Schuler, Canada ... 105 C6
Schumacher, Canada ... 102 C3
Schurz, U.S.A. ... 114 G4
Schuyler, U.S.A. ... 112 E6
Schuylerville, U.S.A. ... 111 C11
Schuylkill →, U.S.A. ... 111 G9
Schuylkill Haven, U.S.A. ... 111 F8
Schwabach, Germany ... 25 F7
Schwaben □, Germany ... 25 G6
Schwäbisch Gmünd,
  Germany ... 25 G5
Schwäbisch Hall, Germany ... 25 F5
Schwäbische Alb, Germany ... 25 G5
Schwabmünchen, Germany ... 25 G6
Schwalmstadt, Germany ... 24 E5
Schwandorf, Germany ... 25 F8
Schwaner, Pegunungan,
  Indonesia ... 62 E4
Schwanewede, Germany ... 24 B4
Schwarmstedt, Germany ... 24 C5
Schwarze Elster →,
  Germany ... 24 D8
Schwarzenberg, Germany ... 24 E8
Schwarzrand, Namibia ... 88 D2
Schwarzwald, Germany ... 25 G4
Schwaz, Austria ... 26 D4
Schwechat, Austria ... 27 C9
Schwedt, Germany ... 24 B10
Schweinfurt, Germany ... 25 E6
Schweizer-Reneke, S. Africa 88 D4
Schwenningen = Villingen-
  Schwenningen, Germany ... 25 G4
Schwerin, Germany ... 24 B7
Schweriner See, Germany ... 24 B7
Schwetzingen, Germany ... 25 F4
Schwyz, Switz. ... 25 H4
Schwyz □, Switz. ... 25 H4
Sciacca, Italy ... 30 E6
Scicli, Italy ... 31 F7
Scilla, Italy ... 31 D8
Scilly, Isles of, U.K. ... 13 H1
Ścinawa, Poland ... 45 G3
Scione, Greece ... 40 G7
Scioto →, U.S.A. ... 108 F4
Scituate, U.S.A. ... 111 D14
Scobey, U.S.A. ... 112 A2
Scone, Australia ... 95 E5
Scordia, Italy ... 31 E7
Scoresbysund =
  Illoqqortoormiit,
  Greenland ... 4 B6
Scornicești, Romania ... 43 F9
Scotia, Calif., U.S.A. ... 114 F1
Scotia, N.Y., U.S.A. ... 111 D11
Scotia Sea, Antarctica ... 5 B18
Scotland, Canada ... 110 C4
Scotland □, U.K. ... 14 E5
Scott, C., Australia ... 92 B4
Scott City, U.S.A. ... 112 F4
Scott Glacier, Antarctica ... 5 C8
Scott I., Antarctica ... 5 C11
Scott Is., Canada ... 104 C3
Scott L., Canada ... 105 B7
Scott Reef, Australia ... 92 B3
Scottburgh, S. Africa ... 89 E5
Scottdale, U.S.A. ... 110 F5
Scottish Borders □, U.K. ... 14 F6
Scottsbluff, U.S.A. ... 112 E3
Scottsboro, U.S.A. ... 109 H3
Scottsburg, U.S.A. ... 108 F3
Scottsdale, Australia ... 94 G4
Scottsdale, U.S.A. ... 115 K7
Scottsville, Ky., U.S.A. ... 109 G2
Scottsville, N.Y., U.S.A. ... 110 C7
Scottville, U.S.A. ... 108 D2
Scranton, U.S.A. ... 111 E9
Scugog, L., Canada ... 110 B6
Sculeni, Moldova ... 43 C12
Scunthorpe, U.K. ... 12 D7
Scuol Schuls, Switz. ... 25 J6
Scutari = Üsküdar, Turkey ... 41 F13
Seabrook, Australia ... 93 F2
Seaford, U.K. ... 13 G8

Seaford, U.S.A. ... 108 F8
Seaforth, Australia ... 94 C4
Seaforth, Canada ... 110 C3
Seaforth, L., U.K. ... 14 D2
Seagraves, U.S.A. ... 113 J3
Seaham, U.K. ... 12 C6
Seal →, Canada ... 105 B10
Seal L., Canada ... 103 B7
Sealy, U.S.A. ... 113 L6
Searchlight, U.S.A. ... 117 K12
Searcy, U.S.A. ... 113 H9
Searles L., U.S.A. ... 117 K9
Seascale, U.K. ... 12 C4
Seaside, Calif., U.S.A. ... 116 J5
Seaside, Oreg., U.S.A. ... 116 E3
Seaspray, Australia ... 95 F4
Seattle, U.S.A. ... 116 C4
Seaview Ra., Australia ... 94 B4
Sebago L., U.S.A. ... 111 C14
Sebago Lake, U.S.A. ... 111 C14
Sebastián Vizcaíno, B.,
  Mexico ... 118 B2
Sebastopol = Sevastopol,
  Ukraine ... 47 K7
Sebastopol, U.S.A. ... 116 G4
Sebba, Burkina Faso ... 83 C5
Sebderat, Eritrea ... 81 D4
Sébékoro, Mali ... 82 C3
Seben, Turkey ... 72 B4
Sebeş, Romania ... 43 E8
Sebeşului, Munţii, Romania 43 E8
Sebewaing, U.S.A. ... 108 D4
Sebezh, Russia ... 46 D5
Sebha = Sabhah, Libya ... 79 C8
Sébi, Mali ... 82 B4
Şebinkarahisar, Turkey ... 73 B8
Sebiş, Romania ... 42 D7
Sebnitz, Germany ... 24 E10
Sebring, Fla., U.S.A. ... 109 M5
Sebring, Ohio, U.S.A. ... 110 F3
Sebringville, Canada ... 110 C3
Sebta = Ceuta, N. Afr. ... 78 A4
Sebuku, Indonesia ... 62 E5
Sebuku, Teluk, Malaysia ... 62 D5
Sečanj, Serbia, Yug. ... 42 E5
Secchia →, Italy ... 28 C8
Sechelt, Canada ... 104 D4
Sechura, Desierto de, Peru ... 124 E2
Seclin, France ... 19 B10
Secondigny, France ... 18 F6
Sečovce, Slovak Rep. ... 27 C14
Secretary I., N.Z. ... 91 L1
Secunderabad, India ... 66 L11
Security-Widefield, U.S.A. ... 112 F2
Sedalia, U.S.A. ... 112 F8
Sedan, France ... 19 C11
Sedan, U.S.A. ... 113 G6
Sedano, Spain ... 34 C7
Seddon, N.Z. ... 91 J5
Seddonville, N.Z. ... 91 J4
Sedé Boqér, Israel ... 75 E3
Sedeh, Fārs, Iran ... 71 D7
Sedeh, Khorāsān, Iran ... 71 C8
Séderon, France ... 21 D9
Sederot, Israel ... 75 D3
Sédhiou, Senegal ... 82 C1
Sedico, Italy ... 29 B9
Sedley, Canada ... 105 C8
Sedona, U.S.A. ... 115 J8
Sędziszów Małopolski,
  Poland ... 45 H8
Seebad Ahlbeck, Germany ... 24 B10
Seefeld in Tirol, Austria ... 26 D4
Seehausen, Germany ... 24 C7
Seeheim, Namibia ... 88 D2
Seeheim-Jugenheim,
  Germany ... 25 F4
Seeis, Namibia ... 88 C2
Seekoei →, S. Africa ... 88 E4
Seeley's Bay, Canada ... 111 B8
Seelow, Germany ... 24 C10
Sées, France ... 18 D7
Seesen, Germany ... 24 D6
Seevetal, Germany ... 24 B6
Sefadu, S. Leone ... 82 D2
Seferihisar, Turkey ... 39 C8
Séfeto, Mali ... 82 C3
Sefwi Bekwai, Ghana ... 82 D4
Segamat, Malaysia ... 65 L4
Segarcea, Romania ... 43 F8
Ségbana, Benin ... 83 C5
Segbwema, S. Leone ... 82 D2
Seget, Indonesia ... 63 E8
Segonzac, France ... 20 C3
Segorbe, Spain ... 33 E4
Ségou, Mali ... 82 C3
Segovia = Coco →,
  Cent. Amer. ... 120 D3
Segovia, Spain ... 34 E6
Segovia □, Spain ... 34 E6
Segré, France ... 18 E6
Séguéla, Ivory C. ... 82 D3
Séguénéga, Burkina Faso ... 83 C4
Seguin, U.S.A. ... 113 L6
Segundo →, Argentina ... 126 C3
Segura →, Spain ... 33 G4
Segura, Sierra de, Spain ... 33 G2
Seh Konj, Kūh-e, Iran ... 71 D8
Sehitwa, Botswana ... 88 C3
Sehore, India ... 68 H7
Sehwan, Pakistan ... 68 F2
Seica Mare, Romania ... 43 D9
Seil, U.K. ... 14 E3
Seiland, Norway ... 8 A20

Seilhac, France 20 C5
Seiling, U.S.A. 113 G5
Seille →, Moselle, France 19 C13
Seille →, Saône-et-Loire, France 19 F11
Sein, Î. de, France 18 D2
Seinäjoki, Finland 9 E20
Seine →, France 18 C7
Seine, B. de la, France 18 C6
Seine-et-Marne □, France 19 D10
Seine-Maritime □, France 18 C7
Seine-St-Denis □, France 19 D9
Seini, Romania 43 C8
Seirijai, Lithuania 44 D10
Sejerø, Denmark 11 J5
Sejerø Bugt, Denmark 11 J5
Sejny, Poland 44 D10
Seka, Ethiopia 81 F4
Sekayu, Indonesia 62 E2
Seke, Tanzania 86 C3
Sekenke, Tanzania 86 C3
Seki, Turkey 39 E11
Sekondi-Takoradi, Ghana 82 E4
Sekota, Ethiopia 81 E4
Seksna, Russia 46 C10
Sekuma, Botswana 88 C3
Selah, U.S.A. 114 C3
Selama, Malaysia 65 K3
Selárgius, Italy 30 C2
Selaru, Indonesia 63 F8
Selb, Germany 25 E8
Selby, U.K. 12 D6
Selby, U.S.A. 112 C4
Selca, Croatia 29 E13
Selçuk, Turkey 39 D9
Selden, U.S.A. 112 F4
Sele →, Italy 31 B7
Selebi-Pikwe, Botswana 89 C4
Selemdzha →, Russia 51 D13
Selendi, Manisa, Turkey 39 C10
Selendi, Manisa, Turkey 39 C9
Selenga = Selenge Mörön →, Asia 60 A5
Selenge Mörön →, Asia 60 A5
Selenica, Albania 40 F3
Selenter See, Germany 24 A6
Sélestat, France 19 D14
Seletan, Tanjung, Indonesia 62 E4
Selevac, Serbia, Yug. 40 B4
Sélibabi, Mauritania 82 B2
Seliger, Ozero, Russia 46 D7
Seligman, U.S.A. 115 J7
Şelim, Turkey 73 B10
Selîma, El Wâhât el, Sudan 80 C2
Selimiye, Turkey 39 D9
Selinda Spillway →, Botswana 88 B3
Selinoús, Greece 38 D3
Selinsgrove, U.S.A. 110 F8
Selizharovo, Russia 46 D7
Selkirk, Canada 105 C9
Selkirk, U.K. 14 F6
Selkirk I., Canada 105 C9
Selkirk Mts., Canada 100 C8
Sellama, Sudan 81 E2
Selliá, Greece 36 D6
Sellières, France 19 F12
Sells, U.S.A. 115 L8
Sellye, Hungary 42 E2
Selma, Ala., U.S.A. 109 J2
Selma, Calif., U.S.A. 116 J7
Selma, N.C., U.S.A. 109 H6
Selmer, U.S.A. 109 H1
Selongey, France 19 E12
Selowandoma Falls, Zimbabwe 87 G3
Selpele, Indonesia 63 E8
Selsey Bill, U.K. 13 G7
Seltso, Russia 46 D7
Seltz, France 19 D15
Selu, Indonesia 63 F8
Sélune →, France 18 D5
Selva = La Selva del Camp, Spain 32 D6
Selva, Argentina 126 B3
Selvas, Brazil 122 D4
Selwyn L., Canada 105 B8
Selwyn Mts., Canada 100 B6
Selwyn Ra., Australia 94 C3
Semani →, Albania 40 F3
Semarang, Indonesia 63 G14
Sembabule, Uganda 86 C3
Şemdinli, Turkey 73 D11
Sémé, Senegal 82 B2
Semeih, Sudan 81 E3
Semenov, Russia 48 B7
Semenovka, Chernihiv, Ukraine 47 F7
Semenovka, Kremenchuk, Ukraine 47 H7
Semeru, Indonesia 63 H15
Semey, Kazakstan 50 D9
Semikarakorskiy, Russia 49 G5
Semiluki, Russia 47 G10
Seminoe Reservoir, U.S.A. 114 F10
Seminole, Okla., U.S.A. 113 H6
Seminole, Tex., U.S.A. 113 J3
Seminole Draw →, U.S.A. 113 J3
Semipalatinsk = Semey, Kazakstan 50 D9
Semirara Is., Phil. 61 F4
Semitau, Indonesia 62 D4
Semiyarka, Kazakstan 50 D8
Semiyarskoye = Semiyarka, Kazakstan 50 D8
Semmering P., Austria 26 D8
Semnān, Iran 71 C7
Semnān □, Iran 71 C7
Semporna, Malaysia 63 D5
Semuda, Indonesia 62 E4
Semur-en-Auxois, France 19 E11

Sen →, Cambodia 62 B3
Senā, Iran 71 D6
Sena, Mozam. 87 F4
Sena Madureira, Brazil 124 E5
Senador Pompeu, Brazil 125 E11
Senaki, Georgia 49 J6
Senanga, Zambia 88 B3
Senatobia, U.S.A. 113 H10
Sencelles, Spain 37 B9
Sendafa, Ethiopia 81 F4
Sendai, Kagoshima, Japan 55 J5
Sendai, Miyagi, Japan 54 E10
Sendai-Wan, Japan 54 E10
Senden, Bayern, Germany 25 G6
Senden, Nordrhein-Westfalen, Germany 24 D3
Sendhwa, India 68 J3
Sene →, Ghana 83 D4
Senec, Slovak Rep. 27 C10
Seneca, U.S.A. 109 H4
Seneca Falls, U.S.A. 111 D8
Seneca L., U.S.A. 110 D8
Senecaville L., U.S.A. 110 G3
Senegal ■, W. Afr. 82 C2
Sénégal →, W. Afr. 82 B1
Senegambia, Africa 76 E2
Senekal, S. Africa 89 D4
Senftenberg, Germany 24 D10
Senga Hill, Zambia 87 D3
Senge Khambab = Indus →, Pakistan 68 G2
Sengiley, Russia 48 D9
Sengua →, Zimbabwe 87 F2
Senhor-do-Bonfim, Brazil 125 F10
Senica, Slovak Rep. 27 C10
Senigállia, Italy 29 E10
Senio →, Italy 29 D9
Senirkent, Turkey 39 C12
Senise, Italy 31 B9
Senj, Croatia 29 D11
Senja, Norway 8 B17
Senkaku-Shotō, Japan 55 L1
Senlis, France 19 C9
Senmonorom, Cambodia 64 F6
Sennâr, Sudan 81 E3
Sennar □, Sudan 81 E3
Senneterre, Canada 102 C4
Senno, Belarus 46 E5
Sénnori, Italy 30 B1
Seno, Laos 64 D5
Senonches, France 18 D8
Senorbì, Italy 30 C2
Senožeče, Slovenia 29 C11
Sens, France 19 D10
Senta, Serbia, Yug. 42 E5
Sentani, Indonesia 63 E10
Sentery, Dem. Rep. of the Congo 86 D2
Sentinel, U.S.A. 115 K7
Şentjur, Slovenia 29 B12
Senya Beraku, Ghana 83 D4
Seo de Urgel = La Seu d'Urgell, Spain 32 C6
Seohara, India 69 E8
Seonath →, India 69 J10
Seondha, India 69 F8
Seoni, India 69 H8
Seoni Malwa, India 68 H8
Seoul = Sŏul, S. Korea 57 F14
Sepīdān, Iran 71 D7
Sepo-ri, N. Korea 57 E14
Sępólno Krajeńskie, Poland 44 E4
Sepone, Laos 64 D6
Sępopol, Poland 44 D8
Sept-Îles, Canada 103 B6
Septemvri, Bulgaria 41 D8
Sepúlveda, Spain 34 D7
Sequeros, Spain 34 E4
Sequim, U.S.A. 116 B3
Sequoia National Park, U.S.A. 116 J8
Serafimovich, Russia 48 F6
Seraing, Belgium 17 D5
Seraja, Indonesia 65 L7
Serakhis →, Cyprus 36 D11
Seram, Indonesia 63 E7
Seram Sea, Indonesia 63 E7
Seranantsara, Madag. 89 B8
Serang, Indonesia 63 G12
Serasan, Indonesia 65 L7
Seravezza, Italy 28 E7
Şerbettar, Turkey 41 E10
Serbia □, Yugoslavia 40 C5
Şercaia, Romania 43 E10
Serdo, Ethiopia 81 E5
Serdobsk, Russia 48 D7
Sered', Slovak Rep. 27 C10
Seredka, Russia 46 C5
Şereflikoçhisar, Turkey 72 C5
Seregno, Italy 28 C6
Seremban, Malaysia 65 L3
Serengeti Plain, Tanzania 86 C4
Serenje, Zambia 87 E3
Sereth = Siret →, Romania 43 E12
Sergach, Russia 48 C7
Serge, Turkey 41 E11
Sergino, Russia 50 C7
Sergipe □, Brazil 125 F11
Sergiyev Posad, Russia 46 D10
Seria, Brunei 62 D4
Serian, Malaysia 62 D4
Seriate, Italy 28 C6
Seribu, Kepulauan, Indonesia 62 F3
Sérifontaine, France 19 C8
Sérifos, Greece 38 D6
Sérignan, France 20 E7
Sérigny →, Canada 103 A6
Serik, Turkey 72 D4
Seringapatam Reef, Australia 92 B3
Serinhisar, Turkey 39 D11

Sermaize-les-Bains, France 19 D11
Sermata, Indonesia 63 F7
Sérmide, Italy 29 D8
Sernovodsk, Russia 48 D10
Sernur, Russia 48 B9
Serock, Poland 45 F8
Serón, Spain 33 H2
Seròs, Spain 32 D5
Serov, Russia 50 D7
Serowe, Botswana 88 C4
Serpa, Portugal 35 H3
Serpeddì, Punta, Italy 30 C2
Serpentara, Italy 30 C2
Serpentine Lakes, Australia 93 E4
Serpis →, Spain 33 G4
Serpukhov, Russia 46 E9
Serra de Outes, Spain 34 C2
Serra do Navio, Brazil 125 C8
Serra San Bruno, Italy 31 D9
Serradilla, Spain 34 F4
Sérrai, Greece 40 E7
Sérrai □, Greece 40 E7
Serramanna, Italy 30 C1
Serravalle Scrívia, Italy 28 D5
Serre-Ponçon, L. de, France 21 D10
Serres, France 21 D9
Serrezuela, Argentina 126 C2
Serrinha, Brazil 125 F11
Sersale, Italy 31 C9
Sertã, Portugal 34 F2
Sertanópolis, Brazil 127 A5
Sêrtar, China 58 A3
Serua, Indonesia 63 F8
Serui, Indonesia 63 E9
Serule, Botswana 88 C4
Sérvia, Greece 40 F6
Serzedelo, Portugal 34 D2
Sese Is., Uganda 86 C3
Sesepe, Indonesia 63 E7
Sesfontein, Namibia 88 B1
Sesheke, Zambia 88 B3
Sésia →, Italy 28 C5
Sesimbra, Portugal 35 G1
S'Espalmador, Spain 37 C7
S'Espardell, Spain 37 C7
Sessa Aurunca, Italy 30 A6
Sestao, Spain 32 B2
Sesto Calende, Italy 28 C5
Sesto San Giovanni, Italy 28 C6
Sestri Levante, Italy 28 D6
Sestriere, Italy 28 D3
Sestroretsk, Russia 46 B6
Sestrunj, Croatia 29 D11
Sestu, Italy 30 C2
Setana, Japan 54 C9
Sète, France 20 E7
Setonaikai, Japan 55 G6
Settat, Morocco 78 B4
Séttimo Torinese, Italy 28 C4
Setting L., Canada 105 C9
Settle, U.K. 12 C5
Settlement Pt., Bahamas 109 M6
Settlers, S. Africa 89 C4
Setúbal, Portugal 35 G2
Setúbal □, Portugal 35 G2
Setúbal, B. de, Portugal 35 G2
Seugne →, France 20 C3
Seul, Lac, Canada 100 C10
Seurre, France 19 F12
Sevan, Armenia 49 K7
Sevan, Ozero = Sevana Lich, Armenia 49 K7
Sevana Lich, Armenia 49 K7
Sevastopol, Ukraine 47 K7
Seven Sisters, Canada 104 C3
Sever →, Spain 35 F3
Sévérac-le-Château, France 20 D7
Severn →, Canada 102 A2
Severn →, U.K. 13 F5
Severn L., Canada 102 B1
Severnaya Zemlya, Russia 51 B10
Severo-Kurilsk, Russia 51 D16
Severo-Yeniseyskiy, Russia 51 C10
Severočeský □, Czech Rep. 26 A7
Severodonetsk = Syeverodonetsk, Ukraine 47 H10
Severodvinsk, Russia 50 C4
Severomoravský □, Czech Rep. 27 B10
Sevier, U.S.A. 115 G7
Sevier →, U.S.A. 115 G7
Sevier Desert, U.S.A. 114 G7
Sevier L., U.S.A. 114 G7
Sevilla, Spain 35 H5
Sevilla □, Spain 35 H5
Seville = Sevilla, Spain 35 H5
Sevlievo, Bulgaria 41 C9
Sevnica, Slovenia 29 B12
Sèvre-Nantaise →, France 18 E5
Sèvre-Niortaise →, France 20 B3
Sevsk, Russia 47 F8
Sewa →, S. Leone 82 D2
Sewani, India 68 E6
Seward, Alaska, U.S.A. 100 B5
Seward, Nebr., U.S.A. 112 E6
Seward, Pa., U.S.A. 110 F5
Seward Peninsula, U.S.A. 100 B3
Sewell, Chile 126 C1
Sewer, Indonesia 63 F8
Sewickley, U.S.A. 110 F4
Sexsmith, Canada 104 B5
Seychelles ■, Ind. Oc. 52 K9
Seyðisfjörður, Iceland 8 D6
Seydişehir, Turkey 72 D4
Seydvān, Iran 70 B5
Seyhan →, Turkey 70 D6
Seyhan Barajı, Turkey 72 D6

Seyitgazi, Turkey 39 B12
Seyitömer, Turkey 39 B11
Seym →, Ukraine 47 G7
Seymen, Turkey 41 E11
Seymour, Australia 95 F4
Seymour, S. Africa 89 E4
Seymour, Conn., U.S.A. 111 E11
Seymour, Ind., U.S.A. 108 F3
Seymour, Tex., U.S.A. 113 J5
Seyne, France 21 D10
Seyssel, France 21 C9
Sežana, Slovenia 29 C10
Sézanne, France 19 D10
Sezze, Italy 30 A6
Sfântu Gheorghe, Covasna, Romania 43 E10
Sfântu Gheorghe, Tulcea, Romania 43 F14
Sfântu Gheorghe, Brațul →, Romania 43 F14
Sfax, Tunisia 79 B8
Sha Xi →, China 59 D12
Sha Xian, China 59 D11
Shaanxi □, China 56 G5
Shaba = Katanga □, Dem. Rep. of the Congo 86 D2
Shabla, Bulgaria 41 C12
Shabogamo L., Canada 103 B6
Shabunda, Dem. Rep. of the Congo 86 C2
Shache, China 60 C2
Shackleton Ice Shelf, Antarctica 5 C8
Shackleton Inlet, Antarctica 5 E11
Shādegān, Iran 71 D6
Shadi, China 59 D10
Shadi, China 69 C7
Shadrinsk, Russia 50 D7
Shadyside, U.S.A. 110 G4
Shaffa, Nigeria 83 C7
Shafter, U.S.A. 117 K7
Shaftesbury, U.K. 13 F5
Shagamu, Nigeria 83 D5
Shagram, Pakistan 69 A5
Shah Alizai, Pakistan 68 E2
Shah Bunder, Pakistan 68 G2
Shahabad, Punjab, India 68 D7
Shahabad, Raj., India 68 G7
Shahabad, Ut. P., India 69 F8
Shahadpur, Pakistan 68 G3
Shahba, Syria 75 C5
Shahdād, Iran 71 D8
Shahdād, Namakzār-e, Iran 71 D8
Shahdadkot, Pakistan 68 F2
Shahdol, India 69 H9
Shahe, China 56 F8
Shahganj, India 69 F10
Shahgarh, India 66 F6
Shahjahanpur, India 69 F8
Shahpur, India 68 H7
Shahpur, Baluchistan, Pakistan 68 E3
Shahpur, Punjab, Pakistan 68 C5
Shahpur, Mad. P., India 69 H9
Shahpur Chakar, Pakistan 68 F3
Shahpura, Mad. P., India 69 H9
Shahpura, Raj., India 68 G6
Shahr-e Bābak, Iran 71 D7
Shahr-e Kord, Iran 71 C6
Shāhrakht, Iran 71 C9
Shahrig, Pakistan 68 D2
Shahukou, China 56 D7
Shaikhabad, Afghan. 68 B3
Shajapur, India 68 H7
Shakargarh, Pakistan 68 C6
Shakawe, Botswana 88 B3
Shaker Heights, U.S.A. 110 E3
Shakhty, Russia 49 G5
Shakhunya, Russia 48 B8
Shaki, Nigeria 83 D5
Shākir, Egypt 80 B3
Shala, L., Ethiopia 81 F4
Shallow Lake, Canada 110 B3
Shalqar, Kazakstan 50 E6
Shalskiy, Russia 46 B8
Shaluli Shan, China 58 B2
Shām, Iran 71 E8
Shām, Bādiyat ash, Asia 70 C3
Shamâl Bahr el Ghazal □, Sudan 81 F2
Shamâl Dârfûr □, Sudan 81 E2
Shamâl Kordofân □, Sudan 81 E3
Shamattawa, Canada 102 A1
Shamattawa →, Canada 102 A2
Shambe, Sudan 81 F3
Shambu, Ethiopia 81 F4
Shamīl, Iran 71 E8
Shamkhor = Şämkir, Azerbaijan 49 K8
Shāmkūh, Iran 71 C8
Shamli, India 68 E7
Shammar, Jabal, Si. Arabia 70 E4
Shamo = Gobi, Asia 56 C6
Shamo, L., Ethiopia 81 F4
Shamokin, U.S.A. 111 F8
Shamrock, U.S.A. 113 H4
Shamva, Zimbabwe 87 F3
Shan □, Burma 67 J21
Shan Xian, China 56 G9
Shanan →, Ethiopia 81 F5
Shanchengzhen, China 57 C13
Shāndak, Iran 71 D9
Shandon, U.S.A. 116 K6
Shandong □, China 57 G10
Shandong Bandao, China 57 F11
Shang Xian = Shangzhou, China 56 H5
Shanga, Nigeria 78 F6
Shangalowe, Dem. Rep. of the Congo 87 E2
Shangani, Zimbabwe 89 B4

Shangani →, Zimbabwe 87 F2
Shangbancheng, China 57 D10
Shangcheng, China 59 B10
Shangchuan Dao, China 59 G9
Shangdu, China 56 D7
Shanggao, China 59 C10
Shanghai, China 59 B13
Shanghai □, China 59 B13
Shanghai Shi □, China 59 B13
Shanghang, China 59 E11
Shanghe, China 57 F9
Shanglin, China 58 F7
Shangnan, China 56 H6
Shangqiu, China 56 G8
Shangrao, China 59 C11
Shangshui, China 56 H8
Shangsi, China 58 F6
Shangyou, China 59 E10
Shangyu, China 59 B13
Shangzhi, China 57 B14
Shangzhou, China 56 H5
Shanhetun, China 57 B14
Shani, Nigeria 83 C7
Shannon →, Ireland 15 D2
Shannon, N.Z. 91 J5
Shannon →, Ireland 15 D2
Shannon, Mouth of the, Ireland 15 D2
Shannon Airport, Ireland 15 D3
Shansi = Shanxi □, China 56 F7
Shantar, Ostrov Bolshoy, Russia 51 D14
Shantipur, India 69 H13
Shantou, China 59 F11
Shantung = Shandong □, China 57 G10
Shanwei, China 59 F10
Shanxi □, China 56 F7
Shanyang, China 56 H5
Shanyin, China 56 E7
Shaodong, China 59 D8
Shaoguan, China 59 E9
Shaoshan, China 59 D8
Shaowu, China 59 D11
Shaoxing, China 59 C13
Shaoyang, Hunan, China 59 D8
Shaoyang, Hunan, China 59 D8
Shap, U.K. 12 C5
Shapinsay, U.K. 14 B6
Shaqq el Gi'eifer →, Sudan 81 D2
Shaqra', Si. Arabia 70 E5
Shaqrā', Yemen 74 E4
Sharafa, Sudan 81 E2
Sharafkhāneh, Iran 70 B5
Sharbot Lake, Canada 111 B8
Shari, Japan 54 C12
Sharjah = Ash Shāriqah, U.A.E. 71 E7
Shark B., Australia 93 E1
Sharm el Sheikh, Egypt 80 B3
Sharon, Mass., U.S.A. 111 D13
Sharon, Pa., U.S.A. 110 E4
Sharon Springs, Kans., U.S.A. 112 F4
Sharon Springs, N.Y., U.S.A. 111 D10
Sharp Pt., Australia 94 A3
Sharpe L., Canada 102 B1
Sharpsville, U.S.A. 110 E4
Sharq el Istiwa'iya □, Sudan 81 G3
Sharya, Russia 48 A7
Shasha, Ethiopia 81 F4
Shashemene, Ethiopia 81 F4
Shashi, Botswana 89 C4
Shashi, China 59 B9
Shashi →, Africa 87 G2
Shasta, Mt., U.S.A. 114 F2
Shasta L., U.S.A. 114 F2
Shatawi, Sudan 81 E3
Shatsk, Russia 48 C5
Shatt al'Arab →, Iraq 71 D6
Shatura, Russia 46 E10
Shaumyani = Shulaveri, Georgia 49 K7
Shaunavon, Canada 105 D7
Shaver L., U.S.A. 116 H7
Shaw →, Australia 92 D2
Shawanaga, Canada 110 A4
Shawangunk Mts., U.S.A. 111 E10
Shawano, U.S.A. 108 C1
Shawinigan, Canada 102 C5
Shawnee, U.S.A. 113 H6
Shay Gap, Australia 92 D3
Shayang, China 59 B9
Shaybārā, Si. Arabia 70 E3
Shayib el Banat, Gebel, Egypt 80 B3
Shaykh, J. ash, Lebanon 75 B4
Shaykh Miskīn, Syria 75 C5
Shaykh Sa'īd, Iraq 70 C5
Shchekino, Russia 46 E9
Shcherbakov = Rybinsk, Russia 46 C10
Shchigry, Russia 47 G9
Shchors, Ukraine 47 F6
Shchuchinsk, Kazakstan 50 D8
She Xian, Anhui, China 59 C12
She Xian, Hebei, China 56 F7
Shebekino, Russia 47 G9
Shebele = Scebeli, Wabi →, Somali Rep. 74 G3
Shebshi Mts., Nigeria 83 D7
Shediac, Canada 103 C7
Sheelin, L., Ireland 15 C4
Sheep Haven, Ireland 15 A4
Sheerness, U.K. 13 F8
Sheet Harbour, Canada 103 D7
Sheffield, U.K. 12 D6
Sheffield, Ala., U.S.A. 109 H2
Sheffield, Mass., U.S.A. 111 D11

Sheffield, Pa., U.S.A.	110	E5
Shehojele, Ethiopia	81	E4
Shehong, China	58	B5
Sheikh Idris, Sudan	81	E3
Sheikhpura, India	69	G11
Shek Hasan, Ethiopia	81	E4
Shekhupura, Pakistan	68	D5
Sheki = Şaki, Azerbaijan	49	K8
Shelburne, N.S., Canada	103	D6
Shelburne, Ont., Canada	102	D3
Shelburne, U.S.A.	111	B11
Shelburne B., Australia	94	A3
Shelburne Falls, U.S.A.	111	D12
Shelby, Mich., U.S.A.	108	D2
Shelby, Miss., U.S.A.	113	J9
Shelby, Mont., U.S.A.	114	B8
Shelby, N.C., U.S.A.	109	H5
Shelby, Ohio, U.S.A.	110	F2
Shelbyville, Ill., U.S.A.	112	F10
Shelbyville, Ind., U.S.A.	108	F3
Shelbyville, Ky., U.S.A.	108	F3
Shelbyville, Tenn., U.S.A.	109	H2
Sheldon, U.S.A.	112	D7
Sheldrake, Canada	103	B7
Shelengo, K. →, Sudan	81	E2
Shelikhova, Zaliv, Russia	51	D16
Shell Lakes, Australia	93	E4
Shellbrook, Canada	105	C7
Shellharbour, Australia	95	E5
Shelon →, Russia	46	C6
Shelter I., U.S.A.	111	E12
Shelton, Conn., U.S.A.	111	E11
Shelton, Wash., U.S.A.	116	C3
Shemakha = Şamaxi, Azerbaijan	49	K9
Shemsi, Sudan	80	D2
Shen Xian, China	56	F8
Shenandoah, Iowa, U.S.A.	112	E7
Shenandoah, Pa., U.S.A.	111	F8
Shenandoah, Va., U.S.A.	108	F6
Shenandoah →, U.S.A.	108	F7
Shenandoah National Park, U.S.A.	108	F6
Shenchi, China	56	E7
Shendam, Nigeria	83	D6
Shendî, Sudan	81	D3
Shenge, S. Leone	82	D2
Shengfang, China	56	E9
Shëngjergji, Albania	40	E4
Shëngjini, Albania	40	E3
Shengzhou, China	59	C13
Shenjingzi, China	57	B13
Shenmëria, Albania	40	D4
Shenmu, China	56	E6
Shennongjia, China	59	B8
Shenqiu, China	56	H8
Shenqiucheng, China	56	H8
Shensi = Shaanxi □, China	56	G5
Shenyang, China	57	D12
Shenzhen, China	59	F10
Sheo, India	68	F4
Sheopur Kalan, India	66	G10
Shepetivka, Ukraine	47	G4
Shepetovka = Shepetivka, Ukraine	47	G4
Shepparton, Australia	95	F4
Sheppey, I. of, U.K.	13	F8
Shepton Mallet, U.K.	13	F5
Sheqi, China	56	H7
Sher Qila, Pakistan	69	A6
Sherab, Sudan	81	E1
Sherborne, U.K	13	G5
Sherbro →, S. Leone	82	D2
Sherbro I., S. Leone	82	D2
Sherbrooke, N.S., Canada	103	C7
Sherbrooke, Qué., Canada	103	C5
Sherburne, U.S.A.	111	D9
Shereik, Sudan	80	D3
Shergarh, India	68	F5
Sherghati, India	69	G11
Sheridan, Ark., U.S.A.	113	H8
Sheridan, Wyo., U.S.A.	114	D10
Sheringham, U.K.	12	E9
Sherkot, India	69	E8
Sherman, U.S.A.	113	J6
Sherpur, India	69	G10
Sherridon, Canada	105	B8
Sherwood Forest, U.K.	12	D6
Sherwood Park, Canada	104	C6
Sheslay →, Canada	104	B2
Shethanei L., Canada	105	B9
Shetland □, U.K.	14	A7
Shetland Is., U.K.	14	A7
Shetrunji →, India	68	J5
Shewa □, Ethiopia	81	F4
Shewa Gimira, Ethiopia	81	F4
Sheyenne →, U.S.A.	112	B6
Shibām, Yemen	74	D4
Shibata, Japan	54	F9
Shibecha, Japan	54	C12
Shibetsu, Japan	54	B11
Shibîn el Kôm, Egypt	80	H7
Shibîn el Qanâtir, Egypt	80	H7
Shibing, China	58	D7
Shibogama L., Canada	102	B2
Shibushi, Japan	55	J5
Shicheng, China	59	D11
Shickshinny, U.S.A.	111	E8
Shickshock Mts. = Chic-Chocs, Mts., Canada	103	C6
Shidao, China	57	F12
Shidian, China	58	E2
Shido, Japan	55	G7
Shiel, L., U.K.	14	E3
Shield, C., Australia	94	A2
Shifang, China	58	B5
Shiga □, Japan	55	G8
Shigu, China	58	D2
Shiguaigou, China	56	D6
Shihchiachuangi = Shijiazhuang, China	56	E8
Shijaku, Albania	40	E3
Shijiazhuang, China	56	E8
Shijiu Hu, China	59	B12
Shikarpur, India	68	E8
Shikarpur, Pakistan	68	F3
Shikohabad, India	69	F8
Shikoku □, Japan	55	H6
Shikoku-Sanchi, Japan	55	H6
Shiliguri, India	67	F16
Shilka, Russia	51	D12
Shilka →, Russia	51	D13
Shillelagh, Ireland	15	D5
Shillington, U.S.A.	111	F9
Shillong, India	67	G17
Shilo, West Bank	75	C4
Shilong, China	59	F9
Shilou, China	56	F6
Shilovo, Russia	48	C5
Shimabara, Japan	55	H5
Shimada, Japan	55	G9
Shimane □, Japan	55	G6
Shimanovsk, Russia	51	D13
Shimen, China	59	C8
Shimenjie, China	59	C11
Shimian, China	58	C4
Shimizu, Japan	55	G9
Shimodate, Japan	55	F9
Shimoga, India	66	N9
Shimoni, Kenya	86	C4
Shimonoseki, Japan	55	H5
Shimpuru Rapids, Angola	88	B2
Shimsk, Russia	46	C6
Shin, L., U.K.	14	C4
Shinan, China	58	F7
Shinano-Gawa →, Japan	55	F9
Shinās, Oman	71	E8
Shindand, Afghan.	66	C3
Shinglehouse, U.S.A.	110	E6
Shingū, Japan	55	H7
Shingwidzi, S. Africa	89	C5
Shinjō, Japan	54	E10
Shinkafe, Nigeria	83	C6
Shinshār, Syria	75	A5
Shinyanga, Tanzania	86	C3
Shinyanga □, Tanzania	86	C3
Shio-no-Misaki, Japan	55	H7
Shiogama, Japan	54	E10
Shiojiri, Japan	55	F8
Shipchenski Prokhod, Bulgaria	41	D9
Shiping, China	58	F4
Shipki La, India	66	D11
Shippegan, Canada	103	C7
Shippensburg, U.S.A.	110	F7
Shippenville, U.S.A.	110	E5
Shiprock, U.S.A.	115	H9
Shiqian, China	58	D7
Shiqma, N. →, Israel	75	D3
Shiquan, China	56	H5
Shiquan He = Indus →, Pakistan	68	G2
Shīr Kūh, Iran	71	D7
Shiragami-Misaki, Japan	54	D10
Shirakawa, Fukushima, Japan	55	F10
Shirakawa, Gifu, Japan	55	F8
Shirane-San, Gumma, Japan	55	F9
Shirane-San, Yamanashi, Japan	55	G9
Shiraoi, Japan	54	C10
Shīrāz, Iran	71	D7
Shirbīn, Egypt	80	H7
Shire →, Africa	87	F4
Shiretoko-Misaki, Japan	54	B12
Shirinab →, Pakistan	68	D2
Shiriya-Zaki, Japan	54	D10
Shiroishi, Japan	54	F10
Shīrvān, Iran	71	B8
Shirwa, L. = Chilwa, L., Malawi	87	F4
Shishi, China	59	E12
Shishou, China	59	C9
Shitai, China	59	B11
Shivpuri, India	68	G7
Shixian, China	57	C15
Shixing, China	59	E10
Shiyan, China	59	A8
Shiyata, Egypt	80	B2
Shizhu, China	58	C7
Shizong, China	58	E5
Shizuishan, China	56	E4
Shizuoka, Japan	55	G9
Shizuoka □, Japan	55	G9
Shklov = Shklow, Belarus	46	E6
Shklow, Belarus	46	E6
Shkoder = Shkodra, Albania	40	D3
Shkodra, Albania	40	D3
Shkumbini →, Albania	40	E3
Shmidta, Ostrov, Russia	51	A10
Shō-Gawa →, Japan	55	F8
Shoal L., Canada	105	D9
Shoal Lake, Canada	105	C8
Shōdo-Shima, Japan	55	G7
Sholapur = Solapur, India	66	L9
Shologontsy, Russia	51	C12
Shōmrōn, West Bank	75	C4
Shoreham by Sea, U.K.	13	G7
Shori →, Pakistan	68	E3
Shorkot Road, Pakistan	68	D5
Shoshone, Calif., U.S.A.	117	K10
Shoshone, Idaho, U.S.A.	114	E6
Shoshone →, U.S.A.	114	D9
Shoshone L., U.S.A.	114	D8
Shoshone Mts., U.S.A.	114	G5
Shoshong, Botswana	88	C4
Shoshoni, U.S.A.	114	E9
Shostka, Ukraine	47	G7
Shou Xian, China	59	A11
Shouchang, China	59	C12
Shouguang, China	57	F10
Shouning, China	59	D12
Shouyang, China	56	F7
Show Low, U.S.A.	115	J9
Shpola, Ukraine	47	H6
Shreveport, U.S.A.	113	J8
Shrewsbury, U.K.	13	E5
Shri Mohangarh, India	68	F4
Shrirampur, India	69	H13
Shropshire □, U.K.	13	E5
Shu, Kazakstan	50	E8
Shu →, Kazakstan	52	E10
Shuangbai, China	58	E3
Shuangcheng, China	57	B14
Shuangfeng, China	59	D9
Shuanggou, China	57	G9
Shuangjiang, China	58	F2
Shuangliao, China	57	C12
Shuangshanzi, China	57	D10
Shuangyang, China	57	C13
Shuangyashan, China	60	B8
Shubra Khit, Egypt	80	H7
Shucheng, China	59	B11
Shugozero, Russia	46	C8
Shuguri Falls, Tanzania	87	D4
Shuiji, China	59	D12
Shuiye, China	56	F8
Shujalpur, India	68	H7
Shukpa Kunzang, India	69	B8
Shulan, China	57	B14
Shulaveri, Georgia	49	K7
Shule, China	60	C2
Shumagin Is., U.S.A.	100	C4
Shumen, Bulgaria	41	C10
Shumerlya, Russia	48	C8
Shumikha, Russia	50	D7
Shunchang, China	59	D11
Shunde, China	59	F9
Shungay, Kazakstan	49	F8
Shuo Xian = Shuozhou, China	56	E7
Shuozhou, China	56	E7
Shūr →, Fārs, Iran	71	D7
Shūr →, Kermān, Iran	71	D8
Shūr →, Yazd, Iran	71	D7
Shūr Āb, Iran	71	C6
Shūr Gaz, Iran	71	D8
Shūrāb, Iran	71	C8
Shurugwi, Zimbabwe	87	F3
Shūsf, Iran	71	D9
Shūsh, Iran	73	F13
Shūshtar, Iran	71	D6
Shuswap L., Canada	104	C5
Shuya, Russia	48	B5
Shuyang, China	57	G10
Shūzū, Iran	71	D7
Shwebo, Burma	67	H19
Shwegu, Burma	67	G20
Shweli →, Burma	67	H20
Shymkent, Kazakstan	50	E7
Shyok, India	69	B8
Shyok →, Pakistan	69	B6
Si Chon, Thailand	65	H2
Si Kiang = Xi Jiang →, China	59	F9
Si-ngan = Xi'an, China	56	G5
Si Prachan, Thailand	64	E3
Si Racha, Thailand	64	F3
Si Xian, China	57	H9
Siahaf →, Pakistan	68	E3
Siahan Range, Pakistan	66	F4
Siaksriindrapura, Indonesia	62	D2
Sialkot, Pakistan	68	C6
Siam = Thailand ■, Asia	64	E4
Sian = Xi'an, China	56	G5
Sianów, Poland	44	D3
Siantan, Indonesia	62	D3
Siāreh, Iran	71	D9
Siargao I., Phil.	61	G7
Siari, Pakistan	69	B7
Siasi, Phil.	63	C6
Siasi I., Phil.	61	J4
Siátista, Greece	40	F5
Siau, Indonesia	63	D7
Šiauliai, Lithuania	9	J20
Šiauliai □, Lithuania	44	C10
Siazan = Siyäzän, Azerbaijan	49	K9
Sibâi, Gebel el, Egypt	70	E2
Sibay, L., S. Africa	89	D5
Sibdu, Sudan	81	E2
Šibenik, Croatia	29	E12
Siberia, Russia	4	D13
Siberut, Indonesia	62	E1
Sibi, Pakistan	68	E2
Sibil = Oksibil, Indonesia	63	E10
Sibiti, Congo	84	E2
Sibiu, Romania	43	E9
Sibiu □, Romania	43	E9
Sibley, U.S.A.	112	D7
Sibolga, Indonesia	62	D1
Sibsagar, India	67	F19
Sibu, Malaysia	62	D4
Sibuco, Phil.	61	H5
Sibuguey B., Phil.	61	H5
Sibut, C.A.R.	84	C3
Sibutu, Phil.	63	D5
Sibutu Group, Phil.	61	J3
Sibutu Passage, E. Indies	63	D5
Sibuyan, Phil.	61	E5
Sibuyan Sea, Phil.	61	E5
Sic, Romania	43	D8
Sicamous, Canada	104	C5
Siccus →, Australia	95	E2
Sichuan □, China	58	B5
Sichuan Pendi, China	58	B5
Sicilia, Italy	31	E7
Sicilia □, Italy	31	E7
Sicily = Sicilia, Italy	31	E7
Sicuani, Peru	124	F4
Šid, Serbia, Yug.	42	E4
Sidamo □, Ethiopia	81	G4
Sidaouet, Niger	83	B6
Sidári, Greece	36	A3
Siddhapur, India	68	H5
Siddipet, India	66	K11
Sidensjö, Sweden	10	A12
Sidéradougou, Burkina Faso	82	C4
Siderno, Italy	31	D9
Sidhauli, India	69	F9
Sídheros, Ákra, Greece	36	D8
Sidhi, India	69	G9
Sidhirókastron, Greece	40	E7
Sîdi Abd el Rahmân, Egypt	80	A2
Sidi-bel-Abbès, Algeria	78	A5
Sidi Haneish, Egypt	80	A2
Sidi Omar, Egypt	80	A1
Sidlaw Hills, U.K.	14	E5
Sidley, Mt., Antarctica	5	D14
Sidmouth, U.K.	13	G4
Sidmouth, C., Australia	94	A3
Sidney, Canada	104	D4
Sidney, Mont., U.S.A.	112	B2
Sidney, N.Y., U.S.A.	111	D9
Sidney, Nebr., U.S.A.	112	E3
Sidney, Ohio, U.S.A.	108	E3
Sidney Lanier L., U.S.A.	109	H4
Sido, Mali	82	C3
Sidoarjo, Indonesia	63	G15
Sidon = Saydā, Lebanon	75	B4
Sidra, G. of = Surt, Khalīj, Libya	79	B9
Siedlce, Poland	45	F9
Sieg →, Germany	24	E3
Siegburg, Germany	24	E3
Siegen, Germany	24	E4
Siem Pang, Cambodia	64	E6
Siem Reap = Siemreab, Cambodia	64	F4
Siemiatycze, Poland	45	F9
Siemreab, Cambodia	64	F4
Siena, Italy	29	E8
Sieniawa, Poland	45	H9
Sieradz, Poland	45	G5
Sieraków, Poland	45	F3
Sierck-les-Bains, France	19	C13
Sierning, Austria	26	C7
Sierpc, Poland	45	F6
Sierra Blanca, U.S.A.	115	L11
Sierra Blanca Peak, U.S.A.	115	K11
Sierra City, U.S.A.	116	F6
Sierra Colorada, Argentina	128	E3
Sierra de Yeguas, Spain	35	H6
Sierra Gorda, Chile	126	A2
Sierra Leone ■, W. Afr.	82	D2
Sierra Madre, Mexico	119	D6
Sierra Mojada, Mexico	118	B4
Sierra Nevada, U.S.A.	116	H8
Sierra Vista, U.S.A.	115	L8
Sierraville, U.S.A.	116	F6
Sierre, Switz.	25	J3
Sifani, Ethiopia	81	E5
Sifié, Ivory C.	82	D3
Sífnos, Greece	38	E6
Sifton, Canada	105	C8
Sifton Pass, Canada	104	B3
Sigean, France	20	E6
Sighetu-Marmației, Romania	43	C8
Sighișoara, Romania	43	D9
Sigli, Indonesia	62	C1
Siglufjörður, Iceland	8	C4
Sigmaringen, Germany	25	G5
Signa, Italy	28	E8
Signakhi = Tsnori, Georgia	49	K7
Signal, U.S.A.	117	L13
Signal Pk., U.S.A.	117	M12
Signy-d'Abbaye, France	19	C11
Sigsig, Ecuador	124	D3
Sigüenza, Spain	32	D2
Siguiri, Guinea	82	C3
Sigulda, Latvia	9	H21
Sihanoukville = Kampong Saom, Cambodia	65	G4
Sihora, India	69	H9
Sihui, China	59	F9
Siikajoki →, Finland	8	D21
Siikainen, Finland	9	F19
Siilinjärvi, Finland	8	E22
Siirt, Turkey	73	D9
Sijarira Ra., Zimbabwe	87	F2
Sika, India	68	H3
Sikao, Thailand	65	J2
Sikar, India	68	F6
Sikasso, Mali	82	C3
Sikeston, U.S.A.	113	G10
Sikhote Alin, Khrebet, Russia	51	E14
Sikhote Alin Ra. = Sikhote Alin, Khrebet, Russia	51	E14
Sikiá, Greece	40	F7
Síkinos, Greece	39	E7
Sikkani Chief →, Canada	104	B4
Sikkim □, India	67	F16
Siklós, Hungary	42	E3
Sikotu-Ko, Japan	54	C10
Sil →, Spain	34	C3
Silacayoapan, Mexico	119	D5
Silale, Lithuania	44	C9
Silandro, Italy	28	B7
Silawad, India	68	J6
Silay, Phil.	61	F5
Silba, Croatia	29	D11
Silchar, India	67	G18
Siler City, U.S.A.	109	H6
Silgarhi Doti, Nepal	69	E9
Silghat, India	67	F18
Sili, Burkina Faso	82	C4
Silifke, Turkey	70	B2
Siliguri = Shiliguri, India	67	F16
Siling Co, China	60	C3
Silistea Nouă, Romania	43	F9
Silistra, Bulgaria	41	B11
Silivri, Turkey	41	E12
Siljan, Sweden	10	D8
Siljansnäs, Sweden	10	D8
Silkeborg, Denmark	11	H3
Silkwood, Australia	94	B4
Silla, Spain	33	F4
Sillajhuay, Cordillera, Chile	124	G5
Sillamäe, Estonia	9	G22
Sillé-le-Guillaume, France	18	D6
Silleda, Spain	34	C2
Silloth, U.K.	12	C4
Sílo, Greece	41	E9
Siloam Springs, U.S.A.	113	G7
Silopi, Turkey	73	D10
Silsbee, U.S.A.	113	K7
Siluko, Nigeria	83	D6
Šilutė, Lithuania	9	J19
Silva Porto = Kuito, Angola	85	G3
Silvan, Turkey	73	C9
Silvani, India	69	H8
Silver City, U.S.A.	115	K9
Silver Cr. →, U.S.A.	114	E4
Silver Creek, U.S.A.	110	D5
Silver L., U.S.A.	116	G6
Silver Lake, Calif., U.S.A.	117	K10
Silver Lake, Oreg., U.S.A.	114	E3
Silverdalen, Sweden	11	G9
Silverton, Colo., U.S.A.	115	H10
Silverton, Tex., U.S.A.	113	H4
Silves, Portugal	35	H2
Silvi Marina, Italy	29	F11
Silvies →, U.S.A.	114	E4
Silvrettahorn, Switz.	28	B7
Silz, Austria	26	D3
Simaltala, India	69	G12
Simanggang = Bandar Sri Aman, Malaysia	62	D4
Simao, China	58	F3
Simard, L., Canada	102	C4
Simav, Turkey	39	B10
Simav →, Turkey	41	F12
Simav Dağları, Turkey	39	B10
Simba, Tanzania	86	C4
Simbach, Germany	25	G9
Simbirsk, Russia	48	C9
Simbo, Tanzania	86	C2
Simcoe, Canada	102	D3
Simcoe, L., Canada	102	D4
Simdega, India	69	H11
Simeonovgrad, Bulgaria	41	D9
Simeria, Romania	42	E8
Simeto →, Italy	31	E8
Simeulue, Indonesia	62	D1
Simferopol, Ukraine	47	K8
Sími, Greece	39	E9
Simi Valley, U.S.A.	117	L8
Simikot, Nepal	69	E9
Simitli, Bulgaria	40	E7
Simla, India	68	D7
Simlångsdalen, Sweden	11	H7
Șimleu-Silvaniei, Romania	42	C7
Simmern, Germany	25	F3
Simmie, Canada	105	D7
Simmler, U.S.A.	117	K7
Simnas, Lithuania	44	D10
Simojoki →, Finland	8	D21
Simojovel, Mexico	119	D6
Simonette →, Canada	104	B5
Simonstown, S. Africa	88	E2
Simontornya, Hungary	42	D3
Simplonpass, Switz.	25	J4
Simplontunnel, Switz.	25	J4
Simpson Desert, Australia	94	D2
Simpson Pen., Canada	101	B11
Simpungdong, N. Korea	57	D15
Simrishamn, Sweden	11	J8
Simsbury, U.S.A.	111	E12
Simushir, Ostrov, Russia	51	E16
Sin Cowe I., S. China Sea	62	C4
Sinabang, Indonesia	62	D1
Sinadogo, Somali Rep.	74	F4
Sinai = Es Sînâ', Egypt	75	F3
Sinai, Mt. = Mûsa, Gebel, Egypt	70	D2
Sinai Peninsula, Egypt	75	F3
Sinaia, Romania	43	E10
Sinaloa □, Mexico	118	C3
Sinaloa de Leyva, Mexico	118	B3
Sinalunga, Italy	29	E8
Sinan, China	58	D7
Sînandrei, Romania	42	E6
Sinarádhes, Greece	36	A3
Sincan, Turkey	72	B5
Sincanlı, Turkey	39	C12
Sincelejo, Colombia	124	B3
Sinch'ang, N. Korea	57	D15
Sinchang-ni, N. Korea	57	E14
Sinclair, U.S.A.	114	F10
Sinclair Mills, Canada	104	C4
Sinclair's B., U.K.	14	C5
Sinclairville, U.S.A.	110	D5
Sincorá, Serra do, Brazil	125	F10
Sind, Pakistan	68	G3
Sind □, Pakistan	68	G3
Sind →, Jammu & Kashmir, India	69	B6
Sind →, Mad. P., India	69	F8
Sind Sagar Doab, Pakistan	68	D4
Sindal, Denmark	11	G4
Sindangan, Phil.	61	G5
Sindangbarang, Indonesia	63	G12
Sinde, Zambia	87	F2
Sindelfingen, Germany	25	G4
Sîndîrgı, Turkey	39	B10
Sindou, Burkina Faso	82	C3
Sindri, India	69	H12
Sine →, Senegal	82	C1
Sinegorskiy, Russia	49	G5

Sinekli, Turkey 41 E12
Sinelnikovo = Synelnykove,
  Ukraine 47 H8
Sinendé, Benin 83 C5
Sines, Portugal 35 H2
Sines, C. de, Portugal ... 35 H2
Sineu, Spain 37 B10
Sinfra, Ivory C. 82 D3
Sing Buri, Thailand 64 E3
Singa, Sudan 81 E3
Singapore ■, Asia 65 M4
Singapore, Straits of, Asia . 65 M5
Singaraja, Indonesia 62 F5
Singen, Germany 25 H4
Singida, Tanzania 86 C3
Singida □, Tanzania 86 D3
Singitikós Kólpos, Greece .. 40 F7
Singkaling Hkamti, Burma .. 67 G19
Singkang, Indonesia 63 E6
Singkawang, Indonesia 62 D3
Singkep, Indonesia 62 E2
Singleton, Australia 95 E5
Singleton, Mt., N. Terr.,
  Australia 92 D5
Singleton, Mt., W. Austral.,
  Australia 93 E2
Singö, Sweden 10 D12
Singoli, India 68 G6
Singora = Songkhla,
  Thailand 65 J3
Singosan, N. Korea 57 E14
Sinhung, N. Korea 57 D14
Siniátsikon, Óros, Greece .. 40 F5
Siniscóla, Italy 30 B2
Sinj, Croatia 29 E13
Sinjai, Indonesia 63 F6
Sinjajevina,
  Montenegro, Yug. 40 D3
Sinjār, Iraq 70 B4
Sinkat, Sudan 80 D4
Sinkiang Uighur = Xinjiang
  Uygur Zizhiqu □, China . 60 D3
Sinmak, N. Korea 57 E14
Sínnai, Italy 30 C2
Sinnamary, Fr. Guiana 125 B8
Sinni →, Italy 31 B9
Sinnuris, Egypt 80 J7
Sinoie, Lacul, Romania ... 43 F13
Sinop, Turkey 72 A6
Sinor, India 68 J5
Sinp'o, N. Korea 57 E15
Sinsheim, Germany 25 F4
Sinsk, Russia 51 C13
Sintang, Indonesia 62 D4
Sinton, U.S.A. 113 L6
Sintra, Portugal 35 G1
Sinŭiju, N. Korea 57 D13
Sinyukha →, Ukraine 47 H6
Sinzig, Germany 24 E3
Sio →, Hungary 42 D3
Siocon, Phil. 61 H5
Siófok, Hungary 42 D3
Sioma, Zambia 88 B3
Sion, Switz. 25 J3
Sion Mills, U.K. 15 B4
Sioux City, U.S.A. 112 D6
Sioux Falls, U.S.A. 112 D6
Sioux Lookout, Canada 102 B1
Sioux Narrows, Canada 105 D10
Sipalay, Phil. 61 G5
Šipan, Croatia 40 D1
Siping, China 57 C13
Sipiwesk L., Canada 105 B9
Šipovo, Bos.-H. 42 F2
Sipra →, India 68 H6
Sipura, Indonesia 62 E1
Siquia →, Nic. 120 D3
Siquijor, Phil. 61 G5
Siquirres, Costa Rica 120 D3
Şīr Banī Yās, U.A.E. 71 E7
Sir Edward Pellew Group,
  Australia 94 B2
Sir Graham Moore Is.,
  Australia 92 B4
Sir James MacBrien, Mt.,
  Canada 100 B7
Sira →, Norway 9 G12
Siracusa, Italy 31 E8
Sirajganj, Bangla. 69 G13
Sirakoro, Mali 82 C3
Şiran, Turkey 73 B8
Sirasso, Ivory C. 82 D3
Sirathu, India 69 G9
Sīrdān, Iran 71 B6
Sirdaryo = Syrdarya →,
  Kazakstan 50 E7
Sire, Ethiopia 81 F4
Siren, U.S.A. 112 C8
Sirer, Spain 37 C7
Siret, Romania 43 C11
Siret →, Romania 43 E12
Sirghāyā, Syria 75 B5
Şiria, Romania 42 D6
Sirino, Mte., Italy 31 B8
Sírmaur, India 69 G9
Sírna, Greece 39 E8
Şirnak, Turkey 73 D10
Sirohi, India 68 G5
Sironj, India 68 G7
Síros, Greece 38 D6
Sirretta Pk., U.S.A. 117 K8
Sīrrī, Iran 71 E7
Sirsa, India 68 E6
Sirsa →, India 69 F8
Siruela, Spain 35 G5
Sisak, Croatia 29 C13
Sisaket, Thailand 64 E5
Sisante, Spain 33 F2
Sisargas, Is., Spain 34 B2
Sishen, S. Africa 88 D3

Sishui, Henan, China 56 G7
Sishui, Shandong, China ... 57 G9
Sisipuk L., Canada 105 B8
Sisophon, Cambodia 64 F4
Sisseton, U.S.A. 112 C6
Sissonne, France 19 C10
Sīstān, Asia 71 D9
Sīstān, Daryācheh-ye, Iran . 66 D2
Sīstān va Balūchestān □,
  Iran 71 E9
Sisters, U.S.A. 114 D3
Siswa Bazar, India 69 F10
Sitakili, Mali 82 C2
Sitamarhi, India 69 F11
Sitampiky, Madag. 89 B8
Sitapur, India 69 F9
Siteki, Swaziland 89 D5
Sitges, Spain 32 D6
Sithoniá, Greece 40 F7
Sitía, Greece 36 D8
Sitka, U.S.A. 104 B1
Sitoti, Botswana 88 C3
Sitra, Egypt →, ... 80 B2
Sittang Myit →, Burma 67 L20
Sittard, Neths. 17 C5
Sittensen, Germany 24 B5
Sittingbourne, U.K. 13 F8
Sittona, Eritrea 81 E4
Sittoung = Sittang Myit →,
  Burma 67 L20
Sittwe, Burma 67 J18
Situbondo, Indonesia 63 G16
Siuna, Nic. 120 D3
Siuri, India 69 H12
Siutghiol, Lacul, Romania . 43 F13
Sīvand, Iran 71 D7
Sivas, Turkey 70 B3
Sivaslı, Turkey 39 C11
Siverek, Turkey 70 B3
Sivrihisar, Turkey 72 C4
Sîwa, Egypt 80 B2
Sīwa, El Wâhât es, Egypt .. 80 B2
Siwa Oasis, Egypt 76 D6
Siwalik Range, Nepal 69 F10
Siwan, India 69 F11
Siwana, India 68 G5
Sixmilebridge, Ireland ... 15 D3
Sixth Cataract, Sudan 81 D3
Siyāl, Jazā'ir, Egypt 80 C4
Siyäzän, Azerbaijan 49 K9
Siziwang Qi, China 56 D6
Sjælland, Denmark 11 J5
Sjællands Odde, Denmark .. 11 J5
Sjenica, Serbia, Yug. 40 C3
Sjöbo, Sweden 11 J7
Sjötofta, Sweden 11 G7
Sjötorp, Sweden 11 F8
Sjumen = Shumen, Bulgaria . 41 C10
Skadarsko Jezero,
  Montenegro, Yug. 40 D3
Skadovsk, Ukraine 47 J7
Skælskør, Denmark 11 J5
Skærbæk, Denmark 11 J2
Skaftafell, Iceland 8 D5
Skagafjörður, Iceland ... 8 D4
Skagaströnd, Iceland 8 D3
Skagen, Denmark 11 G4
Skagern, Sweden 11 F8
Skagerrak, Denmark 11 G2
Skagit →, U.S.A. 116 B4
Skagway, U.S.A. 100 C6
Skala-Podilska, Ukraine .. 47 H4
Skala Podolskaya = Skala-
  Podilska, Ukraine 47 H4
Skalat, Ukraine 47 H3
Skalbmierz, Poland 45 H7
Skälderviken, Sweden 11 H6
Skalica, Slovak Rep. 27 C10
Skalni Dol = Kamenyak,
  Bulgaria 41 C10
Skanderborg, Denmark 11 H3
Skåne, Sweden 11 J7
Skåne län □, Sweden 11 H7
Skaneateles, U.S.A. 111 D8
Skaneateles L., U.S.A. ... 111 D8
Skänninge, Sweden 11 F9
Skanör med Falsterbo,
  Sweden 11 J6
Skantzoúra, Greece 38 B6
Skara, Sweden 11 F7
Skaraborgs län □, Sweden .. 11 F7
Skärblacka, Sweden 11 F9
Skardu, Pakistan 69 B6
Skåre, Sweden 10 E7
Skärhamn, Sweden 11 G5
Skarszewy, Poland 44 D5
Skaryszew, Poland 45 G8
Skarżysko-Kamienna, Poland . 45 G7
Skattkärr, Sweden 10 E7
Skattungbyn, Sweden 10 C8
Skawina, Poland 45 J6
Skebobruk, Sweden 10 E12
Skeena →, Canada 104 C2
Skeena Mts., Canada 104 B3
Skegness, U.K. 12 D8
Skeldon, Guyana 124 B7
Skeleton Coast Park,
  Namibia 88 C1
Skellefte älv →, Sweden .. 8 D19
Skellefteå, Sweden 8 D19
Skelleftehamn, Sweden ... 8 D19
Skender Vakuf, Bos.-H. ... 42 F2
Skerries, The, U.K. 12 D3
Skhíza, Greece 38 E3
Skhoinoúsa, Greece 39 E7
Ski, Norway 9 G14
Skíathos, Greece 38 B5

Skibbereen, Ireland 15 E2
Skiddaw, U.K. 12 C4
Skidegate, Canada 104 C2
Skídhra, Greece 40 F6
Skien, Norway 9 G13
Skierniewice, Poland 45 G7
Skikda, Algeria 78 A7
Skillingaryd, Sweden 11 G8
Skillinge, Sweden 11 J8
Skilloura, Cyprus 36 D12
Skinári, Ákra, Greece ... 38 D2
Skinnskatteberg, Sweden .. 10 E9
Skipton, U.K. 12 D5
Skirmish Pt., Australia .. 94 A1
Skiropoúla, Greece 38 C6
Skíros, Greece 38 C6
Skivarp, Sweden 11 J7
Skive, Denmark 11 H3
Skjálfandafljót →, Iceland . 8 D5
Skjálfandi, Iceland 8 C5
Skjern, Denmark 11 J2
Skoczów, Poland 45 J5
Škofja Loka, Slovenia ... 29 B11
Skoghall, Sweden 10 E7
Skogstorp, Sweden 10 E10
Skoki, Poland 45 F4
Skole, Ukraine 47 H2
Skópelos, Greece 38 B5
Skopí, Greece 36 D8
Skopin, Russia 46 F10
Skopje, Macedonia 40 D5
Skórcz, Poland 44 E5
Skørping, Denmark 11 H3
Skövde, Sweden 11 F7
Skovorodino, Russia 51 D13
Skowhegan, U.S.A. 109 C11
Skradin, Croatia 29 E12
Skrea, Sweden 11 H6
Skrunda, Latvia 44 B9
Skrwa →, Poland 45 F6
Skull, Ireland 15 E2
Skultorp, Sweden 11 F7
Skultuna, Sweden 10 E10
Skunk →, U.S.A. 112 E9
Skuodas, Lithuania 9 H19
Skurup, Sweden 11 J7
Skutskär, Sweden 10 D11
Skvyra, Ukraine 47 H5
Skwierzyna, Poland 45 F2
Skye, U.K. 14 D2
Skykomish, U.S.A. 114 C3
Skyros = Skíros, Greece .. 38 C6
Skyttorp, Sweden 10 D11
Slættaratindur, Færoe Is. . 8 E9
Slagelse, Denmark 11 J5
Slamet, Indonesia 63 G13
Slaney →, Ireland 15 D5
Slangberge, S. Africa ... 88 E3
Slănic, Romania 43 E10
Slano, Croatia 40 D1
Slantsy, Russia 46 C5
Slaný, Czech Rep. 26 A7
Śląskie □, Poland 45 H6
Slätbaken, Sweden 11 F10
Slate Is., Canada 102 C2
Slatina, Croatia 42 E2
Slatina, Romania 43 F9
Slatina Timiş, Romania ... 42 E7
Slatington, U.S.A. 111 F9
Slaton, U.S.A. 113 J4
Slave →, Canada 104 A6
Slave Coast, W. Afr. 83 D5
Slave Lake, Canada 104 B6
Slave Pt., Canada 104 A5
Slavgorod, Russia 50 D8
Slavinja, Serbia, Yug. ... 40 C6
Slavonia = Slavonija,
  Europe 42 E2
Slavonija, Europe 42 E2
Slavonski Brod, Croatia .. 42 E3
Slavuta, Ukraine 47 G4
Slavyanka, Russia 54 C5
Slavyanovo, Bulgaria 41 C8
Slavyansk = Slovyansk,
  Ukraine 47 H9
Slavyansk-na-Kubani, Russia . 47 K10
Sława, Poland 45 G3
Sławharad, Belarus 46 F6
Sławno, Poland 44 D3
Sławoborze, Poland 44 E2
Sleaford, U.K. 12 D7
Sleaford B., Australia ... 95 E2
Sleat, Sd. of, U.K. 14 D3
Sleeper Is., Canada 101 C11
Sleepy Eye, U.S.A. 112 C7
Slemon L., Canada 104 A5
Ślesin, Poland 45 F5
Slide Mt., U.S.A. 111 E10
Slidell, U.S.A. 113 K10
Sliema, Malta 36 D2
Slieve Aughty, Ireland ... 15 C3
Slieve Bloom, Ireland ... 15 C4
Slieve Donard, U.K. 15 B6
Slieve Gamph, Ireland ... 15 B3
Slieve Gullion, U.K. 15 B5
Slieve Mish, Ireland 15 D2
Slievenamon, Ireland 15 D4
Sligeach = Sligo, Ireland . 15 B3
Sligo, Ireland 15 B3
Sligo, U.S.A. 110 E5
Sligo □, Ireland 15 B3
Sligo B., Ireland 15 B3
Slippery Rock, U.S.A. ... 110 E4
Slite, Sweden 11 G12
Sliven, Bulgaria 41 D10
Slivnitsa, Bulgaria 40 D7
Sljeme, Croatia 29 C12
Sloan, U.S.A. 117 K11
Sloansville, U.S.A. 111 D10
Slobozia, Moldova 43 D14
Slobozia, Argeş, Romania .. 43 F10
Slobozia, Ialomiţa, Romania . 43 F12

Slocan, Canada 104 D5
Słomniki, Poland 45 H7
Slonim, Belarus 47 F3
Slough, U.K. 13 F7
Slough □, U.K. 13 F7
Sloughhouse, U.S.A. 116 G5
Slovak Rep. ■, Europe ... 27 C13
Slovakia = Slovak Rep. ■,
  Europe 27 C13
Slovakian Ore Mts. =
  Slovenské Rudohorie,
  Slovak Rep. 27 C12
Slovenia ■, Europe 29 C11
Slovenija = Slovenia ■,
  Europe 29 C11
Slovenj Gradec, Slovenia .. 29 B12
Slovenska Bistrica, Slovenia . 29 B12
Slovenske Konjice, Slovenia . 29 B12
Slovenské Rudohorie,
  Slovak Rep. 27 C12
Slovyansk, Ukraine 47 H9
Słubice, Poland 45 F1
Sluch →, Ukraine 47 G4
Sluis, Neths. 17 C3
Slŭnchev Bryag, Bulgaria .. 41 D11
Slunj, Croatia 29 C12
Słupca, Poland 45 F4
Słupia →, Poland 44 D3
Słupsk, Poland 44 D3
Slurry, S. Africa 88 D4
Slutsk, Belarus 47 F4
Slyne Hd., Ireland 15 C1
Slyudyanka, Russia 51 D11
Småland, Sweden 11 G9
Smålandsfarvandet, Denmark . 11 J5
Smålandsstenar, Sweden ... 11 G7
Smalltree L., Canada 105 A8
Smallwood Res., Canada ... 103 B7
Smara, Morocco 78 B4
Smarhon, Belarus 46 E4
Smarje, Slovenia 29 B12
Smartt Syndicate Dam,
  S. Africa 88 E3
Smartville, U.S.A. 116 F5
Smeaton, Canada 105 C8
Smederevo, Serbia, Yug. .. 40 B4
Smederevska Palanka,
  Serbia, Yug. 40 B4
Smedjebacken, Sweden 10 D9
Smela = Smila, Ukraine ... 47 H6
Smerwick Harbour, Ireland . 15 D1
Smethport, U.S.A. 110 E6
Smidovich, Russia 51 E14
Śmigiel, Poland 45 F3
Smila, Ukraine 47 H6
Smilyan, Bulgaria 41 E8
Smith, Canada 104 B6
Smith Center, U.S.A. 112 F5
Smith Sund, Greenland ... 4 B4
Smithburne →, Australia .. 94 B3
Smithers, Canada 104 C3
Smithfield, S. Africa ... 89 E4
Smithfield, N.C., U.S.A. .. 109 H6
Smithfield, Utah, U.S.A. .. 114 F8
Smiths Falls, Canada 102 D4
Smithton, Australia 94 G4
Smithville, Canada 110 C5
Smithville, U.S.A. 113 K6
Smoky →, Canada 104 B5
Smoky Bay, Australia 95 E1
Smoky Hill →, U.S.A. 112 F6
Smoky Hills, U.S.A. 112 F5
Smoky Lake, Canada 104 C6
Smøla, Norway 8 E13
Smolensk, Russia 46 E7
Smolikas, Óros, Greece ... 40 F4
Smolník, Slovak Rep. 27 C13
Smolyan, Bulgaria 41 E8
Smooth Rock Falls, Canada . 102 C3
Smoothstone L., Canada ... 105 C7
Smorgon = Smarhon,
  Belarus 46 E4
Smulţi, Romania 43 E12
Smyadovo, Bulgaria 41 C11
Smygehamn, Sweden 11 J7
Smyrna = İzmir, Turkey ... 39 C9
Smyrna, U.S.A. 108 F8
Snæfell, Iceland 8 D6
Snaefell, U.K. 12 C3
Snæfellsjökull, Iceland .. 8 D2
Snake →, U.S.A. 114 C4
Snake I., Australia 95 F4
Snake Range, U.S.A. 114 G6
Snake River Plain, U.S.A. . 114 E7
Snåsahögarna, Sweden 10 A6
Snåsavatnet, Norway 8 D14
Snedsted, Denmark 11 H2
Sneek, Neths. 17 A5
Sneeuberge, S. Africa ... 88 E3
Snejbjerg, Denmark 11 H2
Snelling, U.S.A. 116 H6
Snezhnoye, Ukraine 47 J10
Snežnik, Slovenia 29 C11
Śniadowo, Poland 45 E8
Śniardwy, Jezioro, Poland . 44 E8
Śnieżka, Europe 26 A8
Snigirevka = Snihurivka,
  Ukraine 47 J7
Snihurivka, Ukraine 47 J7
Snina, Slovak Rep. 27 C15
Snizort, L., U.K. 14 D2
Snøhetta, Norway 9 E13
Snohomish, U.S.A. 116 C4
Snoul, Cambodia 65 F6
Snow Hill, U.S.A. 108 F8
Snow Lake, Canada 105 C8
Snow Mt., Calif., U.S.A. .. 116 F4
Snow Mt., Maine, U.S.A. ... 111 A14
Snow Shoe, U.S.A. 110 E7
Snowbird L., Canada 105 A8

Snowdon, U.K. 12 D3
Snowdrift →, Canada 105 A6
Snowflake, U.S.A. 115 J8
Snowshoe Pk., U.S.A. 114 B6
Snowtown, Australia 95 E2
Snowville, U.S.A. 114 F7
Snowy →, Australia 95 F4
Snowy Mt., U.S.A. 111 C10
Snowy Mts., Australia ... 95 F4
Snug Corner, Bahamas 121 B5
Snyatyn, Ukraine 47 H3
Snyder, Okla., U.S.A. ... 113 H5
Snyder, Tex., U.S.A. 113 J4
Soahanina, Madag. 89 B7
Soalala, Madag. 89 B8
Soaloka, Madag. 89 B8
Soamanonga, Madag. 89 C7
Soan →, Pakistan 68 C4
Soanierana-Ivongo, Madag. . 89 B8
Soanindraniny, Madag. ... 89 B8
Şoarş, Romania 43 E9
Soavina, Madag. 89 C8
Soavinandriana, Madag. ... 89 B8
Soba, Nigeria 83 C6
Sobat, Nahr →, Sudan 81 F3
Sobeslav, Czech Rep. 26 B7
Sobhapur, India 68 H8
Sobinka, Russia 46 E11
Sobótka, Poland 45 H3
Sobra, Croatia 29 F14
Sobradinho, Reprêsa de,
  Brazil 125 E10
Sobral, Brazil 125 D10
Sobrance, Slovak Rep. ... 27 C15
Sobreira Formosa, Portugal . 34 F3
Soc Giang, Vietnam 58 F6
Soc Trang, Vietnam 65 H5
Soča →, Europe 26 E6
Socastee, U.S.A. 109 J6
Sochaczew, Poland 45 F7
Soch'e = Shache, China ... 60 C2
Sochi, Russia 49 J4
Société, Is. de la, Pac. Oc. . 97 J12
Society Is. = Société, Is. de
  la, Pac. Oc. 97 J12
Socompa, Portezuelo de,
  Chile 126 A2
Socorro, N. Mex., U.S.A. .. 115 J10
Socorro, Tex., U.S.A. ... 115 L10
Socorro, I., Mexico 118 D2
Socotra, Ind. Oc. 74 E5
Socovos, Spain 33 G3
Socuéllamos, Spain 33 F2
Soda L., U.S.A. 115 J5
Soda Plains, India 69 B8
Soda Springs, U.S.A. 114 E8
Sodankylä, Finland 8 C22
Soddy-Daisy, U.S.A. 109 H3
Söderala, Sweden 10 C10
Söderbärke, Sweden 10 D9
Söderfors, Sweden 10 D11
Söderhamn, Sweden 10 C11
Söderköping, Sweden 11 F10
Södermanland, Sweden 9 G17
Södermanlands län □,
  Sweden 10 E10
Södertälje, Sweden 10 E11
Sodiri, Sudan 81 E2
Sodo, Ethiopia 81 F4
Södra Dellen, Sweden 10 C10
Södra Finnskoga, Sweden .. 10 D6
Södra Sandby, Sweden 11 J7
Södra Ulvön, Sweden 10 B12
Södra Vi, Sweden 11 G9
Sodražica, Slovenia 29 C11
Sodus, U.S.A. 110 C7
Soekmekaar, S. Africa ... 89 C4
Soest, Germany 24 D4
Soest, Neths. 17 B5
Sofádhes, Greece 38 B4
Sofala □, Mozam. 89 B5
Sofara, Mali 82 C4
Sofia = Sofiya, Bulgaria .. 40 D7
Sofia →, Madag. 89 B8
Sofievka, Ukraine 47 H7
Sofiya, Bulgaria 40 D7
Sofikón, Greece 38 D5
Sofiya, Bulgaria 40 D7
Sōfu-Gan, Japan 55 K10
Sogakofe, Ghana 83 D5
Sogamoso, Colombia 124 B4
Sogār, Iran 71 E8
Sögel, Germany 24 C3
Sogndalsfjøra, Norway ... 9 F12
Søgne, Norway 9 G12
Sognefjorden, Norway 9 F11
Söğüt, Bilecik, Turkey ... 39 A12
Söğüt, Burdur, Turkey ... 39 D12
Söğüt Dağı, Turkey 39 D12
Söğütköy, Turkey 39 E10
Sŏgwipo, S. Korea 57 H14
Soh, Iran 71 C6
Sohâg, Egypt 80 B3
Sohagpur, India 68 H8
Sŏhori, N. Korea 57 D15
Soignies, Belgium 17 D4
Soira, Eritrea 81 E4
Soissons, France 19 C10
Sōja, Japan 55 G6
Sojat, India 68 G5
Sok →, Russia 48 D10
Sokal, Ukraine 47 G3
Söke, Turkey 39 D9
Sokelo,
  Dem. Rep. of the Congo . 87 D1
Sokhós, Greece 40 F7
Sokhumi, Georgia 49 J5
Soko Banja, Serbia, Yug. .. 40 C5
Sokodé, Togo 83 D5
Sokol, Russia 46 C11

Sokolac, Bos.-H. 42 G3
Sokółka, Poland 44 E10
Sokolo, Mali 82 C3
Sokolo, Mali 82 C3
Sokolov, Czech Rep. 26 A5
Sokołów Małopolski, Poland 45 H9
Sokołów Podlaski, Poland .. 45 F9
Sokoły, Poland 45 F9
Sokoto, Nigeria 83 C6
Sokoto □, Nigeria 83 C6
Sokoto →, Nigeria 83 C5
Sol Iletsk, Russia 50 D6
Sola →, Poland 45 H6
Solai, Kenya 86 B4
Solan, India 68 D7
Solano, Phil. 61 C4
Solapur, India 66 L9
Solca, Romania 43 C10
Solda Gölü, Turkey 39 D11
Soldănești, Moldova 43 C13
Soldotna, U.S.A. 100 B4
Soléa □, Cyprus 36 D12
Solec Kujawski, Poland ... 45 E5
Soledad, Colombia 124 A4
Soledad, U.S.A. 116 J5
Soledad, Venezuela 124 B6
Solent, The, U.K. 13 G6
Solenzara, France 21 G13
Solesmes, France 19 B10
Solfonn, Norway 9 F12
Solhan, Turkey 70 B4
Soligorsk = Salihorsk,
  Belarus 47 F4
Solihull, U.K. 13 E6
Solikamsk, Russia 50 D6
Solila, Madag. 89 C8
Solimões = Amazonas →,
  S. Amer. 122 D5
Solin, Croatia 29 E13
Solingen, Germany 24 D3
Sollebrunn, Sweden 11 F6
Sollefteå, Sweden 10 A11
Sollentuna, Sweden 10 E11
Sóller, Spain 37 B9
Sollerön, Sweden 10 D8
Solling, Germany 24 D5
Solnechnogorsk, Russia .. 46 D9
Solo →, Indonesia 63 G15
Solofra, Italy 31 B7
Sologne, France 19 E8
Solok, Indonesia 62 E2
Sololá, Guatemala 120 D1
Solomon, N. Fork →,
  U.S.A. 112 F5
Solomon, S. Fork →,
  U.S.A. 112 F5
Solomon Is. ■, Pac. Oc. ... 96 H7
Solon, China 60 B7
Solon Springs, U.S.A. ... 112 B9
Solor, Indonesia 63 F6
Solotcha, Russia 46 E10
Solothurn, Switz 25 H3
Solothurn □, Switz. 25 H3
Solsona, Spain 32 C6
Solt, Hungary 42 D2
Šolta, Croatia 29 E13
Solţānābād, Khorāsān, Iran 71 C8
Solţānābād, Khorāsān, Iran 71 B8
Soltau, Germany 24 C5
Soltsy, Russia 46 C6
Solunska Glava, Macedonia 40 E5
Solvang, U.S.A. 117 L6
Solvay, U.S.A. 111 C8
Sölvesborg, Sweden 11 H8
Solway Firth, U.K. 12 C4
Solwezi, Zambia 87 E2
Sōma, Japan 54 F10
Soma, Turkey 39 B9
Somabhula, Zimbabwe .. 89 B4
Somali Pen., Africa 76 F8
Somali Rep. ■, Africa ... 74 F4
Somalia = Somali Rep. ■,
  Africa 74 F4
Sombernon, France 19 E11
Sombor, Serbia, Yug. ... 42 E4
Sombra, Canada 110 D2
Sombrerete, Mexico 118 C4
Sombrero, Anguilla 121 C7
Şomcuta Mare, Romania . 43 C8
Somdari, India 68 G5
Somers, U.S.A. 114 B6
Somerset, Ky., U.S.A. .. 108 G3
Somerset, Mass., U.S.A. 111 E13
Somerset, Pa., U.S.A. .. 110 F5
Somerset □, U.K. 13 F5
Somerset East, S. Africa 88 E4
Somerset I., Canada ... 100 A10
Somerset West, S. Africa 88 E2
Somersworth, U.S.A. ... 111 C14
Somerton, U.S.A. 115 K6
Somerville, U.S.A. 111 F10
Someş →, Romania 42 C7
Someşul Mare →, Romania 43 C8
Somme □, France 19 C9
Somme →, France 19 B8
Somme, B. de la, France .. 18 B8
Sommen, Jönköping, Sweden 11 F8
Sommen, Östergötland,
  Sweden 11 F9
Sommepy-Tahure, France . 19 C11
Sömmerda, Germany 24 D7
Sommesous, France 19 D11
Sommières, France 21 E8
Somnath, India 68 J4
Somogy □, Hungary 42 D2
Somogyszob, Hungary .. 42 D2
Somoto, Nic. 120 D2
Sompolno, Poland 45 F5
Somport, Puerto de, Spain 32 C4
Son →, India 69 G11
Son Ha, Vietnam 64 E7

Son Hoa, Vietnam 64 F7
Son La, Vietnam 58 G4
Son Serra, Spain 37 B10
Son Servera, Spain 32 F8
Son Tay, Vietnam 58 G5
Soná, Panama 120 E3
Sonamarg, India 69 B6
Sonamukhi, India 69 H12
Sonar →, India 69 G8
Sŏnch'ŏn, N. Korea ... 57 E13
Sondags →, S. Africa .. 88 E4
Sønder Felding, Denmark . 11 J2
Sønder Omme, Denmark .. 11 J2
Sønderborg, Denmark ... 11 K3
Sønderjyllands
  Amtskommune □,
  Denmark 11 J3
Sondershausen, Germany . 24 D6
Sóndrio, Italy 28 B6
Sone, Mozam. 87 F3
Sonepur, India 67 J13
Song, Nigeria 83 D7
Song, Thailand 64 C3
Song Cau, Vietnam 64 F7
Song Xian, China 56 G7
Songch'ŏn, N. Korea .. 57 E14
Songea, Tanzania 87 E4
Songeons, France 19 C8
Songhua Hu, China ... 57 C14
Songhua Jiang →, China 60 B8
Songjiang, China 59 B13
Songjin, N. Korea 57 D15
Songjŏng-ni, S. Korea . 57 G14
Songkan, China 58 C6
Songkhla, Thailand ... 65 J3
Songming, China 58 E4
Songnim, N. Korea ... 57 E13
Songo, Mozam. 85 H6
Songo, Sudan 79 G10
Songpan, China 58 A4
Songtao, China 58 C7
Songwe,
  Dem. Rep. of the Congo . 86 C2
Songwe →, Africa 87 D3
Songxi, China 59 D12
Songzi, China 59 B8
Sonhat, India 69 H10
Sonid Youqi, China .. 56 C7
Sonipat, India 68 E7
Sonkach, India 68 H7
Sonkovo, Russia 46 D9
Sonmiani, Pakistan .. 68 G2
Sonmiani B., Pakistan . 68 G2
Sonnino, Italy 30 A6
Sono →, Brazil 125 E9
Sonoma, U.S.A. 116 G4
Sonora, Calif., U.S.A. . 116 H6
Sonora, Tex., U.S.A. .. 113 K4
Sonora □, Mexico ... 118 B2
Sonora →, Mexico ... 118 B2
Sonoran Desert, U.S.A. . 117 L12
Sonoyta, Mexico 118 A2
Sonqor, Iran 73 E12
Sŏnsan, S. Korea 57 F15
Sonseca, Spain 35 F7
Sonsonate, El Salv. ... 120 D2
Sonsorol Is., Pac. Oc. .. 63 C8
Sonstorp, Sweden 11 F9
Sonthofen, Germany .. 25 H6
Soochow = Suzhou, China 59 B13
Sooke, Canada 116 B3
Sop Hao, Laos 58 G5
Sop Prap, Thailand ... 64 D2
Sopelana, Spain 32 B2
Sopi, Indonesia 63 D7
Sopo, Nahr →, Sudan . 81 F2
Sopot, Bulgaria 41 D8
Sopot, Poland 44 D5
Sopot, Serbia, Yug. .. 40 B4
Sopotnica, Macedonia . 40 E5
Sopron, Hungary 42 C1
Sopur, India 69 B6
Sør-Rondane, Antarctica ... 5 D4
Sora, Italy 29 G10
Sorah, Pakistan 68 F3
Söråker, Sweden 10 B11
Sorano, Italy 29 F8
Soraon, India 69 G9
Sorbas, Spain 33 H2
Sörbygden, Sweden .. 10 B10
Sore, France 20 D3
Sorel, Canada 102 C5
Soresina, Italy 28 C6
Sörforsa, Sweden ... 10 C10
Sórgono, Italy 30 B2
Sorgues, France 21 D8
Sorgun, Turkey 72 C6
Soria, Spain 32 D2
Soria □, Spain 32 D2
Soriano, Uruguay .. 126 C4
Soriano nel Cimino, Italy . 29 F9
Sorkh, Kuh-e, Iran . 71 C8
Sorø, Denmark 11 J5
Soro, Guinea 82 C3
Soroca, Moldova ... 43 B13
Sorocaba, Brazil ... 127 A6
Soroki = Soroca, Moldova . 43 B13
Sorol Atoll, Pac. Oc. .. 63 C10
Sorong, Indonesia .. 63 E8
Soroní, Greece 36 C10
Soroti, Uganda 86 B3
Sørøya, Norway 8 A20
Sørøysundet, Norway . 8 A20
Sorraia →, Portugal . 35 G2
Sorrell, Australia ... 94 G4
Sorrento, Italy 31 B7
Sorsele, Sweden 8 D17
Sörsjön, Sweden 10 C7
Sorso, Italy 30 B1

Sorsogon, Phil. 61 E6
Sortavala, Russia 46 B6
Sortino, Italy 31 E8
Sortland, Norway 8 B16
Sorvizhi, Russia 48 B9
Sos = Sos del Rey Católico,
  Spain 32 C3
Sos del Rey Católico, Spain 32 C3
Sŏsan, S. Korea 57 F14
Soscumica, L., Canada .. 102 B4
Sösdala, Sweden 11 H7
Sosna →, Russia 47 F10
Sosnovka, Kirov, Russia . 48 B10
Sosnovka, Tambov, Russia . 48 D5
Sosnovyy Bor, Russia ... 46 C5
Sosnowiec, Poland 45 H6
Sospel, France 21 E11
Sossus Vlei, Namibia ... 88 C2
Sŏsura, N. Korea 57 C16
Sot →, India 69 F8
Sotkamo, Finland 8 D23
Soto del Barco, Spain .. 34 B4
Soto la Marina →, Mexico 119 C5
Soto y Amío, Spain ... 34 C5
Sotrondio, Spain 34 B5
Sotuta, Mexico 119 C7
Souanké, Congo 84 D2
Soubré, Ivory C. 82 D3
Souderton, U.S.A. 111 F9
Soúdha, Greece 36 D6
Soúdhas, Kólpos, Greece . 36 D6
Souflíon, Greece 41 E10
Soufrière, St. Lucia ... 121 D7
Souillac, France 20 D5
Souilly, France 19 C12
Soukhouma, Laos 64 E5
Sŏul, S. Korea 57 F14
Soulac-sur-Mer, France . 20 C2
Soulougou, Burkina Faso . 83 C5
Soultz-sous-Forêts, France .. 19 D14
Sound, The = Øresund,
  Europe 11 J6
Sound, The, U.K. 13 G3
Sources, Mt. aux, Lesotho . 89 D4
Soure, Brazil 125 D9
Soure, Portugal 34 E2
Souris, Man., Canada .. 105 D8
Souris, P.E.I., Canada . 103 C7
Souris →, Canada ... 112 A5
Sourou →, Africa ... 82 C4
Soúrpi, Greece 38 B4
Sousa, Brazil 125 E11
Sousel, Portugal ... 35 G3
Sousse, Tunisia 79 A8
Soustons, France ... 20 E2
Sout →, S. Africa .. 88 E2
South Africa ■, Africa . 88 E3
South America 122 H4
South Atlantic Ocean .. 122 H7
South Aulatsivik I., Canada 103 A7
South Australia □, Australia 95 E2
South Ayrshire □, U.K. . 14 F4
South Baldy, U.S.A. .. 115 J10
South Bass I., U.S.A. . 110 E2
South Bend, Ind., U.S.A. . 108 E2
South Bend, Wash., U.S.A. 116 D3
South Boston, U.S.A. .. 109 G6
South Branch, Canada .. 103 C8
South Brook, Canada .. 103 C8
South Carolina □, U.S.A. . 109 J5
South Charleston, U.S.A. . 108 F5
South China Sea, Asia .. 62 C4
South Dakota □, U.S.A. . 112 C5
South Deerfield, U.S.A. . 111 D12
South Downs, U.K. ... 13 G7
South East C., Australia . 94 G4
South East Is., Australia . 93 F3
South Esk →, U.K. ... 14 E6
South Foreland, U.K. .. 13 F9
South Fork American →,
  U.S.A. 116 G5
South Fork Feather →,
  U.S.A. 116 F5
South Fork Grand →,
  U.S.A. 112 C3
South Fork Republican →,
  U.S.A. 112 E4
South Georgia, Antarctica . 122 J7
South Gloucestershire □,
  U.K. 13 F5
South Hadley, U.S.A. .. 111 D12
South Haven, U.S.A. .. 108 D2
South Henik, L., Canada . 105 A9
South Honshu Ridge,
  Pac. Oc. 96 E6
South Horr, Kenya ... 86 B4
South I., Kenya 86 B4
South I., N.Z. 91 L3
South Indian Lake, Canada 105 B9
South Invercargill, N.Z. . 91 M2
South Knife →, Canada . 105 B10
South Koel →, India .. 69 H11
South Korea ■, Asia .. 57 G15
South Lake Tahoe, U.S.A. . 116 G6
South Lanarkshire □, U.K. 14 F5
South Loup →, U.S.A. . 112 E5
South Magnetic Pole,
  Antarctica 5 C9
South Milwaukee, U.S.A. 108 D2
South Molton, U.K. ... 13 F4
South Moose L., Canada . 105 C8
South Nahanni →, Canada 104 A4
South Nation →, Canada . 111 A9
South Natuna Is. = Natuna
  Selatan, Kepulauan,
  Indonesia 65 L7
South Negril Pt., Jamaica . 120 C4
South Orkney Is., Antarctica 5 C18
South Ossetia □, Georgia . 49 J7

South Pagai, I. = Pagai
  Selatan, Pulau, Indonesia 62 E2
South Paris, U.S.A. 111 B14
South Pittsburg, U.S.A. . 109 H3
South Platte →, U.S.A. . 112 E4
South Pole, Antarctica .. 5 E
South Porcupine, Canada . 102 C3
South Portland, U.S.A. . 109 D10
South Pt., U.S.A. 110 B1
South River, Canada ... 102 C4
South River, U.S.A. ... 111 F10
South Ronaldsay, U.K. . 14 C6
South Sandwich Is.,
  Antarctica 5 B1
South Saskatchewan →,
  Canada 105 C7
South Seal →, Canada . 105 B9
South Shetland Is.,
  Antarctica 5 C18
South Shields, U.K. ... 12 C6
South Sioux City, U.S.A. . 112 D6
South Taranaki Bight, N.Z. 91 H5
South Thompson →,
  Canada 104 C4
South Twin I., Canada .. 102 B4
South Tyne →, U.K. ... 12 C5
South Uist, U.K. 14 D1
South West Africa =
  Namibia ■, Africa ... 88 C2
South West C., Australia . 94 G4
South West Rocks, Australia 95 E5
South Williamsport, U.S.A. 110 E8
South Yorkshire □, U.K. . 12 D6
Southampton, Canada .. 102 D3
Southampton, U.K. 13 G6
Southampton, U.S.A. .. 111 F12
Southampton □, U.K. .. 13 G6
Southampton I., Canada . 101 B11
Southaven, U.S.A. 113 H9
Southbank, Canada ... 104 C3
Southbridge, N.Z. 91 K4
Southbridge, U.S.A. .. 111 D12
Southend, Canada 105 B8
Southend-on-Sea, U.K. . 13 F8
Southend-on-Sea □, U.K. . 13 F8
Southern □, Malawi ... 87 F4
Southern □, S. Leone .. 82 D2
Southern □, Uganda .. 86 C3
Southern □, Zambia ... 87 F2
Southern Alps, N.Z. ... 91 K3
Southern Cross, Australia . 93 F2
Southern Indian L., Canada 105 B9
Southern Ocean, Antarctica 5 C6
Southern Pines, U.S.A. . 109 H6
Southern Uplands, U.K. . 14 F5
Southington, U.S.A. .. 111 E12
Southold, U.S.A. 111 E12
Southport, Australia .. 95 D5
Southport, U.K. 12 D4
Southport, Fla., U.S.A. . 109 K3
Southport, N.Y., U.S.A. . 110 D8
Southwest C., N.Z. 91 M1
Southwold, U.K. 13 E9
Soutpansberg, S. Africa . 89 C4
Souvigny, France 19 F10
Sovata, Romania 43 D10
Soverato, Italy 31 D9
Sovetsk, Kaliningd., Russia 9 J19
Sovetsk, Kirov, Russia .. 48 B9
Sovetskaya Gavan = Vanino,
  Russia 51 E15
Sovicille, Italy 29 E8
Soweto, S. Africa 89 D4
Sōya-Kaikyō = La Perouse
  Str., Asia 54 B11
Sōya-Misaki, Japan ... 54 B10
Soyaux, France 20 C4
Sozh →, Belarus 47 F6
Sozopol, Bulgaria 41 D11
Spa, Belgium 17 D5
Spain ■, Europe 7 H5
Spalding, Australia ... 95 E2
Spalding, U.K. 12 E7
Spangler, U.S.A. 110 F6
Spaniard's Bay, Canada . 103 C9
Spanish, Canada 102 C3
Spanish Fork, U.S.A. . 114 F8
Spanish Town, Jamaica . 120 C4
Sparks, U.S.A. 116 F7
Sparreholm, Sweden .. 10 E10
Sparta = Spárti, Greece . 38 D4
Sparta, Mich., U.S.A. . 108 D3
Sparta, N.J., U.S.A. .. 111 E10
Sparta, Wis., U.S.A. .. 112 D9
Spartanburg, U.S.A. .. 109 H5
Spartansburg, U.S.A. . 110 E5
Spárti, Greece 38 D4
Spartivento, C., Calabria,
  Italy 31 E9
Spartivento, C., Sard., Italy 30 D1
Sparwood, Canada ... 104 D6
Spas-Demensk, Russia . 46 E7
Spas-Klepiki, Russia .. 46 E11
Spassk Dalniy, Russia . 51 E14
Spassk-Ryazanskiy, Russia 46 E11
Spátha, Ákra, Greece .. 36 D5
Spatsizi →, Canada .. 104 B3
Spatsizi Plateau Wilderness
  Park, Canada 104 B3
Spean →, U.K. 14 E4
Spearfish, U.S.A. 112 C3
Spearman, U.S.A. ... 113 G4
Speculator, U.S.A. ... 111 C10
Speia, Moldova 43 D14
Speightstown, Barbados . 121 D8
Speke Gulf, Tanzania . 86 C3
Spello, Italy 29 F9
Spencer, Idaho, U.S.A. . 114 D7
Spencer, Iowa, U.S.A. . 112 D7
Spencer, N.Y., U.S.A. . 111 D8
Spencer, Nebr., U.S.A. . 112 D5
Spencer, C., Australia . 95 F2

Spencer B., Namibia ... 88 D1
Spencer G., Australia .. 95 E2
Spencerville, Canada .. 111 B9
Spences Bridge, Canada . 104 C4
Spennymoor, U.K. 12 C6
Spenser Mts., N.Z. 91 K4
Spentrup, Denmark ... 11 H4
Sperkhiós →, Greece .. 38 C4
Sperrin Mts., U.K. 15 B5
Spessart, Germany 25 F5
Spétsai, Greece 38 D5
Spey →, U.K. 14 D5
Speyer, Germany 25 F4
Spezand, Pakistan ... 68 E2
Spezzano Albanese, Italy . 31 C9
Spickeroog, Germany .. 24 B3
Spiez, Switz. 25 J3
Spíli, Greece 36 D6
Spilimbergo, Italy ... 29 B9
Spīn Būldak, Afghan. . 68 D2
Spinalónga, Greece .. 36 D7
Spinazzola, Italy 31 B9
Spineni, Romania ... 43 F9
Spirit Lake, U.S.A. .. 116 D4
Spirit River, Canada . 104 B5
Spiritwood, Canada . 105 C7
Spišská Nová Ves,
  Slovak Rep. 27 C13
Spišské Podhradie,
  Slovak Rep. 27 B13
Spital, Austria 26 D7
Spithead, U.K. 13 G6
Spittal an der Drau, Austria 26 E6
Spitzbergen = Svalbard,
  Arctic 4 B8
Spjelkavik, Norway .. 9 E12
Split, Croatia 29 E13
Split L., Canada 105 B9
Split Lake, Canada .. 105 B9
Splitski Kanal, Croatia 29 E13
Splügenpass, Switz. . 25 J5
Spofford, U.S.A. ... 113 L4
Spokane, U.S.A. ... 114 C5
Spoleto, Italy 29 F9
Spooner, U.S.A. ... 112 C9
Sporyy Navolok, Mys, Russia 50 B7
Sprague, U.S.A. ... 114 C5
Spratly I., S. China Sea . 62 C4
Spratly Is., S. China Sea . 62 C4
Spray, U.S.A. 114 D4
Spreča →, Bos.-H. .. 42 F3
Spree →, Germany .. 24 C9
Spreewald, Germany . 24 D9
Spremberg, Germany . 24 D10
Sprengisandur, Iceland . 8 D5
Spring City, U.S.A. .. 111 F9
Spring Creek, U.S.A. . 114 F6
Spring Garden, U.S.A. . 116 F6
Spring Hill, U.S.A. .. 109 L4
Spring Mts., U.S.A. . 115 H6
Spring Valley, U.S.A. . 117 N10
Springbok, S. Africa . 88 D2
Springboro, U.S.A. .. 110 E4
Springdale, Canada .. 103 C8
Springdale, U.S.A. .. 113 G7
Springe, Germany ... 24 C5
Springerville, U.S.A. . 115 J9
Springfield, Canada .. 110 D4
Springfield, N.Z. ... 91 K3
Springfield, Colo., U.S.A. 113 G3
Springfield, Ill., U.S.A. 112 F10
Springfield, Mass., U.S.A. 111 D12
Springfield, Mo., U.S.A. 113 G8
Springfield, Ohio, U.S.A. 108 F4
Springfield, Oreg., U.S.A. 114 D2
Springfield, Tenn., U.S.A. 109 G2
Springfield, Vt., U.S.A. 111 C12
Springfontein, S. Africa . 88 E4
Springhill, Canada .. 103 C7
Springhill, U.S.A. .. 113 J8
Springhouse, Canada . 104 C4
Springs, S. Africa ... 89 D4
Springsure, Australia . 94 C4
Springvale, U.S.A. .. 111 C14
Springville, Calif., U.S.A. 116 J8
Springville, N.Y., U.S.A. 110 D6
Springville, Utah, U.S.A. 114 F8
Springwater, U.S.A. . 110 D7
Spruce-Creek, U.S.A. . 110 F6
Spruce Mt., U.S.A. .. 111 B12
Spur, U.S.A. 113 J4
Spurn Hd., U.K. 12 D8
Spuž, Montenegro, Yug. . 40 D3
Spuzzum, Canada .. 104 D4
Squam L., U.S.A. .. 111 C13
Square Islands, Canada . 103 B8
Squillace, G. di, Italy . 31 D9
Squinzano, Italy ... 31 B11
Squires, Mt., Australia . 93 E4
Srbac, Bos.-H. 42 E2
Srbica, Kosovo, Yug. . 40 D4
Srbija = Serbia □,
  Yugoslavia 40 C5
Srbobran, Serbia, Yug. . 42 E4
Sre Ambel, Cambodia . 65 G4
Sre Khtum, Cambodia . 65 F6
Sre Umbell = Sre Ambel,
  Cambodia 65 G4
Srebrenica, Bos.-H. .. 42 F4
Sredinny Ra. = Sredinnyy
  Khrebet, Russia 51 D16
Sredinnyy Khrebet, Russia . 51 D16
Središče, Slovenia .. 29 B13
Sredna Gora, Bulgaria . 41 D8
Srednekolymsk, Russia . 51 C16
Sredni Rodopi, Bulgaria . 41 E8
Srednogorie, Bulgaria . 41 D8
Śrem, Poland 45 F4

Sremska Mitrovica, Serbia, Yug. 42 F4
Sremski Karlovci, Serbia, Yug. 42 E4
Srepok →, Cambodia 64 F6
Sretensk, Russia 51 D12
Sri Lanka ■, Asia 66 R12
Srikakulam, India 67 K13
Srinagar, India 69 B6
Środa Śląska, Poland 45 G3
Środa Wielkopolski, Poland 45 F4
Srpska Crnja, Serbia, Yug. 42 E5
Srpski Itebej, Serbia, Yug. 42 E5
Staaten →, Australia 94 B3
Staberhuk, Germany 24 A7
Stade, Germany 24 B5
Stadskanaal, Neths. 17 A6
Stadtallendorf, Germany 24 E5
Stadthagen, Germany 24 C5
Stadtlohn, Germany 24 D2
Stadtroda, Germany 24 E7
Staffa, U.K. 14 E2
Staffanstorp, Sweden 11 J7
Stafford, U.K. 12 E5
Stafford, U.S.A. 113 G5
Stafford Springs, U.S.A. 111 E12
Staffordshire □, U.K. 12 E5
Stagnone, Italy 30 E5
Staines, U.K. 13 F7
Stainz, Austria 26 E8
Stakhanov, Ukraine 47 H10
Stalać, Serbia, Yug. 40 C5
Stalingrad = Volgograd, Russia 49 F7
Staliniri = Tskhinvali, Georgia 49 J7
Stalino = Donetsk, Ukraine 47 J9
Stalinogorsk = Novomoskovsk, Russia 46 E10
Stalis, Greece 36 D7
Stallarholmen, Sweden 10 E11
Ställdalen, Sweden 10 E8
Stalowa Wola, Poland 45 H9
Stalybridge, U.K. 12 D5
Stamford, Australia 94 C3
Stamford, U.K. 13 E7
Stamford, Conn., U.S.A. 111 E11
Stamford, N.Y., U.S.A. 111 D10
Stamford, Tex., U.S.A. 113 J5
Stampriet, Namibia 88 C2
Stamps, U.S.A. 113 J8
Stančevo = Kalipetrovo, Bulgaria 41 B11
Standerton, S. Africa 89 D4
Standish, U.S.A. 108 D4
Stanford, S. Africa 88 E2
Stanford, U.S.A. 114 C8
Stånga, Sweden 11 G12
Stanger, S. Africa 89 D5
Stanišić, Serbia, Yug. 42 E4
Stanislaus →, U.S.A. 116 H5
Stanislav = Ivano-Frankivsk, Ukraine 47 H3
Stanisławów, Poland 45 F8
Stanley, Australia 94 G4
Stanley, Canada 105 B8
Stanley, Falk. Is. 128 G5
Stanley, U.K. 12 C6
Stanley, Idaho, U.S.A. 114 D6
Stanley, N. Dak., U.S.A. 112 A3
Stanley, N.Y., U.S.A. 110 D7
Stanovoy Khrebet, Russia 51 D13
Stanovoy Ra. = Stanovoy Khrebet, Russia 51 D13
Stansmore Ra., Australia 92 D4
Stanthorpe, Australia 95 D5
Stanton, U.S.A. 113 J4
Stanwood, U.S.A. 116 B4
Staples, U.S.A. 112 B7
Stąporków, Poland 45 G7
Star City, Canada 105 C8
Star Lake, U.S.A. 111 B9
Stará Ľubovňa, Slovak Rep. 27 B13
Stara Moravica, Serbia, Yug. 42 E4
Stara Pazova, Serbia, Yug. 42 F5
Stara Planina, Bulgaria 40 C7
Stará Turá, Slovak Rep. 27 C10
Stara Zagora, Bulgaria 41 D9
Starachowice, Poland 45 G8
Staraya Russa, Russia 46 D6
Starbuck I., Kiribati 97 H12
Starchiojd, Romania 43 E11
Stargard Szczeciński, Poland 44 E2
Stari Bar, Montenegro, Yug. 40 D3
Stari Trg, Slovenia 29 C12
Staritsa, Russia 46 D8
Starke, U.S.A. 109 L4
Starnberg, Germany 25 H7
Starnberger See, Germany 25 H7
Starobilsk, Ukraine 47 H10
Starodub, Russia 47 F7
Starogard Gdański, Poland 44 E5
Starokonstantinov = Starokonstyantyniv, Ukraine 47 H4
Starokonstyantyniv, Ukraine 47 H4
Starominskaya, Russia 47 J10
Staroshcherbinovskaya, Russia 47 J10
Start Pt., U.K. 13 G4
Stary Sącz, Poland 45 J7
Staryy Biryuzyak, Russia 49 H8
Staryy Chartoriysk, Ukraine 47 G3
Staryy Krym, Ukraine 47 K8
Staryy Oskol, Russia 47 G9
Stassfurt, Germany 24 D7
Staszów, Poland 45 H8
State College, U.S.A. 110 F7
Stateline, U.S.A. 116 G7
Staten, I. = Estados, I. de Los, Argentina 122 J4

Staten I., U.S.A. 111 F10
Statesboro, U.S.A. 109 J5
Statesville, U.S.A. 109 H5
Stauffer, U.S.A. 117 L7
Staunton, Ill., U.S.A. 112 F10
Staunton, Va., U.S.A. 108 F6
Stavanger, Norway 9 G11
Staveley, N.Z. 91 K3
Stavelot, Belgium 17 D5
Stavern, Norway 9 G14
Stavoren, Neths. 17 B5
Stavropol, Russia 49 H6
Stavros, Cyprus 36 D11
Stavrós, Greece 36 D6
Stavrós, Ákra, Greece 36 D6
Stavroúpolis, Greece 41 E8
Stawell, Australia 95 F3
Stawell →, Australia 94 C3
Stawiski, Poland 44 E9
Stawiszyn, Poland 45 G5
Stayner, Canada 110 B4
Stayton, Canada 114 D2
Steamboat Springs, U.S.A. 114 F10
Stebleva, Albania 40 E4
Steele, U.S.A. 112 B5
Steelton, U.S.A. 110 F8
Steen River, Canada 104 B5
Steenkool = Bintuni, Indonesia 63 E8
Steens Mt., U.S.A. 114 E4
Steenwijk, Neths. 17 B6
Steep Pt., Australia 93 E1
Steep Rock, Canada 105 C9
Ștefan Vodă, Moldova 43 D14
Ștefănești, Romania 43 C12
Stefanie L. = Chew Bahir, Ethiopia 81 G4
Stefansson Bay, Antarctica 5 C5
Stege, Denmark 11 K6
Ștei, Romania 42 D7
Steiermark □, Austria 26 D8
Steigerwald, Germany 25 F6
Steilacoom, U.S.A. 116 C4
Steilrandberge, Namibia 88 B1
Steinbach, Canada 105 D9
Steinfurt, Germany 24 C3
Steinhausen, Namibia 88 C2
Steinheim, Germany 24 D5
Steinhuder Meer, Germany 24 C5
Steinkjer, Norway 8 D14
Steinkopf, S. Africa 88 D2
Stellarton, Canada 103 C7
Stellenbosch, S. Africa 88 E2
Stelvio, Paso dello, Italy 28 B7
Stenay, France 19 C12
Stendal, Germany 24 C7
Stende, Latvia 44 A9
Stenhamra, Sweden 10 E11
Stenstorp, Sweden 11 F7
Stenungsund, Sweden 11 F5
Steornabhaigh = Stornoway, U.K. 14 C2
Stepanakert = Xankändi, Azerbaijan 70 B5
Stepanavan, Armenia 49 K7
Stephens Creek, Australia 95 E3
Stephens I., Canada 104 C2
Stephens L., Canada 105 B9
Stephenville, Canada 103 C8
Stephenville, U.S.A. 113 J5
Stepnica, Poland 44 E1
Stepnoi = Elista, Russia 49 G7
Steppe, Asia 52 D9
Stereá Ellas □, Greece 38 C4
Sterkstroom, S. Africa 88 E4
Sterling, Colo., U.S.A. 112 E3
Sterling, Ill., U.S.A. 112 E10
Sterling, Kans., U.S.A. 112 F5
Sterling City, U.S.A. 113 K4
Sterling Heights, U.S.A. 108 D4
Sterling Run, U.S.A. 110 E6
Sterlitamak, Russia 50 D6
Sternberg, Germany 24 B7
Šternberk, Czech Rep. 27 B10
Stérnes, Greece 36 D6
Sterzing = Vipiteno, Italy 29 B8
Stettin = Szczecin, Poland 44 E1
Stettiner Haff, Germany 24 B10
Stettler, Canada 104 C6
Steubenville, U.S.A. 110 F4
Stevenage, U.K. 13 F7
Stevens Point, U.S.A. 112 C10
Stevenson, U.S.A. 116 E5
Stevenson L., Canada 105 C9
Stevensville, U.S.A. 114 C6
Stevns Klint, Denmark 11 J6
Stewart, B.C., Canada 104 B3
Stewart, N.W.T., Canada 100 B6
Stewart, I., Chile 128 G2
Stewart →, Canada 116 F7
Stewart, C., Australia 94 A1
Stewart, I., N.Z. 91 M1
Stewarts Point, U.S.A. 116 G3
Stewartville, U.S.A. 112 D8
Stewiacke, Canada 103 C7
Steynsburg, S. Africa 88 E4
Steyr, Austria 26 C7
Steyr →, Austria 26 C7
Steytlerville, S. Africa 88 E3
Stia, Italy 29 E8
Stigler, U.S.A. 113 H7
Stigliano, Italy 31 B9
Stigtomta, Sweden 11 F10
Stikine →, Canada 104 B2
Stilfontein, S. Africa 88 D4
Stilís, Greece 38 C4
Stillwater, N.Z. 91 K3
Stillwater, Minn., U.S.A. 112 C8
Stillwater, N.Y., U.S.A. 111 D11
Stillwater, Okla., U.S.A. 113 G6
Stillwater Range, U.S.A. 114 G4

Stillwater Reservoir, U.S.A. 111 C9
Stilo, Pta., Italy 31 D9
Stilwell, U.S.A. 113 H7
Štip, Macedonia 40 E6
Stíra, Greece 38 C6
Stirling, Canada 110 B7
Stirling, U.K. 14 E5
Stirling □, U.K. 14 E4
Stirling Ra., Australia 93 F2
Stittsville, Canada 111 A9
Stjernøya, Norway 8 A20
Stjørdalshalsen, Norway 8 E14
Stockach, Germany 25 H5
Stockaryd, Sweden 11 G8
Stockerau, Austria 27 C9
Stockholm, Sweden 10 E12
Stockholms län □, Sweden 10 E12
Stockport, U.K. 12 D5
Stocksbridge, U.K. 12 D6
Stockton, Calif., U.S.A. 116 H5
Stockton, Kans., U.S.A. 112 F5
Stockton, Mo., U.S.A. 113 G8
Stockton-on-Tees, U.K. 12 C6
Stockton-on-Tees □, U.K. 12 C6
Stockton Plateau, U.S.A. 113 K3
Stoczek Łukowski, Poland 45 G8
Stöde, Sweden 10 B10
Stogovo, Macedonia 40 E4
Stoholm, Denmark 11 H3
Stoke-on-Trent, U.K. 12 D5
Stoke-on-Trent □, U.K. 12 D5
Stokes Pt., Australia 94 G3
Stokes Ra., Australia 92 C5
Stokksnes, Iceland 8 D6
Stokmarknes, Norway 8 B16
Stolac, Bos.-H. 40 C1
Stolberg, Germany 24 E2
Stolbovoy, Ostrov, Russia 51 D17
Stolbtsy = Stowbtsy, Belarus 46 F4
Stolin, Belarus 47 G4
Stöllet, Sweden 10 D7
Stolnici, Romania 43 F9
Stomíon, Greece 36 D5
Ston, Croatia 29 F14
Stone, U.K. 12 E5
Stoneboro, U.S.A. 110 E4
Stonehaven, U.K. 14 E6
Stonehenge, Australia 94 C3
Stonehenge, U.K. 13 F6
Stonewall, Canada 105 C9
Stony L., Man., Canada 105 B9
Stony L., Ont., Canada 110 B6
Stony Point, U.S.A. 111 E11
Stony Pt., U.S.A. 111 C8
Stony Rapids, Canada 105 B7
Stony Tunguska = Tunguska, Podkamennaya →, Russia 51 C10
Stonyford, U.S.A. 116 F4
Stopnica, Poland 45 H7
Storå, Sweden 10 E9
Storå →, Denmark 11 H2
Stora Gla, Sweden 10 E6
Stora Le, Sweden 10 E5
Stora Lulevatten, Sweden 8 C18
Storavan, Sweden 8 D18
Stord, Norway 9 G11
Store Bælt, Denmark 11 J4
Store Heddinge, Denmark 11 J6
Storebro, Sweden 11 G9
Storfors, Sweden 10 E8
Storlien, Sweden 10 A6
Storm B., Australia 94 G4
Storm Lake, U.S.A. 112 D7
Stormberge, S. Africa 88 E4
Stormsrivier, S. Africa 88 E3
Stornoway, U.K. 14 C2
Storo, Italy 28 C7
Storozhinets = Storozhynets, Ukraine 47 H3
Storozhynets, Ukraine 47 H3
Storrs, U.S.A. 111 E12
Storsjö, Gävleborg, Sweden 10 D10
Storsjön, Jämtland, Sweden 10 B7
Storsjön, Jämtland, Sweden 10 A8
Storstrøms Amtskommune □, Denmark 11 J5
Storuman, Sweden 8 D17
Storuman, sjö, Sweden 8 D17
Storvätteshågna, Sweden 10 B6
Storvik, Sweden 10 D10
Storvreta, Sweden 10 E11
Stouffville, Canada 110 C5
Stoughton, Canada 105 D8
Stour →, Dorset, U.K. 13 G6
Stour →, Kent, U.K. 13 F9
Stour →, Suffolk, U.K. 13 F9
Stourbridge, U.K. 13 E5
Stout L., Canada 105 C10
Stove Pipe Wells Village, U.S.A. 117 J9
Støvring, Denmark 11 H3
Stow, U.S.A. 110 E3
Stowbtsy, Belarus 46 F4
Stowmarket, U.K. 13 E9
Strabane, U.K. 15 B4
Stracin, Macedonia 40 D6
Stradella, Italy 28 C6
Strahan, Australia 94 G4
Strajitsa, Bulgaria 41 C9
Strakonice, Czech Rep. 26 B6
Straldzha, Bulgaria 41 D10
Stralsund, Germany 24 A9
Strand, S. Africa 88 E2
Stranda, Møre og Romsdal, Norway 9 E12
Stranda, Nord-Trøndelag, Norway 8 E14

Strandby, Denmark 11 G4
Strangford L., U.K. 15 B6
Strängnäs, Sweden 10 E11
Stranraer, U.K. 14 G3
Strasbourg, Canada 105 C8
Strasbourg, France 19 D14
Strasburg, Germany 24 B9
Stråseni, Moldova 43 C13
Stråssa, Sweden 10 E9
Stratford, Canada 102 D3
Stratford, N.Z. 91 H5
Stratford, Calif., U.S.A. 116 J7
Stratford, Conn., U.S.A. 111 E11
Stratford, Tex., U.S.A. 113 G3
Stratford-upon-Avon, U.K. 13 E6
Strath Spey, U.K. 14 D5
Strathalbyn, Australia 95 F2
Strathaven, U.K. 14 F4
Strathcona Prov. Park, Canada 104 D3
Strathmore, Canada 104 C6
Strathmore, U.K. 14 E5
Strathmore, U.S.A. 116 J7
Strathnaver, Canada 104 C4
Strathpeffer, U.K. 14 D4
Strathroy, Canada 102 D3
Strathy Pt., U.K. 14 C4
Strattanville, U.S.A. 110 E5
Stratton, U.S.A. 111 A14
Stratton Mt., U.S.A. 111 C12
Straubing, Germany 25 G8
Straumnes, Iceland 8 C2
Strausberg, Germany 24 C9
Strawberry →, U.S.A. 114 F8
Streaky B., Australia 95 E1
Streaky Bay, Australia 95 E1
Streator, U.S.A. 112 E10
Středočeský □, Czech Rep. 26 B7
Streetsboro, U.S.A. 110 E3
Streetsville, Canada 110 C5
Strehaia, Romania 43 F8
Strelcha, Bulgaria 41 D8
Strelka, Russia 51 D10
Streng →, Cambodia 64 F4
Stresa, Italy 28 C5
Streymoy, Færoe Is. 8 E9
Strezhevoy, Russia 50 C8
Stříbro, Czech Rep. 26 A6
Strimón →, Greece 40 F7
Strimonikós Kólpos, Greece 40 F7
Strofádhes, Greece 38 D3
Stroma, U.K. 14 C5
Strómboli, Italy 31 D8
Stromeferry, U.K. 14 D3
Stromness, U.K. 14 C5
Strömsbruk, Sweden 10 C11
Stromsburg, U.S.A. 112 E6
Strömsnäsbruk, Sweden 11 H7
Strömstad, Sweden 11 F5
Strömsund, Sweden 8 E16
Strongili, Greece 39 E11
Stróngoli, Italy 31 C10
Strongsville, U.S.A. 110 E3
Stronie Śląskie, Poland 45 H3
Stronsay, U.K. 14 B6
Stropkov, Slovak Rep. 27 B14
Stroud, U.K. 13 F5
Stroud Road, Australia 95 E5
Stroudsburg, U.S.A. 111 F9
Stroumbi, Cyprus 36 E11
Struer, Denmark 11 H2
Struga, Macedonia 40 E4
Strugi Krasnyye, Russia 46 C5
Strumica, Macedonia 40 E6
Strumica →, Europe 40 E7
Struthers, Canada 102 C2
Struthers, U.S.A. 110 E4
Stryama, Bulgaria 41 D8
Stryker, U.S.A. 114 B6
Stryków, Poland 45 G6
Stryy, Ukraine 47 H2
Strzegom, Poland 45 H3
Strzelce Krajeńskie, Poland 45 F2
Strzelce Opolskie, Poland 45 H5
Strzelecki Cr. →, Australia 95 D2
Strzelin, Poland 45 H4
Strzelno, Poland 45 F5
Strzybnica, Poland 45 H5
Strzyżów, Poland 45 J8
Stuart, Fla., U.S.A. 109 M5
Stuart, Nebr., U.S.A. 112 D5
Stuart →, Canada 104 C4
Stuart Bluff Ra., Australia 92 D5
Stuart L., Canada 104 C4
Stuart Ra., Australia 95 D1
Stubbekøbing, Denmark 11 K6
Stuben, Austria 26 D3
Studen Kladenets, Yazovir, Bulgaria 41 E9
Studenka, Czech Rep. 27 B11
Stugun, Sweden 10 A9
Stuhr, Germany 24 B4
Stull L., Canada 102 B1
Stung Treng = Stoeng Treng, Cambodia 64 F5
Stupart →, Canada 102 A1
Stupava, Slovak Rep. 27 C10
Stupino, Russia 46 D10
Sturgeon B., Canada 105 C9
Sturgeon Bay, U.S.A. 108 C2
Sturgeon Falls, Canada 102 C4
Sturgeon L., Alta., Canada 104 B5
Sturgeon L., Ont., Canada 102 C1
Sturgeon L., Ont., Canada 110 B6
Sturgis, Canada 105 C8
Sturgis, Mich., U.S.A. 108 E3
Sturgis, S. Dak., U.S.A. 112 C3
Sturkö, Sweden 11 H9
Štúrovo, Slovak Rep. 27 D11
Sturt Cr. →, Australia 92 C4

Stutterheim, S. Africa 88 E4
Stuttgart, Germany 25 G5
Stuttgart, U.S.A. 113 H9
Stuyvesant, U.S.A. 111 D11
Stykkishólmur, Iceland 8 D2
Styria = Steiermark □, Austria 26 D8
Styrsö, Sweden 11 G5
Su Xian = Suzhou, China 56 H9
Suakin, Sudan 80 D4
Suan, N. Korea 57 E14
Suaqui, Mexico 118 B3
Suar, India 69 E8
Subang, Indonesia 63 G12
Subansiri →, India 67 F18
Subarnarekha →, India 69 H12
Subayhah, Si. Arabia 70 D3
Subcetate, Romania 42 E8
Subi, Indonesia 65 L7
Subiaco, Italy 29 G10
Subotica, Serbia, Yug. 42 D4
Suca, Ethiopia 81 F4
Suceava, Romania 43 C11
Suceava □, Romania 43 C10
Suceava →, Romania 43 C11
Sucha-Beskidzka, Poland 45 J6
Suchań, Poland 45 E2
Suchan, Russia 54 C6
Suchedniów, Poland 45 G7
Suchitoto, El Salv. 120 D2
Suchou = Suzhou, China 59 B13
Süchow = Xuzhou, China 57 G9
Suchowola, Poland 44 E10
Suck →, Ireland 15 C3
Sucre, Bolivia 124 G5
Sućuraj, Croatia 29 E14
Sucuriú →, Brazil 125 H8
Sud, Pte. du, Canada 103 C7
Sud-Kivu □, Dem. Rep. of the Congo 86 C2
Sud-Ouest, Pte. du, Canada 103 C7
Suda →, Russia 46 C9
Sudak, Ukraine 47 K8
Sudan ■, Africa 81 E3
Sudan, U.S.A. 113 H3
Sudbury, Canada 102 C3
Sudbury, U.K. 13 E8
Sûdd, Sudan 81 F3
Süderbrarup, Germany 24 A5
Süderlügum, Germany 24 A4
Süderoogsand, Germany 24 A4
Sudeten Mts. = Sudety, Europe 27 A9
Sudety, Europe 27 A9
Suðuroy, Færoe Is. 8 F9
Sudi, Tanzania 87 E4
Sudirman, Pegunungan, Indonesia 63 E9
Sudiți, Romania 43 F12
Sudogda, Russia 48 C5
Sudr, Egypt 80 B3
Sudzha, Russia 47 G8
Sue →, Sudan 81 F2
Sueca, Spain 33 F4
Süedinenie, Bulgaria 41 D8
Suemez I., U.S.A. 104 B2
Suez = El Suweis, Egypt 80 J8
Suez, G. of = Suweis, Khalîg el, Egypt 80 J8
Suez Canal = Suweis, Qanâ es, Egypt 80 H8
Suffield, Canada 104 C6
Suffolk, U.S.A. 108 G7
Suffolk □, U.K. 13 E9
Şugag, Romania 43 E8
Sugargrove, U.S.A. 110 E5
Sugarive →, India 69 F12
Suğla Gölü, Turkey 72 D5
Sugluk = Salluit, Canada 101 B12
Suhaia, Lacul, Romania 43 G10
Şuḩār, Oman 71 E8
Sühbaatar □, Mongolia 56 B8
Suhl, Germany 24 E6
Şuhut, Turkey 39 C12
Sui, Pakistan 68 E3
Sui Xian, China 59 B9
Suichang, China 59 C12
Suichuan, China 59 D10
Suide, China 56 F6
Suifenhe, China 57 B16
Suihua, China 60 B7
Suijiang, China 58 C4
Suining, Hunan, China 59 D8
Suining, Jiangsu, China 57 H9
Suining, Sichuan, China 58 B5
Suippes, France 19 C11
Suir →, Ireland 15 D4
Suisun City, U.S.A. 116 G4
Suixi, China 59 G8
Suiyang, Guizhou, China 58 D6
Suiyang, Heilongjiang, China 57 B16
Suizhong, China 57 D11
Suizhou, China 59 B9
Sujangarh, India 68 F6
Sukabumi, Indonesia 63 G12
Sukadana, Indonesia 62 E3
Sukagawa, Japan 55 F10
Sukaraja, Indonesia 62 E4
Sukarnapura = Jayapura, Indonesia 63 E10
Sukhindol, Bulgaria 41 C9
Sukhinichi, Russia 46 E8
Sukhona →, Russia 50 C5
Sukhothai, Thailand 64 D2
Sukhumi = Sokhumi, Georgia 49 J5
Sukkur, Pakistan 68 F3
Sukkur Barrage, Pakistan 68 F3

Tahlequah

Sukovo, Serbia, Yug. 40 C6
Sukri →, India 68 G4
Sukumo, Japan 55 H6
Sukunka →, Canada 104 B4
Sula →, Ukraine 47 H7
Sula, Kepulauan, Indonesia 63 E7
Sulaco →, Honduras 120 C2
Sulaiman Range, Pakistan 68 D3
Sulak →, Russia 49 J8
Sūlār, Iran 71 D6
Sulawesi Sea = Celebes Sea, Indonesia 63 D6
Sulawesi Selatan □, Indonesia 63 E6
Sulawesi Utara □, Indonesia 63 D6
Sulechów, Poland 45 F2
Sulęcin, Poland 45 F2
Sulejów, Poland 45 G6
Sulejówek, Poland 45 F8
Süleymanlı, Turkey 39 C9
Sulima, S. Leone 82 D2
Sulina, Romania 43 E14
Sulina, Braţul →, Romania 43 E14
Sulingen, Germany 24 C4
Suliţa, Romania 43 C11
Sulitjelma, Norway 8 C17
Sułkowice, Poland 45 J6
Sullana, Peru 124 D2
Süller, Turkey 39 C11
Sullivan, Ill., U.S.A. 112 F10
Sullivan, Ind., U.S.A. 108 F2
Sullivan, Mo., U.S.A. 112 F9
Sullivan Bay, Canada 104 C3
Sullivan I. = Lambi Kyun, Burma 65 G2
Sully-sur-Loire, France 19 E9
Sulmierzyce, Poland 45 G4
Sulmona, Italy 29 F10
Süloğlu, Turkey 41 E10
Sulphur, La., U.S.A. 113 K8
Sulphur, Okla., U.S.A. 113 H6
Sulphur Pt., Canada 104 A6
Sulphur Springs, U.S.A. 113 J7
Sultan, Canada 102 C3
Sultan, U.S.A. 116 C5
Sultan Dağları, Turkey 72 C4
Sultanhisar, Turkey 39 D10
Sultaniça, Turkey 41 F10
Sultaniye, Turkey 41 F12
Sultanpur, Mad. P., India 68 H8
Sultanpur, Punjab, India 68 D6
Sultanpur, Ut. P., India 69 F10
Sulu Arch., Phil. 61 J4
Sulu Sea, E. Indies 61 G4
Sülüklü, Turkey 72 C5
Sululta, Ethiopia 81 F4
Suluova, Turkey 72 B6
Suluq, Libya 79 B10
Sulzbach, Germany 25 F3
Sulzbach-Rosenberg, Germany 25 F7
Sulzberger Ice Shelf, Antarctica 5 D10
Sumalata, Indonesia 63 D6
Sumampa, Argentina 126 B3
Sumatera □, Indonesia 62 D2
Sumatera Barat □, Indonesia 62 E2
Sumatera Utara □, Indonesia 62 D1
Sumatra = Sumatera □, Indonesia 62 D2
Sumba, Indonesia 63 F5
Sumba, Selat, Indonesia 63 F5
Sumbawa, Indonesia 62 F5
Sumbawa Besar, Indonesia 62 F5
Sumbawanga □, Tanzania 84 F6
Sumbe, Angola 84 G2
Sumburgh Hd., U.K. 14 B7
Sumdeo, India 69 D8
Sumdo, India 69 B8
Sumedang, Indonesia 63 G12
Sümeg, Hungary 42 D2
Sumeih, Sudan 81 F2
Šumen = Shumen, Bulgaria 41 C10
Sumenep, Indonesia 63 G15
Sumgait = Sumqayıt, Azerbaijan 49 K9
Summer L., U.S.A. 114 E3
Summerland, Canada 104 D5
Summerside, Canada 103 C7
Summersville, U.S.A. 108 F5
Summerville, Ga., U.S.A. 109 H3
Summerville, S.C., U.S.A. 109 J5
Summit Lake, Canada 104 C4
Summit Peak, U.S.A. 115 H10
Sumner, Iowa, U.S.A. 112 D8
Sumner, Wash., U.S.A. 116 C4
Sumoto, Japan 55 G7
Šumperk, Czech Rep. 27 B9
Sumqayıt, Azerbaijan 49 K9
Sumter, U.S.A. 109 J5
Sumy, Ukraine 47 G8
Sun City, Ariz., U.S.A. 115 K7
Sun City, Calif., U.S.A. 117 M9
Sun City Center, U.S.A. 109 M4
Sun Lakes, U.S.A. 115 K8
Sun Valley, U.S.A. 114 E6
Sunagawa, Japan 54 C10
Sunan, N. Korea 57 E13
Sunart, L., U.K. 14 E3
Sunburst, U.S.A. 114 B8
Sunbury, Australia 95 F3
Sunbury, U.S.A. 111 F8
Sunchales, Argentina 126 C3
Suncho Corral, Argentina 126 B3
Sunch'ŏn, S. Korea 57 G14
Suncook, U.S.A. 111 C13
Sunda, Selat, Indonesia 62 F3
Sunda Is., Indonesia 52 K14
Sunda Str. = Sunda, Selat, Indonesia 62 F3
Sundance, Canada 105 B10
Sundance, U.S.A. 112 C2
Sundar Nagar, India 68 D7
Sundarbans, The, Asia 67 J16
Sundargarh, India 67 H14
Sundays = Sondags →, S. Africa 88 E4
Sunderland, Canada 110 B5
Sunderland, U.K. 12 C6
Sundre, Canada 104 C6
Sunds, Denmark 11 H3
Sundsvall, Sweden 10 B11
Sundsvallsbukten, Sweden 10 B11
Sung Hei, Vietnam 65 G6
Sungai Kolok, Thailand 65 J3
Sungai Lembing, Malaysia 65 L4
Sungai Petani, Malaysia 65 K3
Sungaigerong, Indonesia 62 E2
Sungailiat, Indonesia 62 E3
Sungaipenuh, Indonesia 62 E2
Sungari = Songhua Jiang →, China 60 B8
Sunghua Chiang = Songhua Jiang →, China 60 B8
Sungikai, Sudan 81 E2
Sungurlu, Turkey 72 B6
Sunja, Croatia 29 C13
Sunland Park, U.S.A. 115 L10
Sunnansjö, Sweden 10 D8
Sunndalsøra, Norway 9 E13
Sunne, Sweden 10 E7
Sunnemo, Sweden 10 E7
Sunnyside, U.S.A. 114 C3
Sunnyvale, U.S.A. 116 H4
Suntar, Russia 51 C12
Sunyani, Ghana 82 D4
Suomenselkä, Finland 8 E21
Suomussalmi, Finland 8 D23
Suoyarvi, Russia 46 A7
Supai, U.S.A. 115 H7
Supaul, India 69 F12
Superior, Ariz., U.S.A. 115 K8
Superior, Mont., U.S.A. 114 C6
Superior, Nebr., U.S.A. 112 E5
Superior, Wis., U.S.A. 112 B8
Superior, L., N. Amer. 102 C2
Supetar, Croatia 29 E13
Suphan Buri, Thailand 64 E3
Suphan Dağı, Turkey 70 B4
Supiori, Indonesia 63 E9
Supraśl, Poland 45 E10
Supraśl →, Poland 45 E9
Supung Shuiku, China 57 D13
Sūq Suwayq, Si. Arabia 70 E3
Suqian, China 57 H10
Sūr, Lebanon 75 B4
Sūr, Oman 74 C6
Sur, Pt., U.S.A. 116 J5
Sura →, Russia 48 C8
Surab, Pakistan 68 E2
Surabaja = Surabaya, Indonesia 63 G15
Surabaya, Indonesia 63 G15
Surahammar, Sweden 10 E10
Suraia, Romania 43 E12
Surakarta, Indonesia 63 G14
Surakhany, Azerbaijan 49 K10
Šurany, Slovak Rep. 27 C11
Surat, Australia 95 D4
Surat, India 66 J8
Surat Thani, Thailand 65 H2
Suratgarh, India 68 E5
Suraż, Poland 45 F9
Surazh, Belarus 46 E6
Surazh, Russia 47 F7
Surduc, Romania 43 C8
Surduc Pasul, Romania 43 E8
Surdulica, Serbia, Yug. 40 D6
Surendranagar, India 68 H4
Surf, U.S.A. 117 L6
Surgères, France 20 B3
Surgut, Russia 50 C8
Sùria, Spain 32 D6
Suriapet, India 66 L11
Surigao, Phil. 61 G6
Surigao Strait, Phil. 61 F6
Surin, Thailand 64 E4
Surin Nua, Ko, Thailand 65 H1
Surinam ■, S. Amer. 125 C7
Suriname = Surinam ■, S. Amer. 125 C7
Suriname →, Surinam 125 B7
Sürmaq, Iran 71 D7
Sürmene, Turkey 73 B9
Surovikino, Russia 49 F6
Surrey □, U.K. 13 F7
Sursand, India 69 F11
Sursar →, India 69 F12
Sursee, Switz. 25 H4
Sursk, Russia 48 D7
Surskoye, Russia 48 C8
Surt, Libya 79 B9
Surt, Khalīj, Libya 79 B9
Surtanahu, Pakistan 68 F4
Surte, Sweden 11 G6
Surtsey, Iceland 8 E3
Sürüç, Turkey 73 D8
Suruga-Wan, Japan 55 G9
Susa, Italy 28 C4
Suså →, Denmark 11 J5
Sušac, Croatia 29 F13
Susak, Croatia 29 D11
Susaki, Japan 55 H6
Süsangerd, Iran 71 D6
Susanville, U.S.A. 114 F3
Susch, Switz. 25 J6
Suşehri, Turkey 73 B8
Sušice, Czech Rep. 26 B6
Susleni, Moldova 43 C13
Susner, India 68 H7
Susong, China 59 B11
Susquehanna, U.S.A. 111 E9
Susquehanna →, U.S.A. 111 G8
Susques, Argentina 126 A2
Sussex, Canada 103 C6
Sussex, U.S.A. 111 E10
Sussex, E. □, U.K. 13 G8
Sussex, W. □, U.K. 13 G7
Sustut →, Canada 104 B3
Susuman, Russia 51 C15
Susunu, Indonesia 63 E8
Susurluk, Turkey 39 B10
Susuz, Turkey 73 B10
Susz, Poland 44 E6
Sütçüler, Turkey 72 D4
Şuteşti, Romania 43 E12
Sutherland, S. Africa 88 E3
Sutherland, U.S.A. 112 E4
Sutherland Falls, N.Z. 91 L1
Sutherlin, U.S.A. 114 E2
Suthri, India 68 H3
Sutlej →, Pakistan 68 E4
Sutter, U.S.A. 116 F5
Sutter Creek, U.S.A. 116 G6
Sutton, Canada 111 A12
Sutton, Nebr., U.S.A. 112 E6
Sutton, W. Va., U.S.A. 108 F5
Sutton →, Canada 102 A3
Sutton Coldfield, U.K. 13 E6
Sutton in Ashfield, U.K. 12 D6
Sutton L., Canada 102 B3
Suttor →, Australia 94 C4
Suttsu, Japan 54 C10
Suva, Fiji 91 D8
Suva Gora, Macedonia 40 E5
Suva Planina, Serbia, Yug. 40 C6
Suva Reka, Kosovo, Yug. 40 D4
Suvorov, Russia 46 E9
Suvorov Is. = Suwarrow Is., Cook Is. 97 J11
Suvorovo, Bulgaria 41 C11
Suwałki, Poland 44 D9
Suwannaphum, Thailand 64 E4
Suwannee →, U.S.A. 109 L4
Suwanose-Jima, Japan 55 K4
Suwarrow Is., Cook Is. 97 J11
Suwayq aş Şuqban, Iraq 70 D5
Suweis, Khalîg el, Egypt 80 J8
Suweis, Qanâ es, Egypt 80 H8
Suwŏn, S. Korea 57 F14
Suzdal, Russia 46 D11
Suzhou, Anhui, China 56 H9
Suzhou, Jiangsu, China 59 B13
Suzu, Japan 55 F8
Suzu-Misaki, Japan 55 F8
Suzuka, Japan 55 G8
Suzzara, Italy 28 D7
Svalbard, Arctic 4 B8
Svalöv, Sweden 11 J7
Svaneke, Denmark 11 J9
Svängsta, Sweden 11 H8
Svanskog, Sweden 10 E6
Svappavaara, Sweden 8 C19
Svärdsjö, Sweden 10 D9
Svartå, Sweden 10 E8
Svartisen, Norway 8 C15
Svartvik, Sweden 10 B11
Svatove, Ukraine 47 H10
Svatovo = Svatove, Ukraine 47 H10
Svay Chek, Cambodia 64 F4
Svay Rieng, Cambodia 65 G5
Svealand □, Sweden 10 D9
Svedala, Sweden 11 J7
Sveg, Sweden 10 B8
Svendborg, Denmark 11 J4
Svenljunga, Sweden 11 G7
Svenstavik, Sweden 10 B8
Svenstrup, Denmark 11 H3
Sverdlovsk = Yekaterinburg, Russia 50 D7
Sverdlovsk, Ukraine 47 H10
Sverdrup Is., Canada 4 B3
Svetac, Croatia 29 E12
Sveti Nikola, Prokhad, Europe 40 C6
Sveti Nikole, Macedonia 40 E5
Sveti Rok, Croatia 29 D12
Svetlaya, Russia 54 A9
Svetlogorsk = Svyetlahorsk, Belarus 47 F5
Svetlograd, Russia 49 H6
Svetlovodsk = Svitlovodsk, Ukraine 47 H7
Svidník, Slovak Rep. 27 B14
Svilaja Planina, Croatia 29 E13
Svilajnac, Serbia, Yug. 40 B5
Svilengrad, Bulgaria 41 E10
Svir →, Russia 46 B7
Sviritsa, Russia 46 B7
Svishtov, Bulgaria 41 C9
Svislach, Belarus 47 F3
Svitava →, Czech Rep. 27 B9
Svitavy, Czech Rep. 27 B9
Svitlovodsk, Ukraine 47 H7
Svobodnyy, Russia 51 D13
Svoge, Bulgaria 40 D7
Svolvær, Norway 8 B16
Svratka →, Czech Rep. 27 B9
Svrljig, Serbia, Yug. 40 C6
Svyetlahorsk, Belarus 47 F5
Swabian Alps = Schwäbische Alb, Germany 25 G5
Swainsboro, U.S.A. 109 J4
Swakop →, Namibia 88 C2
Swakopmund, Namibia 88 C1
Swale →, U.K. 12 C6
Swan →, Australia 93 F2
Swan →, Canada 105 C8
Swan Hill, Australia 95 F3
Swan Hills, Canada 104 C5
Swan Is., W. Indies 120 C3
Swan L., Canada 105 C8
Swan Peak, U.S.A. 114 C7
Swan Ra., U.S.A. 114 C7
Swan Reach, Australia 95 E2
Swan River, Canada 105 C8
Swanage, U.K. 13 G6
Swansea, Australia 94 G4
Swansea, Canada 110 C5
Swansea, U.K. 13 F4
Swansea □, U.K. 13 F3
Swar →, Pakistan 69 B5
Swartberge, S. Africa 88 E3
Swartmodder, S. Africa 88 D3
Swartnossob →, Namibia 88 C2
Swartruggens, S. Africa 88 D4
Swarzędz, Poland 45 F4
Swastika, Canada 102 C3
Swatow = Shantou, China 59 F11
Swaziland ■, Africa 89 D5
Sweden ■, Europe 9 G16
Swedru, Ghana 83 D4
Sweet Home, U.S.A. 114 D2
Sweetgrass, U.S.A. 114 B8
Sweetwater, Nev., U.S.A. 116 G7
Sweetwater, Tenn., U.S.A. 109 H3
Sweetwater, Tex., U.S.A. 113 J4
Sweetwater →, U.S.A. 114 E10
Swellendam, S. Africa 88 E3
Świder →, Poland 45 F8
Świdnica, Poland 45 H3
Świdnik, Poland 45 G9
Świdwin, Poland 44 E2
Świebodzice, Poland 45 H3
Świebodzin, Poland 45 F2
Świecie, Poland 44 E5
Świerzawa, Poland 45 G2
Świętokrzyskie □, Poland 45 H7
Świętokrzyskie, Góry, Poland 45 H7
Swift Current, Canada 105 C7
Swiftcurrent →, Canada 105 C7
Swilly, L., Ireland 15 A4
Swindon, U.K. 13 F6
Swindon □, U.K. 13 F6
Swinemünde = Świnoujście, Poland 44 E1
Swinford, Ireland 15 C3
Świnoujście, Poland 44 E1
Switzerland ■, Europe 25 J4
Swords, Ireland 15 C5
Swoyerville, U.S.A. 111 E9
Syasstroy, Russia 46 B7
Sychevka, Russia 46 E8
Syców, Poland 45 G4
Sydenham →, Canada 110 D2
Sydney, Australia 95 E5
Sydney, Canada 103 C7
Sydney L., Canada 105 C10
Sydney Mines, Canada 103 C7
Sydprøven = Alluitsup Paa, Greenland 4 C5
Sydra, G. of = Surt, Khalīj, Libya 79 B9
Syeverodonetsk, Ukraine 47 H10
Syke, Germany 24 C4
Sykesville, U.S.A. 110 E6
Syktyvkar, Russia 50 C6
Sylacauga, U.S.A. 109 J2
Sylarna, Sweden 8 E15
Sylhet, Bangla. 67 G17
Sylt, Germany 24 A4
Sylvan Beach, U.S.A. 111 C9
Sylvan Lake, Canada 104 C6
Sylvania, U.S.A. 109 J5
Sylvester, U.S.A. 109 K4
Sym, Russia 50 C9
Symón, Mexico 118 C4
Synelnykove, Ukraine 47 H8
Synnott Ra., Australia 92 C4
Syracuse, Kans., U.S.A. 113 G4
Syracuse, N.Y., U.S.A. 111 C8
Syracuse, Nebr., U.S.A. 112 E6
Syrdarya →, Kazakstan 50 E7
Syria ■, Asia 70 C3
Syrian Desert = Shām, Bādiyat ash, Asia 70 C3
Sysslebäck, Sweden 10 D6
Syzran, Russia 48 D9
Szabolcs-Szatmár-Bereg □, Hungary 42 B6
Szadek, Poland 45 G5
Szamocin, Poland 45 E4
Szamos →, Hungary 42 B7
Szamotuły, Poland 45 F3
Száraz →, Hungary 42 D6
Szarvas, Hungary 42 D5
Százhalombatta, Hungary 42 C3
Szczawnica, Poland 45 J7
Szczebrzeszyn, Poland 45 H9
Szczecin, Poland 44 E1
Szczecinek, Poland 44 E3
Szczeciński, Zalew = Stettiner Haff, Germany 24 B10
Szczekociny, Poland 45 H6
Szczucin, Poland 45 H8
Szczuczyn, Poland 44 E9
Szczyrk, Poland 45 J6
Szczytna, Poland 45 H3
Szczytno, Poland 44 E7
Szechwan = Sichuan □, China 58 B5
Szécsény, Hungary 42 B4
Szeged, Hungary 42 D5
Szeghalom, Hungary 42 C6
Székesfehérvár, Hungary 42 C3
Szekszárd, Hungary 42 D3
Szendrő, Hungary 42 B5
Szentendre, Hungary 42 C4
Szentes, Hungary 42 D5
Szentgotthárd, Hungary 42 D1
Szentlőrinc, Hungary 42 D3
Szerencs, Hungary 42 B6
Szigetszentmiklós, Hungary 42 C4
Szigetvár, Hungary 42 D2
Szikszó, Hungary 42 B5
Szklarska Poreba, Poland 45 H2
Szkwa →, Poland 45 E8
Szlichtyngowa, Poland 45 G3
Szob, Hungary 42 C3
Szolnok, Hungary 42 C5
Szombathely, Hungary 42 C1
Szprotawa, Poland 45 G2
Sztum, Poland 44 E6
Sztutowo, Poland 44 D6
Szubin, Poland 45 E4
Szydłowiec, Poland 45 G7
Szypliszki, Poland 44 D10

T

Ta Khli Khok, Thailand 64 E3
Ta Lai, Vietnam 65 G6
Tab, Hungary 42 D3
Tabacal, Argentina 126 A3
Tabaco, Phil. 61 E5
Tabagné, Ivory C. 82 D4
Ţābah, Si. Arabia 70 E4
Tabankort, Niger 83 B5
Ţabas, Khorāsān, Iran 71 C9
Ţabas, Khorāsān, Iran 71 C8
Tabasará, Serranía de, Panama 120 E3
Tabasco □, Mexico 119 D6
Tabāsīn, Iran 71 D8
Tabatinga, Serra da, Brazil 125 F10
Taber, Canada 104 D6
Taberg, Sweden 11 G8
Taberg, U.S.A. 111 C9
Tabla, Niger 83 C5
Tablas I., Phil. 61 E5
Tablas Strait, Phil. 61 E4
Table B. = Tafelbaai, S. Africa 88 E2
Table B., Canada 103 B8
Table Mt., S. Africa 88 E2
Table Rock L., U.S.A. 113 G8
Tabletop, Mt., Australia 94 C4
Tábor, Czech Rep. 26 B7
Tabora, Tanzania 86 D3
Tabora □, Tanzania 86 D3
Tabou, Ivory C. 82 E3
Tabrīz, Iran 70 B5
Tabuaeran, Pac. Oc. 97 G12
Tabuenca, Spain 32 D3
Tabūk, Si. Arabia 70 D3
Täby, Sweden 10 E12
Tacámbaro de Codallos, Mexico 118 D4
Tacheng, China 60 B3
Tach'i, Taiwan 59 E13
Tachia, Taiwan 59 E13
Tach'ing Shan = Daqing Shan, China 56 D6
Tachov, Czech Rep. 26 B5
Tácina →, Italy 31 D9
Tacloban, Phil. 61 F6
Tacna, Peru 124 G4
Tacoma, U.S.A. 116 C4
Tacuarembó, Uruguay 127 C4
Tademaït, Plateau du, Algeria 78 C6
Tadio, L., Ivory C. 82 D3
Tadjoura, Djibouti 81 E5
Tadjoura, Golfe de, Djibouti 81 E5
Tadmor, N.Z. 91 J4
Tadoule, L., Canada 105 B9
Tadoussac, Canada 103 C6
Tadzhikistan = Tajikistan ■, Asia 50 F8
Taechŏn-ni, S. Korea 57 F14
Taegu, S. Korea 57 G15
Taegwan, N. Korea 57 D13
Taejŏn, S. Korea 57 F14
Tafalla, Spain 32 C3
Tafar, Sudan 81 F2
Tafelbaai, S. Africa 88 E2
Tafermaar, Indonesia 63 F8
Tafí Viejo, Argentina 126 B2
Tafīhān, Iran 71 D7
Tafiré, Ivory C. 82 D3
Tafo, Ghana 83 D4
Tafresh, Iran 71 C6
Taft, Iran 71 D7
Taft, Phil. 61 F6
Taft, U.S.A. 117 K7
Taftān, Kūh-e, Iran 71 D9
Taga Dzong, Bhutan 67 F16
Taganrog, Russia 47 J10
Taganrogskiy Zaliv, Russia 47 J10
Tagânt, Mauritania 82 B2
Tagatay, Phil. 61 D4
Tagbilaran, Phil. 61 G5
Tàggia, Italy 28 E4
Tagish, Canada 104 A2
Tagish L., Canada 104 A2
Tagliacozzo, Italy 29 F10
Tagliamento →, Italy 29 C10
Táglio di Po, Italy 29 D9
Tago, Phil. 61 G7
Tagomago, Spain 37 B8
Tagourāret, Mauritania 82 B3
Taguatinga, Brazil 125 F10
Tagudin, Phil. 61 C4
Tagum, Phil. 61 H6
Tagus = Tejo →, Europe 35 F2
Tahakopa, N.Z. 91 M2
Tahan, Gunong, Malaysia 65 K4
Tahat, Algeria 78 D7
Tāherī, Iran 71 E7
Tahiti, Pac. Oc. 97 J13
Tahlequah, U.S.A. 113 H7

Name	Pg	Ref
Tahoe, L., *U.S.A.*	116	G6
Tahoe City, *U.S.A.*	116	F6
Tahoka, *U.S.A.*	113	J4
Taholah, *U.S.A.*	116	C2
Tahoua, *Niger*	83	C6
Tahrūd, *Iran*	71	D8
Tahsis, *Canada*	104	D3
Tahta, *Egypt*	80	B3
Tahtaköprü, *Turkey*	41	G13
Tahulandang, *Indonesia*	63	D7
Tahuna, *Indonesia*	63	D7
Taï, *Ivory C.*	82	D3
Tai Hu, *China*	59	B12
Tai Shan, *China*	57	F9
Tai'an, *China*	57	F9
Taibei = T'aipei, *Taiwan*	59	E13
Taibique, *Canary Is.*	37	G2
Taibus Qi, *China*	56	D8
Taicang, *China*	59	B13
T'aichung, *Taiwan*	59	E13
Taieri →, *N.Z.*	91	M3
Taigu, *China*	56	F7
Taihang Shan, *China*	56	G7
Taihape, *N.Z.*	91	H5
Taihe, *Anhui, China*	56	H8
Taihe, *Jiangxi, China*	59	D10
Taihu, *China*	59	B11
Taijiang, *China*	58	D7
Taikang, *China*	56	G8
Tailem Bend, *Australia*	95	F2
Tailfingen, *Germany*	25	G5
Tailuko, *Taiwan*	59	E13
Taimyr Peninsula = Taymyr, Poluostrov, *Russia*	51	B11
Tain, *U.K.*	14	D4
T'ainan, *Taiwan*	59	F13
Taínaron, Ákra, *Greece*	38	E4
Taining, *China*	59	D11
T'aipei, *Taiwan*	59	E13
Taiping, *China*	59	B12
Taiping, *Malaysia*	65	K3
Taipingzhen, *China*	56	H6
Tairbeart = Tarbert, *U.K.*	14	D2
Taishan, *China*	59	F9
Taishun, *China*	59	D12
Taita Hills, *Kenya*	86	C4
Taitao, Pen. de, *Chile*	122	H3
T'aitung, *Taiwan*	59	F13
Taivalkoski, *Finland*	8	D23
Taiwan ■, *Asia*	59	F13
Taiwan Strait, *Asia*	59	E12
Taixing, *China*	59	A13
Taiyara, *Sudan*	81	E3
Taïyetos Óros, *Greece*	38	D4
Taiyiba, *Israel*	75	C4
Taiyuan, *China*	56	F7
Taizhong = T'aichung, *Taiwan*	59	E13
Taizhou, *China*	59	A12
Taizhou Liedao, *China*	59	C13
Ta'izz, *Yemen*	74	E3
Tājābād, *Iran*	71	D7
Tajikistan ■, *Asia*	50	F8
Tajima, *Japan*	55	F9
Tajo = Tejo →, *Europe*	35	F2
Tajrīsh, *Iran*	71	C6
Tak, *Thailand*	64	D2
Takāb, *Iran*	70	B5
Takachiho, *Japan*	55	H5
Takachu, *Botswana*	88	C3
Takada, *Japan*	55	F9
Takahagi, *Japan*	55	F10
Takaka, *N.Z.*	91	J4
Takamatsu, *Japan*	55	G7
Takaoka, *Japan*	55	F8
Takapuna, *N.Z.*	91	G5
Takasaki, *Japan*	55	F9
Takatsuki, *Japan*	55	G7
Takaungu, *Kenya*	86	C4
Takayama, *Japan*	55	F8
Take-Shima, *Japan*	55	J5
Takefu, *Japan*	55	G8
Takengon, *Indonesia*	62	D1
Takeo, *Japan*	55	H5
Tåkern, *Sweden*	11	F8
Tākestān, *Iran*	71	C6
Taketa, *Japan*	55	H5
Takev, *Cambodia*	65	G5
Takh, *India*	69	C7
Takht-Sulaiman, *Pakistan*	68	D3
Takikawa, *Japan*	54	C10
Takla L., *Canada*	104	B3
Takla Landing, *Canada*	104	B3
Takla Makan = Taklamakan Shamo, *China*	52	F12
Taklamakan Shamo, *China*	52	F12
Taku →, *Canada*	104	B2
Takum, *Nigeria*	83	D6
Tal Halāl, *Iran*	71	D7
Tala, *Uruguay*	127	C4
Talachyn, *Belarus*	46	E5
Talacogan, *Phil.*	61	G6
Talagang, *Pakistan*	68	C5
Talagante, *Chile*	126	C1
Talak, *Niger*	83	B6
Talamanca, Cordillera de, *Cent. Amer.*	120	E3
Talant, *France*	19	E11
Talara, *Peru*	124	D2
Talas, *Kyrgyzstan*	50	E8
Talas, *Turkey*	72	C6
Talâta, *Egypt*	75	E1
Talata Mafara, *Nigeria*	83	C6
Talaud, Kepulauan, *Indonesia*	63	D7
Talaud Is. = Talaud, Kepulauan, *Indonesia*	63	D7
Talavera de la Reina, *Spain*	34	F6
Talavera la Real, *Spain*	35	G4
Talayan, *Phil.*	61	H6
Talayuela, *Spain*	34	F5
Talbandh, *India*	69	H12
Talbert, Sillon de, *France*	18	D3
Talbot, C., *Australia*	92	B4
Talbragar →, *Australia*	95	E4
Talca, *Chile*	126	D1
Talcahuano, *Chile*	126	D1
Talcher, *India*	67	J14
Talcho, *Niger*	83	C5
Taldy Kurgan = Taldyqorghan, *Kazakhstan*	50	E8
Taldyqorghan, *Kazakhstan*	50	E8
Tälesh, *Iran*	71	B6
Tälesh, Kühhä-ye, *Iran*	71	B6
Talguharai, *Sudan*	80	D4
Tali Post, *Sudan*	81	F3
Taliabu, *Indonesia*	63	E6
Talibon, *Phil.*	63	B6
Talibong, Ko, *Thailand*	65	J2
Talihina, *U.S.A.*	113	H7
Talisayan, *Phil.*	61	G6
Taliwang, *Indonesia*	62	F5
Tall 'Afar, *Iraq*	70	B4
Tall Kalakh, *Syria*	75	A5
Talla, *Egypt*	80	B3
Talladega, *U.S.A.*	109	J2
Tallangatta, *Australia*	95	F4
Tallard, *France*	21	D10
Tällberg, *Sweden*	10	D9
Tallering Pk., *Australia*	93	E2
Talli, *Pakistan*	68	E3
Tallinn, *Estonia*	9	G21
Tallmadge, *U.S.A.*	110	E3
Tallulah, *U.S.A.*	113	J9
Tălmaciu, *Romania*	43	E9
Talmont-St-Hilaire, *France*	20	B2
Talne, *Ukraine*	47	H6
Talnoye = Talne, *Ukraine*	47	H6
Talodi, *Sudan*	81	E3
Talovaya, *Russia*	48	E5
Taloyoak, *Canada*	100	B10
Talpa de Allende, *Mexico*	118	C4
Talsi, *Latvia*	9	H20
Talsi □, *Latvia*	44	A9
Taltal, *Chile*	126	B1
Taltson →, *Canada*	104	A6
Talwood, *Australia*	95	D4
Talyawalka →, *Australia*	95	E3
Tam Chau, *Vietnam*	65	G5
Tam Ky, *Vietnam*	64	E7
Tam Quan, *Vietnam*	64	E7
Tama, *U.S.A.*	112	E8
Tamale, *Ghana*	83	D4
Taman, *Russia*	47	K9
Tamani, *Mali*	82	C3
Tamano, *Japan*	55	G6
Tamanrasset, *Algeria*	78	D7
Tamaqua, *U.S.A.*	111	F9
Tamar →, *U.K.*	13	G3
Tamarinda, *Spain*	37	B10
Tamashima, *Japan*	55	G6
Tamási, *Hungary*	42	D3
Tamaské, *Niger*	83	C6
Tamaulipas □, *Mexico*	119	C5
Tamaulipas, Sierra de, *Mexico*	119	C5
Tamazula, *Mexico*	118	C3
Tamazunchale, *Mexico*	119	C5
Tamba-Dabatou, *Guinea*	82	C2
Tambacounda, *Senegal*	82	C2
Tambelan, Kepulauan, *Indonesia*	62	D3
Tambellup, *Australia*	93	F2
Tambo, *Australia*	94	C4
Tambo de Mora, *Peru*	124	F3
Tambohorano, *Madag.*	89	B7
Tambora, *Indonesia*	62	F5
Tambov, *Russia*	48	D5
Tambre →, *Spain*	34	C2
Tambuku, *Indonesia*	63	G15
Tamburâ, *Sudan*	81	F2
Tâmchekket, *Mauritania*	82	B2
Tâmega →, *Portugal*	34	D2
Tamenglong, *India*	67	G18
Tamgak, Massif du, *Niger*	82	C2
Tamgué, Massif du, *Guinea*	82	C2
Tamiahua, L. de, *Mexico*	119	C5
Tamil Nadu □, *India*	66	P10
Tamis →, *Serbia, Yug.*	42	F5
Tamluk, *India*	69	H12
Tammerfors = Tampere, *Finland*	9	F20
Tammisaari, *Finland*	9	F20
Tämnaren, *Sweden*	10	D11
Tamo Abu, Pegunungan, *Malaysia*	62	D5
Tampa, *U.S.A.*	109	M4
Tampa B., *U.S.A.*	109	M4
Tampere, *Finland*	9	F20
Tampico, *Mexico*	119	C5
Tampin, *Malaysia*	65	L4
Tamsweg, *Austria*	26	D6
Tamu, *Burma*	67	G19
Tamuja →, *Spain*	35	F4
Tamworth, *Australia*	95	E5
Tamworth, *Canada*	110	B8
Tamworth, *U.K.*	13	E6
Tamyang, *S. Korea*	57	G14
Tan An, *Vietnam*	65	G6
Tan-Tan, *Morocco*	78	C3
Tana →, *Kenya*	86	C5
Tana →, *Norway*	8	A23
Tana, L., *Ethiopia*	81	E4
Tana River, *Kenya*	86	C4
Tanabe, *Japan*	55	H7
Tanafjorden, *Norway*	8	A23
Tanaga, Pta., *Canary Is.*	37	G1
Tanahbala, *Indonesia*	62	E1
Tanahgrogot, *Indonesia*	62	E5
Tanahjampea, *Indonesia*	63	F6
Tanahmasa, *Indonesia*	62	E1
Tanahmerah, *Indonesia*	63	F10
Tanakpur, *India*	69	E9
Tanakura, *Japan*	55	F10
Tanami, *Australia*	92	C4
Tanami Desert, *Australia*	92	C5
Tanana →, *U.S.A.*	100	B4
Tananarive = Antananarivo, *Madag.*	89	B8
Tánaro →, *Italy*	28	D5
Tancheng, *China*	57	G10
Tanch'ŏn, *N. Korea*	57	D15
Tanda, *Ut. P., India*	69	F10
Tanda, *Ut. P., India*	69	E8
Tanda, *Ivory C.*	82	D4
Tandag, *Phil.*	61	G7
Tandaia, *Tanzania*	87	D3
Tandârei, *Romania*	43	F12
Tandil, *Argentina*	126	D4
Tandil, Sa. del, *Argentina*	126	D4
Tandlianwala, *Pakistan*	68	D5
Tando Adam, *Pakistan*	68	G3
Tando Allahyar, *Pakistan*	68	G3
Tando Bago, *Pakistan*	68	G3
Tando Mohommed Khan, *Pakistan*	68	G3
Tandou L., *Australia*	95	E3
Tandragee, *U.K.*	15	B5
Tandsjöborg, *Sweden*	10	C8
Tane-ga-Shima, *Japan*	55	J5
Taneatua, *N.Z.*	91	H6
Tanen Tong Dan, *Burma*	64	D2
Tanew →, *Poland*	45	H9
Tanezrouft, *Algeria*	78	D6
Tang, Koh, *Cambodia*	65	G4
Tang, Ra's-e, *Iran*	71	E8
Tang Krasang, *Cambodia*	64	F5
Tanga, *Tanzania*	86	D4
Tanga □, *Tanzania*	86	D4
Tanganyika, L., *Africa*	86	D3
Tangaza, *Nigeria*	83	C5
Tanger = Tangier, *Morocco*	78	A4
Tangerang, *Indonesia*	63	G12
Tangerhütte, *Germany*	24	C7
Tangermünde, *Germany*	24	C7
Tanggu, *China*	57	E9
Tanggula Shan, *China*	60	C4
Tanghe, *China*	56	H7
Tangier, *Morocco*	78	A4
Tangorin, *Australia*	94	C3
Tangorombohitr'i Makay, *Madag.*	89	C8
Tangshan, *China*	57	E10
Tangtou, *China*	57	G10
Tanguiéta, *Benin*	83	C5
Tangxi, *China*	59	C12
Tangyan He →, *China*	58	C7
Tanimbar, Kepulauan, *Indonesia*	63	F8
Tanimbar Is. = Tanimbar, Kepulauan, *Indonesia*	63	F8
Taninthari = Tenasserim □, *Burma*	64	F2
Tanjay, *Phil.*	61	G5
Tanjong Malim, *Malaysia*	65	L3
Tanjore = Thanjavur, *India*	66	P11
Tanjung, *Indonesia*	62	E5
Tanjungbalai, *Indonesia*	62	D1
Tanjungbatu, *Indonesia*	62	D5
Tanjungkarang Telukbetung, *Indonesia*	62	F3
Tanjungpandan, *Indonesia*	62	E3
Tanjungpinang, *Indonesia*	62	D2
Tanjungredeb, *Indonesia*	62	D5
Tanjungselor, *Indonesia*	62	D5
Tank, *Pakistan*	68	C4
Tankhala, *India*	68	J5
Tännäs, *Sweden*	10	B6
Tannersville, *U.S.A.*	111	E9
Tannis Bugt, *Denmark*	11	G4
Tannu-Ola, *Russia*	51	D10
Tannum Sands, *Australia*	94	C5
Tano →, *Ghana*	82	D4
Tanon Str., *Phil.*	61	F5
Tanout, *Niger*	83	C6
Tanshui, *Taiwan*	59	E13
Tantoyuca, *Mexico*	119	C5
Tantung = Dandong, *China*	57	D13
Tanumshede, *Sweden*	11	F5
Tanunda, *Australia*	95	E2
Tanus, *France*	20	D6
Tanzania ■, *Africa*	86	D3
Tanzilla →, *Canada*	104	B2
Tao, Ko, *Thailand*	65	G2
Tao'an = Taonan, *China*	57	B12
Tao'er He →, *China*	57	B13
Taohua Dao, *China*	59	C14
Taolanaro, *Madag.*	89	D8
Taole, *China*	56	E4
Taonan, *China*	57	B12
Taormina, *Italy*	31	E8
Taos, *U.S.A.*	115	H11
Taoudenni, *Mali*	78	D5
Taourirt, *Morocco*	78	B5
T'aoyüan, *Taiwan*	59	E13
Tapa, *Estonia*	9	G21
Tapa Shan = Daba Shan, *China*	58	B7
Tapachula, *Mexico*	119	D6
Tapah, *Malaysia*	65	K3
Tapahoni →, *Surinam*	125	C8
Tapanui, *N.Z.*	91	L2
Tapauá, *Brazil*	124	E6
Tapauá →, *Brazil*	124	E6
Tapes, *Brazil*	127	C5
Tapeta, *Liberia*	82	D3
Taphan Hin, *Thailand*	64	D3
Tapia de Casariego, *Spain*	34	B4
Tapirapecó, Serra, *Venezuela*	124	C6
Tapolca, *Hungary*	42	D2
Tapuaenuku, Mt., *N.Z.*	91	K4
Tapul Group, *Phil.*	61	J4
Tapurucuará, *Brazil*	124	D5
Taquara, *Brazil*	127	B5
Taquari →, *Brazil*	124	G7
Tara, *Australia*	95	D5
Tara, *Canada*	110	B3
Tara, *Russia*	50	D8
Tara, *Zambia*	87	F2
Tara →, *Montenegro, Yug.*	40	C2
Taraba □, *Nigeria*	83	D7
Taraba →, *Nigeria*	83	D7
Tarabagatay, Khrebet, *Kazakhstan*	50	E9
Tarābulus, *Lebanon*	75	A4
Tarābulus, *Libya*	79	B8
Taraclia, *Moldova*	43	D14
Taraclia, *Moldova*	43	E13
Taradehi, *India*	69	H8
Tarajalejo, *Canary Is.*	37	F5
Tarakan, *Indonesia*	62	D5
Tarakit, Mt., *Kenya*	86	B4
Tarama-Jima, *Japan*	55	M2
Taran, Mys, *Russia*	9	J18
Taranagar, *India*	68	E6
Taranaki □, *N.Z.*	91	H5
Tarancón, *Spain*	32	E1
Taranga Hill, *India*	66	H8
Táranto, *Italy*	31	B10
Táranto, G. di, *Italy*	31	B10
Tarapacá, *Colombia*	124	D5
Tarapacá □, *Chile*	126	A2
Tarapoto, *Peru*	124	E3
Tarare, *France*	21	C8
Tararua Ra., *N.Z.*	91	J5
Tarascon-sur-Ariège, *France*	20	F5
Tarashcha, *Ukraine*	47	H6
Tarauacá, *Brazil*	124	E4
Tarauacá →, *Brazil*	124	E5
Taravo →, *France*	21	G12
Tarawa, *Kiribati*	96	G9
Tarawera, *N.Z.*	91	H6
Tarawera L., *N.Z.*	91	H6
Tarazona, *Spain*	32	D3
Tarazona de la Mancha, *Spain*	33	F3
Tarbat Ness, *U.K.*	14	D5
Tarbela Dam, *Pakistan*	68	B5
Tarbert, *Arg. & Bute, U.K.*	14	F3
Tarbert, *W. Isles, U.K.*	14	D2
Tarbes, *France*	20	E4
Tarboro, *U.S.A.*	109	H7
Tărcău, Munţii, *Romania*	43	D11
Tarcento, *Italy*	29	B10
Tarcoola, *Australia*	95	E1
Tarcoon, *Australia*	95	E4
Tardets-Sorholus, *France*	20	E3
Tardoire →, *France*	20	C4
Taree, *Australia*	95	E5
Tarfa, W. el →, *Egypt*	80	B3
Tarfaya, *Morocco*	78	C3
Târgoviște, *Romania*	43	F10
Târgu Bujor, *Romania*	43	E12
Târgu Cărbuneşti, *Romania*	43	F8
Târgu Frumos, *Romania*	43	C12
Târgu-Jiu, *Romania*	43	E8
Târgu Lăpuş, *Romania*	43	C8
Târgu Mureş, *Romania*	43	D9
Târgu Neamţ, *Romania*	43	C11
Târgu Ocna, *Romania*	43	D11
Târgu Secuiesc, *Romania*	43	E11
Târgușor, *Romania*	43	F13
Târhăus, Vf., *Romania*	43	D11
Ţarif, *U.A.E.*	71	E7
Tarifa, *Spain*	35	J5
Tarija, *Bolivia*	126	A3
Tarija □, *Bolivia*	126	A3
Tariku →, *Indonesia*	63	E9
Tarim Basin = Tarim Pendi, *China*	60	C3
Tarim He →, *China*	60	C3
Tarim Pendi, *China*	60	C3
Taritatu →, *Indonesia*	63	E9
Tarka →, *S. Africa*	88	E4
Tarkastad, *S. Africa*	88	E4
Tarkhankut, Mys, *Ukraine*	47	K7
Tarko Sale, *Russia*	50	C8
Tarkwa, *Ghana*	82	D4
Tarlac, *Phil.*	61	D4
Tarm, *Denmark*	11	J2
Tarma, *Peru*	124	F3
Tarn □, *France*	20	E6
Tarn →, *France*	20	D5
Tarn-et-Garonne □, *France*	20	D5
Tarna →, *Hungary*	42	C4
Târnava Mare →, *Romania*	43	D8
Târnava Mică →, *Romania*	43	D8
Târnăveni, *Romania*	43	D9
Tarnica, *Poland*	45	J9
Tarnobrzeg, *Poland*	45	H8
Tarnogród, *Poland*	45	H9
Tarnos, *France*	20	E2
Tarnów, *Poland*	45	H8
Tarnowskie Góry, *Poland*	45	H5
Tärnsjö, *Sweden*	10	D10
Tārom, *Iran*	71	D7
Taroom, *Australia*	95	D4
Taroudannt, *Morocco*	78	B4
Tarp, *Germany*	24	A5
Tarpon Springs, *U.S.A.*	109	L4
Tarquínia, *Italy*	29	F8
Tarragona, *Spain*	32	D6
Tarragona □, *Spain*	32	D6
Tarraleah, *Australia*	94	G4
Tarrasa = Terrassa, *Spain*	32	D7
Tàrrega, *Spain*	32	D6
Tarrytown, *U.S.A.*	111	E11
Tårs, *Denmark*	11	G4
Tarshiha = Me'ona, *Israel*	75	B4
Tarso Emissi, *Chad*	79	D9
Tarsus, *Turkey*	70	B2
Tartagal, *Argentina*	126	A3
Tärtär, *Azerbaijan*	49	K8
Tärtär →, *Azerbaijan*	49	K8
Tartas, *France*	20	E3
Tartu, *Estonia*	9	G22
Ţarţūs, *Syria*	70	C2
Tarumizu, *Japan*	55	J5
Tarussa, *Russia*	46	E9
Tarutao, Ko, *Thailand*	65	J2
Tarutung, *Indonesia*	62	D1
Tarvísio, *Italy*	29	B10
Taseko →, *Canada*	104	C4
Tash-Kömür, *Kyrgyzstan*	50	E8
Tash-Kumyr = Tash-Kömür, *Kyrgyzstan*	50	E8
Tashauz = Dashhowuz, *Turkmenistan*	50	E6
Tashi Chho Dzong = Thimphu, *Bhutan*	67	F16
Tashk, Daryācheh-ye, *Iran*	71	D7
Tashkent = Toshkent, *Uzbekistan*	50	E7
Tashtagol, *Russia*	50	D9
Tasiilaq, *Greenland*	4	C6
Tasikmalaya, *Indonesia*	63	G13
Tåsinge, *Denmark*	11	J4
Tåsjön, *Sweden*	8	D16
Taskan, *Russia*	51	C16
Tasker, *Niger*	83	C7
Taşköprü, *Turkey*	72	B6
Taşlâc, *Moldova*	43	C14
Tasman B., *N.Z.*	91	J4
Tasman Mts., *N.Z.*	91	J4
Tasman Pen., *Australia*	94	G4
Tasman Sea, *Pac. Oc.*	96	L8
Tasmania □, *Australia*	94	G4
Tășnad, *Romania*	42	C7
Tassili n'Ajjer, *Algeria*	78	C7
Tassili Tin-Rerhoh, *Algeria*	83	A5
Tata, *Morocco*	78	C4
Tatabánya, *Hungary*	42	C3
Tatahouine, *Tunisia*	79	B8
Tatar Republic = Tatarstan □, *Russia*	48	C10
Tatarbunary, *Ukraine*	47	K5
Tatarsk, *Russia*	50	D8
Tatarstan □, *Russia*	48	C10
Tateyama, *Japan*	55	G9
Tathlina L., *Canada*	104	A5
Tathra, *Australia*	95	F4
Tati →, *India*	68	J8
Tatinnai L., *Canada*	105	A9
Tatla L., *Canada*	104	C4
Tatlısu, *Turkey*	41	F13
Tatnam, C., *Canada*	105	B10
Tatra = Tatry, *Slovak Rep.*	27	B13
Tatry, *Slovak Rep.*	27	B13
Tatshenshini →, *Canada*	104	B1
Tatsuno, *Japan*	55	G7
Tatta, *Pakistan*	68	G2
Tatuí, *Brazil*	127	A6
Tatum, *U.S.A.*	113	J3
Tat'ung = Datong, *China*	56	D7
Tatvan, *Turkey*	70	B4
Taubaté, *Brazil*	127	A6
Tauberbischofsheim, *Germany*	25	F5
Taucha, *Germany*	24	D8
Tauern-tunnel, *Austria*	26	D6
Taufikia, *Sudan*	81	F3
Taulé, *France*	18	D3
Taumarunui, *N.Z.*	91	H5
Taumaturgo, *Brazil*	124	E4
Taung, *S. Africa*	88	D3
Taungdwingyi, *Burma*	67	J19
Taungup, *Burma*	67	K19
Taungup Pass, *Burma*	67	K19
Taungup Taunggya, *Burma*	67	K18
Taunsa, *Pakistan*	68	D4
Taunsa Barrage, *Pakistan*	68	D4
Taunton, *U.K.*	13	F4
Taunton, *U.S.A.*	111	E13
Taunus, *Germany*	25	E4
Taupo, *N.Z.*	91	H6
Taupo, L., *N.Z.*	91	H5
Tauragė, *Lithuania*	9	J20
Tauragė □, *Lithuania*	44	C9
Tauranga, *N.Z.*	91	G6
Tauranga Harb., *N.Z.*	91	G6
Taurianova, *Italy*	31	D9
Taurus Mts. = Toros Dağları, *Turkey*	70	B2
Tauste, *Spain*	32	D3
Tauz = Tovuz, *Azerbaijan*	49	K7
Tavas, *Turkey*	39	D11
Tavda, *Russia*	50	D7
Tavda →, *Russia*	50	D7
Tavernes de la Valldigna, *Spain*	33	F4
Taveta, *Tanzania*	86	C4
Taveuni, *Fiji*	91	a17
Taviano, *Italy*	31	C11
Tavignano →, *France*	21	F13
Tavira, *Portugal*	35	H3
Tavistock, *Canada*	110	C4
Tavistock, *U.K.*	13	G3
Tavolara, *Italy*	30	B2
Távora →, *Portugal*	34	D3
Tavoy = Dawei, *Burma*	64	E2
Tavşanlı, *Turkey*	39	B11

Taw →, *U.K.* 13 F3
Tawa →, *India* 68 H8
Tawas City, *U.S.A.* 108 C4
Tawau, *Malaysia* 62 D5
Taweisha, *Sudan* 81 E2
Tawitawi, *Phil.* 63 B6
Tawu, *Taiwan* 59 F13
Taxco de Alarcón, *Mexico* . 119 D5
Taxila, *Pakistan* 68 C5
Tay →, *U.K.* 14 E5
Tay, Firth of, *U.K.* 14 E5
Tay, L., *Australia* 93 F3
Tay, L., *U.K.* 14 E4
Tay Ninh, *Vietnam* 65 G6
Tayabamba, *Peru* 124 E3
Tayabas Bay, *Phil.* 61 E4
Taylakova, *Russia* 50 D8
Taylakovy = Taylakova,
   Russia 50 D8
Taylor, *Canada* 104 B4
Taylor, *Nebr., U.S.A.* 112 E5
Taylor, *Pa., U.S.A.* 111 E9
Taylor, *Tex., U.S.A.* 113 K6
Taylor, Mt., *U.S.A.* 115 J10
Taylorville, *U.S.A.* 112 F10
Taymā, *Si. Arabia* 70 E3
Taymyr, Oz., *Russia* 51 B11
Taymyr, Poluostrov, *Russia* 51 B11
Tayport, *U.K.* 14 E6
Tayshet, *Russia* 51 D10
Taytay, *Phil.* 61 F3
Taz →, *Russia* 50 C8
Taza, *Morocco* 78 B5
Tāzah Khurmātū, *Iraq* ... 70 C5
Tazawa-Ko, *Japan* 54 E10
Tazin →, *Canada* 105 B7
Tazin L., *Canada* 105 B7
Tazovskiy, *Russia* 50 C8
Tbilisi, *Georgia* 49 K7
Tchad = Chad ■, *Africa* .. 79 E9
Tchad, L., *Chad* 79 F8
Tchaourou, *Benin* 83 D5
Tch'eng-tou = Chengdu,
   China 58 B5
Tchentlo L., *Canada* 104 B4
Tchetti, *Benin* 83 D5
Tchibanga, *Gabon* 84 E2
Tchien, *Liberia* 82 D3
Tchin Tabaraden, *Niger* .. 83 B6
Tch'ong-k'ing = Chongqing,
   China 58 C6
Tczew, *Poland* 44 D5
Te Anau, L., *N.Z.* 91 L1
Te Aroha, *N.Z.* 91 G5
Te Awamutu, *N.Z.* 91 H5
Te Kuiti, *N.Z.* 91 H5
Te-n-Dghâmcha, Sebkhet,
   Mauritania 82 B1
Te Puke, *N.Z.* 91 G6
Te Waewae B., *N.Z.* 91 M1
Teaca, *Romania* 43 D9
Teague, *U.S.A.* 113 K6
Teano, *Italy* 31 A7
Teapa, *Mexico* 119 D6
Teba, *Spain* 35 J6
Tebakang, *Malaysia* 62 D4
Teberda, *Russia* 49 J5
Tébessa, *Algeria* 78 A7
Tebicuary →, *Paraguay* .. 126 B4
Tebingtinggi, *Indonesia* .. 62 D1
Tebintingii, *Indonesia* ... 62 E2
Tebulos, *Georgia* 49 J7
Tecate, *Mexico* 117 N10
Tecer Dağları, *Turkey* ... 72 C7
Tech →, *France* 20 F7
Techiman, *Ghana* 82 D4
Techirghiol, *Romania* ... 43 F13
Tecka, *Argentina* 128 E2
Tecomán, *Mexico* 118 D4
Tecopa, *Mexico* 117 K10
Tecoripa, *Mexico* 118 B3
Tecuala, *Mexico* 118 C3
Tecuci, *Romania* 43 E12
Tecumseh, *Canada* 110 D2
Tecumseh, *Mich., U.S.A.* . 108 D4
Tecumseh, *Okla., U.S.A.* . 113 H6
Tedzhen =
   Turkmenistan 50 F7
Tees →, *U.K.* 12 C6
Tees B., *U.K.* 12 C6
Teeswater, *Canada* 110 C3
Tefé, *Brazil* 124 D6
Tefenni, *Turkey* 39 D11
Tegal, *Indonesia* 63 G13
Tegernsee, *Germany* 25 H7
Teggiano, *Italy* 31 B8
Tegid, L. = Bala, L., *U.K.* . 12 E4
Tegina, *Nigeria* 83 C6
Tegucigalpa, *Honduras* ... 120 D2
Teguidda i-n-Tessoum, *Niger* 83 B6
Tehachapi, *U.S.A.* 117 K8
Tehachapi Mts., *U.S.A.* .. 117 L8
Tehamiyam, *Sudan* 80 D4
Tehilla, *Sudan* 80 D4
Téhini, *Ivory C.* 82 D4
Tehoru, *Indonesia* 63 E7
Tehrān, *Iran* 71 C6
Tehri, *India* 69 D8
Tehuacán, *Mexico* 119 D5
Tehuantepec, *Mexico* 119 D5
Tehuantepec, G. de, *Mexico* 119 D5
Tehuantepec, Istmo de,
   Mexico 119 D6
Teide, *Canary Is.* 37 F3
Teifi →, *U.K.* 13 E3
Teign →, *U.K.* 13 G4
Teignmouth, *U.K.* 13 G4
Teiuş, *Romania* 43 D8
Teixeira Pinto, *Guinea-Biss.* 82 C1
Tejam, *India* 69 E9
Tejen, *Turkmenistan* 50 F7

Tejen →, *Turkmenistan* ... 71 B9
Tejo →, *Europe* 35 F2
Tejon Pass, *U.S.A.* 117 L8
Tekamah, *U.S.A.* 112 E6
Tekapo, L., *N.Z.* 91 K3
Tekax, *Mexico* 119 C7
Teke, *Turkey* 41 E13
Tekeli, *Kazakstan* 50 E8
Tekeze →, *Ethiopia* 81 E4
Tekija, *Serbia, Yug.* 40 B6
Tekirdağ, *Turkey* 41 F11
Tekirdağ □, *Turkey* 41 E11
Tekirova, *Turkey* 39 E12
Tekkali, *India* 67 K14
Tekke, *Turkey* 72 B7
Tekman, *Turkey* 73 C9
Tekoa, *U.S.A.* 114 C5
Tel Aviv-Yafo, *Israel* 75 C3
Tel Lakhish, *Israel* 75 D3
Tel Megiddo, *Israel* 75 C4
Tela, *Honduras* 120 C2
Telanaipura = Jambi,
   Indonesia 62 E2
Telavi, *Georgia* 49 J7
Telč, *Czech Rep.* 26 B8
Telciu, *Romania* 43 C9
Telde, *Canary Is.* 37 G4
Telegraph Creek, *Canada* . 104 B2
Telekhany = Tsyelyakhany,
   Belarus 47 F3
Telemark, *Norway* 9 G12
Telén, *Argentina* 126 D2
Teleneşti, *Moldova* 43 C13
Teleng, *Iran* 71 E9
Teleño, *Spain* 34 C4
Teleorman □, *Romania* ... 43 G10
Teleorman →, *Romania* .. 43 G10
Teles Pires →, *Brazil* ... 122 D5
Telescope Pk., *U.S.A.* ... 117 J9
Teletaye, *Mali* 83 B5
Telfer Mine, *Australia* ... 92 C3
Telford, *U.K.* 13 E5
Telford and Wrekin □, *U.K.* 12 E5
Telfs, *Austria* 26 D4
Télimélé, *Guinea* 82 C2
Teljo, J., *Sudan* 81 E2
Telkwa, *Canada* 104 C3
Tell City, *U.S.A.* 108 G2
Tellicherry, *India* 66 P9
Telluride, *U.S.A.* 115 H10
Teloloapán, *Mexico* 119 D5
Telpos Iz, *Russia* 6 C17
Telsen, *Argentina* 128 E3
Telšiai, *Lithuania* 9 H20
Telšiai □, *Lithuania* 44 C9
Teltow, *Germany* 24 C9
Teluk Anson = Teluk Intan,
   Malaysia 65 K3
Teluk Betung =
   Tanjungkarang
   Telukbetung, *Indonesia* .. 62 F3
Teluk Intan, *Malaysia* 65 K3
Telukbutun, *Indonesia* ... 65 K7
Telukdalem, *Indonesia* ... 62 D1
Tema, *Ghana* 83 D5
Temax, *Mexico* 119 C7
Temba, *S. Africa* 89 D4
Tembagapura, *Indonesia* .. 63 E9
Tembe,
   Dem. Rep. of the Congo . 86 C2
Tembleque, *Spain* 34 F7
Temblor Range, *U.S.A.* .. 117 K7
Teme →, *U.K.* 13 E5
Temecula, *U.S.A.* 117 M9
Temerloh, *Malaysia* 62 D2
Teminabuan, *Indonesia* .. 63 E8
Temir, *Kazakstan* 50 E6
Temirtau, *Kazakstan* 50 D8
Temirtau, *Russia* 50 D9
Temiscamie →, *Canada* .. 103 B5
Témiscaming, *Canada* ... 102 C4
Témiscamingue, L., *Canada* 102 C4
Temnikov, *Russia* 48 C6
Temo →, *Italy* 30 B1
Temosachic, *Mexico* 118 B3
Tempe, *U.S.A.* 115 K8
Tempio Pausánia, *Italy* ... 30 B2
Tempiute, *U.S.A.* 116 H11
Temple, *U.S.A.* 113 K6
Temple B., *Australia* 94 A3
Templemore, *Ireland* 15 D4
Templeton, *U.S.A.* 116 K6
Templeton →, *Australia* .. 94 C2
Templin, *Germany* 24 B9
Tempoal, *Mexico* 119 C5
Temryuk, *Russia* 47 K9
Temska →, *Serbia, Yug.* .. 40 C6
Temuco, *Chile* 128 D2
Temuka, *N.Z.* 91 L3
Tenabo, *Mexico* 119 C6
Tenaha, *U.S.A.* 113 K7
Tenakee Springs, *U.S.A.* . 104 B1
Tenali, *India* 66 L12
Tenancingo, *Mexico* 119 D5
Tenango, *Mexico* 119 D5
Tenasserim, *Burma* 65 F2
Tenasserim □, *Burma* 64 F2
Tenby, *U.K.* 13 F3
Tenda, Colle di, *France* ... 21 D11
Tendaho, *Ethiopia* 81 E5
Tende, *France* 21 D11
Tendelti, *Sudan* 81 E3
Tendrovskaya Kosa, *Ukraine* 47 J6
Tendukhera, *India* 69 H8
Teneida, *Egypt* 80 B2
Tenenkou, *Mali* 82 C4
Ténéré, *Niger* 83 B7
Tenerife, *Canary Is.* 37 F3
Tenerife, Pico, *Canary Is.* .. 37 G1
Teng Xian,
   Guangxi Zhuangzu, China 59 F8

Teng Xian, *Shandong, China* 57 G9
Tengah □, *Indonesia* 63 E6
Tengah, Kepulauan,
   Indonesia 62 F5
Tengchong, *China* 58 E2
Tengchowfu = Penglai,
   China 57 F11
Tenggara □, *Indonesia* ... 63 E6
Tenggarong, *Indonesia* ... 62 E5
Tenggol, Pulau, *Malaysia* .. 65 K4
Tengiz, Ozero, *Kazakstan* .. 50 D7
Tenhult, *Sweden* 11 G8
Tenino, *U.S.A.* 116 D4
Tenkasi, *India* 66 Q10
Tenke, *Katanga,*
   Dem. Rep. of the Congo . 87 E2
Tenke, *Katanga,*
   Dem. Rep. of the Congo . 87 E2
Tenna →, *Italy* 29 E10
Tennant Creek, *Australia* .. 94 B1
Tennessee □, *U.S.A.* 109 H2
Tennessee →, *U.S.A.* 108 G1
Teno, Pta. de, *Canary Is.* .. 37 F3
Tenom, *Malaysia* 62 C5
Tenosique, *Mexico* 119 D6
Tenryū-Gawa →, *Japan* .. 55 G8
Tenterden, *U.K.* 13 F8
Tenterfield, *Australia* 95 D5
Teo, *Spain* 34 C2
Teófilo Otoni, *Brazil* 125 G10
Tepa, *Indonesia* 63 F7
Tepalcatepec →, *Mexico* .. 118 D4
Tepehuanes, *Mexico* 118 B3
Tepelena, *Albania* 40 F4
Tepetongo, *Mexico* 118 C4
Tepic, *Mexico* 118 C4
Teplá, *Czech Rep.* 26 B5
Teplice, *Czech Rep.* 26 A6
Tepoca, C., *Mexico* 118 A2
Tequila, *Mexico* 118 C4
Ter →, *Spain* 32 C8
Ter Apel, *Neths.* 17 B7
Téra, *Niger* 83 C5
Tera →, *Spain* 34 D5
Teraina, *Kiribati* 97 G11
Terakeka, *Sudan* 81 F3
Téramo, *Italy* 29 F10
Terang, *Australia* 95 F3
Terazit, Massif de, *Niger* ... 83 A6
Tercan, *Turkey* 73 C9
Tercero →, *Argentina* ... 126 C3
Terebovlya, *Ukraine* 47 H3
Teregova, *Romania* 42 E7
Tereina, *Sudan* 81 E3
Terek →, *Russia* 49 J8
Tereshka →, *Russia* 48 E8
Teresina, *Brazil* 125 E10
Terespol, *Poland* 45 F10
Terewah, L., *Australia* ... 95 D4
Terges →, *Portugal* 35 H3
Tergnier, *France* 19 C10
Teridgerie Cr. →, *Australia* 95 E4
Terlizzi, *Italy* 31 A9
Terme, *Turkey* 72 B7
Termez = Termiz,
   Uzbekistan 50 F7
Términi Imerese, *Italy* ... 30 E6
Términos, L. de, *Mexico* .. 119 D6
Termiz, *Uzbekistan* 50 F7
Térmoli, *Italy* 29 F12
Ternate, *Indonesia* 63 D7
Terneuzen, *Neths.* 17 C3
Terney, *Russia* 51 E14
Terni, *Italy* 29 F9
Ternitz, *Austria* 26 D9
Ternopil, *Ukraine* 47 H3
Ternopol = Ternopil,
   Ukraine 47 H3
Terowie, *Australia* 95 E2
Terpní, *Greece* 40 F7
Terra Bella, *U.S.A.* 117 K7
Terra Nova Nat. Park,
   Canada 103 C9
Terrace, *Canada* 104 C3
Terrace Bay, *Canada* 102 C2
Terracina, *Italy* 30 A6
Terralba, *Italy* 30 C1
Terranova = Ólbia, *Italy* .. 30 B2
Terrasini, *Italy* 30 D6
Terrassa, *Spain* 32 D7
Terrasson-la-Villedieu,
   France 20 C5
Terre Haute, *U.S.A.* 108 F2
Terrebonne B., *U.S.A.* ... 113 L9
Terrell, *U.S.A.* 113 J6
Terrenceville, *Canada* 103 C9
Terry, *U.S.A.* 112 B2
Terryville, *U.S.A.* 111 E11
Terschelling, *Neths.* 17 A5
Tersko-Kumskiy Kanal →,
   Russia 49 H7
Tertenía, *Italy* 30 C2
Terter →= Tärtär →,
   Azerbaijan 49 K8
Teruel, *Spain* 32 E4
Teruel □, *Spain* 32 E4
Tervola, *Finland* 8 C21
Teryaweyna L., *Australia* .. 95 E3
Tešanj, *Bos.-H.* 42 F3
Teseney, *Eritrea* 81 D4
Tesha →, *Russia* 48 C6
Teshio, *Japan* 54 B10
Teshio-Gawa →, *Japan* ... 54 B10
Tešica, *Serbia, Yug.* 40 C5
Tesiyn Gol →, *Mongolia* .. 60 A4
Teslić, *Bos.-H.* 42 F2
Teslin, *Canada* 104 A2

Teslin →, *Canada* 104 A2
Teslin L., *Canada* 104 A2
Tessalit, *Mali* 83 A5
Tessaoua, *Niger* 83 C6
Tessin, *Germany* 24 A8
Tessit, *Mali* 83 B5
Test →, *U.K.* 13 G6
Testa del Gargano, *Italy* ... 29 G13
Testigos, Is. Las, *Venezuela* 121 D7
Tét, *Hungary* 42 C2
Têt →, *France* 20 F7
Tetachuck L., *Canada* 104 C3
Tetas, Pta., *Chile* 126 A1
Tete, *Mozam.* 87 F3
Tete □, *Mozam.* 87 F3
Teterev →, *Ukraine* 47 G6
Teterow, *Germany* 24 B8
Teteven, *Bulgaria* 41 D8
Tethul →, *Canada* 104 A6
Tetiyev, *Ukraine* 47 H5
Teton →, *U.S.A.* 114 C8
Tétouan, *Morocco* 78 A4
Tetovo, *Macedonia* 40 D4
Tetyushi, *Russia* 48 C9
Teuco →, *Argentina* 126 B3
Teulada, *Italy* 30 D1
Teulon, *Canada* 105 C9
Teun, *Indonesia* 63 F7
Teutoburger Wald, *Germany* 24 C4
Tevere →, *Italy* 29 G9
Teverya, *Israel* 75 C4
Teviot →, *U.K.* 14 F6
Tewantin, *Australia* 95 D5
Tewkesbury, *U.K.* 13 F5
Texada I., *Canada* 104 D4
Texarkana, *Ark., U.S.A.* .. 113 J8
Texarkana, *Tex., U.S.A.* .. 113 J7
Texas, *Australia* 95 D5
Texas □, *U.S.A.* 113 K5
Texas City, *U.S.A.* 113 L7
Texel, *Neths.* 17 A4
Texline, *U.S.A.* 113 G3
Texoma, L., *U.S.A.* 113 J6
Teykovo, *Russia* 48 C11
Teza →, *Russia* 48 B5
Tezin, *Afghan.* 68 B3
Teziutlán, *Mexico* 119 D5
Tezpur, *India* 67 F18
Tezzeron L., *Canada* 104 C4
Tha-anne →, *Canada* 105 A10
Tha Deua, *Laos* 64 D4
Tha Deua, *Laos* 64 C3
Tha Pla, *Thailand* 64 D3
Tha Rua, *Thailand* 64 E3
Tha Sala, *Thailand* 65 H2
Tha Song Yang, *Thailand* .. 64 D1
Thaba Putsoa, *Lesotho* ... 89 D4
Thabana Ntlenyana, *Lesotho* 89 D4
Thabazimbi, *S. Africa* 89 C4
Thādiq, *Si. Arabia* 70 E5
Thai Binh, *Vietnam* 58 G6
Thai Muang, *Thailand* ... 65 H2
Thai Nguyen, *Vietnam* ... 58 G5
Thailand ■, *Asia* 64 E4
Thailand, G. of, *Asia* 64 G3
Thakhek, *Laos* 64 D5
Thal, *Pakistan* 68 C4
Thal Desert, *Pakistan* 68 D4
Thala La, *Burma* 67 E20
Thalabarivat, *Cambodia* .. 64 F5
Thallon, *Australia* 95 D4
Thalwil, *Switz.* 25 H4
Thames →, *Canada* 102 D3
Thames →, *U.K.* 13 F8
Thames →, *U.S.A.* 111 E12
Thames Estuary, *U.K.* ... 13 F8
Thamesford, *Canada* 110 C4
Thamesville, *Canada* 110 D3
Than, *India* 68 H4
Than Uyen, *Vietnam* 64 B4
Thana Gazi, *India* 68 F7
Thandla, *India* 68 H6
Thane, *India* 66 K8
Thanesar, *India* 68 D7
Thanet, I. of, *U.K.* 13 F9
Thangool, *Australia* 94 C5
Thanh Hoa, *Vietnam* 64 C5
Thanh Hung, *Vietnam* ... 65 H5
Thanh Pho Ho Chi Minh =
   Phanh Bho Ho Chi Minh,
   Vietnam 65 G6
Thanh Thuy, *Vietnam* ... 64 A5
Thanjavur, *India* 66 P11
Thann, *France* 19 E14
Thano Bula Khan, *Pakistan* 68 G2
Thaolinta L., *Canada* 105 A9
Thaon-les-Vosges, *France* . 19 D13
Thap Sakae, *Thailand* 65 G2
Thap Than, *Thailand* 64 E2
Thar Desert, *India* 68 F5
Tharad, *India* 68 G4
Thargomindah, *Australia* .. 95 D3
Tharrawaddy, *Burma* 67 L19
Tharthār, Mileh, *Iraq* ... 70 C4
Tharthār, W. ath →, *Iraq* . 70 C4
Thasopoúla, *Greece* 41 F8
Thásos, *Greece* 41 F8
That Khe, *Vietnam* 58 F6
Thatcher, *Ariz., U.S.A.* .. 115 K9
Thatcher, *Colo., U.S.A.* .. 113 G2
Thaton, *Burma* 67 L20
Thau, Bassin de, *France* .. 20 E7
Thaungdut, *Burma* 67 G19
Thayer, *U.S.A.* 113 G9
Thayetmyo, *Burma* 67 K19
Thazi, *Burma* 67 J20
The Alberga →, *Australia* . 95 D2
The Bight, *Bahamas* 121 B4
The Coorong, *Australia* ... 95 F2
The Dalles, *U.S.A.* 114 D3

The English Company's Is.,
   Australia 94 A2
The Frome →, *Australia* .. 95 D2
The Great Divide = Great
   Dividing Ra., *Australia* .. 94 C4
The Hague = 's-Gravenhage,
   Neths. 17 B4
The Hamilton →, *Australia* 95 D2
The Macumba →, *Australia* 95 D2
The Neales →, *Australia* .. 95 D2
The Officer →, *Australia* .. 93 E5
The Pas, *Canada* 105 C8
The Range, *Zimbabwe* 87 F3
The Rock, *Australia* 95 F4
The Salt L., *Australia* 95 E3
The Sandheads, *India* 69 J13
The Stevenson →, *Australia* 95 D2
The Warburton →, *Australia* 95 D2
The Woodlands, *U.S.A.* ... 113 K7
Thebes = Thívai, *Greece* ... 38 C5
Thebes, *Egypt* 80 B3
Thedford, *Canada* 110 C3
Thedford, *U.S.A.* 112 E4
Theebine, *Australia* 95 D5
Thekulthili L., *Canada* ... 105 A7
Thelon →, *Canada* 105 A8
Thénezay, *France* 18 F6
Thenon, *France* 20 C5
Theodore, *Australia* 94 C5
Theodore, *Canada* 105 C8
Theodore, *U.S.A.* 109 K1
Theodore Roosevelt National
   Memorial Park, *U.S.A.* .. 112 B3
Theodore Roosevelt Res.,
   U.S.A. 115 K8
Thepha, *Thailand* 65 J3
Thérain →, *France* 19 C9
Theresa, *U.S.A.* 111 B9
Thermaïkós Kólpos, *Greece* 40 F6
Thermí, *Greece* 39 B8
Thermopolis, *U.S.A.* 114 E9
Thermopylae P., *Greece* ... 38 C4
Thesprotía □, *Greece* 38 B2
Thessalía □, *Greece* 38 B4
Thessalon, *Canada* 102 C3
Thessaloníki, *Greece* 40 F6
Thessaloníki □, *Greece* ... 40 F7
Thessaloniki, Gulf of =
   Thermaïkós Kólpos,
   Greece 40 F6
Thessaly = Thessalía □,
   Greece 38 B4
Thetford, *U.K.* 13 E8
Thetford Mines, *Canada* .. 103 C5
Theun →, *Laos* 64 C5
Theunissen, *S. Africa* 88 D4
Thevenard, *Australia* 95 E1
Thiámis →, *Greece* 38 B2
Thiberville, *France* 18 C7
Thibodaux, *U.S.A.* 113 L9
Thicket Portage, *Canada* .. 105 B9
Thief River Falls, *U.S.A.* .. 112 A6
Thiel Mts., *Antarctica* ... 5 E16
Thiene, *Italy* 29 C8
Thiérache, *France* 19 C10
Thiers, *France* 20 C7
Thiès, *Senegal* 82 C1
Thiesi, *Italy* 30 B1
Thiet, *Sudan* 81 F2
Thika, *Kenya* 86 C4
Thikombia, *Fiji* 91 B9
Thille-Boubacar, *Senegal* .. 82 B1
Thimphu, *Bhutan* 67 F16
þingvallavatn, *Iceland* 8 D3
Thionville, *France* 19 C13
Thíra, *Greece* 39 E7
Thirasía, *Greece* 39 E7
Third Cataract, *Sudan* 80 D3
Thirsk, *U.K.* 12 C6
Thisted, *Denmark* 11 H2
Thistle I., *Australia* 95 F2
Thívai, *Greece* 38 C5
Thiviers, *France* 20 C4
Thizy, *France* 19 F11
þjórsá →, *Iceland* 8 E3
Thlewiaza →, *Man., Canada* 105 B8
Thlewiaza →, *N.W.T.,*
   Canada 105 A10
Thmar Puok, *Cambodia* ... 64 F4
Tho Vinh, *Vietnam* 64 C5
Thoa →, *Canada* 105 A7
Thoen, *Thailand* 64 D2
Thoeng, *Thailand* 64 C3
Thohoyandou, *S. Africa* ... 85 J6
Tholdi, *Pakistan* 69 B7
Thomas, *U.S.A.* 113 H5
Thomas, L., *Australia* 95 D2
Thomaston, *U.S.A.* 109 J3
Thomasville, *Ala., U.S.A.* .. 109 K2
Thomasville, *Ga., U.S.A.* .. 109 K3
Thomasville, *N.C., U.S.A.* . 109 H5
Thompson, *Canada* 105 B9
Thompson, *U.S.A.* 111 E9
Thompson →, *Canada* ... 104 C4
Thompson Falls, *U.S.A.* ... 114 C6
Thompson Pk., *U.S.A.* ... 114 F2
Thompson Springs, *U.S.A.* . 115 G9
Thompsontown, *U.S.A.* ... 110 F7
Thomson, *U.S.A.* 109 J4
Thomson →, *Australia* ... 94 C3
Thomson's Falls =
   Nyahururu, *Kenya* 86 B4
Thônes, *France* 21 C10
Thonon-les-Bains, *France* . 19 F13
Thorez, *Ukraine* 47 H10
þórisvatn, *Iceland* 8 D4
Thornaby on Tees, *U.K.* .. 12 C6
Thornbury, *Canada* 110 B4
Thorne, *U.K.* 12 D7
Thornhill, *Canada* 104 C3

Thorold, *Canada* 110 C5
þórshöfn, *Iceland* 8 C6
Thouarcé, *France* 18 E6
Thouars, *France* 18 F6
Thouet →, *France* 18 E6
Thouin, C., *Australia* 92 D2
Thousand Oaks, *U.S.A.* .. 117 L8
Thrace, *Turkey* 41 F10
Thrakikón Pélagos, *Greece* . 41 F8
Three Forks, *U.S.A.* 114 D8
Three Gorges Dam, *China* . 59 B8
Three Hills, *Canada* 104 C6
Three Hummock I.,
  Australia 94 G3
Three Points, C., *Ghana* ... 82 E4
Three Rivers, *Calif., U.S.A.* 116 J8
Three Rivers, *Tex., U.S.A.* 113 L5
Three Sisters, *U.S.A.* 114 D3
Three Springs, *Australia* .. 93 E2
Throssell, L., *Australia* 93 E3
Throssell Ra., *Australia* ... 92 D3
Thuan Hoa, *Vietnam* 65 H5
Thubun Lakes, *Canada* ... 105 A6
Thueyts, *France* 21 D8
Thuin, *Belgium* 17 D4
Thuir, *France* 20 F6
Thule = Qaanaaq,
  Greenland 4 B4
Thun, *Switz.* 25 J3
Thunder B., *U.S.A.* 110 B1
Thunder Bay, *Canada* 102 C2
Thunersee, *Switz.* 25 J3
Thung Song, *Thailand* 65 H2
Thunkar, *Bhutan* 67 F17
Thuong Tra, *Vietnam* 64 D6
Thur →, *Switz.* 25 H5
Thurgau □, *Switz.* 25 H5
Thüringen □, *Germany* ... 24 D6
Thüringer Wald, *Germany* . 24 E6
Thurles, *Ireland* 15 D4
Thurn P., *Austria* 26 D5
Thurrock □, *U.K.* 13 F8
Thursday I., *Australia* 94 A3
Thurso, *Canada* 102 C4
Thurso, *U.K.* 14 C5
Thurso →, *U.K.* 14 C5
Thurston I., *Antarctica* 5 D16
Thury-Harcourt, *France* ... 18 D6
Thutade L., *Canada* 104 B3
Thy, *Denmark* 11 H2
Thyborøn, *Denmark* 11 H2
Thyolo, *Malawi* 87 F4
Thysville = Mbanza Ngungu,
  Dem. Rep. of the Congo . 84 F2
Ti-n-Amzi →, *Niger* 83 B5
Ti-n-Barraouene, O. →,
  Africa 83 B5
Ti-n-Zaouatène, *Algeria* ... 83 B5
Ti Tree, *Australia* 94 C1
Tiadiaye, *Senegal* 82 C1
Tian Shan, *Asia* 60 B3
Tianchang, *China* 59 A12
Tiandeng, *China* 58 F6
Tiandong, *China* 58 F6
Tian'e, *China* 58 E6
Tianhe, *China* 58 E7
Tianjin, *China* 57 E9
Tiankoura, *Burkina Faso* .. 82 C4
Tianlin, *China* 58 E6
Tianmen, *China* 59 B9
Tianquan, *China* 58 B4
Tianshui, *China* 56 G3
Tiantai, *China* 59 C13
Tianyang, *China* 58 F6
Tianzhen, *China* 56 D8
Tianzhu, *China* 58 D7
Tianzhuangtai, *China* 57 D12
Tiaret, *Algeria* 78 A6
Tiassalé, *Ivory C.* 82 D4
Tibagi, *Brazil* 127 A5
Tibagi →, *Brazil* 127 A5
Tibati, *Cameroon* 83 D7
Tibe, *Ethiopia* 81 F4
Tiber = Tevere →, *Italy* .. 29 G9
Tiberias = Teverya, *Israel* . 75 C4
Tiberias, L. = Yam
  Kinneret, *Israel* 75 C4
Tibesti, *Chad* 79 D9
Tibet = Xizang Zizhiqu □,
  China 60 C3
Tibet, Plateau of, *Asia* 52 F12
Tibiao, *Phil.* 61 F5
Tibiri, *Niger* 83 C6
Tibleş, Vf., *Romania* 43 C9
Tibleşului, Munţii, *Romania* 43 C9
Tibnī, *Syria* 70 C3
Tibooburra, *Australia* 95 D3
Tibro, *Sweden* 11 F8
Tiburón, I., *Mexico* 118 B2
Ticao, I., *Phil.* 61 E5
Tîchît, *Mauritania* 82 B3
Ticho, *Ethiopia* 81 F4
Ticino □, *Switz.* 25 J4
Ticino →, *Italy* 28 C5
Ticleni, *Romania* 43 F8
Ticonderoga, *U.S.A.* 111 C11
Ticul, *Mexico* 119 C7
Tidaholm, *Sweden* 11 F7
Tidan, *Sweden* 11 F8
Tiddim, *Burma* 67 H18
Tidioute, *U.S.A.* 110 E5
Tidjikja, *Mauritania* 82 B2
Tidore, *Indonesia* 63 D7
Tiébissou, *Ivory C.* 82 D3
Tiel, *Neths.* 17 C5
Tiel, *Senegal* 82 C1
Tieling, *China* 57 C12
Tielt, *Belgium* 17 C3
Tien Shan = Tian Shan, *Asia* 60 B3
Tien-tsin = Tianjin, *China* . 57 E9
Tien Yen, *Vietnam* 64 B6

T'ienching = Tianjin, *China* 57 E9
Tienen, *Belgium* 17 D4
Tiénigbé, *Ivory C.* 82 D3
Tientsin = Tianjin, *China* .. 57 E9
Tieri, *Australia* 94 C4
Tierp, *Sweden* 10 D11
Tierra Amarilla, *Chile* 126 B1
Tierra Amarilla, *U.S.A.* .. 115 H10
Tierra Colorada, *Mexico* .. 119 D5
Tierra de Barros, *Spain* 35 G4
Tierra de Campos, *Spain* .. 34 C6
Tierra del Fuego, I. Gr. de,
  Argentina 122 J4
Tiétar →, *Spain* 34 F4
Tieté →, *Brazil* 127 A5
Tiffin, *U.S.A.* 108 E4
Tiflis = Tbilisi, *Georgia* ... 49 K7
Tifton, *U.S.A.* 109 K4
Tifu, *Indonesia* 63 E7
Tighina, *Moldova* 43 D14
Tigil, *Russia* 51 D16
Tignish, *Canada* 103 C7
Tigray □, *Ethiopia* 81 E4
Tigre →, *Peru* 124 D4
Tigre →, *Venezuela* 124 B6
Tigris = Dijlah, Nahr →,
  Asia 70 D5
Tigveni, *Romania* 43 E9
Tigyaing, *Burma* 67 H20
Tîh, Gebel el, *Egypt* 80 B3
Tijara, *India* 68 F7
Tijuana, *Mexico* 117 N9
Tikal, *Guatemala* 120 C2
Tikamgarh, *India* 69 G8
Tikaré, *Burkina Faso* 83 C4
Tikhoretsk, *Russia* 49 H5
Tikhvin, *Russia* 46 C7
Tiko, *Cameroon* 83 E6
Tikrīt, *Iraq* 70 C4
Tiksi, *Russia* 51 B13
Tilamuta, *Indonesia* 63 D6
Tilburg, *Neths.* 17 C5
Tilbury, *Canada* 102 D3
Tilbury, *U.K.* 13 F8
Tilcara, *Argentina* 126 A2
Tilden, *U.S.A.* 112 D6
Tilemses, *Niger* 83 B5
Tilemsi, Vallée du, *Mali* ... 83 B5
Tilhar, *India* 69 F8
Tilichiki, *Russia* 51 C17
Tílissos, *Greece* 36 D7
Till →, *U.K.* 12 B5
Tillabéri, *Niger* 83 C5
Tillamook, *U.S.A.* 114 D2
Tillberga, *Sweden* 10 E10
Tillia, *Niger* 83 B5
Tillsonburg, *Canada* 102 D3
Tillyeria □, *Cyprus* 36 D11
Tilogne, *Senegal* 82 B2
Tílos, *Greece* 39 E9
Tilpa, *Australia* 95 E3
Tilsit = Sovetsk, *Russia* ... 9 J19
Tilt →, *U.K.* 14 E5
Tilton, *U.S.A.* 111 C13
Tiltonsville, *U.S.A.* 110 F4
Tim, *Denmark* 11 H2
Timagami, L., *Canada* 102 C3
Timaru, *N.Z.* 91 L3
Timashevo, *Russia* 48 D10
Timashevsk, *Russia* 49 H4
Timau, *Kenya* 86 B4
Timbákion, *Greece* 36 D6
Timbedgha, *Mauritania* ... 82 B3
Timber Creek, *Australia* .. 92 C5
Timber Lake, *U.S.A.* 112 C4
Timber Mt., *U.S.A.* 116 H10
Timbo, *Guinea* 82 C2
Timbo, *Liberia* 82 D3
Timbuktu = Tombouctou,
  Mali 82 B4
Timeiaouine, *Algeria* 83 A5
Timétrine, Mts., *Mali* 83 B4
Timfi Óros, *Greece* 38 B2
Timfristós, Óros, *Greece* .. 38 C3
Timi, *Cyprus* 36 E11
Tímia, *Niger* 83 B6
Timimoun, *Algeria* 78 C6
Timiş = Tamiš →,
  Serbia, Yug. 42 F5
Timiş □, *Romania* 42 E6
Timişoara, *Romania* 42 E6
Timmersdala, *Sweden* 11 F7
Timmins, *Canada* 102 C3
Timok →, *Serbia, Yug.* ... 40 B6
Timor, *Indonesia* 63 F7
Timor Sea, *Ind. Oc.* 92 B4
Timor Timur □, *Indonesia* . 63 F7
Timrå, *Sweden* 10 B11
Tin Can Bay, *Australia* ... 95 D5
Tin Ethisane, *Mali* 83 B4
Tin Gornai, *Mali* 83 B4
Tin Mt., *U.S.A.* 116 J9
Tina →, *S. Africa* 89 E4
Tina, Khalîg el, *Egypt* 80 A3
Tinaca Pt., *Phil.* 63 J6
Tinajo, *Canary Is.* 37 E6
Tinca, *Romania* 42 D6
Tindal, *Australia* 92 B5
Tindouf, *Algeria* 78 C4
Tinée →, *France* 21 E11
Tineo, *Spain* 34 B4
Ting Jiang →, *China* 59 E11
Tingi, Pulau, *Malaysia* 65 L5
Tinh Bien, *Vietnam* 65 G5
Tinnevelly = Tirunelveli,
  India 66 Q10

Tinogasta, *Argentina* 126 B2
Tínos, *Greece* 39 D7
Tiñoso, C., *Spain* 33 H3
Tinpahar, *India* 69 G12
Tintina, *Argentina* 126 B3
Tintinara, *Australia* 95 F3
Tioga, N. Dak., *U.S.A.* ... 112 A3
Tioga, Pa., *U.S.A.* 110 E7
Tioman, Pulau, *Malaysia* .. 65 L5
Tione di Trento, *Italy* 28 B7
Tionesta, *U.S.A.* 110 E5
Tipongpani, *India* 67 F19
Tipperary, *Ireland* 15 D3
Tipperary □, *Ireland* 15 D4
Tipton, Calif., *U.S.A.* 116 J7
Tipton, Iowa, *U.S.A.* 112 E9
Tipton Mt., *U.S.A.* 117 K12
Tiptonville, *U.S.A.* 113 G10
Tīrān, *Iran* 71 C6
Tīrān, Si. Arabia* 80 B3
Tirana, *Albania* 40 E3
Tiranë = Tirana, *Albania* . 40 E3
Tirano, *Italy* 28 B7
Tiraspol, *Moldova* 43 D14
Tîrdout, *Mali* 83 B4
Tire, *Turkey* 39 C9
Tirebolu, *Turkey* 73 B8
Tiree, *U.K.* 14 E2
Tiree, Passage of, *U.K.* ... 14 E2
Tîrgovişte = Târgovişte,
  Romania 43 F10
Tîrgu-Jiu = Târgu-Jiu,
  Romania 43 E8
Tîrgu Mureş = Târgu Mureş,
  Romania 43 D9
Tirich Mir, *Pakistan* 66 A7
Tiriolo, *Italy* 31 D9
Tiriro, *Guinea* 82 C3
Tírnavos, *Greece* 38 B4
Tirodi, *India* 66 J11
Tirol □, *Austria* 26 D3
Tirschenreuth, *Germany* .. 25 F8
Tirso →, *Italy* 30 C1
Tirstrup, *Denmark* 11 H4
Tiruchchirappalli, *India* ... 66 P11
Tirunelveli, *India* 66 Q10
Tirupati, *India* 66 N11
Tiruppur, *India* 66 P10
Tiruvannamalai, *India* 66 N11
Tisa, *India* 68 C7
Tisa →, *Serbia, Yug.* 42 E5
Tisdale, *Canada* 105 C8
Tishomingo, *U.S.A.* 113 H6
Tisjön, *Sweden* 10 D7
Tisnaren, *Sweden* 11 F9
Tišnov, *Czech Rep.* 27 B9
Tisovec, *Slovak Rep.* 27 C12
Tisza = Tisa →,
  Serbia, Yug. 42 E5
Tiszaföldvár, *Hungary* 42 D5
Tiszafüred, *Hungary* 42 C5
Tiszalök, *Hungary* 42 B6
Tiszavasvári, *Hungary* 42 C6
Tit-Ary, *Russia* 51 B13
Titaguas, *Spain* 32 F3
Titao, *Burkina Faso* 83 C4
Titel, *Serbia, Yug.* 42 E5
Tithwal, *Pakistan* 69 B5
Titicaca, L., S. Amer.* 122 E4
Titisee, *Germany* 25 H4
Titiwangsa, Banjaran,
  Malaysia 65 K3
Tito, *Italy* 31 B8
Titograd = Podgorica,
  Montenegro, Yug. 40 D3
Titova Korenica, *Croatia* .. 29 D12
Titovo Užice = Užice,
  Serbia, Yug. 42 E5
Titu, *Romania* 43 F10
Titule,
  Dem. Rep. of the Congo . 86 B2
Titusville, Fla., *U.S.A.* 109 L5
Titusville, Pa., *U.S.A.* 110 E5
Tivaouane, *Senegal* 82 C1
Tivat, *Montenegro, Yug.* .. 40 D2
Tiverton, *U.K.* 13 G4
Tívoli, *Italy* 29 G9
Tiyo, *Eritrea* 81 E5
Tizi-Ouzou, *Algeria* 78 A6
Tizimín, *Mexico* 119 C7
Tjæreborg, *Denmark* 11 J2
Tjällmo, *Sweden* 11 F9
Tjeggelvas, *Sweden* 8 C17
Tjirebon = Cirebon,
  Indonesia 63 G13
Tjörn, *Sweden* 11 F5
Tjibuli = Tqibuli, *Georgia* . 49 J6
Tkvarcheli = Tqvarcheli,
  Georgia 49 J5
Tlacotalpan, *Mexico* 119 D5
Tlahualilo, *Mexico* 118 B4
Tlaquepaque, *Mexico* 118 C4
Tlaxcala, *Mexico* 119 D5
Tlaxcala □, *Mexico* 119 D5
Tlaxiaco, *Mexico* 119 D5
Tlemcen, *Algeria* 78 B5
Tłuszcz, *Poland* 45 F8
Tlyarata, *Russia* 49 J8
To Bong, *Vietnam* 64 F7
Toad →, *Canada* 104 B4
Toad River, *Canada* 104 B3
Toamasina, *Madag.* 89 B8
Toamasina □, *Madag.* 89 B8
Toay, *Argentina* 126 D3
Toba, *China* 58 B1
Toba, *Japan* 55 G8
Toba, Danau, *Indonesia* .. 62 D1
Toba Kakar, *Pakistan* 68 D3
Toba Tek Singh, *Pakistan* . 68 D5
Tobago, *W. Indies* 121 D7
Tobarra, *Spain* 33 G3

Tobelo, *Indonesia* 63 D7
Tobermory, *Canada* 102 C3
Tobermory, *U.K.* 14 E2
Tobi, Pac. Oc.* 63 D8
Tobin, *U.S.A.* 116 F5
Tobin, L., *Australia* 92 D4
Tobin L., *Canada* 105 C8
Toboali, *Indonesia* 62 E3
Tobol →, *Russia* 50 D7
Toboli, *Indonesia* 63 E6
Tobolsk, *Russia* 50 D7
Tobruk = Tubruq, *Libya* .. 79 B10
Tobyhanna, *U.S.A.* 111 E9
Tobyl = Tobol →, *Russia* . 50 D7
Tocantinópolis, *Brazil* 125 E9
Tocantins □, *Brazil* 125 F9
Tocantins →, *Brazil* 122 D6
Toccoa, *U.S.A.* 109 H4
Toce →, *Italy* 28 C5
Tochi →, *Pakistan* 68 C4
Tochigi, *Japan* 55 F9
Tochigi □, *Japan* 55 F9
Tocina, *Spain* 35 H5
Töcksfors, *Sweden* 10 E5
Toconao, *Chile* 126 A2
Tocopilla, *Chile* 126 A1
Tocumwal, *Australia* 95 F4
Tocuyo →, *Venezuela* 124 A5
Todd →, *Australia* 94 C2
Todeli, *Indonesia* 63 E6
Todenyang, *Kenya* 86 B4
Todgarh, *India* 68 G5
Todi, *Italy* 29 F9
Todos os Santos, B. de,
  Brazil 125 F11
Todos Santos, *Mexico* 118 C2
Todtnau, *Germany* 25 H3
Toe Hd., *U.K.* 14 D1
Toecé, *Burkina Faso* 83 C4
Tofield, *Canada* 104 C6
Tofino, *Canada* 104 D3
Tofua, *Tonga* 91 D11
Tōgane, *Japan* 55 G10
Togba, *Mauritania* 82 B2
Togian, Kepulauan,
  Indonesia 63 E6
Togliatti, *Russia* 48 D9
Togo ■, *W. Afr.* 83 D5
Togtoh, *China* 56 D6
Tohma →, *Turkey* 72 C7
Tōhoku □, *Japan* 54 E10
Töhöm, *Mongolia* 56 B5
Toinya, *Sudan* 81 F2
Toiyabe Range, *U.S.A.* ... 114 G5
Tojikiston = Tajikistan ■,
  Asia 50 F8
Tojo, *Indonesia* 63 E6
Tōjō, *Japan* 55 G6
Tok, *U.S.A.* 100 B5
Tok-do, *Japan* 55 F5
Tokachi-Dake, *Japan* 54 C11
Tokachi-Gawa →, *Japan* . 54 C11
Tokaj, *Hungary* 42 B6
Tokala, *Indonesia* 63 E6
Tōkamachi, *Japan* 55 F9
Tokanui, *N.Z.* 91 M2
Tokar, *Sudan* 80 D4
Tokara-Rettō, *Japan* 55 K4
Tokarahi, *N.Z.* 91 L3
Tokashiki-Shima, *Japan* .. 55 L3
Tokat, *Turkey* 72 B7
Tŏkch'ŏn, N. Korea* 57 E14
Tokeland, *U.S.A.* 116 D3
Tokelau Is., Pac. Oc.* 96 H10
Tokmak, *Kyrgyzstan* 50 E8
Tokmak, *Ukraine* 47 J8
Toko Ra., *Australia* 94 C2
Tokoro-Gawa →, *Japan* .. 54 B12
Tokuno-Shima, *Japan* 55 L4
Tokushima, *Japan* 55 G7
Tokushima □, *Japan* 55 H7
Tokuyama, *Japan* 55 G5
Tōkyō, *Japan* 55 G9
Tolaga Bay, *N.Z.* 91 H7
Tolbukhin = Dobrich,
  Bulgaria 41 C11
Toledo, *Brazil* 127 A5
Toledo, *Spain* 34 F6
Toledo, Ohio, *U.S.A.* 108 E4
Toledo, Oreg., *U.S.A.* 114 D2
Toledo, Wash., *U.S.A.* ... 114 C2
Toledo, Montes de, *Spain* . 35 F6
Toledo Bend Reservoir,
  U.S.A. 113 K8
Tolentino, *Italy* 29 E10
Tolfa, *Italy* 29 F8
Tolga, *Australia* 94 B4
Toliara, *Madag.* 89 C7
Toliara □, *Madag.* 89 C8
Tolima, *Colombia* 124 C3
Tolitoli, *Indonesia* 63 D6
Tolkmicko, *Poland* 44 D6
Tollarp, *Sweden* 11 J7
Tollensesee, *Germany* 24 B9
Tollhouse, *U.S.A.* 116 H7
Tolmachevo, *Russia* 46 C5
Tolmezzo, *Italy* 29 B10
Tolmin, *Slovenia* 29 B10
Tolna, *Hungary* 42 D3
Tolna □, *Hungary* 42 D3
Tolo, Teluk, *Indonesia* 63 E6
Tolochin = Talachyn,
  Belarus 46 E5
Tolosa, *Spain* 32 B2
Tolox, *Spain* 35 J6
Toluca, *Mexico* 119 D5
Tom Burke, S. Africa* 89 C4
Tom Price, *Australia* 92 D2
Toma, *Burkina Faso* 82 C4

Tomah, *U.S.A.* 112 D9
Tomahawk, *U.S.A.* 112 C10
Tomai, *Moldova* 43 D13
Tomakomai, *Japan* 54 C10
Tomales, *U.S.A.* 116 G4
Tomales B., *U.S.A.* 116 G3
Tomar, *Portugal* 35 F2
Tómaros, Óros, *Greece* ... 38 B2
Tomarza, *Turkey* 72 C6
Tomaszów Lubelski, *Poland* 45 H10
Tomaszów Mazowiecki,
  Poland 45 G7
Tomatlán, *Mexico* 118 D3
Tombadonkéa, *Guinea* 82 C2
Tombador, Serra do, *Brazil* 124 F7
Tombe, *Sudan* 81 F3
Tombigbee →, *U.S.A.* ... 109 K2
Tombouctou, *Mali* 82 B4
Tombstone, *U.S.A.* 115 L8
Tombua, *Angola* 88 B1
Tomé, *Chile* 126 D1
Tomelilla, *Sweden* 11 J7
Tomelloso, *Spain* 35 F7
Tomini, *Indonesia* 63 D6
Tomini, Teluk, *Indonesia* .. 63 E6
Tominian, *Mali* 82 C4
Tomiño, *Spain* 34 D2
Tomintoul, *U.K.* 14 D5
Tomislavgrad, Bos.-H.* ... 42 G2
Tomkinson Ranges, *Australia* 93 E4
Tommot, *Russia* 51 D13
Tomnop Ta Suos, *Cambodia* 65 G5
Tomo →, *Colombia* 124 B5
Toms Place, *U.S.A.* 116 H8
Toms River, *U.S.A.* 111 G10
Tomsk, *Russia* 50 D9
Tomtabacken, *Sweden* ... 11 G8
Tona, *Spain* 32 D7
Tonalá, *Mexico* 119 D6
Tonale, Passo del, *Italy* ... 28 B7
Tonantins, *Brazil* 124 D5
Tonasket, *U.S.A.* 114 B4
Tonawanda, *U.S.A.* 110 D6
Tonbridge, *U.K.* 13 F8
Tondano, *Indonesia* 63 D6
Tondela, *Portugal* 34 E2
Tønder, *Denmark* 11 K2
Tondi Kiwindi, *Niger* 83 C5
Tondibi, *Mali* 83 B4
Tondoro, *Namibia* 88 B2
Tone →, *Australia* 93 F2
Tone-Gawa →, *Japan* 55 F9
Tonekābon, *Iran* 71 B6
Tong Xian, *China* 56 E9
Tonga ■, Pac. Oc.* 91 D11
Tonga Trench, *Pac. Oc.* .. 96 J10
Tong'an, *China* 59 E12
Tongaat, S. Africa* 89 D5
Tongareva, Cook Is.* 97 H12
Tongatapu, *Tonga* 91 E12
Tongbai, *China* 59 A9
Tongcheng, Anhui, *China* . 59 B11
Tongcheng, Hubei, *China* . 59 C9
Tongch'ŏn-ni, N. Korea* ... 57 E14
Tongchuan, *China* 56 G5
Tongdao, *China* 58 D7
Tongeren, *Belgium* 17 D5
Tonggu, *China* 59 C10
Tongguan, *China* 56 G6
Tonghai, *China* 58 E4
Tonghua, *China* 57 D13
Tongjiang, *China* 58 B6
Tongjosŏn Man, N. Korea* . 57 E15
Tongking, G. of, *Asia* 64 C7
Tongking, G. of = Tonkin,
  G. of, *Asia* 64 B7
Tongliang, *China* 58 C6
Tongliao, *China* 57 C12
Tongling, *China* 59 B11
Tonglu, *China* 59 C12
Tongnae, S. Korea* 57 G15
Tongobory, *Madag.* 89 C7
Tongoy, *Chile* 126 C1
Tongren, *China* 58 D7
Tongres = Tongeren,
  Belgium 17 D5
Tongsa Dzong, *Bhutan* ... 67 F17
Tongue, *U.K.* 14 C4
Tongue →, *U.S.A.* 112 B2
Tongwei, *China* 56 G3
Tongxiang, *China* 59 B13
Tongxin, *China* 56 F3
Tongyang, N. Korea* 57 E14
Tongyu, *China* 57 B12
Tongzi, *China* 58 C6
Tonj, *Sudan* 81 F2
Tonj →, *Sudan* 81 F2
Tonk, *India* 68 F6
Tonkawa, *U.S.A.* 113 G6
Tonkin = Bac Phan, *Vietnam* 64 B5
Tonkin, G. of, *Asia* 64 B7
Tonle Sap, *Cambodia* 64 F4
Tonnay-Charente, *France* . 20 C3
Tonneins, *France* 20 D4
Tonnerre, *France* 19 E10
Tönning, *Germany* 24 A4
Tono, *Japan* 54 E10
Tonopah, *U.S.A.* 115 G5
Tonosí, *Panama* 120 E3
Tons →, Haryana, *India* .. 68 D7
Tons →, Ut. P., *India* 69 D8
Tønsberg, *Norway* 9 G14
Tonya, *Turkey* 73 B8
Toobanna, *Australia* 94 B4
Toodyay, *Australia* 93 F2
Tooele, *U.S.A.* 114 F7
Toompine, *Australia* 95 D3
Toora, *Australia* 95 F4
Toora-Khem, *Russia* 51 D10
Toowoomba, *Australia* ... 95 D5

Top Springs, Australia 92 C5
Topalu, Romania 43 F13
Topaz, U.S.A. 116 G7
Topeka, U.S.A. 112 F7
Topl'a →, Slovak Rep. ... 27 C14
Topley, Canada 104 C3
Toplica →, Serbia, Yug. ... 40 C5
Topliţa, Romania 43 D10
Topocalma, Pta., Chile 126 C1
Topock, U.S.A. 117 L12
Topola, Serbia, Yug. 40 B4
Topolčani, Macedonia 40 E5
Topol'čany, Slovak Rep. ... 27 C11
Topolnitsa →, Bulgaria ... 41 D8
Topoloveni, Romania 43 F10
Topolovgrad, Bulgaria 41 D10
Topolvăţu Mare, Romania . 42 E6
Toppenish, U.S.A. 114 C3
Topraisar, Romania 43 F13
Topusko, Croatia 29 C12
Torà, Spain 32 D6
Tora Kit, Sudan 81 E3
Toraka Vestale, Madag. .. 89 B7
Torata, Peru 124 G4
Torbalı, Turkey 39 C9
Torbat-e Heydārīyeh, Iran . 71 C8
Torbat-e Jām, Iran 71 C9
Torbay, Canada 103 C9
Torbay □, U.K. 13 G4
Torbjörntorp, Sweden 11 F7
Tordesillas, Spain 34 D6
Töreboda, Sweden 11 F8
Torekov, Sweden 11 H6
Torellò, Spain 32 C7
Toreno, Spain 34 C4
Torfaen □, U.K. 13 F4
Torgau, Germany 24 D8
Torgelow, Germany 24 B10
Torhamn, Sweden 11 H9
Torhout, Belgium 17 C3
Tori, Ethiopia 81 F3
Tori-Shima, Japan 55 J10
Torigni-sur-Vire, France .. 18 C6
Torija, Spain 32 E1
Torin, Mexico 118 B2
Torino, Italy 28 C4
Torit, Sudan 81 G3
Torkamān, Iran 70 B5
Torkovichi, Russia 46 C6
Tormac, Romania 42 E6
Tormes →, Spain 34 D4
Tornado Mt., Canada 104 D6
Tornal'a, Slovak Rep. 27 C13
Torne älv →, Sweden 8 D21
Torneå = Tornio, Finland .. 8 D21
Torneträsk, Sweden 8 B18
Tornio, Finland 8 D21
Tornionjoki →, Finland .. 8 D21
Tornquist, Argentina 126 D3
Toro, Baleares, Spain 37 B11
Toro, Zamora, Spain 34 D5
Torö, Sweden 11 F11
Toro, Cerro del, Chile 126 B2
Toro, Pk., U.S.A. 117 M10
Torökszentmiklós, Hungary 42 C5
Toroníos Kólpos, Greece .. 40 F7
Toronto, Canada 102 D4
Toronto, U.S.A. 110 F4
Toropets, Russia 46 D6
Tororo, Uganda 86 B3
Toros Dağları, Turkey ... 70 B2
Torpa, India 69 H11
Torquay, Australia 95 F3
Torquay, U.K. 13 G4
Torquemada, Spain 34 C6
Torrance, U.S.A 117 M8
Torrão, Portugal 35 G2
Torre Annunziata, Italy ... 31 B7
Torre de Moncorvo, Portugal 34 D3
Torre del Campo, Spain .. 35 H7
Torre del Greco, Italy 31 B7
Torre del Mar, Spain 35 J6
Torre-Pacheco, Spain 33 H4
Torre Péllice, Italy 28 D4
Torreblanca, Spain 32 E5
Torrecampo, Spain 35 G6
Torrecilla en Cameros, Spain 32 C2
Torredembarra, Spain ... 32 D6
Torredonjimeno, Spain ... 35 H7
Torrejón de Ardoz, Spain . 34 E7
Torrejoncillo, Spain 34 F4
Torrelaguna, Spain 34 E7
Torrelavega, Spain 34 B6
Torremaggiore, Italy 29 G12
Torremolinos, Spain 35 J6
Torrens, L., Australia 95 E2
Torrens Cr. →, Australia . 94 C4
Torrens Creek, Australia .. 94 C4
Torrent, Spain 33 F4
Torrenueva, Spain 35 G7
Torreón, Mexico 118 B4
Torreperogil, Spain 35 G7
Torres, Brazil 127 B5
Torres, Mexico 118 B2
Torres Novas, Portugal .. 35 F2
Torres Strait, Australia .. 96 H6
Torres Vedras, Portugal .. 35 F1
Torrevieja, Spain 33 H4
Torrey, U.S.A. 115 G8
Torridge →, U.K. 13 G3
Torridon, L., U.K. 14 D3
Torrijos, Spain 34 F6
Torring, Denmark 11 J3
Torrington, Conn., U.S.A. . 111 E11
Torrington, Wyo., U.S.A. . 112 D2
Torroella de Montgrì, Spain 32 C8
Torrox, Spain 35 J7
Torsås, Sweden 11 H9
Torsby, Sweden 10 D6
Torshälla, Sweden 10 E10

Tórshavn, Færoe Is. 8 E9
Torslanda, Sweden 11 G5
Torsö, Sweden 11 F7
Tortola, Virgin Is. 121 C7
Tórtoles de Esgueva, Spain . 34 D6
Tortolì, Italy 30 C2
Tortona, Italy 28 D5
Tortosa, Spain 32 E5
Tortosa, C., Spain 32 E5
Tortosendo, Portugal 34 E3
Tortue, I. de la, Haiti 121 B5
Tortum, Turkey 73 B9
Ţorūd, Iran 71 C7
Torul, Turkey 73 B8
Toruń, Poland 45 E5
Torysa →, Slovak Rep. ... 27 C14
Torzhok, Russia 46 D8
Torzym, Poland 45 F2
Tosa, Japan 55 H6
Tosa-Shimizu, Japan 55 H6
Tosa-Wan, Japan 55 H6
Toscana □, Italy 28 E8
Toscano, Arcipelago, Italy . 28 F7
Toshkent, Uzbekistan 50 E7
Tosno, Russia 46 C6
Tossa de Mar, Spain 32 D7
Tostado, Argentina 126 B3
Tostedt, Germany 24 B5
Tostón, Pta. de, Canary Is. . 37 F5
Tosu, Japan 55 H5
Tosya, Turkey 72 B6
Toszek, Poland 45 H5
Totana, Spain 33 H3
Totebo, Sweden 11 G10
Toteng, Botswana 88 C3
Tôtes, France 18 C8
Tótkomlós, Hungary 42 D5
Totma, Russia 50 C5
Totnes, U.K. 13 G4
Totness, Surinam 125 B7
Toto, Nigeria 83 D6
Totonicapán, Guatemala . 120 D1
Totten Glacier, Antarctica . 5 C8
Tottenham, Australia 95 E4
Tottenham, Canada 110 B5
Tottori, Japan 55 G7
Tottori □, Japan 55 G7
Touaret, Niger 83 A6
Touba, Ivory C. 82 D3
Touba, Senegal 82 C1
Toubkal, Djebel, Morocco . 78 B4
Toucy, France 19 E10
Tougan, Burkina Faso ... 82 C4
Touggourt, Algeria 78 B7
Tougué, Guinea 82 C2
Toukoto, Mali 82 C3
Toul, France 19 D12
Toulepleu, Ivory C. 82 D3
Toulon, France 21 E9
Toulouse, France 20 E5
Toummo, Niger 79 D8
Toumodi, Ivory C. 82 D3
Tounan, Taiwan 59 F13
Toungo, Nigeria 83 D7
Toungoo, Burma 67 K20
Touques →, France 18 C7
Touraine, France 18 E7
Tourane = Da Nang,
   Vietnam 64 D7
Tourcoing, France 19 B10
Touriñán, C., Spain 34 B1
Tournai, Belgium 17 D3
Tournan-en-Brie, France .. 19 D9
Tournay, France 20 E4
Tournon-St-Martin, France 18 F7
Tournon-sur-Rhône, France 21 C8
Tournus, France 19 F11
Tours, France 18 E7
Tousidé, Pic, Chad 79 D9
Toussora, Mt., C.A.R. ... 84 C4
Touws →, S. Africa 88 E3
Touwsrivier, S. Africa ... 88 E3
Tovarkovskiy, Russia 46 F10
Tovuz, Azerbaijan 49 K7
Towada, Japan 54 D10
Towada-Ko, Japan 54 D10
Towanda, U.S.A. 111 E8
Towang, India 67 F17
Tower, U.S.A. 112 B8
Towerhill Cr. →, Australia 94 C3
Towner, U.S.A. 112 A4
Townsend, U.S.A. 114 C8
Townshend I., Australia .. 94 C5
Townsville, Australia 94 B4
Towson, U.S.A. 108 F7
Towuti, Danau, Indonesia . 63 E6
Toya-Ko, Japan 54 C10
Toyama, Japan 55 F8
Toyama □, Japan 55 F8
Toyama-Wan, Japan 55 F8
Toyohashi, Japan 55 G8
Toyokawa, Japan 55 G8
Toyonaka, Japan 55 G7
Toyooka, Japan 55 G7
Toyota, Japan 55 G8
Tozeur, Tunisia 78 B7
Tqibuli, Georgia 49 J6
Tqvarcheli, Georgia 49 J5
Trá Li = Tralee, Ireland .. 15 D2
Tra On, Vietnam 65 H5
Trabancos →, Spain 34 D5
Traben-Trarbach, Germany 25 F3
Trabzon, Turkey 73 B8
Tracadie, Canada 103 C7
Tracy, Calif., U.S.A. 116 H5
Tracy, Minn., U.S.A. 112 C7
Tradate, Italy 28 C5

Trade Town, Liberia 82 D3
Trafalgar, C., Spain 35 J4
Traian, Brăila, Romania .. 43 E12
Traian, Tulcea, Romania .. 43 E13
Trail, Canada 104 D5
Trainor L., Canada 104 A4
Trákhonas, Cyprus 36 D12
Tralee, Ireland 15 D2
Tralee B., Ireland 15 D2
Tramore, Ireland 15 D4
Tramore B., Ireland 15 D4
Tran Ninh, Cao Nguyen,
   Laos 64 C4
Tranås, Sweden 11 F8
Tranbjerg, Denmark 11 H4
Trancas, Argentina 126 B2
Trancoso, Portugal 34 E3
Tranebjerg, Denmark ... 11 J4
Tranemo, Sweden 11 G7
Trang, Thailand 65 J2
Trangahy, Madag. 89 B7
Trangan, Indonesia 63 F8
Trangie, Australia 95 E4
Trångsviken, Sweden ... 10 A7
Trani, Italy 31 A9
Tranoroa, Madag. 89 C8
Tranqueras, Uruguay ... 127 C4
Transantarctic Mts.,
   Antarctica 5 E12
Transilvania, Romania .. 43 D9
Transilvanian Alps =
   Carpaţii Meridionali,
   Romania 43 E9
Transtrand, Sweden 10 C7
Transtrandsfjällen, Sweden . 10 C6
Transvaal, S. Africa 85 K5
Transylvania = Transilvania,
   Romania 43 D9
Trápani, Italy 30 D5
Trapper Pk., U.S.A. 114 D6
Traralgon, Australia 95 F4
Trarza, Mauritania 82 B2
Trasacco, Italy 29 G10
Trăscău, Munţii, Romania . 43 D8
Trasimeno, L., Italy 29 E9
Träslövsläge, Sweden ... 11 G6
Trasvase Tajo-Segura, Canal
   de, Spain 32 E2
Trat, Thailand 65 F4
Tratani →, Pakistan 68 E3
Traun, Austria 26 C7
Traun →, Germany 25 H8
Traunreut, Germany 25 H8
Traunsee, Austria 26 D6
Traunstein, Germany ... 25 H8
Travellers L., Australia .. 95 E3
Travemünde, Germany .. 24 B6
Travers, Mt., N.Z. 91 K4
Traverse City, U.S.A. ... 108 C3
Travis, L., U.S.A. 113 K5
Travnik, Bos.-H. 42 F2
Trbovlje, Slovenia 29 B12
Trébbia →, Italy 28 C6
Trebel →, Germany 24 B9
Trébeurden, France 18 D3
Třebíč, Czech Rep. 26 B8
Trebinje, Bos.-H. 40 D2
Trebisacce, Italy 31 C9
Trebišnjica →, Bos.-H. .. 40 D2
Trebišov, Slovak Rep. ... 27 C14
Trebižat →, Bos.-H. 29 E14
Trebnje, Slovenia 29 C12
Třeboň, Czech Rep. 26 B7
Trebonne, Australia 94 B4
Trebujena, Spain 35 J4
Trecate, Italy 28 C5
Tregaron, U.K. 13 E4
Tregnago, Italy 29 C8
Tregrosse Is., Australia .. 94 B5
Tréguier, France 18 D3
Trégunc, France 18 E3
Treherne, Canada 105 D9
Tréia, Italy 29 E10
Treignac, France 20 C5
Treinta y Tres, Uruguay . 127 C5
Treis-karden, Germany .. 25 E3
Treklyano, Bulgaria 40 D6
Trelawney, Zimbabwe .. 89 B5
Trélazé, France 18 E6
Trelew, Argentina 128 E3
Trélissac, France 20 C4
Trelleborg, Sweden 11 J7
Tremadog Bay, U.K. 12 E3
Trémiti, Italy 29 F12
Tremonton, U.S.A. 114 F7
Tremp, Spain 32 C5
Trenche →, Canada 102 C5
Trenčiansky □, Slovak Rep. 27 C11
Trenčín, Slovak Rep. ... 27 C11
Trenggalek, Indonesia ... 63 H14
Trenque Lauquen, Argentina 126 D3
Trent →, Canada 110 B7
Trent →, U.K. 12 D7
Trentino-Alto Adige □, Italy 29 B8
Trento, Italy 28 B8
Trenton, Canada 102 D4
Trenton, Mo., U.S.A. ... 112 E8
Trenton, N.J., U.S.A. ... 111 F10
Trenton, Nebr., U.S.A. .. 112 E4
Trepassey, Canada 103 C9
Trepuzzi, Italy 31 B11
Tres Arroyos, Argentina . 126 D3
Três Corações, Brazil ... 127 A6
Três Lagoas, Brazil 125 H8
Tres Marías, Islas, Mexico . 118 C3
Tres Montes, C., Chile ... 128 F1
Tres Pinos, U.S.A. 116 J5
Três Pontas, Brazil 127 A6
Tres Puentes, Chile 126 B1
Tres Puntas, C., Argentina 128 F3
Três Rios, Brazil 127 A7

Tres Valles, Mexico 119 D5
Tresco, U.K. 13 H1
Treska →, Macedonia ... 40 E5
Treskavica, Bos.-H. 42 G3
Trespaderne, Spain 34 C7
Trets, France 21 E9
Treuchtlingen, Germany .. 25 G6
Treuenbrietzen, Germany . 24 C8
Trevi, Italy 29 F9
Treviglio, Italy 28 C6
Trevínca, Peña, Spain ... 34 C4
Treviso, Italy 29 C9
Trévoux, France 21 C8
Trgovište, Serbia, Yug. ... 40 D6
Triabunna, Australia 94 G4
Triánda, Greece 36 C10
Triangle, Zimbabwe 89 C5
Triaucourt-en-Argonne,
   France 19 D12
Tribsees, Germany 24 A8
Tribulation, C., Australia . 94 B4
Tribune, U.S.A. 112 F4
Tricárico, Italy 31 B9
Tricase, Italy 31 C11
Trichinopoly =
   Tiruchchirappalli, India . 66 P11
Trichur, India 66 P10
Trida, Australia 95 E4
Trier, Germany 25 F2
Trieste, Italy 29 C10
Trieste, G. di, Italy 29 C10
Trieux →, France 18 D3
Triggiano, Italy 31 A9
Triglav, Slovenia 29 B10
Trigno →, Italy 29 F11
Trigueros, Spain 35 H4
Tríkeri, Greece 38 B5
Trikhonís, Límni, Greece . 38 C3
Tríkkala, Greece 38 B3
Tríkkala □, Greece 38 B3
Trikomo, Cyprus 36 D12
Trikora, Puncak, Indonesia . 63 E9
Trilj, Croatia 29 E13
Trillo, Spain 32 E2
Trim, Ireland 15 C5
Trincomalee, Sri Lanka .. 66 Q12
Trindade, Brazil 125 G9
Trindade, I., Atl. Oc. 2 F8
Třinec, Czech Rep. 27 B11
Trinidad, Bolivia 124 F6
Trinidad, Cuba 120 B4
Trinidad, Uruguay 126 C4
Trinidad, U.S.A. 113 G2
Trinidad, W. Indies 121 D7
Trinidad →, Mexico 119 D5
Trinidad & Tobago ■,
   W. Indies 121 D7
Trinitápoli, Italy 31 A9
Trinity, Canada 103 C9
Trinity, U.S.A. 113 K7
Trinity →, Calif., U.S.A. . 114 F2
Trinity →, Tex., U.S.A. .. 113 L7
Trinity B., Canada 103 C9
Trinity Is., U.S.A. 100 C4
Trinity Range, U.S.A. ... 114 F4
Trinkitat, Sudan 80 D4
Trino, Italy 28 C5
Trinway, U.S.A. 110 F2
Trión, Greece 38 C3
Trionto, C., Italy 31 C9
Triora, Italy 28 D4
Tripoli = Tarābulus,
   Lebanon 75 A4
Tripoli = Tarābulus, Libya . 79 B8
Trípolis, Greece 38 D4
Tripolitania, Libya 76 C5
Tripolitania, N. Afr. 79 B8
Tripura □, India 67 H18
Triplyos, Cyprus 36 E11
Trischen, Germany 24 A4
Tristan da Cunha, Atl. Oc. . 77 K2
Trisul, India 69 D8
Trivandrum, India 66 Q10
Trivento, Italy 29 G11
Trnava, Slovak Rep. 27 C10
Trnavský □, Slovak Rep. . 27 C10
Troarn, France 18 C6
Trochu, Canada 104 C6
Trodely I., Canada 102 B4
Troezen, Greece 38 D5
Trogir, Croatia 29 E13
Troglav, Croatia 29 E13
Tróia, Italy 31 A8
Troilus, L., Canada 102 B5
Troina, Italy 31 E7
Trois-Pistoles, Canada .. 103 C6
Trois-Rivières, Canada .. 102 C5
Troisdorf, Germany 24 E3
Troitsk, Russia 50 D7
Troitsko Pechorsk, Russia . 50 C6
Troitskoye, Russia 49 G8
Trölladyngja, Iceland ... 8 D5
Trollhättan, Sweden ... 11 F6
Trollheimen, Norway ... 8 E13
Trombetas →, Brazil ... 125 D7
Tromsø, Norway 8 B18
Trona, U.S.A. 117 K9
Tronador, Mte., Argentina . 128 E2
Trøndelag, Norway 8 D14
Trondheim, Norway 8 E14
Trondheimsfjorden, Norway 8 E14
Trönninge, Sweden 11 H6
Tronto →, Italy 29 F10
Troodos, Cyprus 36 E11
Troon, U.K. 14 F4
Tropea, Italy 31 D8
Tropic, U.S.A. 115 H7
Tropoja, Albania 40 D4
Trosa, Sweden 11 F11
Trostan, U.K. 15 A5
Trostberg, Germany ... 25 G8
Trostyanets, Ukraine ... 47 G8
Trout →, Canada 104 A5

Trout L., N.W.T., Canada . 104 A4
Trout L., Ont., Canada .. 105 C10
Trout Lake, Canada 104 B6
Trout Lake, U.S.A. 116 E5
Trout River, Canada 103 C8
Trout Run, U.S.A. 110 E7
Trouville-sur-Mer, France . 18 C7
Trowbridge, U.K. 13 F5
Troy, Turkey 39 B8
Troy, Ala., U.S.A. 109 K3
Troy, Kans., U.S.A. 112 F7
Troy, Mo., U.S.A. 112 F9
Troy, Mont., U.S.A. 114 B6
Troy, N.Y., U.S.A. 111 D11
Troy, Ohio, U.S.A. 108 E3
Troy, Pa., U.S.A. 111 E8
Troyan, Bulgaria 41 D8
Troyes, France 19 D11
Trpanj, Croatia 29 E14
Trstenik, Serbia, Yug. ... 40 C5
Trubchevsk, Russia 47 F7
Truchas Peak, U.S.A. ... 113 H2
Trucial States = United
   Arab Emirates ■, Asia .. 71 F7
Truckee, U.S.A. 116 F6
Trudfront, Russia 49 H8
Trudovoye, Russia 54 C6
Trujillo, Honduras 120 C2
Trujillo, Peru 124 E3
Trujillo, Spain 35 F5
Trujillo, U.S.A. 113 H2
Trujillo, Venezuela 124 B4
Truk, Micronesia 96 G7
Trumann, U.S.A. 113 H9
Trumansburg, U.S.A. ... 111 D8
Trumbull, Mt., U.S.A. .. 115 H7
Trůn, Bulgaria 40 D6
Trun, France 18 D7
Trundle, Australia 95 E4
Trung-Phan = Annam,
   Vietnam 64 E7
Truro, Canada 103 C7
Truro, U.K. 13 G2
Truskavets, Ukraine ... 47 H2
Trůstenik, Bulgaria 41 C8
Trustrup, Denmark 11 H4
Trutch, Canada 104 B4
Truth or Consequences,
   U.S.A. 115 K10
Trutnov, Czech Rep. ... 26 A8
Truxton, U.S.A. 111 D8
Truyère →, France 20 D6
Tryavna, Bulgaria 41 D9
Tryonville, U.S.A. 110 E5
Trzcianka, Poland 45 E3
Trzciel, Poland 45 F2
Trzcińsko Zdrój, Poland . 45 F1
Trzebiatów, Poland 44 D2
Trzebiez, Poland 44 E1
Trzebnica, Poland 45 G4
Trzemeszno, Poland ... 45 F4
Tržič, Slovenia 29 B11
Tsagan Aman, Russia .. 49 G8
Tsamandás, Greece 38 B2
Tsandi, Namibia 88 B1
Tsaratanana, Madag. ... 89 B8
Tsaratanana, Mt. de, Madag. 89 A8
Tsarevo = Michurin,
   Bulgaria 41 D11
Tsarevo, Bulgaria 41 D9
Tsaritsáni, Greece 38 B4
Tsau, Botswana 88 C3
Tsebrykove, Ukraine ... 47 J6
Tselinograd = Astana,
   Kazakstan 50 D8
Tses, Namibia 88 D2
Tsetserleg, Mongolia ... 60 B5
Tsévié, Togo 83 D5
Tshabong, Botswana ... 88 D3
Tshane, Botswana 88 C3
Tshela,
   Dem. Rep. of the Congo . 84 E2
Tshesebe, Botswana ... 89 C4
Tshibeke,
   Dem. Rep. of the Congo . 86 C2
Tshibinda,
   Dem. Rep. of the Congo . 86 C2
Tshikapa,
   Dem. Rep. of the Congo . 84 F4
Tshilenge,
   Dem. Rep. of the Congo . 86 D1
Tshinsenda,
   Dem. Rep. of the Congo . 87 E2
Tshofa,
   Dem. Rep. of the Congo . 86 D2
Tshwane, Botswana 88 C3
Tsigara, Botswana 88 C4
Tsihombe, Madag. 89 D8
Tsiigehtchic, Canada .. 100 B6
Tsimlyansk, Russia 49 G6
Tsimlyansk Res. =
   Tsimlyanskoye Vdkhr.,
   Russia 49 F6
Tsimlyanskoye Vdkhr.,
   Russia 49 F6
Tsinan = Jinan, China .. 56 F9
Tsineng, S. Africa 88 D3
Tsínga, Greece 41 E8
Tsinghai = Qinghai □, China 60 C4
Tsingtao = Qingdao, China 57 F11
Tsinjoarivo, Madag. ... 89 B8
Tsinjomitondraka, Madag. . 89 B8
Tsiroanomandidy, Madag. . 89 B8
Tsiteli-Tsqaro, Georgia .. 49 K8
Tsivilsk, Russia 48 C8
Tsivory, Madag. 89 C8
Tskhinvali, Georgia 49 J7
Tsna →, Russia 48 C5
Tsnori, Georgia 49 K7
Tso Moriri, L., India ... 69 C8

Tsobis, *Namibia* 88 B2
Tsodilo Hill, *Botswana* 88 B3
Tsogttsetsiy = Baruunsuu, *Mongolia* 56 C3
Tsolo, *S. Africa* 89 E4
Tsomo, *S. Africa* 89 E4
Tsu, *Japan* 55 G8
Tsu L., *Canada* 104 A6
Tsuchiura, *Japan* 55 F10
Tsuen Wan, *H.K.* 59 F10
Tsugaru-Kaikyō, *Japan* 54 D10
Tsumeb, *Namibia* 88 B2
Tsumis, *Namibia* 88 C2
Tsuruga, *Japan* 55 G8
Tsurugi-San, *Japan* 55 H7
Tsuruoka, *Japan* 54 E9
Tsushima, *Gifu, Japan* 55 G8
Tsushima, *Nagasaki, Japan* 55 G4
Tsuyama, *Japan* 55 G7
Tsvetkovo, *Ukraine* 47 H6
Tsyelyakhany, *Belarus* 47 F3
Tua →, *Portugal* 34 D3
Tual, *Indonesia* 63 F8
Tuam, *Ireland* 15 C3
Tuamotu Arch. = Tuamotu Is., *Pac. Oc.* 97 J13
Tuamotu Is., *Pac. Oc.* 97 J13
Tuamotu Ridge, *Pac. Oc.* 97 K14
Tuanfeng, *China* 59 B10
Tuanxi, *China* 58 D6
Tuao, *Phil.* 61 C4
Tuapse, *Russia* 49 H4
Tuatapere, *N.Z.* 91 M1
Tuba City, *U.S.A.* 115 H8
Tuban, *Indonesia* 63 G15
Tubani, *Botswana* 88 C3
Tübingen, *Germany* 25 G5
Tubruq, *Libya* 79 B10
Tubuai Is., *Pac. Oc.* 97 K13
Tuc Trung, *Vietnam* 65 G6
Tucacas, *Venezuela* 124 A5
T'uch'ang, *Taiwan* 59 E13
Tuchodi →, *Canada* 104 B4
Tuchola, *Poland* 44 E4
Tuchów, *Poland* 45 J8
Tuckanarra, *Australia* 93 E2
Tucson, *U.S.A.* 115 K8
Tucumán □, *Argentina* 126 B2
Tucumcari, *U.S.A.* 113 H3
Tucupita, *Venezuela* 124 B6
Tucuruí, *Brazil* 125 D9
Tucuruí, Reprêsa de, *Brazil* 125 D9
Tuczno, *Poland* 45 E3
Tudela, *Spain* 32 C3
Tudmur, *Syria* 70 C3
Tudor, L., *Canada* 103 A6
Tudora, *Romania* 43 C11
Tuella →, *Portugal* 34 D3
Tugela →, *S. Africa* 89 D5
Tuguegarao, *Phil.* 61 C4
Tugur, *Russia* 51 D14
Tui, *Spain* 34 C2
Tuineje, *Canary Is.* 37 F5
Tukangbesi, Kepulauan, *Indonesia* 63 F6
Tukarak I., *Canada* 102 A4
Tukayyid, *Iraq* 70 D5
Tūkh, *Egypt* 80 H7
Tukobo, *Ghana* 82 D4
Tuktoyaktuk, *Canada* 100 B6
Tukums, *Latvia* 9 H20
Tukums □, *Latvia* 44 B10
Tukuyu, *Tanzania* 87 D3
Tula, *Hidalgo, Mexico* 119 C5
Tula, *Tamaulipas, Mexico* 119 C5
Tula, *Nigeria* 83 D7
Tula, *Russia* 46 E9
Tulancingo, *Mexico* 119 C5
Tulare, *Serbia, Yug.* 40 D5
Tulare, *U.S.A.* 116 J7
Tulare Lake Bed, *U.S.A.* 116 K7
Tularosa, *U.S.A.* 115 K10
Tulbagh, *S. Africa* 88 E2
Tulcán, *Ecuador* 124 C3
Tulcea, *Romania* 43 E13
Tulcea □, *Romania* 43 E13
Tulchyn, *Ukraine* 47 H5
Tūleh, *Iran* 71 C7
Tulemalu L., *Canada* 105 A9
Tulgheş, *Romania* 43 D10
Tuli, *Zimbabwe* 87 G2
Tulia, *U.S.A.* 113 H4
Tuliszków, *Poland* 45 F5
Tulita, *Canada* 100 B7
Tülkarm, *West Bank* 75 C4
Tulla, *Ireland* 15 D3
Tullahoma, *U.S.A.* 109 H2
Tullamore, *Australia* 95 E4
Tullamore, *Ireland* 15 C4
Tulle, *France* 20 C5
Tulln, *Austria* 26 C9
Tullow, *Ireland* 15 D5
Tullus, *Sudan* 81 E1
Tully, *Australia* 94 B4
Tully, *U.S.A.* 111 D8
Tulnici, *Romania* 43 E11
Tulovo, *Bulgaria* 41 D9
Tulsa, *U.S.A.* 113 G7
Tulsequah, *Canada* 104 B2
Tulu Milki, *Ethiopia* 81 F4
Tulu Welel, *Ethiopia* 81 F3
Tulua, *Colombia* 124 C3
Tulucești, *Romania* 43 E13
Tulun, *Russia* 51 D11
Tulungagung, *Indonesia* 63 H14
Tuma →, *Nic.* 120 D3
Tuma, *Russia* 46 E11
Tumaco, *Colombia* 124 C3

Tumatumari, *Guyana* 124 B7
Tumba, *Sweden* 10 E11
Tumba, L., *Dem. Rep. of the Congo* 84 E3
Tumbarumba, *Australia* 95 F4
Tumbaya, *Argentina* 126 A2
Tumbes, *Peru* 124 D2
Tumbur, *Sudan* 81 G3
Tumbwe, *Dem. Rep. of the Congo* 87 E2
Tumby Bay, *Australia* 95 E2
Tumd Youqi, *China* 56 D6
Tumen, *China* 57 C15
Tumen Jiang →, *China* 57 C16
Tumeremo, *Venezuela* 124 B6
Tumkur, *India* 66 N10
Tump, *Pakistan* 66 F3
Tumpat, *Malaysia* 65 J4
Tumu, *Ghana* 82 C4
Tumucumaque, Serra, *Brazil* 122 C5
Tumut, *Australia* 95 F4
Tumwater, *U.S.A.* 116 C4
Tuna, *India* 68 H4
Tunadal, *Sweden* 10 B11
Tunas de Zaza, *Cuba* 120 B4
Tunbridge Wells = Royal Tunbridge Wells, *U.K.* 13 F8
Tunçbilek, *Turkey* 39 B11
Tunceli, *Turkey* 73 C8
Tuncurry-Forster, *Australia* 95 E5
Tundla, *India* 68 F8
Tundubai, *Sudan* 80 D2
Tunduru, *Tanzania* 87 E4
Tundzha →, *Bulgaria* 41 E10
Tunga Pass, *India* 67 E19
Tungabhadra →, *India* 66 M11
Tungaru, *Sudan* 81 E3
Tungla, *Nic.* 120 D3
Tungsha Tao, *Taiwan* 59 G11
Tungshih, *Taiwan* 59 E13
Tungsten, *Canada* 104 A3
Tunguska, Nizhnyaya →, *Russia* 51 C9
Tunguska, Podkamennaya →, *Russia* 51 C10
Tunica, *U.S.A.* 113 H9
Tunis, *Tunisia* 79 A8
Tunisia ■, *Africa* 79 A7
Tunja, *Colombia* 124 B4
Tunkhannock, *U.S.A.* 111 E9
Tunliu, *China* 56 F7
Tunnsjøen, *Norway* 8 D15
Tunø, *Denmark* 11 J4
Tunungayualok I., *Canada* 103 A7
Tunuyán, *Argentina* 126 C2
Tunuyán →, *Argentina* 126 C2
Tuo Jiang →, *China* 58 C5
Tuolumne, *U.S.A.* 116 H6
Tuolumne →, *U.S.A.* 116 H5
Tūp Āghāj, *Iran* 70 B5
Tupã, *Brazil* 127 A5
Tupelo, *U.S.A.* 109 H1
Tupik, *Russia* 46 E7
Tupinambaranas, *Brazil* 124 D7
Tupiza, *Bolivia* 126 A2
Tupižnica, *Serbia, Yug.* 40 C6
Tupman, *U.S.A.* 117 K7
Tupper, *Canada* 104 B4
Tupper Lake, *U.S.A.* 111 B10
Tupungato, Cerro, *S. Amer.* 126 C2
Tuquan, *China* 57 B11
Túquerres, *Colombia* 124 C3
Tura, *Russia* 51 C11
Turabah, *Si. Arabia* 70 D4
Turabah, *Si. Arabia* 80 C5
Tūrān, *Iran* 71 C8
Turan, *Russia* 51 D10
Ţurayf, *Si. Arabia* 70 D3
Turbacz, *Poland* 45 J7
Turbe, *Bos.-H.* 42 F2
Turčianske Teplice, *Slovak Rep.* 27 C11
Turcoaia, *Romania* 43 E13
Turda, *Romania* 43 D8
Turek, *Poland* 45 F5
Turen, *Venezuela* 124 B5
Turfan = Turpan, *China* 60 B3
Turfan Depression = Turpan Hami, *China* 52 E12
Turgeon →, *Canada* 102 C4
Tŭrgovishte, *Bulgaria* 41 C10
Turgut, *Turkey* 39 D10
Turgutlu, *Turkey* 39 C9
Turgwe →, *Zimbabwe* 89 C5
Turhal, *Turkey* 72 B7
Turia →, *Spain* 33 F4
Turiaçu, *Brazil* 125 D9
Turiaçu →, *Brazil* 125 D9
Turiec →, *Slovak Rep.* 27 B11
Turin = Torino, *Italy* 28 C4
Turkana, L., *Africa* 86 B4
Türkeli, *Turkey* 41 F11
Turkestan = Türkistan, *Kazakstan* 50 E7
Túrkeve, *Hungary* 42 C5
Turkey ■, *Eurasia* 72 C7
Turkey Creek, *Australia* 92 C4
Turki, *Russia* 48 D6
Türkistan, *Kazakstan* 50 E7
Türkmenbashi, *Turkmenistan* 50 E6
Turkmenistan ■, *Asia* 50 F6
Türkmenli, *Turkey* 39 B8
Türkoğlu, *Turkey* 72 D7
Turks & Caicos Is. ■, *W. Indies* 121 B5
Turks Island Passage, *W. Indies* 121 B5
Turku, *Finland* 9 F20
Turkwel →, *Kenya* 86 B4
Turlock, *U.S.A.* 116 H6

Turnagain →, *Canada* 104 B3
Turnagain, C., *N.Z.* 91 J6
Turneffe Is., *Belize* 119 D7
Turner, *U.S.A.* 114 B9
Turner Pt., *Australia* 94 A1
Turner Valley, *Canada* 104 C6
Turners Falls, *U.S.A.* 111 D12
Turnhout, *Belgium* 17 C4
Türnitz, *Austria* 26 D8
Turnor L., *Canada* 105 B7
Turnov, *Czech Rep.* 26 A8
Tŭrnovo = Veliko Tŭrnovo, *Bulgaria* 41 C9
Turnu Măgurele, *Romania* 43 G9
Turnu Roşu, P., *Romania* 43 E9
Turobin, *Poland* 45 H9
Turpan, *China* 60 B3
Turpan Hami, *China* 52 E12
Turrës, Kalaja e, *Albania* 40 E3
Turriff, *U.K.* 14 D6
Tursāq, *Iraq* 70 C5
Tursi, *Italy* 31 B9
Turtle Head I., *Australia* 94 A3
Turtle Is., *S. Leone* 82 D2
Turtle L., *Canada* 105 C7
Turtle Lake, *U.S.A.* 112 B4
Turtleford, *Canada* 105 C7
Turukhansk, *Russia* 51 C9
Turzovka, *Slovak Rep.* 27 B11
Tuscaloosa, *U.S.A.* 109 J2
Tuscánia, *Italy* 29 F8
Tuscarawas →, *U.S.A.* 110 F3
Tuscarora Mt., *U.S.A.* 110 F7
Tuscola, *Ill., U.S.A.* 108 F1
Tuscola, *Tex., U.S.A.* 113 J5
Tuscumbia, *U.S.A.* 109 H2
Tuskegee, *U.S.A.* 109 J3
Tustin, *U.S.A.* 117 M9
Tuszyn, *Poland* 45 G6
Tutak, *Turkey* 73 C10
Tutayev, *Russia* 46 D10
Tuticorin, *India* 66 Q11
Tutin, *Serbia, Yug.* 40 D4
Tutóia, *Brazil* 125 D10
Tutong, *Brunei* 62 D4
Tutova →, *Romania* 43 D12
Tutrakan, *Bulgaria* 41 B10
Tuttle Creek L., *U.S.A.* 112 F6
Tuttlingen, *Germany* 25 H4
Tutuala, *Indonesia* 63 F7
Tutuila, *Amer. Samoa* 91 B13
Tutume, *Botswana* 85 J5
Tutun, *Egypt* 80 J7
Tututepec, *Mexico* 119 D5
Tuva □, *Russia* 51 D10
Tuvalu ■, *Pac. Oc.* 96 H9
Tuxer Alpen, *Austria* 26 D4
Tuxpan, *Mexico* 119 C5
Tuxtla Gutiérrez, *Mexico* 119 D6
Tuy = Tui, *Spain* 34 C2
Tuy An, *Vietnam* 64 F7
Tuy Duc, *Vietnam* 65 F6
Tuy Hoa, *Vietnam* 64 F7
Tuy Phong, *Vietnam* 65 G7
Tuya L., *Canada* 104 B2
Tuyen Hoa, *Vietnam* 64 D6
Tuyen Quang, *Vietnam* 58 G5
Tūysarkān, *Iran* 71 C6
Tuz Gölü, *Turkey* 72 C5
Ţūz Khurmātū, *Iraq* 70 C5
Tuzi, *Montenegro, Yug.* 40 D3
Tuzla, *Bos.-H.* 42 F3
Tuzlov →, *Russia* 47 J10
Tuzluca, *Turkey* 73 B10
Tvååker, *Sweden* 11 G6
Tvardița, *Moldova* 43 D13
Tver, *Russia* 46 D8
Tvrdošín, *Slovak Rep.* 27 B12
Tvrdošovce, *Slovak Rep.* 27 C11
Tvŭrditsa, *Bulgaria* 41 D9
Twain, *U.S.A.* 116 E5
Twain Harte, *U.S.A.* 116 G6
Twardogóra, *Poland* 45 G4
Tweed, *Canada* 110 B7
Tweed →, *U.K.* 14 F6
Tweed Heads, *Australia* 95 D5
Tweedsmuir Prov. Park, *Canada* 104 C3
Twentynine Palms, *U.S.A.* 117 L10
Twillingate, *Canada* 103 C9
Twin Bridges, *U.S.A.* 114 D7
Twin Falls, *Canada* 103 B7
Twin Falls, *U.S.A.* 114 E6
Twin Valley, *U.S.A.* 112 B6
Twinsburg, *U.S.A.* 110 E3
Twistringen, *Germany* 24 C4
Two Harbors, *U.S.A.* 112 B9
Two Hills, *Canada* 104 C6
Two Rivers, *U.S.A.* 108 C2
Two Rocks, *Australia* 93 F2
Twofold B., *Australia* 95 F4
Tyachiv, *Ukraine* 47 H2
Tychy, *Poland* 45 H5
Tyczyn, *Poland* 45 J9
Tykocin, *Poland* 45 E9
Tyler, *Minn., U.S.A.* 112 C6
Tyler, *Tex., U.S.A.* 113 J7
Tyligul →, *Ukraine* 47 J6
Týn nad Vltavou, *Czech Rep.* 26 B7
Tynda, *Russia* 51 D13
Tyndall, *U.S.A.* 112 D6
Tyne →, *U.K.* 12 C6
Tyne & Wear □, *U.K.* 12 B6
Týnec nad Sázavou, *Czech Rep.* 26 B7
Tynemouth, *U.K.* 12 B6
Tyre = Sūr, *Lebanon* 75 B4

Tyrifjorden, *Norway* 9 F14
Tyringe, *Sweden* 11 H7
Tyrnyauz, *Russia* 49 J6
Tyrol = Tirol □, *Austria* 26 D3
Tyrone, *U.S.A.* 110 F6
Tyrone □, *U.K.* 15 B4
Tyrrell →, *Australia* 95 F3
Tyrrell, L., *Australia* 95 F3
Tyrrell L., *Canada* 105 A7
Tyrrhenian Sea, *Medit. S.* 6 G8
Tysfjorden, *Norway* 8 B17
Tystberga, *Sweden* 11 F11
Tytuvėnai, *Lithuania* 44 C10
Tyub Karagan, Mys, *Kazakstan* 49 H10
Tyuleni, Ostrova, *Kazakstan* 49 H10
Tyuleniy, *Russia* 49 H8
Tyuleniy, Mys, *Azerbaijan* 49 K10
Tyumen, *Russia* 50 D7
Tywi →, *U.K.* 13 F3
Tywyn, *U.K.* 13 E3
Tzaneen, *S. Africa* 89 C5
Tzermiádhes, *Greece* 36 D7
Tzoumérka, Óros, *Greece* 38 B3
Tzukong = Zigong, *China* 58 C5

U

U Taphao, *Thailand* 64 F3
U.S.A. = United States of America ■, *N. Amer.* 106 C7
Uatumã →, *Brazil* 124 D7
Uaupés, *Brazil* 124 D5
Uaupés →, *Brazil* 124 C5
Uaxactún, *Guatemala* 120 C2
Ub, *Serbia, Yug.* 40 B4
Ubá, *Brazil* 127 A7
Uba, *Nigeria* 83 C7
Ubaitaba, *Brazil* 125 F11
Ubangi = Oubangi →, *Dem. Rep. of the Congo* 84 E3
Ubauro, *Pakistan* 68 E3
Ubaye →, *France* 21 D10
Ubayyiḍ, W. al →, *Iraq* 70 C4
Ube, *Japan* 55 H5
Úbeda, *Spain* 35 G7
Uberaba, *Brazil* 125 G9
Uberlândia, *Brazil* 125 G9
Überlingen, *Germany* 25 H5
Ubiaja, *Nigeria* 83 D6
Ubolratna Res., *Thailand* 64 D4
Ubombo, *S. Africa* 89 D5
Ubon Ratchathani, *Thailand* 64 E5
Ubondo, *Dem. Rep. of the Congo* 86 C2
Ubort →, *Belarus* 47 F5
Ubrique, *Spain* 35 J5
Ubundu, *Dem. Rep. of the Congo* 86 C2
Ucayali →, *Peru* 122 D3
Uchab, *Namibia* 88 B2
Uchiura-Wan, *Japan* 54 C10
Uchquduq, *Uzbekistan* 50 E7
Uchte, *Germany* 24 C4
Uchur →, *Russia* 51 D14
Uckermark, *Germany* 24 B9
Ucluelet, *Canada* 104 D3
Uda →, *Russia* 51 D14
Udagamandalam, *India* 66 P10
Udainagar, *India* 68 H7
Udaipur, *India* 68 G5
Udaipur Garhi, *Nepal* 69 F12
Udala, *India* 69 J12
Udbina, *Croatia* 29 D12
Uddeholm, *Sweden* 10 D7
Uddevalla, *Sweden* 11 F5
Uddjaur, *Sweden* 8 D17
Uden, *Neths.* 17 C5
Udgir, *India* 66 K10
Udhampur, *India* 69 C6
Údine, *Italy* 29 B10
Udmurtia □, *Russia* 50 D6
Udon Thani, *Thailand* 64 D4
Udupi, *India* 66 N9
Udvoy Balkan, *Bulgaria* 41 D10
Udzungwa Range, *Tanzania* 87 D4
Ueckermünde, *Germany* 24 B10
Ueda, *Japan* 55 F9
Uedineniya, Os., *Russia* 4 B12
Uele →, *Dem. Rep. of the Congo* 84 D4
Uelen, *Russia* 51 C19
Uelzen, *Germany* 24 C6
Uetersen, *Germany* 24 B5
Uetze, *Germany* 24 C6
Ufa, *Russia* 50 D6
Uffenheim, *Germany* 25 F6
Ugab →, *Namibia* 88 C1
Ugalla →, *Tanzania* 86 D3
Uganda ■, *Africa* 86 B3
Ugento, *Italy* 31 C11
Ugep, *Nigeria* 83 D6
Ugie, *S. Africa* 89 E4
Ughelli, *Nigeria* 83 D6
Ugine, *France* 21 C10
Uglegorsk, *Russia* 51 E15
Uglich, *Russia* 46 D10
Ugljan, *Croatia* 29 D12
Ugljane, *Croatia* 29 E13
Ugra →, *Russia* 46 E9
Uğurchin, *Bulgaria* 41 C8
Uh →, *Slovak Rep.* 27 C15
Uherské Hradiště, *Czech Rep.* 27 B10
Uherský Brod, *Czech Rep.* 27 B10

Úhlava →, *Czech Rep.* 26 B6
Uhlenhorst, *Namibia* 88 C2
Uhrichsville, *U.S.A.* 110 F3
Uibhist a Deas = South Uist, *U.K.* 14 D1
Uibhist a Tuath = North Uist, *U.K.* 14 D1
Uig, *U.K.* 14 D2
Uíge, *Angola* 84 F2
Uijŏngbu, *S. Korea* 57 F14
Ŭiju, *N. Korea* 57 D13
Uinta Mts., *U.S.A.* 114 F8
Uis, *Namibia* 88 B2
Uitenhage, *S. Africa* 88 E4
Uithuizen, *Neths.* 17 A6
Ujazd, *Poland* 45 H5
Újfehértó, *Hungary* 42 C6
Ujh →, *India* 68 C6
Ujhani, *India* 69 F8
Uji-guntō, *Japan* 55 J4
Ujjain, *India* 68 H6
Ujście, *Poland* 45 E3
Újszász, *Hungary* 42 C5
Ujung Pandang, *Indonesia* 63 F5
Uka, *Russia* 51 D17
Ukara I., *Tanzania* 86 C3
Uke-Shima, *Japan* 55 K4
Ukerewe I., *Tanzania* 86 C3
Ukholovo, *Russia* 48 D5
Ukhrul, *India* 67 G19
Ukhta, *Russia* 50 C6
Ukiah, *U.S.A.* 116 F3
Ukki Fort, *India* 69 C7
Ukmergė, *Lithuania* 9 J21
Ukraine ■, *Europe* 47 H7
Ukwi, *Botswana* 88 C3
Ulaan-Uul, *Mongolia* 56 B6
Ulaanbaatar, *Mongolia* 51 E11
Ulaangom, *Mongolia* 60 A4
Ulaanjirem, *Mongolia* 56 B3
Ulamba, *Dem. Rep. of the Congo* 87 D1
Ulan Bator = Ulaanbaatar, *Mongolia* 51 E11
Ulan Erge, *Russia* 49 G7
Ulan Khol, *Russia* 49 H8
Ulan Ude, *Russia* 51 D11
Ulanów, *Poland* 45 H9
Ulaş, *Sivas, Turkey* 72 C7
Ulaş, *Tekirdağ, Turkey* 41 E11
Ulaya, *Morogoro, Tanzania* 86 D4
Ulaya, *Tabora, Tanzania* 86 C3
Ulcinj, *Montenegro, Yug.* 40 E3
Ulco, *S. Africa* 88 D3
Ulefoss, *Norway* 9 G13
Ulëza, *Albania* 40 E3
Ulfborg, *Denmark* 11 H2
Ulhasnagar, *India* 66 K8
Uliastay, *Mongolia* 60 B5
Ulithi Atoll, *Pac. Oc.* 63 B9
Uljma, *Serbia, Yug.* 42 E6
Ulla →, *Spain* 34 C2
Ulladulla, *Australia* 95 F5
Ullapool, *U.K.* 14 D3
Ullared, *Sweden* 11 G6
Ulldecona, *Spain* 32 E5
Ullswater, *U.K.* 12 C5
Ullŭng-do, *S. Korea* 57 F16
Ulm, *Germany* 25 G5
Ulmarra, *Australia* 95 D5
Ulmeni, *Buzău, Romania* 43 E11
Ulmeni, *Maramureş, Romania* 43 C8
Ulonguè, *Mozam.* 87 E3
Ulricehamn, *Sweden* 11 G7
Ulrika, *Sweden* 11 F9
Ulsan, *S. Korea* 57 G15
Ulsta, *U.K.* 14 A7
Ulster □, *U.K.* 15 B5
Ulstrem, *Bulgaria* 41 D10
Ulubat Gölü, *Turkey* 41 F12
Ulubey, *Turkey* 39 C11
Uluborlu, *Turkey* 39 C12
Uluçinar, *Turkey* 72 D6
Uludağ, *Turkey* 41 F13
Uludere, *Turkey* 73 D10
Uluguru Mts., *Tanzania* 86 D4
Ulukışla, *Turkey* 72 D6
Ulungur He →, *China* 60 B3
Uluru = Ayers Rock, *Australia* 93 E5
Uluru Nat. Park, *Australia* 93 E5
Ulutau, *Kazakstan* 50 E7
Ulva, *U.K.* 14 E2
Ulverston, *U.K.* 12 C4
Ulverstone, *Australia* 94 G4
Ulya, *Russia* 51 D15
Ulyanovsk = Simbirsk, *Russia* 48 C9
Ulyasutay = Uliastay, *Mongolia* 60 B5
Ulysses, *U.S.A.* 113 G4
Umag, *Croatia* 29 C10
Umala, *Bolivia* 124 G5
Uman, *Ukraine* 47 H6
Umaria, *India* 67 H12
Umarkot, *Pakistan* 66 G6
Umarpada, *India* 68 J5
Umatilla, *U.S.A.* 114 D4
Umba, *Russia* 50 C5
Umbagog L., *U.S.A.* 111 B13
Umbakumba, *Australia* 94 A2
Umbértide, *Italy* 29 E9
Umbrella Mts., *N.Z.* 91 L2
Umbria □, *Italy* 29 F9
Ume älv →, *Sweden* 8 E19
Umeå, *Sweden* 8 E19
Umera, *Indonesia* 63 E7
Umfuli →, *Zimbabwe* 87 F2
Umgusa, *Zimbabwe* 87 F2
Umim Urūmah, *Si. Arabia* 80 B4

Umka, *Serbia, Yug.* 40 B4
Umkomaas, *S. Africa* 89 E5
Umlazi, *S. Africa* 85 L6
Umm ad Daraj, J., *Jordan* . 75 C4
Umm al Qaywayn, *U.A.E.* . 71 E7
Umm al Qittayn, *Jordan* ... 75 C5
Umm Arda, *Sudan* 81 D3
Umm Badr, *Sudan* 81 E2
Umm Bāb, *Qatar* 71 E6
Umm Baiyud, *Sudan* 81 E3
Umm Bel, *Sudan* 81 E2
Umm Birkah, *Si. Arabia* ... 80 B4
Umm Boim, *Sudan* 81 E2
Umm Dam, *Sudan* 81 E3
Umm Debi, *Sudan* 81 E3
Umm Dubban, *Sudan* 81 D3
Umm el Fahm, *Israel* 75 C4
Umm Gafala, *Sudan* 81 E2
Umm Gimala, *Sudan* 81 E2
Umm Inderaba, *Sudan* 80 D3
Umm Keddada, *Sudan* 81 E2
Umm Koweika, *Sudan* 81 E3
Umm Lajj, *Si. Arabia* 70 E3
Umm Merwa, *Sudan* 80 D3
Umm Qantur, *Sudan* 81 E3
Umm Qurein, *Sudan* 81 F2
Umm Ruwaba, *Sudan* 81 E3
Umm Saiyala, *Sudan* 81 E3
Umm Shanqa, *Sudan* 81 E2
Umm Shutur, *Sudan* 81 F3
Umm Sidr, *Sudan* 81 E2
Umm Zehetir, *Egypt* 80 J8
Umnak I., *U.S.A.* 100 C3
Umniati →, *Zimbabwe* 87 F2
Umpqua →, *U.S.A.* 114 E4
Umreth, *India* 68 H5
Umtata, *S. Africa* 89 E4
Umuahia, *Nigeria* 83 D6
Umuarama, *Brazil* 127 A5
Umurbey, *Turkey* 41 F10
Umvukwe Ra., *Zimbabwe* . 87 F3
Umzingwane →, *Zimbabwe* 87 G2
Umzinto, *S. Africa* 89 E5
Una, *India* 68 J4
Una →, *Bos.-H.* 29 D13
Unac →, *Bos.-H.* 29 D13
Unadilla, *U.S.A.* 111 D9
Unalakleet, *U.S.A.* 100 B3
Unalaska, *U.S.A.* 100 C3
Unalaska I., *U.S.A.* 100 C3
'Unayzah, *Si. Arabia* 70 E4
'Unāzah, J., *Asia* 70 C3
Uncastillo, *Spain* 32 C3
Uncía, *Bolivia* 124 G5
Uncompahgre Peak, *U.S.A.* 115 G10
Uncompahgre Plateau,
 U.S.A. 115 G9
Unden, *Sweden* 11 F8
Underbool, *Australia* 95 F3
Undersaker, *Sweden* 10 A7
Unecha, *Russia* 47 F7
Ungarie, *Australia* 95 E4
Ungarra, *Australia* 95 E2
Ungava, Pén. d', *Canada* .. 101 C12
Ungava B., *Canada* 101 C13
Ungeny = Ungheni,
 Moldova 43 C12
Unggi, *N. Korea* 57 C16
Ungheni, *Moldova* 43 C12
Unguala = Ethiopia 81 F5
Ungwatiri, *Sudan* 81 D4
Uni, *Russia* 48 B10
União da Vitória, *Brazil* . 127 B5
Uničov, *Czech Rep.* 27 B10
Uniejów, *Poland* 45 G5
Unije, *Croatia* 29 D11
Unimak I., *U.S.A.* 100 C3
Union, *Miss., U.S.A.* 113 J10
Union, *Mo., U.S.A.* 112 F9
Union, *S.C., U.S.A.* 109 H5
Union City, *Calif., U.S.A.* 116 H4
Union City, *N.J., U.S.A.* . 111 F10
Union City, *Pa., U.S.A.* . 110 E5
Union City, *Tenn., U.S.A.* 113 G10
Union Gap, *U.S.A.* 114 C3
Union Springs, *U.S.A.* ... 109 J3
Uniondale, *S. Africa* 88 E3
Uniontown, *U.S.A.* 108 F6
Unionville, *U.S.A.* 112 E8
Unirea, *Romania* 43 F12
United Arab Emirates ■,
 Asia 71 F7
United Kingdom ■, *Europe* 7 E5
United States of America ■,
 N. Amer. 106 C7
Unity, *Canada* 105 C7
Universales, Mtes., *Spain* . 32 E3
University Park, *U.S.A.* .. 115 K10
Unjha, *India* 68 H5
Unna, *Germany* 24 D3
Unnao, *India* 69 F9
Uno, Ilha, *Guinea-Biss.* .. 82 C1
Unst, *U.K.* 14 A8
Unstrut →, *Germany* 24 D7
Unterfranken □, *Germany* . 25 F6
Unterschleissheim, *Germany* 25 G7
Unuk →, *Canada* 104 B2
Ünye, *Turkey* 72 B7
Unzha, *Russia* 48 A7
Unzha →, *Russia* 48 B6
Uozu, *Japan* 55 F8
Upata, *Venezuela* 124 B6
Upemba, L.,
 Dem. Rep. of the Congo . 87 D2
Upernavik, *Greenland* 4 B5
Upington, *S. Africa* 88 D3
Upleta, *India* 68 J4
Upolu, *W. Samoa* 91 A13
Upper □, *Ghana* 83 C4

Upper Alkali L., *U.S.A.* ... 114 F3
Upper Arrow L., *Canada* .. 104 C5
Upper Austria =
 Oberösterreich □, *Austria* 26 C7
Upper Foster L., *Canada* .. 105 B7
Upper Hutt, *N.Z.* 91 J5
Upper Klamath L., *U.S.A.* . 114 E3
Upper Lake, *U.S.A.* 116 F4
Upper Musquodoboit,
 Canada 103 C7
Upper Red L., *U.S.A.* 112 A7
Upper Sandusky, *U.S.A.* . 108 E4
Upper Volta = Burkina
 Faso ■, *Africa* 82 C4
Upphärad, *Sweden* 11 F6
Uppland, *Sweden* 10 E11
Upplands-Väsby, *Sweden* . 10 E11
Uppsala, *Sweden* 10 E11
Uppsala län □, *Sweden* .. 10 D11
Upshi, *India* 69 C7
Upstart, C., *Australia* 94 B4
Upton, *U.S.A.* 112 C2
Ur, *Iraq* 70 D5
Urad Qianqi, *China* 56 D5
Urakawa, *Japan* 54 C11
Ural = Zhayyq →,
 Kazakhstan 50 E6
Ural, *Australia* 95 E4
Ural Mts. = Uralskie Gory,
 Eurasia 50 D6
Uralla, *Australia* 95 E5
Uralsk = Oral, *Kazakhstan* .. 48 E10
Uralskie Gory, *Eurasia* .. 50 D6
Urambo, *Tanzania* 86 D3
Urana, *Australia* 95 F4
Urandangi, *Australia* 94 C2
Uranium City, *Canada* ... 105 B7
Uraricoera →, *Brazil* 124 C6
Urawa, *Japan* 55 G9
Uray, *Russia* 50 C7
'Uray'irah, *Si. Arabia* .. 71 E6
Urbana, *Ill., U.S.A.* 108 E1
Urbana, *Ohio, U.S.A.* ... 108 E4
Urbánia, *Italy* 29 E9
Urbel →, *Spain* 34 C7
Urbino, *Italy* 29 E9
Urbión, Picos de, *Spain* .. 32 C2
Urcos, *Peru* 124 F4
Urdinarrain, *Argentina* .. 126 C4
Urdos, *France* 20 F3
Urdzhar, *Kazakhstan* 50 E9
Ure →, *U.K.* 12 C6
Uren, *Russia* 48 B7
Ures, *Mexico* 118 B2
Urfa = Sanliurfa, *Turkey* . 70 B3
Urganch = Urganch,
 Uzbekistan 50 E7
Ürgüp, *Turkey* 70 B2
Uri, *India* 69 B6
Uri □, *Switz.* 25 J4
Uribia, *Colombia* 124 A4
Uricani, *Romania* 42 E8
Uriondo, *Bolivia* 126 A3
Urique, *Mexico* 118 B3
Urique →, *Mexico* 118 B3
Urk, *Neths.* 17 B5
Urla, *Turkey* 39 C8
Urlaţi, *Romania* 43 F11
Urmia = Orūmīyeh, *Iran* . 70 B5
Urmia, L. = Orūmīyeh,
 Daryācheh-ye, *Iran* 70 B5
Uroševac, *Kosovo, Yug.* .. 40 D5
Urshult, *Sweden* 11 H8
Uruaçu, *Brazil* 125 F9
Uruapan, *Mexico* 118 D4
Urubamba →, *Peru* 124 F4
Urubupungá, *Brazil* 127 A5
Uruçara, *Brazil* 124 D7
Uruçuí, *Brazil* 125 E10
Uruguai →, *Brazil* 127 B5
Uruguaiana, *Brazil* 126 B4
Uruguay ■, *S. Amer.* 126 C4
Uruguay →, *S. Amer.* ... 126 C4
Urumchi = Ürümqi, *China* . 50 E9
Ürümqi, *China* 50 E9
Urup →, *Russia* 49 H5
Urup, Ostrov, *Russia* 51 E16
Uryupinsk, *Russia* 48 E5
Urzhum, *Russia* 48 B9
Urziceni, *Romania* 43 F11
Usa →, *Russia* 50 C6
Uşak, *Turkey* 39 C11
Uşak □, *Turkey* 39 C11
Usakos, *Namibia* 88 C2
Ušće, *Serbia, Yug.* 40 C4
Usedom, *Germany* 24 B10
Useless Loop, *Australia* .. 93 E1
'Usfān, *Si. Arabia* 80 C4
Ush-Tobe, *Kazakhstan* ... 50 E8
Ushakova, Ostrov, *Russia* . 4 A12
Ushant = Ouessant, Î. d',
 France 18 D1
Ushashi, *Tanzania* 86 C3
Ushat, *Sudan* 81 F2
'Ushayrah, *Si. Arabia* ... 80 C5
Ushibuka, *Japan* 55 H5
Ushuaia, *Argentina* 128 G3
Ushumun, *Russia* 51 D13
Usk, *Canada* 104 C3
Usk →, *U.K.* 13 F5
Uska, *India* 69 F10
Üsküdar, *Turkey* 41 F13
Uslar, *Germany* 24 D5
Usman, *Russia* 47 F10
Usoke, *Tanzania* 86 D3
Usolye Sibirskoye, *Russia* . 51 D11
Usoro, *Nigeria* 83 D6
Uspallata, P. de, *Argentina* . 126 C2
Uspenskiy, *Kazakhstan* .. 26 E8
Ussel, *France* 20 C6
Usson-du-Poitou, *France* .. 20 B4

Ussuri →, *Asia* 54 A7
Ussuriysk, *Russia* 51 E14
Ussurka, *Russia* 54 B6
Ust-Aldan = Batamay,
 Russia 51 C13
Ust-Amginskoye =
 Khandyga, *Russia* 51 C14
Ust-Bolsheretsk, *Russia* .. 51 D16
Ust-Buzulukskaya, *Russia* . 48 E6
Ust-Chaun, *Russia* 51 C18
Ust-Donetskiy, *Russia* ... 49 G5
Ust-Ilimpeya = Yukta,
 Russia 51 C11
Ust-Ilimsk, *Russia* 51 D11
Ust-Ishim, *Russia* 50 D8
Ust-Kamchatsk, *Russia* .. 51 D17
Ust-Kamenogorsk =
 Öskemen, *Kazakhstan* .. 50 E9
Ust-Khayryuzovo, *Russia* . 51 D16
Ust-Kut, *Russia* 51 D11
Ust-Kuyga, *Russia* 51 B14
Ust-Labinsk, *Russia* 49 H4
Ust-Luga, *Russia* 46 C5
Ust-Maya, *Russia* 51 C14
Ust-Mil, *Russia* 51 D14
Ust-Nera, *Russia* 51 C15
Ust-Nyukzha, *Russia* 51 D13
Ust-Olenek, *Russia* 51 B12
Ust-Omchug, *Russia* 51 C15
Ust-Port, *Russia* 50 C9
Ust-Tsilma, *Russia* 50 C6
Ust Urt = Ustyurt Plateau,
 Asia 50 E6
Ustaritz, *France* 20 E2
Uster, *Switz.* 25 H4
Ústí nad Labem, *Czech Rep.* 26 A7
Ústí nad Orlicí, *Czech Rep.* 27 B9
Ústica, *Italy* 30 D6
Ustinov = Izhevsk, *Russia* . 50 D6
Ustka, *Poland* 44 D3
Ustroń, *Poland* 45 J5
Ustrzyki Dolne, *Poland* .. 45 J9
Ustyurt Plateau, *Asia* 50 E6
Ustyuzhna, *Russia* 46 C9
Usu, *China* 60 B3
Usuki, *Japan* 55 H5
Usulután, *El Salv.* 120 D2
Usumacinta →, *Mexico* .. 119 D6
Usumbura = Bujumbura,
 Burundi 86 C2
Usure, *Tanzania* 86 C3
Usutuo →, *Mozam.* 89 D5
Uta, *Indonesia* 63 E9
Utah □, *U.S.A.* 114 G8
Utah L., *U.S.A.* 114 F8
Utansjö, *Sweden* 10 B11
Utarni, *India* 68 F4
Utatlan, *Guatemala* 120 C1
Ute Creek →, *U.S.A.* 113 H3
Utebo, *Spain* 32 D3
Utena, *Lithuania* 9 J21
Utete, *Tanzania* 86 D4
Uthai Thani, *Thailand* ... 64 E3
Uthal, *Pakistan* 68 G2
Utiariti, *Brazil* 124 F7
Utica, *N.Y., U.S.A.* 111 C9
Utica, *Ohio, U.S.A.* 110 F2
Utikuma L., *Canada* 104 B5
Utö, *Sweden* 10 F12
Utopia, *Australia* 94 C1
Utraula, *India* 69 F10
Utrecht, *Neths.* 17 B5
Utrecht, *S. Africa* 89 D5
Utrecht □, *Neths.* 17 B5
Utrera, *Spain* 35 H5
Utsjoki, *Finland* 8 B22
Utsunomiya, *Japan* 55 F9
Uttar Pradesh □, *India* .. 69 F9
Uttaradit, *Thailand* 64 D3
Uttoxeter, *U.K.* 12 E6
Uummannarsuaq = Nunap
 Isua, *Greenland* 4 D5
Uusikaarlepyy, *Finland* .. 8 E20
Uusikaupunki, *Finland* ... 9 F19
Uva, *Russia* 48 B11
Uvac →, *Serbia, Yug.* ... 40 C3
Uvalde, *U.S.A.* 113 L5
Uvarovo, *Russia* 48 E6
Uvat, *Russia* 50 D7
Uvinza, *Tanzania* 86 D3
Uvira,
 Dem. Rep. of the Congo . 86 C2
Uvs Nuur, *Mongolia* 60 A4
'Uwairidh, Harrat al,
 Si. Arabia 70 E3
Uwajima, *Japan* 55 H6
Uweinat, Jebel, *Sudan* ... 80 D1
Uxbridge, *Canada* 110 B5
Uxin Qi, *China* 56 E5
Uxmal, *Mexico* 119 C7
Üydzin, *Mongolia* 56 B4
Uyo, *Nigeria* 83 D6
Üyüklü Tepe, *Turkey* 39 D9
Uyūn Mūsa, *Egypt* 80 J7
Uyuni, *Bolivia* 124 H5
Uzbekistan ■, *Asia* 50 E7
Uzen, Bolshoi →,
 Kazakhstan 49 F9
Uzen, Mal →, *Kazakhstan* 49 F9
Uzerche, *France* 20 C5
Uzès, *France* 21 D8
Uzh →, *Ukraine* 47 G6
Uzhgorod = Uzhhorod,
 Ukraine 47 H2
Uzhhorod, *Ukraine* 47 H2
Užice, *Serbia, Yug.* 40 C3
Uzlovaya, *Russia* 46 F10
Üzümlü, *Turkey* 39 E11
Uzunköprü, *Turkey* 41 E10
Uzunkuyu, *Turkey* 39 C8

V

Vaal →, *S. Africa* 88 D3
Vaal Dam, *S. Africa* 89 D4
Vaalwater, *S. Africa* 89 C4
Vaasa, *Finland* 8 E19
Vabre, *France* 20 E6
Vác, *Hungary* 42 C4
Vacaria, *Brazil* 127 B5
Vacaville, *U.S.A.* 116 G5
Vaccarès, Étang de, *France* 21 E8
Vach = Vakh →, *Russia* .. 50 C8
Vache, Î. à, *Haiti* 121 C5
Väckelsång, *Sweden* 11 H8
Vadnagar, *India* 68 H5
Vado Lígure, *Italy* 28 D5
Vadodara, *India* 68 H5
Vadsø, *Norway* 8 A23
Vadstena, *Sweden* 11 F8
Vaduz, *Liech.* 25 H5
Værøy, *Norway* 8 C15
Vágar, *Færoe Is.* 8 E9
Vaggeryd, *Sweden* 11 G8
Vagney, *France* 19 D13
Vagnhärad, *Sweden* 11 F11
Vagos, *Portugal* 34 E2
Vågsfjorden, *Norway* 8 B17
Váh →, *Slovak Rep.* 27 D11
Vahsel B., *Antarctica* 5 D1
Vái, *Greece* 36 D8
Vaigach, *Russia* 50 B6
Vaiges, *France* 18 D6
Vaihingen, *Germany* 25 G4
Vail, *U.S.A.* 106 C5
Vailly-sur-Aisne, *France* .. 19 C10
Vaisali →, *India* 69 F8
Vaison-la-Romaine, *France* . 21 D9
Vakarel, *Bulgaria* 40 D7
Vakfıkebir, *Turkey* 73 B8
Vakh →, *Russia* 50 C8
Vakhtan, *Russia* 48 B8
Vál, *Hungary* 42 C3
Val-de-Marne □, *France* .. 19 D9
Val-d'Isère, *France* 21 C10
Val-d'Oise □, *France* 19 C9
Val-d'Or, *Canada* 102 C4
Val Marie, *Canada* 105 D7
Valaam, *Russia* 46 B6
Valadares, *Portugal* 34 D2
Valahia, *Romania* 43 F9
Valais □, *Switz.* 25 J3
Valais, Alpes du, *Switz.* .. 25 J3
Valalta, *Argentina* 128 E3
Valandovo, *Macedonia* .. 40 E6
Valašské Meziříčí,
 Czech Rep. 27 B10
Valáxa, *Greece* 38 C6
Vålberg, *Sweden* 10 E7
Valbo, *Sweden* 10 D10
Valbondione, *Italy* 28 B7
Vâlcani, *Romania* 42 D5
Vâlcea □, *Romania* 43 F9
Valcheta, *Argentina* 128 E3
Valdagno, *Italy* 29 C8
Valdahon, *France* 19 E13
Valdemárrobes, *Spain* ... 32 E5
Valdaj, *U.S.A.* 100 B5
Valdayskaya Vozvyshennost,
 Russia 46 D7
Valdeazogues →, *Spain* .. 35 G6
Valdecañas, Embalse de,
 Spain 34 F5
Valdemarsvik, *Sweden* ... 11 F10
Valdemoro, *Spain* 34 E7
Valdepeñas, *Spain* 35 G7
Valderaduey →, *Spain* ... 34 D5
Valdérice, *Italy* 30 D5
Valderrobres, *Spain* 32 E5
Valdés, Pen., *Argentina* .. 122 H4
Valdez, *U.S.A.* 100 B5
Valdivia, *Chile* 128 D2
Valdobbiádene, *Italy* 29 C8
Valdosta, *U.S.A.* 109 K4
Valdoviño, *Spain* 34 B2
Valdres, *Norway* 9 F13
Vale, *Georgia* 49 K6
Vale, *U.S.A.* 114 E5
Vale of Glamorgan □, *U.K.* 13 F4
Valea lui Mihai, *Romania* . 42 C7
Valea Mărului, *Romania* . 43 E12
Valemount, *Canada* 104 C5
Valença, *Brazil* 125 F11
Valença, *Portugal* 34 C2
Valença do Piauí, *Brazil* . 125 E10
Valençay, *France* 19 E8
Valence = Valence d'Agen,
 France 20 D4
Valence, *France* 21 D8
Valence d'Agen, *France* .. 20 D4
Valencia, *Spain* 33 F4
Valencia, *Venezuela* 124 A5
Valencia □, *Spain* 33 F4
Valencia de Alcántara, *Spain* 35 F3
Valencia de Don Juan, *Spain* 34 C5
Valencia I., *Ireland* 15 E1
Valencia, Albufera de, *Spain* 33 F4
Valenciennes, *France* 19 B10
Vălenii de Munte, *Romania* 43 E11
Valensole, *France* 21 E9
Valentigney, *France* 19 E13
Valentim, Sa. do, *Brazil* .. 125 E10
Valentine, *U.S.A.* 113 K2
Valera, *Venezuela* 124 B4
Valga, *Estonia* 9 H22
Valguarnera Caropepe, *Italy* 31 E7
Valier, *U.S.A.* 114 B7

Valinco, G. de, *France* 21 G12
Valjevo, *Serbia, Yug.* 40 B3
Valka, *Latvia* 9 H21
Valkeakoski, *Finland* 9 F20
Valkenswaard, *Neths.* ... 17 C5
Vall de Uxó = La Vall
 d'Uixó, *Spain* 32 F4
Valla, *Sweden* 10 E10
Valladolid, *Mexico* 119 C7
Valladolid, *Spain* 34 D6
Valladolid □, *Spain* 34 D6
Vallata, *Italy* 31 A8
Valldemossa, *Spain* 37 B9
Valle d'Aosta □, *Italy* ... 28 C4
Valle de Arán, *Spain* 32 C5
Valle de la Pascua,
 Venezuela 124 B5
Valle de las Palmas, *Mexico* 117 N10
Valle de Santiago, *Mexico* . 118 C4
Valle de Suchil, *Mexico* .. 118 C4
Valle de Zaragoza, *Mexico* . 118 B3
Valle Fértil, Sierra del,
 Argentina 126 C2
Valle Hermoso, *Mexico* .. 119 B5
Valledupar, *Colombia* ... 124 A4
Vallehermoso, *Canary Is.* .. 37 F2
Vallejo, *U.S.A.* 116 G4
Vallenar, *Chile* 126 B1
Vallentuna, *Sweden* 10 E12
Valleraugue, *France* 20 D7
Vallet, *France* 18 E5
Valletta, *Malta* 36 D2
Valley Center, *U.S.A.* 117 M9
Valley City, *U.S.A.* 112 B6
Valley Falls, *Oreg., U.S.A.* . 114 E3
Valley Falls, *R.I., U.S.A.* .. 111 E13
Valley Springs, *U.S.A.* ... 116 G6
Valley View, *U.S.A.* 111 F8
Valley Wells, *U.S.A.* 117 K11
Valleyview, *Canada* 104 B5
Valli di Comácchio, *Italy* . 29 D9
Vallimanca, Arroyo,
 Argentina 126 D4
Vallo della Lucánia, *Italy* . 31 B8
Vallon-Pont-d'Arc, *France* . 21 D8
Vallorbe, *Switz.* 25 J2
Valls, *Spain* 32 D6
Valmaseda = Balmaseda,
 Spain 32 B1
Valmiera, *Latvia* 9 H21
Valnera, *Spain* 34 B7
Valognes, *France* 18 C5
Valona = Vlóra, *Albania* .. 40 F3
Valongo, *Portugal* 34 D2
Valozhyn, *Belarus* 46 E4
Valpaços, *Portugal* 34 D3
Valparaíso, *Chile* 126 C1
Valparaíso, *Mexico* 118 C4
Valparaiso, *U.S.A.* 108 E2
Valparaíso □, *Chile* 126 C1
Valpovo, *Croatia* 42 E3
Valréas, *France* 21 D9
Vals, *Switz.* 25 J5
Vals →, *S. Africa* 88 D4
Vals, Tanjung, *Indonesia* . 63 F9
Vals-les-Bains, *France* ... 21 D8
Valsad, *India* 66 J8
Valtellina, *Italy* 28 B6
Valuyki, *Russia* 47 G10
Valverde, *Spain* 37 G2
Valverde del Camino, *Spain* 35 H4
Valverde del Fresno, *Spain* 34 E4
Vama, *Romania* 43 C10
Vamdrup, *Denmark* 11 J3
Våmhus, *Sweden* 10 C8
Vammala, *Finland* 9 F20
Vámos, *Greece* 36 D6
Van, *Turkey* 70 B4
Van, L. = Van Gölü, *Turkey* 70 B4
Van Alstyne, *U.S.A.* 113 J6
Van Blommestein Meer,
 Surinam 125 C7
Van Buren, *Canada* 103 C6
Van Buren, *Ark., U.S.A.* . 113 H7
Van Buren, *Maine, U.S.A.* 109 B11
Van Buren, *Mo., U.S.A.* . 113 G9
Van Canh, *Vietnam* 64 F7
Van Diemen, C., *N. Terr.,
 Australia* 92 B5
Van Diemen, C., *Queens.,
 Australia* 94 B2
Van Diemen G., *Australia* . 92 B5
Van Gölü, *Turkey* 70 B4
Van Horn, *U.S.A.* 113 K2
Van Ninh, *Vietnam* 64 F7
Van Rees, Pegunungan,
 Indonesia 63 E9
Van Wert, *U.S.A.* 108 E3
Van Yen, *Vietnam* 58 G5
Vanadzor, *Armenia* 49 K7
Vanavara, *Russia* 51 C11
Vancouver, *Canada* 104 D4
Vancouver, *U.S.A.* 116 E4
Vancouver, C., *Australia* .. 93 G2
Vancouver I., *Canada* ... 104 D3
Vandalia, *Ill., U.S.A.* 112 F10
Vandalia, *Mo., U.S.A.* ... 112 F9
Vandenburg, *U.S.A.* 117 L6
Vanderbijlpark, *S. Africa* . 89 D4
Vanderhoof, *Canada* 104 C4
Vanderkloof Dam, *S. Africa* 88 E3
Vanderlin I., *Australia* ... 94 B2
Vänern, *Sweden* 11 F7
Vänersborg, *Sweden* 11 F6
Vang Vieng, *Laos* 64 C4
Vanga, *Kenya* 86 C4
Vangaindrano, *Madag.* .. 89 C8
Vanguard, *Canada* 105 D7
Vanino, *Russia* 51 E15

Vanna

Vanna, Norway ... 8 A18
Vännäs, Sweden ... 8 E18
Vannes, France ... 18 E4
Vanoise, France ... 21 C10
Vanrhynsdorp, S. Africa ... 88 E2
Vansbro, Sweden ... 10 D8
Vansittart B., Australia ... 92 B4
Vantaa, Finland ... 9 F21
Vanua Levu, Fiji ... 91 C8
Vanua Mbalavu, Fiji ... 91 C9
Vanuatu ■, Pac. Oc. ... 96 J8
Vanwyksvlei, S. Africa ... 88 E3
Vanzylsrus, S. Africa ... 88 D3
Vapnyarka, Ukraine ... 47 H5
Var □, France ... 21 E10
Var →, France ... 21 E11
Vara, Sweden ... 11 F6
Varades, France ... 18 E5
Varáita →, Italy ... 28 D4
Varallo, Italy ... 28 C5
Varanasi, India ... 69 G10
Varanger-halvøya, Norway . 8 A23
Varangerfjorden, Norway .. 8 A23
Varano, Lago di, Italy ... 29 G12
Varaždin, Croatia ... 29 B13
Varazze, Italy ... 28 D5
Varberg, Sweden ... 11 G6
Vardar = Axiós →, Greece 40 F6
Varde, Denmark ... 11 J2
Varde Å →, Denmark ... 11 J2
Vardø, Norway ... 8 A24
Varel, Germany ... 24 B4
Varella, Mui, Vietnam ... 64 F7
Varéna, Lithuania ... 9 J21
Varennes-sur-Allier, France 19 F10
Varennes-Vauzelles, France 19 E10
Vareš, Bos.-H. ... 42 F3
Varese, Italy ... 28 C5
Vârfurile, Romania ... 42 D7
Vårgårda, Sweden ... 11 F6
Varginha, Brazil ... 127 A6
Vargön, Sweden ... 11 F6
Varillas, Chile ... 126 A1
Varkaus, Finland ... 9 E22
Värmdölandet, Sweden ... 10 E12
Värmeln, Sweden ... 10 E6
Värmlands Bro, Sweden ... 10 E7
Värmlands län □, Sweden .. 10 E6
Varna, Bulgaria ... 41 C11
Varna □, Bulgaria ... 41 C11
Värnamo, Sweden ... 11 G8
Varnsdorf, Czech Rep. ... 26 A7
Várpalota, Hungary ... 42 C3
Vars, Canada ... 111 A9
Vars, France ... 21 D10
Varto, Turkey ... 73 C9
Varvarin, Serbia, Yug. ... 40 C5
Varysburg, U.S.A. ... 110 D6
Varzaneh, Iran ... 71 C7
Varzi, Italy ... 28 D6
Varzo, Italy ... 28 B5
Varzy, France ... 19 E10
Vasa Barris →, Brazil ... 125 F11
Vásárosnamény, Hungary .. 42 B7
Vascão →, Portugal ... 35 H3
Vaşcău, Romania ... 42 D7
Vascongadas = País
Vasco □, Spain ... 32 C2
Vasht = Khāsh, Iran ... 66 E2
Vasilevichi, Belarus ... 47 F5
Vasilikón, Greece ... 38 C5
Vasilkov = Vasylkiv,
Ukraine ... 47 G6
Vaslui, Romania ... 43 D12
Vaslui □, Romania ... 43 D12
Väsman, Sweden ... 10 D9
Vassar, Canada ... 105 D9
Vassar, U.S.A. ... 108 D4
Västerås, Sweden ... 10 E10
Västerbotten, Sweden ... 8 D18
Västerdalälven →, Sweden . 10 D8
Västergötland, Sweden ... 11 F7
Västerhaninge, Sweden ... 10 E12
Västervik, Sweden ... 11 G10
Västmanland, Sweden ... 9 G16
Västmanlands län □, Sweden 10 E10
Vasto, Italy ... 29 F11
Vasvár, Hungary ... 42 C1
Vasylkiv, Ukraine ... 47 G6
Vatan, France ... 19 E8
Vatersay, U.K. ... 14 E1
Váthia, Greece ... 38 E4
Vatican City ■, Europe ... 29 G9
Vaticano, C., Italy ... 31 D8
Vatili, Cyprus ... 36 D12
Vatin, Serbia, Yug. ... 42 E6
Vatnajökull, Iceland ... 8 D5
Vatoa, Fiji ... 91 D9
Vatólakkos, Greece ... 36 D5
Vatoloha, Madag. ... 89 B8
Vatomandry, Madag. ... 89 B8
Vatra-Dornei, Romania ... 43 C10
Vatrak →, India ... 68 H5
Vättern, Sweden ... 11 F8
Vaucluse □, France ... 21 E9
Vaucouleurs, France ... 19 D12
Vaud □, Switz. ... 25 J2
Vaughn, Mont., U.S.A. ... 114 C8
Vaughn, N. Mex., U.S.A. . 115 J11
Vaujours L., France ... 102 A5
Vaupés = Uaupés →, Brazil 124 C5
Vaupes □, Colombia ... 124 C4
Vauvert, France ... 21 E8
Vauxhall, Canada ... 104 C6
Vav, India ... 68 G4
Vavatenina, Madag. ... 89 B8
Vava'u, Tonga ... 91 D12
Vavoua, Ivory C. ... 82 D3
Vawkavysk, Belarus ... 47 F3
Vaxholm, Sweden ... 10 E12

Växjö, Sweden ... 11 H8
Våxtorp, Sweden ... 11 H7
Vaygach, Ostrov, Russia ... 50 C6
Váyia, Greece ... 38 C5
Váyia, Ákra, Greece ... 36 C10
Vechelde, Germany ... 24 C6
Vechta, Germany ... 24 C4
Vechte →, Neths. ... 17 B6
Vecsés, Hungary ... 42 C4
Veddige, Sweden ... 11 G6
Vedea →, Romania ... 43 G10
Vedia, Argentina ... 126 C3
Vedum, Sweden ... 11 F7
Veendam, Neths. ... 17 A6
Veenendaal, Neths. ... 17 B5
Vefsna →, Norway ... 8 D15
Vega, Norway ... 8 D14
Vega, U.S.A. ... 113 H3
Vegadeo, Spain ... 34 B3
Vegorrítis, Límni, Greece .. 40 F5
Vegreville, Canada ... 104 C6
Veinge, Sweden ... 11 H7
Veisiejai, Lithuania ... 44 D10
Vejbystrand, Sweden ... 11 H6
Vejen, Denmark ... 11 J3
Vejer de la Frontera, Spain 35 J5
Vejle, Denmark ... 11 J3
Vejle Amtskommune □,
Denmark ... 11 J3
Vejle Fjord, Denmark ... 11 J3
Vela Luka, Croatia ... 29 F13
Velas, C., Costa Rica ... 120 D2
Velasco, Sierra de, Argentina 126 B2
Velay, Mts. du, France ... 20 D7
Velbert, Germany ... 24 D3
Velddrif, S. Africa ... 88 E2
Velebit Planina, Croatia ... 29 D12
Velebitski Kanal, Croatia .. 29 D11
Veleka →, Bulgaria ... 41 D11
Velenje, Slovenia ... 29 B12
Veles, Macedonia ... 40 E5
Velestínon, Greece ... 38 B4
Vélez-Málaga, Spain ... 35 J6
Vélez Rubio, Spain ... 33 H2
Velhas →, Brazil ... 125 G10
Velika, Croatia ... 42 E2
Velika Gorica, Croatia ... 29 C13
Velika Kapela, Croatia ... 29 C12
Velika Kladuša, Bos.-H. ... 29 C12
Velika Kruša, Kosovo, Yug. 40 D4
Velika Morava →,
Serbia, Yug. ... 40 B5
Velika Plana, Serbia, Yug. . 40 B5
Velikaya →, Russia ... 46 D5
Velikaya Kema, Russia ... 54 B8
Velikaya Lepetikha, Ukraine 47 J7
Veliké Kapušany,
Slovak Rep. ... 27 C15
Velike Lašče, Slovenia ... 29 C11
Veliki Jastrebac,
Serbia, Yug. ... 40 C5
Veliki Kanal, Serbia, Yug. . 42 E4
Veliki Popović, Serbia, Yug. 40 B5
Velikiye Luki, Russia ... 46 D6
Veliko Gradište,
Serbia, Yug. ... 40 B5
Veliko Tŭrnovo, Bulgaria . 41 C9
Velikonda Range, India ... 66 M11
Vélingara, Senegal ... 82 C2
Vélingara, Senegal ... 82 B2
Velingrad, Bulgaria ... 40 D7
Velino, Mte., Italy ... 29 F10
Velizh, Russia ... 46 E6
Velké Karlovice, Czech Rep. 27 B11
Velké Meziříčí, Czech Rep. 26 B9
Vel'ký Javorník, Slovak Rep. 27 B11
Vel'ký Krtíš, Slovak Rep. .. 27 C12
Vel'ký Meder, Slovak Rep. . 27 D10
Vel'ký Tribeč, Slovak Rep. 27 C11
Velletri, Italy ... 30 A5
Vellinge, Sweden ... 11 J6
Vellmar, Germany ... 24 D5
Vellore, India ... 66 N11
Velsk, Russia ... 46 B11
Velten, Germany ... 24 C9
Velva, U.S.A. ... 112 A4
Velvendós, Greece ... 40 F6
Vemb, Denmark ... 11 H2
Vemdalen, Sweden ... 10 B7
Ven, Sweden ... 11 J6
Venaco, France ... 21 F13
Venado Tuerto, Argentina . 126 C3
Venafro, Italy ... 31 A7
Venarey-les-Laumes, France 19 E11
Venaría, Italy ... 28 C4
Venčane, Serbia, Yug. ... 40 B4
Vence, France ... 21 E11
Vendas Novas, Portugal ... 35 G2
Vendée □, France ... 18 F5
Vendée →, France ... 18 F5
Vendéen, Bocage, France .. 20 B2
Vendeuvre-sur-Barse, France 19 D11
Vendôme, France ... 18 E8
Vendrell = El Vendrell,
Spain ... 32 D6
Vendsyssel, Denmark ... 11 G4
Venelles, France ... 21 E9
Véneto □, Italy ... 29 C9
Venev, Russia ... 46 E10
Venézia, Italy ... 29 C9
Venézia, G. di, Italy ... 29 C10
Venezuela ■, S. Amer. ... 124 B5
Venezuela, G. de, Venezuela 122 B3
Vengurla, India ... 66 M8
Venice = Venézia, Italy ... 29 C9
Venice, U.S.A. ... 109 M4
Vénissieux, France ... 21 C8
Venjansjön, Sweden ... 10 D8
Venkatapuram, India ... 67 K12

Venlo, Neths. ... 17 C6
Vennesla, Norway ... 9 G12
Venosa, Italy ... 31 B8
Venray, Neths. ... 17 C6
Venta, Lithuania ... 44 B9
Venta →, Latvia ... 44 A8
Venta de Baños, Spain ... 34 D6
Venta de Cardeña =
Cardeña, Spain ... 35 G6
Ventana, Punta de la,
Mexico ... 118 C3
Ventana, Sa. de la,
Argentina ... 126 D3
Ventersburg, S. Africa ... 88 D4
Venterstad, S. Africa ... 88 E4
Ventimíglia, Italy ... 28 E4
Ventnor, U.K. ... 13 G6
Ventoténe, Italy ... 30 B6
Ventoux, Mt., France ... 21 D9
Ventspils, Latvia ... 9 H19
Ventspils □, Latvia ... 44 A8
Ventuarí →, Venezuela ... 124 C5
Ventucopa, U.S.A. ... 117 L7
Ventura, U.S.A. ... 117 L7
Venus B., Australia ... 95 F4
Vera, Argentina ... 126 B3
Vera, Spain ... 33 H3
Veracruz, Mexico ... 119 D5
Veracruz □, Mexico ... 119 D5
Veraval, India ... 68 J4
Verbánia, Italy ... 28 C5
Verbicaro, Italy ... 31 C8
Verbier, Switz. ... 25 J3
Vercelli, Italy ... 28 C5
Verchovchevo, Ukraine ... 47 H8
Verdalsøra, Norway ... 8 E14
Verde →, Argentina ... 128 E3
Verde →, Goiás, Brazil ... 125 G8
Verde →,
Mato Grosso do Sul,
Brazil ... 125 H8
Verde →, Chihuahua,
Mexico ... 118 B3
Verde →, Oaxaca, Mexico . 119 D5
Verde →, Veracruz, Mexico 118 C4
Verde →, Paraguay ... 126 A4
Verde →, U.S.A. ... 106 D4
Verde, Cay, Bahamas ... 120 B4
Verden, Germany ... 24 C5
Verdhikoúsa, Greece ... 38 B3
Verdi, U.S.A. ... 116 F7
Verdon →, France ... 21 E9
Verdun, France ... 19 C12
Verdun-sur-le-Doubs, France 19 F12
Vereeniging, S. Africa ... 89 D4
Verga, C., Guinea ... 82 C2
Vergara, Uruguay ... 127 C5
Vergato, Italy ... 28 D8
Vergemont Cr. →, Australia 94 C3
Vergennes, U.S.A. ... 111 B11
Vergt, France ... 20 C4
Verín, Spain ... 34 D3
Verkhnedvinsk =
Vyerkhnyadzvinsk, Belarus 46 E4
Verkhnevilyuysk, Russia ... 51 C13
Verkhniy Baskunchak,
Russia ... 49 F8
Verkhovye, Russia ... 47 H9
Verkhoyansk, Russia ... 51 C14
Verkhoyansk Ra. =
Verkhoyanskiy Khrebet,
Russia ... 51 C13
Verkhoyanskiy Khrebet,
Russia ... 51 C13
Vermenton, France ... 19 E10
Vermilion, Canada ... 105 C6
Vermilion, U.S.A. ... 110 E2
Vermilion →, Alta., Canada 105 C6
Vermilion →, Qué., Canada 102 C5
Vermilion, B., U.S.A. ... 113 L9
Vermilion Bay, Canada ... 105 D10
Vermilion L., U.S.A. ... 112 B8
Vermillion, U.S.A. ... 112 D6
Vermont □, U.S.A. ... 111 C12
Vermosh, Albania ... 40 D3
Vernal, U.S.A. ... 114 F9
Vernalis, U.S.A. ... 116 H5
Vernazza, Italy ... 28 D6
Verner, Canada ... 102 C3
Verneuil-sur-Avre, France . 18 D7
Verneukpan, S. Africa ... 88 E3
Vernier, Switz. ... 25 J2
Vernon, Canada ... 104 C5
Vernon, France ... 18 C8
Vernon, U.S.A. ... 113 H5
Vernonia, U.S.A. ... 116 E3
Vernouillet, France ... 18 D8
Vero Beach, U.S.A. ... 109 M5
Véroia, Greece ... 40 F6
Véroli, Italy ... 29 G10
Verona, Canada ... 111 B8
Verona, Italy ... 28 C7
Verona, U.S.A. ... 112 D10
Versailles, France ... 19 D9
Versmold, Germany ... 24 C4
Vert, C., Senegal ... 82 C1
Vertou, France ... 18 E5
Vertus, France ... 19 D11
Verulam, S. Africa ... 89 D5
Verviers, Belgium ... 17 D5
Vervins, France ... 19 C10
Veržej, Slovenia ... 29 B13
Verzy, France ... 19 C11
Vescovato, France ... 21 F13
Veselí nad Lužnicí,
Czech Rep. ... 26 B7
Veselie, Bulgaria ... 41 D11
Veselovskoye Vdkhr., Russia 49 G5

Veshenskaya, Russia ... 48 F5
Vesle →, France ... 19 C10
Vesoul, France ... 19 E13
Vessigebro, Sweden ... 11 H6
Vesterålen, Norway ... 8 B16
Vestfjorden, Norway ... 8 C15
Vestmannaeyjar, Iceland ... 8 E3
Vestsjællands
Amtskommune □,
Denmark ... 11 J5
Vestspitsbergen, Svalbard . 4 B8
Vestvågøy, Norway ... 8 B15
Vesuvio, Italy ... 31 B7
Vesuvius, Mt. = Vesuvio,
Italy ... 31 B7
Vesyegonsk, Russia ... 46 C9
Veszprém, Hungary ... 42 C2
Veszprém □, Hungary ... 42 C2
Vésztő, Hungary ... 42 D6
Vetlanda, Sweden ... 11 G9
Vetluga, Russia ... 48 B7
Vetlugu →, Russia ... 48 B8
Vetluzhskiy, Kostroma,
Russia ... 48 A7
Vetluzhskiy,
Nizhniy Novgorod, Russia 48 B7
Vetovo, Bulgaria ... 41 C10
Vetralla, Italy ... 29 F9
Vetren, Bulgaria ... 41 D8
Vettore, Mte., Italy ... 29 F10
Veurne, Belgium ... 17 C2
Veveno →, Sudan ... 81 F3
Vevey, Switz. ... 25 J2
Vévi, Greece ... 40 F5
Veynes, France ... 21 D9
Veys, Iran ... 71 D6
Vézelay, France ... 19 E10
Vézelise, France ... 19 D13
Vézère →, France ... 20 D4
Vezhen, Bulgaria ... 41 D8
Vezirköprü, Turkey ... 72 B6
Vezzani, France ... 21 F13
Vi Thanh, Vietnam ... 65 H5
Viacha, Bolivia ... 124 G5
Viadana, Italy ... 28 D7
Viamão, Brazil ... 127 C5
Viana, Brazil ... 125 D10
Viana, Spain ... 32 C2
Viana do Alentejo, Portugal 35 G3
Viana do Bolo, Spain ... 34 C3
Viana do Castelo, Portugal . 34 D2
Viana do Castelo □,
Portugal ... 34 D2
Vianden, Lux. ... 17 E6
Vianópolis, Brazil ... 125 G9
Viar →, Spain ... 35 H5
Viaréggio, Italy ... 28 E7
Vibble, Sweden ... 11 G12
Vibo Valéntia, Italy ... 31 D9
Viborg, Denmark ... 11 H3
Viborg Amtskommune □,
Denmark ... 11 H3
Vibraye, France ... 18 D7
Vic, Spain ... 32 D7
Vic, Étang de, France ... 20 E7
Vic-en-Bigorre, France ... 20 E4
Vic-Fézensac, France ... 20 E4
Vic-le-Comte, France ... 19 G10
Vic-sur-Cère, France ... 20 D6
Vícar, Spain ... 33 J2
Vicenza, Italy ... 29 C8
Vichada →, Colombia ... 124 C5
Vichuga, Russia ... 48 B5
Vichy, France ... 19 F10
Vicksburg, Ariz., U.S.A. .. 117 M13
Vicksburg, Miss., U.S.A. .. 113 J9
Vico, France ... 21 F12
Vico del Gargano, Italy ... 29 G12
Vico, L. di, Italy ... 29 F9
Vicovu de Sus, Romania ... 43 C10
Victor, India ... 68 J4
Victor, U.S.A. ... 110 D7
Victor Harbor, Australia ... 95 F2
Victoria = Labuan, Malaysia 62 C5
Victoria, Argentina ... 126 C3
Victoria, Canada ... 104 D4
Victoria, Chile ... 128 D2
Victoria, Guinea ... 82 C2
Victoria, Malta ... 36 C1
Victoria, Phil. ... 61 D4
Victoria □, Australia ... 95 F3
Victoria →, Australia ... 92 C4
Victoria, Grand L., Canada 102 C4
Victoria, L., Africa ... 86 C3
Victoria, L., Australia ... 95 E3
Victoria Beach, Canada ... 105 C9
Victoria de Durango =
Durango, Mexico ... 118 C4
Victoria de las Tunas, Cuba 120 B4
Victoria Falls, Zimbabwe .. 87 F2
Victoria Harbour, Canada .. 110 B5
Victoria I., Canada ... 100 A8
Victoria L., Canada ... 103 C8
Victoria Ld., Antarctica ... 5 D11
Victoria Nile →, Uganda .. 86 B3
Victoria River, Australia ... 92 C4
Victoria Str., Canada ... 100 B9
Victoria Taungdeik, Burma 67 J18
Victoria West, S. Africa ... 88 E3
Victoriaville, Canada ... 103 C5
Victorica, Argentina ... 126 D2
Victorville, U.S.A. ... 117 L9
Vicuña, Chile ... 126 C1
Vicuña Mackenna, Argentina 126 C3
Vidal, U.S.A. ... 117 L12

Vidal Junction, U.S.A. ... 117 L12
Vidalia, U.S.A. ... 109 J4
Vidauban, France ... 21 E10
Videbæk, Denmark ... 11 H2
Videle, Romania ... 43 F10
Vídho, Greece ... 36 A3
Vidigueira, Portugal ... 35 G3
Vidin, Bulgaria ... 40 C6
Vidio, C., Spain ... 34 B4
Vidisha, India ... 68 H7
Vidra, Romania ... 43 E11
Viduša, Bos.-H. ... 40 D2
Vidzy, Belarus ... 9 J22
Viechtach, Germany ... 25 D8
Viedma, Argentina ... 128 E4
Viedma, L., Argentina ... 128 F2
Vieira do Minho, Portugal . 34 D2
Vielha, Spain ... 32 C5
Viella = Vielha, Spain ... 32 C5
Vielsalm, Belgium ... 17 D5
Vienenburg, Germany ... 24 D6
Vieng Pou Kha, Laos ... 58 G3
Vienna = Wien, Austria ... 27 C9
Vienna, Ill., U.S.A. ... 113 G10
Vienna, Mo., U.S.A. ... 112 F9
Vienne, France ... 21 C8
Vienne □, France ... 20 B4
Vienne →, France ... 18 E7
Vientiane, Laos ... 64 D4
Vientos, Paso de los,
Caribbean ... 121 C5
Viernheim, Germany ... 25 F4
Viersen, Germany ... 24 D2
Vierwaldstättersee, Switz. . 25 J4
Vierzon, France ... 19 E9
Vieste, Italy ... 29 G13
Vietnam ■, Asia ... 64 C6
Vieux-Boucau-les-Bains,
France ... 20 E2
Vif, France ... 21 C9
Vigan, Phil. ... 61 C4
Vigévano, Italy ... 28 C5
Vigia, Brazil ... 125 D9
Vigía Chico, Mexico ... 119 D7
Víglas, Ákra, Greece ... 36 D9
Vignemalle, France ... 20 F3
Vigneulles-lès-Hattonchâtel,
France ... 19 D12
Vignola, Italy ... 28 D8
Vigo, Spain ... 34 C2
Vigo, Ría de, Spain ... 34 C2
Vigsø Bugt, Denmark ... 11 G2
Vihiers, France ... 18 E6
Vihowa, Pakistan ... 68 D4
Vihowa →, Pakistan ... 68 D4
Vijayawada, India ... 67 L12
Vík, Iceland ... 8 E4
Vika, Sweden ... 10 D8
Vikarbyn, Sweden ... 10 D8
Vikeke, Indonesia ... 63 F7
Viken, Skåne, Sweden ... 11 H6
Viken, Skaraborg, Sweden . 11 F8
Viking, Canada ... 104 C6
Vikmanshyttan, Sweden ... 10 D9
Vikna, Norway ... 8 D14
Vila da Maganja, Mozam. .. 87 F4
Vila de João Belo = Xai-
Xai, Mozam. ... 89 D5
Vila do Rei, Portugal ... 34 F2
Vila do Bispo, Portugal ... 35 H2
Vila do Conde, Portugal ... 34 D2
Vila Franca de Xira,
Portugal ... 35 G2
Vila Gamito, Mozam. ... 87 E3
Vila Gomes da Costa,
Mozam. ... 89 C5
Vila Machado, Mozam. ... 87 F3
Vila Mouzinho, Mozam. ... 87 E3
Vila Nova de Famalicão,
Portugal ... 34 D2
Vila Nova de Fos Côa,
Portugal ... 34 D3
Vila Nova de Foscôa = Vila
Nova de Fos Côa, Portugal 34 D3
Vila Nova de Gaia, Portugal 34 D2
Vila Nova de Ourém,
Portugal ... 34 F2
Vila Pouca de Aguiar,
Portugal ... 34 D3
Vila Real, Portugal ... 34 D3
Vila Real □, Portugal ... 34 D3
Vila-real de los Infantes,
Spain ... 32 F4
Vila Real de Santo António,
Portugal ... 35 H3
Vila Vasco da Gama,
Mozam. ... 87 E3
Vila Velha, Brazil ... 127 A7
Vila Viçosa, Portugal ... 35 G3
Vilafranca del Maestrat,
Spain ... 32 E4
Vilafranca del Penedès,
Spain ... 32 D6
Vilagarcía de Arousa, Spain 34 C2
Vilaine →, France ... 18 E4
Vilanandro, Tanjona,
Madag. ... 89 B7
Vilanculos, Mozam. ... 89 C6
Vilanova de Castelló, Spain 33 F4
Vilanova i la Geltrú, Spain . 32 D6
Vilar Formoso, Portugal ... 34 E3
Vilaseca-Salou = Vilaseca,
Spain ... 32 D6
Vilaseca, Spain ... 32 D6
Vilbjerg, Denmark ... 11 H2
Vilches, Spain ... 35 G7
Vileyka, Belarus ... 46 E4
Vilhelmina, Sweden ... 8 D17
Vilhena, Brazil ... 124 F6
Viliga, Russia ... 51 C16
Viliya →, Lithuania ... 9 J21

Viljandi, *Estonia* 9 G21
Vilkaviškis, *Lithuania* 44 D10
Vilkija, *Lithuania* 44 C10
Vilkitskogo, Proliv, *Russia* . 51 B11
Vilkovo = Vylkove, *Ukraine* 47 K5
Villa Abecia, *Bolivia* 126 A2
Villa Ahumada, *Mexico* ... 118 A3
Villa Ana, *Argentina* 126 B4
Villa Ángela, *Argentina* ... 126 B3
Villa Bella, *Bolivia* 124 F5
Villa Bens = Tarfaya,
  Morocco 78 C3
Villa Cañás, *Argentina* 126 C3
Villa Cisneros = Dakhla,
  W. Sahara 78 D2
Villa Colón, *Argentina* 126 C2
Villa Constitución, *Argentina* 126 C3
Villa de María, *Argentina* . 126 B3
Villa del Rio, *Spain* 35 H6
Villa Dolores, *Argentina* ... 126 C2
Villa Frontera, *Mexico* 118 B4
Villa Guillermina, *Argentina* 126 B4
Villa Hayes, *Paraguay* ... 126 B4
Villa Iris, *Argentina* 126 D3
Villa Juárez, *Mexico* 118 B4
Villa María, *Argentina* 126 C3
Villa Mazán, *Argentina* ... 126 B2
Villa Minozzo, *Italy* 28 D7
Villa Montes, *Bolivia* 126 A3
Villa Ocampo, *Argentina* .. 126 B4
Villa Ocampo, *Mexico* 118 B3
Villa Ojo de Agua, *Argentina* 126 B3
Villa San Giovanni, *Italy* ... 31 D8
Villa San José, *Argentina* .. 126 C4
Villa San Martín, *Argentina* 126 B3
Villa Santina, *Italy* 29 B9
Villa Unión, *Mexico* 118 C3
Villablino, *Spain* 34 C4
Villacarlos, *Spain* 37 B11
Villacarriedo, *Spain* 34 B7
Villacarrillo, *Spain* 35 G7
Villacastín, *Spain* 34 E6
Villach, *Austria* 26 E6
Villacidro, *Italy* 30 C1
Villada, *Spain* 34 C6
Villadiego, *Spain* 34 C6
Villadóssola, *Italy* 28 B5
Villafeliche, *Spain* 32 D3
Villafranca, *Spain* 32 C3
Villafranca de los Barros,
  Spain 35 G4
Villafranca de los Caballeros,
  Baleares, Spain 37 B10
Villafranca de los Caballeros,
  Toledo, Spain 35 F7
Villafranca del Cid,
  Spain 32 E4
Villafranca del Panadés =
  Vilafranca del Penedès,
  Spain 32 D6
Villafranca di Verona, *Italy* 28 C7
Villafranca Tirrena, *Italy* ... 31 D8
Villagrán, *Mexico* 119 C5
Villaguay, *Argentina* 126 C4
Villaharta, *Spain* 35 G6
Villahermosa, *Mexico* 119 D6
Villahermosa, *Spain* 33 G2
Villaines-la-Juhel, *France* . 18 D6
Villajoyosa, *Spain* 33 G4
Villalba, *Spain* 34 B3
Villalba de Guardo, *Spain* . 34 C6
Villalón de Campos, *Spain* . 34 C5
Villalpando, *Spain* 34 D5
Villaluenga, *Spain* 34 E7
Villamanán, *Spain* 34 C5
Villamartín, *Spain* 35 J5
Villamayor de Santiago,
  Spain 32 F2
Villamblard, *France* 20 C4
Villanova Monteleone, *Italy* 30 B1
Villanueva, *U.S.A.* 113 H2
Villanueva de Castellón =
  Vilanova de Castelló,
  Spain 33 F4
Villanueva de Córdoba,
  Spain 35 G6
Villanueva de la Fuente,
  Spain 33 G2
Villanueva de la Serena,
  Spain 35 G5
Villanueva de la Sierra,
  Spain 34 E4
Villanueva de los Castillejos,
  Spain 35 H3
Villanueva de los Infantes,
  Spain 35 G7
Villanueva del Arzobispo,
  Spain 33 G2
Villanueva del Fresno, *Spain* 35 G3
Villanueva y Geltrú =
  Vilanova i la Geltrú, *Spain* 32 D6
Villaputzu, *Italy* 30 C2
Villaquilambre, *Spain* 34 C5
Villar del Arzobispo, *Spain* . 32 F4
Villar del Rey, *Spain* 35 F4
Villard-de-Lans, *France* ... 21 C9
Villarramiel, *Spain* 34 C6
Villarreal = Vila-real de los
  Infantes, *Spain* 32 F4
Villarrica, *Chile* 128 D2
Villarrica, *Paraguay* 126 B4
Villarrobledo, *Spain* 33 F2
Villarroya de la Sierra, *Spain* 32 D3
Villarrubia de los Ojos,
  Spain 35 F7
Villars-les-Dombes, *France* . 19 F12
Villasayas, *Spain* 32 D2
Villaseco de los Gamitos =
  Villaseco de los Gamitos,
  Spain 34 D4

Villaseco de los Gamitos,
  Spain 34 D4
Villasimíus, *Italy* 30 C2
Villastar, *Spain* 32 E3
Villatobas, *Spain* 34 F7
Villavicencio, *Argentina* ... 126 C2
Villavicencio, *Colombia* ... 124 C4
Villaviciosa, *Spain* 34 B5
Villazón, *Bolivia* 126 A2
Ville-Marie, *Canada* 102 C4
Ville Platte, *U.S.A.* 113 K8
Villedieu-les-Poêles, *France* 18 D5
Villefort, *France* 20 D7
Villefranche-de-Lauragais,
  France 20 E5
Villefranche-de-Rouergue,
  France 20 D6
Villefranche-du-Périgord,
  France 20 D5
Villefranche-sur-Saône,
  France 21 C8
Villel, *Spain* 32 E3
Villemur-sur-Tarn, *France* .. 20 E5
Villena, *Spain* 33 G4
Villenauxe-la-Grande, *France* 19 D10
Villenave-d'Ornon, *France* . 20 D3
Villeneuve-d'Ascq, *France* . 19 B10
Villeneuve-l'Archevêque,
  France 19 D10
Villeneuve-lès-Avignon,
  France 21 E8
Villeneuve-sur-Allier, *France* 19 F10
Villeneuve-sur-Lot, *France* . 20 D4
Villeneuve-sur-Yonne,
  France 19 D10
Villeréal, *France* 20 D4
Villers-Bocage, *France* 18 C6
Villers-Cotterêts, *France* .. 19 C10
Villers-sur-Mer, *France* ... 18 C6
Villersexel, *France* 19 E13
Villerupt, *France* 19 C12
Villeurbanne, *France* 21 C8
Villiers, *S. Africa* 89 D4
Villingen-Schwenningen,
  Germany 25 G4
Vilna, *Canada* 104 C6
Vilnius, *Lithuania* 9 J21
Vils, *Austria* 26 D3
Vils →, *Bayern, Germany* . 25 G9
Vils →, *Bayern, Germany* . 25 F7
Vilsbiburg, *Germany* 25 G8
Vilshofen, *Germany* 25 G9
Vilusi, *Montenegro, Yug.* .. 40 D2
Vilvoorde, *Belgium* 17 D4
Vilyuy →, *Russia* 51 C13
Vilyuysk, *Russia* 51 C13
Vimianzo, *Spain* 34 B1
Vimioso, *Portugal* 34 D4
Vimmerby, *Sweden* 11 G9
Vimoutiers, *France* 18 D7
Vimperk, *Czech Rep.* 26 B6
Viña del Mar, *Chile* 126 C1
Vinarós, *Spain* 32 E5
Vincennes, *U.S.A.* 108 F2
Vincent, *U.S.A.* 117 L8
Vinchina, *Argentina* 126 B2
Vindelälven →, *Sweden* ... 8 E18
Vindeln, *Sweden* 8 D18
Vinderup, *Denmark* 11 H2
Vindhya Ra., *India* 68 H7
Vineland, *U.S.A.* 108 F8
Vineuil, *France* 18
Vinga, *Romania* 42 D6
Vingåker, *Sweden* 10 E9
Vinh, *Vietnam* 64 C5
Vinh Linh, *Vietnam* 64 D6
Vinh Long, *Vietnam* 65 G5
Vinh Yen, *Vietnam* 58 G5
Vinhais, *Portugal* 34 D3
Vinica, *Croatia* 29 B13
Vinica, *Macedonia* 40 E6
Vinica, *Slovenia* 29 C12
Vinita, *U.S.A.* 113 G7
Vinkovci, *Croatia* 42 E3
Vinnitsa = Vinnytsya,
  Ukraine 47 H5
Vinnytsya, *Ukraine* 47 H5
Vinslöv, *Sweden* 11 H7
Vintjärn, *Sweden* 10 D10
Vinton, *Calif., U.S.A.* 116 F6
Vinton, *Iowa, U.S.A.* 112 D8
Vinton, *La., U.S.A.* 113 K8
Vințu de Jos, *Romania* ... 43 D8
Viöl, *Germany* 24 A5
Vipava, *Slovenia* 29 C10
Vipiteno, *Italy* 29 B8
Vir, *Croatia* 29 D12
Virac, *Phil.* 61 E6
Virachei, *Cambodia* 64 F6
Virago Sd., *Canada* 104 C2
Viramgam, *India* 68 H5
Viranşehir, *Turkey* 70 B3
Virawah, *Pakistan* 68 G4
Virden, *Canada* 105 D8
Vire, *France* 18 D6
Vire →, *France* 18 C5
Vírgenes, C., *Argentina* .. 128 G3
Virgin →, *U.S.A.* 115 H6
Virgin Gorda, *Virgin Is.* .. 121 C7
Virgin Is. (British) ■,
  W. Indies 121 C7
Virgin Is. (U.S.) ■,
  W. Indies 121 C7
Virginia, *S. Africa* 88 D4
Virginia, *U.S.A.* 112 B8
Virginia □, *U.S.A.* 108 G7
Virginia Beach, *U.S.A.* ... 108 G8
Virginia City, *Mont., U.S.A.* 114 D8
Virginia City, *Nev., U.S.A.* 116 F7
Virginia Falls, *Canada* 104 A3

Virginiatown, *Canada* 102 C4
Virje, *Croatia* 29 B13
Viroqua, *U.S.A.* 112 D9
Virovitica, *Croatia* 42 E2
Virpazar, *Montenegro, Yug.* 40 D3
Virpur, *India* 68 J4
Virserum, *Sweden* 11 G9
Virton, *Belgium* 17 E5
Virudunagar, *India* 66 Q10
Vis, *Croatia* 29 E13
Visalia, *U.S.A.* 116 J7
Visayan Sea, *Phil.* 61 F5
Visby, *Sweden* 11 G12
Viscount Melville Sd.,
  Canada 4 B2
Visé, *Belgium* 17 D5
Višegrad, *Bos.-H.* 42 G4
Viseu, *Brazil* 125 D9
Viseu, *Portugal* 34 E3
Viseu □, *Portugal* 34 E3
Vișeu de Sus, *Romania* ... 43 C9
Vishakhapatnam, *India* ... 67 L13
Vișina, *Romania* 43 G9
Vișineşti, *Moldova* 43 D13
Visingsö, *Sweden* 11 F8
Viskafors, *Sweden* 11 G6
Viskan →, *Sweden* 11 G6
Viški Kanal, *Croatia* 29 E13
Vislanda, *Sweden* 11 H8
Visnagar, *India* 68 H5
Višnja Gora, *Slovenia* 29 C11
Viso, Mte., *Italy* 28 D4
Viso del Marqués, *Spain* .. 35 G7
Visoko, *Bos.-H.* 42 G3
Visokoi I., *Antarctica* 5 B1
Visp, *Switz.* 25 J3
Vissefjärda, *Sweden* 11 H9
Visselhövede, *Germany* ... 24 C5
Vissenbjerg, *Denmark* 11 J4
Vista, *U.S.A.* 117 M9
Vistonikos, Ormos =
  Vistonís, Límni, *Greece* . 41 E9
Vistonís, Límni, *Greece* ... 41 E9
Vistula = Wisła →, *Poland* 44 D5
Vit →, *Bulgaria* 41 C8
Vitanje, *Slovenia* 29 B12
Vitebsk = Vitsyebsk, *Belarus* 46 E6
Viterbo, *Italy* 29 F9
Vitez, *Bos.-H.* 42 F2
Viti Levu, *Fiji* 91 C7
Vitigudino, *Spain* 34 D4
Vitim, *Russia* 51 D12
Vitim →, *Russia* 51 D12
Vitína, *Bos.-H.* 29 E14
Vitína, *Greece* 38 D4
Vítkov, *Czech Rep.* 27 B10
Vitória, *Brazil* 125 H10
Vitória da Conquista, *Brazil* 125 F10
Vitória de São Antão, *Brazil* 125 E11
Vitoria-Gasteiz, *Spain* 32 C2
Vitré, *France* 18 D5
Vitry-le-François, *France* .. 19 D11
Vitry-sur-Seine, *France* ... 19 D9
Vitsand, *Sweden* 10 D7
Vitsi, Óros, *Greece* 40 F5
Vitsyebsk, *Belarus* 46 E6
Vittaryd, *Sweden* 11 H7
Vitteaux, *France* 19 E11
Vittel, *France* 19 D12
Vittória, *Italy* 31 F7
Vittório Véneto, *Italy* 29 C9
Vittsjö, *Sweden* 11 H7
Viveiro, *Spain* 34 B3
Vivian, *U.S.A.* 113 J8
Viviers, *France* 21 D8
Vivonne, *France* 20 B4
Vizcaíno, Desierto de,
  Mexico 118 B2
Vizcaíno, Sierra, *Mexico* .. 118 B2
Vizcaya □, *Spain* 32 B2
Vize, *Turkey* 41 E11
Vizianagaram, *India* 67 K13
Vizille, *France* 21 C9
Viziñada, *Croatia* 29 C10
Viziru, *Romania* 43 E12
Vizzini, *Italy* 31 E7
Vjosa →, *Albania* 40 F3
Vlaardingen, *Neths.* 17 C4
Vlădeasa, Vf., *Romania* ... 42 D7
Vladičin Han, *Serbia, Yug.* 40 D6
Vladikavkaz, *Russia* 49 J7
Vladimir, *Russia* 46 D11
Vladimir Volynskiy =
  Volodymyr-Volynskyy,
  Ukraine 47 G3
Vladimirci, *Serbia, Yug.* .. 40 B3
Vladimirovac, *Serbia, Yug.* 42 E5
Vladimirovca, *Russia* 49 F8
Vladimirovo, *Bulgaria* 40 C7
Vladimirskaya, *Kazakstan* . 48 E10
Vladislavovka, *Ukraine* ... 47 K8
Vladivostok, *Russia* 51 E14
Vlăhița, *Romania* 43 D10
Vlakhiótis, *Greece* 38 E4
Vlasenica, *Bos.-H.* 42 F3
Vlašić, *Bos.-H.* 42 F2
Vlasinsko Jezero,
  Serbia, Yug. 40 D6
Vlasotince, *Serbia, Yug.* .. 40 D6
Vlieland, *Neths.* 17 A4
Vlissingen, *Neths.* 17 C3
Vlóra, *Albania* 40 F3
Vlóra □, *Albania* 40 F3
Vltava →, *Czech Rep.* 26 A7
Vo Dat, *Vietnam* 65 G6
Voarno, *Italy* 28 C7
Vocin, *Croatia* 42 E2
Vöcklabruck, *Austria* 26 C6
Vodice, *Croatia* 29 E12
Vodňany, *Czech Rep.* 26 B7

Vodnjan, *Croatia* 29 D10
Voe, *U.K.* 14 A7
Vogel Pk., *Nigeria* 83 D7
Vogelkop = Doberai,
  Jazirah, *Indonesia* 63 E8
Vogelsberg, *Germany* 24 E5
Voghera, *Italy* 28 D6
Vohibinany, *Madag.* 89 B8
Vohilava, *Madag.* 89 C8
Vohimarina = Iharana,
  Madag. 89 A9
Vohimena, Tanjon' i,
  Madag. 89 D8
Vohipeno, *Madag.* 89 C8
Voi, *Kenya* 86 C4
Void-Vacon, *France* 19 D12
Voineşti, Iași, *Romania* ... 43 C12
Voineşti, Prahova, *Romania* 43 E10
Voiotía □, *Greece* 38 C5
Voiron, *France* 21 C9
Voisey B., *Canada* 103 A7
Voitsberg, *Austria* 26 D8
Vojens, *Denmark* 11 J3
Vojmsjön, *Sweden* 8 D17
Vojnić, *Croatia* 29 C12
Vojnik, *Italy* 29 B12
Vojvodina □, *Serbia, Yug.* . 42 E5
Vokhtoga, *Russia* 46 C11
Volary, *Czech Rep.* 26 C6
Volborg, *U.S.A.* 112 C2
Volcano Is. = Kazan-Rettō,
  Pac. Oc. 96 E6
Volchansk = Vovchansk,
  Ukraine 47 G9
Volchya →, *Ukraine* 47 H8
Volda, *Norway* 9 E12
Volga, *Russia* 46 C10
Volga →, *Russia* 49 G9
Volga Hts. = Privolzhskaya
  Vozvyshennost, *Russia* .. 48 E7
Volgo-Baltiyskiy Kanal,
  Russia 46 B9
Volgo-Donskoy Kanal,
  Russia 49 F7
Volgodonsk, *Russia* 49 G6
Volgograd, *Russia* 49 F7
Volgogradskoye Vdkhr.,
  Russia 48 E8
Volgorechensk, *Russia* ... 48 B5
Volímai, *Greece* 38 D2
Volintiri, *Moldova* 43 D14
Volissós, *Greece* 39 C7
Volkach, *Germany* 25 F6
Völkermarkt, *Austria* 26 E7
Volkhov, *Russia* 46 C7
Volkhov →, *Russia* 46 B7
Völklingen, *Germany* 25 F2
Volkovysk = Vawkavysk,
  Belarus 47 F3
Volksrust, *S. Africa* 89 D4
Volnansk, *Ukraine* 47 H8
Volnovakha, *Ukraine* 47 J9
Volochanka, *Russia* 51 B10
Volodarsk, *Russia* 48 B6
Volodymyr-Volynskyy,
  Ukraine 47 G3
Vologda, *Russia* 46 C10
Volokolamsk, *Russia* 46 D8
Volokonovka, *Russia* 47 G9
Vólos, *Greece* 38 B4
Volosovo, *Russia* 46 C5
Volovets, *Ukraine* 47 H2
Volovo, *Russia* 46 F10
Volozhin = Valozhyn,
  Belarus 46 E4
Volsk, *Russia* 48 D8
Volta □, *Ghana* 83 D5
Volta →, *Ghana* 83 D5
Volta, L., *Ghana* 83 D5
Volta Blanche = White
  Volta →, *Ghana* 83 D4
Volta Redonda, *Brazil* ... 127 A7
Volterra, *Italy* 28 E7
Voltri, *Italy* 28 D5
Volturno →, *Italy* 30 A6
Vólvi, L., *Greece* 40 F7
Vónitsa, *Greece* 38 C2
Vopnafjörður, *Iceland* ... 8 D6
Vorarlberg □, *Austria* 26 D2
Vóras Óros, *Greece* 40 F5
Vorbasse, *Denmark* 11 J3
Vorchdorf, *Austria* 26 C6
Vorderrhein →, *Switz.* ... 25 J5
Vorë, *Albania* 40 E3
Voreppe, *France* 21 C9
Vórioi Sporádhes, *Greece* . 38 B5
Vórios Aiyaíon □, *Greece* . 39 C7
Vórios Evvoïkos Kólpos,
  Greece 38 C5
Vorkuta, *Russia* 50 C7
Vormsi, *Estonia* 9 G20
Vorona →, *Russia* 48 E6
Voronezh, *Russia* 47 G10
Voronezh →, *Russia* 47 G10
Vorontsovo-
  Aleksandrovskoye =
  Zelenokumsk, *Russia* ... 49 H6
Voroshilovgrad = Luhansk,
  Ukraine 47 H10
Voroshilovsk = Alchevsk,
  Ukraine 47 H10
Vórroi, *Greece* 38 F6
Vorskla →, *Ukraine* 47 H8
Võrts Järv, *Estonia* 9 G22

Võru, *Estonia* 9 H22
Vosges, *France* 19 D14
Vosges □, *France* 19 D13
Voskopoja, *Albania* 40 F4
Voskresensk, *Russia* 46 E10
Voskresenskoye, *Russia* .. 48 B7
Voss, *Norway* 9 F12
Vostok I., *Kiribati* 97 J12
Votice, *Czech Rep.* 26 B7
Votsuri-Shima, *Japan* 55 M1
Vouga →, *Portugal* 34 E2
Vouillé, *France* 18 F7
Voúxa, Ákra, *Greece* 36 D5
Vouzela, *Portugal* 34 E2
Vouziers, *France* 19 C11
Vovchansk, *Ukraine* 47 G9
Vozhe, Ozero, *Russia* 46 B10
Vozhega, *Russia* 46 B11
Voznesensk, *Ukraine* 47 J6
Voznesenye, *Russia* 46 B8
Vrå, *Denmark* 11 G3
Vráble, *Slovak Rep.* 27 C11
Vračevšnica, *Serbia, Yug.* . 40 B4
Vrakhnéïka, *Greece* 38 C3
Vrancea □, *Romania* 43 E11
Vrancei, Munţii, *Romania* . 43 E11
Vrangelya, Ostrov, *Russia* . 51 B19
Vranica, *Bos.-H.* 42 G2
Vranje, *Serbia, Yug.* 40 D5
Vranjska Banja, *Serbia, Yug.* 40 D6
Vranov nad Topl'ou,
  Slovak Rep. 27 C14
Vransko, *Slovenia* 29 B11
Vransko Jezero, *Croatia* ... 29 E12
Vrapčište, *Macedonia* 40 E4
Vratsa, *Bulgaria* 40 C7
Vrbas, *Serbia, Yug.* 42 E4
Vrbas →, *Bos.-H.* 42 F2
Vrbnik, *Croatia* 29 C11
Vrbovec, *Croatia* 29 C13
Vrbovsko, *Croatia* 29 C12
Vrchlabí, *Czech Rep.* 26 A8
Vrede, *S. Africa* 89 D4
Vredefort, *S. Africa* 88 D4
Vreden, *Germany* 24 C2
Vredenburg, *S. Africa* 88 E2
Vredendal, *S. Africa* 88 E2
Vretstorp, *Sweden* 10 E8
Vrgorac, *Croatia* 29 E14
Vrhnika, *Slovenia* 29 C11
Vríði, *Ivory C.* 82 D4
Vrigstad, *Sweden* 11 G8
Vrindavan, *India* 68 F7
Vríses, *Greece* 36 D6
Vrnograč, *Bos.-H.* 29 C12
Vrondádhes, *Greece* 39 C8
Vrpolje, *Croatia* 42 E3
Vršac, *Serbia, Yug.* 42 E6
Vrsacki Kanal, *Serbia, Yug.* 42 E5
Vrútky, *Slovak Rep.* 27 B11
Vryburg, *S. Africa* 88 D3
Vryheid, *S. Africa* 89 D5
Vsetín, *Czech Rep.* 27 B11
Vu Liet, *Vietnam* 64 C5
Vŭcha →, *Bulgaria* 41 D8
Vučitrn, *Kosovo, Yug.* 40 D4
Vukovar, *Croatia* 42 E3
Vulcan, *Canada* 104 C6
Vulcan, *Romania* 43 E8
Vulcaneşti, *Moldova* 43 E13
Vulcano, *Italy* 31 D7
Vŭlchedruma, *Bulgaria* ... 40 C7
Vulkaneshty = Vulcaneşti,
  Moldova 43 E13
Vunduzi →, *Mozam.* 87 F3
Vung Tau, *Vietnam* 65 G6
Vŭrbitsa, *Bulgaria* 41 D10
Vurshets, *Bulgaria* 40 C7
Vutcani, *Romania* 43 D12
Vuya, *Sudan* 81 F2
Vyartsilya, *Russia* 46 A6
Vyatka = Kirov, *Russia* ... 50 D5
Vyatka →, *Russia* 48 C10
Vyatskiye Polyany, *Russia* . 48 B10
Vyazemskiy, *Russia* 51 E14
Vyazma, *Russia* 46 E8
Vyazniki, *Russia* 48 B6
Vyborg, *Russia* 46 B5
Vychegda →, *Russia* 50 C5
Východné Beskydy, *Europe* 27 B15
Východočeský □,
  Czech Rep. 26 E8
Vyerkhnyadzvinsk, *Belarus* 46 E4
Vyksa, *Russia* 48 C6
Vylkove, *Ukraine* 47 K5
Vynohradiv, *Ukraine* 47 H2
Vyrnwy, L., *U.K.* 12 E4
Vyshniy Volochek, *Russia* . 46 D8
Vyshzha = imeni 26
  Bakinskikh Komissarov,
  Turkmenistan 71 B7
Vyškov, *Czech Rep.* 27 B9
Vysoké Mýto, *Czech Rep.* . 27 B9
Vysokovsk, *Russia* 46 D9
Vyšší Brod, *Czech Rep.* ... 26 C7
Vytegra, *Russia* 46 B9

W

W.A.C. Bennett Dam,
  Canada 104 B4
Wa, *Ghana* 82 C4
Waal →, *Neths.* 17 C5
Waalwijk, *Neths.* 17 C5
Waat, *Sudan* 81 F3
Wabana, *Canada* 103 C9
Wabasca →, *Canada* 104 B5
Wabasca-Desmarais, *Canada* 104 B6

Wabash, *U.S.A.* 108 E3
Wabash →, *U.S.A.* 108 G1
Wabi →, *Ethiopia* 81 F5
Wabigoon L., *Canada* 105 D10
Wabowden, *Canada* 105 C9
Wąbrzeźno, *Poland* 45 E5
Wabu Hu, *China* 59 A11
Wabuk Pt., *Canada* 102 A2
Wabush, *Canada* 103 B6
Wąchock, *Poland* 45 K6
Wächtersbach, *Germany* ... 25 E5
Waco, *U.S.A.* 113 K6
Waconichi, L., *Canada* 102 B5
Wad Ban Naqa, *Sudan* ... 81 D3
Wad Banda, *Sudan* 81 E2
Wad el Haddad, *Sudan* ... 81 E3
Wad en Nau, *Sudan* 81 E3
Wad Hamid, *Sudan* 81 D3
Wad Medanî, *Sudan* 81 E3
Wad Thana, *Pakistan* 68 F2
Wadai, *Africa* 76 E5
Wadayama, *Japan* 55 G7
Waddeneilanden, *Neths.* ... 17 A5
Waddenzee, *Neths.* 17 A5
Waddington, *U.S.A.* 111 B9
Waddington, Mt., *Canada* .. 104 C3
Waddy Pt., *Australia* 95 C5
Wadebridge, *U.K.* 13 G3
Wadena, *Canada* 105 C8
Wadena, *U.S.A.* 112 B7
Wädenswil, *Switz.* 25 H4
Wadern, *Germany* 25 F2
Wadeye, *Australia* 92 B4
Wadhams, *Canada* 104 C3
Wādî as Sîr, *Jordan* 75 D4
Wadi Gemâl, *Egypt* 80 C4
Wadi Halfa, *Sudan* 80 C3
Wadian, *China* 59 A9
Wadlew, *Poland* 45 G6
Wadowice, *Poland* 45 J6
Wadsworth, *Nev., U.S.A.* .. 114 G4
Wadsworth, *Ohio, U.S.A.* . 110 E3
Waegwan, *S. Korea* 57 G15
Wafangdian, *China* 57 E11
Wafrah, *Si. Arabia* 70 D5
Wageningen, *Neths.* 17 C5
Wager B., *Canada* 101 B11
Wagga Wagga, *Australia* .. 95 F4
Waghete, *Indonesia* 63 E9
Wagin, *Australia* 93 F2
Wagner, *U.S.A.* 112 D5
Wagon Mound, *U.S.A.* ... 113 G2
Wagoner, *U.S.A.* 113 H7
Wągrowiec, *Poland* 45 F4
Wah, *Pakistan* 68 C5
Wahai, *Indonesia* 63 E7
Wahiawa, *U.S.A.* 106 H15
Wâḥid, *Egypt* 75 E1
Wahnai, *Afghan.* 68 C1
Wahni, *Ethiopia* 81 E4
Wahoo, *U.S.A.* 112 E6
Wahpeton, *U.S.A.* 112 B6
Wai, Koh, *Cambodia* 65 H4
Waiau →, *N.Z.* 91 K4
Waibeem, *Indonesia* 63 E8
Waiblingen, *Germany* 25 G5
Waidhofen an der Thaya,
   Austria 26 C8
Waidhofen an der Ybbs,
   Austria 26 D7
Waigeo, *Indonesia* 63 E8
Waihi, *N.Z.* 91 G5
Waihou →, *N.Z.* 91 G5
Waika,
   Dem. Rep. of the Congo . 86 C2
Waikabubak, *Indonesia* ... 63 F5
Waikari, *N.Z.* 91 K4
Waikato →, *N.Z.* 91 G5
Waikerie, *Australia* 95 E3
Waikokopu, *N.Z.* 91 H6
Waikouaiti, *N.Z.* 91 L3
Wailuku, *U.S.A.* 106 H16
Waimakariri →, *N.Z.* 91 K4
Waimate, *N.Z.* 91 L3
Wainganga →, *India* 66 K11
Waingapu, *Indonesia* 63 F6
Waini →, *Guyana* 124 B7
Wainwright, *Canada* 105 C6
Waiouru, *N.Z.* 91 H5
Waipara, *N.Z.* 91 K4
Waipawa, *N.Z.* 91 H6
Waipiro, *N.Z.* 91 H7
Waipu, *N.Z.* 91 F5
Waipukurau, *N.Z.* 91 J6
Wairakei, *N.Z.* 91 H6
Wairarapa, L., *N.Z.* 91 J5
Wairoa, *N.Z.* 91 H6
Waitaki →, *N.Z.* 91 L3
Waitara, *N.Z.* 91 H5
Waitsburg, *U.S.A.* 114 C5
Waiuku, *N.Z.* 91 G5
Wajima, *Japan* 55 F8
Wajir, *Kenya* 86 B5
Waka, *Ethiopia* 81 F4
Wakasa, *Japan* 55 G7
Wakasa-Wan, *Japan* 55 G7
Wakatipu, L., *N.Z.* 91 L2
Wakaw, *Canada* 105 C7
Wakayama, *Japan* 55 G7
Wakayama □, *Japan* 55 H7
Wake Forest, *U.S.A.* 109 H6
Wake I., *Pac. Oc.* 96 F8
WaKeeney, *U.S.A.* 112 F5
Wakefield, *N.Z.* 91 J4
Wakefield, *U.K.* 12 D6
Wakefield, *Mass., U.S.A.* . 111 D13
Wakefield, *Mich., U.S.A.* . 112 B10
Wakema, *Burma* 67 L19
Wakkanai, *Japan* 54 B10
Wakkerstroom, *S. Africa* . 89 D5
Wakool, *Australia* 95 F3

Wakool →, *Australia* 95 F3
Wakre, *Indonesia* 63 E8
Wakuach, L., *Canada* 103 A6
Walamba, *Zambia* 87 E2
Wałbrzych, *Poland* 45 H3
Walbury Hill, *U.K.* 13 F6
Walcha, *Australia* 95 E5
Walcheren, *Neths.* 17 C3
Walcott, *U.S.A.* 114 F10
Wałcz, *Poland* 45 E3
Waldbröl, *Germany* 24 E3
Waldburg Ra., *Australia* .. 93 D2
Waldeck, *Germany* 24 D5
Walden, *Colo., U.S.A.* ... 114 F10
Walden, *N.Y., U.S.A.* 111 E10
Waldkirch, *Germany* 25 G3
Waldkirchen, *Germany* ... 25 G9
Waldkraiburg, *Germany* .. 25 G8
Waldport, *U.S.A.* 114 D1
Waldron, *U.S.A.* 113 H7
Waldviertel, *Austria* 26 C8
Walebing, *Australia* 93 F2
Walembele, *Ghana* 82 C4
Walensee, *Switz.* 25 H5
Wales □, *U.K.* 13 E3
Walewale, *Ghana* 83 C4
Walgett, *Australia* 95 E4
Walgreen Coast, *Antarctica* .. 5 D15
Walker, *U.S.A.* 112 B7
Walker, L., *Canada* 103 B6
Walker L., *Canada* 105 C9
Walker L., *U.S.A.* 114 G4
Walkerston, *Australia* 94 C4
Walkerton, *Canada* 102 D3
Wall, *U.S.A.* 112 D3
Walla Walla, *U.S.A.* 114 C4
Wallace, *Idaho, U.S.A.* ... 114 C6
Wallace, *N.C., U.S.A.* ... 109 H7
Wallaceburg, *Canada* 102 D3
Wallachia = Valahia,
   Romania 43 F9
Wallal, *Australia* 95 D4
Wallam Cr. →, *Australia* . 95 D4
Wallambin, L., *Australia* . 93 F2
Wallan, *Australia* 95 F3
Wallaroo, *Australia* 95 E2
Walldürn, *Germany* 25 F5
Wallenhorst, *Germany* ... 24 C4
Wallenpaupack, L., *U.S.A.* . 111 E9
Wallingford, *U.S.A.* 111 E12
Wallis & Futuna, Is.,
   Pac. Oc. 96 J10
Wallowa, *U.S.A.* 114 D5
Wallowa Mts., *U.S.A.* ... 114 D5
Walls, *U.K.* 14 A7
Wallula, *U.S.A.* 114 C4
Wallumbilla, *Australia* ... 95 D4
Walmsley, L., *Canada* 105 A7
Walney, I. of, *U.K.* 12 C4
Walnut Creek, *U.S.A.* ... 116 H4
Walnut Ridge, *U.S.A.* ... 113 G9
Walpole, *Australia* 93 F2
Walpole, *U.S.A.* 111 D13
Wals, *Austria* 26 D5
Walsall, *U.K.* 13 E6
Walsenburg, *U.S.A.* 113 G2
Walsh, *U.S.A.* 113 G3
Walsh →, *Australia* 94 B3
Walsrode, *Germany* 24 C5
Walterboro, *U.S.A.* 109 J5
Walters, *U.S.A.* 113 H5
Waltershausen, *Germany* .. 24 E6
Waltham, *U.S.A.* 111 D13
Waltman, *U.S.A.* 114 E10
Walton, *U.S.A.* 111 D9
Walton-on-the-Naze, *U.K.* . 13 F9
Walvis Bay, *Namibia* 88 C1
Walvisbaai = Walvis Bay,
   Namibia 88 C1
Wamba,
   Dem. Rep. of the Congo . 86 B2
Wamba, *Kenya* 86 B4
Wamba, *Nigeria* 83 D6
Wamego, *U.S.A.* 112 F6
Wamena, *Indonesia* 63 E9
Wamsutter, *U.S.A.* 114 F9
Wamulan, *Indonesia* 63 E7
Wan Xian, *China* 56 E6
Wana, *Pakistan* 68 C3
Wanaaring, *Australia* 95 D3
Wanaka, *N.Z.* 91 L2
Wanaka L., *N.Z.* 91 L2
Wan'an, *China* 59 D10
Wanapitei L., *Canada* 102 C3
Wandel Sea = McKinley
   Sea, *Arctic* 4 A7
Wandérama, *Ivory C.* 82 D4
Wanderer, *Zimbabwe* 87 F3
Wandhari, *Pakistan* 68 F2
Wanding, *China* 58 E2
Wandoan, *Australia* 95 D4
Wanfu, *China* 57 D12
Wang →, *Thailand* 64 D2
Wang Kai, *Sudan* 81 F2
Wang Noi, *Thailand* 64 E3
Wang Saphung, *Thailand* . 64 D3
Wang Thong, *Thailand* ... 64 D3
Wanga,
   Dem. Rep. of the Congo . 86 B2
Wangal, *Indonesia* 63 F8
Wanganella, *Australia* ... 95 F3
Wanganui, *N.Z.* 91 H5
Wangaratta, *Australia* ... 95 F4
Wangary, *Australia* 95 E2
Wangcang, *China* 58 A6
Wangcheng, *China* 59 C9
Wangdu, *China* 56 E8
Wangen, *Germany* 25 H5
Wangerooge, *Germany* 24 B3
Wangi, *Kenya* 86 C5

Wangiwangi, *Indonesia* ... 63 F6
Wangjiang, *China* 59 B11
Wangmo, *China* 58 E6
Wangolodougou, *Ivory C.* . 82 D3
Wangqing, *China* 57 C15
Wankaner, *India* 68 H4
Wanless, *Canada* 105 C8
Wannian, *China* 59 C11
Wanning, *China* 64 C8
Wanon Niwat, *Thailand* .. 64 D4
Wanquan, *China* 56 D8
Wanrong, *China* 56 G6
Wanshan, *China* 58 D7
Wanshengchang, *China* ... 58 C6
Wantage, *U.K.* 13 F6
Wanyuan, *China* 58 A7
Wanzai, *China* 59 C10
Wapakoneta, *U.S.A.* 108 E3
Wapato, *U.S.A.* 114 C3
Wapawekka L., *Canada* ... 105 C8
Wapikopa L., *Canada* 102 B2
Wapiti →, *Canada* 104 B5
Wappingers Falls, *U.S.A.* . 111 E11
Wapsipinicon →, *U.S.A.* . 112 E9
Warab □, *Sudan* 81 F2
Warangal, *India* 66 L11
Waraseoni, *India* 69 J9
Waratah, *Australia* 94 G4
Waratah B., *Australia* ... 95 F4
Warburg, *Germany* 24 D5
Warburton, *Vic., Australia* . 95 F4
Warburton, *W. Austral.*,
   Australia 93 E4
Warburton Ra., *Australia* . 93 E4
Ward, *N.Z.* 91 J5
Ward →, *Australia* 95 D4
Ward Mt., *U.S.A.* 116 H8
Warden, *S. Africa* 89 D4
Wardha, *India* 66 J11
Wardha →, *India* 66 K11
Ware, *Canada* 104 B3
Ware, *U.S.A.* 111 D12
Waregem, *Belgium* 17 D3
Wareham, *U.S.A.* 111 E14
Waremme, *Belgium* 17 D5
Waren, *Germany* 24 B8
Warendorf, *Germany* 24 D4
Warialda, *Australia* 95 D5
Wariap, *Indonesia* 63 E8
Warin Chamrap, *Thailand* . 64 E5
Warka, *Poland* 45 G8
Warkopi, *Indonesia* 63 E8
Warm Springs, *U.S.A.* ... 115 G5
Warman, *Canada* 105 C7
Warmbad, *Namibia* 88 D2
Warmbad, *S. Africa* 89 C4
Warmińsko-Mazurskie □,
   Poland 44 D8
Warminster, *U.K.* 13 F5
Warminster, *U.S.A.* 111 F9
Warnemünde, *Germany* ... 24 A8
Warner Mts., *U.S.A.* 114 F3
Warner Robins, *U.S.A.* ... 109 J4
Warnow →, *Germany* 24 A8
Waroona, *Australia* 93 F2
Warracknabeal, *Australia* . 95 F3
Warragul, *Australia* 95 F4
Warrego →, *Australia* ... 95 E4
Warrego Ra., *Australia* .. 94 C4
Warren, *Australia* 95 E4
Warren, *Ark., U.S.A.* 113 J8
Warren, *Mich., U.S.A.* ... 108 D4
Warren, *Minn., U.S.A.* ... 112 A6
Warren, *Ohio, U.S.A.* ... 110 E4
Warren, *Pa., U.S.A.* 110 E5
Warrenpoint, *U.K.* 15 B5
Warrensburg, *Mo., U.S.A.* . 112 F8
Warrensburg, *N.Y., U.S.A.* . 111 C11
Warrenton, *S. Africa* 88 D3
Warrenton, *U.S.A.* 116 D3
Warri, *Nigeria* 83 D6
Warrina, *Australia* 95 D2
Warrington, *U.K.* 12 D5
Warrington, *U.S.A.* 109 K2
Warrington □, *U.K.* 12 D5
Warrnambool, *Australia* .. 95 F3
Warroad, *U.S.A.* 112 A7
Warruwi, *Australia* 94 A1
Warsa, *Indonesia* 63 E9
Warsak Dam, *Pakistan* ... 68 B4
Warsaw = Warszawa,
   Poland 45 F8
Warsaw, *Ind., U.S.A.* 108 E3
Warsaw, *N.Y., U.S.A.* 110 D6
Warsaw, *Ohio, U.S.A.* ... 110 F3
Warstein, *Germany* 24 D4
Warszawa, *Poland* 45 F8
Warta, *Poland* 45 G5
Warta →, *Poland* 45 F1
Warthe = Warta →, *Poland* . 45 F1
Waru, *Indonesia* 63 E8
Warwick, *Australia* 95 D5
Warwick, *U.K.* 13 E6
Warwick, *N.Y., U.S.A.* ... 111 E10
Warwick, *R.I., U.S.A.* ... 111 E13
Warwickshire □, *U.K.* ... 13 E6
Wasaga Beach, *Canada* ... 110 B4
Wasagaming, *Canada* 105 C9
Wasatch Ra., *U.S.A.* 114 F8
Wasbank, *S. Africa* 89 D5
Wasco, *Calif., U.S.A.* 117 K7
Wasco, *Oreg., U.S.A.* 114 D3
Wase, *Nigeria* 83 D6
Waseca, *U.S.A.* 112 C8
Wasekamio L., *Canada* ... 105 B7
Wash, The, *U.K.* 12 E8
Washago, *Canada* 110 B5
Washburn, *N. Dak., U.S.A.* . 112 B4
Washburn, *Wis., U.S.A.* .. 112 B9
Washim, *India* 66 J10
Washington, *U.K.* 12 C6

Washington, *D.C., U.S.A.* . 108 F7
Washington, *Ga., U.S.A.* . 109 J4
Washington, *Ind., U.S.A.* . 108 F2
Washington, *Iowa, U.S.A.* . 112 E9
Washington, *Mo., U.S.A.* . 112 F9
Washington, *N.C., U.S.A.* . 109 H7
Washington, *N.J., U.S.A.* . 111 F10
Washington, *Pa., U.S.A.* .. 110 F4
Washington, *Utah, U.S.A.* . 115 H7
Washington □, *U.S.A.* ... 114 C3
Washington, *Mt., U.S.A.* . 111 B13
Washington Court House,
   U.S.A. 108 F4
Washington I., *U.S.A.* ... 108 C2
Washougal, *U.S.A.* 116 E4
Wasian, *Indonesia* 63 E8
Wasilków, *Poland* 45 E10
Wasilla, *U.S.A.* 100 B5
Wasior, *Indonesia* 63 E8
Waskaganish, *Canada* 102 B4
Waskaiowaka, L., *Canada* . 105 B9
Waskesiu Lake, *Canada* .. 105 C7
Wasserburg, *Germany* 25 G8
Wasserkuppe, *Germany* ... 24 E5
Wassy, *France* 19 D11
Waswanipi, *Canada* 102 C4
Waswanipi, L., *Canada* ... 102 C4
Watampone, *Indonesia* ... 63 E6
Water Park Pt., *Australia* . 94 C5
Water Valley, *U.S.A.* 113 H10
Waterberge, *S. Africa* 89 C4
Waterbury, *Conn., U.S.A.* . 111 E11
Waterbury, *Vt., U.S.A.* ... 111 B12
Waterbury L., *Canada* ... 105 B8
Waterdown, *Canada* 110 C5
Waterford, *Canada* 110 D4
Waterford, *Ireland* 15 D4
Waterford, *Calif., U.S.A.* . 116 H6
Waterford, *Pa., U.S.A.* ... 110 E5
Waterford □, *Ireland* ... 15 D4
Waterford Harbour, *Ireland* . 15 D5
Waterhen L., *Canada* 105 C9
Waterloo, *Belgium* 17 D4
Waterloo, *Ont., Canada* .. 102 D3
Waterloo, *Qué., Canada* .. 111 A12
Waterloo, *S. Leone* 82 D2
Waterloo, *Ill., U.S.A.* ... 112 F9
Waterloo, *Iowa, U.S.A.* .. 112 D8
Waterloo, *N.Y., U.S.A.* .. 110 D7
Watersmeet, *U.S.A.* 112 B10
Waterton Lakes Nat. Park,
   U.S.A. 114 B7
Watertown, *Conn., U.S.A.* . 111 E11
Watertown, *N.Y., U.S.A.* . 111 C9
Watertown, *S. Dak., U.S.A.* . 112 C6
Watertown, *Wis., U.S.A.* . 112 D10
Waterval-Boven, *S. Africa* . 89 D5
Waterville, *Canada* 111 A13
Waterville, *Maine, U.S.A.* . 109 C11
Waterville, *N.Y., U.S.A.* . 111 D9
Waterville, *Pa., U.S.A.* ... 110 E7
Waterville, *Wash., U.S.A.* . 114 C3
Watervliet, *U.S.A.* 111 D11
Wates, *Indonesia* 63 G14
Watford, *Canada* 110 D3
Watford, *U.K.* 13 F7
Watford City, *U.S.A.* 112 B3
Wathaman →, *Canada* ... 105 B8
Wathaman L., *Canada* ... 105 B8
Watheroo, *Australia* 93 F2
Wating, *China* 56 G4
Watkins Glen, *U.S.A.* ... 110 D8
Watling I. = San Salvador I.,
   Bahamas 121 B5
Watonga, *U.S.A.* 113 H5
Watrous, *Canada* 105 C7
Watrous, *U.S.A.* 113 H2
Watsa,
   Dem. Rep. of the Congo . 86 B2
Watseka, *U.S.A.* 108 E2
Watson, *Australia* 93 F5
Watson, *Canada* 105 C8
Watson Lake, *Canada* 104 A3
Watsontown, *U.S.A.* 110 E8
Watsonville, *U.S.A.* 116 J5
Wattiwarriganna Cr. →,
   Australia 95 D2
Wattwil, *Switz.* 25 H5
Watuata = Batuata,
   Indonesia 63 F6
Watubela, Kepulauan,
   Indonesia 63 E8
Watubela Is. = Watubela,
   Kepulauan, *Indonesia* .. 63 E8
Wau, *Sudan* 77 F6
Waubamik, *Canada* 110 A4
Waubay, *U.S.A.* 112 C6
Wauchope, *N.S.W.*,
   Australia 95 E5
Wauchope, *N. Terr.*,
   Australia 94 C1
Waukarlycarly, L., *Australia* . 92 D3
Waukegan, *U.S.A.* 108 D2
Waukesha, *U.S.A.* 108 D1
Waukon, *U.S.A.* 112 D9
Waupaca, *U.S.A.* 112 C10
Waupun, *U.S.A.* 112 D10
Waurika, *U.S.A.* 113 H6
Wausau, *U.S.A.* 112 C10
Wautoma, *U.S.A.* 112 C10
Wauwatosa, *U.S.A.* 108 D2
Waveney →, *U.K.* 13 E9
Waverley, *N.Z.* 91 H5
Waverly, *Iowa, U.S.A.* ... 112 D8
Waverly, *N.Y., U.S.A.* ... 111 E8
Wavre, *Belgium* 17 D4
Wâw, *Sudan* 81 F2
Wâw al Kabîr, *Libya* 79 C9
Wawa, *Canada* 102 C3
Wawa, *Nigeria* 83 D5
Wawa, *Sudan* 80 C3

Wawanesa, *Canada* 105 D9
Wawona, *U.S.A.* 116 H7
Waxahachie, *U.S.A.* 113 J6
Way, L., *Australia* 93 E3
Waycross, *U.S.A.* 109 K4
Wayi, *Sudan* 81 F3
Wayland, *U.S.A.* 110 D7
Wayne, *Nebr., U.S.A.* 112 D6
Wayne, *W. Va., U.S.A.* .. 108 F4
Waynesboro, *Ga., U.S.A.* . 109 J4
Waynesboro, *Miss., U.S.A.* . 109 K1
Waynesboro, *Pa., U.S.A.* . 108 F7
Waynesburg, *U.S.A.* 108 F5
Waynesville, *U.S.A.* 109 H4
Waynoka, *U.S.A.* 113 G5
Wazirabad, *Pakistan* 68 C6
Wda →, *Poland* 44 E5
We, *Indonesia* 62 C1
Weald, The, *U.K.* 13 F8
Wear →, *U.K.* 12 C6
Weatherford, *Okla., U.S.A.* . 113 H5
Weatherford, *Tex., U.S.A.* . 113 J6
Weaverville, *U.S.A.* 114 F2
Webb City, *U.S.A.* 113 G7
Webequie, *Canada* 102 B2
Webo = Nyaake, *Liberia* . 82 E3
Webster, *Mass., U.S.A.* ... 111 D13
Webster, *N.Y., U.S.A.* ... 110 C7
Webster, *S. Dak., U.S.A.* . 112 C6
Webster City, *U.S.A.* 112 D8
Webster Springs, *U.S.A.* . 108 F5
Weda, *Indonesia* 63 D7
Weda, Teluk, *Indonesia* .. 63 D7
Weddell I., *Falk. Is.* 128 G4
Weddell Sea, *Antarctica* .. 5 D1
Wedderburn, *Australia* ... 95 F3
Wedel, *Germany* 24 B5
Wedemark, *Germany* 24 C5
Wedgeport, *Canada* 103 D6
Wedza, *Zimbabwe* 87 F3
Wee Waa, *Australia* 95 E4
Weed, *U.S.A.* 114 F2
Weed Heights, *U.S.A.* ... 116 G7
Weedsport, *U.S.A.* 111 C8
Weedville, *U.S.A.* 110 E6
Weenen, *S. Africa* 89 D5
Weener, *Germany* 24 B3
Weert, *Neths.* 17 C5
Węgierska-Górka, *Poland* . 45 J6
Węgliniec, *Poland* 45 G2
Węgorzewo, *Poland* 44 D8
Węgorzyno, *Poland* 44 E2
Węgrów, *Poland* 45 F9
Wehda □, *Sudan* 81 F3
Wei He →, *Hebei, China* . 56 F8
Wei He →, *Shaanxi, China* . 56 G6
Weichang, *China* 57 D9
Weichuan, *China* 56 G7
Weida, *Germany* 24 E8
Weiden, *Germany* 25 F8
Weifang, *China* 57 F10
Weihai, *China* 57 F12
Weil, *Germany* 25 H3
Weilburg, *Germany* 24 E4
Weilheim, *Germany* 25 H7
Weimar, *Germany* 24 E7
Weinan, *China* 56 G5
Weingarten, *Germany* 25 H5
Weinheim, *Germany* 25 F4
Weining, *China* 58 D5
Weipa, *Australia* 94 A3
Weir →, *Australia* 95 D4
Weir →, *Canada* 105 B10
Weir River, *Canada* 105 B10
Weirton, *U.S.A.* 110 F4
Weiser, *U.S.A.* 114 D5
Weishan, *Shandong, China* . 57 G9
Weishan, *Yunnan, China* . 58 E3
Weissenburg, *Germany* ... 25 F6
Weissenfels, *Germany* 24 D7
Weisswasser, *Germany* ... 24 D10
Wéitra, *Austria* 26 C7
Weixi, *China* 58 D2
Weixin, *China* 58 D5
Weiyuan, *China* 56 G3
Weiz, *Austria* 26 D8
Weizhou Dao, *China* 58 G7
Wejherowo, *Poland* 44 D5
Wekusko L., *Canada* 105 C9
Welch, *U.S.A.* 108 G5
Weldya, *Ethiopia* 81 E4
Welega □, *Ethiopia* 81 F3
Welkite, *Ethiopia* 81 F4
Welkom, *S. Africa* 88 D4
Welland, *Canada* 102 D4
Welland →, *U.K.* 13 E7
Wellesley Is., *Australia* .. 94 B2
Wellingborough, *U.K.* ... 13 E7
Wellington, *Australia* 95 E4
Wellington, *Canada* 110 C7
Wellington, *N.Z.* 91 J5
Wellington, *S. Africa* 88 E2
Wellington, *Somst., U.K.* . 13 G4
Wellington,
   Telford & Wrekin, U.K. . 13 E5
Wellington, *Colo., U.S.A.* . 112 E2
Wellington, *Kans., U.S.A.* . 113 G6
Wellington, *Nev., U.S.A.* . 116 G7
Wellington, *Ohio, U.S.A.* . 110 E2
Wellington, *Tex., U.S.A.* . 113 H4
Wellington, I., *Australia* .. 95 E4
Wellington, L., *Australia* . 95 F4
Wells, *Maine, U.S.A.* 111 C14
Wells, *N.Y., U.S.A.* 111 C10
Wells, *Nev., U.S.A.* 114 F6
Wells, L., *Australia* 93 E3
Wells, Mt., *Australia* 92 C4
Wells Gray Prov. Park,
   Canada 104 C4

Wells-next-the-Sea, U.K. 12 E8
Wells River, U.S.A. 111 B12
Wellsboro, U.S.A. 110 E7
Wellsburg, U.S.A. 110 F4
Wellsville, N.Y., U.S.A. 110 D7
Wellsville, Ohio, U.S.A. ... 110 F4
Wellsville, Utah, U.S.A. ... 114 F8
Wellton, U.S.A. 115 K6
Welmel, Wabi →, Ethiopia . 81 F5
Welo □, Ethiopia 81 E4
Wels, Austria 26 C7
Welshpool, U.K. 13 E4
Welwyn Garden City, U.K. . 13 F7
Wem, U.K. 12 E5
Wembere →, Tanzania ... 86 C3
Wemindji, Canada 102 B4
Wen Xian, China 56 G7
Wenatchee, U.S.A. 114 C3
Wenchang, China 64 C8
Wencheng, China 59 D13
Wenchi, Ghana 82 D4
Wenchow = Wenzhou,
  China 59 D13
Wenchuan, China 58 B4
Wenden, U.S.A. 117 M13
Wendeng, China 57 F12
Wendesi, Indonesia 63 E8
Wendo, Ethiopia 81 F4
Wendover, U.S.A. 114 F6
Weng'an, China 58 D6
Wengcheng, China 59 E9
Wengyuan, China 59 E10
Wenjiang, China 58 B4
Wenling, China 59 C13
Wenlock →, Australia 94 A3
Wenshan, China 58 F5
Wenshang, China 56 G9
Wenshui, Guizhou, China . 58 C6
Wenshui, Shanxi, China .. 56 F7
Wensleydale, U.K. 12 C6
Wensu, China 60 B3
Wensum →, U.K. 12 E8
Wentworth, Australia 95 E3
Wentzel L., Canada 104 B6
Wenut, Indonesia 63 E8
Wenxi, China 56 G6
Wenxian, China 56 H3
Wenzhou, China 59 D13
Weott, U.S.A. 114 F2
Wepener, S. Africa 88 D4
Werda, Botswana 88 D3
Werdau, Germany 24 E8
Werder, Germany 24 C8
Werdohl, Germany 24 D3
Wereilu, Ethiopia 81 E4
Weri, Indonesia 63 E8
Werneck, Germany 25 F6
Wernigerode, Germany ... 24 D6
Werra →, Germany 24 D5
Werrimull, Australia 95 E3
Werris Creek, Australia ... 95 E5
Wertach →, Germany ... 25 G6
Wertheim, Germany 25 F5
Wertingen, Germany 25 G6
Wesel, Germany 24 D2
Weser →, Germany 24 B4
Weser-Ems □, Germany . 24 C3
Weserbergland, Germany . 24 C5
Wesiri, Indonesia 63 F7
Weslemkoon L., Canada . 110 A7
Wesleyville, Canada 103 C9
Wesleyville, U.S.A. 110 D4
Wessel, C., Australia 94 A2
Wessel Is., Australia 94 A2
Wesselburen, Germany .. 24 A4
Wessington Springs, U.S.A. 112 C5
West, U.S.A. 113 K6
West →, U.S.A. 111 D12
West Baines →, Australia . 92 C4
West Bank □, Asia 75 C4
West Bend, U.S.A. 108 D1
West Bengal □, India 69 H13
West Berkshire □, U.K. .. 13 F6
West Beskids = Západné
  Beskydy, Europe 27 B12
West Branch, U.S.A. 108 C3
West Branch
  Susquehanna →, U.S.A. 111 F8
West Bromwich, U.K. 13 E6
West Burra, U.K. 14 A7
West Canada Cr. →, U.S.A. 111 C10
West Cape Howe, Australia 93 G2
West Chazy, U.S.A. 111 B11
West Chester, U.S.A. 111 G9
West Columbia, U.S.A. .. 113 L7
West Covina, U.S.A. 117 L9
West Des Moines, U.S.A. . 112 E8
West Dunbartonshire □,
  U.K. 14 F4
West End, Bahamas 120 A4
West Falkland, Falk. Is. .. 122 J4
West Fargo, U.S.A. 112 B6
West Farmington, U.S.A. . 110 E4
West Fjord = Vestfjorden,
  Norway 8 C15
West Fork Trinity →,
  U.S.A. 113 J6
West Frankfort, U.S.A. .. 112 G10
West Hartford, U.S.A. ... 111 E12
West Haven, U.S.A. 111 E12
West Hazleton, U.S.A. ... 111 F9
West Helena, U.S.A. 113 H9
West Hurley, U.S.A. 111 E10
West Ice Shelf, Antarctica . 5 C7
West Indies, Cent. Amer. . 121 D7
West Jordan, U.S.A. 114 F8
West Lorne, Canada 110 D3
West Lothian □, U.K. 14 F5
West Lunga →, Zambia .. 87 E1
West Memphis, U.S.A. ... 113 H9
West Midlands □, U.K. ... 13 E6

West Mifflin, U.S.A. 110 F5
West Milton, U.S.A. 110 E8
West Monroe, U.S.A. 113 J8
West Newton, U.S.A. 110 F5
West Nicholson, Zimbabwe 87 G2
West Palm Beach, U.S.A. .. 109 M5
West Plains, U.S.A. 113 G9
West Point, N.Y., U.S.A. .. 111 E11
West Point, Nebr., U.S.A. . 112 E6
West Point, Va., U.S.A. ... 108 G7
West Pt. = Ouest, Pte. de l',
  Canada 103 C7
West Pt., Australia 95 F2
West Road →, Canada ... 104 C4
West Rutland, U.S.A. 111 C11
West Schelde =
  Westerschelde →, Neths. 17 C3
West Seneca, U.S.A. 110 D6
West Siberian Plain, Russia 52 C11
West Sussex □, U.K. 13 G7
West-Terschelling, Neths. . 17 A5
West Valley City, U.S.A. .. 114 F8
West Virginia □, U.S.A. ... 108 F5
West-Vlaanderen □, Belgium 17 D2
West Walker →, U.S.A. .. 116 G7
West Wyalong, Australia .. 95 E4
West Yellowstone, U.S.A. . 114 D8
West Yorkshire □, U.K. ... 12 D6
Westall Pt., Australia 95 E1
Westbrook, U.S.A. 109 D10
Westbury, Australia 94 G4
Westby, U.S.A. 112 A2
Westend, U.S.A. 117 K9
Westerland, Germany 9 J13
Westerly, U.S.A. 111 E13
Western □, Ghana 82 D4
Western □, Kenya 86 B3
Western □, S. Leone 82 D2
Western □, Uganda 86 B3
Western □, Zambia 87 F1
Western Australia □,
  Australia 93 E2
Western Cape □, S. Africa . 88 E3
Western Dvina =
  Daugava →, Latvia 9 H21
Western Ghats, India 66 N9
Western Isles □, U.K. 14 D1
Western Sahara ■, Africa . 78 D3
Western Samoa ■, Pac. Oc. 91 B13
Westernport, U.S.A. 108 F6
Westerschelde →, Neths. . 17 C3
Westerstede, Germany ... 24 B3
Westerwald, Germany ... 24 E3
Westfield, Mass., U.S.A. .. 111 D12
Westfield, N.Y., U.S.A. ... 110 D5
Westfield, Pa., U.S.A. 110 E7
Westhill, U.K. 14 D6
Westhope, U.S.A. 112 A4
Westland Bight, N.Z. 91 K3
Westlock, Canada 104 C6
Westmar, Australia 95 D4
Westmeath □, Ireland ... 15 C4
Westminster, U.S.A. 108 F7
Westmont, U.S.A. 110 F6
Westmorland, U.S.A. 117 M11
Weston, Oreg., U.S.A. ... 114 D4
Weston, W. Va., U.S.A. .. 108 F5
Weston I., Canada 102 B4
Weston-super-Mare, U.K. . 13 F5
Westover, U.S.A. 110 F6
Westport, Canada 111 B8
Westport, Ireland 15 C2
Westport, N.Z. 91 J3
Westport, N.Y., U.S.A. ... 111 B11
Westport, Oreg., U.S.A. .. 116 D3
Westport, Wash., U.S.A. . 116 D2
Westray, Canada 105 C8
Westray, U.K. 14 B5
Westree, Canada 102 C3
Westville, U.S.A. 116 F6
Westwood, U.S.A. 114 F3
Wetar, Indonesia 63 F7
Wetaskiwin, Canada 104 C6
Wete, Tanzania 84 F7
Wetherby, U.K. 12 D6
Wethersfield, U.S.A. 111 E12
Wetteren, Belgium 17 D3
Wetzlar, Germany 24 E4
Wewoka, U.S.A. 113 H6
Wexford, Ireland 15 D5
Wexford □, Ireland 15 D5
Wexford Harbour, Ireland . 15 D5
Weyburn, Canada 105 D8
Weyer Markt, Austria ... 26 D7
Weyhe, Germany 24 C4
Weyib →, Ethiopia 81 F5
Weymouth, Canada 103 D6
Weymouth, U.K. 13 G5
Weymouth, U.S.A. 111 D14
Weymouth, C., Australia . 94 A3
Wha Ti, Canada 100 B8
Whakatane, N.Z. 91 G6
Whale →, Canada 103 A6
Whale Cove, Canada 105 A10
Whales, B. of, Antarctica . 5 D12
Whalsay, U.K. 14 A8
Whangamomona, N.Z. ... 91 H5
Whangarei, N.Z. 91 F5
Whangarei Harb., N.Z. ... 91 F5
Wharfe →, U.K. 12 D6
Wharfedale, U.K. 12 C5
Wharton, N.J., U.S.A. ... 111 F10
Wharton, Pa., U.S.A. 110 E6
Wharton, Tex., U.S.A. ... 113 L6
Wheatland, Calif., U.S.A. . 116 F5
Wheatland, Wyo., U.S.A. . 112 D2
Wheatley, U.S.A. 110 D2
Wheaton, Md., U.S.A. ... 108 F7
Wheaton, Minn., U.S.A. .. 112 C6
Wheelbarrow Pk., U.S.A. . 116 H10
Wheeler, Oreg., U.S.A. ... 114 D2

Wheeler, Tex., U.S.A. 113 H4
Wheeler →, Canada 103 A6
Wheeler L., U.S.A. 109 H2
Wheeler Pk., N. Mex.,
  U.S.A. 115 H11
Wheeler Pk., Nev., U.S.A. . 115 G6
Wheeler Ridge, U.S.A. ... 117 L8
Wheeling, U.S.A. 110 F4
Whernside, U.K. 12 C5
Whiskey Jack L., Canada . 105 B8
Whistleduck Cr. →,
  Australia 94 C2
Whistler, Canada 104 C4
Whitby, Canada 110 C6
Whitby, U.K. 12 C7
White →, Ark., U.S.A. ... 113 J9
White →, Ind., U.S.A. ... 108 F2
White →, S. Dak., U.S.A. . 112 D5
White →, Tex., U.S.A. ... 113 J4
White →, Utah, U.S.A. ... 114 F9
White →, Vt., U.S.A. 111 C12
White →, Wash., U.S.A. .. 116 C4
White, L., Australia 92 D4
White B., Canada 103 C8
White Bird, U.S.A. 114 D5
White Butte, U.S.A. 112 B3
White City, U.S.A. 114 E2
White Cliffs, Australia ... 95 E3
White Hall, U.S.A. 112 F9
White Haven, U.S.A. 111 E9
White Horse, Vale of, U.K. 13 F6
White I., N.Z. 91 G6
White L., Canada 111 A8
White L., U.S.A. 113 L8
White Mountain Peak,
  U.S.A. 115 G4
White Mts., Calif., U.S.A. . 116 H8
White Mts., N.H., U.S.A. . 111 B13
White Nile = Nîl el
  Abyad →, Sudan 81 D3
White Nile Dam = Khazzān
  Jabal al Awliyā, Sudan . 81 D3
White Otter L., Canada .. 102 C1
White Pass, U.S.A. 116 D5
White Plains, U.S.A. 111 E11
White River, Canada 102 C2
White River, S. Africa ... 89 D5
White River, U.S.A. 112 D4
White Rock, Canada 116 A4
White Russia = Belarus ■,
  Europe 46 F4
White Sea = Beloye More,
  Russia 50 C4
White Sulphur Springs,
  Mont., U.S.A. 114 C8
White Sulphur Springs,
  W. Va., U.S.A. 108 G5
White Swan, U.S.A. 116 D6
White Volta →, Ghana .. 83 D4
Whitecliffs, N.Z. 91 K3
Whitecourt, Canada 104 C5
Whiteface Mt., U.S.A. ... 111 B11
Whitefield, U.S.A. 111 B13
Whitefish, U.S.A. 114 B6
Whitefish L., Canada 105 A7
Whitefish Point, U.S.A. .. 108 B3
Whitegull, L., Canada ... 103 A7
Whitehall, Mich., U.S.A. . 108 D2
Whitehall, Mont., U.S.A. . 114 D7
Whitehall, N.Y., U.S.A. .. 111 C11
Whitehall, Wis., U.S.A. .. 112 C9
Whitehaven, U.K. 12 C4
Whitehorse, Canada 104 A1
Whitemark, Australia ... 94 G4
Whiteplains, Liberia 82 D2
Whiteriver, U.S.A. 115 K9
Whitesand →, Canada .. 104 A5
Whitesands, S. Africa ... 88 E3
Whitesboro, N.Y., U.S.A. . 111 C9
Whitesboro, Tex., U.S.A. . 113 J6
Whiteshell Prov. Park,
  Canada 105 D9
Whitesville, U.S.A. 110 D7
Whiteville, U.S.A. 109 H6
Whitewater, U.S.A. 108 D1
Whitewater Baldy, U.S.A. . 115 K9
Whitewater L., Canada .. 102 B2
Whitewood, Australia ... 94 C3
Whitewood, Canada 105 C8
Whithorn, U.K. 14 G4
Whitianga, N.Z. 91 G5
Whitman, U.S.A. 111 D14
Whitney, Canada 102 C4
Whitney, Mt., U.S.A. 116 J8
Whitney Point, U.S.A. ... 111 D9
Whitstable, U.K. 13 F9
Whitsunday I., Australia . 94 C4
Whittier, U.S.A. 117 M8
Whittlesea, Australia ... 95 F4
Wholdaia L., Canada 105 A8
Whyalla, Australia 95 E2
Wiarton, Canada 102 D3
Wiawso, Ghana 82 D4
Wiay, U.K. 14 D1
Wiązów, Poland 45 H4
Wibaux, U.S.A. 112 B2
Wichian Buri, Thailand .. 64 E3
Wichita, U.S.A. 113 G6
Wichita Falls, U.S.A. 113 J5
Wick, U.K. 14 C5
Wicked Pt., Canada 110 C7
Wickenburg, U.S.A. 115 K7
Wickepin, Australia 93 F2
Wickham, Australia 92 D2
Wickham, C., Australia .. 94 F3
Wickliffe, U.S.A. 110 E3
Widawa →, Poland 45 G5

Widawka →, Poland 45 G5
Widgeegoara Cr. →,
  Australia 95 D4
Widgiemooltha, Australia . 93 F3
Widnes, U.K. 12 D5
Więcbork, Poland 45 E4
Wiehl, Germany 24 E3
Wiek, Germany 24 A9
Wielbark, Poland 44 E7
Wieleń, Poland 45 F3
Wielichowo, Poland 45 F3
Wieliczka, Poland 45 J7
Wielkopolskie □, Poland . 45 F4
Wieluń, Poland 45 G5
Wien, Austria 27 C9
Wiener Neustadt, Austria . 27 D9
Wieprz →, Poland 45 G8
Wieprza →, Poland 44 D3
Wieruszów, Poland 45 G5
Wiesbaden, Germany ... 25 E4
Wiesental, Germany 25 F4
Wiesloch, Germany 25 F4
Wiesmoor, Germany 24 B3
Wieżyca, Poland 44 D5
Wigan, U.K. 12 D5
Wiggins, Colo., U.S.A. .. 112 E2
Wiggins, Miss., U.S.A. .. 113 K10
Wight, I. of □, U.K. 13 G6
Wigry, Jezioro, Poland .. 44 D10
Wigston, U.K. 13 E6
Wigton, U.K. 12 C4
Wigtown, U.K. 14 G4
Wigtown B., U.K. 14 G4
Wil, Switz. 25 H5
Wilber, U.S.A. 112 E6
Wilberforce, Canada 110 A6
Wilberforce, C., Australia . 94 A2
Wilburton, U.S.A. 113 H7
Wilcannia, Australia 95 E3
Wilcox, U.S.A. 110 E6
Wildbad, Germany 25 G4
Wildeshausen, Germany . 24 C4
Wildon, Austria 26 E8
Wildrose, U.S.A. 117 J9
Wildspitze, Austria 26 E3
Wilga →, Poland 45 G8
Wilge →, S. Africa 89 D4
Wilhelm II Coast, Antarctica 5 C7
Wilhelmsburg, Austria .. 26 C8
Wilhelmshaven, Germany 24 B4
Wilhelmstal, Namibia ... 88 C2
Wilkes-Barre, U.S.A. 111 E9
Wilkie, Canada 105 C7
Wilkinsburg, U.S.A. 110 F5
Wilkinson Lakes, Australia 93 E5
Willandra Creek →,
  Australia 95 E4
Willapa B., U.S.A. 114 C2
Willapa Hills, U.S.A. 116 D3
Willard, N.Y., U.S.A. 110 D8
Willard, Ohio, U.S.A. ... 110 E2
Willcox, U.S.A. 115 K9
Willemstad, Neth. Ant. .. 121 D6
Willet, U.S.A. 111 D9
William →, Canada 105 B7
William 'Bill' Dannely Res.,
  U.S.A. 109 J2
William Creek, Australia . 95 D2
Williams, Australia 93 F2
Williams, Ariz., U.S.A. .. 115 J7
Williams, Calif., U.S.A. .. 116 F4
Williams Harbour, Canada 103 B8
Williams Lake, Canada .. 104 C4
Williamsburg, Ky., U.S.A. 109 G3
Williamsburg, Pa., U.S.A. 110 F6
Williamsburg, Va., U.S.A. 108 G7
Williamson, N.Y., U.S.A. . 110 C7
Williamson, W. Va., U.S.A. 108 G4
Williamsport, U.S.A. 110 E7
Williamston, U.S.A. 109 H7
Williamstown, Australia . 95 F3
Williamstown, Ky., U.S.A. 108 F3
Williamstown, Mass., U.S.A. 111 D11
Williamstown, N.Y., U.S.A. 111 C9
Willimantic, U.S.A. 111 E12
Willingboro, U.S.A. 108 E8
Willis Group, Australia .. 94 B5
Williston, S. Africa 88 E3
Williston, Fla., U.S.A. ... 109 L4
Williston, N. Dak., U.S.A. 112 A3
Williston L., Canada 104 B4
Willits, U.S.A. 114 G2
Willmar, U.S.A. 112 C7
Willoughby, U.S.A. 110 E3
Willow Bunch, Canada .. 105 D7
Willow L., Canada 104 A5
Willow Wall, The, China . 57 C12
Willowick, U.S.A. 110 E3
Willowlake →, Canada .. 104 A4
Willowmore, S. Africa ... 88 E3
Willows, U.S.A. 116 F4
Willowvale = Gatyana,
  S. Africa 89 E4
Wills, L., Australia 92 D4
Wills Cr. →, Australia ... 94 C3
Willsboro, U.S.A. 111 B11
Willunga, Australia 95 F2
Wilmette, U.S.A. 108 D2
Wilmington, Australia ... 95 E2
Wilmington, Del., U.S.A. . 108 F8
Wilmington, N.C., U.S.A. . 109 H7
Wilmington, Ohio, U.S.A. 108 F4
Wilmington, Vt., U.S.A. . 111 D12
Wilmslow, U.K. 12 D5
Wilpena →, Australia ... 95 E2
Wilsall, U.S.A. 114 D8
Wilson, N.C., U.S.A. 109 H7
Wilson, N.Y., U.S.A. 110 C6
Wilson, Pa., U.S.A. 111 F9
Wilson →, Australia 92 C4

Wilson Bluff, Australia 93 F4
Wilson Inlet, Australia 93 G2
Wilsons Promontory,
  Australia 95 F4
Wilster, Germany 24 B5
Wilton, U.S.A. 112 B4
Wilton →, Australia 94 A1
Wiltshire □, U.K. 13 F6
Wiltz, Lux. 17 E5
Wiluna, Australia 93 E3
Wimborne Minster, U.K. . 13 G6
Wimereux, France 19 B8
Wimmera →, Australia .. 95 F3
Winam G., Kenya 86 C3
Winburg, S. Africa 88 D4
Winchendon, U.S.A. 111 D12
Winchester, U.K. 13 F6
Winchester, Conn., U.S.A. 111 E11
Winchester, Idaho, U.S.A. 114 C5
Winchester, Ind., U.S.A. . 108 E3
Winchester, Ky., U.S.A. . 108 G3
Winchester, N.H., U.S.A. 111 D12
Winchester, Nev., U.S.A. 117 J11
Winchester, Tenn., U.S.A. 109 H2
Winchester, Va., U.S.A. . 108 F6
Wind →, U.S.A. 114 E9
Wind River Range, U.S.A. 114 E9
Windau = Ventspils, Latvia 9 H19
Windber, U.S.A. 110 F6
Winder, U.S.A. 109 J4
Windermere, U.K. 12 C5
Windhoek, Namibia 88 C2
Windischgarsten, Austria . 26 D7
Windom, U.S.A. 112 D7
Windorah, Australia 94 D3
Window Rock, U.S.A. ... 115 J9
Windrush →, U.K. 13 F6
Windsor, Australia 95 E5
Windsor, N.S., Canada .. 103 D7
Windsor, Ont., Canada .. 102 D3
Windsor, U.K. 13 F7
Windsor, Colo., U.S.A. .. 112 E2
Windsor, Conn., U.S.A. . 111 E12
Windsor, Mo., U.S.A. ... 112 F8
Windsor, N.Y., U.S.A. ... 111 D9
Windsor, Vt., U.S.A. 111 C12
Windsor & Maidenhead □,
  U.K. 13 F7
Windsorton, S. Africa ... 88 D3
Windward Is., W. Indies . 121 D7
Windward Passage =
  Vientos, Paso de los,
  Caribbean 121 C5
Winefred L., Canada 105 B6
Winejok, Sudan 81 F2
Winfield, U.S.A. 113 G6
Wingate Mts., Australia . 92 B5
Wingham, Australia 95 E5
Wingham, Canada 102 D3
Winisk, Canada 102 A2
Winisk →, Canada 102 A2
Winisk L., Canada 102 B2
Wink, U.S.A. 113 K3
Winkler, Canada 105 D9
Winklern, Austria 26 E5
Winlock, U.S.A. 116 D4
Winneba, Ghana 83 D4
Winnebago, L., U.S.A. .. 108 D1
Winnecke Cr. →, Australia 92 C5
Winnemucca, U.S.A. ... 114 F5
Winnemucca L., U.S.A. . 114 F4
Winnett, U.S.A. 114 C9
Winnfield, U.S.A. 113 K8
Winnibigoshish, L., U.S.A. 112 B7
Winnipeg, Canada 105 D9
Winnipeg →, Canada ... 105 C9
Winnipeg, L., Canada ... 105 C9
Winnipeg Beach, Canada 105 C9
Winnipegosis, Canada .. 105 C9
Winnipegosis L., Canada 105 C9
Winnipesaukee, L., U.S.A. 111 C13
Winnisquam L., U.S.A. .. 111 C13
Winnsboro, La., U.S.A. .. 113 J9
Winnsboro, S.C., U.S.A. . 109 H5
Winnsboro, Tex., U.S.A. . 113 J7
Winokapau, L., Canada .. 103 B7
Winona, Minn., U.S.A. .. 112 C9
Winona, Miss., U.S.A. ... 113 J10
Winooski, U.S.A. 111 B11
Winooski →, U.S.A. 111 B11
Winschoten, Neths. 17 A7
Winsen, Germany 24 B6
Winsford, U.K. 12 D5
Winslow, Ariz., U.S.A. .. 115 J8
Winslow, Wash., U.S.A. . 116 C4
Winsted, U.S.A. 111 E11
Winston-Salem, U.S.A. .. 109 G5
Winter Garden, U.S.A. .. 109 L5
Winter Haven, U.S.A. ... 109 M5
Winter Park, U.S.A. 109 L5
Winterberg, Germany ... 24 D4
Winterhaven, U.S.A. 117 N12
Winters, U.S.A. 116 G5
Wintersville, U.S.A. 110 F4
Winterswijk, Neths. 17 C6
Winterthur, Switz. 25 H4
Winthrop, U.S.A. 114 B3
Winton, Australia 94 C3
Winton, N.Z. 91 M2
Wipper →, Germany ... 24 D7
Wirrulla, Australia 95 E1
Wisbech, U.K. 13 E8
Wisconsin □, U.S.A. 112 C10
Wisconsin →, U.S.A. ... 112 D9
Wisconsin Rapids, U.S.A. 112 C10
Wisdom, U.S.A. 114 D7
Wishaw, U.K. 14 F5
Wishek, U.S.A. 112 B5
Wisła, Poland 45 J5
Wisła →, Poland 44 D5
Wisłok →, Poland 45 H9

Wisłoka →, Poland ... 45 H8
Wismar, Germany ... 24 B7
Wisner, U.S.A. ... 112 E6
Wissant, France ... 19 B8
Wissembourg, France ... 19 C14
Wisznice, Poland ... 45 G10
Witbank, S. Africa ... 89 D4
Witdraai, S. Africa ... 88 D3
Witham, U.K. ... 13 F8
Witham →, U.K. ... 12 E7
Withernsea, U.K. ... 12 D8
Witkowo, Poland ... 45 F4
Witney, U.K. ... 13 F6
Witnica, Poland ... 45 F1
Witnossob →, Namibia ... 88 D3
Witten, Germany ... 24 D3
Wittenberge, Germany ... 24 B7
Wittenburg, Germany ... 24 B7
Wittenheim, France ... 19 E14
Wittenoom, Australia ... 92 D2
Wittingen, Germany ... 24 C6
Wittlich, Germany ... 25 F2
Wittmund, Germany ... 24 B3
Wittow, Germany ... 24 A9
Wittstock, Germany ... 24 B8
Witvlei, Namibia ... 88 C2
Witzenhausen, Germany ... 24 D5
Wkra →, Poland ... 45 F7
Władysławowo, Poland ... 44 D5
Wleń, Poland ... 45 G2
Wlingi, Indonesia ... 63 H15
Włocławek, Poland ... 45 F6
Włodawa, Poland ... 45 G10
Włoszczowa, Poland ... 45 H6
Woburn, U.S.A. ... 111 D13
Wodian, China ... 56 H7
Wodzisław Śląski, Poland ... 45 H5
Wœrth, France ... 19 D14
Woinbogoin, China ... 58 A2
Woippy, France ... 19 C13
Wojcieszów, Poland ... 45 H2
Wokam, Indonesia ... 63 F8
Woking, U.K. ... 13 F7
Wokingham □, U.K. ... 13 F7
Wolbrom, Poland ... 45 H6
Wołczyn, Poland ... 45 G5
Woldegk, Germany ... 24 B9
Wolf →, Canada ... 104 A2
Wolf Creek, U.S.A. ... 114 C7
Wolf L., Canada ... 104 A2
Wolf Point, U.S.A. ... 112 A2
Wolfe I., Canada ... 102 D4
Wolfeboro, U.S.A. ... 111 C13
Wolfen, Germany ... 24 D8
Wolfenbüttel, Germany ... 24 C6
Wolfratshausen, Germany ... 25 H7
Wolfsberg, Austria ... 26 E7
Wolfsburg, Germany ... 24 C6
Wolgast, Germany ... 24 A9
Wolhusen, Switz. ... 25 H4
Wolin, Poland ... 44 E1
Wollaston, Is., Chile ... 128 H3
Wollaston L., Canada ... 105 B8
Wollaston Lake, Canada ... 105 B8
Wollaston Pen., Canada ... 100 B8
Wollongong, Australia ... 95 E5
Wolmaransstad, S. Africa ... 88 D4
Wolmirstedt, Germany ... 24 C7
Wołomin, Poland ... 45 F8
Wołów, Poland ... 45 G3
Wolseley, S. Africa ... 88 E2
Wolsey, U.S.A. ... 112 C5
Wolstenholme, C., Canada ... 98 C12
Wolsztyn, Poland ... 45 F3
Wolvega, Neths. ... 17 B6
Wolverhampton, U.K. ... 13 E5
Wondai, Australia ... 95 D5
Wongalarroo L., Australia ... 95 E3
Wongan Hills, Australia ... 93 F2
Wŏnju, S. Korea ... 57 F14
Wonosari, Indonesia ... 63 G14
Wonosobo, Indonesia ... 63 G13
Wonowon, Canada ... 104 B4
Wŏnsan, N. Korea ... 57 E14
Wonthaggi, Australia ... 95 F4
Wood Buffalo Nat. Park, Canada ... 104 B6
Wood Is., Australia ... 92 C3
Wood L., Canada ... 105 B8
Woodah I., Australia ... 94 A2
Woodbourne, U.S.A. ... 111 E10
Woodbridge, Canada ... 110 C5
Woodbridge, U.K. ... 13 E9
Woodburn, U.S.A. ... 114 D2
Woodenbong, Australia ... 95 D5
Woodend, Australia ... 95 F3
Woodford, Australia ... 95 D5
Woodfords, U.S.A. ... 116 G7
Woodlake, U.S.A. ... 116 J7
Woodland, Calif., U.S.A. ... 116 G5
Woodland, Maine, U.S.A. ... 109 C12
Woodland, Pa., U.S.A. ... 110 F6
Woodland, Wash., U.S.A. ... 116 E4
Woodland Caribou Prov. Park, Canada ... 105 C10
Woodridge, Canada ... 105 D9
Woodroffe, Mt., Australia ... 93 E5
Woods, L., Australia ... 94 B1
Woods, L. of the, Canada ... 105 D10
Woodside, Australia ... 95 F4
Woodstock, Australia ... 94 B4
Woodstock, N.B., Canada ... 103 C6
Woodstock, Ont., Canada ... 102 D3
Woodstock, U.K. ... 13 F6
Woodstock, Ill., U.S.A. ... 112 D10
Woodstock, Vt., U.S.A. ... 111 C12
Woodsville, U.S.A. ... 111 B13
Woodville, N.Z. ... 91 J5
Woodville, Miss., U.S.A. ... 113 K9
Woodville, Tex., U.S.A. ... 113 K7

Woodward, U.S.A. ... 113 G5
Woody, U.S.A. ... 117 K8
Woody →, Canada ... 105 C8
Woolamai, C., Australia ... 95 F4
Wooler, U.K. ... 12 B5
Woolgoolga, Australia ... 95 E5
Woomera, Australia ... 95 E2
Woonsocket, R.I., U.S.A. ... 111 E13
Woonsocket, S. Dak., U.S.A. ... 112 C5
Wooramel →, Australia ... 93 E1
Wooramel Roadhouse, Australia ... 93 E1
Wooster, U.S.A. ... 110 F3
Worcester, S. Africa ... 88 E2
Worcester, U.K. ... 13 E5
Worcester, Mass., U.S.A. ... 111 D13
Worcester, N.Y., U.S.A. ... 111 D10
Worcestershire □, U.K. ... 13 E5
Wörgl, Austria ... 26 D5
Workington, U.K. ... 12 C4
Worksop, U.K. ... 12 D6
Workum, Neths. ... 17 B5
Worland, U.S.A. ... 114 D10
Wormhout, France ... 19 B9
Worms, Germany ... 25 F4
Worsley, Canada ... 104 B5
Wörth, Germany ... 25 F8
Wortham, U.S.A. ... 113 K6
Wörther See, Austria ... 26 E7
Worthing, U.K. ... 13 G7
Worthington, Minn., U.S.A. ... 112 D7
Worthington, Pa., U.S.A. ... 110 F5
Wosi, Indonesia ... 63 E7
Wou-han = Wuhan, China ... 59 B10
Wousi = Wuxi, China ... 59 B13
Wowoni, Indonesia ... 63 E6
Wrangel I. = Vrangelya, Ostrov, Russia ... 51 B19
Wrangell, U.S.A. ... 104 B2
Wrangell Mts., U.S.A. ... 100 B5
Wrath, C., U.K. ... 14 C3
Wray, U.S.A. ... 112 E3
Wrekin, The, U.K. ... 13 E5
Wrens, U.S.A. ... 109 J4
Wrexham, U.K. ... 12 D4
Wrexham □, U.K. ... 12 D5
Wriezen, Germany ... 24 C10
Wright = Paranas, Phil. ... 61 F6
Wright, U.S.A. ... 112 D2
Wright Pt., Canada ... 110 C3
Wrightson Mt., U.S.A. ... 115 L8
Wrightwood, U.S.A. ... 117 L9
Wrigley, Canada ... 100 B7
Wrocław, Poland ... 45 G4
Wronki, Poland ... 45 F3
Września, Poland ... 45 F4
Wschowa, Poland ... 45 G3
Wu Jiang →, China ... 58 C6
Wu'an, China ... 56 F8
Wubin, Australia ... 93 F2
Wubu, China ... 56 F6
Wuchang, China ... 57 B14
Wucheng, China ... 56 F9
Wuchuan, Guangdong, China ... 59 G8
Wuchuan, Guizhou, China ... 58 C7
Wuchuan, Nei Mongol Zizhiqu, China ... 56 D6
Wudi, China ... 57 F9
Wuding, China ... 58 E4
Wuding He →, China ... 56 F6
Wudinna, Australia ... 95 E2
Wudu, China ... 56 H3
Wufeng, China ... 59 B8
Wugang, China ... 59 D8
Wugong Shan, China ... 59 D9
Wuhan, China ... 59 B10
Wuhe, China ... 57 H9
Wuhsi = Wuxi, China ... 59 B13
Wuhu, China ... 59 B12
Wujiang, China ... 59 B13
Wukari, Nigeria ... 83 D6
Wulajie, China ... 57 B14
Wulanbulang, China ... 56 D6
Wular L., India ... 69 B6
Wulehe, Ghana ... 83 D5
Wulian, China ... 57 G10
Wuliang Shan, China ... 58 E3
Wuliaru, Indonesia ... 63 F8
Wuling Shan, China ... 58 C7
Wulong, China ... 58 C6
Wulumuchi = Ürümqi, China ... 50 E9
Wum, Cameroon ... 83 D7
Wuming, China ... 58 F7
Wun Rog, Sudan ... 81 F2
Wundowie, Australia ... 93 F2
Wuning, China ... 59 C10
Wunnummin L., Canada ... 102 B2
Wunsiedel, Germany ... 25 E8
Wunstorf, Germany ... 24 C5
Wuntho, Burma ... 67 H19
Wuping, China ... 59 E11
Wuppertal, Germany ... 24 D3
Wuppertal, S. Africa ... 88 E2
Wuqing, China ... 57 E9
Wurtsboro, U.S.A. ... 111 E10
Würzburg, Germany ... 25 F5
Wurzen, Germany ... 24 D8
Wushan, China ... 56 G3
Wushishi, Nigeria ... 83 D6
Wusuli Jiang = Ussuri →, Asia ... 54 A7
Wutach →, Germany ... 25 H4
Wutai, China ... 56 E7
Wuting = Huimin, China ... 57 F9
Wutong, China ... 59 E8
Wutonghaolai, China ... 57 C11
Wutongqiao, China ... 58 C4

Wuwei, Anhui, China ... 59 B11
Wuwei, Gansu, China ... 60 C5
Wuxi, Jiangsu, China ... 59 B13
Wuxi, Sichuan, China ... 58 B7
Wuxiang, China ... 56 F7
Wuxuan, China ... 58 F7
Wuxue, China ... 59 C10
Wuyang, China ... 56 H7
Wuyi, Hebei, China ... 56 F8
Wuyi, Zhejiang, China ... 59 C12
Wuyi Shan, China ... 59 D11
Wuyishan, China ... 59 D12
Wuyo, Nigeria ... 83 C7
Wuyuan, Jiangxi, China ... 59 C11
Wuyuan, Nei Mongol Zizhiqu, China ... 56 D5
Wuzhai, China ... 56 E6
Wuzhi Shan, China ... 64 C7
Wuzhong, China ... 56 E4
Wuzhou, China ... 59 F8
Wyaaba Cr. →, Australia ... 94 B3
Wyalkatchem, Australia ... 93 F2
Wyalusing, U.S.A. ... 111 E8
Wyandotte, U.S.A. ... 108 D4
Wyandra, Australia ... 95 D4
Wyangala Res., Australia ... 95 E4
Wyara, L., Australia ... 95 D3
Wycheproof, Australia ... 95 F3
Wye →, U.K. ... 13 F5
Wyemandoo, Australia ... 93 E2
Wyk, Germany ... 24 A4
Wymondham, U.K. ... 13 E9
Wymore, U.S.A. ... 112 E6
Wyndham, Australia ... 92 C4
Wyndham, N.Z. ... 91 M2
Wynne, U.S.A. ... 113 H9
Wynyard, Australia ... 94 G4
Wynyard, Canada ... 105 C8
Wyola L., Australia ... 93 E5
Wyoming, Canada ... 110 D2
Wyoming □, U.S.A. ... 114 E10
Wyomissing, U.S.A. ... 111 F9
Wyong, Australia ... 95 E5
Wyrzysk, Poland ... 45 E4
Wyśmierzyce, Poland ... 45 G7
Wysoka, Poland ... 45 E4
Wysokie, Poland ... 45 H9
Wysokie Mazowieckie, Poland ... 45 F9
Wyszków, Poland ... 45 F8
Wyszogród, Poland ... 45 F7
Wytheville, U.S.A. ... 108 G5
Wyżyna Małopolska, Poland ... 45 H7

X

Xaçmaz, Azerbaijan ... 49 K9
Xai-Xai, Mozam. ... 89 D5
Xainza, China ... 60 C3
Xangongo, Angola ... 88 B2
Xankändi, Azerbaijan ... 70 B5
Xanlar, Azerbaijan ... 49 K8
Xanten, Germany ... 24 D2
Xánthi, Greece ... 41 E8
Xánthi □, Greece ... 41 E8
Xanthos, Turkey ... 39 E11
Xanxerê, Brazil ... 127 B5
Xapuri, Brazil ... 124 F5
Xar Moron He →, China ... 57 C11
Xarrë, Albania ... 40 G4
Xátiva, Spain ... 33 G4
Xau, L., Botswana ... 88 C3
Xavantina, Brazil ... 127 A5
Xenia, U.S.A. ... 108 F4
Xeropotamos →, Cyprus ... 36 E11
Xertigny, France ... 19 D13
Xhora, S. Africa ... 89 E4
Xhumo, Botswana ... 88 C3
Xi Jiang →, China ... 59 F9
Xi Xian, Henan, China ... 59 A10
Xi Xian, Shanxi, China ... 56 F6
Xia Xian, China ... 56 G6
Xiachengzi, China ... 57 B16
Xiachuan Dao, China ... 59 G9
Xiaguan, China ... 58 E3
Xiajiang, China ... 59 D10
Xiajin, China ... 56 F9
Xiamen, China ... 59 E12
Xi'an, China ... 56 G5
Xian Xian, China ... 56 E9
Xianfeng, China ... 58 C7
Xiang Jiang →, China ... 59 C9
Xiangcheng, Henan, China ... 56 H8
Xiangcheng, Henan, China ... 56 H7
Xiangcheng, Sichuan, China ... 58 C2
Xiangdu, China ... 58 F6
Xiangfan, China ... 59 A9
Xianggang = Hong Kong □, China ... 59 F10
Xianghuang Qi, China ... 56 C7
Xiangning, China ... 56 G6
Xiangquan, China ... 56 F7
Xiangquan He = Sutlej →, Pakistan ... 68 E4
Xiangshan, China ... 59 C13
Xiangshui, China ... 57 G10
Xiangtan, China ... 59 D9
Xiangxiang, China ... 59 D9
Xiangyin, China ... 59 C9
Xiangyun, China ... 58 E3
Xiangzhou, China ... 58 F7
Xianju, China ... 59 C13
Xianning, China ... 59 C10
Xianshui He →, China ... 58 B3
Xiantao, China ... 59 B9
Xianyang, China ... 56 G5

Xianyou, China ... 59 E12
Xiao Hinggan Ling, China ... 60 B7
Xiao Xian, China ... 56 G9
Xiaofeng, China ... 59 B12
Xiaogan, China ... 59 B9
Xiaojin, China ... 58 B4
Xiaolan, China ... 59 F9
Xiaoshan, China ... 59 B13
Xiaoyi, China ... 56 F6
Xiapu, China ... 59 D12
Xiawa, China ... 57 C11
Xiayi, China ... 56 G9
Xichang, China ... 58 D4
Xichong, China ... 58 B5
Xichou, China ... 58 E5
Xichuan, China ... 56 H6
Xide, China ... 58 D4
Xiemahe, China ... 59 B8
Xieng Khouang, Laos ... 64 C4
Xifei He →, China ... 56 H9
Xifeng, Gansu, China ... 56 G4
Xifeng, Guizhou, China ... 58 D6
Xifeng, Liaoning, China ... 57 C13
Xifengzhen = Xifeng, China ... 56 G4
Xigazê, China ... 60 D3
Xihe, China ... 56 G3
Xihua, China ... 56 H8
Xilaganí, Greece ... 41 F9
Xiliao He →, China ... 57 C12
Xilin, China ... 58 E5
Xilókastron, Greece ... 38 C4
Xime, Guinea-Biss. ... 82 C2
Ximeng, China ... 58 F2
Xin Jiang →, China ... 59 C11
Xin Xian = Xinzhou, China ... 56 E7
Xinavane, Mozam. ... 89 D5
Xinbin, China ... 57 D13
Xincai, China ... 59 A10
Xinchang, China ... 59 C13
Xincheng, Guangxi Zhuangzu, China ... 58 E7
Xincheng, Jiangxi, China ... 59 D10
Xindu, China ... 58 B5
Xinfeng, Guangdong, China ... 59 E10
Xinfeng, Jiangxi, China ... 59 D11
Xinfeng, Jiangxi, China ... 59 E10
Xinfengjiang Skuiku, China ... 59 F10
Xing Xian, China ... 56 E6
Xing'an, Guangxi Zhuangzu, China ... 59 E8
Xingan, Jiangxi, China ... 59 D10
Xingcheng, China ... 57 D11
Xingguo, China ... 59 D10
Xinghe, China ... 56 D7
Xinghua, China ... 57 H10
Xinghua Wan, China ... 59 E12
Xinglong, China ... 57 D9
Xingning, China ... 59 E10
Xingping, China ... 56 G5
Xingren, China ... 58 E5
Xingshan, China ... 59 B8
Xingtai, China ... 56 F8
Xingu →, Brazil ... 122 D5
Xingwen, China ... 58 C5
Xingyang, China ... 56 G7
Xinhe, China ... 56 F8
Xinhua, China ... 59 D8
Xinhuang, China ... 58 D7
Xinhui, China ... 59 F9
Xining, China ... 60 C5
Xinjian, China ... 59 C10
Xinjiang, China ... 56 G6
Xinjiang Uygur Zizhiqu □, China ... 60 B3
Xinjie, China ... 58 D3
Xinjin = Pulandian, China ... 57 E11
Xinjin, China ... 58 B4
Xinkai He →, China ... 57 C12
Xinle, China ... 56 E8
Xinlitun, China ... 57 D12
Xinlong, China ... 58 B3
Xinmin, China ... 57 D12
Xinning, China ... 59 D8
Xinping, China ... 58 E3
Xinshao, China ... 59 D8
Xintai, China ... 57 G9
Xintian, China ... 59 E9
Xinxian, China ... 59 B10
Xinxiang, China ... 56 G7
Xinxing, China ... 59 F9
Xinyang, China ... 59 A10
Xinye, China ... 59 A9
Xinyi, China ... 59 F8
Xinyu, China ... 59 D10
Xinzhan, China ... 57 C14
Xinzheng, China ... 56 G7
Xinzhou, Hubei, China ... 59 B10
Xinzhou, Shanxi, China ... 56 E7
Xinzo de Limia, Spain ... 34 C3
Xiong Xian, China ... 56 E9
Xiongyuecheng, China ... 57 D12
Xiping, Henan, China ... 56 H8
Xiping, Henan, China ... 56 H6
Xiping, Zhejiang, China ... 59 C12
Xique-Xique, Brazil ... 125 F10
Xisha Qundao = Paracel Is., S. China Sea ... 62 A4
Xishui, Guizhou, China ... 58 C6
Xishui, Hubei, China ... 59 B10
Xitole, Guinea-Biss. ... 82 C2
Xiu Shui →, China ... 59 C10
Xiuning, China ... 59 C12
Xiuren, China ... 59 E8
Xiushan, China ... 58 C7
Xiushui, China ... 59 C10
Xiuwen, China ... 58 D6
Xiuyan, China ... 57 D12
Xixabangma Feng, China ... 67 E14
Xixia, China ... 56 H6
Xixiang, China ... 56 H4

Xiyang, China ... 56 F7
Xizang Zizhiqu □, China ... 60 C3
Xlendi, Malta ... 36 C1
Xu Jiang →, China ... 59 D11
Xuan Loc, Vietnam ... 65 G6
Xuan'en, China ... 58 C7
Xuanhan, China ... 58 B6
Xuanhua, China ... 56 D8
Xuanwei, China ... 58 C5
Xuanzhou, China ... 59 B12
Xuchang, China ... 56 G7
Xudat, Azerbaijan ... 49 K9
Xuefeng Shan, China ... 59 D8
Xuejiaping, China ... 59 B8
Xun Jiang →, China ... 59 F8
Xun Xian, China ... 56 G8
Xundian, China ... 58 E4
Xunwu, China ... 59 E10
Xunyang, China ... 56 H5
Xunyi, China ... 56 G5
Xupu, China ... 59 D8
Xúquer →, Spain ... 33 F4
Xushui, China ... 56 E8
Xuwen, China ... 59 G8
Xuyen Moc, Vietnam ... 65 G6
Xuyong, China ... 58 C5
Xuzhou, China ... 57 G9

Y

Ya Xian, China ... 64 C7
Yaamba, Australia ... 94 C5
Ya'an, China ... 58 C4
Yaapeet, Australia ... 95 F3
Yabassi, Cameroon ... 83 E6
Yabelo, Ethiopia ... 81 G4
Yablanitsa, Bulgaria ... 41 C8
Yablonovy Ra. = Yablonovyy Khrebet, Russia ... 51 D12
Yablonovyy Khrebet, Russia ... 51 D12
Yabrai Shan, China ... 56 E2
Yabrūd, Syria ... 75 B5
Yacheng, China ... 64 C7
Yacuiba, Bolivia ... 126 A3
Yacuma →, Bolivia ... 124 F5
Yadgir, India ... 66 L10
Yadkin →, U.S.A. ... 109 H5
Yadrin, Russia ... 48 C8
Yaeyama-Rettō, Japan ... 55 M1
Yagaba, Ghana ... 83 C4
Yağcılar, Turkey ... 39 B10
Yagodnoye, Russia ... 51 C15
Yahila, Dem. Rep. of the Congo ... 86 B1
Yahk, Canada ... 104 D5
Yahotyn, Ukraine ... 47 G6
Yahuma, Dem. Rep. of the Congo ... 84 D4
Yahyalı, Turkey ... 72 C6
Yaita, Japan ... 55 F9
Yaiza, Canary Is. ... 37 F6
Yajiang, China ... 58 B3
Yajua, Nigeria ... 83 C7
Yakima, U.S.A. ... 114 C3
Yakima →, U.S.A. ... 114 C3
Yako, Burkina Faso ... 82 C4
Yakobi I., U.S.A. ... 104 B1
Yakoruda, Bulgaria ... 40 D7
Yakovlevka, Russia ... 54 B6
Yaku-Shima, Japan ... 55 J5
Yakumo, Japan ... 54 C10
Yakutat, U.S.A. ... 100 C6
Yakutia = Sakha □, Russia ... 51 C13
Yakutsk, Russia ... 51 C13
Yala, Thailand ... 65 J3
Yale, U.S.A. ... 110 C2
Yalgoo, Australia ... 93 E2
Yalinga, C.A.R. ... 84 C4
Yalkubul, Punta, Mexico ... 119 C7
Yalleroi, Australia ... 94 C4
Yalobusha →, U.S.A. ... 113 J9
Yalong Jiang →, China ... 58 D3
Yalova, Turkey ... 41 F13
Yalta, Ukraine ... 47 K8
Yalu Jiang →, China ... 57 E13
Yalvaç, Turkey ... 72 C4
Yam Ha Melah = Dead Sea, Asia ... 75 D4
Yam Kinneret, Israel ... 75 C4
Yamada, Japan ... 55 H5
Yamagata, Japan ... 54 E10
Yamagata □, Japan ... 54 E10
Yamaguchi, Japan ... 55 G5
Yamaguchi □, Japan ... 55 G5
Yamal, Poluostrov, Russia ... 50 B8
Yamal Pen. = Yamal, Poluostrov, Russia ... 50 B8
Yamanashi □, Japan ... 55 G9
Yamba, Australia ... 95 D5
Yambarran Ra., Australia ... 92 C5
Yamberra, Guinea ... 82 C2
Yâmbiô, Sudan ... 81 G2
Yambol, Bulgaria ... 41 D10
Yamdena, Indonesia ... 63 F8
Yame, Japan ... 55 H5
Yamethin, Burma ... 67 J20
Yamma-Yamma, L., Australia ... 95 D3
Yamoussoukro, Ivory C. ... 82 D3
Yampa →, U.S.A. ... 114 F9
Yampi Sd., Australia ... 92 C3
Yampil, Moldova ... 47 H5
Yampol = Yampil, Moldova ... 47 H5
Yamrat, Nigeria ... 83 C6
Yamrukchal = Botev, Bulgaria ... 41 D8

Yamuna →, India 69 G9
Yamunanagar, India 68 D7
Yamzho Yumco, China .. 60 D4
Yan, Nigeria 83 C7
Yana →, Russia 51 B14
Yanagawa, Japan 55 H5
Yanai, Japan 55 H6
Yan'an, China 56 F5
Yanbian, China 58 D3
Yanbu 'al Baḥr, Si. Arabia . 70 F3
Yanchang, China 56 F6
Yancheng, Henan, China .. 56 H8
Yancheng, Jiangsu, China . 57 H11
Yanchep Beach, Australia . 93 F2
Yanchi, China 56 F4
Yanchuan, China 56 F6
Yanco, Australia 95 E4
Yanco Cr. →, Australia .. 95 E4
Yandoon, Burma 67 L19
Yanfeng, China 58 E3
Yanfolila, Mali 82 C3
Yang Xian, China 56 H4
Yang-Yang, Senegal 82 B1
Yangambi,
  Dem. Rep. of the Congo . 86 B1
Yangbi, China 58 E2
Yangcheng, China 56 G7
Yangch'ü = Taiyuan, China 56 F7
Yangchun, China 59 F8
Yanggao, China 56 D7
Yanggu, China 56 F8
Yangjiang, China 59 G8
Yangliuqing, China 57 E9
Yangon = Rangoon, Burma 67 L20
Yangping, China 59 B8
Yangpingguan, China ... 56 H4
Yangquan, China 56 F7
Yangshan, China 59 E9
Yangshuo, China 59 E8
Yangtse = Chang Jiang →,
  China 59 B13
Yangtze Kiang = Chang
  Jiang →, China 59 B13
Yangxin, China 59 C10
Yangyang, S. Korea 57 E15
Yangyuan, China 56 D8
Yangzhong, China 59 A12
Yangzhou, China 59 A12
Yanhe, China 58 C7
Yanji, China 57 C15
Yanjin, China 58 C5
Yanjing, China 58 C4
Yankton, U.S.A. 112 D6
Yanonge,
  Dem. Rep. of the Congo . 86 B1
Yanqi, China 60 B3
Yanqing, China 56 D8
Yanshan, Hebei, China .. 57 E9
Yanshan, Jiangxi, China .. 59 C11
Yanshan, Yunnan, China . 58 F5
Yanshou, China 57 B15
Yantabulla, Australia ... 95 D4
Yantai, China 57 F11
Yanting, China 58 B5
Yantra →, Bulgaria 41 C9
Yanwa, China 58 D2
Yanyuan, China 58 D3
Yanzhou, China 56 G9
Yao Xian, China 56 G5
Yao Yai, Ko, Thailand .. 65 J2
Yao'an, China 58 E4
Yaodu, China 58 A5
Yaoundé, Cameroon 83 E7
Yaowan, China 57 G10
Yap I., Pac. Oc. 96 G5
Yapen, Indonesia 63 E9
Yapen, Selat, Indonesia .. 63 E9
Yapero, Indonesia 63 E9
Yappar →, Australia ... 94 B3
Yaqui →, Mexico 118 B3
Yaraka, Australia 94 C3
Yaransk, Russia 48 B8
Yarbasan, Turkey 39 C10
Yardımcı Burnu, Turkey . 39 E12
Yare →, U.K. 13 E9
Yaremcha, Ukraine 47 H3
Yarensk, Russia 50 C5
Yarfa, Si. Arabia 80 C4
Yarí →, Colombia 124 D4
Yarkand = Shache, China . 60 C2
Yarker, Canada 111
Yarkhun →, Pakistan .. 69 A5
Yarmouth, Canada 103 D6
Yarmūk →, Syria 75 C4
Yaroslavl, Russia 46 D10
Yarqa, W. →, Egypt ... 75 F2
Yarra Yarra Lakes, Australia 93 E2
Yarram, Australia 95 F4
Yarraman, Australia 95 D5
Yarras, Australia 95 E5
Yartsevo, Sib., Russia .. 51 C10
Yartsevo, Smolensk, Russia 46 E7
Yarumal, Colombia 124 B3
Yasawa Group, Fiji 91 C7
Yaselda, Belarus 47 F4
Yashi, Nigeria 83 C6
Yashikera, Nigeria 83 D5
Yashkul, Russia 49 G7
Yasin, Pakistan 69 A5
Yasinovataya, Ukraine .. 47 H9
Yasinski, L., Canada ... 102 B4
Yasinya, Ukraine 47 H3
Yasothon, Thailand 64 E5
Yass, Australia 95 E4
Yatağan, Turkey 39 D10
Yatakala, Niger 83 C5
Yates Center, U.S.A. ... 113 G7
Yathkyed L., Canada ... 105 A9
Yatsushiro, Japan 55 H5

Yatta Plateau, Kenya ... 86 C4
Yavari →, Peru 124 D4
Yávaros, Mexico 118 B3
Yavatmal, India 66 J11
Yavne, Israel 75 D3
Yavoriv, Ukraine 47 H2
Yavorov = Yavoriv, Ukraine 47 H2
Yavuzeli, Turkey 72 D7
Yawatahama, Japan 55 H6
Yawri B., S. Leone 82 D2
Yaxi, China 58 D6
Yaxian, China 58 E6
Yazd, Iran 71 D7
Yazd □, Iran 71 D7
Yazd-e Khvāst, Iran ... 71 D7
Yazıköy, Turkey 39 E9
Yazman, Pakistan 68 E4
Yazoo →, U.S.A. 113 J9
Yazoo City, U.S.A. 113 J9
Ybbs, Austria 26 C8
Yding Skovhøj, Denmark . 11 J3
Ye Xian = Laizhou, China . 57 F10
Ye Xian, China 56 H7
Yebyu, Burma 64 E2
Yechŏn, S. Korea 57 F15
Yecla, Spain 33 G3
Yécora, Mexico 118 B3
Yedintsy = Edineţ, Moldova 43 B12
Yedseram →, Nigeria .. 83 C7
Yefremov, Russia 46 F10
Yegorlyk →, Russia ... 49 G5
Yegorlykskaya, Russia .. 49 G5
Yegoryevsk, Russia 46 E10
Yegros, Paraguay 126 B4
Yehuda, Midbar, Israel .. 75 D4
Yei, Sudan 81 G3
Yei, Nahr →, Sudan .. 81 F3
Yejmiadzin, Armenia ... 49 K7
Yekaterinburg, Russia .. 50 D7
Yekaterinodar = Krasnodar,
  Russia 49 H4
Yelabuga, Russia 48 C11
Yelan, Russia 48 E6
Yelarbon, Australia 95 D5
Yelatma, Russia 48 C5
Yelets, Russia 47 F10
Yélimané, Mali 82 B2
Yelizavetgrad = Kirovohrad,
  Ukraine 47 H7
Yell, U.K. 14 A7
Yell Sd., U.K. 14 A7
Yellow Sea, China 57 G12
Yellowhead Pass, Canada . 104 C5
Yellowknife, Canada ... 104 A6
Yellowknife →, Canada . 104 A6
Yellowstone →, U.S.A. . 112 B3
Yellowstone L., U.S.A. .. 114 D8
Yellowstone National Park,
  U.S.A. 114 D9
Yelnya, Russia 46 E7
Yelsk, Belarus 47 G5
Yelwa, Nigeria 83 C5
Yemen ■, Asia 74 E3
Yen Bai, Vietnam 58 G5
Yenagoa, Nigeria 83 E6
Yenakiyeve, Ukraine ... 47 H10
Yenakiyevo = Yenakiyeve,
  Ukraine 47 H10
Yenangyaung, Burma ... 67 J19
Yenbo = Yanbu 'al Baḥr,
  Si. Arabia 70 F3
Yenda, Australia 95 E4
Yende Millimou, Guinea . 82 D2
Yendéré, Burkina Faso .. 82 C4
Yendi, Ghana 83 D4
Yéni, Niger 83 C5
Yenice, Ankara, Turkey .. 72 C5
Yenice, Aydın, Turkey .. 39 D10
Yenice, Çanakkale, Turkey . 39 B9
Yenice, Edirne, Turkey .. 41 F10
Yenice →, Turkey 72 D6
Yenifoça, Turkey 39 C8
Yenihisar, Turkey 39 D9
Yeniköy, Bursa, Turkey .. 41 F13
Yeniköy, Çanakkale, Turkey 39 B8
Yeniköy, Kütahya, Turkey . 39 C11
Yenipazar, Turkey 39 D10
Yenisaía, Greece 41 E8
Yenişehir, Turkey 41 F13
Yenisey →, Russia 50 B9
Yeniseysk, Russia 51 D10
Yeniseyskiy Zaliv, Russia . 50 B9
Yennádhi, Greece 36 C9
Yenne, France 21 C9
Yenotayevka, Russia ... 49 G8
Yenyuka, Russia 51 D13
Yeo →, Australia 93 E3
Yeo, L., Australia 93 E3
Yeo I., Canada 110 A3
Yeola, India 66 J9
Yeoryioúpolis, Greece .. 36 D6
Yeovil, U.K. 13 G5
Yeppoon, Australia 94 C5
Yeráki, Greece 38 D4
Yerbent, Turkmenistan .. 50 F6
Yerbogachen, Russia ... 51 C11
Yerevan, Armenia 49 K7
Yerington, U.S.A. 114 G4
Yerkesik, Turkey 39 D10
Yerköy, Turkey 72 C6
Yermak, Kazakhstan ... 50 D8
Yermo, U.S.A. 117 L10
Yeropol, Russia 51 C17
Yeropótamos →, Greece . 36 D6
Yeroskipos, Cyprus 36 E11
Yershov, Russia 48 E9
Yerushalayim = Jerusalem,
  Israel 75 D4
Yerville, France 18 C7

Yes Tor, U.K. 13 G4
Yesan, S. Korea 57 F14
Yeşilhisar, Turkey 72 C6
Yeşilırmak →, Turkey .. 72 B7
Yeşilkent, Turkey 72 D7
Yeşilköy, Turkey 41 F12
Yeşilova, Turkey 39 D11
Yeşilyurt, Manisa, Turkey . 39 C10
Yeşilyurt, Muğla, Turkey . 39 D10
Yesnogorsk, Russia 46 E9
Yeso, U.S.A. 113 H2
Yessentuki, Russia 49 H6
Yessey, Russia 51 C11
Yeste, Spain 33 G2
Yetman, Australia 95 D5
Yeu, Î. d', France 18 F4
Yevlakh = Yevlax,
  Azerbaijan 49 K8
Yevlax, Azerbaijan 49 K8
Yevpatoriya, Ukraine ... 47 K7
Yeya →, Russia 47 J10
Yeysk, Russia 47 J10
Yezd = Yazd, Iran 71 D7
Yezerishche, Belarus ... 46 E5
Yhati, Paraguay 126 B4
Yhú, Paraguay 127 B4
Yí →, Uruguay 126 C4
Yi 'Allaq, G., Egypt ... 75 E2
Yi He →, China 57 G10
Yi Xian, Anhui, China .. 59 C11
Yi Xian, Hebei, China .. 56 E8
Yi Xian, Liaoning, China . 57 D11
Yialí, Greece 39 E9
Yialiás →, Cyprus 36 D12
Yi'allaq, G., Egypt 80 A3
Yialousa, Cyprus 36 D13
Yiáltra, Greece 38 C4
Yianisádhes, Greece ... 36 D8
Yiannitsa, Greece 40 F6
Yibin, China 58 C5
Yichang, China 59 B8
Yicheng, Henan, China .. 59 B9
Yicheng, Shanxi, China .. 56 G6
Yichuan, China 56 F6
Yichun, Heilongjiang, China 60 B7
Yichun, Jiangxi, China .. 59 D10
Yidu, China 57 F10
Yidun, China 58 B2
Yifag, Ethiopia 81 E4
Yifeng, China 59 C10
Yihuang, China 59 D11
Yijun, China 56 G5
Yıldız Dağları, Turkey .. 41 E11
Yıldızeli, Turkey 72 C7
Yiliang, Yunnan, China . 58 D5
Yiliang, Yunnan, China . 58 E4
Yilong, China 58 B6
Yimen, China 58 E4
Yimianpo, China 57 B15
Yinchuan, China 56 E4
Yindarlgooda, L., Australia 93 F3
Ying He →, China 56 H9
Ying Xian, China 56 E7
Yingcheng, China 59 B9
Yingde, China 59 E9
Yingjiang, China 58 E1
Yingjing, China 58 C4
Yingkou, China 57 D12
Yingshan, Henan, China . 59 B9
Yingshan, Hubei, China . 59 B10
Yingshan, Sichuan, China . 58 B6
Yingshang, China 59 A11
Yingtan, China 59 C11
Yining, China 50 E9
Yinjiang, China 58 C7
Yinmabin, Burma 67 H19
Yiofíros →, China 36 D7
Yíoúra, Nótios Aiyaíon,
  Greece 38 D6
Yíoúra, Thessalía, Greece . 38 B6
Yipinglang, China 58 E3
Yirba Muda, Ethiopia .. 81 F4
Yirga Alem, Ethiopia ... 81 F4
Yirol, Sudan 81 F3
Yirrkala, Australia 94 A2
Yishan, China 58 E7
Yishui, China 57 G10
Yíthion, Greece 38 E4
Yitiaoshan, China 56 F3
Yitong, China 57 C13
Yiwu, China 59 C13
Yixing, China 59 B12
Yiyang, Henan, China .. 56 G7
Yiyang, Hunan, China .. 59 C9
Yiyang, Jiangxi, China .. 59 C11
Yizhang, China 59 E9
Yizre'el, Israel 59 A12
Yli-Kitka, Finland 8 C23
Ylitornio, Finland 8 C20
Ylivieska, Finland 8 D21
Yngaren, Sweden 11 F10
Yoakum, U.S.A. 113 L6
Yobe □, Nigeria 83 C7
Yog Pt., Phil. 63 B6
Yogan, Togo 83 D5
Yoğuntaş, Turkey 41 E11
Yogyakarta, Indonesia .. 63 G14
Yoho Nat. Park, Canada . 104 C5
Yojoa, L. de, Honduras . 120 D2
Yōju, S. Korea 57 F14
Yokadouma, Cameroon . 84 D2
Yokkaichi, Japan 55 G8
Yoko, Cameroon 83 D7
Yokosuka, Japan 55 G9
Yokote, Japan 54 E10
Yola, Nigeria 83 D7
Yolaina, Cordillera de, Nic. 120 D3
Yoloten, Turkmenistan .. 71 B9
Yom →, Thailand 62 A2
Yonago, Japan 55 G6

Yonaguni-Jima, Japan ... 55 M1
Yōnan, N. Korea 57 F14
Yonezawa, Japan 54 F10
Yong Peng, Malaysia ... 65 L4
Yong Sata, Thailand ... 65 J2
Yongamp'o, N. Korea .. 57 E13
Yong'an, China 59 E11
Yongcheng, China 56 H9
Yongch'ŏn, S. Korea .. 57 G15
Yongchuan, China 58 C5
Yongchun, China 59 E12
Yongde, China 58 E2
Yongdeng, China 56 F2
Yongding, China 59 E11
Yŏngdŏk, S. Korea 57 F15
Yŏngdŭngp'o, S. Korea . 57 F14
Yongfeng, China 59 D10
Yongfu, China 58 E7
Yonghe, China 56 F6
Yŏnghŭng, N. Korea ... 57 E14
Yongji, China 56 G6
Yongjia, China 59 C13
Yongjin, S. Korea 57 F15
Yongkang, Yunnan, China . 58 E2
Yongkang, Zhejiang, China 59 C13
Yongnian, China 56 F8
Yongning,
  Guangxi Zhuangzu, China 58 F7
Yongning, Ningxia Huizu,
  China 56 E4
Yongping, China 58 E2
Yongqing, China 56 E9
Yongren, China 58 D3
Yongshan, China 58 C4
Yongsheng, China 58 D3
Yongshun, China 58 C7
Yongtai, China 59 E12
Yongxin, = Jinggangshan,
  China 59 D10
Yongxing, China 59 D9
Yongxiu, China 59 C10
Yongzhou, China 59 D8
Yonibana, S. Leone ... 82 D2
Yonkers, U.S.A. 111 F11
Yonne □, France 19 E10
Yonne →, France 19 D9
York, Australia 93 F2
York, U.K. 12 D6
York, Ala., U.S.A. 113 J10
York, Nebr., U.S.A. ... 112 E6
York, Pa., U.S.A. 108 F7
York, C., Australia 94 A3
York, City of □, U.K. .. 12 D6
York, Kap, Greenland .. 4 B4
York, Vale of, U.K. 12 C6
York Haven, U.S.A. ... 110 F8
York Sd., Australia 92 C4
Yorke Pen., Australia .. 95 E2
Yorketown, Australia ... 95 F2
Yorkshire Wolds, U.K. .. 12 C7
Yorkton, Canada 105 C8
Yorkville, U.S.A. 116 G3
Yoro, Honduras 120 C2
Yoron-Jima, Japan 55 L4
Yorosso, Mali 82 C4
Yos Sudarso, Pulau =
  Dolak, Pulau, Indonesia . 63 F9
Yosemite National Park,
  U.S.A. 116 H7
Yosemite Village, U.S.A. . 116 H7
Yoshkar Ola, Russia ... 48 B8
Yŏsu, S. Korea 57 G14
Yotvata, Israel 75 F4
You Jiang →, China ... 58 F6
You Xian, China 59 D9
Youbou, Canada 116 B2
Youghal, Ireland 15 E4
Youghal B., Ireland ... 15 E4
Youkounkoun, Guinea .. 82 C2
Young, Australia 95 E4
Young, Canada 105 C7
Young, Uruguay 126 C4
Younghusband, L., Australia 95 E2
Younghusband Pen.,
  Australia 95 F2
Youngstown, Canada ... 105 C6
Youngstown, N.Y., U.S.A. 110 C5
Youngstown, Ohio, U.S.A. 110 E4
Youngsville, U.S.A. 110 E5
Youngwood, U.S.A. ... 110 F5
Youxi, China 59 D12
Youyang, China 58 C7
Youyu, China 56 D7
Yozgat, Turkey 72 C6
Ypané →, Paraguay .. 126 A4
Yport, France 18 C7
Ypres = Ieper, Belgium . 17 D2
Yreka, U.S.A. 114 F2
Yssingeaux, France ... 21 C8
Ystad, Sweden 11 J7
Ysyk-Köl, Ozero, Kyrgyzstan 50 E8
Ythan →, U.K. 14 D7
Ytterhogdal, Sweden ... 10 B8
Ytyk Kyuyel, Russia ... 51 C14
Yu Jiang →, China ... 58 F7
Yu Xian, Hebei, China . 56 E8
Yu Xian, Shanxi, China . 56 E7
Yuan Jiang →, Hunan,
  China 59 C8
Yuan Jiang →, Yunnan,
  China 58 F4
Yuanjiang, Hunan, China . 59 C9
Yuanjiang, Yunnan, China . 58 F4
Yuanlin, Taiwan 59 F13
Yuanmou, China 58 E3
Yuanqu, China 56 G6

Yuanyang, Henan, China .. 56 G7
Yuanyang, Yunnan, China . 58 F4
Yuba →, U.S.A. 116 F5
Yuba City, U.S.A. 116 F5
Yūbari, Japan 54 C10
Yubdo, Ethiopia 81 F4
Yūbetsu, Japan 54 B11
Yubo, Sudan 81 F2
Yucatán □, Mexico ... 119 C7
Yucatán, Canal de,
  Caribbean 120 B2
Yucatán, Península de,
  Mexico 98 H11
Yucatán Basin, Cent. Amer. 98 H11
Yucatan Str. = Yucatán,
  Canal de, Caribbean .. 120 B2
Yucca, U.S.A. 117 L12
Yucca Valley, U.S.A. ... 117 L10
Yucheng, China 56 F9
Yuci, China 56 F7
Yudu, China 59 E10
Yuendumu, Australia ... 92 D5
Yueqing, China 59 C13
Yueqing Wan, China ... 59 D13
Yuexi, Anhui, China ... 59 B11
Yuexi, Sichuan, China .. 58 C4
Yueyang, China 59 C9
Yugan, China 59 C11
Yugoslavia ■, Europe .. 40 C4
Yuhuan, China 59 C13
Yŭhuan Dao, China ... 59 C13
Yujiang, China 59 C11
Yukhnov, Russia 46 E8
Yukon →, U.S.A. 100 B3
Yukon Territory □, Canada 100 B6
Yüksekova, Turkey 73 D11
Yukta, Russia 51 C11
Yukuhashi, Japan 55 H5
Yulara, Australia 93 E5
Yule →, Australia 92 D2
Yuleba, Australia 95 D4
Yuli, Nigeria 83 D7
Yuli, Taiwan 59 F13
Yulin, Guangxi Zhuangzu,
  China 59 F8
Yülin, Hainan, China .. 65 C7
Yulin, Shaanxi, China .. 56 E5
Yuma, Ariz., U.S.A. ... 117 N12
Yuma, Colo., U.S.A. ... 112 E3
Yuma, B. de, Dom. Rep. . 121 C6
Yumbe, Uganda 86 B3
Yumbi,
  Dem. Rep. of the Congo . 86 C2
Yumen, China 60 C4
Yumurtalık, Turkey 72 D6
Yun Gui Gaoyuan, China . 58 E3
Yun Ho →, China 57 E9
Yun Ling, China 58 D2
Yun Xian, Hubei, China . 59 A8
Yun Xian, Yunnan, China . 58 E3
Yuna, Australia 93 E2
Yunak, Turkey 72 C4
Yunan, China 59 F8
Yuncheng, Henan, China . 56 G8
Yuncheng, Shanxi, China . 56 G6
Yunfu, China 59 F9
Yungas, Bolivia 124 G5
Yungay, Chile 126 D1
Yunhe, China 59 C12
Yunlin, China 59 F8
Yunlin, Taiwan 59 F13
Yunlong, China 58 E2
Yunmeng, China 59 B9
Yunnan □, China 58 E4
Yunquera de Henares, Spain 32 E1
Yunt Dağı, Turkey 39 C9
Yunta, Australia 95 E2
Yunxi, China 56 H6
Yunxiao, China 59 F11
Yuping, China 58 D7
Yuqing, China 58 D6
Yurga, Russia 50 D9
Yurimaguas, Peru 124 E3
Yuryev-Polskiy, Russia . 46 D10
Yuryevets, Russia 48 B6
Yuryung Kaya, Russia .. 51 B12
Yuscarán, Honduras ... 120 D2
Yushan, China 59 C12
Yushanzhen, China 58 C7
Yushe, China 56 F7
Yushu, Jilin, China 57 B14
Yushu, Qinghai, China . 60 C4
Yusufeli, Turkey 73 B9
Yutai, China 56 G9
Yutian, China 57 E9
Yuxarı Qarabağ = Nagorno-
  Karabakh, Azerbaijan . 70 B5
Yuxi, China 58 E4
Yuyao, China 59 B13
Yuzawa, Japan 54 E10
Yuzha, Russia 48 B6
Yuzhno-Sakhalinsk, Russia 51 E15
Yuzhou, China 56 G7
Yvelines □, France ... 19 D8
Yverdon-les-Bains, Switz. . 25 J2
Yvetot, France 18 C7
Yzeure, France 19 F10

Z

Zaanstad, Neths. 17 B4
Zāb al Kabīr →, Iraq .. 70 C4
Zāb aş Şağīr →, Iraq .. 70 C4
Žabalj, Serbia, Yug. ... 42 E5
Žabari, Serbia, Yug. ... 40 B5
Zabarjad, Egypt 80 C4

Zabaykalsk, *Russia* 51 E12
Ząbki, *Poland* 45 F8
Ząbkowice Śląskie, *Poland* . 45 H3
Žabljak, *Montenegro, Yug.* . 40 C3
Zabłudów, *Poland* 45 F9
Żabno, *Poland* 45 H7
Zābol, *Iran* 71 D9
Zābolī, *Iran* 71 E9
Zabré, *Burkina Faso* 83 C4
Zábřeh, *Czech Rep.* 27 B9
Zabrze, *Poland* 45 H5
Zabzuga, *Ghana* 83 D5
Zacapa, *Guatemala* 120 D2
Zacapu, *Mexico* 118 D4
Zacatecas, *Mexico* 118 C4
Zacatecas □, *Mexico* 118 C4
Zacatecoluca, *El Salv.* ... 120 D2
Zachary, *U.S.A.* 113 K9
Zachodnio-Pomorskie □,
  Poland 44 E2
Zacoalco, *Mexico* 118 C4
Zacualtipán, *Mexico* 119 C5
Zadar, *Croatia* 29 D12
Zadawa, *Nigeria* 83 C7
Zadetkyi Kyun, *Burma* ... 65 G1
Zadonsk, *Russia* 47 F10
Zafarqand, *Iran* 71 C7
Zafora, *Greece* 39 E8
Zafra, *Spain* 35 G4
Zagań, *Poland* 45 G2
Zagaoua, *Chad* 79 E10
Žagarė, *Lithuania* 44 B10
Zagazig, *Egypt* 80 H7
Zägheh, *Iran* 71 C6
Zaglivérion, *Greece* 40 F7
Zaganado, *Benin* 83 D5
Zagorá, *Greece* 38 B5
Zagorje, *Slovenia* 29 B11
Zagórów, *Poland* 45 F4
Zagorsk = Sergiyev Posad,
  Russia 46 D10
Zagórz, *Poland* 45 J9
Zagreb, *Croatia* 29 C12
Zāgros, Kūhhā-ye, *Iran* .. 71 C6
Zagros Mts. = Zāgros,
  Kūhhā-ye, *Iran* 71 C6
Žagubica, *Serbia, Yug.* .. 40 B5
Zaguinaso, *Ivory C.* 82 C3
Zagyva →, *Hungary* 42 C5
Zāhedān, *Fārs, Iran* 71 D7
Zāhedān,
  Sīstān va Balūchestān, Iran 71 D9
Zahlah, *Lebanon* 75 B4
Zahna, *Germany* 24 D8
Záhony, *Hungary* 42 B7
Zainsk, *Russia* 48 C11
Zaïre = Congo →, *Africa* . 84 F2
Zaječar, *Serbia, Yug.* ... 40 C6
Zaka, *Zimbabwe* 89 C5
Zakamensk, *Russia* 51 D11
Zakataly = Zaqatala,
  Azerbaijan 49 K8
Zakháro, *Greece* 38 D3
Zakhodnaya Dzvina =
  Daugava →, *Latvia* .. 9 H21
Zākhū, *Iraq* 70 B4
Zákinthos, *Greece* 38 D2
Zákinthos □, *Greece* .. 38 D2
Zakopane, *Poland* 45 J6
Zakroczym, *Poland* ... 45 F7
Zákros, *Greece* 36 D8
Zala, *Ethiopia* 81 F4
Zala □, *Hungary* 42 D1
Zala →, *Hungary* 42 D2
Zalaegerszeg, *Hungary* . 42 D1
Zalakomár, *Hungary* .. 42 D2
Zalalövö, *Hungary* ... 42 D1
Zalamea de la Serena, *Spain* 35 G5
Zalamea la Real, *Spain* . 35 H4
Zalău, *Romania* 42 C8
Žalec, *Slovenia* 29 B12
Zaleshchiki = Zalishchyky,
  Ukraine 47 H3
Zalew Wiślany, *Poland* . 44 D6
Zalewo, *Poland* 44 E6
Zalingei, *Sudan* 79 F10
Zalishchyky, *Ukraine* . 47 H3
Zama L., *Canada* 104 B5
Zambeke,
  Dem. Rep. of the Congo . 86 B2
Zambeze →, *Africa* ... 87 F4
Zambezi = Zambeze →,
  Africa 87 F4
Zambezi, *Zambia* ... 85 G4
Zambezia □, *Mozam.* . 87 F4
Zambia ■, *Africa* ... 87 F2
Zamboanga, *Phil.* ... 61 H5
Zambrów, *Poland* ... 45 F9
Zametchino, *Russia* .. 48 D6
Zamfara □, *Nigeria* .. 83 C6
Zamfara →, *Nigeria* .. 83 C6
Zamora, *Mexico* 118 D4
Zamora, *Spain* 34 D5
Zamora □, *Spain* ... 34 D5
Zamość, *Poland* 45 H10
Zamtang, *China* 58 A3
Zan, *Ghana* 83 D4
Záncara →, *Spain* ... 33 F1
Zandvoort, *Neths.* .. 17 B4
Zanesville, *U.S.A.* .. 110 G2
Zangābād, *Iran* 70 B5
Zangue →, *Mozam.* .. 87 F4
Zanjān, *Iran* 71 B6
Zanjān □, *Iran* 71 B6
Zannone, *Italy* 30 B6
Zante = Zákinthos, *Greece* 38 D2
Zanthus, *Australia* .. 93 F3
Zanzibar, *Tanzania* .. 86 D4

Zaouiet El-Kala = Bordj
  Omar Driss, *Algeria* ... 78 C7
Zaouiet Reggane, *Algeria* .. 78 C6
Zaoyang, *China* 59 A9
Zaozhuang, *China* 57 G9
Zap Suyu = Zāb al
  Kabīr →, *Iraq* 70 C4
Zapadna Morava →,
  Serbia, Yug. 40 C5
Zapadnaya Dvina =
  Daugava →, *Latvia* .. 9 H21
Zapadnaya Dvina, *Russia* .. 46 D7
Západné Beskydy, *Europe* . 27 B12
Zapadni Rodopi, *Bulgaria* . 40 E7
Západočeský □, *Czech Rep.* 26 B6
Zapala, *Argentina* 128 D2
Zapaleri, Cerro, *Bolivia* .. 126 A2
Zapata, *U.S.A.* 113 M5
Zapatón →, *Spain* 35 F4
Zaporizhzhya, *Ukraine* .. 47 J8
Zaporozhye = Zaporizhzhya,
  Ukraine 47 J8
Zaqatala, *Azerbaijan* ... 49 K8
Zara, *Turkey* 70 B3
Zaragoza, *Coahuila, Mexico* 118 B4
Zaragoza, *Nuevo León,
  Mexico* 119 C5
Zaragoza, *Spain* 32 D4
Zaragoza □, *Spain* 32 D4
Zarand, *Kermān, Iran* .. 71 D8
Zarand, *Markazī, Iran* .. 71 C6
Zărandului, Munţii, *Romania* 42 D7
Zaranj, *Afghan.* 66 D2
Zarasai, *Lithuania* 9 J22
Zárate, *Argentina* 126 C4
Zarautz, *Spain* 32 B2
Zaraysk, *Russia* 46 E10
Zard, Kūh-e, *Iran* ... 71 C6
Zāreh, *Iran* 71 C6
Zari, *Nigeria* 83 C7
Zaria, *Nigeria* 83 C6
Żarki, *Poland* 45 H6
Zárkon, *Greece* 38 B4
Zarneh, *Iran* 70 C5
Zărneşti, *Romania* .. 43 E10
Zárós, *Greece* 36 D6
Zarów, *Poland* 45 H3
Zarqā', Nahr az →, *Jordan* 75 C4
Zarrīn, *Iran* 71 C7
Zaruma, *Ecuador* ... 124 D3
Żary, *Poland* 45 G2
Zarza de Granadilla, *Spain* 34 E4
Zarzis, *Tunisia* 79 B8
Zas, *Spain* 34 B2
Zaskar →, *India* ... 69 B7
Zaskar Mts., *India* . 69 C7
Zástron, *S. Africa* .. 88 E4
Zatec, *Czech Rep.* .. 26 A6
Zaterechnyy, *Russia* . 49 H7
Zator, *Poland* 45 J6
Zavala, *Bos.-H.* 40 D1
Zavāreh, *Iran* 71 C7
Zave, *Zimbabwe* ... 89 B5
Zavetnoye, *Russia* .. 49 G6
Zavidovići, *Bos.-H.* . 42 F3
Zavitinsk, *Russia* .. 51 D13
Zavodovski, I., *Antarctica* . 5 B1
Zavolzhsk, *Russia* .. 48 B6
Zavolzhye, *Russia* .. 48 B6
Zawadzkie, *Poland* . 45 H5
Zawichost, *Poland* . 45 H8
Zawidów, *Poland* .. 45 G2
Zawiercie, *Poland* .. 45 H6
Zāwiyat al Baydā = Al
  Baydā, *Libya* 79 B10
Zāwyet Shammas, *Egypt* ... 80 A2
Zāwyet Um el Rakham,
  Egypt 80 A2
Zāwyet Ungeîla, *Egypt* .. 80 A2
Zāyā, *Iraq* 70 C5
Zāyandeh →, *Iran* .. 71 C7
Zaysan, *Kazakstan* .. 50 E9
Zaysan, Oz., *Kazakstan* . 50 E9
Zayü, *China* 58 C1
Zazafotsy, *Madag.* .. 89 C8
Zázrivá, *Slovak Rep.* . 27 B12
Zbarazh, *Ukraine* .. 47 H3
Zbąszyń, *Poland* ... 45 F2
Zbąszynek, *Poland* . 45 F2
Zblewo, *Poland* ... 44 E5
Ždár nad Sázavov,
  Czech Rep. 26 B8
Zdolbuniv, *Ukraine* . 47 G4
Ždrelo, *Serbia, Yug.* . 40 B5
Zduńska Wola, *Poland* . 45 G5
Zduny, *Poland* 45 G4
Zeballos, *Canada* ... 104 D3
Zebediela, *S. Africa* . 89 C4
Zebila, *Ghana* 83 C4
Zeebrugge, *Belgium* . 17 C3
Zeehan, *Australia* .. 94 G4
Zeeland □, *Neths.* .. 17 C3
Zeerust, *S. Africa* .. 88 D4
Zefat, *Israel* 75 C4
Zege, *Ethiopia* 81 E4
Zeggerene, Iracher, *Mali* . 83 B5
Zégoua, *Mali* 82 C3
Zehdenick, *Germany* . 24 C9
Zeil, Mt., *Australia* .. 92 D5
Zeila, *Somali Rep.* .. 74 E3
Zeist, *Neths.* 17 B5
Zeitz, *Germany* 24 D8
Želechów, *Poland* .. 45 G8
Zelengora, *Bos.-H.* . 40 C2
Zelenodolsk, *Russia* . 48 C9
Zelenogorsk, *Russia* . 46 B5
Zelenograd, *Russia* . 46 D9
Zelenogradsk, *Russia* . 9 J19
Zelenokumsk, *Russia* . 49 H6

Železná Ruda, *Czech Rep.* . 26 B6
Železnik, *Serbia, Yug.* ... 40 B4
Zelienople, *U.S.A.* 110 H4
Želiezovce, *Slovak Rep.* .. 27 C11
Zelina, *Croatia* 29 C13
Zell, *Baden-W., Germany* . 25 H3
Zell, *Rhld-Pfz., Germany* . 25 E3
Zell am See, *Austria* 26 D5
Zella-Mehlis, *Germany* .. 24 E6
Zeltweg, *Austria* 26 D7
Zémio, *C.A.R.* 86 A2
Zempléni-hegység, *Hungary* 42 B6
Zemplínska šírava,
  Slovak Rep. 27 C15
Zemun, *Serbia, Yug.* 40 B4
Zengbé, *Cameroon* 83 D7
Zengcheng, *China* 59 F9
Zenica, *Bos.-H.* 42 F2
Žepče, *Bos.-H.* 42 F3
Zeraf, Bahr ez →, *Sudan* . 81 F3
Zerbst, *Germany* 24 D8
Zerków, *Poland* 45 F4
Zermatt, *Switz.* 25 J3
Zernez, *Switz.* 25 J6
Zernograd, *Russia* 49 G5
Zerqani, *Albania* 40 E4
Zestaponi, *Georgia* ... 49 J6
Zetel, *Germany* 24 B3
Zeulenroda, *Germany* . 24 E7
Zeven, *Germany* 24 B5
Zevenaar, *Neths.* 17 C6
Zévio, *Italy* 28 C8
Zeya, *Russia* 51 D13
Zeya →, *Russia* 51 D13
Zeytinbaği, *Turkey* ... 41 F12
Zeytindağ, *Turkey* ... 39 C9
Zghartā, *Lebanon* ... 75 A4
Zgierz, *Poland* 45 G6
Zgorzelec, *Poland* .. 45 G2
Zguriţa, *Moldova* ... 43 B13
Zhabinka, *Belarus* .. 47 F3
Zhailma, *Kazakstan* . 50 D7
Zhambyl, *Kazakstan* . 50 E8
Zhangaly, *Kazakstan* . 49 G10
Zhangaqazaly, *Kazakstan* . 50 E7
Zhangbei, *China* ... 56 D8
Zhangguangcai Ling, *China* 57 B15
Zhangjiakou, *China* . 56 D8
Zhangping, *China* .. 59 E11
Zhangpu, *China* ... 59 E11
Zhangshu, *China* .. 59 C10
Zhangwu, *China* ... 57 C12
Zhangye, *China* ... 60 C5
Zhangzhou, *China* . 59 E11
Zhanhua, *China* ... 57 F10
Zhanjiang, *China* .. 59 G8
Zhannetty, Ostrov, *Russia* . 51 B16
Zhanyi, *China* 58 E4
Zhanyu, *China* ... 57 B12
Zhao Xian, *China* . 56 F8
Zhao'an, *China* ... 59 F11
Zhaocheng, *China* . 56 F6
Zhaojue, *China* ... 58 C4
Zhaoping, *China* .. 59 E8
Zhaoqing, *China* .. 59 F9
Zhaotong, *China* .. 58 D4
Zhaoyuan, *Heilongjiang,
  China* 57 B13
Zhaoyuan, *Shandong, China* 57 F11
Zharkovsky, *Russia* . 46 E7
Zhashkiv, *Ukraine* . 47 H6
Zhashui, *China* ... 56 H5
Zhayyq →, *Kazakstan* . 50 E6
Zhdanov = Mariupol,
  Ukraine 47 J9
Zhecheng, *China* .. 56 G8
Zhegao, *China* 59 B11
Zhejiang □, *China* . 59 C13
Zheleznogorsk, *Russia* .. 47 F8
Zheleznogorsk-Ilimskiy,
  Russia 51 D11
Zheltyye Vody = Zhovti
  Vody, *Ukraine* 47 H7
Zhen'an, *China* 56 H5
Zhenba, *China* 58 A6
Zhenfeng, *China* ... 58 E5
Zheng'an, *China* ... 58 C6
Zhengding, *China* .. 56 E8
Zhenghe, *China* ... 59 D12
Zhengyang, *China* . 59 A10
Zhengyangguan, *China* . 59 A11
Zhengzhou, *China* . 56 G7
Zhenhai, *China* ... 59 C13
Zhenjiang, *China* .. 59 A12
Zhenkang, *China* .. 58 F2
Zhenlai, *China* ... 57 B12
Zhenning, *China* .. 58 D5
Zhenping, *Henan, China* . 56 H7
Zhenping, *Shaanxi, China* . 58 B7
Zhenxiong, *China* . 58 D5
Zhenyuan, *Gansu, China* . 56 G4
Zhenyuan, *Guizhou, China* 58 D7
Zherdevka, *Russia* . 48 E5
Zherong, *China* ... 59 D12
Zhetiqara, *Kazakstan* . 50 D7
Zhezqazghan, *Kazakstan* . 50 E7
Zhicheng, *China* .. 59 B8
Zhidan, *China* 56 F5
Zhigansk, *Russia* .. 51 C13
Zhigulevsk, *Russia* . 48 D9
Zhijiang, *Hubei, China* . 59 B8
Zhijiang, *Hunan, China* . 58 D7
Zhijin, *China* 58 D5
Zhilinda, *Russia* .. 51 C12
Zhirnovsk, *Russia* . 48 E7
Zhitomir = Zhytomyr,
  Ukraine 47 G5
Zhizdra, *Russia* ... 46 F8
Zhlobin, *Belarus* .. 47 F6

Zhmerinka = Zhmerynka,
  Ukraine 47 H5
Zhmerynka, *Ukraine* . 47 H5
Zhob, *Pakistan* 68 D3
Zhob →, *Pakistan* ... 68 C3
Zhodino = Zhodzina,
  Belarus 46 E5
Zhodzina, *Belarus* .. 46 E5
Zhokhova, Ostrov, *Russia* . 51 B16
Zhongdian, *China* .. 58 D2
Zhongdong, *China* .. 58 F6
Zhongdu, *China* 58 E7
Zhongning, *China* .. 56 F3
Zhongshan, *Guangdong,
  China* 59 F9
Zhongshan,
  Guangxi Zhuangzu, China 59 E8
Zhongtiao Shan, *China* .. 56 G6
Zhongwei, *China* ... 56 F3
Zhongxiang, *China* . 59 B9
Zhongyang, *China* .. 56 F6
Zhoucun, *China* ... 57 F9
Zhouning, *China* ... 59 D12
Zhoushan, *China* .. 59 B14
Zhoushan Dao, *China* . 59 C14
Zhouzhi, *China* ... 56 G5
Zhovti Vody, *Ukraine* . 47 H7
Zhovtneve, *Ukraine* . 47 J7
Zhovtnevoye = Zhovtneve,
  Ukraine 47 J7
Zhu Jiang →, *China* . 59 F9
Zhuanghe, *China* .. 57 E12
Zhucheng, *China* .. 57 G10
Zhugqu, *China* 56 H3
Zhuhai, *China* 59 F9
Zhuji, *China* 59 C13
Zhukovka, *Russia* .. 46 F7
Zhumadian, *China* . 56 H8
Zhuo Xian = Zhuozhou,
  China 56 E8
Zhuolu, *China* 56 D8
Zhuozhou, *China* .. 56 E8
Zhuozi, *China* 56 D7
Zhushan, *China* ... 59 A8
Zhuxi, *China* 58 A7
Zhuzhou, *China* ... 59 D9
Zhytomyr, *Ukraine* . 47 G5
Zi Shui →, *China* .. 59 C9
Ziārān, *Iran* 71 B6
Ziarat, *Pakistan* ... 68 D2
Zibo, *China* 57 F10
Zichang, *China* 56 F5
Zidarovo, *Bulgaria* . 41 D11
Ziębice, *Poland* ... 45 H4
Zielona Góra, *Poland* . 45 G2
Zierikzee, *Neths.* .. 17 C3
Ziesar, *Germany* .. 24 C8
Zifta, *Egypt* 80 H7
Zigey, *Chad* 79 F9
Zigong, *China* 58 C5
Ziguinchor, *Senegal* . 82 C1
Zihuatanejo, *Mexico* . 118 D4
Zijin, *China* 59 F10
Zile, *Turkey* 72 B6
Žilina, *Slovak Rep.* . 27 B11
Žilinský □, *Slovak Rep.* . 27 B12
Zillah, *Libya* 79 C9
Zillertaler Alpen, *Austria* . 26 D4
Zima, *Russia* 51 D11
Zimapán, *Mexico* .. 119 C5
Zimba, *Zambia* ... 87 F2
Zimbabwe, *Zimbabwe* . 87 G3
Zimbabwe ■, *Africa* . 87 F3
Zimi, *S. Leone* ... 82 D2
Zimnicea, *Romania* . 43 G10
Zimovniki, *Russia* . 49 G6
Zinder, *Niger* 83 C6
Zinga, *Tanzania* .. 87 D4
Zingst, *Germany* .. 24 A8
Ziniaré, *Burkina Faso* . 83 C4
Zinnowitz, *Germany* . 24 A9
Zion National Park, *U.S.A.* 115 H7
Zirbitzkogel, *Austria* . 26 D7
Zirc, *Hungary* ... 42 C2
Žiri, *Slovenia* ... 29 B11
Žirje, *Croatia* ... 29 E12
Zirl, *Austria* 26 D4
Zirndorf, *Germany* . 25 F6
Ziros, *Greece* ... 36 D8
Zistersdorf, *Austria* . 27 C9
Zitácuaro, *Mexico* . 118 D4
Žitava →, *Slovak Rep.* . 27 C11
Žitište, *Serbia, Yug.* . 42 E5
Zitong, *China* ... 58 B5
Žitsa, *Greece* ... 38 B2
Zittau, *Germany* . 24 E10
Zitundo, *Mozam.* . 89 D5
Ziway, L., *Ethiopia* . 81 F4
Zixi, *China* 59 D11
Zixing, *China* ... 59 E9
Ziyang, *Shaanxi, China* . 56 H5
Ziyang, *Sichuan, China* . 58 B5
Ziyuan, *China* ... 59 D8
Ziyun, *China* 58 E6
Zizhong, *China* .. 58 C5
Zlarin, *Croatia* .. 29 E12
Zlatar, *Croatia* .. 29 B13
Zlatar, *Serbia, Yug.* . 40 C3
Zlataritsa, *Bulgaria* . 41 C9
Zlatna Panega, *Bulgaria* . 41 C8
Zlatni Pyasŭti, *Bulgaria* . 41 C12
Zlatograd, *Bulgaria* . 41 E9
Zlatoust, *Russia* .. 50 D6

Zletovo, *Macedonia* 40 E6
Zlín, *Czech Rep.* 27 B10
Złocieniec, *Poland* 44 E3
Złoczew, *Poland* 45 G5
Zlot, *Serbia, Yug.* 40 B5
Złotoryja, *Poland* 45 G2
Złotów, *Poland* 44 E4
Zmeinogorsk, *Kazakstan* .. 50 D9
Żmigród, *Poland* 45 G3
Zmiyev, *Ukraine* 47 H9
Znamenka = Znamyanka,
  Ukraine 47 H7
Znamyanka, *Ukraine* ... 47 H7
Żnin, *Poland* 45 F4
Znojmo, *Czech Rep.* .. 26 C9
Zobeyrī, *Iran* 70 C5
Zobia,
  Dem. Rep. of the Congo . 86 B2
Zoetermeer, *Neths.* .. 17 B4
Zogang, *China* 58 C1
Zogno, *Italy* 28 C6
Zogqên, *China* 58 A2
Zolochev = Zolochiv,
  Ukraine 47 H3
Zolochiv, *Ukraine* .. 47 H3
Zolotonosha, *Ukraine* . 47 H7
Zomba, *Malawi* 87 F4
Zongo,
  Dem. Rep. of the Congo . 84 D3
Zonguldak, *Turkey* .. 72 B4
Zongyang, *China* ... 59 B11
Zonqor Pt., *Malta* .. 36 D2
Zonza, *France* 21 G13
Zorgo, *Burkina Faso* . 83 C4
Zorita, *Spain* 35 F5
Zorleni, *Romania* .. 43 D12
Zornitsa, *Bulgaria* . 41 D10
Zorritos, *Peru* 124 D2
Żory, *Poland* 45 H5
Zorzor, *Liberia* ... 82 D3
Zossen, *Germany* . 24 C9
Zou Xiang, *China* . 56 G9
Zouan-Hounien, *Ivory C.* . 82 D3
Zouar, *Chad* 79 D9
Zouérate = Zouîrât,
  Mauritania 78 D3
Zouîrât, *Mauritania* . 78 D3
Zourika, *Niger* ... 83 B6
Zourma, *Burkina Faso* . 83 C4
Zoushan Dao, *China* . 59 B14
Zoutkamp, *Neths.* .. 17 A6
Zrenjanin, *Serbia, Yug.* . 42 E5
Zuarungu, *Ghana* .. 83 C4
Zuba, *Nigeria* 83 D6
Zubayr, *Yemen* ... 81 D5
Zubtsov, *Russia* .. 46 D8
Zuénoula, *Ivory C.* . 82 D3
Zuera, *Spain* 32 D4
Zufār, *Oman* 74 D5
Zug □, *Switz.* ... 25 H4
Zugdidi, *Georgia* . 49 J5
Zugersee, *Switz.* . 25 H4
Zugspitze, *Germany* . 25 H6
Zuid-Holland □, *Neths.* . 17 C4
Zuidbeveland, *Neths.* . 17 C3
Zuidhorn, *Neths.* .. 17 A6
Zújar, *Spain* 35 H4
Zújar →, *Spain* ... 35 G5
Zukowo, *Poland* .. 44 D5
Zula, *Eritrea* 81 D4
Zülpich, *Germany* . 24 E2
Zumaia, *Spain* ... 32 B2
Zumárraga, *Spain* . 32 B2
Zumbo, *Mozam.* .. 87 F3
Zummo, *Nigeria* .. 83 D7
Zumpango, *Mexico* . 119 D5
Zunhua, *China* .. 57 D9
Zuni, *U.S.A.* 115 J9
Zunyi, *China* ... 58 D6
Zuo Jiang →, *China* . 58 F6
Zuozhou, *China* .. 58 F6
Županja, *Croatia* . 42 E3
Žur, *Kosovo, Yug.* . 40 D4
Zurbāţīyah, *Iraq* . 70 C5
Zürich, *Switz.* ... 25 H4
Zürich □, *Switz.* . 25 H4
Zürichsee, *Switz.* . 25 H4
Zuromin, *Poland* . 45 E6
Žut, *Croatia* 29 E12
Zutphen, *Neths.* . 17 B6
Zuwārah, *Libya* . 79 B8
Žūzan, *Iran* 71 C8
Žužemberk, *Slovenia* . 29 C11
Zvenigorodka =
  Zvenyhorodka, *Ukraine* . 47 H6
Zvenyhorodka, *Ukraine* . 47 H6
Zverinogolovskoye, *Russia* . 50 D7
Zvezdets, *Bulgaria* . 41 D11
Zvishavane, *Zimbabwe* . 87 G3
Zvolen, *Slovak Rep.* . 27 C12
Zvonce, *Serbia, Yug.* . 40 D6
Zvornik, *Bos.-H.* . 42 F4
Zwedru = Tchien, *Liberia* . 82 D3
Zweibrücken, *Germany* . 25 F3
Zwenkau, *Germany* . 24 D8
Zwettl, *Austria* . 26 C8
Zwickau, *Germany* . 24 E8
Zwierzyniec, *Poland* . 45 H9
Zwiesel, *Germany* . 25 F9
Zwoleń, *Poland* . 45 G8
Zwolle, *Neths.* . 17 B6
Żychlin, *Poland* . 45 F6
Żyrardów, *Poland* . 45 F7
Zyryan, *Kazakstan* . 50 E9
Zyryanka, *Russia* . 51 C16
Zyryanovsk = Zyryan,
  Kazakstan 50 E9
Żywiec, *Poland* . 45 J6
Zyyi, *Cyprus* . 36 E12